MW01088341

# INGENIX.
## ShopIngenix.com

## Shop Faster. Shop Smarter. Experience ShopIngenix.com.

- **Network with industry peers when you join the Ingenix Coding Circle.** The new ShopIngenix.com eCommunity allows health care professionals to access the latest industry news, share ideas, test coding skills, and connect with colleagues.

- **Navigate the site more efficiently.** Start your product search by selecting either your market type or narrow down resource offerings by specific category.

- **Experience a hassle-free online purchase process.** The new streamlined, easy-to-follow checkout options also give you access to Live Help and a wide variety of self-paced instructions at every step, if needed.

- **Get eSmart:** the ShopIngenix.com frequent buyer program rewards you for every $500 you spend online.**

- **Access your Order History or outstanding Product Renewals.**

- **Create a Wish List.** Create and maintain a Wish List and send it along in an email to others that may need to preapprove purchases, or suggest titles to colleagues or anyone else in your professional network.

- **Get customized product recommendations.** Based on your selections, these recommendations show you items other shoppers have purchased along with the product you've just added to your cart.

CPT is a registered trademark of the American Medical Association.

# SAVE UP TO 20%
### with source code FOBAW9

 Visit **www.shopingenix.com** and enter the source code in the lower right-hand corner and save 20%.

Ingenix | Intelligence for Health Care | Call toll-free 1.800.INGENIX (464.3649), option 1.

**100% Money Back Guarantee** If our merchandise ever fails to meet your expectations, please contact our Customer Service Department toll-free at 1.800.INGENIX (464.3649), option 1, for an immediate response. Software: Credit will be granted for unopened packages only.

FOBA09

# INGENIX®

## 2009 Current Procedural Coding Expert

ISBN: 978-1-60151-196-6
Item Number: CE09
Available: December 2008
Price: $99.95

ISBN: 978-1-60151-197-3
Item Number: CEC09
Available: December 2008
Price: $89.95

### CPT® Codes with Medicare Essentials Enhanced for Accuracy.

Understanding and accurately coding CPT® codes is easier with this refurbished and expanded guide for effective coding. This reference combines CPT® codes with billing and Medicare regulatory information in one volume, clarifies annual CPT® code changes and describes the implications of changes.

← Identify Medicare rules and regulations that impact coding

← Save time researching the coding guidelines behind outpatient procedures

← Quickly and accurately locate CPT® codes

### New Features

- Body system headings on each page header
- Ingenix subheadings for each section
- Global/follow-up days
- Unlisted codes returned to the body of the code set where they belong
- Brand name vaccinations associated with CPT® codes
- Additional illustrations
- Improved index providing terms in a variety of ways to make it easier to find codes

### Key Features and Benefits

- **PQRI Ready.** Identify codes and their associated quality measure with PQRI icons and appendix.

- **Up-to-date and comprehensive.** New, revised and deleted codes plus the latest medicare information.

- **Comprehensive, code-specific definitions, rules and references exclusive to Ingenix.** Compiled from AMA, CMS, Ingenix and other sources to help you accelerate coding and speed reimbursement.

- **IngenixEdge®—Medicare Coverage Rules highlighted by icons and Pub. 100 references.** Know at a glance what policies apply to CPT® codes prior to claim submission.

- **IngenixEdge®—New information from the Pub. 100 and LCDs.** Better identification of national coverage manual and local coverage determinations that affect coding.

- **Color illustrations and modifier icons.** Quickly locate CPT® codes and apply modifiers correctly from the start to protect yourself from this prime cause for CPT® coding inaccuracies.

CPT is a registered trademark of the American Medical Association.

Ingenix | Intelligence for Health Care | Call toll-free 1.800.INGENIX (464.3649), option 1.

# INGENIX.

## Four simple ways to place an order.

### Call
1.800.ingenix (464.3649), option 1. Mention source code FOBA09 when ordering.

### Mail
PO Box 27116
Salt Lake City, UT 84127-0116
With payment and/or purchase order.

### Fax
801.982.4033
With credit card information and/or purchase order.

### Click
www.shopingenix.com
*Save 20% when you order online today—use source code FOBAW9.*

### ingenix *e*smart

GET REWARDS FOR SHOPPING ONLINE!
To find out more, visit www.shopingenix.com
eSmart program available only to Ingenix customers who are not part of Medallion, Gold Medallion or Partner Accounts programs. You must be registered at ShopIngenix.com to have your online purchases tracked for rewards purposes. Shipping charges and taxes still apply and cannot be used for rewards. Offer valid online only.

### 100% Money Back Guarantee
If our merchandise* ever fails to meet your expectations, please contact our Customer Service Department toll-free at 1.800.ingenix (464.3649), option 1 for an immediate response.
*Software: Credit will be granted for unopened packages only.

### Customer Service Hours
7:00 am - 5:00 pm Mountain Time
9:00 am - 7:00 pm Eastern Time

### Shipping and Handling

| no. of items | fee |
|---|---|
| 1 | $10.95 |
| 2-4 | $12.95 |
| 5-7 | $14.95 |
| 8-10 | $19.95 |
| 11+ | Call |

## Order Form

### Information

Customer No. _____ Contact No. _____

Source Code _____

Contact Name _____

Title _____ Specialty _____

Company _____

Street Address _____
NO PO BOXES, PLEASE
City _____ State _____ Zip _____

Telephone ( ) _____ Fax ( ) _____
IN CASE WE HAVE QUESTIONS ABOUT YOUR ORDER
E-mail _____ @ _____
REQUIRED FOR ORDER CONFIRMATION AND SELECT PRODUCT DELIVERY

Ingenix respects your right to privacy. We will not sell or rent your e-mail address or fax number to anyone outside Ingenix and its business partners. If you would like to remove your name from Ingenix promotion, please call 1.800.ingenix (464.3649), option 1.

### Product

| Item No. | Qty | Description | Price | Total |
|---|---|---|---|---|
| | | | | |
| | | | | |
| | | | | |
| | | | | |
| | | | | |
| | | | | |
| | | | | |
| | | | | |
| | | | | |
| | | | | |
| | | | | |
| | | | | |
| | | | | |
| | | | | |
| | | | | |

Subtotal _____

UT, VA, TN, OH, CT, IA, MD, MN, NC & NJ residents, please add applicable  Sales tax _____

(See chart on the left)  Shipping & handling charges _____

*All foreign orders, please call for shipping costs*

Total _____

### Payment

○ Please bill my credit card  ○ MasterCard  ○ VISA  ○ Amex  ○ Discover

Card No. | | | | | | | | | | | | | | | |  Expires | |
MONTH   YEAR

Signature _____

○ Check enclosed, made payable to: Ingenix, Inc.  ○ Please bill my office

Purchase Order No. _____
ATTACH COPY OF PURCHASE ORDER

©2009 Ingenix. All prices subject to change without notice

FOBA09

# HCPCS Level II
# Expert

2009

## Publisher's Notice

The Ingenix *2009 HCPCS* is designed to be an accurate and authoritative source of information about this government coding system. Every effort has been made to verify the accuracy of the listings, and all information is believed reliable at the time of publication. Absolute accuracy cannot be guaranteed, however. This publication is made available with the understanding that the publisher is not engaged in rendering legal or other services that require a professional license.

## For Answers to Coding Questions Try Our New Ingenix Coding Answers

**Validate your coding accuracy and reduce denials.** Find answers to those difficult coding questions in 48 to 72 hours.

**Increase your productivity.** Access the tool and submit your questions online 24 hours a day, seven days a week.

**Save time and money associated with researching those hard to code procedures.**

**Use existing site content as a research tool.** Quickly access previously submitted questions and answers by other users.

**Always know where your questions stand during the Q&A process.** Access real-time status of pending questions and receive email notifications when a question is answered.

**No subscription necessary.** Take advantage of the flexible pricing options based on the number of questions you purchase.

For information, please visit www.shopingenix.com or call customer service at 1.800.INGENIX (464.3649), option 1.

## Copyright

Made in the USA

HEC     ISBN 978-1-60151-157-7

## Acknowledgments

Steven Woodward, *Product Manager*
Karen Schmidt, BSN, *Technical Director*
Stacy Perry, *Manager, Desktop Publishing*
Lisa Singley, *Project Manager*
Wendy Gabbert, CPC, CPC-H, PCS, FCS, *Clinical/Technical Editor*
Temeka Lewis, *Clinical/Technical Editor*
Tracy Betzler, *Desktop Publishing Specialist*
Jean Parkinson, *Editor*

## Technical Editors

### Wendy Gabbert, CPC, CPC-H, PCS, FCS

**Clinical/Technical Editor**

Ms. Gabbert has more than 25 years of experience in the health care field. She has extensive background in CPT/HCPCS and ICD-9-CM coding. She served several years as a coding consultant. Her areas of expertise include physician and hospital CPT coding assessments, chargemaster reviews, and the outpatient prospective payment system (OPPS). She is a member of the American Academy of Professional Coders and American College of Medical Coding Specialists.

### Temeka Lewis, MBA, CCS

**Clinical/Technical Editor**

Ms. Lewis is a clinical/technical editor for Ingenix with expertise in hospital inpatient and outpatient coding. Her areas of expertise include ICD-9-CM, CPT, and HCPCS coding. Ms Lewis' past experience includes conducting coding audits and physician education, teaching ICD-9-CM and CPT coding, functioning as a member of a revenue cycle team, chargemaster maintenance, and writing compliance newsletters. Most recently she was responsible for coding and compliance in a specialty hospital. She is an active member of the American Health Information Management Association (AHIMA).

## Our Commitment to Accuracy

Ingenix is committed to producing accurate and reliable materials. To report corrections, please visit www.shopingenix.com/accuracy or email accuracy@ingenix.com. You can also reach customer service by calling 1.800.INGENIX (464.3649), option 1.

# Introduction

## ORGANIZATION OF HCPCS

The Ingenix 2009 *HCPCS Level II* book contains mandated changes and new codes for use as of January 1, 2009. Deleted codes have also been indicated and cross-referenced to active codes when possible. New codes have been added to the appropriate sections, eliminating the time-consuming step of looking in two places for a code. However, keep in mind that the information in this book is a reproduction of the 2009 HCPCS; additional information on coverage issues may have been provided to Medicare contractors after publication. All contractors periodically update their systems and records throughout the year. If this book does not agree with your contractor, it is either because of a mid-year update or correction or a specific local or regional coverage policy.

We have included codes noted in addendum B of the 2009 Outpatient Prospective Payment System (OPPS) update as published in the *Federal Register* and from transmittals through 2008 that include codes not discussed in other Centers for Medicare and Medicaid Services (CMS) documents. The sources for these codes are often noted in blue beneath the description.

## HOW TO USE INGENIX HCPCS LEVEL II BOOK

### Index

Because HCPCS is organized by code number rather than by service or supply name, the index enables the coder to locate any code without looking through individual ranges of codes. Just look up the medical or surgical supply, service, orthotic, prosthetic, or generic or brand name drug in question to find the appropriate codes. This index also refers to many of the brand names by which these items are known.

### Table of Drugs

The brand names of drugs listed are examples only and may not include all products available for that type of drug. Our table of drugs lists HCPCS codes from any available sections including A codes, C codes, J codes, S codes, and Q codes under brand and generic drug names with amount, route of administration, and code numbers. While we try to make the table comprehensive, it is not all-inclusive.

### Color-coded Coverage Instructions

The Ingenix *HCPCS Level II* book provides colored symbols for each coverage and reimbursement instruction. A legend to these symbols is provided on the bottom of each two-page spread.

---

**Blue Color Bar—Special Coverage Instructions**
A blue bar for "special coverage instructions" over a code means that special coverage instructions apply to that code. These special instructions are also typically given in the form of Medicare Pub.100 reference numbers. The appendixes provide the full text of the cited Medicare Pub.100 references.

**A4211** Supplies for self-administered injections

---

**Yellow Color Bar—Contractor Discretion**
Issues that are left to "contractor discretion" are covered with a yellow bar. Contact the contractor for specific coverage information on those codes.

**A4248** Chlorhexidine containing anti-septic, 1 ml

---

**Red Color Bar—Not Covered by or Invalid for Medicare**
Codes that are not covered by or are invalid for Medicare are covered by a red bar. The pertinent Medicare internet-only manuals (Pub. 100) reference numbers are also given explaining why a particular code is not covered. These numbers refer to the appendixes, where we have listed the Medicare references.

**A4232** Syringe with needle for external insulin pump, sterile, 3cc

---

Codes in the Ingenix *HCPCS Level II* follow the AMA CPT book conventions to indicate new, revised, and deleted codes.

- A black circle (●) precedes a new code.
- A black triangle (▲) precedes a code with revised terminology or rules.
- A circle (○) precedes a reissued code.
- Codes deleted from the 2009 active codes appear with a strike-out.

● J0641 Injection, levoleucovorin calcium, 0.5 mg

▲ A6010 Collagen based wound filler, dry form, sterile, per gram of collagen

○ J7611 Albuterol, inhalation solution, FDA-approved final product, noncompounded, administered through DME, concentrated form, 1 mg

~~C9003 Palivizumab-RSV-IgM, per 50 mg~~

## ☑ Quantity Alert

Many codes in HCPCS report quantities that may not coincide with quantities available in the marketplace. For instance, a HCPCS code for an ostomy pouch with skin barrier reports each pouch, but the product is generally sold in a package of 10; "10" must be indicated in the quantity box on the CMS claim form to ensure proper reimbursement. This symbol indicates that care should be taken to verify quantities in this code. These quantity alerts do not represent Medicare Unlikely Edits (MUEs) and should not be used for MUEs. An appendix of the MUE's can be found in appendix 8 of the *Expert* editions only.

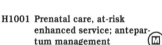 A4207 Syringe with needle, sterile 2 cc, each

A4280 Adhesive skin support attachment for use with external breast prosthesis, each ♀

## ♀ Female Only

This icon identifies procedures that should only be reported for female patients.

## ♂ Male Only

This icon identifies procedures that should only be reported for male patients.

A4326 Male external catheter specialty type with integral collection chamber, anytype, each ♂

## ▲ Age Edit

This icon denotes codes intended for use with a specific age group, such as neonate, newborn, pediatric, and adult. Carefully review the code description to ensure that the code you report most appropriately reflects the patient's age.

D6985 Pediatric partial denture, fixed ▲

## ⓜ Maternity

This icon identifies procedures that by definition should only be used for maternity patients generally between 12 and 55 years of age.

H1001 Prenatal care, at-risk enhanced service; antepartum management ⓜ

## ⒜²-⒵³ ASC Payment Indicators

Codes designated as being paid by ASC groupings that were effective at the time of printing are denoted by the group number.

G0105 Colorectal cancer screening; colonoscopy on individual at high risk ⒜²

A4600 Sleeve for intermittent limb compression device, replacement only, each ♿

## ♿ DMEPOS

Use this icon to identify when to consult the CMS durable medical equipment, prosthetics, orthotics, and supplies (DMEPOS) for payment of this durable medical item.

## ⊘ Skilled Nursing Facility (SNF)

Use this icon to identify certain items and services excluded from SNF consolidated billing. These items may be billed directly to the Medicare contractor by the provider or supplier of the service or item.

A4653 Peritoneal dialysis catheter anchoring device, belt, each

Drugs commonly reported with a code are listed underneath by brand or generic name.

J7310 Ganciclovir, 4.5 mg, long-acting implant

Use this code for Vitasert.

CMS does not use consistent terminology when a code for a specific procedure is not listed. The code description may include any of the following terms: unlisted, not otherwise classified (NOC), unspecified, unclassified, other, and miscellaneous. If you are sure there is no code for the service or supply provided or used, be sure to provide adequate documentation to the payer. Check with the payer for more information.

A0999 Unlisted ambulance service

## OPPS Status Indicators

A-Y OPPS status indicators
Status indicators identify how individual HCPCS Level II codes are paid or not paid under the OPPS. The same status indicator is assigned to all the codes within an ambulatory payment classification (APC). Consult the payer or resource to learn which CPT codes fall within various APCs. Status indicators for HCPCS and their definitions follow:

A Services furnished to a hospital outpatient that are paid under a fee schedule or payment system other than OPPS, for example:

- Ambulance Services
- Clinical Diagnostic Laboratory Services
- Non-Implantable Prosthetic and Orthotic Devices
- EPO for ESRD Patients
- Physical, Occupational, and Speech Therapy
- Routine Dialysis Services for ESRD Patients Provided in a Certified Dialysis Unit of a Hospital
- Diagnostic Mammography
- Screening Mammography

B Codes that are not recognized by OPPS when submitted on an outpatient hospital Part B bill type (12x and 13x)

C Inpatient Procedures

E Items, Codes, and Services:

- That are not covered by any Medicare outpatient benefit based on statutory exclusion.
- That are not covered by any Medicare outpatient benefit for reasons other than statutory exclusion
- That are not recognized by Medicare for outpatient claims but for which an alternate code for the same item or service may be available
- For which separate payment is not provided on outpatient claims

F Corneal Tissue Acquisition; Certain CRNA Services and Hepatitis B Vaccines

G Pass-Through Drugs and Biologicals

H Pass-Through Device Categories and Therapeutic Radiopharmaceuticals

K Nonpass-Through Drugs and Biologicals

L Influenza Vaccine; Pneumococcal Pneumonia Vaccine

M Items and Services Not Billable to the Fiscal Intermediary/MAC

N Items and Services Packaged into APC Rates

P Partial Hospitalization

01 STVX-Packaged Codes

02 T-Packaged Codes

03 Codes That May Be Paid Through a Composite APC

R Blood and Blood Products

S Significant Procedure, Not Discounted when Multiple

T Significant Procedure, Multiple Reduction Applies

U Brachytherapy Sources

V Clinic or Emergency Department Visit

X Ancillary Services

Y Non-Implantable Durable Medical Equipment

A A4321 Therapeutic agent for urinary catheter irrigation

B Q4005 Cast supplies, long arm cast, adult (11 years +), plaster

C G0341 Percutaneous islet cell transplant, includes portal vein catheterization and infusion

E A0021 Ambulance service, outside state per mile, transport (Medicaid only)

F V2785 Processingm, preserving and transporting corneal tissue

G J1300 Injection, eculizumab, 10 mg

H C1821 Interspinous process distraction device (implantable)

K J7501 Azathioprine, parenteral, 100 mg

M G0333 Dispense fee initial 30 day

N A4220 Refill kit for implantable infusion pump

P G0129 Occupational therapy requiring the skills of a qualified occupational therapist, furnished as a component of a partial hospitalization treatment program, per day

03 G0379 Direct admission of patient for hospital observation care

S G0251 Linear accelerator based stereotactic radiosurgery, delivery including collimator changes and custom plugging, fractionated treatment, all lesions, per session, maximum five sessions per course of treatment

T C9724 Endoscopic full-thickness plication in the gastric cardia using endoscopic plication system (EPS); includes endoscopy

V G0101 Cervical or vaginal cancer screening; pelvic and clinical breast examination

X Q0035 Cardiokymography

Y A4222 Infusion supplies for external drug infusion pump, per cassette or bag (list drugs separately)

# INTRODUCTION

**A2 – Z3 ASC Payment Indicators**

This icon identifies the new ASC status payment indicators, effective January 1, 2009. They indicate how the ASC payment rate was derived and/or how the procedure, item, or service is treated under the revised ASC payment system. For more information about these new indicators and how they affect billing, consult Ingenix's *Outpatient Billing Editor*.

**A2** Surgical procedure on ASC list in CY 2007; payment based on OPPS relative payment weight

**F4** Corneal tissue acquisition, hepatitis B vaccine; paid at reasonable cost

**G2** Nonoffice-based surgical procedure added in CY 2008 or later; payment based on OPPS relative payment weight

**H2** Brachytherapy source paid separately when provided integral to a surgical procedure on ASC list; payment contractor-priced

**H8** Device-intensive procedure on ASC list in CY 2007; paid at adjusted rate

**J7** OPPS pass-through device paid separately when provided integral to a surgical procedure on ASC list; payment contractor-priced

**J8** Device-intensive procedure added to ASC list in CY 2008 or later; paid at adjusted rate

**K2** Drugs and biologicals paid separately when provided integral to a surgical procedure on ASC list; payment based on OPPS rate

**K7** Unclassified drugs and biologicals; payment contractor-priced

**L1** Influenza vaccine; pneumococcal vaccine; packaged item/service; no separate payment made

**L6** New Technology Intraocular Lens (NTIOL); special payment

**N1** Packaged service/item; no separate payment made

**P2** Office-based surgical procedure added to ASC list in CY 2008 or later with MPFS nonfacility PE RVUs; payment based on OPPS relative payment weight

**P3** Office-based surgical procedure added to ASC list in CY 2008 or later with MPFS nonfacility PE RVUs; payment based on MPFS nonfacility PE RVUs

**R2** Office-based surgical procedure added to ASC list in CY 2008 or later without MPFS nonfacility PE RVUs; payment based on OPPS relative payment weight

**Z2** Radiology service paid separately when provided integral to a surgical procedure on ASC list; payment based on OPPS relative payment weight

**Z3** Radiology service paid separately when provided integral to a surgical procedure on ASC list; payment based on MPFS nonfacility PE RVUs

**A2** G0105 Coloerectal cancer screening; colonoscopy on individual at high risk **A2 ⊘**

**F4** V2785 Processing, preserving and transporting corneal tissue **F4**

**G2** C9716 Creations of thermal anal lesions by radiofrequency energy **G2**

**H2** A9527 Iodine I-125, sodium iodide solution, therapeutic per millicurie **H2**

**N1** L8690 Auditory osseointegrated device, includes all internal and external components **N1**

**K2** J0128 Injection, abarelix, 10 mg **K2**

**K7** C9399 Unclassified drugs or biologicals **K7**

**MED:** This notation precedes an instruction pertaining to this code in the CMS Publication 100 (Pub 100) electronic manual or in a National Coverage Determination (NCD). These CMS sources, formerly called the Medicare Carriers Manual (MCM) and Coverage Issues Manual (CIM), present the rules for submitting these services to the federal government or its contractors and are included in the appendix of this book.

**AHA:** American Hospital Association Coding Clinic for HCPCS citations help you find expanded information about specific codes and their usage.

A4300 Implantable access catheter, (e.g., venous, arterial, epidural subarachnoid, or peritoneal, etc.) external access
MED: 100-2, 15, 120

A4290 Sacral nerve stimulation test lead, each
AHA: 1Q, '02, 9

# ABOUT HCPCS CODES

Ingenix does not develop or maintain HCPCS Level II codes. The federal government does.

Any supplier or manufacturer can submit a request for coding modification to the HCPCS Level II national codes. A document explaining the HCPCS modification process, as well as a detailed format for submitting a recommendation for a modification to HCPCS Level II codes, is available on the HCPCS website at http://www.cms.hhs.gov/MedHCPCSGenInfo/Downloads/2008_ALPHA.pdf. Besides the information requested in this format, a requestor should also submit any additional descriptive material, including the manufacturer's product literature and information that is believed would be helpful in furthering CMS's understanding of the medical features of the item for which a coding modification is being recommended. The HCPCS coding review process is an ongoing, continuous process.

Requests for coding modifications should be sent to the following address:

Felicia Eggleston, CMS HCPCS Workgroup Coordinatorr
Center for Medicare Management
Centers for Medicare and Medicaid Services
C5-08-27
7500 Security Boulevard
Baltimore, MD 21244-1850

# HOW TO USE HCPCS LEVEL II

Coders should keep in mind, however, that the insurance companies and government do not base payment solely on what was done for the patient. They need to know why the services were performed. In addition to using the HCPCS coding system for procedures and supplies, coders must also use the ICD-9-CM coding system to denote the diagnosis. This book will not discuss ICD-9-CM codes, which can be found in a current ICD-9-CM code book for diagnosis codes. To locate a HCPCS Level II code, follow these steps:

1.  Identify the services or procedures that the patient received.

    Example:

    Patient administered PSA exam.

2.  Look up the appropriate term in the index.

    Example:

    Screening
      prostate

    Coding Tip: Coders who are unable to find the procedure or service in the index can look in the table of contents for the type of procedure or device to narrow the code choices. Also, coders should remember to check the unlisted procedure guidelines for additional choices.

3.  Assign a tentative code.

    Example:

    Code G0103

    Coding Tip: To the right of the terminology, there may be a single code or multiple codes, a cross-reference, or an indication that the code has been deleted. Tentatively assign all codes listed.

4.  Locate the code or codes in the appropriate section. When multiple codes are listed in the index, be sure to read the narrative of all codes listed to find the appropriate code based on the service performed.

    Example:

    **G0103  Prostate cancer screening; prostate specific antigen test (PSA)**

5.  Check for color bars, symbols, notes, and references.

    Example:

    A        **G0103  Prostate cancer screening; prostate specific antigen test (PSA)**♂

            **MED:** 100-3, 210.1; 100-4, 18, 50

# INTRODUCTION

6. Review the appendixes for the reference definitions and other guidelines for coverage issues that apply.

7. Determine whether any modifiers should be used.

8. Assign the code.

    Example:

    The code assigned is G0103.

# CODING STANDARDS

## Levels of Use

Coders may find that the same procedure is coded at two or even three levels. Which code is correct? There are certain rules to follow if this should occur.

When both a CPT and a HCPCS Level II code have virtually identical narratives for a procedure or service, the CPT code should be used. If, however, the narratives are not identical (e.g., the CPT code narrative is generic, whereas the HCPCS Level II code is specific), the Level II code should be used.

Be sure to check for a national code when a CPT code description contains an instruction to include additional information, such as describing a specific medication. For example, when billing Medicare or Medicaid for supplies, avoid using CPT code 99070 Supplies and materials (except spectacles), provided by the physician over and above those usually included with the office visit or other services rendered (list drugs, trays, supplies, or materials provided). There are many HCPCS Level II codes that specify supplies in more detail.

## Special Reports

Submit a special report with the claim when a new, unusual, or variable procedure is provided or a modifier is used. Include the following information:

- A copy of the appropriate report (e.g., operative, x-ray), explaining the nature, extent, and need for the procedure
- Documentation of the medical necessity of the procedure
- Documentation of the time and effort necessary to perform the procedure

**10% LMD**, J7100
**5% dextrose/normal saline**, J7042
**5% dextrose/water**, J7060

## A

**Abarelix**, J0128
**Abatacept**, J0129
**Abbokinase**, J3364, J3365
**Abciximab**, J0130
**Abdomen/abdominal**
dressing holder/binder, A4461, A4463
pad, low profile, L1270
**Abduction**
control, each, L2624
pillow, E1399
rotation bar, foot, L3140-L3170
**Abortion**, S2260-S2267
**Abscess, incision and drainage**, D7510-D7520
**Absorption dressing**, A6251-A6256
**Abutments**
for implants, D6056-D6057
retainers for resin bonded "Maryland bridge", D6545
**Accession of brush biopsy sample**, D0486
**Accession of tissue, dental**, D0472-D0474
**Accessories**
ambulation devices, E0153-E0159
artifcial kidney and machine (see also ESRD), E1510-E1699
beds, E0271-E0280, E0305-E0326
oxygen, E1354-E1358
wheelchairs, E0950-E1010, E1050-E1298, E2201-E2231, E2295, E2300-E2367, K0001-K0108
**Access system**, A4301
**AccuChek**
blood glucose meter, E0607
test strips, box of 50, A4253
**Accurate**
prosthetic sock, L8420-L8435
stump sock, L8470-L8485
**Acetate concentrate for hemodialysis**, A4708
**Acetazolamide sodium**, J1120
**Acetylcysteine**
inhalation solution, J7608
injection, J0132
**Achromycin**, J0120
**Acid concentrate for hemodialysis**, A4709
**ACTH**, J0800
**Acthar**, J0800
**Actimmune**, J9216
**Action neoprene supports**, L1825
**Action Patriot manual wheelchair**, K0004
**Action Xtra, Action MVP, Action Pro-T, manual wheelchair**, K0005

**Active Life**
convex one-piece urostomy pouch, A4421
flush away, A5051
one-piece
drainable custom pouch, A5061
pre-cut closed-end pouch, A5051
stoma cap, A5055
**Activity therapy**, G0176
**Acyclovir**, J0133
**Adalimumab**, J0135
**Adaptor**
neurostimulator, C1883
pacing lead, C1883
**Addition**
cushion AK, L5648
cushion BK, L5646
harness upper extremity, L6675-L6676
to lower extremity orthotic, K0672
to lower extremity prosthesis, L5970-L5990
wrist, flexion, extension, L6620
**Adenocard**, J0150
**Adenosine**, J0150-J0152
**Adhesive**
barrier, C1765
catheter, A4364
disc or foam pad, A5126
medical, A4364
Nu-Hope
1 oz bottle with applicator, A4364
3 oz bottle with applicator, A4364
ostomy, A4364
pads, A6203-A6205, A6212-A6214, A6219-A6221, A6237-A6239, A6245-A6247, A6254-A6256
remover, A4365, A4455
support, breast prosthesis, A4280
tape, A4450, A4452
tissue, G0168
**Adjunctive services, dental**, D9220-D9310
**Adjustabrace 3**, L2999
**Adjustment, bariatric band**, S2083
**Administration**
hepatitis B vaccine, G0010
influenza virus vaccine, G0008
medication, T1502-T1503
direct observation, H0033
pneumococcal vaccine, G0009
**Adoptive immunotherapy**, S2107
**Adrenalin**, J0170
**Adrenal transplant**, S2103
**Adriamycin**, J9000
**Adrucil**, J9190
**AdvantaJet**, A4210
**AFO**, E1815, E1830, L1900-L1990, L4392, L4396
**Agalsidase beta**, J0180
**Aimsco Ultra Thin syringe, 1 cc or 1/2 cc, each**, A4206

**Air ambulance** — see also Ambulance
**Air bubble detector, dialysis**, E1530
**Aircast**, L4350-L4380
**Aircast air stirrup ankle brace**, L1906
**Air fluidized bed**, E0194
**Airlife Brand Misty-Neb nebulizer**, E0580
**Air pressure pad/mattress**, E0186, E0197
**AirSep**, E0601
**Air travel and nonemergency transportation**, A0140
**Airway device**, E0485-E0486
**Akineton**, J0190
**Alarm**
enuresis, S8270
pressure, dialysis, E1540
**Alatrofloxacin mesylate**, J0200
**Albumarc**, P9041
**Albumin, human**, P9041, P9045-P9047
**Albuterol**, J7611, J7613
**Alcohol**
abuse service, G0396, G0397, H0047
pint, A4244
testing, H0048
wipes, A4245
**Aldesleukin**, J9015
**Aldomet**, J0210
**Aldurazyme**, J1931
**Alefacept**, J0215
**Alemtuzumab**, J9010
injection, S0088
**Alferon N**, J9215
**Algiderm, alginate dressing**, A6196-A6199
**Alginate dressing**, A6196-A6199
**Alglucerase**, J0205
**Algosteril, alginate dressing**, A6196-A6199
**Alimta**, J9305
**Alkaban-AQ**, J9360
**Alkaline battery for blood glucose monitor**, A4233-A4236
**Alkeran**, J8600
**Allogenic cord blood harvest**, S2140
**Allograft**
Cymetra, Q4112
GRAFTJACKET, Q4113
small intestine and liver, S2053
soft dental tissue, D4275
**Alpha 1-proteinase inhibitor, human**, J0256
**Alteplase recombinant**, J2997
**Alternating pressure mattress/pad**, E0181, E0277
pump, E0182
**Alternative communication device, i.e., communication board**, E1902
**Alveoloplasty**
with extraction(s), D7310-D7311
without extractions, D7320-D7321
**Alveolus, fracture**, D7770

Amalgam, restoration, dental — Assessment

**Amalgam, restoration, dental,**
  D2140-D2161
**Amantadine hydrochloride,**
  G9017, G9033
**Ambulance,** A0021-A0999
  air, A0436
  disposable supplies, A0382-
    A0398
  oxygen, A0422
  response, treatment, no trans-
    port, A0998
**Ambulation device,** E0100-E0159
**Ambulation stimulator**
  spinal cord injured, E0762
**Amcort,** J3302
**A-methaPred,** J2920, J2930
**Amevive,** J0215
**Amifostine,** J0207
**Amikacin sulfate,** J0278
**Aminaid, enteral nutrition,** B4154
**Aminolevulinic acid, topical,**
  J7308
**Aminophylline,** J0280
**Amiodarone hydrochloride,** J0282
**Amirosyn-RF, parenteral nutri-
  tion,** B5000
**Amitriptyline HCl,** J1320
**Ammonia N-13**
  diagnostic imaging agent, A9526
**Ammonia test paper,** A4774
**Amobarbital,** J0300
**Amphocin,** J0285
**Amphotericin B,** J0285
  cholesterol sulfate, J0288
  lipid complex, J0287
  liposome, J0289
**Ampicillin sodium,** J0290
  sodium/sulbactam sodium,
    J0295
**Amputee**
  adapter, wheelchair, E0959
  prosthesis, L5000-L7510,
    L7520, L7900, L8400-
    L8465
  stump sock, L8470
  wheelchair, E1170-E1190,
    E1200
**Amygdalin,** J3570
**Amytal,** J0300
**Anabolin LA 100,** J2320-J2322
**Analgesia, dental,** D9230, D9241,
  D9242
  nonintravenous conscious seda-
    tion, D9248
**Analysis**
  saliva sample, D0418
**Anastrozole,** S0170
**Ancef,** J0690
**Anchor, screw,** C1713
**Andrest 90-4,** J0900
**Andro-Cyp,** J1070-J1080
**Andro-Estro 90-4,** J0900
**Androgyn L.A.,** J0900
**Andro L.A. 200,** J3130
**Androlone**
  -D 100, J2321
**Andronaq**
  -LA, J1070
**Andronate**
  -100, J1070

**Andronate** — *continued*
  -200, J1080
**Andropository 100,** J3120
**Andryl 200,** J3130
**Anectine,** J0330
**Anergan (25, 50),** J2550
**Anesthesia**
  dental, D9210-D9221
  dialysis, A4736-A4737
**Angiography**
  iliac artery, G0278
  magnetic resonance, C8901-
    C8914, C8918-C8920
  reconstruction, G0288
  renal artery, G0275
**Angioplasty**
  percutaneous, G0392-G0393
**Anidulafungin,** J0348
**Anistreplase,** J0350
**Ankle–foot orthotic AFO,** L1900-
  L1990, L2106-L2116
  Dorsiwedge Night Splint, L4398
    or A4570 or, L2999
  Specialist
    Ankle Foot Orthotic, L1930
    Tibial Pre-formed Fracture
      Brace, L2116
    Surround Ankle Stirrup Braces
      with Floam, L1906
**Antagon,** S0132
**Anterior-posterior orthotic**
  lateral orthotic, L0700, L0710
**Antibiotic home infusion therapy,**
  S9494-S9504
**Antibody testing, HIV-1,** S3645
**Anticeptic**
  chlorhexidine, A4248
**Anticoagulation clinic,** S9401
**Antiemetic drug, prescription**
  oral, Q0163-Q0181
**Antifungal home infusion thera-
  py,** S9494-S9504
**Anti-hemophilic factor (Factor
  VIII),** J7190-J7192
**Anti-hemophilic factor (Factor
  VIIa) recombinant,** J7189
**Anti-inhibitors,** J7198
**Anti-neoplastic drug, NOC,** J9999
**Antispas,** J0500
**Antithrombin III,** J7197
**Antiviral home infusion therapy,**
  S9494-S9504
**Anzemet,** J1260
**Apexifcation, dental,** D3351-
  D3353
**Apicoectomy, dental,** D3410-
  D3426
**A.P.L.,** J0725
**Apligraf,** Q4101
**Apnea monitor,** E0618-E0619
  with recording feature, E0619
  electrodes, A4556
  lead wires, A4557
**Apomorphine hydrochloride,**
  J0364
**Appliance**
  cleaner, A5131
  orthodontic
    fixed, D8220
    removable, D8210

**Appliance** — *continued*
  orthodontic — *continued*
    removal, D7997
    pneumatic, E0655-E0673
**Application**
  fluoride, D1203-D1206
**Aprepitant,** J8501
**Apresoline,** J0360
**Aprotinin,** J0365
**AquaMEPHYTON,** J3430
**AquaPedic sectional gel flotation,**
  E0196
**Aqueous**
  shunt, L8612
**Ara-C,** J9100
**Aralen,** J0390
**Aramine,** J0380
**Aranesp**
  ESRD, J0882
  non-ESRD, J0881
**Arbutamine HCl,** J0395
**Arch support,** L3040-L3100
**Aredia,** J2430
**Argatroban,** C9121
**Argyle Sentinel Seal chest
  drainage unit,** E0460
**Aristocort**
  forte, J3302
  intralesional, J3302
**Aristospan**
  Intra-articular, J3303
  Intralesional, J3303
**Arm**
  sling
    deluxe, A4565
    mesh cradle, A4565
    universal
      arm, A4565
      elevator, A4565
    wheelchair, E0973
**Arrestin,** J3250
**Arrow, power wheelchair,** K0014
**Arsenic trioxide,** J9017
**Arthrocentesis, dental,** D7870
**Arthroereisis**
  subtalar, S2117
**Arthroplasty, dental,** D7865
**Arthroscopy**
  dental, D7872-D7877
  knee
    harvest of cartilage, S2112
    removal loose body, FB,
      G0289
  shoulder
    with capsulorrhaphy, S2300
**Arthrotomy, dental,** D7860
**Artifcial**
  kidney machines and acces-
    sories (*see also* Dialysis),
    E1510-E1699
  larynx, L8500
  saliva, A9155
**Asparaginase,** J9020
**Aspart insulin,** S5551
**Aspiration, bone marrow,** G0364
**Assertive community treatment,**
  H0039-H0040
**Assessment**
  alcohol and/or substance,
    G0396-G0397

**Drainage** — *continued*
  bottle, A4911, A5102
**Dramamine**, J1240
**Dramanate**, J1240
**Dramilin**, J1240
**Dramocen**, J1240
**Dramoject**, J1240
**Dressing** — *see also* Bandage,
  A6021-A6404
  alginate, A6196-A6199
  composite, A6200-A6205
  contact layer, A6206-A6208
  film, A6257-A6259
  foam, A6209-A6215
  gauze, A6216-A6230, A6402-
    A6404
  holder/binder, A4461, A4463
  hydrocolloid, A6234-A6241
  hydrogel, A6242-A6248
  specialty absorptive, A6251-
    A6256
  tape, A4450, A4452
  transparent film, A6257-A6259
  tubular, A6457
**Dronabinol**, Q0167-Q0168
**Droperidol**, J1790
  and fentanyl citrate, J1810
**Dropper**, A4649
**Drug delivery system**
  controlled dose delivery system,
    K0730
  disposable, A4306
**Drugs** — *see also* Table of Drugs
  administered through a metered
    dose inhaler, J3535
  chemotherapy, J8999-J9999
  dental
    injection, D9610
    other, D9910
  disposable delivery system, 50
    ml or greater per hour,
    A4305
  disposable delivery system, 5 ml
    or less per hour, A4306
  immunosuppressive, J7500-
    J7599
  infusion supplies, A4221,
    A4222, A4230-A4232
  injections (*see also* drug name),
    J0120-J8999
  not otherwise classifed, J3490,
    J7599, J7699, J7799,
    J8499, J8999, J9999
  prescription, oral, J8499, J8999
**Dry pressure pad/mattress**,
    E0184, E0199
**Dry socket, localized osteitis**,
    D9930
**DTIC-Dome**, J9130
**Dunlap**
  heating pad, E0210
  hot water bottle, E0220
**Duo-Gen L.A.**, J0900
**Duolock curved tail closures**,
    A4421
**Durable medical equipment
    (DME)**, E0100-E8002
**Duracillin A.S.**, J2510
**Duraclon**, J0735

**Duragen (-10, -20, -40)**, J0970,
    J1380, J1390
**Duralone**
  -40, J1030
  -80, J1040
**Duramorph**, J2275
**Duratest**
  -100, J1070
  -200, J1080
**Duratestrin**, J1060
**Durathate-200**, J3130
**Durr-Fillauer**
  cervical collar, L0140
  Pavlik harness, L1620
**Dymenate**, J1240
**Dyphylline**, J1180

## E

**Ear wax removal**, G0268
**Easy Care**
  folding walker, E0143
  quad cane, E0105
**ECG**
  initial Medicare ECG, G0403-
    G0405
  monitor, S0345-S0347
**Echocardiogram**
  transesophageal, C8925-C8928
  transthoracic, C8921-C8924,
    C8929-C8930
**Echosclerotherapy**, S2202
**Economy knee splint**, L1830
**Edetate**
  calcium disodium, J0600
  edetate disodium, J3520
**Education**
  asthma, S9441
  birthing, S9436-S9439, S9442
  diabetes, S9145
  exercise, S9451
  family planning, individualized
    programs, school based,
    T1018
  infant safety, S9447
  lactation, S9443
  Lamaze, S9436
  parenting, S9444
  smoking cessation, S9453
  stress management, S9454
  weight management, S9449
**Efalizumab**, S0162
**Eggcrate dry pressure pad/mat-
    tress**, E0184, E0199
**Elastic support**, A6530-A6549
**Elavil**, J1320
**Elbow**
  brace, universal rehabilitation,
    L3720
  disarticulation, endoskeletal,
    L6450
  Masterhinge Elbow Brace 3,
    L3999
  orthotic (EO), E1800, L3700-
    L3740
  protector, E0191
**Electrical work, dialysis equip-
    ment**, A4870
**Electric hand**
  adult, L7007

**Electric hand** — *continued*
  pediatric, L7008
**Electric heat pad for peritoneal
    dialysis**, E0210
**Electric hook**, L7009
**Electric stimulator supplies**,
    A4595
**Electrocardiographic monitoring**,
    S0345-S0347
**Electrodes, per pair**, A4556
**Electrodiagnostic Testing**, S3905
**Electromagnetic therapy**, G0295,
    G0329
**Electron beam computed tomog-
    raphy**, S8092
**Electron microscopy - diagnostic**,
    D0481
**Elevating leg rest**, K0195
**Elevator, air pressure, heel**,
    E0370
**Ellence**, J9178
**Elliotts B solution**, J9175
**Eloxatin**, J9263
**Elspar**, J9020
**Embolization, protection system**,
    C1884
  for tumor destruction, S2095
**Embryo**
  cryopreserved transferred,
    S4037
  monitor/store cryopreserved,
    S4040
**Emergency**
  dental treatment, D9430
  facility visit, G0380-G0384
**EMG**, E0746
**Eminase**, J0350
**Enameloplasty**, D9971
**Enbrel**, J1438
**Encounter, clinic**, T1015
**Endarterectomy, chemical**,
    M0300
**Endodontic procedures**, D3110-
    D3999
**End of life care planning**, S0257
**Endoscope sheath**, A4270
**Endoscopy**
  full thickness plication gastric
    cardia, C9724
  nasal, S2344
**Endoskeletal system, addition**,
    L5925, L5984
**Enema**
  bag, reusable, A4458
  barium, G0106
  cancer screening, G0120
**Enfuvirtide**, J1324
**Enovil**, J1320
**Enoxaparin sodium**, J1650
**Enrich, enteral nutrition**, B4150
**Ensure, enteral nutrition**, B4150
  HN, B4150
  Plus, B4152
  Plus HN, B4152
  powder, B4150
**Enteral**
  administration services, feeding,
    S9340-S9343

**Heparin**
  infusion pump (for dialysis), E1520
  lock flush, J1642
  sodium, J1644
**HepatAmine, parenteral nutrition**, B5100
**Hepatic-aid, enteral nutrition**, B4154
**Hep-Lock (U/P)**, J1642
**Herceptin**, J9355
**Hexadrol phosphate**, J1100
**Hexalite**, A4590
**Hexior power wheelchair**, K0014
**High Frequency chest wall oscillation equipment**, A7025-A7026, E0483
**High osmolar contrast**
  up to 149 mgs iodine, Q9958
  150-199 mgs iodine, Q9959
  200-249 mgs iodine, Q9960
  250-299 mgs iodine, Q9961
  300-349 mgs iodine, Q9962
  350-399 mgs iodine, Q9963
  400 or greater mgs iodine, Q9964
**Hip**
  Custom Masterhinge Hip Hinge 3, L2999
  disarticulation prosthesis, L5250, L5270
  Masterhinge Hip Hinge 3, L2999
  orthotic (HO), L1600-L1686
**Hip-knee-ankle-foot orthotic (HKAFO)**, L2040-L2090
**Histaject**, J0945
**Histerone (-50, -100)**, J3140
**History and physical**
  related to surgical procedure, S0260
**Histrelin**
  acetate injection, J1675
  implant, J9225
**HIV-1 antibody testing**, S3645
**HKAFO**, L2040-L2090
**HN2**, J9230
**Holder**
  heel, E0951
  surgical dressing, A4461, A4463
  toe, E0952
**Hole cutter tool**, A4421
**Hollister**
  belt adapter, A4421
  closed pouch, A5051, A5052
  colostomy/ileostomy kit, A5061
  drainable pouches, A5061
    with flange, A5063
  medical adhesive, A4364
  pediatric ostomy belt, A4367
  remover, adhesive, A4455
  skin barrier, A4362, A5122
  skin cleanser, A4335
  skin conditioning creme, A4335
  skin gel protective dressing wipes, A5120
  stoma cap, A5055
  two-piece pediatric ostomy system, A5054, A5063, A5073
  urostomy pouch, A5071, A5072

**Home health**
  aide, S9122, T1030-T1031
    home health setting, G0156
  care
    certified nurse assistant, S9122, T1021
    home health aide, S9122, T1021
    management
      episodic, S0272
      hospice, S0271
      standard, S0270
    nursing care, S9122-S9124, T1030-T1031
    outside capitation arrangement, S0273-S0274
    re-certification, G0179-G0180
  gestational
    assessment, T1028
    delivery suppies, S8415
    diabetes, S9214
    hypertension, S9211
    pre-eclampsia, S9213
    preterm labor, S9208-S9209
  hydration therapy, S9373-S9379
  infusion therapy, S9325-S9379, S9494-S9497, S9537-S9810
  insertion midline venous catheter, S5523
  nursing services, S0274, S9212-S9213
  physician services, S0270-S0273
  postpartum hypertension, S9212
  services of
    clinical social worker, G0155
    occupational therapist, G0152
    physical therapist, G0151
    skilled nurse, G0154
    speech/language pathologist, G0153
  transfusion, blood products, S9538
  wound care, S9097
**Home uterine monitor**, S9001
**Hook**
  electric, L7009
  mechanical, L6706-L6707
**Hospice**
  care, Q5001-Q5008, S9126, T2041-T2046
  evaluation and counseling services, G0337
  referral visit, S0255
**Hospital**
  call
    dental, D9420
  observation
    direct admit, G0379
    per hour, G0378
**Hot water bottle**, E0220
**Houdini security suit**, E0700
**House call, dental**, D9410
**Housing, supported**, H0043-H0044

**Hoyer patient lifts**, E0621, E0625, E0630
**H-Tron insulin pump**, E0784
**H-Tron Plus insulin pump**, E0784
**Hudson**
  adult multi-vent venturi style mask, A4620
  nasal cannula, A4615
  oxygen supply tubing, A4616
  UC-BL type shoe insert, L3000
**Humalog**, J1815, J1817, S5550
**Human insulin**, J1815, J1817
**Humidifer**, E0550-E0560
  water chamber, A7046
**Humira**, J0135
**Humulin insulin**, J1815, J1817
**Hyaluronidase**
  bovine, J3470
  ovine, up to 150 units, J3471
  ovine,up to 999 units, J3472
  recombinant, J3473
**Hyate**, J7191
**Hybolin**
  decanoate, J2321
**Hycamtin**, J9350
**Hydralazine HCl**, J0360
**Hydrate**, J1240
**Hydration therapy**, S9373-S9379
**Hydraulic patient lift**, E0630
**Hydrocollator**, E0225, E0239
**Hydrocolloid dressing**, A6234-A6241
**Hydrocortisone**
  acetate, J1700
  sodium phosphate, J1710
  sodium succinate, J1720
**Hydrocortone**
  acetate, J1700
  phosphate, J1710
**Hydrogel dressing**, A6242-A6248
**Hydromorphone**, J1170, S0092
**Hydroxyurea**, S0176
**Hydroxyzine HCl**, J3410
  pamoate, Q0177-Q0178
**Hyoscyamine sulfate**, J1980
**Hyperbaric oxygen chamber, topical**, A4575
**Hyperstat IV**, J1730
**Hypertonic saline solution**, J7130
**Hypo-Let lancet device**, A4258
**Hypothermia**
  intragastric, M0100
**HypRho-D**, J2790
**Hyrexin-50**, J1200
**Hyzine-;50**, J3410

### I

**I-125 sodium iothalamate**, A9554
**I-131**
  sodium iodide, A9531
    capsule, A9517, A9528
    solution, A9529-A9530
  tositumomab, A9544-A9545
**I&D**
  Intraoral, D7511, D7521
**Ibandronate sodium injection**, J1740
**Ibutilide fumarate**, J1742
**Ice cap or collar**, E0230

**Injectable**
allograft, Q4112-Q4113
bulking agent, urinary tract,
L8606
flowable wound matrix, Q4114
**Injection** — *see also* Table of Drugs
contrast material, during MRI,
A9576-A9579, Q9953
dental service, D9610, D9630
sacroiliac joint, G0259-G0260
supplies for self-administered,
A4211
**Injection adjustment, bariatric
band**, S2083
**Inlay, dental**
fixed partial denture retainers
metallic, D6545-D6615
porcelain/ceramic, D6548-
D6609
metallic, D2510-D2530
porcelain/ceramic, D2610-
D2630
recement inlay, D2910
intentional replantation,
D3470, D7270
resin-based composite, D2650-
D2652
titanium, D6624
**Innovar**, J1810
**Insert**
convex, for ostomy, A5093
diabetic, for shoe, A5512-A5513
implant
soft palate, C9727
vaginal cylinder for brachytherapy, S2270
**Insertion**
tray, A4310-A4316
vaginal cylinder, S2270
**In-situ tissue hybridization**,
D0479
**Insulin**, J1815, J1817
delivery device, A9274, E0784,
S5565-S5571
home infusion administration,
S9353
intermediate acting, S5552
long acting, S5553
NPH, J1815, S5552
rapid onset, S5550-S5551
**Intal**, J7631
**Integra**
bilayer matrix wound dressing,
Q4104
dermal regeneration template,
Q4105
flowable wound matrix, Q4114
matrix, Q4108
**Interferon**
Alfa, J9212-J9215
Alfacon-1, J9212
Beta-1a, J1825, Q3025-Q3026
Beta-1b, J1830
Gamma, J9216
home injection, S9559
**Intergrilin injection**, J1327
**Intermittent**
limb compression device, E0676
peritoneal dialysis system,
E1592

**Intermittent** — *continued*
positive pressure breathing
(IPPB) machine, E0500
**Interphalangeal joint, prosthetic
implant**, L8658
**Interscapular thoracic prosthesis**
endoskeletal, L6570
upper limb, L6350-L6370
**Interspinous process distraction
device**, C1821
**Intervention**
alcohol and/or drug, H0050
**Intrafallopian transfer**
complete cycle, gamete, S4013
complete cycle, zygote, S4014
donor egg cycle, S4023
incomplete cycle, S4017
**Intraocular lenses**, C1780, Q1003-
Q1005, V2630-V2632
new technology
category 3, Q1003
category 4, Q1004
category 5, Q1005
presbyopia correcting function,
V2788
**Intraoral radiographs**, D0210-
D0240
**Intrauterine device**
copper contraceptive, J7300
other, S4989
Progestacert, S4989
**Intravenous sedation/analgesia,
dental**, D9241-D9242
**Introducer sheath**
guiding, C1766, C1892, C1893
other than guiding, C1894,
C2629, C2629
**Intron A**, J9214
**Iodine 125**, A9527, A9532, C2638-
C2639
**Iodine I-123**, A9509, A9516
**Iodine I-131**
albumin, A9524
iobenguane sulfate, A9508
sodium iodide, A9517
**Iodine swabs/wipes**, A4247
**IPD**
system, E1592
**IPPB machine**, E0500
**Ipratropium bromide**
administered through DME,
J7644-J7645
**Iressa**, J8565
**Irinotecan**, J9206
**Iris Preventix pressure relief/re-
duction mattress**, E0184
**Iris therapeutic overlays**, E0199
**IRM ankle-foot orthotic**, L1950
**Iron**
sucrose, J1756
**Irrigation/evacuation system,
bowel**
control unit, E0350
disposable supplies for, E0352
**Irrigation supplies**, A4320, A4322,
A4355, A4397-A4400
Surfit
irrigation sleeve, A4397
night drainage container set,
A5102

**Irrigation supplies** — *continued*
Visi-flow irrigator, A4398,
A4399
**Islet cell transplant**
laparoscopy, G0342
laparotomy, G0343
percutaneous, G0341
**Isocaine HCl**, J0670
**Isocal, enteral nutrition**, B4150
HCN, B4152
**Isoetharine**
inhalation solution
concentrated, J7647
unit dose, J7649-J7650
**Isolates**, B4150, B4152
**Isoproterenol HCl**
administered through DME,
J7657-J7660
**Isotein, enteral nutrition**, B4153
**Isuprel**, J7658-J7659
**Itraconazole**, J1835
**IUD**, J7300
**IV**
infusion, OPPS, C8957
pole, E0776, K0105
solution
5% dextrose/normal saline,
J7042
10% LMD, J7100
D-5-W, J7070
dextran, J7100, J7110
Gentran, J7100, J7110
normal saline, A4217,
J7030-J7040, J7050
Rheomacrodex, J7100
Ringer's lactate, J7120

## J

**Jace tribrace**, L1832
**Jacket**
scoliosis, L1300, L1310
**J-cell battery, replacement for
blood glucose monitor**,
A4234
**Jejunostomy tube**, B4087-B4088
**Jenamicin**, J1580
**Joint device**, C1776
transcutaneous electrical stimu-
lation, E0762

## K

**Kabikinase**, J2995
**Kaleinate**, J0610
**Kaltostat, alginate dressing**,
A6196-A6199
**Kanamycin sulfate**, J1840, J1850
**Kantrex**, J1840, J1850
**Kartop Patient Lift, toilet or
bathroom** (*see also* Lift),
E0625
**Keflin**, J1890
**Kefurox**, J0697
**Kefzol**, J0690
**Kenaject -40**, J3301
**Kenalog (-10, -40)**, J3301
**Keratectomy photorefractive**,
S0810
**Keratoprosthesis**, C1818

**Kestrone-5**, J1435
**Keto-Diastix, box of 100 glucose/ketone urine test strips**, A4250
**Ketorolac thomethamine**, J1885
**Key-Pred**
-25,-50, J2650
**K-Flex**, J2360
**Kidney**
ESRD supply, A4651-A4913
system, E1510
wearable artifcial, E1632
**Kingsley gloves, above hands**, L6890
**Kits**
enteral feeding supply (syringe) (pump) (gravity), B4034-B4036
fistula cannulation (set), A4730
parenteral nutrition, B4220-B4224
surgical dressing (tray), A4550
tracheostomy, A4625
**Klebcil**, J1840, J1850
**Knee**
Adjustabrace 3, L2999
disarticulation, prosthesis, L5150-L5160
extension/fexion device, E1812
immobilizer, L1830
joint, miniature, L5826
Knee-O-Prene Hinged Knee Sleeve, L1810
Knee-O-Prene Hinged Wraparound Knee Support, L1810
locks, L2405-L2425
Masterbrace 3, L2999
Masterhinge Adjustabrace 3, L2999
orthotic (KO), E1810, L1800-L1846
Performance Wrap (KO), L1825
**Knee-ankle-foot orthotic (KAFO)**, L2000-L2038, L2126-L2136
**Knee-O-Prene Hinged Knee Sleeve**, L1810
**Knee-O-Prene Hinged Wraparound Knee Support**, L1810
**KnitRite**
prosthetic
sheath, L8400-L8415
sock, L8420-L8435
stump sock, L8470-L8485
**Kodel clavicle splint**, L3660
**Kogenate**, J7192
**Konakion**, J3430
**Konyne-HT**, J7194
**K-Y Lubricating Jelly**, A4332, A4402
**Kyphosis pad**, L1020, L1025
**Kytril**, J1626

**L**

**Laboratory tests**
chemistry, P2028-P2038
microbiology, P7001
miscellaneous, P9010-P9615, Q0111-Q0115

**Laboratory tests** — *continued*
toxicology, P3000-P3001, Q0091
**Labor care (not resulting in delivery)**, S4005
**Lacrimal duct implant**
permanent, A4263
temporary, A4262
**Lactated Ringer's infusion**, J7120
**LAE 20**, J0970, J1380, J1390
**Laetrile**, J3570
**Lancet**, A4258, A4259
**Lanoxin**, J1160
**Laparoscopy, surgical**
esophagomyotomy, S2079
repair
**Laronidase**, J1931
**Laryngectomy**
tube, A7520-A7522
**Larynx, artifcial**, L8500
**Laser**
application, S8948
assisted uvulopalatoplasty (LAUP), S2080
in situ keratomileusis, S0800
myringotomy, S2225
**Laser skin piercing device, for blood collection**, E0620
replacement lens, A4257
**Lasix**, J1940
**LAUP**, S2080
**Lead**
adaptor
neurostimulator, C1883
pacing, C1883
cardioverter, defibrillator, C1777, C1895, C1896
environmental, home evaluation, T1029
neurostimulator, C1778
neurostimulator/test kit, C1897
pacemaker, C1779, C1898, C1899
**Lederle**, J8610
**LeFort**
I osteotomy, D7946-D7947
II osteotomy, D7948-D7949
III osteotomy, D7948-D7949
**Leg**
bag, A4358, A5112
extensions for walker, E0158
Nextep Contour Lower Leg Walker, L2999
Nextep Low Silhouette Lower Leg Walkers, L2999
rest, elevating, K0195
rest, wheelchair, E0990
strap, A5113, A5114, K0038, K0039
**Legg Perthes orthotic**, A4565, L1700-L1755
**Lens**
aniseikonic, V2118, V2318
contact, V2500-V2599
deluxe feature, V2702
eye, S0504-S0508, S0580-S0590, V2100-V2615, V2700-V2799
intraocular, C1780, V2630-V2632
low vision, V2600-V2615

**Lens** — *continued*
mirror coating, V2761
occupational multifocal, V2786
polarization, V2762
polycarbonate, V2784
progressive, V2781
skin piercing device, replacement, A4257
tint, V2744
addition, V2745
**Lente insulin**, J1815, S5552
**Lenticular lens**
bifocal, V2221
single vision, V2121
trifocal, V2321
**Lepirudin**, J1945
**Lerman Minerva spinal orthotic**, L0174
**Lesions, surgical excision, dental**, D7410-D7465
**Leucovorin calcium**, J0640
**Leukocyte**
poor blood, each unit, P9016
**Leuprolide acetate**, J1950, J9217, J9218
**Leuprolide acetate implant**, J9219
**Leustat**, J9065
**Leustatin**, J9065
**Levamisole HCl**, S0177
**Levaquin I.U.**, J1956
**Levine, stomach tube**, B4087-B4088
**Levocarnitine**, J1955
**Levo-Dromoran**, J1960
**Levofloxacin**, J1956
**Levonorgestrel, contraceptive implants and supplies**, J7302, J7306
**Levorphanol tartrate**, J1960
**Librium**, J1990
**Lice infestation treatment**, A9180
**Lidocaine HCl for intravenous infusion**, J2001
**Lifescan lancets, box of 100**, A4259
**Lifestand manual wheelchair**, K0009
**Lifestyle modification program, coronary heart disease**, S0340-S0342
**Lift**
combination, E0637
patient, and seat, E0621-E0635
Hoyer
Home Care, E0621
Partner All-Purpose, hydraulic, E0630
Partner Power Multifunction, E0625
shoe, L3300-L3334
standing frame system, E0638
**Lift-Aid patient lifts**, E0621
**Light box**, E0203
**Lincocin**, J2010
**Lincomycin HCl**, J2010
**Lioresal**, J0475
**Liquaemin sodium**, J1644
**Lispro insulin**, S5551

Metacarpophalangeal joint prosthesis, L8630
Metaraminol bitartrate, J0380
Metatarsal joint, prosthetic implant, L8641
Meter, bath conductivity, dialysis, E1550
Methacholine chloride, J7674
Methadone, J1230
oral, S0109
Methergine, J2210
Methocarbamol, J2800
Methotrexate, oral, J8610
sodium, J9250, J9260
Methyldopa HCl, J0210
Methylene blue injection, A9535
Methylergonovine maleate, J2210
Methylprednisolone
acetate, J1020-J1040
oral, J7509
sodium succinate, J2920, J2930
Metoclopramide HCl, J2765
Metronidazole, S0030
Meunster Suspension, socket prosthesis, L6110
Miacalcin, J0630
Micafungin sodium, J2248
Microabrasion, enamel, D9970
Microbiology test, P7001
Microcapillary tube, A4651
sealant, A4652
Micro-Fine
disposable insulin syringes, up to 1 cc, per syringe, A4206
lancets, box of 100, A4259
Microlipids, enteral nutrition, B4155
Microspirometer, S8190
Midazolam HCl, J2250
Mileage, ambulance, A0380, A0390
Milk, breast
processing, T2101
Milrinone lactate, J2260
Milwaukee spinal orthotic, L1000
Minerva, spinal orthotic, L0700, L0710
Mini-bus, nonemergency transportation, A0120
Minimed
3 cc syringe, A4232
506 insulin pump, E0784
insulin infusion set with bent needle wings, each, A4231
Sof-Set 24" insulin infusion set, each, A4230
Minoxidil, S0139
Mitomycin, J9280-J9291
Mitoxantrone HCl, J9293
Mobilite hospital beds, E0293, E0295, E0297
Moducal, enteral nutrition, B4155
Moisture exchanger for use with invasive mechanical ventilation, A4483
Moisturizer, skin, A6250
Monarc-M, J7190
Monitor
apnea, E0618

Monitor — *continued*
blood glucose, E0607
Accu-Check, E0607
Tracer II, E0607
blood pressure, A4670
device, A9279
ECG, S0345-S0347
pacemaker, E0610, E0615
ventilator, E0450
Monitoring
electrocardiographic, S0345-S0347
Monoclonal antibodies, J7505
Monoject disposable insulin syringes, up to 1 cc, per syringe, A4206
Monojector lancet device, A4258
Morcellator, C1782
Morphine sulfate, J2270, J2271, S0093
sterile, preservative-free, J2275
Moulage, facial, D5911-D5912
Mouth exam, athletic, D9941
Mouthpiece (for respiratory equipment), A4617
Moxifloxacin, J2280
M-Prednisol-40, J1030
-80, J1040
MRI
contrast material, A9576-A9579, Q9954
low field, S8042
Mucoprotein, blood, P2038
Multifetal pregnancy reduction, ultrasound guidance, S8055
Multiple post collar, cervical, L0180-L0200
Multipositional patient support system, E0636
Muscular dystrophy, genetic test, S3853
Muse, J0275
Mutamycin, J9280
Mycophenolate mofetil, J7517
Mycophenolic acid, J7518
Mylotarg, J9300
Myochrysine, J1600
Myolin, J2360
Myotonic muscular dystrophy, genetic test, S3853
Myringotomy, S2225

# N

Nabilone, oral, J8650
Nafcillin sodium, S0032
Nail trim, G0127, S0390
Nalbuphine HCl, J2300
Naloxone HCl, J2310
Naltrexone depot injection, J2315
Nandrobolic L.A., J2321
Nandrolone
decanoate, J2320-J2322
Narcan, J2310
Narrowing device, wheelchair, E0969
Nasahist B, J0945
Nasal
application device (for CPAP device), A7032-A7034

Nasal — *continued*
vaccine inhalation, J3530
Nasogastric tubing, B4081, B4082
Navelbine, J9390
ND Stat, J0945
Nebcin, J3260
Nebulizer, E0570-E0585
aerosol compressor, E0571
aerosol mask, A7015
aerosols, E0580
Airlife Brand Misty-Neb, E0580
Power-Mist, E0580
Up-Draft Neb-U-Mist, E0580
Up-Mist hand-held nebulizer, E0580
compressor, with, E0570
Madamist II medication compressor/nebulizer, E0570
Pulmo-Aide compressor/nebulizer, E0570
Schuco Mist nebulizer system, E0570
corrugated tubing
disposable, A7010, A7018
non-disposable, A7011
distilled water, A7018
filter
disposable, A7013
non-disposable, A7014
heater, E1372
large volume
disposable, prefilled, A7008
disposable, unfilled, A7007
not used with oxygen
durable glass, A7017
pneumatic, administration set, A7003, A7005, A7006
pneumatic, nonfiltered, A7004
portable, E0570
small volume, E0574
spacer or nebulizer, S8100
with mask, S8101
ultrasonic, dome and mouthpiece, A7016
ultrasonic, reservoir bottle nondisposable, A7009
water, A7018
water collection device large volume nebulizer, A7012
distilled water, A7018
NebuPent, J2545
Needle, A4215
with syringe, A4206-A4209
brachytherapy, C1715
non-coring, A4212
Negative pressure wound therapy
dressing set, A6550
pump, E2402
Nelarabine, J9261
Nembutal sodium solution, J2515
Neocyten, J2360
Neo-Durabolic, J2320-J2322
Neomax knee support, L1800
Neoplasms, dental, D7410-D7465
Neoquess, J0500
Neosar, J9070-J9092
Neostigmine methylsulfate, J2710

Neo-Synephrine, J2370
NephrAmine, parenteral nutrition, B5000
Nesacaine MPF, J2400
Nesiritide, J2325
Neulasta, J2505
Neumega, J2355
Neuromuscular stimulator, E0745
  ambulation of spinal cord injured, E0762
Neuro-Pulse, E0720
Neurostimulator
  functional transcutaneous, E0764
  generator, C1767, C1820
  implantable
    electrode, L8680
    pulse generator, L8685-L8688
    receiver, L8682
  lead, C1778
  patient programmer, L8681
  receiver and/or transmitter, C1816
  transmitter
    external, L8683-L8684
Neutrexin, J3305
Newington
  Legg Perthes orthotic, L1710
  mobility frame, L1500
Newport Lite hip orthotic, L1685
Nextep Contour Lower Leg Walker, L2999
Nextep Low Silhouette Lower Leg Walkers, L2999
Nicotine
  gum, S4995
  patches, S4990-S4991
Niemann-Pick disease, genetic test, S3849
Nightguard, D9940
Nipent, J9268
Nitrogen mustard, J9230
Nitrous oxide, dental analgesia, D9230
Nonchemotherapy drug, oral, J8499
Noncovered services, A9270, G0293-G0294
Nonemergency transportation, A0080-A0210
Nonimpregnated gauze dressing, A6216, A6221, A6402, A6404
Nonintravenous conscious sedation, dental, D9248
Nonprescription drug, A9150
Nonthermal pulsed high frequency radiowaves treatment device, E0761
Nordryl, J1200
Norflex, J2360
Normal saline, A4216-A4217, J7030, J7040, J7042, J7050, J7130
Norplant System contraceptive, J7306
Northwestern Suspension, socket prosthesis, L6110

Not otherwise classifed drug, J3490, J7599, J7699, J7799, J8499, J8999, J9999, Q0181
Novantrone, J9293
Novo Nordisk insulin, J1815, J1817
Novo Seven, J7189
NPH insulin, J1815, S5552
Nubain, J2300
NuHope
  adhesive, 1 oz bottle with applicator, A4364
  adhesive, 3 oz bottle with applicator, A4364
  cleaning solvent, 16 oz bottle, A4455
  cleaning solvent, 4 oz bottle, A4455
  hole cutter tool, A4421
Numorphan H.P., J2410
Nursing care, in home
  licensed practical nurse, S9124
  registered nurse, S9123
Nursing home visit, dental, D9410
Nursing services, S9211-S9212, T1000-T1004
Nutri-Source, enteral nutrition, B4155
Nutrition
  counseling
    dental, D1310, D1320
    dietary, S9452
  enteral formulae, B4150-B4162
  enteral infusion pump, B9002
  medical food, S9433
  parenteral infusion pump, B9004, B9006
  parenteral solution, B4164-B5200
Nutritional counseling, dietition visit, S9470

# O

O&P Express
  above knee, L5210
  ankle-foot orthotic with bilateral uprights, L1990
  anterior floor reaction orthotic, L1945
  below knee, L5105
  elbow disarticulation, L6200
  hip disarticulation, L5250
  hip-knee-ankle-foot orthotic, L2080
  interscapular thoracic, L6370
  knee-ankle-foot orthotic, L2000, L2010, L2020, L2036
  knee disarticulation, L5150, L5160
  Legg Perthes orthotic, Patten bottom type, L1755
  Legg Perthes orthotic, Scottish Rite, L1730
  partial foot, L5000, L5020
  plastic foot drop brace, L1960
  supply/accessory/service, L9900

Oasis
  burn matrix, Q4103
  wound matrix, Q4102
Observation service
  direct admission, G0379
  per hour, G0378
Obturator prosthesis
  definitive, D5932
  dental
    postsurgical, D5932
    refitting, D5933
    surgical, D5931
  interim, D5936
  surgical, D5931
Occipital/mandibular support, cervical, L0160
Occlusal
  adjustment, dental, D9951-D9952
  guard, dental, D9940
  orthotic device, D7877
Occlusion/analysis, D9950
Occupational multifocal lens, V2786
Occupational therapist
  home health setting, G0152
Occupational therapy, S9129
Octafluoropropae microspheres, Q9956
Octreotide
  intramuscular form, J2353
  subcutaneous or intravenous form, J2354
Ocular device, C1784
Ocular prosthetic implant, L8610
Oculinum, J0585
Odansetron HCl, J2405, Q0179
Odontoplasty (enameloplasty), D9971
Office service, M0064
Offobock cosmetic gloves, L6895
O-Flex, J2360
Ofloxacin, S0034
Ohio Willow
  prosthetic sheath
    above knee, L8410
    below knee, L8400
    upper limb, L8415
  prosthetic sock, L8420-L8435
  stump sock, L8470-L8485
Olanzapine, S0166
Omalizumab, J2357
Omnipen-N, J0290
Oncaspar, J9266
Oncology
  breast cancer, G9071-G9073, G9131
  chronic myelogenous leukemia, G9139
  colon cancer, G9083-G9089
  coordination of care, G9054
  demonstration project, G9056
  esophageal cancer, G9096-G9099
  evaluation, G9050
  expectant management, G9053
  gastric cancer, G9100-G9104
  head and neck, G9110-G9112
  management
    adheres to guidelines, G9056

**Parapodium, mobility frame,** L1500
**Parenteral nutrition**
administration kit, B4224
home infusion therapy, S9364-S9368
pump, B9004, B9006
solution, B4164-B5200
supplies, not otherwise classified, B9999
supply kit, B4220, B4222
**Parenting class,** S9444
infant safety, S9447
**Paricalcitol,** J2501
**Parking fee, nonemergency transport,** A0170
**Partial dentures**
fixed
implant/adjustment-supported retainers, D6068-D6077
pontic, D6210-D6252
retainers, D6545-D6792
removable, D5211-D5281
**PASRR,** T2010-T2011
**Passive motion**
continuous exercise device, E0936
**Paste, conductive,** A4558
conductive, A4558
coupling for ultrasound, A4559
**Pathology and laboratory tests,** P9010-P9615
surgical
prostate, G0416-G0419
**Patient lift,** E0625, E0637, E0639, E0640
**Patten Bottom, Legg Perthes orthotic,** L1755
**Pavlik harness, hip orthotic,** L1650
**Peak flow meter,** S8110
portable, S8096
**Pediatric hip abduction splint**
Orthomedics, L1640
Orthomerica, L1640
**Pediculosis treatment,** A9180
**PEFR, peak expiratory flow rate meter,** A4614
**Pegademase bovine,** J2504
**Pegaspargase,** J9266
**Pegasys,** S0145
**Pegfilgrastrim,** J2505
**Peg-L-asparaginase,** J9266
**Pelvic and breast exam,** G0101
**Pelvic belt/harness/boot,** E0944
**Pemetrexed,** J9305
**Penicillin G**
benzathine and penicillin G procaine, J0530-J0580
potassium, J2540
procaine, aqueous, J2510
**Penlet II lancet device,** A4258
**Penlet lancet device,** A4258
**Pentamidine isethionate,** J2545, S0080
**Pentastarch,** J2513
**Pentazocine HCl,** J3070
**Pentobarbital sodium,** J2515
**Pentostatin,** J9268

**Percussor,** E0480
**Percutaneous**
access system, A4301
**Perflexane lipid microspheres,** Q9955
**Perflutren lipid microsphere,** Q9957
**Performance Wrap (KO),** L1825
**Periapical service,** D3410-D3470
**Periodontal procedures,** D4210-D4999
**Periradicular/apicoectomy,** D3410-D3426
**Perlstein, ankle-foot orthotic,** L1920
**Permapen,** J0560-J0580
**Peroneal strap,** L0980
**Peroxide,** A4244
**Perphenazine,** J3310, Q0175-Q0176
**Persantine,** J1245
**Personal care services,** T1019-T1020
**Pessary,** A4561-A4562
**PET imaging**
any site, NOS, G0235
breast, G0252
whole body, G0219
**Pfzerpen,** J2540
**A.S.,** J2510
**PGE1,** J0270
**Phamacologicals, dental,** D9610, D9630
**Pharmacy**
compounding and dispensing, S9430
dispensing fee
inhalation drugs
per 30 days, Q0513
per 90 days, Q0514
supply fee
imitial immunosuppressive drugs, Q0510
oral anticancer antiemetic or immunosuppressive drug, Q0511-Q0512
**Pharmaplast disposable insulin syringes, per syringe,** A4206
**Phelps, ankle-foot orthotic,** L1920
**Phenazine (25, 50),** J2550
**Phenergan,** J2550
**Phenobarbital sodium,** J2560
**Phentolamine mesylate,** J2760
**Phenylephrine HCl,** J2370
**Phenytoin sodium,** J1165
**Philadelphia tracheotomy cervical collar,** L0172
**Philly One-piece Extrication collar,** L0150
**pHisoHex solution,** A4246
**Photofrin,** J9600
**Photographs, dental, diagnostic,** D0350
**Phototherapy**
home visit service (Bili-Lite), S9098
keratectomy (PKT), S0812
light (bilirubin), E0202
**Physical exam**
for college, S0622

**Physical exam** — *continued*
related to surgical procedure, S0260
**Physical therapy,** S8990
shoulder stretch device, E1841
**Physical therapy/therapist**
home health setting, G0151, S9131
**Physician management**
home care
episodic, S0272
hospice monthly, S0271
standard monthly, S0270
**Physician quality reporting indicators (PQRI)**
ABI, G8407-G8409, G8513-G8515
ACE or ARB therapy, G8472-G8475, G8479-G8481, G8506
alarm symptoms, G8248, G8274
antibiotic prophylaxis, G8152-G8196, G8527-G8529
anticoagulant, G8226
antidepressant medication, G8126-G8131
antiplatelet therapy, G8226, G8521-G8523
antivirals, G8458-G8463
asthma, G8370, G8391
atrial fibrillation, G8183-G8184
AV fistula, G8530-G8532
back pain, G8493, G8502
beta-blocker, G8450-G8452
blood pressure, G8476-G8478
BMI, G8417-G8422
breast cancer, G8376, G8380-G8381
cancer stage
lung and esophageal, G8518-G8520
CEA, G8523-G8526
chemotherapy, G8371-G8374
cognitive impairment, G8434-G8436
colon cancer, G8371-G8372, G8377
chemotherapy, G8373
COPD, G8093-G8094
coronary artery bypass graft (CABG), G8159-G8167, G8497, G8544
coronary artery disease (CAD), G8036-G8041, G8182, G8489, G8498
CT or MRI, G8243
deep vein thrombosis prophylactic, G8217
depression, G8431-G8433, G8466-G8467, G8510-G8511
DEXA, G8399-G8400
diabetes, G8016-G8026, G8385-G8386, G8390, G8485, G8494
dysphagia screening, G8234
elder maltreatment, G8534-G8538
EMR/CCHIT, G8447-G8449

**Physician quality reporting indicators (PQRI) —** *continued*
endoscopy
end stage renal disease measure reporting, G8488
ESRD, G8075-G8082, G8085, G8387-G8388
fall risk, G8516-G8517
footwear evaluation, G8410, G8415-G8416
functional outcome, G8539-G8543
glaucoma, G8305-G8308
hearing assessment, G8057-G8059
heart failure patient, G8027-G8032, G8183-G8184
HIV/AIDS, G8491, G8500
influenza vaccination, G8108-G8110, G8423-G8426, G8482-G8484
intraocular pressure, G8302-G8304
kidney disease, G8487, G8495
left ventricular ejection fraction (LVEF), G8395-G8396, G8450-G8452, G8468-G8472
leukemia, G8375, G8384
mammogram, G8111-G8114
medication list/review, G8427-G8430
mole assessment, G8246
multiple myeloma, G8382
mycardial infarction, G8006-G8011, G8033-G8035
myelodysplastic syndrome (MDS), G8384, G8389
neurological exam, G8404-G8406
osteoporosis, G8051-G8053, G8099-G8100, G8103-G8104, G8106-G8107, G8185-G8186, G8401
pain, G8440-G8442, G8508-G8509, G8512
perioperative care, G8492, G8501
pneumococcal vaccination, G8115-G8117
pneumonia, G8012-G8014
prescriptiona, G8443-G8446
preventive care, G8486, G8496
prophylactic antibiotic, G8503-G8505
prostate cancer, G8464-G8465
radiation therapy, G8378-G8379, G8383
rehabilitation, G8238
retinopathy, G8397-G8398
rheumatoid arthritis, G8490, G8499
systemic clinical database registry, G8533
thromboembolism prophylaxis, G8155-G8157
tobacco use, G8402-G8403, G8453-G8457
TPA, G8231

**Physician quality reporting indicators (PQRI) —** *continued*
treatment plan, G8437-G8439
urinary incontinence assessment, G8060-G8062
verification of medication, G8507
warfarin therapy, G8183-G8184
**Phytonadione**, J3430
**Pillo pump**, E0182
**Pillow**
abduction, E1399
decubitus care, E0190
nasal, A7029
positioning, E0190
**Pin retention, per tooth**, D2951
**Pinworm examination**, Q0113
**Piperacillin sodium**, S0081
**Pit and fissure sealant**, D1351
**Pitocin**, J2590
**Placement**
applicator, breast, C9726
fixation device, D7998
interim implant body, D6012
interstitial device radiotherapy, other than prostate, C9728
temporary anchorage device, D7292-D7294
**Planing, dental root**, D0350
**Plasma**
frozen, P9058-P9060
multiple donor, pooled, frozen, P9023
protein fraction, P9048
single donor, fresh frozen, P9017
**Plastazote**, L3002, L3252, L3253, L3265, L5654-L5658
**Plaster**
bandages
Orthoflex Elastic Plaster Bandages, A4580
Specialist Plaster Bandages, A4580
Genmould Creamy Plaster, A4580
Specialist J-Splint Plaster Roll Immobilizer, A4580
Specialist Plaster Roll Immobilizer, A4580
Specialist Plaster Splints, A4580
**Platelet**
concentrate, each unit, P9019
rich plasma, each unit, P9020
**Platelets**, P9032-P9040, P9052-P9053
**Platform attachment**
forearm crutch, E0153
walker, E0154
**Platform, for home blood glucose monitor**, A4255
**Platinol**, J9060, J9062
**Plenaxis**, J0128
**Pleural catheter**, A7042
drainage bottle, A7043
**Plicamycin**, J9270
**Plumbing, for home ESRD equipment**, A4870

**PMD**
See power mobility device
**Pneumatic**
appliance, E0655-E0673, L4350-L4380
compressor, E0650-E0652, E0675
splint, L4350-L4380
tire, wheelchair, E2211, E2214
insert, E2213
tube, E2212, E2215
**Pneumatic nebulizer**
administration set
small volume
filtered, A7006
non-filtered, A7003
non-disposable, A7005
small volume, disposable, A7004
**Pneumococcal conjugate vaccine**, S0195
**Polaris**, E0601
**Polaris Lt**, E0601
**Polocaine**, J0670
**Polycillin-N**, J0290
**Polycose, enteral nutrition**
liquid, B4155
powder, B4155
**Poly-l-lactic acid**, S0196
**Pontic**
indirect resin based composite, D6205
titanium, D6214
**Poor blood, each unit**, P9016
**Porfimer**, J9600
**Pork insulin**, J1815, J1817
**Port**
indwelling, C1788
**Portable**
equipment transfer, R0070-R0076
hemodialyzer system, E1635
nebulizer, E0570
x-ray equipment, Q0092
**Portagen Powder, enteral nutrition**, B4150
**Posey restraints**, E0700
**Positive airway pressure device supply**, A7046
**Post and core, dental**, D2952-D2954, D2957, D6970-D6972, D6976-D6977
**Post-coital examination**, Q0115
**Postdischarge services**
LVRS surgery, G0305
**Post removal, dental**, D2955
**Postural drainage board**, E0606
**Potassium**
chloride, J3480
hydroxide (KOH) preparation, Q0112
**Pouch**
Active Life convex one-piece urostomy, A4421
closed, A4387, A5052
drainable, A4388-A4389, A5061
fecal collection, A4330
Little Ones Sur-fit mini, A5054

Index

Recement — Ropivacaine hydrochloride

**Recement** — *continued*
retainers, D8693
**Recombinant**
ankle splints, L4392-L4398
DNA insulin, J1815, J1817
**Recombinate**, J7192
**Reconstruction**
breast, S2066-S2067
**Red blood cells**, P9038-P9040
**Red blood cells, each unit**, P9021, P9022
**Red Dot**
crutches, E0114
folding walkers, E0135, E0143
**Redisol**, J3420
**Regitine**, J2760
**Reglan**, J2765
**Regular insulin**, J1815
**Regulator, oxygen**, E1353
**Rehabilitation**
program, H2001
service
juveniles, H2033
mental health clubhouse, H2030-H2031
psychosocial, H2017-H2018
social work and psychological, G0409
substance abuse, H2034-H2036
supported employment, H2023-H2024
vestibular, S9476
**Reimplantation, dental**
accidentally evulsed, D7270
intentional, D3470
**Relefact TRH**, J2725
**Relenza**, G9018
**Remicade**, J1745
**Removal**
applicator, breast, C9726
fixed space maintainer, D1555
**RemRes**, E0601
**REMStar**, E0601
**Renacidin**, Q2004
**RenAmin, parenteral nutrition**, B5000
**Renu, enteral nutrition**, B4150
**ReoPro, TRH**, J0130
**Repair**
contract, ERSD, A4890
dental, D2980, D3351-D3353, D5510-D5630, D6090, D6980, D7852, D7955
durable medical equipment, E1340
hearing aid, V5014, V5336
hernia
diphragmatic
fetus, S2400
laparoscopy
home dialysis equipment, A4890
occlusal guard, dental, D9942
orthotic, L4000-L4130
prosthetic, L7500, L7510, L7520
skilled technical, E1340
**Replacement**
battery, A4233-A4236, A4630
ear pulse generator, A4638

**Replacement** — *continued*
battery — *continued*
external infusion pump, K0601-K0605
handgrip for cane, crutch, walker, A4636
implant/abutment prosthesis, D6091
ostomy filters, A4421
sleeve, intermittent limb compression device, A4600
tip for cane, crutch, walker, A4637
underarm pad for crutch, A4635
**Repositioning device, mandibular**, S8262
**Rep-Pred**
40, J1030
80, J1040
**ResCap headgear**, A7035
**Reservoir**
metered dose inhaler, A4627
**Residential care**, T2032-T2033
**Resin dental restoration**, D2330-D2394
**Resipiradyne II Plus pulmonary function/ventilation monitor**, E0450
**ResMed Sb Elite**, E0601
**RespiGam**, J1565
**Respiratory syncytial virus immune globulin**, J1565
**Respiratory therapy**, G0237-G0238
**Respite care**, T1005
in home, S9125
not in home, H0045
**Restorations, dental**
amalgam, D2140-D2161
gold foil, D2410-D2430
inlay/onlay, D2510-D2664, D6600-D6615
resin-based composite, D2330-D2394
**Restorative**
dental work, D2330-D2999
injection
face, S0196
**Restorative injection, face**, S0196
**Restraint**
any type, E0710
belts
Posey, E0700
Secure-All, E0700
Bite disposable jaw locks, E0700
body holders
Houdini security suit, E0700
Quick Release, one piece, E0700
Secure-All, one piece, E0700
System2 zippered, E0700
UltraCare vest-style with sleeves, E0700
hand
Secure-All finger control mit, E0700
limb holders
Posey, E0700
Quick Release, E0700

**Restraint** — *continued*
limb holders — *continued*
Secure-All, E0700
pelvic
Secure-All, E0700
**Resurfacing**
total hip, S2118
**Retail therapy item, miscellaneous**, T1999
**Retainers, dental**
fixed partial denture, D6545-D6792
implant/abutment supported, D6068-D6077
orthodontic, D8680
**Retinal**
device, intraoperative, C1784
exam for diabetes, S3000
tamponade, C1814
telescreening, S0625
**Retinoblastoma, genetic test**, S3841
**Retrieval device, insertable**, C1773
**Retrograde dental filling**, D3430
**Rhesonativ**, J2790
**Rheumatrex**, J8610
**RhoGAM**, J2790
**Rho(D) immune globulin, human**, J2790, J2792
minidose, J2788
**Rib belt**
thoracic, L0210, L0220
Don-Joy, L0210
**Rice ankle splint**, L1904
**Richfoam convoluted&flat overlays**, E0199
**Ride Lite 200, Ride Lite 9000, manual wheelchair**, K0004
**Ridge augmentation/sinus lift, dental**, D7950
**Rimantadine HCl**, G9020, G9036
**Rimso**, J1212
**Ringer's lactate infusion**, J7120
**Ring, ostomy**, A4404
**Risperidone, long acting**, J2794
**Rituxan**, J9310
**Rituximab**, J9310
**Riveton, foot orthotic**, L3140, L3150
**RN services**, T1002
**Road Savage power wheelchair**, K0011
**Road Warrior power wheelchair**, K0011
**Robaxin**, J2800
**Robin-Aids, prosthesis**
partial hand, L6000-L6020
**Robotic surgical system**, S2900
**Rocephin**, J0696
**Rocking bed**, E0462
**Rollabout chair**, E1031
**Root canal therapy**, D3310-D3353
**Root planning and scaling, dental**, D4341
**Root removal, dental**, D7140, D7250
**Root resection/amputation, dental**, D3450
**Ropivacaine hydrochloride**, J2795

**Yttrium 90**
  ibritumomab tiuxeton, A9543
  microsphere
    brachytherapy, C2616
    procedure, S2095

## Z

**Zanamivir**, G9018, G9034
**Zantac**, J2780
**Zenapax**, J7513

**Zetran**, J3360
**Zidovudine**, J3485
**ZIFT**, S4014
**Zinacef**, J0697
**Zinecard**, J1190
**Ziprasidone mesylate**, J3486
**Zithromax**
  I.V., J0456
  oral, Q0144
**Zofran**, J2405
  oral, S0181

**Zoladex**, J9202
**Zoledronic acid**, J3487
**Zolicef**, J0690
**Zosyn**, J2543
**Zygomatic arch, fracture treatment**, D7650, D7660, D7750, D7760
**Zyprexa**, S0166
**Zyvok**, J2020

## TRANSPORTATION SERVICES INCLUDING AMBULANCE A0000-A0999

This code range includes ground and air ambulance, nonemergency transportation (taxi, bus, automobile, wheelchair van), and ancillary transportation-related fees.

HCPCS Level II codes for ambulance services must be reported with modifiers that indicate pick-up origins and destinations. The modifier describing the arrangement (QM, QN) is listed first. The modifiers describing the origin and destination are listed second. Origin and destination modifiers are created by combining two alpha characters from the following list. Each alpha character, with the exception of X, represents either an origin or a destination. Each pair of alpha characters creates one modifier. The first position represents the origin and the second the destination. The modifiers most commonly used are:

**D**    Diagnostic or therapeutic site other than "P" or "H" when these are used as origin codes

**E**    Residential, domiciliary, custodial facility (other than 1819 facility)

**G**    Hospital-based ESRD facility

**H**    Hospital

**I**    Site of transfer (e.g., airport or helicopter pad) between modes of ambulance transport

**J**    Free standing ESRD facility

**N**    Skilled nursing facility (SNF)

**P**    Physician's office

**R**    Residence

**S**    Scene of accident or acute event

**X**    Intermediate stop at physician's office on way to hospital (destination code only)

Note: Modifier X can only be used as a destination code in the second position of a modifier.

See S0215. For Medicaid, see T codes and T modifiers.

| | | |
|---|---|---|
| E | **A0021** | **Ambulance service, outside state per mile, transport (Medicaid only)** |
| E | **A0080** | **Nonemergency transportation, per mile — vehicle provided by volunteer (individual or organization), with no vested interest** |
| E | **A0090** | **Nonemergency transportation, per mile — vehicle provided by individual (family member, self, neighbor) with vested interest** |
| E | **A0100** | **Nonemergency transportation; taxi** |
| E | **A0110** | **Nonemergency transportation and bus, intra- or interstate carrier** |
| E | **A0120** | **Nonemergency transportation: mini-bus, mountain area transports, or other transportation systems** |
| E | **A0130** | **Nonemergency transportation: wheelchair van** |
| E | **A0140** | **Nonemergency transportation and air travel (private or commercial) intra- or interstate** |
| E | **A0160** | **Nonemergency transportation: per mile — caseworker or social worker** |
| E | **A0170** | **Transportation ancillary: parking fees, tolls, other** |
| E | **A0180** | **Nonemergency transportation: ancillary: lodging, recipient** |
| E | **A0190** | **Nonemergency transportation: ancillary: meals, recipient** |
| E | **A0200** | **Nonemergency transportation: ancillary: lodging, escort** |
| E | **A0210** | **Nonemergency transportation: ancillary: meals, escort** |

**Transportation Services Including Ambulance**

**A0225 — A0426**

| | | | |
|---|---|---|---|
| E | | A0225 | Ambulance service, neonatal transport, base rate, emergency transport, one way |

MED: 100-4,1,10.1.4.1

| | | | |
|---|---|---|---|
| E | ☑ | A0380 | BLS mileage (per mile)<br>See code(s): A0425 |

MED: 100-2,6,10; 100-4,1,10.1.4.1

| | | |
|---|---|---|
| A | A0382 | BLS routine disposable supplies |

| | | |
|---|---|---|
| A | A0384 | BLS specialized service disposable supplies; defibrillation (used by ALS ambulances and BLS ambulances in jurisdictions where defibrillation is permitted in BLS ambulances) |

| | | | |
|---|---|---|---|
| E | ☑ | A0390 | ALS mileage (per mile)<br>See code(s): A0425 |

MED: 100-4,1,10.1.4.1

| | | |
|---|---|---|
| A | A0392 | ALS specialized service disposable supplies; defibrillation (to be used only in jurisdictions where defibrillation cannot be performed in BLS ambulances) |

| | | |
|---|---|---|
| A | A0394 | ALS specialized service disposable supplies; IV drug therapy |

| | | |
|---|---|---|
| A | A0396 | ALS specialized service disposable supplies; esophageal intubation |

| | | |
|---|---|---|
| A | A0398 | ALS routine disposable supplies |

### WAITING TIME TABLE

| Units | Time |
|---|---|
| 1 | 1/2 to 1 hr. |
| 2 | 1 to 1-1/2 hrs. |
| 3 | 1-1/2 to 2 hrs. |
| 4 | 2 to 2-1/2 hrs. |
| 5 | 2-1/2 to 3 hrs. |
| 6 | 3 to 3-1/2 hrs. |
| 7 | 3-1/2 to 4 hrs. |
| 8 | 4 to 4-1/2 hrs. |
| 9 | 4-1/2 to 5 hrs. |
| 10 | 5 to 5-1/2 hrs. |

| | | |
|---|---|---|
| A | A0420 | Ambulance waiting time (ALS or BLS), one-half (1/2) hour increments ⊘ |

| | | |
|---|---|---|
| A | A0422 | Ambulance (ALS or BLS) oxygen and oxygen supplies, life sustaining situation ⊘ |

| | | |
|---|---|---|
| A | A0424 | Extra ambulance attendant, ground (ALS or BLS) or air (fixed or rotary winged); (requires medical review) ⊘<br>Pertinent documentation to evaluate medical appropriateness should be included when this code is reported. |

| | | |
|---|---|---|
| A | A0425 | Ground mileage, per statute mile |

MED: 100-2,6,10; 100-2,10,20; 100-4,1,10.1.4.1

| | | |
|---|---|---|
| A | A0426 | Ambulance service, advanced life support, nonemergency transport, level 1 (ALS 1) |

MED: 100-2,6,10; 100-2,10,20; 100-4,1,10.1.4.1

| | | |
|---|---|---|
| Ⓐ | **A0427** | Ambulance service, advanced life support, emergency transport, level 1 (ALS 1 — emergency) |
| | | MED: 100-2,6,10; 100-2,10,20; 100-4,1,10.1.4.1 |
| Ⓐ | **A0428** | Ambulance service, basic life support, nonemergency transport, (BLS) |
| | | MED: 100-2,6,10; 100-2,10,20; 100-4,1,10.1.4.1 |
| Ⓐ | **A0429** | Ambulance service, basic life support, emergency transport (BLS, emergency) |
| | | MED: 100-2,6,10; 100-2,10,20; 100-4,1,10.1.4.1 |
| Ⓐ | **A0430** | Ambulance service, conventional air services, transport, one way (fixed wing) |
| | | MED: 100-2,6,10; 100-2,10,20; 100-4,1,10.1.4.1 |
| Ⓐ | **A0431** | Ambulance service, conventional air services, transport, one way (rotary wing) |
| | | MED: 100-2,6,10; 100-2,10,20; 100-4,1,10.1.4.1 |
| Ⓐ | **A0432** | Paramedic intercept (PI), rural area, transport furnished by a volunteer ambulance company which is prohibited by state law from billing third-party payers |
| | | MED: 100-2,10,20 |
| Ⓐ | **A0433** | Advanced life support, level 2 (ALS 2) |
| | | MED: 100-2,10,20 |
| Ⓐ | **A0434** | Specialty care transport (SCT) |
| | | MED: 100-2,10,20 |
| Ⓐ | **A0435** | Fixed wing air mileage, per statute mile |
| | | MED: 100-2,10,20 |
| Ⓐ | **A0436** | Rotary wing air mileage, per statute mile |
| | | MED: 100-2,10,20 |
| Ⓔ | **A0888** | Noncovered ambulance mileage, per mile (e.g., for miles traveled beyond closest appropriate facility) |
| | | MED: 100-2,10,20 |
| Ⓔ | **A0998** | Ambulance response and treatment, no transport |
| Ⓐ | **A0999** | Unlisted ambulance service ⊘ |
| | | Determine if an alternative HCPCS Level II or a CPT code better describes the service being reported. This code should be used only if a more specific code is unavailable. |
| | | MED: 100-2,10,20; 100-4,1,10.1.4.1 |

## MEDICAL AND SURGICAL SUPPLIES A4000-A8999

This section covers a wide variety of medical, surgical, and some durable medical equipment (DME) related supplies and accessories. DME-related supplies, accessories, maintenance, and repair required to ensure the proper functioning of this equipment is generally covered by Medicare under the prosthetic devices provision.

## MISCELLANEOUS SUPPLIES

These codes are to be filed with the Medicare local contractor, unless otherwise noted (if incident to a physicians' services, not separately billable) unless they represent incidental services or supplies which are referred to the DME Medicare Administrative Contractor (DME MAC).

| | | | |
|---|---|---|---|
| Ⓔ | ☑ | **A4206** | Syringe with needle, sterile, 1 cc or less, each |
| Ⓔ | ☑ | **A4207** | Syringe with needle, sterile 2 cc, each |

---

☑ Quantity Alert   ● New Code   ○ Recycled/Reinstated   ▲ Revised Code   ⅙ DMEPOS Paid   ⊘ SNF Excluded

**Medical and Surgical Supplies**

**A4208 — A4234**

| | | | |
|---|---|---|---|
| E ☑ | A4208 | Syringe with needle, sterile 3 cc, each | |
| E ☑ | A4209 | Syringe with needle, sterile 5 cc or greater, each | |
| E ☑ | A4210 | Needle-free injection device, each | |

Sometimes covered by commercial payers with preauthorization and physician letter stating need (e.g., for insulin injection in young children).

MED: 100-3,280.1

E    A4211    Supplies for self-administered injections

When a drug that is usually injected by the patient (e.g., insulin or calcitonin) is injected by the physician, it is excluded from Medicare coverage unless administered in an emergency situation (e.g., diabetic coma).

MED: 100-2,15,50

| | | | |
|---|---|---|---|
| B | A4212 | Noncoring needle or stylet with or without catheter | |
| E | A4213 | Syringe, sterile, 20 cc or greater, each | |
| E | A4215 | Needle, sterile, any size, each | |
| A ☑ | A4216 | Sterile water, saline and/or dextrose, diluent/flush, 10 ml | ठ |

MED: 100-2,15,50

A ☑    A4217    Sterile water/saline, 500 ml    ठ

MED: 100-2,15,50

N    A4218    Sterile saline or water, metered dose dispenser, 10 ml    🔟

N    A4220    Refill kit for implantable infusion pump    🔟

Implantable infusion pumps are covered by Medicare for 5-FUdR therapy for unresected liver or colorectal cancer and for opioid drug therapy for intractable pain. They are not covered by Medicare for heparin therapy for thromboembolic disease. Report drugs separately.

MED: 100-3,280.14

Y    A4221    Supplies for maintenance of drug infusion catheter, per week (list drug separately)    ठ

Y    A4222    Infusion supplies for external drug infusion pump, per cassette or bag (list drugs separately)    ठ

E ☑    A4223    Infusion supplies not used with external infusion pump, per cassette or bag (list drugs separately)

N ☑    A4230    Infusion set for external insulin pump, nonneedle cannula type

Covered by some commercial payers as ongoing supply to preauthorized pump.

MED: 100-3,280.14

N ☑    A4231    Infusion set for external insulin pump, needle type

Covered by some commercial payers as ongoing supply to preauthorized pump.

MED: 100-3,280.14

E ☑    A4232    Syringe with needle for external insulin pump, sterile, 3 cc

Covered by some commercial payers as ongoing supply to preauthorized pump.

MED: 100-3,280.14

Y ☑    A4233    Replacement battery, alkaline (other than J cell), for use with medically necessary home blood glucose monitor owned by patient, each

Y ☑    A4234    Replacement battery, alkaline, J cell, for use with medically necessary home blood glucose monitor owned by patient, each

Y ☑ **A4235** Replacement battery, lithium, for use with medically necessary home blood glucose monitor owned by patient, each

Y ☑ **A4236** Replacement battery, silver oxide, for use with medically necessary home blood glucose monitor owned by patient, each

E ☑ **A4244** Alcohol or peroxide, per pint

E ☑ **A4245** Alcohol wipes, per box

E ☑ **A4246** Betadine or pHisoHex solution, per pint

E ☑ **A4247** Betadine or iodine swabs/wipes, per box

N ☑ **A4248** Chlorhexidine containing antiseptic, 1 ml ▥

Reference chart

— pH
— Protein
— Glucose
— Ketones
— Bilirubin
— Hemoglobin

Dipstick urinalysis: The strip is dipped and color-coded squares are read at timed intervals (e.g., pH immediately; ketones at 15 sec., etc.). Results are compared against a reference chart

Tablet reagents turn specific colors when urine droplets are placed on them

E ☑ **A4250** Urine test or reagent strips or tablets (100 tablets or strips)
MED: 100-2,15,110

E ☑ **A4252** Blood ketone test or reagent strip, each

Y ☑ **A4253** Blood glucose test or reagent strips for home blood glucose monitor, per 50 strips &
Medicare covers glucose strips for diabetic patients using home glucose monitoring devices prescribed by their physicians.
MED: 100-3,40.2

Y ☑ **A4255** Platforms for home blood glucose monitor, 50 per box &
Some Medicare contractors cover monitor platforms for diabetic patients using home glucose monitoring devices prescribed by their physicians. Some commercial payers also provide this coverage to noninsulin dependent diabetics.
MED: 100-3,40.2

Y **A4256** Normal, low, and high calibrator solution/chips &
Some Medicare contractors cover calibration solutions or chips for diabetic patients using home glucose monitoring devices prescribed by their physicians. Some commercial payers also provide this coverage to noninsulin dependent diabetics.
MED: 100-3,40.2

Y ☑ **A4257** Replacement lens shield cartridge for use with laser skin piercing device, each &

Y ☑ **A4258** Spring-powered device for lancet, each &
Some Medicare contractors cover lancing devices for diabetic patients using home glucose monitoring devices prescribed by their physicians. Medicare jurisdiction: DME regional contractor. Some commercial payers also provide this coverage to noninsulin dependent diabetics.
MED: 100-3,40.2

---

☑ Quantity Alert ● New Code ○ Recycled/Reinstated ▲ Revised Code & DMEPOS Paid ⊘ SNF Excluded

**Medical and Surgical Supplies**

**A4259 — A4290**

| Y ☑ | **A4259** | Lancets, per box of 100   &#9855; |
| | | Medicare covers lancets for diabetic patients using home glucose monitoring devices prescribed by their physicians. Medicare jurisdiction: DME regional contractor. Some commercial payers also provide this coverage to noninsulin dependent diabetics. |
| | | MED: 100-3,40.2 |
| E | **A4261** | Cervical cap for contraceptive use   ♀ |
| N ☑ | **A4262** | Temporary, absorbable lacrimal duct implant, each   ▣ |
| | | Always report concurrent to the implant procedure. |
| N ☑ | **A4263** | Permanent, long-term, nondissolvable lacrimal duct implant, each   ▣ |
| | | Always report concurrent to the implant procedure. |
| Y ☑ | **A4265** | Paraffin, per pound   &#9855; |
| | | MED: 100-3,280.1 |
| E | **A4266** | Diaphragm for contraceptive use   ♀ |
| E ☑ | **A4267** | Contraceptive supply, condom, male, each   ♂ |
| E ☑ | **A4268** | Contraceptive supply, condom, female, each   ♀ |
| E ☑ | **A4269** | Contraceptive supply, spermicide (e.g., foam, gel), each   ♀ |
| N ☑ | **A4270** | Disposable endoscope sheath, each   ▣ |

Two part prosthesis

Adhesive skin support (A4280)

Any of several breast prostheses fits over skin support

| A ☑ | **A4280** | Adhesive skin support attachment for use with external breast prosthesis, each   ▣♀&#9855; |
| E | **A4281** | Tubing for breast pump, replacement   Ⓜ♀ |
| E | **A4282** | Adapter for breast pump, replacement   Ⓜ♀ |
| E | **A4283** | Cap for breast pump bottle, replacement   Ⓜ♀ |
| E | **A4284** | Breast shield and splash protector for use with breast pump, replacement   Ⓜ♀ |
| E | **A4285** | Polycarbonate bottle for use with breast pump, replacement   Ⓜ♀ |
| E | **A4286** | Locking ring for breast pump, replacement   Ⓜ♀ |
| B ☑ | **A4290** | Sacral nerve stimulation test lead, each |
| | | AHA: 1Q,'02,9 |

## VASCULAR CATHETERS

| Special Coverage Instructions | Noncovered by Medicare | Carrier Discretion |

Ⓜ Maternity Edit   &#9651; Age Edit   ▣ PQRI   Ⓐ-Ⓨ OPPS Status   **2009 HCPCS**

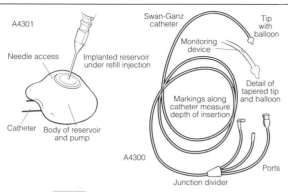

- A4301
- Needle access
- Implanted reservoir under refill injection
- Catheter
- Body of reservoir and pump
- A4300
- Junction divider
- Swan-Ganz catheter
- Monitoring device
- Tip with balloon
- Detail of tapered tip and balloon
- Markings along catheter measure depth of insertion
- Ports

**A4300** Implantable access catheter, (e.g., venous, arterial, epidural subarachnoid, or peritoneal, etc.) external access

MED: 100-2,15,120

**A4301** Implantable access total catheter, port/reservoir (e.g., venous, arterial, epidural, subarachnoid, peritoneal, etc.)

☑ **A4305** Disposable drug delivery system, flow rate of 50 ml or greater per hour

**A4306** Disposable drug delivery system, flow rate of less than 50 ml per hour

## INCONTINENCE APPLIANCES AND CARE SUPPLIES

Covered by Medicare when the medical record indicates incontinence is permanent, or of long and indefinite duration.

**A4310** Insertion tray without drainage bag and without catheter (accessories only) ♿

MED: 100-2,15,120

**A4311** Insertion tray without drainage bag with indwelling catheter, Foley type, 2-way latex with coating (Teflon, silicone, silicone elastomer or hydrophilic, etc.) ♿

MED: 100-2,15,120

**A4312** Insertion tray without drainage bag with indwelling catheter, Foley type, 2-way, all silicone ♿

MED: 100-2,15,120

**A4313** Insertion tray without drainage bag with indwelling catheter, Foley type, 3-way, for continuous irrigation ♿

MED: 100-2,15,120

**A4314** Insertion tray with drainage bag with indwelling catheter, Foley type, 2-way latex with coating (Teflon, silicone, silicone elastomer or hydrophilic, etc.) ♿

MED: 100-2,15,120

**A4315** Insertion tray with drainage bag with indwelling catheter, Foley type, 2-way, all silicone ♿

MED: 100-2,15,120

**A4316** Insertion tray with drainage bag with indwelling catheter, Foley type, 3-way, for continuous irrigation ♿

MED: 100-2,15,120

**A4320** Irrigation tray with bulb or piston syringe, any purpose ♿

MED: 100-2,15,120

---

☑ Quantity Alert   ● New Code   ○ Recycled/Reinstated   ▲ Revised Code   ♿ DMEPOS Paid   ⊘ SNF Excluded

A    **A4321**    Therapeutic agent for urinary catheter irrigation    &
MED: 100-2,15,120

A ☑    **A4322**    Irrigation syringe, bulb or piston, each    &
MED: 100-2,15,120

A ☑    **A4326**    Male external catheter with integral collection chamber, any type, each    ♂ &
MED: 100-2,15,120

A ☑    **A4327**    Female external urinary collection device; meatal cup, each    ♀ &
MED: 100-2,15,120

A ☑    **A4328**    Female external urinary collection device; pouch, each    ♀ &
MED: 100-2,15,120

A ☑    **A4330**    Perianal fecal collection pouch with adhesive, each    &
MED: 100-2,15,120

A ☑    **A4331**    Extension drainage tubing, any type, any length, with connector/adaptor, for use with urinary leg bag or urostomy pouch, each    &
MED: 100-2,15,120

A ☑    **A4332**    Lubricant, individual sterile packet, each    &
MED: 100-2,15,120

A ☑    **A4333**    Urinary catheter anchoring device, adhesive skin attachment, each    &
MED: 100-2,15,120

A ☑    **A4334**    Urinary catheter anchoring device, leg strap, each    &
MED: 100-2,15,120

A    **A4335**    Incontinence supply; miscellaneous
MED: 100-2,15,120

A ☑    **A4338**    Indwelling catheter; Foley type, 2-way latex with coating (Teflon, silicone, silicone elastomer, or hydrophilic, etc.), each    &
MED: 100-2,15,120

A ☑    **A4340**    Indwelling catheter; specialty type, (e.g., Coude, mushroom, wing, etc.), each    &
MED: 100-2,15,120

A ☑    **A4344**    Indwelling catheter, Foley type, 2-way, all silicone, each    &
MED: 100-2,15,120

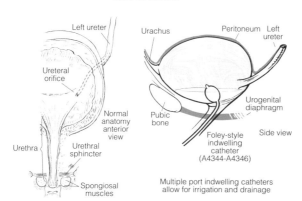

Left ureter
Ureteral orifice
Urethra
Urethral sphincter
Spongiosal muscles
Normal anatomy anterior view

Urachus
Peritoneum
Left ureter
Pubic bone
Urogenital diaphragm
Foley-style indwelling catheter (A4344-A4346)
Side view

Multiple port indwelling catheters allow for irrigation and drainage

A ☑    **A4346**    Indwelling catheter; Foley type, 3-way for continuous irrigation, each &
MED: 100-2,15,120

---

Ⓐ ☑ **A4349** Male external catheter, with or without adhesive, disposable, each ♂
MED: 100-2,15,120

Ⓐ ☑ **A4351** Intermittent urinary catheter; straight tip, with or without coating (Teflon, silicone, silicone elastomer, or hydrophilic, etc.), each &
MED: 100-2,15,120

Ⓐ ☑ **A4352** Intermittent urinary catheter; Coude (curved) tip, with or without coating (Teflon, silicone, silicone elastomeric, or hydrophilic, etc.), each &
MED: 100-2,15,120

Ⓐ **A4353** Intermittent urinary catheter, with insertion supplies &
MED: 100-2,15,120

Ⓐ **A4354** Insertion tray with drainage bag but without catheter &
MED: 100-2,15,120

Ⓐ ☑ **A4355** Irrigation tubing set for continuous bladder irrigation through a 3-way indwelling Foley catheter, each &
MED: 100-2,15,120

## EXTERNAL URINARY SUPPLIES

Ⓐ ☑ **A4356** External urethral clamp or compression device (not to be used for catheter clamp), each &
MED: 100-2,15,120

Ⓐ ☑ **A4357** Bedside drainage bag, day or night, with or without antireflux device, with or without tube, each &
MED: 100-2,15,120

Ⓐ ☑ **A4358** Urinary drainage bag, leg or abdomen, vinyl, with or without tube, with straps, each &
MED: 100-2,15,120

## OSTOMY SUPPLIES

Ⓐ ☑ **A4361** Ostomy faceplate, each &
MED: 100-2,15,120

Ⓐ ☑ **A4362** Skin barrier; solid, 4 x 4 or equivalent; each &
See code(s) A4461 or A4463

Ⓐ **A4363** Ostomy clamp, any type, replacement only, each &

Ⓐ ☑ **A4364** Adhesive, liquid or equal, any type, per oz &
MED: 100-2,15,120

Ⓐ ☑ **A4365** Adhesive remover wipes, any type, per 50 &
MED: 100-2,15,120

Ⓐ ☑ **A4366** Ostomy vent, any type, each &

Ⓐ ☑ **A4367** Ostomy belt, each &
MED: 100-2,15,120

Ⓐ ☑ **A4368** Ostomy filter, any type, each &

Ⓐ ☑ **A4369** Ostomy skin barrier, liquid (spray, brush, etc.), per oz &
MED: 100-2,15,120

Ⓐ ☑ **A4371** Ostomy skin barrier, powder, per oz &
MED: 100-2,15,120

A △ ☑　**A4372**　Ostomy skin barrier, solid 4 x 4 or equivalent, standard wear, with built-in convexity, each　　&
MED: 100-2,15,120

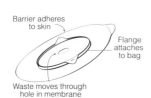

Barrier adheres to skin

Flange attaches to bag

Waste moves through hole in membrane

Faceplate flange and skin barrier combination (A4373)

A △ ☑　**A4373**　Ostomy skin barrier, with flange (solid, flexible or accordian), with built-in convexity, any size, each　　&
MED: 100-2,15,120

A △ ☑　**A4375**　Ostomy pouch, drainable, with faceplate attached, plastic, each　　&
MED: 100-2,15,120

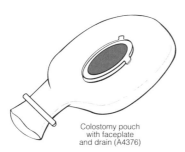

Colostomy pouch with faceplate and drain (A4376)

A △ ☑　**A4376**　Ostomy pouch, drainable, with faceplate attached, rubber, each　　&
MED: 100-2,15,120

A △ ☑　**A4377**　Ostomy pouch, drainable, for use on faceplate, plastic, each　　&
MED: 100-2,15,120

A △ ☑　**A4378**　Ostomy pouch, drainable, for use on faceplate, rubber, each　　&
MED: 100-2,15,120

A △ ☑　**A4379**　Ostomy pouch, urinary, with faceplate attached, plastic, each　　&
MED: 100-2,15,120

A △ ☑　**A4380**　Ostomy pouch, urinary, with faceplate attached, rubber, each　　&
MED: 100-2,15,120

A △ ☑　**A4381**　Ostomy pouch, urinary, for use on faceplate, plastic, each　　&
MED: 100-2,15,120

A △ ☑　**A4382**　Ostomy pouch, urinary, for use on faceplate, heavy plastic, each　　&
MED: 100-2,15,120

A △ ☑　**A4383**　Ostomy pouch, urinary, for use on faceplate, rubber, each　　&
MED: 100-2,15,120

A △ ☑　**A4384**　Ostomy faceplate equivalent, silicone ring, each　　&
MED: 100-2,15,120

Ⓐ ☑ **A4385**   Ostomy skin barrier, solid 4 x 4 or equivalent, extended wear, without built-in convexity, each   ♿
MED: 100-2,15,120

Ⓐ ☑ **A4387**   Ostomy pouch, closed, with barrier attached, with built-in convexity (1 piece), each   ♿
MED: 100-2,15,120

Ⓐ ☑ **A4388**   Ostomy pouch, drainable, with extended wear barrier attached, (1 piece), each   ♿
MED: 100-2,15,120

Ⓐ ☑ **A4389**   Ostomy pouch, drainable, with barrier attached, with built-in convexity (1 piece), each   ♿
MED: 100-2,15,120

Ⓐ ☑ **A4390**   Ostomy pouch, drainable, with extended wear barrier attached, with built-in convexity (1 piece), each   ♿
MED: 100-2,15,120

Ⓐ ☑ **A4391**   Ostomy pouch, urinary, with extended wear barrier attached (1 piece), each   ♿
MED: 100-2,15,120

Ⓐ ☑ **A4392**   Ostomy pouch, urinary, with standard wear barrier attached, with built-in convexity (1 piece), each   ♿
MED: 100-2,15,120

Ⓐ ☑ **A4393**   Ostomy pouch, urinary, with extended wear barrier attached, with built-in convexity (1 piece), each   ♿
MED: 100-2,15,120

Ⓐ ☑ **A4394**   Ostomy deodorant, with or without lubricant, for use in ostomy pouch, per fl oz   ♿
MED: 100-2,15,120

Ⓐ ☑ **A4395**   Ostomy deodorant for use in ostomy pouch, solid, per tablet   ♿
MED: 100-2,15,120

Ⓐ   **A4396**   Ostomy belt with peristomal hernia support   ♿
MED: 100-2,15,120

Ⓐ ☑ **A4397**   Irrigation supply; sleeve, each   ♿
MED: 100-2,15,120

Ⓐ ☑ **A4398**   Ostomy irrigation supply; bag, each   ♿
MED: 100-2,15,120

Ⓐ   **A4399**   Ostomy irrigation supply; cone/catheter, including brush   ♿
MED: 100-2,15,120

Ⓐ   **A4400**   Ostomy irrigation set   ♿
MED: 100-2,15,120

Ⓐ ☑ **A4402**   Lubricant, per oz   ♿
MED: 100-2,15,120

Ⓐ ☑ **A4404**   Ostomy ring, each   ♿
MED: 100-2,15,120

Ⓐ ☑ **A4405**   Ostomy skin barrier, nonpectin-based, paste, per oz   ♿
MED: 100-2,15,120

Ⓐ ☑ **A4406**   Ostomy skin barrier, pectin-based, paste, per oz   ♿
MED: 100-2,15,120

**Medical and Surgical Supplies**

**A4407 — A4424**

| | | | |
|---|---|---|---|
| A ☑ | A4407 | Ostomy skin barrier, with flange (solid, flexible, or accordion), extended wear, with built-in convexity, 4 x 4 in or smaller, each ♿ | |
| | | MED: 100-2,15,120 | |
| A ☑ | A4408 | Ostomy skin barrier, with flange (solid, flexible or accordion), extended wear, with built-in convexity, larger than 4 x 4 in, each ♿ | |
| | | MED: 100-2,15,120 | |
| A ☑ | A4409 | Ostomy skin barrier, with flange (solid, flexible or accordion), extended wear, without built-in convexity, 4 x 4 in or smaller, each ♿ | |
| | | MED: 100-2,15,120 | |
| A ☑ | A4410 | Ostomy skin barrier, with flange (solid, flexible or accordion), extended wear, without built-in convexity, larger than 4 x 4 in, each ♿ | |
| | | MED: 100-2,15,120 | |
| A ☑ | A4411 | Ostomy skin barrier, solid 4 x 4 or equivalent, extended wear, with built-in convexity, each | |
| A ☑ | A4412 | Ostomy pouch, drainable, high output, for use on a barrier with flange (2 piece system), without filter, each | |
| | | MED: 100-2,15,120 | |
| A ☑ | A4413 | Ostomy pouch, drainable, high output, for use on a barrier with flange (2-piece system), with filter, each ♿ | |
| | | MED: 100-2,15,120 | |
| A ☑ | A4414 | Ostomy skin barrier, with flange (solid, flexible or accordion), without built-in convexity, 4 x 4 in or smaller, each ♿ | |
| | | MED: 100-2,15,120 | |
| A ☑ | A4415 | Ostomy skin barrier, with flange (solid, flexible or accordion), without built-in convexity, larger than 4 x 4 in, each ♿ | |
| | | MED: 100-2,15,120 | |
| A ☑ | A4416 | Ostomy pouch, closed, with barrier attached, with filter (1 piece), each ♿ | |
| A ☑ | A4417 | Ostomy pouch, closed, with barrier attached, with built-in convexity, with filter (1 piece), each ♿ | |
| A ☑ | A4418 | Ostomy pouch, closed; without barrier attached, with filter (1 piece), each ♿ | |
| A ☑ | A4419 | Ostomy pouch, closed; for use on barrier with nonlocking flange, with filter (2 piece), each ♿ | |
| A ☑ | A4420 | Ostomy pouch, closed; for use on barrier with locking flange (2 piece), each ♿ | |
| E | A4421 | Ostomy supply; miscellaneous | |
| | | **Determine if an alternative HCPCS Level II or a CPT code better describes the service being reported. This code should be used only if a more specific code is unavailable.** | |
| | | MED: 100-2,15,120 | |
| A ☑ | A4422 | Ostomy absorbent material (sheet/pad/crystal packet) for use in ostomy pouch to thicken liquid stomal output, each ♿ | |
| | | MED: 100-2,15,120 | |
| A ☑ | A4423 | Ostomy pouch, closed; for use on barrier with locking flange, with filter (2 piece), each ♿ | |
| A ☑ | A4424 | Ostomy pouch, drainable, with barrier attached, with filter (1 piece), each ♿ | |

| A | ☑ | A4425 | Ostomy pouch, drainable; for use on barrier with nonlocking flange, with filter (2-piece system), each   &#9855; |
|---|---|-------|---|
| A | ☑ | A4426 | Ostomy pouch, drainable; for use on barrier with locking flange (2-piece system), each   &#9855; |
| A | ☑ | A4427 | Ostomy pouch, drainable; for use on barrier with locking flange, with filter (2-piece system), each   &#9855; |
| A | ☑ | A4428 | Ostomy pouch, urinary, with extended wear barrier attached, with faucet-type tap with valve (1 piece), each   &#9855; |
| A | ☑ | A4429 | Ostomy pouch, urinary, with barrier attached, with built-in convexity, with faucet-type tap with valve (1 piece), each   &#9855; |
| A | ☑ | A4430 | Ostomy pouch, urinary, with extended wear barrier attached, with built-in convexity, with faucet-type tap with valve (1 piece), each   &#9855; |
| A | ☑ | A4431 | Ostomy pouch, urinary; with barrier attached, with faucet-type tap with valve (1 piece), each   &#9855; |
| A | ☑ | A4432 | Ostomy pouch, urinary; for use on barrier with nonlocking flange, with faucet-type tap with valve (2 piece), each   &#9855; |
| A | ☑ | A4433 | Ostomy pouch, urinary; for use on barrier with locking flange (2 piece), each   &#9855; |
| A | ☑ | A4434 | Ostomy pouch, urinary; for use on barrier with locking flange, with faucet-type tap with valve (2 piece), each   &#9855; |

## ADDITIONAL MISCELLANEOUS SUPPLIES

| A | ☑ | A4450 | Tape, nonwaterproof, per 18 sq in   &#9855;<br>See also code A4452.<br>MED: 100-2,15,120 |
|---|---|-------|---|
| A | ☑ | A4452 | Tape, waterproof, per 18 sq in   &#9855;<br>See also code A4450.<br>MED: 100-2,15,120 |
| A | ☑ | A4455 | Adhesive remover or solvent (for tape, cement or other adhesive), per oz   &#9855;<br>MED: 100-2,15,120 |
| E | | A4458 | Enema bag with tubing, reusable |
| A | ☑ | A4461 | Surgical dressing holder, nonreusable, each · |
| A | ☑ | A4463 | Surgical dressing holder, reusable, each |
| N | | A4465 | Nonelastic binder for extremity |
| N | | A4470 | Gravlee jet washer<br>MED: 100-2,16,90; 100-3,230.5 |
| N | | A4480 | VABRA aspirator   ♀<br>MED: 100-2,16,90; 100-3,230.6 |
| A | ☑ | A4481 | Tracheostoma filter, any type, any size, each   &#9855;<br>MED: 100-2,15,120 |
| A | | A4483 | Moisture exchanger, disposable, for use with invasive mechanical ventilation   &#9855;<br>MED: 100-2,15,120 |
| E | ☑ | A4490 | Surgical stockings above knee length, each<br>MED: 100-2,15,100; 100-2,15,110; 100-3,280.1 |

E ☑ **A4495**  Surgical stockings thigh length, each
MED: 100-2,15,100; 100-2,15,110; 100-3,280.1

E ☑ **A4500**  Surgical stockings below knee length, each
MED: 100-2,15,100; 100-2,15,110; 100-3,280.1

E ☑ **A4510**  Surgical stockings full-length, each
MED: 100-2,15,100; 100-2,15,110; 100-3,280.1

E ☑ **A4520**  Incontinence garment, any type, (e.g., brief, diaper), each
MED: 100-3,280.1

B **A4550**  Surgical trays

E ☑ **A4554**  Disposable underpads, all sizes
MED: 100-2,15,120; 100-3,280.1

Y ☑ **A4556**  Electrodes (e.g., apnea monitor), per pair  &

Y ☑ **A4557**  Lead wires (e.g., apnea monitor), per pair  &

Y ☑ **A4558**  Conductive gel or paste, for use with electrical device (e.g., TENS, NMES), per oz  &

Y ☑ **A4559**  Coupling gel or paste, for use with ultrasound device, per oz  &

N **A4561**  Pessary, rubber, any type  △ ♀ &

N **A4562**  Pessary, nonrubber, any type  △ ♀ &
Medicare jurisdiction: DME regional contractor.

N **A4565**  Slings
Dressings applied by a physician are included as part of the professional service. Surgical dressings obtained by the patient to perform homecare as prescribed by the physician are covered.

E **A4570**  Splint
Dressings applied by a physician are included as part of the professional service.
MED: 100-2,6,10; 100-2,15,100; 100-4,4,240

E **A4575**  Topical hyperbaric oxygen chamber, disposable
MED: 100-3,20.29

E **A4580**  Cast supplies (e.g., plaster)
See Q4001-Q4048.
MED: 100-2,6,10; 100-2,15,100; 100-4,4,240

E **A4590**  Special casting material (e.g., fiberglass)
See Q4001-Q4048.
MED: 100-2,6,10; 100-2,15,100; 100-4,4,240

Y **A4595**  Electrical stimulator supplies, 2 lead, per month, (e.g., TENS, NMES)  &
MED: 100-3,160.13

Y ☑ **A4600**  Sleeve for intermittent limb compression device, replacement only, each  &

Y **A4601**  Lithium ion battery for nonprosthetic use, replacement  &

Y **A4604**  Tubing with integrated heating element for use with positive airway pressure device

Y ☑ **A4605**  Tracheal suction catheter, closed system, each

A **A4606**  Oxygen probe for use with oximeter device, replacement

Y ☑ **A4608**  Transtracheal oxygen catheter, each  &

---

## SUPPLIES FOR OXYGEN AND RELATED RESPIRATORY EQUIPMENT

| | | | |
|---|---|---|---|
| Y | | A4611 | Battery, heavy-duty; replacement for patient-owned ventilator 　&. |
| Y | | A4612 | Battery cables; replacement for patient-owned ventilator 　&. |
| Y | ☑ | A4613 | Battery charger; replacement for patient-owned ventilator 　&. |
| Y | | A4614 | Peak expiratory flow rate meter, hand held 　&. |
| Y | | A4615 | Cannula, nasal 　&. |

MED: 100-3,160.6; 100-4,20,100.2

| | | | |
|---|---|---|---|
| Y | ☑ | A4616 | Tubing (oxygen), per foot 　&. |

MED: 100-3,160.6; 100-4,20,100.2

| | | | |
|---|---|---|---|
| Y | | A4617 | Mouthpiece 　&. |

MED: 100-3,160.6; 100-4,20,100.2

| | | | |
|---|---|---|---|
| Y | | A4618 | Breathing circuits 　&. |

MED: 100-3,160.6; 100-4,20,100.2

| | | | |
|---|---|---|---|
| Y | | A4619 | Face tent 　&. |

MED: 100-3,160.6; 100-4,20,100.2

| | | | |
|---|---|---|---|
| Y | | A4620 | Variable concentration mask 　&. |

MED: 100-3,160.6; 100-4,20,100.2

| | | | |
|---|---|---|---|
| A | | A4623 | Tracheostomy, inner cannula 　&. |

MED: 100-2,15,120; 100-3,20.9

| | | | |
|---|---|---|---|
| Y | ☑ | A4624 | Tracheal suction catheter, any type other than closed system, each 　&. |
| A | | A4625 | Tracheostomy care kit for new tracheostomy 　&. |

MED: 100-2,15,120

| | | | |
|---|---|---|---|
| A | ☑ | A4626 | Tracheostomy cleaning brush, each 　&. |

MED: 100-2,15,120

| | | | |
|---|---|---|---|
| E | | A4627 | Spacer, bag or reservoir, with or without mask, for use with metered dose inhaler |

MED: 100-2,15,110

| | | | |
|---|---|---|---|
| Y | ☑ | A4628 | Oropharyngeal suction catheter, each 　&. |
| A | | A4629 | Tracheostomy care kit for established tracheostomy 　&. |

MED: 100-2,15,120

## SUPPLIES FOR OTHER DURABLE MEDICAL EQUIPMENT

| | | | |
|---|---|---|---|
| Y | ☑ | A4630 | Replacement batteries, medically necessary, transcutaneous electrical stimulator, owned by patient 　&. |

MED: 100-3,160.7

| | | | |
|---|---|---|---|
| Y | ☑ | A4633 | Replacement bulb/lamp for ultraviolet light therapy system, each 　&. |
| A | | A4634 | Replacement bulb for therapeutic light box, tabletop model |
| Y | ☑ | A4635 | Underarm pad, crutch, replacement, each 　&. |

MED: 100-3,280.1

| | | | |
|---|---|---|---|
| Y | ☑ | A4636 | Replacement, handgrip, cane, crutch, or walker, each 　&. |

MED: 100-3,280.1

| | | | |
|---|---|---|---|
| Y | ☑ | A4637 | Replacement, tip, cane, crutch, walker, each 　&. |

MED: 100-3,280.1

| | | | |
|---|---|---|---|
| Y | ☑ | A4638 | Replacement battery for patient-owned ear pulse generator, each 　&. |

Medical and Surgical Supplies

A4611 — A4638

| Y | ☑ | A4639 | Replacement pad for infrared heating pad system, each | 🔥 |
| Y | | A4640 | Replacement pad for use with medically necessary alternating pressure pad owned by patient | 🔥 |
| | | | MED: 100-3,280.1; 100-8,5,5.2.3 | |

## SUPPLIES FOR RADIOLOGIC PROCEDURES

| N | | A4641 | Radiopharmaceutical, diagnostic, not otherwise classified | Ⅲ |
| | | | MED: 100-4,13,60.3.1 | |
| N | ☑ | A4642 | Indium In-111 satumomab pendetide, diagnostic, per study dose, up to 6 millicuries | Ⅲ |
| | | | Use this code for Oncoscint. | |

## MISCELLANEOUS SUPPLIES

| N | ☑ | A4648 | Tissue marker, implantable, any type, each | Ⅲ |
| N | | A4649 | Surgical supply; miscellaneous | |
| | | | Determine if an alternative HCPCS Level II or a CPT code better describes the service being reported. This code should be used only if a more specific code is unavailable. | |
| N | ☑ | A4650 | Implantable radiation dosimeter, each | Ⅲ |
| A | ☑ | A4651 | Calibrated microcapillary tube, each | ⊘ |
| A | | A4652 | Microcapillary tube sealant | ⊘ |

## DIALYSIS SUPPLIES

| A | ☑ | A4653 | Peritoneal dialysis catheter anchoring device, belt, each | ⊘ |
| N | ☑ | A4657 | Syringe, with or without needle, each | ⊘ |
| N | | A4660 | Sphygmomanometer/blood pressure apparatus with cuff and stethoscope | ⊘ |
| N | | A4663 | Blood pressure cuff only | ⊘ |
| E | | A4670 | Automatic blood pressure monitor | ⊘ |
| | | | MED: 100-3,20.19 | |
| B | ☑ | A4671 | Disposable cycler set used with cycler dialysis machine, each | ⊘ |
| B | ☑ | A4672 | Drainage extension line, sterile, for dialysis, each | ⊘ |
| B | | A4673 | Extension line with easy lock connectors, used with dialysis | ⊘ |
| B | ☑ | A4674 | Chemicals/antiseptics solution used to clean/sterilize dialysis equipment, per 8 oz | ⊘ |
| N | ☑ | A4680 | Activated carbon filter for hemodialysis, each | ⊘ |
| | | | MED: 100-3,230.7 | |
| N | ☑ | A4690 | Dialyzer (artificial kidneys), all types, all sizes, for hemodialysis, each | ⊘ |
| N | ☑ | A4706 | Bicarbonate concentrate, solution, for hemodialysis, per gallon | ⊘ |
| N | ☑ | A4707 | Bicarbonate concentrate, powder, for hemodialysis, per packet | ⊘ |
| N | ☑ | A4708 | Acetate concentrate solution, for hemodialysis, per gallon | ⊘ |
| N | ☑ | A4709 | Acid concentrate, solution, for hemodialysis, per gallon | ⊘ |
| N | ☑ | A4714 | Treated water (deionized, distilled, or reverse osmosis) for peritoneal dialysis, per gallon | ⊘ |
| | | | MED: 100-3,230.7 | |

| | | | | |
|---|---|---|---|---|
| N | | A4719 | "Y set" tubing for peritoneal dialysis | ⊘ |
| N | ☑ | A4720 | Dialysate solution, any concentration of dextrose, fluid volume greater than 249 cc, but less than or equal to 999 cc, for peritoneal dialysis | ⊘ |
| N | ☑ | A4721 | Dialysate solution, any concentration of dextrose, fluid volume greater than 999 cc but less than or equal to 1999 cc, for peritoneal dialysis | ⊘ |
| N | ☑ | A4722 | Dialysate solution, any concentration of dextrose, fluid volume greater than 1999 cc but less than or equal to 2999 cc, for peritoneal dialysis | ⊘ |
| N | ☑ | A4723 | Dialysate solution, any concentration of dextrose, fluid volume greater than 2999 cc but less than or equal to 3999 cc, for peritoneal dialysis | ⊘ |
| N | ☑ | A4724 | Dialysate solution, any concentration of dextrose, fluid volume greater than 3999 cc but less than or equal to 4999 cc, for peritoneal dialysis | ⊘ |
| N | ☑ | A4725 | Dialysate solution, any concentration of dextrose, fluid volume greater than 4999 cc but less than or equal to 5999 cc, for peritoneal dialysis | ⊘ |
| N | ☑ | A4726 | Dialysate solution, any concentration of dextrose, fluid volume greater than 5999 cc, for peritoneal dialysis | ⊘ |
| B | ☑ | A4728 | Dialysate solution, nondextrose containing, 500 ml | ⊘ |
| N | ☑ | A4730 | Fistula cannulation set for hemodialysis, each | ⊘ |
| N | ☑ | A4736 | Topical anesthetic, for dialysis, per gram | ⊘ |
| N | ☑ | A4737 | Injectable anesthetic, for dialysis, per 10 ml | ⊘ |
| N | | A4740 | Shunt accessory, for hemodialysis, any type, each | ⊘ |
| N | ☑ | A4750 | Blood tubing, arterial or venous, for hemodialysis, each | ⊘ |
| N | ☑ | A4755 | Blood tubing, arterial and venous combined, for hemodialysis, each | ⊘ |
| N | ☑ | A4760 | Dialysate solution test kit, for peritoneal dialysis, any type, each | ⊘ |
| N | ☑ | A4765 | Dialysate concentrate, powder, additive for peritoneal dialysis, per packet | ⊘ |
| N | ☑ | A4766 | Dialysate concentrate, solution, additive for peritoneal dialysis, per 10 ml | ⊘ |
| N | ☑ | A4770 | Blood collection tube, vacuum, for dialysis, per 50 | ⊘ |
| N | ☑ | A4771 | Serum clotting time tube, for dialysis, per 50 | ⊘ |
| N | ☑ | A4772 | Blood glucose test strips, for dialysis, per 50 | ⊘ |
| N | ☑ | A4773 | Occult blood test strips, for dialysis, per 50 | ⊘ |
| N | ☑ | A4774 | Ammonia test strips, for dialysis, per 50 | ⊘ |
| N | ☑ | A4802 | Protamine sulfate, for hemodialysis, per 50 mg | ⊘ |
| N | ☑ | A4860 | Disposable catheter tips for peritoneal dialysis, per 10 | ⊘ |
| N | | A4870 | Plumbing and/or electrical work for home hemodialysis equipment | ⊘ |
| N | | A4890 | Contracts, repair and maintenance, for hemodialysis equipment | ⊘ |
| | | | MED: 100-2,15,110.2 | |
| N | ☑ | A4911 | Drain bag/bottle, for dialysis, each | ⊘ |
| N | | A4913 | Miscellaneous dialysis supplies, not otherwise specified | ⊘ |
| | | | Pertinent documentation to evaluate medical appropriateness should be included when this code is reported. Determine if an alternative HCPCS Level II or a CPT code better describes the service being reported. This code should be used only if a more specific code is unavailable. | |
| N | ☑ | A4918 | Venous pressure clamp, for hemodialysis, each | ⊘ |

Medical and Surgical Supplies

A4719 — A4918

Medical and Surgical Supplies

A4927 — A5105

| | | | | |
|---|---|---|---|---|
| N | ☑ | A4927 | Gloves, nonsterile, per 100 | ⊘ |
| N | ☑ | A4928 | Surgical mask, per 20 | ⊘ |
| N | ☑ | A4929 | Tourniquet for dialysis, each | ⊘ |
| N | ☑ | A4930 | Gloves, sterile, per pair | ⊘ |
| N | ☑ | A4931 | Oral thermometer, reusable, any type, each | ⊘ |
| E | ☑ | A4932 | Rectal thermometer, reusable, any type, each | |

## ADDITIONAL OSTOMY SUPPLIES

| | | | | |
|---|---|---|---|---|
| A | ☑ | A5051 | Ostomy pouch, closed; with barrier attached (1 piece), each<br>MED: 100-2,15,120 | ♿ |
| A | ☑ | A5052 | Ostomy pouch, closed; without barrier attached (1 piece), each<br>MED: 100-2,15,120 | ♿ |
| A | ☑ | A5053 | Ostomy pouch, closed; for use on faceplate, each<br>MED: 100-2,15,120 | ♿ |
| A | ☑ | A5054 | Ostomy pouch, closed; for use on barrier with flange (2 piece), each<br>MED: 100-2,15,120 | ♿ |
| A | | A5055 | Stoma cap<br>MED: 100-2,15,120 | ♿ |
| A | ☑ | A5061 | Ostomy pouch, drainable; with barrier attached, (1 piece), each | ♿ |
| A | ☑ | A5062 | Ostomy pouch, drainable; without barrier attached (1 piece), each<br>MED: 100-2,15,120 | ♿ |
| A | ☑ | A5063 | Ostomy pouch, drainable; for use on barrier with flange (2-piece system), each<br>MED: 100-2,15,120 | ♿ |
| A | ☑ | A5071 | Ostomy pouch, urinary; with barrier attached (1 piece), each<br>MED: 100-2,15,120 | ♿ |
| A | ☑ | A5072 | Ostomy pouch, urinary; without barrier attached (1 piece), each<br>MED: 100-2,15,120 | ♿ |
| A | ☑ | A5073 | Ostomy pouch, urinary; for use on barrier with flange (2 piece), each<br>MED: 100-2,15,120 | ♿ |
| A | | A5081 | Continent device; plug for continent stoma<br>MED: 100-2,15,120 | ♿ |
| A | | A5082 | Continent device; catheter for continent stoma<br>MED: 100-2,15,120 | ♿ |
| A | | A5083 | Continent device, stoma absorptive cover for continent stoma | ♿ |
| A | | A5093 | Ostomy accessory; convex insert<br>MED: 100-2,15,120 | ♿ |

## ADDITIONAL INCONTINENCE APPLIANCES/SUPPLIES

| | | | | |
|---|---|---|---|---|
| A | ☑ | A5102 | Bedside drainage bottle with or without tubing, rigid or expandable, each<br>MED: 100-2,15,120 | ♿ |
| A | ☑ | A5105 | Urinary suspensory with leg bag, with or without tube, each<br>MED: 100-2,15,120 | ♿ |

---

| A | | A5112 | Urinary leg bag; latex | ප |
|---|---|---|---|---|
| | | | MED: 100-2,15,120 | |
| A | ☑ | A5113 | Leg strap; latex, replacement only, per set | ප |
| | | | MED: 100-2,15,120 | |
| A | ☑ | A5114 | Leg strap; foam or fabric, replacement only, per set | ප |
| | | | MED: 100-2,15,120 | |

## SUPPLIES FOR EITHER INCONTINENCE OR OSTOMY APPLIANCES

For additional skin barrier codes see codes A4405-A4411.

| A | ☑ | A5120 | Skin barrier, wipes or swabs, each | |
|---|---|---|---|---|
| | | | MED: 100-2,15,120 | |
| A | ☑ | A5121 | Skin barrier; solid, 6 x 6 or equivalent, each | ප |
| | | | MED: 100-2,15,120 | |
| A | ☑ | A5122 | Skin barrier; solid, 8 x 8 or equivalent, each | ප |
| | | | MED: 100-2,15,120 | |
| A | | A5126 | Adhesive or nonadhesive; disk or foam pad | ප |
| | | | MED: 100-2,15,120 | |
| A | ☑ | A5131 | Appliance cleaner, incontinence and ostomy appliances, per 16 oz | ප |
| | | | MED: 100-2,15,120 | |
| A | | A5200 | Percutaneous catheter/tube anchoring device, adhesive skin attachment | ප |
| | | | MED: 100-2,15,120 | |

## DIABETIC SHOES, FITTING, AND MODIFICATIONS

According to Medicare, documentation from the prescribing physician must certify the diabetic patient has one of the following conditions: peripheral neuropathy with evidence of callus formation; history of preulcerative calluses; history of ulceration; foot deformity; previous amputation; or poor circulation. The footwear must be fitted and furnished by a podiatrist, pedorthist, orthotist, or prosthetist.

| Y | ☑ | A5500 | For diabetics only, fitting (including follow-up), custom preparation and supply of off-the-shelf depth-inlay shoe manufactured to accommodate multidensity insert(s), per shoe | |
|---|---|---|---|---|
| | | | MED: 100-2,15,140 | |
| Y | ☑ | A5501 | For diabetics only, fitting (including follow-up), custom preparation and supply of shoe molded from cast(s) of patient's foot (custom molded shoe), per shoe | |
| | | | MED: 100-2,15,140 | |
| Y | ☑ | A5503 | For diabetics only, modification (including fitting) of off-the-shelf depth-inlay shoe or custom molded shoe with roller or rigid rocker bottom, per shoe | |
| | | | MED: 100-2,15,140 | |
| Y | ☑ | A5504 | For diabetics only, modification (including fitting) of off-the-shelf depth-inlay shoe or custom molded shoe with wedge(s), per shoe | |
| | | | MED: 100-2,15,140 | |
| Y | ☑ | A5505 | For diabetics only, modification (including fitting) of off-the-shelf depth-inlay shoe or custom molded shoe with metatarsal bar, per shoe | |
| | | | MED: 100-2,15,140 | |

| | | | |
|---|---|---|---|
| Ⓨ ☑ | **A5506** | For diabetics only, modification (including fitting) of off-the-shelf depth-inlay shoe or custom molded shoe with off-set heel(s), per shoe | |
| | | MED: 100-2,15,140 | |
| Ⓨ ☑ | **A5507** | For diabetics only, not otherwise specified modification (including fitting) of off-the-shelf depth-inlay shoe or custom molded shoe, per shoe | |
| | | MED: 100-2,15,140 | |
| Ⓨ ☑ | **A5508** | For diabetics only, deluxe feature of off-the-shelf depth-inlay shoe or custom molded shoe, per shoe | |
| | | MED: 100-2,15,140 | |
| Ⓔ ☑ | **A5510** | For diabetics only, direct formed, compression molded to patient's foot without external heat source, multiple-density insert(s) prefabricated, per shoe | |
| | | MED: 100-2,15,140 | |
| Ⓨ ☑ | **A5512** | For diabetics only, multiple density insert, direct formed, molded to foot after external heat source of 230 degrees Fahrenheit or higher, total contact with patient's foot, including arch, base layer minimum of 1/4 inch material of shore a 35 durometer or 3/16 inch material of shore a 40 durometer (or higher), prefabricated, each ♿ | |
| Ⓨ ☑ | **A5513** | For diabetics only, multiple density insert, custom molded from model of patient's foot, total contact with patient's foot, including arch, base layer minimum of 3/16 inch material of shore a 35 durometer or higher), includes arch filler and other shaping material, custom fabricated, each ♿ | |

## DRESSINGS

| | | | |
|---|---|---|---|
| Ⓔ | **A6000** | Noncontact wound-warming wound cover for use with the noncontact wound-warming device and warming card | |
| | | MED: 100-2,16,20 | |
| ▲ Ⓐ ☑ | **A6010** | Collagen based wound filler, dry form, sterile, per gram of collagen ♿ | |
| | | MED: 100-2,15,100 | |
| ▲ Ⓐ ☑ | **A6011** | Collagen based wound filler, gel/paste, sterile, per gram of collagen ♿ | |
| | | MED: 100-2,15,100 | |
| ▲ Ⓐ ☑ | **A6021** | Collagen dressing, sterile, pad size 16 sq in or less, each ♿ | |
| | | MED: 100-2,15,100; 100-4,4,240 | |
| ▲ Ⓐ ☑ | **A6022** | Collagen dressing, sterile, pad size more than 16 sq in but less than or equal to 48 sq in, each ♿ | |
| | | MED: 100-2,15,100; 100-4,4,240 | |
| ▲ Ⓐ ☑ | **A6023** | Collagen dressing, sterile, pad size more than 48 sq in, each ♿ | |
| | | MED: 100-2,15,100; 100-4,4,240 | |
| ▲ Ⓐ ☑ | **A6024** | Collagen dressing wound filler, sterile, per 6 in ♿ | |
| | | MED: 100-2,15,100; 100-4,4,240 | |
| Ⓔ ☑ | **A6025** | Gel sheet for dermal or epidermal application, (e.g., silicone, hydrogel, other), each | |
| Ⓐ ☑ | **A6154** | Wound pouch, each ♿ | |
| | | MED: 100-2,15,100 | |
| ▲ Ⓐ ☑ | **A6196** | Alginate or other fiber gelling dressing, wound cover, sterile, pad size 16 sq in or less, each dressing ♿ | |
| | | MED: 100-2,15,100; 100-4,4,240 | |

---

▨ Special Coverage Instructions　　　▨ Noncovered by Medicare　　　▨ Carrier Discretion

▲ Ⓐ ☑ **A6197** Alginate or other fiber gelling dressing, wound cover, sterile, pad size more than 16 sq in but less than or equal to 48 sq in, each dressing ♿
MED: 100-2,15,100; 100-4,4,240

▲ Ⓐ ☑ **A6198** Alginate or other fiber gelling dressing, wound cover, sterile, pad size more than 48 sq in, each dressing
MED: 100-2,15,100; 100-4,4,240

▲ Ⓐ ☑ **A6199** Alginate or other fiber gelling dressing, wound filler, sterile, per 6 in ♿
MED: 100-2,15,100; 100-4,4,240

Ⓔ ☑ **A6200** Composite dressing, pad size 16 sq in or less, without adhesive border, each dressing ♿
MED: 100-2,15,100; 100-4,4,240

Ⓔ ☑ **A6201** Composite dressing, pad size more than 16 sq in but less than or equal to 48 sq in, without adhesive border, each dressing ♿
MED: 100-2,15,100; 100-4,4,240

Ⓔ ☑ **A6202** Composite dressing, pad size more than 48 sq in, without adhesive border, each dressing ♿
MED: 100-2,15,100; 100-4,4,240

▲ Ⓐ ☑ **A6203** Composite dressing, sterile, pad size 16 sq in or less, with any size adhesive border, each dressing ♿
MED: 100-2,15,100; 100-4,4,240

▲ Ⓐ ☑ **A6204** Composite dressing, sterile, pad size more than 16 sq in, but less than or equal to 48 sq in, with any size adhesive border, each dressing ♿
MED: 100-2,15,100; 100-4,4,240

▲ Ⓐ ☑ **A6205** Composite dressing, sterile, pad size more than 48 sq in, with any size adhesive border, each dressing
MED: 100-2,15,100; 100-4,4,240

▲ Ⓐ ☑ **A6206** Contact layer, sterile, 16 sq in or less, each dressing
MED: 100-2,15,100; 100-4,4,240

▲ Ⓐ ☑ **A6207** Contact layer, sterile, more than 16 sq in but less than or equal to 48 sq in, each dressing ♿
MED: 100-2,15,100; 100-4,4,240

▲ Ⓐ ☑ **A6208** Contact layer, sterile, more than 48 sq in, each dressing
MED: 100-2,15,100; 100-4,4,240

▲ Ⓐ ☑ **A6209** Foam dressing, wound cover, sterile, pad size 16 sq in or less, without adhesive border, each dressing ♿
MED: 100-2,15,100; 100-4,4,240

▲ Ⓐ ☑ **A6210** Foam dressing, wound cover, sterile, pad size more than 16 sq in but less than or equal to 48 sq in, without adhesive border, each dressing ♿
MED: 100-2,15,100; 100-4,4,240

▲ Ⓐ ☑ **A6211** Foam dressing, wound cover, sterile, pad size more than 48 sq in, without adhesive border, each dressing ♿
MED: 100-2,15,100; 100-4,4,240

▲ Ⓐ ☑ **A6212** Foam dressing, wound cover, sterile, pad size 16 sq in or less, with any size adhesive border, each dressing ♿
MED: 100-2,15,100; 100-4,4,240

▲ Ⓐ ☑ **A6213** Foam dressing, wound cover, sterile, pad size more than 16 sq in but less than or equal to 48 sq in, with any size adhesive border, each dressing
MED: 100-2,15,100; 100-4,4,240

*Medical and Surgical Supplies*

**A6197 — A6213**

▲ Ⓐ ☑ **A6214** Foam dressing, wound cover, sterile, pad size more than 48 sq in, with any size adhesive border, each dressing    ♿
MED: 100-2,15,100; 100-4,4,240

▲ Ⓐ ☑ **A6215** Foam dressing, wound filler, sterile, per gram
MED: 100-2,15,100; 100-4,4,240

Ⓐ ☑ **A6216** Gauze, nonimpregnated, nonsterile, pad size 16 sq in or less, without adhesive border, each dressing    ♿
MED: 100-2,15,100; 100-4,4,240

Ⓐ ☑ **A6217** Gauze, nonimpregnated, nonsterile, pad size more than 16 sq in but less than or equal to 48 sq in, without adhesive border, each dressing    ♿
MED: 100-2,15,100; 100-4,4,240

Ⓐ ☑ **A6218** Gauze, nonimpregnated, nonsterile, pad size more than 48 sq in, without adhesive border, each dressing
MED: 100-2,15,100; 100-4,4,240

▲ Ⓐ ☑ **A6219** Gauze, nonimpregnated, sterile, pad size 16 sq in or less, with any size adhesive border, each dressing    ♿
MED: 100-2,15,100; 100-4,4,240

▲ Ⓐ ☑ **A6220** Gauze, nonimpregnated, sterile, pad size more than 16 sq in but less than or equal to 48 sq in, with any size adhesive border, each dressing    ♿
MED: 100-2,15,100; 100-4,4,240

▲ Ⓐ ☑ **A6221** Gauze, nonimpregnated, sterile, pad size more than 48 sq in, with any size adhesive border, each dressing
MED: 100-2,15,100; 100-4,4,240

▲ Ⓐ ☑ **A6222** Gauze, impregnated with other than water, normal saline, or hydrogel, sterile, pad size 16 sq in or less, without adhesive border, each dressing    ♿
MED: 100-2,15,100; 100-4,4,240

▲ Ⓐ ☑ **A6223** Gauze, impregnated with other than water, normal saline, or hydrogel, sterile, pad size more than 16 sq in, but less than or equal to 48 sq in, without adhesive border, each dressing    ♿
MED: 100-2,15,100; 100-4,4,240

▲ Ⓐ ☑ **A6224** Gauze, impregnated with other than water, normal saline, or hydrogel, sterile, pad size more than 48 sq in, without adhesive border, each dressing    ♿
MED: 100-2,15,100; 100-4,4,240

▲ Ⓐ ☑ **A6228** Gauze, impregnated, water or normal saline, sterile, pad size 16 sq in or less, without adhesive border, each dressing
MED: 100-2,15,100; 100-4,4,240

▲ Ⓐ ☑ **A6229** Gauze, impregnated, water or normal saline, sterile, pad size more than 16 sq in but less than or equal to 48 sq in, without adhesive border, each dressing    ♿
MED: 100-2,15,100; 100-4,4,240

▲ Ⓐ ☑ **A6230** Gauze, impregnated, water or normal saline, sterile, pad size more than 48 sq in, without adhesive border, each dressing
MED: 100-2,15,100; 100-4,4,240

▲ Ⓐ ☑ **A6231** Gauze, impregnated, hydrogel, for direct wound contact, sterile, pad size 16 sq in or less, each dressing    ♿
MED: 100-2,15,100; 100-4,4,240

▲ Ⓐ ☑ **A6232** Gauze, impregnated, hydrogel, for direct wound contact, sterile, pad size greater than 16 sq in, but less than or equal to 48 sq in, each dressing ♿

MED: 100-2,15,100; 100-4,4,240

▲ Ⓐ ☑ **A6233** Gauze, impregnated, hydrogel, for direct wound contact, sterile, pad size more than 48 sq in, each dressing ♿

MED: 100-2,15,100; 100-4,4,240

▲ Ⓐ ☑ **A6234** Hydrocolloid dressing, wound cover, sterile, pad size 16 sq in or less, without adhesive border, each dressing ♿

MED: 100-2,15,100; 100-4,4,240

▲ Ⓐ ☑ **A6235** Hydrocolloid dressing, wound cover, sterile, pad size more than 16 sq in but less than or equal to 48 sq in, without adhesive border, each dressing ♿

MED: 100-2,15,100; 100-4,4,240

▲ Ⓐ ☑ **A6236** Hydrocolloid dressing, wound cover, sterile, pad size more than 48 sq in, without adhesive border, each dressing ♿

MED: 100-2,15,100; 100-4,4,240

▲ Ⓐ ☑ **A6237** Hydrocolloid dressing, wound cover, sterile, pad size 16 sq in or less, with any size adhesive border, each dressing ♿

MED: 100-2,15,100; 100-4,4,240

▲ Ⓐ ☑ **A6238** Hydrocolloid dressing, wound cover, sterile, pad size more than 16 sq in but less than or equal to 48 sq in, with any size adhesive border, each dressing ♿

MED: 100-2,15,100; 100-4,4,240

▲ Ⓐ ☑ **A6239** Hydrocolloid dressing, wound cover, sterile, pad size more than 48 sq in, with any size adhesive border, each dressing

MED: 100-2,15,100; 100-4,4,240

▲ Ⓐ ☑ **A6240** Hydrocolloid dressing, wound filler, paste, sterile, per oz ♿

MED: 100-2,15,100; 100-4,4,240

▲ Ⓐ ☑ **A6241** Hydrocolloid dressing, wound filler, dry form, sterile, per gram ♿

MED: 100-2,15,100; 100-4,4,240

▲ Ⓐ ☑ **A6242** Hydrogel dressing, wound cover, sterile, pad size 16 sq in or less, without adhesive border, each dressing ♿

MED: 100-2,15,100; 100-4,4,240

▲ Ⓐ ☑ **A6243** Hydrogel dressing, wound cover, sterile, pad size more than 16 sq in but less than or equal to 48 sq in, without adhesive border, each dressing ♿

MED: 100-2,15,100; 100-4,4,240

▲ Ⓐ ☑ **A6244** Hydrogel dressing, wound cover, sterile, pad size more than 48 sq in, without adhesive border, each dressing ♿

MED: 100-2,15,100; 100-4,4,240

▲ Ⓐ ☑ **A6245** Hydrogel dressing, wound cover, sterile, pad size 16 sq in or less, with any size adhesive border, each dressing ♿

MED: 100-2,15,100; 100-4,4,240

▲ Ⓐ ☑ **A6246** Hydrogel dressing, wound cover, sterile, pad size more than 16 sq in but less than or equal to 48 sq in, with any size adhesive border, each dressing ♿

MED: 100-2,15,100; 100-4,4,240

▲ Ⓐ ☑ **A6247** Hydrogel dressing, wound cover, sterile, pad size more than 48 sq in, with any size adhesive border, each dressing ♿

MED: 100-2,15,100; 100-4,4,240

▲ A ☑ **A6248** Hydrogel dressing, wound filler, gel, sterile, per fl oz &#x267f;
MED: 100-2,15,100; 100-4,4,240

A **A6250** Skin sealants, protectants, moisturizers, ointments, any type, any size
Surgical dressings applied by a physician are included as part of the professional service. Surgical dressings obtained by the patient to perform homecare as prescribed by the physician are covered.
MED: 100-2,15,100; 100-4,4,240

▲ A ☑ **A6251** Specialty absorptive dressing, wound cover, sterile, pad size 16 sq in or less, without adhesive border, each dressing &#x267f;
MED: 100-2,15,100; 100-4,4,240

▲ A ☑ **A6252** Specialty absorptive dressing, wound cover, sterile, pad size more than 16 sq in but less than or equal to 48 sq in, without adhesive border, each dressing &#x267f;
MED: 100-2,15,100; 100-4,4,240

▲ A ☑ **A6253** Specialty absorptive dressing, wound cover, sterile, pad size more than 48 sq in, without adhesive border, each dressing &#x267f;
MED: 100-2,15,100; 100-4,4,240

▲ A ☑ **A6254** Specialty absorptive dressing, wound cover, sterile, pad size 16 sq in or less, with any size adhesive border, each dressing &#x267f;
MED: 100-2,15,100; 100-4,4,240

▲ A ☑ **A6255** Specialty absorptive dressing, wound cover, sterile, pad size more than 16 sq in but less than or equal to 48 sq in, with any size adhesive border, each dressing &#x267f;
MED: 100-2,15,100; 100-4,4,240

▲ A ☑ **A6256** Specialty absorptive dressing, wound cover, sterile, pad size more than 48 sq in, with any size adhesive border, each dressing
MED: 100-2,15,100; 100-4,4,240

▲ A ☑ **A6257** Transparent film, sterile, 16 sq in or less, each dressing &#x267f;
Surgical dressings applied by a physician are included as part of the professional service. Surgical dressings obtained by the patient to perform homecare as prescribed by the physician are covered. Use this code for Polyskin, Tegaderm, and Tegaderm HP.
MED: 100-2,15,100; 100-4,4,240

▲ A ☑ **A6258** Transparent film, sterile, more than 16 sq in but less than or equal to 48 sq in, each dressing &#x267f;
Surgical dressings applied by a physician are included as part of the professional service. Surgical dressings obtained by the patient to perform homecare as prescribed by the physician are covered.
MED: 100-2,15,100; 100-4,4,240

▲ A ☑ **A6259** Transparent film, sterile, more than 48 sq in, each dressing &#x267f;
Surgical dressings applied by a physician are included as part of the professional service. Surgical dressings obtained by the patient to perform homecare as prescribed by the physician are covered.
MED: 100-2,15,100; 100-4,4,240

▲ A **A6260** Wound cleansers, sterile, any type, any size
Surgical dressings applied by a physician are included as part of the professional service. Surgical dressings obtained by the patient to perform homecare as prescribed by the physician are covered.
MED: 100-2,15,100; 100-4,4,240

▲ Ⓐ ☑ **A6261** Wound filler, gel/paste, sterile, per fl oz, not otherwise specified
Surgical dressings applied by a physician are included as part of the professional service. Surgical dressings obtained by the patient to perform homecare as prescribed by the physician are covered.
MED: 100-2,15,100; 100-4,4,240

▲ Ⓐ ☑ **A6262** Wound filler, dry form, sterile, per gram, not otherwise specified
MED: 100-2,15,100; 100-4,4,240

▲ Ⓐ ☑ **A6266** Gauze, impregnated, other than water, normal saline, or zinc paste, sterile, any width, per linear yd                                             ᵭ
Surgical dressings applied by a physician are included as part of the professional service. Surgical dressings obtained by the patient to perform homecare as prescribed by the physician are covered.
MED: 100-2,15,100; 100-4,4,240

Ⓐ ☑ **A6402** Gauze, nonimpregnated, sterile, pad size 16 sq in or less, without adhesive border, each dressing       ᵭ
Surgical dressings applied by a physician are included as part of the professional service. Surgical dressings obtained by the patient to perform homecare as prescribed by the physician are covered.
MED: 100-2,15,100; 100-4,4,240

Ⓐ ☑ **A6403** Gauze, nonimpregnated, sterile, pad size more than 16 sq in, less than or equal to 48 sq in, without adhesive border, each dressing    ᵭ
Surgical dressings applied by a physician are included as part of the professional service. Surgical dressings obtained by the patient to perform homecare as prescribed by the physician are covered.
MED: 100-2,15,100; 100-4,4,240

Ⓐ ☑ **A6404** Gauze, nonimpregnated, sterile, pad size more than 48 sq in, without adhesive border, each dressing
MED: 100-2,15,100; 100-4,4,240

▲ Ⓐ ☑ **A6407** Packing strips, nonimpregnated, sterile, up to 2 in in width, per linear yd       ᵭ

Ⓐ ☑ **A6410** Eye pad, sterile, each       ᵭ
MED: 100-2,15,100

Ⓐ ☑ **A6411** Eye pad, nonsterile, each       ᵭ
MED: 100-2,15,100

Ⓔ ☑ **A6412** Eye patch, occlusive, each

Ⓔ ☑ **A6413** Adhesive bandage, first aid type, any size, each

Ⓐ ☑ **A6441** Padding bandage, nonelastic, nonwoven/nonknitted, width greater than or equal to 3 in and less than 5 in, per yd       ᵭ

Ⓐ ☑ **A6442** Conforming bandage, nonelastic, knitted/woven, nonsterile, width less than 3 in, per yd       ᵭ

Ⓐ ☑ **A6443** Conforming bandage, nonelastic, knitted/woven, nonsterile, width greater than or equal to 3 in and less than 5 in, per yd       ᵭ

Ⓐ ☑ **A6444** Conforming bandage, nonelastic, knitted/woven, nonsterile, width greater than or equal to 5 in, per yd       ᵭ

Ⓐ ☑ **A6445** Conforming bandage, nonelastic, knitted/woven, sterile, width less than 3 in, per yd       ᵭ

Ⓐ ☑ **A6446** Conforming bandage, nonelastic, knitted/woven, sterile, width greater than or equal to 3 in and less than 5 in, per yd       ᵭ

---

☑ Quantity Alert    ● New Code    ○ Recycled/Reinstated    ▲ Revised Code    ᵭ DMEPOS Paid    ⊘ SNF Excluded

| | | | |
|---|---|---|---|
| Ⓐ | ☑ | **A6447** | Conforming bandage, nonelastic, knitted/woven, sterile, width greater than or equal to 5 in, per yd   ♿ |
| Ⓐ | ☑ | **A6448** | Light compression bandage, elastic, knitted/woven, width less than 3 in, per yd   ♿ |
| Ⓐ | ☑ | **A6449** | Light compression bandage, elastic, knitted/woven, width greater than or equal to 3 in and less than 5 in, per yd   ♿ |
| Ⓐ | ☑ | **A6450** | Light compression bandage, elastic, knitted/woven, width greater than or equal to 5 in, per yd   ♿ |
| Ⓐ | ☑ | **A6451** | Moderate compression bandage, elastic, knitted/woven, load resistance of 1.25 to 1.34 ft lbs at 50% maximum stretch, width greater than or equal to 3 in and less than 5 in, per yd   ♿ |
| Ⓐ | ☑ | **A6452** | High compression bandage, elastic, knitted/woven, load resistance greater than or equal to 1.35 ft lbs at 50% maximum stretch, width greater than or equal to 3 in and less than 5 in, per yd   ♿ |
| Ⓐ | ☑ | **A6453** | Self-adherent bandage, elastic, nonknitted/nonwoven, width less than 3 in, per yd   ♿ |
| Ⓐ | ☑ | **A6454** | Self-adherent bandage, elastic, nonknitted/nonwoven, width greater than or equal to 3 in and less than 5 in, per yd   ♿ |
| Ⓐ | ☑ | **A6455** | Self-adherent bandage, elastic, nonknitted/nonwoven, width greater than or equal to 5 in, per yd   ♿ |
| Ⓐ | ☑ | **A6456** | Zinc paste impregnated bandage, nonelastic, knitted/woven, width greater than or equal to 3 in and less than 5 in, per yd   ♿ |
| Ⓐ | | **A6457** | Tubular dressing with or without elastic, any width, per linear yard |
| Ⓐ | | **A6501** | Compression burn garment, bodysuit (head to foot), custom fabricated   ♿<br>MED: 100-2,15,100 |
| Ⓐ | | **A6502** | Compression burn garment, chin strap, custom fabricated   ♿<br>MED: 100-2,15,100 |
| Ⓐ | | **A6503** | Compression burn garment, facial hood, custom fabricated   ♿<br>MED: 100-2,15,100 |
| Ⓐ | | **A6504** | Compression burn garment, glove to wrist, custom fabricated   ♿<br>MED: 100-2,15,100 |
| Ⓐ | | **A6505** | Compression burn garment, glove to elbow, custom fabricated   ♿<br>MED: 100-2,15,100 |
| Ⓐ | | **A6506** | Compression burn garment, glove to axilla, custom fabricated   ♿<br>MED: 100-2,15,100 |
| Ⓐ | | **A6507** | Compression burn garment, foot to knee length, custom fabricated   ♿<br>MED: 100-2,15,100 |
| Ⓐ | | **A6508** | Compression burn garment, foot to thigh length, custom fabricated   ♿<br>MED: 100-2,15,100 |
| Ⓐ | | **A6509** | Compression burn garment, upper trunk to waist including arm openings (vest), custom fabricated   ♿<br>MED: 100-2,15,100 |
| Ⓐ | | **A6510** | Compression burn garment, trunk, including arms down to leg openings (leotard), custom fabricated   ♿<br>MED: 100-2,15,100 |

| | | | |
|---|---|---|---|
| Ⓐ | | A6511 | Compression burn garment, lower trunk including leg openings (panty), custom fabricated ♿<br>MED: 100-2,15,100 |
| Ⓐ | | A6512 | Compression burn garment, not otherwise classified<br>MED: 100-2,15,100 |
| Ⓑ | | A6513 | Compression burn mask, face and/or neck, plastic or equal, custom fabricated |
| Ⓔ | ☑ | A6530 | Gradient compression stocking, below knee, 18-30 mm Hg, each |
| Ⓐ | ☑ | A6531 | Gradient compression stocking, below knee, 30-40 mm Hg, each<br>MED: 100-2,15,100 |
| Ⓐ | ☑ | A6532 | Gradient compression stocking, below knee, 40-50 mm Hg, each<br>MED: 100-2,15,100 |
| Ⓔ | ☑ | A6533 | Gradient compression stocking, thigh length, 18-30 mm Hg, each<br>MED: 100-2,15,130 |
| Ⓔ | ☑ | A6534 | Gradient compression stocking, thigh length, 30-40 mm Hg, each<br>MED: 100-2,15,130 |
| Ⓔ | ☑ | A6535 | Gradient compression stocking, thigh length, 40-50 mm Hg, each<br>MED: 100-2,15,130 |
| Ⓔ | ☑ | A6536 | Gradient compression stocking, full-length/chap style, 18-30 mm Hg, each<br>MED: 100-2,15,130 |
| Ⓔ | ☑ | A6537 | Gradient compression stocking, full-length/chap style, 30-40 mm Hg, each<br>MED: 100-2,15,130 |
| Ⓔ | ☑ | A6538 | Gradient compression stocking, full-length/chap style, 40-50 mm Hg, each<br>MED: 100-2,15,130 |
| Ⓔ | ☑ | A6539 | Gradient compression stocking, waist length, 18-30 mm Hg, each<br>MED: 100-2,15,130 |
| Ⓔ | ☑ | A6540 | Gradient compression stocking, waist length, 30-40 mm Hg, each<br>MED: 100-2,15,130 |
| Ⓔ | ☑ | A6541 | Gradient compression stocking, waist length, 40-50 mm Hg, each<br>MED: 100-2,15,130 |
| Ⓔ | | A6542 | Gradient compression stocking, custom made<br>MED: 100-2,15,130 |
| Ⓔ | | A6543 | Gradient compression stocking, lymphedema<br>MED: 100-2,15,130 |
| Ⓔ | | A6544 | Gradient compression stocking, garter belt<br>MED: 100-2,15,130 |
| ● Ⓐ | ☑ | A6545 | Gradient compression wrap, nonelastic, below knee, 30-50 mm Hg, each |
| Ⓔ | | A6549 | Gradient compression stocking, not otherwise specified<br>MED: 100-2,15,130 |
| Ⓨ | ☑ | A6550 | Wound care set, for negative pressure wound therapy electrical pump, includes all supplies and accessories ♿ |

## MISCELLANEOUS SUPPLIES

| | | | |
|---|---|---|---|
| Ⓨ | ☑ | A7000 | Canister, disposable, used with suction pump, each ♿ |

**Medical and Surgical Supplies**

**A7001 — A7036**

| | | | | |
|---|---|---|---|---|
| Ⓨ | ☑ | A7001 | Canister, nondisposable, used with suction pump, each | ㅅ |
| Ⓨ | ☑ | A7002 | Tubing, used with suction pump, each | ㅅ |
| Ⓨ | | A7003 | Administration set, with small volume nonfiltered pneumatic nebulizer, disposable | ㅅ |
| Ⓨ | | A7004 | Small volume nonfiltered pneumatic nebulizer, disposable | ㅅ |
| Ⓨ | | A7005 | Administration set, with small volume nonfiltered pneumatic nebulizer, nondisposable | ㅅ |
| Ⓨ | | A7006 | Administration set, with small volume filtered pneumatic nebulizer | ㅅ |
| Ⓨ | | A7007 | Large volume nebulizer, disposable, unfilled, used with aerosol compressor | ㅅ |
| Ⓨ | | A7008 | Large volume nebulizer, disposable, prefilled, used with aerosol compressor | ㅅ |
| Ⓨ | | A7009 | Reservoir bottle, nondisposable, used with large volume ultrasonic nebulizer | ㅅ |
| Ⓨ | ☑ | A7010 | Corrugated tubing, disposable, used with large volume nebulizer, 100 ft | ㅅ |
| Ⓨ | ☑ | A7011 | Corrugated tubing, nondisposable, used with large volume nebulizer, 10 ft | ㅅ |
| Ⓨ | | A7012 | Water collection device, used with large volume nebulizer | ㅅ |
| Ⓨ | | A7013 | Filter, disposable, used with aerosol compressor | ㅅ |
| Ⓨ | | A7014 | Filter, nondisposable, used with aerosol compressor or ultrasonic generator | ㅅ |
| Ⓨ | | A7015 | Aerosol mask, used with DME nebulizer | ㅅ |
| Ⓨ | | A7016 | Dome and mouthpiece, used with small volume ultrasonic nebulizer | ㅅ |
| Ⓨ | | A7017 | Nebulizer, durable, glass or autoclavable plastic, bottle type, not used with oxygen | ㅅ |
| | | | MED: 100-3,280.1 | |
| Ⓨ | ☑ | A7018 | Water, distilled, used with large volume nebulizer, 1000 ml | ㅅ |
| Ⓨ | ☑ | A7025 | High frequency chest wall oscillation system vest, replacement for use with patient-owned equipment, each | ㅅ |
| Ⓨ | ☑ | A7026 | High frequency chest wall oscillation system hose, replacement for use with patient-owned equipment, each | ㅅ |
| Ⓨ | ☑ | A7027 | Combination oral/nasal mask, used with continuous positive airway pressure device, each | |
| Ⓨ | ☑ | A7028 | Oral cushion for combination oral/nasal mask, replacement only, each | |
| Ⓨ | ☑ | A7029 | Nasal pillows for combination oral/nasal mask, replacement only, pair | |
| Ⓨ | ☑ | A7030 | Full face mask used with positive airway pressure device, each | ㅅ |
| Ⓨ | ☑ | A7031 | Face mask interface, replacement for full face mask, each | ㅅ |
| Ⓨ | ☑ | A7032 | Cushion for use on nasal mask interface, replacement only, each | ㅅ |
| Ⓨ | ☑ | A7033 | Pillow for use on nasal cannula type interface, replacement only, pair | ㅅ |
| Ⓨ | | A7034 | Nasal interface (mask or cannula type) used with positive airway pressure device, with or without head strap | ㅅ |
| Ⓨ | | A7035 | Headgear used with positive airway pressure device | ㅅ |
| Ⓨ | | A7036 | Chinstrap used with positive airway pressure device | ㅅ |

| | | | | |
|---|---|---|---|---|
| Y | | A7037 | Tubing used with positive airway pressure device | &. |
| Y | | A7038 | Filter, disposable, used with positive airway pressure device | &. |
| Y | | A7039 | Filter, nondisposable, used with positive airway pressure device | &. |
| A | | A7040 | One way chest drain valve | |
| A | | A7041 | Water seal drainage container and tubing for use with implanted chest tube | |
| N | ☑ | A7042 | Implanted pleural catheter, each | &. |
| A | | A7043 | Vacuum drainage bottle and tubing for use with implanted catheter | &. |
| Y | ☑ | A7044 | Oral interface used with positive airway pressure device, each | &. |
| Y | | A7045 | Exhalation port with or without swivel used with accessories for positive airway devices, replacement only | |
| | | | MED: 100-3,230.17 | |
| Y | ☑ | A7046 | Water chamber for humidifier, used with positive airway pressure device, replacement, each | &. |
| | | | MED: 100-3,230.17 | |
| A | ☑ | A7501 | Tracheostoma valve, including diaphragm, each | &. |
| | | | MED: 100-2,15,120 | |
| A | ☑ | A7502 | Replacement diaphragm/faceplate for tracheostoma valve, each | &. |
| | | | MED: 100-2,15,120 | |
| A | ☑ | A7503 | Filter holder or filter cap, reusable, for use in a tracheostoma heat and moisture exchange system, each | &. |
| | | | MED: 100-2,15,120 | |
| A | ☑ | A7504 | Filter for use in a tracheostoma heat and moisture exchange system, each | &. |
| | | | MED: 100-2,15,120 | |
| A | ☑ | A7505 | Housing, reusable without adhesive, for use in a heat and moisture exchange system and/or with a tracheostoma valve, each | &. |
| | | | MED: 100-2,15,120 | |
| A | ☑ | A7506 | Adhesive disc for use in a heat and moisture exchange system and/or with tracheostoma valve, any type each | &. |
| | | | MED: 100-2,15,120 | |
| A | ☑ | A7507 | Filter holder and integrated filter without adhesive, for use in a tracheostoma heat and moisture exchange system, each | &. |
| | | | MED: 100-2,15,120 | |
| A | ☑ | A7508 | Housing and integrated adhesive, for use in a tracheostoma heat and moisture exchange system and/or with a tracheostoma valve, each | &. |
| | | | MED: 100-2,15,120 | |
| A | ☑ | A7509 | Filter holder and integrated filter housing, and adhesive, for use as a tracheostoma heat and moisture exchange system, each | &. |
| | | | MED: 100-2,15,120 | |
| A | ☑ | A7520 | Tracheostomy/laryngectomy tube, noncuffed, polyvinylchloride (PVC), silicone or equal, each | &. |
| A | ☑ | A7521 | Tracheostomy/laryngectomy tube, cuffed, polyvinylchloride (PVC), silicone or equal, each | &. |
| A | ☑ | A7522 | Tracheostomy/laryngectomy tube, stainless steel or equal (sterilizable and reusable), each | &. |
| A | ☑ | A7523 | Tracheostomy shower protector, each | |

*Medical and Surgical Supplies*

*A7037 — A7523*

| | | | | |
|---|---|---|---|---|
| Ⓐ ☑ | A7524 | Tracheostoma stent/stud/button, each | ↻ |
| Ⓐ ☑ | A7525 | Tracheostomy mask, each | ↻ |
| Ⓐ ☑ | A7526 | Tracheostomy tube collar/holder, each | ↻ |
| Ⓐ ☑ | A7527 | Tracheostomy/laryngectomy tube plug/stop, each | |
| Ⓨ | A8000 | Helmet, protective, soft, prefabricated, includes all components and accessories | ↻ |
| Ⓨ | A8001 | Helmet, protective, hard, prefabricated, includes all components and accessories | ↻ |
| Ⓨ | A8002 | Helmet, protective, soft, custom fabricated, includes all components and accessories | ↻ |
| Ⓨ | A8003 | Helmet, protective, hard, custom fabricated, includes all components and accessories | ↻ |
| Ⓨ | A8004 | Soft interface for helmet, replacement only | ↻ |

## ADMINISTRATIVE, MISCELLANEOUS & INVESTIGATIONAL A9000-A9999

This section of codes reports items such as nonprescription drugs, noncovered items/services, exercise equipment and, most notably, radiopharmaceutical diagnostic imaging agents.

| | | | |
|---|---|---|---|
| Ⓑ | A9150 | **Nonprescription drugs** <br> MED: 100-2,15,50 | |
| Ⓔ ☑ | A9152 | Single vitamin/mineral/trace element, oral, per dose, not otherwise specified | |
| Ⓔ ☑ | A9153 | Multiple vitamins, with or without minerals and trace elements, oral, per dose, not otherwise specified | |
| Ⓑ | A9155 | Artificial saliva, 30 ml | |
| Ⓔ | A9180 | Pediculosis (lice infestation) treatment, topical, for administration by patient/caretaker | |
| Ⓔ | A9270 | Noncovered item or service <br> MED: 100-2,16,20 | |
| Ⓔ ☑ | A9274 | External ambulatory insulin delivery system, disposable, each, includes all supplies and accessories | |
| Ⓔ | A9275 | Home glucose disposable monitor, includes test strips | |
| Ⓔ ☑ | A9276 | Sensor; invasive (e.g., subcutaneous), disposable, for use with interstitial continuous glucose monitoring system, 1 unit = 1 day supply | |
| Ⓔ | A9277 | Transmitter; external, for use with interstitial continuous glucose monitoring system | |
| Ⓔ | A9278 | Receiver (monitor); external, for use with interstitial continuous glucose monitoring system | |
| Ⓔ | A9279 | Monitoring feature/device, stand-alone or integrated, any type, includes all accessories, components and electronics, not otherwise classified | |
| Ⓔ | A9280 | Alert or alarm device, not otherwise classified | |
| Ⓔ ☑ | A9281 | Reaching/grabbing device, any type, any length, each | |
| Ⓔ ☑ | A9282 | Wig, any type, each | |
| Ⓔ ☑ | A9283 | Foot pressure off loading/supportive device, any type, each | |
| ● Ⓝ | A9284 | Spirometer, nonelectronic, includes all accessories | |

| E | | A9300 | Exercise equipment |
|---|---|---|---|
| | | | MED: 100-2,15,110.1; 100-3,280.1 |

## RADIOPHARMACEUTICALS

| | | | | |
|---|---|---|---|---|
| N ☑ | | A9500 | Technetium Tc-99m sestamibi, diagnostic, per study dose, up to 40 millicuries | N |
| | | | Use this code for Cardiolite. | |
| N ☑ | | A9501 | Technetium Tc-99m teboroxime, diagnostic, per study dose | N |
| ▲ N ☑ | | A9502 | Technetium Tc-99m tetrofosmin, diagnostic, per study dose | N |
| | | | Use this code for Myoview. | |
| N ☑ | | A9503 | Technetium Tc-99m medronate, diagnostic, per study dose, up to 30 millicuries | N |
| | | | Use this code for CIS-MDP, Draximage MDP-10, Draximage MDP-25, MDP-Bracco, Technetium Tc-99m MPI-MDP | |
| | | | AHA: 2Q,'02,9 | |
| N ☑ | | A9504 | Technetium Tc-99m apcitide, diagnostic, per study dose, up to 20 millicuries | N |
| | | | Use this code for Acutect | |
| | | | AHA: 2Q,'02,9; 4Q,'01,5 | |
| N ☑ | | A9505 | Thallium Tl-201 thallous chloride, diagnostic, per millicurie | N |
| | | | Use this code for MIBG, Thallous Chloride USP. | |
| | | | AHA: 2Q,'02,9 | |
| N ☑ | | A9507 | Indium In-111 capromab pendetide, diagnostic, per study dose, up to 10 millicuries | N |
| | | | Use this code for Prostascint. | |
| N ☑ | | A9508 | Iodine I-131 iobenguane sulfate, diagnostic, per 0.5 millicurie | N |
| | | | Use this code for MIBG. | |
| | | | AHA: 2Q,'02,9 | |
| N ☑ | | A9509 | Iodine I-123 sodium iodide, diagnostic, per millicurie | N |
| N ☑ | | A9510 | Technetium Tc-99m disofenin, diagnostic, per study dose, up to 15 millicuries | N |
| | | | Use this code for Hepatolite. | |
| N ☑ | | A9512 | Technetium Tc-99m pertechnetate, diagnostic, per millicurie | N |
| | | | Use this code for Technelite, Ultra-Technelow. | |
| N ☑ | | A9516 | Iodine I-123 sodium iodide, diagnostic, per 100 microcuries, up to 999 microcuries | N |
| H ☑ | | A9517 | Iodine I-131 sodium iodide capsule(s), therapeutic, per millicurie | |
| N ☑ | | A9521 | Technetium Tc-99m exametazime, diagnostic, per study dose, up to 25 millicuries | N |
| | | | Use this code for Ceretec. | |
| N ☑ | | A9524 | Iodine I-131 iodinated serum albumin, diagnostic, per 5 microcuries | N |
| N ☑ | | A9526 | Nitrogen N-13 ammonia, diagnostic, per study dose, up to 40 millicuries | N |
| | | | MED: 100-3,220.6; 100-4,13,60.3.1; 100-4,13,60.3.2 | |
| U ☑ | | A9527 | Iodine I-125, sodium iodide solution, therapeutic, per millicurie | |
| N ☑ | | A9528 | Iodine I-131 sodium iodide capsule(s), diagnostic, per millicurie | N |
| N ☑ | | A9529 | Iodine I-131 sodium iodide solution, diagnostic, per millicurie | N |
| H ☑ | | A9530 | Iodine I-131 sodium iodide solution, therapeutic, per millicurie | ⊘ |

---

☑ Quantity Alert    ● New Code    ○ Recycled/Reinstated    ▲ Revised Code    ⅙ DMEPOS Paid    ⊘ SNF Excluded

| | | | | |
|---|---|---|---|---|
| N | ☑ | A9531 | Iodine I-131 sodium iodide, diagnostic, per microcurie (up to 100 microcuries) | NI |
| N | ☑ | A9532 | Iodine I-125 serum albumin, diagnostic, per 5 microcuries | NI |
| N | ☑ | A9535 | Injection, methylene blue, 1 ml | NI |
| N | ☑ | A9536 | Technetium Tc-99m depreotide, diagnostic, per study dose, up to 35 millicuries | NI |
| N | ☑ | A9537 | Technetium Tc-99m mebrofenin, diagnostic, per study dose, up to 15 millicuries | NI |
| N | ☑ | A9538 | Technetium Tc-99m pyrophosphate, diagnostic, per study dose, up to 25 millicuries<br>Use this code for CIS-PYRO, Phosphostec, Technescan Pyp Kit | NI |
| N | ☑ | A9539 | Technetium Tc-99m pentetate, diagnostic, per study dose, up to 25 millicuries<br>Use this code for AN-DTPA, DTPA, Magnavist, MPI-DTPA Kit-Chelate, MPI Indium DTPA IN-111, Pentate Calcium Trisodium, Pentate Zinc Trisodium | NI |
| N | ☑ | A9540 | Technetium Tc-99m macroaggregated albumin, diagnostic, per study dose, up to 10 millicuries | NI |
| N | ☑ | A9541 | Technetium Tc-99m sulfur colloid, diagnostic, per study dose, up to 20 millicuries | NI |
| N | ☑ | A9542 | Indium In-111 ibritumomab tiuxetan, diagnostic, per study dose, up to 5 millicuries<br>Use this code for Zevalin | NI ⃠ |
| H | ☑ | A9543 | Yttrium Y-90 ibritumomab tiuxetan, therapeutic, per treatment dose, up to 40 millicuries | ⃠ |
| N | ☑ | A9544 | Iodine I-131 tositumomab, diagnostic, per study dose | NI ⃠ |
| H | ☑ | A9545 | Iodine I-131 tositumomab, therapeutic, per treatment dose<br>Use this code for Bexxar. | ⃠ |
| N | ☑ | A9546 | Cobalt Co-57/58, cyanocobalamin, diagnostic, per study dose, up to 1 microcurie | NI |
| N | ☑ | A9547 | Indium In-111 oxyquinoline, diagnostic, per 0.5 millicurie | NI |
| N | ☑ | A9548 | Indium In-111 pentetate, diagnostic, per 0.5 millicurie | NI |
| N | ☑ | A9550 | Technetium Tc-99m sodium gluceptate, diagnostic, per study dose, up to 25 millicurie | NI |
| N | ☑ | A9551 | Technetium Tc-99m succimer, diagnostic, per study dose, up to 10 millicuries<br>Use this code for MPI-DMSA Kidney Reagent. | NI |
| N | ☑ | A9552 | Fluorodeoxyglucose F-18 FDG, diagnostic, per study dose, up to 45 millicuries | NI |
| N | ☑ | A9553 | Chromium Cr-51 sodium chromate, diagnostic, per study dose, up to 250 microcuries<br>Use this code for Chromitope Sodium. | NI |
| N | ☑ | A9554 | Iodine I-125 sodium iothalamate, diagnostic, per study dose, up to 10 microcuries<br>Use this code for Glofil-125. | NI |
| N | ☑ | A9555 | Rubidium Rb-82, diagnostic, per study dose, up to 60 millicuries<br>Use this code for Cardiogen 82. | NI |

N ☑ **A9556** Gallium Ga-67 citrate, diagnostic, per millicurie ⅏
Use this code for Ganite.

N ☑ **A9557** Technetium Tc-99m bicisate, diagnostic, per study dose, up to 25 millicuries ⅏
Use this code for Neurolite.

N ☑ **A9558** Xenon Xe-133 gas, diagnostic, per 10 millicuries ⅏

N ☑ **A9559** Cobalt Co-57 cyanocobalamin, oral, diagnostic, per study dose, up to 1 microcurie ⅏

N ☑ **A9560** Technetium Tc-99m labeled red blood cells, diagnostic, per study dose, up to 30 millicuries ⅏

N ☑ **A9561** Technetium Tc-99m oxidronate, diagnostic, per study dose, up to 30 millicuries ⅏
Use this code for TechneScan.

N ☑ **A9562** Technetium Tc-99m mertiatide, diagnostic, per study dose, up to 15 millicuries ⅏
Use this code for TechneScan MAG-3.

H ☑ **A9563** Sodium phosphate P-32, therapeutic, per millicurie

H ☑ **A9564** Chromic phosphate P-32 suspension, therapeutic, per millicurie
Use this code for Phosphocol (P32).

N ☑ **A9566** Technetium Tc-99m fanolesomab, diagnostic, per study dose, up to 25 millicuries ⅏

N ☑ **A9567** Technetium Tc-99m pentetate, diagnostic, aerosol, per study dose, up to 75 millicuries ⅏
Use this code for AN-DTPA, DTPA, MPI-DTPA Kit-Chelate, MPI Indium DTPA IN-111, Pentate Calcium Trisodium, Pentate Zinc Trisodium.

N ☑ **A9568** Technetium Tc-99m arcitumomab, diagnostic, per study dose, up to 45 millicuries ⅏
Use this code for CEA Scan.

N ☑ **A9569** Technetium Tc-99m exametazime labeled autologous white blood cells, diagnostic, per study dose ⅏
Use this code for Ceretec.

N ☑ **A9570** Indium In-111 labeled autologous white blood cells, diagnostic, per study dose ⅏

N ☑ **A9571** Indium In-111 labeled autologous platelets, diagnostic, per study dose ⅏

N ☑ **A9572** Indium In-111 pentetreotide, diagnostic, per study dose, up to 6 millicuries ⅏
Use this code for Ostreoscan.

N ☑ **A9576** Injection, gadoteridol, (ProHance multipack), per ml ⅏

N ☑ **A9577** Injection, gadobenate dimeglumine (MultiHance), per ml ⅏

N ☑ **A9578** Injection, gadobenate dimeglumine (MultiHance multipack), per ml ⅏

N ☑ **A9579** Injection, gadolinium-based magnetic resonance contrast agent, not otherwise specified (NOS), per ml ⅏
Use this code for Omniscan.

● N **A9580** Sodium fluoride F-18, diagnostic, per study dose, up to 30 millicuries ⅏

**Administrative, Misc., Investigational**

**A9600 — A9999**

| | | | |
|---|---|---|---|
| H ☑ | A9600 | Strontium Sr-89 chloride, therapeutic, per millicurie | |

Use this code for Metastron.

AHA: 2Q,'02,9

| H ☑ | A9605 | Samarium Sm-153 lexidronamm, therapeutic, per 50 millicuries |

Use this code for Quadramet.

AHA: 2Q,'02,9

| N | A9698 | Nonradioactive contrast imaging material, not otherwise classified, per study    ▥ |

| N | A9699 | Radiopharmaceutical, therapeutic, not otherwise classified |

| B | A9700 | Supply of injectable contrast material for use in echocardiography, per study |

AHA: 4Q,'01,5

## MISCELLANEOUS

| Y | A9900 | Miscellaneous DME supply, accessory, and/or service component of another HCPCS code    ♿ |

| A | A9901 | DME delivery, set up, and/or dispensing service component of another HCPCS code |

| Y | A9999 | Miscellaneous DME supply or accessory, not otherwise specified |

## ENTERAL AND PARENTERAL THERAPY B4000-B9999

This section includes codes for supplies, formulae, nutritional solutions, and infusion pumps.

## ENTERAL FORMULAE AND ENTERAL MEDICAL SUPPLIES

**Certification of medical necessity is required for coverage. Submit a revision to the certification of medical necessity if the patient's daily volume changes by more than one liter; if there is a change in infusion method; or if there is a change from premix to home mix or parenteral to enteral therapy.**

Y ☑   **B4034**   Enteral feeding supply kit; syringe fed, per day   ♿
      MED: 100-2,15,120; 100-3,180.2; 100-4,20,100.2.2; 100-4,20,160.1

Y ☑   **B4035**   Enteral feeding supply kit; pump fed, per day   ♿
      MED: 100-2,15,120; 100-3,180.2; 100-4,20,100.2.2; 100-4,20,160.1

Y ☑   **B4036**   Enteral feeding supply kit; gravity fed, per day   ♿
      MED: 100-2,15,120; 100-3,180.2; 100-4,20,100.2.2; 100-4,20,160.1

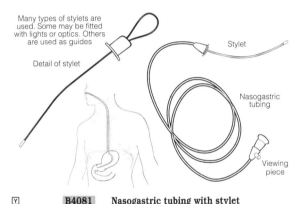

Many types of stylets are used. Some may be fitted with lights or optics. Others are used as guides

Detail of stylet

Stylet

Nasogastric tubing

Viewing piece

Y   **B4081**   Nasogastric tubing with stylet   ♿
      MED: 100-2,15,120; 100-3,180.2; 100-4,20,100.2.2; 100-4,20,160.1

Y   **B4082**   Nasogastric tubing without stylet   ♿
      MED: 100-2,15,120; 100-3,180.2; 100-4,20,100.2.2; 100-4,20,160.1

Y   **B4083**   Stomach tube — Levine type   ♿
      MED: 100-2,15,120; 100-3,180.2; 100-4,20,100.2.2

A ☑   **B4087**   Gastrostomy/jejunostomy tube, standard, any material, any type, each

A ☑   **B4088**   Gastrostomy/jejunostomy tube, low-profile, any material, any type, each

E ☑   **B4100**   Food thickener, administered orally, per oz

Y ☑   **B4102**   Enteral formula, for adults, used to replace fluids and electrolytes (e.g., clear liquids), 500 ml = 1 unit   ♿
      MED: 100-3,180.2; 100-4,20,160.1

Y ☑   **B4103**   Enteral formula, for pediatrics, used to replace fluids and electrolytes (e.g., clear liquids), 500 ml = 1 unit   ♿
      MED: 100-3,180.2; 100-4,20,160.1

E   **B4104**   Additive for enteral formula (e.g., fiber)
      MED: 100-3,180.2; 100-4,20,160.1

Ⓨ ☑ **B4149** Enteral formula, manufactured blenderized natural foods with intact nutrients, includes proteins, fats, carbohydrates, vitamins and minerals, may include fiber, administered through an enteral feeding tube, 100 calories = 1 unit ♿

MED: 100-2,15,120; 100-3,180.2; 100-4,20,100.2.2; 100-4,20,160.1

Ⓨ ☑ **B4150** Enteral formula, nutritionally complete with intact nutrients, includes proteins, fats, carbohydrates, vitamins and minerals, may include fiber, administered through an enteral feeding tube, 100 calories = 1 unit ♿

Use this code for Enrich, Ensure, Ensure HN, Ensure Powder, Isocal, Lonalac Powder, Meritene, Meritene Powder, Osmolite, Osmolite HN, Portagen Powder, Sustacal, Renu, Sustagen Powder, Travasorb.

MED: 100-2,15,120; 100-3,180.2; 100-4,20,100.2.2; 100-4,20,160.1

Ⓨ ☑ **B4152** Enteral formula, nutritionally complete, calorically dense (equal to or greater than 1.5 kcal/ml) with intact nutrients, includes proteins, fats, carbohydrates, vitamins and minerals, may include fiber, administered through an enteral feeding tube, 100 calories = 1 unit ♿

Use this code for Magnacal, Isocal HCN, Sustacal HC, Ensure Plus, Ensure Plus HN.

MED: 100-2,15,120; 100-3,180.2; 100-4,20,100.2.2; 100-4,20,160.1

Ⓨ ☑ **B4153** Enteral formula, nutritionally complete, hydrolyzed proteins (amino acids and peptide chain), includes fats, carbohydrates, vitamins and minerals, may include fiber, administered through an enteral feeding tube, 100 calories = 1 unit ♿

Use this code for Criticare HN, Vivonex t.e.n. (Total Enteral Nutrition), Vivonex HN, Vital (Vital HN), Travasorb HN, Isotein HN, Precision HN, Precision Isotonic.

MED: 100-2,15,120; 100-3,180.2; 100-4,20,100.2.2; 100-4,20,160.1

Ⓨ ☑ **B4154** Enteral formula, nutritionally complete, for special metabolic needs, excludes inherited disease of metabolism, includes altered composition of proteins, fats, carbohydrates, vitamins and/or minerals, may include fiber, administered through an enteral feeding tube, 100 calories = 1 unit ♿

Use this code for Hepatic-aid, Travasorb Hepatic, Travasorb MCT, Travasorb Renal, Traum-aid, Tramacal, Aminaid.

MED: 100-2,15,120; 100-3,180.2; 100-4,20,100.2.2; 100-4,20,160.1

Ⓨ ☑ **B4155** Enteral formula, nutritionally incomplete/modular nutrients, includes specific nutrients, carbohydrates (e.g., glucose polymers), proteins/amino acids (e.g., glutamine, arginine), fat (e.g., medium chain triglycerides) or combination, administered through an enteral feeding tube, 100 calories = 1 unit ♿

Use this code for Propac, Gerval Protein, Promix, Casec, Moducal, Controlyte, Polycose Liquid or Powder, Sumacal, Microlipids, MCT Oil, Nutri-source.

MED: 100-2,15,120; 100-3,180.2; 100-4,20,100.2.2; 100-4,20,160.1

Ⓨ ☑ **B4157** Enteral formula, nutritionally complete, for special metabolic needs for inherited disease of metabolism, includes proteins, fats, carbohydrates, vitamins and minerals, may include fiber, administered through an enteral feeding tube, 100 calories = 1 unit ♿

MED: 100-3,180.2; 100-4,20,160.1

Ⓨ ☑ **B4158** Enteral formula, for pediatrics, nutritionally complete with intact nutrients, includes proteins, fats, carbohydrates, vitamins and minerals, may include fiber and/or iron, administered through an enteral feeding tube, 100 calories = 1 unit ♿

MED: 100-3,180.2; 100-4,20,160.1

---

Ⓨ ☑ **B4159** Enteral formula, for pediatrics, nutritionally complete soy based with intact nutrients, includes proteins, fats, carbohydrates, vitamins and minerals, may include fiber and/or iron, administered through an enteral feeding tube, 100 calories = 1 unit    ♿

MED: 100-3,180.2; 100-4,20,160.1

Ⓨ ☑ **B4160** Enteral formula, for pediatrics, nutritionally complete calorically dense (equal to or greater than 0.7 kcal/ml) with intact nutrients, includes proteins, fats, carbohydrates, vitamins and minerals, may include fiber, administered through an enteral feeding tube, 100 calories = 1 unit   ♿

MED: 100-3,180.2; 100-4,20,160.1

Ⓨ ☑ **B4161** Enteral formula, for pediatrics, hydrolyzed/amino acids and peptide chain proteins, includes fats, carbohydrates, vitamins and minerals, may include fiber, administered through an enteral feeding tube, 100 calories = 1 unit   ♿

MED: 100-3,180.2; 100-4,20,160.1

Ⓨ ☑ **B4162** Enteral formula, for pediatrics, special metabolic needs for inherited disease of metabolism, includes proteins, fats, carbohydrates, vitamins and minerals, may include fiber, administered through an enteral feeding tube, 100 calories = 1 unit   ♿

MED: 100-3,180.2; 100-4,20,160.1

## PARENTERAL NUTRITION SOLUTIONS AND SUPPLIES

Ⓨ ☑ **B4164** Parenteral nutrition solution: carbohydrates (dextrose), 50% or less (500 ml = 1 unit), home mix   ♿

MED: 100-2,15,120; 100-3,180.2; 100-4,3,10.4; 100-4,20,100.2.2

Ⓨ ☑ **B4168** Parenteral nutrition solution; amino acid, 3.5%, (500 ml = 1 unit) — home mix   ♿

MED: 100-2,15,120; 100-3,180.2; 100-4,3,10.4; 100-4,20,100.2.2

Ⓨ ☑ **B4172** Parenteral nutrition solution; amino acid, 5.5% through 7%, (500 ml = 1 unit) — home mix   ♿

MED: 100-2,15,120; 100-3,180.2; 100-4,3,10.4; 100-4,20,100.2.2

Ⓨ ☑ **B4176** Parenteral nutrition solution; amino acid, 7% through 8.5%, (500 ml = 1 unit) — home mix   ♿

MED: 100-2,15,120; 100-3,180.2; 100-4,3,10.4; 100-4,20,100.2.2

Ⓨ ☑ **B4178** Parenteral nutrition solution: amino acid, greater than 8.5% (500 ml = 1 unit), home mix   ♿

MED: 100-2,15,120; 100-3,180.2; 100-4,3,10.4; 100-4,20,100.2.2

Ⓨ ☑ **B4180** Parenteral nutrition solution: carbohydrates (dextrose), greater than 50% (500 ml = 1 unit), home mix   ♿

MED: 100-2,15,120; 100-3,180.2; 100-4,3,10.4; 100-4,20,100.2.2

Ⓑ ☑ **B4185** Parenteral nutrition solution, per 10 grams lipids

Ⓨ ☑ **B4189** Parenteral nutrition solution: compounded amino acid and carbohydrates with electrolytes, trace elements, and vitamins, including preparation, any strength, 10 to 51 g of protein, premix   ♿

MED: 100-2,15,120; 100-3,180.2; 100-4,3,10.4; 100-4,20,100.2.2

Ⓨ ☑ **B4193** Parenteral nutrition solution: compounded amino acid and carbohydrates with electrolytes, trace elements, and vitamins, including preparation, any strength, 52 to 73 g of protein, premix   ♿

MED: 100-2,15,120; 100-3,180.2; 100-4,3,10.4; 100-4,20,100.2.2

---

☑ Quantity Alert    ● New Code    ○ Recycled/Reinstated    ▲ Revised Code    ♿ DMEPOS Paid    ⊘ SNF Excluded

**Enteral and Parenteral Therapy**

**B4197 — B9998**

| | | | |
|---|---|---|---|
| Y ☑ | **B4197** | Parenteral nutrition solution; compounded amino acid and carbohydrates with electrolytes, trace elements and vitamins, including preparation, any strength, 74 to 100 grams of protein — premix | ♿ |
| | | MED: 100-2,15,120; 100-3,180.2; 100-4,3,10.4; 100-4,20,100.2.2 | |
| Y ☑ | **B4199** | Parenteral nutrition solution; compounded amino acid and carbohydrates with electrolytes, trace elements and vitamins, including preparation, any strength, over 100 grams of protein — premix | ♿ |
| | | MED: 100-2,15,120; 100-3,180.2; 100-4,3,10.4; 100-4,20,100.2.2 | |
| Y | **B4216** | Parenteral nutrition; additives (vitamins, trace elements, Heparin, electrolytes), home mix, per day | ♿ |
| | | MED: 100-2,15,120; 100-3,180.2; 100-4,3,10.4; 100-4,20,100.2.2 | |
| Y | **B4220** | Parenteral nutrition supply kit; premix, per day | ♿ |
| | | MED: 100-2,15,120; 100-3,180.2; 100-4,3,10.4; 100-4,20,100.2.2 | |
| Y | **B4222** | Parenteral nutrition supply kit; home mix, per day | ♿ |
| | | MED: 100-2,15,120; 100-3,180.2; 100-4,3,10.4; 100-4,20,100.2.2 | |
| Y | **B4224** | Parenteral nutrition administration kit, per day | ♿ |
| | | MED: 100-2,15,120; 100-3,180.2; 100-4,3,10.4; 100-4,20,100.2.2 | |
| Y | **B5000** | Parenteral nutrition solution: compounded amino acid and carbohydrates with electrolytes, trace elements, and vitamins, including preparation, any strength, renal - Amirosyn RF, NephrAmine, RenAmine - premix | ♿ |
| | | Use this code for Amirosyn-RF, NephrAmine, RenAmin. | |
| | | MED: 100-2,15,120; 100-3,180.2; 100-4,3,10.4; 100-4,20,100.2.2 | |
| Y | **B5100** | Parenteral nutrition solution: compounded amino acid and carbohydrates with electrolytes, trace elements, and vitamins, including preparation, any strength, hepatic - FreAmine HBC, HepatAmine - premix | ♿ |
| | | Use this code for FreAmine HBC, HepatAmine. | |
| | | MED: 100-2,15,120; 100-3,180.2; 100-4,3,10.4; 100-4,20,100.2.2 | |
| Y | **B5200** | Parenteral nutrition solution: compounded amino acid and carbohydrates with electrolytes, trace elements, and vitamins, including preparation, any strength, stress - branch chain amino acids - premix | ♿ |
| | | MED: 100-2,15,120; 100-3,180.2; 100-4,3,10.4; 100-4,20,100.2.2 | |

## ENTERAL AND PARENTERAL PUMPS

Submit documentation of the need for the infusion pump. Medicare will reimburse for the simplest model that meets the patient's needs.

| | | | |
|---|---|---|---|
| Y | **B9000** | Enteral nutrition infusion pump — without alarm | ♿ |
| | | MED: 100-2,15,120; 100-3,180.2; 100-4,20,100.2.2 | |
| Y | **B9002** | Enteral nutrition infusion pump — with alarm | ♿ |
| | | MED: 100-2,15,120; 100-3,180.2; 100-4,20,100.2.2 | |
| Y | **B9004** | Parenteral nutrition infusion pump, portable | ♿ |
| | | MED: 100-2,15,120; 100-3,180.2; 100-4,3,10.4; 100-4,20,100.2.2 | |
| Y | **B9006** | Parenteral nutrition infusion pump, stationary | ♿ |
| | | MED: 100-2,15,120; 100-3,180.2; 100-4,3,10.4; 100-4,20,100.2.2 | |
| Y | **B9998** | NOC for enteral supplies | ♿ |
| | | MED: 100-2,15,120; 100-3,180.2; 100-4,3,10.4; 100-4,20,100.2.2 | |

| Ⓨ | B9999 | NOC for parenteral supplies       ໒ |
|---|---|---|

Determine if an alternative HCPCS Level II or a CPT code better describes the service being reported. This code should be used only if a more specific code is unavailable.

MED: 100-2,15,120; 100-3,180.2; 100-4,3,10.4; 100-4,20,100.2.2

## OUTPATIENT PPS C1000-C9999

This section reports drugs, biologicals, and devices codes that must be used by OPPS hospitals. Non-OPPS hospitals, Critical Access Hospitals (CAHs), Indian Health Service Hospitals (HIS), hospitals located in American Samoa, Guam, Saipan, or the Virgin Islands, and Maryland waiver hospitals may report these codes at their discretion. The codes can only be reported for facility (technical) services.

The C series of HCPCS may include device catagories, new technology procedures, and drugs, biologicals and radiopharmaceuticals that do not have other HCPCS codes assigned. Some of these items and services are eligible for transitional pass-through payments for OPPS hospitals, have separate APC payments, or are items that are packaged. Hospitals are encouraged to report all appropriate C codes regardless of payment status.

S ☑ **C1300** **Hyperbaric oxygen under pressure, full body chamber, per 30 minute interval**
    MED: 100-4,32,30.1

N **C1713** **Anchor/screw for opposing bone-to-bone or soft tissue-to-bone (implantable)** ⚕
    MED: 100-4,4,61.1
    AHA: 3Q,'02,5; 1Q,'01,5

N **C1714** **Catheter, transluminal atherectomy, directional** ⚕
    MED: 100-4,4,61.1
    AHA: 4Q,'03,8; 3Q,'02,5; 1Q,'01,5

N **C1715** **Brachytherapy needle** ⚕ ⊘
    MED: 100-4,4,61.1
    AHA: 3Q,'02,5; 1Q,'01,5

U ☑ **C1716** **Brachytherapy source, nonstranded, gold-198, per source** ⊘
    MED: 100-4,4,61.1
    AHA: 3Q,'02,5; 1Q,'01,5

U ☑ **C1717** **Brachytherapy source, nonstranded, high dose rate iridium-192, per source** ⊘
    MED: 100-4,4,61.1
    AHA: 3Q,'02,5; 1Q,'01,5

U ☑ **C1719** **Brachytherapy source, nonstranded, nonhigh dose rate iridium-192, per source** ⊘
    MED: 100-4,4,61.1
    AHA: 3Q,'02,5; 1Q,'01,5

N **C1721** **Cardioverter-defibrillator, dual chamber (implantable)** ⚕
    MED: 100-4,4,61.1
    AHA: 3Q,'02,5; 1Q,'01,5

N **C1722** **Cardioverter-defibrillator, single chamber (implantable)** ⚕
    MED: 100-4,4,61.1
    AHA: 3Q,'02,5; 1Q,'01,5

N **C1724** **Catheter, transluminal atherectomy, rotational** ⚕
    MED: 100-4,4,61.1
    AHA: 4Q,'03,8; 3Q,'02,5; 1Q,'01,5

N **C1725** **Catheter, transluminal angioplasty, nonlaser (may include guidance, infusion/perfusion capability)** ⚕
    MED: 100-4,4,61.1
    AHA: 4Q,'03,8; 3Q,'02,5; 1Q,'01,5

N **C1726** **Catheter, balloon dilatation, nonvascular** ⚕
    MED: 100-4,4,61.1
    AHA: 3Q,'02,5; 1Q,'01,5

| | | | | |
|---|---|---|---|---|
| N | **C1727** | Catheter, balloon tissue dissector, nonvascular (insertable) | N1 | |
| | | MED: 100-4,4,61.1 | | |
| | | AHA: 3Q,'02,5; 1Q,'01,5 | | |
| ○ N | **C1728** | Catheter, brachytherapy seed administration | N1 ⊘ | |
| | | MED: 100-4,4,61.1 | | |
| | | AHA: 3Q,'02,5; 1Q,'01,5 | | |
| N | **C1729** | Catheter, drainage | N1 | |
| | | MED: 100-4,4,61.1 | | |
| | | AHA: 3Q,'02,5; 1Q,'01,5 | | |
| N | **C1730** | Catheter, electrophysiology, diagnostic, other than 3D mapping (19 or fewer electrodes) | N1 | |
| | | MED: 100-4,4,61.1 | | |
| | | AHA: 3Q,'02,5; 1Q,'01,5 | | |
| N | **C1731** | Catheter, electrophysiology, diagnostic, other than 3D mapping (20 or more electrodes) | N1 | |
| | | MED: 100-4,4,61.1 | | |
| | | AHA: 3Q,'02,5; 1Q,'01,5 | | |
| N | **C1732** | Catheter, electrophysiology, diagnostic/ablation, 3D or vector mapping | N1 | |
| | | MED: 100-4,4,61.1 | | |
| | | AHA: 1Q,'01,5 | | |
| N | **C1733** | Catheter, electrophysiology, diagnostic/ablation, other than 3D or vector mapping, other than cool-tip | N1 | |
| | | MED: 100-4,4,61.1 | | |
| | | AHA: 3Q,'02,5; 1Q,'01,5 | | |
| N | **C1750** | Catheter, hemodialysis/peritoneal, long-term | N1 | |
| | | MED: 100-4,4,61.1 | | |
| | | AHA: 4Q,'03,8; 3Q,'02,5; 1Q,'01,5 | | |
| N | **C1751** | Catheter, infusion, inserted peripherally, centrally or midline (other than hemodialysis) | N1 | |
| | | MED: 100-4,4,61.1 | | |
| | | AHA: 4Q,'03,8; 3Q,'02,5; 3Q,'01,5 | | |
| N | **C1752** | Catheter, hemodialysis/peritoneal, short-term | N1 | |
| | | MED: 100-4,4,61.1 | | |
| | | AHA: 4Q,'03,8; 3Q,'02,5; 1Q,'01,5 | | |
| N | **C1753** | Catheter, intravascular ultrasound | N1 | |
| | | MED: 100-4,4,61.1 | | |
| | | AHA: 4Q,'03,8; 3Q,'02,5; 1Q,'01,5 | | |
| N | **C1754** | Catheter, intradiscal | N1 | |
| | | MED: 100-4,4,61.1 | | |
| | | AHA: 4Q,'03,8; 3Q,'02,5; 1Q,'01,5 | | |
| N | **C1755** | Catheter, intraspinal | N1 | |
| | | MED: 100-4,4,61.1 | | |
| | | AHA: 4Q,'03,8; 3Q,'02,5; 1Q,'01,5 | | |
| N | **C1756** | Catheter, pacing, transesophageal | N1 | |
| | | MED: 100-4,4,61.1 | | |
| | | AHA: 4Q,'03,8; 3Q,'02,5; 1Q,'01,5 | | |
| N | **C1757** | Catheter, thrombectomy/embolectomy | N1 | |
| | | MED: 100-4,4,61.1 | | |
| | | AHA: 4Q,'03,8; 3Q,'02,5; 1Q,'01,5 | | |

**Outpatient PPS**

**C1758 — C1776**

N [C1758] Catheter, ureteral □N
MED: 100-4,4,61.1
AHA: 4Q,'03,8; 3Q,'02,5; 1Q,'01,6

N [C1759] Catheter, intracardiac echocardiography □N
MED: 100-4,4,61.1
AHA: 4Q,'03,8; 3Q,'02,5; 1Q,'01,5; 3Q,'01,4

N [C1760] Closure device, vascular (implantable/insertable) □N
MED: 100-4,4,61.1
AHA: 4Q,'03,8; 3Q,'02,5; 1Q,'01,6

N [C1762] Connective tissue, human (includes fascia lata) □N
MED: 100-4,4,61.1
AHA: 3Q,'03,12; 4Q,'03,8; 3Q,'02,5; 1Q,'01,6

N [C1763] Connective tissue, nonhuman (includes synthetic) □N
MED: 100-4,4,61.1
AHA: 3Q,'03,12; 4Q,'03,8; 3Q,'02,5; 1Q,'01,6

N [C1764] Event recorder, cardiac (implantable) □N
MED: 100-4,4,61.1
AHA: 4Q,'03,8; 3Q,'02,5; 1Q,'01,6

N [C1765] Adhesion barrier □N
MED: 100-4,4,61.1

N [C1766] Introducer/sheath, guiding, intracardiac electrophysiological, steerable, other than peel-away □N
MED: 100-4,4,61.1
AHA: 3Q,'02,5; 3Q,'01,5

N [C1767] Generator, neurostimulator (implantable), nonrechargeable □N
MED: 100-4,4,61.1
AHA: 4Q,'03,8; 1Q,'02,9; 3Q,'02,5

N [C1768] Graft, vascular □N
MED: 100-4,4,61.1
AHA: 4Q,'03,8; 3Q,'02,5; 1Q,'01,6

N [C1769] Guide wire □N
MED: 100-4,4,61.1
AHA: 4Q,'03,8; 3Q,'02,5; 1Q,'01,6; 3Q,'01,4

N [C1770] Imaging coil, magnetic resonance (insertable) □N
MED: 100-4,4,61.1
AHA: 4Q,'03,8; 3Q,'02,5; 1Q,'01,6

N [C1771] Repair device, urinary, incontinence, with sling graft □N
MED: 100-4,4,61.1
AHA: 4Q,'03,8; 3Q,'02,5; 1Q,'01,6

N [C1772] Infusion pump, programmable (implantable) □N
MED: 100-4,4,61.1
AHA: 3Q,'02,5; 1Q,'01,6

N [C1773] Retrieval device, insertable (used to retrieve fractured medical devices) □N
MED: 100-4,4,61.1
AHA: 4Q,'03,8; 3Q,'02,5; 1Q,'01,6

N [C1776] Joint device (implantable) □N
MED: 100-4,4,61.1
AHA: 3Q,'02,5; 1Q,'01,6; 3Q,'01,5

---

Special Coverage Instructions    Noncovered by Medicare    Carrier Discretion

| N | C1777 | Lead, cardioverter-defibrillator, endocardial single coil (implantable) | N1 |
|---|---|---|---|

MED: 100-4,4,61.1
AHA: 3Q,'02,5; 1Q,'01,6

| N | C1778 | Lead, neurostimulator (implantable) | N1 |
|---|---|---|---|

MED: 100-4,4,61.1
AHA: 3Q,'02,5; 1Q,'02,9

| N | C1779 | Lead, pacemaker, transvenous VDD single pass | N1 |
|---|---|---|---|

MED: 100-4,4,61.1
AHA: 3Q,'02,5; 1Q,'01,6

| N | C1780 | Lens, intraocular (new technology) | N1 |
|---|---|---|---|

MED: 100-4,4,61.1
AHA: 3Q,'02,5; 1Q,'01,6

| N | C1781 | Mesh (implantable) | N1 |
|---|---|---|---|

MED: 100-4,4,61.1
AHA: 3Q,'02,5; 1Q,'01,6

| N | C1782 | Morcellator | N1 |
|---|---|---|---|

MED: 100-4,4,61.1
AHA: 3Q,'02,5; 1Q,'01,6

| N | C1783 | Ocular implant, aqueous drainage assist device | N1 |
|---|---|---|---|

MED: 100-4,4,61.1

| N | C1784 | Ocular device, intraoperative, detached retina | N1 |
|---|---|---|---|

MED: 100-4,4,61.1
AHA: 3Q,'02,5; 1Q,'01,6

| N | C1785 | Pacemaker, dual chamber, rate-responsive (implantable) | N1 |
|---|---|---|---|

MED: 100-4,3,10.4; 100-4,4,61.1
AHA: 4Q,'03,8; 3Q,'02,5; 1Q,'01,6

| N | C1786 | Pacemaker, single chamber, rate-responsive (implantable) | N1 |
|---|---|---|---|

MED: 100-4,4,61.1
AHA: 4Q,'03,8; 3Q,'02,5; 1Q,'01,6

| N | C1787 | Patient programmer, neurostimulator | N1 |
|---|---|---|---|

MED: 100-4,4,61.1
AHA: 4Q,'03,8; 3Q,'02,5; 1Q,'01,6

| N | C1788 | Port, indwelling (implantable) | N1 |
|---|---|---|---|

MED: 100-4,4,61.1
AHA: 4Q,'03,8; 3Q,'02,5; 1Q,'01,6; 3Q,'01,4

| N | C1789 | Prosthesis, breast (implantable) | N1 |
|---|---|---|---|

MED: 100-4,4,61.1
AHA: 4Q,'03,8; 3Q,'02,5; 1Q,'01,6

| N | C1813 | Prosthesis, penile, inflatable | N1 |
|---|---|---|---|

MED: 100-4,4,61.1
AHA: 4Q,'03,8; 3Q,'02,5; 1Q,'01,6

| N | C1814 | Retinal tamponade device, silicone oil | N1 |
|---|---|---|---|

MED: 100-4,4,61.1

| N | C1815 | Prosthesis, urinary sphincter (implantable) | N1 |
|---|---|---|---|

MED: 100-4,4,61.1
AHA: 4Q,'03,8; 3Q,'02,5; 1Q,'01,6

| N | C1816 | Receiver and/or transmitter, neurostimulator (implantable) | N1 |
|---|---|---|---|

MED: 100-4,4,61.1
AHA: 4Q,'03,8; 3Q,'02,5; 1Q,'01,6

---

☑ Quantity Alert    ● New Code    ○ Recycled/Reinstated    ▲ Revised Code    ☒ DMEPOS Paid    ⊘ SNF Excluded

| N | C1817 | Septal defect implant system, intracardiac | NI |
|---|---|---|---|

MED: 100-4,4,61.1

AHA: 4Q,'03,8; 3Q,'02,5; 1Q,'01,6

| N | C1818 | Integrated keratoprosthesis | NI |
|---|---|---|---|

MED: 100-4,4,61.1

AHA: 4Q,'03,4

| N | C1819 | Surgical tissue localization and excision device (implantable) | NI |
|---|---|---|---|

MED: 100-4,4,61.1

| N | C1820 | Generator, neurostimulator (implantable), with rechargeable battery and charging system | NI |
|---|---|---|---|

MED: 100-4,4,10.12

| N | C1821 | Interspinous process distraction device (implantable) | NI |
|---|---|---|---|

| N | C1874 | Stent, coated/covered, with delivery system | NI |
|---|---|---|---|

MED: 100-4,4,61.1

AHA: 4Q,'03,8; 1Q,'01,6

| N | C1875 | Stent, coated/covered, without delivery system | NI |
|---|---|---|---|

MED: 100-4,4,61.1

AHA: 4Q,'03,8; 1Q,'01,6

| N | C1876 | Stent, noncoated/noncovered, with delivery system | NI |
|---|---|---|---|

MED: 100-4,4,61.1

AHA: 4Q,'03,8; 3Q,'02,5; 1Q,'01,6; 3Q,'01,4

| N | C1877 | Stent, noncoated/noncovered, without delivery system | NI |
|---|---|---|---|

MED: 100-4,4,61.1

AHA: 4Q,'03,8; 3Q,'02,5; 1Q,'01,6; 3Q,'01,4

| N | C1878 | Material for vocal cord medialization, synthetic (implantable) | NI |
|---|---|---|---|

MED: 100-4,4,61.1

AHA: 3Q,'02,5; 1Q,'01,6

| N | C1879 | Tissue marker (implantable) | NI |
|---|---|---|---|

MED: 100-4,4,61.1

AHA: 4Q,'03,8; 3Q,'02,5; 1Q,'01,6

| N | C1880 | Vena cava filter | NI |
|---|---|---|---|

MED: 100-4,4,61.1

AHA: 4Q,'03,8; 3Q,'02,5; 1Q,'01,6

| N | C1881 | Dialysis access system (implantable) | NI |
|---|---|---|---|

MED: 100-4,4,61.1

AHA: 4Q,'03,8; 3Q,'02,5; 1Q,'01,6

| N | C1882 | Cardioverter-defibrillator, other than single or dual chamber (implantable) | NI |
|---|---|---|---|

MED: 100-4,4,61.1

AHA: 3Q,'02,5; 1Q,'01,5

| N | C1883 | Adaptor/extension, pacing lead or neurostimulator lead (implantable) | NI |
|---|---|---|---|

MED: 100-4,4,61.1

AHA: 1Q,'02,9; 3Q,'02,5; 1Q,'01,5

| N | C1884 | Embolization protective system | NI |
|---|---|---|---|

MED: 100-4,4,61.1

| N | C1885 | Catheter, transluminal angioplasty, laser | NI |
|---|---|---|---|

MED: 100-4,4,61.1

AHA: 4Q,'03,8; 3Q,'02,5; 1Q,'01,5

| N | C1887 | Catheter, guiding (may include infusion/perfusion capability) | N1 |

MED: 100-4,4,61.1

AHA: 3Q,'02,5; 1Q,'01,5

| N | C1888 | Catheter, ablation, noncardiac, endovascular (implantable) | N1 |

MED: 100-4,4,61.1

| N | C1891 | Infusion pump, nonprogrammable, permanent (implantable) | N1 |

MED: 100-4,4,61.1

AHA: 4Q,'03,8; 3Q,'02,5; 1Q,'01,6

| N | C1892 | Introducer/sheath, guiding, intracardiac electrophysiological, fixed-curve, peel-away | N1 |

MED: 100-4,4,61.1

AHA: 3Q,'02,5; 1Q,'01,6

| N | C1893 | Introducer/sheath, guiding, intracardiac electrophysiological, fixed-curve, other than peel-away | N1 |

MED: 100-4,4,61.1

AHA: 3Q,'02,5; 1Q,'01,6; 3Q,'01,4

| N | C1894 | Introducer/sheath, other than guiding, other than intracardiac electrophysiological, nonlaser | N1 |

MED: 100-4,4,61.1

AHA: 3Q,'02,5

| N | C1895 | Lead, cardioverter-defibrillator, endocardial dual coil (implantable) | N1 |

MED: 100-4,4,61.1

AHA: 3Q,'02,5; 1Q,'01,6

| N | C1896 | Lead, cardioverter-defibrillator, other than endocardial single or dual coil (implantable) | N1 |

MED: 100-4,4,61.1

AHA: 3Q,'02,5; 1Q,'01,6

| N | C1897 | Lead, neurostimulator test kit (implantable) | N1 |

MED: 100-4,4,61.1

AHA: 1Q,'02,9; 3Q,'02,5; 1Q,'01,6

| N | C1898 | Lead, pacemaker, other than transvenous VDD single pass | N1 |

MED: 100-4,4,61.1

AHA: 1Q,'01,6; 3Q,'01,4

| N | C1899 | Lead, pacemaker/cardioverter-defibrillator combination (implantable) | N1 |

MED: 100-4,4,61.1

AHA: 3Q,'02,5; 1Q,'01,6

| N | C1900 | Lead, left ventricular coronary venous system | N1 |

MED: 100-4,4,61.1

| N | C2614 | Probe, percutaneous lumbar discectomy | N1 |

MED: 100-4,4,61.1

| N | C2615 | Sealant, pulmonary, liquid | N1 |

MED: 100-4,4,61.1

AHA: 3Q,'02,5; 1Q,'01,6

| U | ☑ | C2616 | Brachytherapy source, nonstranded, yttrium-90, per source | ⊘ |

MED: 100-4,4,61.1

AHA: 3Q,'03,11; 3Q,'02,5

| N | C2617 | Stent, noncoronary, temporary, without delivery system | N1 |

MED: 100-4,4,61.1

AHA: 4Q,'03,8; 3Q,'02,5; 1Q,'01,6

---

☑ Quantity Alert ● New Code ○ Recycled/Reinstated ▲ Revised Code ♿ DMEPOS Paid ⊘ SNF Excluded

| | | | |
|---|---|---|---|
| N | | C2618 | Probe, cryoablation ▯ |
| | | | MED: 100-4,4,61.1 |
| | | | AHA: 4Q,'03,8; 3Q,'02,5; 1Q,'01,6 |
| N | | C2619 | Pacemaker, dual chamber, nonrate-responsive (implantable) ▯ |
| | | | MED: 100-4,4,61.1 |
| | | | AHA: 3Q,'02,5; 1Q,'01,6; 3Q,'01,4 |
| N | | C2620 | Pacemaker, single chamber, nonrate-responsive (implantable) ▯ |
| | | | MED: 100-4,3,10.4; 100-4,4,61.1 |
| | | | AHA: 4Q,'03,8; 3Q,'02,5; 1Q,'01,6 |
| N | | C2621 | Pacemaker, other than single or dual chamber (implantable) ▯ |
| | | | MED: 100-4,3,10.4; 100-4,4,61.1 |
| | | | AHA: 4Q,'03,8; 1Q,'01,6 |
| N | | C2622 | Prosthesis, penile, noninflatable ▯ |
| | | | MED: 100-4,4,61.1 |
| | | | AHA: 4Q,'03,8; 3Q,'02,5; 1Q,'01,6 |
| N | | C2625 | Stent, noncoronary, temporary, with delivery system ▯ |
| | | | MED: 100-4,4,61.1 |
| | | | AHA: 4Q,'03,8; 3Q,'02,5; 1Q,'01,6 |
| N | | C2626 | Infusion pump, nonprogrammable, temporary (implantable) ▯ |
| | | | MED: 100-4,4,61.1 |
| | | | AHA: 3Q,'02,5; 1Q,'01,6 |
| N | | C2627 | Catheter, suprapubic/cystoscopic ▯ |
| | | | MED: 100-4,4,61.1 |
| | | | AHA: 4Q,'03,8; 3Q,'02,5; 1Q,'01,5 |
| N | | C2628 | Catheter, occlusion ▯ |
| | | | MED: 100-4,4,61.1 |
| | | | AHA: 4Q,'03,8; 3Q,'02,5; 1Q,'01,5 |
| N | | C2629 | Introducer/sheath, other than guiding, intracardiac electrophysiological, laser ▯ |
| | | | MED: 100-4,4,61.1 |
| | | | AHA: 3Q,'02,5; 1Q,'01,6 |
| N | | C2630 | Catheter, electrophysiology, diagnostic/ablation, other than 3D or vector mapping, cool-tip ▯ |
| | | | MED: 100-4,4,61.1 |
| | | | AHA: 3Q,'02,5; 1Q,'01,5 |
| N | | C2631 | Repair device, urinary, incontinence, without sling graft ▯ |
| | | | MED: 100-4,4,61.1 |
| | | | AHA: 4Q,'03,8; 3Q,'02,5; 1Q,'01,6 |
| U | ☑ | C2634 | Brachytherapy source, nonstranded, high activity, iodine-125, greater than 1.01 mCi (NIST), per source ⊘ |
| | | | MED: 100-4,4,61.1 |
| | | | AHA: 2Q,'05,8 |
| U | ☑ | C2635 | Brachytherapy source, nonstranded, high activity, palladium-103, greater than 2.2 mCi (NIST), per source ⊘ |
| | | | MED: 100-4,4,61.1 |
| | | | AHA: 2Q,'05,8 |
| U | ☑ | C2636 | Brachytherapy linear source, nonstranded, palladium-103, per 1 mm ⊘ |
| | | | MED: 100-4,4,61.1 |
| B | ☑ | C2637 | Brachytherapy source, nonstranded, ytterbium-169, per source ⊘ |
| | | | AHA: 3Q,'05,7 |
| U | ☑ | C2638 | Brachytherapy source, stranded, iodine-125, per source |

| | | | |
|---|---|---|---|
| U ☑ | C2639 | Brachytherapy source, nonstranded, iodine-125, per source | |
| U ☑ | C2640 | Brachytherapy source, stranded, palladium-103, per source | |
| U ☑ | C2641 | Brachytherapy source, nonstranded, palladium-103, per source | |
| U ☑ | C2642 | Brachytherapy source, stranded, cesium-131, per source | |
| U ☑ | C2643 | Brachytherapy source, nonstranded, cesium-131, per source | |
| U ☑ | C2698 | Brachytherapy source, stranded, not otherwise specified, per source | |
| U ☑ | C2699 | Brachytherapy source, nonstranded, not otherwise specified, per source | |
| Q3 | C8900 | Magnetic resonance angiography with contrast, abdomen | Z2 ⊘ |
| Q3 | C8901 | Magnetic resonance angiography without contrast, abdomen | Z2 ⊘ |
| Q3 | C8902 | Magnetic resonance angiography without contrast followed by with contrast, abdomen | Z2 ⊘ |
| Q3 | C8903 | Magnetic resonance imaging with contrast, breast; unilateral | Z2 ⊘ |
| Q3 | C8904 | Magnetic resonance imaging without contrast, breast; unilateral | Z2 ⊘ |
| Q3 | C8905 | Magnetic resonance imaging without contrast followed by with contrast, breast; unilateral | Z2 ⊘ |
| Q3 | C8906 | Magnetic resonance imaging with contrast, breast; bilateral | Z2 ⊘ |
| Q3 | C8907 | Magnetic resonance imaging without contrast, breast; bilateral | Z2 ⊘ |
| Q3 | C8908 | Magnetic resonance imaging without contrast followed by with contrast, breast; bilateral | Z2 ⊘ |
| Q3 | C8909 | Magnetic resonance angiography with contrast, chest (excluding myocardium) | Z2 ⊘ |
| Q3 | C8910 | Magnetic resonance angiography without contrast, chest (excluding myocardium) | Z2 ⊘ |
| Q3 | C8911 | Magnetic resonance angiography without contrast followed by with contrast, chest (excluding myocardium) | Z2 ⊘ |
| Q3 | C8912 | Magnetic resonance angiography with contrast, lower extremity | Z2 ⊘ |
| Q3 | C8913 | Magnetic resonance angiography without contrast, lower extremity | Z2 ⊘ |
| Q3 | C8914 | Magnetic resonance angiography without contrast followed by with contrast, lower extremity | Z2 ⊘ |
| Q3 | C8918 | Magnetic resonance angiography with contrast, pelvis | Z2 ⊘ |
| | | AHA: 4Q,'03,4 | |
| Q3 | C8919 | Magnetic resonance angiography without contrast, pelvis | Z2 ⊘ |
| | | AHA: 4Q,'03,4 | |
| Q3 | C8920 | Magnetic resonance angiography without contrast followed by with contrast, pelvis | Z2 ⊘ |
| | | AHA: 4Q,'03,4 | |
| ▲ S | C8921 | Transthoracic echocardiography with contrast, or without contrast followed by with contrast, for congenital cardiac anomalies; complete | |
| ▲ S | C8922 | Transthoracic echocardiography with contrast, or without contrast followed by with contrast, for congenital cardiac anomalies; follow-up or limited study | |
| ▲ S | C8923 | Transthoracic echocardiography with contrast, or without contrast followed by with contrast, real-time with image documentation (2D) with or without M-mode recording; complete | |

**Outpatient PPS**

**C8924 — C9241**

▲ Ⓢ **C8924** Transthoracic echocardiography with contrast, or without contrast followed by with contrast, real-time with image documentation (2D) with or without M-mode recording; follow-up or limited study

▲ Ⓢ **C8925** Transesophageal echocardiography (TEE) with contrast, or without contrast followed by with contrast, real time with image documentation (2D) (with or without M-mode recording); including probe placement, image acquisition, interpretation and report

▲ Ⓢ **C8926** Transesophageal echocardiography (TEE) with contrast, or without contrast followed by with contrast, for congenital cardiac anomalies; including probe placement, image acquisition, interpretation and report

▲ Ⓢ **C8927** Transesophageal echocardiography (TEE) with contrast, or without contrast followed by with contrast, for monitoring purposes, including probe placement, real time 2-dimensional image acquisition and interpretation leading to ongoing (continuous) assessment of (dynamically changing) cardiac pumping function and to therapeutic measures on an immediate time basis

▲ Ⓢ **C8928** Transthoracic echocardiography with contrast, or without contrast followed by with contrast, real-time with image documentation (2D), with or without M-mode recording, during rest and cardiovascular stress test using treadmill, bicycle exercise and/or pharmacologically induced stress, with interpretation and report

● Ⓢ **C8929** Transthoracic echocardiography with contrast, or without contrast followed by with contrast, real-time with image documentation (2D), includes M-mode recording, when performed, complete, with spectral doppler echocardiography, and with color flow doppler echocardiography

● Ⓢ **C8930** Transthoracic echocardiography, with contrast, or without contrast followed by with contrast, real-time with image documentation (2D), includes M-mode recording, when performed, during rest and cardiovascular stress test using treadmill, bicycle exercise and/or pharmacologically induced stress, with interpretation and report; including performance of continuous electrocardiographic monitoring, with physician supervision

Ⓢ **C8957** Intravenous infusion for therapy/diagnosis; initiation of prolonged infusion (more than 8 hours), requiring use of portable or implantable pump
MED: 100-4,4,230.2.1; 100-4,4,230.2.3

~~C9003~~ ~~Palivizumab-RSV-IgM, per 50 mg~~

Ⓝ **C9113** Injection, pantoprazole sodium, per vial ⬛N1
Use this code for Protonix.

Ⓚ ☑ **C9121** Injection, argatroban, per 5 mg ⬛K2

~~C9237~~ ~~Injection, lanreotide acetate, 1 mg~~
See J1930

~~C9238~~ ~~Injection, levetiracetam, 10 mg~~
See J1953

~~C9239~~ ~~Injection, temsirolimus, 1 mg~~
See J9330

~~C9240~~ ~~Injection, ixabepilone, 1 mg~~
See J9207

~~C9241~~ ~~Injection, doripenem, 10 mg~~
See J1267

~~C9242~~ ~~Injection, fosaprepitant, 1 mg~~
See J1453

~~C9243~~ ~~Injection, bendamustine hcl, 1 mg~~
See J9033

~~C9244~~ ~~Injection, regadenoson, 0.4 mg~~
See J2785

● G ☑ C9245 Injection, romiplostim, 10 mcg K2
Use this code for Nplate

● G ☑ C9246 Injection, gadoxetate disodium, per ml K2
Use this code for Eovist

● N C9247 Iobenguane, I-123, diagnostic, per study dose, up to 10 millicuries N1

● G ☑ C9248 Injection, clevidipine butyrate, 1 mg K2
Use this code for Cleviprex

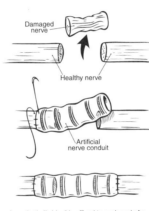

Damaged nerve

Healthy nerve

Artificial nerve conduit

A synthetic "bridge" is affixed to each end of a severed nerve with sutures
This procedure is performed using an operating microscope

N ☑ C9352 Microporous collagen implantable tube (NeuraGen Nerve Guide), per cm length N1

N ☑ C9353 Microporous collagen implantable slit tube (NeuraWrap Nerve Protector), per cm length N1

G ☑ C9354 Acellular pericardial tissue matrix of nonhuman origin (Veritas), per sq cm K2

G ☑ C9355 Collagen nerve cuff (NeuroMatrix), per 0.5 cm length K2

● G ☑ C9356 Tendon, porous matrix of cross-linked collagen and glycosaminoglycan matrix (TenoGlide Tendon Protector Sheet), per sq cm K2

~~C9357~~ ~~Dermal substitute, granulated cross-linked collagen and glycosaminoglycan matrix (Flowable Wound Matrix), 1 cc~~
See Q4114

**Outpatient PPS**

**C9358 — C9899**

| | | | | |
|---|---|---|---|---|
| ● | G ☑ | **C9358** | Dermal substitute, native, nondenatured collagen (SurgiMend Collagen Matrix), per 0.5 square cm | K2 |
| ● | G ☑ | **C9359** | Porous purified collagen matrix bone void filler (Integra Mozaik Osteoconductive Scaffold Putty, Integra OS Osteoconductive Scaffold Putty), per 0.5 cc | K2 |
| | A | **C9399** | Unclassified drugs or biologicals | K7 |
| | T | **C9716** | Creations of thermal anal lesions by radiofrequency energy | G2 |
| | | ~~C9723~~ | ~~Dynamic infrared blood perfusion imaging (DIRI)~~ | |
| | T | **C9724** | Endoscopic full-thickness plication in the gastric cardia using endoscopic plication system (EPS); includes endoscopy | G2 |
| | T | **C9725** | Placement of endorectal intracavitary applicator for high intensity brachytherapy | G2 ⊘ |

AHA: 3Q,'05,7

| | | | | |
|---|---|---|---|---|
| | T | **C9726** | Placement and removal (if performed) of applicator into breast for radiation therapy | G2 |
| | T ☑ | **C9727** | Insertion of implants into the soft palate; minimum of 3 implants | G2 |
| | X | **C9728** | Placement of interstitial device(s) for radiation therapy/surgery guidance (e.g., fiducial markers, dosimeter), other than prostate (any approach), single or multiple | R2 |
| ● | N | **C9898** | Radiolabeled product provided during a hospital inpatient stay | |
| ● | A | **C9899** | Implanted prosthetic device, payable only for inpatients who do not have inpatient coverage | |

Special Coverage Instructions     Noncovered by Medicare     Carrier Discretion

## DENTAL PROCEDURES D0000-D9999

The D, or dental, codes are a separate category of national codes. The Current Dental Terminology code set is copyrighted by the American Dental Association (ADA). CDT is included in HCPCS Level II. Decisions regarding the modification, deletion, or addition of CDT codes are made by the ADA and not the national panel responsible for the administration of HCPCS.

The Department of Health and Human Services has an agreement with the AMA pertaining to the use of the CPT codes for physician services; it also has an agreement with the ADA to include as a set of HCPCS Level II codes for use in billing for dental services.

Please refer to you CPT book for possible alternate code(s).

## DIAGNOSTIC D0100-D0999

### CLINICAL ORAL EVALUATION

| | | | |
|---|---|---|---|
| E | D0120 | Periodic oral evaluation — established patient | |

This procedure is covered if its purpose is to identify a patient's existing infections prior to kidney transplantation.

E   **D0140**   Limited oral evaluation — problem focused

E   **D0145**   Oral evaluation for a patient under 3 years of age and counseling with primary caregiver

S   **D0150**   Comprehensive oral evaluation — new or established patient   ⊘

This procedure is covered if its purpose is to identify a patient's existing infections prior to kidney transplantation.

MED: 100-2,15,150; 100-2,16,140; 100-3,260.6

E   **D0160**   Detailed and extensive oral evaluation — problem focused, by report

Pertinent documentation to evaluate medical appropriateness should be included when this code is reported.

E   **D0170**   Re-evaluation, limited, problem-focused (established patient, not postoperative visit)

E   **D0180**   Comprehensive periodontal evaluation — new or established patient

### RADIOGRAPHS

E   **D0210**   Intraoral, complete series (including bitewings)

E ☑   **D0220**   Intraoral, periapical, first film

E ☑   **D0230**   Intraoral, periapical, each additional film

S   **D0240**   Intraoral — occlusal film   ⊘

MED: 100-2,15,150; 100-2,16,140

S ☑   **D0250**   Extraoral, first film   ⊘

MED: 100-2,15,150; 100-2,16,140

S ☑   **D0260**   Extraoral, each additional film   ⊘

MED: 100-2,15,150; 100-2,16,140

S ☑   **D0270**   Bitewing, single film   ⊘

MED: 100-2,15,150; 100-2,16,140

S ☑   **D0272**   Bitewings, 2 films   ⊘

MED: 100-2,15,150; 100-2,16,140

E   **D0273**   Bitewings, 3 films

---

**Dental Procedures**

| | | | |
|---|---|---|---|
| S ☑ | **D0274** | Bitewings, 4 films | ⊘ |
| | | MED: 100-2,15,150; 100-2,16,140 | |
| S ☑ | **D0277** | Vertical bitewings - 7 to 8 films | |
| | | MED: 100-2,15,150; 100-2,16,140 | |
| E | **D0290** | Posterior-anterior or lateral skull and facial bone survey film | |
| E | **D0310** | Sialography | |
| E | **D0320** | Temporomandibular joint arthrogram, including injection | |
| E | **D0321** | Other temporomandibular joint films, by report | |
| E | **D0322** | Tomographic survey | |
| | | MED: 100-3,260.6 | |
| E | **D0330** | Panoramic film | |
| E | **D0340** | Cephalometric film | |
| E | **D0350** | Oral/facial photographic images<br>This code excludes conventional radiographs. | |
| E | **D0360** | Cone beam CT — craniofacial data capture | |
| E | **D0362** | Cone beam, 2-dimensional image reconstruction using existing data, includes multiple images | |
| E | **D0363** | Cone beam, 3-dimensional image reconstruction using existing data, includes multiple images | |

## TEST AND LABORATORY EXAMINATIONS

| | | |
|---|---|---|
| E | **D0415** | Collection of microorganisms for culture and sensitivity<br>This procedure is covered if its purpose is to identify a patient's existing infections prior to kidney transplantation.<br><br>See code(s): D0410 |
| B | **D0416** | Viral culture |
| ● | D0417 | Collection and preparation of saliva sample for laboratory diagnostic testing |
| ● | D0418 | Analysis of saliva sample |
| B | **D0421** | Genetic test for susceptibility to oral diseases |
| E | **D0425** | Caries susceptibility tests<br>This procedure is covered by Medicare if its purpose is to identify a patient's existing infections prior to kidney transplantation. |
| B | **D0431** | Adjunctive prediagnostic test that aids in detection of mucosal abnormalities including premalignant and malignant lesions, not to include cytology or biopsy procedures |
| S | **D0460** | Pulp vitality tests ⊘<br>This procedure is covered by Medicare if its purpose is to identify a patient's existing infections prior to kidney transplantation.<br>MED: 100-2,15,150; 100-2,16,140; 100-3,260.6 |
| E | **D0470** | Diagnostic casts |
| B | **D0472** | Accession of tissue, gross examination, preparation, and transmission of written report<br>MED: 100-2,15,150; 100-2,16,140; 100-3,260.6 |
| B | **D0473** | Accession of tissue, gross and microscopic examination, preparation and transmission of written report<br>MED: 100-2,15,150; 100-2,16,140; 100-3,260.6 |

**D0274 — D0473**

| | | |
|---|---|---|
| B | D0474 | Accession of tissue, gross and microscopic examination, including assessment of surgical margins for presence of disease, preparation and transmission of written report |
| | | MED: 100-2,15,150; 100-2,16,140; 100-3,260.6 |
| B | D0475 | Decalcification procedure |
| B | D0476 | Special stains for microorganisms |
| B | D0477 | Special stains, not for microorganisms |
| B | D0478 | Immunohistochemical stains |
| B | D0479 | Tissue in-situ hybridization, including interpretation |
| B | D0480 | Accession of exfoliative cytologic smears, microscopic examination, preparation and transmission of written report |
| | | MED: 100-2,15,150; 100-2,16,140; 100-3,260.6 |
| B | D0481 | Electron microscopy - diagnostic |
| B | D0482 | Direct immunofluorescence |
| B | D0483 | Indirect immunofluorescence |
| B | D0484 | Consultation on slides prepared elsewhere |
| B | D0485 | Consultation, including preparation of slides from biopsy material supplied by referring source |
| ▲ E | D0486 | Laboratory accession of brush biopsy sample, microscopic examination, preparation and transmission of written report |
| B | D0502 | Other oral pathology procedures, by report    ⊘ |
| | | Pertinent documentation to evaluate medical appropriateness should be included when this code is reported. This procedure is covered by Medicare if its purpose is to identify a patient's existing infections prior to kidney transplantation. |
| | | MED: 100-2,15,150; 100-2,16,140; 100-3,260.6 |
| B | D0999 | Unspecified diagnostic procedure, by report    ⊘ |
| | | Determine if an alternative HCPCS Level II or a CPT code better describes the service being reported. This code should be used only if a more specific code is unavailable. |
| | | MED: 100-2,15,150; 100-2,16,140; 100-3,260.6 |

## PREVENTIVE D1000-D1999

## DENTAL PROPHYLAXIS

| | | | |
|---|---|---|---|
| E | D1110 | Prophylaxis, adult | A |
| E | D1120 | Prophylaxis, child | A |

## TOPICAL FLUORIDE TREATMENT (OFFICE PROCEDURE)

| | | | | |
|---|---|---|---|---|
| ▲ | E | D1203 | Topical application of fluoride, child | A |
| ▲ | E | D1204 | Topical application of fluoride, adult | A |
| | E | D1206 | Topical fluoride varnish; therapeutic application for moderate to high caries risk patients | |

## OTHER PREVENTIVE SERVICES

| | | |
|---|---|---|
| E | D1310 | Nutritional counseling for the control of dental disease |
| | | MED: 100-2,16,10 |

---

| E | | D1320 | Tobacco counseling for the control and prevention of oral disease | |
|---|---|---|---|---|
| | | | MED: 100-2,16,10 | |
| E | | D1330 | Oral hygiene instruction | |
| | | | MED: 100-2,16,10 | |
| E | ☑ | D1351 | Sealant, per tooth | |

## SPACE MAINTENANCE (PASSIVE APPLIANCES)

| S | | D1510 | Space maintainer, fixed unilateral | ⊘ |
|---|---|---|---|---|
| | | | MED: 100-2,16,140 | |
| S | | D1515 | Space maintainer, fixed bilateral | ⊘ |
| | | | MED: 100-2,15,150; 100-2,16,140 | |
| S | | D1520 | Space maintainer, removable unilateral | ⊘ |
| | | | MED: 100-2,15,150; 100-2,16,140 | |
| S | | D1525 | Space maintainer, removable bilateral | ⊘ |
| | | | MED: 100-2,15,150; 100-2,16,140 | |
| S | | D1550 | Recementation of space maintainer | ⊘ |
| | | | MED: 100-2,15,150; 100-2,16,140 | |
| E | | D1555 | Removal of fixed space maintainer | |
| E | ☑ | D2140 | Amalgam—one surface, primary or permanent | |
| E | ☑ | D2150 | Amalgam, 2 surfaces, primary or permanent | |
| E | ☑ | D2160 | Amalgam, 3 surfaces, primary or permanent | |
| E | ☑ | D2161 | Amalgam, 4 or more surfaces, primary or permanent | |

## RESIN RESTORATIONS

| E | ☑ | D2330 | Resin, one surface, anterior |
|---|---|---|---|
| E | ☑ | D2331 | Resin, 2 surfaces, anterior |
| E | ☑ | D2332 | Resin, 3 surfaces, anterior |
| E | ☑ | D2335 | Resin, 4 or more surfaces or involving incisal angle (anterior) |
| E | ☑ | D2390 | Resin-based composite crown, anterior |
| E | ☑ | D2391 | Resin-based composite — one surface, posterior |
| E | ☑ | D2392 | Resin-based composite, 2 surfaces, posterior |
| E | ☑ | D2393 | Resin-based composite, 3 surfaces, posterior |
| E | ☑ | D2394 | Resin-based composite, 4 or more surfaces, posterior |

## GOLD FOIL RESTORATIONS

| E | ☑ | D2410 | Gold foil, one surface |
|---|---|---|---|
| E | ☑ | D2420 | Gold foil, 2 surfaces |
| E | ☑ | D2430 | Gold foil, 3 surfaces |

## INLAY/ONLAY RESTORATIONS

| E | ☑ | D2510 | Inlay, metallic, one surface |
|---|---|---|---|
| E | ☑ | D2520 | Inlay, metallic, 2 surfaces |
| E | ☑ | D2530 | Inlay, metallic, 3 or more surfaces |
| E | ☑ | D2542 | Onlay, metallic, 2 surfaces |
| E | ☑ | D2543 | Onlay, metallic, 3 surfaces |

| | | | |
|---|---|---|---|
| E | ☑ | D2544 | Onlay, metallic, 4 or more surfaces |
| E | ☑ | D2610 | Inlay, porcelain/ceramic, one surface |
| E | ☑ | D2620 | Inlay, porcelain/ceramic, 2 surfaces |
| E | ☑ | D2630 | Inlay, porcelain/ceramic, 3 or more surfaces |
| E | ☑ | D2642 | Onlay, porcelain/ceramic, 2 surfaces |
| E | ☑ | D2643 | Onlay, porcelain/ceramic, 3 surfaces |
| E | ☑ | D2644 | Onlay, porcelain/ceramic, 4 or more surfaces |
| E | ☑ | D2650 | Inlay — resin-based composite — one surface |
| E | ☑ | D2651 | Inlay, resin-based composite, 2 surfaces |
| E | ☑ | D2652 | Inlay, resin-based composite, 3 or more surfaces |
| E | ☑ | D2662 | Onlay, resin-based composite, 2 surfaces |
| E | ☑ | D2663 | Onlay, resin-based composite, 3 surfaces |
| E | ☑ | D2664 | Onlay, resin-based composite, 4 or more surfaces |

## CROWNS - SINGLE RESTORATION ONLY

| | | |
|---|---|---|
| E | D2710 | Crown — resin-based composite (indirect) |
| E | D2712 | Crown — 3/4 resin-based composite (indirect) |
| E | D2720 | Crown, resin with high noble metal |
| E | D2721 | Crown, resin with predominantly base metal |
| E | D2722 | Crown, resin with noble metal |
| E | D2740 | Crown, porcelain/ceramic substrate |
| E | D2750 | Crown, porcelain fused to high noble metal |
| E | D2751 | Crown — porcelain fused to predominantly base metal |
| E | D2752 | Crown, porcelain fused to noble metal |
| E | D2780 | Crown — 3/4 cast high noble metal |
| E | D2781 | Crown - 3/4 cast predominantly base metal |
| E | D2782 | Crown — 3/4 cast noble metal |
| E | D2783 | Crown - 3/4 porcelain/ceramic |
| E | D2790 | Crown, full cast high noble metal |
| E | D2791 | Crown, full cast predominantly base metal |
| E | D2792 | Crown, full cast noble metal |
| E | D2794 | Crown, titanium |
| E | D2799 | Provisional crown<br>Do not use this code to report a temporary crown for routine prosthetic restoration. |

## OTHER RESTORATIVE SERVICES

| | | |
|---|---|---|
| E | D2910 | Recement inlay, onlay or partial coverage restoration |
| E | D2915 | Recement cast or prefabricated post and core |
| E | D2920 | Recement crown |
| E | D2930 | Prefabricated stainless steel crown, primary tooth |
| E | D2931 | Prefabricated stainless steel crown, permanent tooth |
| E | D2932 | Prefabricated resin crown |

| | | |
|---|---|---|
| E | D2933 | Prefabricated stainless steel crown with resin window |
| E | D2934 | Prefabricated esthetic coated stainless steel crown - primary tooth |
| E | D2940 | Sedative filling |
| E | D2950 | Core buildup, including any pins |
| E | D2951 | Pin retention, per tooth, in addition to restoration |
| E | D2952 | Post and core in addition to crown, indirectly fabricated |
| E | D2953 | Each additional indirectly fabricated post — same tooth<br>Report in addition to code D2952. |
| E | D2954 | Prefabricated post and core in addition to crown |
| E | D2955 | Post removal (not in conjunction with endodontic therapy) |
| E | D2957 | Each additional prefabricated post — same tooth<br>Report in addition to code D2954. |
| E | D2960 | Labial veneer (laminate)-chairside |
| E | D2961 | Labial veneer (resin laminate), laboratory |
| E | D2962 | Labial veneer (porcelain laminate), laboratory |
| ○ E | D2970 | Temporary crown (fractured tooth) |
| E | D2971 | Additional procedures to construct new crown under existing partial denture framework |
| E | D2975 | Coping |
| E | D2980 | Crown repair, by report<br>*Pertinent documentation to evaluate medical appropriateness should be included when this code is reported.* |
| S | D2999 | Unspecified restorative procedure, by report      ⊘<br>*Determine if an alternative HCPCS Level II or a CPT code better describes the service being reported. This code should be used only if a more specific code is unavailable.*<br>MED: 100-2,15,150; 100-2,16,140 |

## ENDODONTICS D3000-D3999

### PULP CAPPING

| | | |
|---|---|---|
| E | D3110 | Pulp cap, direct (excluding final restoration) |
| E | D3120 | Pulp cap, indirect (excluding final restoration) |

### PULPOTOMY

| | | |
|---|---|---|
| E | D3220 | Therapeutic pulpotomy (excluding final restoration), removal of pulp coronal to the dentinocemental junction and application of medicament<br>*Do not use this code to report the first stage of root canal therapy.* |
| E | D3221 | Pulpal debridement, primary and permanent teeth |
| ● | D3222 | Partial pulpotomy for apexogenesis, permanent tooth with incomplete root development |

### PULPAL THERAPY ON PRIMARY TEETH (INCLUDES PRIMARY TEETH WITH SUCCEDANEOUS TEETH AND PLACEMENT OF RESORBABLE FILLING)

| | | |
|---|---|---|
| E | D3230 | Pulpal therapy (resorbable filling), anterior, primary tooth (excluding final restoration) |

*Side tab:* Dental Procedures — D2933 — D3230

Dental Procedures

| | | | |
|---|---|---|---|
| E | | D3240 | Pulpal therapy (resorbable filling), posterior, primary tooth (excluding final restoration) |

## ROOT CANAL THERAPY (INCLUDING TREATMENT PLAN, CLINICAL PROCEDURES, AND FOLLOW-UP CARE, INCLUDES PRIMARY TEETH WITHOUT SUCCEDANEOUS TEETH AND PERMANENT TEETH)

| | | | |
|---|---|---|---|
| ▲ E | | D3310 | Endodontic therapy, anterior tooth (excluding final restoration) |
| ▲ E | | D3320 | Endodontic therapy, bicuspid tooth (excluding final restoration) |
| ▲ E | | D3330 | Endodontic therapy, molar (excluding final restoration) |
| E | | D3331 | Treatment of root canal obstruction; nonsurgical access |
| E | | D3332 | Incomplete endodontic therapy; inoperable, unrestorable or fractured tooth |
| E | | D3333 | Internal root repair of perforation defects |
| E | | D3346 | Retreatment of previous root canal therapy, anterior |
| E | | D3347 | Retreatment of previous root canal therapy, bicuspid |
| E | | D3348 | Retreatment of previous root canal therapy, molar |
| E | | D3351 | Apexification/recalcification, initial visit (apical closure/calcific repair of perforations, root resorption, etc.) |
| E | | D3352 | Apexification/recalcification, interim medication replacement (apical closure/calcific repair of perforations, root resorption, etc.) |
| E | | D3353 | Apexification/recalcification, final visit (includes completed root canal therapy, apical closure/calcific repair of perforations, root resorption, etc.) |

## APICOECTOMY/PERIRADICULAR SERVICES

| | | | | |
|---|---|---|---|---|
| E | | D3410 | Apicoectomy/periradicular surgery, anterior | |
| E | | D3421 | Apicoectomy/periradicular surgery, bicuspid (first root) | |
| E | | D3425 | Apicoectomy/periradicular surgery, molar (first root) | |
| E | ☑ | D3426 | Apicoectomy/periradicular surgery (each additional root) | |
| E | ☑ | D3430 | Retrograde filling, per root | |
| E | ☑ | D3450 | Root amputation, per root | |
| S | | D3460 | Endodontic endosseous implant | ⊘ |
| | | | MED: 100-2,15,150; 100-2,16,140 | |
| E | | D3470 | Intentional replantation (including necessary splinting) | |

## OTHER ENDODONTIC PROCEDURES

| | | | | |
|---|---|---|---|---|
| E | | D3910 | Surgical procedure for isolation of tooth with rubber dam | |
| E | | D3920 | Hemisection (including any root removal), not including root canal therapy | |
| E | | D3950 | Canal preparation and fitting of preformed dowel or post | |
| S | | D3999 | Unspecified endodontic procedure, by report | ⊘ |
| | | | Determine if an alternative HCPCS Level II or a CPT code better describes the service being reported. This code should be used only if a more specific code is unavailable. | |
| | | | MED: 100-2,15,150; 100-2,16,140 | |

D3240 — D3999

**Dental Procedures**

**D4210 — D4341**

## PERIODONTICS D4000-D4999

### SURGICAL SERVICES (INCLUDING USUAL POSTOPERATIVE SERVICES)

▲ E ☑ **D4210** Gingivectomy or gingivoplasty, 4 or more contiguous teeth or tooth bounded spaces per quadrant

▲ E ☑ **D4211** Gingivectomy or gingivoplasty, 1 to 3 contiguous teeth or tooth bounded spaces per quadrant

E **D4230** Anatomical crown exposure, 4 or more contiguous teeth per quadrant

E **D4231** Anatomical crown exposure, 1 to 3 teeth per quadrant

▲ E ☑ **D4240** Gingival flap procedure, including root planing, 4 or more contiguous teeth or tooth bounded spaces per quadrant

▲ E **D4241** Gingival flap procedure, including root planing, 1 to 3 contiguous teeth or tooth bounded spaces per quadrant

E **D4245** Apically positioned flap

E **D4249** Clinical crown lengthening, hard tissue

▲ S ☑ **D4260** Osseous surgery (including flap entry and closure), 4 or more contiguous teeth or tooth bounded spaces per quadrant    ⊘
MED: 100-2,15,150; 100-2,16,140

▲ E **D4261** Osseous surgery (including flap entry and closure), 1 to 3 contiguous teeth or tooth bounded spaces per quadrant

S ☑ **D4263** Bone replacement graft — first site in quadrant    ⊘
MED: 100-2,15,150; 100-2,16,140; 100-3,260.6

S ☑ **D4264** Bone replacement graft — each additional site in quadrant    ⊘
MED: 100-2,15,150; 100-2,16,140; 100-3,260.6

E **D4265** Biologic materials to aid in soft and osseous tissue regeneration

E ☑ **D4266** Guided tissue regeneration — resorbable barrier, per site

E ☑ **D4267** Guided tissue regeneration, nonresorbable barrier, per site (includes membrane removal)

S ☑ **D4268** Surgical revision procedure, per tooth
MED: 100-2,15,150; 100-2,16,140

S **D4270** Pedicle soft tissue graft procedure    ⊘
MED: 100-2,15,150; 100-2,16,140

S **D4271** Free soft tissue graft procedure (including donor site surgery)    ⊘
MED: 100-2,15,150; 100-2,16,140

S **D4273** Subepithelial connective tissue graft procedures, per tooth    ⊘
MED: 100-2,15,150; 100-2,16,140; 100-3,260.6

E **D4274** Distal or proximal wedge procedure (when not performed in conjunction with surgical procedures in the same anatomical area)

E **D4275** Soft tissue allograft

E **D4276** Combined connective tissue and double pedicle graft, per tooth

### ADJUNCTIVE PERIODONTAL SERVICES

E **D4320** Provisional splinting, intracoronal

E **D4321** Provisional splinting, extracoronal

E ☑ **D4341** Periodontal scaling and root planing, 4 or more teeth per quadrant

---

| | | | |
|---|---|---|---|
| E | ☑ | **D4342** | Periodontal scaling and root planing, 1 to 3 teeth, per quadrant |
| S | | **D4355** | Full mouth debridement to enable comprehensive evaluation and diagnosis ⊘ |

This procedure is covered by Medicare if its purpose is to identify a patient's existing infections prior to kidney transplantation.

MED: 100-2,15,150; 100-2,16,140; 100-3,260.6

| | | |
|---|---|---|
| S | **D4381** | Localized delivery of antimicrobial agents via a controlled release vehicle into diseased crevicular tissue, per tooth, by report ⊘ |

Pertinent documentation to evaluate medical appropriateness should be included when this code is reported.

MED: 100-2,15,150; 100-2,16,140; 100-3,260.6

## OTHER PERIODONTAL SERVICES

| | | |
|---|---|---|
| E | **D4910** | Periodontal maintenance |
| E | **D4920** | Unscheduled dressing change (by someone other than treating dentist) |
| E | **D4999** | Unspecified periodontal procedure, by report |

Determine if an alternative HCPCS Level II or a CPT code better describes the service being reported. This code should be used only if a more specific code is unavailable.

## PROSTHODONTICS (REMOVABLE) D5000-D5899

## COMPLETE DENTURES (INCLUDING ROUTINE POST DELIVERY CARE)

| | | |
|---|---|---|
| E | **D5110** | Complete denture — maxillary |
| E | **D5120** | Complete denture — mandibular |
| E | **D5130** | Immediate denture — maxillary |
| E | **D5140** | Immediate denture — mandibular |

## PARTIAL DENTURES (INCLUDING ROUTINE POST DELIVERY CARE)

| | | | |
|---|---|---|---|
| ▲ | E | **D5211** | Upper partial denture - resin base (including any conventional clasps, rests and teeth) |
| ▲ | E | **D5212** | Lower partial denture - resin base (including any conventional clasps, rests and teeth) |
| | E | **D5213** | Maxillary partial denture — cast metal framework with resin denture bases (including any conventional clasps, rests and teeth) |
| | E | **D5214** | Mandibular partial denture, cast metal framework with resin denture bases (including any conventional clasps, rests, and teeth) |
| | E | **D5225** | Maxillary partial denture - flexible base (including any clasps, rests and teeth) |
| | E | **D5226** | Mandibular partial denture — flexible base (including any clasps, rests and teeth) |
| | E | **D5281** | Removable unilateral partial denture, 1 piece cast metal (including clasps and teeth) |

## ADJUSTMENTS TO REMOVABLE PROSTHESES

| | | |
|---|---|---|
| E | **D5410** | Adjust complete denture — maxillary |
| E | **D5411** | Adjust complete denture — mandibular |
| E | **D5421** | Adjust partial denture — maxillary |
| E | **D5422** | Adjust partial denture — mandibular |

*Dental Procedures*

*D5510 — D5861*

## REPAIRS TO COMPLETE DENTURES

| | | |
|---|---|---|
| E | D5510 | Repair broken complete denture base |
| E | D5520 | Replace missing or broken teeth, complete denture (each tooth) |

## REPAIRS TO PARTIAL DENTURES

| | | | |
|---|---|---|---|
| E | | D5610 | Repair resin denture base |
| E | | D5620 | Repair cast framework |
| E | | D5630 | Repair or replace broken clasp |
| E | ☑ | D5640 | Replace broken teeth, per tooth |
| E | | D5650 | Add tooth to existing partial denture |
| E | | D5660 | Add clasp to existing partial denture |
| E | | D5670 | Replace all teeth and acrylic on cast metal framework (maxillary) |
| E | | D5671 | Replace all teeth and acrylic on cast metal framework (mandibular) |

## DENTURE REBASE PROCEDURES

| | | |
|---|---|---|
| E | D5710 | Rebase complete maxillary denture |
| E | D5711 | Rebase complete mandibular denture |
| E | D5720 | Rebase maxillary partial denture |
| E | D5721 | Rebase mandibular partial denture |

## DENTURE RELINE PROCEDURES

| | | |
|---|---|---|
| E | D5730 | Reline complete maxillary denture (chairside) |
| E | D5731 | Reline lower complete mandibular denture (chairside) |
| E | D5740 | Reline maxillary partial denture (chairside) |
| E | D5741 | Reline mandibular partial denture (chairside) |
| E | D5750 | Reline complete maxillary denture (laboratory) |
| E | D5751 | Reline complete mandibular denture (laboratory) |
| E | D5760 | Reline maxillary partial denture (laboratory) |
| E | D5761 | Reline mandibular partial denture (laboratory) |

## OTHER REMOVABLE PROSTHETIC SERVICES

| | | |
|---|---|---|
| E | D5810 | Interim complete denture (maxillary) |
| E | D5811 | Interim complete denture (mandibular) |
| E | D5820 | Interim partial denture (maxillary) |
| E | D5821 | Interim partial denture (mandibular) |
| E | D5850 | Tissue conditioning, maxillary |
| E | D5851 | Tissue conditioning, mandibular |
| E | D5860 | Overdenture, complete, by report<br>Pertinent documentation to evaluate medical appropriateness should be included when this code is reported. |
| E | D5861 | Overdenture, partial, by report<br>Pertinent documentation to evaluate medical appropriateness should be included when this code is reported. |

| | | |
|---|---|---|
| E | D5862 | **Precision attachment, by report** |
| | | Pertinent documentation to evaluate medical appropriateness should be included when this code is reported. |
| E | D5867 | **Replacement of replaceable part of semi-precision or precision attachment (male or female component)** |
| E | D5875 | **Modification of removable prosthesis following implant surgery** |
| E | D5899 | **Unspecified removable prosthodontic procedure, by report** |
| | | Determine if an alternative HCPCS Level II or a CPT code better describes the service being reported. This code should be used only if a more specific code is unavailable. |

## MAXILLOFACIAL PROSTHETICS D5900-D5999

| | | | |
|---|---|---|---|
| S | D5911 | **Facial moulage (sectional)** | ⊘ |
| | | MED: 100-2,15,120; 100-2,15,150 | |
| S | D5912 | **Facial moulage (complete)** | ⊘ |
| | | MED: 100-2,15,120 | |
| E | D5913 | **Nasal prosthesis** | |
| E | D5914 | **Auricular prosthesis** | |
| E | D5915 | **Orbital prosthesis** | |
| | | See code(s): L8611 | |
| E | D5916 | **Ocular prosthesis** | |
| | | See code(s): V2623, V2629 | |
| E | D5919 | **Facial prosthesis** | |
| E | D5922 | **Nasal septal prosthesis** | |
| E | D5923 | **Ocular prosthesis, interim** | |
| E | D5924 | **Cranial prosthesis** | |
| E | D5925 | **Facial augmentation implant prosthesis** | |
| E | D5926 | **Nasal prosthesis, replacement** | |
| E | D5927 | **Auricular prosthesis, replacement** | |
| E | D5928 | **Orbital prosthesis, replacement** | |
| E | D5929 | **Facial prosthesis, replacement** | |
| E | D5931 | **Obturator prosthesis, surgical** | |
| E | D5932 | **Obturator prosthesis, definitive** | |
| E | D5933 | **Obturator prosthesis, modification** | |
| E | D5934 | **Mandibular resection prosthesis with guide flange** | |
| E | D5935 | **Mandibular resection prosthesis without guide flange** | |
| E | D5936 | **Obturator/prosthesis, interim** | |
| E | D5937 | **Trismus appliance (not for TM treatment)** | |
| | | MED: 100-2,15,120 | |
| E | D5951 | **Feeding aid** | ⊘ |
| | | MED: 100-2,15,120; 100-2,16,140 | |
| E | D5952 | **Speech aid prosthesis, pediatric** | |
| E | D5953 | **Speech aid prosthesis, adult** | |
| E | D5954 | **Palatal augmentation prosthesis** | |

Dental Procedures

D5862 — D5954

**Dental Procedures**

| | | | |
|---|---|---|---|
| E | D5955 | Palatal lift prosthesis, definitive | |
| E | D5958 | Palatal lift prosthesis, interim | |
| E | D5959 | Palatal lift prosthesis, modification | |
| E | D5960 | Speech aid prosthesis, modification | |
| E | D5982 | Surgical stent | |
| S | D5983 | Radiation carrier | ⊘ |
| | | MED: 100-2,15,150; 100-2,16,140 | |
| S | D5984 | Radiation shield | ⊘ |
| | | MED: 100-2,15,150; 100-2,16,140 | |
| S | D5985 | Radiation cone locator | ⊘ |
| | | MED: 100-2,15,150; 100-2,16,140 | |
| E | D5986 | Fluoride gel carrier | |
| S | D5987 | Commissure splint | ⊘ |
| | | MED: 100-2,15,150; 100-2,16,140; 100-4,4,240 | |
| E | D5988 | Surgical splint | |
| | | MED: 100-4,4,240 | |
| ● | D5991 | Topical medicament carrier | |
| E | D5999 | Unspecified maxillofacial prosthesis, by report | |

D5999: Determine if an alternative HCPCS Level II or a CPT code better describes the service being reported. This code should be used only if a more specific code is unavailable.

## IMPLANT SERVICES D6000-D6199

| | | |
|---|---|---|
| E | D6010 | Surgical placement of implant body: endosteal implant |
| E | D6012 | Surgical placement of interim implant body for transitional prosthesis: endosteal implant |
| E | D6040 | Surgical placement: eposteal implant |
| E | D6050 | Surgical placement: transosteal implant |
| E | D6053 | Implant/abutment supported removable denture for completely edentulous arch |
| | | MED: 100-2,15,150 |
| E | D6054 | Implant/abutment supported removable denture for partially edentulous arch |
| | | MED: 100-2,15,150 |
| E | D6055 | Dental implant supported connecting bar |
| | | MED: 100-2,15,150 |
| E | D6056 | Prefabricated abutment - includes placement |
| | | MED: 100-2,15,150 |
| E | D6057 | Custom abutment — includes placement |
| | | MED: 100-2,15,150 |
| E | D6058 | Abutment supported porcelain/ceramic crown |
| | | MED: 100-2,15,150 |
| E | D6059 | Abutment supported porcelain fused to metal crown (high noble metal) |
| | | MED: 100-2,15,150 |

**D5955 — D6059**

| | | |
|---|---|---|
| E | D6060 | Abutment supported porcelain fused to metal crown (predominantly base metal) |
| | | MED: 100-2,15,150 |
| E | D6061 | Abutment supported porcelain fused to metal crown (noble metal) |
| | | MED: 100-2,15,150 |
| E | D6062 | Abutment supported cast metal crown (high noble metal) |
| | | MED: 100-2,15,150 |
| E | D6063 | Abutment supported cast metal crown (predominantly base metal) |
| | | MED: 100-2,15,150 |
| E | D6064 | Abutment supported cast metal crown (noble metal) |
| | | MED: 100-2,15,150 |
| E | D6065 | Implant supported porcelain/ceramic crown |
| | | MED: 100-2,15,150 |
| E | D6066 | Implant supported porcelain fused to metal crown (titanium, titanium alloy, high noble metal) |
| | | MED: 100-2,15,150 |
| E | D6067 | Implant supported metal crown (titanium, titanium alloy, high noble metal) |
| | | MED: 100-2,15,150 |
| E | D6068 | Abutment supported retainer for porcelain/ceramic FPD |
| | | MED: 100-2,15,150 |
| E | D6069 | Abutment supported retainer for porcelain fused to metal FPD (high noble metal) |
| | | MED: 100-2,15,150 |
| E | D6070 | Abutment supported retainer for porcelain fused to metal FPD (predominantly base metal) |
| | | MED: 100-2,15,150 |
| E | D6071 | Abutment supported retainer for porcelain fused to metal FPD (noble metal) |
| | | MED: 100-2,15,150 |
| E | D6072 | Abutment supported retainer for cast metal FPD (high noble metal) |
| | | MED: 100-2,15,150 |
| E | D6073 | Abutment supported retainer for cast metal FPD (predominantly base metal) |
| | | MED: 100-2,15,150 |
| E | D6074 | Abutment supported retainer for cast metal FPD (noble metal) |
| | | MED: 100-2,15,150 |
| E | D6075 | Implant supported retainer for ceramic FPD |
| | | MED: 100-2,15,150 |
| E | D6076 | Implant supported retainer for porcelain fused to metal FPD (titanium, titanium alloy, or high noble metal) |
| | | MED: 100-2,15,150 |
| E | D6077 | Implant supported retainer for cast metal FPD (titanium, titanium alloy, or high noble metal) |
| | | MED: 100-2,15,150 |
| E | D6078 | Implant/abutment supported fixed denture for completely edentulous arch |
| | | MED: 100-2,15,150 |

| | | |
|---|---|---|
| E | D6079 | Implant/abutment supported fixed denture for partially edentulous arch |
| | | MED: 100-2,15,150 |
| E | D6080 | Implant maintenance procedures, including removal of prosthesis, cleansing of prosthesis and abutments, reinsertion of prosthesis |
| | | MED: 100-2,15,150 |
| E | D6090 | Repair implant-supported prosthesis, by report |
| | | Pertinent documentation to evaluate medical appropriateness should be included when this code is reported. |
| E | D6091 | Replacement of semi-precision or precision attachment (male or female component) of implant/abutment supported prosthesis, per attachment |
| E | D6092 | Recement implant/abutment supported crown |
| E | D6093 | Recement implant/abutment supported fixed partial denture |
| E | D6094 | Abutment supported crown - (titanium) |
| E | D6095 | Repair implant abutment, by report |
| | | Pertinent documentation to evaluate medical appropriateness should be included when this code is reported. |
| E | D6100 | Implant removal, by report |
| | | Pertinent documentation to evaluate medical appropriateness should be included when this code is reported. |
| E | D6190 | Radiographic/surgical implant index, by report |
| E | D6194 | Abutment supported retainer crown for FPD - (titanium) |
| E | D6199 | Unspecified implant procedure, by report |
| E | D6205 | Pontic — indirect resin based composite |

## PROSTHODONTICS (FIXED) D6200-D6999

### FIXED PARTIAL DENTURE PONTICS

| | | |
|---|---|---|
| E | D6210 | Pontic, cast high noble metal |
| | | Each abutment and each pontic constitute a unit in a prosthesis. An alloy of at least 60 percent gold (Au), palladium (Pd), or platinum (Pt) is considered a high noble metal. |
| E | D6211 | Pontic, cast predominantly base metal |
| | | Each abutment and each pontic constitute a unit in a prosthesis. An alloy of less than 25 percent gold (Au), palladium (Pd), or platinum (Pt) is considered a high noble metal. |
| E | D6212 | Pontic, cast noble metal |
| | | Each abutment and each pontic constitute a unit in a prosthesis. An alloy of at least 25 percent gold (Au), palladium (Pd), or platinum (Pt) is considered a high noble metal. |
| E | D6214 | Pontic — titanium |
| E | D6240 | Pontic, porcelain fused to high noble metal |
| | | Each abutment and each pontic constitute a unit in a prosthesis. An alloy of at least 60 percent gold (Au), palladium (Pd), or platinum (Pt) is considered a high noble metal. |
| E | D6241 | Pontic, porcelain fused to predominantly base metal |
| | | Each abutment and each pontic constitute a unit in a prosthesis. An alloy of less than 25 percent gold (Au), palladium (Pd), or platinum (Pt) is considered a high noble metal. |

| | | |
|---|---|---|
| E | **D6242** | **Pontic, porcelain fused to noble metal**<br>Each abutment and each pontic constitute a unit in a prosthesis. An alloy of at least 60 percent gold (Au), palladium (Pd), or platinum (Pt) is considered a high noble metal. |
| E | **D6245** | **Pontic — porcelain/ceramic**<br>MED: 100-2,15,150 |
| E | **D6250** | **Pontic, resin with high noble metal**<br>Each abutment and each pontic constitute a unit in a prosthesis. An alloy of at least 60 percent gold (Au), palladium (Pd), or platinum (Pt) is considered a high noble metal. |
| E | **D6251** | **Pontic, resin with predominantly base metal**<br>Each abutment and each pontic constitute a unit in a prosthesis. An alloy of less than 25 percent gold (Au), palladium (Pd), or platinum (Pt) is considered a high noble metal. |
| E | **D6252** | **Pontic, resin with noble metal**<br>Each abutment and each pontic constitute a unit in a prosthesis. An alloy of at least 25 percent gold (Au), palladium (Pd), or platinum (Pt) is considered a high noble metal. |
| E | **D6253** | **Provisional pontic** |
| E | **D6545** | **Retainer, cast metal for resin bonded fixed prosthesis** |
| E | **D6548** | **Retainer — porcelain/ceramic for resin bonded fixed prosthesis**<br>MED: 100-2,15,150 |
| E | **D6600** | **Inlay, porcelain/ceramic, 2 surfaces**<br>MED: 100-2,15,150 |
| E | **D6601** | **Inlay, porcelain/ceramic, 3 or more surfaces**<br>MED: 100-2,15,150 |
| E | **D6602** | **Inlay, cast high noble metal, 2 surfaces**<br>MED: 100-2,15,150 |
| E | **D6603** | **Inlay, cast high noble metal, 3 or more surfaces**<br>MED: 100-2,15,150 |
| E | **D6604** | **Inlay, cast predominantly base metal, 2 surfaces**<br>MED: 100-2,15,150 |
| E | **D6605** | **Inlay, cast predominantly base metal, 3 or more surfaces**<br>MED: 100-2,15,150 |
| E | **D6606** | **Inlay, cast noble metal, 2 surfaces**<br>MED: 100-2,15,150 |
| E | **D6607** | **Inlay, cast noble metal, 3 or more surfaces**<br>MED: 100-2,15,150 |
| E | **D6608** | **Onlay, porcelain/ceramic, 2 surfaces**<br>MED: 100-2,15,150 |
| E | **D6609** | **Onlay, porcelain/ceramic, 3 or more surfaces**<br>MED: 100-2,15,150 |
| E | **D6610** | **Onlay, cast high noble metal, 2 surfaces**<br>MED: 100-2,15,150 |
| E | **D6611** | **Onlay, cast high noble metal, 3 or more surfaces**<br>MED: 100-2,15,150 |
| E | **D6612** | **Onlay, cast predominantly base metal, 2 surfaces**<br>MED: 100-2,15,150 |

**Dental Procedures**

**D6613 — D6790**

| E | D6613 | Onlay, cast predominantly base metal, 3 or more surfaces |
|---|---|---|
| | | MED: 100-2,15,150 |
| E | D6614 | Onlay, cast noble metal, 2 surfaces |
| | | MED: 100-2,15,150 |
| E | D6615 | Onlay, cast noble metal, 3 or more surfaces |
| | | MED: 100-2,15,150 |
| E | D6624 | Inlay — titanium |
| E | D6634 | Onlay — titanium |
| E | D6710 | Crown — indirect resin based composite |

## FIXED PARTIAL DENTURE RETAINERS - CROWNS

| E | D6720 | Crown, resin with high noble metal |
|---|---|---|
| | | An alloy of at least 60 percent gold (Au), palladium (Pd), or platinum (Pt) is considered a high noble metal. |
| E | D6721 | Crown, resin with predominantly base metal |
| | | An alloy of less than 25 percent gold (Au), palladium (Pd), or platinum (Pt) is considered a base metal. |
| E | D6722 | Crown, resin with noble metal |
| | | An alloy of at least 25 percent gold (Au), palladium (Pd), or platinum (Pt) is considered a noble metal. |
| E | D6740 | Crown — porcelain/ceramic |
| | | MED: 100-2,15,150 |
| E | D6750 | Crown, porcelain fused to high noble metal |
| | | An alloy of at least 60 percent gold (Au), palladium (Pd), or platinum (Pt) is considered a high noble metal. |
| E | D6751 | Crown, porcelain fused to predominantly base metal |
| | | An alloy of less than 25 percent gold (Au), palladium (Pd), or platinum (Pt) is considered a base metal. |
| E | D6752 | Crown, porcelain fused to noble metal |
| | | An alloy of at least 25 percent gold (Au), palladium (Pd), or platinum (Pt) is considered a noble metal. |
| E | D6780 | Crown, 3/4 cast high noble metal |
| | | An alloy of at least 60 percent gold (Au), palladium (Pd), or platinum (Pt) is considered a high noble metal. |
| E | D6781 | Crown - 3/4 cast predominantly base metal |
| | | An alloy of less than 25 percent gold (Au), palladium (Pd), or platinum (Pt) is considered a base metal. |
| | | MED: 100-2,15,150 |
| E | D6782 | Crown — 3/4 cast noble metal |
| | | An alloy of at least 25 percent gold (Au), palladium (Pd), or platinum (Pt) is considered a noble metal. |
| | | MED: 100-2,15,150 |
| E | D6783 | Crown — 3/4 porcelain/ceramic |
| | | MED: 100-2,15,150 |
| E | D6790 | Crown, full cast high noble metal |
| | | An alloy of at least 60 percent gold (Au), palladium (Pd), or platinum (Pt) is considered a high noble metal. |

| | | |
|---|---|---|
| E | **D6791** | Crown, full cast predominantly base metal |

An alloy of less than 25 percent gold (Au), palladium (Pd), or platinum (Pt) is considered a base metal.

| | | |
|---|---|---|
| E | **D6792** | Crown, full cast noble metal |

An alloy of at least 25 percent gold (Au), palladium (Pd), or platinum (Pt) is considered a noble metal.

| | | |
|---|---|---|
| E | **D6793** | Provisional retainer crown |
| E | **D6794** | Crown — titanium |

## OTHER FIXED PARTIAL DENTURE SERVICES

| | | |
|---|---|---|
| S | **D6920** | Connector bar ⊘ |

MED: 100-2,15,150; 100-2,16,140; 100-3,260.6

| | | |
|---|---|---|
| E | **D6930** | Recement bridge |
| E | **D6940** | Stress breaker |
| E | **D6950** | Precision attachment |
| E | **D6970** | Post and core in addition to fixed partial denture retainer, indirectly fabricated |
| E | **D6972** | Prefabricated post and core in addition to bridge retainer |
| E | **D6973** | Core build up for retainer, including any pins |
| E | **D6975** | Coping, metal |
| E | **D6976** | Each additional indirectly fabricated post — same tooth |

Report this code in addition to codes D6970.

MED: 100-2,15,150

| | | |
|---|---|---|
| E | **D6977** | Each additional prefabricated post — same tooth |

Report this code in addition to code D6972.

MED: 100-2,15,150

| | | |
|---|---|---|
| E | **D6980** | Bridge repair, by report |

Pertinent documentation to evaluate medical appropriateness should be included when this code is reported.

| | | |
|---|---|---|
| E | **D6985** | Pediatric partial denture, fixed |
| E | **D6999** | Unspecified fixed prosthodontic procedure, by report |

Determine if an alternative HCPCS Level II or a CPT code better describes the service being reported. This code should be used only if a more specific code is unavailable.

## SURGICAL EXTRACTIONS (INCLUDES LOCAL ANESTHESIA AND ROUTINE POSTOPERATIVE CARE)

| | | |
|---|---|---|
| S | **D7111** | Extraction, coronal remnants — deciduous tooth |

MED: 100-2,16,140

| | | |
|---|---|---|
| S | **D7140** | Extraction, erupted tooth or exposed root (elevation and/or forceps removal) |

MED: 100-2,16,140

| | | |
|---|---|---|
| S | **D7210** | Surgical removal of erupted tooth requiring elevation of mucoperiosteal flap and removal of bone and/or section of tooth ⊘ |

MED: 100-2,15,150; 100-2,16,140

| | | |
|---|---|---|
| S | **D7220** | Removal of impacted tooth, soft tissue ⊘ |

MED: 100-2,15,150; 100-2,16,140

---

Dental Procedures

D7230 — D7321

| | | | |
|---|---|---|---|
| S | D7230 | Removal of impacted tooth, partially bony | ⊘ |
| | | MED: 100-2,15,150; 100-2,16,140 | |
| S | D7240 | Removal of impacted tooth, completely bony | ⊘ |
| | | MED: 100-2,15,150; 100-2,16,140 | |
| S | D7241 | Removal of impacted tooth, completely bony, with unusual surgical complications | ⊘ |
| | | MED: 100-2,15,150; 100-2,16,140 | |
| S | D7250 | Surgical removal of residual tooth roots (cutting procedure) | ⊘ |
| | | MED: 100-2,15,150; 100-2,16,140 | |

## OTHER SURGICAL PROCEDURES

| | | | |
|---|---|---|---|
| S | D7260 | Oral antral fistula closure | ⊘ |
| | | MED: 100-2,15,150; 100-2,16,140 | |
| S | D7261 | Primary closure of a sinus perforation | |
| | | See equivalent CPT code for repair of mucous membranes. | |
| | | MED: 100-2,16,140 | |
| E | D7270 | Tooth reimplantation and/or stabilization of accidentally evulsed or displaced tooth | |
| E | D7272 | Tooth transplantation (includes reimplantation from one site to another and splinting and/or stabilization) | |
| E | D7280 | Surgical access of an unerupted tooth | |
| E | D7282 | Mobilization of erupted or malpositioned tooth to aid eruption | |
| B | D7283 | Placement of device to facilitate eruption of impacted tooth | |
| E | D7285 | Biopsy of oral tissue — hard (bone, tooth) | |
| E | D7286 | Biopsy of oral tissue — soft | |
| E | D7287 | Exfoliative cytological sample collection | |
| B | D7288 | Brush biopsy — transepithelial sample collection | |
| E | D7290 | Surgical repositioning of teeth | |
| S | D7291 | Transseptal fiberotomy/supra crestal fiberotomy, by report | ⊘ |
| | | Pertinent documentation to evaluate medical appropriateness should be included when this code is reported. | |
| | | MED: 100-2,15,150; 100-2,16,140 | |
| E | D7292 | Surgical placement: temporary anchorage device (screw retained plate) requiring surgical flap | |
| E | D7293 | Surgical placement: temporary anchorage device requiring surgical flap | |
| E | D7294 | Surgical placement: temporary anchorage device without surgical flap | |

## ALVEOLOPLASTY - SURGICAL PREPARATION OF RIDGE FOR DENTURES

| | | | |
|---|---|---|
| E ☑ | D7310 | Alveoloplasty in conjunction with extractions, 4 or more teeth or tooth spaces, per quadrant |
| E ☑ | D7311 | Alveoloplasty in conjunction with extractions, 1 to 3 teeth or tooth spaces, per quadrant |
| E ☑ | D7320 | Alveoloplasty not in conjunction with extractions, 4 or more teeth or tooth spaces, per quadrant |
| B ☑ | D7321 | Alveoloplasty not in conjunction with extractions, 1 to 3 teeth or tooth spaces, per quadrant |

## VESTIBULOPLASTY

E    **D7340**    Vestibuloplasty, ridge extension (second epithelialization)

E    **D7350**    Vestibuloplasty, ridge extension (including soft tissue grafts, muscle re-attachments, revision of soft tissue attachment, and management of hypertrophied and hyperplastic tissue)

## SURGICAL EXCISION OF REACTIVE INFLAMMATORY LESIONS (SCAR TISSUE OR LOCALIZED CONGENITAL LESIONS)

E    **D7410**    Excision of benign lesion up to 1.25 cm

E    **D7411**    Excision of benign lesion greater than 1.25 cm

E    **D7412**    Excision of benign lesion, complicated

E    **D7413**    Excision of malignant lesion up to 1.25 cm

E    **D7414**    Excision of malignant lesion greater than 1.25 cm

E    **D7415**    Excision of malignant lesion, complicated

E ☑    **D7440**    Excision of malignant tumor, lesion diameter up to 1.25 cm

E ☑    **D7441**    Excision of malignant tumor, lesion diameter greater than 1.25 cm

E ☑    **D7450**    Removal of benign odontogenic cyst or tumor — lesion diameter up to 1.25 cm

E ☑    **D7451**    Removal of benign odontogenic cyst or tumor, lesion diameter greater than 1.25 cm

E ☑    **D7460**    Removal of benign nonodontogenic cyst or tumor, lesion diameter up to 1.25 cm

E ☑    **D7461**    Removal of benign nonodontogenic cyst or tumor, lesion diameter greater than 1.25 cm

E    **D7465**    Destruction of lesion(s) by physical or chemical methods, by report
Pertinent documentation to evaluate medical appropriateness should be included when this code is reported.

E ☑    **D7471**    Removal of lateral exostosis (maxilla or mandible)

E    **D7472**    Removal of torus palatinus

E    **D7473**    Removal of torus mandibularis

E    **D7485**    Surgical reduction of osseous tuberosity

E    **D7490**    Radical resection of maxilla or mandible

## SURGICAL INCISION

E    **D7510**    Incision and drainage of abscess, intraoral soft tissue

B    **D7511**    Incision and drainage of abscess — intraoral soft tissue — complicated (includes drainage of multiple fascial spaces)

E    **D7520**    Incision and drainage of abscess, extraoral soft tissue

B    **D7521**    Incision and drainage of abscess — extraoral soft tissue — complicated (includes drainage of multiple fascial spaces)

E    **D7530**    Removal of foreign body from mucosa, skin, or subcutaneous alveolar tissue

E    **D7540**    Removal of reaction-producing foreign bodies, musculoskeletal system

E    **D7550**    Partial ostectomy/sequestrectomy for removal of nonvital bone

E    **D7560**    Maxillary sinusotomy for removal of tooth fragment or foreign body

---

**Dental Procedures**

**D7610 — D7873**

## TREATMENT OF FRACTURES - SIMPLE

| | | |
|---|---|---|
| E | D7610 | Maxilla, open reduction (teeth immobilized if present) |
| E | D7620 | Maxilla, closed reduction (teeth immobilized if present) |
| E | D7630 | Mandible, open reduction (teeth immobilized if present) |
| E | D7640 | Mandible, closed reduction (teeth immobilized if present) |
| E | D7650 | Malar and/or zygomatic arch, open reduction |
| E | D7660 | Malar and/or zygomatic arch, closed reduction |
| E | D7670 | Alveolus - closed reduction, may include stabilization of teeth |
| E | D7671 | Alveolus - open reduction, may include stabilization of teeth |
| E | D7680 | Facial bones, complicated reduction with fixation and multiple surgical approaches |

## TREATMENT OF FRACTURES - COMPOUND

| | | |
|---|---|---|
| E | D7710 | Maxilla, open reduction |
| E | D7720 | Maxilla, closed reduction |
| E | D7730 | Mandible, open reduction |
| E | D7740 | Mandible, closed reduction |
| E | D7750 | Malar and/or zygomatic arch, open reduction |
| E | D7760 | Malar and/or zygomatic arch, closed reduction |
| E | D7770 | Alveolus — open reduction stabilization of teeth |
| E | D7771 | Alveolus, closed reduction stabilization of teeth |
| E | D7780 | Facial bones, complicated reduction with fixation and multiple surgical approaches |

## REDUCTION OF DISLOCATION AND MANAGEMENT OF OTHER TEMPOROMANDIBULAR JOINT DYSFUNCTIONS

Procedures which are an integral part of a primary procedure should not be reported separately.

| | | |
|---|---|---|
| E | D7810 | Open reduction of dislocation |
| E | D7820 | Closed reduction of dislocation |
| E | D7830 | Manipulation under anesthesia |
| E | D7840 | Condylectomy |
| E | D7850 | Surgical discectomy; with/without implant |
| E | D7852 | Disc repair |
| E | D7854 | Synovectomy |
| E | D7856 | Myotomy |
| E | D7858 | Joint reconstruction |
| E | D7860 | Arthrotomy |
| | | MED: 100-2,15,150; 100-2,16,140 |
| E | D7865 | Arthroplasty |
| E | D7870 | Arthrocentesis |
| E | D7871 | Nonarthroscopic lysis and lavage |
| E | D7872 | Arthroscopy, diagnosis, with or without biopsy |
| E | D7873 | Arthroscopy, surgical: lavage and lysis of adhesions |

| | | | |
|---|---|---|---|
| E | | D7874 | Arthroscopy, surgical: disc repositioning and stabilization |
| E | | D7875 | Arthroscopy, surgical: synovectomy |
| E | | D7876 | Arthroscopy, surgical: discectomy |
| E | | D7877 | Arthroscopy, surgical: debridement |
| E | | D7880 | Occlusal orthotic appliance |
| E | | D7899 | Unspecified TMD therapy, by report |

Determine if an alternative HCPCS Level II or a CPT code better describes the service being reported. This code should be used only if a more specific code is unavailable.

## REPAIR OF TRAUMATIC WOUNDS

| | | | |
|---|---|---|---|
| E | ☑ | D7910 | Suture of recent small wounds up to 5 cm |

## COMPLICATED SUTURING (RECONSTRUCTION REQUIRING DELICATE HANDLING OF TISSUES AND WIDE UNDERMINING FOR METICULOUS CLOSURE)

| | | | |
|---|---|---|---|
| E | | D7911 | Complicated suture, up to 5 cm |
| E | | D7912 | Complicated suture, greater than 5 cm |

## OTHER REPAIR PROCEDURES

| | | | |
|---|---|---|---|
| E | | D7920 | Skin graft (identify defect covered, location, and type of graft) |
| S | | D7940 | Osteoplasty, for orthognathic deformities ⊘ |

MED: 100-2,15,150; 100-2,16,140

| | | | |
|---|---|---|---|
| E | | D7941 | Osteotomy — mandibular rami |
| E | | D7943 | Osteotomy — mandibular rami with bone graft; includes obtaining the graft |
| E | ☑ | D7944 | Osteotomy-segmented or subapical |
| E | | D7945 | Osteotomy, body of mandible |
| E | | D7946 | LeFort I (maxilla, total) |
| E | | D7947 | LeFort I (maxilla, segmented) |
| E | | D7948 | LeFort II or LeFort III (osteoplasty of facial bones for midface hypoplasia or retrusion), without bone graft |
| E | | D7949 | LeFort II or LeFort III, with bone graft |
| E | | D7950 | Osseous, osteoperiosteal, or cartilage graft of the mandible or maxilla, autogenous or nonautogenous, by report |

Pertinent documentation to evaluate medical appropriateness should be included when this code is reported.

| | | | |
|---|---|---|---|
| E | | D7951 | Sinus augmentation with bone or bone substitutes |
| E | ☑ | D7953 | Bone replacement graft for ridge preservation - per site |
| E | | D7955 | Repair of maxillofacial soft and/or hard tissue defect |
| E | | D7960 | Frenulectomy (frenectomy or frenotomy), separate procedure |
| E | | D7963 | Frenuloplasty |
| E | ☑ | D7970 | Excision of hyperplastic tissue, per arch |
| E | | D7971 | Excision of pericoronal gingiva |
| E | | D7972 | Surgical reduction of fibrous tuberosity |
| E | | D7980 | Sialolithotomy |

---

**Dental Procedures**

| | E | D7981 | Excision of salivary gland, by report<br>Pertinent documentation to evaluate medical appropriateness should be included when this code is reported. | |
|---|---|---|---|---|
| | E | D7982 | Sialodochoplasty | |
| | E | D7983 | Closure of salivary fistula | |
| | E | D7990 | Emergency tracheotomy | |
| | E | D7991 | Coronoidectomy | |
| | E | D7995 | Synthetic graft, mandible or facial bones, by report<br>Pertinent documentation to evaluate medical appropriateness should be included when this code is reported. | |
| | E | D7996 | Implant, mandible for augmentation purposes (excluding alveolar ridge), by report<br>Pertinent documentation to evaluate medical appropriateness should be included when this code is reported. | |
| | E | D7997 | Appliance removal (not by dentist who placed appliance), includes removal of archbar | |
| | E | D7998 | Intraoral placement of a fixation device not in conjunction with a fracture | |
| | E | D7999 | Unspecified oral surgery procedure, by report<br>Determine if an alternative HCPCS Level II or a CPT code better describes the service being reported. This code should be used only if a more specific code is unavailable. | |

## ORTHODONTICS D8000-D8999

| | E | D8010 | Limited orthodontic treatment of the primary dentition | A |
|---|---|---|---|---|
| | E | D8020 | Limited orthodontic treatment of the transitional dentition | |
| | E | D8030 | Limited orthodontic treatment of the adolescent dentition | A |
| | E | D8040 | Limited orthodontic treatment of the adult dentition | A |
| | E | D8050 | Interceptive orthodontic treatment of the primary dentition | A |
| | E | D8060 | Interceptive orthodontic treatment of the transitional dentition | |
| | E | D8070 | Comprehensive orthodontic treatment of the transitional dentition | |
| | E | D8080 | Comprehensive orthodontic treatment of the adolescent dentition | A |
| | E | D8090 | Comprehensive orthodontic treatment of the adult dentition | A |

## MINOR TREATMENT TO CONTROL HARMFUL HABITS

| | E | D8210 | Removable appliance therapy | |
|---|---|---|---|---|
| | E | D8220 | Fixed appliance therapy | |

## OTHER ORTHODONTIC SERVICES

| | E | D8660 | Orthodontic treatment (alternative billing to a contract fee) | |
|---|---|---|---|---|
| | E | D8670 | Periodic orthodontic treatment visit (as part of contract) | |
| | E | D8680 | Orthodontic retention (removal of appliances, construction and placement of retainer(s)) | |
| | E | D8690 | Orthodontic treatment (alternative billing to a contract fee) | |
| | E | D8691 | Repair of orthodontic appliance | |

---

| E | D8692 | Replacement of lost or broken retainer |
| E | D8693 | Rebonding or recementing; and/or repair, as required, of fixed retainers |
| E | D8999 | Unspecified orthodontic procedure, by report |

Determine if an alternative HCPCS Level II or a CPT code better describes the service being reported. This code should be used only if a more specific code is unavailable.

## ADJUNCTIVE GENERAL SERVICES D9110-D9999

### UNCLASSIFIED TREATMENT

| N | D9110 | Palliative (emergency) treatment of dental pain-minor procedures | ⊘ |

MED: 100-2,15,150; 100-2,16,140

| E | D9120 | Fixed partial denture sectioning |

### ANESTHESIA

| E | D9210 | Local anesthesia not in conjunction with operative or surgical procedures |
| E | D9211 | Regional block anesthesia |
| E | D9212 | Trigeminal division block anesthesia |
| E | D9215 | Local anesthesia |
| E ☑ | D9220 | Deep sedation/general anesthesia, first 30 minutes |
| E ☑ | D9221 | Deep sedation/general anesthesia, each additional 15 minutes |

MED: 100-2,15,150; 100-2,16,140

| N | D9230 | Analgesia, anxiolysis, inhalation of nitrous oxide | ⊘ |

MED: 100-2,15,150; 100-2,16,140

| E ☑ | D9241 | Intravenous conscious sedation/analgesia — first 30 minutes |
| E ☑ | D9242 | Intravenous conscious sedation/analgesia — each additional 15 minutes |
| N | D9248 | Nonintravenous conscious sedation |

### PROFESSIONAL CONSULTATION

| E | D9310 | Consultation, diagnostic service provided by dentist or physician other than requesting dentist or physician |

### PROFESSIONAL VISITS

| E | D9410 | House/extended care facility call |
| E | D9420 | Hospital call |
| E | D9430 | Office visit for observation (during regularly scheduled hours), no other services performed |
| E | D9440 | Office visit, after regularly scheduled hours |
| E | D9450 | Case presentation, detailed and extensive treatment planning |

### DRUGS

| E | D9610 | Therapeutic parenteral drug, single administration |

Pertinent documentation to evaluate medical appropriateness should be included when this code is reported.

| E | D9612 | Therapeutic parenteral drugs, 2 or more administrations, different medications |

---

☑ Quantity Alert    ● New Code    ○ Recycled/Reinstated    ▲ Revised Code    ⚕ DMEPOS Paid    ⊘ SNF Excluded

Dental Procedures

D9630 — D9999

⑤      **D9630**    Other drugs and/or medicaments, by report        ⊘
                             Determine if an alternative HCPCS Level II or a CPT code better describes the service being reported. This code should be used only if a more specific code is unavailable.
                             MED: 100-2,15,150; 100-2,16,140

## MISCELLANEOUS SERVICES

Ⓔ          **D9910**    Application of desensitizing medicament

Ⓔ   ☑    **D9911**    Application of desensitizing resin for cervical and/or root surface, per tooth

Ⓔ          **D9920**    Behavior management, by report
                             Pertinent documentation to evaluate medical appropriateness should be included when this code is reported.

⑤          **D9930**    Treatment of complications (postsurgical) — unusual circumstances, by report                            ⊘
                             MED: 100-2,15,150; 100-2,16,140

⑤          **D9940**    Occlusal guards, by report                          ⊘
                             Pertinent documentation to evaluate medical appropriateness should be included when this code is reported.
                             MED: 100-2,15,150; 100-2,16,140

Ⓔ          **D9941**    Fabrication of athletic mouthguard

Ⓔ          **D9942**    Repair and/or reline of occlusal guard

⑤          **D9950**    Occlusion analysis, mounted case                    ⊘
                             MED: 100-2,15,150; 100-2,16,140

⑤          **D9951**    Occlusal adjustment, limited                       ⊘
                             MED: 100-2,15,150; 100-2,16,140

⑤          **D9952**    Occlusal adjustment, complete                     ⊘
                             MED: 100-2,15,150; 100-2,16,140

Ⓔ          **D9970**    Enamel microabrasion

Ⓔ   ☑    **D9971**    Odontoplasty 1-2 teeth; includes removal of enamel projections

Ⓔ   ☑    **D9972**    External bleaching — per arch

Ⓔ   ☑    **D9973**    External bleaching — per tooth

Ⓔ   ☑    **D9974**    Internal bleaching — per tooth

Ⓔ          **D9999**    Unspecified adjunctive procedure, by report
                             Determine if an alternative HCPCS Level II or a CPT code better describes the service being reported. This code should be used only if a more specific code is unavailable.

## DURABLE MEDICAL EQUIPMENT E0100-E9999

E codes include durable medical equipment such as canes, crutches, walkers, commodes, decubitus care, bath and toilet aids, hospital beds, oxygen and related respiratory equipment, monitoring equipment, pacemakers, patient lifts, safety equipment, restraints, traction equipment, fracture frames, wheelchairs, and artificial kidney machines.

## CANES

Y    **E0100**    **Cane, includes canes of all materials, adjustable or fixed, with tip**   ⅅ
**White canes for the blind are not covered under Medicare.**
MED: 100-2,15,110.1; 100-3,280.1; 100-3,280.2

Y    **E0105**    **Cane, quad or 3-prong, includes canes of all materials, adjustable or fixed, with tips**   ⅅ
MED: 100-2,15,110.1; 100-3,280.1; 100-3,280.5

## CRUTCHES

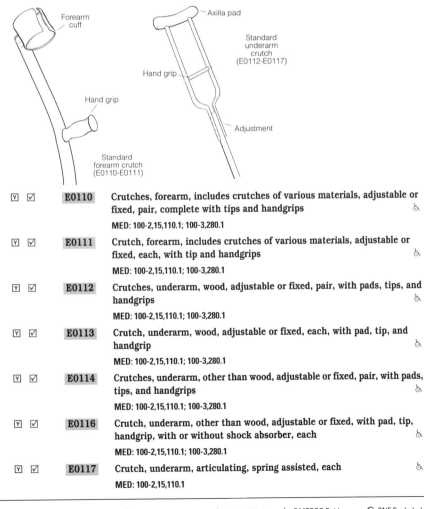

Forearm cuff

Axilla pad

Standard underarm crutch (E0112-E0117)

Hand grip

Hand grip

Adjustment

Standard forearm crutch (E0110-E0111)

Y ☑    **E0110**    **Crutches, forearm, includes crutches of various materials, adjustable or fixed, pair, complete with tips and handgrips**   ⅅ
MED: 100-2,15,110.1; 100-3,280.1

Y ☑    **E0111**    **Crutch, forearm, includes crutches of various materials, adjustable or fixed, each, with tip and handgrips**   ⅅ
MED: 100-2,15,110.1; 100-3,280.1

Y ☑    **E0112**    **Crutches, underarm, wood, adjustable or fixed, pair, with pads, tips, and handgrips**   ⅅ
MED: 100-2,15,110.1; 100-3,280.1

Y ☑    **E0113**    **Crutch, underarm, wood, adjustable or fixed, each, with pad, tip, and handgrip**   ⅅ
MED: 100-2,15,110.1; 100-3,280.1

Y ☑    **E0114**    **Crutches, underarm, other than wood, adjustable or fixed, pair, with pads, tips, and handgrips**   ⅅ
MED: 100-2,15,110.1; 100-3,280.1

Y ☑    **E0116**    **Crutch, underarm, other than wood, adjustable or fixed, with pad, tip, handgrip, with or without shock absorber, each**   ⅅ
MED: 100-2,15,110.1; 100-3,280.1

Y ☑    **E0117**    **Crutch, underarm, articulating, spring assisted, each**   ⅅ
MED: 100-2,15,110.1

Ⓔ ☑   **E0118**   Crutch substitute, lower leg platform, with or without wheels, each
Medicare covers walkers if patient's ambulation is impaired.

## WALKERS

Ⓨ   **E0130**   Walker, rigid (pickup), adjustable or fixed height
MED: 100-2,15,110.1; 100-3,280.1

Ⓨ   **E0135**   Walker, folding (pickup), adjustable or fixed height    ⅄
Medicare covers walkers if patient's ambulation is impaired.
MED: 100-2,15,110.1; 100-3,280.1

Ⓨ   **E0140**   Walker, with trunk support, adjustable or fixed height, any type   ⅄
MED: 100-2,15,110.1; 100-3,280.1

Ⓨ   **E0141**   Walker, rigid, wheeled, adjustable or fixed height   ⅄
Medicare covers walkers if patient's ambulation is impaired.
MED: 100-2,15,110.1; 100-3,280.1

Ⓨ   **E0143**   Walker, folding, wheeled, adjustable or fixed height   ⅄
Medicare covers walkers if patient's ambulation is impaired.
MED: 100-2,15,110.1; 100-3,280.1

Ⓨ   **E0144**   Walker, enclosed, 4 sided framed, rigid or folding, wheeled with posterior
seat   ⅄
MED: 100-2,15,110.1; 100-3,280.1

Ⓨ   **E0147**   Walker, heavy duty, multiple braking system, variable wheel
resistance   ⅄
Medicare covers safety roller walkers only in patients with severe
neurological disorders or restricted use of one hand. In some cases, coverage
will be extended to patients with a weight exceeding the limits of a standard
wheeled walker.
MED: 100-2,15,110.1; 100-3,280.5

Ⓨ   **E0148**   Walker, heavy-duty, without wheels, rigid or folding, any type, each   ⅄

Ⓨ   **E0149**   Walker, heavy-duty, wheeled, rigid or folding, any type   ⅄

## ATTACHMENTS

Ⓨ ☑   **E0153**   Platform attachment, forearm crutch, each   ⅄

Ⓨ ☑   **E0154**   Platform attachment, walker, each   ⅄

Ⓨ   **E0155**   Wheel attachment, rigid pick-up walker, per pair   ⅄

Ⓨ   **E0156**   Seat attachment, walker   ⅄

Ⓨ ☑   **E0157**   Crutch attachment, walker, each   ⅄

Ⓨ ☑   **E0158**   Leg extensions for walker, per set of 4   ⅄

Ⓨ ☑   **E0159**   Brake attachment for wheeled walker, replacement, each   ⅄

## COMMODES

Ⓨ   **E0160**   Sitz type bath or equipment, portable, used with or without commode ⅄
Medicare covers sitz baths if medical record indicates that the patient has
an infection or injury of the perineal area and the sitz bath is prescribed by
the physician.
MED: 100-3,280.1

---

Special Coverage Instructions      Noncovered by Medicare      Carrier Discretion

| ☒ | | E0161 | Sitz type bath or equipment, portable, used with or without commode, with faucet attachment(s)    ♿ |
|---|---|---|---|

Medicare covers sitz baths if medical record indicates that the patient has an infection or injury of the perineal area and the sitz bath is prescribed by the physician.

**MED: 100-3,280.1**

| ☒ | | E0162 | Sitz bath chair    ♿ |
|---|---|---|---|

Medicare covers sitz baths if medical record indicates that the patient has an infection or injury of the perineal area and the sitz bath is prescribed by the physician.

**MED: 100-3,280.1**

| ☒ | | E0163 | Commode chair, mobile or stationary, with fixed arms    ♿ |
|---|---|---|---|

Medicare covers commodes for patients confined to their beds or rooms, for patients without indoor bathroom facilities, and to patients who cannot climb or descend the stairs necessary to reach the bathrooms in their homes.

**MED: 100-2,15,110.1; 100-3,280.1**

| ☒ | | E0165 | Commode chair, mobile or stationary, with detachable arms    ♿ |
|---|---|---|---|

Medicare covers commodes for patients confined to their beds or rooms, for patients without indoor bathroom facilities, and to patients who cannot climb or descend the stairs necessary to reach the bathrooms in their homes.

**MED: 100-2,15,110.1; 100-3,280.1**

| ☒ | | E0167 | Pail or pan for use with commode chair, replacement only    ♿ |
|---|---|---|---|

Medicare covers commodes for patients confined to their beds or rooms, for patients without indoor bathroom facilities, and to patients who cannot climb or descend the stairs necessary to reach the bathrooms in their homes.

**MED: 100-3,280.1**

| ☒ | | E0168 | Commode chair, extra wide and/or heavy-duty, stationary or mobile, with or without arms, any type, each    ♿ |
|---|---|---|---|
| ☒ | | E0170 | Commode chair with integrated seat lift mechanism, electric, any type |
| ☒ | | E0171 | Commode chair with integrated seat lift mechanism, nonelectric, any type |
| ☒ | | E0172 | Seat lift mechanism placed over or on top of toilet, any type |
| ☒ | ☑ | E0175 | Footrest, for use with commode chair, each    ♿ |

## DECUBITUS CARE EQUIPMENT

| ☒ | | E0181 | Powered pressure reducing mattress overlay/pad, alternating, with pump, includes heavy-duty    ♿ |
|---|---|---|---|

Medicare covers pads if physicians supervise their use in patients who have decubitus ulcers or susceptibility to them. Prior authorization is required by Medicare for this item.

**MED: 100-3,280.1; 100-8,5,5.2.3**

| ☒ | | E0182 | Pump for alternating pressure pad, for replacement only    ♿ |
|---|---|---|---|

Medicare covers pads if physicians supervise their use in patients who have decubitus ulcers or susceptibility to them. Prior authorization is required by Medicare for this item.

**MED: 100-3,280.1; 100-8,5,5.2.3**

| ☒ | | E0184 | Dry pressure mattress    ♿ |
|---|---|---|---|

Medicare covers pads if physicians supervise their use in patients who have decubitus ulcers or susceptibility to them. Prior authorization is required by Medicare for this item.

**MED: 100-3,280.1; 100-8,5,5.2.3**

---

Y    **E0185**    Gel or gel-like pressure pad for mattress, standard mattress length and width

Medicare covers pads if physicians supervise their use in patients who have decubitus ulcers or susceptibility to them. Prior authorization is required by Medicare for this item.

MED: 100-3,280.1; 100-8,5,5.2.3

Y    **E0186**    Air pressure mattress

Medicare covers pads if physicians supervise their use in patients who have decubitus ulcers or susceptibility to them.

MED: 100-3,280.1

Y    **E0187**    Water pressure mattress

Medicare covers pads if physicians supervise their use in patients who have decubitus ulcers or susceptibility to them.

MED: 100-3,280.1

Y    **E0188**    Synthetic sheepskin pad

Medicare covers pads if physicians supervise their use in patients who have decubitus ulcers or susceptibility to them. Prior authorization is required by Medicare for this item.

MED: 100-3,280.1; 100-8,5,5.2.3

Y    **E0189**    Lambswool sheepskin pad, any size

Medicare covers pads if physicians supervise their use in patients who have decubitus ulcers or susceptibility to them. Prior authorization is required by Medicare for this item.

MED: 100-3,280.1; 100-8,5,5.2.3

E    **E0190**    Positioning cushion/pillow/wedge, any shape or size, includes all components and accessories

MED: 100-2,15,110.1

Y ☑    **E0191**    Heel or elbow protector, each

Y    **E0193**    Powered air flotation bed (low air loss therapy)

Y    **E0194**    Air fluidized bed

An air fluidized bed is covered by Medicare if the patient has a stage 3 or stage 4 pressure sore and, without the bed, would require institutionalization. A physician's prescription is required.

MED: 100-3,280.8

Y    **E0196**    Gel pressure mattress

Medicare covers pads if physicians supervise their use in patients who have decubitus ulcers or susceptibility to them.

MED: 100-3,280.1

Y    **E0197**    Air pressure pad for mattress, standard mattress length and width

Medicare covers pads if physicians supervise their use in patients who have decubitus ulcers or susceptibility to them.

MED: 100-3,280.1

Y    **E0198**    Water pressure pad for mattress, standard mattress length and width

Medicare covers pads if physicians supervise their use in patients who have decubitus ulcers or susceptibility to them.

MED: 100-3,280.1

Y    **E0199**    Dry pressure pad for mattress, standard mattress length and width

Medicare covers pads if physicians supervise their use in patients who have decubitus ulcers or susceptibility to them.

MED: 100-3,280.1

## HEAT/COLD APPLICATION

| Y | E0200 | Heat lamp, without stand (table model), includes bulb, or infrared element | &#x267F; |
| | | MED: 100-2,15,110.1; 100-3,280.1 | |
| Y | E0202 | Phototherapy (bilirubin) light with photometer | &#x267F; |
| E | E0203 | Therapeutic lightbox, minimum 10,000 lux, table top model | |
| Y | E0205 | Heat lamp, with stand, includes bulb, or infrared element | &#x267F; |
| | | MED: 100-2,15,110.1; 100-3,280.1 | |
| Y | E0210 | Electric heat pad, standard | &#x267F; |
| | | MED: 100-3,280.1 | |
| Y | E0215 | Electric heat pad, moist | &#x267F; |
| | | MED: 100-3,280.1 | |
| Y | E0217 | Water circulating heat pad with pump | &#x267F; |
| | | MED: 100-3,280.1 | |
| Y | E0218 | Water circulating cold pad with pump | |
| | | MED: 100-3,280.1 | |
| Y | E0220 | Hot water bottle | &#x267F; |
| Y | E0221 | Infrared heating pad system | &#x267F; |
| | | MED: 100-3,270.2 | |
| Y | E0225 | Hydrocollator unit, includes pads | &#x267F; |
| | | MED: 100-2,15,230; 100-3,280.1 | |
| Y | E0230 | Ice cap or collar | &#x267F; |
| E | E0231 | Noncontact wound-warming device (temperature control unit, AC adapter and power cord) for use with warming card and wound cover | |
| | | MED: 100-2,16,20 | |
| E | E0232 | Warming card for use with the noncontact wound-warming device and noncontact wound-warming wound cover | |
| | | MED: 100-2,16,20 | |
| Y | E0235 | Paraffin bath unit, portable (see medical supply code A4265 for paraffin) | &#x267F; |
| | | MED: 100-2,15,230; 100-3,280.1 | |
| Y | E0236 | Pump for water circulating pad | &#x267F; |
| | | MED: 100-3,280.1 | |
| Y | E0238 | Nonelectric heat pad, moist | &#x267F; |
| | | MED: 100-3,280.1 | |
| Y | E0239 | Hydrocollator unit, portable | &#x267F; |
| | | MED: 100-2,15,230; 100-3,280.1 | |

## BATH AND TOILET AIDS

| E | E0240 | Bath/shower chair, with or without wheels, any size | |
| | | MED: 100-3,280.1 | |
| E ☑ | E0241 | Bathtub wall rail, each | |
| | | MED: 100-2,15,110.1; 100-3,280.1 | |
| E | E0242 | Bathtub rail, floor base | |
| | | MED: 100-2,15,110.1; 100-3,280.1 | |

Durable Medical Equipment

E0243 — E0273

| | | | |
|---|---|---|---|
| E ☑ | E0243 | Toilet rail, each | |
| | | MED: 100-2,15,110.1; 100-3,280.1 | |
| E | E0244 | Raised toilet seat | |
| | | MED: 100-3,280.1 | |
| E | E0245 | Tub stool or bench | |
| | | MED: 100-3,280.1 | |
| E | E0246 | Transfer tub rail attachment | |
| E | E0247 | Transfer bench for tub or toilet with or without commode opening | |
| | | MED: 100-3,280.1 | |
| E | E0248 | Transfer bench, heavy-duty, for tub or toilet with or without commode opening | |
| | | MED: 100-3,280.1 | |
| Y | E0249 | Pad for water circulating heat unit | ♿ |
| | | MED: 100-3,280.1 | |

## HOSPITAL BEDS AND ACCESSORIES

| | | | |
|---|---|---|---|
| E | E0250 | Hospital bed, fixed height, with any type side rails, with mattress | ♿ |
| | | MED: 100-2,15,110.1; 100-3,280.7 | |
| E | E0251 | Hospital bed, fixed height, with any type side rails, without mattress | ♿ |
| | | MED: 100-2,15,110.1; 100-3,280.7 | |
| E | E0255 | Hospital bed, variable height, hi-lo, with any type side rails, with mattress | ♿ |
| | | MED: 100-2,15,110.1; 100-3,280.7 | |
| E | E0256 | Hospital bed, variable height, hi-lo, with any type side rails, without mattress | ♿ |
| | | MED: 100-2,15,110.1; 100-3,280.7 | |
| E | E0260 | Hospital bed, semi-electric (head and foot adjustment), with any type side rails, with mattress | ♿ |
| | | MED: 100-2,15,110.1; 100-3,280.7 | |
| E | E0261 | Hospital bed, semi-electric (head and foot adjustment), with any type side rails, without mattress | ♿ |
| | | MED: 100-2,15,110.1; 100-3,280.7 | |
| E | E0265 | Hospital bed, total electric (head, foot, and height adjustments), with any type side rails, with mattress | ♿ |
| | | MED: 100-2,15,110.1; 100-3,280.7 | |
| E | E0266 | Hospital bed, total electric (head, foot, and height adjustments), with any type side rails, without mattress | ♿ |
| | | MED: 100-2,15,110.1; 100-3,280.7 | |
| E | E0270 | Hospital bed, institutional type includes: oscillating, circulating and Stryker frame, with mattress | |
| | | MED: 100-3,280.1 | |
| E | E0271 | Mattress, innerspring | ♿ |
| | | MED: 100-3,280.1; 100-3,280.7 | |
| E | E0272 | Mattress, foam rubber | ♿ |
| | | MED: 100-3,280.1; 100-3,280.7 | |
| E | E0273 | Bed board | |
| | | MED: 100-3,280.1 | |

| | | |
|---|---|---|
| E | E0274 | Over-bed table |
| | | MED: 100-3,280.1 |
| Y | E0275 | Bed pan, standard, metal or plastic     &#9855; |
| | | Reusable, autoclavable bedpans are covered by Medicare for bed-confined patients. |
| | | MED: 100-3,280.1 |
| Y | E0276 | Bed pan, fracture, metal or plastic     &#9855; |
| | | Reusable, autoclavable bedpans are covered by Medicare for bed-confined patients. |
| | | MED: 100-3,280.1 |
| Y | E0277 | Powered pressure-reducing air mattress     &#9855; |
| | | MED: 100-3,280.1 |
| Y | E0280 | Bed cradle, any type     &#9855; |
| E | E0290 | Hospital bed, fixed height, without side rails, with mattress   &#9855; |
| | | MED: 100-2,15,110.1; 100-3,280.7 |
| Y | E0291 | Hospital bed, fixed height, without side rails, without mattress   &#9855; |
| | | MED: 100-2,15,110.1; 100-3,280.7 |
| E | E0292 | Hospital bed, variable height, hi-lo, without side rails, with mattress  &#9855; |
| | | MED: 100-2,15,110.1; 100-3,280.7 |
| Y | E0293 | Hospital bed, variable height, hi-lo, without side rails, without mattress  &#9855; |
| | | MED: 100-2,15,110.1; 100-3,280.7 |
| E | E0294 | Hospital bed, semi-electric (head and foot adjustment), without side rails, with mattress  &#9855; |
| | | MED: 100-2,15,110.1; 100-3,280.7 |
| Y | E0295 | Hospital bed, semi-electric (head and foot adjustment), without side rails, without mattress  &#9855; |
| | | MED: 100-2,15,110.1; 100-3,280.7 |
| E | E0296 | Hospital bed, total electric (head, foot, and height adjustments), without side rails, with mattress  &#9855; |
| | | MED: 100-2,15,110.1; 100-3,280.7 |
| Y | E0297 | Hospital bed, total electric (head, foot, and height adjustments), without side rails, without mattress  &#9855; |
| | | MED: 100-2,15,110.1; 100-3,280.7 |
| Y | E0300 | Pediatric crib, hospital grade, fully enclosed   &#9855; |
| Y | E0301 | Hospital bed, heavy-duty, extra wide, with weight capacity greater than 350 pounds, but less than or equal to 600 pounds, with any type side rails, without mattress  &#9855; |
| | | MED: 100-3,280.7 |
| Y | E0302 | Hospital bed, extra heavy-duty, extra wide, with weight capacity greater than 600 pounds, with any type side rails, without mattress  &#9855; |
| | | MED: 100-3,280.7 |
| E | E0303 | Hospital bed, heavy-duty, extra wide, with weight capacity greater than 350 pounds, but less than or equal to 600 pounds, with any type side rails, with mattress  &#9855; |
| | | MED: 100-3,280.7 |
| E | E0304 | Hospital bed, extra heavy-duty, extra wide, with weight capacity greater than 600 pounds, with any type side rails, with mattress  &#9855; |
| | | MED: 100-3,280.7 |

---

| | | | |
|---|---|---|---|
| E | **E0305** | Bedside rails, half-length | 🦽 |
| | | MED: 100-3,280.7 | |
| E | **E0310** | Bedside rails, full-length | 🦽 |
| | | MED: 100-3,280.7 | |
| E | **E0315** | Bed accessory: board, table, or support device, any type | |
| | | MED: 100-3,280.1 | |
| Y | **E0316** | Safety enclosure frame/canopy for use with hospital bed, any type | 🦽 |
| Y | **E0325** | Urinal; male, jug-type, any material | ♂🦽 |
| | | MED: 100-3,280.1 | |
| Y | **E0326** | Urinal; female, jug-type, any material | ♀🦽 |
| | | MED: 100-3,280.1 | |
| Y | **E0328** | Hospital bed, pediatric, manual, 360 degree side enclosures, top of headboard, footboard and side rails up to 24 inches above the spring, includes mattress | |
| Y | **E0329** | Hospital bed, pediatric, electric or semi-electric, 360 degree side enclosures, top of headboard, footboard and side rails up to 24 inches above the spring, includes mattress | |
| E | **E0350** | Control unit for electronic bowel irrigation/evacuation system | |
| E | **E0352** | Disposable pack (water reservoir bag, speculum, valving mechanism, and collection bag/box) for use with the electronic bowel irrigation/evacuation system | |
| E | **E0370** | Air pressure elevator for heel | |
| Y | **E0371** | Nonpowered advanced pressure reducing overlay for mattress, standard mattress length and width | 🦽 |
| Y | **E0372** | Powered air overlay for mattress, standard mattress length and width | 🦽 |
| Y | **E0373** | Nonpowered advanced pressure reducing mattress | 🦽 |

## OXYGEN AND RELATED RESPIRATORY EQUIPMENT

| | | | |
|---|---|---|---|
| Y | **E0424** | Stationary compressed gaseous oxygen system, rental; includes container, contents, regulator, flowmeter, humidifier, nebulizer, cannula or mask, and tubing | 🦽 |
| | | For the first claim filed for home oxygen equipment or therapy, submit a certificate of medical necessity that includes the oxygen flow rate, anticipated frequency and duration of oxygen therapy, and physician signature. Medicare accepts oxygen therapy as medically necessary in cases documenting any of the following: erythocythemia with a hematocrit greater than 56 percent; a P pulmonale on EKG; or dependent edema consistent with congestive heart failure. | |
| | | MED: 100-3,240.2 | |
| E | **E0425** | Stationary compressed gas system, purchase; includes regulator, flowmeter, humidifier, nebulizer, cannula or mask, and tubing | |
| | | MED: 100-3,240.2 | |
| E | **E0430** | Portable gaseous oxygen system, purchase; includes regulator, flowmeter, humidifier, cannula or mask, and tubing | |
| | | MED: 100-3,240.2 | |
| Y | **E0431** | Portable gaseous oxygen system, rental; includes portable container, regulator, flowmeter, humidifier, cannula or mask, and tubing | 🦽 |
| | | MED: 100-3,240.2 | |

| Y | | E0434 | Portable liquid oxygen system, rental; includes portable container, supply reservoir, humidifier, flowmeter, refill adaptor, contents gauge, cannula or mask, and tubing   ♿ |
| | | | MED: 100-3,240.2 |
| E | | E0435 | Portable liquid oxygen system, purchase; includes portable container, supply reservoir, flowmeter, humidifier, contents gauge, cannula or mask, tubing and refill adaptor |
| | | | MED: 100-3,240.2 |
| Y | | E0439 | Stationary liquid oxygen system, rental; includes container, contents, regulator, flowmeter, humidifier, nebulizer, cannula or mask, & tubing   ♿ |
| | | | MED: 100-3,240.2 |
| E | | E0440 | Stationary liquid oxygen system, purchase; includes use of reservoir, contents indicator, regulator, flowmeter, humidifier, nebulizer, cannula or mask, and tubing |
| | | | MED: 100-3,240.2 |
| Y | ☑ | E0441 | Oxygen contents, gaseous (for use with owned gaseous stationary systems or when both a stationary and portable gaseous system are owned), 1 month's supply = 1 unit   ♿ |
| | | | MED: 100-3,240.2 |
| Y | ☑ | E0442 | Oxygen contents, liquid (for use with owned liquid stationary systems or when both a stationary and portable liquid system are owned), 1 month's supply = 1 unit   ♿ |
| | | | MED: 100-3,240.2 |
| Y | ☑ | E0443 | Portable oxygen contents, gaseous (for use only with portable gaseous systems when no stationary gas or liquid system is used), 1 month's supply = 1 unit   ♿ |
| | | | MED: 100-3,240.2 |
| Y | ☑ | E0444 | Portable oxygen contents, liquid (for use only with portable liquid systems when no stationary gas or liquid system is used), 1 month's supply = 1 unit   ♿ |
| | | | MED: 100-3,240.2 |
| N | | E0445 | Oximeter device for measuring blood oxygen levels noninvasively |
| Y | | E0450 | Volume control ventilator, without pressure support mode, may include pressure control mode, used with invasive interface (e.g., tracheostomy tube)   ♿ |
| | | | MED: 100-3,280.1 |
| Y | | E0455 | Oxygen tent, excluding croup or pediatric tents |
| | | | MED: 100-3,240.2 |
| Y | | E0457 | Chest shell (cuirass)   ♿ |
| Y | | E0459 | Chest wrap   ♿ |
| Y | | E0460 | Negative pressure ventilator; portable or stationary   ♿ |
| | | | MED: 100-3,280.1 |
| Y | | E0461 | Volume control ventilator, without pressure support mode, may include pressure control mode, used with noninvasive interface (e.g., mask)   ♿ |
| | | | MED: 100-3,280.1 |
| Y | | E0462 | Rocking bed, with or without side rails   ♿ |
| Y | | E0463 | Pressure support ventilator with volume control mode, may include pressure control mode, used with invasive interface (e.g., tracheostomy tube) |

| | | | |
|---|---|---|---|
| Y | | E0464 | Pressure support ventilator with volume control mode, may include pressure control mode, used with noninvasive interface (e.g., mask) |
| Y | | E0470 | Respiratory assist device, bi-level pressure capability, without backup rate feature, used with noninvasive interface, e.g., nasal or facial mask (intermittent assist device with continuous positive airway pressure device) ♿ |
| | | | MED: 100-3,280.1 |
| Y | | E0471 | Respiratory assist device, bi-level pressure capability, with back-up rate feature, used with noninvasive interface, e.g., nasal or facial mask (intermittent assist device with continuous positive airway pressure device) ♿ |
| | | | MED: 100-3,280.1 |
| Y | | E0472 | Respiratory assist device, bi-level pressure capability, with backup rate feature, used with invasive interface, e.g., tracheostomy tube (intermittent assist device with continuous positive airway pressure device) ♿ |
| | | | MED: 100-3,280.1 |
| Y | | E0480 | Percussor, electric or pneumatic, home model ♿ |
| | | | MED: 100-3,280.1 |
| E | | E0481 | Intrapulmonary percussive ventilation system and related accessories |
| | | | MED: 100-3,240.5 |
| Y | | E0482 | Cough stimulating device, alternating positive and negative airway pressure ♿ |
| Y | ✓ | E0483 | High frequency chest wall oscillation air-pulse generator system, (includes hoses and vest), each ♿ |
| Y | ✓ | E0484 | Oscillatory positive expiratory pressure device, nonelectric, any type, each ♿ |
| Y | | E0485 | Oral device/appliance used to reduce upper airway collapsibility, adjustable or nonadjustable, prefabricated, includes fitting and adjustment |
| Y | | E0486 | Oral device/appliance used to reduce upper airway collapsibility, adjustable or nonadjustable, custom fabricated, includes fitting and adjustment |
| ● N | | E0487 | Spirometer, electronic, includes all accessories |

## IPPB MACHINES

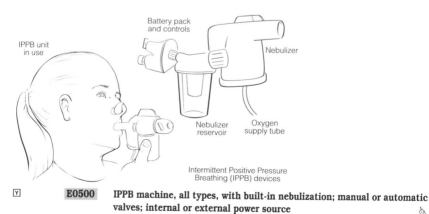

Battery pack and controls

IPPB unit in use

Nebulizer

Nebulizer reservoir

Oxygen supply tube

Intermittent Positive Pressure Breathing (IPPB) devices

| | | |
|---|---|---|
| Y | E0500 | IPPB machine, all types, with built-in nebulization; manual or automatic valves; internal or external power source ♿ |
| | | MED: 100-3,280.1 |

## HUMIDIFIERS/COMPRESSORS/NEBULIZERS FOR USE WITH OXYGEN IPPB EQUIPMENT

| | | | |
|---|---|---|---|
| Ⓨ | E0550 | Humidifier, durable for extensive supplemental humidification during IPPB treatments or oxygen delivery | ♿ |
| | | MED: 100-3,280.1 | |
| Ⓨ | E0555 | Humidifier, durable, glass or autoclavable plastic bottle type, for use with regulator or flowmeter | ♿ |
| | | MED: 100-3,280.1 | |
| Ⓨ | E0560 | Humidifier, durable for supplemental humidification during IPPB treatment or oxygen delivery | ♿ |
| | | MED: 100-3,280.1 | |
| Ⓨ | E0561 | Humidifier, nonheated, used with positive airway pressure device | ♿ |
| Ⓨ | E0562 | Humidifier, heated, used with positive airway pressure device | ♿ |
| Ⓨ | E0565 | Compressor, air power source for equipment which is not self-contained or cylinder driven | ♿ |
| Ⓨ | E0570 | Nebulizer, with compressor | ♿ |
| | | MED: 100-3,280.1 | |
| Ⓨ | E0571 | Aerosol compressor, battery powered, for use with small volume nebulizer | ♿ |
| | | MED: 100-3,280.1 | |
| Ⓨ | E0572 | Aerosol compressor, adjustable pressure, light duty for intermittent use | ♿ |
| Ⓨ | E0574 | Ultrasonic/electronic aerosol generator with small volume nebulizer | ♿ |
| Ⓨ | E0575 | Nebulizer, ultrasonic, large volume | ♿ |
| | | MED: 100-3,280.1 | |
| Ⓨ | E0580 | Nebulizer, durable, glass or autoclavable plastic, bottle type, for use with regulator or flowmeter | ♿ |
| | | MED: 100-3,280.1 | |
| Ⓨ | E0585 | Nebulizer, with compressor and heater | ♿ |
| | | MED: 100-3,280.1 | |

## SUCTION PUMP/ROOM VAPORIZERS

| | | | |
|---|---|---|---|
| Ⓨ | E0600 | Respiratory suction pump, home model, portable or stationary, electric | ♿ |
| | | MED: 100-3,280.1 | |
| Ⓨ | E0601 | Continuous airway pressure (CPAP) device | ♿ |
| | | MED: 100-3,240.4 | |
| Ⓨ | E0602 | Breast pump, manual, any type | Ⓜ ♀ ♿ |
| Ⓝ | E0603 | Breast pump, electric (AC and/or DC), any type | Ⓜ ♀ |
| Ⓐ | E0604 | Breast pump, hospital grade, electric (AC and/or DC), any type | Ⓜ ♀ |
| Ⓨ | E0605 | Vaporizer, room type | ♿ |
| | | MED: 100-3,280.1 | |
| Ⓨ | E0606 | Postural drainage board | ♿ |
| | | MED: 100-3,280.1 | |

## MONITORING EQUIPMENT

Y    E0607    Home blood glucose monitor    &

Medicare covers home blood testing devices for diabetic patients when the devices are prescribed by the patients' physicians. Many commercial payers provide this coverage to non-insulin dependent diabetics as well.

MED: 100.3,230.16

## PACEMAKER MONITOR

Y    E0610    Pacemaker monitor, self-contained, (checks battery depletion, includes audible and visible check systems)    &

MED: 100-3,20.8; 100-3,20.8.1; 100-3,20.8.2

Y    E0615    Pacemaker monitor, self-contained, checks battery depletion and other pacemaker components, includes digital/visible check systems    &

MED: 100-3,20.8; 100-3,20.8.1; 100-3,20.8.2

N    E0616    Implantable cardiac event recorder with memory, activator, and programmer    M

Y    E0617    External defibrillator with integrated electrocardiogram analysis    &

Y    E0618    Apnea monitor, without recording feature

Y    E0619    Apnea monitor, with recording feature

Y    E0620    Skin piercing device for collection of capillary blood, laser, each    &

## PATIENT LIFTS

Y    E0621    Sling or seat, patient lift, canvas or nylon    &

MED: 100-3,280.1

E    E0625    Patient lift, bathroom or toilet, not otherwise classified

MED: 100-3,280.1

Y    E0627    Seat lift mechanism incorporated into a combination lift-chair mechanism    &

MED: 100-3,280.4; 100-4,20,100; 100-4,20,130.2; 100-4,20,130.3; 100-4,20,130.4; 100-4,20,130.5

Y    E0628    Separate seat lift mechanism for use with patient-owned furniture, electric    &

MED: 100-3,280.4; 100-4,20,100; 100-4,20,130.2; 100-4,20,130.3; 100-4,20,130.4; 100-4,20,130.5

Y    E0629    Separate seat lift mechanism for use with patient-owned furniture, nonelectric    &

MED: 100-4,20,100; 100-4,20,130.2; 100-4,20,130.3; 100-4,20,130.4; 100-4,20,130.5

Y    E0630    Patient lift, hydraulic or mechanical, includes any seat, sling, strap(s), or pad(s)    &

MED: 100-3,280.1

Y    E0635    Patient lift, electric, with seat or sling    &

MED: 100-3,280.1

Y    E0636    Multipositional patient support system, with integrated lift, patient accessible controls    &

E    E0637    Combination sit to stand system, any size including pediatric, with seatlift feature, with or without wheels    &

MED: 100-3,280.1

Durable Medical Equipment

| | | |
|---|---|---|
| E | E0638 | Standing frame system, one position (e.g., upright, supine, or prone stander), any size including pediatric, with or without wheels    ♿ |
| | | MED: 100-3,280.1 |
| E | E0639 | Patient lift, moveable from room to room with disassembly and reassembly, includes all components/accessories |
| E | E0640 | Patient lift, fixed system, includes all components/accessories |
| E | E0641 | Standing frame system, multi-position (e.g., 3-way stander), any size including pediatric, with or without wheels |
| E | E0642 | Standing frame system, mobile (dynamic stander), any size including pediatric |

## PNEUMATIC COMPRESSOR AND APPLIANCES

| | | | |
|---|---|---|---|
| | Y | E0650 | Pneumatic compressor, nonsegmental home model    ♿ |
| | | | MED: 100-3,280.6 |
| | Y | E0651 | Pneumatic compressor, segmental home model without calibrated gradient pressure    ♿ |
| | | | MED: 100-3,280.6 |
| | Y | E0652 | Pneumatic compressor, segmental home model with calibrated gradient pressure    ♿ |
| | | | MED: 100-3,280.6 |
| | Y | E0655 | Nonsegmental pneumatic appliance for use with pneumatic compressor, half arm    ♿ |
| | | | MED: 100-3,280.6 |
| ● | Y | E0656 | Segmental pneumatic appliance for use with pneumatic compressor, trunk |
| ● | Y | E0657 | Segmental pneumatic appliance for use with pneumatic compressor, chest |
| | Y | E0660 | Nonsegmental pneumatic appliance for use with pneumatic compressor, full leg    ♿ |
| | | | MED: 100-3,280.6 |
| | Y | E0665 | Nonsegmental pneumatic appliance for use with pneumatic compressor, full arm    ♿ |
| | | | MED: 100-3,280.6 |
| | Y | E0666 | Nonsegmental pneumatic appliance for use with pneumatic compressor, half leg    ♿ |
| | | | MED: 100-3,280.6 |
| | Y | E0667 | Segmental pneumatic appliance for use with pneumatic compressor, full leg    ♿ |
| | | | MED: 100-3,280.6 |
| | Y | E0668 | Segmental pneumatic appliance for use with pneumatic compressor, full arm    ♿ |
| | | | MED: 100-3,280.6 |
| | Y | E0669 | Segmental pneumatic appliance for use with pneumatic compressor, half leg    ♿ |
| | | | MED: 100-3,280.6 |
| | Y | E0671 | Segmental gradient pressure pneumatic appliance, full leg    ♿ |
| | | | MED: 100-3,280.6 |

E0638 — E0671

---

Ⓨ    **E0672**    Segmental gradient pressure pneumatic appliance, full arm    ♿
MED: 100-3,280.6

Ⓨ    **E0673**    Segmental gradient pressure pneumatic appliance, half leg    ♿
MED: 100-3,280.6

Ⓨ    **E0675**    Pneumatic compression device, high pressure, rapid inflation/deflation cycle, for arterial insufficiency (unilateral or bilateral system)    ♿

Ⓨ    **E0676**    Intermittent limb compression device (includes all accessories), not otherwise specified    ♿

Ⓨ    **E0691**    Ultraviolet light therapy system panel, includes bulbs/lamps, timer and eye protection, treatment area 2 sq ft or less    ♿

Ⓨ    **E0692**    Ultraviolet light therapy system panel, includes bulbs/lamps, timer and eye protection, 4 ft panel    ♿

Ⓨ    **E0693**    Ultraviolet light therapy system panel, includes bulbs/lamps, timer and eye protection, 6 ft panel    ♿

Ⓨ    **E0694**    Ultraviolet multidirectional light therapy system in 6 ft cabinet, includes bulbs/lamps, timer, and eye protection    ♿

## SAFETY EQUIPMENT

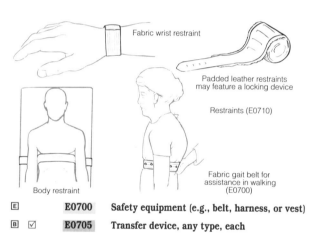

Fabric wrist restraint

Padded leather restraints may feature a locking device

Restraints (E0710)

Body restraint

Fabric gait belt for assistance in walking (E0700)

Ⓔ    **E0700**    Safety equipment (e.g., belt, harness, or vest)

Ⓑ ☑    **E0705**    Transfer device, any type, each

## RESTRAINTS

Ⓔ    **E0710**    Restraints, any type (body, chest, wrist, or ankle)

## TRANSCUTANEOUS AND/OR NEUROMUSCULAR ELECTRICAL NERVE STIMULATORS - TENS

Ⓨ    **E0720**    Transcutaneous electrical nerve stimulation (TENS) device, 2 lead, localized stimulation    ♿
While TENS is covered when employed to control chronic pain, it is not covered for experimental treatment, as in motor function disorders like MS. Prior authorization is required by Medicare for this item.
MED: 100-3,40.5; 100-3,130.5; 100-3,130.6; 100-3,160.2; 100-3,160.7.1; 100-3,230.1; 100-8,5,5.2.3

Durable Medical Equipment

| | | |
|---|---|---|
| Y | E0730 | **Transcutaneous electrical nerve stimulation (TENS) device, 4 or more leads, for multiple nerve stimulation**   ᵟ<br>While TENS is covered when employed to control chronic pain, it is not covered for experimental treatment, as in motor function disorders like MS. Prior authorization is required by Medicare for this item.<br>MED: 100-3,40.5; 100-3,130.5; 100-3,130.6; 100-3,160.2; 100-3,160.7.1; 100-3,230.1; 100-8,5,5.2.3 |
| Y | E0731 | **Form-fitting conductive garment for delivery of TENS or NMES (with conductive fibers separated from the patient's skin by layers of fabric)** ᵟ<br>MED: 100-3,160.13 |
| Y | E0740 | **Incontinence treatment system, pelvic floor stimulator, monitor, sensor, and/or trainer**   ᵟ<br>MED: 100-3,230.8 |
| Y | E0744 | **Neuromuscular stimulator for scoliosis**   ᵟ |
| Y | E0745 | **Neuromuscular stimulator, electronic shock unit**   ᵟ<br>MED: 100-3,160.12 |
| N | E0746 | **Electromyography (EMG), biofeedback device**<br>Biofeedback therapy is covered by Medicare only for re-education of specific muscles or for treatment of incapacitating muscle spasm or weakness. Medicare jurisdiction: local contractor.<br>MED: 100-3,30.1; 100-3,30.1.1 |
| Y | E0747 | **Osteogenesis stimulator, electrical, noninvasive, other than spinal applications**   ᵟ<br>Medicare covers noninvasive osteogenic stimulation for nonunion of long bone fractures, failed fusion, or congenital pseudoarthroses.<br>MED: 100-3,150.2 |
| Y | E0748 | **Osteogenesis stimulator, electrical, noninvasive, spinal applications**   ᵟ<br>Medicare covers noninvasive osteogenic stimulation as an adjunct to spinal fusion surgery for patients at high risk of pseudoarthroses due to previously failed spinal fusion, or for those undergoing fusion of three or more vertebrae.<br>MED: 100-3,150.2 |
| N | E0749 | **Osteogenesis stimulator, electrical, surgically implanted**   ◫ ᵟ<br>Medicare covers invasive osteogenic stimulation for nonunion of long bone fractures or as an adjunct to spinal fusion surgery for patients at high risk of pseudoarthroses due to previously failed spinal fusion, or for those undergoing fusion of three or more vertebrae.<br>MED: 100-3,150.2 |
| E | E0755 | **Electronic salivary reflex stimulator (intraoral/noninvasive)** |
| Y | E0760 | **Osteogenesis stimulator, low intensity ultrasound, noninvasive**   ᵟ<br>MED: 100-3,150.2 |
| E | E0761 | **Nonthermal pulsed high frequency radiowaves, high peak power electromagnetic energy treatment device** |
| B | E0762 | **Transcutaneous electrical joint stimulation device system, includes all accessories**   ᵟ |
| ▲ Y | E0764 | **Functional neuromuscular stimulation, transcutaneous stimulation of sequential muscle groups of ambulation with computer control, used for walking by spinal cord injured, entire system, after completion of training program** |
| Y | E0765 | **FDA approved nerve stimulator, with replaceable batteries, for treatment of nausea and vomiting**   ᵟ |

E0730 — E0765

---

| | | |
|---|---|---|
| ☒ | E0769 | Electrical stimulation or electromagnetic wound treatment device, not otherwise classified |
| | | MED: 100-4,32,11.1 |
| ● ☒ | E0770 | Functional electrical stimulator, transcutaneous stimulation of nerve and/or muscle groups, any type, complete system, not otherwise specified |

## INFUSION SUPPLIES

| | | |
|---|---|---|
| ☒ | E0776 | IV pole      占 |
| ☒ | E0779 | Ambulatory infusion pump, mechanical, reusable, for infusion 8 hours or greater      占 |
| ☒ | E0780 | Ambulatory infusion pump, mechanical, reusable, for infusion less than 8 hours      占 |
| ☒ | E0781 | Ambulatory infusion pump, single or multiple channels, electric or battery operated, with administrative equipment, worn by patient      占 |
| | | MED: 100-3,280.14 |
| ☒ | E0782 | Infusion pump, implantable, nonprogrammable (includes all components, e.g., pump, catheter, connectors, etc.)      Ⓜ 占 |
| | | MED: 100-3,280.14 |
| ☒ | E0783 | Infusion pump system, implantable, programmable (includes all components, e.g., pump, catheter, connectors, etc.)      Ⓜ 占 |
| | | MED: 100-3,280.14 |
| ☒ | E0784 | External ambulatory infusion pump, insulin      占 |
| | | Covered by some commercial payers with preauthorization. |
| | | MED: 100-3,280.14 |
| ☒ | E0785 | Implantable intraspinal (epidural/intrathecal) catheter used with implantable infusion pump, replacement      Ⓜ 占 |
| | | Medicare jurisdiction: local contractor. |
| | | MED: 100-3,280.14 |
| ☒ | E0786 | Implantable programmable infusion pump, replacement (excludes implantable intraspinal catheter)      Ⓜ 占 |
| | | Medicare jurisdiction: local contractor. |
| | | MED: 100-3,280.14 |
| ☒ | E0791 | Parenteral infusion pump, stationary, single, or multichannel      占 |
| | | MED: 100-2,15,120; 100-3,180.2; 100-4,20,100.2.2 |

## TRACTION - ALL TYPES

| | | |
|---|---|---|
| ☒ | E0830 | Ambulatory traction device, all types, each |
| | | MED: 100-3,280.1 |

## TRACTION - CERVICAL

| | | |
|---|---|---|
| ☒ | E0840 | Traction frame, attached to headboard, cervical traction      占 |
| | | MED: 100-3,280.1 |
| ☒ | E0849 | Traction equipment, cervical, free-standing stand/frame, pneumatic, applying traction force to other than mandible |
| ☒ | E0850 | Traction stand, freestanding, cervical traction      占 |
| | | MED: 100-3,280.1 |
| ☒ | E0855 | Cervical traction equipment not requiring additional stand or frame      占 |

| Y | E0856 | Cervical traction device, cervical collar with inflatable air bladder |

## TRACTION - OVERDOOR

| Y | E0860 | Traction equipment, overdoor, cervical | &. |
MED: 100-3,280.1

## TRACTION - EXTREMITY

| Y | E0870 | Traction frame, attached to footboard, extremity traction (e.g., Buck's) | &. |
MED: 100-3,280.1

| Y | E0880 | Traction stand, freestanding, extremity traction (e.g., Buck's) | &. |
MED: 100-3,280.1

## TRACTION - PELVIC

| Y | E0890 | Traction frame, attached to footboard, pelvic traction | &. |
MED: 100-3,280.1

| Y | E0900 | Traction stand, freestanding, pelvic traction (e.g., Buck's) | &. |
MED: 100-3,280.1

## TRAPEZE EQUIPMENT, FRACTURE FRAME, AND OTHER ORTHOPEDIC DEVICES

| Y | E0910 | Trapeze bars, also known as Patient Helper, attached to bed, with grab bar | &. |
MED: 100-3,280.1

| Y | E0911 | Trapeze bar, heavy-duty, for patient weight capacity greater than 250 pounds, attached to bed, with grab bar |

| Y | E0912 | Trapeze bar, heavy-duty, for patient weight capacity greater than 250 pounds, freestanding, complete with grab bar |

| Y | E0920 | Fracture frame, attached to bed, includes weights | &. |
MED: 100-3,280.1

| Y | E0930 | Fracture frame, freestanding, includes weights | &. |
MED: 100-3,280.1

| Y | E0935 | Continuous passive motion exercise device for use on knee only | &. |
MED: 100-3,280.1

| E | E0936 | Continuous passive motion exercise device for use other than knee |

| Y | E0940 | Trapeze bar, freestanding, complete with grab bar | &. |
MED: 100-3,280.1

| Y | E0941 | Gravity assisted traction device, any type | &. |
MED: 100-3,280.1

| Y | E0942 | Cervical head harness/halter | &. |

| Y | E0944 | Pelvic belt/harness/boot | &. |

| Y | E0945 | Extremity belt/harness | &. |

| Y | E0946 | Fracture frame, dual with cross bars, attached to bed (e.g., Balken, Four Poster) | &. |
MED: 100-3,280.1

| Y | E0947 | Fracture frame, attachments for complex pelvic traction | &. |
MED: 100-3,280.1

---

☑ Quantity Alert   ● New Code   ○ Recycled/Reinstated   ▲ Revised Code   &. DMEPOS Paid   ⊘ SNF Excluded

| | | | | |
|---|---|---|---|---|
| Y | | E0948 | Fracture frame, attachments for complex cervical traction | ♿ |
| | | | MED: 100-3,280.1 | |

## WHEELCHAIR ACCESSORIES

| | | | | |
|---|---|---|---|---|
| Y | | E0950 | Wheelchair accessory, tray, each | |
| | | | MED: 100-3,280.1 | |
| Y | ☑ | E0951 | Heel loop/holder, any type, with or without ankle strap, each | |
| Y | ☑ | E0952 | Toe loop/holder, any type, each | ♿ |
| | | | MED: 100-3,280.1 | |
| Y | ☑ | E0955 | Wheelchair accessory, headrest, cushioned, any type, including fixed mounting hardware, each | ♿ |
| Y | ☑ | E0956 | Wheelchair accessory, lateral trunk or hip support, any type, including fixed mounting hardware, each | ♿ |
| Y | ☑ | E0957 | Wheelchair accessory, medial thigh support, any type, including fixed mounting hardware, each | ♿ |
| Y | ☑ | E0958 | Manual wheelchair accessory, one-arm drive attachment, each | |
| | | | MED: 100-3,280.1 | |
| B | ☑ | E0959 | Manual wheelchair accessory, adapter for amputee, each | ♿ |
| | | | MED: 100-3,280.1 | |
| Y | | E0960 | Wheelchair accessory, shoulder harness/straps or chest strap, including any type mounting hardware | ♿ |
| B | ☑ | E0961 | Manual wheelchair accessory, wheel lock brake extension (handle), each | ♿ |
| | | | MED: 100-3,280.1 | |
| B | ☑ | E0966 | Manual wheelchair accessory, headrest extension, each | ♿ |
| | | | MED: 100-3,280.1 | |
| Y | ☑ | E0967 | Manual wheelchair accessory, hand rim with projections, any type, each | ♿ |
| | | | MED: 100-3,280.1 | |
| Y | | E0968 | Commode seat, wheelchair | ♿ |
| | | | MED: 100-3,280.1 | |
| Y | | E0969 | Narrowing device, wheelchair | ♿ |
| | | | MED: 100-3,280.1 | |
| E | | E0970 | No. 2 footplates, except for elevating legrest | ♿ |
| | | | See code(s): K0037, K0042 | |
| | | | MED: 100-3,280.1 | |
| B | ☑ | E0971 | Manual wheelchair accessory, antitipping device, each | ♿ |
| | | | DME fee schedule reflects a base billing unit of each. | |
| | | | MED: 100-3,280.1 | |
| B | ☑ | E0973 | Wheelchair accessory, adjustable height, detachable armrest, complete assembly, each | ♿ |
| | | | MED: 100-3,280.1 | |
| B | ☑ | E0974 | Manual wheelchair accessory, antirollback device, each | ♿ |
| | | | MED: 100-3,280.1 | |
| B | ☑ | E0978 | Wheelchair accessory, positioning belt/safety belt/pelvic strap, each | ♿ |
| Y | | E0980 | Safety vest, wheelchair | ♿ |
| Y | ☑ | E0981 | Wheelchair accessory, seat upholstery, replacement only, each | ♿ |

---

| Special Coverage Instructions | Noncovered by Medicare | Carrier Discretion |
|---|---|---|

| | | | | |
|---|---|---|---|---|
| Y | ☑ | E0982 | Wheelchair accessory, back upholstery, replacement only, each | ♿ |
| Y | | E0983 | Manual wheelchair accessory, power add-on to convert manual wheelchair to motorized wheelchair, joystick control | |
| Y | | E0984 | Manual wheelchair accessory, power add-on to convert manual wheelchair to motorized wheelchair, tiller control | ♿ |
| Y | | E0985 | Wheelchair accessory, seat lift mechanism | ♿ |
| Y | ☑ | E0986 | Manual wheelchair accessory, push activated power assist, each | ♿ |
| B | ☑ | E0990 | Wheelchair accessory, elevating legrest, complete assembly, each | ♿ |
| | | | MED: 100-3,280.1 | |
| B | | E0992 | Manual wheelchair accessory, solid seat insert | ♿ |
| Y | ☑ | E0994 | Armrest, each | ♿ |
| | | | MED: 100-3,280.1 | |
| B | ☑ | E0995 | Wheelchair accessory, calf rest/pad, each | ♿ |
| | | | MED: 100-3,280.1 | |
| Y | | E1002 | Wheelchair accessory, power seating system, tilt only | ♿ |
| Y | | E1003 | Wheelchair accessory, power seating system, recline only, without shear reduction | |
| Y | | E1004 | Wheelchair accessory, power seating system, recline only, with mechanical shear reduction | ♿ |
| Y | | E1005 | Wheelchair accessory, power seatng System, recline only, with power shear reduction | ♿ |
| Y | | E1006 | Wheelchair accessory, power seating system, combination tilt and recline, without shear reduction | ♿ |
| Y | | E1007 | Wheelchair accessory, power seating system, combination tilt and recline, with mechanical shear reduction | ♿ |
| Y | | E1008 | Wheelchair accessory, power seating system, combination tilt and recline, with power shear reduction | ♿ |
| Y | ☑ | E1009 | Wheelchair accessory, addition to power seating system, mechanically linked leg elevation system, including pushrod and legrest, each | ♿ |
| Y | ☑ | E1010 | Wheelchair accessory, addition to power seating system, power leg elevation system, including legrest, pair | ♿ |
| Y | | E1011 | Modification to pediatric size wheelchair, width adjustment package (not to be dispensed with initial chair) | ♿ |
| | | | MED: 100-3,280.1 | |
| Y | | E1014 | Reclining back, addition to pediatric size wheelchair | ♿ |
| | | | MED: 100-3,280.1 | |
| Y | | E1015 | Shock absorber for manual wheelchair, each | ♿ |
| | | | MED: 100-3,280.1 | |
| Y | | E1016 | Shock absorber for power wheelchair, each | ♿ |
| | | | MED: 100-3,280.1 | |
| Y | ☑ | E1017 | Heavy-duty shock absorber for heavy-duty or extra heavy-duty manual wheelchair, each | ♿ |
| | | | MED: 100-3,280.1 | |
| Y | ☑ | E1018 | Heavy-duty shock absorber for heavy-duty or extra heavy-duty power wheelchair, each | ♿ |
| | | | MED: 100-3,280.1 | |

Durable Medical Equipment

E1020 — E1087

| | | |
|---|---|---|
| Y | **E1020** | Residual limb support system for wheelchair ♿ |
| | | MED: 100-3,280.3 |
| Y | **E1028** | Wheelchair accessory, manual swingaway, retractable or removable mounting hardware for joystick, other control interface or positioning accessory ♿ |
| Y | **E1029** | Wheelchair accessory, ventilator tray, fixed ♿ |
| Y | **E1030** | Wheelchair accessory, ventilator tray, gimbaled ♿ |

## ROLLABOUT CHAIR

| | | |
|---|---|---|
| Y | **E1031** | Rollabout chair, any and all types with castors 5 in or greater ♿ |
| | | MED: 100-3,280.1 |
| Y | **E1035** | Multi-positional patient transfer system, with integrated seat, operated by care giver ♿ |
| | | MED: 100-2,15,110 |
| Y | **E1037** | Transport chair, pediatric size ♿ |
| | | MED: 100-3,280.1 |
| Y | **E1038** | Transport chair, adult size, patient weight capacity up to and including 300 pounds ♿ |
| | | MED: 100-3,280.1 |
| Y | **E1039** | Transport chair, adult size, heavy-duty, patient weight capacity greater than 300 pounds ♿ |

## WHEELCHAIRS - FULLY RECLINING

| | | |
|---|---|---|
| Y | **E1050** | Fully-reclining wheelchair, fixed full-length arms, swing-away detachable elevating legrests |
| | | MED: 100-3,280.1 |
| Y | **E1060** | Fully-reclining wheelchair, detachable arms, desk or full-length, swing-away detachable elevating legrests |
| | | MED: 100-3,280.1 |
| Y | **E1070** | Fully-reclining wheelchair, detachable arms (desk or full-length) swing-away detachable footrest |
| | | MED: 100-3,280.1 |
| Y | **E1083** | Hemi-wheelchair; fixed full-length arms, swing-away, detachable, elevating legrests |
| | | MED: 100-3,280.1 |
| Y | **E1084** | Hemi-wheelchair, detachable arms desk or full-length arms, swing-away detachable elevating legrests |
| | | MED: 100-3,280.1 |
| E | **E1085** | Hemi-wheelchair, fixed full-length arms, swing-away detachable footrests |
| | | See code(s): K0002 |
| | | MED: 100-3,280.1 |
| E | **E1086** | Hemi-wheelchair, detachable arms, desk or full-length, swing-away detachable footrests |
| | | See code(s): K0002 |
| | | MED: 100-3,280.1 |
| Y | **E1087** | High strength lightweight wheelchair, fixed full-length arms, swing-away detachable elevating legrests |
| | | MED: 100-3,280.1 |

| Y | E1088 | High strength lightweight wheelchair, detachable arms desk or full-length, swing-away detachable elevating legrests |
|---|---|---|
| | | MED: 100-3,280.1 |
| E | E1089 | High-strength lightweight wheelchair, fixed-length arms, swing-away detachable footrest |
| | | See code(s): K0004 |
| | | MED: 100-3,280.1 |
| E | E1090 | High-strength lightweight wheelchair, detachable arms, desk or full-length, swing-away detachable footrests |
| | | See code(s): K0004 |
| | | MED: 100-3,280.1 |
| Y | E1092 | Wide heavy-duty wheel chair, detachable arms (desk or full-length), swing-away detachable elevating legrests |
| | | MED: 100-3,280.1 |
| Y | E1093 | Wide heavy-duty wheelchair, detachable arms, desk or full-length, swing-away detachable footrests |
| | | MED: 100-3,280.1 |

## WHEELCHAIR - SEMI-RECLINING

| Y | E1100 | Semi-reclining wheelchair, fixed full-length arms, swing-away detachable elevating legrests |
|---|---|---|
| | | MED: 100-3,280.1 |
| Y | E1110 | Semi-reclining wheelchair, detachable arms (desk or full-length) elevating legrest |
| | | MED: 100-3,280.1 |

## WHEELCHAIR - STANDARD

| E | E1130 | Standard wheelchair, fixed full-length arms, fixed or swing-away detachable footrests |
|---|---|---|
| | | See code(s): K0001 |
| | | MED: 100-3,280.1 |
| E | E1140 | Wheelchair, detachable arms, desk or full-length, swing-away detachable footrests |
| | | See code(s): K0001 |
| | | MED: 100-3,280.1 |
| Y | E1150 | Wheelchair, detachable arms, desk or full-length swing-away detachable elevating legrests       &#9855; |
| | | MED: 100-3,280.1 |
| Y | E1160 | Wheelchair, fixed full-length arms, swing-away detachable elevating legrests |
| | | MED: 100-3,280.1 |
| Y | E1161 | Manual adult size wheelchair, includes tilt in space |

## WHEELCHAIR - AMPUTEE

| Y | E1170 | Amputee wheelchair, fixed full-length arms, swing-away detachable elevating legrests |
|---|---|---|
| | | MED: 100-3,280.1 |
| Y | E1171 | Amputee wheelchair, fixed full-length arms, without footrests or legrest |
| | | MED: 100-3,280.1 |

☑    E1172    Amputee wheelchair, detachable arms (desk or full-length) without
              footrests or legrest
              MED: 100-3,280.1

☑    E1180    Amputee wheelchair, detachable arms (desk or full-length) swing-away
              detachable footrests
              MED: 100-3,280.1

☑    E1190    Amputee wheelchair, detachable arms (desk or full-length) swing-away
              detachable elevating legrests
              MED: 100-3,280.1

☑    E1195    Heavy-duty wheelchair, fixed full-length arms, swing-away detachable
              elevating legrests
              MED: 100-3,280.1

☑    E1200    Amputee wheelchair, fixed full-length arms, swing-away detachable
              footrest
              MED: 100-3,280.1

## WHEELCHAIR - SPECIAL SIZE

☑    E1220    Wheelchair, specially sized or constructed (indicate brand name, model
              number, if any, and justification)
              MED: 100-3,280.3

☑    E1221    Wheelchair with fixed arm, footrests
              MED: 100-3,280.3

☑    E1222    Wheelchair with fixed arm, elevating legrests
              MED: 100-3,280.3

☑    E1223    Wheelchair with detachable arms, footrests
              MED: 100-3,280.3

☑    E1224    Wheelchair with detachable arms, elevating legrests
              MED: 100-3,280.3

☑    E1225    Wheelchair accessory, manual semi-reclining back, (recline greater than
              15 degrees, but less than 80 degrees), each                          ♿
              MED: 100-3,280.3

☑    E1226    Wheelchair accessory, manual fully reclining back, (recline greater than
              80 degrees), each                                                     ♿
              See also K0028
              MED: 100-3,280.1

☑    E1227    Special height arms for wheelchair                                    ♿
              MED: 100-3,280.3

☑    E1228    Special back height for wheelchair                                    ♿
              MED: 100-3,280.3

☑    E1229    Wheelchair, pediatric size, not otherwise specified

☑    E1230    Power operated vehicle (3- or 4-wheel nonhighway, specify brand name
              and model number                                                     ♿
              Prior authorization is required by Medicare for this item.
              MED: 100-8,5,5.2.3

☑    E1231    Wheelchair, pediatric size, tilt-in-space, rigid, adjustable, with seating
              system                                                                ♿
              MED: 100-3,280.1

Ⓨ     **E1232**     Wheelchair, pediatric size, tilt-in-space, folding, adjustable, with seating system    ♿
MED: 100-3,280.1

Ⓨ     **E1233**     Wheelchair, pediatric size, tilt-in-space, rigid, adjustable, without seating system    ♿
MED: 100-3,280.1

Ⓨ     **E1234**     Wheelchair, pediatric size, tilt-in-space, folding, adjustable, without seating system    ♿
MED: 100-3,280.1

Ⓨ     **E1235**     Wheelchair, pediatric size, rigid, adjustable, with seating system    ♿
MED: 100-3,280.1

Ⓨ     **E1236**     Wheelchair, pediatric size, folding, adjustable, with seating system    ♿
MED: 100-3,280.1

Ⓨ     **E1237**     Wheelchair, pediatric size, rigid, adjustable, without seating system    ♿
MED: 100-3,280.1

Ⓨ     **E1238**     Wheelchair, pediatric size, folding, adjustable, without seating system ♿
MED: 100-3,280.1

Ⓨ     **E1239**     Power wheelchair, pediatric size, not otherwise specified

## WHEELCHAIR - LIGHTWEIGHT

Ⓨ     **E1240**     Lightweight wheelchair, detachable arms, (desk or full-length) swing-away detachable, elevating legrest
MED: 100-3,280.1

Ⓔ     **E1250**     Lightweight wheelchair, fixed full-length arms, swing-away detachable footrest
See code(s): K0003
MED: 100-3,280.1

Ⓔ     **E1260**     Lightweight wheelchair, detachable arms (desk or full-length) swing-away detachable footrest
See code(s): K0003
MED: 100-3,280.1

Ⓨ     **E1270**     Lightweight wheelchair, fixed full-length arms, swing-away detachable elevating legrests
MED: 100-3,280.1

## WHEELCHAIR - HEAVY-DUTY

Ⓨ     **E1280**     Heavy-duty wheelchair, detachable arms (desk or full-length) elevating legrests
MED: 100-3,280.1

Ⓔ     **E1285**     Heavy-duty wheelchair, fixed full-length arms, swing-away detachable footrest
See code(s): K0006
MED: 100-3,280.1

Ⓔ     **E1290**     Heavy-duty wheelchair, detachable arms (desk or full-length) swing-away detachable footrest
See code(s): K0006
MED: 100-3,280.1

Ⓨ     **E1295**     Heavy-duty wheelchair, fixed full-length arms, elevating legrest
MED: 100-3,280.1

Durable Medical Equipment

E1232 — E1295

| ☑ | | E1296 | Special wheelchair seat height from floor   ♿ |
| | | | MED: 100-3,280.3 |
| ☑ | | E1297 | Special wheelchair seat depth, by upholstery   ♿ |
| | | | MED: 100-3,280.3 |
| ☑ | | E1298 | Special wheelchair seat depth and/or width, by construction   ♿ |
| | | | MED: 100-3,280.3 |

## WHIRLPOOL - EQUIPMENT

| Ⓔ | | E1300 | Whirlpool, portable (overtub type) |
| | | | MED: 100-3,280.1 |
| ☑ | | E1310 | Whirlpool, nonportable (built-in type)   ♿ |
| | | | MED: 100-3,280.1 |

## REPAIRS AND REPLACEMENT SUPPLIES

| ☑ | ☑ | E1340 | Repair or nonroutine service for durable medical equipment requiring the skill of a technician, labor component, per 15 minutes |
| | | | Medicare jurisdiction: local contractor if repair or implanted DME. |
| | | | MED: 100-2,15,110.2 |

## ADDITIONAL OXYGEN RELATED EQUIPMENT

| | ☑ | | E1353 | Regulator   ♿ |
| | | | | MED: 100-3,240.2 |
| ● | ☑ | | E1354 | Oxygen accessory, wheeled cart for portable cylinder or portable concentrator, any type, replacement only, each |
| | ☑ | | E1355 | Stand/rack   ♿ |
| | | | | MED: 100-3,240.2 |
| ● | ☑ | | E1356 | Oxygen accessory, battery pack/cartridge for portable concentrator, any type, replacement only, each |
| ● | ☑ | | E1357 | Oxygen accessory, battery charger for portable concentrator, any type, replacement only, each |
| ● | ☑ | | E1358 | Oxygen accessory, DC power adapter for portable concentrator, any type, replacement only, each |
| | ☑ | | E1372 | Immersion external heater for nebulizer   ♿ |
| | | | | MED: 100-3,240.2 |
| | ☑ | | E1390 | Oxygen concentrator, single delivery port, capable of delivering 85 percent or greater oxygen concentration at the prescribed flow rate   ♿ |
| | | | | MED: 100-3,240.2 |
| | ☑ | ☑ | E1391 | Oxygen concentrator, dual delivery port, capable of delivering 85 percent or greater oxygen concentration at the prescribed flow rate, each   ♿ |
| | | | | MED: 100-3,240.2 |
| | ☑ | | E1392 | Portable oxygen concentrator, rental   ♿ |
| | ☑ | | E1399 | Durable medical equipment, miscellaneous   ♿ |
| | | | | Determine if an alternative HCPCS Level II or a CPT code better describes the service being reported. This code should be used only if a more specific code is unavailable. Medicare jurisdiction: local contractor if repair or implanted DME. |
| | ☑ | | E1405 | Oxygen and water vapor enriching system with heated delivery   ♿ |
| | | | | MED: 100-3,240.2; 100-4,20,20; 100-4,20,20.4 |

| | | | | |
|---|---|---|---|---|
| Y | E1406 | Oxygen and water vapor enriching system without heated delivery | &#575; |
| | | MED: 100-3,240.2; 100-4,20,20; 100-4,20,20.4 | |

## ARTIFICIAL KIDNEY MACHINES AND ACCESSORIES

| | | | | |
|---|---|---|---|---|
| A | | E1500 | Centrifuge, for dialysis | ⊘ |
| A | | E1510 | Kidney, dialysate delivery system kidney machine, pump recirculating, air removal system, flowrate meter, power off, heater and temp control with alarm, IV poles, pressure gauge, concentrate container | ⊘ |
| A | | E1520 | Heparin infusion pump for hemodialysis | ⊘ |
| A | ☑ | E1530 | Air bubble detector for hemodialysis, each, replacement | ⊘ |
| A | ☑ | E1540 | Pressure alarm for hemodialysis, each, replacement | ⊘ |
| A | ☑ | E1550 | Bath conductivity meter for hemodialysis, each | ⊘ |
| A | ☑ | E1560 | Blood leak detector for hemodialysis, each, replacement | ⊘ |
| A | | E1570 | Adjustable chair, for ESRD patients | ⊘ |
| A | ☑ | E1575 | Transducer protectors/fluid barriers, for hemodialysis, any size, per 10 | ⊘ |
| A | | E1580 | Unipuncture control system for hemodialysis | ⊘ |
| A | | E1590 | Hemodialysis machine | ⊘ |
| A | | E1592 | Automatic intermittent peritoneal dialysis system | ⊘ |
| A | | E1594 | Cycler dialysis machine for peritoneal dialysis | ⊘ |
| A | | E1600 | Delivery and/or installation charges for hemodialysis equipment | ⊘ |
| A | | E1610 | Reverse osmosis water purification system, for hemodialysis | ⊘ |
| | | | MED: 100-3,230.7 | |
| A | | E1615 | Deionizer water purification system, for hemodialysis | ⊘ |
| | | | MED: 100-3,230.7 | |
| A | | E1620 | Blood pump for hemodialysis, replacement | ⊘ |
| A | | E1625 | Water softening system, for hemodialysis | ⊘ |
| | | | MED: 100-3,230.7 | |
| A | | E1630 | Reciprocating peritoneal dialysis system | ⊘ |
| A | ☑ | E1632 | Wearable artificial kidney, each | ⊘ |
| B | ☑ | E1634 | Peritoneal dialysis clamps, each | ⊘ |
| A | | E1635 | Compact (portable) travel hemodialyzer system | ⊘ |
| A | ☑ | E1636 | Sorbent cartridges, for hemodialysis, per 10 | ⊘ |
| A | ☑ | E1637 | Hemostats, each | ⊘ |
| A | ☑ | E1639 | Scale, each | ⊘ |
| A | | E1699 | Dialysis equipment, not otherwise specified | ⊘ |
| | | | Determine if an alternative HCPCS Level II or a CPT code better describes the service being reported. This code should be used only if a more specific code is unavailable. Pertinent documentation to evaluate medical appropriateness should be included when this code is reported. | |

## JAW MOTION REHABILITATION SYSTEM AND ACCESSORIES

| | | | | |
|---|---|---|---|---|
| Y | E1700 | Jaw motion rehabilitation system | &#575; |
| | | Medicare jurisdiction: local contractor. | |

| | | | |
|---|---|---|---|
| Y ☑ | E1701 | Replacement cushions for jaw motion rehabilitation system, package of 6 Medicare jurisdiction: local contractor. | ♿ |
| Y ☑ | E1702 | Replacement measuring scales for jaw motion rehabilitation system, package of 200 Medicare jurisdiction: local contractor. | ♿ |

## OTHER ORTHOPEDIC DEVICES

| | | | |
|---|---|---|---|
| Y | E1800 | Dynamic adjustable elbow extension/flexion device, includes soft interface material | ♿ |
| Y | E1801 | Static progressive stretch elbow device, extension and/or flexion, with or without range of motion adjustment, includes all components and accessories | ♿ |
| Y | E1802 | Dynamic adjustable forearm pronation/supination device, includes soft interface material | ♿ |
| Y | E1805 | Dynamic adjustable wrist extension/flexion device, includes soft interface material | ♿ |
| Y | E1806 | Static progressive stretch wrist device, flexion and/or extension, with or without range of motion adjustment, includes all components and accessories | ♿ |
| Y | E1810 | Dynamic adjustable knee extension/flexion device, includes soft interface material | ♿ |
| Y | E1811 | Static progressive stretch knee device, extension and/or flexion, with or without range of motion adjustment, includes all components and accessories | ♿ |
| Y | E1812 | Dynamic knee, extension/flexion device with active resistance control | |
| Y | E1815 | Dynamic adjustable ankle extension/flexion device, includes soft interface material | ♿ |
| Y | E1816 | Static progressive stretch ankle device, flexion and/or extension, with or without range of motion adjustment, includes all components and accessories | ♿ |
| Y | E1818 | Static progressive stretch forearm pronation/supination device, with or without range of motion adjustment, includes all components and accessories | ♿ |
| Y | E1820 | Replacement soft interface material, dynamic adjustable extension/flexion device | ♿ |
| Y | E1821 | Replacement soft interface material/cuffs for bi-directional static progressive stretch device | ♿ |
| Y | E1825 | Dynamic adjustable finger extension/flexion device, includes soft interface material | ♿ |
| Y | E1830 | Dynamic adjustable toe extension/flexion device, includes soft interface material | ♿ |
| Y | E1840 | Dynamic adjustable shoulder flexion/abduction/rotation device, includes soft interface material | ♿ |
| Y | E1841 | Static progressive stretch shoulder device, with or without range of motion adjustment, includes all components and accessories | |
| Y | E1902 | Communication board, nonelectronic augmentative or alternative communication device | |

| | | | | |
|---|---|---|---|---|
| Y | | E2000 | Gastric suction pump, home model, portable or stationary, electric | &#9855; |
| Y | | E2100 | Blood glucose monitor with integrated voice synthesizer | &#9855; |
| | | | MED: 100.3,230.16 | |
| Y | | E2101 | Blood glucose monitor with integrated lancing/blood sample | &#9855; |
| | | | MED: 100.3,230.16 | |
| Y | | E2120 | Pulse generator system for tympanic treatment of inner ear endolymphatic fluid | &#9855; |

## WHEELCHAIR ACCESSORY

| | | | | |
|---|---|---|---|---|
| Y | ☑ | E2201 | Manual wheelchair accessory, nonstandard seat frame, width greater than or equal to 20 in and less than 24 in | &#9855; |
| Y | ☑ | E2202 | Manual wheelchair accessory, nonstandard seat frame width, 24-27 in | &#9855; |
| Y | ☑ | E2203 | Manual wheelchair accessory, nonstandard seat frame depth, 20 to less than 22 in | &#9855; |
| Y | ☑ | E2204 | Manual wheelchair accessory, nonstandard seat frame depth, 22 to 25 in | &#9855; |
| Y | ☑ | E2205 | Manual wheelchair accessory, handrim without projections (includes ergonomic or contoured), any type, replacement only, each | |
| Y | ☑ | E2206 | Manual wheelchair accessory, wheel Lock assembly, complete, each | |
| Y | ☑ | E2207 | Wheelchair accessory, crutch and cane holder, each | |
| Y | ☑ | E2208 | Wheelchair accessory, cylinder tank carrier, each | |
| Y | ☑ | E2209 | Accessory, arm trough, with or without hand support, each | |
| Y | ☑ | E2210 | Wheelchair accessory, bearings, any type, replacement only, each | |
| Y | ☑ | E2211 | Manual wheelchair accessory, pneumatic propulsion tire, any size, each | |
| Y | ☑ | E2212 | Manual wheelchair accessory, tube for pneumatic propulsion tire, any size, each | |
| Y | ☑ | E2213 | Manual wheelchair accessory, insert for pneumatic propulsion tire (removable), any type, any size, each | |
| Y | ☑ | E2214 | Manual wheelchair accessory, pneumatic caster tire, any size, each | |
| Y | ☑ | E2215 | Manual wheelchair accessory, tube for pneumatic caster tire, any size, each | |
| Y | ☑ | E2216 | Manual wheelchair accessory, foam filled propulsion tire, any size, each | |
| Y | ☑ | E2217 | Manual wheelchair accessory, foam filled caster tire, any size, each | |
| Y | ☑ | E2218 | Manual wheelchair accessory, foam propulsion tire, any size, each | |
| Y | ☑ | E2219 | Manual wheelchair accessory, foam caster tire, any size, each | |
| Y | ☑ | E2220 | Manual wheelchair accessory, solid (rubber/plastic) propulsion tire, any size, each | |
| Y | ☑ | E2221 | Manual wheelchair accessory, solid (rubber/plastic) caster tire (removable), any size, each | |
| Y | ☑ | E2222 | Manual wheelchair accessory, solid (rubber/plastic) caster tire with integrated wheel, any size, each | |
| Y | ☑ | E2223 | Manual wheelchair accessory, valve, any type, replacement only, each | |
| Y | ☑ | E2224 | Manual wheelchair accessory, propulsion wheel excludes tire, any size, each | |

---

☑ Quantity Alert    ● New Code    ○ Recycled/Reinstated    ▲ Revised Code    &#9855; DMEPOS Paid    ⊘ SNF Excluded

Durable Medical Equipment

E2225 — E2325

| | | | |
|---|---|---|---|
| Ⓨ ☑ | E2225 | Manual wheelchair accessory, caster wheel excludes tire, any size, replacement only, each | |
| Ⓨ ☑ | E2226 | Manual wheelchair accessory, caster fork, any size, replacement only, each | |
| Ⓨ ☑ | E2227 | Manual wheelchair accessory, gear reduction drive wheel, each | ♿ |
| Ⓨ ☑ | E2228 | Manual wheelchair accessory, wheel braking system and lock, complete, each | ♿ |
| ● Ⓔ | E2230 | Manual wheelchair accessory, manual standing system | |
| ● Ⓨ | E2231 | Manual wheelchair accessory, solid seat support base (replaces sling seat), includes any type mounting hardware | |
| Ⓨ | E2291 | Back, planar, for pediatric size wheelchair including fixed attaching hardware | |
| Ⓨ | E2292 | Seat, planar, for pediatric size wheelchair including fixed attaching hardware | |
| Ⓨ | E2293 | Back, contoured, for pediatric size wheelchair including fixed attaching hardware | |
| Ⓨ | E2294 | Seat, contoured, for pediatric size wheelchair including fixed attaching hardware | |
| ● Ⓨ | E2295 | Manual wheelchair accessory, for pediatric size wheelchair, dynamic seating frame, allows coordinated movement of multiple positioning features | |
| Ⓨ | E2300 | Power wheelchair accessory, power seat elevation system | |
| Ⓨ | E2301 | Power wheelchair accessory, power standing system | |
| Ⓨ | E2310 | Power wheelchair accessory, electronic connection between wheelchair controller and one power seating system motor, including all related electronics, indicator feature, mechanical function selection switch, and fixed mounting hardware | ♿ |
| Ⓨ | E2311 | Power wheelchair accessory, electronic connection between wheelchair controller and 2 or more power seating system motors, including all related electronics, indicator feature, mechanical function selection switch, and fixed mounting hardware | ♿ |
| Ⓨ | E2312 | Power wheelchair accessory, hand or chin control interface, mini-proportional remote joystick, proportional, including fixed mounting hardware | |
| Ⓨ | E2313 | Power wheelchair accessory, harness for upgrade to expandable controller, including all fasteners, connectors and mounting hardware, each | ♿ |
| Ⓨ | E2321 | Power wheelchair accessory, hand control interface, remote joystick, nonproportional, including all related electronics, mechanical stop switch, and fixed mounting hardware | ♿ |
| Ⓨ | E2322 | Power wheelchair accessory, hand control interface, multiple mechanical switches, nonproportional, including all related electronics, mechanical stop switch, and fixed mounting hardware | ♿ |
| Ⓨ | E2323 | Power wheelchair accessory, specialty joystick handle for hand control interface, prefabricated | ♿ |
| Ⓨ | E2324 | Power wheelchair accessory, chin cup for chin control interface | ♿ |
| Ⓨ | E2325 | Power wheelchair accessory, sip and puff interface, nonproportional, including all related electronics, mechanical stop switch, and manual swingaway mounting hardware | ♿ |

| | | | |
|---|---|---|---|
| Y | | E2326 | Power wheelchair accessory, breath tube kit for sip and puff interface ☟ |
| Y | | E2327 | Power wheelchair accessory, head control interface, mechanical, proportional, including all related electronics, mechanical direction change switch, and fixed mounting hardware ☟ |
| Y | | E2328 | Power wheelchair accessory, head control or extremity control interface, electronic, proportional, including all related electronics and fixed mounting hardware ☟ |
| Y | | E2329 | Power wheelchair accessory, head control interface, contact switch mechanism, nonproportional, including all related electronics, mechanical stop switch, mechanical direction change switch, head array, and fixed mounting hardware ☟ |
| Y | | E2330 | Power wheelchair accessory, head control interface, proximity switch mechanism, nonproportional, including all related electronics, mechanical stop switch, mechanical direction change switch, head array, and fixed mounting hardware ☟ |
| Y | | E2331 | Power wheelchair accessory, attendant control, proportional, including all related electronics and fixed mounting hardware |
| Y | ☑ | E2340 | Power wheelchair accessory, nonstandard seat frame width, 20-23 in ☟ |
| Y | ☑ | E2341 | Power wheelchair accessory, nonstandard seat frame width, 24-27 in ☟ |
| Y | ☑ | E2342 | Power wheelchair accessory, nonstandard seat frame depth, 20 or 21 in ☟ |
| Y | ☑ | E2343 | Power wheelchair accessory, nonstandard seat frame depth, 22-25 in ☟ |
| Y | | E2351 | Power wheelchair accessory, electronic interface to operate speech generating device using power wheelchair control interface ☟ |
| Y | ☑ | E2360 | Power wheelchair accessory, 22 NF nonsealed lead acid battery, each ☟ |
| Y | ☑ | E2361 | Power wheelchair accessory, 22 NF sealed lead acid battery, each (e.g., gel cell, absorbed glassmat) ☟ |
| Y | ☑ | E2362 | Power wheelchair accessory, group 24 nonsealed lead acid battery, each ☟ |
| Y | ☑ | E2363 | Power wheelchair accessory, group 24 sealed lead acid battery, each (e.g., gel cell, absorbed glassmat) ☟ |
| Y | ☑ | E2364 | Power wheelchair accessory, U-1 nonsealed lead acid battery, each ☟ |
| Y | ☑ | E2365 | Power wheelchair accessory, U-1 sealed lead acid battery, each (e.g., gel cell, absorbed glassmat) ☟ |
| Y | ☑ | E2366 | Power wheelchair accessory, battery charger, single mode, for use with only one battery type, sealed or nonsealed, each ☟ |
| Y | ☑ | E2367 | Power wheelchair accessory, battery charger, dual mode, for use with either battery type, sealed or nonsealed, each |
| Y | | E2368 | Power wheelchair component, motor, replacement only |
| Y | | E2369 | Power wheelchair component, gear box, replacement only |
| Y | | E2370 | Power wheelchair component, motor and gear box combination, replacement only |
| Y | ☑ | E2371 | Power wheelchair accessory, group 27 sealed lead acid battery, (e.g., gel cell, absorbed glassmat), each |
| Y | ☑ | E2372 | Power wheelchair accessory, group 27 nonsealed lead acid battery, each |
| Y | | E2373 | Power wheelchair accessory, hand or chin control interface, compact remote joystick, proportional, including fixed mounting hardware ☟ |

| | | | |
|---|---|---|---|
| Y | | **E2374** | Power wheelchair accessory, hand or chin control interface, standard remote joystick (not including controller), proportional, including all related electronics and fixed mounting hardware, replacement only &#9855; |
| Y | | **E2375** | Power wheelchair accessory, nonexpandable controller, including all related electronics and mounting hardware, replacement only &#9855; |
| Y | | **E2376** | Power wheelchair accessory, expandable controller, including all related electronics and mounting hardware, replacement only &#9855; |
| Y | | **E2377** | Power wheelchair accessory, expandable controller, including all related electronics and mounting hardware, upgrade provided at initial issue &#9855; |
| Y | ☑ | **E2381** | Power wheelchair accessory, pneumatic drive wheel tire, any size, replacement only, each &#9855; |
| Y | ☑ | **E2382** | Power wheelchair accessory, tube for pneumatic drive wheel tire, any size, replacement only, each &#9855; |
| Y | ☑ | **E2383** | Power wheelchair accessory, insert for pneumatic drive wheel tire (removable), any type, any size, replacement only, each &#9855; |
| Y | ☑ | **E2384** | Power wheelchair accessory, pneumatic caster tire, any size, replacement only, each &#9855; |
| Y | ☑ | **E2385** | Power wheelchair accessory, tube for pneumatic caster tire, any size, replacement only, each &#9855; |
| Y | ☑ | **E2386** | Power wheelchair accessory, foam filled drive wheel tire, any size, replacement only, each &#9855; |
| Y | ☑ | **E2387** | Power wheelchair accessory, foam filled caster tire, any size, replacement only, each &#9855; |
| Y | ☑ | **E2388** | Power wheelchair accessory, foam drive wheel tire, any size, replacement only, each &#9855; |
| Y | ☑ | **E2389** | Power wheelchair accessory, foam caster tire, any size, replacement only, each &#9855; |
| Y | ☑ | **E2390** | Power wheelchair accessory, solid (rubber/plastic) drive wheel tire, any size, replacement only, each &#9855; |
| Y | ☑ | **E2391** | Power wheelchair accessory, solid (rubber/plastic) caster tire (removable), any size, replacement only, each &#9855; |
| Y | ☑ | **E2392** | Power wheelchair accessory, solid (rubber/plastic) caster tire with integrated wheel, any size, replacement only, each &#9855; |
| Y | ☑ | **E2393** | Power wheelchair accessory, valve for pneumatic tire tube, any type, replacement only, each &#9855; |
| Y | ☑ | **E2394** | Power wheelchair accessory, drive wheel excludes tire, any size, replacement only, each &#9855; |
| Y | ☑ | **E2395** | Power wheelchair accessory, caster wheel excludes tire, any size, replacement only, each &#9855; |
| Y | ☑ | **E2396** | Power wheelchair accessory, caster fork, any size, replacement only, each &#9855; |
| Y | ☑ | **E2397** | Power wheelchair accessory, lithium-based battery, each &#9855; |
| Y | | **E2399** | Power wheelchair accessory, not otherwise classified interface, including all related electronics and any type mounting hardware &#9855; |

## WOUND THERAPY

| | | | |
|---|---|---|---|
| Y | | **E2402** | Negative pressure wound therapy electrical pump, stationary or portable &#9855; |

## SPEECH GENERATING DEVICE

Ⓨ ☑ **E2500** Speech generating device, digitized speech, using pre-recorded messages, less than or equal to eight minutes recording time      ♿
MED: 100-3,50.1

Ⓨ ☑ **E2502** Speech generating device, digitized speech, using prerecorded messages, greater than 8 minutes but less than or equal to 20 minutes recording time      ♿
MED: 100-3,50.1

Ⓨ ☑ **E2504** Speech generating device, digitized speech, using prerecorded messages, greater than 20 minutes but less than or equal to 40 minutes recording time      ♿
MED: 100-3,50.1

Ⓨ ☑ **E2506** Speech generating device, digitized speech, using prerecorded messages, greater than 40 minutes recording time      ♿
MED: 100-3,50.1

Ⓨ **E2508** Speech generating device, synthesized speech, requiring message formulation by spelling and access by physical contact with the device      ♿
MED: 100-3,50.1

Ⓨ **E2510** Speech generating device, synthesized speech, permitting multiple methods of message formulation and multiple methods of device access      ♿
MED: 100-3,50.1

Ⓨ **E2511** Speech generating software program, for personal computer or personal digital assistant      ♿
MED: 100-3,50.1

Ⓨ **E2512** Accessory for speech generating device, mounting system      ♿
MED: 100-3,50.1

Ⓨ **E2599** Accessory for speech generating device, not otherwise classified
MED: 100-3,50.1

## WHEELCHAIR CUSHION

Ⓨ **E2601** General use wheelchair seat cushion, width less than 22 in, any depth

Ⓨ **E2602** General use wheelchair seat cushion, width 22 in or greater, any depth

Ⓨ **E2603** Skin protection wheelchair seat cushion, width less than 22 in, any depth

Ⓨ **E2604** Skin protection wheelchair seat cushion, width 22 in or greater, any depth

Ⓨ **E2605** Positioning wheelchair seat cushion, width less than 22 in, any depth

Ⓨ **E2606** Positioning wheelchair seat cushion, width 22 in or greater, any depth

Ⓨ **E2607** Skin protection and positioning wheelchair seat cushion, width less than 22 in, any depth

Ⓨ **E2608** Skin protection and positioning wheelchair seat cushion, width 22 in or greater, any depth

Ⓨ **E2609** Custom fabricated wheelchair seat cushion, any size

Ⓑ **E2610** Wheelchair seat cushion, powered

---

☑ Quantity Alert    ● New Code    ○ Recycled/Reinstated    ▲ Revised Code    ♿ DMEPOS Paid    ⊘ SNF Excluded

Ⓨ     **E2611**     General use wheelchair back cushion, width less than 22 in, any height, including any type mounting hardware

Ⓨ     **E2612**     General use wheelchair back cushion, width 22 in or greater, any height, including any type mounting hardware

Ⓨ     **E2613**     Positioning wheelchair back cushion, posterior, width less than 22 in, any height, including any type mounting hardware

Ⓨ     **E2614**     Positioning wheelchair back cushion, posterior, width 22 in or greater, any height, including any type mounting hardware

Ⓨ     **E2615**     Positioning wheelchair back cushion, posterior-lateral, width less than 22 in, any height, including any type mounting hardware

Ⓨ     **E2616**     Positioning wheelchair back cushion, posterior-lateral, width 22 in or greater, any height, including any type mounting hardware

Ⓨ     **E2617**     Custom fabricated wheelchair back cushion, any size, including any type mounting hardware

Ⓨ     **E2619**     Replacement cover for wheelchair seat cushion or back cushion, each

Ⓨ     **E2620**     Positioning wheelchair back cushion, planar back with lateral supports, width less than 22 in, any height, including any type mounting hardware

Ⓨ     **E2621**     Positioning wheelchair back cushion, planar back with lateral supports, width 22 in or greater, any height, including any type mounting hardware

## GAIT TRAINER

Ⓔ     **E8000**     Gait trainer, pediatric size, posterior support, includes all accessories and components

Ⓔ     **E8001**     Gait trainer, pediatric size, upright support, includes all accessories and components

Ⓔ     **E8002**     Gait trainer, pediatric size, anterior support, includes all accessories and components

## PROCEDURES/PROFESSIONAL SERVICES (TEMPORARY) G0000-G9999

The G codes are used to identify professional health care procedures and services that would otherwise be coded in CPT but for which there are no CPT codes.

Please refer to you CPT book for possible alternate code(s).

### VACCINE ADMINISTRATION

S      **G0008**      **Administration of influenza virus vaccine**      ⊘
MED: 100-2,6,10; 100-4,4,240

S      **G0009**      **Administration of pneumococcal vaccine**      ⊘
MED: 100-2,6,10; 100-4,4,240

B      **G0010**      **Administration of hepatitis B vaccine**      ⊘
MED: 100-2,6,10; 100-4,4,240

### SEMEN ANALYSIS

A      **G0027**      **Semen analysis; presence and/or motility of sperm excluding huhner** ♂

### SCREENING SERVICES

V      **G0101**      **Cervical or vaginal cancer screening; pelvic and clinical breast examination**   ♀⊘
G0101 can be reported with an E/M code when a separately identifiable E/M service was provided.
MED: 100-2,6,10; 100-4,4,240
AHA: 4Q,'02,8; 3Q,'01,6

N      **G0102**      **Prostate cancer screening; digital rectal examination**   ♂⊘
MED: 100-2,6,10; 100-3,210.1; 100-4,4,240

A      **G0103**      **Prostate cancer screening; prostate specific antigen test (PSA)**   ♂⊘
MED: 100-2,6,10; 100-3,210.1; 100-4,4,240

S      **G0104**      **Colorectal cancer screening; flexible sigmoidoscopy**   P3⊘
Medicare covers colorectal screening for cancer via flexible sigmoidoscopy once every four years for patients 50 years or older.
MED: 100-2,6,10; 100-4,4,240; 100-4,18,60.1

T      **G0105**      **Colorectal cancer screening; colonoscopy on individual at high risk** M2⊘
An individual with ulcerative enteritis or a history of a malignant neoplasm of the lower gastrointestinal tract is considered at high-risk for colorectal cancer, as defined by CMS.
MED: 100-2,6,10; 100-4,4,240; 100-4,18,60.1
AHA: 3Q,'01,6

S      **G0106**      **Colorectal cancer screening; alternative to G0104, screening sigmoidoscopy, barium enema**   ⊘
MED: 100-2,6,10; 100-4,4,240; 100-4,18,60.1

A  ☑    **G0108**      **Diabetes outpatient self-management training services, individual, per 30 minutes**   ⊘
MED: 100-2,6,10; 100-4,4,240

A  ☑    **G0109**      **Diabetes outpatient self-management training services, group session (2 or more), per 30 minutes**   ⊘
MED: 100-2,6,10; 100-4,4,240

---

| | | | |
|---|---|---|---|
| S | G0117 | Glaucoma screening for high risk patients furnished by an optometrist or ophthalmologist | ⊘ |

MED: 100-2,15,280.1
AHA: 1Q,'02,4; 3Q,'01,12

| S | G0118 | Glaucoma screening for high risk patient furnished under the direct supervision of an optometrist or ophthalmologist | ⊘ |

MED: 100-2,15,280.1
AHA: 1Q,'02,4; 3Q,'01,12

| S | G0120 | Colorectal cancer screening; alternative to G0105, screening colonoscopy, barium enema | ⊘ |

MED: 100-2,6,10; 100-4,18,60.1

| T | G0121 | Colorectal cancer screening; colonoscopy on individual not meeting criteria for high risk | A2 ⊘ |

MED: 100-2,6,10; 100-4,4,240; 100-4,18,60.1
AHA: 1Q,'02,4; 3Q,'01,12

| E | G0122 | Colorectal cancer screening; barium enema | |

| A | G0123 | Screening cytopathology, cervical or vaginal (any reporting system), collected in preservative fluid, automated thin layer preparation, screening by cytotechnologist under physician supervision | ♀⊘ |

See also P3000-P3001.

MED: 100-2,6,10; 100-3,190.2; 100-4,4,240

| B | G0124 | Screening cytopathology, cervical or vaginal (any reporting system), collected in preservative fluid, automated thin layer preparation, requiring interpretation by physician | ♀⊘ |

See also P3000-P3001.

MED: 100-2,6,10; 100-3,190.2; 100-4,4,240

| T | G0127 | Trimming of dystrophic nails, any number | P3 ⊘ |

MED: 100-2,15,290

| B ☑ | G0128 | Direct (face-to-face with patient) skilled nursing services of a registered nurse provided in a comprehensive outpatient rehabilitation facility, each 10 minutes beyond the first 5 minutes | ⊘ |

MED: 100-4,5,100.3

| ▲ P | G0129 | Occupational therapy services requiring the skills of a qualified occupational therapist, furnished as a component of a partial hospitalization treatment program, per session (45 minutes or more) | |

| X | G0130 | Single energy x-ray absorptiometry (SEXA) bone density study, one or more sites; appendicular skeleton (peripheral) (e.g., radius, wrist, heel) | Z3 |

MED: 100-2,6,10; 100-3,150.3; 100-4,4,240; 100-4,13,140

| B | G0141 | Screening cytopathology smears, cervical or vaginal, performed by automated system, with manual rescreening, requiring interpretation by physician | ♀⊘ |

MED: 100-2,6,10

| A | G0143 | Screening cytopathology, cervical or vaginal (any reporting system), collected in preservative fluid, automated thin layer preparation, with manual screening and rescreening by cytotechnologist under physician supervision | ♀⊘ |

MED: 100-2,6,10

---

■ Special Coverage Instructions      ■ Noncovered by Medicare      ■ Carrier Discretion

| | | | |
|---|---|---|---|
| A | | G0144 | Screening cytopathology, cervical or vaginal (any reporting system), collected in preservative fluid, automated thin layer preparation, with screening by automated system, under physician supervision ♀⊘ |
| | | | MED: 100-2,6,10 |
| A | | G0145 | Screening cytopathology, cervical or vaginal (any reporting system), collected in preservative fluid, automated thin layer preparation, with screening by automated system and manual rescreening under physician supervision ♀⊘ |
| | | | MED: 100-2,6,10 |
| A | | G0147 | Screening cytopathology smears, cervical or vaginal, performed by automated system under physician supervision ♀⊘ |
| | | | MED: 100-2,6,10 |
| A | | G0148 | Screening cytopathology smears, cervical or vaginal, performed by automated system with manual rescreening ♀⊘ |
| | | | MED: 100-2,6,10 |
| B | ☑ | G0151 | Services of physical therapist in home health setting, each 15 minutes |
| B | ☑ | G0152 | Services of occupational therapist in home health setting, each 15 minutes |
| B | ☑ | G0153 | Services of speech and language pathologist in home health setting, each 15 minutes |
| B | ☑ | G0154 | Services of skilled nurse in home health setting, each 15 minutes |
| B | ☑ | G0155 | Services of clinical social worker in home health setting, each 15 minutes |
| B | ☑ | G0156 | Services of home health aide in home health setting, each 15 minutes |
| T | ☑ | G0166 | External counterpulsation, per treatment session ⊘ |
| | | | MED: 100-3,20.20 |
| B | | G0168 | Wound closure utilizing tissue adhesive(s) only ⊘ |
| | | | AHA: 3Q,'01,13; 4Q,'01,12 |
| S | | G0173 | Linear accelerator based stereotactic radiosurgery, complete course of therapy in one session ⊠⊘ |
| V | | G0175 | Scheduled interdisciplinary team conference (minimum of 3 exclusive of patient care nursing staff) with patient present |
| P | | G0176 | Activity therapy, such as music, dance, art or play therapies not for recreation, related to the care and treatment of patient's disabling mental health problems, per session (45 minutes or more) |
| N | | G0177 | Training and educational services related to the care and treatment of patient's disabling mental health problems per session (45 minutes or more) |
| M | | G0179 | Physician re-certification for Medicare-covered home health services under a home health plan of care (patient not present), including contacts with home health agency and review of reports of patient status required by physicians to affirm the initial implementation of the plan of care that meets patient's needs, per re-certification period ⊘ |
| | | | MED: 100-4,11,40.1.3.1; 100-4,12,180; 100-4,12,180.1 |
| M | | G0180 | Physician certification for Medicare-covered home health services under a home health plan of care (patient not present), including contacts with home health agency and review of reports of patient status required by physicians to affirm the initial implementation of the plan of care that meets patient's needs, per certification period ⊘ |
| | | | MED: 100-4,11,40.1.3.1; 100-4,12,180; 100-4,12,180.1 |

[M]    **G0181**    Physician supervision of a patient receiving Medicare-covered services provided by a participating home health agency (patient not present) requiring complex and multidisciplinary care modalities involving regular physician development and/or revision of care plans, review of subsequent reports of patient status, review of laboratory and other studies, communication (including telephone calls) with other health care professionals involved in the patient's care, integration of new information into the medical treatment plan and/or adjustment of medical therapy, within a calendar month, 30 minutes or more   ⊘

       MED: 100-4,11,40.1.3.1; 100-4,12,180; 100-4,12,180.1

[M]    **G0182**    Physician supervision of a patient under a Medicare-approved hospice (patient not present) requiring complex and multidisciplinary care modalities involving regular physician development and/or revision of care plans, review of subsequent reports of patient status, review of laboratory and other studies, communication (including telephone calls) with other health care professionals involved in the patient's care, integration of new information into the medical treatment plan and/or adjustment of medical therapy, within a calendar month, 30 minutes or more   ⊘

       MED: 100-4,11,40.1.3.1; 100-4,12,180; 100-4,12,180.1

[T]    **G0186**    Destruction of localized lesion of choroid (for example, choroidal neovascularization); photocoagulation, feeder vessel technique (one or more sessions)   [R2] ⊘

[A]    **G0202**    Screening mammography, producing direct digital image, bilateral, all views   ♀⊘

       MED: 100-2,6,10; 100-4,4,240
       AHA: 1Q,'02,3

[A]    **G0204**    Diagnostic mammography, producing direct digital image, bilateral, all views

       AHA: 1Q,'03,7

[A]    **G0206**    Diagnostic mammography, producing direct digital image, unilateral, all views

       AHA: 1Q,'03,7

[E]    **G0219**    PET imaging whole body; melanoma for noncovered indications

       MED: 100-3,220.6
       AHA: 1Q,'02,10

[E]    **G0235**    PET imaging, any site, not otherwise specified

[S] ☑    **G0237**    Therapeutic procedures to increase strength or endurance of respiratory muscles, face-to-face, one-on-one, each 15 minutes (includes monitoring)

[S] ☑    **G0238**    Therapeutic procedures to improve respiratory function, other than described by G0237, one-on-one, face-to-face, per 15 minutes (includes monitoring)

[S]    **G0239**    Therapeutic procedures to improve respiratory function or increase strength or endurance of respiratory muscles, 2 or more individuals (includes monitoring)

▽     **G0245**     Initial physician evaluation and management of a diabetic patient with diabetic sensory neuropathy resulting in a loss of protective sensation (LOPS) which must include: (1) the diagnosis of LOPS, (2) a patient history, (3) a physical examination that consists of at least the following elements: (a) visual inspection of the forefoot, hindfoot, and toe web spaces, (b) evaluation of a protective sensation, (c) evaluation of foot structure and biomechanics, (d) evaluation of vascular status and skin integrity, and (e) evaluation and recommendation of footwear, and (4) patient education     ⊘

MED: 100-3,70.2.1

AHA: 4Q,'02,9

▽     **G0246**     Follow-up physician evaluation and management of a diabetic patient with diabetic sensory neuropathy resulting in a loss of protective sensation (LOPS) to include at least the following: (1) a patient history, (2) a physical examination that includes: (a) visual inspection of the forefoot, hindfoot, and toe web spaces, (b) evaluation of protective sensation, (c) evaluation of foot structure and biomechanics, (d) evaluation of vascular status and skin integrity, and (e) evaluation and recommendation of footwear, and (3) patient education     ⊘

MED: 100-3,70.2.1

AHA: 4Q,'02,9

▽     **G0247**     Routine foot care by a physician of a diabetic patient with diabetic sensory neuropathy resulting in a loss of protective sensation (LOPS) to include the local care of superficial wounds (i.e., superficial to muscle and fascia) and at least the following, if present: (1) local care of superficial wounds, (2) debridement of corns and calluses, and (3) trimming and debridement of nails     P3 ⊘

MED: 100-3,70.2.1

AHA: 4Q,'02,9

▲ ▽     **G0248**     Demonstration, prior to initial use, of home INR monitoring for patient with either mechanical heart valve(s), chronic atrial fibrillation, or venous thromboembolism who meets Medicare coverage criteria, under the direction of a physician; includes: face-to-face demonstration of use and care of the INR monitor, obtaining at least one blood sample, provision of instructions for reporting home INR test results, and documentation of patient ability to perform testing prior to its use

MED: 100-3,210.1

AHA: 4Q,'02,9

▽     **G0249**     Provision of test materials and equipment for home INR monitoring of patient with either mechanical heart valve(s), chronic atrial fibrillation, or venous thromboembolism who meets Medicare coverage criteria; includes provision of materials for use in the home and reporting of test results to physician; not occurring more frequently than once a week

MED: 100-3,210.1

AHA: 4Q,'02,9

▲ Ⓜ     **G0250**     Physician review, interpretation, and patient management of home INR testing for a patient with either mechanical heart valve(s), chronic atrial fibrillation, or venous thromboembolism who meets Medicare coverage criteria; includes face-to-face verification by the physician at least once a year (e.g., during an evaluation and management service) that the patient uses the device in the context of the management of the anticoagulation therapy following initiation of the home INR monitoring; not occurring more frequently than once a week.     ⊘

MED: 100-3,210.1

AHA: 4Q,'02,9

---

⑤ ☑ **G0251** Linear accelerator based stereotactic radiosurgery, delivery including collimator changes and custom plugging, fractionated treatment, all lesions, per session, maximum 5 sessions per course of treatment  ⓩ ⊘

Ⓔ **G0252** PET imaging, full and partial-ring PET scanners only, for initial diagnosis of breast cancer and/or surgical planning for breast cancer (e.g., initial staging of axillary lymph nodes)
MED: 100-3,220.6

Ⓔ **G0255** Current perception threshold/sensory nerve conduction test, (SNCT) per limb, any nerve
MED: 100-3,160.23
AHA: 4Q,'02,9

⑤ **G0257** Unscheduled or emergency dialysis treatment for an ESRD patient in a hospital outpatient department that is not certified as an ESRD facility
AHA: 1Q,'03,9; 4Q,'02,9

Ⓝ **G0259** Injection procedure for sacroiliac joint; arthrography  Ⓝ
AHA: 4Q,'02,9

Ⓣ **G0260** Injection procedure for sacroiliac joint; provision of anesthetic, steroid and/or other therapeutic agent, with or without arthrography  Ⓐ2
AHA: 4Q,'02,9

Ⓝ **G0268** Removal of impacted cerumen (one or both ears) by physician on same date of service as audiologic function testing  Ⓝ ⊘
AHA: 1Q,'03,12

Ⓝ **G0269** Placement of occlusive device into either a venous or arterial access site, postsurgical or interventional procedure (e.g., angioseal plug, vascular plug)  Ⓝ ⊘

Ⓐ ☑ **G0270** Medical nutrition therapy; reassessment and subsequent intervention(s) following second referral in same year for change in diagnosis, medical condition or treatment regimen (including additional hours needed for renal disease), individual, face-to-face with the patient, each 15 minutes  ⊘ Ⓟ

Ⓐ ☑ **G0271** Medical nutrition therapy, reassessment and subsequent intervention(s) following second referral in same year for change in diagnosis, medical condition, or treatment regimen (including additional hours needed for renal disease), group (2 or more individuals), each 30 minutes  ⊘ Ⓟ

▲ Ⓝ **G0275** Renal angiography, nonselective, one or both kidneys, performed at the same time as cardiac catheterization and/or coronary angiography, includes positioning or placement of any catheter in the abdominal aorta at or near the origins (ostia) of the renal arteries, injection of dye, flush aortogram, production of permanent images, and radiologic supervision and interpretation (List separately in addition to primary procedure)  ⊘

▲ Ⓝ **G0278** Iliac and/or femoral artery angiography, nonselective, bilateral or ipsilateral to catheter insertion, performed at the same time as cardiac catheterization and/or coronary angiography, includes positioning or placement of the catheter in the distal aorta or ipsilateral femoral or iliac artery, injection of dye, production of permanent images, and radiologic supervision and interpretation (List separately in addition to primary procedure)  ⊘

Ⓐ **G0281** Electrical stimulation, (unattended), to one or more areas, for chronic Stage III and Stage IV pressure ulcers, arterial ulcers, diabetic ulcers, and venous stasis ulcers not demonstrating measurable signs of healing after 30 days of conventional care, as part of a therapy plan of care
MED: 100-4,32,11.1
AHA: 1Q,'03,7; 2Q,'03,7

---

⬜ Special Coverage Instructions   ⬜ Noncovered by Medicare   ⬜ Carrier Discretion

| | | | |
|---|---|---|---|
| E | **G0282** | Electrical stimulation, (unattended), to one or more areas, for wound care other than described in G0281   ⊘ | |

MED: 100-3,270.1

AHA: 1Q,'03,7; 2Q,'03,7

| | | | |
|---|---|---|---|
| A | **G0283** | Electrical stimulation (unattended), to one or more areas for indication(s) other than wound care, as part of a therapy plan of care | |

AHA: 1Q,'03,7; 2Q,'03,7

| | | | |
|---|---|---|---|
| N | **G0288** | Reconstruction, computed tomographic angiography of aorta for surgical planning for vascular surgery   N | |

| | | | |
|---|---|---|---|
| N | **G0289** | Arthroscopy, knee, surgical, for removal of loose body, foreign body, debridement/shaving of articular cartilage (chondroplasty) at the time of other surgical knee arthroscopy in a different compartment of the same knee   N ⊘ | |

| | | | |
|---|---|---|---|
| T | **G0290** | Transcatheter placement of a drug eluting intracoronary stent(s), percutaneous, with or without other therapeutic intervention, any method; single vessel   ⊘ | |

AHA: 3Q,'03,11; 4Q,'03,7; 4Q,'02,9

| | | | |
|---|---|---|---|
| T | **G0291** | Transcatheter placement of a drug eluting intracoronary stent(s), percutaneous, with or without other therapeutic intervention, any method; each additional vessel   ⊘ | |

AHA: 3Q,'03,11; 4Q,'03,7; 4Q,'02,9

| | | | |
|---|---|---|---|
| X ☑ | **G0293** | Noncovered surgical procedure(s) using conscious sedation, regional, general, or spinal anesthesia in a Medicare qualifying clinical trial, per day   ⊘ | |

AHA: 4Q,'02,9

| | | | |
|---|---|---|---|
| X ☑ | **G0294** | Noncovered procedure(s) using either no anesthesia or local anesthesia only, in a Medicare qualifying clinical trial, per day   ⊘ | |

AHA: 4Q,'02,9

| | | | |
|---|---|---|---|
| E | **G0295** | Electromagnetic therapy, to one or more areas, for wound care other than described in G0329 or for other uses | |

MED: 100-3,270.1

AHA: 1Q,'03,7

| | | | |
|---|---|---|---|
| S ☑ | **G0302** | Preoperative pulmonary surgery services for preparation for LVRS, complete course of services, to include a minimum of 16 days of services | |

| | | | |
|---|---|---|---|
| S ☑ | **G0303** | Preoperative pulmonary surgery services for preparation for LVRS, 10 to 15 days of services | |

| | | | |
|---|---|---|---|
| S ☑ | **G0304** | Preoperative pulmonary surgery services for preparation for LVRS, 1 to 9 days of services | |

| | | | |
|---|---|---|---|
| S ☑ | **G0305** | Postdischarge pulmonary surgery services after LVRS, minimum of 6 days of services | |

| | | | |
|---|---|---|---|
| A | **G0306** | Complete CBC, automated (HgB, HCT, RBC, WBC, without platelet count) and automated WBC differential count | |

| | | | |
|---|---|---|---|
| A | **G0307** | Complete (CBC), automated (HgB, HCT, RBC, WBC, without platelet count) | |

| | | | |
|---|---|---|---|
| | ~~G0308~~ | ~~ESRD related services during the course of treatment, for patients under 2 years of age to include monitoring for the adequacy of nutrition, assessment of growth and development, and counseling of parents; with 4 or more face-to-face physician visits per month.~~ | |

Procedures/Professional Services (Temporary)   G0282 — G0308

G0309     ESRD related services during the course of treatment, for patients under 2 years of age to include monitoring for the adequacy of nutrition, assessment of growth and development, and counseling of parents; with 2 or 3 face-to-face physician visits per month.

G0310     ESRD related services during the course of treatment, for patients under 2 years of age to include monitoring for the adequacy of nutrition, assessment of growth and development, and counseling of parents; with 1 face-to-face physician visit per month

G0311     ESRD related services during the course of treatment, for patients between 2 and 11 years of age to include monitoring for the adequacy of nutrition, assessment of growth and development, and counseling of parents; with 4 or more face-to-face physician visits per month

G0312     ESRD related services during the course of treatment, for patients between 2 and 11 years of age to include monitoring for the adequacy of nutrition, assessment of growth and development, and counseling of parents; with 2 or 3 face-to-face physician visits per month

G0313     ESRD related services during the course of treatment, for patients between 2 and 11 years of age to include monitoring for the adequacy of nutrition, assessment of growth and development, and counseling of parents; with 1 face-to-face physician visit per month

G0314     ESRD related services during the course of treatment, for patients between 12 and 19 years of age to include monitoring for the adequacy of nutrition, assessment of growth and development, and counseling of parents; with 4 or more face-to-face physician visits per month

G0315     End Stage Renal disease (ESRD) related services during the course of treatment, for patients between 12 and 19 years of age to include monitoring for the adequacy of nutrition, assessment of growth and development, and counseling of parents; with two or three face-to-face physician visits per month

G0316     End Stage Renal disease (ESRD) related services during the course of treatment, for patients between 12 and 19 years of age to include monitoring for the adequacy of nutrition, assessment of growth and development, and counseling of parents; with one face-to-face physician visit per month

G0317     End Stage Renal disease (ESRD) related services during the course of treatment, for patients 20 years of age and over; with four or more face-to-face physician visits per month

G0318     ESRD related services during the course of treatment, for patients 20 years of age and over; with 2 or 3 face-to-face physician visits per month

G0319     End Stage Renal disease (ESRD) related services during the course of treatment, for patients 20 years of age and over; with one face-to-face physician visit per month

G0320     ESRD related services for home dialysis patients per full month; for patients under 2 years of age to include monitoring for adequacy of nutrition, assessment of growth and development, and counseling of parents

G0321     ESRD related services for home dialysis patients per full month; for patients 2 to 11 years of age to include monitoring for adequacy of nutrition, assessment of growth and development, and counseling of parents

G0322     End Stage Renal disease (ESRD) related services for home dialysis patients per full month; for patients 12 to 19 years of age to include monitoring for adequacy of nutrition, assessment of growth and development, and counseling of parents

G0323 ~~End Stage Renal disease (ESRD) related services for home dialysis patients per full month; for patients 20 years of age and older~~

G0324 ~~ESRD related services for home dialysis (less than full month), per day; for patients under 2 years of age~~

G0325 ~~ESRD related services for home dialysis (less than full month), per day; for patients between 2 and 11 years of age~~

G0326 ~~ESRD related services for home dialysis (less than full month), per day; for patients between twelve and nineteen years of age~~

G0327 ~~ESRD related services for home dialysis (less than full month), per day; for patients twenty years of age and over~~

[A] G0328 Colorectal cancer screening; fecal occult blood test, immunoassay, 1-3 simultaneous determinations ⊘

MED: 100-4,18,60.1

[A] G0329 Electromagnetic therapy, to one or more areas for chronic Stage III and Stage IV pressure ulcers, arterial ulcers, diabetic ulcers and venous stasis ulcers not demonstrating measurable signs of healing after 30 days of conventional care as part of a therapy plan of care ⊘

MED: 100-4,32,11.2

G0332 ~~Services for intravenous infusion of immunoglobulin prior to administration (this service is to be billed in conjunction with administration of immunoglobulin)~~

[M] G0333 Pharmacy dispensing fee for inhalation drug(s); initial 30-day supply as a beneficiary

[B] G0337 Hospice evaluation and counseling services, preelection

[S] G0339 Image guided robotic linear accelerator-based stereotactic radiosurgery, complete course of therapy in one session, or first session of fractionated treatment　　ZZ ⊘

[S] G0340 Image guided robotic linear accelerator-based stereotactic radiosurgery, delivery including collimator changes and custom plugging, fractionated treatment, all lesions, per session, second through fifth sessions, maximum 5 sessions per course of treatment　　ZZ ⊘

[C] G0341 Percutaneous islet cell transplant, includes portal vein catheterization and infusion ⊘

MED: 100-3,260.3; 100-4,32,70

[C] G0342 Laparoscopy for islet cell transplant, includes portal vein catheterization and infusion ⊘

MED: 100-3,260.3; 100-4,32,70

[C] G0343 Laparotomy for islet cell transplant, includes portal vein catheterization and infusion ⊘

MED: 100-3,260.3; 100-4,32,70

G0344 ~~Initial preventive physical examination; face-to-face visit, services limited to new beneficiary during the first six months of Medicare enrollment~~
See G0402

[X] G0364 Bone marrow aspiration performed with bone marrow biopsy through the same incision on the same date of service　　P3 ⊘

[S] G0365 Vessel mapping of vessels for hemodialysis access (services for preoperative vessel mapping prior to creation of hemodialysis access using an autogenous hemodialysis conduit, including arterial inflow and venous outflow)

---

☑ Quantity Alert　●  New Code　○ Recycled/Reinstated　▲ Revised Code　🖦 DMEPOS Paid　⊘ SNF Excluded

| | | G0366 | ~~Electrocardiogram, routine ECG with 12 leads; performed as a component of the initial preventive examination with interpretation and report~~ |
|---|---|---|---|
| | | | See G0403 |

     G0367    ~~Tracing only, without interpretation and report, performed as a component of the initial preventive examination~~
See G0404

     G0368    ~~Interpretation and report only, performed as a component of the initial preventive examination~~
See G0405

[M]    **G0372**    Physician service required to establish and document the need for a power mobility device      ⊘

[N]    **G0378**    Hospital observation service, per hour
MED: 100-2,6,20.6

[03]    **G0379**    Direct admission of patient for hospital observation care
MED: 100-2,6,20.6

▲ [V]    **G0380**    Level 1 hospital emergency department visit provided in a type B emergency department; (the ED must meet at least one of the following requirements: (1) it is licensed by the state in which it is located under applicable state law as an emergency room or emergency department; (2) it is held out to the public (by name, posted signs, advertising, or other means) as a place that provides care for emergency medical conditions on an urgent basis without requiring a previously scheduled appointment; or (3) during the calendar year immediately preceding the calendar year in which a determination under 42 CFR 489.24 is being made, based on a representative sample of patient visits that occurred during that calendar year, it provides at least one-third of all of its outpatient visits for the treatment of emergency medical conditions on an urgent basis without requiring a previously scheduled appointment)
MED: 100-4,4,160

▲ [V]    **G0381**    Level 2 hospital emergency department visit provided in a type B emergency department; (the ED must meet at least one of the following requirements: (1) it is licensed by the state in which it is located under applicable state law as an emergency room or emergency department; (2) it is held out to the public (by name, posted signs, advertising, or other means) as a place that provides care for emergency medical conditions on an urgent basis without requiring a previously scheduled appointment; or (3) during the calendar year immediately preceding the calendar year in which a determination under 42 CFR 489.24 is being made, based on a representative sample of patient visits that occurred during that calendar year, it provides at least one-third of all of its outpatient visits for the treatment of emergency medical conditions on an urgent basis without requiring a previously scheduled appointment)
MED: 100-4,4,160

▲ Ⓥ    **G0382**    Level 3 hospital emergency department visit provided in a type B emergency department; (the ED must meet at least one of the following requirements: (1) it is licensed by the state in which it is located under applicable state law as an emergency room or emergency department; (2) it is held out to the public (by name, posted signs, advertising, or other means) as a place that provides care for emergency medical conditions on an urgent basis without requiring a previously scheduled appointment; or (3) during the calendar year immediately preceding the calendar year in which a determination under 42 CFR 489.24 is being made, based on a representative sample of patient visits that occurred during that calendar year, it provides at least one-third of all of its outpatient visits for the treatment of emergency medical conditions on an urgent basis without requiring a previously scheduled appointment)

MED: 100-4,4,160

Ⓥ    **G0383**    Level 4 hospital emergency department visit provided in a type B emergency department; (the ED must meet at least one of the following requirements: (1) it is licensed by the state in which it is located under applicable state law as an emergency room or emergency department; (2) it is held out to the public (by name, posted signs, advertising, or other means) as a place that provides care for emergency medical conditions on an urgent basis without requiring a previously scheduled appointment; or (3) during the calendar year immediately preceding the calendar year in which a determination under 42 CFR 489.24 is being made, based on a representative sample of patient visits that occurred during that calendar year, it provides at least one-third of all of its outpatient visits for the treatment of emergency medical conditions on an urgent basis without requiring a previously scheduled appointment)

MED: 100-4,4,160

▲ ⓪③    **G0384**    Level 5 hospital emergency department visit provided in a type B emergency department; (the ED must meet at least one of the following requirements: (1) it is licensed by the state in which it is located under applicable state law as an emergency room or emergency department; (2) it is held out to the public (by name, posted signs, advertising, or other means) as a place that provides care for emergency medical conditions on an urgent basis without requiring a previously scheduled appointment; or (3) during the calendar year immediately preceding the calendar year in which a determination under 42 CFR 489.24 is being made, based on a representative sample of patient visits that occurred during that calendar year, it provides at least one-third of all of its outpatient visits for the treatment of emergency medical conditions on an urgent basis without requiring a previously scheduled appointment)

MED: 100-4,4,160

Ⓢ    **G0389**    Ultrasound B-scan and/or real time with image documentation; for abdominal aortic aneurysm (AAA) screening    ⊘

Ⓢ    **G0390**    Trauma response team associated with hospital critical care service

Ⓣ    **G0392**    Transluminal balloon angioplasty, percutaneous; for maintenance of hemodialysis access, arteriovenous fistula or graft; arterial    A2

Ⓣ    **G0393**    Transluminal balloon angioplasty, percutaneous; for maintenance of hemodialysis access, arteriovenous fistula or graft; venous    A2

~~G0394~~    ~~Blood occult test (e.g., guaiac), feces, for single determination for colorectal neoplasm (e.g., patient was provided three cards or single triple card for consecutive collection)~~

Ⓢ    **G0396**    Alcohol and/or substance (other than tobacco) abuse structured assessment (e.g., AUDIT, DAST), and brief intervention 15 to 30 minutes

Procedures/Professional Services (Temporary)

G0397 — G0414

| | | |
|---|---|---|
| ⑤ | G0397 | Alcohol and/or substance (other than tobacco) abuse structured assessment (e.g., AUDIT, DAST), and intervention, greater than 30 minutes |
| ● ⑤ | G0398 | Home sleep study test (HST) with type II portable monitor, unattended; minimum of 7 channels: EEG, EOG, EMG, ECG/heart rate, airflow, respiratory effort and oxygen saturation |
| ● ⑤ | G0399 | Home sleep test (HST) with type III portable monitor, unattended; minimum of 4 channels: 2 respiratory movement/airflow, 1 ECG/heart rate and 1 oxygen saturation |
| ● ⑤ | G0400 | Home sleep test (HST) with type IV portable monitor, unattended; minimum of 3 channels |
| ● ⓥ | G0402 | Initial preventive physical examination; face-to-face visit, services limited to new beneficiary during the first 12 months of Medicare enrollment |
| ● ⓜ | G0403 | Electrocardiogram, routine ECG with 12 leads; performed as a screening for the initial preventive physical examination with interpretation and report |
| ● ⑤ | G0404 | Electrocardiogram, routine ECG with 12 leads; tracing only, without interpretation and report, performed as a screening for the initial preventive physical examination |
| ● ⑧ | G0405 | Electrocardiogram, routine ECG with 12 leads; interpretation and report only, performed as a screening for the initial preventive physical examination |
| ● ⓒ | G0406 | Follow-up inpatient telehealth consultation, limited, physicians typically spend 15 minutes communicating with the patient via telehealth |
| ● ⓒ | G0407 | Follow-up inpatient telehealth consultation, intermediate, physicians typically spend 25 minutes communicating with the patient via telehealth |
| ● ⓒ | G0408 | Follow-up inpatient telehealth consultation, complex, physicians typically spend 35 minutes or more communicating with the patient via telehealth |
| ● ⓜ | G0409 | Social work and psychological services, directly relating to and/or furthering the patient's rehabilitation goals, each 15 minutes, face-to-face; individual (services provided by a CORF qualified social worker or psychologist in a CORF) |
| ● ⓟ | G0410 | Group psychotherapy other than of a multiple family group, in a partial hospitalization setting, approximately 45 to 50 minutes |
| ● ⓟ | G0411 | Interactive group psychotherapy, in a partial hospitalization setting, approximately 45 to 50 minutes |
| ● ⓒ | G0412 | Open treatment of iliac spine(s), tuberosity avulsion, or iliac wing fracture(s), unilateral or bilateral for pelvic bone fracture patterns which do not disrupt the pelvic ring, includes internal fixation, when performed |
| ● ⓣ | G0413 | Percutaneous skeletal fixation of posterior pelvic bone fracture and/or dislocation, for fracture patterns which disrupt the pelvic ring, unilateral or bilateral, (includes ilium, sacroiliac joint and/or sacrum) |
| ● ⓒ | G0414 | Open treatment of anterior pelvic bone fracture and/or dislocation for fracture patterns which disrupt the pelvic ring, unilateral or bilateral, includes internal fixation when performed (includes pubic symphysis and/or superior/inferior rami) |

● ⓒ  **G0415**  Open treatment of posterior pelvic bone fracture and/or dislocation, for fracture patterns which disrupt the pelvic ring, unilateral or bilateral, includes internal fixation, when performed (includes ilium, sacroiliac joint and/or sacrum)

● Ⓢ  **G0416**  Surgical pathology, gross and microscopic examination for prostate needle saturation biopsy sampling, 1-20 specimens

● Ⓢ  **G0417**  Surgical pathology, gross and microscopic examination for prostate needle saturation biopsy sampling, 21-40 specimens

● Ⓢ  **G0418**  Surgical pathology, gross and microscopic examination for prostate needle saturation biopsy sampling, 41-60 specimens

● Ⓢ  **G0419**  Surgical pathology, gross and microscopic examination for prostate needle saturation biopsy sampling, greater than 60 specimens

Ⓢ ☑  **G3001**  Administration and supply of tositumomab, 450 mg    ⊘

## PHYSICIAN QUALITY REPORTING INDICATOR CODE (PQRI)

Physician Quality Reporting Indicator Codes (PQRI) are to be used for the physician Quality Reporting Indicator Code (PQRI) program in which CMS seeks to analyze the quality of care provided to Medicare beneficiaries. Reporting of these codes is voluntary. Physicians should not charge for these codes. Unless otherwise indicated, report these codes in addition to office visit, home visit, nursing facility, and domiciliary evaluation and management codes. For additional information, please visit the following website: http://www.cms.hhs.gov/providers/PQRI

Ⓜ  **G8006**  Acute myocardial infarction: patient documented to have received aspirin at arrival

Ⓜ  **G8007**  Acute myocardial infarction: patient not documented to have received aspirin at arrival

Ⓜ  **G8008**  Clinician documented that acute myocardial infarction patient was not an eligible candidate to receive aspirin at arrival measure

Ⓜ  **G8009**  Acute myocardial infarction: patient documented to have received beta-blocker at arrival    PQ

Ⓜ  **G8010**  Acute myocardial infarction: patient not documented to have received beta-blocker at arrival    PQ

Ⓜ  **G8011**  Clinician documented that acute myocardial infarction patient was not an eligible candidate for beta-blocker at arrival measure    PQ

Ⓜ  **G8012**  Pneumonia: patient documented to have received antibiotic within 4 hours of presentation

Ⓜ  **G8013**  Pneumonia: patient not documented to have received antibiotic within 4 hours of presentation

Ⓜ  **G8014**  Clinician documented that pneumonia patient was not an eligible candidate for antibiotic within 4 hours of presentation measure

Ⓜ  **G8015**  Diabetic patient with most recent hemoglobin A1c level (within the last 6 months) documented as greater than 9%

Ⓜ  **G8016**  Diabetic patient with most recent hemoglobin A1c level (within the last 6 months) documented as less than or equal to 9%

Ⓜ  **G8017**  Clinician documented that diabetic patient was not eligible candidate for hemoglobin A1c measure

Ⓜ  **G8018**  Clinician has not provided care for the diabetic patient for the required time for hemoglobin A1c measure (6 months)

Ⓜ  **G8019**  Diabetic patient with most recent low-density lipoprotein (within the last 12 months) documented as greater than or equal to 100 mg/dl

Procedures/Professional Services (Temporary)

G8020 — G8041

| | | |
|---|---|---|
| M | G8020 | Diabetic patient with most recent low-density lipoprotein (within the last 12 months) documented as less than 100 mg/dl |
| M | G8021 | Clinician documented that diabetic patient was not eligible candidate for low-density lipoprotein measure |
| M | G8022 | Clinician has not provided care for the diabetic patient for the required time for low-density lipoprotein measure (12 months) |
| M | G8023 | Diabetic patient with most recent blood pressure (within the last 6 months) documented as equal to or greater than 140 systolic or equal to or greater than 80 mm Hg diastolic |
| M | G8024 | Diabetic patient with most recent blood pressure (within the last 6 months) documented as less than 140 systolic and less than 80 diastolic |
| M | G8025 | Clinician documented that the diabetic patient was not eligible candidate for blood pressure measure |
| M | G8026 | Clinician has not provided care for the diabetic patient for the required time for blood pressure measure (within the last 6 months) |
| M | G8027 | Heart failure patient with left ventricular systolic dysfunction (LVSD) documented to be on either angiotensin-converting enzyme-inhibitor or angiotensin-receptor blocker (ACE-1 or ARB) therapy |
| M | G8028 | Heart failure patient with left ventricular systolic dysfunction (LVSD) not documented to be on either angiotensin-converting enzyme-inhibitor or angiotensin-receptor blocker (ACE-1 or ARB) therapy |
| M | G8029 | Clinician documented that heart failure patient was not an eligible candidate for either angiotensin-converting enzyme-inhibitor or angiotensin-receptor blocker (ACE-1 or ARB) therapy measure |
| M | G8030 | Heart failure patient with left ventricular systolic dysfunction (LVSD) documented to be on beta-blocker therapy |
| M | G8031 | Heart failure patient with left ventricular systolic dysfunction (LVSD) not documented to be on beta-blocker therapy |
| M | G8032 | Clinician documented that heart failure patient was not eligible candidate for beta-blocker therapy measure |
| M | G8033 | Prior myocardial infarction, coronary artery disease patient documented to be on beta-blocker therapy |
| M | G8034 | Prior myocardial infarction, coronary artery disease patient not documented to be on beta-blocker therapy |
| M | G8035 | Clinician documented that prior myocardial infarction, coronary artery disease patient was not eligible candidate for beta-blocker therapy measure |
| M | G8036 | Coronary artery disease patient documented to be on antiplatelet therapy |
| M | G8037 | Coronary artery disease patient not documented to be on antiplatelet therapy |
| M | G8038 | Clinician documented that coronary artery disease patient was not eligible candidate for antiplatelet therapy measure |
| M | G8039 | Coronary artery disease patient with low-density lipoprotein documented to be greater than 100 mg/dl |
| M | G8040 | Coronary artery disease patient with low-density lipoprotein documented to be less than or equal to 100 mg/dl |
| M | G8041 | Clinician documented that coronary artery disease patient was not eligible candidate for low-density lipoprotein measure ♀ |

| | | |
|---|---|---|
| Ⓜ | **G8051** | Patient (female) documented to have been assessed for osteoporosis ♀ |
| Ⓜ | **G8052** | Patient (female) not documented to have been assessed for osteoporosis ♀ |
| Ⓜ | **G8053** | Clinician documented that (female) patient was not an eligible candidate for osteoporosis assessment measure ♀ |
| Ⓜ | **G8054** | Patient not documented for the assessment for falls within last 12 months |
| Ⓜ | **G8055** | Patient documented for the assessment for falls within last 12 months |
| Ⓜ | **G8056** | Clinician documented that patient was not an eligible candidate for the falls assessment measure within the last 12 months |
| Ⓜ | **G8057** | Patient documented to have received hearing assessment |
| Ⓜ | **G8058** | Patient not documented to have received hearing assessment |
| Ⓜ | **G8059** | Clinician documented that patient was not an eligible candidate for hearing assessment measure |
| Ⓜ | **G8060** | Patient documented for the assessment of urinary incontinence |
| Ⓜ | **G8061** | Patient not documented for the assessment of urinary incontinence |
| Ⓜ | **G8062** | Clinician documented that patient was not an eligible candidate for urinary incontinence assessment measure |
| Ⓜ | **G8075** | ESRD patient with documented dialysis dose of URR greater than or equal to 65% (or Kt/ V greater than or equal to 1.2) Ⓐ 🄿🄾 |
| Ⓜ | **G8076** | ESRD patient with documented dialysis dose of URR less than 65% (or Kt/V less than 1.2) Ⓐ 🄿🄾 |
| Ⓜ | **G8077** | Clinician documented that ESRD patient was not an eligible candidate for URR or Kt/V measure Ⓐ 🄿🄾 |
| Ⓜ | **G8078** | ESRD patient with documented hematocrit greater than or equal to 33 (or hemoglobin greater than or equal to 11) Ⓐ 🄿🄾 |
| Ⓜ | **G8079** | ESRD patient with documented hematocrit less than 33 (or hemoglobin less than 11) Ⓐ 🄿🄾 |
| Ⓜ | **G8080** | Clinician documented that ESRD patient was not an eligible candidate for hematocrit (hemoglobin) measure Ⓐ 🄿🄾 |
| Ⓜ | **G8081** | ESRD patient requiring hemodialysis vascular access documented to have received autogenous AV fistula |
| Ⓜ | **G8082** | ESRD patient requiring hemodialysis documented to have received vascular access other than autogenous AV fistula |
| Ⓜ | **G8085** | ESRD patient requiring hemodialysis vascular access was not an eligible candidate for autogenous AV fistula |
| Ⓜ | **G8093** | Newly diagnosed chronic obstructive pulmonary disease (COPD) patient documented to have received smoking cessation intervention, within 3 months of diagnosis |
| Ⓜ | **G8094** | Newly diagnosed chronic obstructive pulmonary disease (COPD) patient not documented to have received smoking cessation intervention, within 3 months of diagnosis |
| Ⓜ | **G8099** | Osteoporosis patient documented to have been prescribed calcium and vitamin D supplements |
| Ⓜ | **G8100** | Clinician documented that osteoporosis patient was not an eligible candidate for calcium and vitamin D supplement measure |

Procedures/Professional Services (Temporary)

G8103 — G8153

| | | |
|---|---|---|
| Ⓜ | G8103 | Newly diagnosed osteoporosis patients documented to have been treated with antiresorptive therapy and/or PTH within 3 months of diagnosis |
| Ⓜ | G8104 | Clinician documented that newly diagnosed osteoporosis patient was not an eligible candidate for antiresorptive therapy and/or PTH treatment measure within 3 months of diagnosis |
| Ⓜ | G8106 | Within 6 months of suffering a nontraumatic fracture, female patient 65 years of age or older documented to have undergone bone mineral density testing or to have been prescribed a drug to treat or prevent osteoporosis |
| Ⓜ | G8107 | Clinician documented that female patient 65 years of age or older who suffered a nontraumatic fracture within the last 6 months was not an eligible candidate for measure to test bone mineral density or drug to treat or prevent osteoporosis |
| Ⓜ | G8108 | Patient documented to have received influenza vaccination during influenza season Ⓐ |
| Ⓜ | G8109 | Patient not documented to have received influenza vaccination during influenza season Ⓐ |
| Ⓜ | G8110 | Clinician documented that patient was not an eligible candidate for influenza vaccination measure Ⓐ |
| Ⓜ | G8111 | Patient (female) documented to have received a mammogram during the measurement year or prior year to the measurement year Ⓐ♀ |
| Ⓜ | G8112 | Patient (female) not documented to have received a mammogram during the measurement year or prior year to the measurement year Ⓐ♀ |
| Ⓜ | G8113 | Clinician documented that female patient was not an eligible candidate for mammography measure Ⓐ |
| Ⓜ | G8114 | Clinician did not provide care to patient for the required time of mammography measure (i.e., measurement year or prior year) Ⓐ |
| Ⓜ | G8115 | Patient documented to have received pneumococcal vaccination Ⓐ |
| Ⓜ | G8116 | Patient not documented to have received pneumococcal vaccination Ⓐ |
| Ⓜ | G8117 | Clinician documented that patient was not an eligible candidate for pneumococcal vaccination measure Ⓐ |
| Ⓜ | G8126 | Patient documented as being treated with antidepressant medication during the entire 12 week acute treatment phase Ⓐ PQ |
| Ⓜ | G8127 | Patient not documented as being treated with antidepressant medication during the entire 12 weeks acute treatment phase Ⓐ PQ |
| Ⓜ | G8128 | Clinician documented that patient was not an eligible candidate for antidepressant medication during the entire 12 week acute treatment phase measure Ⓐ PQ |
| Ⓜ | G8129 | Patient documented as being treated with antidepressant medication for at least 6 months continuous treatment phase Ⓐ |
| Ⓜ | G8130 | Patient not documented as being treated with antidepressant medication for at least 6 months continuous treatment phase Ⓐ |
| Ⓜ | G8131 | Clinician documented that patient was not an eligible candidate for antidepressant medication for continuous treatment phase Ⓐ |
| Ⓜ | G8152 | Patient documented to have received antibiotic prophylaxis one hour prior to incision time (2 hours for vancomycin) |
| Ⓜ | G8153 | Patient not documented to have received antibiotic prophylaxis one hour prior to incision time (2 hours for vancomycin) |

| | | |
|---|---|---|
| Ⓜ | G8154 | Clinician documented that patient was not an eligible candidate for antibiotic prophylaxis one hour prior to incision time (2 hours for vancomycin) measure |
| Ⓜ | G8155 | Patient with documented receipt of thromboembolism prophylaxis |
| Ⓜ | G8156 | Patient without documented receipt of thromboembolism prophylaxis |
| Ⓜ | G8157 | Clinician documented that patient was not an eligible candidate for thromboembolism prophylaxis measure |
| Ⓜ | G8159 | Patient documented to have received coronary artery bypass graft without use of internal mammary artery |
| Ⓜ | G8162 | Patient with isolated coronary artery bypass graft not documented to have received preoperative beta-blockade |
| Ⓜ | G8164 | Patient with isolated coronary artery bypass graft documented to have prolonged intubation |
| Ⓜ | G8165 | Patient with isolated coronary artery bypass graft not documented to have prolonged intubation |
| Ⓜ | G8166 | Patient with isolated coronary artery bypass graft documented to have required surgical re-exploration |
| Ⓜ | G8167 | Patient with isolated coronary artery bypass graft did not require surgical re-exploration |
| Ⓜ | G8170 | Patient with isolated coronary artery bypass graft documented to have been discharged on aspirin or clopidogrel |
| Ⓜ | G8171 | Patient with isolated coronary artery bypass graft not documented to have been discharged on aspirin or clopidogrel |
| Ⓜ | G8172 | Clinician documented that patient with isolated coronary artery bypass graft was not an eligible candidate for antiplatelet therapy at discharge measure |
| Ⓜ | G8182 | Clinician has not provided care for the cardiac patient for the required time for low-density lipoprotein measure (6 months) |
| Ⓜ | G8183 | Patient with heart failure and atrial fibrillation documented to be on warfarin therapy |
| Ⓜ | G8184 | Clinician documented that patient with heart failure and atrial fibrillation was not an eligible candidate for warfarin therapy measure |
| Ⓜ | G8185 | Patients diagnosed with symptomatic osteoarthritis with documented annual assessment of function and pain |
| Ⓜ | G8186 | Clinician documented that symptomatic osteoarthritis patient was not an eligible candidate for annual assessment of function and pain measure |
| Ⓜ | G8193 | Clinician did not document that an order for prophylactic antibiotic to be given within one hour (if vancomycin, 2 hours) prior to surgical incision (or start of procedure when no incision is required) was given |
| Ⓜ | G8196 | Clinician did not document a prophylactic antibiotic was administered within one hour (if vancomycin, 2 hours) prior to surgical incision (or start of procedure when no incision is required) |
| Ⓜ | G8200 | Order for cefazolin or cefuroxime for antimicrobial prophylaxis not documented |
| Ⓜ | G8204 | Clinician did not document an order was given to discontinue prophylactic antibiotics within 24 hours of surgical end time |
| Ⓜ | G8209 | Clinician did not document an order was given to discontinue prophylactic antibiotics within 48 hours of surgical end time |

Procedures/Professional Services (Temporary)

G8214 — G8274

| | | |
|---|---|---|
| Ⓜ | G8214 | Clinician did not document an order was given for appropriate venous thromboembolism (VTE) prophylaxis to be given within 24 hrs prior to incision time or 24 hours after surgery end time |
| Ⓜ | G8217 | Patient not documented to have received DVT prophylaxis by end of hospital day 2 |
| Ⓜ | G8219 | Patient documented to have received DVT prophylaxis by end of hospital day 2 |
| Ⓜ | G8220 | Patient not documented to have received DVT prophylaxis by end of hospital day 2 |
| Ⓜ | G8221 | Clinician documented that patient was not an eligible candidate for DVT prophylaxis by the end of hospital day 2, including physician documentation that patient is ambulatory |
| Ⓜ | G8223 | Patient not documented to have received prescription for antiplatelet therapy at discharge |
| Ⓜ | G8226 | Patient not documented to have received prescription for anticoagulant therapy at discharge |
| Ⓜ | G8231 | Patient not documented to have received T-PA or not documented to have been considered a candidate for T-PA administration |
| Ⓜ | G8234 | Patient not documented to have received dysphagia screening |
| Ⓜ | G8238 | Patient not documented to have received order for or consideration for rehabilitation services |
| Ⓜ | G8240 | Internal carotid stenosis patient in the 30-99% range, and no documentation of reference to measurements of distal internal carotid diameter as the denominator for stenosis measurement |
| Ⓜ | G8243 | Patient not documented to have received CT or MRI and the presence or absence of hemorrhage, mass lesion and acute infarction not documented in the final report |
| Ⓜ | G8246 | Patient was not an eligible candidate for medical history review with assessment of new or changing moles |
| Ⓜ | G8248 | Patient with at least one alarm symptom not documented to have had upper endoscopy or referral for upper endoscopy |
| Ⓜ | G8251 | Patient not documented to have received an esophageal biopsy when suspicion of Barrett's esophagus is indicated in the endoscopy report |
| Ⓜ | G8254 | Patient with no documentation order for barium swallow test |
| Ⓜ | G8257 | Clinician has not documented reconciliation of discharge medications with current medication list in medical record |
| Ⓜ | G8260 | Patient not documented to have surrogate decision maker or advance care plan in medical record |
| Ⓜ | G8263 | Patient not documented to have been assessed for presence or absence of urinary incontinence |
| Ⓜ | G8266 | Patient not documented to have received characterization of urinary incontinence |
| Ⓜ | G8268 | Patient not documented to have received plan of care for urinary incontinence |
| Ⓜ | G8271 | Patient with no documentation of screening for fall risks (2 or more falls in the past year or any fall with injury in the past year) |
| Ⓜ | G8274 | Clinician has not documented presence or absence of alarm symptoms |

| | | |
|---|---|---|
| M | G8276 | Patient not documented to have received medical history with assessment of new or changing moles |
| M | G8279 | Patient not documented to have received a complete physical skin exam |
| M | G8282 | Patient not documented to have received counseling to perform a self-examination |
| M | G8285 | Patient not documented to have received pharmacologic therapy |
| M | G8289 | Patient with no documentation of calcium and vitamin D use or counseling regarding both calcium and vitamin D use, or exercise |
| M | G8293 | COPD patient without spirometry results documented |
| M | G8296 | COPD patient not documented to have inhaled bronchodilator therapy prescribed |
| M | G8298 | Patient documented to have received optic nerve head evaluation |
| M | G8299 | Patient not documented to have received optic nerve head evaluation |
| M | G8302 | Patient documented to have a specific target intraocular pressure range goal |
| M | G8303 | Patient not documented to have a specific target intraocular pressure range goal |
| M | G8304 | Clinician documented that patient was not an eligible candidate for a specific target intraocular pressure range goal |
| M | G8305 | Clinician has not provided care for the primary open-angle glaucoma patient for the required time for treatment range goal documentation measurement |
| M | G8306 | Primary open-angle glaucoma patient with intraocular pressure above the target range goal documented to have received plan of care |
| M | G8307 | Primary open-angle glaucoma patient with intraocular pressure at or below goal, no plan of care necessary |
| M | G8308 | Primary open-angle glaucoma patient with intraocular pressure above the target range goal, and not documented to have received plan of care during the reporting year |
| M | G8310 | Patient not documented to have been prescribed/recommended at least one antioxidant vitamin or mineral supplement during the reporting year |
| M | G8314 | Patient not documented to have received macular exam with documentation of presence or absence of macular thickening or hemorrhage and no documentation of Level of macular degeneration severity |
| M | G8318 | Patient documented not to have visual functional status assessed |
| M | G8322 | Patient not documented to have had presurgical axial length, corneal power measurement and method of intraocular lens power calculation |
| M | G8326 | Patient not documented to have received fundus evaluation within 6 months prior to cataract surgery |
| M | G8330 | Patient not documented to have received dilated macular or fundus exam with level of severity of retinopathy and the presence or absence of macular edema not documented |
| M | G8334 | Documentation of findings of macular or fundus exam not communicated to the physician managing the patient's ongoing diabetes care |

Procedures/Professional Services (Temporary)

G8338 — G8383

| | | |
|---|---|---|
| Ⓜ | G8338 | Clinician has not documented that communication was sent to the physician managing ongoing care of patient that a fracture occurred and that the patient was or should be tested or treated for osteoporosis |
| Ⓜ | G8341 | Patient not documented to have had central DEXA measurement or pharmacologic therapy |
| Ⓜ | G8345 | Patient not documented to have had central DEXA measurement ordered or performed or pharmacologic therapy |
| Ⓜ | G8351 | Patient not documented to have had ECG |
| Ⓜ | G8354 | Patient not documented to have received or taken aspirin 24 hours before emergency department arrival or during emergency department stay |
| Ⓜ | G8357 | Patient not documented to have had ECG |
| Ⓜ | G8360 | Patient not documented to have vital signs recorded and reviewed |
| Ⓜ | G8362 | Patient not documented to have oxygen saturation assessed |
| Ⓜ | G8365 | Patient not documented to have mental status assessed |
| Ⓜ | G8367 | Patient not documented to have appropriate empiric antibiotic prescribed |
| Ⓜ | G8370 | Asthma patients with numeric frequency of symptoms or patient completion of an asthma assessment tool/survey/questionnaire not documented |
| Ⓜ | G8371 | Chemotherapy documented as not received or prescribed for Stage III colon cancer patients Ⓐ 🄿 |
| Ⓜ | G8372 | Chemotherapy documented as received or prescribed for Stage III colon cancer patients Ⓐ 🄿 |
| Ⓜ | G8373 | Chemotherapy plan documented prior to chemotherapy administration 🄿 |
| Ⓜ | G8374 | Chemotherapy plan not documented prior to chemotherapy administration 🄿 |
| Ⓜ | G8375 | Chronic lymphocytic leukemia (CLL) patient with no documentation of baseline flow cytometry performed |
| Ⓜ | G8376 | Clinician documentation that breast cancer patient was not eligible for tamoxifen or aromatase inhibitor therapy measure Ⓐ ♀ 🄿 |
| Ⓜ | G8377 | Clinician documentation that colon cancer patient is not eligible for chemotherapy measure Ⓐ 🄿 |
| Ⓜ | G8378 | Clinician documentation that patient was not an eligible candidate for radiation therapy measure Ⓐ 🄿 |
| Ⓜ | G8379 | Documentation of radiation therapy recommended within 12 months of first office visit Ⓐ 🄿 |
| Ⓜ | G8380 | For patients with ER or PR positive, Stage IC-III breast cancer, clinician did not document that the patient received or was prescribed tamoxifen or aromatase inhibitor Ⓐ ♀ 🄿 |
| Ⓜ | G8381 | For patients with ER or PR positive, Stage IC-III breast cancer, clinician documented or prescribed that the patient is receiving tamoxifen or aromatase inhibitor Ⓐ ♀ 🄿 |
| Ⓜ | G8382 | Multiple myeloma patients with no documentation of prescribed or received intravenous bisphosphonate therapy |
| Ⓜ | G8383 | No documentation of radiation therapy recommended within 12 months of first office visit Ⓐ 🄿 |

| | | |
|---|---|---|
| M | G8384 | Baseline cytogenetic testing not performed in patients with myelodysplastic syndrome (MDS) or acute leukemias |
| M | G8385 | Diabetic patients with no documentation of hemoglobin A1c level (within the last 12 months) |
| M | G8386 | Diabetic patients with no documentation of low-density lipoprotein (within the last 12 months) |
| M | G8387 | ESRD patient with a hematocrit or hemoglobin not documented　A PO |
| M | G8388 | ESRD patient with URR or Kt/V value not documented, but otherwise eligible for measure　A PO |
| M | G8389 | Myelodysplastic syndrome (MDS) patients with no documentation of iron stores prior to receiving erythropoietin therapy |
| M | G8390 | Diabetic patients with no documentation of blood pressure measurement (within the last 12 months) |
| M | G8391 | Patients with persistent asthma, no documentation of preferred long-term control medication or acceptable alternative treatment prescribed |
| M | G8395 | Left ventricular ejection fraction (LVEF) >= 40% or documentation as normal or mildly depressed left ventricular systolic function |
| M | G8396 | Left ventricular ejection fraction (LVEF) not performed or documented |
| M | G8397 | Dilated macular or fundus exam performed, including documentation of the presence or absence of macular edema and level of severity of retinopathy |
| M | G8398 | Dilated macular or fundus exam not performed |
| M | G8399 | Patient with central dual-energy x-ray absorptiometry (DXA) results documented or ordered or pharmacologic therapy (other than minerals/vitamins) for osteoporosis prescribed |
| M | G8400 | Patient with central dual-energy x-ray absorptiometry (DXA) results not documented or not ordered or pharmacologic therapy (other than minerals/vitamins) for osteoporosis not prescribed |
| M | G8401 | Clinician documented that patient was not an eligible candidate for screening or therapy for osteoporosis for women measure　♀ |
| M | G8402 | Tobacco (smoke) use cessation intervention, counseling |
| M | G8403 | Tobacco (smoke) use cessation intervention not counseled |
| M | G8404 | Lower extremity neurological exam performed and documented |
| M | G8405 | Lower extremity neurological exam not performed |
| M | G8406 | Clinician documented that patient was not an eligible candidate for lower extremity neurological exam measure |
| M | G8407 | ABI measured and documented |
| M | G8408 | ABI measurement was not obtained |
| M | G8409 | Clinician documented that patient was not an eligible candidate for ABI measurement measure |
| M | G8410 | Footwear evaluation performed and documented |
| M | G8415 | Footwear evaluation was not performed |
| M | G8416 | Clinician documented that patient was not an eligible candidate for footwear evaluation measure |
| ▲ M | G8417 | Calculated BMI above the upper parameter and a follow-up plan was documented in the medical record |

| | | | |
|---|---|---|---|
| ▲ Ⓜ | G8418 | Calculated BMI below the lower parameter and a follow-up plan was documented in the medical record |
| ▲ Ⓜ | G8419 | Calculated BMI outside normal parameters, no follow-up plan was documented in the medical record |
| ▲ Ⓜ | G8420 | Calculated BMI within normal parameters and documented |
| Ⓜ | G8421 | BMI not calculated |
| Ⓜ | G8422 | Patient not eligible for BMI calculation |
| Ⓜ | G8423 | Documented that patient was screened and either influenza vaccination status is current or patient was counseled |
| Ⓜ | G8424 | Influenza vaccine status was not screened |
| Ⓜ | G8425 | Influenza vaccine status screened, patient not current and counseling was not provided |
| Ⓜ | G8426 | Documented that patient was not appropriate for screening and/or counseling about the influenza vaccine (e.g., allergy to eggs) |
| ▲ Ⓜ | G8427 | List of current medications with dosages (includes prescription, over-the-counter, herbals, vitamin/mineral/dietary nutritional supplements) and verification with the patient or authorized representative documented by the provider |
| ▲ Ⓜ | G8428 | Provider documentation of current medications with dosages (includes prescription, over-the-counter, herbals, vitamin/mineral/dietary nutritional supplements) without documented patient verification |
| ▲ Ⓜ | G8429 | Incomplete or no provider documentation that patient's current medications with dosages (includes prescription, over-the-counter, herbals, vitamin/mineral/dietary nutritional supplements were assessed |
| ▲ Ⓜ | G8430 | Provider documentation that patient is not eligible for medication assessment |
| ▲ Ⓜ | G8431 | Positive screen for clinical depression using a standardized tool and a follow-up plan documented |
| Ⓜ | G8432 | No documentation of clinical depression screening using a standardized tool |
| ▲ Ⓜ | G8433 | Screening for clinical depression using a standardized tool not documented, patient not eligible/appropriate |
| Ⓜ | G8434 | Documentation of cognitive impairment screening using a standardized tool |
| Ⓜ | G8435 | No documentation of cognitive impairment screening using a standardized tool |
| Ⓜ | G8436 | Patient not eligible/not appropriate for cognitive impairment screening |
| ▲ Ⓜ | G8437 | Documentation of clinician and patient involvement with the development of a plan of care including signature by the practitioner/therapist and either a co-signature by the patient or documented verbal agreement obtained from the patient or, when necessary, an authorized representative |
| ▲ Ⓜ | G8438 | No documentation of clinician and patient involvement with the development of a plan of care including signature by the practitioner/therapist and either a co-signature by the patient or documented verbal agreement obtained from the patient or, when necessary, an authorized representative |

▲ Ⓜ    **G8439**    Documentation that patient is not eligible for co-developing a plan of care including signature by the practitioner/therapist and either a co-signature by the patient or documented verbal agreement obtained from the patient or, when necessary, an authorized representative

▲ Ⓜ    **G8440**    Documentation of pain assessment (including location, intensity and description) prior to initiation of treatment or documentation of the absence of pain as a result of assessment through discussion with the patient including the use of a standardized tool and a follow-up plan is documented

Ⓜ    **G8441**    No documentation of pain assessment (including location, intensity and description) prior to initiation of treatment

Ⓜ    **G8442**    Documentation that patient is not eligible for pain assessment

Ⓜ    **G8443**    All prescriptions created during the encounter were generated using a qualified e-prescribing system

Ⓜ    **G8445**    No prescriptions were generated during the encounter, provider does have access to a qualified e-prescribing system

▲ Ⓜ    **G8446**    Provider does have access to a qualified e-prescribing system and some or all of the prescriptions generated during the encounter were printed or phoned in as required by state or Federal law or regulations, patient request or pharmacy system being unable to receive electronic transmission; or because they were for narcotics or other controlled substances

▲ Ⓜ    **G8447**    Patient encounter was documented using a CCHIT certified EHR

▲ Ⓜ    **G8448**    Patient encounter was documented using a qualified (non-CCHIT certified) EHR

Ⓜ    **G8449**    Patient encounter was not documented using an EMR due to system reasons such as, the system being inoperable at the time of the visit; use of this code implies that an EMR is in place and generally available

Ⓜ    **G8450**    Beta-blocker therapy prescribed for patients with left ventricular ejection fraction (LVEF) <40% or documentation as moderately or severely depressed left ventricular systolic function

Ⓜ    **G8451**    Clinician documented patient with left ventricular ejection fraction (LVEF) <40% or documentation as moderately or severely depressed left ventricular systolic function was not eligible candidate for beta-blocker therapy

Ⓜ    **G8452**    Beta-blocker therapy not prescribed for patients with left ventricular ejection fraction (LVEF) <40% or documentation as moderately or severely depressed left ventricular systolic function

Ⓜ    **G8453**    Tobacco use cessation intervention, counseling

Ⓜ    **G8454**    Tobacco use cessation intervention not counseled, reason not specified

Ⓜ    **G8455**    Current tobacco smoker

Ⓜ    **G8456**    Current smokeless tobacco user

▲ Ⓜ    **G8457**    Current tobacco nonuser

Ⓜ    **G8458**    Clinician documented that patient is not an eligible candidate for genotype testing; patient not receiving antiviral treatment for hepatitis C

Ⓜ    **G8459**    Clinician documented that patient is receiving antiviral treatment for hepatitis C

Ⓜ    **G8460**    Clinician documented that patient is not an eligible candidate for quantitative RNA testing at week 12; patient not receiving antiviral treatment for hepatitis C

---

☑ Quantity Alert    ● New Code    ○ Recycled/Reinstated    ▲ Revised Code    ዽ DMEPOS Paid    ⊘ SNF Excluded

Procedures/Professional Services (Temporary)

G8461 — G8480

M    **G8461**    Patient receiving antiviral treatment for hepatitis C

M    **G8462**    Clinician documented that patient is not an eligible candidate for counseling regarding contraception prior to antiviral treatment; patient not receiving antiviral treatment for hepatitis C

M    **G8463**    Patient receiving antiviral treatment for hepatitis C documented

M    **G8464**    Clinician documented that prostate cancer patient is not an eligible candidate for adjuvant hormonal therapy; low or intermediate risk of recurrence or risk of recurrence not determined

M    **G8465**    High risk of recurrence of prostate cancer

M    **G8466**    Clinician documented that patient is not an eligible candidate for suicide risk assessment; major depressive disorder, in remission

M    **G8467**    Documentation of new diagnosis of initial or recurrent episode of major depressive disorder

M    **G8468**    Angiotensin converting enzyme (ACE) inhibitor or angiotensin receptor blocker (ARB) therapy prescribed for patients with a left ventricular ejection fraction (LVEF) <40% or documentation of moderately or severely depressed left ventricular systolic function

M    **G8469**    Clinician documented that patient with a left ventricular ejection fraction (LVEF) <40% or documentation of moderately or severely depressed left ventricular systolic function was not an eligible candidate for angiotensin converting enzyme (ACE) inhibitor or angiotensin receptor blocker (ARB) therapy

M    **G8470**    Patient with left ventricular ejection fraction (LVEF) >=40% or documentation as normal or mildly depressed left ventricular systolic function

M    **G8471**    Left ventricular ejection fraction (LVEF) was not performed or documented

M    **G8472**    Angiotensin converting enzyme (ACE) inhibitor or angiotensin receptor blocker (ARB) therapy not prescribed for patients with a left ventricular ejection fraction (LVEF) <40% or documentation of moderately or severely depressed left ventricular systolic function, reason not specified

M    **G8473**    Angiotensin converting enzyme (ACE) inhibitor or angiotensin receptor blocker (ARB) therapy prescribed

M    **G8474**    Angiotensin converting enzyme (ACE) inhibitor or angiotensin receptor blocker (ARB) therapy not prescribed for reasons documented by the clinician

M    **G8475**    Angiotensin converting enzyme (ACE) inhibitor or angiotensin receptor blocker (ARB) therapy not prescribed, reason not specified

M    **G8476**    Most recent blood pressure has a systolic measurement of <130 mm/Hg and a diastolic measurement of <80 mm/Hg

M    **G8477**    Most recent blood pressure has a systolic measurement of >=130 mm/Hg and/or a diastolic measurement of >=80 mm/Hg

M    **G8478**    Blood pressure measurement not performed or documented, reason not specified

M    **G8479**    Clinician prescribed angiotensin converting enzyme (ACE) inhibitor or angiotensin receptor blocker (ARB) therapy

M    **G8480**    Clinician documented that patient was not an eligible candidate for angiotensin converting enzyme (ACE) inhibitor or angiotensin receptor blocker (ARB) therapy

| | | |
|---|---|---|
| Ⓜ | G8481 | Clinician did not prescribe angiotensin converting enzyme (ACE) inhibitor or angiotensin receptor blocker (ARB) therapy, reason not specified |
| Ⓜ | G8482 | Influenza immunization was ordered or administered |
| Ⓜ | G8483 | Influenza immunization was not ordered or administered for reasons documented by clinician |
| Ⓜ | G8484 | Influenza immunization was not ordered or administered, reason not specified |
| ● Ⓜ | G8485 | I intend to report the diabetes mellitus measures group  PQ |
| ● Ⓜ | G8486 | I intend to report the preventive care measures group  PQ |
| ● Ⓜ | G8487 | I intend to report the chronic kidney disease (CKD) measures group  PQ |
| ● Ⓜ | G8488 | Clinician intends to report the ESRD measure group  PQ |
| ● Ⓜ | G8489 | I intend to report the coronary artery disease (CAD) measures group |
| ● Ⓜ | G8490 | I intend to report the rheumatoid arthritis measures group |
| ● Ⓜ | G8491 | I intend to report the HIV/AIDS measures group |
| ● Ⓜ | G8492 | I intend to report the perioperative care measures group |
| ● Ⓜ | G8493 | I intend to report the back pain measures group |
| ● Ⓜ | G8494 | All quality actions for the applicable measures in the diabetes mellitus measures group have been performed for this patient |
| ● Ⓜ | G8495 | All quality actions for the applicable measures in the CKD measures group have been performed for this patient |
| ● Ⓜ | G8496 | All quality actions for the applicable measures in the preventive care measures group have been performed for this patient |
| ● Ⓜ | G8497 | All quality actions for the applicable measures in the coronary artery bypass graft (CABG) measures group have been performed for this patient |
| ● Ⓜ | G8498 | All quality actions for the applicable measures in the coronary artery disease (CAD) measures group have been performed for this patient |
| ● Ⓜ | G8499 | All quality actions for the applicable measures in the rheumatoid arthritis measures group have been performed for this patient |
| ● Ⓜ | G8500 | All quality actions for the applicable measures in the HIV/AIDS measures group have been performed for this patient |
| ● Ⓜ | G8501 | All quality actions for the applicable measures in the perioperative care measures group have been performed for this patient |
| ● Ⓜ | G8502 | All quality actions for the applicable measures in the back pain measures group have been performed for this patient |
| ● Ⓜ | G8503 | Documentation that prophylactic antibiotic was given within one hour (if fluoroquinolone or vancomycin, two hours) prior to surgical incision (or start of procedure when no incision is required) |
| ● Ⓜ | G8504 | Documentation of order for prophylactic antibiotics to be given within one hour (if fluoroquinolone or vancomycin, two hours) prior to surgical incision (or start of procedure when no incision is required) |
| ● Ⓜ | G8505 | Documentation that prophylactic antibiotic was not given within one hour (if fluoroquinolone or vancomycin, two hours) prior to surgical incision (or start of procedure when no incision is required), reason not specified |
| ● Ⓜ | G8506 | Patient receiving angiotensin converting enzyme (ACE) inhibitor or angiotensin receptor blocker (ARB) therapy |

**Procedures/Professional Services (Temporary)**

**G8507 — G8529**

| | | |
|---|---|---|
| ● Ⓜ | **G8507** | Provider documentation that patient is not eligible for patient verification of current medications |
| ● Ⓜ | **G8508** | Documentation of pain assessment (including location, intensity and description) prior to initiation of treatment or documentation of the absence of pain as a result of assessment through discussion with the patient including the use of a standardized tool; no documentation of a follow-up plan, patient not eligible |
| ● Ⓜ | **G8509** | Documentation of pain assessment (including location, intensity and description) prior to initiation of treatment or documentation of the absence of pain as a result of assessment through discussion with the patient including the use of a standardized tool; no documentation of a follow-up plan, reason not specified |
| ● Ⓜ | **G8510** | Negative screen for clinical depression using a standardized tool, patient not eligible/appropriate for follow-up plan documented |
| ● Ⓜ | **G8511** | Screen for clinical depression using a standardized tool documented, follow up plan not documented, reason not specified |
| ● Ⓜ | **G8512** | Pain severity quantified; pain present |
| ● Ⓜ | **G8513** | ABI measured and documented |
| ● Ⓜ | **G8514** | Clinician documented that patient was not an eligible candidate for ABI measurement measure |
| ● Ⓜ | **G8515** | ABI measurement was not obtained |
| ● Ⓜ | **G8516** | Patient screened for future falls risk; documentation of two or more falls in the past year or any fall with injury in the past year |
| ● Ⓜ | **G8517** | Patient screened for future fall risk; documentation of no falls in the past year or only one fall without injury in the past year |
| ● Ⓜ | **G8518** | Clinical stage prior to surgery for lung cancer and esophageal cancer resection was recorded |
| ● Ⓜ | **G8519** | Clinician documented that patient was not eligible for clinical stage prior to surgery for lung cancer and esophageal cancer resection measure |
| ● Ⓜ | **G8520** | Clinician stage prior to surgery for lung cancer and esophageal cancer resection was not recorded, reason not specified |
| ● Ⓜ | **G8521** | Antiplatelet therapy received (ASA [81-325 mg/day] and/or clopidogrel [75 mg/day]) within 48 hours of the initiation of surgery and at discharge |
| ● Ⓜ | **G8522** | Clinician documented that patient was not an eligible candidate for antiplatelet therapy |
| ● Ⓜ | **G8523** | Antiplatelet therapy not received 48 hours prior to CEA and at discharge, reason not specified |
| ● Ⓜ | **G8524** | Patch closure used for patient undergoing conventional CEA |
| ● Ⓜ | **G8525** | Clinician documented that patient did not receive conventional CEA |
| ● Ⓜ | **G8526** | Patch closure not used for patient undergoing conventional CEA, reason not specified |
| ● Ⓜ | **G8527** | Documentation of order for cefazolin or cefuroxime for antimicrobial prophylaxis |
| ● Ⓜ | **G8528** | Clinician documented that patient was ineligible for prophylactic antibiotic selection measure |
| ● Ⓜ | **G8529** | Order for cefazolin or cefuroxime for antimicrobial prophylaxis not documented, reason not specified |

| | | | |
|---|---|---|---|
| ● | Ⓜ | G8530 | Autogenous AV fistula received |
| ● | Ⓜ | G8531 | Clinician documented that patient was not an eligible candidate for autogenous AV fistula |
| ● | Ⓜ | G8532 | Clinician documented that patient received vascular access other than autogenous AV fistula, reason not specified |
| ● | Ⓜ | G8533 | Participation by a physician or other clinician in systematic clinical database registry that includes consensus-endorsed quality measures |
| ● | Ⓜ | G8534 | Documentation of an elder maltreatment screen and follow-up plan |
| ● | Ⓜ | G8535 | No documentation of an elder maltreatment screen, patient not eligible |
| ● | Ⓜ | G8536 | No documentation of an elder maltreatment screen, reason not specified |
| ● | Ⓜ | G8537 | Elder maltreatment screen documented, follow-up plan not documented, patient not eligible |
| ● | Ⓜ | G8538 | Elder maltreatment screen documented, follow-up plan not documented, reason not specified |
| ● | Ⓜ | G8539 | Documentation of a current functional outcome assessment using a standardized tool and care plan based on identified deficiencies |
| ● | Ⓜ | G8540 | Documentation that the patient is not eligible for a functional outcome assessment using a standardized tool |
| ● | Ⓜ | G8541 | No documentation of a current functional outcome assessment using a standardized tool, reason not specified |
| ● | Ⓜ | G8542 | Documentation of a current functional outcome assessment using a standardized tool; no documentation of a care plan, patient not eligible |
| ● | Ⓜ | G8543 | Documentation of a current functional outcome assessment using a standardized tool; no documentation of a care plan, reason not specified |
| ● | Ⓜ | G8544 | I intend to report the coronary artery bypass graft (CABG) measures group |
| | Ⓑ | G9001 | Coordinated care fee, initial rate ⊘ |
| | Ⓑ | G9002 | Coordinated care fee, maintenance rate ⊘ |
| | Ⓑ | G9003 | Coordinated care fee, risk adjusted high, initial ⊘ |
| | Ⓑ | G9004 | Coordinated care fee, risk adjusted low, initial ⊘ |
| | Ⓑ | G9005 | Coordinated care fee, risk adjusted maintenance ⊘ |
| | Ⓑ | G9006 | Coordinated care fee, home monitoring ⊘ |
| | Ⓑ | G9007 | Coordinated care fee, scheduled team conference ⊘ |
| | Ⓑ | G9008 | Coordinated care fee, physician coordinated care oversight services ⊘ |
| | Ⓑ | G9009 | Coordinated care fee, risk adjusted maintenance, Level 3 |
| | Ⓑ | G9010 | Coordinated care fee, risk adjusted maintenance, Level 4 ⊘ |
| | Ⓑ | G9011 | Coordinated care fee, risk adjusted maintenance, Level 5 ⊘ |
| | Ⓑ | G9012 | Other specified case management service not elsewhere classified ⊘ |
| | Ⓔ | G9013 | ESRD demo basic bundle Level I |
| | Ⓔ | G9014 | ESRD demo expanded bundle including venous access and related services |

Procedures/Professional Services (Temporary)

G9016 — G9054

| | | |
|---|---|---|
| E | G9016 | Smoking cessation counseling, individual, in the absence of or in addition to any other evaluation and management service, per session (6-10 minutes) [demo project code only] ⊘ |
| A | G9017 | Amantadine HCl, oral, per 100 mg (for use in a Medicare-approved demonstration project) |
| A | G9018 | Zanamivir, inhalation powder, administered through inhaler, generic, per 10 mg (for use in a Medicare-approved demonstration project) |
| A | G9019 | Oseltamivir phosphate, oral, generic, per 75 mg (for use in a Medicare-approved demonstration project) |
| A | G9020 | Rimantadine HCl, oral, per 100 mg (for use in a Medicare-approved demonstration project) |
| A | G9033 | Amantadine HCl, oral brand, per 100 mg (for use in a Medicare-approved demonstration project) |
| A | G9034 | Zanamivir, inhalation powder, administered through inhaler, brand name, per 10 mg (for use in a Medicare-approved demonstration project) |
| A | G9035 | Oseltamivir phosphate, oral, brand name, per 75 mg (for use in a Medicare-approved demonstration project) |
| A | G9036 | Rimantadine HCl, oral, brand name, per 100 mg (for use in a Medicare-approved demonstration project) |
| A | G9041 | Rehabilitation services for low vision by qualified occupational therapist, direct one-on-one contact, each 15 minutes |
| A | G9042 | Rehabilitation services for low vision by certified orientation and mobility specialists, direct one-on-one contact, each 15 minutes |
| A | G9043 | Rehabilitation services for low vision by certified low vision rehabilitation therapist, direct one-on-one contact, each 15 minutes |
| A | G9044 | Rehabilitation services for low vision by certified low vision rehabilitation teacher, direct one-on-one contact, each 15 minutes |
| E | G9050 | Oncology; primary focus of visit; work-up, evaluation, or staging at the time of cancer diagnosis or recurrence (for use in a Medicare-approved demonstration project) |
| E | G9051 | Oncology; primary focus of visit; treatment decision-making after disease is staged or restaged, discussion of treatment options, supervising/coordinating active cancer-directed therapy or managing consequences of cancer-directed therapy (for use in a Medicare-approved demonstration project) |
| E | G9052 | Oncology; primary focus of visit; surveillance for disease recurrence for patient who has completed definitive cancer-directed therapy and currently lacks evidence of recurrent disease; cancer-directed therapy might be considered in the future (for use in a Medicare-approved demonstration project) |
| E | G9053 | Oncology; primary focus of visit; expectant management of patient with evidence of cancer for whom no cancer-directed therapy is being administered or arranged at present; cancer-directed therapy might be considered in the future (for use in a Medicare-approved demonstration project) |
| E | G9054 | Oncology; primary focus of visit; supervising, coordinating or managing care of patient with terminal cancer or for whom other medical illness prevents further cancer treatment; includes symptom management, end-of-life care planning, management of palliative therapies (for use in a Medicare-approved demonstration project) |

| | | |
|---|---|---|
| E | G9055 | Oncology; primary focus of visit; other, unspecified service not otherwise listed (for use in a Medicare-approved demonstration project) |
| E | G9056 | Oncology; practice guidelines; management adheres to guidelines (for use in a Medicare-approved demonstration project) |
| E | G9057 | Oncology; practice guidelines; management differs from guidelines as a result of patient enrollment in an institutional review board-approved clinical trial (for use in a Medicare-approved demonstration project) |
| E | G9058 | Oncology; practice guidelines; management differs from guidelines because the treating physician disagrees with guideline recommendations (for use in a Medicare-approved demonstration project) |
| E | G9059 | Oncology; practice guidelines; management differs from guidelines because the patient, after being offered treatment consistent with guidelines, has opted for alternative treatment or management, including no treatment (for use in a Medicare-approved demonstration project) |
| E | G9060 | Oncology; practice guidelines; management differs from guidelines for reason(s) associated with patient comorbid illness or performance status not factored into guidelines (for use in a Medicare-approved demonstration project) |
| E | G9061 | Oncology; practice guidelines; patient's condition not addressed by available guidelines (for use in a Medicare-approved demonstration project) |
| E | G9062 | Oncology; practice guidelines; management differs from guidelines for other reason(s) not listed (for use in a Medicare-approved demonstration project) |
| M | G9063 | Oncology; disease status; limited to nonsmall cell lung cancer; extent of disease initially established as Stage I (prior to neoadjuvant therapy, if any) with no evidence of disease progression, recurrence, or metastases (for use in a Medicare-approved demonstration project) |
| M | G9064 | Oncology; disease status; limited to nonsmall cell lung cancer; extent of disease initially established as Stage II (prior to neoadjuvant therapy, if any) with no evidence of disease progression, recurrence, or metastases (for use in a Medicare-approved demonstration project) |
| M | G9065 | Oncology; disease status; limited to nonsmall cell lung cancer; extent of disease initially established as Stage III a (prior to neoadjuvant therapy, if any) with no evidence of disease progression, recurrence, or metastases (for use in a Medicare-approved demonstration project) |
| M | G9066 | Oncology; disease status; limited to nonsmall cell lung cancer; Stage III B-IV at diagnosis, metastatic, locally recurrent, or progressive (for use in a Medicare-approved demonstration project) |
| M | G9067 | Oncology; disease status; limited to nonsmall cell lung cancer; extent of disease unknown, staging in progress, or not listed (for use in a Medicare-approved demonstration project) |
| M | G9068 | Oncology; disease status; limited to small cell and combined small cell/nonsmall cell; extent of disease initially established as limited with no evidence of disease progression, recurrence, or metastases (for use in a Medicare-approved demonstration project) |
| M | G9069 | Oncology; disease status; small cell lung cancer, limited to small cell and combined small cell/nonsmall cell; extensive Stage at diagnosis, metastatic, locally recurrent, or progressive (for use in a Medicare-approved demonstration project) |

**Procedures/Professional Services (Temporary)**

**G9070 — G9084**

| | | |
|---|---|---|
| M | **G9070** | Oncology; disease status; small cell lung cancer, limited to small cell and combined small cell/nonsmall; extent of disease unknown, staging in progress, or not listed (for use in a Medicare-approved demonstration project) |
| M | **G9071** | Oncology; disease status; invasive female breast cancer (does not include ductal carcinoma in situ); adenocarcinoma as predominant cell type; stage I or stage IIA-IIB; or T3, N1, M0; and ER and/or PR positive; with no evidence of disease progression, recurrence, or metastases (for use in a Medicare-approved demonstration project) ♀ |
| M | **G9072** | Oncology; disease status; invasive female breast cancer (does not include ductal carcinoma in situ); adenocarcinoma as predominant cell type; stage I, or stage IIA-IIB; or T3, N1, M0; and ER and PR negative; with no evidence of disease progression, recurrence, or metastases (for use in a Medicare-approved demonstration project) ♀ |
| M | **G9073** | Oncology; disease status; invasive female breast cancer (does not include ductal carcinoma in situ); adenocarcinoma as predominant cell type; stage IIIA-IIIB; and not T3, N1, M0; and ER and/or PR positive; with no evidence of disease progression, recurrence, or metastases (for use in a Medicare-approved demonstration project) ♀ |
| M | **G9074** | Oncology; disease status; invasive female breast cancer (does not include ductal carcinoma in situ); adenocarcinoma as predominant cell type; stage IIIA-IIIB; and not T3, N1, M0; and ER and PR negative; with no evidence of disease progression, recurrence, or metastases (for use in a Medicare-approved demonstration project) ♀ |
| M | **G9075** | Oncology; disease status; invasive female breast cancer (does not include ductal carcinoma in situ); adenocarcinoma as predominant cell type; M1 at diagnosis, metastatic locally recurrent, or progressive (for use in a Medicare-approved demonstration project) ♀ |
| M | **G9077** | Oncology; disease status; prostate cancer, limited to adenocarcinoma as predominant cell type; T1-T2C and Gleason 2-7 and PSA < or equal to 20 at diagnosis with no evidence of disease progression, recurrence, or metastases (for use in a Medicare-approved demonstration project) ♂ |
| M | **G9078** | Oncology; disease status; prostate cancer, limited to adenocarcinoma as predominant cell type; T2 or T3a Gleason 8-10 or PSA >20 at diagnosis with no evidence of disease progression, recurrence, or metastases (for use in a Medicare-approved demonstration project) ♂ |
| M | **G9079** | Oncology; disease status; prostate cancer, limited to adenocarcinoma as predominant cell type; T3B-T4, any N; any T, N1 at diagnosis with no evidence of disease progression, recurrence, or metastases (for use in a Medicare-approved demonstration project) ♂ |
| M | **G9080** | Oncology; disease status; prostate cancer, limited to adenocarcinoma; after initial treatment with rising PSA or failure of PSA decline (for use in a Medicare-approved demonstration project) ♂ |
| M | **G9083** | Oncology; disease status; prostate cancer, limited to adenocarcinoma; extent of disease unknown, staging in progress, or not listed (for use in a Medicare-approved demonstration project) ♂ |
| M | **G9084** | Oncology; disease status; colon cancer, limited to invasive cancer, adenocarcinoma as predominant cell type; extent of disease initially established as T1-3, N0, M0 with no evidence of disease progression, recurrence or metastases (for use in a Medicare-approved demonstration project) |

| M | G9085 | Oncology; disease status; colon cancer, limited to invasive cancer, adenocarcinoma as predominant cell type; extent of disease initially established as T4, N0, M0 with no evidence of disease progression, recurrence, or metastases (for use in a Medicare-approved demonstration project) |
|---|-------|---|
| M | G9086 | Oncology; disease status; colon cancer, limited to invasive cancer, adenocarcinoma as predominant cell type; extent of disease initially established as T1-4, N1-2, M0 with no evidence of disease progression, recurrence, or metastases (for use in a Medicare-approved demonstration project) |
| M | G9087 | Oncology; disease status; colon cancer, limited to invasive cancer, adenocarcinoma as predominant cell type; M1 at diagnosis, metastatic locally recurrent, or progressive with current clinical, radiologic, or biochemical evidence of disease (for use in a Medicare-approved demonstration project) |
| M | G9088 | Oncology; disease status; colon cancer, limited to invasive cancer, adenocarcinoma as predominant cell type; M1 at diagnosis, metastatic, locally recurrent, or progressive without current clinical, radiologic, or biochemical evidence of disease (for use in a Medicare-approved demonstration project) |
| M | G9089 | Oncology; disease status; colon cancer, limited to invasive cancer, adenocarcinoma as predominant cell type; extent of disease unknown, staging in progress or not listed (for use in a Medicare-approved demonstration project) |
| M | G9090 | Oncology; disease status; rectal cancer, limited to invasive cancer, adenocarcinoma as predominant cell type; extent of disease initially established as T1-2, N0, M0 (prior to neoadjuvant therapy, if any) with no evidence of disease progression, recurrence, or metastases (for use in a Medicare-approved demonstration project) |
| M | G9091 | Oncology; disease status; rectal cancer, limited to invasive cancer, adenocarcinoma as predominant cell type; extent of disease initially established as T3, N0, M0 (prior to neoadjuvant therapy, if any) with no evidence of disease progression, recurrence, or metastases (for use in a Medicare-approved demonstration project) |
| M | G9092 | Oncology; disease status; rectal cancer, limited to invasive cancer, adenocarcinoma as predominant cell type; extent of disease initially established as T1-3, N1-2, M0 (prior to neoadjuvant therapy, if any) with no evidence of disease progression, recurrence or metastases (for use in a Medicare-approved demonstration project) |
| M | G9093 | Oncology; disease status; rectal cancer, limited to invasive cancer, adenocarcinoma as predominant cell type; extent of disease initially established as T4, any N, M0 (prior to neoadjuvant therapy, if any) with no evidence of disease progression, recurrence, or metastases (for use in a Medicare-approved demonstration project) |
| M | G9094 | Oncology; disease status; rectal cancer, limited to invasive cancer, adenocarcinoma as predominant cell type; M1 at diagnosis, metastatic, locally recurrent, or progressive (for use in a Medicare-approved demonstration project) |
| M | G9095 | Oncology; disease status; rectal cancer, limited to invasive cancer, adenocarcinoma as predominant cell type; extent of disease unknown, staging in progress or not listed (for use in a Medicare-approved demonstration project) |

Procedures/Professional Services (Temporary)

G9096 — G9108

| M | **G9096** | Oncology; disease status; esophageal cancer, limited to adenocarcinoma or squamous cell carcinoma as predominant cell type; extent of disease initially established as T1-T3, N0-N1 or NX (prior to neoadjuvant therapy, if any) with no evidence of disease progression, recurrence, or metastases (for use in a Medicare-approved demonstration project) |
|---|---|---|
| M | **G9097** | Oncology; disease status; esophageal cancer, limited to adenocarcinoma or squamous cell carcinoma as predominant cell type; extent of disease initially established as T4, any N, M0 (prior to neoadjuvant therapy, if any) with no evidence of disease progression, recurrence, or metastases (for use in a Medicare-approved demonstration project) |
| M | **G9098** | Oncology; disease status; esophageal cancer, limited to adenocarcinoma or squamous cell carcinoma as predominant cell type; M1 at diagnosis, metastatic, locally recurrent, or progressive (for use in a Medicare-approved demonstration project) |
| M | **G9099** | Oncology; disease status; esophageal cancer, limited to adenocarcinoma or squamous cell carcinoma as predominant cell type; extent of disease unknown, staging in progress, or not listed (for use in a Medicare-approved demonstration project) |
| M | **G9100** | Oncology; disease status; gastric cancer, limited to adenocarcinoma as predominant cell type; post R0 resection (with or without neoadjuvant therapy) with no evidence of disease recurrence, progression, or metastases (for use in a Medicare-approved demonstration project) |
| M | **G9101** | Oncology; disease status; gastric cancer, limited to adenocarcinoma as predominant cell type; post R1 or R2 resection (with or without neoadjuvant therapy) with no evidence of disease progression, or metastases (for use in a Medicare-approved demonstration project) |
| M | **G9102** | Oncology; disease status; gastric cancer, limited to adenocarcinoma as predominant cell type; clinical or pathologic M0, unresectable with no evidence of disease progression, or metastases (for use in a Medicare-approved demonstration project) |
| M | **G9103** | Oncology; disease status; gastric cancer, limited to adenocarcinoma as predominant cell type; clinical or pathologic M1 at diagnosis, metastatic, locally recurrent, or progressive (for use in a Medicare-approved demonstration project) |
| M | **G9104** | Oncology; disease status; gastric cancer, limited to adenocarcinoma as predominant cell type; extent of disease unknown, staging in progress, or not listed (for use in a Medicare-approved demonstration project) |
| M | **G9105** | Oncology; disease status; pancreatic cancer, limited to adenocarcinoma as predominant cell type; post R0 resection without evidence of disease progression, recurrence, or metastases (for use in a Medicare-approved demonstration project) |
| M | **G9106** | Oncology; disease status; pancreatic cancer, limited to adenocarcinoma; post R1 or R2 resection with no evidence of disease progression, or metastases (for use in a Medicare-approved demonstration project) |
| M | **G9107** | Oncology; disease status; pancreatic cancer, limited to adenocarcinoma; unresectable at diagnosis, M1 at diagnosis, metastatic, locally recurrent, or progressive (for use in a Medicare-approved demonstration project) |
| M | **G9108** | Oncology; disease status; pancreatic cancer, limited to adenocarcinoma; extent of disease unknown, staging in progress, or not listed (for use in a Medicare-approved demonstration project) |

Special Coverage Instructions     Noncovered by Medicare     Carrier Discretion

| M | G9109 | Oncology; disease status; head and neck cancer, limited to cancers of oral cavity, pharynx and larynx with squamous cell as predominant cell type; extent of disease initially established as T1-T2 and N0, M0 (prior to neoadjuvant therapy, if any) with no evidence of disease progression, recurrence, or metastases (for use in a Medicare-approved demonstration project) |
| M | G9110 | Oncology; disease status; head and neck cancer, limited to cancers of oral cavity, pharynx and larynx with squamous cell as predominant cell type; extent of disease initially established as T3-4 and/or N1-3, M0 (prior to neoadjuvant therapy, if any) with no evidence of disease progression, recurrence, or metastases (for use in a Medicare-approved demonstration project) |
| M | G9111 | Oncology; disease status; head and neck cancer, limited to cancers of oral cavity, pharynx and larynx with squamous cell as predominant cell type; M1 at diagnosis, metastatic, locally recurrent, or progressive (for use in a Medicare-approved demonstration project) |
| M | G9112 | Oncology; disease status; head and neck cancer, limited to cancers of oral cavity, pharynx and larynx with squamous cell as predominant cell type; extent of disease unknown, staging in progress, or not listed (for use in a Medicare-approved demonstration project) |
| M | G9113 | Oncology; disease status; ovarian cancer, limited to epithelial cancer; pathologic stage 1A-B (Grade 1) without evidence of disease progression, recurrence, or metastases (for use in a Medicare-approved demonstration project) ♀ |
| M | G9114 | Oncology; disease status; ovarian cancer, limited to epithelial cancer; pathologic stage IA-B (grade 2-3); or stage IC (all grades); or stage II; without evidence of disease progression, recurrence, or metastases (for use in a Medicare-approved demonstration project) ♀ |
| M | G9115 | Oncology; disease status; ovarian cancer, limited to epithelial cancer; pathologic stage III-IV; without evidence of progression, recurrence, or metastases (for use in a Medicare-approved demonstration project) ♀ |
| M | G9116 | Oncology; disease status; ovarian cancer, limited to epithelial cancer; evidence of disease progression, or recurrence, and/or platinum resistance (for use in a Medicare-approved demonstration project) ♀ |
| M | G9117 | Oncology; disease status; ovarian cancer, limited to epithelial cancer; extent of disease unknown, staging in progress, or not listed (for use in a Medicare-approved demonstration project) ♀ |
| M | G9123 | Oncology; disease status; chronic myelogenous leukemia, limited to Philadelphia chromosome positive and/or BCR-ABL positive; chronic phase not in hematologic, cytogenetic, or molecular remission (for use in a Medicare-approved demonstration project) |
| M | G9124 | Oncology; disease status; chronic myelogenous leukemia, limited to Philadelphia chromosome positive and /or BCR-ABL positive; accelerated phase not in hematologic cytogenetic, or molecular remission (for use in a Medicare-approved demonstration project) |
| M | G9125 | Oncology; disease status; chronic myelogenous leukemia, limited to Philadelphia chromosome positive and/or BCR-ABL positive; blast phase not in hematologic, cytogenetic, or molecular remission (for use in a Medicare-approved demonstration project) |
| M | G9126 | Oncology; disease status; chronic myelogenous leukemia, limited to Philadelphia chromosome positive and/or BCR-ABL positive; in hematologic, cytogenetic, or molecular remission (for use in a Medicare-approved demonstration project) |

Ⓜ     **G9128**     Oncology; disease status; limited to multiple myeloma, systemic disease; smoldering, stage I (for use in a Medicare-approved demonstration project)

Ⓜ     **G9129**     Oncology; disease status; limited to multiple myeloma, systemic disease; stage II or higher (for use in a Medicare-approved demonstration project)

Ⓜ     **G9130**     Oncology; disease status; limited to multiple myeloma, systemic disease; extent of disease unknown, staging in progress, or not listed (for use in a Medicare-approved demonstration project)

Ⓜ     **G9131**     Oncology; disease status; invasive female breast cancer (does not include ductal carcinoma in situ); adenocarcinoma as predominant cell type; extent of disease unknown, staging in progress, or not listed (for use in a Medicare-approved demonstration project)     ♀

Ⓜ     **G9132**     Oncology; disease status; prostate cancer, limited to adenocarcinoma; hormone-refractory/androgen-independent (e.g., rising PSA on antiandrogen therapy or postorchiectomy); clinical metastases (for use in a Medicare-approved demonstration project)     ♂

Ⓜ     **G9133**     Oncology; disease status; prostate cancer, limited to adenocarcinoma; hormone-responsive; clinical metastases or M1 at diagnosis (for use in a Medicare-approved demonstration project)     ♂

Ⓜ     **G9134**     Oncology; disease status; non-Hodgkin's lymphoma, any cellular classification; Stage I, II at diagnosis, not relapsed, not refractory (for use in a Medicare-approved demonstration project)

Ⓜ     **G9135**     Oncology; disease status; non-Hodgkin's lymphoma, any cellular classification; Stage III, IV, not relapsed, not refractory (for use in a Medicare-approved demonstration project)

Ⓜ     **G9136**     Oncology; disease status; non-Hodgkin's lymphoma, transformed from original cellular diagnosis to a second cellular classification (for use in a medicare-approved demonstration project)

Ⓜ     **G9137**     Oncology; disease status; non-Hodgkin's lymphoma, any cellular classification; relapsed/refractory (for use in a medicare-approved demonstration project)

Ⓜ     **G9138**     Oncology; disease status; non-Hodgkin's lymphoma, any cellular classification; diagnostic evaluation, stage not determined, evaluation of possible relapse or nonresponse to therapy, or not listed (for use in a Medicare-approved demonstration project)

Ⓜ     **G9139**     Oncology; disease status; chronic myelogenous leukemia, limited to Philadelphia chromosome positive and/or BCR-ABL positive; extent of disease unknown, staging in progress, not listed (for use in a Medicare-approved demonstration project)

Ⓐ ☑     **G9140**     Frontier extended stay clinic demonstration; for a patient stay in a clinic approved for the CMS demonstration project; the following measures should be present: the stay must be equal to or greater than 4 hours; weather or other conditions must prevent transfer or the case falls into a category of monitoring and observation cases that are permitted by the rules of the demonstration; there is a maximum frontier extended stay clinic (FESC) visit of 48 hours, except in the case when weather or other conditions prevent transfer; payment is made on each period up to 4 hours, after the first 4 hours

## ALCOHOL AND DRUG ABUSE TREATMENT SERVICES H0001–H2037

The H codes are used by those state Medicaid agencies that are mandated by state law to establish separate codes for identifying mental health services that include alcohol and drug treatment services.

| | | |
|---|---|---|
| | H0001 | Alcohol and/or drug assessment |
| | H0002 | Behavioral health screening to determine eligibility for admission to treatment program |
| | H0003 | Alcohol and/or drug screening; laboratory analysis of specimens for presence of alcohol and/or drugs |
| ☑ | H0004 | Behavioral health counseling and therapy, per 15 minutes |
| | H0005 | Alcohol and/or drug services; group counseling by a clinician |
| | H0006 | Alcohol and/or drug services; case management |
| | H0007 | Alcohol and/or drug services; crisis intervention (outpatient) |
| | H0008 | Alcohol and/or drug services; subacute detoxification (hospital inpatient) |
| | H0009 | Alcohol and/or drug services; acute detoxification (hospital inpatient) |
| | H0010 | Alcohol and/or drug services; subacute detoxification (residential addiction program inpatient) |
| | H0011 | Alcohol and/or drug services; acute detoxification (residential addiction program inpatient) |
| | H0012 | Alcohol and/or drug services; subacute detoxification (residential addiction program outpatient) |
| | H0013 | Alcohol and/or drug services; acute detoxification (residential addiction program outpatient) |
| | H0014 | Alcohol and/or drug services; ambulatory detoxification |
| | H0015 | Alcohol and/or drug services; intensive outpatient (treatment program that operates at least 3 hours/day and at least 3 days/week and is based on an individualized treatment plan), including assessment, counseling; crisis intervention, and activity therapies or education |
| | H0016 | Alcohol and/or drug services; medical/somatic (medical intervention in ambulatory setting) |
| ☑ | H0017 | Behavioral health; residential (hospital residential treatment program), without room and board, per diem |
| ☑ | H0018 | Behavioral health; short-term residential (nonhospital residential treatment program), without room and board, per diem |
| ☑ | H0019 | Behavioral health; long-term residential (nonmedical, nonacute care in a residential treatment program where stay is typically longer than 30 days), without room and board, per diem |
| | H0020 | Alcohol and/or drug services; methadone administration and/or service (provision of the drug by a licensed program) |
| | H0021 | Alcohol and/or drug training service (for staff and personnel not employed by providers) |
| | H0022 | Alcohol and/or drug intervention service (planned facilitation) |
| | H0023 | Behavioral health outreach service (planned approach to reach a targeted population) |

| | | |
|---|---|---|
| | H0024 | Behavioral health prevention information dissemination service (one-way direct or nondirect contact with service audiences to affect knowledge and attitude) |
| | H0025 | Behavioral health prevention education service (delivery of services with target population to affect knowledge, attitude and/or behavior) |
| | H0026 | Alcohol and/or drug prevention process service, community-based (delivery of services to develop skills of impactors) |
| | H0027 | Alcohol and/or drug prevention environmental service (broad range of external activities geared toward modifying systems in order to mainstream prevention through policy and law) |
| | H0028 | Alcohol and/or drug prevention problem identification and referral service (e.g., student assistance and employee assistance programs), does not include assessment |
| | H0029 | Alcohol and/or drug prevention alternatives service (services for populations that exclude alcohol and other drug use e.g., alcohol free social events) |
| | H0030 | Behavioral health hotline service |
| | H0031 | Mental health assessment, by nonphysician |
| | H0032 | Mental health service plan development by nonphysician |
| | H0033 | Oral medication administration, direct observation |
| ☑ | H0034 | Medication training and support, per 15 minutes |
| ☑ | H0035 | Mental health partial hospitalization, treatment, less than 24 hours |
| ☑ | H0036 | Community psychiatric supportive treatment, face-to-face, per 15 minutes |
| ☑ | H0037 | Community psychiatric supportive treatment program, per diem |
| ☑ | H0038 | Self-help/peer services, per 15 minutes |
| ☑ | H0039 | Assertive community treatment, face-to-face, per 15 minutes |
| ☑ | H0040 | Assertive community treatment program, per diem |
| ☑ | H0041 | Foster care, child, nontherapeutic, per diem    🅐 |
| ☑ | H0042 | Foster care, child, nontherapeutic, per month    🅐 |
| ☑ | H0043 | Supported housing, per diem |
| ☑ | H0044 | Supported housing, per month |
| ☑ | H0045 | Respite care services, not in the home, per diem |
| | H0046 | Mental health services, not otherwise specified |
| | H0047 | Alcohol and/or other drug abuse services, not otherwise specified |
| | H0048 | Alcohol and/or other drug testing: collection and handling only, specimens other than blood |
| | H0049 | Alcohol and/or drug screening |
| ☑ | H0050 | Alcohol and/or drug services, brief intervention, per 15 minutes |
| | H1000 | Prenatal care, at-risk assessment    Ⓜ ♀ |
| | H1001 | Prenatal care, at-risk enhanced service; antepartum management    Ⓜ ♀ |
| | H1002 | Prenatal care, at risk enhanced service; care coordination    Ⓜ ♀ |
| | H1003 | Prenatal care, at-risk enhanced service; education    Ⓜ ♀ |
| | H1004 | Prenatal care, at-risk enhanced service; follow-up home visit    Ⓜ ♀ |

| | | |
|---|---|---|
| | H1005 | Prenatal care, at-risk enhanced service package (includes H1001–H1004)     Ⓜ ♀ |
| ☑ | H1010 | Nonmedical family planning education, per session |
| | H1011 | Family assessment by licensed behavioral health professional for state defined purposes |
| | H2000 | Comprehensive multidisciplinary evaluation |
| ☑ | H2001 | Rehabilitation program, per 1/2 day |
| ☑ | H2010 | Comprehensive medication services, per 15 minutes |
| ☑ | H2011 | Crisis intervention service, per 15 minutes |
| ☑ | H2012 | Behavioral health day treatment, per hour |
| ☑ | H2013 | Psychiatric health facility service, per diem |
| ☑ | H2014 | Skills training and development, per 15 minutes |
| ☑ | H2015 | Comprehensive community support services, per 15 minutes |
| ☑ | H2016 | Comprehensive community support services, per diem |
| ☑ | H2017 | Psychosocial rehabilitation services, per 15 minutes |
| ☑ | H2018 | Psychosocial rehabilitation services, per diem |
| ☑ | H2019 | Therapeutic behavioral services, per 15 minutes |
| ☑ | H2020 | Therapeutic behavioral services, per diem |
| ☑ | H2021 | Community-based wrap-around services, per 15 minutes |
| ☑ | H2022 | Community-based wrap-around services, per diem |
| ☑ | H2023 | Supported employment, per 15 minutes |
| ☑ | H2024 | Supported employment, per diem |
| ☑ | H2025 | Ongoing support to maintain employment, per 15 minutes |
| ☑ | H2026 | Ongoing support to maintain employment, per diem |
| ☑ | H2027 | Psychoeducational service, per 15 minutes |
| ☑ | H2028 | Sexual offender treatment service, per 15 minutes |
| ☑ | H2029 | Sexual offender treatment service, per diem |
| ☑ | H2030 | Mental health clubhouse services, per 15 minutes |
| ☑ | H2031 | Mental health clubhouse services, per diem |
| ☑ | H2032 | Activity therapy, per 15 minutes |
| ☑ | H2033 | Multisystemic therapy for juveniles, per 15 minutes |
| ☑ | H2034 | Alcohol and/or drug abuse halfway house services, per diem |
| ☑ | H2035 | Alcohol and/or other drug treatment program, per hour |
| ☑ | H2036 | Alcohol and/or other drug treatment program, per diem |
| ☑ | H2037 | Developmental delay prevention activities, dependent child of client, per 15 minutes     Ⓐ |

**Drugs Administered Other Than Oral Method**

**J0120 — J0210**

## DRUGS ADMINISTERED OTHER THAN ORAL METHOD J0000-J9999

J codes include drugs that ordinarily cannot be self-administered, chemotherapy drugs, immunosuppressive drugs, inhalation solutions, and other miscellaneous drugs and solutions.

N ☑ **J0120** Injection, tetracycline, up to 250 mg    N1
MED: 100-2,15,50

K ☑ **J0128** Injection, abarelix, 10 mg    ♂ K2
Use this code for Planaxis.

K ☑ **J0129** Injection, abatacept, 10 mg    K2
Use this code for Orencia

K ☑ **J0130** Injection abciximab, 10 mg    K2
Use this code for ReoPro.
MED: 100-2,15,50

K ☑ **J0132** Injection, acetylcysteine, 100 mg    K2
Use this code for Acetadote.

N ☑ **J0133** Injection, acyclovir, 5 mg    N1
Use this code for Zovirax

K ☑ **J0135** Injection, adalimumab, 20 mg    K2
Use this code for Humira.

K ☑ **J0150** Injection, adenosine for therapeutic use, 6 mg (not to be used to report any adenosine phosphate compounds, instead use A9270)    K2
Use this code for Adenocard.
MED: 100-2,15,50
AHA: 2Q,'02,10

K ☑ **J0152** Injection, adenosine for diagnostic use, 30 mg (not to be used to report any adenosine phosphate compounds; instead use A9270)    K2
Use this code for Adenoscan.

N ☑ **J0170** Injection, adrenalin, epinephrine, up to 1 ml ampule    N1
Use this code for Adrenalin Chloride, Epipen, Sus-Phrine.
MED: 100-2,15,50

K ☑ **J0180** Injection, agalsidase beta, 1 mg    K2
Use this code for Fabrazyme.

N ☑ **J0190** Injection, biperiden lactate, per 5 mg    N1
MED: 100-2,15,50

N ☑ **J0200** Injection, alatrofloxacin mesylate, 100 mg    N1
MED: 100-2,15,50.5

K ☑ **J0205** Injection, alglucerase, per 10 units    K2
Use this code for Ceredase.
MED: 100-2,15,50

K ☑ **J0207** Injection, amifostine, 500 mg    K2
Use this code for Ethyol.
MED: 100-2,15,50

K ☑ **J0210** Injection, methyldopa HCl, up to 250 mg    K2
Use this code for Aldomet.
MED: 100-2,15,50

---

Special Coverage Instructions    Noncovered by Medicare    Carrier Discretion

K ☑ **J0215**    Injection, alefacept, 0.5 mg    K2
Use this for Amevive.

K ☑ **J0220**    Injection, alglucosidase alfa, 10 mg    K2
Use this code for Myozime

K ☑ **J0256**    Injection, alpha 1-proteinase inhibitor — human, 10 mg    K2
Use this code for Prolastin, Zemira.
MED: 100-2,15,50

▲ B    **J0270**    Injection, alprostadil, 1.25 mcg (code may be used for Medicare when drug administered under the direct supervision of a physician, not for use when drug is self-administered)
Use this code for Alprostadil, Caverject, Edex, Prostin VR Pediatric.
MED: 100-2,15,50

B    **J0275**    Alprostadil urethral suppository (code may be used for Medicare when drug administered under the direct supervision of a physician, not for use when drug is self-administered)
Use this code for Muse.
MED: 100-2,15,50

N ☑ **J0278**    Injection, amikacin sulfate, 100 mg    N1
Use this code for Amikin.

N ☑ **J0280**    Injection, aminophyllin, up to 250 mg    N1
MED: 100-2,15,50

N ☑ **J0282**    Injection, amiodarone HCl, 30 mg    N1
Use this code for Cordarone IV.
MED: 100-2,15,50

N ☑ **J0285**    Injection, amphotericin B, 50 mg    N1
Use this for Abelcet, Amphocin, Fungizone
MED: 100-2,15,50

K ☑ **J0287**    Injection, amphotericin B lipid complex, 10 mg    K2
MED: 100-2,15,50

K ☑ **J0288**    Injection, amphotericin B cholesteryl sulfate complex, 10 mg    K2
Use this code for Amphotec.
MED: 100-2,15,50

K ☑ **J0289**    Injection, amphotericin B liposome, 10 mg    K2
Use this code for Ambisome.
MED: 100-2,15,50

N ☑ **J0290**    Injection, ampicillin sodium, 500 mg    N1
MED: 100-2,15,50

N ☑ **J0295**    Injection, ampicillin sodium/sulbactam sodium, per 1.5 g    N1
Use this code for Unasyn.
MED: 100-2,15,50

N ☑ **J0300**    Injection, amobarbital, up to 125 mg    N1
Use this code for Amytal.
MED: 100-2,15,50

N ☑ **J0330**    Injection, succinylcholine chloride, up to 20 mg    N1
Use this code for Anectine, Quelicin.
MED: 100-2,15,50

▲ K ☑ **J0348**    Injection, anidulafungin, 1 mg    K2
Use this code for Eraxis.

---

| N | ☑ | **J0350** | Injection, anistreplase, per 30 units | N1 |

Use this code for Eminase.

MED: 100-2,15,50

| N | ☑ | **J0360** | Injection, hydralazine HCl, up to 20 mg | N1 |

MED: 100-2,15,50

| N | ☑ | **J0364** | Injection, apomorphine HCl, 1 mg | N1 |

Use this code for Apokyn.

| K | ☑ | **J0365** | Injection, aprotonin, 10,000 kiu | K2 |

Use this code for Trasylol.

MED: 100-2,15,50

| N | ☑ | **J0380** | Injection, metaraminol bitartrate, per 10 mg | N1 |

Use this code for Aramine.

MED: 100-2,15,50

| N | ☑ | **J0390** | Injection, chloroquine HCl, up to 250 mg | N1 |

Use this code for Aralen.

MED: 100-2,15,50

| N | ☑ | **J0395** | Injection, arbutamine HCl, 1 mg | N1 |

MED: 100-2,15,50

| N | ☑ | **J0400** | Injection, aripiprazole, intramuscular, 0.25 mg | N1 |

Use this code for Abilify.

| N | ☑ | **J0456** | Injection, azithromycin, 500 mg | N1 |

Use this code for Zithromax.

MED: 100-2,15,50.5

| N | ☑ | **J0460** | Injection, atropine sulfate, up to 0.3 mg | N1 |

Use this code for Atropen.

MED: 100-2,15,50

| K | ☑ | **J0470** | Injection, dimercaprol, per 100 mg | K2 |

Use this code for BAL.

MED: 100-2,15,50

| K | ☑ | **J0475** | Injection, baclofen, 10 mg | K2 |

Use this code for Lioresal.

MED: 100-2,15,50

| K | ☑ | **J0476** | Injection, baclofen, 50 mcg for intrathecal trial | K2 |

Use this code for Lioresal for intrathecal trial.

MED: 100-2,15,50

| K | | **J0480** | Injection, basiliximab, 20 mg | K2 |

Use this code for Simulect.

MED: 100-2,15,50; 100-4,4,240

| N | ☑ | **J0500** | Injection, dicyclomine HCl, up to 20 mg | N1 |

Use this code for Bentyl.

MED: 100-2,15,50

| N | ☑ | **J0515** | Injection, benztropine mesylate, per 1 mg | N1 |

Use this code for Cogentin.

MED: 100-2,15,50

| N | ☑ | **J0520** | Injection, bethanechol chloride, Myotonachol or Urecholine, up to 5 mg | N1 |

MED: 100-2,15,50

---

| | | | |
|---|---|---|---|
| N ☑ | J0530 | Injection, penicillin G benzathine and penicillin G procaine, up to 600,000 units | N1 |

Use this code for Bicillin C-R.

MED: 100-2,15,50

| | | | |
|---|---|---|---|
| N ☑ | J0540 | Injection, penicillin G benzathine and penicillin G procaine, up to 1,200,000 units | N1 |

Use this code for Bicillin C-R, Bicillin C-R 900/300.

MED: 100-2,15,50

| | | | |
|---|---|---|---|
| K ☑ | J0550 | Injection, penicillin G benzathine and penicillin G procaine, up to 2,400,000 units | K2 |

Use this code for Bicillin C-R.

MED: 100-2,15,50

| | | | |
|---|---|---|---|
| N ☑ | J0560 | Injection, penicillin G benzathine, up to 600,000 units | N1 |

Use this code for Bicillin L-A, Permapen.

MED: 100-2,15,50

| | | | |
|---|---|---|---|
| N ☑ | J0570 | Injection, penicillin G benzathine, up to 1,200,000 units | N1 |

Use this code for Bicillin L-A, Permapen.

MED: 100-2,15,50

| | | | |
|---|---|---|---|
| N ☑ | J0580 | Injection, penicillin G benzathine, up to 2,400,000 units | N1 |

Use this code for Bicillin L-A, Permapen.

MED: 100-2,15,50

| | | | |
|---|---|---|---|
| K ☑ | J0583 | Injection, bivalirudin, 1 mg | K2 |

Use this code for Angiomax.

| | | | |
|---|---|---|---|
| K ☑ | J0585 | Botulinum toxin type A, per unit | K2 |

Use this code for Botox.

MED: 100-2,15,50

| | | | |
|---|---|---|---|
| K ☑ | J0587 | Botulinum toxin type B, per 100 units | K2 |

Use this code for Myobloc.

MED: 100-2,15,50

AHA: 2Q,'02,8

| | | | |
|---|---|---|---|
| N ☑ | J0592 | Injection, buprenorphine HCl, 0.1 mg | N1 |

Use this code for Buprenex.

MED: 100-2,15,50

| | | | |
|---|---|---|---|
| K ☑ | J0594 | Injection, busulfan, 1 mg | K2 |

Use this code for Busulfex.

| | | | |
|---|---|---|---|
| N ☑ | J0595 | Injection, butorphanol tartrate, 1 mg | N1 |

Use this code for Stadol.

| | | | |
|---|---|---|---|
| K ☑ | J0600 | Injection, edetate calcium disodium, up to 1,000 mg | K2 |

Use this code for Calcium Disodium Versenate, Calcium EDTA.

MED: 100-2,15,50

| | | | |
|---|---|---|---|
| N ☑ | J0610 | Injection, calcium gluconate, per 10 ml | N1 |

MED: 100-2,15,50

| | | | |
|---|---|---|---|
| N ☑ | J0620 | Injection, calcium glycerophosphate and calcium lactate, per 10 ml | N1 |

MED: 100-2,15,50

| | | | |
|---|---|---|---|
| K ☑ | J0630 | Injection, calcitonin salmon, up to 400 units | K2 |

Use this code for Calcimar, Miacalcin.

MED: 100-2,15,50

Drugs Administered Other Than Oral Method J0530 — J0630

N ☑ **J0636**　Injection, calcitriol, 0.1 mcg　　　　　　　　　　　　N1
Use this code for Calcijex.
MED: 100-2,15,50

K 　　**J0637**　Injection, caspofungin acetate, 5 mg　　　　　　　　　K2
Use this code for Cancidas.

N ☑ **J0640**　Injection, leucovorin calcium, per 50 mg　　　　　　　N1
MED: 100-2,15,50

● K ☑ **J0641**　Injection, levoleucovorin calcium, 0.5 mg　　　　　　K2
Use this code for Fusilev

N ☑ **J0670**　Injection, mepivacaine HCl, per 10 ml　　　　　　　　N1
Use this code for Carbocaine, Polocaine, Isocaine HCl, Scandonest
MED: 100-2,15,50

N ☑ **J0690**　Injection, cefazolin sodium, 500 mg　　　　　　　　　N1
Use this code for Ancef, Kefzol
MED: 100-2,15,50

N ☑ **J0692**　Injection, cefepime HCl, 500 mg　　　　　　　　　　　N1
Use this code for Maxipime.

N ☑ **J0694**　Injection, cefoxitin sodium, 1 g　　　　　　　　　　　N1
MED: 100-2,15,50

N ☑ **J0696**　Injection, ceftriaxone sodium, per 250 mg　　　　　　　N1
Use this code for Rocephin.
MED: 100-2,15,50

N ☑ **J0697**　Injection, sterile cefuroxime sodium, per 750 mg　　　　N1
Use this code for Zinacef.
MED: 100-2,15,50

N ☑ **J0698**　Injection, cefotaxime sodium, per g　　　　　　　　　N1
Use this code for Claforan.
MED: 100-2,15,50

N ☑ **J0702**　Injection, betamethasone acetate 3 mg and betamethasone sodium
phosphate 3 mg　　　　　　　　　　　　　　　　　　N1
Use this code for Celestone Soluspan.
MED: 100-2,15,50

N ☑ **J0704**　Injection, betamethasone sodium phosphate, per 4 mg　　N1
MED: 100-2,15,50

N ☑ **J0706**　Injection, caffeine citrate, 5 mg　　　　　　　　　　　N1
Use this code for Cafcit.
AHA: 2Q,'02,8

N ☑ **J0710**　Injection, cephapirin sodium, up to 1 g　　　　　　　　N1
MED: 100-2,15,50

N ☑ **J0713**　Injection, ceftazidime, per 500 mg　　　　　　　　　　N1
Use this code for Ceptax, Fortaz, Tazicef
MED: 100-2,15,50

N ☑ **J0715**　Injection, ceftizoxime sodium, per 500 mg　　　　　　　N1
Use this code for Cefizox.
MED: 100-2,15,50

N ☑ **J0720**　Injection, chloramphenicol sodium succinate, up to 1 g　　N1
Use this code for Chlormycetin.
MED: 100-2,15,50

| | | | | |
|---|---|---|---|---|
| N ☑ | **J0725** | Injection, chorionic gonadotropin, per 1,000 USP units | | N1 |
| | | MED: 100-2,15,50 | | |
| K ☑ | **J0735** | Injection, clonidine HCl, 1 mg | | K2 |
| | | Use this code for Clorpres, Duraclon, Iopidine | | |
| | | MED: 100-2,15,50 | | |
| K ☑ | **J0740** | Injection, cidofovir, 375 mg | | K2 |
| | | Use this code for Vistide. | | |
| | | MED: 100-2,15,50 | | |
| N ☑ | **J0743** | Injection, cilastatin sodium; imipenem, per 250 mg | | N1 |
| | | Use this code for Primaxin I.M., Primaxin I.V. | | |
| | | MED: 100-2,15,50 | | |
| N ☑ | **J0744** | Injection, ciprofloxacin for intravenous infusion, 200 mg | | N1 |
| | | Use this code for Cipro. | | |
| N ☑ | **J0745** | Injection, codeine phosphate, per 30 mg | | N1 |
| | | MED: 100-2,15,50 | | |
| N ☑ | **J0760** | Injection, colchicine, per 1 mg | | N1 |
| | | MED: 100-2,15,50 | | |
| N ☑ | **J0770** | Injection, colistimethate sodium, up to 150 mg | | N1 |
| | | Use this code for Coly-Mycin M. | | |
| | | MED: 100-2,15,50 | | |
| N ☑ | **J0780** | Injection, prochlorperazine, up to 10 mg | | N1 |
| | | Use this code for Compazine, Cotranzine, Compa-Z, Ultrazine-10. | | |
| | | MED: 100-2,15,50 | | |
| K ☑ | **J0795** | Injection, corticorelin ovine triflutate, 1 mcg | | K2 |
| | | Use this code for Acthrel. | | |
| | | MED: 100-2,15,50 | | |
| K ☑ | **J0800** | Injection, corticotropin, up to 40 units | | K2 |
| | | Use this code for H.P. Acthar gel | | |
| | | MED: 100-2,15,50 | | |
| K ☑ | **J0835** | Injection, cosyntropin, per 0.25 mg | | K2 |
| | | Use this code for Cortrosyn. | | |
| | | MED: 100-2,15,50 | | |
| K ☑ | **J0850** | Injection, cytomegalovirus immune globulin intravenous (human), per vial | | K2 |
| | | Use this code for Cytogam. | | |
| | | MED: 100-2,15,50; 100-4,4,240 | | |
| K ☑ | **J0878** | Injection, daptomycin, 1 mg | | K2 |
| | | Use this code for Cubicin. | | |
| K ☑ | **J0881** | Injection, darbepoetin alfa, 1 mcg (non-ESRD use) | | K2 |
| | | Use this code for Aranesp. | | |
| | | MED: 100-2,6,10; 100-4,4,240 | | |
| A ☑ | **J0882** | Injection, darbepoetin alfa, 1 mcg (for ESRD on dialysis) | | ⊘ |
| | | Use this code for Aranesp. | | |
| | | MED: 100-2,6,10; 100-4,4,240 | | |
| K ☑ | **J0885** | Injection, epoetin alfa, (for non-ESRD use), 1000 units | | K2 |
| | | Use this code for Epogen/Procrit. | | |
| | | MED: 100-2,6,10; 100-2,15,50; 100-4,4,240 | | |

---

☑ Quantity Alert   ● New Code   ○ Recycled/Reinstated   ▲ Revised Code   ᕳ DMEPOS Paid   ⊘ SNF Excluded

[A] ☑  **J0886**  Injection, epoetin alfa, 1000 units (for ESRD on dialysis)          ⊘
Use this code for Epogen/Procrit.
MED: 100-2,6,10; 100-4,4,240

[K] ☑  **J0894**  Injection, decitabine, 1 mg                                          [K2]
Use this code for Dacogen.

[N] ☑  **J0895**  Injection, deferoxamine mesylate, 500 mg                             [N1]
Use this code for Desferal.
MED: 100-2,15,50

[N] ☑  **J0900**  Injection, testosterone enanthate and estradiol valerate, up to 1 cc  [N1]
MED: 100-2,15,50

[N] ☑  **J0945**  Injection, brompheniramine maleate, per 10 mg                        [N1]
MED: 100-2,15,50

[N] ☑  **J0970**  Injection, estradiol valerate, up to 40 mg                           [N1]
Use this code for Clinagen LA, Clinagen, LA-10, Clinagen LA-20, Clinagen
LA-40, Delestrogen
MED: 100-2,15,50

[N] ☑  **J1000**  Injection, depo-estradiol cypionate, up to 5 mg                      [N1]
Use this code for depGynogen, Depogen, Estradiol Cypionate
MED: 100-2,15,50

[N] ☑  **J1020**  Injection, methylprednisolone acetate, 20 mg                         [N1]
Use this code for Depo-Medrol.
MED: 100-2,15,50; 100-4,4,240

[N] ☑  **J1030**  Injection, methylprednisolone acetate, 40 mg                         [N1]
Use this code for DepoMedalone40, Depo-Medrol, Sano-Drol
MED: 100-2,15,50; 100-4,4,240

[N] ☑  **J1040**  Injection, methylprednisolone acetate, 80 mg                         [N1]
Use this code for Cortimed, DepMedalone, DepoMedalone 80, Depo-Medrol,
Duro Cort, Methylcotolone, Pri-Methylate, Sano-Drol
MED: 100-2,15,50; 100-4,4,240

[N] ☑  **J1051**  Injection, medroxyprogesterone acetate, 50 mg                  ♀ [N1]
Use this code for Depo-Provera.
MED: 100-2,15,50

[E]     **J1055**  Injection, medroxyprogesterone acetate for contraceptive use, 150 mg ♀
Use this code for Depo-Provera.

[E]     **J1056**  Injection, medroxyprogesterone acetate/estradiol cypionate, 5 mg/25
mg                                                                       ♀
Use this code for Lunelle monthly contraceptive.

[N] ☑  **J1060**  Injection, testosterone cypionate and estradiol cypionate, up to 1 ml [N1]
Use this code for Depo-Testadiol, Duo-Span, Duo-Span II.
MED: 100-2,15,50

[N] ☑  **J1070**  Injection, testosterone cypionate, up to 100 mg                      [N1]
Use this code for Depo Testosterone Cypionate
MED: 100-2,15,50

[N] ☑  **J1080**  Injection, testosterone cypionate, 1 cc, 200 mg                      [N1]
Use this code for Depandrante, Depo-Testosterone, Virilon
MED: 100-2,15,50

---

N    **J1094**    Injection, dexamethasone acetate, 1 mg    N1
Use this code for Cortastat LA, Dalalone L.A., Dexamethasone Acetate Anhydrous, Dexone LA.
MED: 100-2,15,50

N ☑   **J1100**    Injection, dexamethasone sodium phosphate, 1 mg    N1
Use this code for Cortastat, Dalalone, Decaject, Dexone, Solurex, Adrenocort, Primethasone, Dexasone, Dexim, Medidex, Spectro-Dex.
MED: 100-2,15,50

N ☑   **J1110**    Injection, dihydroergotamine mesylate, per 1 mg    N1
Use this code for D.H.E. 45.
MED: 100-2,15,50

N ☑   **J1120**    Injection, acetazolamide sodium, up to 500 mg    N1
Use this code for Diamox.
MED: 100-2,15,50

N ☑   **J1160**    Injection, digoxin, up to 0.5 mg    N1
Use this code for Lanoxin.
MED: 100-2,15,50

K ☑   **J1162**    Injection, digoxin immune fab (ovine), per vial    K2
Use this code for Digibind, Digifab.
MED: 100-2,15,50

N ☑   **J1165**    Injection, phenytoin sodium, per 50 mg    N1
Use this code for Dilantin.
MED: 100-2,15,50

N ☑   **J1170**    Injection, hydromorphone, up to 4 mg    N1
Use this code for Dilaudid, Dilaudid-HP.
MED: 100-2,15,50

N ☑   **J1180**    Injection, dyphylline, up to 500 mg    N1
MED: 100-2,15,50

K ☑   **J1190**    Injection, dexrazoxane HCl, per 250 mg    K2
Use this code for Totect, Zinecard.
MED: 100-2,15,50

N ☑   **J1200**    Injection, diphenhydramine HCl, up to 50 mg    N1
Use this code for Benadryl, Benahist 10, Benahist 50, Benoject-10, Benoject-50, Bena-D 10, Bena-D 50, Nordryl, Dihydrex, Dimine, Diphenacen-50, Hyrexin-50, Truxadryl, Wehdryl.
MED: 100-2,15,50
AHA: 1Q,'02,2

K ☑   **J1205**    Injection, chlorothiazide sodium, per 500 mg    K2
Use this code for Diuril Sodium.
MED: 100-2,15,50

K ☑   **J1212**    Injection, DMSO, dimethyl sulfoxide, 50%, 50 ml    K2
Use this code for Rimso 50. DMSO is covered only as a treatment of interstitial cystitis.
MED: 100-2,15,50; 100-3,230.12

N ☑   **J1230**    Injection, methadone HCl, up to 10 mg    N1
Use this code for Dolophine HCl.
MED: 100-2,15,50

---

☑ Quantity Alert    ● New Code    ○ Recycled/Reinstated    ▲ Revised Code    ⅋ DMEPOS Paid    ⊘ SNF Excluded

N ☑ **J1240** Injection, dimenhydrinate, up to 50 mg     N1
Use this code for Dramamine, Dinate, Dommanate, Dramanate, Dramilin, Dramocen, Dramoject, Dymenate, Hydrate, Marmine, Wehamine.
MED: 100-2,15,50

N ☑ **J1245** Injection, dipyridamole, per 10 mg     N1
Use this code for Persantine IV.
MED: 100-2,15,50

N ☑ **J1250** Injection, Dobutamine HCl, per 250 mg     N1
MED: 100-2,15,50

K ☑ **J1260** Injection, dolasetron mesylate, 10 mg     K2
Use this code for Anzemet.
MED: 100-2,15,50

N ☑ **J1265** Injection, dopamine HCl, 40 mg     N1

● G **J1267** Injection, doripenem, 10 mg     K2
Use this code for Doribax.

N ☑ **J1270** Injection, doxercalciferol, 1 mcg     N1
Use this code for Hectorol.

G ☑ **J1300** Injection, eculizumab, 10 mg     K2
Use this code for Soliris.

N ☑ **J1320** Injection, amitriptyline HCl, up to 20 mg     N1
Use this code for Elavil.
MED: 100-2,15,50

N ☑ **J1324** Injection, enfuvirtide, 1 mg     N1
Use this code for Fuzeon.

N ☑ **J1325** Injection, epoprostenol, 0.5 mg     N1
Use this code for Flolan. See K0455 for infusion pump for epoprosterol.
MED: 100-2,15,50

K ☑ **J1327** Injection, eptifibatide, 5 mg     K2
Use this code for Integrilin.
MED: 100-2,15,50

N ☑ **J1330** Injection, ergonovine maleate, up to 0.2 mg     N1
Medicare jurisdiction: local contractor. Use this code for Ergotrate Maleate.
MED: 100-2,15,50

N ☑ **J1335** Injection, ertapenem sodium, 500 mg     N1
Use this code for Invanz.

N ☑ **J1364** Injection, erythromycin lactobionate, per 500 mg     N1
MED: 100-2,15,50

N ☑ **J1380** Injection, estradiol valerate, up to 10 mg     N1
Use this code for Delestrogen, Dioval, Dioval XX, Dioval 40, Duragen-10, Duragen-20, Duragen-40, Estradiol L.A., Estradiol L.A. 20, Estradiol L.A. 40, Gynogen L.A. 10, Gynogen L.A. 20, Gynogen L.A. 40, Valergen 10, Valergen 20, Valergen 40, Estra-L 20, Estra-L 40, L.A.E. 20.
MED: 100-2,15,50

N ☑ **J1390** Injection, estradiol valerate, up to 20 mg    N1
Use this code for Delestrogen, Dioval, Dioval XX, Dioval 40, Duragen-10, Duragen-20, Duragen-40, Estradiol L.A., Estradiol L.A. 20, Estradiol L.A. 40, Gynogen L.A. 10, Gynogen L.A. 20, Gynogen L.A. 40, Valergen 10, Valergen 20, Valergen 40, Estra-L 20, Estra-L 40, L.A.E. 20.
MED: 100-2,15,50

K ☑ **J1410** Injection, estrogen conjugated, per 25 mg    K2
Use this code for Natural Estrogenic Substance, Premarin Intravenous, Primestrin Aqueous.
MED: 100-2,15,50

K    **J1430** Injection, ethanolamine oleate, 100 mg    K2
Use this code for Ethamiolin.
MED: 100-2,15,50

N ☑ **J1435** Injection, estrone, per 1 mg    N1
Use this code for Estone Aqueous, Estragyn, Estro-A, Estrone, Estronol, Theelin Aqueous, Estone 5, Kestrone 5.
MED: 100-2,15,50

K ☑ **J1436** Injection, etidronate disodium, per 300 mg    K2
Use this code for Didronel.
MED: 100-2,15,50

K ☑ **J1438** Injection, etanercept, 25 mg (code may be used for Medicare when drug administered under the direct supervision of a physician, not for use when drug is self-administered)    K2
Use this code for Enbrel.
MED: 100-2,15,50

K ☑ **J1440** Injection, filgrastim (G-CSF), 300 mcg    K2
Use this code for Neupogen.
MED: 100-2,15,50

K ☑ **J1441** Injection, filgrastim (G-CSF), 480 mcg    K2
Use this code for Neupogen.
MED: 100-2,15,50

N ☑ **J1450** Injection, fluconazole, 200 mg    N1
Use this code for Diflucan.
MED: 100-2,15,50.5

K ☑ **J1451** Injection, fomepizole, 15 mg    K2
Use this code for Antizol.
MED: 100-2,15,50

N ☑ **J1452** Injection, fomivirsen sodium, intraocular, 1.65 mg    N1
Use this code for Vitavene.
MED: 100-2,15,50.4.2

● G **J1453** Injection, fosaprepitant, 1 mg    K2
Use this code for Emend

K ☑ **J1455** Injection, foscarnet sodium, per 1,000 mg    K2
Use this code for Foscavir.

K ☑ **J1457** Injection, gallium nitrate, 1 mg    K2
Use this code for Ganite.

K ☑ **J1458** Injection, galsulfase, 1 mg    K2
Use this code for Naglazyme.

---

☑ Quantity Alert    ● New Code    ○ Recycled/Reinstated    ▲ Revised Code    ᕲ DMEPOS Paid    ⊘ SNF Excluded

Drugs Administered Other Than Oral Method

J1459 — J1568

● Ⓖ **J1459** Injection, immune globulin (Privigen), intravenous, nonlyophilized (e.g., liquid), 500 mg     K2

Ⓚ ☑ **J1460** Injection, gamma globulin, intramuscular, 1 cc     K2
Use this code for GamaSTAN SD.
MED: 100-2,15,50

Ⓚ ☑ **J1470** Injection, gamma globulin, intramuscular, 2 cc     K2
Use this code for GamaSTAN SD.
MED: 100-2,15,50

Ⓚ ☑ **J1480** Injection, gamma globulin, intramuscular, 3 cc     K2
Use this code for GamaSTAN SD.
MED: 100-2,15,50

Ⓚ ☑ **J1490** Injection, gamma globulin, intramuscular, 4 cc     K2
Use this code for GamaSTAN SD.
MED: 100-2,15,50

Ⓚ ☑ **J1500** Injection, gamma globulin, intramuscular, 5 cc     K2
Use this code for GamaSTAN SD.
MED: 100-2,15,50

Ⓚ ☑ **J1510** Injection, gamma globulin, intramuscular, 6 cc     K2
Use this code for GamaSTAN SD.
MED: 100-2,15,50

Ⓚ ☑ **J1520** Injection, gamma globulin, intramuscular, 7 cc     K2
Use this code for GamaSTAN SD.
MED: 100-2,15,50

Ⓚ ☑ **J1530** Injection, gamma globulin, intramuscular, 8 cc     K2
Use this code for GamaSTAN SD.
MED: 100-2,15,50

Ⓚ ☑ **J1540** Injection, gamma globulin, intramuscular, 9 cc     K2
Use this code for GamaSTAN SD.
MED: 100-2,15,50

Ⓚ ☑ **J1550** Injection, gamma globulin, intramuscular, 10 cc     K2
Use this code for GamaSTAN SD.
MED: 100-2,15,50

Ⓚ ☑ **J1560** Injection, gamma globulin, intramuscular, over 10 cc     K2
Use this code for GamaSTAN SD.
MED: 100-2,15,50

Ⓚ ☑ **J1561** Injection, immune globulin, (Gamunex), intravenous, nonlyophilized (e.g., liquid), 500 mg     K2

Ⓚ ☑ **J1562** Injection, immune globulin (Vivaglobin), 100 mg     K2

Ⓚ ☑ **J1565** Injection, respiratory syncytial virus immune globulin, intravenous, 50 mg     K2
Use this code for Respigam.
MED: 100-2,15,50

Ⓚ ☑ **J1566** Injection, immune globulin, intravenous, lyophilized (e.g., powder), not otherwise specified, 500 mg     K2
Use this code for Carimune.
MED: 100-2,15,50

Ⓚ ☑ **J1568** Injection, immune globulin, (Octagam), intravenous, nonlyophilized (e.g., liquid), 500 mg     K2

---

Special Coverage Instructions      Noncovered by Medicare      Carrier Discretion

| | | | |
|---|---|---|---|
| K ☑ | **J1569** | Injection, immune globulin, (Gammagard liquid), intravenous, nonlyophilized, (e.g., liquid), 500 mg | K2 |
| N ☑ | **J1570** | Injection, ganciclovir sodium, 500 mg<br>Use this code for Cytovene.<br>MED: 100-2,15,50 | N1 |
| G ☑ | **J1571** | Injection, hepatitis B immune globulin (Hepagam B), intramuscular, 0.5 ml | K2 |
| ▲ K ☑ | **J1572** | Injection, immune globulin, (Flebogamma/Flebogamma Dif), intravenous, nonlyophilized (e.g., liquid), 500 mg | K2 |
| G ☑ | **J1573** | Injection, hepatitis B immune globulin (Hepagam B), intravenous, 0.5 ml | K2 |
| N ☑ | **J1580** | Injection, garamycin, gentamicin, up to 80 mg<br>Use this code for Gentamicin Sulfate, Jenamicin.<br>MED: 100-2,15,50 | N1 |
| N ☑ | **J1590** | Injection, gatifloxacin, 10 mg | N1 |
| K ☑ | **J1595** | Injection, glatiramer acetate, 20 mg<br>Use this code for Copaxone.<br>MED: 100-2,15,50 | K2 |
| N ☑ | **J1600** | Injection, gold sodium thiomalate, up to 50 mg<br>Use this code for Myochrysine.<br>MED: 100-2,15,50 | N1 |
| K ☑ | **J1610** | Injection, glucagon HCl, per 1 mg<br>Use this code for Glucagen.<br>MED: 100-2,15,50 | K2 |
| K ☑ | **J1620** | Injection, gonadorelin HCl, per 100 mcg<br>Use this code for Factrel, Lutrepulse.<br>MED: 100-2,15,50 | K2 |
| K ☑ | **J1626** | Injection, granisetron HCl, 100 mcg<br>Use this code for Kytril.<br>MED: 100-2,15,50 | K2 |
| N ☑ | **J1630** | Injection, haloperidol, up to 5 mg<br>Use this code for Haldol.<br>MED: 100-2,15,50 | N1 |
| N ☑ | **J1631** | Injection, haloperidol decanoate, per 50 mg<br>Use this code for Haldol Decanoate-50.<br>MED: 100-2,15,50 | N1 |
| K ☑ | **J1640** | Injection, hemin, 1 mg<br>Use this code for Panhematin.<br>MED: 100-2,15,50 | K2 |
| N ☑ | **J1642** | Injection, heparin sodium, (heparin lock flush), per 10 units<br>Use this code for Hep-Lock, Hep-Lock U/P, Hep-Pak, Lok-Pak.<br>MED: 100-2,15,50 | N1 |
| N ☑ | **J1644** | Injection, Heparin sodium, per 1000 units<br>Use this code for Heparin Sodium, Liquaemin Sodium.<br>MED: 100-2,15,50 | N1 |
| N ☑ | **J1645** | Injection, dalteparin sodium, per 2500 IU<br>Use this code for Fragmin.<br>MED: 100-2,15,50 | N1 |

☑ Quantity Alert  ● New Code  ○ Recycled/Reinstated  ▲ Revised Code  ა DMEPOS Paid  ⊘ SNF Excluded

N ☑ **J1650** Injection, enoxaparin sodium, 10 mg   N1
Use this code for Lovenox.

K ☑ **J1652** Injection, fondaparinux sodium, 0.5 mg   K2
Use this code for Atrixtra.
MED: 100-2,15,50

N ☑ **J1655** Injection, tinzaparin sodium, 1000 IU   N1
Use this code for Innohep.

K ☑ **J1670** Injection, tetanus immune globulin, human, up to 250 units   K2
Use this code for HyperTET SD.
MED: 100-2,15,50

B **J1675** Injection, histrelin acetate, 10 mcg
Use this code for Supprelin LA.
MED: 100-2,15,50

N ☑ **J1700** Injection, hydrocortisone acetate, up to 25 mg   N1
Use this code for Hydrocortone Acetate.
MED: 100-2,15,50

N ☑ **J1710** Injection, hydrocortisone sodium phosphate, up to 50 mg   N1
Use this code for Hydrocortone Phosphate.
MED: 100-2,15,50

N ☑ **J1720** Injection, hydrocortisone sodium succinate, up to 100 mg   N1
Use this code for Solu-Cortef, A-Hydrocort.
MED: 100-2,15,50

K ☑ **J1730** Injection, diazoxide, up to 300 mg   K2
MED: 100-2,15,50

K ☑ **J1740** Injection, ibandronate sodium, 1 mg   K2
Use this code for Boniva.

K ☑ **J1742** Injection, ibutilide fumarate, 1 mg   K2
Use this code for Corvert.
MED: 100-2,15,50

K **J1743** Injection, idursulfase, 1 mg   K2
Use this code for Elaprase.

K ☑ **J1745** Injection infliximab, 10 mg   K2
Use this code for Remicade.
MED: 100-2,15,50

○ K **J1750** Injection, iron dextran, 50 mg   K2
Use this code for INFeD.

~~J1751~~ ~~Injection, iron dextran 165, 50 mg~~
See J1750

~~J1752~~ ~~Injection, iron dextran 267, 50 mg~~
See J1750

K ☑ **J1756** Injection, iron sucrose, 1 mg   K2
Use this code for Venofer.

K ☑ **J1785** Injection, imiglucerase, per unit   K2
Use this code for Cerezyme.
MED: 100-2,15,50

N ☑ **J1790** Injection, droperidol, up to 5 mg  N1
Use this code for Inapsine.
MED: 100-2,15,50

N ☑ **J1800** Injection, propranolol HCl, up to 1 mg  N1
Use this code for Inderal.
MED: 100-2,15,50

E ☑ **J1810** Injection, droperidol and fentanyl citrate, up to 2 ml ampule
MED: 100-2,15,50
AHA: 2Q,'02,8

N ☑ **J1815** Injection, insulin, per 5 units  N1
Use this code for Humalog, Humulin, Iletin, Insulin Lispo, Novo Nordisk, NPH, Pork insulin, Regular insulin, Ultralente, Velosulin, Humulin R, Iletin II Regular Port, Insulin Purified Pork, Relion, Lente Iletin I, Novolin R, Humulin R U-500.
MED: 100-2,15,50; 100-3,280.14

N ☑ **J1817** Insulin for administration through DME (i.e., insulin pump) per 50 units  N1
Use this code for Humalog, Humulin, Vesolin BR, Iletin II NPH Pork, Lantus, Lispro-PFC, Novolin, Novolog, Novolog Flexpen, Novolog Mix, Relion Novolin.

E ☑ **J1825** Injection, interferon beta-1a, 33 mcg
Use this code for Avonex, Rebif.

K ☑ **J1830** Injection interferon beta-1b, 0.25 mg (code may be used for Medicare when drug administered under the direct supervision of a physician, not for use when drug is self-administered)  K2
Use this code for Betaseron.
MED: 100-2,15,50

K ☑ **J1835** Injection, itraconazole, 50 mg  K2
Use this code for Sporonox IV.

N ☑ **J1840** Injection, kanamycin sulfate, up to 500 mg  N1
Use this code for Kantrex.
MED: 100-2,15,50

N ☑ **J1850** Injection, kanamycin sulfate, up to 75 mg  N1
Use this code for Kantrex.
MED: 100-2,15,50

N ☑ **J1885** Injection, ketorolac tromethamine, per 15 mg  N1
MED: 100-2,15,50

N ☑ **J1890** Injection, cephalothin sodium, up to 1 g  N1
MED: 100-2,15,50

● K ☑ **J1930** Injection, lanreotide, 1 mg  K2
Use this code for Somatuline.

K ☑ **J1931** Injection, laronidase, 0.1 mg  K2
Use this code for Aldurazyme.

N ☑ **J1940** Injection, furosemide, up to 20 mg  N1
Use this code for Lasix.
MED: 100-2,15,50

K ☑ **J1945** Injection, lepirudin, 50 mg  K2
Use this code for Refludan.
This drug is used for patients with heparin induced thrombocytopenia.
MED: 100-2,15,50

---

☑ Quantity Alert   ● New Code   ○ Recycled/Reinstated   ▲ Revised Code   ⅙ DMEPOS Paid   ⊘ SNF Excluded

K ☑ **J1950** Injection, leuprolide acetate (for depot suspension), per 3.75 mg    K2
Use this code for Eliguard, Lupron, Lupron-3, Lupron-4, Lupron Depot.
MED: 100-2,15,50

● G ☑ **J1953** Injection, levetiracetam, 10 mg    K2
Use this code for Keppra

B ☑ **J1955** Injection, levocarnitine, per 1 g
Use this code for Carnitor
MED: 100-2,15,50

N ☑ **J1956** Injection, levofloxacin, 250 mg    N1
Use this code for Levaquin.
MED: 100-2,15,50

N ☑ **J1960** Injection, levorphanol tartrate, up to 2 mg    N1
Use this code for Levo-Dromoran.
MED: 100-2,15,50

N ☑ **J1980** Injection, hyoscyamine sulfate, up to 0.25 mg    N1
Use this code for Levsin.
MED: 100-2,15,50

N ☑ **J1990** Injection, chlordiazepoxide HCl, up to 100 mg    N1
Use this code for Librium.
MED: 100-2,15,50

N ☑ **J2001** Injection, lidocaine HCl for intravenous infusion, 10 mg    N1
Use this code for Xylocaine.
MED: 100-2,15,50

N ☑ **J2010** Injection, lincomycin HCl, up to 300 mg    N1
Use this code for Lincocin
MED: 100-2,15,50

K ☑ **J2020** Injection, linezolid, 200 mg    K2
Use this code for Zyvok.
AHA: 2Q,'02,8

N ☑ **J2060** Injection, lorazepam, 2 mg    N1
Use this code for Ativan.
MED: 100-2,15,50

N ☑ **J2150** Injection, mannitol, 25% in 50 ml    N1
Use this code for Osmitrol.
MED: 100-2,15,50

N ☑ **J2170** Injection, mecasermin, 1 mg    N1
Use this code for Iplex, Increlex.

N ☑ **J2175** Injection, meperidine HCl, per 100 mg    N1
Use this code for Demerol.
MED: 100-2,15,50

N ☑ **J2180** Injection, meperidine and promethazine HCl, up to 50 mg    N1
Use this code for Mepergan Injection.
MED: 100-2,15,50

N ☑ **J2185** Injection, meropenem, 100 mg    N1
Use this code for Merrem

N ☑ **J2210** Injection, methylergonovine maleate, up to 0.2 mg    N1
Use this code for Methergine.
MED: 100-2,15,50

Special Coverage Instructions      Noncovered by Medicare      Carrier Discretion

| | | | | |
|---|---|---|---|---|
| K | ☑ | J2248 | Injection, micafungin sodium, 1 mg<br>Use this code for Mycamine. | K2 |
| N | ☑ | J2250 | Injection, midazolam HCl, per 1 mg<br>Use this code for Versed.<br>MED: 100-2,15,50 | N1 |
| N | ☑ | J2260 | Injection, milrinone lactate, 5 mg<br>Use this code for Primacor.<br>MED: 100-2,15,50 | N1 |
| N | ☑ | J2270 | Injection, morphine sulfate, up to 10 mg<br>Use this code for Depodur, Infumorph<br>MED: 100-2,15,50 | N1 |
| N | ☑ | J2271 | Injection, morphine sulfate, 100 mg<br>Use this code for Depodur, Infumorph<br>MED: 100-2,15,50; 100-3,280.14 | N1 |
| N | ☑ | J2275 | Injection, morphine sulfate (preservative-free sterile solution), per 10 mg<br>Use this code for Astramorph PF, Duramorph, Infumorph.<br>MED: 100-2,15,50; 100-3,280.14 | N1 |
| K | ☑ | J2278 | Injection, ziconotide, 1 mcg<br>Use this code for Prialt | K2 |
| N | ☑ | J2280 | Injection, moxifloxacin, 100 mg<br>Use this code for Avelox. | N1 |
| N | ☑ | J2300 | Injection, nalbuphine HCl, per 10 mg<br>Use this code for Nubain.<br>MED: 100-2,15,50 | N1 |
| N | ☑ | J2310 | Injection, naloxone HCl, per 1 mg<br>Use this code for Narcan.<br>MED: 100-2,15,50 | N1 |
| K | ☑ | J2315 | Injection, naltrexone, depot form, 1 mg<br>Use this code for Vivitrol. | K2 |
| N | ☑ | J2320 | Injection, nandrolone decanoate, up to 50 mg<br>MED: 100-2,15,50 | N1 |
| N | ☑ | J2321 | Injection, nandrolone decanoate, up to 100 mg<br>MED: 100-2,15,50 | N1 |
| N | ☑ | J2322 | Injection, nandrolone decanoate, up to 200 mg<br>MED: 100-2,15,50 | N1 |
| K | | J2323 | Injection, natalizumab, 1 mg<br>Use this code for Tysabri. | K2 |
| K | ☑ | J2325 | Injection, nesiritide, 0.1 mg<br>Use this code for Natrecor.<br>MED: 100-2,15,50 | K2 |
| K | ☑ | J2353 | Injection, octreotide, depot form for intramuscular injection, 1 mg<br>Use this code for Sandostatin LAR. | K2 |
| N | ☑ | J2354 | Injection, octreotide, nondepot form for subcutaneous or intravenous injection, 25 mcg<br>Use this code for Sandostatin. | N1 |

K ☑   **J2355**   Injection, oprelvekin, 5 mg    K2
Use this code for Neumega.
MED: 100-2,15,50

K ☑   **J2357**   Injection, omalizumab, 5 mg    K2
Use this code for Xolair.

N ☑   **J2360**   Injection, orphenadrine citrate, up to 60 mg    N1
Use this code for Norflex
MED: 100-2,15,50

N ☑   **J2370**   Injection, phenylephrine HCl, up to 1 ml    N1
MED: 100-2,15,50

N ☑   **J2400**   Injection, chloroprocaine HCl, per 30 ml    N1
Use this code for Nesacaine, Nesacaine-MPF.
MED: 100-2,15,50

K ☑   **J2405**   Injection, ondansetron HCl, per 1 mg    K2
Use this code for Zofran.
MED: 100-2,15,50

N ☑   **J2410**   Injection, oxymorphone HCl, up to 1 mg    N1
Use this code for Numorphan, Oxymorphone HCl.
MED: 100-2,15,50

K ☑   **J2425**   Injection, palifermin, 50 mcg    K2
Use this code for Kepivance.

K ☑   **J2430**   Injection, pamidronate disodium, per 30 mg    K2
Use this code for Aredia
MED: 100-2,15,50

N ☑   **J2440**   Injection, papaverine HCl, up to 60 mg    N1
MED: 100-2,15,50

K ☑   **J2460**   Injection, oxytetracycline HCl, up to 50 mg    K2
Use this code for Terramycin IM.
MED: 100-2,15,50

K ☑   **J2469**   Injection, palonosetron HCl, 25 mcg    K2
Use this code for Aloxi.

N ☑   **J2501**   Injection, paricalcitol, 1 mcg    N1
Use this code For Zemplar.
MED: 100-2,15,50

K   **J2503**   Injection, pegaptanib sodium, 0.3 mg    K2
Use this code for Mucagen.

K ☑   **J2504**   Injection, pegademase bovine, 25 IU    K2
Use this code for Adagen.
MED: 100-2,15,50

K ☑   **J2505**   Injection, pegfilgrastim, 6 mg    K2
Use this code for Neulasta.

N ☑   **J2510**   Injection, penicillin G procaine, aqueous, up to 600,000 units    N1
Use this code for Wycillin, Duracillin A.S., Pfizerpen A.S., Crysticillin 300
A.S., Crysticillin 600 A.S.
MED: 100-2,15,50

K   **J2513**   Injection, pentastarch, 10% solution, 100 ml    K2
MED: 100-2,15,50

---

| | | | | |
|---|---|---|---|---|
| K ☑ | | **J2515** | Injection, pentobarbital sodium, per 50 mg | K2 |
| | | | Use this code for Nembutal Sodium Solution. | |
| | | | MED: 100-2,15,50 | |
| N ☑ | | **J2540** | Injection, penicillin G potassium, up to 600,000 units | N1 |
| | | | Use this code for Pfizerpen. | |
| | | | MED: 100-2,15,50 | |
| N ☑ | | **J2543** | Injection, piperacillin sodium/tazobactam sodium, 1 g/0.125 g (1.125 g) | N1 |
| | | | Use this code for Zosyn. | |
| | | | MED: 100-2,15,50 | |
| B ☑ | | **J2545** | Pentamidine isethionate, inhalation solution, FDA-approved final product, noncompounded, administered through DME, unit dose form, per 300 mg | |
| | | | Use this code for Nebupent, Pentam 300 | |
| N ☑ | | **J2550** | Injection, promethazine HCl, up to 50 mg | N1 |
| | | | Use this code for Phenergan | |
| | | | MED: 100-2,15,50 | |
| N ☑ | | **J2560** | Injection, phenobarbital sodium, up to 120 mg | N1 |
| | | | MED: 100-2,15,50 | |
| N ☑ | | **J2590** | Injection, oxytocin, up to 10 units | N1 |
| | | | Use this code for Pitocin, Syntocinon. | |
| | | | MED: 100-2,15,50 | |
| N ☑ | | **J2597** | Injection, desmopressin acetate, per 1 mcg | N1 |
| | | | Use this code for DDAVP. | |
| | | | MED: 100-2,15,50 | |
| N ☑ | | **J2650** | Injection, prednisolone acetate, up to 1 ml | N1 |
| | | | MED: 100-2,15,50; 100-4,4,240 | |
| N ☑ | | **J2670** | Injection, tolazoline HCl, up to 25 mg | N1 |
| | | | MED: 100-2,15,50 | |
| N | | **J2675** | Injection, progesterone, per 50 mg | N1 |
| | | | Use this code for Gesterone, Gestrin. | |
| | | | MED: 100-2,15,50 | |
| N ☑ | | **J2680** | Injection, fluphenazine decanoate, up to 25 mg | N1 |
| | | | MED: 100-2,15,50 | |
| N ☑ | | **J2690** | Injection, procainamide HCl, up to 1 g | N1 |
| | | | Use this code for Pronestyl. | |
| | | | MED: 100-2,15,50 | |
| N ☑ | | **J2700** | Injection, oxacillin sodium, up to 250 mg | N1 |
| | | | Use this code for Bactocill | |
| | | | MED: 100-2,15,50 | |
| N ☑ | | **J2710** | Injection, neostigmine methylsulfate, up to 0.5 mg | N1 |
| | | | Use this code for Prostigmin. | |
| | | | MED: 100-2,15,50 | |
| N ☑ | | **J2720** | Injection, protamine sulfate, per 10 mg | N1 |
| | | | MED: 100-2,15,50 | |
| K | | **J2724** | Injection, protein C concentrate, intravenous, human, 10 IU | K2 |

---

☑ Quantity Alert   ● New Code   ○ Recycled/Reinstated   ▲ Revised Code   ప DMEPOS Paid   ⊘ SNF Excluded

N ☑ **J2725** Injection, protirelin, per 250 mcg     N1
Use this code for Thyrel TRH
MED: 100-2,15,50

K ☑ **J2730** Injection, pralidoxime chloride, up to 1 g     K2
Use this code for Protopam Chloride.
MED: 100-2,15,50

N ☑ **J2760** Injection, phentolamine mesylate, up to 5 mg     N1
Use this code for Regitine.
MED: 100-2,15,50

N ☑ **J2765** Injection, metoclopramide HCl, up to 10 mg     N1
Use this code for Reglan
MED: 100-2,15,50

K ☑ **J2770** Injection, quinupristin/dalfopristin, 500 mg (150/350)     K2
Use this code for Synercid.
MED: 100-2,15,50

K ☑ **J2778** Injection, ranibizumab, 0.1 mg     K2
Use this code for Lucentis.

N ☑ **J2780** Injection, ranitidine HCl, 25 mg     N1
Use this code for Zantac.
MED: 100-2,15,50

K ☑ **J2783** Injection, rasburicase, 0.5 mg     K2
Use this code for Elitek.

● G ☑ **J2785** Injection, regadenoson, 0.1 mg     K2
Use this code for Lexiscan

▲ K ☑ **J2788** Injection, Rho D immune globulin, human, minidose, 50 mcg (250 i.u.)     K2
Use this code for RhoGam, MiCRhoGAM.
MED: 100-2,15,50

▲ K ☑ **J2790** Injection, Rho D immune globulin, human, full dose, 300 mcg (1500 i.u.)     K2
Use this code for RhoGam, Rhophylac.
MED: 100-2,15,50

K    **J2791** Injection, Rho( D) immune globulin (human), (Rhophylac), intramuscular or intravenous, 100 IU     K2
Use this for HypRho SD, WINRho SDF.

K ☑ **J2792** Injection, Rho D immune globulin, intravenous, human, solvent detergent, 100 IU     K2
MED: 100-2,15,50

K ☑ **J2794** Injection, risperidone, long acting, 0.5 mg     K2
Use this code for Risperidal Consta Long Acting.

N ☑ **J2795** Injection, ropivacaine HCl, 1 mg     N1
Use this code for Naropin.

N ☑ **J2800** Injection, methocarbamol, up to 10 ml     N1
Use this code for Robaxin
MED: 100-2,15,50

K    **J2805** Injection, sincalide, 5 mcg     K2
Use this code for Kinevac.

| | | | | |
|---|---|---|---|---|
| N | ☑ | **J2810** | Injection, theophylline, per 40 mg | N1 |
| | | | MED: 100-2,15,50 | |
| K | ☑ | **J2820** | Injection, sargramostim (GM-CSF), 50 mcg | K2 |
| | | | Use this code for Leukine | |
| | | | MED: 100-2,15,50 | |
| K | ☑ | **J2850** | Injection, secretin, synthetic, human, 1 mcg | K2 |
| | | | MED: 100-2,15,50 | |
| N | ☑ | **J2910** | Injection, aurothioglucose, up to 50 mg | N1 |
| | | | Use this code for Solganal. | |
| | | | MED: 100-2,15,50 | |
| N | ☑ | **J2916** | Injection, sodium ferric gluconate complex in sucrose injection, 12.5 mg | N1 |
| | | | MED: 100-2,15,50.2 | |
| N | ☑ | **J2920** | Injection, methylprednisolone sodium succinate, up to 40 mg | N1 |
| | | | Use this code for Solu-Medrol, A-methaPred. | |
| | | | MED: 100-2,15,50; 100-4,4,240 | |
| N | ☑ | **J2930** | Injection, methylprednisolone sodium succinate, up to 125 mg | N1 |
| | | | Use this code for Solu-Medrol, A-methaPred. | |
| | | | MED: 100-2,15,50; 100-4,4,240 | |
| K | ☑ | **J2940** | Injection, somatrem, 1 mg | K2 |
| | | | Use this code for Protropin. | |
| | | | MED: 100-2,15,50 | |
| | | | AHA: 2Q,'02,8 | |
| K | ☑ | **J2941** | Injection, somatropin, 1 mg | K2 |
| | | | Use this code for Humatrope, Genotropin Nutropin, Biotropin, Genotropin, Genotropin Miniquick, Norditropin, Nutropin, Nutropin AQ, Saizen, Saizen Somatropin RDNA Origin, Serostim, Serostim RDNA Origin, Zorbtive. | |
| | | | MED: 100-2,15,50 | |
| | | | AHA: 2Q,'02,8 | |
| N | ☑ | **J2950** | Injection, promazine HCl, up to 25 mg | N1 |
| | | | Use this code for Sparine, Prozine-50. | |
| | | | MED: 100-2,15,50 | |
| K | ☑ | **J2993** | Injection, reteplase, 18.1 mg | K2 |
| | | | Use this code for Retavase | |
| | | | MED: 100-2,15,50 | |
| K | ☑ | **J2995** | Injection, streptokinase, per 250,000 IU | K2 |
| | | | Use this code for Streptase | |
| | | | MED: 100-2,15,50 | |
| K | ☑ | **J2997** | Injection, alteplase recombinant, 1 mg | K2 |
| | | | Use this code for Activase, Cathflo. | |
| | | | MED: 100-2,15,50 | |
| N | ☑ | **J3000** | Injection, streptomycin, up to 1 g | N1 |
| | | | Use this code for Streptomycin Sulfate. | |
| | | | MED: 100-2,15,50 | |
| N | ☑ | **J3010** | Injection, fentanyl citrate, 0.1 mg | N1 |
| | | | Use this code for Sublimaze. | |
| | | | MED: 100-2,15,50 | |

---

☑ Quantity Alert   ● New Code   ○ Recycled/Reinstated   ▲ Revised Code    & DMEPOS Paid   ⊘ SNF Excluded

K ☑ **J3030** Injection, sumatriptan succinate, 6 mg (code may be used for Medicare when drug administered under the direct supervision of a physician, not for use when drug is self-administered)  K2
Use this code for Imitrex.

MED: 100-2,15,50

N ☑ **J3070** Injection, pentazocine, 30 mg  N1
Use this code for Talwin.

MED: 100-2,15,50

~~J3100~~ ~~Injection, tenecteplase, 50 mg~~
See J3101

● K ☑ **J3101** Injection, tenecteplase, 1 mg  K2
Use this code for TNKase.

N ☑ **J3105** Injection, terbutaline sulfate, up to 1 mg  N1
For terbutaline in inhalation solution, see K0525 and K0526.

MED: 100-2,15,50

B ☑ **J3110** Injection, teriparatide, 10 mcg
Use this code for Forteo.

N ☑ **J3120** Injection, testosterone enanthate, up to 100 mg  N1
Use this code for Delatestryl.

MED: 100-2,15,50

N ☑ **J3130** Injection, testosterone enanthate, up to 200 mg  N1
Use this code for Delatestryl.

MED: 100-2,15,50

N ☑ **J3140** Injection, testosterone suspension, up to 50 mg  N1

MED: 100-2,15,50

N ☑ **J3150** Injection, testosterone propionate, up to 100 mg  N1

MED: 100-2,15,50

N ☑ **J3230** Injection, chlorpromazine HCl, up to 50 mg  N1
Use this code for Thorazine.

MED: 100-2,15,50

K ☑ **J3240** Injection, thyrotropin alpha, 0.9 mg, provided in 1.1 mg vial  K2
Use this code for Thyrogen.

MED: 100-2,15,50

K ☑ **J3243** Injection, tigecycline, 1 mg  K2
Use this code for Tygacil.

K ☑ **J3246** Injection, tirofiban HCl, 0.25 mg  K2
Use this code for Aggrastat.

N ☑ **J3250** Injection, trimethobenzamide HCl, up to 200 mg  N1
Use this code for Tigan, Tiject-20, Arrestin.

MED: 100-2,15,50

N ☑ **J3260** Injection, tobramycin sulfate, up to 80 mg  N1
Use this code for Nebcin.

MED: 100-2,15,50

N ☑ **J3265** Injection, torsemide, 10 mg/ml  N1
Use this code for Demadex, Torsemide.

MED: 100-2,15,50

N ☑ **J3280** Injection, thiethylperazine maleate, up to 10 mg    N1
MED: 100-2,15,50

K ☑ **J3285** Injection, treprostinil, 1 mg    K2
Use this code for Remodulin.

● N **J3300** Injection, triamcinolone acetonide, preservative free, 1 mg    N1
Use this code for TRIVARIS.

▲ N ☑ **J3301** Injection, triamcinolone acetonide, not otherwise specified, 10 mg    N1
Use this code for Kenalog-10, Kenalog-40, Tri-Kort, Kenaject-40, Cenacort A-40, Triam-A, Trilog.
MED: 100-2,15,50

N ☑ **J3302** Injection, triamcinolone diacetate, per 5 mg    N1
Use this code for Aristocort, Aristocort Intralesional, Aristocort Forte, Amcort, Trilone, Cenacort Forte.
MED: 100-2,15,50

N ☑ **J3303** Injection, triamcinolone hexacetonide, per 5 mg    N1
Use this code for Aristospan Intralesional, Aristospan Intra-articular.
MED: 100-2,15,50

K ☑ **J3305** Injection, trimetrexate glucuronate, per 25 mg    K2
Use this code for Neutrexin.
MED: 100-2,15,50

N ☑ **J3310** Injection, perphenazine, up to 5 mg    N1
Use this code for Trilafon.
MED: 100-2,15,50

K ☑ **J3315** Injection, triptorelin pamoate, 3.75 mg    ♂ K2
Use this code for Trelstar Depot, Trelstar Depot Plus Debioclip Kit, Trelstar LA.
MED: 100-2,15,50

N ☑ **J3320** Injection, spectinomycin dihydrochloride, up to 2 g    N1
Use this code for Trobicin.
MED: 100-2,15,50

K ☑ **J3350** Injection, urea, up to 40 g    K2
MED: 100-2,15,50

K **J3355** Injection, urofollitropin, 75 IU    K2
Use this code for Metrodin, Bravelle, Fertinex.
MED: 100-2,15,50

N ☑ **J3360** Injection, diazepam, up to 5 mg    N1
Use this code for Diastat, Dizac, Valium.
MED: 100-2,15,50

N ☑ **J3364** Injection, urokinase, 5,000 IU vial    N1
Use this code for Kinlytic
MED: 100-2,15,50

K ☑ **J3365** Injection, IV, urokinase, 250,000 IU vial    K2
Use this code for Kinlytic
MED: 100-2,15,50

N ☑ **J3370** Injection, vancomycin HCl, 500 mg    N1
Use this code for Vancocin.
MED: 100-2,15,50; 100-3,280.14

---

☑ Quantity Alert    ● New Code    ○ Recycled/Reinstated    ▲ Revised Code    ఈ DMEPOS Paid    ⊘ SNF Excluded

| | | | | |
|---|---|---|---|---|
| K | ☑ | **J3396** | Injection, verteporfin, 0.1 mg | K2 |
| | | | Use this code for Visudyne. | |
| | | | MED: 100-3,80.2; 100-3,80.3 | |
| K | ☑ | **J3400** | Injection, triflupromazine HCl, up to 20 mg | K2 |
| | | | MED: 100-2,15,50 | |
| N | ☑ | **J3410** | Injection, hydroxyzine HCl, up to 25 mg | N1 |
| | | | Use this code for Vistaril, Vistaject-25, Hyzine, Hyzine-50. | |
| | | | MED: 100-2,15,50 | |
| N | ☑ | **J3411** | Injection, thiamine HCl, 100 mg | N1 |
| N | ☑ | **J3415** | Injection, pyridoxine HCl, 100 mg | N1 |
| N | ☑ | **J3420** | Injection, vitamin B-12 cyanocobalamin, up to 1,000 mcg | N1 |
| | | | Use this code for Sytobex, Redisol, Rubramin PC, Betalin 12, Berubigen, Cobex, Cobal, Crystal B12, Cyano, Cyanocobalamin, Hydroxocobalamin, Hydroxycobal, Nutri-Twelve. | |
| | | | MED: 100-2,15,50; 100-3,150.6 | |
| N | ☑ | **J3430** | Injection, phytonadione (vitamin K), per 1 mg | N1 |
| | | | Use this code for AquaMephyton, Konakion, Menadione, Phytonadione. | |
| | | | MED: 100-2,15,50 | |
| K | ☑ | **J3465** | Injection, voriconazole, 10 mg | K2 |
| | | | MED: 100-2,15,50 | |
| N | ☑ | **J3470** | Injection, hyaluronidase, up to 150 units | N1 |
| | | | MED: 100-2,15,50 | |
| N | ☑ | **J3471** | Injection, hyaluronidase, ovine, preservative free, per 1 USP unit (up to 999 USP units) | N1 |
| K | ☑ | **J3472** | Injection, hyaluronidase, ovine, preservative free, per 1,000 USP units | K2 |
| K | ☑ | **J3473** | Injection, hyaluronidase, recombinant, 1 USP unit | K2 |
| N | ☑ | **J3475** | Injection, magnesium sulfate, per 500 mg | N1 |
| | | | Use this code for Mag Sul, Sulfa Mag. | |
| | | | MED: 100-2,15,50 | |
| N | ☑ | **J3480** | Injection, potassium chloride, per 2 mEq | N1 |
| | | | MED: 100-2,15,50 | |
| N | ☑ | **J3485** | Injection, zidovudine, 10 mg | N1 |
| | | | Use this code for Retrovir, Zidovudine. | |
| | | | MED: 100-2,15,50 | |
| N | ☑ | **J3486** | Injection, ziprasidone mesylate, 10 mg | N1 |
| | | | Use this code for Geodon. | |
| K | ☑ | **J3487** | Injection, zoledronic acid (Zometa), 1 mg | K2 |
| G | ☑ | **J3488** | Injection, zoledronic acid (Reclast), 1 mg | K2 |
| N | | **J3490** | Unclassified drugs | N1 |
| | | | MED: 100-2,15,50 | |
| E | ☑ | **J3520** | Edetate disodium, per 150 mg | |
| | | | Use this code for Endrate, Disotate, Meritate, Chealamide, E.D.T.A. This drug is used in chelation therapy, a treatment for atherosclerosis that is not covered by Medicare. | |
| | | | MED: 100-3,20.21; 100-3,20.22 | |

| | | | |
|---|---|---|---|
| N | | J3530 | Nasal vaccine inhalation     N1 |
| | | | MED: 100-2,15,50 |
| E | | J3535 | Drug administered through a metered dose inhaler |
| | | | MED: 100-2,15,50 |
| E | | J3570 | Laetrile, amygdalin, vitamin B-17 |
| | | | The FDA has found Laetrile to have no safe or effective therapeutic purpose. |
| | | | MED: 100-3,30.7 |
| N | | J3590 | Unclassified biologics     N1 |

## MISCELLANEOUS DRUGS AND SOLUTIONS

| | | | |
|---|---|---|---|
| N | ☑ | J7030 | Infusion, normal saline solution, 1,000 cc     N1 |
| | | | MED: 100-2,15,50 |
| N | ☑ | J7040 | Infusion, normal saline solution, sterile (500 ml=1 unit)     N1 |
| | | | MED: 100-2,15,50 |
| N | ☑ | J7042 | 5% dextrose/normal saline (500 ml = 1 unit)     N1 |
| | | | MED: 100-2,15,50 |
| N | ☑ | J7050 | Infusion, normal saline solution, 250 cc     N1 |
| | | | MED: 100-2,15,50 |
| N | ☑ | J7060 | 5% dextrose/water (500 ml = 1 unit)     N1 |
| | | | MED: 100-2,15,50 |
| N | ☑ | J7070 | Infusion, D-5-W, 1,000 cc     N1 |
| | | | MED: 100-2,15,50 |
| N | ☑ | J7100 | Infusion, dextran 40, 500 ml     N1 |
| | | | Use this code for Gentran, 10% LMD, Rheomacrodex. |
| | | | MED: 100-2,15,50 |
| N | ☑ | J7110 | Infusion, dextran 75, 500 ml     N1 |
| | | | Use this code for Gentran 75. |
| | | | MED: 100-2,15,50 |
| N | ☑ | J7120 | Ringers lactate infusion, up to 1,000 cc     N1 |
| | | | MED: 100-2,15,50 |
| N | ☑ | J7130 | Hypertonic saline solution, 50 or 100 mEq, 20 cc vial     N1 |
| | | | MED: 100-2,15,50 |
| ● K | | J7186 | Injection, antihemophilic factor VIII/von Willebrand factor complex (human), per factor VIII i.u.     K2 |
| | | | Use this code for Alphanate. |
| K | | J7187 | Injection, von Willebrand factor complex (Humate-P), per IU vWF-RCO K2 |
| K | ☑ | J7189 | Factor VIIa (antihemophilic factor, recombinant), per 1 mcg     K2 |
| | | | MED: 100-1,1,10.1; 100-2,6,10; 100-2,15,50; 100-4,3,20.7.3 |
| K | ☑ | J7190 | Factor VIII (antihemophilic factor, human) per IU     K2 |
| | | | Use this code for Koate-DVI, Monarc-M, Monoclate-P. |
| | | | MED: 100-1,1,10.1; 100-2,6,10; 100-2,15,50; 100-4,3,20.7.3; 100-4,4,240; 100-4,17,80.4 |
| K | ☑ | J7191 | Factor VIII (antihemophilic factor (porcine)), per IU     K2 |
| | | | MED: 100-1,1,10.1; 100-2,6,10; 100-2,15,50; 100-4,3,20.7.3; 100-4,4,240; 100-4,17,80.4 |
| K | ☑ | J7192 | Factor VIII (antihemophilic factor, recombinant) per IU     K2 |
| | | | Use this code for Recombinate, Kogenate FS, Helixate FX, Advate rAHF-PFM, Antihemophilic Factor Human Method M Monoclonal Purified, Refacto. |
| | | | MED: 100-1,1,10.1; 100-2,6,10; 100-2,15,50; 100-4,3,20.7.3; 100-4,4,240; 100-4,17,80.4 |

Drugs Administered Other Than Oral Method    J3530 — J7192

---

☑ Quantity Alert    ● New Code    ○ Recycled/Reinstated    ▲ Revised Code    ⅄ DMEPOS Paid    ⊘ SNF Excluded

| K ☑ | **J7193** | Factor IX (antihemophilic factor, purified, nonrecombinant) per IU   K2 |
| | | Use this code for AlphaNine SD, Mononine. |
| | | MED: 100-1,1,10.1; 100-2,6,10; 100-2,15,50; 100-4,3,20.7.3; 100-4,4,240; 100-4,17,80.4 |
| | | AHA: 2Q,'02,8 |

| K ☑ | **J7194** | Factor IX complex, per IU   K2 |
| | | Use this code for Konyne-80, Profilnine SD, Proplex T, Proplex T, Bebulin VH, factor IX+ complex, Profilnine SD. |
| | | MED: 100-1,1,10.1; 100-2,6,10; 100-2,15,50; 100-4,3,20.7.3; 100-4,4,240; 100-4,17,80.4 |

| K ☑ | **J7195** | Factor IX (antihemophilic factor, recombinant) per IU   K2 |
| | | Use this code for Benefix. |
| | | MED: 100-1,1,10.1; 100-2,6,10; 100-2,15,50; 100-4,3,20.7.3; 100-4,4,240; 100-4,17,80.4 |
| | | AHA: 2Q,'02,8 |

| N ☑ | **J7197** | Antithrombin III (human), per IU   N1 |
| | | Use this code for Thrombate III, ATnativ. |
| | | MED: 100-2,15,50 |

| K ☑ | **J7198** | Antiinhibitor, per IU   K2 |
| | | Medicare jurisdiction: local contractor. Use this code for Autoplex T, Feiba VH AICC. |

| B | **J7199** | Hemophilia clotting factor, not otherwise classified |
| | | Medicare jurisdiction: local contractor. |

| E | **J7300** | Intrauterine copper contraceptive |
| | | Use this code for Paragard T380A. |

| E ☑ | **J7302** | Levonorgestrel-releasing intrauterine contraceptive system, 52 mg   ♀ |
| | | Use this code for Mirena. |

| E ☑ | **J7303** | Contraceptive supply, hormone containing vaginal ring, each   ♀ |
| | | Use this code for Nuvaring Vaginal Ring. |

| E ☑ | **J7304** | Contraceptive supply, hormone containing patch, each |

| E | **J7306** | Levonorgestrel (contraceptive) implant system, including implants and supplies |
| | | Use this code for Norplant II. |

| E | **J7307** | Etonogestrel (contraceptive) implant system, including implant and supplies |
| | | Use this code for Implanon. |

| K ☑ | **J7308** | Aminolevulinic acid HCl for topical administration, 20%, single unit dosage form (354 mg)   K2 |

| K ☑ | **J7310** | Ganciclovir, 4.5 mg, long-acting implant   K2 |
| | | Use this code for Vitrasert. |
| | | MED: 100-2,15,50 |

| K | **J7311** | Fluocinolone acetonide, intravitreal implant   K2 |
| | | Use this code for Retisert. |

| K ☑ | **J7321** | Hyaluronan or derivative, Hyalgan or Supartz, for intra-articular injection, per dose   K2 |

| K ☑ | **J7322** | Hyaluronan or derivative, Synvisc, for intra-articular injection, per dose   K2 |

| K ☑ | **J7323** | Hyaluronan or derivative, Euflexxa, for intra-articular injection, per dose   K2 |

| K ☑ | **J7324** | Hyaluronan or derivative, Orthovisc, for intra-articular injection, per dose   K2 |

---

B ☑   **J7330**   Autologous cultured chondrocytes, implant
Medicare jurisdiction: local contractor. Use this code for Carticel.

J7340   ~~Dermal and epidermal, (substitute) tissue of human origin, with or without bioengineered or processed elements, with metabolically active elements, per square centimeter~~
See Q4100-Q4111

J7341   ~~Dermal (substitute) tissue of nonhuman origin, with or without other bioengineered or processed elements, with metabolically active elements, per square centimeter~~
See Q4100-Q4111

J7342   ~~Dermal (substitute) tissue of human origin, with or without other bioengineered or processed elements, with metabolically active elements, per square centimeter~~
See Q4100-Q4111

J7343   ~~Dermal and epidermal, (substitute) tissue of nonhuman origin, with or without other bioengineered or processed elements, without metabolically active elements, per square centimeter~~
See Q4100-Q4111

J7344   ~~Dermal (substitute) tissue of human origin, with or without other bioengineered or processed elements, without metabolically active elements, per square centimeter~~
See Q4100-Q4111

J7346   ~~Dermal (substitute) tissue of human origin, injectable, with or without other bioengineered or processed elements, but without metabolically active elements, 1 cc~~
See Q4100-Q4111

J7347   ~~Dermal (substitute) tissue of nonhuman origin, with or without other bioengineered or processed elements, without metabolically active elements (Integra Matrix), per sq. cm.~~
See Q4100-Q4111

J7348   ~~Dermal (substitute) tissue of nonhuman origin, with or without other bioengineered or processed elements, without metabolically active elements (TissueMend), per sq. cm.~~
See Q4100-Q4111

J7349   ~~Dermal (substitute) tissue of nonhuman origin, with or without other bioengineered or processed elements, without metabolically active elements (PriMatrix), per sq. cm.~~
See Q4100-Q4111

N ☑   **J7500**   Azathioprine, oral, 50 mg    N1
Use this code for Azasan, Imuran.
MED: 100-2,15,50.5; 100-4,4,240; 100-4,17,80.3

K ☑   **J7501**   Azathioprine, parenteral, 100 mg    K2
MED: 100-2,6,10; 100-2,15,50; 100-4,4,240; 100-4,17,80.3

K ☑   **J7502**   Cyclosporine, oral, 100 mg    K2
Use this code for Neoral, Sandimmune, Gengraf, Sangcya
MED: 100-2,15,50.5; 100-4,4,240; 100-4,17,80.3

K ☑   **J7504**   Lymphocyte immune globulin, antithymocyte globulin, equine, parenteral, 250 mg    K2
Use this code for Atgam.
MED: 100-2,6,10; 100-2,15,50; 100-3,260.7; 100-4,4,240; 100-4,17,80.3

---

K ☑ **J7505**    Muromonab-CD3, parenteral, 5 mg    K2
Use this code for Orthoclone OKT3.
MED: 100-2,6,10; 100-2,15,50; 100-4,4,240; 100-4,17,80.3

N ☑ **J7506**    Prednisone, oral, per 5 mg    N1
Use this code for Deltasone, Liquid Pred Syrup, Levoxyl, Predone, Prednicot, Sterapred.
MED: 100-2,15,50.5; 100-4,4,240; 100-4,17,80.3

K ☑ **J7507**    Tacrolimus, oral, per 1 mg    K2
Use this code for Prograf.
MED: 100-2,15,50.5; 100-4,4,240; 100-4,17,80.3

N ☑ **J7509**    Methylprednisolone, oral, per 4 mg    N1
Use this code for Medrol, Methylpred.
MED: 100-2,15,50.5; 100-4,4,240; 100-4,17,80.3

N ☑ **J7510**    Prednisolone, oral, per 5 mg    N1
Use this code for Delta-Cortef, Cotolone, Pediapred, Prednoral, Prelone.
MED: 100-2,15,50.5; 100-4,4,240; 100-4,17,80.3

K ☑ **J7511**    Lymphocyte immune globulin, antithymocyte globulin, rabbit, parenteral, 25 mg    K2
Use this code for Thymoglobulin.
MED: 100-2,6,10; 100-4,4,240; 100-4,17,80.3
AHA: 2Q,'02,8

K ☑ **J7513**    Daclizumab, parenteral, 25 mg    K2
Use this code for Zenapax.
MED: 100-2,6,10; 100-2,15,50.5; 100-4,4,240; 100-4,17,80.3

N ☑ **J7515**    Cyclosporine, oral, 25 mg    N1
Use this code for Neoral, Sandimmune, Gengraf, Sangcya.
MED: 100-4,4,240; 100-4,17,80.3

K ☑ **J7516**    Cyclosporine, parenteral, 250 mg    K2
Use this code for Neoral, Sandimmune, Gengraf, Sangcya.
MED: 100-2,6,10; 100-4,4,240; 100-4,17,80.3

K ☑ **J7517**    Mycophenolate mofetil, oral, 250 mg    K2
Use this code for CellCept.
MED: 100-4,4,240; 100-4,17,80.3

K ☑ **J7518**    Mycophenolic acid, oral, 180 mg    K2
Use this code for Myfortic Delayed Release.
MED: 100-4,4,240; 100-4,17,80.3.1

K ☑ **J7520**    Sirolimus, oral, 1 mg    K2
Use this code for Rapamune.
MED: 100-2,15,50.5; 100-4,4,240; 100-4,17,80.3

K ☑ **J7525**    Tacrolimus, parenteral, 5 mg    K2
Use this code for Prograf.
MED: 100-2,6,10; 100-2,15,50.5; 100-4,4,240; 100-4,17,80.3

N    **J7599**    Immunosuppressive drug, not otherwise classified    N1
Determine if an alternative HCPCS Level II or a CPT code better describes the service being reported. This code should be used only if a more specific code is unavailable.
MED: 100-2,6,10; 100-2,15,50.5; 100-4,4,240; 100-4,17,80.3

Special Coverage Instructions      Noncovered by Medicare      Carrier Discretion

## INHALATION SOLUTIONS

~~J7602~~  ~~Albuterol, all formulations including separated isomers, inhalation solution, FDA-approved final product, noncompounded, administered through DME, concentrated form, per 1 mg (Albuterol) or per 0.5 mg Levalbuterol)~~

~~J7603~~  ~~Albuterol, all formulations including separated isomers, inhalation solution, FDA-approved final product, noncompounded, administered through DME, unit dose, per 1 mg (Albuterol) or per 0.5 mg Levalbuterol)~~

Ⓜ ☑ **J7604** Acetylcysteine, inhalation solution, compounded product, administered through DME, unit dose form, per g

Ⓜ ☑ **J7605** Arformoterol, inhalation solution, FDA approved final product, noncompounded, administered through DME, unit dose form, 15 mcg

● Ⓜ **J7606** Formoterol fumarate, inhalation solution, FDA approved final product, noncompounded, administered through DME, unit dose form, 20 mcg
Use this code for Perforomist.

Ⓜ ☑ **J7607** Levalbuterol, inhalation solution, compounded product, administered through DME, concentrated form, 0.5 mg

Ⓜ ☑ **J7608** Acetylcysteine, inhalation solution, FDA-approved final product, noncompounded, administered through DME, unit dose form, per g
Use this code for Acetadote, Mucomyst, Mucosil.
MED: 100-2,15,110.3

Ⓜ ☑ **J7609** Albuterol, inhalation solution, compounded product, administered through DME, unit dose, 1 mg

Ⓜ ☑ **J7610** Albuterol, inhalation solution, compounded product, administered through DME, concentrated form, 1 mg

○ Ⓜ ☑ **J7611** Albuterol, inhalation solution, FDA-approved final product, noncompounded, administered through DME, concentrated form, 1 mg
Use this code for Accuneb, Proventil, Respirol, Ventolin.
MED: 100-2,15,110.3

○ Ⓜ ☑ **J7612** Levalbuterol, inhalation solution, FDA-approved final product, noncompounded, administered through DME, concentrated form, 0.5 mg
Use this code for Xopenex HFA.
MED: 100-2,15,110.3

○ Ⓜ ☑ **J7613** Albuterol, inhalation solution, FDA-approved final product, noncompounded, administered through DME, unit dose, 1 mg
Use this code for Accuneb, Proventil, Respirol, Ventolin.
MED: 100-2,15,110.3

○ Ⓜ ☑ **J7614** Levalbuterol, inhalation solution, FDA-approved final product, noncompounded, administered through DME, unit dose, 0.5 mg
Use this code for Xopenex.
MED: 100-2,15,110.3

Ⓜ ☑ **J7615** Levalbuterol, inhalation solution, compounded product, administered through DME, unit dose, 0.5 mg

Ⓜ ☑ **J7620** Albuterol, up to 2.5 mg and ipratropium bromide, up to 0.5 mg, FDA-approved final product, noncompounded, administered through DME
MED: 100-2,15,110.3

**Drugs Administered Other Than Oral Method**

**J7622 — J7640**

M ☑ **J7622** Beclomethasone, inhalation solution, compounded product, administered through DME, unit dose form, per mg
Use this code for Beclovent, Beconase.

M ☑ **J7624** Betamethasone, inhalation solution, compounded product, administered through DME, unit dose form, per mg

M ☑ **J7626** Budesonide, inhalation solution, FDA-approved final product, noncompounded, administered through DME, unit dose form, up to 0.5 mg
Use this code for Pulmicort, Pulmicort Flexhaler, Pulmicort Respules, Vanceril.

M ☑ **J7627** Budesonide, inhalation solution, compounded product, administered through DME, unit dose form, up to 0.5 mg

M ☑ **J7628** Bitolterol mesylate, inhalation solution, compounded product, administered through DME, concentrated form, per mg
MED: 100-2,15,110.3

M ☑ **J7629** Bitolterol mesylate, inhalation solution, compounded product, administered through DME, unit dose form, per mg
MED: 100-2,15,110.3

M ☑ **J7631** Cromolyn sodium, inhalation solution, FDA-approved final product, noncompounded, administered through DME, unit dose form, per 10 mg
Use this code for Intal, Nasalcrom
MED: 100-2,15,110.3

M ☑ **J7632** Cromolyn sodium, inhalation solution, compounded product, administered through DME, unit dose form, per 10 mg

M ☑ **J7633** Budesonide, inhalation solution, FDA-approved final product, noncompounded, administered through DME, concentrated form, per 0.25 mg
Use this code for Pulmicort, Pulmicort Flexhaler, Pulmicort Respules, Vanceril

M ☑ **J7634** Budesonide, inhalation solution, compounded product, administered through DME, concentrated form, per 0.25 mg

M ☑ **J7635** Atropine, inhalation solution, compounded product, administered through DME, concentrated form, per mg
MED: 100-2,15,110.3

M ☑ **J7636** Atropine, inhalation solution, compounded product, administered through DME, unit dose form, per mg
MED: 100-2,15,110.3

M ☑ **J7637** Dexamethasone, inhalation solution, compounded product, administered through DME, concentrated form, per mg
MED: 100-2,15,110.3

M ☑ **J7638** Dexamethasone, inhalation solution, compounded product, administered through DME, unit dose form, per mg
MED: 100-2,15,110.3

▲ M ☑ **J7639** Dornase alfa, inhalation solution, FDA-approved final product, noncompounded, administered through DME, unit dose form, per mg
Use this code for Pulmozyme.
MED: 100-2,15,110.3

E ☑ **J7640** Formoterol, inhalation solution, compounded product, administered through DME, unit dose form, 12 mcg

---

Special Coverage Instructions     Noncovered by Medicare     Carrier Discretion

Ⓜ ☑ **J7641** Flunisolide, inhalation solution, compounded product, administered through DME, unit dose, per mg
Use this code for Aerobid, Flunisolide.

Ⓜ ☑ **J7642** Glycopyrrolate, inhalation solution, compounded product, administered through DME, concentrated form, per mg
MED: 100-2,15,110.3

Ⓜ ☑ **J7643** Glycopyrrolate, inhalation solution, compounded product, administered through DME, unit dose form, per mg
MED: 100-2,15,110.3

Ⓜ ☑ **J7644** Ipratropium bromide, inhalation solution, FDA-approved final product, noncompounded, administered through DME, unit dose form, per mg
Use this code for Atrovent.
MED: 100-2,15,110.3

Ⓜ ☑ **J7645** Ipratropium bromide, inhalation solution, compounded product, administered through DME, unit dose form, per mg

Ⓜ ☑ **J7647** Isoetharine HCl, inhalation solution, compounded product, administered through DME, concentrated form, per mg

Ⓜ ☑ **J7648** Isoetharine HCl, inhalation solution, FDA-approved final product, noncompounded, administered through DME, concentrated form, per mg
Use this code for Beta-2.
MED: 100-2,15,110.3

Ⓜ ☑ **J7649** Isoetharine HCl, inhalation solution, FDA-approved final product, noncompounded, administered through DME, unit dose form, per mg
MED: 100-2,15,110.3

Ⓜ ☑ **J7650** Isoetharine HCl, inhalation solution, compounded product, administered through DME, unit dose form, per mg

Ⓜ ☑ **J7657** Isoproterenol HCl, inhalation solution, compounded product, administered through DME, concentrated form, per mg

Ⓜ ☑ **J7658** Isoproterenol HCl, inhalation solution, FDA-approved final product, noncompounded, administered through DME, concentrated form, per mg
Use this code for Isuprel HCl.
MED: 100-2,15,110.3

Ⓜ ☑ **J7659** Isoproterenol HCl, inhalation solution, FDA-approved final product, noncompounded, administered through DME, unit dose form, per mg
Use this code for Isuprel HCl
MED: 100-2,15,110.3

Ⓜ ☑ **J7660** Isoproterenol HCl, inhalation solution, compounded product, administered through DME, unit dose form, per mg

Ⓜ ☑ **J7667** Metaproterenol sulfate, inhalation solution, compounded product, concentrated form, per 10 mg

Ⓜ ☑ **J7668** Metaproterenol sulfate, inhalation solution, FDA-approved final product, noncompounded, administered through DME, concentrated form, per 10 mg
Use this code for Alupent
MED: 100-2,15,110.3

☑ Quantity Alert   ● New Code   ○ Recycled/Reinstated   ▲ Revised Code   ⅋ DMEPOS Paid   ⊘ SNF Excluded

**2009 HCPCS**   Ⓐ-Ⓩ ASC Payment Indicators   **MED:** Pub 100/NCD References   ♀ Female Only   ♂ Male Only   **173**

| M ☑ | **J7669** | Metaproterenol sulfate, inhalation solution, FDA-approved final product, noncompounded, administered through DME, unit dose form, per 10 mg |
| | | Use this code for Alupent. |
| | | MED: 100-2,15,110.3 |

| M ☑ | **J7670** | Metaproterenol sulfate, inhalation solution, compounded product, administered through DME, unit dose form, per 10 mg |

| N ☑ | **J7674** | Methacholine chloride administered as inhalation solution through a nebulizer, per 1 mg    🔲 |

| M ☑ | **J7676** | Pentamidine isethionate, inhalation solution, compounded product, administered through DME, unit dose form, per 300 mg |

| M ☑ | **J7680** | Terbutaline sulfate, inhalation solution, compounded product, administered through DME, concentrated form, per mg |
| | | Use this code for Brethine. |
| | | MED: 100-2,15,110.3 |

| M ☑ | **J7681** | Terbutaline sulfate, inhalation solution, compounded product, administered through DME, unit dose form, per mg |
| | | Use this code for Brethine. |
| | | MED: 100-2,15,110.3 |

| M ☑ | **J7682** | Tobramycin, inhalation solution, FDA-approved final product, noncompounded, unit dose form, administered through DME, per 300 mg |
| | | Use this code for Tobi. |
| | | MED: 100-2,15,110.3 |

| M ☑ | **J7683** | Triamcinolone, inhalation solution, compounded product, administered through DME, concentrated form, per mg |
| | | Use this code for Azmacort. |
| | | MED: 100-2,15,110.3 |

| M ☑ | **J7684** | Triamcinolone, inhalation solution, compounded product, administered through DME, unit dose form, per mg |
| | | Use this code for Azmacort. |
| | | MED: 100-2,15,110.3 |

| M ☑ | **J7685** | Tobramycin, inhalation solution, compounded product, administered through DME, unit dose form, per 300 mg |

| M | **J7699** | NOC drugs, inhalation solution administered through DME |
| | | MED: 100-2,15,110.3 |

| N | **J7799** | NOC drugs, other than inhalation drugs, administered through DME    🔲 |
| | | MED: 100-2,15,110.3 |

| B | **J8498** | Antiemetic drug, rectal/suppository, not otherwise specified |

| E | **J8499** | Prescription drug, oral, nonchemotherapeutic, NOS |
| | | MED: 100-2,15,50 |

| K ☑ | **J8501** | Aprepitant, oral, 5 mg    K2 |
| | | Use this code for Emend. |
| | | MED: 100-4,4,240; 100-4,17,80.2; 100-4,17,80.2.1; 100-4,17,80.2.4 |

| K ☑ | **J8510** | Busulfan; oral, 2 mg    K2 |
| | | Use this code for Busulfex, Myleran. |
| | | MED: 100-2,15,50.5; 100-4,4,240; 100-4,17,80.1.1 |

---

| E | ☑ | **J8515** | Cabergoline, oral, 0.25 mg |
|---|---|---|---|
| | | | Use this code for Dostinex. |
| | | | MED: 100-2,15,50.5; 100-4,4,240 |

| K | ☑ | **J8520** | Capecitabine, oral, 150 mg | K2 |
|---|---|---|---|---|
| | | | Use this code for Xeloda. |
| | | | MED: 100-2,15,50.5; 100-4,4,240; 100-4,17,80.1.1 |

| K | ☑ | **J8521** | Capecitabine, oral, 500 mg | K2 |
|---|---|---|---|---|
| | | | Use this code for Xeloda. |
| | | | MED: 100-2,15,50.5; 100-4,4,240; 100-4,17,80.1.1 |

| N | ☑ | **J8530** | Cyclophosphamide; oral, 25 mg | N1 |
|---|---|---|---|---|
| | | | Use this code for Cytoxan. |
| | | | MED: 100-2,15,50.5; 100-4,4,240; 100-4,17,80.1.1 |

| N | ☑ | **J8540** | Dexamethasone, oral, 0.25 mg | N1 |
|---|---|---|---|---|
| | | | Use this code for Decadron. |

| K | ☑ | **J8560** | Etoposide; oral, 50 mg | K2 |
|---|---|---|---|---|
| | | | Use this code for VePesid. |
| | | | MED: 100-2,15,50.5; 100-4,4,240; 100-4,17,80.1.1 |

| E | ☑ | **J8565** | Gefitinib, oral, 250 mg |
|---|---|---|---|
| | | | Use this code for Iressa. |
| | | | MED: 100-4,4,240; 100-4,17,80.1.1 |

| N | | **J8597** | Antiemetic drug, oral, not otherwise specified | N1 |
|---|---|---|---|---|

| N | ☑ | **J8600** | Melphalan; oral, 2 mg | N1 |
|---|---|---|---|---|
| | | | Use this code for Alkeran. |
| | | | MED: 100-2,15,50.5; 100-4,4,240; 100-4,17,80.1.1 |

| N | ☑ | **J8610** | Methotrexate; oral, 2.5 mg | N1 |
|---|---|---|---|---|
| | | | Use this code for Trexall. |

Methotrexate is an anti-metabolite used in the treatment of certain neoplastic diseases, severe psoriasis, and adult rheumatoid arthritis.

MED: 100-2,15,50.5; 100-4,4,240; 100-4,17,80.1.1

| K | ☑ | **J8650** | Nabilone, oral, 1 mg | K2 |
|---|---|---|---|---|
| | | | Use this code for Cesamet |

| K | ☑ | **J8700** | Temozolomide, oral, 5 mg | K2 |
|---|---|---|---|---|
| | | | Use this code for Temodar. |
| | | | MED: 100-2,15,50.5; 100-4,4,240 |

| ● | K | ☑ | **J8705** | Topotecan, oral, 0.25 mg | K2 |
|---|---|---|---|---|---|
| | | | | Use this code for Hycamtin. |

| B | | **J8999** | Prescription drug, oral, chemotherapeutic, NOS |
|---|---|---|---|

Determine if an alternative HCPCS Level II or a CPT code better describes the service being reported. This code should be used only if a more specific code is unavailable.

MED: 100-2,15,50.5; 100-4,4,240; 100-4,17,80.1.1; 100-4,17,80.1.2

## CHEMOTHERAPY DRUGS J9000-J9999

These codes cover the cost of the chemotherapy drug only, not the administration.

| ▲ | N | ☑ | **J9000** | Injection, doxorubicin HCl, 10 mg | N1 ⊘ |
|---|---|---|---|---|---|
| | | | | Use this code for Adriamycin PFS, Adriamycin RDF, Rubex. |
| | | | | MED: 100-2,15,50; 100-4,17,80.2 |

**Chemotherapy Drugs**

**J9001 — J9065**

▲ ☒K ☑ **J9001** Injection, doxorubicin HCl, all lipid formulations, 10 mg    K2 ⊘
Use this code for Doxil.
MED: 100-2,15,50; 100-4,17,80.2

▲ ☒K ☑ **J9010** Injection, alemtuzumab, 10 mg    K2 ⊘
Use this code for Campath.

▲ ☒K ☑ **J9015** Injection, aldesleukin, per single use vial    K2 ⊘
Use this code for Proleukin, IL-2, Interleukin.
MED: 100-2,15,50

▲ ☒K ☑ **J9017** Injection, arsenic trioxide, 1 mg    K2 ⊘
Use this code for Trisenox.
AHA: 2Q,'02,8

▲ ☒K ☑ **J9020** Injection, asparaginase, 10,000 units    K2 ⊘
Use this code for Elspar.
MED: 100-2,15,50

☒K ☑ **J9025** Injection, azacitidine, 1 mg    K2 ⊘
Use this code for Vidaza.

☒K ☑ **J9027** Injection, clofarabine, 1 mg    K2 ⊘
Use this code for Clolar.

☒K ☑ **J9031** BCG (intravesical) per instillation    K2
Use this code for Tice BCG, PACIS BCG, TheraCys.
MED: 100-2,15,50

● ☒G ☑ **J9033** Injection, bendamustine HCl, 1 mg    K2
Use this code for TREANDA.

☒K ☑ **J9035** Injection, bevacizumab, 10 mg    K2 ⊘
Use this code for Avastin.

▲ ☒N ☑ **J9040** Injection, bleomycin sulfate, 15 units    N1 ⊘
Use this code for Blenoxane.
MED: 100-2,15,50

☒K ☑ **J9041** Injection, bortezomib, 0.1 mg    K2 ⊘
Use this code for Velcade.

▲ ☒N ☑ **J9045** Injection, carboplatin, 50 mg    N1 ⊘
Use this code for Paraplatin, Platinol AQ.
MED: 100-2,15,50

▲ ☒K ☑ **J9050** Injection, carmustine, 100 mg    K2 ⊘
Use this code for BiCNU.
MED: 100-2,15,50; 100-4,17,80.2

☒K ☑ **J9055** Injection, cetuximab, 10 mg    K2 ⊘
Use this code for Erbitux.

☒N ☑ **J9060** Cisplatin, powder or solution, per 10 mg    N1 ⊘
Use this code for Plantinol AQ.
MED: 100-2,15,50; 100-4,17,80.2

☒N ☑ **J9062** Cisplatin, 50 mg    N1 ⊘
Use this code for Plantinol AQ.
MED: 100-2,15,50; 100-4,17,80.2

☒K ☑ **J9065** Injection, cladribine, per 1 mg    K2 ⊘
Use this code for Leustatin.
MED: 100-2,15,50

▨ Special Coverage Instructions     ▨ Noncovered by Medicare     ▨ Carrier Discretion

| | | | | |
|---|---|---|---|---|
| N ☑ | **J9070** | Cyclophosphamide, 100 mg<br>Use this code for Endoxan-Asta.<br>MED: 100-2,15,50; 100-4,17,80.2 | N1 ⊘ |
| N ☑ | **J9080** | Cyclophosphamide, 200 mg<br>Use this code for Cytoxan, Neosar.<br>MED: 100-2,15,50; 100-4,17,80.2 | N1 ⊘ |
| N ☑ | **J9090** | Cyclophosphamide, 500 mg<br>Use this code for Cytoxan, Neosar.<br>MED: 100-2,15,50; 100-4,17,80.2 | N1 ⊘ |
| N ☑ | **J9091** | Cyclophosphamide, 1 g<br>Use this code for Cytoxan, Neosar.<br>MED: 100-2,15,50; 100-4,17,80.2 | N1 ⊘ |
| N ☑ | **J9092** | Cyclophosphamide, 2 g<br>Use this code for Cytoxan, Neosar.<br>MED: 100-2,15,50; 100-4,17,80.2 | N1 ⊘ |
| N ☑ | **J9093** | Cyclophosphamide, lyophilized, 100 mg<br>Use this code for Cytoxan Lyophilized.<br>MED: 100-2,15,50; 100-4,17,80.2 | N1 ⊘ |
| N ☑ | **J9094** | Cyclophosphamide, lyophilized, 200 mg<br>Use this code for Cytoxan Lyophilized.<br>MED: 100-2,15,50; 100-4,17,80.2 | N1 ⊘ |
| N ☑ | **J9095** | Cyclophosphamide, lyophilized, 500 mg<br>Use this code for Cytoxan Lyophilized.<br>MED: 100-2,15,50; 100-4,17,80.2 | N1 ⊘ |
| N ☑ | **J9096** | Cyclophosphamide, lyophilized, 1 g<br>Use this code for Cytoxan Lyophilized.<br>MED: 100-2,15,50; 100-4,17,80.2 | N1 ⊘ |
| N ☑ | **J9097** | Cyclophosphamide, lyophilized, 2 g<br>Use this code for Cytoxan Lyophilized.<br>MED: 100-2,15,50; 100-4,17,80.2 | N1 ⊘ |
| ▲ K ☑ | **J9098** | Injection, cytarabine liposome, 10 mg<br>Use this code for Depocyt. | K2 ⊘ |
| ▲ N ☑ | **J9100** | Injection, cytarabine, 100 mg<br>Use this code for Cytosar-U, Ara-C, Tarabin CFS.<br>MED: 100-2,15,50 | N1 ⊘ |
| ▲ N ☑ | **J9110** | Injection cytarabine 500 mg<br>Use this code for Cytosar-U.<br>MED: 100-2,15,50 | N1 ⊘ |
| ▲ K ☑ | **J9120** | Injection, dactinomycin, 0.5 mg<br>Use this code for Cosmegen.<br>MED: 100-2,15,50 | K2 ⊘ |
| N ☑ | **J9130** | Dacarbazine, 100 mg<br>Use this code for DTIC-Dome.<br>MED: 100-2,15,50; 100-4,17,80.2 | N1 ⊘ |
| N ☑ | **J9140** | Dacarbazine, 200 mg<br>Use this code for DTIC-Dome.<br>MED: 100-2,15,50; 100-4,17,80.2 | N1 ⊘ |

▲ K ☑ **J9150** Injection, daunorubicin, 10 mg K2 ⊘
Use this code for Cerubidine.
MED: 100-2,15,50

▲ K ☑ **J9151** Injection, daunorubicin citrate, liposomal formulation, 10 mg K2 ⊘
Use this code for Daunoxome.
MED: 100-2,15,50

▲ K ☑ **J9160** Injection, denileukin diftitox, 300 mcg K2 ⊘
Use this code for Ontak.

▲ K ☑ **J9165** Injection, diethylstilbestrol diphosphate, 250 mg K2
MED: 100-2,15,50

▲ K ☑ **J9170** Injection, docetaxel, 20 mg K2 ⊘
Use this code for Taxotere.
MED: 100-2,15,50

N ☑ **J9175** Injection, Elliotts' B solution, 1 ml N1
MED: 100-2,15,50

K ☑ **J9178** Injection, epirubicin HCl, 2 mg K2 ⊘
Use this code for Ellence.
MED: 100-4,17,80.2

▲ N ☑ **J9181** Injection, etoposide, 10 mg N1 ⊘
Use this code for VePesid, Toposar.
MED: 100-2,15,50

~~J9182~~ ~~Etoposide, 100 mg~~
See J9181

▲ K ☑ **J9185** Injection, fludarabine phosphate, 50 mg K2 ⊘
Use this code for Fludara.
MED: 100-2,15,50

▲ N ☑ **J9190** Injection, fluorouracil, 500 mg N1
Use this code for Adrucil.
MED: 100-2,15,50

▲ K ☑ **J9200** Injection, floxuridine, 500 mg K2 ⊘
Use this code for FUDR.
MED: 100-2,15,50

▲ K ☑ **J9201** Injection, gemcitabine HCl, 200 mg K2 ⊘
Use this code for Gemzar.
MED: 100-2,15,50

K ☑ **J9202** Goserelin acetate implant, per 3.6 mg K2
Use this code for Zoladex.
MED: 100-2,15,50

▲ K ☑ **J9206** Injection, irinotecan, 20 mg K2 ⊘
Use this code for Camptosar.
MED: 100-2,15,50

● G ☑ **J9207** Injection, ixabepilone, 1 mg K2
Use this code for IXEMPRA.

▲ K ☑ **J9208** Injection, ifosfamide, 1 g K2 ⊘
Use this code for IFEX, Mitoxana.
MED: 100-2,15,50

---

▲ K ☑ **J9209** Injection, mesna, 200 mg K2
Use this code for Mesnex.
MED: 100-2,15,50

▲ K ☑ **J9211** Injection, idarubicin HCl, 5 mg K2 ⊘
Use this code for Idamycin.
MED: 100-2,15,50

N ☑ **J9212** Injection, interferon alfacon-1, recombinant, 1 mcg N1
Use this code for Infergen.
MED: 100-2,15,50

▲ K ☑ **J9213** Injection, interferon, alfa-2a, recombinant, 3 million units K2
Use this code for Roferon-A.
MED: 100-2,15,50

▲ K ☑ **J9214** Injection, interferon, alfa-2b, recombinant, 1 million units K2
Use this code for Intron A, Rebetron Kit.
MED: 100-2,15,50

▲ K ☑ **J9215** Injection, interferon, alfa-N3, (human leukocyte derived), 250,000 IU K2
Use this code for Alferon N.
MED: 100-2,15,50

▲ K ☑ **J9216** Injection, interferon, gamma-1b, 3 million units K2
Use this code for Actimmune.
MED: 100-2,15,50

K ☑ **J9217** Leuprolide acetate (for depot suspension), 7.5 mg K2
Use this code for Lupron Depot, Eligard.
MED: 100-2,15,50

K ☑ **J9218** Leuprolide acetate, per 1 mg K2
Use this code for Lupron.
MED: 100-2,15,50

K ☑ **J9219** Leuprolide acetate implant, 65 mg K2
Use this code for Lupron Implant.
MED: 100-2,15,50
AHA: 4Q,'01,5

G ☑ **J9225** Histrelin implant (Vantas), 50 mg K2 ⊘
MED: 100-2,15,50

G ☑ **J9226** Histrelin implant (Supprelin LA), 50 mg K2

▲ K ☑ **J9230** Injection, mechlorethamine HCl, (nitrogen mustard), 10 mg K2 ⊘
Use this code for Mustargen.
MED: 100-2,15,50; 100-4,17,80.2

K ☑ **J9245** Injection, melphalan HCl, 50 mg K2 ⊘
Use this code for Alkeran, L-phenylalanine mustard.
MED: 100-2,15,50

N ☑ **J9250** Methotrexate sodium, 5 mg N1
Use this code for Folex, Folex PFS, Methotrexate LPF.
MED: 100-2,15,50

N ☑ **J9260** Methotrexate sodium, 50 mg N1
Use this code for Folex, Folex PFS, Methotrexate LPF.
MED: 100-2,15,50

G ☑ **J9261** Injection, nelarabine, 50 mg K2 ⊘
Use this code for Arranon

---

☑ Quantity Alert   ● New Code   ○ Recycled/Reinstated   ▲ Revised Code   ⅙ DMEPOS Paid   ⊘ SNF Excluded

K ☑ **J9263** Injection, oxaliplatin, 0.5 mg    K2 ⊘
Use this code for Eloxatin.

K ☑ **J9264** Injection, paclitaxel protein-bound particles, 1 mg    K2 ⊘
Use this code for Abraxane.

▲ K ☑ **J9265** Injection, paclitaxel, 30 mg    K2 ⊘
Use this code for Taxol, Nov-Onxol.
MED: 100-2,15,50

▲ K ☑ **J9266** Injection, pegaspargase, per single dose vial    K2 ⊘
Use this code for Oncaspar.
MED: 100-2,15,50
AHA: 2Q,'02,8

▲ K ☑ **J9268** Injection, pentostatin, 10 mg    K2 ⊘
Use this code for Nipent.
MED: 100-2,15,50

▲ K ☑ **J9270** Injection, plicamycin, 2.5 mg    K2 ⊘
Use this code for Mithacin.
MED: 100-2,15,50

K ☑ **J9280** Mitomycin, 5 mg    K2 ⊘
Use this code for Mutamycin.
MED: 100-2,15,50

K ☑ **J9290** Mitomycin, 20 mg    K2 ⊘
Use this code for Mutamycin.
MED: 100-2,15,50

K ☑ **J9291** Mitomycin, 40 mg    K2 ⊘
Use this code for Mutamycin.
MED: 100-2,15,50

K ☑ **J9293** Injection, mitoxantrone HCl, per 5 mg    K2 ⊘
Use this code for Navantrone.
MED: 100-2,15,50

▲ K ☑ **J9300** Injection, gemtuzumab ozogamicin, 5 mg    K2 ⊘
Use this code for Mylotarg.
AHA: 2Q,'02,8

K ☑ **J9303** Injection, panitumumab, 10 mg    K2 ⊘
Use this code for Vectibix.

K ☑ **J9305** Injection, pemetrexed, 10 mg    K2 ⊘
Use this code for Alimta.

▲ K ☑ **J9310** Injection, rituximab, 100 mg    K2 ⊘
Use this code for RituXan.
MED: 100-2,15,50

▲ K ☑ **J9320** Injection, streptozocin, 1 g    K2 ⊘
Use this code for Zanosar.
MED: 100-2,15,50; 100-4,17,80.2

● G ☑ **J9330** Injection, temsirolimus, 1 mg    K2
Use this code for TORISEL.

▲ K ☑ **J9340** Injection, thiotepa, 15 mg    K2 ⊘
Use this code for Thioplex.
MED: 100-2,15,50

---

▲ K ☑ **J9350** Injection, topotecan, 4 mg  K2 ⊘
Use this code for Hycamtin.
MED: 100-2,15,50

▲ K ☑ **J9355** Injection, trastuzumab, 10 mg  K2 ⊘
Use this code for Herceptin.

▲ K ☑ **J9357** Injection, valrubicin, intravesical, 200 mg  K2 ⊘
Use this code for Valstar.
MED: 100-2,15,50

▲ N ☑ **J9360** Injection, vinblastine sulfate, 1 mg  N1 ⊘
Use this code for Velban.
MED: 100-2,15,50

N ☑ **J9370** Vincristine sulfate, 1 mg  N1 ⊘
Use this code for Oncovin, Vincasar PFS.
MED: 100-2,15,50

N ☑ **J9375** Vincristine sulfate, 2 mg  N1 ⊘
Use this code for Oncovin, Vincasar PFS.
MED: 100-2,15,50

N ☑ **J9380** Vincristine sulfate, 5 mg  N1 ⊘
Use this code for Oncovin.
MED: 100-2,15,50

▲ K ☑ **J9390** Injection, vinorelbine tartrate, 10 mg  K2 ⊘
Use this code for Navelbine.
MED: 100-2,15,50

K ☑ **J9395** Injection, fulvestrant, 25 mg  K2 ⊘
Use this code for Fastodex.

▲ K ☑ **J9600** Injection, porfimer sodium, 75 mg  K2 ⊘
Use this code for Photofrin.
MED: 100-2,15,50

N **J9999** Not otherwise classified, antineoplastic drugs  N1
Determine if an alternative HCPCS Level II or a CPT code better describes
the service being reported. This code should be used only if a more specific
code is unavailable.
MED: 100-2,15,50; 100-3,110.2

---

☑ Quantity Alert  ● New Code  ○ Recycled/Reinstated  ▲ Revised Code  ♿ DMEPOS Paid  ⊘ SNF Excluded

## TEMPORARY CODES K0000-K9999

The K codes were established for use by the DME Medicare Administrative Contractors (DME MACs). The K codes are developed when the currently existing permanent national codes for supplies and certain product categories do not include the codes needed to implement a DME MAC medical review policy.

## K CODES ASSIGNED TO DURABLE MEDICAL EQUIPMENT ADMINISTRATIVE CONTRACTORS (DME MACS)

### WHEELCHAIR AND WHEELCHAIR ACCESSORIES

| | | | | |
|---|---|---|---|---|
| Y | | K0001 | Standard wheelchair | ⊘ ৬ |
| Y | | K0002 | Standard hemi (low seat) wheelchair | ⊘ ৬ |
| Y | | K0003 | Lightweight wheelchair | ⊘ ৬ |
| Y | | K0004 | High strength, lightweight wheelchair | ⊘ ৬ |
| Y | | K0005 | Ultralightweight wheelchair | ⊘ ৬ |
| Y | | K0006 | Heavy-duty wheelchair | ⊘ ৬ |
| Y | | K0007 | Extra heavy-duty wheelchair | ⊘ ৬ |
| Y | | K0009 | Other manual wheelchair/base | ⊘ |
| Y | | K0010 | Standard-weight frame motorized/power wheelchair | ⊘ ৬ |
| Y | | K0011 | Standard-weight frame motorized/power wheelchair with programmable control parameters for speed adjustment, tremor dampening, acceleration control and braking | ⊘ ৬ |
| Y | | K0012 | Lightweight portable motorized/power wheelchair | ⊘ ৬ |
| Y | | K0014 | Other motorized/power wheelchair base | ⊘ |
| Y | ☑ | K0015 | Detachable, nonadjustable height armrest, each | ⊘ ৬ |
| Y | ☑ | K0017 | Detachable, adjustable height armrest, base, each | ⊘ ৬ |
| Y | ☑ | K0018 | Detachable, adjustable height armrest, upper portion, each | ⊘ ৬ |
| Y | ☑ | K0019 | Arm pad, each | ⊘ ৬ |
| Y | ☑ | K0020 | Fixed, adjustable height armrest, pair | ⊘ ৬ |
| Y | ☑ | K0037 | High mount flip-up footrest, each | ⊘ ৬ |
| Y | ☑ | K0038 | Leg strap, each | ⊘ ৬ |
| Y | ☑ | K0039 | Leg strap, H style, each | ⊘ ৬ |
| Y | ☑ | K0040 | Adjustable angle footplate, each | ⊘ ৬ |
| Y | ☑ | K0041 | Large size footplate, each | ⊘ ৬ |
| Y | ☑ | K0042 | Standard size footplate, each | ⊘ ৬ |
| Y | ☑ | K0043 | Footrest, lower extension tube, each | ⊘ ৬ |
| Y | ☑ | K0044 | Footrest, upper hanger bracket, each | ⊘ ৬ |
| Y | | K0045 | Footrest, complete assembly | ⊘ ৬ |
| Y | ☑ | K0046 | Elevating legrest, lower extension tube, each | ⊘ ৬ |
| Y | ☑ | K0047 | Elevating legrest, upper hanger bracket, each | ⊘ ৬ |
| Y | | K0050 | Ratchet assembly | ⊘ ৬ |
| Y | ☑ | K0051 | Cam release assembly, footrest or legrest, each | ⊘ ৬ |

| | | | | |
|---|---|---|---|---|
| Y | ☑ | **K0052** | Swingaway, detachable footrests, each | ⊘ ⅄ |
| Y | ☑ | **K0053** | Elevating footrests, articulating (telescoping), each | ⊘ ⅄ |
| Y | ☑ | **K0056** | Seat height less than 17 in or equal to or greater than 21 in for a high-strength, lightweight, or ultralightweight wheelchair | ⊘ ⅄ |
| Y | ☑ | **K0065** | Spoke protectors, each | ⊘ ⅄ |
| Y | ☑ | **K0069** | Rear wheel assembly, complete, with solid tire, spokes or molded, each | ⊘ ⅄ |
| Y | ☑ | **K0070** | Rear wheel assembly, complete, with pneumatic tire, spokes or molded, each | ⊘ ⅄ |
| Y | ☑ | **K0071** | Front caster assembly, complete, with pneumatic tire, each | ⊘ ⅄ |
| Y | ☑ | **K0072** | Front caster assembly, complete, with semipneumatic tire, each | ⊘ ⅄ |
| Y | ☑ | **K0073** | Caster pin lock, each | ⊘ ⅄ |
| Y | ☑ | **K0077** | Front caster assembly, complete, with solid tire, each | ⊘ ⅄ |
| Y | | **K0098** | Drive belt for power wheelchair | ⊘ ⅄ |
| Y | ☑ | **K0105** | IV hanger, each | ⊘ ⅄ |
| Y | | **K0108** | Wheelchair component or accessory, not otherwise specified | ⊘ |
| Y | | **K0195** | Elevating legrests, pair (for use with capped rental wheelchair base) ⊘ ⅄ |
| | | | MED: 100-3,230.10 | |
| Y | | **K0455** | Infusion pump used for uninterrupted parenteral administration of medication, (e.g., epoprostenol or treprostinol) | ⊘ ⅄ |
| | | | MED: 100-3,280.14 | |
| Y | | **K0462** | Temporary replacement for patient-owned equipment being repaired, any type | ⊘ |
| | | | MED: 100-4,20,40.1 | |
| Y | ☑ | **K0552** | Supplies for external drug infusion pump, syringe type cartridge, sterile, each | ⊘ ⅄ |
| | | | MED: 100-3,280.14 | |
| Y | ☑ | **K0601** | Replacement battery for external infusion pump owned by patient, silver oxide, 1.5 volt, each | ⊘ ⅄ |
| | | | AHA: 2Q,'03,7 | |
| Y | ☑ | **K0602** | Replacement battery for external infusion pump owned by patient, silver oxide, 3 volt, each | ⊘ ⅄ |
| | | | AHA: 2Q,'03,7 | |
| Y | ☑ | **K0603** | Replacement battery for external infusion pump owned by patient, alkaline, 1.5 volt, each | ⊘ ⅄ |
| | | | AHA: 2Q,'03,7 | |
| Y | ☑ | **K0604** | Replacement battery for external infusion pump owned by patient, lithium, 3.6 volt, each | ⊘ ⅄ |
| | | | AHA: 2Q,'03,7 | |
| Y | ☑ | **K0605** | Replacement battery for external infusion pump owned by patient, lithium, 4.5 volt, each | ⊘ ⅄ |
| | | | AHA: 2Q,'03,7 | |
| Y | | **K0606** | Automatic external defibrillator, with integrated electrocardiogram analysis, garment type | ⊘ ⅄ |
| | | | AHA: 4Q,'03,4 | |
| Y | ☑ | **K0607** | Replacement battery for automated external defibrillator, garment type only, each | ⊘ ⅄ |
| | | | AHA: 4Q,'03,4 | |

---

☑ Quantity Alert  ● New Code  ○ Recycled/Reinstated  ▲ Revised Code  ⅄ DMEPOS Paid  ⊘ SNF Excluded

Ⓨ ☑ **K0608** Replacement garment for use with automated external defibrillator, each      ⊘ ♿

AHA: 4Q,'03,4

Ⓨ ☑ **K0609** Replacement electrodes for use with automated external defibrillator, garment type only, each      ⊘ ♿

AHA: 4Q,'03,4

▲ Ⓨ **K0669** Wheelchair accessory, wheelchair seat or back cushion, does not meet specific code criteria or no written coding verification from DME PDAC

● Ⓐ ☑ **K0672** Addition to lower extremity orthotic, removable soft interface, all components, replacement only, each      ♿

Ⓨ **K0730** Controlled dose inhalation drug delivery system

Ⓨ **K0733** Power wheelchair accessory, 12 to 24 amp hour sealed lead acid battery, each (e.g., gel cell, absorbed glassmat)      ♿

Ⓨ **K0734** Skin protection wheelchair seat cushion, adjustable, width less than 22 in, any depth

Ⓨ **K0735** Skin protection wheelchair seat cushion, adjustable, width 22 in or greater, any depth

Ⓨ **K0736** Skin protection and positioning wheelchair seat cushion, adjustable, width less than 22 in, any depth

Ⓨ **K0737** Skin protection and positioning wheelchair seat cushion, adjustable, width 22 in or greater, any depth

Ⓨ **K0738** Portable gaseous oxygen system, rental; home compressor used to fill portable oxygen cylinders; includes portable containers, regulator, flowmeter, humidifier, cannula or mask, and tubing

Ⓨ **K0800** Power operated vehicle, group 1 standard, patient weight capacity up to and including 300 pounds      ♿

Ⓨ **K0801** Power operated vehicle, group 1 heavy-duty, patient weight capacity 301 to 450 pounds      ♿

Ⓨ **K0802** Power operated vehicle, group 1 very heavy-duty, patient weight capacity 451 to 600 pounds      ♿

Ⓨ **K0806** Power operated vehicle, group 2 standard, patient weight capacity up to and including 300 pounds      ♿

Ⓨ **K0807** Power operated vehicle, group 2 heavy-duty, patient weight capacity 301 to 450 pounds      ♿

Ⓨ **K0808** Power operated vehicle, group 2 very heavy-duty, patient weight capacity 451 to 600 pounds      ♿

Ⓨ **K0812** Power operated vehicle, not otherwise classified      ♿

Ⓨ **K0813** Power wheelchair, group 1 standard, portable, sling/solid seat and back, patient weight capacity up to and including 300 pounds      ♿

Ⓨ **K0814** Power wheelchair, group 1 standard, portable, captain's chair, patient weight capacity up to and including 300 pounds      ♿

Ⓨ **K0815** Power wheelchair, group 1 standard, sling/solid seat and back, patient weight capacity up to and including 300 pounds      ♿

Ⓨ **K0816** Power wheelchair, group 1 standard, captain's chair, patient weight capacity up to and including 300 pounds      ♿

Ⓨ **K0820** Power wheelchair, group 2 standard, portable, sling/solid seat/back, patient weight capacity up to and including 300 pounds      ♿

| ☑ | K0821 | Power wheelchair, group 2 standard, portable, captain's chair, patient weight capacity up to and including 300 pounds   🦽 |
| ☑ | K0822 | Power wheelchair, group 2 standard, sling/solid seat/back, patient weight capacity up to and including 300 pounds   🦽 |
| ☑ | K0823 | Power wheelchair, group 2 standard, captain's chair, patient weight capacity up to and including 300 pounds   🦽 |
| ☑ | K0824 | Power wheelchair, group 2 heavy-duty, sling/solid seat/back, patient weight capacity 301 to 450 pounds   🦽 |
| ☑ | K0825 | Power wheelchair, group 2 heavy-duty, captain's chair, patient weight capacity 301 to 450 pounds   🦽 |
| ☑ | K0826 | Power wheelchair, group 2 very heavy-duty, sling/solid seat/back, patient weight capacity 451 to 600 pounds   🦽 |
| ☑ | K0827 | Power wheelchair, group 2 very heavy-duty, captain's chair, patient weight capacity 451 to 600 pounds   🦽 |
| ☑ | K0828 | Power wheelchair, group 2 extra heavy-duty, sling/solid seat/back, patient weight capacity 601 pounds or more   🦽 |
| ☑ | K0829 | Power wheelchair, group 2 extra heavy-duty, captain's chair, patient weight 601 pounds or more   🦽 |
| ☑ | K0830 | Power wheelchair, group 2 standard, seat elevator, sling/solid seat/back, patient weight capacity up to and including 300 pounds   🦽 |
| ☑ | K0831 | Power wheelchair, group 2 standard, seat elevator, captain's chair, patient weight capacity up to and including 300 pounds   🦽 |
| ☑ | K0835 | Power wheelchair, group 2 standard, single power option, sling/solid seat/back, patient weight capacity up to and including 300 pounds   🦽 |
| ☑ | K0836 | Power wheelchair, group 2 standard, single power option, captain's chair, patient weight capacity up to and including 300 pounds   🦽 |
| ☑ | K0837 | Power wheelchair, group 2 heavy-duty, single power option, sling/solid seat/back, patient weight capacity 301 to 450 pounds   🦽 |
| ☑ | K0838 | Power wheelchair, group 2 heavy-duty, single power option, captain's chair, patient weight capacity 301 to 450 pounds   🦽 |
| ☑ | K0839 | Power wheelchair, group 2 very heavy-duty, single power option sling/solid seat/back, patient weight capacity 451 to 600 pounds   🦽 |
| ☑ | K0840 | Power wheelchair, group 2 extra heavy-duty, single power option, sling/solid seat/back, patient weight capacity 601 pounds or more   🦽 |
| ☑ | K0841 | Power wheelchair, group 2 standard, multiple power option, sling/solid seat/back, patient weight capacity up to and including 300 pounds   🦽 |
| ☑ | K0842 | Power wheelchair, group 2 standard, multiple power option, captain's chair, patient weight capacity up to and including 300 pounds   🦽 |
| ☑ | K0843 | Power wheelchair, group 2 heavy-duty, multiple power option, sling/solid seat/back, patient weight capacity 301 to 450 pounds   🦽 |
| ☑ | K0848 | Power wheelchair, group 3 standard, sling/solid seat/back, patient weight capacity up to and including 300 pounds   🦽 |
| ☑ | K0849 | Power wheelchair, group 3 standard, captain's chair, patient weight capacity up to and including 300 pounds   🦽 |
| ☑ | K0850 | Power wheelchair, group 3 heavy-duty, sling/solid seat/back, patient weight capacity 301 to 450 pounds   🦽 |

---

☑ Quantity Alert    ● New Code    ○ Recycled/Reinstated    ▲ Revised Code    🦽 DMEPOS Paid    ⊘ SNF Excluded

Temporary Codes

K0851 — K0884

| | | | |
|---|---|---|---|
| Ⓨ | **K0851** | Power wheelchair, group 3 heavy-duty, captain's chair, patient weight capacity 301 to 450 pounds | ♿ |
| Ⓨ | **K0852** | Power wheelchair, group 3 very heavy-duty, sling/solid seat/back, patient weight capacity 451 to 600 pounds | ♿ |
| Ⓨ | **K0853** | Power wheelchair, group 3 very heavy-duty, captain's chair, patient weight capacity 451 to 600 pounds | ♿ |
| Ⓨ | **K0854** | Power wheelchair, group 3 extra heavy-duty, sling/solid seat/back, patient weight capacity 601 pounds or more | ♿ |
| Ⓨ | **K0855** | Power wheelchair, group 3 extra heavy duty, captain's chair, patient weight capacity 601 pounds or more | ♿ |
| Ⓨ | **K0856** | Power wheelchair, group 3 standard, single power option, sling/solid seat/back, patient weight capacity up to and including 300 pounds | ♿ |
| Ⓨ | **K0857** | Power wheelchair, group 3 standard, single power option, captain's chair, patient weight capacity up to and including 300 pounds | ♿ |
| Ⓨ | **K0858** | Power wheelchair, group 3 heavy-duty, single power option, sling/solid seat/back, patient weight 301 to 450 pounds | ♿ |
| Ⓨ | **K0859** | Power wheelchair, group 3 heavy-duty, single power option, captain's chair, patient weight capacity 301 to 450 pounds | ♿ |
| Ⓨ | **K0860** | Power wheelchair, group 3 very heavy-duty, single power option, sling/solid seat/back, patient weight capacity 451 to 600 pounds | ♿ |
| Ⓨ | **K0861** | Power wheelchair, group 3 standard, multiple power option, sling/solid seat/back, patient weight capacity up to and including 300 pounds | ♿ |
| Ⓨ | **K0862** | Power wheelchair, group 3 heavy-duty, multiple power option, sling/solid seat/back, patient weight capacity 301 to 450 pounds | ♿ |
| Ⓨ | **K0863** | Power wheelchair, group 3 very heavy-duty, multiple power option, sling/solid seat/back, patient weight capacity 451 to 600 pounds | ♿ |
| Ⓨ | **K0864** | Power wheelchair, group 3 extra heavy-duty, multiple power option, sling/solid seat/back, patient weight capacity 601 pounds or more | ♿ |
| Ⓨ | **K0868** | Power wheelchair, group 4 standard, sling/solid seat/back, patient weight capacity up to and including 300 pounds | ♿ |
| Ⓨ | **K0869** | Power wheelchair, group 4 standard, captain's chair, patient weight capacity up to and including 300 pounds | ♿ |
| Ⓨ | **K0870** | Power wheelchair, group 4 heavy-duty, sling/solid seat/back, patient weight capacity 301 to 450 pounds | ♿ |
| Ⓨ | **K0871** | Power wheelchair, group 4 very heavy-duty, sling/solid seat/back, patient weight capacity 451 to 600 pounds | ♿ |
| Ⓨ | **K0877** | Power wheelchair, group 4 standard, single power option, sling/solid seat/back, patient weight capacity up to and including 300 pounds | ♿ |
| Ⓨ | **K0878** | Power wheelchair, group 4 standard, single power option, captain's chair, patient weight capacity up to and including 300 pounds | ♿ |
| Ⓨ | **K0879** | Power wheelchair, group 4 heavy-duty, single power option, sling/solid seat/back, patient weight capacity 301 to 450 pounds | ♿ |
| Ⓨ | **K0880** | Power wheelchair, group 4 very heavy-duty, single power option, sling/solid seat/back, patient weight 451 to 600 pounds | ♿ |
| Ⓨ | **K0884** | Power wheelchair, group 4 standard, multiple power option, sling/solid seat/back, patient weight capacity up to and including 300 pounds | ♿ |

| | | | |
|---|---|---|---|
| Y | K0885 | Power wheelchair, group 4 standard, multiple power option, captain's chair, patient weight capacity up to and including 300 pounds | &#9855; |
| Y | K0886 | Power wheelchair, group 4 heavy-duty, multiple power option, sling/solid seat/back, patient weight capacity 301 to 450 pounds | &#9855; |
| Y | K0890 | Power wheelchair, group 5 pediatric, single power option, sling/solid seat/back, patient weight capacity up to and including 125 pounds | &#9855; |
| Y | K0891 | Power wheelchair, group 5 pediatric, multiple power option, sling/solid seat/back, patient weight capacity up to and including 125 pounds | &#9855; |
| Y | K0898 | Power wheelchair, not otherwise classified | &#9855; |
| ▲ Y | K0899 | Power mobility device, not coded by DME PDAC or does not meet criteria | &#9855; |

Orthotic Procedures

L0112 — L0430

## ORTHOTIC PROCEDURES AND DEVICES L0000-L4999

L codes include orthotic and prosthetic procedures and devices, as well as scoliosis equipment, orthopedic shoes, and prosthetic implants.

## ORTHOTIC DEVICES - SPINAL

### CERVICAL

| | | | |
|---|---|---|---|
| Ⓐ | L0112 | Cranial cervical orthotic, congenital torticollis type, with or without soft interface material, adjustable range of motion joint, custom fabricated |
| ● Ⓐ | L0113 | Cranial cervical orthotic, torticollis type, with or without joint, with or without soft interface material, prefabricated, includes fitting and adjustment |
| Ⓐ | L0120 | Cervical, flexible, nonadjustable (foam collar) |
| Ⓐ | L0130 | Cervical, flexible, thermoplastic collar, molded to patient |
| Ⓐ | L0140 | Cervical, semi-rigid, adjustable (plastic collar) |
| Ⓐ | L0150 | Cervical, semi-rigid, adjustable molded chin cup (plastic collar with mandibular/occipital piece) |
| Ⓐ | L0160 | Cervical, semi-rigid, wire frame occipital/mandibular support |
| Ⓐ | L0170 | Cervical, collar, molded to patient model |
| Ⓐ | L0172 | Cervical, collar, semi-rigid thermoplastic foam, 2 piece |
| Ⓐ | L0174 | Cervical, collar, semi-rigid, thermoplastic foam, 2 piece with thoracic extension |

### MULTIPLE POST COLLAR

| | | | |
|---|---|---|---|
| Ⓐ | L0180 | Cervical, multiple post collar, occipital/mandibular supports, adjustable |
| Ⓐ | L0190 | Cervical, multiple post collar, occipital/mandibular supports, adjustable cervical bars (SOMI, Guilford, Taylor types) |
| Ⓐ | L0200 | Cervical, multiple post collar, occipital/mandibular supports, adjustable cervical bars, and thoracic extension |

### THORACIC

| | | | |
|---|---|---|---|
| Ⓐ | L0210 | Thoracic, rib belt |
| Ⓐ | L0220 | Thoracic, rib belt, custom fabricated |
| Ⓐ | L0430 | Spinal orthotic, anterior-posterior-lateral control, with interface material, custom fitted (DeWall Posture Protector only) |

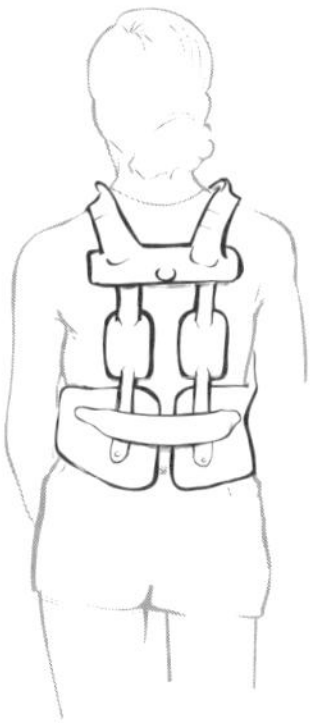

TLSO brace with adjustable straps and pads (L0450). The model at right and similar devices such as the Boston brace are molded polymer over foam and may be bivalve (front and back components)

Thoracic lumbar sacral orthosis (TLSO)

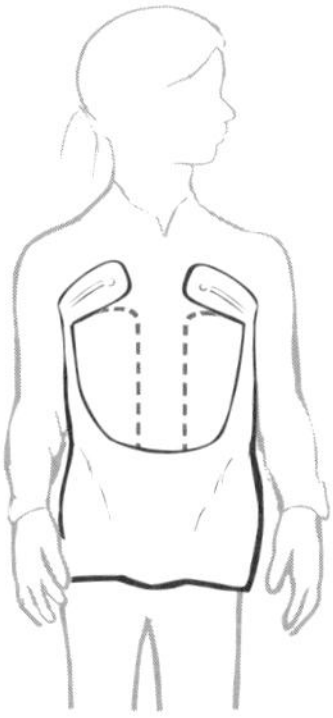



[A] **L0450** **Thoracic-lumbar-sacral orthotic (TLSO), flexible, provides trunk support, upper thoracic region, produces intracavitary pressure to reduce load on the intervertebral disks with rigid stays or panel(s), includes shoulder straps and closures, prefabricated, includes fitting and adjustment**

[A] **L0452** **Thoracic-lumbar-sacral orthotic (TLSO), flexible, provides trunk support, upper thoracic region, produces intracavitary pressure to reduce load on the intervertebral disks with rigid stays or panel(s), includes shoulder straps and closures, custom fabricated**

[A] **L0454** **Thoracic-lumbar-sacral orthotic (TLSO) flexible, provides trunk support, extends from sacrococcygeal junction to above T-9 vertebra, restricts gross trunk motion in the sagittal plane, produces intracavitary pressure to reduce load on the intervertebral disks with rigid stays or panel(s), includes shoulder straps and closures, prefabricated, includes fitting and adjustment**

[A] **L0456** **Thoracic-lumbar-sacral orthotic (TLSO), flexible, provides trunk support, thoracic region, rigid posterior panel and soft anterior apron, extends from the sacrococcygeal junction and terminates just inferior to the scapular spine, restricts gross trunk motion in the sagittal plane, produces intracavitary pressure to reduce load on the intervertebral disks, includes straps and closures, prefabricated, includes fitting and adjustment**

[A] **L0458** **Thoracic-lumbar-sacral orthotic (TLSO), triplanar control, modular segmented spinal system, 2 rigid plastic shells, posterior extends from the sacrococcygeal junction and terminates just inferior to the scapular spine, anterior extends from the symphysis pubis to the xiphoid, soft liner, restricts gross trunk motion in the sagittal, coronal, and transverse planes, lateral strength is provided by overlapping plastic and stabilizing closures, includes straps and closures, prefabricated, includes fitting and adjustment**

[A] **L0460** **Thoracic-lumbar-sacral orthotic (TLSO), triplanar control, modular segmented spinal system, 2 rigid plastic shells, posterior extends from the sacrococcygeal junction and terminates just inferior to the scapular spine, anterior extends from the symphysis pubis to the sternal notch, soft liner, restricts gross trunk motion in the sagittal, coronal, and transverse planes, lateral strength is provided by overlapping plastic and stabilizing closures, includes straps and closures, prefabricated, includes fitting and adjustment** ♿

**Orthotic Procedures**

**L0462 — L0480**

[A]   **L0462**   Thoracic-lumbar-sacral orthotic (TLSO), triplanar control, modular segmented spinal system, 3 rigid plastic shells, posterior extends from the sacrococcygeal junction and terminates just inferior to the scapular spine, anterior extends from the symphysis pubis to the sternal notch, soft liner, restricts gross trunk motion in the sagittal, coronal, and transverse planes, lateral strength is provided by overlapping plastic and stabilizing closures, includes straps and closures, prefabricated, includes fitting and adjustment    &#9851;

[A]   **L0464**   Thoracic-lumbar-sacral orthotic (TLSO), triplanar control, modular segmented spinal system, 4 rigid plastic shells, posterior extends from sacrococcygeal junction and terminates just inferior to scapular spine, anterior extends from symphysis pubis to the sternal notch, soft liner, restricts gross trunk motion in sagittal, coronal, and transverse planes, lateral strength is provided by overlapping plastic and stabilizing closures, includes straps and closures, prefabricated, includes fitting and adjustment    &#9851;

[A]   **L0466**   Thoracic-lumbar-sacral orthotic (TLSO), sagittal control, rigid posterior frame and flexible soft anterior apron with straps, closures and padding, restricts gross trunk motion in sagittal plane, produces intracavitary pressure to reduce load on intervertebral disks, includes fitting and shaping the frame, prefabricated, includes fitting and adjustment    &#9851;

[A]   **L0468**   Thoracic-lumbar-sacral orthotic (TLSO), sagittal-coronal control, rigid posterior frame and flexible soft anterior apron with straps, closures and padding, extends from sacrococcygeal junction over scapulae, lateral strength provided by pelvic, thoracic, and lateral frame pieces, restricts gross trunk motion in sagittal, and coronal planes, produces intracavitary pressure to reduce load on intervertebral disks, includes fitting and shaping the frame, prefabricated, includes fitting and adjustment    &#9851;

[A]   **L0470**   Thoracic-lumbar-sacral orthotic (TLSO), triplanar control, rigid posterior frame and flexible soft anterior apron with straps, closures and padding, extends from sacrococcygeal junction to scapula, lateral strength provided by pelvic, thoracic, and lateral frame pieces, rotational strength provided by subclavicular extensions, restricts gross trunk motion in sagittal, coronal, and transverse planes, produces intracavitary pressure to reduce load on the intervertebral disks, includes fitting and shaping the frame, prefabricated, includes fitting and adjustment    &#9851;

[A]   **L0472**   Thoracic-lumbar-sacral orthotic (TLSO), triplanar control, hyperextension, rigid anterior and lateral frame extends from symphysis pubis to sternal notch with 2 anterior components (one pubic and one sternal), posterior and lateral pads with straps and closures, limits spinal flexion, restricts gross trunk motion in sagittal, coronal, and transverse planes, includes fitting and shaping the frame, prefabricated, includes fitting and adjustment    &#9851;

[A]   **L0480**   Thoracic-lumbar-sacral orthotic (TLSO), triplanar control, 1 piece rigid plastic shell without interface liner, with multiple straps and closures, posterior extends from sacrococcygeal junction and terminates just inferior to scapular spine, anterior extends from symphysis pubis to sternal notch, anterior or posterior opening, restricts gross trunk motion in sagittal, coronal, and transverse planes, includes a carved plaster or CAD-CAM model, custom fabricated    &#9851;

| | | |
|---|---|---|
| A | L0482 | Thoracic-lumbar-sacral orthotic (TLSO), triplanar control, 1 piece rigid plastic shell with interface liner, multiple straps and closures, posterior extends from sacrococcygeal junction and terminates just inferior to scapular spine, anterior extends from symphysis pubis to sternal notch, anterior or posterior opening, restricts gross trunk motion in sagittal, coronal, and transverse planes, includes a carved plaster or CAD-CAM model, custom fabricated ♿ |
| A | L0484 | Thoracic-lumbar-sacral orthotic TLSO, triplanar control, 2 piece rigid plastic shell without interface liner, with multiple straps and closures, posterior extends from sacrococcygeal junction and terminates just inferior to scapular spine, anterior extends from symphysis pubis to sternal notch, lateral strength is enhanced by overlapping plastic, restricts gross trunk motion in the sagittal, coronal, and transverse planes, includes a carved plaster or CAD-CAM model, custom fabricated ♿ |
| A | L0486 | Thoracic-lumbar-sacral orthotic (TLSO), triplanar control, 2 piece rigid plastic shell with interface liner, multiple straps and closures, posterior extends from sacrococcygeal junction and terminates just inferior to scapular spine, anterior extends from symphysis pubis to sternal notch, lateral strength is enhanced by overlapping plastic, restricts gross trunk motion in the sagittal, coronal, and transverse planes, includes a carved plaster or CAD-CAM model, custom fabricated ♿ |
| A | L0488 | Thoracic-lumbar-sacral orthotic (TLSO), triplanar control, 1 piece rigid plastic shell with interface liner, multiple straps and closures, posterior extends from sacrococcygeal junction and terminates just inferior to scapular spine, anterior extends from symphysis pubis to sternal notch, anterior or posterior opening, restricts gross trunk motion in sagittal, coronal, and transverse planes, prefabricated, includes fitting and adjustment ♿ |
| A | L0490 | Thoracic-lumbar-sacral orthotic (TLSO), sagittal-coronal control, 1 piece rigid plastic shell, with overlapping reinforced anterior, with multiple straps and closures, posterior extends from sacrococcygeal junction and terminates at or before the T-9 vertebra, anterior extends from symphysis pubis to xiphoid, anterior opening, restricts gross trunk motion in sagittal and coronal planes, prefabricated, includes fitting and adjustment ♿ |
| A | L0491 | Thoracic-lumbar-sacral orthotic (TLSO), sagittal-coronal control, modular segmented spinal system, 2 rigid plastic shells, posterior extends from the sacrococcygeal junction and terminates just inferior to the scapular spine, anterior extends from the symphysis pubis to the xiphoid, soft liner, restricts gross trunk motion in the sagittal and coronal planes, lateral strength is provided by overlapping plastic and stabilizing closures, includes straps and closures, prefabricated, includes fitting and adjustment |
| A | L0492 | Thoracic-lumbar-sacral orthotic (TLSO), sagittal-coronal control, modular segmented spinal system, 3 rigid plastic shells, posterior extends from the sacrococcygeal junction and terminates just inferior to the scapular spine, anterior extends from the symphysis pubis to the xiphoid, soft liner, restricts gross trunk motion in the sagittal and coronal planes, lateral strength is provided by overlapping plastic and stabilizing closures, includes straps and closures, prefabricated, includes fitting and adjustment |

## CERVICAL-THORACIC-LUMBAR-SACRAL ORTHOTIC (CTLSO)

Ⓐ **L0621** Sacroiliac orthotic, flexible, provides pelvic-sacral support, reduces motion about the sacroiliac joint, includes straps, closures, may include pendulous abdomen design, prefabricated, includes fitting and adjustment

Ⓐ **L0622** Sacroiliac orthotic, flexible, provides pelvic-sacral support, reduces motion about the sacroiliac joint, includes straps, closures, may include pendulous abdomen design, custom fabricated

Ⓐ **L0623** Sacroiliac orthotic, provides pelvic-sacral support, with rigid or semi-rigid panels over the sacrum and abdomen, reduces motion about the sacroiliac joint, includes straps, closures, may include pendulous abdomen design, prefabricated, includes fitting and adjustment

Ⓐ **L0624** Sacroiliac orthotic, provides pelvic-sacral support, with rigid or semi-rigid panels placed over the sacrum and abdomen, reduces motion about the sacroiliac joint, includes straps, closures, may include pendulous abdomen design, custom fabricated

Ⓐ **L0625** Lumbar orthotic, flexible, provides lumbar support, posterior extends from L-1 to below L-5 vertebra, produces intracavitary pressure to reduce load on the intervertebral discs, includes straps, closures, may include pendulous abdomen design, shoulder straps, stays, prefabricated, includes fitting and adjustment

Ⓐ **L0626** Lumbar orthotic, sagittal control, with rigid posterior panel(s), posterior extends from L-1 to below L-5 vertebra, produces intracavitary pressure to reduce load on the intervertebral discs, includes straps, closures, may include padding, stays, shoulder straps, pendulous abdomen design, prefabricated, includes fitting and adjustment

Ⓐ **L0627** Lumbar orthotic, sagittal control, with rigid anterior and posterior panels, posterior extends from L-1 to below L-5 vertebra, produces intracavitary pressure to reduce load on the intervertebral discs, includes straps, closures, may include padding, shoulder straps, pendulous abdomen design, prefabricated, includes fitting and adjustment

Ⓐ **L0628** Lumbar-sacral orthotic, flexible, provides lumbo-sacral support, posterior extends from sacrococcygeal junction to T-9 vertebra, produces intracavitary pressure to reduce load on the intervertebral discs, includes straps, closures, may include stays, shoulder straps, pendulous abdomen design, prefabricated, includes fitting and adjustment

Ⓐ **L0629** Lumbar-sacral orthotic, flexible, provides lumbo-sacral support, posterior extends from sacrococcygeal junction to T-9 vertebra, produces intracavitary pressure to reduce load on the intervertebral discs, includes straps, closures, may include stays, shoulder straps, pendulous abdomen design, custom fabricated

Ⓐ **L0630** Lumbar-sacral orthotic, sagittal control, with rigid posterior panel(s), posterior extends from sacrococcygeal junction to T-9 vertebra, produces intracavitary pressure to reduce load on the intervertebral discs, includes straps, closures, may include padding, stays, shoulder straps, pendulous abdomen design, prefabricated, includes fitting and adjustment

Ⓐ **L0631** Lumbar-sacral orthotic, sagittal control, with rigid anterior and posterior panels, posterior extends from sacrococcygeal junction to T-9 vertebra, produces intracavitary pressure to reduce load on the intervertebral discs, includes straps, closures, may include padding, shoulder straps, pendulous abdomen design, prefabricated, includes fitting and adjustment

Ⓐ **L0632** Lumbar-sacral orthotic (LSO), sagittal control, with rigid anterior and posterior panels, posterior extends from sacrococcygeal junction to T-9 vertebra, produces intracavitary pressure to reduce load on the intervertebral discs, includes straps, closures, may include padding, shoulder straps, pendulous abdomen design, custom fabricated

Ⓐ **L0633** Lumbar-sacral orthotic (LSO), sagittal-coronal control, with rigid posterior frame/panel(s), posterior extends from sacrococcygeal junction to T-9 vertebra, lateral strength provided by rigid lateral frame/panels, produces intracavitary pressure to reduce load on intervertebral discs, includes straps, closures, may include padding, stays, shoulder straps, pendulous abdomen design, prefabricated, includes fitting and adjustment

Ⓐ **L0634** Lumbar-sacral orthotic (LSO), sagittal-coronal control, with rigid posterior frame/panel(s), posterior extends from sacrococcygeal junction to T-9 vertebra, lateral strength provided by rigid lateral frame/panel(s), produces intracavitary pressure to reduce load on intervertebral discs, includes straps, closures, may include padding, stays, shoulder straps, pendulous abdomen design, custom fabricated

Ⓐ **L0635** Lumbar-sacral orthotic (LSO), sagittal-coronal control, lumbar flexion, rigid posterior frame/panel(s), lateral articulating design to flex the lumbar spine, posterior extends from sacrococcygeal junction to T-9 vertebra, lateral strength provided by rigid lateral frame/panel(s), produces intracavitary pressure to reduce load on intervertebral discs, includes straps, closures, may include padding, anterior panel, pendulous abdomen design, prefabricated, includes fitting and adjustment

Ⓐ **L0636** Lumbar-sacral orthotic (LSO), sagittal-coronal control, lumbar flexion, rigid posterior frame/panels, lateral articulating design to flex the lumbar spine, posterior extends from sacrococcygeal junction to T-9 vertebra, lateral strength provided by rigid lateral frame/panels, produces intracavitary pressure to reduce load on intervertebral discs, includes straps, closures, may include padding, anterior panel, pendulous abdomen design, custom fabricated

Ⓐ **L0637** Lumbar-sacral orthotic (LSO), sagittal-coronal control, with rigid anterior and posterior frame/panels, posterior extends from sacrococcygeal junction to T-9 vertebra, lateral strength provided by rigid lateral frame/panels, produces intracavitary pressure to reduce load on intervertebral discs, includes straps, closures, may include padding, shoulder straps, pendulous abdomen design, prefabricated, includes fitting and adjustment

Ⓐ **L0638** Lumbar-sacral orthotic (LSO), sagittal-coronal control, with rigid anterior and posterior frame/panels, posterior extends from sacrococcygeal junction to T-9 vertebra, lateral strength provided by rigid lateral frame/panels, produces intracavitary pressure to reduce load on intervertebral discs, includes straps, closures, may include padding, shoulder straps, pendulous abdomen design, custom fabricated

Ⓐ **L0639** Lumbar-sacral orthotic (LSO), sagittal-coronal control, rigid shell(s)/panel(s), posterior extends from sacrococcygeal junction to T-9 vertebra, anterior extends from symphysis pubis to xyphoid, produces intracavitary pressure to reduce load on the intervertebral discs, overall strength is provided by overlapping rigid material and stabilizing closures, includes straps, closures, may include soft interface, pendulous abdomen design, prefabricated, includes fitting and adjustment

| Ⓐ | **L0640** | Lumbar-sacral orthotic (LSO), sagittal-coronal control, rigid shell(s)/panel(s), posterior extends from sacrococcygeal junction to T-9 vertebra, anterior extends from symphysis pubis to xyphoid, produces intracavitary pressure to reduce load on the intervertebral discs, overall strength is provided by overlapping rigid material and stabilizing closures, includes straps, closures, may include soft interface, pendulous abdomen design, custom fabricated |

## ANTERIOR-POSTERIOR-LATERAL CONTROL

| Ⓐ | **L0700** | Cervical-thoracic-lumbar-sacral orthosis (CTLSO), anterior-posterior-lateral control, molded to patient model, (Minerva type)    ☒ |
| Ⓐ | **L0710** | Cervical-thoracic-lumbar-sacral orthotic (CTLSO), anterior-posterior-lateral-control, molded to patient model, with interface material, (Minerva type)    ☒ |

## HALO PROCEDURE

| Ⓐ | **L0810** | Halo procedure, cervical halo incorporated into jacket vest    ☒ |
| Ⓐ | **L0820** | Halo procedure, cervical halo incorporated into plaster body jacket    ☒ |
| Ⓐ | **L0830** | Halo procedure, cervical halo incorporated into Milwaukee type orthotic    ☒ |
| Ⓐ | **L0859** | Addition to halo procedure, magnetic resonance image compatible systems, rings and pins, any material |
| Ⓐ | **L0861** | Addition to halo procedure, replacement liner/interface material    ☒ |

## ADDITIONS TO SPINAL ORTHOTIC

| Ⓐ | | **L0970** | Thoracic-lumbar-sacral orthotic (TLSO), corset front    ☒ |
| Ⓐ | | **L0972** | Lumbar-sacral orthotic (LSO), corset front    ☒ |
| Ⓐ | | **L0974** | Thoracic-lumbar-sacral orthotic (TLSO), full corset    ☒ |
| Ⓐ | | **L0976** | Lumbar-sacral orthotic (LSO), full corset    ☒ |
| Ⓐ | | **L0978** | Axillary crutch extension    ☒ |
| Ⓐ | ☑ | **L0980** | Peroneal straps, pair    ☒ |
| Ⓐ | ☑ | **L0982** | Stocking supporter grips, set of 4    ☒ |
| Ⓐ | ☑ | **L0984** | Protective body sock, each    ☒ |
| Ⓐ | | **L0999** | Addition to spinal orthotic, not otherwise specified |

**Determine if an alternative HCPCS Level II or a CPT code better describes the service being reported. This code should be used only if a more specific code is unavailable.**

## ORTHOTIC DEVICES - SCOLIOSIS PROCEDURES

The orthotic care of scoliosis differs from other orthotic care in that the treatment is more dynamic in nature and uses continual modification of the orthosis to the patient's changing condition. This coding structure uses the proper names - or eponyms - of the procedures because they have historic and universal acceptance in the profession. It should be recognized that variations to the basic procedures described by the founders/developers are accepted in various medical and orthotic practices throughout the country. All procedures include model of patient when indicated.

## CERVICAL-THORACIC-LUMBAR-SACRAL ORTHOTIC (CTLSO)

Cervical component

A variety of configurations are available for the Milwaukee brace (L1000)

Thoracic component

Axilla sling (L1010)

Lumbar-sacral component

Milwaukee-style braces; cervical thoracic lumbar sacral orthosis (CTSLO)

| | | | |
|---|---|---|---|
| Ⓐ | | L1000 | Cervical-thoracic-lumbar-sacral orthotic (CTLSO) (Milwaukee), inclusive of furnishing initial orthotic, including model    ♿ |
| Ⓐ | | L1001 | Cervical-thoracic-lumbar-sacral orthotic (CTLSO), immobilizer, infant size, prefabricated, includes fitting and adjustment    Ⓐ |
| Ⓐ | | L1005 | Tension based scoliosis orthotic and accessory pads, includes fitting and adjustment    ♿ |
| Ⓐ | | L1010 | Addition to cervical-thoracic-lumbar-sacral orthotic (CTLSO) or scoliosis orthotic, axilla sling    ♿ |
| Ⓐ | | L1020 | Addition to cervical-thoracic-lumbar-sacral orthotic (CTLSO) or scoliosis orthotic, kyphosis pad    ♿ |
| Ⓐ | | L1025 | Addition to cervical-thoracic-lumbar-sacral orthotic (CTLSO) or scoliosis orthotic, kyphosis pad, floating    ♿ |
| Ⓐ | | L1030 | Addition to cervical-thoracic-lumbar-sacral orthotic (CTLSO) or scoliosis orthotic, lumbar bolster pad    ♿ |
| Ⓐ | | L1040 | Addition to cervical-thoracic-lumbar-sacral orthotic (CTLSO) or scoliosis orthotic, lumbar or lumbar rib pad    ♿ |
| Ⓐ | | L1050 | Addition to cervical-thoracic-lumbar-sacral orthotic (CTLSO) or scoliosis orthotic, sternal pad    ♿ |
| Ⓐ | | L1060 | Addition to cervical-thoracic-lumbar-sacral orthotic (CTLSO) or scoliosis orthotic, thoracic pad    ♿ |
| Ⓐ | | L1070 | Addition to cervical-thoracic-lumbar-sacral orthotic (CTLSO) or scoliosis orthotic, trapezius sling    ♿ |
| Ⓐ | | L1080 | Addition to cervical-thoracic-lumbar-sacral orthotic (CTLSO) or scoliosis orthotic, outrigger    ♿ |
| Ⓐ | | L1085 | Addition to cervical-thoracic-lumbar-sacral orthotic (CTLSO) or scoliosis orthotic, outrigger, bilateral with vertical extensions    ♿ |
| Ⓐ | | L1090 | Addition to cervical-thoracic-lumbar-sacral orthotic (CTLSO) or scoliosis orthotic, lumbar sling    ♿ |
| Ⓐ | | L1100 | Addition to cervical-thoracic-lumbar-sacral orthotic (CTLSO) or scoliosis orthotic, ring flange, plastic or leather    ♿ |
| Ⓐ | | L1110 | Addition to cervical-thoracic-lumbar-sacral orthotic (CTLSO) or scoliosis orthotic, ring flange, plastic or leather, molded to patient model    ♿ |
| Ⓐ | ☑ | L1120 | Addition to cervical-thoracic-lumbar-sacral orthotic (CTLSO), scoliosis orthotic, cover for upright, each    ♿ |

Orthotic Procedures

L1000 — L1120

*Orthotic Procedures*

*L1200 — L1620*

## THORACIC-LUMBAR-SACRAL ORTHOSIS (TLSO) (LOW PROFILE)

| | | | |
|---|---|---|---|
| Ⓐ | | L1200 | Thoracic-lumbar-sacral orthotic (TLSO), inclusive of furnishing initial orthotic only    ♿ |
| Ⓐ | | L1210 | Addition to thoracic-lumbar-sacral orthotic (TLSO), (low profile), lateral thoracic extension    ♿ |
| Ⓐ | | L1220 | Addition to thoracic-lumbar-sacral orthotic (TLSO), (low profile), anterior thoracic extension    ♿ |
| Ⓐ | | L1230 | Addition to thoracic-lumbar-sacral orthotic (TLSO), (low profile), Milwaukee type superstructure    ♿ |
| Ⓐ | | L1240 | Addition to thoracic-lumbar-sacral orthotic (TLSO), (low profile), lumbar derotation pad    ♿ |
| Ⓐ | | L1250 | Addition to thoracic-lumbar-sacral orthotic (TLSO), (low profile), anterior ASIS pad    ♿ |
| Ⓐ | | L1260 | Addition to thoracic-lumbar-sacral orthotic (TLSO), (low profile), anterior thoracic derotation pad    ♿ |
| Ⓐ | | L1270 | Addition to thoracic-lumbar-sacral orthotic (TLSO), (low profile), abdominal pad    ♿ |
| Ⓐ ☑ | | L1280 | Addition to thoracic-lumbar-sacral orthotic (TLSO), (low profile), rib gusset (elastic), each    ♿ |
| Ⓐ | | L1290 | Addition to thoracic-lumbar-sacral orthotic (TLSO), (low profile), lateral trochanteric pad    ♿ |

## OTHER SCOLIOSIS PROCEDURES

| | | | |
|---|---|---|---|
| Ⓐ | L1300 | Other scoliosis procedure, body jacket molded to patient model    ♿ |
| Ⓐ | L1310 | Other scoliosis procedure, postoperative body jacket    ♿ |
| Ⓐ | L1499 | Spinal orthotic, not otherwise specified |

L1499 Determine if an alternative HCPCS Level II or a CPT code better describes the service being reported. This code should be used only if a more specific code is unavailable.

## THORACIC-HIP-KNEE-ANKLE ORTHOTIC (THKAO)

| | | | |
|---|---|---|---|
| Ⓐ | L1500 | Thoracic-hip-knee-ankle orthotic (THKAO), mobility frame (Newington, Parapodium types)    ♿ |
| Ⓐ | L1510 | Thoracic-hip-knee-ankle orthotic (THKAO), standing frame, with or without tray and accessories    ♿ |
| Ⓐ | L1520 | Thoracic-hip-knee-ankle orthotic (THKAO), swivel walker    ♿ |

# ORTHOTIC DEVICES - LOWER LIMB

The procedures in L1600-L2999 are considered as "base" or "basic procedures" and may be modified by listing procedure from the "additions" sections and adding them to the base procedures.

## HIP ORTHOTIC (HO) - FLEXIBLE

| | | | |
|---|---|---|---|
| Ⓐ | L1600 | Hip orthotic (HO), abduction control of hip joints, flexible, Frejka type with cover, prefabricated, includes fitting and adjustment    ♿ |
| Ⓐ | L1610 | Hip orthotic (HO), abduction control of hip joints, flexible, (Frejka cover only), prefabricated, includes fitting and adjustment    ♿ |
| Ⓐ | L1620 | Hip orthosis (HO), abduction control of hip joints, flexible, (Pavlik harness), prefabricated, includes fitting and adjustment    ♿ |

*Orthotic Procedures*

| | | |
|---|---|---|
| A | **L1630** | Hip orthotic (HO), abduction control of hip joints, semi-flexible (Von Rosen type), custom fabricated    &#9855; |
| A | **L1640** | Hip orthotic (HO), abduction control of hip joints, static, pelvic band or spreader bar, thigh cuffs, custom fabricated    &#9855; |
| A | **L1650** | Hip orthotic (HO), abduction control of hip joints, static, adjustable, (Ilfled type), prefabricated, includes fitting and adjustment    &#9855; |
| A | **L1652** | Hip orthotic, bilateral thigh cuffs with adjustable abductor spreader bar, adult size, prefabricated, includes fitting and adjustment, any type    &#9855; |
| A | **L1660** | Hip orthotic (HO), abduction control of hip joints, static, plastic, prefabricated, includes fitting and adjustment    &#9855; |
| A | **L1680** | Hip orthotic (HO), abduction control of hip joints, dynamic, pelvic control, adjustable hip motion control, thigh cuffs (Rancho hip action type), custom fabricated    &#9855; |
| A | **L1685** | Hip orthosis (HO), abduction control of hip joint, postoperative hip abduction type, custom fabricated    &#9855; |
| A | **L1686** | Hip orthotic (HO), abduction control of hip joint, postoperative hip abduction type, prefabricated, includes fitting and adjustment    &#9855; |
| A | **L1690** | Combination, bilateral, lumbo-sacral, hip, femur orthotic providing adduction and internal rotation control, prefabricated, includes fitting and adjustment    &#9855; |

## LEGG PERTHES

| | | |
|---|---|---|
| A | **L1700** | Legg Perthes orthotic, (Toronto type), custom fabricated    &#9855; |
| A | **L1710** | Legg Perthes orthotic, (Newington type), custom fabricated    &#9855; |
| A | **L1720** | Legg Perthes orthotic, trilateral, (Tachdijan type), custom fabricated    &#9855; |
| A | **L1730** | Legg Perthes orthotic, (Scottish Rite type), custom fabricated    &#9855; |
| A | **L1755** | Legg Perthes orthotic, (Patten bottom type), custom fabricated    &#9855; |

## KNEE ORTHOTIC (KO)

| | | |
|---|---|---|
| A | **L1800** | Knee orthotic (KO), elastic with stays, prefabricated, includes fitting and adjustment    &#9855; |
| A | **L1810** | Knee orthotic (KO), elastic with joints, prefabricated, includes fitting and adjustment    &#9855; |
| A | **L1815** | Knee orthotic (KO), elastic or other elastic type material with condylar pad(s), prefabricated, includes fitting and adjustment    &#9855; |
| A | **L1820** | Knee orthotic, elastic with condylar pads and joints, with or without patellar control, prefabricated, includes fitting and adjustment    &#9855; |
| A | **L1825** | Knee orthotic (KO), elastic knee cap, prefabricated, includes fitting and adjustment    &#9855; |
| A | **L1830** | Knee orthotic (KO), immobilizer, canvas longitudinal, prefabricated, includes fitting and adjustment    &#9855; |
| A | **L1831** | Knee orthotic, locking knee joint(s), positional orthotic, prefabricated, includes fitting and adjustment    &#9855; |
| A | **L1832** | Knee orthotic, adjustable knee joints (unicentric or polycentric), positional orthotic, rigid support, prefabricated, includes fitting and adjustment &#9855; |
| A | **L1834** | Knee orthotic (KO), without knee joint, rigid, custom fabricated    &#9855; |

*L1630 — L1834*

| | | |
|---|---|---|
| A | **L1836** | Knee orthotic, rigid, without joint(s), includes soft interface material, prefabricated, includes fitting and adjustment ♿ |
| A | **L1840** | Knee orthotic (KO), derotation, medial-lateral, anterior cruciate ligament, custom fabricated ♿ |
| A | **L1843** | Knee orthotic (KO), single upright, thigh and calf, with adjustable flexion and extension joint (unicentric or polycentric), medial-lateral and rotation control, with or without varus/valgus adjustment, prefabricated, includes fitting and adjustment ♿ |
| A | **L1844** | Knee orthotic (KO), single upright, thigh and calf, with adjustable flexion and extension joint (unicentric or polycentric), medial-lateral and rotation control, with or without varus/valgus adjustment, custom fabricated ♿ |
| A | **L1845** | Knee orthotic, double upright, thigh and calf, with adjustable flexion and extension joint (unicentric or polycentric), medial-lateral and rotation control, with or without varus/valgus adjustment, prefabricated, includes fitting and adjustment ♿ |
| A | **L1846** | Knee orthotic, double upright, thigh and calf, with adjustable flexion and extension joint (unicentric or polycentric), medial-lateral and rotation control, with or without varus/valgus adjustment, custom fabricated ♿ |
| A | **L1847** | Knee orthotic (KO), double upright with adjustable joint, with inflatable air support chamber(s), prefabricated, includes fitting and adjustment ♿ |
| A | **L1850** | Knee orthotic (KO), Swedish type, prefabricated, includes fitting and adjustment ♿ |
| A | **L1860** | Knee orthotic (KO), modification of supracondylar prosthetic socket, custom fabricated (SK) ♿ |

## ANKLE-FOOT ORTHOTIC (AFO)

| | | |
|---|---|---|
| A | **L1900** | Ankle-foot orthotic (AFO), spring wire, dorsiflexion assist calf band, custom fabricated ♿ |
| A | **L1901** | Ankle orthotic, elastic, prefabricated, includes fitting and adjustment (e.g., neoprene, Lycra) ♿ |
| A | **L1902** | Ankle-foot orthotic (AFO), ankle gauntlet, prefabricated, includes fitting and adjustment ♿ |
| A | **L1904** | Ankle-foot orthotic (AFO), molded ankle gauntlet, custom fabricated ♿ |
| A | **L1906** | Ankle-foot orthosis (AFO), multiligamentus ankle support, prefabricated, includes fitting and adjustment ♿ |
| A | **L1907** | AFO, supramalleolar with straps, with or without interface/pads, custom fabricated ♿ |

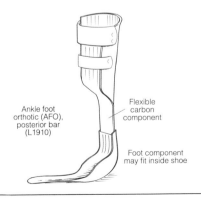

Ankle foot
orthotic (AFO),
posterior bar
(L1910)

Flexible
carbon
component

Foot component
may fit inside shoe

| A | **L1910** | Ankle-foot orthotic (AFO), posterior, single bar, clasp attachment to shoe counter, prefabricated, includes fitting and adjustment &#9855; |
|---|---|---|
| A | **L1920** | Ankle-foot orthotic (AFO), single upright with static or adjustable stop (Phelps or Perlstein type), custom fabricated &#9855; |
| A | **L1930** | Ankle-foot orthotic (AFO), plastic or other material, prefabricated, includes fitting and adjustment &#9855; |
| A | **L1932** | AFO, rigid anterior tibial section, total carbon fiber or equal material, prefabricated, includes fitting and adjustment |
| A | **L1940** | Ankle-foot orthotic (AFO), plastic or other material, custom fabricated &#9855; |

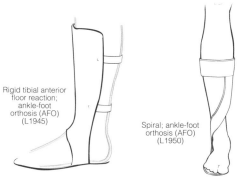

Rigid tibial anterior floor reaction; ankle-foot orthosis (AFO) (L1945)

Spiral; ankle-foot orthosis (AFO) (L1950)

| A | **L1945** | Ankle-foot orthotic (AFO), plastic, rigid anterior tibial section (floor reaction), custom fabricated &#9855; |
|---|---|---|
| A | **L1950** | Ankle-foot orthotic (AFO), spiral, (Institute of Rehabilitative Medicine type), plastic, custom fabricated &#9855; |
| A | **L1951** | Ankle-foot orthotic (AFO), spiral, (Institute of rehabilitative Medicine type), plastic or other material, prefabricated, includes fitting and adjustment &#9855; |
| A | **L1960** | Ankle-foot orthotic (AFO), posterior solid ankle, plastic, custom fabricated &#9855; |
| A | **L1970** | Ankle-foot orthotic (AFO), plastic with ankle joint, custom fabricated &#9855; |
| A | **L1971** | Ankle-foot orthotic (AFO), plastic or other material with ankle joint, prefabricated, includes fitting and adjustment &#9855; |
| A | **L1980** | Ankle-foot orthotic (AFO), single upright free plantar dorsiflexion, solid stirrup, calf band/cuff (single bar 'BK' orthotic), custom fabricated &#9855; |
| A | **L1990** | Ankle-foot orthotic (AFO), double upright free plantar dorsiflexion, solid stirrup, calf band/cuff (double bar 'BK' orthotic), custom fabricated &#9855; |

## KNEE-ANKLE-FOOT ORTHOTIC (KAFO) - OR ANY COMBINATION

| A | **L2000** | Knee-ankle-foot orthotic (KAFO), single upright, free knee, free ankle, solid stirrup, thigh and calf bands/cuffs (single bar 'AK' orthotic), custom fabricated &#9855; |
|---|---|---|
| A | **L2005** | Knee-ankle-foot orthotic (KAFO), any material, single or double upright, stance control, automatic lock and swing phase release, mechanical activation, includes ankle joint, any type, custom fabricated |
| A | **L2010** | Knee-ankle-foot orthotic (KAFO), single upright, free ankle, solid stirrup, thigh and calf bands/cuffs (single bar 'AK' orthotic), without knee joint, custom fabricated &#9855; |

---

**Orthotic Procedures**

**L2020 — L2132**

| | | |
|---|---|---|
| [A] | L2020 | Knee-ankle-foot orthotic (KAFO), double upright, free ankle, solid stirrup, thigh and calf bands/cuffs (double bar 'AK' orthotic), custom fabricated   ♿ |
| [A] | L2030 | Knee-ankle-foot orthotic (KAFO), double upright, free ankle, solid stirrup, thigh and calf bands/cuffs, (double bar 'AK' orthotic), without knee joint, custom fabricated   ♿ |
| [A] | L2034 | Knee-ankle-foot orthotic (KAFO), full plastic, single upright, with or without free motion knee, medial-lateral rotation control, with or without free motion ankle, custom fabricated |
| [A] | L2035 | Knee-ankle-foot orthotic (KAFO), full plastic, static (pediatric size), without free motion ankle, prefabricated, includes fitting and adjustment   ♿ |
| [A] | L2036 | Knee-ankle-foot orthotic (KAFO), full plastic, double upright, with or without free motion knee, with or without free motion ankle, custom fabricated   ♿ |
| [A] | L2037 | Knee-ankle-foot orthotic (KAFO), full plastic, single upright, with or without free motion knee, with or without free motion ankle, custom fabricated   ♿ |
| [A] | L2038 | Knee-ankle-foot orthotic (KAFO), full plastic, with or without free motion knee, multi-axis ankle, custom fabricated   ♿ |

### TORSION CONTROL: HIP-KNEE-ANKLE-FOOT ORTHOTIC (HKAFO)

| | | |
|---|---|---|
| [A] | L2040 | Hip-knee-ankle-foot orthotic (HKAFO), torsion control, bilateral rotation straps, pelvic band/belt, custom fabricated   ♿ |
| [A] | L2050 | Hip-knee-ankle-foot orthotic (HKAFO), torsion control, bilateral torsion cables, hip joint, pelvic band/belt, custom fabricated   ♿ |
| [A] | L2060 | Hip-knee-ankle-foot orthotic (HKAFO), torsion control, bilateral torsion cables, ball bearing hip joint, pelvic band/ belt, custom fabricated   ♿ |
| [A] | L2070 | Hip-knee-ankle-foot orthotic (HKAFO), torsion control, unilateral rotation straps, pelvic band/belt, custom fabricated   ♿ |
| [A] | L2080 | Hip-knee-ankle-foot orthotic (HKAFO), torsion control, unilateral torsion cable, hip joint, pelvic band/belt, custom fabricated   ♿ |
| [A] | L2090 | Hip-knee-ankle-foot orthotic (HKAFO), torsion control, unilateral torsion cable, ball bearing hip joint, pelvic band/ belt, custom fabricated   ♿ |
| [A] | L2106 | Ankle-foot orthotic (AFO), fracture orthotic, tibial fracture cast orthotic, thermoplastic type casting material, custom fabricated   ♿ |
| [A] | L2108 | Ankle-foot orthotic (AFO), fracture orthotic, tibial fracture cast orthotic, custom fabricated   ♿ |
| [A] | L2112 | Ankle-foot orthotic (AFO), fracture orthotic, tibial fracture orthotic, soft, prefabricated, includes fitting and adjustment   ♿ |
| [A] | L2114 | Ankle-foot orthosis (AFO), fracture orthosis, tibial fracture orthosis, semi-rigid, prefabricated, includes fitting and adjustment   ♿ |
| [A] | L2116 | Ankle-foot orthotic (AFO), fracture orthotic, tibial fracture orthotic, rigid, prefabricated, includes fitting and adjustment   ♿ |
| [A] | L2126 | Knee-ankle-foot orthotic (KAFO), fracture orthotic, femoral fracture cast orthotic, thermoplastic type casting material, custom fabricated   ♿ |
| [A] | L2128 | Knee-ankle-foot orthotic (KAFO), fracture orthotic, femoral fracture cast orthotic, custom fabricated   ♿ |
| [A] | L2132 | Knee-ankle-foot orthotic (KAFO), fracture orthotic, femoral fracture cast orthotic, soft, prefabricated, includes fitting and adjustment   ♿ |

| | | | |
|---|---|---|---|
| A | | L2134 | Knee-ankle-foot orthotic (KAFO), fracture orthotic, femoral fracture cast orthotic, semi-rigid, prefabricated, includes fitting and adjustment ♿ |
| A | | L2136 | KAFO, fracture orthotic, femoral fracture cast orthotic, rigid, prefabricated, includes fitting and adjustment ♿ |

## ADDITIONS TO FRACTURE ORTHOTIC

| | | | |
|---|---|---|---|
| A | | L2180 | Addition to lower extremity fracture orthotic, plastic shoe insert with ankle joints ♿ |
| A | | L2182 | Addition to lower extremity fracture orthotic, drop lock knee joint ♿ |
| A | | L2184 | Addition to lower extremity fracture orthotic, limited motion knee joint ♿ |
| A | | L2186 | Addition to lower extremity fracture orthotic, adjustable motion knee joint, Lerman type ♿ |
| A | | L2188 | Addition to lower extremity fracture orthotic, quadrilateral brim ♿ |
| A | | L2190 | Addition to lower extremity fracture orthotic, waist belt ♿ |
| A | | L2192 | Addition to lower extremity fracture orthotic, hip joint, pelvic band, thigh flange, and pelvic belt ♿ |

## ADDITIONS TO LOWER EXTREMITY ORTHOTIC: SHOE-ANKLE-SHIN-KNEE

| | | | |
|---|---|---|---|
| A | ☑ | L2200 | Addition to lower extremity, limited ankle motion, each joint ♿ |
| A | ☑ | L2210 | Addition to lower extremity, dorsiflexion assist (plantar flexion resist), each joint ♿ |
| A | ☑ | L2220 | Addition to lower extremity, dorsiflexion and plantar flexion assist/resist, each joint ♿ |
| A | | L2230 | Addition to lower extremity, split flat caliper stirrups and plate attachment ♿ |
| A | | L2232 | Addition to lower extremity orthotic, rocker bottom for total contact ankle-foot orthotic (AFO), for custom fabricated orthotic only |
| A | | L2240 | Addition to lower extremity, round caliper and plate attachment ♿ |
| A | | L2250 | Addition to lower extremity, foot plate, molded to patient model, stirrup attachment ♿ |
| A | | L2260 | Addition to lower extremity, reinforced solid stirrup (Scott-Craig type) ♿ |
| A | | L2265 | Addition to lower extremity, long tongue stirrup ♿ |
| A | | L2270 | Addition to lower extremity, varus/valgus correction (T) strap, padded/lined or malleolus pad ♿ |
| A | | L2275 | Addition to lower extremity, varus/valgus correction, plastic modification, padded/lined ♿ |
| A | | L2280 | Addition to lower extremity, molded inner boot ♿ |
| A | | L2300 | Addition to lower extremity, abduction bar (bilateral hip involvement), jointed, adjustable ♿ |
| A | | L2310 | Addition to lower extremity, abduction bar, straight ♿ |
| A | | L2320 | Addition to lower extremity, nonmolded lacer, for custom fabricated orthotic only ♿ |
| A | | L2330 | Addition to lower extremity, lacer molded to patient model, for custom fabricated orthotic only ♿ |
| A | | L2335 | Addition to lower extremity, anterior swing band ♿ |

| | | | |
|---|---|---|---|
| A | | L2340 | Addition to lower extremity, pretibial shell, molded to patient model ♿ |
| A | | L2350 | Addition to lower extremity, prosthetic type, (BK) socket, molded to patient model, (used for PTB, AFO orthoses) ♿ |
| A | | L2360 | Addition to lower extremity, extended steel shank ♿ |
| A | | L2370 | Addition to lower extremity, Patten bottom ♿ |
| A | | L2375 | Addition to lower extremity, torsion control, ankle joint and half solid stirrup ♿ |
| A | ☑ | L2380 | Addition to lower extremity, torsion control, straight knee joint, each joint ♿ |
| A | ☑ | L2385 | Addition to lower extremity, straight knee joint, heavy-duty, each joint ♿ |
| A | | L2387 | Addition to lower extremity, polycentric knee joint, for custom fabricated knee-ankle-foot orthotic(KAFO), each joint |
| A | ☑ | L2390 | Addition to lower extremity, offset knee joint, each joint ♿ |
| A | ☑ | L2395 | Addition to lower extremity, offset knee joint, heavy-duty, each joint ♿ |
| A | | L2397 | Addition to lower extremity orthotic, suspension sleeve ♿ |

## ADDITIONS TO STRAIGHT KNEE OR OFFSET KNEE JOINTS

| | | | |
|---|---|---|---|
| A | ☑ | L2405 | Addition to knee joint, drop lock, each ♿ |
| A | ☑ | L2415 | Addition to knee lock with integrated release mechanism (bail, cable, or equal), any material, each joint ♿ |
| A | ☑ | L2425 | Addition to knee joint, disc or dial lock for adjustable knee flexion, each joint ♿ |
| A | ☑ | L2430 | Addition to knee joint, ratchet lock for active and progressive knee extension, each joint ♿ |
| A | | L2492 | Addition to knee joint, lift loop for drop lock ring ♿ |

## ADDITIONS: THIGH/WEIGHT BEARING - GLUTEAL/ISCHIAL WEIGHT BEARING

| | | | |
|---|---|---|---|
| A | | L2500 | Addition to lower extremity, thigh/weight bearing, gluteal/ischial weight bearing, ring ♿ |
| A | | L2510 | Addition to lower extremity, thigh/weight bearing, quadri-lateral brim, molded to patient model ♿ |
| A | | L2520 | Addition to lower extremity, thigh/weight bearing, quadri-lateral brim, custom fitted ♿ |
| A | | L2525 | Addition to lower extremity, thigh/weight bearing, ischial containment/narrow M-L brim molded to patient model ♿ |
| A | | L2526 | Addition to lower extremity, thigh/weight bearing, ischial containment/narrow M-L brim, custom fitted ♿ |
| A | | L2530 | Addition to lower extremity, thigh/weight bearing, lacer, nonmolded ♿ |
| A | | L2540 | Addition to lower extremity, thigh/weight bearing, lacer, molded to patient model ♿ |
| A | | L2550 | Addition to lower extremity, thigh/weight bearing, high roll cuff ♿ |

## ADDITIONS: PELVIC AND THORACIC CONTROL

| | | | |
|---|---|---|---|
| A | ☑ | L2570 | Addition to lower extremity, pelvic control, hip joint, Clevis type, 2-position joint, each ♿ |
| A | | L2580 | Addition to lower extremity, pelvic control, pelvic sling ♿ |

| | | |
|---|---|---|
| A ☑ | L2600 | Addition to lower extremity, pelvic control, hip joint, Clevis type, or thrust bearing, free, each ♿ |
| A ☑ | L2610 | Addition to lower extremity, pelvic control, hip joint, Clevis or thrust bearing, lock, each ♿ |
| A ☑ | L2620 | Addition to lower extremity, pelvic control, hip joint, heavy-duty, each ♿ |
| A ☑ | L2622 | Addition to lower extremity, pelvic control, hip joint, adjustable flexion, each ♿ |
| A ☑ | L2624 | Addition to lower extremity, pelvic control, hip joint, adjustable flexion, extension, abduction control, each ♿ |
| A | L2627 | Addition to lower extremity, pelvic control, plastic, molded to patient model, reciprocating hip joint and cables ♿ |
| A | L2628 | Addition to lower extremity, pelvic control, metal frame, reciprocating hip joint and cables ♿ |
| A | L2630 | Addition to lower extremity, pelvic control, band and belt, unilateral ♿ |
| A | L2640 | Addition to lower extremity, pelvic control, band and belt, bilateral ♿ |
| A ☑ | L2650 | Addition to lower extremity, pelvic and thoracic control, gluteal pad, each ♿ |
| A | L2660 | Addition to lower extremity, thoracic control, thoracic band ♿ |
| A | L2670 | Addition to lower extremity, thoracic control, paraspinal uprights ♿ |
| A | L2680 | Addition to lower extremity, thoracic control, lateral support uprights ♿ |

## ADDITIONS: GENERAL

| | | |
|---|---|---|
| A ☑ | L2750 | Addition to lower extremity orthotic, plating chrome or nickel, per bar ♿ |
| A | L2755 | Addition to lower extremity orthotic, high strength, lightweight material, all hybrid lamination/prepreg composite, per segment, for custom fabricated orthotic only ♿ |
| A ☑ | L2760 | Addition to lower extremity orthotic, extension, per extension, per bar (for lineal adjustment for growth) ♿ |
| A ☑ | L2768 | Orthotic side bar disconnect device, per bar ♿ |
| A ☑ | L2770 | Addition to lower extremity orthotic, any material, per bar or joint ♿ |
| A ☑ | L2780 | Addition to lower extremity orthotic, noncorrosive finish, per bar ♿ |
| A ☑ | L2785 | Addition to lower extremity orthotic, drop lock retainer, each ♿ |
| A | L2795 | Addition to lower extremity orthotic, knee control, full kneecap ♿ |
| A | L2800 | Addition to lower extremity orthotic, knee control, knee cap, medial or lateral pull, for use with custom fabricated orthotic only ♿ |
| A | L2810 | Addition to lower extremity orthotic, knee control, condylar pad ♿ |
| A | L2820 | Addition to lower extremity orthotic, soft interface for molded plastic, below knee section ♿ |
| A | L2830 | Addition to lower extremity orthotic, soft interface for molded plastic, above knee section ♿ |
| A ☑ | L2840 | Addition to lower extremity orthotic, tibial length sock, fracture or equal, each ♿ |
| A ☑ | L2850 | Addition to lower extremity orthotic, femoral length sock, fracture or equal, each ♿ |

Orthotic Procedures

L2860 — L3090

| | | L2860 | ~~Addition to lower extremity joint, knee or ankle, concentric adjustable torsion style mechanism, each~~ |

Ⓐ  L2999  Lower extremity orthoses, not otherwise specified
Determine if an alternative HCPCS Level II or a CPT code better describes the service being reported. This code should be used only if a more specific code is unavailable.

## ORTHOPEDIC SHOES

### INSERTS

Ⓐ ☑  **L3000**  Foot insert, removable, molded to patient model, UCB type, Berkeley shell, each
MED: 100-2,15,290

Ⓐ ☑  **L3001**  Foot, insert, removable, molded to patient model, Spenco, each
MED: 100-2,15,290

Ⓐ ☑  **L3002**  Foot insert, removable, molded to patient model, Plastazote or equal, each
MED: 100-2,15,290

Ⓐ ☑  **L3003**  Foot insert, removable, molded to patient model, silicone gel, each
MED: 100-2,15,290

Ⓐ ☑  **L3010**  Foot insert, removable, molded to patient model, longitudinal arch support, each
MED: 100-2,15,290

Ⓐ ☑  **L3020**  Foot insert, removable, molded to patient model, longitudinal/metatarsal support, each
MED: 100-2,15,290

Ⓐ ☑  **L3030**  Foot insert, removable, formed to patient foot, each
MED: 100-2,15,290

Ⓐ ☑  **L3031**  Foot, insert/plate, removable, addition to lower extremity orthotic, high strength, lightweight material, all hybrid lamination/prepreg composite, each

### ARCH SUPPORT, REMOVABLE, PREMOLDED

Ⓐ ☑  **L3040**  Foot, arch support, removable, premolded, longitudinal, each
MED: 100-2,15,290

Ⓐ ☑  **L3050**  Foot, arch support, removable, premolded, metatarsal, each
MED: 100-2,15,290

Ⓐ ☑  **L3060**  Foot, arch support, removable, premolded, longitudinal/metatarsal, each
MED: 100-2,15,290

### ARCH SUPPORT, NONREMOVABLE, ATTACHED TO SHOE

Ⓐ ☑  **L3070**  Foot, arch support, nonremovable, attached to shoe, longitudinal, each
MED: 100-2,15,290

Ⓐ ☑  **L3080**  Foot, arch support, nonremovable, attached to shoe, metatarsal, each
MED: 100-2,15,290

Ⓐ ☑  **L3090**  Foot, arch support, nonremovable, attached to shoe, longitudinal/metatarsal, each
MED: 100-2,15,290

Ⓐ     L3100   Hallus-valgus night dynamic splint

MED: 100-2,15,290; 100-4,4,240

## ABDUCTION AND ROTATION BARS

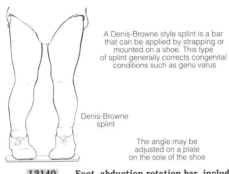

A Denis-Browne style splint is a bar that can be applied by strapping or mounted on a shoe. This type of splint generally corrects congenital conditions such as genu varus

Denis-Browne splint

The angle may be adjusted on a plate on the sole of the shoe

Ⓐ     L3140   Foot, abduction rotation bar, including shoes

MED: 100-2,15,290

Ⓐ     L3150   Foot, abduction rotation bar, without shoes

MED: 100-2,15,290

Ⓐ     L3160   Foot, adjustable shoe-styled positioning device

Ⓐ     L3170   Foot, plastic, silicone or equal, heel stabilizer, each

MED: 100-2,15,290

## ORTHOPEDIC FOOTWEAR

Ⓐ     L3201   Orthopedic shoe, Oxford with supinator or pronator, infant     Ⓐ

MED: 100-2,15,290

Ⓐ     L3202   Orthopedic shoe, Oxford with supinator or pronator, child     Ⓐ

MED: 100-2,15,290

Ⓐ     L3203   Orthopedic shoe, Oxford with supinator or pronator, junior     Ⓐ

MED: 100-2,15,290

Ⓐ     L3204   Orthopedic shoe, hightop with supinator or pronator, infant     Ⓐ

MED: 100-2,15,290

Ⓐ     L3206   Orthopedic shoe, hightop with supinator or pronator, child     Ⓐ

MED: 100-2,15,290

Ⓐ     L3207   Orthopedic shoe, hightop with supinator or pronator, junior     Ⓐ

MED: 100-2,15,290

Ⓐ  ☑   L3208   Surgical boot, each, infant     Ⓐ

MED: 100-2,15,100

Ⓐ  ☑   L3209   Surgical boot, each, child     Ⓐ

MED: 100-2,15,100

Ⓐ  ☑   L3211   Surgical boot, each, junior     Ⓐ

MED: 100-2,15,100

Ⓐ  ☑   L3212   Benesch boot, pair, infant     Ⓐ

MED: 100-2,15,100

Ⓐ  ☑   L3213   Benesch boot, pair, child     Ⓐ

MED: 100-2,15,100

---

Ⓐ ☑ **L3214** Benesch boot, pair, junior Ⓐ
MED: 100-2,15,100

Ⓔ ☑ **L3215** Orthopedic footwear, ladies shoe, oxford, each Ⓐ♀

Ⓔ ☑ **L3216** Orthopedic footwear, ladies shoe, depth inlay, each Ⓐ♀

Ⓔ ☑ **L3217** Orthopedic footwear, ladies shoe, hightop, depth inlay, each Ⓐ♀

Ⓔ ☑ **L3219** Orthopedic footwear, mens shoe, oxford, each Ⓐ♂

Ⓔ ☑ **L3221** Orthopedic footwear, mens shoe, depth inlay, each Ⓐ♂

Ⓔ ☑ **L3222** Orthopedic footwear, mens shoe, hightop, depth inlay, each Ⓐ♂

Ⓐ **L3224** Orthopedic footwear, woman's shoe, oxford, used as an integral part of a
brace (orthotic) ♀♿
MED: 100-2,15,290

Ⓐ **L3225** Orthopedic footwear, man's shoe, oxford, used as an integral part of a
brace (orthotic) ♂♿
MED: 100-2,15,290

Ⓐ **L3230** Orthopedic footwear, custom shoe, depth inlay, each
MED: 100-2,15,290

Ⓐ ☑ **L3250** Orthopedic footwear, custom molded shoe, removable inner mold,
prosthetic shoe, each
MED: 100-2,15,290

Ⓐ ☑ **L3251** Foot, shoe molded to patient model, silicone shoe, each
MED: 100-2,15,290

Ⓐ ☑ **L3252** Foot, shoe molded to patient model, Plastazote (or similar), custom
fabricated, each
MED: 100-2,15,290

Ⓐ ☑ **L3253** Foot, molded shoe, Plastazote (or similar), custom fitted, each
MED: 100-2,15,290

Ⓐ **L3254** Nonstandard size or width
MED: 100-2,15,290

Ⓐ **L3255** Nonstandard size or length
MED: 100-2,15,290

Ⓐ **L3257** Orthopedic footwear, additional charge for split size
MED: 100-2,15,290

Ⓔ ☑ **L3260** Surgical boot/shoe, each
MED: 100-2,15,100

Ⓐ ☑ **L3265** Plastazote sandal, each

## SHOE MODIFICATION - LIFTS

Ⓐ ☑ **L3300** Lift, elevation, heel, tapered to metatarsals, per in
MED: 100-2,15,290

Ⓐ ☑ **L3310** Lift, elevation, heel and sole, neoprene, per in
MED: 100-2,15,290

Ⓐ ☑ **L3320** Lift, elevation, heel and sole, cork, per in
MED: 100-2,15,290

Ⓐ **L3330** Lift, elevation, metal extension (skate)
MED: 100-2,15,290

Ⓐ ☑ **L3332** Lift, elevation, inside shoe, tapered, up to one-half in
MED: 100-2,15,290

Ⓐ ☑ **L3334**  Lift, elevation, heel, per in
MED: 100-2,15,290

## SHOE MODIFICATION - WEDGES

Ⓐ **L3340**  Heel wedge, SACH
MED: 100-2,15,290

Ⓐ **L3350**  Heel wedge
MED: 100-2,15,290

Ⓐ **L3360**  Sole wedge, outside sole
MED: 100-2,15,290

Ⓐ **L3370**  Sole wedge, between sole
MED: 100-2,15,290

Ⓐ **L3380**  Clubfoot wedge
MED: 100-2,15,290

Ⓐ **L3390**  Outflare wedge
MED: 100-2,15,290

Ⓐ **L3400**  Metatarsal bar wedge, rocker
MED: 100-2,15,290

Ⓐ **L3410**  Metatarsal bar wedge, between sole
MED: 100-2,15,290

Ⓐ **L3420**  Full sole and heel wedge, between sole
MED: 100-2,15,290

## SHOE MODIFICATIONS - HEELS

Ⓐ **L3430**  Heel, counter, plastic reinforced
MED: 100-2,15,290

Ⓐ **L3440**  Heel, counter, leather reinforced
MED: 100-2,15,290

Ⓐ **L3450**  Heel, SACH cushion type
MED: 100-2,15,290

Ⓐ **L3455**  Heel, new leather, standard
MED: 100-2,15,290

Ⓐ **L3460**  Heel, new rubber, standard
MED: 100-2,15,290

Ⓐ **L3465**  Heel, Thomas with wedge
MED: 100-2,15,290

Ⓐ **L3470**  Heel, Thomas extended to ball
MED: 100-2,15,290

Ⓐ **L3480**  Heel, pad and depression for spur
MED: 100-2,15,290

Ⓐ **L3485**  Heel, pad, removable for spur
MED: 100-2,15,290

## MISCELLANEOUS SHOE ADDITIONS

Ⓐ **L3500**  Orthopedic shoe addition, insole, leather
MED: 100-2,15,290

Ⓐ **L3510**  Orthopedic shoe addition, insole, rubber
MED: 100-2,15,290

---

☑ Quantity Alert    ● New Code    ○ Recycled/Reinstated    ▲ Revised Code    ♿ DMEPOS Paid    ⊘ SNF Excluded

Orthotic Procedures

L3520 — L3651

| | | |
|---|---|---|
| A | **L3520** | Orthopedic shoe addition, insole, felt covered with leather |
| | | MED: 100-2,15,290 |
| A | **L3530** | Orthopedic shoe addition, sole, half |
| | | MED: 100-2,15,290 |
| A | **L3540** | Orthopedic shoe addition, sole, full |
| | | MED: 100-2,15,290 |
| A | **L3550** | Orthopedic shoe addition, toe tap, standard |
| | | MED: 100-2,15,290 |
| A | **L3560** | Orthopedic shoe addition, toe tap, horseshoe |
| | | MED: 100-2,15,290 |
| A | **L3570** | Orthopedic shoe addition, special extension to instep (leather with eyelets) |
| | | MED: 100-2,15,290 |
| A | **L3580** | Orthopedic shoe addition, convert instep to Velcro closure |
| | | MED: 100-2,15,290 |
| A | **L3590** | Orthopedic shoe addition, convert firm shoe counter to soft counter |
| | | MED: 100-2,15,290 |
| A | **L3595** | Orthopedic shoe addition, March bar |
| | | MED: 100-2,15,290 |

## TRANSFER OR REPLACEMENT

| | | |
|---|---|---|
| A | **L3600** | Transfer of an orthotic from one shoe to another, caliper plate, existing |
| | | MED: 100-2,15,290 |
| A | **L3610** | Transfer of an orthotic from one shoe to another, caliper plate, new |
| | | MED: 100-2,15,290 |
| A | **L3620** | Transfer of an orthotic from one shoe to another, solid stirrup, existing |
| | | MED: 100-2,15,290 |
| A | **L3630** | Transfer of an orthotic from one shoe to another, solid stirrup, new |
| | | MED: 100-2,15,290 |
| A | **L3640** | Transfer of an orthotic from one shoe to another, Dennis Browne splint (Riveton), both shoes |
| | | MED: 100-2,15,290 |
| A | **L3649** | Orthopedic shoe, modification, addition or transfer, not otherwise specified |
| | | Determine if an alternative HCPCS Level II or a CPT code better describes the service being reported. This code should be used only if a more specific code is unavailable. |
| | | MED: 100-2,15,290 |

## ORTHOTIC DEVICES - UPPER LIMB

The procedures in this section are considered as "base" or "basic procedures" and may be modified by listing procedures from the "additions" sections and adding them to the base procedure.

### SHOULDER ORTHOTIC (SO)

| | | |
|---|---|---|
| A | **L3650** | Shoulder orthotic (SO), figure of eight design abduction restrainer, prefabricated, includes fitting and adjustment   ♿ |
| A | **L3651** | Shoulder orthotic (SO), single shoulder, elastic, prefabricated, includes fitting and adjustment (e.g., neoprene, Lycra)   ♿ |

| | | |
|---|---|---|
| A | **L3652** | Shoulder orthotic (SO), double shoulder, elastic, prefabricated, includes fitting and adjustment (e.g., neoprene, Lycra)   &#x262F; |
| A | **L3660** | Shoulder orthotic (SO), figure of eight design abduction restrainer, canvas and webbing, prefabricated, includes fitting and adjustment   &#x262F; |
| A | **L3670** | Shoulder orthotic (SO), acromio/clavicular (canvas and webbing type), prefabricated, includes fitting and adjustment   &#x262F; |
| A | **L3671** | Shoulder orthotic (SO), shoulder cap design, without joints, may include soft interface, straps, custom fabricated, includes fitting and adjustment |
| A | **L3672** | Shoulder orthotic (SO), abduction positioning (airplane design), thoracic component and support bar, without joints, may inlcude soft interface, straps, custom fabricated, includes fitting and adjustment |
| A | **L3673** | Shoulder orthotic (SO), abduction positioning (airplane design), thoracic component and support bar, includes nontorsion joint/turnbuckle, may include soft interface, straps, custom fabricated, includes fitting and adjustment |
| A | **L3675** | Shoulder orthotic (SO), vest type abduction restrainer, canvas webbing type or equal, prefabricated, includes fitting and adjustment   &#x262F; |
| E | **L3677** | Shoulder orthotic (SO), hard plastic, shoulder stabilizer, prefabricated, includes fitting and adjustment <br> MED: 100-2,15,120 |

## ELBOW ORTHOTIC (EO)

| | | |
|---|---|---|
| A | **L3700** | Elbow orthotic (EO), elastic with stays, prefabricated, includes fitting and adjustment   &#x262F; |
| A | **L3701** | Elbow orthotic (EO), elastic, prefabricated, includes fitting and adjustment (e.g., neoprene, Lycra)   &#x262F; |
| A | **L3702** | Elbow orthotic (EO), without joints, may include soft interface, straps, custom fabricated, includes fitting and adjustment |
| A | **L3710** | Elbow orthotic (EO), elastic with metal joints, prefabricated, includes fitting and adjustment   &#x262F; |
| A | **L3720** | Elbow orthotic (EO), double upright with forearm/arm cuffs, free motion, custom fabricated   &#x262F; |
| A | **L3730** | Elbow orthotic (EO), double upright with forearm/arm cuffs, extension/flexion assist, custom fabricated   &#x262F; |
| A | **L3740** | Elbow orthotic (EO), double upright with forearm/arm cuffs, adjustable position lock with active control, custom fabricated   &#x262F; |
| A | **L3760** | Elbow orthotic (EO), with adjustable position locking joint(s), prefabricated, includes fitting and adjustments, any type   &#x262F; |
| A | **L3762** | Elbow orthotic (EO), rigid, without joints, includes soft interface material, prefabricated, includes fitting and adjustment   &#x262F; |
| A | **L3763** | Elbow-wrist-hand orthotic (EWHO), rigid, without joints, may include soft interface, straps, custom fabricated, includes fitting and adjustment |
| A | **L3764** | Elbow-wrist-hand orthotic (EWHO), includes one or more nontorsion joints, elastic bands, turnbuckles, may include soft interface, straps, custom fabricated, includes fitting and adjustment |
| A | **L3765** | Elbow-wrist-hand-finger orthotic (EWHFO), rigid, without joints, may include soft interface, straps, custom fabricated, includes fitting and adjustment |

---

Orthotic Procedures

L3766 — L3915

[A]   L3766   Elbow-wrist-hand-finger orthotic, includes one or more nontorsion joints, elastic bands (EWHFO), turnbuckles, may include soft interface, straps, custom fabricated, includes fitting and adjustment

## WRIST-HAND-FINGER ORTHOTIC (WHFO)

[A]   L3806   Wrist-hand-finger orthotic (WHFO), includes one or more nontorsion joint(s), turnbuckles, elastic bands/springs, may include soft interface material, straps, custom fabricated, includes fitting and adjustment   &#x267F;

[A]   L3807   Wrist-hand-finger orthotic (WHFO), without joint(s), prefabricated, includes fitting and adjustments, any type   &#x267F;

[A]   L3808   Wrist-hand-finger orthotic (WHFO), rigid without joints, may include soft interface material; straps, custom fabricated, includes fitting and adjustment   &#x267F;

## ADDITIONS

~~L3890~~   ~~Addition to upper extremity joint, wrist or elbow, concentric adjustable torsion style mechanism, each~~

## DYNAMIC FLEXOR HINGE, RECIPROCAL WRIST EXTENSION/FLEXION, FINGER FLEXION/EXTENSION

[A]   L3900   Wrist-hand-finger orthotic (WHFO), dynamic flexor hinge, reciprocal wrist extension/ flexion, finger flexion/extension, wrist or finger driven, custom fabricated   &#x267F;

[A]   L3901   Wrist-hand-finger orthotic (WHFO), dynamic flexor hinge, reciprocal wrist extension/ flexion, finger flexion/extension, cable driven, custom fabricated   &#x267F;

## EXTERNAL POWER

[A]   L3904   Wrist-hand-finger orthotic (WHFO), external powered, electric, custom fabricated   &#x267F;

## OTHER - CUSTOM FITTED

▲ [A]   L3905   Wrist-hand orthotic (WHO), includes one or more nontorsion joints, elastic bands, turnbuckles, may include soft interface, straps, custom fabricated, includes fitting and adjustment

[A]   L3906   Wrist-hand orthosis (WHO), without joints, may include soft interface, straps, custom fabricated, includes fitting and adjustment   &#x267F;

[A]   L3908   Wrist-hand orthotic (WHO), wrist extension control cock-up, nonmolded, prefabricated, includes fitting and adjustment   &#x267F;

[A]   L3909   Wrist orthotic (WO), elastic, prefabricated, includes fitting and adjustment (e.g., neoprene, Lycra)   &#x267F;

[A]   L3911   Wrist hand finger orthotic (WHFO), elastic, prefabricated, includes fitting and adjustment (e.g., neoprene, Lycra)   &#x267F;

[A]   L3912   Hand-finger orthotic (HFO), flexion glove with elastic finger control, prefabricated, includes fitting and adjustment   &#x267F;

[A]   L3913   Hand finger orthotic (HFO), without joints, may include soft interface, straps, custom fabricated, includes fitting and adjustment

[A]   L3915   Wrist hand orthotic (WHO), includes one or more nontorsion joint(s), elastic bands, turnbuckles, may include soft interface, straps, prefabricated, includes fitting and adjustment   &#x267F;

Orthotic Procedures

| A | | L3917 | Hand orthotic (HO), metacarpal fracture orthotic, prefabricated, includes fitting and adjustment   &#9981; |
|---|---|---|---|
| A | | L3919 | Hand orthotic (HO), without joints, may include soft interface, straps, custom fabricated, includes fitting and adjustment |
| A | | L3921 | Hand finger orthotic (HFO), includes one or more nontorsion joints, elastic bands, turnbuckles, may include soft interface, straps, custom fabricated, includes fitting and adjustment |
| A | | L3923 | Hand finger orthotic (HFO), without joints, may include soft interface, straps, prefabricated, includes fitting and adjustment   &#9981; |
| A | | L3925 | Finger orthotic (FO), proximal interphalangeal (PIP)/distal interphalangeal (DIP), nontorsion joint/spring, extension/flexion, may include soft interface material, prefabricated, includes fitting and adjustment |
| ☑ | | L3927 | Finger orthotic (FO), proximal interphalangeal (PIP)/distal interphalangeal (DIP), without joint/spring, extension/flexion (e.g., static or ring type), may include soft interface material, prefabricated, includes fitting and adjustment |
| A | | L3929 | Hand-finger orthotic (HFO), includes one or more nontorsion joint(s), turnbuckles, elastic bands/springs, may include soft interface material, straps, prefabricated, includes fitting and adjustment |
| A | | L3931 | Wrist-hand-finger orthotic (WHFO), includes one or more nontorsion joint(s), turnbuckles, elastic bands/springs, may include soft interface material, straps, prefabricated, includes fitting and adjustment |
| A | | L3933 | Finger orthotic (FO), without joints, may include soft interface, custom fabricated, includes fitting and adjustment |
| A | | L3935 | Finger orthotic, nontorsion joint, may include soft interface, custom fabricated, includes fitting and adjustment |
| A | ☑ | L3956 | Addition of joint to upper extremity orthotic, any material; per joint &#9981; |

## SHOULDER-ELBOW-WRIST-HAND ORTHOTIC (SEWHO)

### ABDUCTION POSITION, CUSTOM FITTED

| A | L3960 | Shoulder-elbow-wrist-hand orthotic (SEWHO), abduction positioning, airplane design, prefabricated, includes fitting and adjustment   &#9981; |
|---|---|---|
| A | L3961 | Shoulder elbow wrist hand orthotic (SEWHO), shoulder cap design, without joints, may include soft interface, straps, custom fabricated, includes fitting and adjustment |
| A | L3962 | Shoulder-elbow-wrist-hand orthotic (SEWHO), abduction positioning, Erb's palsy design, prefabricated, includes fitting and adjustment   &#9981; |
| Y | L3964 | Shoulder-elbow orthotic (SEO), mobile arm support attached to wheelchair, balanced, adjustable, prefabricated, includes fitting and adjustment   &#9981; |
| Y | L3965 | Shoulder-elbow orthotic (SEO), mobile arm support attached to wheelchair, balanced, adjustable Rancho type, prefabricated, includes fitting and adjustment   &#9981; |
| Y | L3966 | Shoulder-elbow orthotic (SEO), mobile arm support attached to wheelchair, balanced, reclining, prefabricated, includes fitting and adjustment   &#9981; |
| A | L3967 | Shoulder-elbow-wrist-hand orthotic (SEWHO), abduction positioning (airplane design), thoracic component and support bar, without joints, may include soft interface, straps, custom fabricated, includes fitting and adjustment |

L3917 — L3967

---

☑ Quantity Alert    ● New Code    ○ Recycled/Reinstated    ▲ Revised Code    &#9981; DMEPOS Paid    ⊘ SNF Excluded

**Orthotic Procedures**

**L3968 — L4000**

| | | | |
|---|---|---|---|
| Ⓨ | **L3968** | Shoulder-elbow orthotic (SEO), mobile arm support attached to wheelchair, balanced, friction arm support (friction dampening to proximal and distal joints), prefabricated, includes fitting and adjustment | ♿ |
| Ⓨ | **L3969** | Shoulder-elbow orthotic (SEO), mobile arm support, monosuspension arm and hand support, overhead elbow forearm hand sling support, yoke type suspension support, prefabricated, includes fitting and adjustment | ♿ |

## ADDITIONS TO MOBILE ARM SUPPORTS

| | | | |
|---|---|---|---|
| Ⓨ | **L3970** | Shoulder-elbow orthotic (SEO), addition to mobile arm support, elevating proximal arm | ♿ |
| Ⓐ | **L3971** | Shoulder-elbow-wrist-hand orthotic (SEWHO), shoulder cap design, includes one or more nontorsion joints, elastic bands, turnbuckles, may include soft interface, straps, custom fabricated, includes fitting and adjustment | |
| Ⓨ | **L3972** | Shoulder-elbow orthotic (SEO), addition to mobile arm support, offset or lateral rocker arm with elastic balance control | ♿ |
| Ⓐ | **L3973** | Shoulder-elbow-wrist-hand orthotic (SEWHO), abduction positioning (airplane design), thoracic component and support bar, includes one or more nontorsion joints, elastic bands, turnbuckles, may include soft interface, straps, custom fabricated, includes fitting and adjustment | |
| Ⓨ | **L3974** | Shoulder-elbow orthotic (SEO), addition to mobile arm support, supinator | ♿ |
| Ⓐ | **L3975** | Shoulder-elbow-wrist-hand-finger orthotic (SEWHO), shoulder cap design, without joints, may include soft interface, straps, custom fabricated, includes fitting and adjustment | |
| Ⓐ | **L3976** | Shoulder-elbow-wrist-hand-finger orthotic (SEWHO), abduction positioning (airplane design), thoracic component and support bar, without joints, may include soft interface, straps, custom fabricated, includes fitting and adjustment | |
| Ⓐ | **L3977** | Shoulder-elbow-wrist-hand-finger orthotic (SEWHO), shoulder cap design, includes one or more nontorsion joints, elastic bands, turnbuckles, may include soft interface, straps, custom fabricated, includes fitting and adjustment | |
| Ⓐ | **L3978** | Shoulder-elbow-wrist-hand-finger orthotic (SEWHO), abduction positioning (airplane design), thoracic component and support bar, includes one or more nontorsion joints, elastic bands, turnbuckles, may include soft interface, straps, custom fabricated, includes fitting and adjustment | |

## FRACTURE ORTHOTIC

| | | | |
|---|---|---|---|
| Ⓐ | **L3980** | Upper extremity fracture orthotic, humeral, prefabricated, includes fitting and adjustment | ♿ |
| Ⓐ | **L3982** | Upper extremity fracture orthotic, radius/ulnar, prefabricated, includes fitting and adjustment | ♿ |
| Ⓐ | **L3984** | Upper extremity fracture orthotic, wrist, prefabricated, includes fitting and adjustment | ♿ |
| Ⓐ ☑ | **L3995** | Addition to upper extremity orthotic, sock, fracture or equal, each | ♿ |
| Ⓐ | **L3999** | Upper limb orthosis, not otherwise specified | |

## SPECIFIC REPAIR

| | | | |
|---|---|---|---|
| Ⓐ | **L4000** | Replace girdle for spinal orthotic (cervical-thoracic-lumbar-sacral orthotic (CTLSO) or spinal orthotic SO) | ♿ |

| | | | |
|---|---|---|---|
| Ⓐ | L4002 | Replacement strap, any orthotic, includes all components, any length, any type | |
| Ⓐ | L4010 | Replace trilateral socket brim | & |
| Ⓐ | L4020 | Replace quadrilateral socket brim, molded to patient model | & |
| Ⓐ | L4030 | Replace quadrilateral socket brim, custom fitted | & |
| Ⓐ | L4040 | Replace molded thigh lacer, for custom fabricated orthotic only | & |
| Ⓐ | L4045 | Replace nonmolded thigh lacer, for custom fabricated orthotic only | & |
| Ⓐ | L4050 | Replace molded calf lacer, for custom fabricated orthotic only | & |
| Ⓐ | L4055 | Replace nonmolded calf lacer, for custom fabricated orthotic only | & |
| Ⓐ | L4060 | Replace high roll cuff | & |
| Ⓐ | L4070 | Replace proximal and distal upright for KAFO | & |
| Ⓐ | L4080 | Replace metal bands KAFO, proximal thigh | & |
| Ⓐ | L4090 | Replace metal bands KAFO-AFO, calf or distal thigh | & |
| Ⓐ | L4100 | Replace leather cuff KAFO, proximal thigh | & |
| Ⓐ | L4110 | Replace leather cuff KAFO-AFO, calf or distal thigh | & |
| Ⓐ | L4130 | Replace pretibial shell | & |

## REPAIRS

| | | | | |
|---|---|---|---|---|
| Ⓐ | ☑ | L4205 | Repair of orthotic device, labor component, per 15 minutes | |
| | | | MED: 100-2,15,110.2 | |
| Ⓐ | | L4210 | Repair of orthotic device, repair or replace minor parts | |
| | | | MED: 100-2,15,110.2; 100-2,15,120 | |
| Ⓐ | | L4350 | Ankle control orthotic, stirrup style, rigid, includes any type interface (e.g., pneumatic, gel), prefabricated, includes fitting and adjustment | & |
| ▲ Ⓐ | | L4360 | Walking boot, pneumatic and/or vacuum, with or without joints, with or without interface material, prefabricated, includes fitting and adjustment | & |
| Ⓐ | | L4370 | Pneumatic full leg splint, prefabricated, includes fitting and adjustment | & |
| | | | MED: 100-4,4,240 | |
| Ⓐ | | L4380 | Pneumatic knee splint, prefabricated, includes fitting and adjustment | & |
| | | | MED: 100-4,4,240 | |
| Ⓐ | | L4386 | Walking boot, nonpneumatic, with or without joints, with or without interface material, prefabricated, includes fitting and adjustment | & |
| Ⓐ | | L4392 | Replacement, soft interface material, static AFO | & |
| Ⓐ | | L4394 | Replace soft interface material, foot drop splint | & |
| Ⓐ | | L4396 | Static ankle-foot orthotic (AFO), including soft interface material, adjustable for fit, for positioning, pressure reduction, may be used for minimal ambulation, prefabricated, includes fitting and adjustment | & |
| Ⓐ | | L4398 | Foot drop splint, recumbent positioning device, prefabricated, includes fitting and adjustment | & |
| | | | MED: 100-4,4,240 | |

---

# PROSTHETIC PROCEDURES L5000-L9999

## LOWER LIMB

The procedures in this section are considered as "base" or "basic procedures" and may be modified by listing items/procedures or special materials from the "additions" sections and adding them to the base procedure.

### PARTIAL FOOT

A **L5000** Partial foot, shoe insert with longitudinal arch, toe filler
MED: 100-2,15,290; 100-4,3,10.4

A **L5010** Partial foot, molded socket, ankle height, with toe filler
MED: 100-2,15,290; 100-4,3,10.4

A **L5020** Partial foot, molded socket, tibial tubercle height, with toe filler
MED: 100-2,15,290; 100-4,3,10.4

### ANKLE

A **L5050** Ankle, Symes, molded socket, SACH foot ⃠ ♿
MED: 100-4,3,10.4

A **L5060** Ankle, Symes, metal frame, molded leather socket, articulated ankle/foot ⃠ ♿
MED: 100-4,3,10.4

### BELOW KNEE

A **L5100** Below knee, molded socket, shin, SACH foot ⃠ ♿
MED: 100-4,3,10.4

A **L5105** Below knee, plastic socket, joints and thigh lacer, SACH foot ⃠ ♿
MED: 100-4,3,10.4

### KNEE DISARTICULATION

A **L5150** Knee disarticulation (or through knee), molded socket, external knee joints, shin, SACH foot ⃠ ♿
MED: 100-4,3,10.4

A **L5160** Knee disarticulation (or through knee), molded socket, bent knee configuration, external knee joints, shin, SACH foot ⃠ ♿
MED: 100-4,3,10.4

### ABOVE KNEE

A **L5200** Above knee, molded socket, single axis constant friction knee, shin, SACH foot ⃠ ♿
MED: 100-4,3,10.4

A ☑ **L5210** Above knee, short prosthesis, no knee joint (stubbies), with foot blocks, no ankle joints, each ⃠ ♿
MED: 100-4,3,10.4

A ☑ **L5220** Above knee, short prosthesis, no knee joint (stubbies), with articulated ankle/foot, dynamically aligned, each ⃠ ♿
MED: 100-4,3,10.4

A **L5230** Above knee, for proximal femoral focal deficiency, constant friction knee, shin, SACH foot ⃠ ♿
MED: 100-4,3,10.4

### HIP DISARTICULATION

A   **L5250**   Hip disarticulation, Canadian type; molded socket, hip joint, single axis constant friction knee, shin, SACH foot ⊘ ຢ
MED: 100-4,3,10.4

A   **L5270**   Hip disarticulation, tilt table type; molded socket, locking hip joint, single axis constant friction knee, shin, SACH foot ⊘ ຢ
MED: 100-4,3,10.4

### HEMIPELVECTOMY

A   **L5280**   Hemipelvectomy, Canadian type; molded socket, hip joint, single axis constant friction knee, shin, SACH foot ⊘ ຢ
MED: 100-4,3,10.4

A   **L5301**   Below knee, molded socket, shin, SACH foot, endoskeletal system ⊘ ຢ
MED: 100-4,3,10.4

A   **L5311**   Knee disarticulation (or through knee), molded socket, external knee joints, shin, SACH foot, endoskeletal system ⊘ ຢ
MED: 100-4,3,10.4

A   **L5321**   Above knee, molded socket, open end, SACH foot, endoskeletal system, single axis knee ⊘ ຢ
MED: 100-4,3,10.4

A   **L5331**   Hip disarticulation, Canadian type, molded socket, endoskeletal system, hip joint, single axis knee, SACH foot ⊘ ຢ
MED: 100-4,3,10.4

A   **L5341**   Hemipelvectomy, Canadian type, molded socket, endoskeletal system, hip joint, single axis knee, SACH foot ⊘ ຢ
MED: 100-4,3,10.4

### IMMEDIATE POSTSURGICAL OR EARLY FITTING PROCEDURES

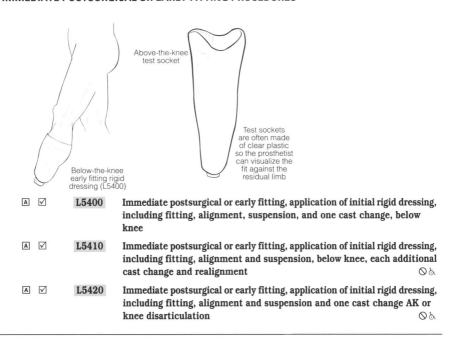

Above-the-knee test socket

Test sockets are often made of clear plastic so the prosthetist can visualize the fit against the residual limb

Below-the-knee early fitting rigid dressing (L5400)

A ☑   **L5400**   Immediate postsurgical or early fitting, application of initial rigid dressing, including fitting, alignment, suspension, and one cast change, below knee

A ☑   **L5410**   Immediate postsurgical or early fitting, application of initial rigid dressing, including fitting, alignment and suspension, below knee, each additional cast change and realignment ⊘ ຢ

A ☑   **L5420**   Immediate postsurgical or early fitting, application of initial rigid dressing, including fitting, alignment and suspension and one cast change AK or knee disarticulation ⊘ ຢ

A ☑ **L5430**    Immediate postsurgical or early fitting, application of initial rigid dressing, including fitting, alignment and suspension, AK or knee disarticulation, each additional cast change and realignment                                        ⊘ ஃ

A **L5450**    Immediate postsurgical or early fitting, application of nonweight bearing rigid dressing, below knee                                                    ⊘ ஃ

A **L5460**    Immediate postsurgical or early fitting, application of nonweight bearing rigid dressing, above knee                                                    ⊘ ஃ

## INITIAL PROSTHESIS

A **L5500**    Initial, below knee PTB type socket, nonalignable system, pylon, no cover, SACH foot, plaster socket, direct formed                                        ⊘ ஃ

MED: 100-4,3,10.4

A **L5505**    Initial, above knee, knee disarticulation, ischial level socket, nonalignable system, pylon, no cover, SACH foot, plaster socket, direct formed    ⊘ ஃ

MED: 100-4,3,10.4

## PREPARATORY PROSTHESIS

A **L5510**    Preparatory, below knee PTB type socket, nonalignable system, pylon, no cover, SACH foot, plaster socket, molded to model                              ⊘ ஃ

A **L5520**    Preparatory, below knee PTB type socket, nonalignable system, pylon, no cover, SACH foot, thermoplastic or equal, direct formed                        ⊘ ஃ

A **L5530**    Preparatory, below knee PTB type socket, nonalignable system, pylon, no cover, SACH foot, thermoplastic or equal, molded to model                      ⊘ ஃ

A **L5535**    Preparatory, below knee PTB type socket, nonalignable system, pylon, no cover, SACH foot, prefabricated, adjustable open end socket                     ⊘ ஃ

A **L5540**    Preparatory, below knee PTB type socket, nonalignable system, pylon, no cover, SACH foot, laminated socket, molded to model                            ⊘ ஃ

A **L5560**    Preparatory, above knee, knee disarticulation, ischial level socket, nonalignable system, pylon, no cover, SACH foot, plaster socket, molded to model                                                                      ⊘ ஃ

A **L5570**    Preparatory, above knee — knee disarticulation, ischial level socket, nonalignable system, pylon, no cover, SACH foot, thermoplastic or equal, direct formed                                                                  ⊘ ஃ

A **L5580**    Preparatory, above knee, knee disarticulation, ischial level socket, nonalignable system, pylon, no cover, SACH foot, thermoplastic or equal, molded to model                                                                  ⊘ ஃ

A **L5585**    Preparatory, above knee — knee disarticulation, ischial level socket, nonalignable system, pylon, no cover, SACH foot, prefabricated adjustable open end socket                                                              ⊘ ஃ

A **L5590**    Preparatory, above knee, knee disarticulation, ischial level socket, nonalignable system, pylon, no cover, SACH foot, laminated socket, molded to model                                                                      ⊘ ஃ

A **L5595**    Preparatory, hip disarticulation/hemipelvectomy, pylon, no cover, SACH foot, thermoplastic or equal, molded to patient model                              ⊘ ஃ

A **L5600**    Preparatory, hip disarticulation/hemipelvectomy, pylon, no cover, SACH foot, laminated socket, molded to patient model                                    ⊘ ஃ

## ADDITIONS: LOWER EXTREMITY

A **L5610**    Addition to lower extremity, endoskeletal system, above knee, hydracadence system                                                                    ⊘ ஃ

| | | | |
|---|---|---|---|
| A | | L5611 | Addition to lower extremity, endoskeletal system, above knee, knee disarticulation, 4-bar linkage, with friction swing phase control ⊘ ♿ |
| A | | L5613 | Addition to lower extremity, endoskeletal system, above knee, knee disarticulation, 4-bar linkage, with hydraulic swing phase control ⊘ ♿ |
| A | | L5614 | Addition to lower extremity, exoskeletal system, above knee-knee disarticulation, 4 bar linkage, with pneumatic swing phase control ⊘ ♿ |
| A | | L5616 | Addition to lower extremity, endoskeletal system, above knee, universal multiplex system, friction swing phase control ⊘ ♿ |
| A | ☑ | L5617 | Addition to lower extremity, quick change self-aligning unit, above knee or below knee, each ⊘ ♿ |

## ADDITIONS: TEST SOCKETS

| | | | |
|---|---|---|---|
| A | | L5618 | Addition to lower extremity, test socket, Symes ⊘ ♿ |
| A | | L5620 | Addition to lower extremity, test socket, below knee ⊘ ♿ |
| A | | L5622 | Addition to lower extremity, test socket, knee disarticulation ⊘ ♿ |
| A | | L5624 | Addition to lower extremity, test socket, above knee ⊘ ♿ |
| A | | L5626 | Addition to lower extremity, test socket, hip disarticulation ⊘ ♿ |
| A | | L5628 | Addition to lower extremity, test socket, hemipelvectomy ⊘ ♿ |
| A | | L5629 | Addition to lower extremity, below knee, acrylic socket ⊘ ♿ |

## ADDITIONS: SOCKET VARIATIONS

| | | | |
|---|---|---|---|
| A | | L5630 | Addition to lower extremity, Symes type, expandable wall socket ⊘ ♿ |
| A | | L5631 | Addition to lower extremity, above knee or knee disarticulation, acrylic socket ⊘ ♿ |
| A | | L5632 | Addition to lower extremity, Symes type, PTB brim design socket ⊘ ♿ |
| A | | L5634 | Addition to lower extremity, Symes type, posterior opening (Canadian) socket ⊘ ♿ |
| A | | L5636 | Addition to lower extremity, Symes type, medial opening socket ⊘ ♿ |
| A | | L5637 | Addition to lower extremity, below knee, total contact ⊘ ♿ |
| A | | L5638 | Addition to lower extremity, below knee, leather socket ⊘ ♿ |
| A | | L5639 | Addition to lower extremity, below knee, wood socket ⊘ ♿ |
| A | | L5640 | Addition to lower extremity, knee disarticulation, leather socket ⊘ ♿ |
| A | | L5642 | Addition to lower extremity, above knee, leather socket ⊘ ♿ |
| A | | L5643 | Addition to lower extremity, hip disarticulation, flexible inner socket, external frame ⊘ ♿ |
| A | | L5644 | Addition to lower extremity, above knee, wood socket ⊘ ♿ |
| A | | L5645 | Addition to lower extremity, below knee, flexible inner socket, external frame ⊘ ♿ |
| A | | L5646 | Addition to lower extremity, below knee, air, fluid, gel or equal, cushion socket ⊘ ♿ |
| A | | L5647 | Addition to lower extremity, below knee, suction socket ⊘ ♿ |
| A | | L5648 | Addition to lower extremity, above knee, air, fluid, gel or equal, cushion socket ⊘ ♿ |
| A | | L5649 | Addition to lower extremity, ischial containment/narrow M-L socket ⊘ ♿ |

**Prosthetic Procedures**

**L5650 — L5676**

A | **L5650** | Additions to lower extremity, total contact, above knee or knee disarticulation socket ⊘ &

A | **L5651** | Addition to lower extremity, above knee, flexible inner socket, external frame ⊘ &

A | **L5652** | Addition to lower extremity, suction suspension, above knee or knee disarticulation socket ⊘ &

A | **L5653** | Addition to lower extremity, knee disarticulation, expandable wall socket ⊘ &

## ADDITIONS: SOCKET INSERT AND SUSPENSION

A | **L5654** | Addition to lower extremity, socket insert, Symes, (Kemblo, Pelite, Aliplast, Plastazote) or equal ⊘ &

A | **L5655** | Addition to lower extremity, socket insert, below knee (Kemblo, Pelite, Aliplast, Plastazote or equal) ⊘ &

A | **L5656** | Addition to lower extremity, socket insert, knee disarticulation (Kemblo, Pelite, Aliplast, Plastazote or equal) ⊘ &

A | **L5658** | Addition to lower extremity, socket insert, above knee (Kemblo, Pelite, Aliplast, Plastazote or equal) ⊘ &

A | **L5661** | Addition to lower extremity, socket insert, multidurometer Symes ⊘ &

A | **L5665** | Addition to lower extremity, socket insert, multidurometer, below knee ⊘ &

A | **L5666** | Addition to lower extremity, below knee, cuff suspension ⊘ &

A | **L5668** | Addition to lower extremity, below knee, molded distal cushion ⊘ &

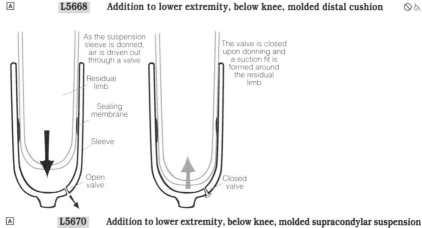

As the suspension sleeve is donned, air is driven out through a valve

The valve is closed upon donning and a suction fit is formed around the residual limb

Residual limb

Sealing membrane

Sleeve

Open valve

Closed valve

A | **L5670** | Addition to lower extremity, below knee, molded supracondylar suspension (PTS or similar) ⊘ &

A | **L5671** | Addition to lower extremity, below knee / above knee suspension locking mechanism (shuttle, lanyard, or equal), excludes socket insert ⊘ &

A | **L5672** | Addition to lower extremity, below knee, removable medial brim suspension ⊘ &

A | **L5673** | Addition to lower extremity, below knee/above knee, custom fabricated from existing mold or prefabricated, socket insert, silicone gel, elastomeric or equal, for use with locking mechanism ⊘ &

A ☑ | **L5676** | Additions to lower extremity, below knee, knee joints, single axis, pair ⊘ &

| | | | |
|---|---|---|---|
| Ⓐ ☑ | L5677 | Additions to lower extremity, below knee, knee joints, polycentric, pair | ⊘ ᕱ |
| Ⓐ ☑ | L5678 | Additions to lower extremity, below knee, joint covers, pair | ⊘ ᕱ |
| Ⓐ | L5679 | Addition to lower extremity, below knee/above knee, custom fabricated from existing mold or prefabricated, socket insert, silicone gel, elastomeric or equal, not for use with locking mechanism | ⊘ ᕱ |
| Ⓐ | L5680 | Addition to lower extremity, below knee, thigh lacer, nonmolded | ⊘ ᕱ |
| Ⓐ | L5681 | Addition to lower extremity, below knee/above knee, custom fabricated socket insert for congenital or atypical traumatic amputee, silicone gel, elastomeric or equal, for use with or without locking mechanism, initial only (for other than initial, use code L5673 or L5679) | ⊘ ᕱ |
| Ⓐ | L5682 | Addition to lower extremity, below knee, thigh lacer, gluteal/ischial, molded | ⊘ ᕱ |
| Ⓐ | L5683 | Addition to lower extremity, below knee/above knee, custom fabricated socket insert for other than congenital or atypical traumatic amputee, silicone gel, elastomeric or equal, for use with or without locking mechanism, initial only (for other than initial, use code L5673 or L5679) | ⊘ ᕱ |
| Ⓐ | L5684 | Addition to lower extremity, below knee, fork strap | ⊘ ᕱ |
| Ⓐ | L5685 | Addition to lower extremity prosthesis, below knee, suspension/sealing sleeve, with or without valve, any material, each | ⊘ |
| Ⓐ | L5686 | Addition to lower extremity, below knee, back check (extension control) | ⊘ ᕱ |
| Ⓐ | L5688 | Addition to lower extremity, below knee, waist belt, webbing | ⊘ ᕱ |
| Ⓐ | L5690 | Addition to lower extremity, below knee, waist belt, padded and lined | ⊘ ᕱ |
| Ⓐ | L5692 | Addition to lower extremity, above knee, pelvic control belt, light | ⊘ ᕱ |
| Ⓐ | L5694 | Addition to lower extremity, above knee, pelvic control belt, padded and lined | ⊘ ᕱ |
| Ⓐ ☑ | L5695 | Addition to lower extremity, above knee, pelvic control, sleeve suspension, neoprene or equal, each | ⊘ |
| Ⓐ | L5696 | Addition to lower extremity, above knee or knee disarticulation, pelvic joint | ⊘ |
| Ⓐ | L5697 | Addition to lower extremity, above knee or knee disarticulation, pelvic band | ⊘ |
| Ⓐ | L5698 | Addition to lower extremity, above knee or knee disarticulation, Silesian bandage | ⊘ |
| Ⓐ | L5699 | All lower extremity prostheses, shoulder harness | ⊘ |

## REPLACEMENTS

| | | | |
|---|---|---|---|
| Ⓐ | L5700 | Replacement, socket, below knee, molded to patient model | ⊘ |
| Ⓐ | L5701 | Replacement, socket, above knee/knee disarticulation, including attachment plate, molded to patient model | ⊘ |
| Ⓐ | L5702 | Replacement, socket, hip disarticulation, including hip joint, molded to patient model | ⊘ |
| Ⓐ | L5703 | Ankle, Symes, molded to patient model, socket without solid ankle cushion heel (SACH) foot, replacement only | ⊘ |

Prosthetic Procedures

L5704 — L5812

| | | | |
|---|---|---|---|
| A | **L5704** | Custom shaped protective cover, below knee | ⊘ |
| A | **L5705** | Custom shaped protective cover, above knee | ⊘ |
| A | **L5706** | Custom shaped protective cover, knee disarticulation | ⊘ |
| A | **L5707** | Custom shaped protective cover, hip disarticulation | ⊘ |

## ADDITIONS: EXOSKELETAL KNEE-SHIN SYSTEM

| | | | |
|---|---|---|---|
| A | **L5710** | Addition, exoskeletal knee-shin system, single axis, manual lock | ⊘ |
| A | **L5711** | Additions exoskeletal knee-shin system, single axis, manual lock, ultra-light material | ⊘ |
| A | **L5712** | Addition, exoskeletal knee-shin system, single axis, friction swing and stance phase control (safety knee) | ⊘ |
| A | **L5714** | Addition, exoskeletal knee-shin system, single axis, variable friction swing phase control | ⊘ |
| A | **L5716** | Addition, exoskeletal knee-shin system, polycentric, mechanical stance phase lock | ⊘ |
| A | **L5718** | Addition, exoskeletal knee-shin system, polycentric, friction swing and stance phase control | ⊘ |
| A | **L5722** | Addition, exoskeletal knee-shin system, single axis, pneumatic swing, friction stance phase control | ⊘ |
| A | **L5724** | Addition, exoskeletal knee-shin system, single axis, fluid swing phase control | ⊘ |
| A | **L5726** | Addition, exoskeletal knee/shin system, single axis, external joints, fluid swing phase control | ⊘ |
| A | **L5728** | Addition, exoskeletal knee-shin system, single axis, fluid swing and stance phase control | ⊘ |
| A | **L5780** | Addition, exoskeletal knee-shin system, single axis, pneumatic/hydra pneumatic swing phase control | ⊘ |
| A | **L5781** | Addition to lower limb prosthesis, vacuum pump, residual limb volume management and moisture evacuation system | ⊘ |
| A | **L5782** | Addition to lower limb prosthesis, vacuum pump, residual limb volume management and moisture evacuation system, heavy-duty | ⊘ |

## COMPONENT MODIFICATION

| | | | |
|---|---|---|---|
| A | **L5785** | Addition, exoskeletal system, below knee, ultra-light material (titanium, carbon fiber or equal) | ⊘ |
| A | **L5790** | Addition, exoskeletal system, above knee, ultra-light material (titanium, carbon fiber or equal) | ⊘ |
| A | **L5795** | Addition, exoskeletal system, hip disarticulation, ultra-light material (titanium, carbon fiber or equal) | ⊘ |

## ADDITIONS: ENDOSKELETAL KNEE-SHIN SYSTEM

| | | | |
|---|---|---|---|
| A | **L5810** | Addition, endoskeletal knee-shin system, single axis, manual lock | ⊘ |
| A | **L5811** | Addition, endoskeletal knee-shin system, single axis, manual lock, ultra-light material | ⊘ |
| A | **L5812** | Addition, endoskeletal knee-shin system, single axis, friction swing and stance phase control (safety knee) | ⊘ |

| Ⓐ | **L5814** | Addition, endoskeletal knee-shin system, polycentric, hydraulic swing phase control, mechanical stance phase lock ⊘ |
|---|---|---|
| Ⓐ | **L5816** | Addition, endoskeletal knee-shin system, polycentric, mechanical stance phase lock ⊘ |
| Ⓐ | **L5818** | Addition, endoskeletal knee/shin system, polycentric, friction swing and stance phase control ⊘ |
| Ⓐ | **L5822** | Addition, endoskeletal knee-shin system, single axis, pneumatic swing, friction stance phase control ⊘ |
| Ⓐ | **L5824** | Addition, endoskeletal knee-shin system, single axis, fluid swing phase control ⊘ |
| Ⓐ | **L5826** | Addition, endoskeletal knee-shin system, single axis, hydraulic swing phase control, with miniature high activity frame ⊘ |
| Ⓐ | **L5828** | Addition, endoskeletal knee-shin system, single axis, fluid swing and stance phase control ⊘ |
| Ⓐ | **L5830** | Addition, endoskeletal knee/shin system, single axis, pneumatic/swing phase control ⊘ |
| Ⓐ | **L5840** | Addition, endoskeletal knee/shin system, 4-bar linkage or multiaxial, pneumatic swing phase control ⊘ |
| Ⓐ | **L5845** | Addition, endoskeletal knee/shin system, stance flexion feature, adjustable ⊘ |
| Ⓐ | **L5848** | Addition to endoskeletal knee-shin system, fluid stance extension, dampening feature, with or without adjustability ⊘ |
| Ⓐ | **L5850** | Addition, endoskeletal system, above knee or hip disarticulation, knee extension assist ⊘ |
| Ⓐ | **L5855** | Addition, endoskeletal system, hip disarticulation, mechanical hip extension assist ⊘ |
| Ⓐ | **L5856** | Addition to lower extremity prosthesis, endoskeletal knee-shin system, microprocessor control feature, swing and stance phase, includes electronic sensor(s), any type ⊘ |
| Ⓐ | **L5857** | Addition to lower extremity prosthesis, endoskeletal knee-shin system, microprocessor control feature, swing phase only, includes electronic sensor(s), any type ⊘ |
| Ⓐ | **L5858** | Addition to lower extremity prosthesis, endoskeletal knee shin system, microprocessor control feature, stance phase only, includes electronic sensor(s), any type ⊘ |
| Ⓐ | **L5910** | Addition, endoskeletal system, below knee, alignable system ⊘ |
| Ⓐ | **L5920** | Addition, endoskeletal system, above knee or hip disarticulation, alignable system ⊘ |
| Ⓐ | **L5925** | Addition, endoskeletal system, above knee, knee disarticulation or hip disarticulation, manual lock ⊘ |
| Ⓐ | **L5930** | Addition, endoskeletal system, high activity knee control frame ⊘ |
| Ⓐ | **L5940** | Addition, endoskeletal system, below knee, ultra-light material (titanium, carbon fiber or equal) ⊘ |
| Ⓐ | **L5950** | Addition, endoskeletal system, above knee, ultra-light material (titanium, carbon fiber or equal) ⊘ |
| Ⓐ | **L5960** | Addition, endoskeletal system, hip disarticulation, ultra-light material (titanium, carbon fiber or equal) ⊘ |

☑ Quantity Alert   ● New Code   ○ Recycled/Reinstated   ▲ Revised Code   ↳ DMEPOS Paid   ⊘ SNF Excluded

Ⓐ    **L5962**    Addition, endoskeletal system, below knee, flexible protective outer surface covering system    ⊘

Ⓐ    **L5964**    Addition, endoskeletal system, above knee, flexible protective outer surface covering system    ⊘

Ⓐ    **L5966**    Addition, endoskeletal system, hip disarticulation, flexible protective outer surface covering system    ⊘

Ⓐ    **L5968**    Addition to lower limb prosthesis, multiaxial ankle with swing phase active dorsiflexion feature    ⊘

Ⓐ    **L5970**    All lower extremity prostheses, foot, external keel, SACH foot    ⊘

Ⓐ    **L5971**    All lower extremity prosthesis, solid ankle cushion heel (SACH) foot, replacement only    ⊘

Ⓐ    **L5972**    All lower extremity prostheses, flexible keel foot (SAFE, STEN, Bock Dynamic or equal)    ⊘

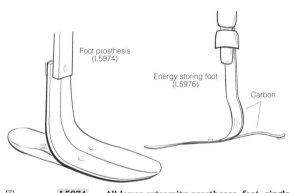

Foot prosthesis
(L5974)

Energy storing foot
(L5976)

Carbon

Ⓐ    **L5974**    All lower extremity prostheses, foot, single axis ankle/foot    ⊘

Ⓐ    **L5975**    All lower extremity prosthesis, combination single axis ankle and flexible keel foot    ⊘

Ⓐ    **L5976**    All lower extremity prostheses, energy storing foot (Seattle Carbon Copy II or equal)    ⊘

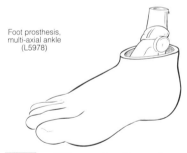

Foot prosthesis,
multi-axial ankle
(L5978)

Ⓐ    **L5978**    All lower extremity prostheses, foot, multiaxial ankle/foot    ⊘

Ⓐ    **L5979**    All lower extremity prostheses, multiaxial ankle, dynamic response foot, one piece system    ⊘

Ⓐ    **L5980**    All lower extremity prostheses, flex-foot system    ⊘

Ⓐ    **L5981**    All lower extremity prostheses, flex-walk system or equal    ⊘

Ⓐ    **L5982**    All exoskeletal lower extremity prostheses, axial rotation unit    ⊘

| | | |
|---|---|---|
| Ⓐ | **L5984** | All endoskeletal lower extremity prosthesis, axial rotation unit, with or without adjustability ⊘ |
| Ⓐ | **L5985** | All endoskeletal lower extremity prostheses, dynamic prosthetic pylon ⊘ |
| Ⓐ | **L5986** | All lower extremity prostheses, multiaxial rotation unit (MCP or equal) ⊘ |
| Ⓐ | **L5987** | All lower extremity prosthesis, shank foot system with vertical loading pylon |
| Ⓐ | **L5988** | Addition to lower limb prosthesis, vertical shock reducing pylon feature ⊘ |
| Ⓐ | **L5990** | Addition to lower extremity prosthesis, user adjustable heel height ⊘ |
| | ~~L5993~~ | ~~Addition to lower extremity prosthesis, heavy duty feature, foot only, (for patient weight greater than 300 lbs)~~ |
| | ~~L5994~~ | ~~Addition to lower extremity prosthesis, heavy duty feature, knee only, (for patient weight greater than 300 lbs)~~ |
| | ~~L5995~~ | ~~Addition to lower extremity prosthesis, heavy duty feature, other than foot or knee, (for patient weight greater than 300 lbs)~~ |
| Ⓐ | **L5999** | Lower extremity prosthesis, not otherwise specified |
| | | Determine if an alternative HCPCS Level II or a CPT code better describes the service being reported. This code should be used only if a more specific code is unavailable. |

## UPPER LIMB

The procedures in L6000-L6590 are considered as "base" or "basic procedures" and may be modified by listing procedures from the "addition" sections. The base procedures include only standard friction wrist and control cable system unless otherwise specified.

### PARTIAL HAND

| | | |
|---|---|---|
| Ⓐ | **L6000** | Partial hand, Robin-Aids, thumb remaining (or equal) |
| Ⓐ | **L6010** | Partial hand, Robin-Aids, little and/or ring finger remaining (or equal) |
| Ⓐ | **L6020** | Partial hand, Robin-Aids, no finger remaining (or equal) |
| Ⓐ | **L6025** | Transcarpal/metacarpal or partial hand disarticulation prosthesis, external power, self-suspended, inner socket with removable forearm section, electrodes and cables, 2 batteries, charger, myoelectric control of terminal device |

### WRIST DISARTICULATION

| | | |
|---|---|---|
| Ⓐ | **L6050** | Wrist disarticulation, molded socket, flexible elbow hinges, triceps pad ⊘ |
| Ⓐ | **L6055** | Wrist disarticulation, molded socket with expandable interface, flexible elbow hinges, triceps pad ⊘ |

### BELOW ELBOW

| | | |
|---|---|---|
| Ⓐ | **L6100** | Below elbow, molded socket, flexible elbow hinge, triceps pad ⊘ |
| Ⓐ | **L6110** | Below elbow, molded socket (Muenster or Northwestern suspension types) ⊘ |
| Ⓐ | **L6120** | Below elbow, molded double wall split socket, step-up hinges, half cuff ⊘ |

Ⓐ    L6130    Below elbow, molded double wall split socket, stump activated locking hinge, half cuff    ⊘

## ELBOW DISARTICULATION

Ⓐ    L6200    Elbow disarticulation, molded socket, outside locking hinge, forearm    ⊘

Ⓐ    L6205    Elbow disarticulation, molded socket with expandable interface, outside locking hinges, forearm    ⊘ &

## ABOVE ELBOW

Ⓐ    L6250    Above elbow, molded double wall socket, internal locking elbow, forearm    ⊘ &

## SHOULDER DISARTICULATION

Ⓐ    L6300    Shoulder disarticulation, molded socket, shoulder bulkhead, humeral section, internal locking elbow, forearm    ⊘ &

Ⓐ    L6310    Shoulder disarticulation, passive restoration (complete prosthesis)    ⊘ &

Ⓐ    L6320    Shoulder disarticulation, passive restoration (shoulder cap only)    ⊘ &

## INTERSCAPULAR THORACIC

Ⓐ    L6350    Interscapular thoracic, molded socket, shoulder bulkhead, humeral section, internal locking elbow, forearm    ⊘ &

Ⓐ    L6360    Interscapular thoracic, passive restoration (complete prosthesis)    ⊘ &

Ⓐ    L6370    Interscapular thoracic, passive restoration (shoulder cap only)    ⊘ &

## IMMEDIATE AND EARLY POSTSURGICAL PROCEDURES

Ⓐ    L6380    Immediate postsurgical or early fitting, application of initial rigid dressing, including fitting alignment and suspension of components, and one cast change, wrist disarticulation or below elbow    &

Ⓐ ☑    L6382    Immediate postsurgical or early fitting, application of initial rigid dressing including fitting alignment and suspension of components, and one cast change, elbow disarticulation or above elbow    &

Ⓐ ☑    L6384    Immediate postsurgical or early fitting, application of initial rigid dressing including fitting alignment and suspension of components, and one cast change, shoulder disarticulation or interscapular thoracic    &

Ⓐ ☑    L6386    Immediate postsurgical or early fitting, each additional cast change and realignment    &

Ⓐ    L6388    Immediate postsurgical or early fitting, application of rigid dressing only    &

## ENDOSKELETAL: BELOW ELBOW

Ⓐ    L6400    Below elbow, molded socket, endoskeletal system, including soft prosthetic tissue shaping    ⊘ &

## ENDOSKELETAL: ELBOW DISARTICULATION

Ⓐ    L6450    Elbow disarticulation, molded socket, endoskeletal system, including soft prosthetic tissue shaping    ⊘ &

## ENDOSKELETAL: ABOVE ELBOW

Ⓐ    L6500    Above elbow, molded socket, endoskeletal system, including soft prosthetic tissue shaping    ⊘ &

## ENDOSKELETAL: SHOULDER DISARTICULATION

Ⓐ    **L6550**    Shoulder disarticulation, molded socket, endoskeletal system, including soft prosthetic tissue shaping     ⊘ ♿

## ENDOSKELETAL: INTERSCAPULAR THORACIC

Ⓐ    **L6570**    Interscapular thoracic, molded socket, endoskeletal system, including soft prosthetic tissue shaping     ⊘ ♿

Ⓐ    **L6580**    Preparatory, wrist disarticulation or below elbow, single wall plastic socket, friction wrist, flexible elbow hinges, figure of eight harness, humeral cuff, Bowden cable control, USMC or equal pylon, no cover, molded to patient model     ⊘ ♿

Ⓐ    **L6582**    Preparatory, wrist disarticulation or below elbow, single wall socket, friction wrist, flexible elbow hinges, figure of eight harness, humeral cuff, Bowden cable control, USMC or equal pylon, no cover, direct formed     ⊘ ♿

Ⓐ    **L6584**    Preparatory, elbow disarticulation or above elbow, single wall plastic socket, friction wrist, locking elbow, figure of eight harness, fair lead cable control, USMC or equal pylon, no cover, molded to patient model    ⊘ ♿

Ⓐ    **L6586**    Preparatory, elbow disarticulation or above elbow, single wall socket, friction wrist, locking elbow, figure of eight harness, fair lead cable control, USMC or equal pylon, no cover, direct formed     ⊘ ♿

Ⓐ    **L6588**    Preparatory, shoulder disarticulation or interscapular thoracic, single wall plastic socket, shoulder joint, locking elbow, friction wrist, chest strap, fair lead cable control, USMC or equal pylon, no cover, molded to patient model     ⊘ ♿

Ⓐ    **L6590**    Preparatory, shoulder disarticulation or interscapular thoracic, single wall socket, shoulder joint, locking elbow, friction wrist, chest strap, fair lead cable control, USMC or equal pylon, no cover, direct formed     ⊘ ♿

## ADDITIONS: UPPER LIMB

The following procedures/modifications/components may be added to other base procedures. The items in this section should reflect the additional complexity of each modification procedure, in addition to the base procedure, at the time of the original order.

Ⓐ ☑    **L6600**    Upper extremity additions, polycentric hinge, pair     ⊘ ♿

Ⓐ ☑    **L6605**    Upper extremity additions, single pivot hinge, pair     ⊘ ♿

Ⓐ ☑    **L6610**    Upper extremity additions, flexible metal hinge, pair     ⊘ ♿

Ⓐ    **L6611**    Addition to upper extremity prosthesis, external powered, additional switch, any type     ⊘ ♿

Ⓐ    **L6615**    Upper extremity addition, disconnect locking wrist unit     ⊘ ♿

Ⓐ ☑    **L6616**    Upper extremity addition, additional disconnect insert for locking wrist unit, each     ⊘ ♿

Ⓐ    **L6620**    Upper extremity addition, flexion/extension wrist unit, with or without friction     ⊘ ♿

Ⓐ    **L6621**    Upper extremity prosthesis addition, flexion/extension wrist with or without friction, for use with external powered terminal device    ⊘

Ⓐ    **L6623**    Upper extremity addition, spring assisted rotational wrist unit with latch release     ⊘ ♿

Ⓐ    **L6624**    Upper extremity addition, flexion/extension and rotation wrist unit ⊘ ♿

---

| | | | |
|---|---|---|---|
| Ⓐ | | L6625 | Upper extremity addition, rotation wrist unit with cable lock ⊘ ♿ |
| Ⓐ | | L6628 | Upper extremity addition, quick disconnect hook adapter, Otto Bock or equal ⊘ ♿ |
| Ⓐ | | L6629 | Upper extremity addition, quick disconnect lamination collar with coupling piece, Otto Bock or equal ⊘ ♿ |
| Ⓐ | | L6630 | Upper extremity addition, stainless steel, any wrist ⊘ ♿ |
| Ⓐ | ☑ | L6632 | Upper extremity addition, latex suspension sleeve, each ⊘ ♿ |
| Ⓐ | | L6635 | Upper extremity addition, lift assist for elbow ⊘ ♿ |
| Ⓐ | | L6637 | Upper extremity addition, nudge control elbow lock ⊘ ♿ |
| Ⓐ | | L6638 | Upper extremity addition to prosthesis, electric locking feature, only for use with manually powered elbow ⊘ ♿ |
| Ⓐ | | L6639 | Upper extremity addition, heavy-duty feature, any elbow ⊘ ♿ |
| Ⓐ | ☑ | L6640 | Upper extremity additions, shoulder abduction joint, pair ⊘ ♿ |
| Ⓐ | | L6641 | Upper extremity addition, excursion amplifier, pulley type ⊘ ♿ |
| Ⓐ | | L6642 | Upper extremity addition, excursion amplifier, lever type ⊘ ♿ |
| Ⓐ | ☑ | L6645 | Upper extremity addition, shoulder flexion-abduction joint, each ⊘ ♿ |
| Ⓐ | | L6646 | Upper extremity addition, shoulder joint, multipositional locking, flexion, adjustable abduction friction control, for use with body powered or external powered system ⊘ ♿ |
| Ⓐ | | L6647 | Upper extremity addition, shoulder lock mechanism, body powered actuator ⊘ ♿ |
| Ⓐ | | L6648 | Upper extremity addition, shoulder lock mechanism, external powered actuator ⊘ ♿ |
| Ⓐ | ☑ | L6650 | Upper extremity addition, shoulder universal joint, each ⊘ ♿ |
| Ⓐ | | L6655 | Upper extremity addition, standard control cable, extra ⊘ ♿ |
| Ⓐ | | L6660 | Upper extremity addition, heavy-duty control cable ⊘ ♿ |
| Ⓐ | | L6665 | Upper extremity addition, Teflon, or equal, cable lining ⊘ ♿ |
| Ⓐ | | L6670 | Upper extremity addition, hook to hand, cable adapter ⊘ ♿ |
| Ⓐ | | L6672 | Upper extremity addition, harness, chest or shoulder, saddle type ⊘ ♿ |
| Ⓐ | | L6675 | Upper extremity addition, harness, (e.g., figure of eight type), single cable design ⊘ ♿ |
| Ⓐ | | L6676 | Upper extremity addition, harness, (e.g., figure of eight type), dual cable design ⊘ ♿ |
| Ⓐ | | L6677 | Upper extremity addition, harness, triple control, simultaneous operation of terminal device and elbow ⊘ |
| Ⓐ | | L6680 | Upper extremity addition, test socket, wrist disarticulation or below elbow ⊘ ♿ |
| Ⓐ | | L6682 | Upper extremity addition, test socket, elbow disarticulation or above elbow ⊘ ♿ |
| Ⓐ | | L6684 | Upper extremity addition, test socket, shoulder disarticulation or interscapular thoracic ⊘ ♿ |
| Ⓐ | | L6686 | Upper extremity addition, suction socket ⊘ ♿ |
| Ⓐ | | L6687 | Upper extremity addition, frame type socket, below elbow or wrist disarticulation ⊘ ♿ |

---

| | | | | |
|---|---|---|---|---|
| Ⓐ | | L6688 | Upper extremity addition, frame type socket, above elbow or elbow disarticulation | ⊘ & |
| Ⓐ | | L6689 | Upper extremity addition, frame type socket, shoulder disarticulation | ⊘ & |
| Ⓐ | | L6690 | Upper extremity addition, frame type socket, interscapular-thoracic | ⊘ & |
| Ⓐ | ☑ | L6691 | Upper extremity addition, removable insert, each | ⊘ & |
| Ⓐ | ☑ | L6692 | Upper extremity addition, silicone gel insert or equal, each | ⊘ & |
| Ⓐ | | L6693 | Upper extremity addition, locking elbow, forearm counterbalance | ⊘ & |
| Ⓐ | | L6694 | Addition to upper extremity prosthesis, below elbow/above elbow, custom fabricated from existing mold or prefabricated, socket insert, silicone gel, elastomeric or equal, for use with locking mechanism | ⊘ |
| Ⓐ | | L6695 | Addition to upper extremity prosthesis, below elbow/above elbow, custom fabricated from existing mold or prefabricated, socket insert, silicone gel, elastomeric or equal, not for use with locking mechanism | ⊘ |
| Ⓐ | | L6696 | Addition to upper extremity prosthesis, below elbow/above elbow, custom fabricated socket insert for congenital or atypical traumatic amputee, silicone gel, elastomeric or equal, for use with or without locking mechanism, initial only (for other than initial, use code L6694 or L6695) | ⊘ |
| Ⓐ | | L6697 | Addition to upper extremity prosthesis, below elbow/above elbow, custom fabricated socket insert for other than congenital or atypical traumatic amputee, silicone gel, elastomeric or equal, for use with or without locking mechanism, initial only (for other than initial, use code L6694 or L6695) | ⊘ |
| Ⓐ | | L6698 | Addition to upper extremity prosthesis, below elbow/above elbow, lock mechanism, excludes socket insert | ⊘ |

## TERMINAL DEVICES

## HOOKS AND HANDS

| | | | | |
|---|---|---|---|---|
| | Ⓐ | L6703 | Terminal device, passive hand/mitt, any material, any size | ⊘ |
| | Ⓐ | L6704 | Terminal device, sport/recreational/work attachment, any material, any size | ⊘ |
| | Ⓐ | L6706 | Terminal device, hook, mechanical, voluntary opening, any material, any size, lined or unlined | ⊘ |
| | Ⓐ | L6707 | Terminal device, hook, mechanical, voluntary closing, any material, any size, lined or unlined | ⊘ |
| | Ⓐ | L6708 | Terminal device, hand, mechanical, voluntary opening, any material, any size | ⊘ |
| | Ⓐ | L6709 | Terminal device, hand, mechanical, voluntary closing, any material, any size | ⊘ |
| ● | Ⓐ | L6711 | Terminal device, hook, mechanical, voluntary opening, any material, any size, lined or unlined, pediatric | |
| ● | Ⓐ | L6712 | Terminal device, hook, mechanical, voluntary closing, any material, any size, lined or unlined, pediatric | |
| ● | Ⓐ | L6713 | Terminal device, hand, mechanical, voluntary opening, any material, any size, pediatric | |

---

☑ Quantity Alert    ● New Code    ○ Recycled/Reinstated    ▲ Revised Code    & DMEPOS Paid    ⊘ SNF Excluded

● Ⓐ **L6714** Terminal device, hand, mechanical, voluntary closing, any material, any size, pediatric

● Ⓐ **L6721** Terminal device, hook or hand, heavy-duty, mechanical, voluntary opening, any material, any size, lined or unlined

● Ⓐ **L6722** Terminal device, hook or hand, heavy-duty, mechanical, voluntary closing, any material, any size, lined or unlined

Ⓐ **L6805** Addition to terminal device, modifier wrist unit   ⊘&
MED: 100-2,15,120; 100-4,3,10.4

Ⓐ **L6810** Addition to terminal device, precision pinch device   ⊘&
MED: 100-2,15,120; 100-4,3,10.4

Ⓐ **L6881** Automatic grasp feature, addition to upper limb electric prosthetic terminal device   ⊘&

Ⓐ **L6882** Microprocessor control feature, addition to upper limb prosthetic terminal device   ⊘&
MED: 100-2,15,120; 100-4,3,10.4

Ⓐ **L6883** Replacement socket, below elbow/wrist disarticulation, molded to patient model, for use with or without external power

Ⓐ **L6884** Replacement socket, above elbow/elbow disarticulation, molded to patient model, for use with or without external power

Ⓐ **L6885** Replacement socket, shoulder disarticulation/interscapular thoracic, molded to patient model, for use with or without external power

## GLOVES FOR ABOVE HANDS

Ⓐ **L6890** Addition to upper extremity prosthesis, glove for terminal device, any material, prefabricated, includes fitting and adjustment   &

Ⓐ **L6895** Addition to upper extremity prosthesis, glove for terminal device, any material, custom fabricated   &

## HAND RESTORATION

Ⓐ **L6900** Hand restoration (casts, shading and measurements included), partial hand, with glove, thumb or one finger remaining   &

Ⓐ **L6905** Hand restoration (casts, shading and measurements included), partial hand, with glove, multiple fingers remaining   &

Ⓐ **L6910** Hand restoration (casts, shading and measurements included), partial hand, with glove, no fingers remaining   &

Ⓐ **L6915** Hand restoration (shading and measurements included), replacement glove for above   &

## EXTERNAL POWER

## BASE DEVICES

Ⓐ **L6920** Wrist disarticulation, external power, self-suspended inner socket, removable forearm shell, Otto Bock or equal switch, cables, 2 batteries and 1 charger, switch control of terminal device   ⊘&

Ⓐ **L6925** Wrist disarticulation, external power, self-suspended inner socket, removable forearm shell, Otto Bock or equal electrodes, cables, 2 batteries and one charger, myoelectronic control of terminal device   ⊘&

| | | | |
|---|---|---|---|
| A | L6930 | Below elbow, external power, self-suspended inner socket, removable forearm shell, Otto Bock or equal switch, cables, 2 batteries and one charger, switch control of terminal device | ⃠ ♿ |
| A | L6935 | Below elbow, external power, self-suspended inner socket, removable forearm shell, Otto Bock or equal electrodes, cables, 2 batteries and one charger, myoelectronic control of terminal device | ⃠ ♿ |
| A | L6940 | Elbow disarticulation, external power, molded inner socket, removable humeral shell, outside locking hinges, forearm, Otto Bock or equal switch, cables, 2 batteries and one charger, switch control of terminal device | ⃠ ♿ |
| A | L6945 | Elbow disarticulation, external power, molded inner socket, removable humeral shell, outside locking hinges, forearm, Otto Bock or equal electrodes, cables, 2 batteries and one charger, myoelectronic control of terminal device | ⃠ ♿ |
| A | L6950 | Above elbow, external power, molded inner socket, removable humeral shell, internal locking elbow, forearm, Otto Bock or equal switch, cables, 2 batteries and one charger, switch control of terminal device | ⃠ ♿ |
| A | L6955 | Above elbow, external power, molded inner socket, removable humeral shell, internal locking elbow, forearm, Otto Bock or equal electrodes, cables, 2 batteries and one charger, myoelectronic control of terminal device | ⃠ ♿ |
| A | L6960 | Shoulder disarticulation, external power, molded inner socket, removable shoulder shell, shoulder bulkhead, humeral section, mechanical elbow, forearm, Otto Bock or equal switch, cables, 2 batteries and one charger, switch control of terminal device | ⃠ ♿ |
| A | L6965 | Shoulder disarticulation, external power, molded inner socket, removable shoulder shell, shoulder bulkhead, humeral section, mechanical elbow, forearm, Otto Bock or equal electrodes, cables, 2 batteries and one charger, myoelectronic control of terminal device | ⃠ ♿ |
| A | L6970 | Interscapular-thoracic, external power, molded inner socket, removable shoulder shell, shoulder bulkhead, humeral section, mechanical elbow, forearm, Otto Bock or equal switch, cables, 2 batteries and one charger, switch control of terminal device | ⃠ ♿ |
| A | L6975 | Interscapular-thoracic, external power, molded inner socket, removable shoulder shell, shoulder bulkhead, humeral section, mechanical elbow, forearm, Otto Bock or equal electrodes, cables, 2 batteries and one charger, myoelectronic control of terminal device | ⃠ ♿ |
| A | L7007 | Electric hand, switch or myoelectric controlled, adult | A |
| A | L7008 | Electric hand, switch or myoelectric, controlled, pediatric | A |
| A | L7009 | Electric hook, switch or myoelectric controlled, adult | A |
| A | L7040 | Prehensile actuator, switch controlled | ⃠ ♿ |
| A | L7045 | Electric hook, switch or myoelectric controlled, pediatric | ⃠ ♿ |

## ELBOW

| | | | |
|---|---|---|---|
| A | L7170 | Electronic elbow, Hosmer or equal, switch controlled | ⃠ ♿ |
| A | L7180 | Electronic elbow, microprocessor sequential control of elbow and terminal device | ⃠ ♿ |
| A | L7181 | Electronic elbow, microprocessor simultaneous control of elbow and terminal device | ⃠ |

**Prosthetic Procedures**

**L7185 — L7510**

| | | | |
|---|---|---|---|
| Ⓐ | L7185 | Electronic elbow, adolescent, Variety Village or equal, switch controlled | ⊘ & |
| Ⓐ | L7186 | Electronic elbow, child, Variety Village or equal, switch controlled | ⊘ & |
| Ⓐ | L7190 | Electronic elbow, adolescent, Variety Village or equal, myoelectronically controlled | ⊘ & |
| Ⓐ | L7191 | Electronic elbow, child, Variety Village or equal, myoelectronically controlled | ⊘ & |
| Ⓐ | L7260 | Electronic wrist rotator, Otto Bock or equal | ⊘ & |
| Ⓐ | L7261 | Electronic wrist rotator, for Utah arm | ⊘ & |
| Ⓐ | L7266 | Servo control, Steeper or equal | ⊘ & |
| Ⓐ | L7272 | Analogue control, UNB or equal | ⊘ & |
| Ⓐ | L7274 | Proportional control, 6–12 volt, Liberty, Utah or equal | ⊘ & |

## BATTERY COMPONENTS

| | | | | |
|---|---|---|---|---|
| Ⓐ | ☑ | L7360 | Six volt battery, each | & |
| Ⓐ | ☑ | L7362 | Battery charger, 6 volt, each | ⊘ & |
| Ⓐ | ☑ | L7364 | Twelve volt battery, each | & |
| Ⓐ | ☑ | L7366 | Battery charger, twelve volt, each | ⊘ & |
| Ⓐ | | L7367 | Lithium ion battery, replacement | ⊘ & |
| Ⓐ | | L7368 | Lithium ion battery charger | ⊘ & |
| Ⓐ | | L7400 | Addition to upper extremity prosthesis, below elbow/wrist disarticulation, ultralight material (titanium, carbon fiber or equal) | ⊘ |
| Ⓐ | | L7401 | Addition to upper extremity prosthesis, above elbow disarticulation, ultralight material (titanium, carbon fiber or equal) | ⊘ |
| Ⓐ | | L7402 | Addition to upper extremity prosthesis, shoulder disarticulation/interscapular thoracic, ultralight material (titanium, carbon fiber or equal) | ⊘ |
| Ⓐ | | L7403 | Addition to upper extremity prosthesis, below elbow/wrist disarticulation, acrylic material | ⊘ |
| Ⓐ | | L7404 | Addition to upper extremity prosthesis, above elbow disarticulation, acrylic material | ⊘ |
| Ⓐ | | L7405 | Addition to upper extremity prosthesis, shoulder disarticulation/interscapular thoracic, acrylic material | ⊘ |
| Ⓐ | | L7499 | Upper extremity prosthesis, not otherwise specified | |

## REPAIRS

Ⓐ    L7500    Repair of prosthetic device, hourly rate (excludes V5335 repair of oral or laryngeal prosthesis or artificial larynx)
Medicare jurisdiction: local contractor if repair of implanted prosthetic device.
**MED:** 100-2,15,110.2; 100-2,15,120; 100-4,32,100

Ⓐ    L7510    Repair of prosthetic device, repair or replace minor parts
Medicare jurisdiction: local contractor if repair of implanted prosthetic device.
**MED:** 100-2,15,110.2; 100-2,15,120; 100-4,32,100

Prosthetic Procedures

| | | | |
|---|---|---|---|
| A | ☑ | **L7520** | Repair prosthetic device, labor component, per 15 minutes |

Medicare jurisdiction: local contractor if repair of implanted prosthetic device.

| | | | |
|---|---|---|---|
| E | ☑ | **L7600** | Prosthetic donning sleeve, any material, each |

## TERMINAL DEVICES

**L7611** ~~Terminal device, hook, mechanical, voluntary opening, any material, any size, lined or unlined, pediatric~~
See L6711

**L7612** ~~Terminal device, hook, mechanical, voluntary closing, any material, any size, lined or unlined, pediatric~~
See L6712

**L7613** ~~Terminal device, hand, mechanical, voluntary opening, any material, any size, pediatric~~
See L6713

**L7614** ~~Terminal device, hand, mechanical, voluntary closing, any material, any size, pediatric~~
See L6714

**L7621** ~~Terminal device, hook or hand, heavy duty, mechanical, voluntary opening, any material, any size, lined or unlined~~
See L6721

**L7622** ~~Terminal device, hook or hand, heavy duty, mechanical, voluntary closing, any material, any size, lined or unlined~~
See L6722

## GENERAL

| | | |
|---|---|---|
| A | **L7900** | Male vacuum erection system     A ♂ ⅄ |

## PROSTHESIS

| | | |
|---|---|---|
| A | **L8000** | Breast prosthesis, mastectomy bra     A ♀ ⅄ |

MED: 100-2,15,120

| | | |
|---|---|---|
| A | **L8001** | Breast prosthesis, mastectomy bra, with integrated breast prosthesis form, unilateral     A ♀ ⅄ |

MED: 100-2,15,120

| | | |
|---|---|---|
| A | **L8002** | Breast prosthesis, mastectomy bra, with integrated breast prosthesis form, bilateral     A ♀ ⅄ |

MED: 100-2,15,120

| | | |
|---|---|---|
| A | **L8010** | Breast prosthesis, mastectomy sleeve     A ♀ |

MED: 100-2,15,120

| | | |
|---|---|---|
| A | **L8015** | External breast prosthesis garment, with mastectomy form, postmastectomy     A ♀ ⅄ |

MED: 100-2,15,120

| | | |
|---|---|---|
| A | **L8020** | Breast prosthesis, mastectomy form     A ♀ ⅄ |

MED: 100-2,15,120

| | | |
|---|---|---|
| A | **L8030** | Breast prosthesis, silicone or equal     A ♀ ⅄ |

MED: 100-2,15,120

Prosthetic Procedures

L7520 — L8030

---

Prosthetic Procedures

L8035 — L8415

| A | | **L8035** | Custom breast prosthesis, post mastectomy, molded to patient model | Ⓐ♀♿ |
| | | | MED: 100-2,15,120 | |
| A | | **L8039** | Breast prosthesis, not otherwise specified | Ⓐ♀ |

Orbital and midfacial prosthesis (L8041-L8042)

Nasal prosthesis (L8040)

Frontal bone

Nasal bone

Maxilla

Zygoma

(L8043-L8044)

Facial prosthetics are typically custom manufactured from polymers and carefully matched to the original features. The maxilla, zygoma, frontal, and nasal bones are often involved, either singly or in combination (L8040-L8044)

| A | | **L8040** | Nasal prosthesis, provided by a nonphysician | ♿ |
| A | | **L8041** | Midfacial prosthesis, provided by a nonphysician | ♿ |
| A | | **L8042** | Orbital prosthesis, provided by a nonphysician | ♿ |
| A | | **L8043** | Upper facial prosthesis, provided by a nonphysician | ♿ |
| A | | **L8044** | Hemi-facial prosthesis, provided by a nonphysician | ♿ |
| A | | **L8045** | Auricular prosthesis, provided by a nonphysician | ♿ |
| A | | **L8046** | Partial facial prosthesis, provided by a nonphysician | ♿ |
| A | | **L8047** | Nasal septal prosthesis, provided by a nonphysician | ♿ |
| A | | **L8048** | Unspecified maxillofacial prosthesis, by report, provided by a nonphysician | |
| A | | **L8049** | Repair or modification of maxillofacial prosthesis, labor component, 15 minute increments, provided by a nonphysician | |

## TRUSSES

| A | | **L8300** | Truss, single with standard pad | ♿ |
| | | | MED: 100-2,15,120; 100-3,280.11; 100-3,280.12; 100-4,4,240 | |
| A | | **L8310** | Truss, double with standard pads | ♿ |
| | | | MED: 100-2,15,120; 100-3,280.11; 100-3,280.12; 100-4,4,240 | |
| A | | **L8320** | Truss, addition to standard pad, water pad | ♿ |
| | | | MED: 100-2,15,120; 100-3,280.11; 100-3,280.12; 100-4,4,240 | |
| A | | **L8330** | Truss, addition to standard pad, scrotal pad | ♂♿ |
| | | | MED: 100-2,15,120; 100-3,280.11; 100-3,280.12; 100-4,4,240 | |

## PROSTHETIC SOCKS

| A | ☑ | **L8400** | Prosthetic sheath, below knee, each | ♿ |
| | | | MED: 100-2,15,120 | |
| A | ☑ | **L8410** | Prosthetic sheath, above knee, each | ♿ |
| | | | MED: 100-2,15,120 | |
| A | ☑ | **L8415** | Prosthetic sheath, upper limb, each | ♿ |
| | | | MED: 100-2,15,120 | |

Special Coverage Instructions    Noncovered by Medicare    Carrier Discretion

Ⓐ ☑ **L8417** Prosthetic sheath/sock, including a gel cushion layer, below knee or above knee, each ♿

Ⓐ ☑ **L8420** Prosthetic sock, multiple ply, below knee, each ♿
MED: 100-2,15,120

Ⓐ ☑ **L8430** Prosthetic sock, multiple ply, above knee, each ♿
MED: 100-2,15,120

Ⓐ ☑ **L8435** Prosthetic sock, multiple ply, upper limb, each ♿
MED: 100-2,15,120

Ⓐ ☑ **L8440** Prosthetic shrinker, below knee, each ♿
MED: 100-2,15,120

Ⓐ ☑ **L8460** Prosthetic shrinker, above knee, each ♿
MED: 100-2,15,120

Ⓐ ☑ **L8465** Prosthetic shrinker, upper limb, each ♿
MED: 100-2,15,120

Ⓐ ☑ **L8470** Prosthetic sock, single ply, fitting, below knee, each ♿
MED: 100-2,15,120

Ⓐ ☑ **L8480** Prosthetic sock, single ply, fitting, above knee, each ♿
MED: 100-2,15,120

Ⓐ ☑ **L8485** Prosthetic sock, single ply, fitting, upper limb, each ♿
MED: 100-2,15,120

Ⓐ **L8499** Unlisted procedure for miscellaneous prosthetic services
Determine if an alternative HCPCS Level II or a CPT code better describes the service being reported. This code should be used only if a more specific code is unavailable.

## PROSTHETIC IMPLANTS

### INTEGUMENTARY SYSTEM

Ⓐ **L8500** Artificial larynx, any type ♿
MED: 100-2,15,120; 100-3,50.2; 100-4,4,240

Ⓐ **L8501** Tracheostomy speaking valve ♿
MED: 100-3,50.4

Ⓐ **L8505** Artificial larynx replacement battery/accessory, any type

Ⓐ ☑ **L8507** Tracheo-esophageal voice prosthesis, patient inserted, any type, each ♿

Ⓐ **L8509** Tracheo-esophageal voice prosthesis, inserted by a licensed health care provider, any type ♿

Ⓐ **L8510** Voice amplifier ♿
MED: 100-3,50.2

Ⓐ ☑ **L8511** Insert for indwelling tracheoesophageal prosthesis, with or without valve, replacement only, each ♿

Ⓐ ☑ **L8512** Gelatin capsules or equivalent, for use with tracheoesophageal voice prosthesis, replacement only, per 10 ♿

Ⓐ ☑ **L8513** Cleaning device used with tracheoesophageal voice prosthesis, pipet, brush, or equal, replacement only, each ♿

Ⓐ ☑ **L8514** Tracheoesophageal puncture dilator, replacement only, each ♿

Ⓐ ☑ **L8515** Gelatin capsule, application device for use with tracheoesophageal voice prosthesis, each

☑ Quantity Alert ● New Code ○ Recycled/Reinstated ▲ Revised Code ♿ DMEPOS Paid ⊘ SNF Excluded

Prosthetic Procedures

L8600 — L8621

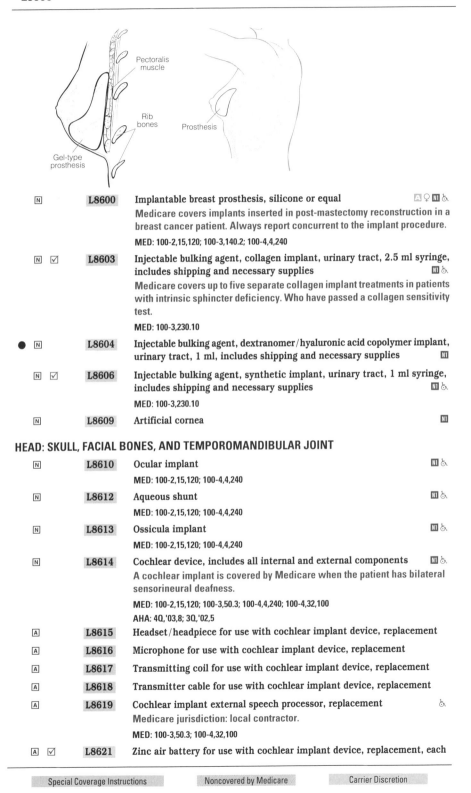

Pectoralis
muscle

Rib
bones    Prosthesis

Gel-type
prosthesis

[N]  **L8600**  Implantable breast prosthesis, silicone or equal    [A] [♀] [M] [&]
Medicare covers implants inserted in post-mastectomy reconstruction in a breast cancer patient. Always report concurrent to the implant procedure.
MED: 100-2,15,120; 100-3,140.2; 100-4,4,240

[N] [☑]  **L8603**  Injectable bulking agent, collagen implant, urinary tract, 2.5 ml syringe, includes shipping and necessary supplies    [M] [&]
Medicare covers up to five separate collagen implant treatments in patients with intrinsic sphincter deficiency. Who have passed a collagen sensitivity test.
MED: 100-3,230.10

● [N]  **L8604**  Injectable bulking agent, dextranomer/hyaluronic acid copolymer implant, urinary tract, 1 ml, includes shipping and necessary supplies    [M]

[N] [☑]  **L8606**  Injectable bulking agent, synthetic implant, urinary tract, 1 ml syringe, includes shipping and necessary supplies    [M] [&]
MED: 100-3,230.10

[N]  **L8609**  Artificial cornea    [M]

## HEAD: SKULL, FACIAL BONES, AND TEMPOROMANDIBULAR JOINT

[N]  **L8610**  Ocular implant    [M] [&]
MED: 100-2,15,120; 100-4,4,240

[N]  **L8612**  Aqueous shunt    [M] [&]
MED: 100-2,15,120; 100-4,4,240

[N]  **L8613**  Ossicula implant    [M] [&]
MED: 100-2,15,120; 100-4,4,240

[N]  **L8614**  Cochlear device, includes all internal and external components    [M] [&]
A cochlear implant is covered by Medicare when the patient has bilateral sensorineural deafness.
MED: 100-2,15,120; 100-3,50.3; 100-4,4,240; 100-4,32,100
AHA: 4Q,'03,8; 3Q,'02,5

[A]  **L8615**  Headset/headpiece for use with cochlear implant device, replacement

[A]  **L8616**  Microphone for use with cochlear implant device, replacement

[A]  **L8617**  Transmitting coil for use with cochlear implant device, replacement

[A]  **L8618**  Transmitter cable for use with cochlear implant device, replacement

[A]  **L8619**  Cochlear implant external speech processor, replacement    [&]
Medicare jurisdiction: local contractor.
MED: 100-3,50.3; 100-4,32,100

[A] [☑]  **L8621**  Zinc air battery for use with cochlear implant device, replacement, each

---

Special Coverage Instructions   Noncovered by Medicare   Carrier Discretion

| | | | |
|---|---|---|---|
| A ☑ | **L8622** | Alkaline battery for use with cochlear implant device, any size, replacement, each | |
| A ☑ | **L8623** | Lithium ion battery for use with cochlear implant device speech processor, other than ear level, replacement, each | ⅋ |
| A ☑ | **L8624** | Lithium ion battery for use with cochlear implant device speech processor, ear level, replacement, each | ⅋ |

## UPPER EXTREMITY

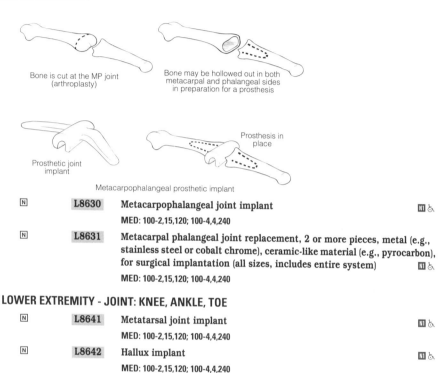

Bone is cut at the MP joint (arthroplasty)

Bone may be hollowed out in both metacarpal and phalangeal sides in preparation for a prosthesis

Prosthetic joint implant

Prosthesis in place

Metacarpophalangeal prosthetic implant

| | | | |
|---|---|---|---|
| N | **L8630** | Metacarpophalangeal joint implant | N ⅋ |
| | | MED: 100-2,15,120; 100-4,4,240 | |
| N | **L8631** | Metacarpal phalangeal joint replacement, 2 or more pieces, metal (e.g., stainless steel or cobalt chrome), ceramic-like material (e.g., pyrocarbon), for surgical implantation (all sizes, includes entire system) | N ⅋ |
| | | MED: 100-2,15,120; 100-4,4,240 | |

## LOWER EXTREMITY - JOINT: KNEE, ANKLE, TOE

| | | | |
|---|---|---|---|
| N | **L8641** | Metatarsal joint implant | N ⅋ |
| | | MED: 100-2,15,120; 100-4,4,240 | |
| N | **L8642** | Hallux implant | N ⅋ |
| | | MED: 100-2,15,120; 100-4,4,240 | |

## MISCELLANEOUS MUSCULAR-SKELETAL

| | | | |
|---|---|---|---|
| N ☑ | **L8658** | Interphalangeal joint spacer, silicone or equal, each | N ⅋ |
| | | MED: 100-2,15,120; 100-4,4,240 | |
| N | **L8659** | Interphalangeal finger joint replacement, 2 or more pieces, metal (e.g., stainless steel or cobalt chrome), ceramic-like material (e.g., pyrocarbon) for surgical implantation, any size | N ⅋ |
| | | MED: 100-2,15,120; 100-4,4,240 | |

## CARDIOVASCULAR SYSTEM

| | | | |
|---|---|---|---|
| N | **L8670** | Vascular graft material, synthetic, implant | N ⅋ |
| | | MED: 100-2,15,120; 100-4,4,240 | |

## GENERAL

| | | | |
|---|---|---|---|
| B ☑ | **L8680** | Implantable neurostimulator electrode, each | |
| | | MED: 100-4,32,50 | |
| ▲ A | **L8681** | Patient programmer (external) for use with implantable programmable neurostimulator pulse generator, replacement only | |

Prosthetic Procedures

L8682 — L9900

| N | L8682 | Implantable neurostimulator radiofrequency receiver ▣ |
| A | L8683 | Radiofrequency transmitter (external) for use with implantable neurostimulator radiofrequency receiver |
| A | L8684 | Radiofrequency transmitter (external) for use with implantable sacral root neurostimulator receiver for bowel and bladder management, replacement |
| N | L8685 | Implantable neurostimulator pulse generator, single array, rechargeable, includes extension |

MED: 100-4,32,50

| N | L8686 | Implantable neurostimulator pulse generator, single array, nonrechargeable, includes extension |

MED: 100-4,32,50

| N | L8687 | Implantable neurostimulator pulse generator, dual array, rechargeable, includes extension |

MED: 100-4,32,50

| N | L8688 | Implantable neurostimulator pulse generator, dual array, nonrechargeable, includes extension |

MED: 100-4,32,50

| ▲ A | L8689 | External recharging system for battery (internal) for use with implantable neurostimulator, replacement only |
| N | L8690 | Auditory osseointegrated device, includes all internal and external components ▣ |
| A | L8691 | Auditory osseointegrated device, external sound processor, replacement |
| ▲ A | L8695 | External recharging system for battery (external) for use with implantable neurostimulator, replacement only |
| N | L8699 | Prosthetic implant, not otherwise specified ▣ |

Determine if an alternative HCPCS Level II or a CPT code better describes the service being reported. This code should be used only if a more specific code is unavailable.

| N | L9900 | Orthotic and prosthetic supply, accessory, and/or service component of another HCPCS L code |

## MEDICAL SERVICES M0000-M0301

### OTHER MEDICAL SERVICES

M codes include office services, cellular therapy, prolotherapy, intragastric hypothermia, IV chelation therapy, and fabric wrapping of an abdominal aneurysm.

[03] **M0064** Brief office visit for the sole purpose of monitoring or changing drug prescriptions used in the treatment of mental psychoneurotic and personality disorders ⊘
MED: 100-4,12,210.1

[E] **M0075** Cellular therapy
The therapeutic efficacy of injecting foreign proteins has not been established.
MED: 100-3,30.8

[E] **M0076** Prolotherapy
The therapeutic efficacy of prolotherapy and joint sclerotherapy has not been established.
MED: 100-3,150.7

[E] **M0100** Intragastric hypothermia using gastric freezing
Code with caution: This procedure is considered obsolete.
MED: 100-3,100.6

### CARDIOVASCULAR SERVICES

[E] **M0300** IV chelation therapy (chemical endarterectomy)
Chelation therapy is considered experimental in the United States.
MED: 100-3,20.21

[E] **M0301** Fabric wrapping of abdominal aneurysm
Code with caution: This procedure has largely been replaced with more effective treatment modalities. Submit documentation.
MED: 100-3,20.23

**Pathology And Laboratory Services**

**P2028 — P9016**

# PATHOLOGY AND LABORATORY SERVICES P0000-P9999

P codes include chemistry, toxicology, and microbiology tests, screening Papanicolaou procedures, and various blood products.

## CHEMISTRY AND TOXICOLOGY TESTS

[A]  **P2028**  Cephalin floculation, blood
Code with caution: This test is considered obsolete. Submit documentation.
MED: 100-3,300.1

[A]  **P2029**  Congo red, blood
Code with caution: This test is considered obsolete. Submit documentation.
MED: 100-3,300.1

[E]  **P2031**  Hair analysis (excluding arsenic)
MED: 100-3,190.6

[A]  **P2033**  Thymol turbidity, blood
Code with caution: This test is considered obsolete. Submit documentation.
MED: 100-3,300.1

[A]  **P2038**  Mucoprotein, blood (seromucoid) (medical necessity procedure)
Code with caution: This test is considered obsolete. Submit documentation.
MED: 100-3,300.1

## PATHOLOGY SCREENING TESTS

[A]  **P3000**  Screening Papanicolaou smear, cervical or vaginal, up to 3 smears, by technician under physician supervision  [A] ♀ ⊘
One Pap test is covered by Medicare every two years, unless the physician suspects cervical abnormalities and shortens the interval. See also G0123-G0124.
MED: 100-2,6,10; 100-3,190.2; 100-4,4,240

[B]  **P3001**  Screening Papanicolaou smear, cervical or vaginal, up to 3 smears, requiring interpretation by physician  [A] ♀ ⊘
One Pap test is covered by Medicare every two years, unless the physician suspects cervical abnormalities and shortens the interval. See also G0123-G0124.
MED: 100-2,6,10; 100-3,190.2; 100-4,4,240

## MICROBIOLOGY TESTS

[E]  **P7001**  Culture, bacterial, urine; quantitative, sensitivity study

## MISCELLANEOUS

[R] ☑  **P9010**  Blood (whole), for transfusion, per unit
MED: 100-1,3,20.5; 100-2,1,10; 100-4,3,40.2.2

[R] ☑  **P9011**  Blood, split unit
MED: 100-1,3,20.5; 100-2,1,10; 100-4,3,40.2.2

[R] ☑  **P9012**  Cryoprecipitate, each unit
MED: 100-1,3,20.5; 100-2,1,10; 100-4,3,40.2.2

[R] ☑  **P9016**  Red blood cells, leukocytes reduced, each unit
MED: 100-1,3,20.5; 100-2,1,10; 100-4,3,40.2.2

Pathology And Laboratory Services

P9017 — P9046

☒ ☑ **P9017** Fresh frozen plasma (single donor), frozen within 8 hours of collection, each unit
MED: 100-1,3,20.5; 100-2,1,10; 100-4,3,40.2.2

☒ ☑ **P9019** Platelets, each unit
MED: 100-1,3,20.5; 100-2,1,10; 100-4,3,40.2.2

☒ ☑ **P9020** Platelet rich plasma, each unit
MED: 100-1,3,20.5; 100-4,3,40.2.2

☒ ☑ **P9021** Red blood cells, each unit
MED: 100-1,3,20.5; 100-2,1,10; 100-4,3,40.2.2

☒ ☑ **P9022** Red blood cells, washed, each unit
MED: 100-1,3,20.5; 100-2,1,10; 100-4,3,40.2.2

☒ ☑ **P9023** Plasma, pooled multiple donor, solvent/detergent treated, frozen, each unit
MED: 100-1,3,20.5; 100-2,1,10; 100-4,3,40.2.2

☒ ☑ **P9031** Platelets, leukocytes reduced, each unit
MED: 100-1,3,20.5; 100-1,3,20.5.2; 100-1,3,20.5.3; 100-2,1,10; 100-4,3,40.2.2

☒ ☑ **P9032** Platelets, irradiated, each unit
MED: 100-1,3,20.5; 100-1,3,20.5.2; 100-1,3,20.5.3; 100-2,1,10; 100-4,3,40.2.2

☒ ☑ **P9033** Platelets, leukocytes reduced, irradiated, each unit
MED: 100-1,3,20.5; 100-1,3,20.5.2; 100-1,3,20.5.3; 100-2,1,10; 100-4,3,40.2.2

☒ ☑ **P9034** Platelets, pheresis, each unit
MED: 100-1,3,20.5; 100-1,3,20.5.2; 100-1,3,20.5.3; 100-2,1,10; 100-4,3,40.2.2

☒ ☑ **P9035** Platelets, pheresis, leukocytes reduced, each unit
MED: 100-1,3,20.5; 100-1,3,20.5.2; 100-1,3,20.5.3; 100-2,1,10; 100-4,3,40.2.2

☒ ☑ **P9036** Platelets, pheresis, irradiated, each unit
MED: 100-1,3,20.5; 100-1,3,20.5.2; 100-1,3,20.5.3; 100-2,1,10; 100-4,3,40.2.2

☒ ☑ **P9037** Platelets, pheresis, leukocytes reduced, irradiated, each unit
MED: 100-1,3,20.5; 100-1,3,20.5.2; 100-1,3,20.5.3; 100-2,1,10; 100-4,3,40.2.2

☒ ☑ **P9038** Red blood cells, irradiated, each unit
MED: 100-1,3,20.5; 100-1,3,20.5.2; 100-1,3,20.5.3; 100-2,1,10; 100-4,3,40.2.2

☒ ☑ **P9039** Red blood cells, deglycerolized, each unit
MED: 100-1,3,20.5; 100-1,3,20.5.2; 100-1,3,20.5.3; 100-2,1,10; 100-4,3,40.2.2

☒ ☑ **P9040** Red blood cells, leukocytes reduced, irradiated, each unit
MED: 100-1,3,20.5; 100-1,3,20.5.2; 100-1,3,20.5.3; 100-2,1,10; 100-4,3,40.2.2

☒ ☑ **P9041** Infusion, albumin (human), 5%, 50 ml ⟨K2⟩
Not considered a blood product for OPPS effective July 1, 2005.
MED: 100-2,1,10; 100-4,3,40.2.2

☒ ☑ **P9043** Infusion, plasma protein fraction (human), 5%, 50 ml
MED: 100-1,3,20.5; 100-2,1,10; 100-4,3,40.2.2

☒ ☑ **P9044** Plasma, cryoprecipitate reduced, each unit
MED: 100-1,3,20.5; 100-2,1,10; 100-4,3,40.2.2

☒ ☑ **P9045** Infusion, albumin (human), 5%, 250 ml ⟨K2⟩
Not considered a blood product for OPPS effective July 1, 2005.
MED: 100-2,1,10; 100-4,3,40.2.2

☒ ☑ **P9046** Infusion, albumin (human), 25%, 20 ml ⟨K2⟩
Not considered a blood product for OPPS effective July 1, 2005.
MED: 100-2,1,10; 100-4,3,40.2.2

---

☑ Quantity Alert    ● New Code    ○ Recycled/Reinstated    ▲ Revised Code    ⅍ DMEPOS Paid    ⊘ SNF Excluded

Pathology And Laboratory Services

P9047 — P9615

K ☑ **P9047** Infusion, albumin (human), 25%, 50 ml  K2
Not considered a blood product for OPPS effective July 1, 2005.
MED: 100-2,1,10; 100-4,3,40.2.2

R ☑ **P9048** Infusion, plasma protein fraction (human), 5%, 250 ml
MED: 100-2,1,10; 100-4,3,40.2.2

R ☑ **P9050** Granulocytes, pheresis, each unit
MED: 100-2,1,10; 100-4,3,40.2.2

R ☑ **P9051** Whole blood or red blood cells, leukocytes reduced, CMV-negative, each unit
MED: 100-2,1,10; 100-4,3,40.2.2

R ☑ **P9052** Platelets, HLA-matched leukocytes reduced, apheresis/pheresis, each unit
MED: 100-2,1,10; 100-4,3,40.2.2

R ☑ **P9053** Platelets, pheresis, leukocytes reduced, CMV-negative, irradiated, each unit
MED: 100-2,1,10; 100-4,3,40.2.2

R ☑ **P9054** Whole blood or red blood cells, leukocytes reduced, frozen, deglycerol, washed, each unit
MED: 100-2,1,10; 100-4,3,40.2.2

R ☑ **P9055** Platelets, leukocytes reduced, CMV-negative, apheresis/pheresis, each unit
MED: 100-2,1,10; 100-4,3,40.2.2

R ☑ **P9056** Whole blood, leukocytes reduced, irradiated, each unit
MED: 100-2,1,10; 100-4,3,40.2.2

R ☑ **P9057** Red blood cells, frozen/deglycerolized/washed, leukocytes reduced, irradiated, each unit
MED: 100-2,1,10; 100-4,3,40.2.2

R ☑ **P9058** Red blood cells, leukocytes reduced, CMV-negative, irradiated, each unit
MED: 100-2,1,10; 100-4,3,40.2.2

R ☑ **P9059** Fresh frozen plasma between 8-24 hours of collection, each unit
MED: 100-2,1,10; 100-4,3,40.2.2

R ☑ **P9060** Fresh frozen plasma, donor retested, each unit
MED: 100-2,1,10; 100-4,3,40.2.2

A ☑ **P9603** Travel allowance, one way in connection with medically necessary laboratory specimen collection drawn from homebound or nursing homebound patient; prorated miles actually travelled.
MED: 100-4,16,60

A ☑ **P9604** Travel allowance, one way in connection with medically necessary laboratory specimen collection drawn from homebound or nursing homebound patient; prorated trip charge
MED: 100-4,16,60

A **P9612** Catheterization for collection of specimen, single patient, all places of service
MED: 100-4,16,60

N **P9615** Catheterization for collection of specimen(s) (multiple patients)
MED: 100-4,16,60

Special Coverage Instructions    Noncovered by Medicare    Carrier Discretion

Ⓜ Maternity Edit   Ⓐ Age Edit   PQ PQRI   A-Y OPPS Status   **2009 HCPCS**

## Q CODES (TEMPORARY) Q0000-Q9999

New temporary Q codes to pay health care providers for the supplies used in creating casts were established to replace the removal of the practice expense for all HCPCS codes, including the CPT codes for fracture management and for casts and splints. Coders should continue to use the appropriate CPT code to report the work and practice expenses involved with creating the cast or splint; the temporary Q codes replace less specific coding for the casting and splinting supplies.

| | | | |
|---|---|---|---|
| ☒ | | **Q0035** | **Cardiokymography**<br>Covered only in conjunction with electrocardiographic stress testing in male patients with atypical angina or nonischemic chest pain, or female patients with angina.<br>MED: 100-3,20.24 |
| ☑ | | **Q0081** | **Infusion therapy, using other than chemotherapeutic drugs, per visit**<br>MED: 100-3,280.14<br>AHA: 1Q,'02,7; 4Q,'02,7 |
| ☑ ☑ | | **Q0083** | **Chemotherapy administration by other than infusion technique only (e.g., subcutaneous, intramuscular, push), per visit** ⊘ |
| ☑ ☑ | | **Q0084** | **Chemotherapy administration by infusion technique only, per visit** ⊘<br>MED: 100-3,280.14 |
| ☑ ☑ | | **Q0085** | **Chemotherapy administration by both infusion technique and other technique(s) (e.g., subcutaneous, intramuscular, push), per visit** ⊘ |
| ☑ | | **Q0091** | **Screening Papanicolaou smear; obtaining, preparing and conveyance of cervical or vaginal smear to laboratory** ▣ ♀ ⊘<br>One pap test is covered by Medicare every two years for low risk patients and every one year for high risk patients. Q0091 can be reported with an E/M code when a separately identifiable E/M service is provided.<br>MED: 100-3,190.2<br>AHA: 4Q,'02,8 |
| ☑ | | **Q0092** | **Set-up portable x-ray equipment** |
| ☑ | | **Q0111** | **Wet mounts, including preparations of vaginal, cervical or skin specimens** |
| ☑ | | **Q0112** | **All potassium hydroxide (KOH) preparations** |
| ☑ | | **Q0113** | **Pinworm examinations** |
| ☑ | | **Q0114** | **Fern test** ♀ |
| ☑ | | **Q0115** | **Postcoital direct, qualitative examinations of vaginal or cervical mucous** ▣ ♀ |
| ☑ ☑ | | **Q0144** | **Azithromycin dihydrate, oral, capsules/powder, 1 g**<br>Use this code for Zithromax, Zithromax Z-PAK. |
| ☑ ☑ | | **Q0163** | **Diphenhydramine HCl, 50 mg, oral, FDA approved prescription antiemetic, for use as a complete therapeutic substitute for an IV antiemetic at time of chemotherapy treatment not to exceed a 48-hour dosage regimen** ▥<br>See also J1200. Medicare covers at the time of chemotherapy if regimen doesn't exceed 48 hours. Submit on the same claim as the chemotherapy. Use this code for Truxadryl.<br>MED: 100-2,6,10; 100-4,4,240; 100-4,17,80.2<br>AHA: 1Q,'02,2 |

N ☑ **Q0164** Prochlorperazine maleate, 5 mg, oral, FDA approved prescription antiemetic, for use as a complete therapeutic substitute for an IV antiemetic at the time of chemotherapy treatment, not to exceed a 48-hour dosage regimen ▥

Medicare covers at the time of chemotherapy if regimen doesn't exceed 48 hours. Submit on the same claim as the chemotherapy. Use this code for Compazine.

MED: 100-2,6,10; 100-4,4,240; 100-4,17,80.2

N ☑ **Q0165** Prochlorperazine maleate, 10 mg, oral, FDA approved prescription antiemetic, for use as a complete therapeutic substitute for an IV antiemetic at the time of chemotherapy treatment, not to exceed a 48-hour dosage regimen

Medicare covers at the time of chemotherapy if regimen doesn't exceed 48 hours. Submit on the same claim as the chemotherapy. Use this code for Compazine.

MED: 100-2,6,10; 100-4,4,240; 100-4,17,80.2

K ☑ **Q0166** Granisetron HCl, 1 mg, oral, FDA approved prescription antiemetic, for use as a complete therapeutic substitute for an IV antiemetic at the time of chemotherapy treatment, not to exceed a 24-hour dosage regimen ▥

Medicare covers at the time of chemotherapy if regimen doesn't exceed 48 hours. Submit on the same claim as the chemotherapy. Use this code for Kytril.

MED: 100-2,6,10; 100-4,4,240; 100-4,17,80.2

N ☑ **Q0167** Dronabinol, 2.5 mg, oral, FDA approved prescription antiemetic, for use as a complete therapeutic substitute for an IV antiemetic at the time of chemotherapy treatment, not to exceed a 48-hour dosage regimen ▥

Medicare covers at the time of chemotherapy if regimen doesn't exceed 48 hours. Submit on the same claim as the chemotherapy. Use this code for Marinol.

MED: 100-2,6,10; 100-4,4,240; 100-4,17,80.2

N ☑ **Q0168** Dronabinol, 5 mg, oral, FDA approved prescription antiemetic, for use as a complete therapeutic substitute for an IV antiemetic at the time of chemotherapy treatment, not to exceed a 48-hour dosage regimen

Use this code for Marinol.

MED: 100-2,6,10; 100-4,4,240; 100-4,17,80.2

N ☑ **Q0169** Promethazine HCl, 12.5 mg, oral, FDA approved prescription antiemetic, for use as a complete therapeutic substitute for an IV antiemetic at the time of chemotherapy treatment, not to exceed a 48-hour dosage regimen ▥

Medicare covers at the time of chemotherapy if regimen doesn't exceed 48 hours. Submit on the same claim as the chemotherapy. Use this code for Phenergan, Amergan.

MED: 100-2,6,10; 100-4,4,240; 100-4,17,80.2

N ☑ **Q0170** Promethazine HCl, 25 mg, oral, FDA approved prescription antiemetic, for use as a complete therapeutic substitute for an IV antiemetic at the time of chemotherapy treatment, not to exceed a 48-hour dosage regimen

Medicare covers at the time of chemotherapy if regimen doesn't exceed 48 hours. Submit on the same claim as the chemotherapy. Use this code for Phenergan, Amergan.

MED: 100-2,6,10; 100-4,4,240; 100-4,17,80.2

Special Coverage Instructions     Noncovered by Medicare     Carrier Discretion

N ☑ **Q0171** Chlorpromazine HCl, 10 mg, oral, FDA approved prescription antiemetic, for use as a complete therapeutic substitute for an IV antiemetic at the time of chemotherapy treatment, not to exceed a 48-hour dosage regimen ▪️

Medicare covers at the time of chemotherapy if regimen doesn't exceed 48 hours. Submit on the same claim as the chemotherapy. Use this code for Thorazine.

MED: 100-2,6,10; 100-4,4,240; 100-4,17,80.2

N ☑ **Q0172** Chlorpromazine HCl, 25 mg, oral, FDA approved prescription antiemetic, for use as a complete therapeutic substitute for an IV antiemetic at the time of chemotherapy treatment, not to exceed a 48-hour dosage regimen

Medicare covers at the time of chemotherapy if regimen doesn't exceed 48 hours. Submit on the same claim as the chemotherapy. Use this code for Thorazine.

MED: 100-2,6,10; 100-4,4,240; 100-4,17,80.2

N ☑ **Q0173** Trimethobenzamide HCl, 250 mg, oral, FDA approved prescription antiemetic, for use as a complete therapeutic substitute for an IV antiemetic at the time of chemotherapy treatment, not to exceed a 48-hour dosage regimen ▪️

Medicare covers at the time of chemotherapy if regimen doesn't exceed 48 hours. Submit on the same claim as the chemotherapy. Use this code for Tebamide, T-Gen, Ticon, Tigan, Triban, Thimazide.

MED: 100-2,6,10; 100-4,4,240; 100-4,17,80.2

N ☑ **Q0174** Thiethylperazine maleate, 10 mg, oral, FDA approved prescription antiemetic, for use as a complete therapeutic substitute for an IV antiemetic at the time of chemotherapy treatment, not to exceed a 48-hour dosage regimen ▪️

Medicare covers at the time of chemotherapy if regimen doesn't exceed 48 hours. Submit on the same claim as the chemotherapy. Use this code for Torecan.

MED: 100-2,6,10; 100-4,4,240; 100-4,17,80.2

N ☑ **Q0175** Perphenazine, 4 mg, oral, FDA approved prescription antiemetic, for use as a complete therapeutic substitute for an IV antiemetic at the time of chemotherapy treatment, not to exceed a 48 hour dosage regimen ▪️

Medicare covers at the time of chemotherapy if regimen doesn't exceed 48 hours. Submit on the same claim as the chemotherapy. Use this code for Trilifon.

MED: 100-2,6,10; 100-4,4,240; 100-4,17,80.2

N ☑ **Q0176** Perphenazine, 8 mg, oral, FDA approved prescription antiemetic, for use as a complete therapeutic substitute for an IV antiemetic at the time of chemotherapy treatment, not to exceed a 48 hour dosage regimen

Medicare covers at the time of chemotherapy if regimen doesn't exceed 48 hours. Submit on the same claim as the chemotherapy. Use this code for Trilifon.

MED: 100-2,6,10; 100-4,4,240; 100-4,17,80.2

N ☑ **Q0177** Hydroxyzine pamoate, 25 mg, oral, FDA approved prescription antiemetic, for use as a complete therapeutic substitute for an IV antiemetic at the time of chemotherapy treatment, not to exceed a 48-hour dosage regimen ▪️

Medicare covers at the time of chemotherapy if regimen doesn't exceed 48 hours. Submit on the same claim as the chemotherapy. Use this code for Vistaril.

MED: 100-2,6,10; 100-4,4,240; 100-4,17,80.2

N ☑ **Q0178** Hydroxyzine pamoate, 50 mg, oral, FDA approved prescription antiemetic, for use as a complete therapeutic substitute for an IV antiemetic at the time of chemotherapy treatment, not to exceed a 48-hour dosage regimen
Medicare covers at the time of chemotherapy if regimen doesn't exceed 48 hours. Submit on the same claim as the chemotherapy.

MED: 100-2,6,10; 100-4,4,240; 100-4,17,80.2

K ☑ **Q0179** Ondansetron HCl 8 mg, oral, FDA approved prescription antiemetic, for use as a complete therapeutic substitute for an IV antiemetic at the time of chemotherapy treatment, not to exceed a 48-hour dosage regimen K2
Medicare covers at the time of chemotherapy if regimen doesn't exceed 48 hours. Submit on the same claim as the chemotherapy. Use this code for Zofran.

MED: 100-2,6,10; 100-4,4,240; 100-4,17,80.2

K ☑ **Q0180** Dolasetron mesylate, 100 mg, oral, FDA approved prescription antiemetic, for use as a complete therapeutic substitute for an IV antiemetic at the time of chemotherapy treatment, not to exceed a 24-hour dosage regimen K2
Medicare covers at the time of chemotherapy if regimen doesn't exceed 24 hours. Submit on the same claim as the chemotherapy. Use this code for Anzemet.

MED: 100-2,6,10; 100-4,4,240; 100-4,17,80.2

E ☑ **Q0181** Unspecified oral dosage form, FDA approved prescription antiemetic, for use as a complete therapeutic substitute for an IV antiemetic at the time of chemotherapy treatment, not to exceed a 48-hour dosage regimen
Medicare covers at the time of chemotherapy if regimen doesn't exceed 48-hours. Submit on the same claim as the chemotherapy.

MED: 100-2,6,10; 100-4,4,240; 100-4,17,80.2

A **Q0480** Driver for use with pneumatic ventricular assist device, replacement only ♿

AHA: 3Q,'05,2

A **Q0481** Microprocessor control unit for use with electric ventricular assist device, replacement only ♿

AHA: 3Q,'05,2

A **Q0482** Microprocessor control unit for use with electric/pneumatic combination ventricular assist device, replacement only ♿

AHA: 3Q,'05,2

A **Q0483** Monitor/display module for use with electric ventricular assist device, replacement only ♿

AHA: 3Q,'05,2

A **Q0484** Monitor/display module for use with electric or electric/pneumatic ventricular assist device, replacement only ♿

AHA: 3Q,'05,2

A **Q0485** Monitor control cable for use with electric ventricular assist device, replacement only ♿

AHA: 3Q,'05,2

A **Q0486** Monitor control cable for use with electric/pneumatic ventricular assist device, replacement only ♿

AHA: 3Q,'05,2

A **Q0487** Leads (pneumatic/electrical) for use with any type electric/pneumatic ventricular assist device, replacement only ♿

AHA: 3Q,'05,2

Ⓐ       **Q0488** Power pack base for use with electric ventricular assist device, replacement only

AHA: 3Q,'05,2

Ⓐ       **Q0489** Power pack base for use with electric/pneumatic ventricular assist device, replacement only    ♿

AHA: 3Q,'05,2

Ⓐ       **Q0490** Emergency power source for use with electric ventricular assist device, replacement only    ♿

AHA: 3Q,'05,2

Ⓐ       **Q0491** Emergency power source for use with electric/pneumatic ventricular assist device, replacement only    ♿

AHA: 3Q,'05,2

Ⓐ       **Q0492** Emergency power supply cable for use with electric ventricular assist device, replacement only    ♿

AHA: 3Q,'05,2

Ⓐ       **Q0493** Emergency power supply cable for use with electric/pneumatic ventricular assist device, replacement only    ♿

AHA: 3Q,'05,2

Ⓐ       **Q0494** Emergency hand pump for use with electric or electric/pneumatic ventricular assist device, replacement only    ♿

AHA: 3Q,'05,2

Ⓐ       **Q0495** Battery/power pack charger for use with electric or electric/pneumatic ventricular assist device, replacement only    ♿

AHA: 3Q,'05,2

Ⓐ       **Q0496** Battery for use with electric or electric/pneumatic ventricular assist device, replacement only    ♿

AHA: 3Q,'05,2

Ⓐ       **Q0497** Battery clips for use with electric or electric/pneumatic ventricular assist device, replacement only    ♿

AHA: 3Q,'05,2

Ⓐ       **Q0498** Holster for use with electric or electric/pneumatic ventricular assist device, replacement only    ♿

AHA: 3Q,'05,2

Ⓐ       **Q0499** Belt/vest for use with electric or electric/pneumatic ventricular assist device, replacement only    ♿

AHA: 3Q,'05,2

Ⓐ ☑    **Q0500** Filters for use with electric or electric/pneumatic ventricular assist device, replacement only    ♿

The base unit for this code is for each filter.

AHA: 3Q,'05,2

Ⓐ       **Q0501** Shower cover for use with electric or electric/pneumatic ventricular assist device, replacement only    ♿

AHA: 3Q,'05,2

Ⓐ       **Q0502** Mobility cart for pneumatic ventricular assist device, replacement only    ♿

AHA: 3Q,'05,2

Ⓐ ☑    **Q0503** Battery for pneumatic ventricular assist device, replacement only, each    ♿

AHA: 3Q,'05,2

Ⓐ       **Q0504** Power adapter for pneumatic ventricular assist device, replacement only, vehicle type    ♿

AHA: 3Q,'05,2

---

Q Codes (Temporary)

Q0505 — Q4004

| | | | |
|---|---|---|---|
| [A] | | Q0505 | Miscellaneous supply or accessory for use with ventricular assist device |
| | | | AHA: 3Q,'05,2 |
| [B] | | Q0510 | Pharmacy supply fee for initial immunosuppressive drug(s), first month following transplant |
| | | | MED: 100-4,4,240 |
| [B] | | Q0511 | Pharmacy supply fee for oral anticancer, oral antiemetic, or immunosuppressive drug(s); for the first prescription in a 30-day period |
| | | | MED: 100-4,4,240 |
| [B] | | Q0512 | Pharmacy supply fee for oral anticancer, oral antiemetic, or immunosuppressive drug(s); for a subsequent prescription in a 30-day period |
| | | | MED: 100-4,4,240 |
| [B] | | Q0513 | Pharmacy dispensing fee for inhalation drug(s); per 30 days |
| [B] | | Q0514 | Pharmacy dispensing fee for inhalation drug(s); per 90 days |
| [K] | ☑ | Q0515 | Injection, sermorelin acetate, 1 mcg    [K2] |
| | | | MED: 100-2,15,50 |
| [N] | | Q1003 | New technology, intraocular lens, category 3 (reduced spherical aberration)    [L6] ⊘ |
| [E] | | Q1004 | New technology intraocular lens category 4 as defined in Federal Register notice |
| [E] | | Q1005 | New technology intraocular lens category 5 as defined in Federal Register notice |
| [N] | ☑ | Q2004 | Irrigation solution for treatment of bladder calculi, for example renacidin, per 500 ml    [N1] |
| | | | MED: 100-2,15,50 |
| [N] | ☑ | Q2009 | Injection, fosphenytoin, 50 mg    [N1] |
| | | | Use this code for Cerebyx. |
| [K] | ☑ | Q2017 | Injection, teniposide, 50 mg    [K2] |
| | | | Use this code for Vumon. |
| | | | MED: 100-2,15,50 |
| [B] | ☑ | Q3001 | Radioelements for brachytherapy, any type, each    ⊘ |
| [A] | | Q3014 | Telehealth originating site facility fee |
| [K] | ☑ | Q3025 | Injection, interferon beta-1a, 11 mcg for intramuscular use    [K2] |
| | | | Use this code for Avonex, Rebif. See also J1825. |
| | | | MED: 100-2,15,50 |
| [E] | ☑ | Q3026 | Injection, interferon beta-1a, 11 mcg for subcutaneous use |
| | | | Use this code for Avonex, Rebif. See also J1825. |
| [N] | | Q3031 | Collagen skin test |
| | | | MED: 100-3,230.10 |
| [B] | | Q4001 | Casting supplies, body cast adult, with or without head, plaster    [A] |
| | | | MED: 100-4,4,240; 100-4,20,170 |
| [B] | | Q4002 | Cast supplies, body cast adult, with or without head, fiberglass    [A] |
| | | | MED: 100-4,4,240; 100-4,20,170 |
| [B] | | Q4003 | Cast supplies, shoulder cast, adult (11 years +), plaster    [A] |
| | | | MED: 100-4,4,240; 100-4,20,170 |
| [B] | | Q4004 | Cast supplies, shoulder cast, adult (11 years +), fiberglass    [A] |
| | | | MED: 100-4,4,240; 100-4,20,170 |

| | | | |
|---|---|---|---|
| ⓑ | Q4005 | Cast supplies, long arm cast, adult (11 years +), plaster | Ⓐ |
| | | MED: 100-4,4,240; 100-4,20,170 | |
| ⓑ | Q4006 | Cast supplies, long arm cast, adult (11 years +), fiberglass | Ⓐ |
| | | MED: 100-4,4,240; 100-4,20,170 | |
| ⓑ | Q4007 | Cast supplies, long arm cast, pediatric (0–10 years), plaster | Ⓐ |
| | | MED: 100-4,4,240; 100-4,20,170 | |
| ⓑ | Q4008 | Cast supplies, long arm cast, pediatric (0–10 years), fiberglass | Ⓐ |
| | | MED: 100-4,4,240; 100-4,20,170 | |
| ⓑ | Q4009 | Cast supplies, short arm cast, adult (11 years +), plaster | Ⓐ |
| | | MED: 100-4,4,240; 100-4,20,170 | |
| ⓑ | Q4010 | Cast supplies, short arm cast, adult (11 years +), fiberglass | Ⓐ |
| | | MED: 100-4,4,240; 100-4,20,170 | |
| ⓑ | Q4011 | Cast supplies, short arm cast, pediatric (0–10 years), plaster | Ⓐ |
| | | MED: 100-4,4,240; 100-4,20,170 | |
| ⓑ | Q4012 | Cast supplies, short arm cast, pediatric (0–10 years), fiberglass | Ⓐ |
| | | MED: 100-4,4,240; 100-4,20,170 | |
| ⓑ | Q4013 | Cast supplies, gauntlet cast (includes lower forearm and hand), adult (11 years +), plaster | Ⓐ |
| | | MED: 100-4,4,240; 100-4,20,170 | |
| ⓑ | Q4014 | Cast supplies, gauntlet cast (includes lower forearm and hand), adult (11 years +), fiberglass | Ⓐ |
| | | MED: 100-4,4,240; 100-4,20,170 | |
| ⓑ | Q4015 | Cast supplies, gauntlet cast (includes lower forearm and hand), pediatric (0–10 years), plaster | Ⓐ |
| | | MED: 100-4,4,240; 100-4,20,170 | |
| ⓑ | Q4016 | Cast supplies, gauntlet cast (includes lower forearm and hand), pediatric (0–10 years), fiberglass | Ⓐ |
| | | MED: 100-4,4,240; 100-4,20,170 | |
| ⓑ | Q4017 | Cast supplies, long arm splint, adult (11 years +), plaster | Ⓐ |
| | | MED: 100-4,4,240; 100-4,20,170 | |
| ⓑ | Q4018 | Cast supplies, long arm splint, adult (11 years +), fiberglass | Ⓐ |
| | | MED: 100-4,4,240; 100-4,20,170 | |
| ⓑ | Q4019 | Cast supplies, long arm splint, pediatric (0–10 years), plaster | Ⓐ |
| | | MED: 100-4,4,240; 100-4,20,170 | |
| ⓑ | Q4020 | Cast supplies, long arm splint, pediatric (0–10 years), fiberglass | Ⓐ |
| | | MED: 100-4,4,240; 100-4,20,170 | |
| ⓑ | Q4021 | Cast supplies, short arm splint, adult (11 years +), plaster | Ⓐ |
| | | MED: 100-4,4,240; 100-4,20,170 | |
| ⓑ | Q4022 | Cast supplies, short arm splint, adult (11 years +), fiberglass | Ⓐ |
| | | MED: 100-4,4,240; 100-4,20,170 | |
| ⓑ | Q4023 | Cast supplies, short arm splint, pediatric (0–10 years), plaster | Ⓐ |
| | | MED: 100-4,4,240; 100-4,20,170 | |
| ⓑ | Q4024 | Cast supplies, short arm splint, pediatric (0–10 years), fiberglass | Ⓐ |
| | | MED: 100-4,4,240; 100-4,20,170 | |
| ⓑ | Q4025 | Cast supplies, hip spica (one or both legs), adult (11 years +), plaster | Ⓐ |
| | | MED: 100-4,4,240; 100-4,20,170 | |

*Q Codes (Temporary)*

*Q4026 — Q4046*

| | | |
|---|---|---|
| B | **Q4026** | Cast supplies, hip spica (one or both legs), adult (11 years +), fiberglass A |
| | | MED: 100-4,4,240; 100-4,20,170 |
| B | **Q4027** | Cast supplies, hip spica (one or both legs), pediatric (0–10 years), plaster A |
| | | MED: 100-4,4,240; 100-4,20,170 |
| B | **Q4028** | Cast supplies, hip spica (one or both legs), pediatric (0–10 years), fiberglass A |
| | | MED: 100-4,4,240; 100-4,20,170 |
| B | **Q4029** | Cast supplies, long leg cast, adult (11 years +), plaster A |
| | | MED: 100-4,4,240; 100-4,20,170 |
| B | **Q4030** | Cast supplies, long leg cast, adult (11 years +), fiberglass A |
| | | MED: 100-4,4,240; 100-4,20,170 |
| B | **Q4031** | Cast supplies, long leg cast, pediatric (0–10 years), plaster A |
| | | MED: 100-4,4,240; 100-4,20,170 |
| B | **Q4032** | Cast supplies, long leg cast, pediatric (0–10 years), fiberglass A |
| | | MED: 100-4,4,240; 100-4,20,170 |
| B | **Q4033** | Cast supplies, long leg cylinder cast, adult (11 years +), plaster A |
| | | MED: 100-4,4,240; 100-4,20,170 |
| B | **Q4034** | Cast supplies, long leg cylinder cast, adult (11 years +), fiberglass A |
| | | MED: 100-4,4,240; 100-4,20,170 |
| B | **Q4035** | Cast supplies, long leg cylinder cast, pediatric (0–10 years), plaster A |
| | | MED: 100-4,4,240; 100-4,20,170 |
| B | **Q4036** | Cast supplies, long leg cylinder cast, pediatric (0–10 years), fiberglass A |
| | | MED: 100-4,4,240; 100-4,20,170 |
| B | **Q4037** | Cast supplies, short leg cast, adult (11 years +), plaster A |
| | | MED: 100-4,4,240; 100-4,20,170 |
| B | **Q4038** | Cast supplies, short leg cast, adult (11 years +), fiberglass A |
| | | MED: 100-4,4,240; 100-4,20,170 |
| B | **Q4039** | Cast supplies, short leg cast, pediatric (0–10 years), plaster A |
| | | MED: 100-4,4,240; 100-4,20,170 |
| B | **Q4040** | Cast supplies, short leg cast, pediatric (0–10 years), fiberglass A |
| | | MED: 100-4,4,240; 100-4,20,170 |
| B | **Q4041** | Cast supplies, long leg splint, adult (11 years +), plaster A |
| | | MED: 100-4,4,240; 100-4,20,170 |
| B | **Q4042** | Cast supplies, long leg splint, adult (11 years +), fiberglass A |
| | | MED: 100-4,4,240; 100-4,20,170 |
| B | **Q4043** | Cast supplies, long leg splint, pediatric (0–10 years), plaster A |
| | | MED: 100-4,4,240; 100-4,20,170 |
| B | **Q4044** | Cast supplies, long leg splint, pediatric (0–10 years), fiberglass A |
| | | MED: 100-4,4,240; 100-4,20,170 |
| B | **Q4045** | Cast supplies, short leg splint, adult (11 years +), plaster A |
| | | MED: 100-4,4,240; 100-4,20,170 |
| B | **Q4046** | Cast supplies, short leg splint, adult (11 years +), fiberglass A |
| | | MED: 100-4,4,240; 100-4,20,170 |

| | | | |
|---|---|---|---|
| B | Q4047 | Cast supplies, short leg splint, pediatric (0–10 years), plaster | A |
| | | MED: 100-4,4,240; 100-4,20,170 | |
| B | Q4048 | Cast supplies, short leg splint, pediatric (0–10 years), fiberglass | A |
| | | MED: 100-4,4,240; 100-4,20,170 | |
| B | Q4049 | Finger splint, static | |
| | | MED: 100-4,4,240; 100-4,20,170 | |
| B | Q4050 | Cast supplies, for unlisted types and materials of casts | |
| | | MED: 100-4,4,240; 100-4,20,170 | |
| B | Q4051 | Splint supplies, miscellaneous (includes thermoplastics, strapping, fasteners, padding and other supplies) | |
| | | MED: 100-4,4,240; 100-4,20,170 | |
| Y ☑ | Q4080 | Iloprost, inhalation solution, FDA-approved final product, noncompounded, administered through DME, unit dose form, 20 mcg | |
| | | AHA: 3Q,'05,7 | |
| A ☑ | Q4081 | Injection, epoetin alfa, 100 units (for ESRD on dialysis) | |
| B | Q4082 | Drug or biological, not otherwise classified, Part B drug competitive acquisition program (CAP) | |
| | ~~Q4096~~ | ~~Injection, von Willebrand factor complex human, ristocetin cofactor (not otherwise specified), per I.U. VWF:RCO~~ | |
| | ~~Q4097~~ | ~~Injection, immune globulin (Privigen), intravenous, nonlyophilized (e.g., liquid), 500 mg~~ | |
| | | See J1459 | |
| | ~~Q4098~~ | ~~Injection, iron dextran, 50 mg~~ | |
| | | See J1750 | |
| | ~~Q4099~~ | ~~Formoterol fumarate,inhalation solution, FDA approved final product, noncompounded, administered through DME, unit dose form, 20 micrograms~~ | |
| | | See J7606 | |
| ● N | Q4100 | Skin substitute, not otherwise specified | N1 |
| ● K | Q4101 | Skin substitute, Apligraf, per sq cm | K2 |
| ● K | Q4102 | Skin substitute, Oasis wound matrix, per sq cm | K2 |
| ● K | Q4103 | Skin substitute, Oasis burn matrix, per sq cm | K2 |
| ● K | Q4104 | Skin substitute, Integra bilayer matrix wound dressing (BMWD), per sq cm | K2 |
| ● K | Q4105 | Skin substitute, Integra dermal regeneration template (DRT), per sq cm | K2 |
| ● K | Q4106 | Skin substitute, Dermagraft, per sq cm | K2 |
| ● K | Q4107 | Skin substitute, GRAFTJACKET, per sq cm | K2 |
| ● K | Q4108 | Skin substitute, Integra matrix, per sq cm | K2 |
| ● N | Q4109 | Skin substitute, TissueMend, per sq cm | N1 |
| ● K | Q4110 | Skin substitute, PriMatrix, per sq cm | K2 |
| ● | Q4111 | Skin substitute, GammaGraft, per sq cm | |
| ● K | Q4112 | Allograft, Cymetra, injectable, 1 cc | K2 |
| ● K | Q4113 | Allograft, GRAFTJACKET express, injectable, 1cc | K2 |
| ● G | Q4114 | Integra flowable wound matrix, injectable, 1 cc | K2 |

Q Codes (Temporary)

Q4047 — Q4114

Q Codes (Temporary)

Q5001 — Q9967

| | | | |
|---|---|---|---|
| B | | Q5001 | Hospice care provided in patient's home/residence |
| B | | Q5002 | Hospice care provided in assisted living facility |
| B | | Q5003 | Hospice care provided in nursing long-term care facility (LTC) or nonskilled nursing facility (NF) |
| B | | Q5004 | Hospice care provided in skilled nursing facility (SNF) |
| B | | Q5005 | Hospice care provided in inpatient hospital |
| B | | Q5006 | Hospice care provided in inpatient hospice facility |
| B | | Q5007 | Hospice care provided in long-term care facility |
| B | | Q5008 | Hospice care provided in inpatient psychiatric facility |
| B | | Q5009 | Hospice care provided in place not otherwise specified (NOS) |
| N | ☑ | Q9951 | Low osmolar contrast material, 400 or greater mg/ml iodine concentration, per ml   N1 |
| N | ☑ | Q9953 | Injection, iron-based magnetic resonance contrast agent, per ml   N1 |
| N | ☑ | Q9954 | Oral magnetic resonance contrast agent, per 100 ml   N1 |
| N | ☑ | Q9955 | Injection, perflexane lipid microspheres, per ml   N1 |
| N | ☑ | Q9956 | Injection, octafluoropropane microspheres, per ml   N1 |
| N | ☑ | Q9957 | Injection, perflutren lipid microspheres, per ml   N1 |
| N | ☑ | Q9958 | High osmolar contrast material, up to 149 mg/ml iodine concentration, per ml   N1 <br> AHA: 3Q,'05,7 |
| N | ☑ | Q9959 | High osmolar contrast material, 150–199 mg/ml iodine concentration, per ml   N1 <br> AHA: 3Q,'05,7 |
| N | ☑ | Q9960 | High osmolar contrast material, 200–249 mg/ml iodine concentration, per ml   N1 <br> AHA: 3Q,'05,7 |
| N | ☑ | Q9961 | High osmolar contrast material, 250–299 mg/ml iodine concentration, per ml   N1 <br> AHA: 3Q,'05,7 |
| N | ☑ | Q9962 | High osmolar contrast material, 300–349 mg/ml iodine concentration, per ml   N1 <br> AHA: 3Q,'05,7 |
| N | ☑ | Q9963 | High osmolar contrast material, 350–399 mg/ml iodine concentration, per ml   N1 <br> AHA: 3Q,'05,7 |
| N | ☑ | Q9964 | High osmolar contrast material, 400 or greater mg/ml iodine concentration, per ml   N1 <br> AHA: 3Q,'05,7 |
| N | ☑ | Q9965 | Low osmolar contrast material, 100–199 mg/ml iodine concentration, per ml   N1 <br> Use this code for Omnipaque 140, Omnipaque 180, Optiray 160, Optiray 140. |
| N | ☑ | Q9966 | Low osmolar contrast material, 200–299 mg/ml iodine concentration, per ml   N1 <br> Use this code for Omnipaque 240, Optiray 240. |
| N | ☑ | Q9967 | Low osmolar contrast material, 300–399 mg/ml iodine concentration, per ml   N1 <br> Use this code for Omnipaque 300, Omnipaque 350, Optiray, Optiray 300, Optiray 320, Oxilan 300, Oxilan 350. |

## DIAGNOSTIC RADIOLOGY SERVICES R0000-R5999

R codes are used for the transportation of portable x-ray and/or EKG equipment.

Ⓑ ☑ **R0070** **Transportation of portable x-ray equipment and personnel to home or nursing home, per trip to facility or location, one patient seen**
Only a single, reasonable transportation charge is allowed for each trip the portable x-ray supplier makes to a location. When more than one patient is x-rayed at the same location, prorate the single allowable transport charge among all patients.

Ⓑ ☑ **R0075** **Transportation of portable x-ray equipment and personnel to home or nursing home, per trip to facility or location, more than one patient seen**
Only a single, reasonable transportation charge is allowed for each trip the portable x-ray supplier makes to a location. When more than one patient is x-rayed at the same location, prorate the single allowable transport charge among all patients.

Ⓑ ☑ **R0076** **Transportation of portable EKG to facility or location, per patient**
Only a single, reasonable transportation charge is allowed for each trip the portable EKG supplier makes to a location. When more than one patient is tested at the same location, prorate the single allowable transport charge among all patients.
**MED: 100-1,5,90.2; 100-3,20.15**

## TEMPORARY NATIONAL CODES (NON-MEDICARE) S0000-S9999

The S codes are used by the Blue Cross/Blue Shield Association (BCBSA) and the Health Insurance Association of America (HIAA) to report drugs, services, and supplies for which there are no national codes but for which codes are needed by the private sector to implement policies, programs, or claims processing. They are for the purpose of meeting the particular needs of the private sector. These codes are also used by the Medicaid program, but they are not payable by Medicare.

☑ **S0012** **Butorphanol tartrate, nasal spray, 25 mg**
Use this code for Stadol NS.

☑ **S0014** **Tacrine HCl, 10 mg**
Use this code for Cognex.

☑ **S0017** **Injection, aminocaproic acid, 5 g**
Use this code for Amicar.

☑ **S0020** **Injection, bupivicaine HCl, 30 ml**
Use this code for Marcaine, Sensorcaine.

☑ **S0021** **Injection, cefoperazone sodium, 1 g**
Use this code for Cefobid.

☑ **S0023** **Injection, cimetidine HCl, 300 mg**
Use this code for Tagamet HCl.

☑ **S0028** **Injection, famotidine, 20 mg**
Use this code for Pepcid.

☑ **S0030** **Injection, metronidazole, 500 mg**
Use this code for Flagyl IV RTU.

☑ **S0032** **Injection, nafcillin sodium, 2 g**
Use this code for Nallpen, Unipen.

☑ **S0034** **Injection, ofloxacin, 400 mg**
Use this code for Floxin IV.

☑ **S0039** **Injection, sulfamethoxazole and trimethoprim, 10 ml**
Use this code for Bactrim IV, Septra IV, SMZ-TMP, Sulfutrim.

☑ **S0040** **Injection, ticarcillin disodium and clavulanate potassium, 3.1 g**
Use this code for Timentin.

☑ **S0073** **Injection, aztreonam, 500 mg**
Use this code for Azactam.

☑ **S0074** **Injection, cefotetan disodium, 500 mg**
Use this code for Cefotan.

☑ **S0077** **Injection, clindamycin phosphate, 300 mg**
Use this code for Cleocin Phosphate.

☑ **S0078** **Injection, fosphenytoin sodium, 750 mg**
Use this code for Cerebryx.

☑ **S0080** **Injection, pentamidine isethionate, 300 mg**
Use this code for NebuPent, Pentam 300, Pentacarinat. See also code J2545.

☑ **S0081** **Injection, piperacillin sodium, 500 mg**
Use this code for Pipracil.

▲ ☑ **S0088** **Imatinib, 100 mg**
Use this code for Gleevec.

☑ **S0090** **Sildenafil citrate, 25 mg** Ⓐ
Use this code for Viagra.

---

☑ **S0091** Granisetron HCl, 1 mg (for circumstances falling under the Medicare statute, use Q0166)
Use this code for Kytril.

☑ **S0092** Injection, hydromorphone HCl, 250 mg (loading dose for infusion pump)
Use this code for Dilaudid, Hydromophone. See also J1170.

☑ **S0093** Injection, morphine sulfate, 500 mg (loading dose for infusion pump)
Use this code for Duramorph, MS Contin, Morphine Sulfate. See also J2270, J2271, J2275.

**S0104** Zidovudine, oral, 100 mg
See also J3485 for Retrovir.

☑ **S0106** Bupropion HCl sustained release tablet, 150 mg, per bottle of 60 tablets
Use this code for Wellbutrin SR tablets.

☑ **S0108** Mercaptopurine, oral, 50 mg
Use this code for Purinethol oral.

☑ **S0109** Methadone, oral, 5 mg
Use this code for Dolophine.

☑ **S0117** Tretinoin, topical, 5 g

☑ **S0122** Injection, menotropins, 75 IU
Use this code for Humegon, Pergonal, Repronex.

☑ **S0126** Injection, follitropin alfa, 75 IU
Use this code for Gonal-F.

☑ **S0128** Injection, follitropin beta, 75 IU ♀
Use this code for Follistim.

☑ **S0132** Injection, ganirelix acetate, 250 mcg ♀
Use this code for Antagon.

☑ **S0136** Clozapine, 25 mg
Use this code for Clozaril.

☑ **S0137** Didanosine (ddI), 25 mg
Use this code for Videx.

☑ **S0138** Finasteride, 5 mg ♂
Use this code for Propecia (oral), Proscar (oral).

☑ **S0139** Minoxidil, 10 mg
Use this code for Loniten (oral).

☑ **S0140** Saquinavir, 200 mg
Use this code for Fortovase (oral), Invirase (oral).

~~**S0141** Zalcitabine (ddC), 0.375 mg~~

☑ **S0142** Colistimethate sodium, inhalation solution administered through DME, concentrated form, per mg

~~**S0143** Aztreonam, inhalation solution administered through DME, concentrated form, per g~~

☑ **S0145** Injection, pegylated interferon alfa-2a, 180 mcg per ml
Use this code for Pegasys.

☑ **S0146** Injection, pegylated interferon alfa-2b, 10 mcg per 0.5 ml

☑ **S0155** Sterile dilutant for epoprostenol, 50 ml
Use this code for Flolan.

☑ **S0156** Exemestane, 25 mg
Use this code for Aromasin.

---

☑   **S0157**   Becaplermin gel 0.01%, 0.5 gm
Use this code for Regraex Gel.

☑   **S0160**   Dextroamphetamine sulfate, 5 mg

☑   **S0161**   Calcitrol, 0.25 mg

☑   **S0162**   Injection, efalizumab, 125 mg
Use this code for Raptiva.

☑   **S0164**   Injection, pantoprazole sodium, 40 mg
Use this code for Protonix IV.

☑   **S0166**   Injection, olanzapine, 2.5 mg
Use this code for Zyprexa.

☑   **S0170**   Anastrozole, oral, 1 mg
Use this code for Arimidex.

☑   **S0171**   Injection, bumetanide, 0.5 mg
Use this code for Bumex.

☑   **S0172**   Chlorambucil, oral, 2 mg
Use this code for Leukeran.

☑   **S0174**   Dolasetron mesylate, oral 50 mg (for circumstances falling under the Medicare statute, use Q0180)
Use this code for Anzemet.

☑   **S0175**   Flutamide, oral, 125 mg
Use this code for Eulexin.

☑   **S0176**   Hydroxyurea, oral, 500 mg
Use this code for Droxia, Hydrea, Mylocel.

☑   **S0177**   Levamisole HCl, oral, 50 mg
Use this code for Ergamisol.

☑   **S0178**   Lomustine, oral, 10 mg
Use this code for Ceenu.
MED: 100-4,17,80.2

☑   **S0179**   Megestrol acetate, oral, 20 mg
Use this code for Megace.

☑   **S0181**   Ondansetron HCl, oral, 4 mg (for circumstances falling under the Medicare statute, use Q0179)
Use this code for Zofran.

☑   **S0182**   Procarbazine HCl, oral, 50 mg
Use this code for Matulane.

☑   **S0183**   Prochlorperazine maleate, oral, 5 mg (for circumstances falling under the Medicare statute, use Q0164-Q0165)
Use this code for Compazine.

☑   **S0187**   Tamoxifen citrate, oral, 10 mg
Use this code for Nolvadex.

☑   **S0189**   Testosterone pellet, 75 mg

☑   **S0190**   Mifepristone, oral, 200 mg   ♀
Use this code for Mifoprex 200 mg oral.

☑   **S0191**   Misoprostol, oral, 200 mcg

☑   **S0194**   Dialysis/stress vitamin supplement, oral, 100 capsules

Special Coverage Instructions    Noncovered by Medicare    Carrier Discretion

**S0195** Pneumococcal conjugate vaccine, polyvalent, intramuscular, for children from 5 years to 9 years of age who have not previously received the vaccine ▣
Use this code for Pneumovax II.

☑ **S0196** Injectable poly-l-lactic acid, restorative implant, 1 ml, face (deep dermis, subcutaneous layers)

☑ **S0197** Prenatal vitamins, 30-day supply Ⓜ ♀

**S0199** Medically induced abortion by oral ingestion of medication including all associated services and supplies (e.g., patient counseling, office visits, confirmation of pregnancy by HCG, ultrasound to confirm duration of pregnancy, ultrasound to confirm completion of abortion) except drugs ♀

**S0201** Partial hospitalization services, less than 24 hours, per diem

**S0207** Paramedic intercept, nonhospital-based ALS service (nonvoluntary), nontransport

**S0208** Paramedic intercept, hospital-based ALS service (nonvoluntary), nontransport

**S0209** Wheelchair van, mileage, per mile

☑ **S0215** Nonemergency transportation; mileage, per mile
See also codes A0021-A0999 for transportation.

☑ **S0220** Medical conference by a physician with interdisciplinary team of health professionals or representatives of community agencies to coordinate activities of patient care (patient is present); approximately 30 minutes

☑ **S0221** Medical conference by a physician with interdisciplinary team of health professionals or representatives of community agencies to coordinate activities of patient care (patient is present); approximately 60 minutes

**S0250** Comprehensive geriatric assessment and treatment planning performed by assessment team ▣

**S0255** Hospice referral visit (advising patient and family of care options) performed by nurse, social worker, or other designated staff

**S0257** Counseling and discussion regarding advance directives or end of life care planning and decisions, with patient and/or surrogate (list separately in addition to code for appropriate evaluation and management service)

**S0260** History and physical (outpatient or office) related to surgical procedure (list separately in addition to code for appropriate evaluation and management service)

☑ **S0265** Genetic counseling, under physician supervision, each 15 minutes

☑ **S0270** Physician management of patient home care, standard monthly case rate (per 30 days)

☑ **S0271** Physician management of patient home care, hospice monthly case rate (per 30 days)

☑ **S0272** Physician management of patient home care, episodic care monthly case rate (per 30 days)

**S0273** Physician visit at member's home, outside of a capitation arrangement

**S0274** Nurse practitioner visit at member's home, outside of a capitation arrangement

**S0302** Completed early periodic screening diagnosis and treatment (EPSDT) service (list in addition to code for appropriate evaluation and management service)

| | | |
|---|---|---|
| | S0310 | Hospitalist services (list separately in addition to code for appropriate evaluation and management service) |
| | S0315 | Disease management program; initial assessment and initiation of the program |
| | S0316 | Disease management program, follow-up/reassessment |
| ☑ | S0317 | Disease management program; per diem |
| | S0320 | Telephone calls by a registered nurse to a disease management program member for monitoring purposes; per month |
| | S0340 | Lifestyle modification program for management of coronary artery disease, including all supportive services; first quarter/stage |
| | S0341 | Lifestyle modification program for management of coronary artery disease, including all supportive services; second or third quarter/stage |
| | S0342 | Lifestyle modification program for management of coronary artery disease, including all supportive services; 4th quarter / stage |
| ☑ | S0345 | Electrocardiographic monitoring utilizing a home computerized telemetry station with automatic activation and real-time notification of monitoring station, 24-hour attended monitoring, including recording, monitoring, receipt of transmissions, analysis, and physician review and interpretation; per 24-hour period |
| ☑ | S0346 | Electrocardiographic monitoring utilizing a home computerized telemetry station with automatic activation and real-time notification of monitoring station, 24-hour attended monitoring, including recording, monitoring, receipt of transmissions, and analysis; per 24-hour period |
| ☑ | S0347 | Electrocardiographic monitoring utilizing a home computerized telemetry station with automatic activation and real-time notification of monitoring station, 24-hour attended monitoring, including physician review and interpretation; 24-hour period |
| | S0390 | Routine foot care; removal and/or trimming of corns, calluses and/or nails and preventive maintenance in specific medical conditions (e.g., diabetes), per visit |
| | S0395 | Impression casting of a foot performed by a practitioner other than the manufacturer of the orthotic |
| | S0400 | Global fee for extracorporeal shock wave lithotripsy treatment of kidney stone(s) |
| ☑ | S0500 | Disposable contact lens, per lens |
| ☑ | S0504 | Single vision prescription lens (safety, athletic, or sunglass), per lens |
| ☑ | S0506 | Bifocal vision prescription lens (safety, athletic, or sunglass), per lens |
| ☑ | S0508 | Trifocal vision prescription lens (safety, athletic, or sunglass), per lens |
| ☑ | S0510 | Nonprescription lens (safety, athletic, or sunglass), per lens |
| ☑ | S0512 | Daily wear specialty contact lens, per lens |
| ☑ | S0514 | Color contact lens, per lens |
| | S0515 | Scleral lens, liquid bandage device, per lens |
| | S0516 | Safety eyeglass frames |
| | S0518 | Sunglasses frames |
| | S0580 | Polycarbonate lens (list this code in addition to the basic code for the lens) |
| | S0581 | Nonstandard lens (list this code in addition to the basic code for the lens) |

---

Special Coverage Instructions    Noncovered by Medicare    Carrier Discretion

Ⓜ Maternity Edit   Ⓐ Age Edit   PQI PQRI   Ⓐ-Ⓨ OPPS Status   **2009 HCPCS**

| | | |
|---|---|---|
| S0590 | Integral lens service, miscellaneous services reported separately | |
| S0592 | Comprehensive contact lens evaluation | |
| S0595 | Dispensing new spectacle lenses for patient supplied frame | |
| S0601 | Screening proctoscopy | ♂ |
| | MED: 100-4,4,240 | |
| S0605 | Digital rectal examination, annual | |
| S0610 | Annual gynecological examination, new patient | ♀ |
| | MED: 100-4,4,240 | |
| S0612 | Annual gynecological examination, established patient | ♀ |
| | MED: 100-4,4,240 | |
| S0613 | Annual gynecological examination; clinical breast examination without pelvic evaluation | ♀ |
| S0618 | Audiometry for hearing aid evaluation to determine the level and degree of hearing loss | |
| S0620 | Routine ophthalmological examination including refraction; new patient | |
| S0621 | Routine ophthalmological examination including refraction; established patient | |
| S0622 | Physical exam for college, new or established patient (list separately in addition to appropriate evaluation and management code) | A |
| S0625 | Retinal telescreening by digital imaging of multiple different fundus areas to screen for vision-threatening conditions, including imaging, interpretation and report | |
| S0630 | Removal of sutures; by a physician other than the physician who originally closed the wound | |
| S0800 | Laser in situ keratomileusis (LASIK) | |
| S0810 | Photorefractive keratectomy (PRK) | |
| S0812 | Phototherapeutic keratectomy (PTK) | |
| S1001 | Deluxe item, patient aware (list in addition to code for basic item) | |
| | MED: 100-2,1,10.1.4 | |
| S1002 | Customized item (list in addition to code for basic item) | |
| S1015 | IV tubing extension set | |
| S1016 | Non-PVC (polyvinyl chloride) intravenous administration set, for use with drugs that are not stable in PVC e.g., Paclitaxel | |
| S1030 | Continuous noninvasive glucose monitoring device, purchase (for physician interpretation of data, use CPT code) | |
| S1031 | Continuous noninvasive glucose monitoring device, rental, including sensor, sensor replacement, and download to monitor (for physician interpretation of data, use CPT code) | |
| S1040 | Cranial remolding orthotic, pediatric, rigid, with soft interface material, custom fabricated, includes fitting and adjustment(s) | |
| S2053 | Transplantation of small intestine and liver allografts | |
| S2054 | Transplantation of multivisceral organs | |
| S2055 | Harvesting of donor multivisceral organs, with preparation and maintenance of allografts; from cadaver donor | |
| S2060 | Lobar lung transplantation | |

| | |
|---|---|
| S2061 | Donor lobectomy (lung) for transplantation, living donor |
| S2065 | Simultaneous pancreas kidney transplantation |
| S2066 | Breast reconstruction with gluteal artery perforator (GAP) flap, including harvesting of the flap, microvascular transfer, closure of donor site and shaping the flap into a breast, unilateral  ♀ |
| S2067 | Breast reconstruction of a single breast with "stacked" deep inferior epigastric perforator (DIEP) flap(s) and/or gluteal artery perforator (GAP) flap(s), including harvesting of the flap(s), microvascular transfer, closure of donor site(s) and shaping the flap into a breast, unilateral  ♀ |
| S2068 | Breast reconstruction with deep inferior epigastric perforator (DIEP) flap or superficial inferior epigastric artery (SIEA) flap, including harvesting of the flap, microvascular transfer, closure of donor site and shaping the flap into a breast, unilateral  ♀ |
| S2070 | Cystourethroscopy, with ureteroscopy and/or pyeloscopy; with endoscopic laser treatment of ureteral calculi (includes ureteral catheterization) |
| ~~S2075~~ | ~~Laparoscopy, surgical; repair incisional or ventral hernia~~ |
| ~~S2076~~ | ~~Laparoscopy, surgical; repair umbilical hernia~~ |
| ~~S2077~~ | ~~Laparoscopy, surgical; implantation of mesh or other prosthesis for incisional or ventral hernia repair (List separately in addition to code for the incisional or ventral hernia repair)~~ |
| S2079 | Laparoscopic esophagomyotomy (Heller type) |
| S2080 | Laser-assisted uvulopalatoplasty (LAUP) |
| S2083 | Adjustment of gastric band diameter via subcutaneous port by injection or aspiration of saline |
| S2095 | Transcatheter occlusion or embolization for tumor destruction, percutaneous, any method, using yttrium-90 microspheres |
| S2102 | Islet cell tissue transplant from pancreas; allogeneic |
| S2103 | Adrenal tissue transplant to brain |
| S2107 | Adoptive immunotherapy i.e. development of specific antitumor reactivity (e.g., tumor-infiltrating lymphocyte therapy) per course of treatment |
| S2112 | Arthroscopy, knee, surgical for harvesting of cartilage (chondrocyte cells) |
| S2115 | Osteotomy, periacetabular, with internal fixation |
| S2117 | Arthroereisis, subtalar |
| ● S2118 | Metal-on-metal total hip resurfacing, including acetabular and femoral components |
| S2120 | Low density lipoprotein (LDL) apheresis using heparin-induced extracorporeal LDL precipitation |
| ~~S2135~~ | ~~Neurolysis, by injection, of metatarsal neuroma/interdigital neuritis, any interspace of the foot~~ |
| S2140 | Cord blood harvesting for transplantation, allogeneic |
| S2142 | Cord blood-derived stem-cell transplantation, allogeneic |
| S2150 | Bone marrow or blood-derived stem cells (peripheral or umbilical), allogeneic or autologous, harvesting, transplantation, and related complications including pheresis and cell preparation/storage; marrow ablative therapy; drugs, supplies, hospitalization with outpatient follow-up; medical/surgical, diagnostic, emergency, and rehabilitative services; and the number of days of pre- and posttransplant care in the global definition |

Special Coverage Instructions    Noncovered by Medicare    Carrier Discretion

| | |
|---|---|
| **S2152** | Solid organ(s), complete or segmental, single organ or combination of organs; deceased or living donor (s), procurement, transplantation, and related complications; including: drugs; supplies; hospitalization with outpatient follow-up; medical/surgical, diagnostic, emergency, and rehabilitative services, and the number of days of pre and posttransplant care in the global definition |
| **S2202** | Echosclerotherapy |
| **S2205** | Minimally invasive direct coronary artery bypass surgery involving mini-thoracotomy or mini-sternotomy surgery, performed under direct vision; using arterial graft(s), single coronary arterial graft |
| **S2206** | Minimally invasive direct coronary artery bypass surgery involving mini-thoracotomy or mini-sternotomy surgery, performed under direct vision; using arterial graft(s), 2 coronary arterial grafts |
| **S2207** | Minimally invasive direct coronary artery bypass surgery involving mini-thoracotomy or mini-sternotomy surgery, performed under direct vision; using venous graft only, single coronary venous graft |
| **S2208** | Minimally invasive direct coronary artery bypass surgery involving mini-thoracotomy or mini-sternotomy surgery, performed under direct vision; using single arterial and venous graft(s), single venous graft |
| **S2209** | Minimally invasive direct coronary artery bypass surgery involving mini-thoracotomy or mini-sternotomy surgery, performed under direct vision; using 2 arterial grafts and single venous graft |
| **S2225** | Myringotomy, laser-assisted |
| **S2230** | Implantation of magnetic component of semi-implantable hearing device on ossicles in middle ear |
| **S2235** | Implantation of auditory brain stem implant |
| **S2260** | Induced abortion, 17 to 24 weeks   M ♀ |
| **S2265** | Induced abortion, 25 to 28 weeks   M ♀ |
| **S2266** | Induced abortion, 29 to 31 weeks   M ♀ |
| **S2267** | Induced abortion, 32 weeks or greater   M ♀ |
| **S2270** | Insertion of vaginal cylinder for application of radiation source or clinical brachytherapy (report separately in addition to radiation source delivery) |
| **S2300** | Arthroscopy, shoulder, surgical; with thermally-induced capsulorrhaphy |
| **S2325** | Hip core decompression |
| **S2340** | Chemodenervation of abductor muscle(s) of vocal cord |
| **S2341** | Chemodenervation of adductor muscle(s) of vocal cord |
| **S2342** | Nasal endoscopy for postoperative debridement following functional endoscopic sinus surgery, nasal and/or sinus cavity(s), unilateral or bilateral |
| **S2344** | Nasal/sinus endoscopy, surgical; with enlargement of sinus ostium opening using inflatable device (i.e., balloon sinuplasty) |
| **S2348** | Decompression procedure, percutaneous, of nucleus pulposus of intervertebral disc, using radiofrequency energy, single or multiple levels, lumbar |
| **S2350** | Diskectomy, anterior, with decompression of spinal cord and/or nerve root(s), including osteophytectomy; lumbar, single interspace |

---

| | |
|---|---|
| S2351 | Diskectomy, anterior, with decompression of spinal cord and/or nerve root(s), including osteophytectomy; lumbar, each additional interspace (list separately in addition to code for primary procedure) |
| S2360 | Percutaneous vertebroplasty, one vertebral body, unilateral or bilateral injection; cervical |
| S2361 | Each additional cervical vertebral body (list separately in addition to code for primary procedure) |
| S2400 | Repair, congenital diaphragmatic hernia in the fetus using temporary tracheal occlusion, procedure performed in utero Ⓜ♀ |
| S2401 | Repair, urinary tract obstruction in the fetus, procedure performed in utero Ⓜ♀ |
| S2402 | Repair, congenital cystic adenomatoid malformation in the fetus, procedure performed in utero Ⓜ♀ |
| S2403 | Repair, extralobar pulmonary sequestration in the fetus, procedure performed in utero Ⓜ♀ |
| S2404 | Repair, myelomeningocele in the fetus, procedure performed in utero Ⓜ♀ |
| S2405 | Repair of sacrococcygeal teratoma in the fetus, procedure performed in utero Ⓜ♀ |
| S2409 | Repair, congenital malformation of fetus, procedure performed in utero, not otherwise classified Ⓜ♀ |
| S2411 | Fetoscopic laser therapy for treatment of twin-to-twin transfusion syndrome Ⓜ♀ |
| S2900 | Surgical techniques requiring use of robotic surgical system (list separately in addition to code for primary procedure) |
| S3000 | Diabetic indicator; retinal eye exam, dilated, bilateral |
| S3005 | Performance measurement, evaluation of patient self assessment, depression |
| S3600 | STAT laboratory request (situations other than S3601) |
| S3601 | Emergency STAT laboratory charge for patient who is homebound or residing in a nursing facility |
| S3620 | Newborn metabolic screening panel, includes test kit, postage and the laboratory tests specified by the state for inclusion in this panel (e.g., galactose; hemoglobin, electrophoresis; hydroxyprogesterone, 17-d; phenylanine (PKU); and thyroxine, total) Ⓐ |
| S3625 | Maternal serum triple marker screen including alpha-fetoprotein (AFP), estriol, and human chorionic gonadotropin (HCG) Ⓜ♀ |
| S3626 | Maternal serum quadruple marker screen including alpha-fetoprotein (AFP), estriol, human chorionic gonadotropin hCG) and inhibin A |
| ● S3628 | Placental alpha microglobulin-1 rapid immunoassay for detection of rupture of fetal membranes Ⓜ♀ |
| S3630 | Eosinophil count, blood, direct |
| S3645 | HIV-1 antibody testing of oral mucosal transudate |
| S3650 | Saliva test, hormone level; during menopause Ⓐ♀ |
| S3652 | Saliva test, hormone level; to assess preterm labor risk Ⓜ♀ |
| S3655 | Antisperm antibodies test (immunobead) Ⓐ♀ |
| S3708 | Gastrointestinal fat absorption study |

● | **S3711** | Circulating tumor cell test
| **S3800** | Genetic testing for amyotrophic lateral sclerosis (ALS)
| **S3818** | Complete gene sequence analysis; BRCA1 gene
| **S3819** | Complete gene sequence analysis; BRCA2 gene
| **S3820** | Complete BRCA1 and BRCA2 gene sequence analysis for susceptibility to breast and ovarian cancer ♀
| **S3822** | Single mutation analysis (in individual with a known BRCA1 or BRCA2 mutation in the family) for susceptibility to breast and ovarian cancer ♀
| **S3823** | Three-mutation BRCA1 and BRCA2 analysis for susceptibility to breast and ovarian cancer in Ashkenazi individuals ♀
| **S3828** | Complete gene sequence analysis; MLH1 gene
| **S3829** | Complete gene sequence analysis; MLH2 gene
| **S3830** | Complete MLH1 and MLH2 gene sequence analysis for hereditary nonpolyposis colorectal cancer (HNPCC) genetic testing
| **S3831** | Single-mutation analysis (in individual with a known MLH1 and MLH2 mutation in the family) for hereditary nonpolyposis colorectal cancer (HNPCC) genetic testing
| **S3833** | Complete APC gene sequence analysis for susceptibility to familial adenomatous polyposis (FAP) and attenuated fap
| **S3834** | Single-mutation analysis (in individual with a known APC mutation in the family) for susceptibility to familial adenomatous polyposis (FAP) and attenuated FAP
| **S3835** | Complete gene sequence analysis for cystic fibrosis genetic testing
| **S3837** | Complete gene sequence analysis for hemochromatosis genetic testing
| **S3840** | DNA analysis for germline mutations of the RET proto-oncogene for susceptibility to multiple endocrine neoplasia type 2
| **S3841** | Genetic testing for retinoblastoma
| **S3842** | Genetic testing for Von Hippel-Lindau disease
| **S3843** | DNA analysis of the F5 gene for susceptibility to factor V Leiden thrombophilia
| **S3844** | DNA analysis of the connexin 26 gene (GJB2) for susceptibility to congenital, profound deafness
| **S3845** | Genetic testing for alpha-thalassemia
| **S3846** | Genetic testing for hemoglobin E beta-thalassemia
| **S3847** | Genetic testing for Tay-Sachs disease
| **S3848** | Genetic testing for Gaucher disease
| **S3849** | Genetic testing for Niemann-Pick disease
| **S3850** | Genetic testing for sickle cell anemia
| **S3851** | Genetic testing for Canavan disease
| **S3852** | DNA analysis for APOE epsilon 4 allele for susceptibility to Alzheimer's disease
| **S3853** | Genetic testing for myotonic muscular dystrophy
| **S3854** | Gene expression profiling panel for use in the management of breast cancer treatment
| **S3855** | Genetic testing for detection of mutations in the presenilin - 1 gene

●    **S3860**    Genetic testing, comprehensive cardiac ion channel analysis, for variants in 5 major cardiac ion channel genes for individuals with high index of suspicion for familial long QT syndrome (LQTS) or related syndromes

●    **S3861**    Genetic testing, sodium channel, voltage-gated, type V, alpha subunit (SCN5A) and variants for suspected Brugada Syndrome

●    **S3862**    Genetic testing, family-specific ion channel analysis, for blood-relatives of individuals (index case) who have previously tested positive for a genetic variant of a cardiac ion channel syndrome using either one of the above test configurations or confirmed results from another laboratory

**S3890**    DNA analysis, fecal, for colorectal cancer screening

**S3900**    Surface electromyography (EMG)

**S3902**    Ballistocardiogram

**S3904**    Masters 2 step

**S3905**    Noninvasive electrodiagnostic testing with automatic computerized hand-held device to stimulate and measure neuromuscular signals in diagnosing and evaluating systemic and entrapment neuropathies

**S4005**    Interim labor facility global (labor occurring but not resulting in delivery)    Ⓜ ♀

**S4011**    In vitro fertilization; including but not limited to identification and incubation of mature oocytes, fertilization with sperm, incubation of embryo(s), and subsequent visualization for determination of development    Ⓜ ♀

**S4013**    Complete cycle, gamete intrafallopian transfer (GIFT), case rate    Ⓜ ♀

**S4014**    Complete cycle, zygote intrafallopian transfer (ZIFT), case rate    Ⓜ ♀

**S4015**    Complete in vitro fertilization cycle, not otherwise specified, case rate    Ⓜ ♀

**S4016**    Frozen in vitro fertilization cycle, case rate    ♀

**S4017**    Incomplete cycle, treatment cancelled prior to stimulation, case rate    ♀

**S4018**    Frozen embryo transfer procedure cancelled before transfer, case rate    ♀

**S4020**    In vitro fertilization procedure cancelled before aspiration, case rate    ♀

**S4021**    In vitro fertilization procedure cancelled after aspiration, case rate    ♀

**S4022**    Assisted oocyte fertilization, case rate    ♀

**S4023**    Donor egg cycle, incomplete, case rate    ♀

**S4025**    Donor services for in vitro fertilization (sperm or embryo), case rate    Ⓐ

**S4026**    Procurement of donor sperm from sperm bank    ♂

**S4027**    Storage of previously frozen embryos    ♀

**S4028**    Microsurgical epididymal sperm aspiration (MESA)    Ⓐ ♂

**S4030**    Sperm procurement and cryopreservation services; initial visit    Ⓐ ♂

**S4031**    Sperm procurement and cryopreservation services; subsequent visit    Ⓐ ♂

**S4035**    Stimulated intrauterine insemination (IUI), case rate    ♀

**S4037**    Cryopreserved embryo transfer, case rate    ♀

**S4040**    Monitoring and storage of cryopreserved embryos, per 30 days    ♀

---

| | Code | Description | |
|---|---|---|---|
| | S4042 | Management of ovulation induction (interpretation of diagnostic tests and studies, nonface-to-face medical management of the patient), per cycle | |
| | S4981 | Insertion of levonorgestrel-releasing intrauterine system | ♀ |
| | S4989 | Contraceptive intrauterine device (e.g., Progestacert IUD), including implants and supplies | ♀ |
| ☑ | S4990 | Nicotine patches, legend | |
| ☑ | S4991 | Nicotine patches, nonlegend | |
| | S4993 | Contraceptive pills for birth control | ♀ |
| | S4995 | Smoking cessation gum | |
| ☑ | S5000 | Prescription drug, generic | |
| ☑ | S5001 | Prescription drug, brand name | |
| ☑ | S5010 | 5% dextrose and 0.45% normal saline, 1000 ml | |
| ☑ | S5011 | 5% dextrose in lactated ringer's, 1000 ml | |
| ☑ | S5012 | 5% dextrose with potassium chloride, 1000 ml | |
| ☑ | S5013 | 5% dextrose/0.45% normal saline with potassium chloride and magnesium sulfate, 1000 ml | |
| ☑ | S5014 | 5% dextrose/0.45% normal saline with potassium chloride and magnesium sulfate, 1500 ml | |
| | S5035 | Home infusion therapy, routine service of infusion device (e.g., pump maintenance) | |
| | S5036 | Home infusion therapy, repair of infusion device (e.g., pump repair) | |
| ☑ | S5100 | Day care services, adult; per 15 minutes | A |
| ☑ | S5101 | Day care services, adult; per half day | A |
| ☑ | S5102 | Day care services, adult; per diem | A |
| ☑ | S5105 | Day care services, center-based; services not included in program fee, per diem | |
| ☑ | S5108 | Home care training to home care client, per 15 minutes | |
| ☑ | S5109 | Home care training to home care client, per session | |
| ☑ | S5110 | Home care training, family; per 15 minutes | |
| | S5111 | Home care training, family; per session | |
| ☑ | S5115 | Home care training, nonfamily; per 15 minutes | |
| ☑ | S5116 | Home care training, nonfamily; per session | |
| ☑ | S5120 | Chore services; per 15 minutes | |
| ☑ | S5121 | Chore services; per diem | |
| ☑ | S5125 | Attendant care services; per 15 minutes | |
| ☑ | S5126 | Attendant care services; per diem | |
| ☑ | S5130 | Homemaker service, NOS; per 15 minutes | |
| ☑ | S5131 | Homemaker service, NOS; per diem | |
| ☑ | S5135 | Companion care, adult (e.g., IADL/ADL); per 15 minutes | A |
| ☑ | S5136 | Companion care, adult (e.g., IADL/ADL); per diem | A |
| ☑ | S5140 | Foster care, adult; per diem | A |
| | S5141 | Foster care, adult; per month | A |

| | | | |
|---|---|---|---|
| | S5145 | Foster care, therapeutic, child; per diem | Ⓐ |
| | S5146 | Foster care, therapeutic, child; per month | Ⓐ |
| ☑ | S5150 | Unskilled respite care, not hospice; per 15 minutes | |
| | S5151 | Unskilled respite care, not hospice; per diem | |
| | S5160 | Emergency response system; installation and testing | |
| | S5161 | Emergency response system; service fee, per month (excludes installation and testing) | |
| | S5162 | Emergency response system; purchase only | |
| | S5165 | Home modifications; per service | |
| | S5170 | Home delivered meals, including preparation; per meal | |
| | S5175 | Laundry service, external, professional; per order | |
| | S5180 | Home health respiratory therapy, initial evaluation | |
| | S5181 | Home health respiratory therapy, NOS, per diem | |
| | S5185 | Medication reminder service, nonface-to-face; per month | |
| | S5190 | Wellness assessment, performed by nonphysician | |
| | S5199 | Personal care item, NOS, each | |
| | S5497 | Home infusion therapy, catheter care/maintenance, not otherwise classified; includes administrative services, professional pharmacy services, care coordination, and all necessary supplies and equipment (drugs and nursing visits coded separately), per diem | |
| | S5498 | Home infusion therapy, catheter care/maintenance, simple (single lumen), includes administrative services, professional pharmacy services, care coordination and all necessary supplies and equipment, (drugs and nursing visits coded separately), per diem | |
| | S5501 | Home infusion therapy, catheter care/maintenance, complex (more than one lumen), includes administrative services, professional pharmacy services, care coordination, and all necessary supplies and equipment (drugs and nursing visits coded separately), per diem | |
| | S5502 | Home infusion therapy, catheter care/maintenance, implanted access device, includes administrative services, professional pharmacy services, care coordination and all necessary supplies and equipment (drugs and nursing visits coded separately), per diem (use this code for interim maintenance of vascular access not currently in use) | |
| | S5517 | Home infusion therapy, all supplies necessary for restoration of catheter patency or declotting | |
| | S5518 | Home infusion therapy, all supplies necessary for catheter repair | |
| | S5520 | Home infusion therapy, all supplies (including catheter) necessary for a peripherally inserted central venous catheter (PICC) line insertion | |
| | S5521 | Home infusion therapy, all supplies (including catheter) necessary for a midline catheter insertion | |
| | S5522 | Home infusion therapy, insertion of peripherally inserted central venous catheter (PICC), nursing services only (no supplies or catheter included) | |
| | S5523 | Home infusion therapy, insertion of midline venous catheter, nursing services only (no supplies or catheter included) | |
| ☑ | S5550 | Insulin, rapid onset, 5 units | |
| ☑ | S5551 | Insulin, most rapid onset (Lispro or Aspart); 5 units | |
| ☑ | S5552 | Insulin, intermediate acting (NPH or LENTE); 5 units | |

| | | |
|---|---|---|
| ☑ | S5553 | Insulin, long acting; 5 units |
| ☑ | S5560 | Insulin delivery device, reusable pen; 1.5 ml size |
| ☑ | S5561 | Insulin delivery device, reusable pen; 3 ml size |
| ☑ | S5565 | Insulin cartridge for use in insulin delivery device other than pump; 150 units |
| ☑ | S5566 | Insulin cartridge for use in insulin delivery device other than pump; 300 units |
| ☑ | S5570 | Insulin delivery device, disposable pen (including insulin); 1.5 ml size |
| ☑ | S5571 | Insulin delivery device, disposable pen (including insulin); 3 ml size |
| | S8030 | Scleral application of tantalum ring(s) for localization of lesions for proton beam therapy |
| | S8035 | Magnetic source imaging |
| | S8037 | Magnetic resonance cholangiopancreatography (MRCP) |
| | S8040 | Topographic brain mapping |
| | S8042 | Magnetic resonance imaging (MRI), low-field |
| | S8049 | Intraoperative radiation therapy (single administration) |
| | S8055 | Ultrasound guidance for multifetal pregnancy reduction(s), technical component (only to be used when the physician doing the reduction procedure does not perform the ultrasound, guidance is included in the CPT code for multifetal pregnancy reduction (59866)      Ⓜ ♀ |
| | S8080 | Scintimammography (radioimmunoscintigraphy of the breast), unilateral, including supply of radiopharmaceutical |
| | S8085 | Fluorine-18 fluorodeoxyglucose (F-18 FDG) imaging using dual-head coincidence detection system (nondedicated PET scan) |
| | S8092 | Electron beam computed tomography (also known as ultrafast CT, cine CT) |
| | S8096 | Portable peak flow meter |
| ☑ | S8097 | Asthma kit (including but not limited to portable peak expiratory flow meter, instructional video, brochure, and/or spacer) |
| | S8100 | Holding chamber or spacer for use with an inhaler or nebulizer; without mask |
| | S8101 | Holding chamber or spacer for use with an inhaler or nebulizer; with mask |
| | S8110 | Peak expiratory flow rate (physician services) |
| ☑ | S8120 | Oxygen contents, gaseous, 1 unit equals 1 cubic foot |
| ☑ | S8121 | Oxygen contents, liquid, 1 unit equals 1 pound |
| | S8185 | Flutter device |
| | S8186 | Swivel adaptor |
| | S8189 | Tracheostomy supply, not otherwise classified |
| | S8190 | Electronic spirometer (or microspirometer) |
| | S8210 | Mucus trap |
| | S8262 | Mandibular orthopedic repositioning device, each |
| | S8265 | Haberman feeder for cleft lip/palate |
| | S8270 | Enuresis alarm, using auditory buzzer and/or vibration device |
| | S8301 | Infection control supplies, not otherwise specified |

| | | |
|---|---|---|
| | S8415 | Supplies for home delivery of infant Ⓜ♀ |
| | S8420 | Gradient pressure aid (sleeve and glove combination), custom made |
| | S8421 | Gradient pressure aid (sleeve and glove combination), ready made |
| | S8422 | Gradient pressure aid (sleeve), custom made, medium weight |
| | S8423 | Gradient pressure aid (sleeve), custom made, heavy weight |
| | S8424 | Gradient pressure aid (sleeve), ready made |
| | S8425 | Gradient pressure aid (glove), custom made, medium weight |
| | S8426 | Gradient pressure aid (glove), custom made, heavy weight |
| | S8427 | Gradient pressure aid (glove), ready made |
| | S8428 | Gradient pressure aid (gauntlet), ready made |
| | S8429 | Gradient pressure exterior wrap |
| ☑ | S8430 | Padding for compression bandage, roll |
| ☑ | S8431 | Compression bandage, roll |

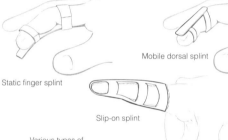

Mobile dorsal splint

Static finger splint

Slip-on splint

Various types of
digit splints (S8450)

| | | |
|---|---|---|
| ☑ | S8450 | Splint, prefabricated, digit (specify digit by use of modifier) |
| ☑ | S8451 | Splint, prefabricated, wrist or ankle |
| ☑ | S8452 | Splint, prefabricated, elbow |
| | S8460 | Camisole, postmastectomy |
| ☑ | S8490 | Insulin syringes (100 syringes, any size) |
| | S8940 | Equestrian/hippotherapy, per session |
| ☑ | S8948 | Application of a modality (requiring constant provider attendance) to one or more areas; low-level laser; each 15 minutes |
| ☑ | S8950 | Complex lymphedema therapy, each 15 minutes |
| | S8990 | Physical or manipulative therapy performed for maintenance rather than restoration |
| | S8999 | Resuscitation bag (for use by patient on artificial respiration during power failure or other catastrophic event) |
| | S9001 | Home uterine monitor with or without associated nursing services Ⓜ♀ |
| | S9007 | Ultrafiltration monitor |
| | S9015 | Automated EEG monitoring |
| | S9024 | Paranasal sinus ultrasound |
| | S9025 | Omnicardiogram/cardiointegram |

---

| | | |
|---|---|---|
| | S9034 | Extracorporeal shockwave lithotripsy for gall stones (if performed with ERCP, use 43265) |
| | S9055 | Procuren or other growth factor preparation to promote wound healing |
| | S9056 | Coma stimulation per diem |
| | S9061 | Home administration of aerosolized drug therapy (e.g., Pentamidine); administrative services, professional pharmacy services, care coordination, all necessary supplies and equipment (drugs and nursing visits coded separately), per diem |
| | S9075 | Smoking cessation treatment |
| | S9083 | Global fee urgent care centers |
| | S9088 | Services provided in an urgent care center (list in addition to code for service) |
| ☑ | S9090 | Vertebral axial decompression, per session |
| | ~~S9092~~ | ~~Canolith repositioning, per visit~~ |
| | S9097 | Home visit for wound care |
| | S9098 | Home visit, phototherapy services (e.g., Bili-lite), including equipment rental, nursing services, blood draw, supplies, and other services, per diem |
| | S9109 | Congestive heart failure telemonitoring, equipment rental, including telescale, computer system and software, telephone connections, and maintenance, per month |
| ☑ | S9117 | Back school, per visit |
| ☑ | S9122 | Home health aide or certified nurse assistant, providing care in the home; per hour |
| ☑ | S9123 | Nursing care, in the home; by registered nurse, per hour (use for general nursing care only, not to be used when CPT codes 99500-99602 can be used) |
| ☑ | S9124 | Nursing care, in the home; by licensed practical nurse, per hour |
| ☑ | S9125 | Respite care, in the home, per diem |
| ☑ | S9126 | Hospice care, in the home, per diem |
| ☑ | S9127 | Social work visit, in the home, per diem |
| ☑ | S9128 | Speech therapy, in the home, per diem |
| ☑ | S9129 | Occupational therapy, in the home, per diem |
| ☑ | S9131 | Physical therapy; in the home, per diem |
| ☑ | S9140 | Diabetic management program, follow-up visit to non-MD provider |
| ☑ | S9141 | Diabetic management program, follow-up visit to MD provider |
| | S9145 | Insulin pump initiation, instruction in initial use of pump (pump not included) |
| | S9150 | Evaluation by ocularist |
| | S9152 | Speech therapy, re-evaluation |
| | S9208 | Home management of preterm labor, including administrative services, professional pharmacy services, care coordination, and all necessary supplies or equipment (drugs and nursing visits coded separately), per diem (do not use this code with any home infusion per diem code) Ⓜ ♀ |

S9209    Home management of preterm premature rupture of membranes (PPROM), including administrative services, professional pharmacy services, care coordination, and all necessary supplies or equipment (drugs and nursing visits coded separately), per diem (do not use this code with any home infusion per diem code)    Ⓜ ♀

S9211    Home management of gestational hypertension, includes administrative services, professional pharmacy services, care coordination and all necessary supplies and equipment (drugs and nursing visits coded separately); per diem (do not use this code with any home infusion per diem code)    Ⓜ ♀

S9212    Home management of postpartum hypertension, includes administrative services, professional pharmacy services, care coordination, and all necessary supplies and equipment (drugs and nursing visits coded separately), per diem (do not use this code with any home infusion per diem code)    ♀

S9213    Home management of preeclampsia, includes administrative services, professional pharmacy services, care coordination, and all necessary supplies and equipment (drugs and nursing services coded separately); per diem (do not use this code with any home infusion per diem code)    Ⓜ ♀

S9214    Home management of gestational diabetes, includes administrative services, professional pharmacy services, care coordination, and all necessary supplies and equipment (drugs and nursing visits coded separately); per diem (do not use this code with any home infusion per diem code)    Ⓜ ♀

S9325    Home infusion therapy, pain management infusion; administrative services, professional pharmacy services, care coordination, and all necessary supplies and equipment, (drugs and nursing visits coded separately), per diem (do not use this code with S9326, S9327 or S9328)

S9326    Home infusion therapy, continuous (24 hours or more) pain management infusion; administrative services, professional pharmacy services, care coordination and all necessary supplies and equipment (drugs and nursing visits coded separately), per diem

S9327    Home infusion therapy, intermittent (less than 24 hours) pain management infusion; administrative services, professional pharmacy services, care coordination, and all necessary supplies and equipment (drugs and nursing visits coded separately), per diem

S9328    Home infusion therapy, implanted pump pain management infusion; administrative services, professional pharmacy services, care coordination, and all necessary supplies and equipment (drugs and nursing visits coded separately), per diem

S9329    Home infusion therapy, chemotherapy infusion; administrative services, professional pharmacy services, care coordination, and all necessary supplies and equipment (drugs and nursing visits coded separately), per diem (do not use this code with S9330 or S9331)

S9330    Home infusion therapy, continuous (24 hours or more) chemotherapy infusion; administrative services, professional pharmacy services, care coordination, and all necessary supplies and equipment (drugs and nursing visits coded separately), per diem

**S9331**    Home infusion therapy, intermittent (less than 24 hours) chemotherapy infusion; administrative services, professional pharmacy services, care coordination, and all necessary supplies and equipment (drugs and nursing visits coded separately), per diem

**S9335**    Home therapy, hemodialysis; administrative services, professional pharmacy services, care coordination, and all necessary supplies and equipment (drugs and nursing services coded separately), per diem

**S9336**    Home infusion therapy, continuous anticoagulant infusion therapy (e.g., Heparin), administrative services, professional pharmacy services, care coordination and all necessary supplies and equipment (drugs and nursing visits coded separately), per diem

**S9338**    Home infusion therapy, immunotherapy, administrative services, professional pharmacy services, care coordination, and all necessary supplies and equipment (drugs and nursing visits coded separately), per diem

**S9339**    Home therapy; peritoneal dialysis, administrative services, professional pharmacy services, care coordination and all necessary supplies and equipment (drugs and nursing visits coded separately), per diem

**S9340**    Home therapy; enteral nutrition; administrative services, professional pharmacy services, care coordination, and all necessary supplies and equipment (enteral formula and nursing visits coded separately), per diem

**S9341**    Home therapy; enteral nutrition via gravity; administrative services, professional pharmacy services, care coordination, and all necessary supplies and equipment (enteral formula and nursing visits coded separately), per diem

**S9342**    Home therapy; enteral nutrition via pump; administrative services, professional pharmacy services, care coordination, and all necessary supplies and equipment (enteral formula and nursing visits coded separately), per diem

**S9343**    Home therapy; enteral nutrition via bolus; administrative services, professional pharmacy services, care coordination, and all necessary supplies and equipment (enteral formula and nursing visits coded separately), per diem

**S9345**    Home infusion therapy, antihemophilic agent infusion therapy (e.g., factor VIII); administrative services, professional pharmacy services, care coordination, and all necessary supplies and equipment (drugs and nursing visits coded separately), per diem

**S9346**    Home infusion therapy, alpha-1-proteinase inhibitor (e.g., Prolastin); administrative services, professional pharmacy services, care coordination, and all necessary supplies and equipment (drugs and nursing visits coded separately), per diem

**S9347**    Home infusion therapy, uninterrupted, long-term, controlled rate intravenous or subcutaneous infusion therapy (e.g., epoprostenol); administrative services, professional pharmacy services, care coordination, and all necessary supplies and equipment (drugs and nursing visits coded separately), per diem

**S9348**    Home infusion therapy, sympathomimetic/inotropic agent infusion therapy (e.g., Dobutamine); administrative services, professional pharmacy services, care coordination, all necessary supplies and equipment (drugs and nursing visits coded separately), per diem

**S9349**    Home infusion therapy, tocolytic infusion therapy; administrative services, professional pharmacy services, care coordination, and all necessary supplies and equipment (drugs and nursing visits coded separately), per diem    Ⓜ ♀

**S9351**    Home infusion therapy, continuous or intermittent antiemetic infusion therapy; administrative services, professional pharmacy services, care coordination, and all necessary supplies and equipment (drugs and visits coded separately), per diem

**S9353**    Home infusion therapy, continuous insulin infusion therapy; administrative services, professional pharmacy services, care coordination, and all necessary supplies and equipment (drugs and nursing visits coded separately), per diem

**S9355**    Home infusion therapy, chelation therapy; administrative services, professional pharmacy services, care coordination, and all necessary supplies and equipment (drugs and nursing visits coded separately), per diem

**S9357**    Home infusion therapy, enzyme replacement intravenous therapy; (e.g., Imiglucerase); administrative services, professional pharmacy services, care coordination, and all necessary supplies and equipment (drugs and nursing visits coded separately), per diem

**S9359**    Home infusion therapy, antitumor necrosis factor intravenous therapy; (e.g., Infliximab); administrative services, professional pharmacy services, care coordination, and all necessary supplies and equipment (drugs and nursing visits coded separately), per diem

**S9361**    Home infusion therapy, diuretic intravenous therapy; administrative services, professional pharmacy services, care coordination, and all necessary supplies and equipment (drugs and nursing visits coded separately), per diem

**S9363**    Home infusion therapy, antispasmotic therapy; administrative services, professional pharmacy services, care coordination, and all necessary supplies and equipment (drugs and nursing visits coded separately), per diem

**S9364**    Home infusion therapy, total parenteral nutrition (TPN); administrative services, professional pharmacy services, care coordination, and all necessary supplies and equipment including standard TPN formula (lipids, specialty amino acid formulas, drugs other than in standard formula and nursing visits coded separately), per diem (do not use with home infusion codes S9365–S9368 using daily volume scales)

**S9365**    Home infusion therapy, total parenteral nutrition (TPN); 1 liter per day, administrative services, professional pharmacy services, care coordination, and all necessary supplies and equipment including standard TPN formula (lipids, specialty amino acid formulas, drugs other than in standard formula and nursing visits coded separately), per diem

**S9366**    Home infusion therapy, total parenteral nutrition (TPN); more than 1 liter but no more than 2 liters per day, administrative services, professional pharmacy services, care coordination, and all necessary supplies and equipment including standard TPN formula (lipids, specialty amino acid formulas, drugs other than in standard formula and nursing visits coded separately), per diem

**S9367**   Home infusion therapy, total parenteral nutrition (TPN); more than 2 liters but no more than 3 liters per day, administrative services, professional pharmacy services, care coordination, and all necessary supplies and equipment including standard TPN formula (lipids, specialty amino acid formulas, drugs other than in standard formula and nursing visits coded separately), per diem

**S9368**   Home infusion therapy, total parenteral nutrition (TPN); more than 3 liters per day, administrative services, professional pharmacy services, care coordination, and all necessary supplies and equipment including standard TPN formula (lipids, specialty amino acid formulas, drugs other than in standard formula and nursing visits coded separately), per diem

**S9370**   Home therapy, intermittent antiemetic injection therapy; administrative services, professional pharmacy services, care coordination, and all necessary supplies and equipment (drugs and nursing visits coded separately), per diem

**S9372**   Home therapy; intermittent anticoagulant injection therapy (e.g., Heparin); administrative services, professional pharmacy services, care coordination, and all necessary supplies and equipment (drugs and nursing visits coded separately), per diem (do not use this code for flushing of infusion devices with Heparin to maintain patency)

**S9373**   Home infusion therapy, hydration therapy; administrative services, professional pharmacy services, care coordination, and all necessary supplies and equipment (drugs and nursing visits coded separately), per diem (do not use with hydration therapy codes S9374–S9377 using daily volume scales)

**S9374**   Home infusion therapy, hydration therapy; 1 liter per day, administrative services, professional pharmacy services, care coordination, and all necessary supplies and equipment (drugs and nursing visits coded separately), per diem

**S9375**   Home infusion therapy, hydration therapy; more than 1 liter but no more than 2 liters per day, administrative services, professional pharmacy services, care coordination, and all necessary supplies and equipment (drugs and nursing visits coded separately), per diem

**S9376**   Home infusion therapy, hydration therapy; more than 2 liters but no more than 3 liters per day, administrative services, professional pharmacy services, care coordination, and all necessary supplies and equipment (drugs and nursing visits coded separately), per diem

**S9377**   Home infusion therapy, hydration therapy; more than 3 liters per day, administrative services, professional pharmacy services, care coordination, and all necessary supplies (drugs and nursing visits coded separately), per diem

**S9379**   Home infusion therapy, infusion therapy, not otherwise classified; administrative services, professional pharmacy services, care coordination, and all necessary supplies and equipment (drugs and nursing visits coded separately), per diem

**S9381**   Delivery or service to high risk areas requiring escort or extra protection, per visit

**S9401**   Anticoagulation clinic, inclusive of all services except laboratory tests, per session

**S9430**   Pharmacy compounding and dispensing services

● **S9433**   Medical food nutritionally complete, administered orally, providing 100% of nutritional intake

**Temporary National Codes (Non-Medicare)**

**S9434 — S9490**

| | | |
|---|---|---|
| | S9434 | Modified solid food supplements for inborn errors of metabolism |
| | S9435 | Medical foods for inborn errors of metabolism |
| ☑ | S9436 | Childbirth preparation/Lamaze classes, nonphysician provider, per session ⅏♀ |
| | S9437 | Childbirth refresher classes, nonphysician provider, per session ⅏♀ |
| ☑ | S9438 | Cesarean birth classes, nonphysician provider, per session ⅏♀ |
| ☑ | S9439 | VBAC (vaginal birth after cesarean) classes, nonphysician provider, per session ⅏♀ |
| ☑ | S9441 | Asthma education, nonphysician provider, per session |
| ☑ | S9442 | Birthing classes, nonphysician provider, per session ⅏♀ |
| ☑ | S9443 | Lactation classes, nonphysician provider, per session ⅏♀ |
| ☑ | S9444 | Parenting classes, nonphysician provider, per session |
| ☑ | S9445 | Patient education, not otherwise classified, nonphysician provider, individual, per session |
| ☑ | S9446 | Patient education, not otherwise classified, nonphysician provider, group, per session |
| ☑ | S9447 | Infant safety (including CPR) classes, nonphysician provider, per session |
| ☑ | S9449 | Weight management classes, nonphysician provider, per session |
| | S9451 | Exercise classes, nonphysician provider, per session |
| | S9452 | Nutrition classes, nonphysician provider, per session |
| | S9453 | Smoking cessation classes, nonphysician provider, per session |
| | S9454 | Stress management classes, nonphysician provider, per session |
| | S9455 | Diabetic management program, group session |
| | S9460 | Diabetic management program, nurse visit |
| | S9465 | Diabetic management program, dietitian visit |
| | S9470 | Nutritional counseling, dietitian visit |
| | S9472 | Cardiac rehabilitation program, nonphysician provider, per diem |
| | S9473 | Pulmonary rehabilitation program, nonphysician provider, per diem |
| | S9474 | Enterostomal therapy by a registered nurse certified in enterostomal therapy, per diem |
| | S9475 | Ambulatory setting substance abuse treatment or detoxification services, per diem |
| | S9476 | Vestibular rehabilitation program, nonphysician provider, per diem |
| | S9480 | Intensive outpatient psychiatric services, per diem |
| ☑ | S9482 | Family stabilization services, per 15 minutes |
| ☑ | S9484 | Crisis intervention mental health services, per hour |
| | S9485 | Crisis intervention mental health services, per diem |
| | S9490 | Home infusion therapy, corticosteroid infusion; administrative services, professional pharmacy services, care coordination, and all necessary supplies and equipment (drugs and nursing visits coded separately), per diem |

**S9494**   Home infusion therapy, antibiotic, antiviral, or antifungal therapy; administrative services, professional pharmacy services, care coordination, and all necessary supplies and equipment (drugs and nursing visits coded separately, per diem) (do not use this code with home infusion codes for hourly dosing schedules S9497–S9504)

**S9497**   Home infusion therapy, antibiotic, antiviral, or antifungal therapy; once every 3 hours; administrative services, professional pharmacy services, care coordination, and all necessary supplies and equipment (drugs and nursing visits coded separately), per diem

**S9500**   Home infusion therapy, antibiotic, antiviral, or antifungal therapy; once every 24 hours; administrative services, professional pharmacy services, care coordination, and all necessary supplies and equipment (drugs and nursing visits coded separately), per diem

**S9501**   Home infusion therapy, antibiotic, antiviral, or antifungal therapy; once every 12 hours; administrative services, professional pharmacy services, care coordination, and all necessary supplies and equipment (drugs and nursing visits coded separately), per diem

**S9502**   Home infusion therapy, antibiotic, antiviral, or antifungal therapy; once every 8 hours, administrative services, professional pharmacy services, care coordination, and all necessary supplies and equipment (drugs and nursing visits coded separately), per diem

**S9503**   Home infusion therapy, antibiotic, antiviral, or antifungal; once every 6 hours; administrative services, professional pharmacy services, care coordination, and all necessary supplies and equipment (drugs and nursing visits coded separately), per diem

**S9504**   Home infusion therapy, antibiotic, antiviral, or antifungal; once every 4 hours; administrative services, professional pharmacy services, care coordination, and all necessary supplies and equipment (drugs and nursing visits coded separately), per diem

**S9529**   Routine venipuncture for collection of specimen(s), single homebound, nursing home, or skilled nursing facility patient

**S9537**   Home therapy; hematopoietic hormone injection therapy (e.g., erythropoietin, G-CSF, GM-CSF); administrative services, professional pharmacy services, care coordination, and all necessary supplies and equipment (drugs and nursing visits coded separately), per diem

**S9538**   Home transfusion of blood product(s); administrative services, professional pharmacy services, care coordination and all necessary supplies and equipment (blood products, drugs, and nursing visits coded separately), per diem

**S9542**   Home injectable therapy, not otherwise classified, including administrative services, professional pharmacy services, care coordination, and all necessary supplies and equipment (drugs and nursing visits coded separately), per diem

**S9558**   Home injectable therapy; growth hormone, including administrative services, professional pharmacy services, care coordination, and all necessary supplies and equipment (drugs and nursing visits coded separately), per diem

**S9559**   Home injectable therapy, interferon, including administrative services, professional pharmacy services, care coordination, and all necessary supplies and equipment (drugs and nursing visits coded separately), per diem

---

☑ Quantity Alert    ● New Code    ○ Recycled/Reinstated    ▲ Revised Code    ⅋ DMEPOS Paid    ⊘ SNF Excluded

| | |
|---|---|
| **S9560** | Home injectable therapy; hormonal therapy (e.g., leuprolide, goserelin), including administrative services, professional pharmacy services, care coordination, and all necessary supplies and equipment (drugs and nursing visits coded separately), per diem |
| **S9562** | Home injectable therapy, palivizumab, including administrative services, professional pharmacy services, care coordination, and all necessary supplies and equipment (drugs and nursing visits coded separately), per diem |
| **S9590** | Home therapy, irrigation therapy (e.g., sterile irrigation of an organ or anatomical cavity); including administrative services, professional pharmacy services, care coordination, and all necessary supplies and equipment (drugs and nursing visits coded separately), per diem |
| **S9810** | Home therapy; professional pharmacy services for provision of infusion, specialty drug administration, and/or disease state management, not otherwise classified, per hour (do not use this code with any per diem code) |
| **S9900** | Services by authorized Christian Science practitioner for the process of healing, per diem; not to be used for rest or study; excludes in-patient services |
| **S9970** | Health club membership, annual |
| **S9975** | Transplant related lodging, meals and transportation, per diem |
| **S9976** | Lodging, per diem, not otherwise classified |
| **S9977** | Meals, per diem, not otherwise specified |
| **S9981** | Medical records copying fee, administrative |
| ☑ **S9982** | Medical records copying fee, per page |
| **S9986** | Not medically necessary service (patient is aware that service not medically necessary) |
| **S9988** | Services provided as part of a Phase I clinical trial |
| **S9989** | Services provided outside of the United States of America (list in addition to code(s) for services(s)) |
| **S9990** | Services provided as part of a Phase II clinical trial |
| **S9991** | Services provided as part of a Phase III clinical trial |
| **S9992** | Transportation costs to and from trial location and local transportation costs (e.g., fares for taxicab or bus) for clinical trial participant and one caregiver/companion |
| **S9994** | Lodging costs (e.g., hotel charges) for clinical trial participant and one caregiver/companion |
| **S9996** | Meals for clinical trial participant and one caregiver/companion |
| **S9999** | Sales tax |

## NATIONAL T CODES ESTABLISHED FOR STATE MEDICAID AGENCIES T1000-T9999

The T codes are designed for use by Medicaid state agencies to establish codes for items for which there are no permanent national codes but for which codes are necessary to administer the Medicaid program (T codes are not accepted by Medicare but can be used by private insurers). This range of codes describes nursing and home health-related services, substance abuse treatment, and certain training-related procedures.

☑ **T1000** Private duty/independent nursing service(s), licensed, up to 15 minutes

**T1001** Nursing assessment/evaluation

☑ **T1002** RN services, up to 15 minutes

☑ **T1003** LPN/LVN services, up to 15 minutes

☑ **T1004** Services of a qualified nursing aide, up to 15 minutes

☑ **T1005** Respite care services, up to 15 minutes

**T1006** Alcohol and/or substance abuse services, family/couple counseling

**T1007** Alcohol and/or substance abuse services, treatment plan development and/or modification

**T1009** Child sitting services for children of the individual receiving alcohol and/or substance abuse services

**T1010** Meals for individuals receiving alcohol and/or substance abuse services (when meals not included in the program)

**T1012** Alcohol and/or substance abuse services, skills development

☑ **T1013** Sign language or oral interpretive services, per 15 minutes

**T1014** Telehealth transmission, per minute, professional services bill separately

**T1015** Clinic visit/encounter, all-inclusive

☑ **T1016** Case management, each 15 minutes

☑ **T1017** Targeted case management, each 15 minutes

**T1018** School-based individualized education program (IEP) services, bundled

☑ **T1019** Personal care services, per 15 minutes, not for an inpatient or resident of a hospital, nursing facility, ICF/MR or IMD, part of the individualized plan of treatment (code may not be used to identify services provided by home health aide or certified nurse assistant)

**T1020** Personal care services, per diem, not for an inpatient or resident of a hospital, nursing facility, ICF/MR or IMD, part of the individualized plan of treatment (code may not be used to identify services provided by home health aide or certified nurse assistant)

**T1021** Home health aide or certified nurse assistant, per visit

**T1022** Contracted home health agency services, all services provided under contract, per day

**T1023** Screening to determine the appropriateness of consideration of an individual for participation in a specified program, project or treatment protocol, per encounter

**T1024** Evaluation and treatment by an integrated, specialty team contracted to provide coordinated care to multiple or severely handicapped children, per encounter   Ⓐ

**T1025** Intensive, extended multidisciplinary services provided in a clinic setting to children with complex medical, physical, mental and psychosocial impairments, per diem   Ⓐ

**National T Codes**

**T1026 — T2028**

| | | |
|---|---|---|
| | T1026 | Intensive, extended multidisciplinary services provided in a clinic setting to children with complex medical, physical, medical and psychosocial impairments, per hour ▣ |
| ☑ | T1027 | Family training and counseling for child development, per 15 minutes |
| | T1028 | Assessment of home, physical and family environment, to determine suitability to meet patient's medical needs |
| | T1029 | Comprehensive environmental lead investigation, not including laboratory analysis, per dwelling |
| ☑ | T1030 | Nursing care, in the home, by registered nurse, per diem |
| ☑ | T1031 | Nursing care, in the home, by licensed practical nurse, per diem |
| ☑ | T1502 | Administration of oral, intramuscular and/or subcutaneous medication by health care agency/professional, per visit |
| ☑ | T1503 | Administration of medication, other than oral and/or injectable, by a health care agency/professional, per visit |
| | T1999 | Miscellaneous therapeutic items and supplies, retail purchases, not otherwise classified; identify product in "remarks" |
| | T2001 | Nonemergency transportation; patient attendant/escort |
| ☑ | T2002 | Nonemergency transportation; per diem |
| | T2003 | Nonemergency transportation; encounter/trip |
| | T2004 | Nonemergency transport; commercial carrier, multipass |
| | T2005 | Nonemergency transportation; stretcher van |
| ☑ | T2007 | Transportation waiting time, air ambulance and nonemergency vehicle, one-half (1/2) hour increments |
| ☑ | T2010 | Preadmission screening and resident review (PASRR) level I identification screening, per screen |
| | T2011 | Preadmission screening and resident review (PASRR) level II evaluation, per evaluation |
| ☑ | T2012 | Habilitation, educational; waiver, per diem |
| ☑ | T2013 | Habilitation, educational, waiver; per hour |
| ☑ | T2014 | Habilitation, prevocational, waiver; per diem |
| ☑ | T2015 | Habilitation, prevocational, waiver; per hour |
| ☑ | T2016 | Habilitation, residential, waiver; per diem |
| ☑ | T2017 | Habilitation, residential, waiver; 15 minutes |
| ☑ | T2018 | Habilitation, supported employment, waiver; per diem |
| ☑ | T2019 | Habilitation, supported employment, waiver; per 15 minutes |
| ☑ | T2020 | Day habilitation, waiver; per diem |
| ☑ | T2021 | Day habilitation, waiver; per 15 minutes |
| ☑ | T2022 | Case management, per month |
| ☑ | T2023 | Targeted case management; per month |
| | T2024 | Service assessment/plan of care development, waiver |
| | T2025 | Waiver services; not otherwise specified (NOS) |
| ☑ | T2026 | Specialized childcare, waiver; per diem |
| ☑ | T2027 | Specialized childcare, waiver; per 15 minutes |
| | T2028 | Specialized supply, not otherwise specified, waiver |

National T Codes

| | T2029 | Specialized medical equipment, not otherwise specified, waiver |
|---|---|---|
| ☑ | T2030 | Assisted living, waiver; per month |
| ☑ | T2031 | Assisted living; waiver, per diem |
| ☑ | T2032 | Residential care, not otherwise specified (NOS), waiver; per month |
| ☑ | T2033 | Residential care, not otherwise specified (NOS), waiver; per diem |
| ☑ | T2034 | Crisis intervention, waiver; per diem |
| | T2035 | Utility services to support medical equipment and assistive technology/devices, waiver |
| ☑ | T2036 | Therapeutic camping, overnight, waiver; each session |
| ☑ | T2037 | Therapeutic camping, day, waiver; each session |
| ☑ | T2038 | Community transition, waiver; per service |
| ☑ | T2039 | Vehicle modifications, waiver; per service |
| ☑ | T2040 | Financial management, self-directed, waiver; per 15 minutes |
| ☑ | T2041 | Supports brokerage, self-directed, waiver; per 15 minutes |
| ☑ | T2042 | Hospice routine home care; per diem |
| ☑ | T2043 | Hospice continuous home care; per hour |
| ☑ | T2044 | Hospice inpatient respite care; per diem |
| ☑ | T2045 | Hospice general inpatient care; per diem |
| ☑ | T2046 | Hospice long-term care, room and board only; per diem |
| ☑ | T2048 | Behavioral health; long-term care residential (nonacute care in a residential treatment program where stay is typically longer than 30 days), with room and board, per diem |
| ☑ | T2049 | Nonemergency transportation; stretcher van, mileage; per mile |
| | T2101 | Human breast milk processing, storage and distribution only ♀ |
| ☑ | T4521 | Adult sized disposable incontinence product, brief/diaper, small, each <br> MED: 100-3,230.10 |
| ☑ | T4522 | Adult sized disposable incontinence product, brief/diaper, medium, each <br> MED: 100-3,230.10 |
| ☑ | T4523 | Adult sized disposable incontinence product, brief/diaper, large, each <br> MED: 100-3,230.10 |
| ☑ | T4524 | Adult sized disposable incontinence product, brief/diaper, extra large, each <br> MED: 100-3,230.10 |
| ☑ | T4525 | Adult sized disposable incontinence product, protective underwear/pull-on, small size, each <br> MED: 100-3,230.10 |
| ☑ | T4526 | Adult sized disposable incontinence product, protective underwear/pull-on, medium size, each <br> MED: 100-3,230.10 |
| ☑ | T4527 | Adult sized disposable incontinence product, protective underwear/pull-on, large size, each <br> MED: 100-3,230.10 |
| ☑ | T4528 | Adult sized disposable incontinence product, protective underwear/pull-on, extra large size, each <br> MED: 100-3,230.10 |

National T Codes

T2029 — T4528

☑ | T4529 | Pediatric sized disposable incontinence product, brief/diaper, small/medium size, each
MED: 100-3,230.10

☑ | T4530 | Pediatric sized disposable incontinence product, brief/diaper, large size, each
MED: 100-3,230.10

☑ | T4531 | Pediatric sized disposable incontinence product, protective underwear/pull-on, small/medium size, each
MED: 100-3,230.10

☑ | T4532 | Pediatric sized disposable incontinence product, protective underwear/pull-on, large size, each
MED: 100-3,230.10

☑ | T4533 | Youth sized disposable incontinence product, brief/diaper, each
MED: 100-3,230.10

☑ | T4534 | Youth sized disposable incontinence product, protective underwear/pull-on, each
MED: 100-3,230.10

☑ | T4535 | Disposable liner/shield/guard/pad/undergarment, for incontinence, each
MED: 100-3,230.10

☑ | T4536 | Incontinence product, protective underwear/pull-on, reusable, any size, each
MED: 100-3,230.10

☑ | T4537 | Incontinence product, protective underpad, reusable, bed size, each
MED: 100-3,230.10

☑ | T4538 | Diaper service, reusable diaper, each diaper
MED: 100-3,230.10

☑ | T4539 | Incontinence product, diaper/brief, reusable, any size, each
MED: 100-3,230.10

☑ | T4540 | Incontinence product, protective underpad, reusable, chair size, each
MED: 100-3,230.10

☑ | T4541 | Incontinence product, disposable underpad, large, each

☑ | T4542 | Incontinence product, disposable underpad, small size, each

☑ | T4543 | Disposable incontinence product, brief/diaper, bariatric, each

| T5001 | Positioning seat for persons with special orthopedic needs

| T5999 | Supply, not otherwise specified

## VISION SERVICES V0000-V2999

These V codes include vision-related supplies, including spectacles, lenses, contact lenses, prostheses, intraocular lenses, and miscellaneous lenses.

## FRAMES

| | | | |
|---|---|---|---|
| Ⓐ | **V2020** | Frames, purchases | ㅤ♿ |
| | | MED: 100-2,15,120; 100-4,3,10.4 | |
| Ⓔ | **V2025** | Deluxe frame | |
| | | MED: 100-4,1,30.3.5 | |

## SPECTACLE LENSES

See S0500-S0592 for temporary vision codes.

## SINGLE VISION, GLASS, OR PLASTIC

Monofocal spectacles (V2100-V2114)

Trifocal spectacles (V2300-V2314)

Low vision aids mounted to spectacles (V2610)

Telescopic or other compound lens fitted on spectacles as a low vision aid (V2615)

| | | | | |
|---|---|---|---|---|
| Ⓐ | ☑ | **V2100** | Sphere, single vision, plano to plus or minus 4.00, per lens | ♿ |
| Ⓐ | ☑ | **V2101** | Sphere, single vision, plus or minus 4.12 to plus or minus 7.00d, per lens | ♿ |
| Ⓐ | ☑ | **V2102** | Sphere, single vision, plus or minus 7.12 to plus or minus 20.00d, per lens | ♿ |
| Ⓐ | ☑ | **V2103** | Spherocylinder, single vision, plano to plus or minus 4.00d sphere, 0.12 to 2.00d cylinder, per lens | ♿ |
| Ⓐ | ☑ | **V2104** | Spherocylinder, single vision, plano to plus or minus 4.00d sphere, 2.12 to 4.00d cylinder, per lens | ♿ |
| Ⓐ | ☑ | **V2105** | Spherocylinder, single vision, plano to plus or minus 4.00d sphere, 4.25 to 6.00d cylinder, per lens | ♿ |
| Ⓐ | ☑ | **V2106** | Spherocylinder, single vision, plano to plus or minus 4.00d sphere, over 6.00d cylinder, per lens | ♿ |
| Ⓐ | ☑ | **V2107** | Spherocylinder, single vision, plus or minus 4.25 to plus or minus 7.00 sphere, 0.12 to 2.00d cylinder, per lens | ♿ |
| Ⓐ | ☑ | **V2108** | Spherocylinder, single vision, plus or minus 4.25d to plus or minus 7.00d sphere, 2.12 to 4.00d cylinder, per lens | ♿ |
| Ⓐ | ☑ | **V2109** | Spherocylinder, single vision, plus or minus 4.25 to plus or minus 7.00d sphere, 4.25 to 6.00d cylinder, per lens | ♿ |

Vision Services

V2020 — V2109

Vision Services

| | | | |
|---|---|---|---|
| A | ☑ | **V2110** | Spherocylinder, single vision, plus or minus 4.25 to 7.00d sphere, over 6.00d cylinder, per lens ♿ |
| A | ☑ | **V2111** | Spherocylinder, single vision, plus or minus 7.25 to plus or minus 12.00d sphere, 0.25 to 2.25d cylinder, per lens ♿ |
| A | ☑ | **V2112** | Spherocylinder, single vision, plus or minus 7.25 to plus or minus 12.00d sphere, 2.25d to 4.00d cylinder, per lens ♿ |
| A | ☑ | **V2113** | Spherocylinder, single vision, plus or minus 7.25 to plus or minus 12.00d sphere, 4.25 to 6.00d cylinder, per lens ♿ |
| A | ☑ | **V2114** | Spherocylinder, single vision, sphere over plus or minus 12.00d, per lens ♿ |
| A | ☑ | **V2115** | Lenticular (myodisc), per lens, single vision ♿ |
| A | | **V2118** | Aniseikonic lens, single vision ♿ |
| A | ☑ | **V2121** | Lenticular lens, per lens, single ♿ |
| | | | MED: 100-2,15,120; 100-4,3,10.4 |
| A | | **V2199** | Not otherwise classified, single vision lens |

## BIFOCAL, GLASS, OR PLASTIC

| | | | |
|---|---|---|---|
| A | ☑ | **V2200** | Sphere, bifocal, plano to plus or minus 4.00d, per lens ♿ |
| A | ☑ | **V2201** | Sphere, bifocal, plus or minus 4.12 to plus or minus 7.00d, per lens ♿ |
| A | ☑ | **V2202** | Sphere, bifocal, plus or minus 7.12 to plus or minus 20.00d, per lens ♿ |
| A | ☑ | **V2203** | Spherocylinder, bifocal, plano to plus or minus 4.00d sphere, 0.12 to 2.00d cylinder, per lens ♿ |
| A | ☑ | **V2204** | Spherocylinder, bifocal, plano to plus or minus 4.00d sphere, 2.12 to 4.00d cylinder, per lens ♿ |
| A | ☑ | **V2205** | Spherocylinder, bifocal, plano to plus or minus 4.00d sphere, 4.25 to 6.00d cylinder, per lens ♿ |
| A | ☑ | **V2206** | Spherocylinder, bifocal, plano to plus or minus 4.00d sphere, over 6.00d cylinder, per lens ♿ |
| A | ☑ | **V2207** | Spherocylinder, bifocal, plus or minus 4.25 to plus or minus 7.00d sphere, 0.12 to 2.00d cylinder, per lens ♿ |
| A | ☑ | **V2208** | Spherocylinder, bifocal, plus or minus 4.25 to plus or minus 7.00d sphere, 2.12 to 4.00d cylinder, per lens ♿ |
| A | ☑ | **V2209** | Spherocylinder, bifocal, plus or minus 4.25 to plus or minus 7.00d sphere, 4.25 to 6.00d cylinder, per lens ♿ |
| A | ☑ | **V2210** | Spherocylinder, bifocal, plus or minus 4.25 to plus or minus 7.00d sphere, over 6.00d cylinder, per lens ♿ |
| A | ☑ | **V2211** | Spherocylinder, bifocal, plus or minus 7.25 to plus or minus 12.00d sphere, 0.25 to 2.25d cylinder, per lens ♿ |
| A | ☑ | **V2212** | Spherocylinder, bifocal, plus or minus 7.25 to plus or minus 12.00d sphere, 2.25 to 4.00d cylinder, per lens ♿ |
| A | ☑ | **V2213** | Spherocylinder, bifocal, plus or minus 7.25 to plus or minus 12.00d sphere, 4.25 to 6.00d cylinder, per lens ♿ |
| A | ☑ | **V2214** | Spherocylinder, bifocal, sphere over plus or minus 12.00d, per lens ♿ |
| A | ☑ | **V2215** | Lenticular (myodisc), per lens, bifocal ♿ |
| A | ☑ | **V2218** | Aniseikonic, per lens, bifocal ♿ |
| A | ☑ | **V2219** | Bifocal seg width over 28mm ♿ |

| | | | |
|---|---|---|---|
| A ☑ | V2220 | Bifocal add over 3.25d | ♿ |
| A | V2221 | Lenticular lens, per lens, bifocal | ♿ |
| | | MED: 100-2,15,120; 100-4,3,10.4 | |
| A | V2299 | Specialty bifocal (by report) | |
| | | Pertinent documentation to evaluate medical appropriateness should be included when this code is reported. | |

## TRIFOCAL, GLASS, OR PLASTIC

| | | | |
|---|---|---|---|
| A ☑ | V2300 | Sphere, trifocal, plano to plus or minus 4.00d, per lens | ♿ |
| A ☑ | V2301 | Sphere, trifocal, plus or minus 4.12 to plus or minus 7.00d per lens | ♿ |
| A ☑ | V2302 | Sphere, trifocal, plus or minus 7.12 to plus or minus 20.00, per lens | ♿ |
| A ☑ | V2303 | Spherocylinder, trifocal, plano to plus or minus 4.00d sphere, 0.12 to 2.00d cylinder, per lens | ♿ |
| A ☑ | V2304 | Spherocylinder, trifocal, plano to plus or minus 4.00d sphere, 2.25 to 4.00d cylinder, per lens | ♿ |
| A ☑ | V2305 | Spherocylinder, trifocal, plano to plus or minus 4.00d sphere, 4.25 to 6.00 cylinder, per lens | ♿ |
| A ☑ | V2306 | Spherocylinder, trifocal, plano to plus or minus 4.00d sphere, over 6.00d cylinder, per lens | ♿ |
| A ☑ | V2307 | Spherocylinder, trifocal, plus or minus 4.25 to plus or minus 7.00d sphere, 0.12 to 2.00d cylinder, per lens | ♿ |
| A ☑ | V2308 | Spherocylinder, trifocal, plus or minus 4.25 to plus or minus 7.00d sphere, 2.12 to 4.00d cylinder, per lens | ♿ |
| A ☑ | V2309 | Spherocylinder, trifocal, plus or minus 4.25 to plus or minus 7.00d sphere, 4.25 to 6.00d cylinder, per lens | ♿ |
| A ☑ | V2310 | Spherocylinder, trifocal, plus or minus 4.25 to plus or minus 7.00d sphere, over 6.00d cylinder, per lens | ♿ |
| A ☑ | V2311 | Spherocylinder, trifocal, plus or minus 7.25 to plus or minus 12.00d sphere, 0.25 to 2.25d cylinder, per lens | ♿ |
| A ☑ | V2312 | Spherocylinder, trifocal, plus or minus 7.25 to plus or minus 12.00d sphere, 2.25 to 4.00d cylinder, per lens | ♿ |
| A ☑ | V2313 | Spherocylinder, trifocal, plus or minus 7.25 to plus or minus 12.00d sphere, 4.25 to 6.00d cylinder, per lens | ♿ |
| A ☑ | V2314 | Spherocylinder, trifocal, sphere over plus or minus 12.00d, per lens | ♿ |
| A ☑ | V2315 | Lenticular, (myodisc), per lens, trifocal | ♿ |
| A | V2318 | Aniseikonic lens, trifocal | ♿ |
| A ☑ | V2319 | Trifocal seg width over 28 mm | ♿ |
| A ☑ | V2320 | Trifocal add over 3.25d | ♿ |
| A | V2321 | Lenticular lens, per lens, trifocal | ♿ |
| | | MED: 100-2,15,120; 100-4,3,10.4 | |
| A | V2399 | Specialty trifocal (by report) | |
| | | Pertinent documentation to evaluate medical appropriateness should be included when this code is reported. | |

## VARIABLE ASPHERICITY LENS, GLASS, OR PLASTIC

| | | | |
|---|---|---|---|
| A ☑ | V2410 | Variable asphericity lens, single vision, full field, glass or plastic, per lens | ♿ |

**Vision Services**

**V2430 — V2615**

| | | | |
|---|---|---|---|
| Ⓐ | ☑ | **V2430** | Variable asphericity lens, bifocal, full field, glass or plastic, per lens   ♿ |
| Ⓐ | | **V2499** | Variable sphericity lens, other type |

## CONTACT LENS

If procedure code 92391 or 92396 is reported, recode with specific lens type listed below (per lens).

| | | | |
|---|---|---|---|
| Ⓐ | ☑ | **V2500** | Contact lens, PMMA, spherical, per lens   ♿ |
| Ⓐ | ☑ | **V2501** | Contact lens, PMMA, toric or prism ballast, per lens   ♿ |
| Ⓐ | ☑ | **V2502** | Contact lens PMMA, bifocal, per lens   ♿ |
| Ⓐ | ☑ | **V2503** | Contact lens, PMMA, color vision deficiency, per lens   ♿ |
| Ⓐ | ☑ | **V2510** | Contact lens, gas permeable, spherical, per lens   ♿ |
| Ⓐ | ☑ | **V2511** | Contact lens, gas permeable, toric, prism ballast, per lens   ♿ |
| Ⓐ | ☑ | **V2512** | Contact lens, gas permeable, bifocal, per lens   ♿ |
| Ⓐ | ☑ | **V2513** | Contact lens, gas permeable, extended wear, per lens   ♿ |
| Ⓐ | ☑ | **V2520** | Contact lens, hydrophilic, spherical, per lens   ♿ |
| | | | **Hydrophilic contact lenses are covered by Medicare only for aphakic patients. Local contractor if incident to physician services.** |
| | | | **MED: 100-3,80.1; 100-3,80.4** |
| Ⓐ | ☑ | **V2521** | Contact lens, hydrophilic, toric, or prism ballast, per lens   ♿ |
| | | | **Hydrophilic contact lenses are covered by Medicare only for aphakic patients. Local contractor if incident to physician services.** |
| | | | **MED: 100-3,80.1; 100-3,80.4** |
| Ⓐ | ☑ | **V2522** | Contact lens, hydrophilic, bifocal, per lens   ♿ |
| | | | **Hydrophilic contact lenses are covered by Medicare only for aphakic patients. Local contractor if incident to physician services.** |
| | | | **MED: 100-3,80.1; 100-3,80.4** |
| Ⓐ | ☑ | **V2523** | Contact lens, hydrophilic, extended wear, per lens   ♿ |
| | | | **Hydrophilic contact lenses are covered by Medicare only for aphakic patients.** |
| | | | **MED: 100-3,80.1; 100-3,80.4** |
| Ⓐ | ☑ | **V2530** | Contact lens, scleral, gas impermeable, per lens (for contact lens modification, see 92325)   ♿ |
| Ⓐ | ☑ | **V2531** | Contact lens, scleral, gas permeable, per lens (for contact lens modification, see 92325)   ♿ |
| | | | **MED: 100-3,80.5** |
| Ⓐ | | **V2599** | Contact lens, other type |
| | | | **Local contractor if incident to physician services.** |

## VISION AIDS

| | | | |
|---|---|---|---|
| Ⓐ | | **V2600** | Hand held low vision aids and other nonspectacle mounted aids |
| Ⓐ | | **V2610** | Single lens spectacle mounted low vision aids |
| Ⓐ | | **V2615** | Telescopic and other compound lens system, including distance vision telescopic, near vision telescopes and compound microscopic lens system |

## PROSTHETIC EYE

---

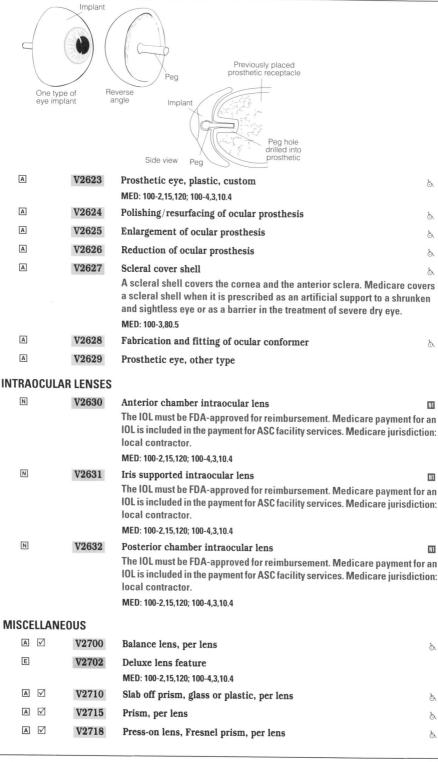

Implant

One type of eye implant

Reverse angle

Peg

Previously placed prosthetic receptacle

Implant

Peg hole drilled into prosthetic

Side view   Peg

| A | **V2623** | Prosthetic eye, plastic, custom | 占 |
|---|---|---|---|
| | | MED: 100-2,15,120; 100-4,3,10.4 | |
| A | **V2624** | Polishing/resurfacing of ocular prosthesis | 占 |
| A | **V2625** | Enlargement of ocular prosthesis | 占 |
| A | **V2626** | Reduction of ocular prosthesis | 占 |
| A | **V2627** | Scleral cover shell | 占 |

**A scleral shell covers the cornea and the anterior sclera. Medicare covers a scleral shell when it is prescribed as an artificial support to a shrunken and sightless eye or as a barrier in the treatment of severe dry eye.**

MED: 100-3,80.5

| A | **V2628** | Fabrication and fitting of ocular conformer | 占 |
|---|---|---|---|
| A | **V2629** | Prosthetic eye, other type | |

## INTRAOCULAR LENSES

| N | **V2630** | Anterior chamber intraocular lens | N1 |
|---|---|---|---|

**The IOL must be FDA-approved for reimbursement. Medicare payment for an IOL is included in the payment for ASC facility services. Medicare jurisdiction: local contractor.**

MED: 100-2,15,120; 100-4,3,10.4

| N | **V2631** | Iris supported intraocular lens | N1 |
|---|---|---|---|

**The IOL must be FDA-approved for reimbursement. Medicare payment for an IOL is included in the payment for ASC facility services. Medicare jurisdiction: local contractor.**

MED: 100-2,15,120; 100-4,3,10.4

| N | **V2632** | Posterior chamber intraocular lens | N1 |
|---|---|---|---|

**The IOL must be FDA-approved for reimbursement. Medicare payment for an IOL is included in the payment for ASC facility services. Medicare jurisdiction: local contractor.**

MED: 100-2,15,120; 100-4,3,10.4

## MISCELLANEOUS

| A ☑ | **V2700** | Balance lens, per lens | 占 |
|---|---|---|---|
| E | **V2702** | Deluxe lens feature | |
| | | MED: 100-2,15,120; 100-4,3,10.4 | |
| A ☑ | **V2710** | Slab off prism, glass or plastic, per lens | 占 |
| A ☑ | **V2715** | Prism, per lens | 占 |
| A ☑ | **V2718** | Press-on lens, Fresnel prism, per lens | 占 |

A ☑ **V2730** Special base curve, glass or plastic, per lens ♿

A ☑ **V2744** Tint, photochromatic, per lens ♿
MED: 100-2,15,120; 100-4,3,10.4

A ☑ **V2745** Addition to lens; tint, any color, solid, gradient or equal, excludes photochromatic, any lens material, per lens ♿
MED: 100-2,15,120; 100-4,3,10.4

A ☑ **V2750** Antireflective coating, per lens ♿
MED: 100-2,15,120; 100-4,3,10.4

A ☑ **V2755** U-V lens, per lens ♿
MED: 100-2,15,120; 100-4,3,10.4

E **V2756** Eye glass case

A ☑ **V2760** Scratch resistant coating, per lens ♿

B ☑ **V2761** Mirror coating, any type, solid, gradient or equal, any lens material, per lens
MED: 100-2,15,120; 100-4,3,10.4

A ☑ **V2762** Polarization, any lens material, per lens ♿
MED: 100-2,15,120; 100-4,3,10.4

A ☑ **V2770** Occluder lens, per lens ♿

A ☑ **V2780** Oversize lens, per lens ♿

B ☑ **V2781** Progressive lens, per lens

A ☑ **V2782** Lens, index 1.54 to 1.65 plastic or 1.60 to 1.79 glass, excludes polycarbonate, per lens ♿
MED: 100-2,15,120; 100-4,3,10.4

A ☑ **V2783** Lens, index greater than or equal to 1.66 plastic or greater than or equal to 1.80 glass, excludes polycarbonate, per lens ♿
MED: 100-2,15,120; 100-4,3,10.4

A ☑ **V2784** Lens, polycarbonate or equal, any index, per lens ♿
MED: 100-2,15,120; 100-4,3,10.4

F **V2785** Processing, preserving and transporting corneal tissue F4
Medicare jurisdiction: local contractor.

A ☑ **V2786** Specialty occupational multifocal lens, per lens ♿
MED: 100-2,15,120; 100-4,3,10.4

E **V2787** Astigmatism correcting function of intraocular lens

E **V2788** Presbyopia correcting function of intraocular lens

N **V2790** Amniotic membrane for surgical reconstruction, per procedure N1
Medicare jurisdiction: local contractor.

A **V2797** Vision supply, accessory and/or service component of another HCPCS vision code

A **V2799** Vision service, miscellaneous
Determine if an alternative HCPCS Level II or a CPT code better describes the service being reported. This code should be used only if a more specific code is unavailable.

## HEARING SERVICES V5000-V5999

This range of codes describes hearing tests and related supplies and equipment, speech-language pathology screenings, and repair of augmentative communicative system.

| | | |
|---|---|---|
| E | V5008 | Hearing screening |
| | | MED: 100-2,16,90 |
| E | V5010 | Assessment for hearing aid |
| E | V5011 | Fitting/orientation/checking of hearing aid |
| E | V5014 | Repair/modification of a hearing aid |
| E | V5020 | Conformity evaluation |
| E | V5030 | Hearing aid, monaural, body worn, air conduction |
| E | V5040 | Hearing aid, monaural, body worn, bone conduction |
| E | V5050 | Hearing aid, monaural, in the ear |
| E | V5060 | Hearing aid, monaural, behind the ear |
| E | V5070 | Glasses, air conduction |
| E | V5080 | Glasses, bone conduction |
| E | V5090 | Dispensing fee, unspecified hearing aid |
| E | V5095 | Semi-implantable middle ear hearing prosthesis |
| E | V5100 | Hearing aid, bilateral, body worn |
| E | V5110 | Dispensing fee, bilateral |
| E | V5120 | Binaural, body |
| E | V5130 | Binaural, in the ear |
| E | V5140 | Binaural, behind the ear |
| E | V5150 | Binaural, glasses |
| E | V5160 | Dispensing fee, binaural |
| E | V5170 | Hearing aid, CROS, in the ear |
| E | V5180 | Hearing aid, CROS, behind the ear |
| E | V5190 | Hearing aid, CROS, glasses |
| E | V5200 | Dispensing fee, CROS |
| E | V5210 | Hearing aid, BICROS, in the ear |
| E | V5220 | Hearing aid, BICROS, behind the ear |
| E | V5230 | Hearing aid, BICROS, glasses |
| E | V5240 | Dispensing fee, BICROS |
| E | V5241 | Dispensing fee, monaural hearing aid, any type |
| E | V5242 | Hearing aid, analog, monaural, CIC (completely in the ear canal) |
| E | V5243 | Hearing aid, analog, monaural, ITC (in the canal) |
| E | V5244 | Hearing aid, digitally programmable analog, monaural, CIC |
| E | V5245 | Hearing aid, digitally programmable, analog, monaural, ITC |
| E | V5246 | Hearing aid, digitally programmable analog, monaural, ITE (in the ear) |
| E | V5247 | Hearing aid, digitally programmable analog, monaural, BTE (behind the ear) |

---

Hearing Services

V5248 — V5364

| | | | |
|---|---|---|---|
| E | | V5248 | Hearing aid, analog, binaural, CIC |
| E | | V5249 | Hearing aid, analog, binaural, ITC |
| E | | V5250 | Hearing aid, digitally programmable analog, binaural, CIC |
| E | | V5251 | Hearing aid, digitally programmable analog, binaural, ITC |
| E | | V5252 | Hearing aid, digitally programmable, binaural, ITE |
| E | | V5253 | Hearing aid, digitally programmable, binaural, BTE |
| E | | V5254 | Hearing aid, digital, monaural, CIC |
| E | | V5255 | Hearing aid, digital, monaural, ITC |
| E | | V5256 | Hearing aid, digital, monaural, ITE |
| E | | V5257 | Hearing aid, digital, monaural, BTE |
| E | | V5258 | Hearing aid, digital, binaural, CIC |
| E | | V5259 | Hearing aid, digital, binaural, ITC |
| E | | V5260 | Hearing aid, digital, binaural, ITE |
| E | | V5261 | Hearing aid, digital, binaural, BTE |
| E | | V5262 | Hearing aid, disposable, any type, monaural |
| E | | V5263 | Hearing aid, disposable, any type, binaural |
| E | | V5264 | Ear mold/insert, not disposable, any type |
| E | | V5265 | Ear mold/insert, disposable, any type |
| E | | V5266 | Battery for use in hearing device |
| E | | V5267 | Hearing aid supplies/accessories |
| E | | V5268 | Assistive listening device, telephone amplifier, any type |
| E | | V5269 | Assistive listening device, alerting, any type |
| E | | V5270 | Assistive listening device, television amplifier, any type |
| E | | V5271 | Assistive listening device, television caption decoder |
| E | | V5272 | Assistive listening device, TDD |
| E | | V5273 | Assistive listening device, for use with cochlear implant |
| E | | V5274 | Assistive listening device, not otherwise specified |
| E | ☑ | V5275 | Ear impression, each |
| E | | V5298 | Hearing aid, not otherwise classified |
| B | | V5299 | Hearing service, miscellaneous ⊘ |

Determine if an alternative HCPCS Level II or a CPT code better describes the service being reported. This code should be used only if a more specific code is unavailable.

MED: 100-2,16,90

## SPEECH-LANGUAGE PATHOLOGY SERVICES

| | | |
|---|---|---|
| E | V5336 | Repair/modification of augmentative communicative system or device (excludes adaptive hearing aid) |

Medicare jurisdiction: DME regional contractor.

| | | |
|---|---|---|
| E | V5362 | Speech screening |
| E | V5363 | Language screening |
| E | V5364 | Dysphagia screening |

# APPENDIX 1 — TABLE OF DRUGS

## Introduction and Directions

The HCPCS 2009 Table of Drugs is designed to quickly and easily direct the user to drug names and their corresponding codes. Both generic and brand or trade names are alphabetically listed in the "Drug Name" column of the table. The associated A, C, J, K, Q, or S code is given only for the generic name of the drug.

The "Unit Per" column lists the stated amount for the referenced generic drug as provided by CMS. "Up to" listings are inclusive of all quantities up to and including the listed amount. All other listings are for the amount of the drug as listed. The editors recognize that the availability of some drugs in the quantities listed is dependent on many variables beyond the control of the clinical ordering clerk. The availability in your area of regularly used drugs in the most cost-effective quantities should be relayed to your third-party payers.

The "Route of Administration" column addresses the most common methods of delivering the referenced generic drug as described in current pharmaceutical literature. The official definitions for Level II drug codes generally describe administration other than by oral method. Therefore, with a handful of exceptions, oral-delivered options for most drugs are omitted from the Route of Administration column.

Intravenous administration includes all methods, such as gravity infusion, injections, and timed pushes. When several routes of administration are listed, the first listing is simply the first, or most common, method as described in current reference literature. The "VAR" posting denotes various routes of administration and is used for drugs that are commonly administered into joints, cavities, tissues, or topical applications, in addition to other parenteral administrations. Listings posted with "OTH" alert the user to other administration methods, such as suppositories or catheter injections.

Please be reminded that the Table of Drugs, as well as all HCPCS Level II national definitions and listings, constitutes a post-treatment medical reference for billing purposes only. Although the editors have exercised all normal precautions to ensure the accuracy of the table and related material, the use of any of this information to select medical treatment is entirely inappropriate. Do not code directly from the table of drugs. Refer to the tabular section for complete information.

See Appendix 3 for abbreviations.

| Drug Name | Unit Per | Route | Code |
|---|---|---|---|
| 10% LMD | 500 ML | IV | J7100 |
| 5% DEXTROSE/NORMAL SALINE | 5% | VAR | J7042 |
| 5% DEXTROSE/WATER | 500 ML | IV | J7060 |
| ABARELIX | 10 MG | IM | J0128 |
| ABATACEPT | 10 MG | IV | J0129 |
| ABCIXIMAB | 10 MG | IV | J0130 |
| ABELCET | 50 MG | IV | J0285 |
| ABILIFY | 0.25 MG | IM | J0400 |
| ABRAXANE | 1 MG | IV | J9264 |
| ACCELULAR PERICARDIAL TISSUE MATRIX NONHUMAN | SQ CM | OTH | C9354 |
| ACCUNEB NONCOMPOUNDED, CONCENTRATED | 1 MG | INH | J7611 |
| ACCUNEB NONCOMPOUNDED, UNIT DOSE | 1 MG | INH | J7613 |
| ACETADOTE | 1 G | INH | J7608 |
| ACETADOTE | 100 MG | IV | J0132 |
| ACETAZOLAMIDE SODIUM | 500 MG | IM, IV | J1120 |
| ACETYLCYSTEINE COMPOUNDED | PER G | INH | J7604 |
| ACETYLCYSTEINE NONCOMPOUNDED | 1 G | INH | J7608 |
| ACTHREL | 1 MCG | IV | J0795 |
| ACTIMMUNE | 0.25 MG | SC | J1830 |
| ACTIMMUNE | 3 MU | SC | J9216 |
| ACTIVASE | 1 MG | IV | J2997 |
| ACUTECT | DOSE | IV | A9504 |
| ACYCLOVIR | 5 MG | IV | J0133 |
| ADAGEN | 25 IU | IM | J2504 |
| ADALIMUMAB | 20 MG | SC | J0135 |

**Appendix 1 — Table of Drugs**

| Drug Name | Unit Per | Route | Code |
|---|---|---|---|
| ADBEON | 4 MG | IM, IV | J0704 |
| ADENOCARD | 6 MG | IV | J0150 |
| ADENOSCAN | 30 MG | IV | J0152 |
| ADENOSINE | 30 MG | IV | J0152 |
| ADENOSINE | 6 MG | IV | J0150 |
| ADRENALIN | 1 MG | IM, IV, SC | J0170 |
| ADRENALIN CHLORIDE | 1 MG | IM, IV, SC | J0170 |
| ADRENOCORT | 1 MG | IM, IV, OTH | J1100 |
| ADRIAMYCIN | 10 MG | IV | J9000 |
| ADRUCIL | 500 MG | IV | J9190 |
| AEROBID | 1 MG | INH | J7641 |
| AGALSIDASE BETA | 1 MG | IV | J0180 |
| AGGRASTAT | 12.5 MG | IM, IV | J3246 |
| A-HYDROCORT | 100 MG | IV, IM, SC | J1720 |
| ALATROFLOXACIN MESYLATE | 100 MG | IV | J0200 |
| ALBUTEROL AND IPRATROPIUM BROMIDE NONCOMPOUNDED | 2.5MG/0.5 MG | INH | J7620 |
| ALBUTEROL COMPOUNDED, CONCENTRATED | 1 MG | INH | J7610 |
| ALBUTEROL COMPOUNDED, UNIT DOSE | 1 MG | INH | J7609 |
| ~~ALBUTEROL NONCOMPOUNDED, UNIT DOSE~~ | ~~PER 1 MG~~ | ~~INH~~ | ~~J7603~~ |
| ALBUTEROL NONCOMPOUNDED, UNIT DOSE | PER 1 MG | INH | J7613 |
| ~~ALBUTEROL, NONCOMPOUNDED, CONCENTRATED FORM~~ | ~~PER 1 MG~~ | ~~INH~~ | ~~J7602~~ |
| ALBUTEROL, NONCOMPOUNDED, CONCENTRATED FORM | PER 1 MG | INH | J7611 |
| ALDESLEUKIN | 1 VIAL | IV | J9015 |
| ALDURAZYME | 0.1 MG | IV | J1931 |
| ALEFACEPT | 0.5 MG | IV, IM | J0215 |
| ALEMTUZUMAB | 10 MG | IV | J9010 |
| ALFERON N | 250,000 IU | IM | J9215 |
| ALGLUCERASE | 10 U | IV | J0205 |
| ALGLUCOSIDASE ALFA | 10 MG | IV | J0220 |
| ALIMTA | 10 MG | IV | J9305 |
| ALKERAN | 2 MG | ORAL | J8600 |
| ALKERAN | 50 MG | IV | J9245 |
| ALLOGRAFT, CYMETRA | 1 CC | INJ | Q4112 |
| ALLOGRAFT, GRAFTJACKET EXPRESS | 1 CC | INJ | Q4113 |
| ALOXI | 25 MCG | IV | J2469 |
| ALPHA 1 - PROTEINASE INHIBITOR — HUMAN | 10 MG | IV | J0256 |
| ALPHANATE | PER FACTOR IU | IV | J7186 |
| ALPHANINE SD | 1 IU | IV | J7193 |
| ALPROSTADIL | 1.25 MCG | INJ | J0270 |
| ALPROSTADIL | EA | OTH | J0275 |
| ALTEPLASE RECOMBINANT | 1 MG | IV | J2997 |
| ALUPENT, NONCOMPOUNDED, CONCENTRATED | 10 MG | INH | J7668 |
| ALUPENT, NONCOMPOUNDED, UNIT DOSE | 10 MG | INH | J7669 |
| AMANTADINE HYDROCHLORIDE (BRAND NAME) | 100 MG | ORAL | G9033 |
| AMANTADINE HYDROCHLORIDE (GENERIC) | 100 MG | ORAL | G9017 |
| AMBISOME | 10 MG | IV | J0289 |
| AMCORT | 5 MG | IM | J3302 |
| AMERGAN | 12.5 MG | ORAL | Q0169 |
| A-METHAPRED | 125 MG | IM, IV | J2930 |

| Drug Name | Unit Per | Route | Code |
|---|---|---|---|
| A-METHAPRED | 40 MG | IM, IV | J2920 |
| AMEVIVE | 0.5 MG | IV, IM | J0215 |
| AMICAR | 5 G | IV | S0017 |
| AMIFOSTINE | 500 MG | IV | J0207 |
| AMIKACIN SULFATE | 100 MG | IM, IV | J0278 |
| AMIKIN | 100 MG | IM, IV | |
| AMINOCAPRIOC ACID | 5 G | IV | S0017 |
| AMINOPHYLLINE | 250 MG | IV | J0280 |
| AMIODARONE HCL | 30 MG | IV | J0282 |
| AMITRIPTYLINE HCL | 20 MG | IM | J1320 |
| AMMONIA N-13 | DOSE | IV | A9526 |
| AMOBARBITAL | 125 MG | IM, IV | J0300 |
| AMPHOCIN | 50 MG | IV | J0285 |
| AMPHOTEC | 10 MG | IV | J0287 |
| AMPHOTERICIN B | 50 MG | IV | J0285 |
| AMPHOTERICIN B CHOLESTERYL SULFATE COMPLEX | 10 MG | IV | J0288 |
| AMPHOTERICIN B LIPID COMPLEX | 10 MG | IV | J0287 |
| AMPHOTERICIN B LIPOSOME | 10 MG | IV | J0289 |
| AMPICILLIN SODIUM | 500 MG | IM, IV | J0290 |
| AMPICILLIN SODIUM/SULBACTAM SODIUM | 1.5 G | IM, IV | J0295 |
| AMYTAL | 125 MG | IM, IV | J0300 |
| ANASTROZOLE | 1 MG | ORAL | S0170 |
| ANCEF | 500 MG | IV, IM | J0690 |
| AN-DTPA DIAGNOSTIC | UP TO 25 MCI | IV | A9539 |
| AN-DTPA THERAPEUTIC | UP TO 25 MCI | IV | A9567 |
| ANECTINE | 20 MG | IM, IV | J0330 |
| ANGIOMAX | 1 MG | IV | J0583 |
| ANIDULAFUNGIN | 1 MG | IV | J0348 |
| ANISTREPLASE | 30 U | IV | J0350 |
| ANTAGON | 250 MCG | SC | S0132 |
| ANTIHEMOPHILIC FACTOR HUMAN METHOD M MONOCLONAL PURIFIED | 1 IU | IV | J7192 |
| ANTIHEMOPHILIC FACTOR PORCINE | 1 IU | IV | J7191 |
| ANTIHEMOPHILIC FACTOR VIII/VON WILLEBRAND FACTOR COMPLEX, HUMAN | PER FACTOR VIII IU | IV | J7186 |
| ANTI-INHIBITOR | 1 IU | IV | J7198 |
| ANTITHROMBIN III | 1 IU | IV | J7195 |
| ANTI-THYMOCYTE GLOBULIN,EQUINE | 250 MG | OTH | J7504 |
| ANTIZOL | 15 MG | IV | J1451 |
| ANZEMET | 10 MG | IV | J1260 |
| ANZEMET | 50 MG | ORAL | S0174 |
| ANZEMET | 100 MG | ORAL | Q0180 |
| APLIGRAF | SQ CM | OTH | J7340 |
| APLIGRAF | SQ CM | OTH | Q4101 |
| APOKYN | 1 MG | SC | J0364 |
| APOKYN | 1 MG | SC | |
| APOMORPHINE HYDROCHLORIDE | 1 MG | SC | |
| APOMORPHINE HYDROCHLORIDE | 1 MG | SC | J0364 |
| APREPITANT, ORAL, 5 MG | 5 MG | ORAL | J8501 |
| APROTININ | 10,000 KIU | IV | J0365 |

# APPENDIX 1 — TABLE OF DRUGS

| Drug Name | Unit Per | Route | Code |
|---|---|---|---|
| AQUAMEPHYTON | 1 MG | IM, SC, IV | J3430 |
| ARA-C | 100 MG | SC, IV | J9100 |
| ARAMINE | 10 MG | IV, IM, SC | J0380 |
| ARANESP, ESRD USE | 1 MCG | SC, IV | J0882 |
| ARANESP, NON-ESRD USE | 1 MCG | SC, IV | J0881 |
| ARBUTAMINE HCL | 1 MG | IV | J0395 |
| AREDIA | 30 MG | IV | J2430 |
| ARFORMOTEROL | 15 MCG | INH | J7605 |
| ARIMIDEX | 1 MG | ORAL | S0170 |
| ARIPIPRAZOLE | 0.25 MG | IM | J0400 |
| ARISTOCORT | 5 MG | IM | J3302 |
| ARISTOCORTE FORTE | 5 MG | IM | J3302 |
| ARISTOCORTE INTRALESIONAL | 5 MG | OTH | J3302 |
| ARISTOSPAN | 5 MG | VAR | J3303 |
| ARIXTRA | 0.5 MG | SC | J1652 |
| AROMASIN | 25 MG | ORAL | S0156 |
| ARRANON | 50 MG | IV | J9261 |
| ARRESTIN | 200 MG | IM | J3250 |
| ARSENIC TRIOXIDE | 1 MG | IV | J9017 |
| ASPARAGINASE | 10,000 U | VAR | J9020 |
| ASTRAMORPH PF | 10 MG | IM, IV, SC | J2275 |
| ATGAM | 250 MG | OTH | J7504 |
| ATIVAN | 2 MG | IM, IV | J2060 |
| ATOPICLAIR | ANY SIZE | OTH | A6250 |
| ATROPEN | 0.3 MG | IV, IM, SC | J0460 |
| ATROPINE SULFATE | 0.3 MG | IV, IM, SC | J0460 |
| ATROPINE, COMPOUNDED, CONCENTRATED | 1 MG | INH | J7635 |
| ATROPINE, COMPOUNDED, UNIT DOSE | 1 MG | INH | J7636 |
| ATROVENT, NONCOMPOUNDED, UNIT DOSE | 1 MG | INH | J7644 |
| AUROTHIOGLUCOSE | 50 MG | IM | J2910 |
| AUTOPLEX T | 1 IU | IV | J7198 |
| AVASTIN | 10 MG | IV | J9035 |
| AVELOX | 100 MG | IV | J2280 |
| AVONEX | 11 MCG | IM | Q3025 |
| AVONEX | 33 MCG | IM | J1825 |
| AZACITIDINE | 1 MG | SC | J9025 |
| AZACTAM | 500 MG | IV | S0073 |
| AZASAN | 50 MG | ORAL | J7500 |
| AZATHIOPRINE | 100 MG | OTH | J7501 |
| AZATHIOPRINE | 50 MG | ORAL | J7500 |
| AZITHROMYCIN | 500 MG | IV | J0456 |
| AZMACORT | PER MG | INH | J7684 |
| AZMACORT CONCENTRATED | PER MG | INH | J7683 |
| AZTREONAM | 500 MG | IV | S0073 |
| ~~AZTREONAM~~ | ~~PER MG~~ | ~~INH~~ | ~~S0143~~ |
| BACLOFEN | 10 MG | IT | J0475 |
| BACLOFEN | 50 MCG | OTH | J0476 |
| ~~BACTERIOSTATIC WATER~~ | ~~5%~~ | ~~VAR~~ | |
| BACTOCILL | 250 MG | IM, IV | J2700 |

| Drug Name | Unit Per | Route | Code |
|---|---|---|---|
| BACTRIM IV | 10 ML | IV | S0039 |
| BAL | 100 MG | IM | J0470 |
| BASILIXIMAB | 20 MG | IV | J0480 |
| BAYGAM | 1 CC | IM | J1460 |
| BAYRHO-D | 300 MCG | IM | J2790 |
| BAYTET | 250 U | IM | J1670 |
| BCG VACCINE LIVE | VIAL | IV | J9031 |
| BEBULIN VH | 1 IU | IV | J7194 |
| BECAPLERMIN GEL 0.01% | 0.5 G | OTH | S0157 |
| BECLOMETHASONE COMPOUNDED | 1 MG | INH | J7622 |
| BECLOVENT COMPOUNDED | 1 MG | INH | J7622 |
| BECONASE COMPOUNDED | 1 MG | INH | J7622 |
| BENA-D 10 | 50 MG | IV, IM | J1200 |
| BENA-D 50 | 50 MG | IV, IM | J1200 |
| BENADRYL | 50 MG | IV, IM | J1200 |
| BENAHIST 10 | 50 MG | IV, IM | J1200 |
| BENAHIST 50 | 50 MG | IV, IM | J1200 |
| BENDAMUSTINE HCL | 1 MG | IV | C9243 |
| BENDAMUSTINE HCL | 1 MG | IV | J9033 |
| BENEFIX | 1 IU | IV | J7195 |
| BENOJECT-10 | 50 MG | IV, IM | J1200 |
| BENOJECT-50 | 50 MG | IV, IM | J1200 |
| BENTYL | 20 MG | IM | J0500 |
| BENZTROPINE MESYLATE | 1 MG | IM, IV | J0515 |
| BERUBIGEN | 1,000 MCG | SC, IM | J3420 |
| BETA-2 | 1 MG | INH | J7648 |
| BETALIN 12 | 1,000 MCG | SC, IM | J3420 |
| BETAMETHASONE ACETATE AND BETAMETHASONE SODIUM PHOSPHATE | 3 MG, OF EACH | IM | J0702 |
| BETAMETHASONE COMPOUNDED, UNIT DOSE | 1 MG | INH | J7624 |
| BETAMETHASONE SODIUM PHOSPHATE | 4 MG | IM, IV | J0704 |
| BETASERON | 0.25 MG | SC | J1830 |
| BETHANECHOL CHLORIDE, MYOTONACHOL OR URECHOLINE | 5 MG | SC | J0520 |
| BEVACIZUMAB | 10 MG | IV | J9035 |
| BEXXAR THERAPEUTIC | TX DOSE | IV | A9545 |
| BICILLIN CR | 1,200,000 U | IM | J0540 |
| BICILLIN CR | 600,000 U | IM | J0530 |
| BICILLIN CR 900/300 | 1,200,000 U | IM, IV | J0540 |
| BICILLIN CR 900/300 | 2,400,000 U | IM, IV | J0550 |
| BICILLIN LA | 1,200,000 U | IM | J0570 |
| BICILLIN LA | 600,000 U | IM | J0560 |
| BICILLIN LA | 2,400,000 U | INJ | J0580 |
| BICNU | 100 MG | IV | J9050 |
| BIOCLATE | 1 IU | IV | J7192 |
| BIOTROPIN | 1 MG | SC | J2941 |
| BITOLTEROL MESYLATE, COMPOUNDED CONCENTRATED | PER MG | INH | J7628 |
| BITOLTEROL MESYLATE, COMPOUNDED UNIT DOSE | PER MG | INH | J7629 |
| BIVALIRUDIN | 1 MG | IV | J0583 |
| BLENOXANE | 15 U | IM, IV, SC | J9040 |

Appendix 1 — Table of Drugs

| Drug Name | Unit Per | Route | Code |
|---|---|---|---|
| BLEOMYCIN LYOPHILLIZED | 15 U | IM, IV, SC | J9040 |
| BLEOMYCIN SULFATE | 15 U | IM, IV, SC | J9040 |
| BONIVA | 1 MG | IV | J1740 |
| BORTEZOMIB | 0.1 MG | IV | J9041 |
| BOTOX | 1 U | IM | J0585 |
| BOTULINUM TOXIN TYPE A | 1 U | OTH | J0585 |
| BOTULINUM TOXIN TYPE B | 100 U | OTH | J0587 |
| BRAVELLE | 75 IU | SC, IM | J3355 |
| BRETHINE | PER MG | INH | J7681 |
| BRETHINE CONCENTRATED | PER MG | INH | J7680 |
| BRICANYL | PER MG | INH | J7681 |
| BRICANYL CONCENTRATED | PER MG | INH | J7680 |
| BROM-A-COT | 10 MG | IM, SC, IV | J0945 |
| BROMPHENIRAMINE MALEATE | 10 MG | IM, SC, IV | J0945 |
| ~~BRONCHO SALINE~~ | ~~5 CC~~ | ~~VAR~~ | |
| BUDESONIDE COMPOUNDED, CONCETRATED | 0.25 MG | INH | J7634 |
| BUDESONIDE, COMPOUNDED, UNIT DOSE | 0.5 MG | INH | J7627 |
| BUDESONIDE, NONCOMPOUNDED, CONCENTRATED | 0.25 MG | INH | J7633 |
| BUDESONIDE, NONCOMPOUNDED, UNIT DOSE | 0.5 MG | INH | J7626 |
| BUMETANIDE | 0.5 MG | IM, IV | S0171 |
| BUPIVACAINE HCL | 30 ML | OTH | S0020 |
| BUPRENEX | 0.1 MG | IM, IV | J0592 |
| BUPRENORPHINE HCL | 0.1 MG | IM, IV | J0592 |
| BUPROPION HCL | 150 MG | ORAL | S0106 |
| BUSULFAN | 1 MG | IV | J0594 |
| BUSULFAN | 2 MG | OTH | J8510 |
| BUSULFEX | 1 MG | IV | J0594 |
| BUSULFEX | 2 MG | ORAL | J8510 |
| BUTORPHANOL TARTRATE | 2 MG | IM, IV | J0595 |
| BUTORPHANOL TARTRATE | 25 MG | OTH | S0012 |
| CABERGOLINE | 0.25 MG | ORAL | J8515 |
| CAFCIT | 5 MG | IV | J0706 |
| CAFFEINE CITRATE | 5 MG | IV | J0706 |
| CALCIJEX | 0.1 MCG | IM | J0636 |
| CALCIMAR | UP TO 400 U | SC, IM | J0630 |
| CALCITONIN SALMON | 400 U | SC, IM | J0630 |
| CALCITRIOL | 0.1 MCG | IM | J0636 |
| CALCITROL | 0.25 MG | IM | S0161 |
| CALCIUM DISODIUM VERSENATE | 1,000 MG | IV, SC, IM | J0600 |
| CALCIUM GLUCONATE | 10 ML | IV | J0610 |
| CALCIUM GLYCEROPHOSPHATE AND CALCIUM LACTATE | 10 ML | IM, SC | J0620 |
| CAMPATH | 10 MG | IV | J9010 |
| CAMPTOSAR | 20 MG | IV | J9206 |
| CANCIDAS | 5 MG | IV | J0637 |
| CAPECITABINE | 150 MG | ORAL | J8520 |
| CAPROMAB PENDETIDE | DOSE | IV | A9507 |
| CARBOCAINE | 10 ML | VAR | J0670 |
| CARBOPLATIN | 50 MG | IV | J9045 |
| CARDIOGEN 82 | 60 MCI | IV | A9555 |

| Drug Name | Unit Per | Route | Code |
|---|---|---|---|
| CARDIOLITE | DOSE | IV | A9500 |
| CARIMUNE | 500 MG | IV | J1566 |
| CARMUSTINE | 100 MG | IV | J9050 |
| CARNITOR | 1 G | IV | J1955 |
| CARTICEL | | OTH | J7330 |
| CASPOFUNGIN ACETATE | 5 MG | IV | J0637 |
| CATAPRES | 1 MG | OTH | J0735 |
| CATHFLO | 1 MG | IV | J2997 |
| CAVERJECT | 1.25 MCG | VAR | J0270 |
| CEA SCAN | UP TO 45 MCI | IV | A9568 |
| CEENU | 10 MG | ORAL | S0178 |
| CEFEPIME HCL | 500 MG | IV | J0692 |
| CEFIZOX | 500 MG | IV, IM | J0715 |
| CEFOBID | 1 G | IV | S0021 |
| CEFOPERAZONE SODIUM | 1 G | IV | S0021 |
| CEFOTAN | 500 MG | IM, IV | S0074 |
| CEFOTAXIME SODIUM | 1 GM | IV, IM | J0698 |
| CEFOTETAN DISODIUM | 500 MG | IM. IV | S0074 |
| CEFOXITIN SODIUM | 1 GM | IV, IM | J0694 |
| CEFTAZIDIME | 500 MG | IM, IV | J0713 |
| CEFTIZOXIME SODIUM | 500 MG | IV, IM | J0715 |
| CEFTRIAXONE | 250 MG | IV, IM | J0696 |
| CEFTRIAXONE SODIUM | 250 MG | IV, IM | J0696 |
| CEFUROXIME | 750 MG | IM, IV | J0697 |
| CEFUROXIME SODIUM STERILE | 750 MG | IM, IV | J0697 |
| CELESTONE SOLUSPAN | 3 MG | IM | J0702 |
| CELLCEPT | 250 MG | ORAL | J7517 |
| CENACORT A-40 | 10 MG | IM | J3301 |
| CENACORT FORTE | 5 MG | IM | J3302 |
| CEPHAPIRIN SODIUM | 1 G | IV | J0710 |
| CEPTAZ | 500 MG | IM, IV | J0713 |
| CEREBRYX | 50 MG | IM, IV | Q2009 |
| CEREBRYX | 750 MG | IM, IV | S0078 |
| CEREDASE | 10 U | IV | J0205 |
| CERETEC | DOSE | IV | A9521 |
| CERETEC | PER STUDY DOSE | IV | A9569 |
| CEREZYME | 1 U | IV | J1785 |
| CERUBIDINE | 10 MG | IV | J9150 |
| CESAMET | 1 MG | ORAL | J8650 |
| CETUXIMAB | 10 MG | IV | J9055 |
| CHEALAMIDE | 150 MG | IV | J3520 |
| CHLORAMBUCIL | 2 MG | ORAL | S0172 |
| CHLORAMPHENICOL SODIUM SUCCINATE | 1 G | IV | J0720 |
| CHLORDIAZEPOXIDE HCL | 100 MG | IM, IV | J1990 |
| CHLOROMYCETIN | 1 G | IV | J0720 |
| CHLOROPROCAINE HCL | 30 ML | VAR | J2400 |
| CHLOROTHIAZIDE SODIUM | 500 MG | IV | J1205 |
| CHLORPROMAZINE HCL | 10 MG | ORAL | Q0171 |

# APPENDIX 1 — TABLE OF DRUGS

| Drug Name | Unit Per | Route | Code |
|---|---|---|---|
| CHLORPROMAZINE HCL | 50 MG | IM, IV | J3230 |
| CHLORPROMAZINE HCL | 25 MG | ORAL | Q0172 |
| CHOLETEC | UP TO 35 MCI | IV | A9537 |
| CHORIONIC GONADOTROPIN | 1,000 USP U | IM | J0725 |
| CHROMIC PHOSPHATE P32 | 1 MCI | IV | A9564 |
| CHROMITOPE SODIUM | 250 UCI | IV | A9553 |
| CHROMIUM CR-51 SODIUM IOTHALAMATE, DIAGNOSTIC | 10 UCI | IV | A9553 |
| CIDOFOVIR | 375 MG | IV | J0740 |
| CILASTATIN SODIUM | 250 MG | IV, IM | J0743 |
| CIMETIDINE HCL | 300 MG | IM, IV | S0023 |
| CIPRO | 200 MG | IV | J0744 |
| CIPROFLOXACIN FOR INTRAVENOUS INFUSION | 200 MG | IV | J0744 |
| CIS-MDP | 30 MCI | IV | A9503 |
| CISPLATIN | 10 MG | IV | J9060 |
| CIS-PYRO | UP TO 25 MCI | IV | A9538 |
| CLADRIBINE | 1 MG | IV | J9065 |
| CLAFORAN | 1 GM | IV, IM | J0698 |
| CLEOCIN PHOSPHATE | 300 MG | IV | S0077 |
| CLEVIDIPINE BUTYRATE | 1 MG | IV | C9248 |
| CLEVIPREX | 1 MG | IV | C9248 |
| CLINAGEN LA | UP TO 40 MG | IM | J0970 |
| CLINDAMYCIN PHOSPHATE | 300 MG | IV | S0077 |
| CLOFARABINE | 1 MG | IV | J9027 |
| CLOLAR | 1 MG | IV | J9027 |
| CLONIDINE HCL | 1 MG | OTH | J0735 |
| CLOSTRIDIUM BOTULINUM TOXIN | 1 U | OTH | J0585 |
| CLOZAPINE | 25 MG | ORAL | S0136 |
| CLOZARIL | 25 MG | ORAL | S0136 |
| COBAL | 1,000 MCG | IM, SC | J3420 |
| COBALT CO-57 CYNOCOBALAMIN, DIAGNOSTIC | 1 UCI | ORAL | A9559 |
| COBATOPE 57 | 1 UCI | ORAL | A9559 |
| COBEX | 1,000 MCG | SC, IM | J3420 |
| CODEINE PHOSPHATE | 30 MG | IM, IV, SC | J0745 |
| COGENTIN | 1 MG | IM, IV | J0515 |
| COGNEX | 10 MG | ORAL | S0014 |
| COLCHICINE | 1 MG | IV | J0760 |
| COLHIST | 10 MG | IM, SC, IV | J0945 |
| COLISTIMETHATE SODIUM | 150 MG | IM, IV | J0770 |
| COLISTIMETHATE SODIUM | PER MG | INH | S0142 |
| COLLAGEN BASED WOUND FILLER DRY FOAM | 1 GM | OTH | A6010 |
| COLLAGEN NERVE CUFF | 0.5 CM LENGTH | OTH | C9355 |
| ~~COLLAGEN, MICROPOROUS NONHUMAN~~ | ~~SQ CM~~ | ~~OTH~~ | |
| ~~COLLAGEN-GLYCOSAMINOGLYCAN SKIN SUBSTITUTE~~ | ~~SQ CM~~ | ~~OTH~~ | ~~J7343~~ |
| COLLAGEN BASED WOUND FILLER, GEL/PASTE | 1 GM | OTH | A6011 |
| COLY-MYCIN M | 150 MG | IM, IV | J0770 |
| COMPAZINE | 10 MG | IM, IV | J0780 |
| COMPAZINE | 5 MG | ORAL | S0183 |
| COMPAZINE | 10 MG | ORAL | Q0165 |
| COMPAZINE | 5 MG | ORAL | Q0164 |

| Drug Name | Unit Per | Route | Code |
|---|---|---|---|
| CONTRACEPTIVE SUPPLY, HORMONE CONTAINING PATCH | EACH | OTH | J7304 |
| COPAXONE | 20 MG | SC | J1595 |
| COPPER T MODEL TCU380A IUD COPPER WIRE/COPPER COLLAR | EA | OTH | J7300 |
| CORDARONE | 30 MG | IV | J0282 |
| CORTASTAT | 1 MG | IM, IV, OTH | J1100 |
| CORTASTAT LA | 1 MG | IM | J1094 |
| CORTICORELIN OVINE TRIFLUTATE | 1 MCG | IV | J0795 |
| CORTICOTROPIN | 40 U | IV, IM, SC | J0800 |
| CORTIMED | 80 MG | IM | J1040 |
| CORTROSYN | 0.25 MG | IM, IV | J0835 |
| CORVERT | 1 MG | IV | J1742 |
| COSMEGEN | 0.5 MG | IV | J9120 |
| COSYNTROPIN | 0.25 MG | IM, IV | J0835 |
| COTOLONE | 5 MG | ORAL | J7510 |
| CROMOLYN SODIUM COMPOUNDED | PER 10 MG | INH | J7632 |
| CROMOLYN SODIUM NONCOMPOUNDED | 10 MG | INH | J7631 |
| CRYSTAL B12 | 1,000 MCG | IM, SC | J3420 |
| CRYSTICILLIN 300 A.S. | 600,000 UNITS | IM, IV | J2510 |
| CRYSTICILLIN 600 A.S. | 600,000 UNITS | IM, IV | J2510 |
| CUBICIN | 1 MG | IV | J0878 |
| CYANO | 1,000 MCG | IM, SC | J3420 |
| CYANOCOBALAMIN | 1,000 MCG | IM, SC | J3420 |
| CYANOCOBALAMIN COBALT 58/57 | 1 UCI | IV | A9546 |
| CYANOCOBALAMIN COBALT CO-57 | 1 UCI | ORAL | A9559 |
| CYCLOPHOSPHAMIDE | 1 G | IV | J9091 |
| CYCLOPHOSPHAMIDE | 200 MG | IV | J9080 |
| CYCLOPHOSPHAMIDE | 25 MG | ORAL | J8530 |
| CYCLOPHOSPHAMIDE | 500 MG | IV | J9090 |
| CYCLOPHOSPHAMIDE | 2 G | IV | J9092 |
| CYCLOPHOSPHAMIDE | 100 MG | IV | J9070 |
| CYCLOPHOSPHAMIDE LYOPHILIZED | 1 G | IV | J9096 |
| CYCLOPHOSPHAMIDE LYOPHILIZED | 2 G | IV | J9097 |
| CYCLOPHOSPHAMIDE LYOPHILIZED | 500 MG | IV | J9095 |
| CYCLOPHOSPHAMIDE LYOPHILIZED | 100 MG | IV | J9093 |
| CYCLOPHOSPHAMIDE LYOPHILIZED | 200 MG | IV | J9094 |
| CYCLOSPORINE | 100 MG | ORAL | J7502 |
| CYCLOSPORINE | 25 MG | ORAL | J7515 |
| CYCLOSPORINE | 250 MG | IV | J7516 |
| CYMETRA | 1 CC | INJ | Q4112 |
| CYTARABINE | 100 MG | SC, IV | J9100 |
| CYTARABINE | 500 MG | SC, IV | J9110 |
| CYTARABINE LIPOSOME | 10 MG | IT | J9098 |
| CYTOGAM | VIAL | IV | J0850 |
| CYTOMEGALOVIRUS IMMUNE GLOB | VIAL | IV | J0850 |
| CYTOSAR-U | 100 MG | SC, IV | J9100 |
| CYTOSAR-U | 500 MG | SC, IV | J9110 |
| CYTOTEC | 200 MCG | ORAL | S0191 |
| CYTOVENE | 500 MG | IV | J1570 |

# APPENDIX 1 — TABLE OF DRUGS

| Drug Name | Unit Per | Route | Code |
|---|---|---|---|
| CYTOXAN | 1 G | IV | J9091 |
| CYTOXAN | 100 MG | IV | J9070 |
| CYTOXAN | 500 MG | IV | J9090 |
| CYTOXAN | 200 MG | IV | J9080 |
| CYTOXAN | 2 G | IV | J9092 |
| CYTOXAN | 25 MG | ORAL | J8530 |
| CYTOXAN LYOPHILIZED | 1 G | IV | J9096 |
| CYTOXAN LYOPHILIZED | 500 MG | IV | J9095 |
| CYTOXAN LYOPHILIZED | 2 G | IV | J9097 |
| CYTOXAN LYOPHILIZED | 200 MG | IV | J9094 |
| CYTOXAN LYOPHILIZED | 100 MG | IV | J9093 |
| D.H.E. 45 | 1 MG | IM, IV | J1110 |
| DACARBAZINE | 100 MG | IV | J9130 |
| DACARBAZINE | 200 MG | IV | J9140 |
| DACLIZUMAB | 25 MG | OTH | J7513 |
| DACOGEN | 1 MG | IV | J0894 |
| DACTINOMYCIN | 0.5 MG | IV | J9120 |
| DALALONE | 1 MG | IM, IV, OTH | J1100 |
| DALALONE LA | 1 MG | IM | J1094 |
| DALTEPARIN SODIUM | 2,500 IU | SC | J1645 |
| DAPTOMYCIN | 1 MG | IV | J0878 |
| DARBEPOETIN ALFA, ESRD USE | 1 MCG | SC, IV | J0882 |
| DARBEPOETIN ALFA, NON-ESRD USE | 1 MCG | SC, IV | J0881 |
| DAUNORUBICIN | 10 MG | IV | J9150 |
| DAUNORUBICIN CITRATE, LIPOOSOMAL FORMULATION | 10 MG | IV | J9151 |
| DAUNOXOME | 10 MG | IV | J9151 |
| DDAVP | 1 MCG | IV, SC | J2597 |
| DECADRON | 0.25 MG | ORAL | J8540 |
| DECAJECT | 1 MG | IM, IV, OTH | J1100 |
| DECITABINE | 1 MG | IV | J0894 |
| DECOLONE-50 | 50 MG | IM | J2320 |
| DEFEROXAMINE MESYLATE | 500 MG | IM, SC, IV | J0895 |
| DELATESTRYL | 100 MG | IM | J3120 |
| DELATESTRYL | 200 MG | IM | J3130 |
| DELESTROGEN | 10 MG | IM | J1380 |
| DELESTROGEN | 20 MG | IM | J1390 |
| DELESTROGEN | UP TO 40 MG | IM | J0970 |
| DELTA-CORTEF | 5 MG | ORAL | J7510 |
| DELTASONE | 5 MG | ORAL | J7506 |
| DELTASONE | 5 MG | OTH | J7506 |
| DEMADEX | 10 MG | IV | J3265 |
| DEMEROL | 100 MG | IM, IV, SC | J2175 |
| DENILEUKIN DIFTITOX | 300 MCG | IV | J9160 |
| DEPANDRATE | 1 CC, 200 MG | IM | J1080 |
| DEPANDROGYN | 1 ML | IM | J1060 |
| DEPGYNOGEN | UP TO 5 MG | IM | J1000 |
| DEPHENACEN-50 | 50 MG | IM, IV | J1200 |
| DEPMEDALONE | 40 MG | IM | J1030 |
| DEPMEDALONE | 80 MG | IM | J1040 |

| Drug Name | Unit Per | Route | Code |
|---|---|---|---|
| DEPOCYT | 10 MG | IT | J9098 |
| DEPODUR | UP TO 10 MG | IV | J2270 |
| DEPODUR | UP TO 10 MG | IV | J2271 |
| DEPO-ESTRADIOL CYPIONATE | UP TO 5 MG | IM | J1000 |
| DEPOGEN | UP TO 5 MG | IM | J1000 |
| DEPO-MEDROL | 20 MG | IM | J1020 |
| DEPO-MEDROL | 40 MG | IM | J1030 |
| DEPO-MEDROL | 80 MG | IM | J1040 |
| DEPO-PROVERA | 150 MG | IM | J1055 |
| DEPO-PROVERA | 50 MG | IM | J1051 |
| DEPO-TESTADIOL | 1 ML | IM | J1060 |
| DEPO-TESTOSTERONE | 1 CC, 200 MG | IM | J1080 |
| DEPO-TESTOSTERONE | UP TO 100 MG | IM | J1070 |
| DEPO-TESTOSTERONE CYPIONATE | UP TO 100 MG | IM | J1070 |
| DEPTESTROGEN | UP TO 100 MG | IM | J1070 |
| ~~DERMAGRAFT~~ | ~~SQ CM~~ | ~~OTH~~ | ~~J7342~~ |
| DERMAGRAFT | SQ CM | OTH | Q4106 |
| ~~DERMAL (SUBSTITUTE) TISSUE OF NONHUMAN ORIGIN, WITH OR WITHOUT OTHER BIOENGINEERED OR PROCESSED ELEMENTS, WITHOUT METABOLICALLY ACTIVE ELEMENTS (INTEGRA MATRIX)~~ | ~~UNIT PER SQ CM~~ | ~~OTH~~ | ~~J7347~~ |
| ~~DERMAL (SUBSTITUTE) TISSUE OF NONHUMAN ORIGIN, WITH OR WITHOUT OTHER BIOENGINEERED OR PROCESSED ELEMENTS, WITHOUT METABOLICALLY ACTIVE ELEMENTS (PRIMATRIX)~~ | ~~SQ CM~~ | ~~OTH~~ | ~~J7349~~ |
| ~~DERMAL (SUBSTITUTE) TISSUE OF NONHUMAN ORIGIN, WITH OR WITHOUT OTHER BIOENGINEERED OR PROCESSED ELEMENTS, WITHOUT METABOLICALLY ACTIVE ELEMENTS (TISSUEMEND)~~ | ~~SQ CM~~ | ~~OTH~~ | ~~J7348~~ |
| ~~DERMAL AND EPIDERMAL, TISSUE OF NONHUMAN ORIGIN, WITH OR WITHOUT OTHER BIOENGINEERED OR PROCESSED ELEMENTS, WITHOUT METABOLICALLY ACTIVE ELEMENTS~~ | ~~SQ CM~~ | ~~OTH~~ | ~~J7343~~ |
| ~~DERMAL SUBSTITUTE, GRANULATED CROSS-LINKED COLLAGEN AND GLYCOSAMINOGLYCAN MATRIX~~ | ~~1 CC~~ | ~~OTH~~ | ~~C9357~~ |
| DERMAL SUBSTITUTE, NATIVE, NONDENATURED | 0.5 SQ CM | OTH | C9358 |
| DERMAL SUBSTITUTE, NATIVE, NONDENTURED COLLAGEN | 0.5 SQ CM | OTH | C9358 |
| ~~DERMAL TISSUE, OF HUMAN ORIGIN, WITH OR WITHOUT OTHER BIOENGINEERED OR PROCESSED ELEMENTS, WITH METABOLICALLY ACTIVE ELEMENTS~~ | ~~SQ CM~~ | ~~OTH~~ | ~~J7342~~ |
| DERMAL TISSUE, OF HUMAN ORIGIN, WITH OR WITHOUT OTHER BIOENGINEERED OR PROCESSED ELEMENTS, WITHOUT METABOLICALLY ACTIVE ELEMENTS | SQ CM | OTH | J7344 |
| DESFERAL | 500 MG | IM, SC, IV | J0895 |
| DESMOPRESSIN ACETATE | 1 MCG | IV, SC | J2597 |
| DEXAMETHASONE | 0.25 MG | ORAL | J8540 |
| DEXAMETHASONE ACETATE | 1 MG | IM | J1094 |
| DEXAMETHASONE ACETATE ANHYDROUS | 1 MG | IM | J1094 |
| DEXAMETHASONE SODIUM PHOSPHATE | 1 MG | IM, IV, OTH | J1100 |
| DEXAMETHASONE, COMPOUNDED, CONCENTRATED | PER MG | INH | J7637 |
| DEXAMETHASONE, COMPOUNDED, UNIT DOSE | PER MG | INH | J7638 |
| DEXASONE | 1 MG | IM, IV, OTH | J1100 |
| DEXEDRINE | 5 MG | ORAL | S0160 |
| ~~DEXFERRUM~~ | ~~50 MG~~ | ~~IM, IV~~ | ~~J1752~~ |
| DEXIM | 1 MG | IM, IV, OTH | J1100 |

# APPENDIX 1 — TABLE OF DRUGS

| Drug Name | Unit Per | Route | Code |
|---|---|---|---|
| DEXONE | 0.25 MG | ORAL | J8540 |
| DEXONE | 1 MG | IM, IV, OTH | J1100 |
| DEXONE LA | 1 MG | IM | J1094 |
| DEXRAZOXANE | 250 MG | IV | J1190 |
| DEXRAZOXANE HYDROCHLORIDE | 250 MG | IV | J1190 |
| DEXTRAN 40 | 500 ML | IV | J7100 |
| DEXTROAMPHETAMINE SULFATE | 5 MG | ORAL | S0160 |
| DEXTROSE | 500 ML | IV | J7060 |
| DEXTROSE, STERILE WATER, AND/OR DEXTROSE DILUENT/FLUSH | 10 ML | VAR | A4216 |
| DEXTROSE/SODIUM CHLORIDE | 5% | VAR | J7042 |
| DEXTROSE/THEOPHYLLINE | 40 MG | IV | J2810 |
| DEXTROSTAT | 5 MG | ORAL | S0160 |
| DIALYSIS/STRESS VITAMINS | 100 CAPS | ORAL | S0194 |
| DIAMOX | 500 MG | IM, IV | J1120 |
| DIASTAT | 5 MG | IV, IM | J3360 |
| DIAZEPAM | 5 MG | IV, IM | J3360 |
| DIAZOXIDE | 300 MG | IV | J1730 |
| DICYCLOMINE HCL | 20 MG | IM | J0500 |
| DIDANOSINE (DDI) | 25 MG | ORAL | S0137 |
| DIDRONEL | 300 MG | IV | J1436 |
| DIETHYLSTILBESTROL DIPHOSPHATE | 250 MG | INJ | J9165 |
| DIFLUCAN | 200 MG | IV | J1450 |
| DIGIBIND | VIAL | IV | J1162 |
| DIGIFAB | VIAL | IV | J1162 |
| DIGOXIN | 0.5 MG | IM, IV | J1160 |
| DIGOXIN IMMUNE FAB | VIAL | IV | J1162 |
| DIHYDROERGOTAMINE MESYLATE | 1 MG | IM, IV | J1110 |
| DILANTIN | 50 MG | IM, IV | J1165 |
| DILAUDID | 250 MG | OTH | S0092 |
| DILAUDID | 4 MG | SC, IM, IV | J1170 |
| DIMENHYDRINATE | 50 MG | IM, IV | J1240 |
| DIMERCAPROL | 100 MG | IM | J0470 |
| DIMINE | 50 MG | IV, IM | J1200 |
| DINATE | 50 MG | IM, IV | J1240 |
| DIOVAL | 10 MG | IM | J1380 |
| DIOVAL | 20 MG | IM | J1390 |
| DIOVAL 40 | 10 MG | IM | J1380 |
| DIOVAL 40 | 20 MG | IM | J1390 |
| DIOVAL XX | 10 MG | IM | J1380 |
| DIOVAL XX | 20 MG | IM | J1390 |
| DIPHENHYDRAMINE HCL | 50 MG | IV, IM | J1200 |
| DIPHENHYDRAMINE HCL | 50 MG | ORAL | Q0163 |
| DIPYRIDAMOLE | 10 MG | IV | J1245 |
| DISOTATE | 150 MG | IV | J3520 |
| DIURIL | 500 MG | IV | J1205 |
| DIURIL SODIUM | 500 MG | IV | J1205 |
| DIZAC | 5 MG | IV, IM | J3360 |
| ~~DMSA~~ | ~~VIAL~~ | ~~IV~~ | |
| ~~DMSA KIT~~ | ~~VIAL~~ | ~~IV~~ | |

| Drug Name | Unit Per | Route | Code |
|---|---|---|---|
| DMSO, DIMETHYL SULFOXIDE | 50%, 50 ML | OTH | J1212 |
| DOBUTAMINE HCL | 250 MG | IV | J1250 |
| DOCETAXEL | 20 MG | IV | J9170 |
| DOLASETRON MESYLATE | 10 MG | IV | J1260 |
| DOLASETRON MESYLATE | 50 MG | ORAL | S0174 |
| DOLASETRON MESYLATE | 100 MG | ORAL | Q0180 |
| DOLOPHINE | 5 MG | ORAL | S0109 |
| DOLOPHINE HCL | 10 MG | IM, SC | J1230 |
| DOMMANATE | 50 MG | IM, IV | J1240 |
| DOPAMINE HCL | 40 MG | IV | J1265 |
| DORIBAX | 10 MG | IV | J1267 |
| DORIPENEM | 10 MG | IV | J1267 |
| DORNASE ALPHA, NONCOMPOUNDED, UNIT DOSE | PER MG | INH | J7639 |
| DOSTINEX | 0.25 MG | ORAL | J8515 |
| DOXERCALCIFEROL | 1 MG | IV | J1270 |
| DOXIL | 10 MG | IV | J9001 |
| DOXORUBICIN HCL | 10 MG | IV | J9000 |
| DOXORUBICIN HCL, ALL LIPID FORMULATIONS | 10 MG | IV | J9001 |
| DRAMAMINE | 50 MG | IM, IV | J1240 |
| DRAMILIN | 50 MG | IM, IV | J1240 |
| DRAMOCEN | 50 MG | IM, IV | J1240 |
| DRAMOJECT | 50 MG | IM, IV | J1240 |
| DRAXIMAGE MDP-10 | 30 MCI | IV | A9503 |
| DRAXIMAGE MDP-25 | 30 MCI | IV | A9503 |
| DRONABINAL | 2.5 MG | ORAL | Q0167 |
| DRONABINAL | 5 MG | ORAL | Q0168 |
| DROPERIDOL | 5 MG | IM, IV | J1790 |
| DROPERIDOL AND FENTANYL CITRATE | 2 ML | IM, IV | J1810 |
| DROXIA | 500 MG | ORAL | S0176 |
| DTIC-DOME | 100 MG | IV | J9130 |
| DTIC-DOME | 200 MG | IV | J9140 |
| DTPA | UP TO 25 MCI | IV | A9539 |
| DTPA | UP TO 25 MCI | INH | A9567 |
| DUO-SPAN | 1 ML | IM | J1060 |
| DUO-SPAN II | 1 ML | IM | J1060 |
| DURACILLIN A.S. | 600,000 UNITS | IM, IV | J2510 |
| DURACLON | 1 MG | OTH | J0735 |
| DURAGEN-10 | 10 MG | IM | J1380 |
| DURAGEN-10 | 20 MG | IM | J1390 |
| DURAGEN-20 | 10 MG | IM | J1380 |
| DURAGEN-20 | 20 MG | IM | J1390 |
| DURAGEN-40 | 10 MG | IM | J1380 |
| DURAGEN-40 | 20 MG | IM | J1390 |
| DURAMORPH | 10 MG | IM, IV, SC | J2275 |
| DURAMORPH | 500 MG | OTH | S0093 |
| DURO CORT | 80 MG | IM | J1040 |
| DYMENATE | 50 MG | IM, IV | J1240 |
| DYPHYLLINE | 500 MG | IM | J1180 |

# APPENDIX 1 — TABLE OF DRUGS

| Drug Name | Unit Per | Route | Code |
|---|---|---|---|
| E.D.T.A | 150 MG | IV | J3520 |
| ECHOCARDIOGRAM IMAGE ENHANCER | 1 ML | IV | Q9955 |
| ECHOCARDIOGRAM IMAGE ENHANCER | 1 ML | INJ | Q9956 |
| ECULIZUMAB | 10 MG | IV | J1300 |
| EDETATE CALCIUM DISODIUM | 1,000 MG | IV, SC, IM | J0600 |
| EDETATE DISODIUM | 150 MG | IV | J3520 |
| EDEX | 1.25 MCG | VAR | J0270 |
| EFALIZUMAB | 125 MG | SC | S0162 |
| ~~ELAPRASE~~ | ~~1 MG~~ | ~~IV~~ | ~~99205~~ |
| ELAPRASE | 1 MG | IV | J1743 |
| ELAVIL | 20 MG | IM | J1320 |
| ELIGARD | 7.5 MG | IM | J9217 |
| ELIGARD | PER 3.75 MG | SC | J1950 |
| ELITEK | 50 MCG | IM | J2783 |
| ELLENCE | 2 MG | IV | J9178 |
| ELLIOTTS B SOLUTION | 1 ML | IV, IT | J9175 |
| ELOXATIN | 0.5 MG | IV | J9263 |
| ELSPAR | 10,000 U | VAR | J9020 |
| EMEND | 5 MG | ORAL | J8501 |
| EMEND | 1 MG | IV | J1453 |
| EMINASE | 30 U | IV | J0350 |
| ENBREL | 25 MG | IM, IV | J1438 |
| ENDOXAN-ASTA | 1 G | IV | J9091 |
| ENDOXAN-ASTA | 200 MG | IV | J9080 |
| ENDOXAN-ASTA | 100 MG | IV | J9070 |
| ENDOXAN-ASTA | 500 MG | IV | J9090 |
| ENDRATE | 150 MG | IV | J3520 |
| ENFUVIRTIDE | 1 MG | SC | J1324 |
| ENOXAPARIN SODIUM | 10 MG | SC | J1650 |
| EOVIST | 1 ML | IV | C9246 |
| EPINEPHRINE | 1 MG | IM, IV, SC, VAR | J0170 |
| EPIPEN | 0.3 MG | IM | J0170 |
| EPIRUBICIN HCL | 2 MG | IV | J9178 |
| EPOETIN ALFA, ESRD USE | 1,000 U | SC, IV | J0886 |
| EPOETIN ALFA, NON-ESRD USE | 1,000 U | SC, IV | J0885 |
| EPOGEN/ESRD | 1,000 U | SC, IV | J0886 |
| EPOGEN/NON-ESRD | 1,000 U | SC, IV | J0885 |
| EPOPROSTENOL | 0.5 MG | IV | J1325 |
| EPOPROSTENOL STERILE DILUTANT | 50 ML | IV | S0155 |
| EPTIFIBATIDE | 5 MG | IM, IV | J1327 |
| ERAXIS | 1 MG | IV | J0348 |
| ERBITUX | 10 MG | IV | J9055 |
| ERGAMISOL | 50 MG | ORAL | S0177 |
| ERGONOVINE MALEATE | 0.2 MG | IM, IV | J1330 |
| ERTAPENEM SODIUM | 500 MG | IM, IV | J1335 |
| ERYTHROCIN LACTOBIONATE | 500 MG | IV | J1364 |
| ESTONE AQUEOUS | 1 MG | IM, IV | J1435 |
| ESTRADIOL CYPIONATE | UP TO 5 MG | IM | J1000 |
| ESTRADIOL L.A. | 10 MG | IM | J1380 |

| Drug Name | Unit Per | Route | Code |
|---|---|---|---|
| ESTRADIOL L.A. | 20 MG | IM | J1390 |
| ESTRADIOL L.A. 20 | 10 MG | IM | J1380 |
| ESTRADIOL L.A. 20 | 20 MG | IM | J1390 |
| ESTRADIOL L.A. 40 | 10 MG | IM | J1380 |
| ESTRADIOL L.A. 40 | 20 MG | IM | J1390 |
| ESTRADIOL VALERATE | 10 MG | IM | J1380 |
| ESTRADIOL VALERATE | UP TO 40 MG | IM | J0970 |
| ESTRADIOL VALERATE | 20 MG | IM | J1390 |
| ESTRAGYN | 1 MG | IV, IM | J1435 |
| ESTRA-L 20 | 10 MG | IM | J1380 |
| ESTRA-L 20 | 20 MG | IM | J1390 |
| ESTRA-L 40 | 10 MG | IM | J1380 |
| ESTRA-L 40 | 20 MG | IM | J1390 |
| ESTRO-A | 1 MG | IV, IM | J1435 |
| ESTROGEN CONJUGATED | 25 MG | IV, IM | J1410 |
| ESTRONE | 1 MG | IV, IM | J1435 |
| ESTRONOL | 1 MG | IM, IV | J1435 |
| ETANERCEPT | 25 MG | IM, IV | J1438 |
| ETHAMOLIN | 100 MG | IV | J1430 |
| ETHANOLAMINE OLEATE | 100 MG | IV | J1430 |
| ETHYOL | 500 MG | IV | J0207 |
| ETIDRONATE DISODIUM | 300 MG | IV | J1436 |
| ETONOGESTREL | PER IMPLANT | OTH | J7307 |
| ETOPOSIDE | 10 MG | IV | J9181 |
| ~~ETOPOSIDE~~ | ~~100 MG~~ | ~~IV~~ | ~~J9182~~ |
| ETOPOSIDE | 50 MG | ORAL | J8560 |
| EUFLEXXA | PER DOSE | OTH | J7323 |
| EULEXIN | 125 MG | ORAL | S0175 |
| EXAMETAZIME LABELED AUTOLOGOUS WHITE BLOOD CELLS, TECHNETIUM TC-99M | PER STUDY DOSE | IV | A9569 |
| EXMESTANE | 25 MG | ORAL | S0156 |
| FABRAZYME | 1 MG | IV | J0180 |
| FACTOR IX NON-RECOMBINANT | 1 IU | IV | J7193 |
| FACTOR IX RECOMBINANT | 1 IU | IV | J7195 |
| FACTOR IX+ COMPLEX | 1 IU | IV | J7194 |
| FACTOR VIIA RECOMBINANT | 1 MCG | IV | J7189 |
| FACTOR VIII PORCINE | 1 IU | IV | J7191 |
| FACTOR VIII RECOMBINANT | 1 IU | IV | J7192 |
| FACTOR VIII, HUMAN | 1 IU | IV | J7190 |
| FACTREL | 100 MCG | SC, IV | J1620 |
| FAMOTIDINE | 20 MG | IV | S0028 |
| FASLODEX | 25 MG | IM | J9395 |
| FDG | STUDY DOSE | | A9552 |
| FEIBA-VH AICC | 1 IU | IV | J7198 |
| FENTANYL CITRATE | 0.1 MG | IM, IV | J3010 |
| FERIDEX IV | 1 ML | IV | Q9953 |
| FERRLECIT | 12.5 MG | IV | J2916 |
| FERTINEX | 75 IU | SC | J3355 |
| FILGRASTIM | 300 MCG | SC, IV | J1440 |

# APPENDIX 1 — TABLE OF DRUGS

| Drug Name | Unit Per | Route | Code |
|---|---|---|---|
| FILGRASTIM | 480 MCG | SC, IV | J1441 |
| FINASTERIDE | 5 MG | ORAL | S0138 |
| FLAGYL | 500 MG | IV | S0030 |
| FLEBOGAMMA | 500 MG | IV | J1572 |
| FLEXON | 60 MG | IV, IM | J2360 |
| FLOLAN | 0.5 MG | IV | J1325 |
| ~~FLOWABLE WOUND MATRIX~~ | ~~1 CC~~ | ~~OTH~~ | ~~C9357~~ |
| FLOXIN IV | 400 MG | IV | S0034 |
| FLOXURIDINE | 500 MG | IV | J9200 |
| FLUCONAZOLE | 200 MG | IV | J1450 |
| FLUDARA | 50 MG | IV | J9185 |
| FLUDARABINE PHOSPHATE | 50 MG | IV | J9185 |
| FLUDEOXYGLUCOSE F18 | STUDY DOSE | IV | A9552 |
| FLUNISOLIDE, COMPOUNDED, UNIT DOSE | 1 MG | INH | J7641 |
| FLUOCINOLONE ACETONIDE INTRAVITREAL | IMPLANT | OTH | J7311 |
| FLUORODEOXYGLUCOSE F-18 FDG, DIAGNOSTIC | 45 MCI | IV | A9552 |
| FLUOROURACIL | 500 MG | IV | J9190 |
| FLUPHENAZINE DECANOATE | 25 MG | SC, IM | J2680 |
| FLUTAMIDE | 125 MG | ORAL | S0175 |
| FOLEX | 5 MG | IV, IM, IT, IA | J9250 |
| FOLEX | 50 MG | IV, IM, IT, IA | J9260 |
| FOLEX PFS | 5 MG | IV, IM, IT, IA | J9250 |
| FOLEX PFS | 50 MG | IV, IM, IT, IA | J9260 |
| FOLLISTIM | 75 IU | SC, IM | S0128 |
| FOLLITROPIN ALFA | 75 IU | SC | S0126 |
| FOLLITROPIN BETA | 75 IU | SC, IM | S0128 |
| FOMEPIZOLE | 15 MG | IV | J1451 |
| FOMIVIRSEN SODIUM | 1.65 MG | OTH | J1452 |
| FONDAPARINUX SODIUM | 0.5 MG | SC | J1652 |
| ~~FORMOTEROL FUMARATE~~ | ~~20 MCG~~ | ~~INH~~ | ~~Q4099~~ |
| FORMOTEROL FUMARATE NONCOMPOUNDED UNIT DOSE FORM | 20 MCG | INH | J7606 |
| FORMOTEROL, COMPOUNDED, UNIT DOSE | 12 MCG | INH | J7640 |
| FORTAZ | 500 MG | IM, IV | J0713 |
| FORTEO | 10 MCG | SC | J3110 |
| FORTOVASE | 200 MG | ORAL | S0140 |
| FOSAPREPITANT | 1 MG | IV | J1453 |
| FOSCARNET SODIUM | 1,000 MG | IV | J1455 |
| FOSCAVIR | 1,000 MG | IV | J1455 |
| FOSPHENYTOIN | 50 MG | IM, IV | Q2009 |
| FOSPHENYTOIN SODIUM | 750 MCG | IM, IV | S0078 |
| FRAGMIN | 2,500 IU | SC | J1645 |
| FUDR | 500 MG | IV | J9200 |
| FULVESTRANT | 25 MG | IM | J9395 |
| FUNGIZONE | 50 MG | IV | J0285 |
| FUROSEMIDE | 20 MG | IM, IV | J1940 |
| FUSILEV | 0.5 MG | IV | J0641 |
| FUZEON | 1 MG | SC | J1324 |
| GADOBENATE DIMEGLUMINE (MULTIHANCE MULTIPACK) | PER ML | IV | A9577 |
| GADOTERIDOL (PROHANCE MULTIPACK) | PER ML | IV | A9576 |

| Drug Name | Unit Per | Route | Code |
|---|---|---|---|
| GADOXETATE DISODIUM | 1 ML | IV | C9246 |
| GALLIUM GA-67 | 1 MCI | IV | A9556 |
| GALLIUM NITRATE | 1 MG | IV | J1457 |
| GALSULFASE | 1 MG | IV | J1458 |
| GAMASTAN | 1 CC | IM | J1460 |
| GAMASTAN | 2 CC | IM | J1470 |
| GAMASTAN | 5 CC | IM | J1500 |
| GAMASTAN | 6 CC | IM | J1510 |
| GAMASTAN | 4 CC | IM | J1490 |
| GAMASTAN | 3 CC | IM | J1480 |
| GAMASTAN | 7 CC | IM | J1520 |
| GAMASTAN | 9 CC | IM | J1540 |
| GAMASTAN | OVER 10 CC | IM | J1560 |
| GAMASTAN | 10 CC | IM | J1550 |
| GAMASTAN | 8 CC | IM | J1530 |
| GAMASTAN SD | 1 CC | IM | J1460 |
| GAMASTAN SD | OVER 10 CC | IM | J1560 |
| GAMASTAN SD | 10 CC | IM | J1550 |
| GAMASTAN SD | 9 CC | IM | J1540 |
| GAMASTAN SD | 4 CC | IM | J1490 |
| GAMASTAN SD | 5 CC | IM | J1500 |
| GAMASTAN SD | 6 CC | IM | J1510 |
| GAMASTAN SD | 8 CC | IM | J1530 |
| GAMASTAN SD | 7 CC | IM | J1520 |
| GAMASTAN SD | 3 CC | IM | J1480 |
| GAMASTAN SD | 2 CC | IM | J1470 |
| ~~GAMIMMUNE N~~ | ~~500 MG~~ | ~~IV~~ | |
| GAMMA GLOBULIN | 1 CC | IM | J1460 |
| GAMMA GLOBULIN | 2 CC | IM | J1470 |
| GAMMA GLOBULIN | 3 CC | IM | J1480 |
| GAMMA GLOBULIN | 5 CC | IM | J1500 |
| GAMMA GLOBULIN | OVER 10 CC | IM | J1560 |
| GAMMA GLOBULIN | 10 CC | IM | J1550 |
| GAMMA GLOBULIN | 9 CC | IM | J1540 |
| GAMMA GLOBULIN | 8 CC | IM | J1530 |
| GAMMA GLOBULIN | 7 CC | IM | J1520 |
| GAMMA GLOBULIN | 6 CC | IM | J1510 |
| GAMMA GLOBULIN | 4 CC | IM | J1490 |
| GAMMAGARD | 500 MG | IV | J1569 |
| GAMMAGARD S/D | 500 MG | IV | J1566 |
| GAMMAGRAFT | SQ CM | OTH | Q4111 |
| ~~GAMMAR~~ | ~~1 CC~~ | ~~IM~~ | ~~J1460~~ |
| ~~GAMMAR~~ | ~~2 CC~~ | ~~IM~~ | ~~J1470~~ |
| ~~GAMMAR~~ | ~~4 CC~~ | ~~IM~~ | ~~J1490~~ |
| ~~GAMMAR~~ | ~~7 CC~~ | ~~IM~~ | ~~J1520~~ |
| ~~GAMMAR~~ | ~~6 CC~~ | ~~IM~~ | ~~J1510~~ |
| ~~GAMMAR~~ | ~~5 CC~~ | ~~IM~~ | ~~J1500~~ |
| ~~GAMMAR~~ | ~~3 CC~~ | ~~IM~~ | ~~J1480~~ |
| ~~GAMMAR~~ | ~~8 CC~~ | ~~IM~~ | ~~J1530~~ |

# APPENDIX 1 — TABLE OF DRUGS

| Drug Name | Unit Per | Route | Code |
|---|---|---|---|
| GAMMAR | OVER 10 CC | IM | J1560 |
| GAMMAR | 10 CC | IM | J1550 |
| GAMMAR | 9 CC | IM | J1540 |
| GAMMAR P | 500 MG | IV | J1566 |
| GAMULIN RH | 300 MCG | IM | J2790 |
| GAMUNEX | 500 MG | IV | |
| GAMUNEX | 500 MG | IV | J1561 |
| GANCICLOVIR | 4.5 MG | OTH | J7310 |
| GANCICLOVIR SODIUM | 500 MG | IV | J1570 |
| GANIRELIX ACETATE | 250 MCG | SC | S0132 |
| GANITE | 1 MG | IV | J1457 |
| GANITE | PER MCI | IV | A9556 |
| GARAMYCIN | 80 MG | IM, IV | J1580 |
| GASTROCROM | 10 MG | INH | J7631 |
| GASTROMARK | 1 ML | ORAL | Q9954 |
| GATIFLOXACIN | 10 MG | IV | J1590 |
| GEFITINIB | 250 MG | ORAL | J8565 |
| GEMCITABINE HCL | 200 MG | IV | J9201 |
| GEMTUZUMAB | 5 MG | IV | J9300 |
| GEMZAR | 200 MG | IV | J9201 |
| GENARC | 1 IU | IV | J7192 |
| GENGRAF | 100 MG | ORAL | J7502 |
| GENGRAF | 25 MG | ORAL | J7515 |
| GENOTROPIN | 1 MG | SC | J2941 |
| GENOTROPIN MINIQUICK | 1 MG | SC | J2941 |
| GENOTROPIN NUTROPIN | 1 MG | SC | J2941 |
| GENTAMICIN | 80 MG | IM, IV | J1580 |
| GENTRAN | 500 ML | IV | J7100 |
| GENTRAN 75 | 500 ML | IV | J7110 |
| GEODON | 10 MG | IM | J3486 |
| GEREF | 1MCG | SC | Q0515 |
| GLATIRAMER ACETATE | 20 MG | SC | J1595 |
| GLEEVEC | 100 MG | ORAL | S0088 |
| GLOFIL-125 | 10 UCI | IV | A9554 |
| GLUCAGEN | 1 MG | SC, IM, IV | J1610 |
| GLUCAGON | 1 MG | SC, IM, IV | J1610 |
| GLUCOTOPE | STUDY DOSE | IV | A9552 |
| GLYCOPYRROLATE, COMPOUNDED CONCENTRATED | PER MG | INH | J7642 |
| GLYCOPYRROLATE, COMPOUNDED, UNIT DOSE | 1 MG | INH | J7643 |
| GOLD SODIUM THIOMALATE | 50 MG | IM | J1600 |
| GONADORELIN HCL | 100 MCG | SC, IV | J1620 |
| GONAL-F | 75 IU | SC | S0126 |
| GOSERELIN ACETATE | 3.6 MG | SC | J9202 |
| GRAFTJACKET | SQ CM | OTH | Q4107 |
| GRAFTJACKET EXPRESS | 1 CC | INJ | Q4113 |
| GRAFTJACKET REGULAR MATRIX | PER 16 SQ CM | OTH | |
| GRAFTJACKET SOFT TISSUE MATRIX | 1 CC | OTH | |
| GRANISETRON HCL | 1 MG | ORAL | Q0166 |
| GRANISETRON HCL | 1 MG | IV | S0091 |

| Drug Name | Unit Per | Route | Code |
|---|---|---|---|
| GRANISETRON HCL | 100 MCG | IV | J1626 |
| GYNOGEN L.A. 10 | 10 MG | IM | J1380 |
| GYNOGEN L.A. 10 | 20 MG | IM | J1390 |
| GYNOGEN L.A. 20 | 10 MG | IM | J1380 |
| GYNOGEN L.A. 20 | 20 MG | IM | J1390 |
| GYNOGEN L.A. 40 | 10 MG | IM | J1380 |
| GYNOGEN L.A. 40 | 20 MG | IM | J1390 |
| GYNOGEN LA | 20 MG | IM | J1390 |
| H.P. ACTHAR GEL | UP TO 40 UNITS | OTH | J0800 |
| HALDOL | 5 MG | IM, IV | J1630 |
| HALDOL DECANOATE | 50 MG | IM | J1631 |
| HALOPERIDOL | 5 MG | IM, IV | J1630 |
| ~~HAVID~~ | ~~0.375 MG~~ | ~~ORAL~~ | ~~S0141~~ |
| HECTOROL | 1 MG | IV | J1270 |
| HELIXATE FS | 1 IU | IV | J7192 |
| HEMIN | 1 MG | IV | J1640 |
| HEMOFIL-M | 1 IU | IV | J7190 |
| HEP LOCK | 10 U | IV | J1642 |
| HEPAGAM B | 0.5 ML | IM | J1571 |
| HEPAGAM B | 0.5 ML | IV | J1571 |
| HEPARIN SODIUM | 1,000 U | IV, SC | J1644 |
| HEPARIN SODIUM | 10 U | IV | J1642 |
| HEPATOLITE | UP TO 15 MCI | IV | A9510 |
| HEP-PAK | 10 UNITS | IV | J1642 |
| HERCEPTIN | 10 MG | IV | J9355 |
| ~~HEXABRIX 320~~ | ~~1 ML~~ | ~~IV~~ | ~~99201~~ |
| HEXADROL | 0.25 MG | ORAL | J8540 |
| HIGH OSMOLAR CONTRAST MATERIAL, UP TO 149 MG/ML IODINE CONCENTRATION | 1 ML | IV | Q9958 |
| HIGH OSMOLAR CONTRAST MATERIAL, UP TO 150-199 MG/ML IODINE CONCENTRATION | 1 ML | IV | Q9959 |
| HIGH OSMOLAR CONTRAST MATERIAL, UP TO 200-249 MG/ML IODINE CONCENTRATION | 1 ML | IV | Q9960 |
| HIGH OSMOLAR CONTRAST MATERIAL, UP TO 250-299 MG/ML IODINE CONCENTRATION | 1 ML | IV | Q9961 |
| HIGH OSMOLAR CONTRAST MATERIAL, UP TO 300-349 MG/ML IODINE CONCENTRATION | 1 ML | IV | Q9962 |
| HIGH OSMOLAR CONTRAST MATERIAL, UP TO 350-399 MG/ML IODINE CONCENTRATION | 1 ML | IV | Q9963 |
| HIGH OSMOLAR CONTRAST MATERIAL, UP TO 400 OR GREATER MG/ML IODINE CONCENTRATION | 1 ML | IV | Q9964 |
| HISTERLIN IMPLANT | 50 MG | OTH | J9225 |
| HISTRELIN ACETATE | 10 MG | INJ | J1675 |
| HUMALOG | 5 U | SC | J1815 |
| HUMALOG | 5 U | SC | S5551 |
| HUMALOG | 50 U | SC | J1817 |
| HUMATE-P | 1 IU | IV | J7187 |
| HUMATROPE | 1 MG | SC | J2941 |
| HUMIRA | 20 MG | SC | J0135 |
| HUMULIN | 5 U | SC | J1815 |

# APPENDIX 1 — TABLE OF DRUGS

| Drug Name | Unit Per | Route | Code |
|---|---|---|---|
| HUMULIN | 50 U | SC | J1817 |
| HUMULIN R | 5 U | SC | J1815 |
| HUMULIN R U-500 | 5 U | SC | J1815 |
| HYALGAN | DOSE | OTH | J7321 |
| HYALURONAN, EUFLEXXA | PER DOSE | OTH | J7323 |
| HYALURONAN, HYALGAN OR SUPARTZ | PER DOSE | OTH | J7321 |
| HYALURONAN, ORTHOVISC | PER DOSE | OTH | J7324 |
| HYALURONAN, SYNVISC | PER DOSE | OTH | J7322 |
| HYALURONIDASE | 150 UNITS | VAR | J3470 |
| HYALURONIDASE RECOMBINANT | 1 USP UNIT | SC | J3473 |
| HYALURONIDASE, OVINE, PRESERVATIVE FREE | 1 USP | OTH | J3471 |
| HYALURONIDASE, OVINE, PRESERVATIVE FREE | 1000 USP | OTH | J3472 |
| ~~HYATE C~~ | ~~1 IU~~ | ~~IV~~ | ~~J7191~~ |
| HYCAMTIN | 4 MG | IV | J9350 |
| HYCAMTIN | 0.25 MG | ORAL | J8705 |
| HYCAMTIN | 0.25 MG | ORAL | J8705 |
| HYDRALAZINE HCL | 20 MG | IV, IM | J0360 |
| HYDRATE | 50 MG | IM, IV | J1240 |
| HYDREA | 500 MG | ORAL | S0176 |
| HYDROCORTISONE ACETATE | 25 MG | IV, IM, SC | J1700 |
| HYDROCORTISONE SODIUM PHOSPHATE | 50 MG | IV, IM, SC | J1710 |
| HYDROCORTISONE SODIUM SUCCINATE | 100 MG | IV, IM, SC | J1720 |
| HYDROCORTONE PHOSPHATE | 50 MG | SC, IM, IV | J1710 |
| HYDROMORPHONE HCL | 4 MG | SC, IM, IV | J1170 |
| HYDROMORPHONE HYDROCHLORIDE | 250 MG | OTH | S0092 |
| HYDROXOCOBALAMIN | 1,000 MCG | IM, SC | J3420 |
| HYDROXYCOBAL | 1,000 MCG | IM, SC | J3420 |
| HYDROXYUREA | 500 MG | ORAL | S0176 |
| HYDROXYZINE HCL | 25 MG | IM | J3410 |
| HYDROXYZINE PAMOATE | 25 MG | ORAL | Q0177 |
| HYDROXYZINE PAMOATE | 50 MG | ORAL | Q0178 |
| HYOSCYAMINE SULFATE | 0.25 MG | SC, IM, IV | J1980 |
| HYPERTET SD | UP TO 250 MG | IM | J1670 |
| ~~HYPRHO-D~~ | ~~300 MCG~~ | ~~IM~~ | ~~J2790~~ |
| HYREXIN | 50 MG | IV, IM | J1200 |
| HYZINE | 25 MG | IM | J3410 |
| HYZINE-50 | 25 MG | IM | J3410 |
| I-131 TOSITUMOMAB DIAGNOSTIC | DOSE | IV | A9544 |
| I-131 TOSITUMOMAB THERAPEUTIC | DOSE | IV | A9545 |
| IBANDRONATE SODIUM | 1 MG | IV | J1740 |
| IBRITUMOMAB TUXETAN | 5 MCI | IV | A9542 |
| IBUTILIDE FUMARATE | 1 MG | IV | J1742 |
| IDAMYCIN | 5 MG | IV | J9211 |
| IDAMYCIN PFS | 5 MG | IV | J9211 |
| IDARUBICIN HCL | 5 MG | IV | J9211 |
| IDURSULFASE | 1 MG | IV | J1743 |
| IFEX | 1 G | IV | J9208 |
| IFOSFAMIDE | 1 G | IV | J9208 |
| IL-2 | 1 VIAL | IV | J9015 |

| Drug Name | Unit Per | Route | Code |
|---|---|---|---|
| ILETIN | 5 UNITS | SC | J1815 |
| ILETIN II NPH PORK | 50 U | SC | J1817 |
| ILETIN II REGULAR PORK | 5 U | SC | J1815 |
| ILOPROST INHALATION SOLUTION | 20 UCI | INH | Q4080 |
| IMAGENT | 1 ML | IV | Q9955 |
| IMATINIB | 100 MG | ORAL | S0088 |
| IMIGLUCERASE | 1 U | IV | J1785 |
| IMITREX | 6 MG | SC | J3030 |
| IMMUNE GLOBULIN (FLEBOGAMMA, FLEBOGAMMA DIF | 500 MG | IV | J1572 |
| IMMUNE GLOBULIN (GAMMAGARD LIQUID) | 500 MG | IV | J1569 |
| IMMUNE GLOBULIN (GAMUNEX) | 500 MG | IV | J1561 |
| IMMUNE GLOBULIN (OCTAGAM) | 500 MG | IV | J1568 |
| IMMUNE GLOBULIN (PRIVIGEN) NONLYOPHILIZED | 500 MG | IV | J1459 |
| IMMUNE GLOBULIN (RHOPHYLAC) | 100 IU | IM, IV | J2791 |
| IMMUNE GLOBULIN LYOPHILIZED | 500 MG | IV | J1566 |
| IMMUNE GLOBULIN SUBCUTANEOUS | 100 MG | SC | J1562 |
| IMPLANON | PER IMPLANT | OTH | J7307 |
| IMURAN | 50 MG | ORAL | J7500 |
| IN-111 SATUMOMAB PENDETIDE | DOSE | IV | A4642 |
| INAPSINE | 5 MG | IM, IV | J1790 |
| INDERAL | 1 MG | IV | J1800 |
| INDIUM IN-111 IBRITUMOMAB TIUXETAN, DIAGNOSTIC | 5 MCI | IV | A9542 |
| INDIUM IN-111 LABELED AUTOLOGOUS PLATELETS | PER STUDY DOSAGE | IV | A9571 |
| INDIUM IN-111 LABELED AUTOLOGOUS WHITE BLOOD CELLS | PER STUDY DOSE | IV | A9570 |
| INDIUM IN-111 OXYQUINOLINE | 0.5 MCI | IV | A9547 |
| INDIUM IN-111PENTETREOTIDE | PER STUDY DOSE | IV | A9572 |
| INDURSALFASE | 1 MG | IV | J1743 |
| ~~INFED~~ | ~~50 MG~~ | ~~IM, IV~~ | ~~J1751~~ |
| INFED | 50 MG | IM, IV | J1750 |
| INFERGEN | 1 MCG | SC | J9212 |
| INFLIXIMAB | 100 MG | IV | J1745 |
| INFUMORPH | 10 MG | IM, IV, SC | J2270 |
| INFUMORPH | 10 MG | OTH | J2275 |
| INFUMORPH PRESERVATIVE FREE | 100 MG | IM, IV, SC | J2271 |
| INNOHEP | 1,000 IU | SC | J1655 |
| INSULIN | 5 U | SC | J1815 |
| INSULIN | 50 U | SC | J1817 |
| INSULIN LISPRO | 5 U | SC | J1815 |
| INSULIN LISPRO | 5 U | SC | S5551 |
| INSULIN PURIFIED REGULAR PORK | 5 U | SC | J1815 |
| INTAL | 10 MG | INH | J7631 |
| INTEGRA BILAYER MATRIX DRESSING | SQ CM | OTH | Q4104 |
| INTEGRA DERMAL REGENERATION TEMPLATE | SQ CM | OTH | Q4105 |
| INTEGRA FLOWABLE WOUND MATRIC | 1 CC | INJ | Q4114 |
| INTEGRA FLOWABLE WOUND MATRIX | 1 CC | INJ | Q4114 |
| INTEGRA MATRIX | PER SQ. CM. | OTH | J7347 |
| INTEGRA MATRIX | SQ CM | OTH | Q4108 |

# APPENDIX 1 — TABLE OF DRUGS

| Drug Name | Unit Per | Route | Code |
|---|---|---|---|
| INTEGRA MOZAIK OSTEOCONDUCTIVE SCAFFOLD PUTTY | 0.5 CC | OTH | C9359 |
| INTEGRA MOZAIK OSTEOCONDUCTIVE SCAFFOLD PUTTY | 0.5 CC | OTH | C9359 |
| INTEGRA OS OSTEOCONDUCTIVE SCAFFOLD PUTTY | 0.5 CC | OTH | C9359 |
| INTEGRA OS OSTEOCONDUCTIVE SCAFFOLD PUTTY | 0.5 CC | OTH | C9359 |
| INTEGRILIN | 5 MG | IM, IV | J1327 |
| INTERFERON ALFA-2A | 3,000,000 U | SC, IM | J9213 |
| INTERFERON ALFA-2B | 1,000,000 U | SC, IM | J9214 |
| INTERFERON ALFACON-1 | 1 MCG | SC | J9212 |
| INTERFERON ALFA-N3 | 250,000 IU | IM | J9215 |
| INTERFERON BETA-1A | 11 MCG | IM | Q3025 |
| INTERFERON BETA-1A | 33 MCG | IM | J1825 |
| INTERFERON BETA-1A | 11 MCG | SC | Q3026 |
| INTERFERON BETA-1B | 0.25 MG | SC | J1830 |
| INTERFERON, ALFA-2A, RECOMBINANT | 3,000,000 U | SC, IM | J9213 |
| INTERFERON, ALFA-2B, RECOMBINANT | 1,000,000 U | SC, IM | J9214 |
| INTERFERON, ALFA-N3, (HUMAN LEUKOCYTE DERIVED) | 250,000 IU | IM | J9215 |
| INTERFERON, GAMMA 1-B | 3,000,000 U | SC | J9216 |
| INTERLUEKIN | 1 VIAL | IV | J9015 |
| INTRON A | 1,000,000 U | SC, IM | J9214 |
| INVANZ | 500 MG | IM, IV | J1335 |
| INVIRASE | 200 MG | ORAL | S0140 |
| IOBENGUANE SULFATE I-131 | 0.5 MCI | IV | A9508 |
| IOBENGUANE, I-123, DIAGNOSTIC | PER STUDY DOSE UP TO 10 MCI | IV | C9247 |
| IODINE I-123 SODIUM IODIDE | PER MCI | IV | A9509 |
| IODINE I-123 SODIUM IODIDE CAPSULE(S), DIAGNOSTIC | 100 UCI | ORAL | A9516 |
| IODINE I-125 SERUM ALBUMIN, DIAGNOSTIC | 10 UCI | IV | A9554 |
| IODINE I-125 SODIUM IOTHALAMATE, DIAGNOSTIC | 10 UCI | IV | A9554 |
| IODINE I-125, SODIUM IODIDE SOLUTION, THERAPEUTIC | 1 UCI | ORAL | A9527 |
| IODINE I-131 IODINATED SERIUM ALBUMIN, DIAGNOSTIC | PER 5 UCI | ORAL | A9524 |
| IODINE I-131 SERUM ALBUMIN, DIAGNOSTIC | 5 UCI | IV | A9532 |
| IODINE I-131 SODIUM IODIDE CAPSULE(S), DIAGNOSTIC | 1 MCI | ORAL | A9528 |
| IODINE I-131 SODIUM IODIDE CAPSULE(S), THERAPEUTIC | 1 MCI | ORAL | A9517 |
| IODINE I-131 SODIUM IODIDE SOLUTION, DIAGNOSTIC | 1 MCI | ORAL | A9529 |
| IODINE I-131 SODIUM IODIDE SOLUTION, THERAPEUTIC | 1 MCI | ORAL | A9530 |
| IODINE I-131 SODIUM IODIDE, DIAGNOSTIC | 100 UCI | IV | A9531 |
| IODINE I-131 TOSITUMOMAB, DIAGNOSTIC | STUDY DOSE | IV | A9544 |
| IODINE I-131 TOSITUMOMAB, THERAPEUTIC | STUDY DOSE | IV | A9545 |
| IODOTOPE THERAPEUTIC CAPSULE(S) | 1 MCI | ORAL | A9517 |
| IODOTOPE THERAPEUTIC SOLUTION | 1 MCI | ORAL | A9530 |
| ION-BASED MAGNETIC RESONANCE CONTRAST AGENT | 1 ML | IV | Q9953 |
| IOTHALAMATE SODIUM I-125 | STUDY DOSE | IV | A9554 |
| IPLEX | 1 MG | SC | J2170 |
| IPRATROPIUM BROMIDE, NONCOMPOUNDED, UNIT DOSE | 1 MG | INH | J7644 |
| IPTRATROPIUM BROMIDE COMPOUNDED, UNIT DOSE | 1 MG | INH | J7645 |
| IRESSA | 250 MG | ORAL | J8565 |
| IRINOTECAN | 20 MG | IV | J9206 |
| ~~IRON DEXTRAN 165~~ | ~~50 MG~~ | ~~IM, IV~~ | ~~J1751~~ |
| ~~IRON DEXTRAN 237~~ | ~~50 MG~~ | ~~IM, IV~~ | ~~J1752~~ |

| Drug Name | Unit Per | Route | Code |
|---|---|---|---|
| IRON DEXTRAN, 50 MG | 50 MG | IM, IV | J1750 |
| IRON SUCROSE | 1 MG | IV | J1756 |
| ISOCAINE | 10 ML | VAR | J0670 |
| ISOETHARINE HCL COMPOUNDED, CONCENTRATED | 1 MG | INH | J7647 |
| ISOETHARINE HCL NONCOMPOUNDED, CONCENTRATED | 1 MG | INH | J7650 |
| ISOETHARINE HCL, NONCOMPOUNDED CONCENTRATED | PER MG | INH | J7648 |
| ISOETHARINE HCL, NONCOMPOUNDED, UNIT DOSE | 1 MG | INH | J7649 |
| ISOJEX | 5 MCI | IV | A9532 |
| ISOPROTERENOL HCL COMPOUNDED, CONCENTRATED | 1 MG | INH | J7657 |
| ISOPROTERENOL HCL COMPOUNDED, UNIT DOSE | 1 MG | INH | J7660 |
| ISOPROTERENOL HCL, NONCOMPOUNDED CONCENTRATED | 1 MG | INH | J7658 |
| ISOPROTERNOL HCL, NONCOMPOUNDED, UNIT DOSE | PER MG | INH | J7659 |
| ITRACONAZOLE | 50 MG | IV | J1835 |
| IVEEGAM | 500 MG | IV | J1566 |
| IXABEPILONE | 1 MG | IV | J9207 |
| IXEMPRA | 1 MG | IV | J9207 |
| KANAMYCIN | 500 MG | IM, IV | J1840 |
| KANTREX | 500 MG | IM, IV | J1840 |
| KANTREX | 75 MG | IM, IV | J1850 |
| KEFZOL | 500 MG | IV, IM | J0690 |
| KENAJECT-40 | 10 MG | IM | J3301 |
| KENALOG-10 | 10 MG | IM | J3301 |
| KENALOG-40 | 10 MG | IM | J3301 |
| KEPIVANCE | 50 MCG | IV | J2425 |
| KEPIVANCE | 60 MCG | IV | J2425 |
| KEPPRA | 10 MG | IV | J1953 |
| KESTRONE | 1 MG | IV, IM | J1435 |
| KETOROLAC TROMETHAMINE | 15 MG | IM, IV | J1885 |
| KINEVAC | 5 MCG | IV | J2805 |
| KOATE-DVI | 1 IU | IV | J7190 |
| ~~KOGENATE~~ | ~~1 IU~~ | ~~IV~~ | ~~J7190~~ |
| KOGENATE FS | 1 IU | IV | J7192 |
| KONAKION | 1 MG | SC, IM, IV | J3430 |
| KONYNE 80 | 1 IU | IV | J7194 |
| KYTRIL | 1 MG | ORAL | Q0166 |
| KYTRIL | 1 MG | IV | S0091 |
| KYTRIL | 100 MCG | IV | J1626 |
| L.A.E. 20 | 10 MG | IM | J1380 |
| L.A.E. 20 | 20 MG | IM | J1390 |
| LANOXIN | 0.5 MG | IM, IV | J1160 |
| LANREOTIDE | 1 MG | SC | J1930 |
| LANTUS | 50 U | SC | J1817 |
| LARONIDASE | 0.1 MG | IV | J1931 |
| LASIX | 20 MG | IM, IV | J1940 |
| LENTE ILETIN I | 5 U | SC | J1815 |
| LEPIRUDIN | 50 MG | IV | J1945 |
| LEUCOVORIN CALCIUM | 50 MG | IM, IV | J0640 |
| LEUKERAN | 2 MG | ORAL | S0172 |
| LEUKINE | 50 MCG | IV | J2820 |

# APPENDIX 1 — TABLE OF DRUGS

| Drug Name | Unit Per | Route | Code |
|---|---|---|---|
| LEUPROLIDE ACETATE | 1 MG | IM | J9218 |
| LEUPROLIDE ACETATE | 7.5 MG | IM | J9217 |
| LEUPROLIDE ACETATE (FOR DEPOT SUSPENSION) | 3.75 MG | IM | J1950 |
| LEUPROLIDE ACETATE DEPOT | 7.5 MG | IM | J9217 |
| LEUPROLIDE ACETATE IMPLANT | 65 MG | OTH | J9219 |
| LEUSTATIN | 1 MG | IV | J9065 |
| LEVABUTEROL COMPOUNDED, UNIT DOSE | 1 MG | INH | J7615 |
| LEVABUTEROL, COMPOUNDED, CONCENTRATED | 0.5 MG | INH | J7607 |
| LEVALBUTEROL NONCOMPOUNDED, CONCENTRATED FORM | 0.5 MG | INH | J7612 |
| ~~LEVALBUTEROL, NONCOMPOUNDED, CONCENTRATED FORM~~ | ~~PER 0.5 MG~~ | ~~INH~~ | ~~J7602~~ |
| LEVALBUTEROL, NONCOMPOUNDED, CONCENTRATED FORM | PER 0.5 MG | INH | J7612 |
| ~~LEVALBUTEROL, NONCOMPOUNDED, UNIT DOSE~~ | ~~PER 0.5 MG~~ | ~~INH~~ | ~~J7603~~ |
| LEVALBUTEROL, NONCOMPOUNDED, UNIT DOSE | PER 0.5 MG | INH | J7614 |
| LEVAMISOLE HCL | 50 MG | ORAL | S0177 |
| LEVAQUIN | 250 MG | IV | J1956 |
| LEVETIRACETAM | 10 MG | IV | J1953 |
| LEVOCARNITINE | 1 G | IV | J1955 |
| LEVOFLOXACIN | 250 MG | IV | J1956 |
| LEVOLEUCOVORIN CALCIUM | 0.5 MG | IV | J0641 |
| LEVONORGESTREL | 52 MG | OTH | J7302 |
| LEVORPHANOL TARTRATE | 2 MG | SC, IV, IM | J1960 |
| LEVOXYL | 5 MG | ORAL | J7506 |
| LEVSIN | 0.25 MG | SC, IM, IV | J1980 |
| LEVULAN KERASTICK | SINGLE UNIT DOSE (354 MG) | OTH | J7308 |
| ~~LEXISCAN~~ | ~~0.4 MG~~ | ~~IV~~ | ~~C9244~~ |
| LEXISCAN | 0.1 MG | IV | J2785 |
| LIBRIUM | 100 MG | IM, IV | J1990 |
| LIDOCAINE HCL | 10 MG | IV | J2001 |
| LINCOCIN HCL | 300 MG | IV | J2010 |
| LINCOMYCIN HCL | 300 MG | IM, IV | J2010 |
| LINEZOLID | 200 MG | IV | J2020 |
| LIORESAL | 10 MG | IT | J0475 |
| LIORESAL INTRATHECAL REFILL | 50 MCG | IT | J0476 |
| LIQUAEMIN SODIUM | 1,000 UNITS | SC, IV | J1644 |
| LIQUID PRED SYRUP | 5 MG | OTH | J7506 |
| LISPRO-PFC | 50 U | SC | J1817 |
| LOK-PAK | 10 UNITS | IV | J1642 |
| LOMUSTINE | 10 MG | ORAL | S0178 |
| LONITEN | 10 MG | ORAL | S0139 |
| LORAZEPAM | 2 MG | IM, IV | J2060 |
| LOVENOX | 10 MG | SC | J1650 |
| LOW OSMOLAR CONTRAST MATERIAL, 100-199 MG/ML IODINE CONCENTRATIONS | PER ML | IV | Q9965 |
| LOW OSMOLAR CONTRAST MATERIAL, 200-299 MG/ML IODINE CONCENTRATION | PER ML | IV | Q9966 |
| LOW OSMOLAR CONTRAST MATERIAL, 300-399 MG/ML IODINE CONCENTRATION | PER ML | IV | Q9967 |
| LOW OSMOLAR CONTRAST MATERIAL, 400 OR GREATER MG/ML IODINE CONCENTRATION | 1 ML | IV | Q9951 |

| Drug Name | Unit Per | Route | Code |
|---|---|---|---|
| L-PHENYLALANINE MUSTARD | 50 MG | IV | J9245 |
| LUCENTIS | 0.1 MG | IV | J2778 |
| LUNELLE | 5 MG/25 MG | IM | J1056 |
| LUPRON | 1 MG | IM | J9218 |
| LUPRON | PER 3.75 MG | SC | J1950 |
| LUPRON | 7.5 MG | IM | J9217 |
| LUPRON DEPOT | 3.75 MG | IM | J1950 |
| LUPRON DEPOT | 7.5 MG | IM | J9217 |
| LUPRON IMPLANT | 65 MG | OTH | J9219 |
| LUPRON-3 | PER 3.75 MG | SC | J1950 |
| LUPRON-4 | PER 3.75 MG | SC | J1950 |
| LUTREPULSE | 100 MCG | SC, IV | J1620 |
| LYMPHOCYTE IMMUNE GLOBULIN, ANTITHYMOCYTE GLOBULIN, EQUINE | 250 MG | OTH | J7504 |
| LYMPHOCYTE IMMUNE GLOBULIN, ANTITHYMOCYTE GLOBULIN, RABBIT | 25 MG | OTH | J7511 |
| MACUGEN | 0.3 MG | OTH | J2503 |
| MAGNAVIST | UP TO 25 MCI | INH | A9567 |
| MAGNESIUM SULFATE | 500 MG | IV | J3475 |
| MAGNETIC RESONANCE CONTRAST AGENT | 1 ML | ORAL | Q9954 |
| MAGNEVIST | UP TO 25 MCI | IV | A9539 |
| MAGROTEC | 10 MCI | IV | A9540 |
| MANNITOL | 25% IN 50 ML | IV | J2150 |
| MARCAINE HCL | 30 ML | VAR | S0020 |
| MARINOL | 2.5 MG | ORAL | Q0167 |
| MARINOL | 5 MG | ORAL | Q0168 |
| MARMINE | 50 MG | IM, IV | J1240 |
| MATULANE | 50 MG | ORAL | S0182 |
| MAXIPIME | 500 MG | IV | J0692 |
| MDP-BRACCO | 30 MCI | IV | A9503 |
| MECASERMIN | 1 MG | SC | J2170 |
| MECHLORETHAMINE HYDROCHLORIDE (NITROGEN MUSTARD) | 10 MG | IV | J9230 |
| MEDIDEX | 1 MG | IM, IV, OTH | J1100 |
| MEDROL | 4 MG | ORAL | J7509 |
| MEDROXYPROGESTERONE ACETATE | 150 MG | IM | J1055 |
| MEDROXYPROGESTERONE ACETATE | 50 MG | IM | J1051 |
| MEDROXYPROGESTERONE ACETATE/ESTRADIOL CYPIONATE | 5 MG/25 MG | IM | J1056 |
| MEFOXIN | 1 G | IV | J0694 |
| MEGACE | 20 MG | ORAL | S0179 |
| MEGESTROL ACETATE | 20 MG | ORAL | S0179 |
| MELPHALAN HCL | 2 MG | ORAL | J8600 |
| MELPHALAN HCL | 50 MG | IV | J9245 |
| MENADIONE | 1 MG | IM, SC, IV | J3430 |
| MENOTROPINS | 75 IU | SC, IM, IV | S0122 |
| MEPERGAN | 50 MG | IM, IV | J2180 |
| MEPERIDINE AND PROMETHAZINE HCL | 50 MG | IM, IV | J2180 |
| MEPERIDINE HCL | 100 MG | IM, IV, SC | J2175 |
| MEPIVACAINE HCL | 10 ML | VAR | J0670 |
| MERCAPTOPURINE | 50 MG | ORAL | S0108 |
| MERITATE | 150 MG | IV | J3520 |

Appendix 1 — Table of Drugs

**Appendix 1 — Table of Drugs**

| Drug Name | Unit Per | Route | Code |
|---|---|---|---|
| MEROPENEM | 100 MG | IV | J2185 |
| MERREM | 100 MG | IV | J2185 |
| MESNA | 200 MG | IV | J9209 |
| MESNEX | 200 MG | IV | J9209 |
| METAPROTERENOL SULFATE COMPOUNDED, UNIT DOSE | 10 MG | INH | J7670 |
| METAPROTERENOL SULFATE, NONCOMPOUNDED, CONCENTRATED | 10 MG | INH | J7668 |
| METAPROTERENOL SULFATE, NONCOMPOUNDED, UNIT DOSE | 10 MG | INH | J7669 |
| METARAMINOL BITARTRATE | 10 MG | IV, IM, SC | J0380 |
| METASTRON STRONTIUM 89 CHLORIDE | 1 MCI | IV | A9600 |
| METATRACE | STUDY DOSE | IV | A9552 |
| METHACHOLINE CHLORIDE | 1 MG | INH | J7674 |
| METHADONE | 5 MG | ORAL | S0109 |
| METHADONE HCL | 10 MG | IM, SC | J1230 |
| METHAPREL, COMPOUNDED, UNIT DOSE | 10 MG | INH | J7670 |
| METHAPREL, NONCOMPOUNDED, CONCENTRATED | 10 MG | INH | J7668 |
| METHAPREL, NONCOMPOUNDED, UNIT DOSE | 10 MG | INH | J7669 |
| METHERGINE | 0.2 MG | IM, IV | J2210 |
| METHOTREXATE | 5 MG | IV, IM, IT, IA | J9250 |
| METHOTREXATE | 50 MG | IV, IM, IT, IA | J9260 |
| METHOTREXATE LPF | 5 MG | IV, IM, IT, IA | J9250 |
| METHOTREXATE LPF | 50 MG | IV, IM, IT, IA | J9260 |
| METHOTREXATE SODIUM | 2.5 MG | ORAL | J8610 |
| METHOTREXATE SODIUM | 5 MG | IV, IM, IT, IA | J9250 |
| METHOTREXATE SODIUM | 50 MG | IV, IM, IT, IA | J9260 |
| METHYLCOTOLONE | 80 MG | IM | J1040 |
| METHYLDOPA HCL | 250 MG | IV | J0210 |
| METHYLDOPATE HCL | 5 MG | IV | J0210 |
| METHYLENE BLUE | 1 ML | IV | A9535 |
| METHYLERGONOVINE MALEATE | 0.2 MG | IM, IV | J2210 |
| METHYLPRED | 4 MG | ORAL | J7509 |
| METHYLPREDNISOLONE | 125 MG | IM, IV | J2930 |
| METHYLPREDNISOLONE | 4 MG | ORAL | J7509 |
| METHYLPREDNISOLONE | UP TO 40 MG | IM, IV | J2920 |
| METHYLPREDNISOLONE ACETATE | 20 MG | IM | J1020 |
| METHYLPREDNISOLONE ACETATE | 40 MG | IM | J1030 |
| METHYLPREDNISOLONE ACETATE | 80 MG | IM | J1040 |
| METOCLOPRAMIDE | 10 MG | IV | J2765 |
| METRONIDAZOLE | 500 MG | IV | S0030 |
| MIACALCIN | 400 U | SC, IM | J0630 |
| MIBG | 0.5 MCI | IV | A9508 |
| MICAFUNGIN SODIUM | 1 MG | IV | J2248 |
| MICRHOGAM | 50 MCG | IV | J2788 |
| MICROPOROUS COLLAGEN IMPLANTABLE SLIT TUBE | 1 CM LENGTH | OTH | C9353 |
| MICROPOROUS COLLAGGEN IMPLANTABLE TUBE | 1 CM LENGTH | OTH | C9352 |
| MIDAZOLAM HCl | 1 MG | IM, IV | J2250 |
| MIFEPRISTONE | 200 MG | ORAL | S0190 |
| MILRINONE LACTATE | 5 MG | IV | J2260 |
| MINOXIDIL | 10 MG | ORAL | S0139 |
| MIRENA | 52 MG | OTH | J7302 |

| Drug Name | Unit Per | Route | Code |
|---|---|---|---|
| MISOPROSTOL | 200 MG | ORAL | S0191 |
| MITHRACIN | 2.5 MG | IV | J9270 |
| MITOMYCIN | 20 MG | IV | J9290 |
| MITOMYCIN | 5 MG | IV | J9280 |
| MITOMYCIN | 40 MG | IV | J9291 |
| MITOXANA | 1 G | IV | J9208 |
| MITOXANTRONE HYDROCHLORIDE | 5 MG | IV | J9293 |
| MONARC-M | 1 IU | IV | J7190 |
| MONOCLATE-P | 1 IU | IV | J7190 |
| MONONINE | 1 IU | IV | J7193 |
| MONOPUR | 75 IU | SC, IM | S0122 |
| MORPHINE SULFATE | 10 MG | IM, IV, SC | J2270 |
| MORPHINE SULFATE | 500 MG | OTH | S0093 |
| MORPHINE SULFATE | 100 MG | IM, IV, SC | J2271 |
| MORPHINE SULFATE, PRESERVATIVE FREE, STERILE SOLUTION | 10 MG | IM, IV, SC | J2275 |
| MOXIFLOXACIN | 100 MG | IV | J2280 |
| MPI INDIUM DTPA | 0.5 MCI | IV | A9548 |
| MS CONTIN | 500 MG | OTH | S0093 |
| MUCOMYST | 1 G | INH | J7608 |
| MUCOSIL | 1 G | INH | J7608 |
| MULTIHANCE | 1 ML | IV | A9577 |
| MULTIHANCE MULTIPACK | 1 ML | IV | A9578 |
| MUROMONAB-CD3 | 5 MG | OTH | J7505 |
| MUSE | EA | OTH | J0275 |
| MUSTARGEN | 10 MG | IV | J9230 |
| MUTAMYCIN | 20 MG | IV | J9290 |
| MUTAMYCIN | 5 MG | IV | J9280 |
| MUTAMYCIN | 40 MG | IV | J9291 |
| MYCAMINE | 1 MG | IV | J2248 |
| MYCOPHENOLATE MOFETIL | 250 MG | ORAL | J7517 |
| MYCOPHENOLIC ACID | 180 MG | ORAL | J7518 |
| MYFORTIC DELAYED RELEASE | 180 MG | ORAL | J7518 |
| MYLERAN | 2 MG | ORAL | J8510 |
| MYLOCEL | 500 MG | ORAL | S0176 |
| MYLOTARG | 5 MG | IV | J9300 |
| MYOBLOC | 100 U | IM | J0587 |
| MYOCHRYSINE | 50 MG | IM | J1600 |
| NABILONE | 1 MG | ORAL | J8650 |
| NAFCILLIN SODIUM | 2 GM | IM, IV | S0032 |
| NAGLAZYME | 1 MG | IV | J1458 |
| NALBUPHINE HCL | 10 MG | IM, IV, SC | J2300 |
| NALLPEN | 2 GM | IM, IV | S0032 |
| NALOXONE HCL | 1 MG | IM, IV, SC | J2310 |
| NALTREXONE, DEPOT FORM | 1 MG | IM | J2315 |
| NANDROLONE DECANOATE | 100 MG | IM | J2321 |
| NANDROLONE DECANOATE | 200 MG | IM | J2322 |
| NANDROLONE DECANOATE | 50 MG | IM | J2320 |
| NARCAN | 1 MG | IM, IV, SC | J2310 |
| NAROPIN | 1 MG | VAR | J2795 |

# APPENDIX 1 — TABLE OF DRUGS

| Drug Name | Unit Per | Route | Code |
|---|---|---|---|
| NASAHIST B | 10 MG | IM | J0945 |
| NASALCROM | 10 MG | INH | J7631 |
| NATALIZUMAB | 1 MG | IV | J2323 |
| NATRECOR | 0.1 MG | IV | J2325 |
| NATURAL ESTROGENIC SUBSTANCE | 1 MG | IM, IV | J1410 |
| NAVELBINE | 10 MG | IV | J9390 |
| ND-STAT | 10 MG | IM, SC, IV | J0945 |
| NEBCIN | 80 MG | IM, IV | J3260 |
| NEBUPENT | 300 MG | INH | J2545 |
| NEBUPENT | 300 MG | IM, IV | S0080 |
| NELARABINE | 50 MG | IV | J9261 |
| NEMBUTAL SODIUM | 50 MG | IM, IV, OTH | J2515 |
| NEORAL | 25 MG | ORAL | J7515 |
| NEORAL | 250 MG | ORAL | J7516 |
| NEOSAR | 1 G | IV | J9091 |
| NEOSAR | 2 G | IV | J9092 |
| NEOSAR | 200 MG | IV | J9080 |
| NEOSAR | 100 MG | IV | J9070 |
| NEOSAR | 500 MG | IV | J9090 |
| NEOSCAN | 1 MCI | IV | A9556 |
| NEOSTIGMINE METHYLSULFATE | 250 MG | IM, IV | J2710 |
| NEOTECT | STUDY DOSE | IV | A9536 |
| NESACAINE | 30 ML | VAR | J2400 |
| NESACAINE-MPF | 30 ML | VAR | J2400 |
| NESIRITIDE | 0.1 MG | IV | J2325 |
| NEULASTA | 6 MG | SC, SQ | J2505 |
| NEUMEGA | 5 MG | SC | J2355 |
| NEUPOGEN | 300 MCG | SC, IV | J1440 |
| NEUPOGEN | 480 MCG | SC, IV | J1441 |
| NEURAGEN NERVE GUIDE | 1 CM LENGTH | OTH | C9352 |
| NEUROLITE | 25 MCI | IV | A9557 |
| NEUROMATRIX | 0.5 CM LENGTH | OTH | C9355 |
| NEUROWRAP NERVE PROTECTOR | 1 CM LENGTH | OTH | C9353 |
| NEUTREXIN | 25 MG | IV | J3305 |
| NEUTROSPEC | 25 MCI | IV | A9566 |
| NIPENT | 10 MG | IV | J9268 |
| NITROGEN MUSTARD | 10 MG | IV | J9230 |
| NITROGEN N-13 AMMONIA, DIAGNOSTIC | STUDY DOSE, UP TO 40 MCI | INJ | A9526 |
| NOC DRUGS, INHALATION SOLUTION ADMINISTERED THROUGH DME | 1 EA | | J7699 |
| NOLVADEX | 10 MG | ORAL | S0187 |
| NOLVADEX | 10 MG | ORAL | S0187 |
| NORDITROPIN | 1 MG | SC | J2941 |
| NORDYL | 50 MG | IV, IM | J1200 |
| NORFLEX | 60 MG | IV, IM | J2360 |
| NORPLANT II | PER IMPLANT | OTH | J7306 |
| NOT OTHERWISE CLASSIFIED, ANTINEOPLASTIC DRUGS | | | J9999 |
| NOVANTRONE | 5 MG | IV | J9293 |

| Drug Name | Unit Per | Route | Code |
|---|---|---|---|
| NOVAREL | 1,000 USP U | IM | J0725 |
| NOVASTAN | 5 MG | IV | C9121 |
| NOVO NORDISK | 5 UNITS | SC | J1815 |
| NOVOLIN | 50 U | SC | J1817 |
| NOVOLIN R | 5 U | SC | J1815 |
| NOVOLOG | 50 U | SC | J1817 |
| NOV-ONXOL | 30 MG | IV | J9265 |
| NOVOSEVEN | 1 MCG | IV | J7189 |
| NPH | 5 UNITS | SC | J1815 |
| NPLATE | 10 MCG | SC | C9245 |
| NUBAIN | 10 MG | IM, IV, SC | J2300 |
| NUMORPHAN | 1 MG | IV, SC, IM | J2410 |
| NUTRI-TWELVE | 1,000 MCG | IM, SC | J3420 |
| NUTROPIN | 1 MG | SC | J2941 |
| NUTROPIN A.Q. | 1 MG | SC | J2941 |
| NUVARING VAGINAL RING | EA | OTH | J7303 |
| OASIS BURN MATRIX | SQ CM | OTH | Q4103 |
| OASIS WOUND MATRIX | SQ CM | OTH | Q4102 |
| OCTAFLUOROPROPANE UCISPHERES | 1 ML | IV | Q9956 |
| OCTAGAM | 500 MG | IV | J1568 |
| ~~OCTAGAM IMMUNE GLOBULIN~~ | ~~1 GM~~ | ~~IV~~ | |
| OCTREOSCAN | 1 MCI | IV | A9572 |
| OCTREOTIDE ACETATE DEPOT | 1 MG | IM | J2353 |
| OCTREOTIDE, NON-DEPOT FORM | 25 MCG | SC, IV | J2354 |
| OFLOXACIN | 400 MG | IV | S0034 |
| OLANZAPINE | 2.5 MG | IM | S0166 |
| OMALIZUMAB | 5 MG | SC | J2357 |
| OMNIPAQUE 140 | PER ML | IV | Q9965 |
| OMNIPAQUE 180 | PER ML | IV | Q9965 |
| OMNIPAQUE 240 | PER ML | IV | Q9966 |
| OMNIPAQUE 300 | PER ML | IV | Q9966 |
| OMNIPAQUE 350 | PER ML | IV | Q9967 |
| OMNISCAN | PER ML | IV | A9579 |
| ONCASPAR | VIAL | IM, IV | J9266 |
| ONCOSCINT | DOSE | IV | A4642 |
| ONDANSETRON HCL | 4 MG | ORAL | S0181 |
| ONDANSETRON HCL | 8 MG | ORAL | Q0179 |
| ONDANSETRON HYDROCHLORIDE | 1 MG | IV | J2405 |
| ONTAK | 300 MCG | IV | J9160 |
| ONXOL | 30 MG | IV | J9265 |
| OPRELVEKIN | 5 MG | SC | J2355 |
| OPTIRAY | PER ML | IV | Q9967 |
| OPTIRAY 160 | PER ML | IV | Q9965 |
| OPTIRAY 240 | PER ML | IV | Q9966 |
| OPTIRAY 300 | PER ML | IV | Q9967 |
| OPTIRAY 320 | PER ML | IV | Q9967 |
| OPTISON | 1 ML | IV | Q9957 |
| ORAL MAGNETIC RESONANCE CONTRAST AGENT, PER 100 ML | 100 ML | ORAL | Q9954 |
| ~~ORCEL~~ | ~~SQ CM~~ | ~~OTH~~ | ~~J7340~~ |

# APPENDIX 1 — TABLE OF DRUGS

| Drug Name | Unit Per | Route | Code |
|---|---|---|---|
| ORENCIA | 10 MG | IV | J0129 |
| ORPHENADRINE CITRATE | 60 MG | IV, IM | J2360 |
| ORTHOCLONE OKT3 | 5 MG | OTH | J7505 |
| ORTHOVISC | PER DOSE | OTH | J7324 |
| OSELTAMIVIR PHOSPHATE (BRAND NAME) | 75 MG | ORAL | G9035 |
| OSELTAMIVIR PHOSPHATE (GENERIC) | 75 MG | ORAL | G9019 |
| OSMITROL | 25% IN 50 ML | IV | J2150 |
| OSTREOSCAN | UP TO 6 MCI | IV | A9572 |
| OXACILLIN SODIUM | 250 MG | IM, IV | J2700 |
| OXALIPLATIN | 0.5 MG | IV | J9263 |
| OXILAN 300 | PER ML | IV | Q9967 |
| OXILAN 350 | PER ML | IV | Q9967 |
| OXYMORPHONE HCL | 1 MG | IV, SC, IM | J2410 |
| OXYTETRACYCLINE HCL | 50 MG | IM | J2460 |
| OXYTOCIN | 10 U | IV, IM | J2590 |
| PACIS BCG | VIAL | OTH | J9031 |
| PACLITAXEL | 30 MG | IV | J9265 |
| PACLITAXEL PROTEIN-BOUND PARTICLES | 1 MG | IV | J9264 |
| PALIFERMIN | 50 MCG | IV | J2425 |
| ~~PALIVIZUMAB-RSV-IGM~~ | ~~50 MG~~ | ~~IM~~ | ~~C9003~~ |
| PALONOSETRON HCL | 25 MCG | IV | J2469 |
| PAMIDRONATE DISODIUM | 30 MG | IV | J2430 |
| ~~PANGLOBULIN~~ | ~~1 G~~ | ~~IV~~ | ~~S0045~~ |
| PANHEMATIN | 1 MG | IV | J1640 |
| PANITUMUMAB | 10 MG | IV | J9303 |
| PANTOPRAZOLE SODIUM | 40 MG | IV | S0164 |
| PANTOPRAZOLE SODIUM | VIAL | IV | C9113 |
| PAPAVERINE HCL | 60 MG | IV, IM | J2440 |
| PARAGARD T380A | EA | OTH | J7300 |
| PARAPLANTIN | 50 MG | IV | J9045 |
| PARICALCITOL | 1 MCG | IV, IM | J2501 |
| PEDIAPRED | 5 MG | ORAL | J7510 |
| PEGADEMASE BOVINE | 25 IU | IM | J2504 |
| PEGAPTANIB SODIUM | 0.3 MG | OTH | J2503 |
| PEGASPARGASE | VIAL | IM, IV | J9266 |
| PEGASYS | 10 MCG | SC | S0146 |
| PEGFILGRASTIM | 6 MG | SC | J2505 |
| PEGINTERFERON ALFA-2A | 180 MCG | SC | S0145 |
| PEG-INTRON | 10 MCG | SC | S0146 |
| PEG-INTRON | 180 MCG | SC | S0145 |
| PEGYLATED INTERFERON ALFA-2A | 180 MCG | SC | S0145 |
| PEGYLATED INTERFERON ALFA-2B | 10 MCG | SC | S0146 |
| PEMETREXED | 10 MG | IV | J9305 |
| PEN G BENZ/PEN G PROCAINE | 600,000 U | IM | J0530 |
| PENICILLIN G BENZATHINE | 1,200,000 U | IM | J0570 |
| PENICILLIN G BENZATHINE | 600,000 U | IM | J0560 |
| PENICILLIN G BENZATHINE | 2,400,000 U | IM | J0580 |
| PENICILLIN G BENZATHINE AND PENICILLIN G PROCAINE | 1,200,000 U | IM | J0540 |
| PENICILLIN G POTASSIUM | 600,000 U | IM, IV | J2540 |

| Drug Name | Unit Per | Route | Code |
|-----------|----------|-------|------|
| PENICILLIN G PROCAINE | 600,000 U | IM, IV | J2510 |
| PENTACARINAT | 300 MG | INH | S0080 |
| PENTAM | 300 MG | IM, IV | J2545 |
| PENTAM 300 | 300 MG | IM, IV | S0080 |
| PENTAMIDINE ISETHIONATE | 300 MG | IM, IV | S0080 |
| PENTAMIDINE ISETHIONATE COMPOUNDED | PER 300 MG | INH | J7676 |
| PENTAMIDINE ISETHIONATE NONCOMPOUNDED | 300 MG | INH | J2545 |
| PENTASPAN | 100 ML | IV | J2513 |
| PENTASTARCH 10% SOLUTION | 100 ML | IV | J2513 |
| PENTATE CALCIUM TRISODIUM | UP TO 25 MCI | IV | A9539 |
| PENTATE CALCIUM TRISODIUM | UP TO 25 MCI | INH | A9567 |
| PENTATE ZINC TRISODIUM | UP TO 25 MCI | IV | A9539 |
| PENTATE ZINC TRISODIUM | UP TO 25 MCI | INH | A9567 |
| PENTAZOCINE | 30 MG | IM, SC, IV | J3070 |
| PENTOBARBITAL SODIUM | 50 MG | IM, IV, OTH | J2515 |
| PENTOSTATIN | 10 MG | IV | J9268 |
| PEPCID | 20 MG | IV | S0028 |
| PERFLEXANE LIPID UCISPHERE | 1 ML | IV | Q9955 |
| PERFLUTREN LIPID UCISPHERE | 1 ML | IV | Q9957 |
| PERFOROMIST | 20 MCG | INH | J7606 |
| ~~PERFOROMIST~~ | ~~20 MCG~~ | ~~INH~~ | ~~Q4099~~ |
| PERMAPEN | >1,200,000 U | IM | J0570 |
| PERMAPEN | 600,000 | IM | J0560 |
| PERMAPEN | > 2,400,000 U | IM | J0580 |
| PERPHENAZINE | 4 MG | ORAL | Q0175 |
| PERPHENAZINE | 5 MG | IM, IV | J3310 |
| PERSANTINE | 10 MG | IV | J1245 |
| PFIZERPEN A.S. | 600,000 U | IM, IV | J2510 |
| PHENERGAN | 12.5 MG | ORAL | Q0169 |
| PHENERGAN | 50 MG | IM, IV | J2550 |
| PHENOBARBITAL SODIUM | 120 MG | IM, IV | J2560 |
| PHENTOLAMINE MESYLATE | 5 MG | IM, IV | J2760 |
| PHENYLEPHRINE HCL | 1 ML | SC, IM, IV | J2370 |
| PHENYTOIN SODIUM | 50 MG | IM, IV | J1165 |
| PHOSPHOCOL | 1 MCI | IV | A9563 |
| PHOSPHOTEC | 25 MCI | IV | A9538 |
| PHOTOFRIN | 75 MG | IV | J9600 |
| PHYTONADIONE | 1 MG | IM, SC, IV | J3430 |
| PIPERACILLIN SODIUM | 500 MG | IM, IV | S0081 |
| PIPERACILLIN SODIUM/TAZOBACTAM SODIUM | 1 G/1.125 GM | IV | J2543 |
| PITOCIN | 10 U | IV, IM | J2590 |
| PLATINOL AQ | 10 MG | IV | J9060 |
| PLATINOL AQ | 50 MG | IV | J9062 |
| PLENAXIS | 10 MG | IM | J0128 |
| PLICAMYCIN | 2.5 MG | IV | J9270 |
| PNEUMOCOCCAL CONJUGATE | EA | IM | S0195 |
| PNEUMOVAX II | EA | IM | S0195 |
| POLOCAINE | 10 ML | VAR | J0670 |
| POLYGAM | 500 MG | IV | J1566 |

# APPENDIX 1 — TABLE OF DRUGS

| Drug Name | Unit Per | Route | Code |
|---|---|---|---|
| POLYGAM S/D | 500 MG | IV | J1566 |
| POLY-L-LACTIC ACID | 1 ML | SC | S0196 |
| PORFIMER SODIUM | 75 MG | IV | J9600 |
| PORK INSULIN | 5 U | SC | J1815 |
| POROUS PURIFIED COLLAGEN MATRIX BONE VOID FILLER | 0.5 CC | OTH | C9359 |
| POROUS PURIFIED COLLAGEN MATRIX BONE VOID FILLER | 0.5 CC | OTH | C9359 |
| POTASSIUM CHLORIDE | 2 MEQ | IV | J3480 |
| PRALIDOXIME CHLORIDE | 1 MG | IV, IM, SC | J2730 |
| PREDNICOT | 5 ML | ORAL | J7506 |
| PREDNISOLONE | 5 MG | ORAL | J7510 |
| PREDNISOLONE ACETATE | 1 ML | IM | J2650 |
| PREDNISONE | 5 MG | ORAL | J7506 |
| PREDNORAL | 5 MG | ORAL | J7510 |
| PREDONE | 5 MG | ORAL | J7506 |
| PREGNYL | 1,000 USP U | IM | J0725 |
| PRELONE | 5 MG | ORAL | J7510 |
| PREMARIN | 25 MG | IV, IM | J1410 |
| PRENATAL VITAMINS | 30 TABS | ORAL | S0197 |
| PRIALT | 1 MCG | OTH | J2278 |
| PRIMACOR | 5 MG | IV | J2260 |
| ~~PRIMATRIX~~ | ~~PER SQ. CM.~~ | ~~OTH~~ | ~~J7349~~ |
| PRIMATRIX | SQ CM | OTH | Q4110 |
| PRIMAXIN | 250 MG | IV, IM | J0743 |
| PRIMESTRIN AQUEOUS | 1 MG | IM, IV | J1410 |
| PRIMETHASONE | 1 MG | IM, IV, OTH | J1100 |
| PRI-METHYLATE | 80 MG | IM | J1040 |
| PRIVIGEN | 500 MG | IV | J1459 |
| PROCAINAMIDE HCL | 1 G | IM, IV | J2690 |
| PROCARBAZINE HCL | 50 MG | ORAL | S0182 |
| PROCHLOPERAZINE MALEATE | 5 MG | ORAL | S0183 |
| PROCHLORPERAZINE | 10 MG | IM, IV | J0780 |
| PROCHLORPERAZINE MALEATE | 10 MG | ORAL | Q0165 |
| PROCHLORPERAZINE MALEATE | 5 MG | ORAL | Q0164 |
| PROCRIT, ESRD USE | 1,000 U | SC, IV | J0886 |
| PROCRIT, NON-ESRD USE | 1,000 U | SC, IV | J0885 |
| PROFILNINE HEAT-TREATED | 1 IU | IV | J7194 |
| PROFILNINE SD | 1 IU | IV | J7194 |
| PROFONIX | VIAL | INJ | C9113 |
| PROGESTERONE | 50 MG | IM | J2675 |
| PROGRAF | 1 MG | ORAL | J7507 |
| PROGRAF | 5 MG | OTH | J7525 |
| PROHANCE | 1 ML | IV | 5005F |
| ~~PROHANCE MULTIPACK (GADOTERIDOL)~~ | ~~PER ML~~ | ~~IV~~ | ~~A9576~~ |
| PROLASTIN | 10 MG | IV | J0256 |
| PROLEUKIN | 1 VIAL | VAR | J9015 |
| PROLIXIN DECANOATE | 25 MG | SC, IM | J2680 |
| PROMAZINE HCL | 25 MG | IM | J2950 |
| PROMETHAZINE HCL | 12.5 MG | ORAL | Q0169 |
| PROMETHAZINE HCL | 50 MG | IM, IV | J2550 |

| Drug Name | Unit Per | Route | Code |
|---|---|---|---|
| PRONESTYL | 1 G | IM, IV | J2690 |
| PROPECIA | 5 MG | ORAL | S0138 |
| PROPLEX SX-T | 1 IU | IV | J7194 |
| PROPLEX T | 1 IU | IV | J7194 |
| PROPRANOLOL HCL | 1 MG | IV | J1800 |
| PROREX | 50 MG | IM, IV | J2550 |
| PROSCAR | 5 MG | ORAL | S0138 |
| PROSTASCINT | DOSE | IV | A9507 |
| PROSTIGMIN | 0.5 MG | IM, IV | J2710 |
| PROSTIN VR | 1.25 MCG | INJ | J0270 |
| PROTAMINE SULFATE | 10 MG | IV | J2720 |
| PROTEIN C CONCENTRATE | 10 IU | IV | J2724 |
| PROTEINASE INHIBITOR (HUMAN) | 10 MG | IV | J0256 |
| PROTIRELIN | 250 MCG | IV | J2725 |
| PROTONIX IV | 40 MG | IV | S0164 |
| PROTONIX IV | VIAL | IV | C9113 |
| PROTOPAM CHLORIDE | 1 G | SC, IM, IV | J2730 |
| PROTROPIN | 1 MG | SC, IM | J2940 |
| PROVENTIL NONCOMPOUNDED, CONCENTRATED | 1 MG | INH | J7611 |
| PROVENTIL NONCOMPOUNDED, UNIT DOSE | 1 MG | INH | J7613 |
| PROVOCHOLINE POWDER | 1 MG | INH | J7674 |
| PROZINE-50 | 25 MG | IM | J2950 |
| PULMICORT | 0.25 MG | INH | J7633 |
| PULMICORT RESPULES | 0.5 MG | INH | J7627 |
| PULMICORT RESPULES NONCOMPOUNDED, CONCETRATED | 0.25 MG | INH | J7626 |
| PULMOZYME | 1 MG | INH | J7639 |
| PURINETHOL | 50 MG | ORAL | S0108 |
| PYRIDOXINE HCL | 100 MG | INJ | J3415 |
| QUADRAMET | 50 MCI | IV | A9605 |
| QUELICIN | 20 MG | IM, IV | J0330 |
| QUINUPRISTIN/DALFOPRISTIN | 500 MG | IV | J2770 |
| RANIBIZUMAB | 0.5 MG | OTH | J2778 |
| RANITIDINE HCL | 25 MG | INJ | J2780 |
| RAPAMUNE | 1 MG | ORAL | J7520 |
| RAPTIVA | 125 MG | SC | S0162 |
| RASBURICASE | 50 MCG | IM | J2783 |
| REBETRON KIT | 1,000,000 U | SC, IM | J9214 |
| REBIF | 11 MCG | SC | Q3026 |
| REBIF | 33 MCG | SC | J1825 |
| RECLAST | 1 MG | IV | J3488 |
| RECOMBINATE | 1 IU | IV | J7192 |
| REDISOL | 1,000 MCG | SC. IM | J3420 |
| REFACTO | 1 IU | IV | J7192 |
| REFLUDAN | 50 MG | IM, IV | J1945 |
| ~~REGADENOSON~~ | ~~0.4 MG~~ | ~~IV~~ | ~~C9244~~ |
| REGADENOSON | 0.1 MG | IV | J2785 |
| REGITINE | 5 MG | IM, IV | J2760 |
| REGLAN | 10 MG | IV | J2765 |
| ~~REGRANEX GEL~~ | ~~0.5 G~~ | ~~OTH~~ | ~~50065~~ |

| Drug Name | Unit Per | Route | Code |
|---|---|---|---|
| REGRANEX GEL | 0.5 G | OTH | S0157 |
| REGULAR INSULIN | 5 UNITS | SC | J1815 |
| RELAXIN | 10 ML | IV, IM | J2800 |
| RELION | 5 U | SC | J1815 |
| RELION NOVOLIN | 50 U | SC | J1817 |
| REMICADE | 10 MG | IV | J1745 |
| REMODULIN | 1 MG | SC | J3285 |
| REODULIN | 1 MG | SC | J3285 |
| REOPRO | 10 MG | IV | J0130 |
| REPRONEX | 75 IU | SC, IM, IV | S0122 |
| RESP SYNCYTIAL VIR IMMUNE GLOB | 50 MG | IV | J1565 |
| RESPIGAM | 50 MG | IV | J1565 |
| RESPIROL NONCOMPOUNDED, CONCENTRATED | 1 MG | INH | J7611 |
| RESPIROL NONCOMPOUNDED, UNIT DOSE | 1 MG | INH | J7613 |
| RETAVASE | 18.1 MG | IV | J2993 |
| RETEPLASE | 18.1 MG | IV | J2993 |
| RETISERT | IMPLANT | OTH | J7311 |
| RETROVIR | 10 MG | IV | J3485 |
| RETROVIR | 100 MG | ORAL | S0104 |
| RHEOMACRODEX | 500 ML | IV | J7100 |
| RHEUMATREX DOSE PACK | 2.5 MG | ORAL | J8610 |
| RHO D IMMUNE GLOBULIN | 300 MCG | IV | J2790 |
| RHO D IMMUNE GLOBULIN (RHOPHYLAC) | 100 IU | IM, IV | J2791 |
| RHO D IMMUNE GLOBULIN MINIDOSE | 50 MCG | IM | J2788 |
| RHO D IMMUNE GLOBULIN SOLVENT DETERGENT | 100 IU | IV | J2792 |
| RHOGAM | 300 MCG | IM | J2790 |
| RHOGAM | 50 MCG | IM | J2788 |
| RHOPHYLAC | 100 IU | IM, IV | J2791 |
| RIMANTADINE HYDROCHLORIDE | 100 MG | ORAL | G9036 |
| RIMANTADINE HYDROCHLORIDE (GENERIC) | 100 MG | ORAL | G9020 |
| RIMSO 50 | 50 ML | IV | J1212 |
| RINGERS LACTATE INFUSION | 1,000 ML | VAR | J7120 |
| RISPERDAL COSTA LONG ACTING | 0.5 MG | IM | J2794 |
| RISPERIDONE, LONG ACTING | 0.5 MG | IM | J2794 |
| RITUXAN | 100 MG | IV | J9310 |
| RITUXIMAB | 100 MG | IV | J9310 |
| ROBAXIN | 10 ML | IV, IM | J2800 |
| ROCEPHIN | 250 MG | IV, IM | J0696 |
| ROFERON-A | 3,000,000 U | SC, IM | J9213 |
| ROMIPLOSTIM | 10 MCG | SC | C9245 |
| ROPIVACAINE HYDROCHLORIDE | 1 MG | VAR | J2795 |
| RUBEX | 10 MG | IV | J9000 |
| RUBIDIUM RB-82 | 60 MCI | IV | A9555 |
| RUBRAMIN PC | 1,000 MCG | SC, IM | J3420 |
| RUBRATOPE 57 | 1 MCI | ORAL | A9559 |
| SAIZEN | 1 MG | SC | J2941 |
| SAIZEN SOMATROPIN RDNA ORIGIN | 1 MG | SC | J2941 |
| SALINE OR STERILE WATER, METERED DOSE DISPENSER | 10 ML | INH | A4218 |
| SALINE, STERILE WATER, AND/OR DEXTROSE DILUENT/FLUSH | 10 ML | VAR | A4216 |

| Drug Name | Unit Per | Route | Code |
|---|---|---|---|
| SALINE/STERILE WATER | 500 ML | VAR | A4217 |
| SAMARIUM LEXIDRONAMM | 50 MCI | IV | A9605 |
| SANDIMMUNE | 100 MG | ORAL | J7502 |
| SANDIMMUNE | 25 MG | ORAL | J7515 |
| SANDIMMUNE | 250 MG | IV | J7516 |
| ~~SANDOGLOBULIN~~ | ~~1 G~~ | ~~IV~~ | ~~50045~~ |
| SANDOSTATIN | 25 MCG | SC, IV | J2354 |
| SANDOSTATIN LAR | 1 MG | IM | J2353 |
| SANGCYA | 100 MG | ORAL | J7502 |
| SANO-DROL | 40 MG | IM | J1030 |
| SANO-DROL | 80 MG | IM | J1040 |
| SAQUINAVIR | 200 MG | ORAL | S0140 |
| SARGRAMOSTIM (GM-CSF) | 50 MCG | IV | J2820 |
| SCANDONEST | PER 10 ML | IV | J0670 |
| SECREFLO | 1 MCG | IV | J2850 |
| SECRETIN, SYNTHETIC, HUMAN | 1 MCG | IV | J2850 |
| SENSORCAINE | 30 ML | VAR | S0020 |
| SEPTRA IV | 10 ML | IV | S0039 |
| SERMORELIN ACETATE | 1 MCG | IV | Q0515 |
| SEROSTIM | 1 MG | SC | J2941 |
| SEROSTIM RDNA ORIGIN | 1 MG | SC | J2941 |
| SILDENAFIL CITRATE | 25 MG | ORAL | S0090 |
| SIMULECT | 20 MG | IV | J0480 |
| SINCALIDE | 5 MCG | IV | J2805 |
| SIROLIMUS | 1 MG | ORAL | J7520 |
| SKIN SUBSTITUTE, APLIGRAF | SQ CM | OTH | Q4101 |
| SKIN SUBSTITUTE, DERMAGRAFT | SQ CM | OTH | Q4106 |
| SKIN SUBSTITUTE, GAMMAGRAFT | SQ CM | OTH | Q4111 |
| SKIN SUBSTITUTE, GRAFTJACKET | SQ CM | OTH | Q4107 |
| SKIN SUBSTITUTE, INTEGRA BILAYER MATRIX WOUND DRESSING | SQ CM | OTH | Q4104 |
| SKIN SUBSTITUTE, INTEGRA DERMAL REGENERATION TEMPLATE | SQ CM | OTH | Q4105 |
| SKIN SUBSTITUTE, INTEGRA MATRIX | SQ CM | OTH | Q4108 |
| SKIN SUBSTITUTE, OASIS BURN MATRIX | SQ CM | OTH | Q4103 |
| SKIN SUBSTITUTE, OASIS WOUND MATRIX | SQ CM | OTH | Q4102 |
| SKIN SUBSTITUTE, PRIMATRIX | SQ CM | OTH | Q4110 |
| SKIN SUBSTITUTE, TISSUEMEND | SQ CM | OTH | Q4109 |
| SMZ-TMP | 10 ML | IV | S0039 |
| SODIUM FERRIC GLUCONATE COMPLEX IN SUCROSE | 12.5 MG | IV | J2916 |
| SODIUM FLUORIDE F-18, DIAGNOSTIC | STUDY DOSE UP TO 30 MCI | IV | A9580 |
| ~~SODIUM HYALURONATE~~ | ~~1 MG~~ | ~~OTH~~ | ~~60000~~ |
| ~~SODIUM HYALURONATE~~ | ~~INJ~~ | ~~OTH~~ | ~~60000~~ |
| SODIUM IODIDE I-131 CAPSULE DIAGNOSTIC | 1 MCI | ORAL | A9528 |
| SODIUM IODIDE I-131 CAPSULE THERAPEUTIC | 1 MCI | ORAL | A9517 |
| SODIUM IODIDE I-131 SOLUTION THERAPEUTIC | 1 MCI | ORAL | A9530 |
| SODIUM PHOSPHATE P32 | 1 MCI | IV | A9563 |
| SOLGANAL | 50 MG | IM | J2910 |
| SOLIRIS | 10 MG | IV | J1300 |

# APPENDIX 1 — TABLE OF DRUGS

| Drug Name | Unit Per | Route | Code |
|---|---|---|---|
| SOLTAMOX | 10 MG | ORAL | S0187 |
| SOLU-CORTEF | 100 MG | IV, IM, SC | J1720 |
| SOLU-MEDROL | 125 MG | IM, IV | J2930 |
| SOLU-MEDROL | 40 MG | IM, IV | J2920 |
| SOLUREX | 1 MG | IM, IV, OTH | J1100 |
| SOMATREM | 1 MG | SC, IM | J2940 |
| SOMATROPIN | 1 MG | SC | J2941 |
| ~~SOMATULINE~~ | ~~1 MG~~ | ~~INJ~~ | ~~C9237~~ |
| SOMATULINE | 1 MG | SC | J1930 |
| SPECTINOMYCIN DIHYDROCHLORIDE | 2 G | IM | J3320 |
| SPECTRO-DEX | 1 MG | IM, IV, OTH | J1100 |
| SPORANOX | 50 MG | IV | J1835 |
| STADOL | 1 MG | IM, IV | J0595 |
| STADOL NS | 25 MG | OTH | S0012 |
| STERAPRED | 5 MG | ORAL | J7506 |
| STERILE WATER OR SALINE, METERED DOSE DISPENSER | 10 ML | INH | A4218 |
| STERILE WATER, SALINE, AND/OR DEXTROSE DILUENT/FLUSH | 10 ML | VAR | A4216 |
| STERILE WATER/SALINE | 500 ML | VAR | A4217 |
| STREPTASE | 250,000 IU | IV | J2995 |
| STREPTOKINASE | 250,000 IU | IV | J2995 |
| STREPTOMYCIN | 1 G | IM | J3000 |
| STREPTOZOCIN | 1 GM | IV | J9320 |
| STRONTIUM 89 CHLORIDE | 1 MCI | IV | A9600 |
| SUBLIMAZE | 0.1 MG | IM, IV | J3010 |
| SUCCINYLCHOLINE CHLORIDE | 20 MG | IM, IV | J0330 |
| SULFAMETHOXAZOLE AND TRIMETHOPRIM | 10 ML | IV | S0039 |
| SULFAMETHOXAZOLE-TRIMETHOPRIM | 400-80 MG | ORAL | J8499 |
| SULFUTRIM | 10 ML | IV | S0039 |
| SUMATRIPTAN SUCCINATE | 6 MG | SC | J3030 |
| SUPARTZ | PER DOSE | OTH | J7321 |
| SUPPRELIN LA | 10 MCG | OTH | J1675 |
| SURGIMEND COLLAGEN MATRIX | 0.5 SQ CM | OTH | C9358 |
| SUS-PHRINE | UP TO 1 ML | VAR | J0170 |
| ~~SYNAGIS~~ | ~~50 MG~~ | ~~IM~~ | ~~C9003~~ |
| SYNERCID | 500 MG | IV | J2770 |
| SYNTOCINON | 10 UNITS | IV | J2590 |
| SYNVISC | PER DOSE | OTH | J7322 |
| SYTOBEX | 1,000 MCG | SC, IM | J3420 |
| TACRINE HCL | 10 MG | ORAL | S0014 |
| TACROLIMUS | 1 MG | ORAL | J7507 |
| TACROLIMUS | 5 MG | OTH | J7525 |
| TAGAMET HCL | 300 MG | IM, IV | S0023 |
| TALWIN | 30 MG | IM, SC, IV | J3070 |
| TAMOXIFEN CITRATE | 10 MG | ORAL | S0187 |
| TAXOL | 30 MG | IV | J9265 |
| TAXOTERE | 20 MG | IV | J9170 |
| TAZICEF | 500 MG | IM, IV | J0713 |
| TEBAMIDE | 250 MG | ORAL | Q0173 |
| TEBOROXIME TECHNETIUM TC 99 | PER STUDY DOSE | IV | A9501 |

| Drug Name | Unit Per | Route | Code |
|---|---|---|---|
| TEBOROXIME, TECHNETIUM | PER STUDY DOSE | IV | A9501 |
| TECHNEPLEX | 25 MCI | IV | A9539 |
| TECHNESCAN | UP TO 30 MCI | IV | A9561 |
| TECHNESCAN FANOLESOMAB | STUDY DOSE | IV | A9566 |
| TECHNESCAN MAA | 10 MCI | IV | A9540 |
| TECHNESCAN MAG3 | STUDY DOSE | IV | A9562 |
| TECHNESCAN PYP | 25 MCI | IV | A9538 |
| TECHNESCAN PYP KIT | UP TO 25 MCI | IV | A9538 |
| TECHNETIUM SESTAMBI | 40 MCI | IV | A9500 |
| ~~TECHNETIUM TC 99M ACRCITUMOMAB~~ | ~~PER STUDY DOSE~~ | ~~IV~~ | ~~A9568~~ |
| TECHNETIUM TC 99M APCITIDE | 20 MCI | IV | A9504 |
| TECHNETIUM TC 99M ARCITUMOMAB, DIAGNOSTIC | 45 MCI | IV | A9568 |
| TECHNETIUM TC 99M BICISATE | 25 MCI | IV | A9557 |
| TECHNETIUM TC 99M DEPREOTIDE | 35 MCI | IV | A9536 |
| TECHNETIUM TC 99M EXAMETAZIME | 25 MCI | IV | A9521 |
| TECHNETIUM TC 99M FANOLESOMAB | 25 MCI | IV | A9566 |
| TECHNETIUM TC 99M LABELED RED BLOOD CELLS | 30 MCI | IV | A9560 |
| TECHNETIUM TC 99M MACROAGGREGATED ALBUMIN | 10 MCI | IV | A9540 |
| TECHNETIUM TC 99M MDI-MDP | 30 MCI | IV | A9503 |
| TECHNETIUM TC 99M MEBROFENIN | 15 MCI | IV | A9537 |
| TECHNETIUM TC 99M MEDRONATE | 30 MCI | IV | A9503 |
| TECHNETIUM TC 99M MERTIATIDE | 15 MCI | IV | A9562 |
| TECHNETIUM TC 99M OXIDRONATE | 30 MCI | IV | A9561 |
| TECHNETIUM TC 99M PENTETATE | 75 MCI | INH | A9539 |
| TECHNETIUM TC 99M PENTETATE | 25 MCI | IV | A9539 |
| TECHNETIUM TC 99M PYROPHOSPHATE | 25 MCI | IV | A9538 |
| TECHNETIUM TC 99M SODIUM GLUCEPATATE | 25 MCI | IV | A9550 |
| TECHNETIUM TC 99M SUCCIMER | 10 MCI | IV | A9551 |
| TECHNETIUM TC 99M SULFUR COLLOID | 20 MCI | IV | A9541 |
| TECHNETIUM TC 99M TETROFOSMIN, DIAGNOSTIC | STUDY DOSE | IV | A9502 |
| TECHNETIUM TC-99M EXAMETAZIME LABELED AUTOLOGOUS WHITE BLOOD CELLS | PER STUDY DOSE | IV | A9569 |
| TECHNETIUM TC-99M TEBOROXIME | PER STUDY DOSE | IV | A9501 |
| TECHNILITE | PER MCI | IV | A9512 |
| TEMODAR | 100 MG | ORAL | J8700 |
| TEMOZOLOMIDE | 100 MG | ORAL | J8700 |
| TEMSIROLIMUS | 1 MG | IV | J9330 |
| TENDON, POROUS MATRIX | 1 SQ CM | OTH | C9356 |
| TENDON, POROUS MATRIX CROSS-LINKED AND GLYCOSAMINOGLYCAN MATRIX | SQ CM | OTH | C9356 |
| ~~TENECTEPLASE~~ | ~~50 MG~~ | ~~IV~~ | ~~J3100~~ |
| TENECTEPLASE | 1 MG | IV | J3101 |
| TENIPOSIDE | 50 MG | IV | Q2017 |
| TENOGLIDE TENDON PROTECTOR | 1 SQ CM | OTH | C9356 |
| TENOGLIDE TENDON PROTECTOR SHEET | SQ CM | OTH | C9356 |
| TEQUIN | 10 MG | IV | J1590 |
| TERBUTALINE SULFATE | 1 MG | SC, IV | J3105 |
| TERBUTALINE SULFATE, COMPOUNDED, CONCENTRATED | 1 MG | INH | J7680 |

# APPENDIX 1 — TABLE OF DRUGS

| Drug Name | Unit Per | Route | Code |
|---|---|---|---|
| TERBUTALINE SULFATE, COMPOUNDED, UNIT DOSE | 1 MG | INH | J7681 |
| TERIPARATIDE | 10 MCG | SC | J3110 |
| TERRAMYCIN | 50 MG | IM | J2460 |
| TESTERONE | 50 MG | IM | J3140 |
| TESTOSTERONE CYPIONATE | 1 CC, 200 MG | IM | J1080 |
| TESTOSTERONE CYPIONATE | UP TO 100 MG | IM | J1070 |
| TESTOSTERONE CYPIONATE & ESTRADIOL CYPIONATE | 1 ML | IM | J1060 |
| TESTOSTERONE ENANTHATE | 100 MG | IM | J3120 |
| TESTOSTERONE ENANTHATE | 200 MG | IM | J3130 |
| TESTOSTERONE ENANTHATE & ESTRADIOL VALERATE | UP TO 1 CC | IM | J0900 |
| TESTOSTERONE PELLET | 75 MG | OTH | S0189 |
| TESTOSTERONE PROPIONATE | 100 MG | IM | J3150 |
| TESTOSTERONE SUSPENSION | 50 MG | IM | J3140 |
| TESTRO AQ | 50 MG | IM | J3140 |
| TETANUS IMMUNE GLOBULIN | 250 U | IM | J1670 |
| TETRACYCLINE HCL | 250 MG | IV | J0120 |
| T-GEN | 250 MG | ORAL | Q0173 |
| THALLOUS CHLORIDE | 1 MCI | IV | A9505 |
| THALLOUS CHLORIDE TL-201 | 1 MCI | IV | A9505 |
| THALLOUS CHLORIDE USP | 1 MCI | IV | A9505 |
| THEELIN AQUEOUS | 1 MG | IM, IV | J1435 |
| THEOPHYLLINE | 40 MG | IV | J2810 |
| THERACYS | VIAL | IV | J9031 |
| THIAMINE HCL | 100 MG | INJ | J3411 |
| THIETHYLPERAZINE MALEATE | 10 MG | IM | J3280 |
| THIETHYLPERAZINE MALEATE | 10 MG | ORAL | Q0174 |
| THIMAZIDE | 250 MG | ORAL | Q0173 |
| THIOTEPA | 15 MG | IV | J9340 |
| THORAZINE | 10 MG | ORAL | Q0171 |
| THORAZINE | 25 MG | ORAL | Q0172 |
| THORAZINE | 50 MG | IM, IV | J3230 |
| THROMBATE III | 1 IU | IV | J7197 |
| THYMOGLOBULIN | 25 MG | OTH | J7511 |
| THYROGEN | 0.9 MG | IM, SC | J3240 |
| THYROTROPIN ALPHA | 0.9 MG | IM, SC | J3240 |
| TICARCILLIN DISODIUM AND CLAVULANATE | 3.1 G | IV | S0040 |
| TICE BCG | VIAL | OTH | J9031 |
| TICON | 250 MG | IM | Q0173 |
| TIGAN | 200 MG | IM | J3250 |
| TIGECYCLINE | 1 MG | IV | J3243 |
| TIJECT-20 | 200 MG | IM | J3250 |
| TIMENTIN | 3.1 G | IV | S0040 |
| TINZAPARIN | 1,000 IU | SC | J1655 |
| TIROFIBAN HCL | 0.25 MG | IM, IV | J3246 |
| ~~TISSUEMEND~~ | ~~PER SQ. CM.~~ | ~~OTH~~ | ~~J7348~~ |
| TISSUEMEND | SQ CM | OTH | Q4109 |
| ~~TNKASE~~ | ~~50 MG~~ | ~~IV~~ | ~~J3100~~ |
| TNKASE | 1 MG | IV | J3101 |
| TOBI | 300 MG | INH | J7682 |

| Drug Name | Unit Per | Route | Code |
|-----------|----------|-------|------|
| TOBRAMYCIN COMPOUNDED, UNIT DOSE | 300 MG | INH | J7685 |
| TOBRAMYCIN SULFATE | 80 MG | IM, IV | J3260 |
| TOBRAMYCIN, NONCOMPOUNDED, UNIT DOSE | 300 MG | INH | J7682 |
| TOLAZOLINE HCL | 25 MG | IV | J2670 |
| TOPOSAR | 10 MG | IV | J9181 |
| ~~TOPOSAR~~ | ~~100 MG~~ | ~~IV~~ | ~~J9182~~ |
| TOPOTECAN | 4 MG | IV | J9350 |
| TOPOTECAN | 0.25 MG | ORAL | J8705 |
| TORECAN | 10 MG | ORAL | Q0174 |
| TORISEL | 1 MG | IV | J9330 |
| TORISEL | 1 MG | IV | J9330 |
| TORNALATE | PER MG | INH | J7629 |
| TORNALATE CONCENTRATE | PER MG | INH | J7628 |
| TORSEMIDE | 10 MG | IV | J3265 |
| TOSITUMOMAB DIAGNOSTIC | DOSE | IV | A9544 |
| TOSITUMOMAB THERAPEUTIC | DOSE | IV | A9545 |
| TOTECT | PER 250 MG | IV | J1190 |
| ~~TRANSCYTE~~ | ~~PER 247 SQ CM~~ | ~~OTH~~ | ~~J7340~~ |
| TRASTUZUMAB | 10 MG | IV | J9355 |
| TRASYLOL | 10,000 KIU | IV | J0365 |
| ~~TREANDA~~ | ~~1 MG~~ | ~~IV~~ | ~~C9243~~ |
| TREANDA | 1 MG | IV | J9033 |
| TRELSTAR DEPOT | 3.75 MG | IM | J3315 |
| TRELSTAR DEPOT PLUS DEBIOCLIP KIT | 3.75 MG | IM | J3315 |
| TRELSTAR LA | 3.75 MG | IM | J3315 |
| TREPROSTINIL | 1 MG | SC | J3285 |
| TRETINOIN | 5 G | OTH | S0117 |
| TRIAM-A | 10 MG | IM | J3301 |
| TRIAMCINOLONE ACETONIDE | 10 MG | IM | J3301 |
| TRIAMCINOLONE ACETONIDE, PRESERVATIVE FREE | 1 MG | INJ | J3300 |
| TRIAMCINOLONE DIACETATE | 5 MG | IM | J3302 |
| TRIAMCINOLONE HEXACETONIDE | 5 MG | VAR | J3303 |
| TRIAMCINOLONE, COMPOUNDED, CONCENTRATED | 1 MG | INH | J7683 |
| TRIAMCINOLONE, COMPOUNDED, UNIT DOSE | 1 MG | INH | J7684 |
| TRIBAN | 250 MG | ORAL | Q0173 |
| TRI-KORT | 10 MG | IM | J3301 |
| TRILIFON | 4 MG | ORAL | Q0175 |
| TRILOG | 10 MG | IM | J3301 |
| TRILONE | 5 MG | IM | J3302 |
| TRIMETHOBENZAMIDE HCL | 200 MG | IM | J3250 |
| TRIMETHOBENZAMIDE HCL | 250 MG | ORAL | Q0173 |
| TRIMETREXATE GLUCURONATE | 25 MG | IV | J3305 |
| TRIPTORELIN PAMOATE | 3.75 MG | IM | J3315 |
| TRISENOX | 1 MG | IV | J9017 |
| TRIVARIS | 1 MG | VAR | J3300 |
| TROBICIN | 2 G | IM | J3320 |
| TRUXADRYL | 50 MG | IV, IM | J1200 |
| TYGACIL | 1 MG | IV | J3243 |

Appendix 1 — Table of Drugs

| Drug Name | Unit Per | Route | Code |
|---|---|---|---|
| TYPE A BOTOX | 1 U | OTH | J0585 |
| TYSABRI | 1 MG | IV | J2323 |
| ULTRALENTE | 5 U | SC | J1815 |
| ULTRATAG | 30 MCI | IV | A9560 |
| ULTRA-TECHNEKOW | PER MCI | IV | A9512 |
| ~~ULTRAVIST~~ | ~~1 ML~~ | ~~IV~~ | ~~50020~~ |
| ~~ULTRAVIST 150~~ | ~~1 ML~~ | ~~IV~~ | ~~70010~~ |
| ~~ULTRAVIST 240~~ | ~~1 ML~~ | ~~IV~~ | ~~70015~~ |
| ~~ULTRAVIST 370~~ | ~~1 ML~~ | ~~IV~~ | ~~70015~~ |
| UNASYN | 1.5 G | IM, IV | J0295 |
| UNCLASSIFIED BIOLOGICS | | | J3590 |
| UREA | 40 G | IV | J3350 |
| UROFOLLITROPIN | 75 IU | SC, IM | J3355 |
| UROKINASE | 250,000 IU | IV | J3365 |
| UROKINASE | 5,000 IU | IV | J3364 |
| VALERGEN | 10 MG | IM | J1380 |
| VALERGEN | 20 MG | IM | J1390 |
| VALIUM | 5 MG | IV, IM | J3360 |
| VALRUBICIN INTRAVESICAL | 200 MG | OTH | J9357 |
| VALSTAR | 200 MG | OTH | J9357 |
| VANCOCIN | 500 MG | IM, IV | J3370 |
| VANCOMYCIN HCL | 500 MG | IV, IM | J3370 |
| VANTAS | 50 MG | OTH | J9225 |
| ~~VECTIBIX~~ | ~~10 MG~~ | ~~IV~~ | ~~70015~~ |
| VECTIBIX | 10 MG | IV | J9303 |
| VELCADE | 0.1 MG | IV | J9041 |
| VELOSULIN | 5 U | SC | J1815 |
| VELOSULIN BR | 5 U | SC | J1815 |
| VENOFER | 1 MG | IV | J1756 |
| ~~VENOGLOBULIN-S~~ | ~~1 G~~ | ~~IV~~ | ~~50045~~ |
| VENTOLIN NONCOMPOUNDED, CONCENTRATED | 1 MG | INH | J7611 |
| VENTOLIN NONCOMPOUNDED, UNIT DOSE | 1 MG | INH | J7613 |
| VEPESID | 10 MG | IV | J9181 |
| ~~VEPESID~~ | ~~100 MG~~ | ~~IV~~ | ~~J9182~~ |
| VEPESID | 50 MG | ORAL | J8560 |
| VERITAS | SQ CM | OTH | C9354 |
| VERSED | 1 MG | IM, IV | J2250 |
| VERTEPORFIN | 0.1 MG | IV | J3396 |
| VFEND | 200 MG | IV | J3465 |
| VIAGRA | 25 MG | ORAL | S0090 |
| VIDAZA | 1 MG | SC | J9025 |
| VIDEX | 25 MG | ORAL | S0137 |
| VINBLASTINE SULFATE | 1 MG | IV | J9360 |
| VINCRISTINE SULFATE | 1 MG | IV | J9370 |
| VINCRISTINE SULFATE | 2 MG | IV | J9375 |
| VINORELBINE TARTRATE | 10 MG | IV | J9390 |
| VIRILON | 1 CC, 200 MG | IM | J1080 |
| ~~VISIPAQUE 270~~ | ~~1 ML~~ | ~~IV~~ | ~~70015~~ |
| ~~VISIPAQUE 320~~ | ~~1 ML~~ | ~~IV~~ | ~~50020~~ |

| Drug Name | Unit Per | Route | Code |
|---|---|---|---|
| VISTAJECT-25 | 25 MG | IM | J3410 |
| VISTARIL | 25 MG | IM | J3410 |
| VISTARIL | 25 MG | ORAL | Q0177 |
| VISTIDE | 375 MG | IV | J0740 |
| VISUDYNE | 0.1 MG | IV | J3396 |
| VITAMIN B-12 CYANOCOBALAMIN | 1,000 MCG | IM, SC | J3420 |
| VITRASE | 1 USP | OTH | J3471 |
| VITRASE | 1,000 USP | OTH | J3472 |
| VITRASERT | 4.5 MG | OTH | J7310 |
| VITRAVENE | 1.65 MG | OTH | J1452 |
| VIVITROL | 1 MG | IM | J2315 |
| VON WILLEBAND FACTOR VIII COMPLEX, HUMAN | PER FACTOR VIII IU | IV | J7186 |
| VON WILLEBRAND FACTOR COMPLEX, HUMATE-P | IU | IV | J7187 |
| ~~VON WILLEBRAND FACTOR COMPLEX, RISTOCETIN COFACTOR~~ | ~~IU~~ | ~~IV~~ | ~~Q4096~~ |
| VORICONAZOLE | 200 MG | IV | J3465 |
| VUMON | 50 MG | IV | Q2017 |
| WEHAMINE | 50 MG | IM, IV | J1240 |
| WEHDRYL | 50 MG | IM, IV | J1200 |
| WELBUTRIN SR | 150 MG | ORAL | S0106 |
| WINRHO SDF | 100 IU | IV | J2792 |
| WYCILLIN | 600,000 U | IM, IV | J2510 |
| XELODA | 150 MG | ORAL | J8520 |
| XELODA | 500 MG | ORAL | J8521 |
| XENON XE-133 | 10 MCI | OTH | A9558 |
| XOLAIR | 5 MG | SC | J2357 |
| XYLOCAINE | 10 MG | IV | J2001 |
| YTTRIUM 90 IBRITUMOMAB TIUXETAN | TX DOSE | IV | A9543 |
| ~~ZALCITABINE (DDC)~~ | ~~0.375 MG~~ | ~~ORAL~~ | ~~S0141~~ |
| ZANAMIVIR (BRAND NAME) | 10 MG | INH | G9034 |
| ZANAMIVIR (GENERIC) | 10 MG | INH | G9018 |
| ZANOSAR | 1 GM | IV | J9320 |
| ZANTAC | 25 MG | INJ | J2780 |
| ZEMAIRA | 10 MG | IV | J0256 |
| ZEMPLAR | 1 MCG | IV, IM | J2501 |
| ZENAPAX | 25 MG | OTH | J7513 |
| ZEVALIN | UP TO 5 MCI | IV | A9542 |
| ZEVALIN DIAGNOSTIC | TX DOSE | IV | A9542 |
| ZEVALIN THERAPEUTIC | TX DOSE | IV | A9543 |
| ZICONOTIDE | 1 MCG | IT | J2278 |
| ZIDOVUDINE | 10 MG | IV | J3485 |
| ZIDOVUDINE | 100 MG | ORAL | S0104 |
| ZINACEFT | PER 750 MG | IM, IV | J0697 |
| ZINECARD | 250 MG | IV | J1190 |
| ZIPRASIDONE MESYLATE | 10 MG | IM | J3486 |
| ZITHROMAX | 1 G | ORAL | Q0144 |
| ZITHROMAX | 500 MG | IV | J0456 |
| ZOFRAN | 1 MG | IV | J2405 |
| ZOFRAN | 8 MG | ORAL | Q0179 |

# APPENDIX 1 — TABLE OF DRUGS

| Drug Name | Unit Per | Route | Code |
|---|---|---|---|
| ZOFRAN | 4 MG | ORAL | S0181 |
| ZOLADEX | 3.6 MG | SC | J9202 |
| ZOLEDRONIC ACID | 1 MG | IV | J3487 |
| ZOLEDRONIC ACID (RECLAST) | 1 MG | IV | J3488 |
| ~~ZOLEDRONIC ACID FOR PAGET'S DISEASE~~ | ~~1 MG~~ | ~~IV~~ | ~~70015~~ |
| ZOMETA | 1 MG | IV | J3487 |
| ZORBTIVE | 1 MG | SC | J2941 |
| ZOSYN | 1 G/1.125 GM | IV | J2543 |
| ZOVIRAX | 5 MG | IV | J0133 |
| ~~ZOVIRAX~~ | ~~50 MG~~ | ~~IV~~ | ~~70015~~ |
| ZYPREXA | 2.5 MG | IM | S0166 |
| ZYVOX | 200 MG | IV | J2020 |

## NOT OTHERWISE CLASSIFIED DRUGS

| Drug Name | Unit Per | Route | Code |
|---|---|---|---|
| ALFENTANIL | 500 MCG | IV | J3490 |
| ~~ALGUCOSIDE ALFA~~ | ~~1 MG~~ | ~~IV~~ | ~~J3490~~ |
| ALLOPURINOL SODIUM | 500 MG | IV | J3490 |
| AMINOCAPROIC ACID | 250 MG | IV | J3490 |
| ~~ARFORMOTEROL TATRATE~~ | ~~15 MCG~~ | ~~INH~~ | ~~J3490~~ |
| ARGININE HYDROCHLORIDE | 300 ML | IV | J3490 |
| ASCORBIC ACID | 250 MG | IV | J3490 |
| ATROPINE SULFATE/EDROPHONIUM CHLORIDE | 10 MG | IV | J3490 |
| AZTREONAM | 500 MG | IV | J3490 |
| ~~BENDAMUSTINE HCL~~ | ~~1 MG~~ | ~~IV~~ | ~~J3490~~ |
| BUMETANIDE | 0.25 MG | IM, IV | J3490 |
| BUPIVACAINE, 0.25% | 1 ML | OTH | J3490 |
| BUPIVACAINE, 0.50% | 1 ML | OTH | J3490 |
| BUPIVACAINE, 0.75% | 1 ML | OTH | J3490 |
| CALCIUM CHLORIDE | 100 MG | IV | J3490 |
| CIMETIDINE HCL | 150 MG | IM, IV | J3490 |
| CLAVULANTE POTASSIUM/TICARCILLIN DISODIUM | 0.1-3 GM | IV | J3490 |
| CLINDAMYCIN PHOSPHATE | 150 MG | IV | J3490 |
| COPPER SULFATE | 0.4 MG | INJ | J3490 |
| DEXTROSE 50% | 50 ML | IV | J3490 |
| DILTIAZEM HCL | 5 MG | IV | J3490 |
| DILTIAZEM HCL | 5 MG | IV | J3490 |
| DOXAPRAM HCL | 20 MG | IV | J3490 |
| DOXYCYCLINE HYCLATE | 100 MG | INJ | J3490 |
| ~~ECULIZUMAB~~ | ~~1 MG~~ | ~~IV~~ | ~~J3490~~ |
| EDROPHONIUM CHLORIDE | 10 MG | IM, IV | J3490 |
| ENALAPRILAT | 1.25 MG | IV | J3490 |
| ESMOLOL HCL | 10 MG | IV | J3490 |
| ESOMEPRAZOLE SODIUM | 20 MG | IV | J3490 |
| ETOMIDATE | 2 MG | IV | J3490 |
| FAMOTIDINE | 10 MG | IV | J3490 |
| FLUMAZENIL | 0.1 MG | IV | J3490 |
| FOLIC ACID | 5 MG | SC, IM, IV | J3490 |
| GLYCOPYRROLATE | 0.2 MG | IM, IV | J3490 |

| Drug Name | Unit Per | Route | Code |
|---|---|---|---|
| HEPAGAMB INTRAVENOUS | 0.5 ML | IV | J3490 |
| IDURSULFASE | 1 MG | IV | J3490 |
| IXABEPILONE | 1 MG | IV | J3490 |
| KETAMINE HCL | 10 MG | IM, IV | J3490 |
| LABETALOL HCL | 5 MG | INJ | J3490 |
| LEVETIRACETAM (KEPPRA INTRAVENOUS) | 10 MG | IV | J3490 |
| LIDOCAINE | 1 ML | VAR | J3490 |
| METOPROLOL TARTRATE | 1 MG | IV | J3490 |
| METRONIDAZOLE INJ | 500 MG | IV | J3490 |
| MORRHUATE SODIUM | 50 MG | OTH | J3490 |
| NAFCILLIN SODIUM | 1 GM | IM, IV | J3490 |
| NALMEFENE HCL | 10 MCG | IV | J3490 |
| NITROGLYCERIN | 5 MG | IV | J3490 |
| OLANZAPINE | 0.5 MG | IM | J3490 |
| PANITUMUMAB | 1 MG | IV | J3490 |
| PANITUMUMAB | 1MG | IV | J3490 |
| PEGASYS | 180 MCG | SC | J3490 |
| PEGINTERFERON ALFA-2A | 180 MCG | SC | J3490 |
| POTASSIUM ACETATE | 2 MEQ | IV | J3490 |
| POTASSIUM POSPHATE | 3 MMOL | IV | J3490 |
| PROPOFOL | 10 MG | IV | J3490 |
| PROTONIX | 40 MG | IV | J3490 |
| RANIBIZUMAB INJ | 0.5 MG | OTH | J3490 |
| RIFAMPIN | 600 MG | IV | J3490 |
| SARRACENIA PURPURA | 1 ML | INJ | J3490 |
| SODIUM ACETATE | 2 MEQ | | J3490 |
| SODIUM BICARBONATE, 8.4% | 50 ML | IV | J3490 |
| SODIUM CHLORIDE, HYPERTONIC | 250 CC | IV | J3490 |
| SODIUM THIOSULFATE | 100 MG | IV | J3490 |
| SURGIMEND | 0.5 SQ CM | OTH | J3490 |
| TEMSIROLIMUS | 1 MG | IV | J9330 |
| TRIAMCINOLONE ACETONIDE, PRESERVATIVE FREE | 1 MG | INJ | J3490 |
| VALPROATE SODIUM | 100 MG | IV | J3490 |
| VASOPRESSIN | 20 UNITS | SC, IM | J3490 |
| VECURONIUM BROMIDE | 1 MG | IV | J3490 |
| VERAPAMIL HCL | 2.5 MG | IV | J3490 |

# APPENDIX 2 — MODIFIERS

A modifier is a two-position alpha or numeric code that is added to the end of a CPT code to clarify the services being billed. Modifiers provide a means by which a service can be altered without changing the procedure code. They add more information, such as the anatomical site, to the code. In addition, they help to eliminate the appearance of duplicate billing and unbundling. Modifiers are used to increase accuracy in reimbursement, coding consistency, editing, and to capture payment data.

| | |
|---|---|
| A1 | Dressing for one wound |
| A2 | Dressing for 2 wounds |
| A3 | Dressing for 3 wounds |
| A4 | Dressing for 4 wounds |
| A5 | Dressing for 5 wounds |
| A6 | Dressing for 6 wounds |
| A7 | Dressing for 7 wounds |
| A8 | Dressing for 8 wounds |
| A9 | Dressing for 9 or more wounds |
| AA | Anesthesia services performed personally by anesthesiologist |
| AD | Medical supervision by a physician: more than 4 concurrent anesthesia procedures |
| AE | Registered dietician |
| AF | Specialty physician |
| AG | Primary physician |
| AH | Clinical psychologist |
| AJ | Clinical social worker |
| AK | Non participating physician |
| AM | Physician, team member service |
| AP | Determination of refractive state was not performed in the course of diagnostic ophthalmological examination |
| AQ | Physician providing a service in an unlisted health professional shortage area (HPSA) |
| AR | Physician provider services in a physician scarcity area |
| AS | Physician assistant, nurse practitioner, or clinical nurse specialist services for assistant at surgery |
| AT | Acute treatment (this modifier should be used when reporting service 98940, 98941, 98942) |
| AU | Item furnished in conjunction with a urological, ostomy, or tracheostomy supply |
| AV | Item furnished in conjunction with a prosthetic device, prosthetic or orthotic |
| AW | Item furnished in conjunction with a surgical dressing |
| AX | Item furnished in conjunction with dialysis services |
| BA | Item furnished in conjunction with parenteral enteral nutrition (PEN) services |
| BL | Special acquisition of blood and blood products |
| BO | Orally administered nutrition, not by feeding tube |

| | |
|---|---|
| BP | The beneficiary has been informed of the purchase and rental options and has elected to purchase the item |
| BR | The beneficiary has been informed of the purchase and rental options and has elected to rent the item |
| BU | The beneficiary has been informed of the purchase and rental options and after 30 days has not informed the supplier of his/her decision |
| CA | Procedure payable only in the inpatient setting when performed emergently on an outpatient who expires prior to admission |
| CB | Service ordered by a renal dialysis facility (RDF) physician as part of the ESRD beneficiary's dialysis benefit, is not part of the composite rate, and is separately reimbursable |
| CC | Procedure code change (use CC when the procedure code submitted was changed either for administrative reasons or because an incorrect code was filed) |
| CD | AMCC test has been ordered by an ESRD facility or MCP physician that is part of the composite rate and is not separately billable |
| CE | AMCC test has been ordered by an ESRD facility or MCP physician that is a composite rate test but is beyond the normal frequency covered under the rate and is separately reimbursable based on medical necessity |
| CF | AMCC test has been ordered by an ESRD facility or MCP physician that is not part of the composite rate and is separately billable |
| CG | Policy criteria applied |
| CR | Catastrophe/Disaster related |
| E1 | Upper left, eyelid |
| E2 | Lower left, eyelid |
| E3 | Upper right, eyelid |
| E4 | Lower right, eyelid |
| EA | Erythropoetic stimulating agent (ESA) administered to treat anemia due to anticancer chemotherapy |
| EB | Erythropoetic stimulating agent (ESA) administered to treat anemia due to anticancer radiotherapy |
| EC | Erythropoetic stimulating agent (ESA) administered to treat anemia not due to anticancer radiotherapy or anticancer chemotherapy |
| ED | Hematocrit level has exceeded 39% (or hemoglobin level has exceeded 13.0 G/dl) for 3 or more consecutive billing cycles immediately prior to and including the current cycle |
| EE | Hematocrit level has not exceeded 39% (or hemoglobin level has not exceeded 13.0 G/dl) for 3 or more consecutive billing cycles immediately prior to and including the current cycle |

**EJ** Subsequent claims for a defined course of therapy, e.g., EPO, sodium hyaluronate, infliximab

**EM** Emergency reserve supply (for ESRD benefit only)

**EP** Service provided as part of Medicaid early periodic screening diagnosis and treatment (EPSDT) program

**ET** Emergency services

**EY** No physician or other licensed health care provider order for this item or service

**F1** Left hand, 2nd digit

**F2** Left hand, third digit

**F3** Left hand, 4th digit

**F4** Left hand, fifth digit

**F5** Right hand, thumb

**F6** Right hand, 2nd digit

**F7** Right hand, third digit

**F8** Right hand, 4th digit

**F9** Right hand, 5th digit

**FA** Left hand, thumb

**FB** Item provided without cost to provider, supplier or practitioner, or full credit received for replaced device (examples, but not limited to, covered under warranty, replaced due to defect, free samples)

**FC** Partial credit received for replaced device

**FP** Service provided as part of family planning program

**G1** Most recent URR reading of less than 60

**G2** Most recent URR reading of 60 to 64.9

**G3** Most recent URR reading of 65 to 69.9

**G4** Most recent URR reading of 70 to 74.9

**G5** Most recent URR reading of 75 or greater

**G6** ESRD patient for whom less than 6 dialysis sessions have been provided in a month

**G7** Pregnancy resulted from rape or incest or pregnancy certified by physician as life threatening

**G8** Monitored anesthesia care (MAC) for deep complex, complicated, or markedly invasive surgical procedure

**G9** Monitored anesthesia care for patient who has history of severe cardiopulmonary condition

**GA** Waiver of liability statement on file

**GB** Claim being resubmitted for payment because it is no longer covered under a global payment demonstration

**GC** This service has been performed in part by a resident under the direction of a teaching physician

**GD** Units of service exceeds medically unlikely edit value and represents reasonable and necessary services

**GE** This service has been performed by a resident without the presence of a teaching physician under the primary care exception

**GF** Nonphysician (e.g., nurse practitioner (NP), certified registered nurse anesthetist (CRNA), certified registered nurse (CRN), clinical nurse specialist (CNS), physician assistant (PA)) services in a critical access hospital

**GG** Performance and payment of a screening mammogram and diagnostic mammogram on the same patient, same day

**GH** Diagnostic mammogram converted from screening mammogram on same day

**GJ** Opt out physician or practitioner emergency or urgent service

**GK** Reasonable and necessary item/service associated with GA or GZ modifier

**GL** Medically unnecessary upgrade provided instead of nonupgraded item, no charge, no advance beneficiary notice (ABN)

**GM** Multiple patients on one ambulance trip

**GN** Services delivered under an outpatient speech language pathology plan of care

**GO** Services delivered under an outpatient occupational therapy plan of care

**GP** Services delivered under an outpatient physical therapy plan of care

**GQ** Via asynchronous telecommunications system

**GR** This service was performed in whole or in part by a resident in a department of veterans affairs medical center or clinic, supervised in accordance with VA policy

**GS** Dosage of EPO or darbepoetin alfa has been reduced and maintained in response to hematocrit or hemoglobin level

**GT** Via interactive audio and video telecommunication systems

**GV** Attending physician not employed or paid under arrangement by the patient's hospice provider

**GW** Service not related to the hospice patient's terminal condition

**GY** Item or service statutorily excluded, does not meet the definition of any Medicare benefit or for non-Medicare insurers, is not a contract benefit

**GZ** Item or service expected to be denied as not reasonable and necessary

**H9** Court-ordered

**HA** Child/adolescent program

**HB** Adult program, nongeriatric

**HC** Adult program, geriatric

**HD** Pregnant/parenting women's program

**HE** Mental health program

**HF** Substance abuse program

**HG** Opioid addiction treatment program

**HH** Integrated mental health/substance abuse program

**HI** Integrated mental health and mental retardation/developmental disabilities program

| | |
|---|---|
| HJ | Employee assistance program |
| HK | Specialized mental health programs for high-risk populations |
| HL | Intern |
| HM | Less than bachelor degree level |
| HN | Bachelors degree level |
| HO | Masters degree level |
| HP | Doctoral level |
| HQ | Group setting |
| HR | Family/couple with client present |
| HS | Family/couple without client present |
| HT | Multi-disciplinary team |
| HU | Funded by child welfare agency |
| HV | Funded state addictions agency |
| HW | Funded by state mental health agency |
| HX | Funded by county/local agency |
| HY | Funded by juvenile justice agency |
| HZ | Funded by criminal justice agency |
| J1 | Competitive acquisition program no-pay submission for a prescription number |
| J2 | Competitive acquisition program, restocking of emergency drugs after emergency administration |
| J3 | Competitive acquisition program (CAP), drug not available through CAP as written, reimbursed under average sales price methodology |
| JA | Administered intravenously |
| JB | Administered subcutaneously |
| JC | Skin substitute used as a graft |
| JD | Skin substitute not used as a graft |
| JW | Drug amount discarded/not administered to any patient |
| K0 | Lower extremity prosthesis functional level 0—does not have the ability or potential to ambulate or transfer safely with or without assistance and a prosthesis does not enhance their quality of life or mobility |
| K1 | Lower extremity prosthesis functional level 1 - has the ability or potential to use a prosthesis for transfers or ambulation on level surfaces at fixed cadence, typical of the limited and unlimited household ambulator. |
| K2 | Lower extremity prosthesis functional level 2 - has the ability or potential for ambulation with the ability to traverse low level environmental barriers such as curbs, stairs or uneven surfaces. typical of the limited community ambulator. |
| K3 | Lower extremity prosthesis functional level 3—has the ability or potential for ambulation with variable cadence, typical of the community ambulator who has the ability to traverse most environmental barriers and may have vocational, therapeutic, or exercise activity that demands prosthetic utilization beyond simple locomotion |

| | |
|---|---|
| K4 | Lower extremity prosthesis functional level 4 - has the ability or potential for prosthetic ambulation that exceeds the basic ambulation skills, exhibiting high impact, stress, or energy levels, typical of the prosthetic demands of the child, active adult, or athlete. |
| KA | Add on option/accessory for wheelchair |
| KB | Beneficiary requested upgrade for ABN, more than 4 modifiers identified on claim |
| KC | Replacement of special power wheelchair interface |
| KD | Drug or biological infused through DME |
| KE | Bid under round one of the DMEPOS competitive bidding program for use with noncompetitive bid base equipment |
| KF | Item designated by FDA as class III device |
| KG | DMEPOS item subject to DMEPOS competitive bidding program number 1 |
| KH | DMEPOS item, initial claim, purchase or first month rental |
| KI | DMEPOS item, 2nd or 3rd month rental |
| KJ | DMEPOS item, parenteral enteral nutrition (PEN) pump or capped rental, months 4 to 15 |
| KK | DMEPOS item subject to DMEPOS competitive bidding program number 2 |
| KL | DMEPOS item delivered via mail |
| KM | Replacement of facial prosthesis including new impression/moulage |
| KN | Replacement of facial prosthesis using previous master model |
| KO | Single drug unit dose formulation |
| KP | First drug of a multiple drug unit dose formulation |
| KQ | Second or subsequent drug of a multiple drug unit dose formulation |
| KR | Rental item, billing for partial month |
| KS | Glucose monitor supply for diabetic beneficiary not treated with insulin |
| KT | Beneficiary resides in a competitive bidding area and travels outside that competitive bidding area and receives a competitive bid item. |
| KU | DMEPOS item subject to DMEPOS competitive bidding program number 3 |
| KV | DMEPOS item subject to DMEPOS competitive bidding program that is furnished as part of a professional service |
| KW | DMEPOS item subject to DMEPOS competitive bidding program number 4 |
| KX | Requirements specified in the medical policy have been met |
| KY | DMEPOS item subject to DMEPOS competitive bidding program number 5 |
| KZ | New coverage not implemented by managed care |
| LC | Left circumflex coronary artery |
| LD | Left anterior descending coronary artery |

**LL** Lease/rental (use the LL modifier when DME equipment rental is to be applied against the purchase price)

**LR** Laboratory round trip

**LS** FDA-monitored intraocular lens implant

**LT** Left side (used to identify procedures performed on the left side of the body)

**M2** Medicare secondary payer (MSP)

**MS** Six month maintenance and servicing fee for reasonable and necessary parts and labor which are not covered under any manufacturer or supplier warranty

**NR** New when rented (use the NR modifier when DME which was new at the time of rental is subsequently purchased)

**NU** New equipment

**P1** A normal healthy patient

**P2** A patient with mild systemic disease

**P3** A patient with severe systemic disease

**P4** A patient with severe systemic disease that is a constant threat to life

**P5** A moribund patient who is not expected to survive without the operation

**P6** A declared brain-dead patient whose organs are being removed for donor purposes

**PL** Progressive addition lenses

**PR** Ambulance transportation from physician's office (includes HMO non-hospital facility, clinic, etc.)to residence

**Q0** Investigational clinical service provided in a clinical research study that is in an approved clinical research study

**Q1** Routine clinical service provided in a clinical research study that is in an approved clinical research study

**Q2** HCFA/ORD demonstration project procedure/service

**Q3** Live kidney donor surgery and related services

**Q4** Service for ordering/referring physician qualifies as a service exemption

**Q5** Service furnished by a substitute physician under a reciprocal billing arrangement

**Q6** Service furnished by a locum tenens physician

**Q7** One Class A finding

**Q8** Two Class B findings

**Q9** One class B and 2 class C findings

**QB** Physician providing service in a rural HPSA

**QC** Single channel monitoring

**QD** Recording and storage in solid state memory by a digital recorder

**QE** Prescribed amount of oxygen is less than 1 liter per minute (LPM)

**QF** Prescribed amount of oxygen exceeds 4 liters per minute (LPM) and portable oxygen is prescribed

**QG** Prescribed amount of oxygen is greater than 4 liters per minute (LPM)

**QH** Oxygen conserving device is being used with an oxygen delivery system

**QJ** Services/items provided to a prisoner or patient in state or local custody, however the state or local government, as applicable, meets the requirements in 42 CFR 411.4(B)

**QK** Medical direction of 2, 3, or 4 concurrent anesthesia procedures involving qualified individuals

**QL** Patient pronounced dead after ambulance called

**QM** Ambulance service provided under arrangement by a provider of services

**QN** Ambulance service furnished directly by a provider of services

**QP** Documentation is on file showing that the laboratory test(s) was ordered individually or ordered as a CPT-recognized panel other than automated profile codes 80002-80019, G0058, G0059, and G0060

**QQ** Claim submitted with a written statement of intent

**QS** Monitored anesthesia care service

**QT** Recording and storage on tape by an analog tape recorder

**QU** Physician providing service in an urban HPSA

**QW** CLIA waived test

**QX** CRNA service: with medical direction by a physician

**QY** Medical direction of one certified registered nurse anesthetist (CRNA) by an anesthesiologist

**QZ** CRNA service: without medical direction by a physician

**RA** Replacement of a DME item

**RB** Replacement of a part of DME furnished as part of a repair

**RC** Right coronary artery

**RD** Drug provided to beneficiary, but not administered "incident-to"

**RE** Furnished in full compliance with FDA-mandated risk evaluation and mitigation strategy (REMS)

**RR** Rental (use the RR modifier when DME is to be rented)

**RT** Right side (used to identify procedures performed on the right side of the body)

**SA** Nurse practitioner rendering service in collaboration with a physician

**SB** Nurse midwife

**SC** Medically necessary service or supply

**SD** Services provided by registered nurse with specialized, highly technical home infusion training

**SE** State and/or federally-funded programs/services

**SF** Second opinion ordered by a professional review organization (PRO) per section 9401, p.l. 99-272 (100% reimbursement - no Medicare deductible or coinsurance)

# APPENDIX 2 — MODIFIERS

**SG** Ambulatory surgical center (ASC) facility service

**SH** Second concurrently administered infusion therapy

**SJ** Third or more concurrently administered infusion therapy

**SK** Member of high risk population (use only with codes for immunization)

**SL** State supplied vaccine

**SM** Second surgical opinion

**SN** Third surgical opinion

**SQ** Item ordered by home health

**SS** Home infusion services provided in the infusion suite of the IV therapy provider

**ST** Related to trauma or injury

**SU** Procedure performed in physician's office (to denote use of facility and equipment)

**SV** Pharmaceuticals delivered to patient's home but not utilized

**SW** Services provided by a certified diabetic educator

**SY** Persons who are in close contact with member of high-risk population (use only with codes for immunization)

**T1** Left foot, 2nd digit

**T2** Left foot, 3rd digit

**T3** Left foot, 4th digit

**T4** Left foot, 5th digit

**T5** Right foot, great toe

**T6** Right foot, 2nd digit

**T7** Right foot, 3rd digit

**T8** Right foot, 4th digit

**T9** Right foot, 5th digit

**TA** Left foot, great toe

**TC** Technical component. Under certain circumstances, a charge may be made for the technical component alone. Under those circumstances the technical component charge is identified by adding modifier 'TC' to the usual procedure number. Technical component charges are institutional charges and not billed separately by physicians. However, portable x-ray suppliers only bill for technical component and should utilize modifier TC. The charge data from portable x-ray suppliers will then be used to build customary and prevailing profiles.

**TD** RN

**TE** LPN/LVN

**TF** Intermediate level of care

**TG** Complex/high tech level of care

**TH** Obstetrical treatment/services, prenatal or postpartum

**TJ** Program group, child and/or adolescent

**TK** Extra patient or passenger, nonambulance

**TL** Early intervention/individualized family service plan (IFSP)

**TM** Individualized education program (IEP)

**TN** Rural/outside providers' customary service area

**TP** Medical transport, unloaded vehicle

**TQ** Basic life support (BSL) transport by a volunteer ambulance provider

**TR** School-based individualized education program (IEP) services provided outside the public school district responsible for the student

**TS** Follow-up service

**TT** Individualized service provided to more than one patient in same setting

**TU** Special payment rate, overtime

**TV** Special payment rates, holidays/weekends

**TW** Back-up equipment

**U1** Medicaid level of care 1, as defined by each state

**U2** Medicaid level of care 2, as defined by each state

**U3** Medicaid level of care 3, as defined by each state

**U4** Medicaid level of care 4, as defined by each state

**U5** Medicaid level of care 5, as defined by each state

**U6** Medicaid level of care 6, as defined by each state

**U7** Medicaid level of care 7, as defined by each state

**U8** Medicaid level of care 8, as defined by each state

**U9** Medicaid level of care 9, as defined by each state

**UA** Medicaid level of care 10, as defined by each state

**UB** Medicaid level of care 11, as defined by each state

**UC** Medicaid level of care 12, as defined by each state

**UD** Medicaid level of care 13, as defined by each state

**UE** Used durable medical equipment

**UF** Services provided in the morning

**UG** Services provided in the afternoon

**UH** Services provided in the evening

**UJ** Services provided at night

**UK** Services provided on behalf of the client to someone other than the client (collateral relationship)

**UN** Two patients served

**UP** Three patients served

**UQ** Four patients served

**UR** Five patients served

**US** Six or more patients served

**VP** Aphakic patient

# APPENDIX 3 — ABBREVIATIONS AND ACRONYMS

## HCPCS Abbreviations and Acronyms

The following abbreviations and acronyms are used in the HCPCS descriptions:

| | |
|---|---|
| / | or |
| < | less than |
| <= | less than equal to |
| > | greater than |
| >= | greater than equal to |
| AC | alternating current |
| AFO | ankle-foot orthosis |
| AICC | anti-inhibitor coagulant complex |
| AK | above the knee |
| AKA | above knee amputation |
| ALS | advanced life support |
| AMP | ampule |
| ART | artery |
| ART | Arterial |
| ASC | ambulatory surgery center |
| ATT | attached |
| A-V | Arteriovenous |
| AVF | arteriovenous fistula |
| BICROS | bilateral routing of signals |
| BK | below the knee |
| BLS | basic life support |
| BMI | body mass index |
| BP | blood pressure |
| BTE | behind the ear (hearing aid) |
| CAPD | continuous ambulatory peritoneal dialysis |
| Carb | carbohydrate |
| CBC | complete blood count |
| cc | cubic centimeter |
| CCPD | continuous cycling peritoneal analysis |
| CHF | congestive heart failure |
| CIC | completely in the canal (hearing aid) |
| CIM | Coverage Issue Manual |
| Clsd | closed |
| cm | centimeter |
| CMN | certificate of medical necessity |
| CMS | Centers for Medicare and Medicaid Services |
| CMV | Cytomegalovirus |
| Conc | concentrate |
| Conc | concentrated |
| Cont | continuous |
| CP | clinical psychologist |
| CPAP | continuous positive airway pressure |
| CPT | Current Procedural Terminology |
| CRF | chronic renal failure |
| CRNA | certified registered nurse anesthetist |
| CROS | contralateral routing of signals |
| CSW | clinical social worker |
| CT | computed tomography |
| CTLSO | cervical-thoracic-lumbar-sacral orthosis |
| cu | cubic |
| DC | direct current |
| DI | diurnal rhythm |
| Dx | diagnosis |
| DLI | donor leukocyte infusion |
| DME | durable medical equipment |
| DME MAC | durable medical equipment Medicare administrative contractor |
| DMEPOS | Durable Medical Equipment, Prosthestics, Orthotics and Other Supplies |
| DMERC | durable medical equipment regional carrier |
| DR | diagnostic radiology |
| DX | diagnostic |
| e.g. | for example |
| Ea | each |
| ECF | extended care facility |
| EEG | electroencephalogram |
| EKG | electrocardiogram |
| EMG | electromyography |
| EO | elbow orthosis |
| EP | electrophysiologic |
| EPO | epoetin alfa |
| EPSDT | early periodic screening, diagnosis and treatment |
| ESRD | end-stage renal disease |
| Ex | extended |
| Exper | experimental |
| Ext | external |
| F | french |
| FDA | Food and Drug Administration |
| FDG-PET | Positron emission with tomography with 18 fluorodeoxyglucose |
| Fem | female |
| FO | finger orthosis |
| FPD | fixed partial denture |
| Fr | french |
| ft | foot |
| G-CSF | filgrastim (granulocyte colony-stimulating factor) |
| gm | gram (g) |
| H2O | water |
| HCl | hydrochloric acid, hydrochloride |
| HCPCS | Healthcare Common Procedural Coding System |
| HCT | hematocrit |
| HFO | hand-finger orthosis |
| HHA | home health agency |
| HI | high |
| HI-LO | high-low |
| HIT | home infusion therapy |
| HKAFO | hip-knee-ankle foot orthosis |
| HLA | human leukocyte antigen |
| HMES | heat and moisture exchange system |
| HNPCC | hereditary non-polyposis colorectal cancer |
| HO | hip orthosis |
| HPSA | health professional shortage area |
| HST | home sleep test |
| IA | intra-arterial administration |
| ip | interphalangeal |
| I-131 | Iodine 131 |
| ICF | intermediate care facility |
| ICU | intensive care facility |
| IM | intramuscular |
| in | inch |
| INF | infusion |
| INH | inhalation solution |
| INJ | injection |
| IOL | intraocular lens |
| IPD | intermittent peritoneal dialysis |

| | |
|---|---|
| IPPB | intermittent positive pressure breathing |
| IT | intrathecal administration |
| ITC | in the canal (hearing aid) |
| ITE | in the ear (hearing aid) |
| IU | international units |
| IV | intravenous |
| IVF | in vitro fertilization |
| KAFO | knee-ankle-foot orthosis |
| KO | knee orthosis |
| KOH | potassium hydroxide |
| L | left |
| LASIK | laser in situ keratomileusis |
| LAUP | laser assisted uvulopalatoplasty |
| lbs | pounds |
| LDL | low density lipoprotein |
| Lo | low |
| LPM | liters per minute |
| LPN/LVN | Licensed Practical Nurse/Licensed Vocational Nurse |
| LSO | lumbar-sacral orthosis |
| MAC | Medicare administrative contractor |
| mp | metacarpophalangeal |
| mcg | microgram |
| mCi | millicurie |
| MCM | Medicare Carriers Manual |
| MCP | metacarparpophalangeal joint |
| MCP | monthly capitation payment |
| mEq | milliequivalent |
| MESA | microsurgical epididymal sperm aspiration |
| mg | milligram |
| mgs | milligrams |
| MHT | megahertz |
| ml | milliliter |
| mm | millimeter |
| mmHg | millimeters of Mercury |
| MRA | magnetic resonance angiography |
| MRI | magnetic resonance imaging |
| NA | sodium |
| NCI | National Cancer Institute |
| NEC | not elsewhere classified |
| NG | nasogastric |
| NH | nursing home |
| NMES | neuromuscular electrical stimulation |
| NOC | not otherwise classified |
| NOS | not otherwise specified |
| O2 | oxygen |
| OBRA | Omnibus Budget Reconciliation Act |
| OMT | osteopathic manipulation therapy |
| OPPS | outpatient prospective payment system |
| ORAL | oral administration |
| OSA | obstructive sleep apnea |
| Ost | ostomy |
| OTH | other routes of administration |
| oz | ounce |
| PA | physician's assistant |
| PAR | parenteral |
| PCA | patient controlled analgesia |
| PCH | pouch |
| PEN | parenteral and enteral nutrition |
| PENS | percutaneous electrical nerve stimulation |
| PET | positron emission tomography |
| PHP | pre-paid health plan |

| | |
|---|---|
| PHP | physician hospital plan |
| PI | paramedic intercept |
| PICC | peripherally inserted central venous catheter |
| PKR | photorefractive keratotomy |
| Pow | powder |
| PRK | photoreactive keratectomy |
| PRO | peer review organization |
| PSA | prostate specific antigen |
| PTB | patellar tendon bearing |
| PTK | phototherapeutic keratectomy |
| PVC | polyvinyl chloride |
| R | right |
| Repl | replace |
| RN | registered nurse |
| RP | retrograde pyelogram |
| Rx | prescription |
| SACH | solid ankle, cushion heel |
| SC | subcutaneous |
| SCT | specialty care transport |
| SEO | shoulder-elbow orthosis |
| SEWHO | shoulder-elbow-wrist-hand orthosis |
| SEXA | single energy x-ray absorptiometry |
| SGD | speech generating device |
| SGD | sinus rhythm |
| SM | samarium |
| SNCT | sensory nerve conduction test |
| SNF | skilled nursing facility |
| SO | sacroilliac othrosis |
| SO | shoulder orthosis |
| Sol | solution |
| SQ | square |
| SR | screen |
| ST | standard |
| ST | sustained release |
| Syr | syrup |
| TABS | tablets |
| Tc | Technetium |
| Tc 99m | technetium isotope |
| TENS | transcutaneous electrical nerve stimulator |
| THKAO | thoracic-hip-knee-ankle orthosis |
| TLSO | thoracic-lumbar-sacral-orthosis |
| TM | temporomandibular |
| TMJ | temporomandibular joint |
| TPN | total parenteral nutrition |
| U | unit |
| uCi | microcurie |
| VAR | various routes of administration |
| w | with |
| w/ | with |
| w/o | with or without |
| WAK | wearable artificial kidney |
| wc | wheelchair |
| WHFO | wrist-hand-finger orthotic |
| Wk | week |
| w/o | without |
| Xe | xenon (isotope mass of xenon 133) |

# APPENDIX 4 — PUB 100 REFERENCES

The Centers for Medicare and Medicaid Services restructured its paper-based manual system as a web-based system on October 1, 2003. Called the online CMS manual system, it combines all of the various program instructions into internet-only manuals (IOMs), which are used by all CMS programs and contractors. Complete versions of all of the manuals can be found at http://www.cms.hhs.gov/manuals.

Effective September 30, 2003, the former method of publishing program memoranda (PMs) to communicate program instructions was replaced by the following four templates:

• One-time notification

• Manual revisions

• Business requirements

• Confidential requirements

The web-based system has been organized by functional area (e.g., eligibility, entitlement, claims processing, benefit policy, program integrity) in an effort to eliminate redundancy within the manuals, simplify updating, and make CMS program instructions available more quickly. The web-based system contains the functional areas included below:

Pub. 100    Introduction

Pub. 100-1    Medicare General Information, Eligibility, and Entitlement Manual

Pub. 100-2    Medicare Benefit Policy Manual

Pub. 100-3    Medicare National Coverage Determinations Manual

Pub. 100-4    Medicare Claims Processing Manual

Pub. 100-5    Medicare Secondary Payer Manual

Pub. 100-6    Medicare Financial Management Manual

Pub. 100-7    State Operations Manual

Pub. 100-8    Medicare Program Integrity Manual

Pub. 100-9    Medicare Contractor Beneficiary and Provider Communications Manual

Pub. 100-10    Quality Improvement Organization Manual

Pub. 100-11    Reserved

Pub. 100-12    State Medicaid Manual (under development)

Pub. 100-13    Medicaid State Children's Health Insurance Program (under development)

Pub. 100-14    Medicare ESRD Network Organizations Manual

Pub. 100-15    State Buy-In Manual

Pub. 100-16    Medicare Managed Care Manual

Pub. 100-17    CMS/Business Partners Systems Security Manual

Pub. 100-18    Reserved

Pub. 100-19    Demonstrations

Pub. 100-20    One-Time Notification

Pub. 100-21    Recurring Update Notification

A brief description of the Medicare manuals primarily used for *CPC Expert* follows:

The **National Coverage Determinations Manual** (NCD), is organized according to categories such as diagnostic services, supplies, and medical procedures. The table of contents lists each category and subject within that category. Revision transmittals identify any new or background material, recap the changes, and provide an effective date for the change.

When complete, the manual will contain two chapters. Chapter 1 currently includes a description of CMS's national coverage determinations. When available, chapter 2 will contain a list of HCPCS codes related to each coverage determination. The manual is organized in accordance with CPT category sequences.

The **Medicare Benefit Policy Manual** contains Medicare general coverage instructions that are not national coverage determinations. As a general rule, in the past these instructions have been found in chapter II of the **Medicare Carriers Manual**, the **Medicare Intermediary Manual**, other provider manuals, and program memoranda.

The **Medicare Claims Processing Manual** contains instructions for processing claims for contractors and providers.

The **Medicare Program Integrity Manual** communicates the priorities and standards for the Medicare integrity programs.

## 100-1,1,10.1

### Hospital Insurance (Part A) for Inpatient Hospital, Hospice, Home Health and Skilled Nursing Facility (SNF) Services - A Brief Description

Hospital insurance is designed to help patients defray the expenses incurred by hospitalization and related care. In addition to inpatient hospital benefits, hospital insurance covers post hospital extended care in SNFs and post hospital care furnished by a home health agency in the patient's home. Blood clotting factors, for hemophilia patients competent to use such factors to control bleeding without medical or other supervision, and items related to the administration of such factors, are also a Part A benefit for beneficiaries in a covered Part A stay. The purpose of these additional benefits is to provide continued treatment after hospitalization and to encourage the appropriate use of more economical alternatives to inpatient hospital care. Program payments for services rendered to beneficiaries by providers (i.e., hospitals, SNFs, and home health agencies) are generally made to the provider. In each benefit period, payment may be made for up to 90 inpatient hospital days, and 100 days of post hospital extended care services .Hospices also provide Part A hospital insurance services such as short-term inpatient care. In order to be eligible to elect hospice care under Medicare, an individual must be entitled to Part A of Medicare and be certified as being terminally ill. An individual is considered to be terminally ill if the individual has a medical prognosis that his or her life expectancy is 6 months or less if the illness runs its normal course.

### 100-1,3,20.5
#### Blood Deductibles (Part A and Part B)
Program payment may not be made for the first 3 pints of whole blood or equivalent units of packed red cells received under Part A and Part B combined in a calendar year. However, blood processing (e.g., administration, storage) is not subject to the deductible.

The blood deductibles are in addition to any other applicable deductible and coinsurance amounts for which the patient is responsible.

The deductible applies only to the first 3 pints of blood furnished in a calendar year, even if more than one provider furnished blood.

### 100-1,3,20.5.2
#### Part B Blood Deductible
Blood is furnished on an outpatient basis or is subject to the Part B blood deductible and is counted toward the combined limit. It should be noted that payment for blood may be made to the hospital under Part B only for blood furnished in an outpatient setting. Blood is not covered for inpatient Part B services.

### 100-1,3,20.5.3
#### Items Subject to Blood Deductibles
The blood deductibles apply only to whole blood and packed red cells. The term whole blood means human blood from which none of the liquid or cellular components have been removed. Where packed red cells are furnished, a unit of packed red cells is considered equivalent to a pint of whole blood. Other components of blood such as platelets, fibrinogen, plasma, gamma globulin, and serum albumin are not subject to the blood deductible. However, these components of blood are covered as biologicals.

Refer to Pub. 100-04, Medicare Claims Processing Manual, chapter 4, Sec.231 regarding billing for blood and blood products under the Hospital Outpatient Prospective Payment System (OPPS).

### 100-1,5,90.2
#### Laboratory Defined
Laboratory means a facility for the biological, microbiological, serological, chemical, immuno-hematological, hematological, biophysical, cytological, pathological, or other examination of materials derived from the human body for the purpose of providing information for the diagnosis, prevention, or treatment of any disease or impairment of, or the assessment of the health of, human beings. These examinations also include procedures to determine, measure, or otherwise describe the presence or absence of various substances or organisms in the body. Facilities only collecting or preparing specimens (or both) or only serving as a mailing service and not performing testing are not considered laboratories.

### 100-2,1,10
#### Covered Inpatient Hospital Services Covered Under Part A
A3-3101, HO-210

Patients covered under hospital insurance are entitled to have payment made on their behalf for inpatient hospital services. (Inpatient hospital services do not include extended care services provided by hospitals pursuant to swing bed approvals. See Pub. 100-1, Chapter 8, Sec.10.1, "Hospital Providers of Extended Care Services."). However, both inpatient hospital and inpatient SNF benefits are provided under Part A - Hospital Insurance Benefits for the Aged and Disabled, of Title XVIII).

Additional information concerning the following topics can be found in the following manual chapters:

- Benefit periods is found in Chapter 3, "Duration of Covered Inpatient Services";
- Copayment days is found in Chapter 2, "Duration of Covered Inpatient Services";
- Lifetime reserve days is found in Chapter 5, "Lifetime Reserve Days";
- Related payment information is housed in the Provider Reimbursement Manual.

Blood must be furnished on a day which counts as a day of inpatient hospital services to be covered as a Part A service and to count toward the blood deductible. Thus, blood is not covered under Part A and does not count toward the Part A blood deductible when furnished to an inpatient after the inpatient has exhausted all benefit days in a benefit period, or where the individual has elected not to use lifetime reserve days. However, where the patient is discharged on their first day of entitlement or on the hospital's first day of participation, the hospital is permitted to submit a billing form with no accommodation charge, but with ancillary charges including blood.

The records for all Medicare hospital inpatient discharges are maintained in CMS for statistical analysis and use in determining future PPS DRG classifications and rates.

Non-PPS hospitals do not pay for noncovered services generally excluded from coverage in the Medicare Program. This may result in denial of a part of the billed charges or in denial of the entire admission, depending upon circumstance. In PPS hospitals, the following are also possible:

1. In appropriately admitted cases where a noncovered procedure was performed, denied services may result in payment of a different DRG (i.e., one which excludes payment for the noncovered procedure); or

2. In appropriately admitted cases that become cost outlier cases, denied services may lead to denial of some or all of an outlier payment.

The following examples illustrate this principle. If care is noncovered because a patient does not need to be hospitalized, the intermediary denies the admission and makes no Part A (i.e., PPS) payment unless paid under limitation on liability. Under limitation on liability, Medicare payment may be made when the provider and the beneficiary were not aware the services were not necessary and could not reasonably be expected to know that he services were not necessary. For detailed instructions, see the Medicare Claims Processing Manual, Chapter 30,"Limitation on Liability." If a patient is appropriately hospitalized but receives (beyond routine services) only noncovered care, the admission is denied.

NOTE: The intermediary does not deny an admission that includes covered care, even if noncovered care was also rendered. Under PPS, Medicare assumes that it is paying for only the covered care rendered whenever covered services needed to treat and/or diagnose the illness were in fact provided.

If a noncovered procedure is provided along with covered nonroutine care, a DRG change rather than an admission denial might occur. If noncovered procedures are elevating costs into the cost outlier category, outlier payment is denied in whole or in part.

When the hospital is included in PPS, most of the subsequent discussion regarding coverage of inpatient hospital services is relevant only in the context of determining the appropriateness of admissions, which DRG, if any, to pay, and the appropriateness of payment for any outlier cases.

If a patient receives items or services in excess of, or more expensive than, those for which payment can be made, payment is made only for the covered items or services or for only the appropriate prospective payment amount. This provision applies not only to inpatient services, but also to all hospital services under Parts A and B of the program. If the items or services were requested by the patient, the hospital may charge him the difference between the amount customarily charged for the services requested and the amount customarily charged for covered services.

An inpatient is a person who has been admitted to a hospital for bed occupancy for purposes of receiving inpatient hospital services. Generally, a patient is considered an inpatient if formally admitted as inpatient with the expectation that he or she will remain at least overnight and occupy a bed even though it later develops that the patient can be discharged or transferred to another hospital and not actually use a hospital bed overnight.

The physician or other practitioner responsible for a patient's care at the hospital is also responsible for deciding whether the patient should be admitted as an inpatient. Physicians should use a 24-hour period as a benchmark, i.e., they should order admission for patients who are expected to need hospital care for 24 hours or more, and treat other patients on an outpatient basis. However, the decision to admit a patient is a complex medical judgment which can be made only after the physician has considered a number of factors, including the patient's medical history and current medical needs, the types of facilities available to inpatients and to outpatients, the hospital's by-laws and admissions policies, and the relative appropriateness of treatment in each setting. Factors to be considered when making the decision to admit include such things as:

The severity of the signs and symptoms exhibited by the patient;

The medical predictability of something adverse happening to the patient;

The need for diagnostic studies that appropriately are outpatient services (i.e., their performance does not ordinarily require the patient to remain at the hospital for 24 hours or more) to assist in assessing whether the patient should be admitted; and

The availability of diagnostic procedures at the time when and at the location where the patient presents.

Admissions of particular patients are not covered or noncovered solely on the basis of the length of time the patient actually spends in the hospital. In certain specific situations coverage of services on an inpatient or outpatient basis is determined by the following rules:

Minor Surgery or Other Treatment - When patients with known diagnoses enter a hospital for a specific minor surgical procedure or other treatment that is expected to keep them in the hospital for only a few hours (less than 24), they are considered outpatients for coverage purposes regardless of: the hour they came to the hospital, whether they used a bed, and whether they remained in the hospital past midnight.

Renal Dialysis - Renal dialysis treatments are usually covered only as outpatient services but may under certain circumstances be covered as inpatient services depending on the patient's condition. Patients staying at home, who are ambulatory, whose conditions are stable and who come to the hospital for routine chronic dialysis treatments, and not for a diagnostic workup or a change in therapy, are considered outpatients. On the other hand, patients undergoing short-term dialysis until their kidneys recover from an acute illness (acute dialysis), or persons with borderline renal failure who develop acute renal failure every time they have an illness and require dialysis (episodic dialysis) are usually inpatients. A patient may begin dialysis as an inpatient and then progress to an outpatient status.

Under original Medicare, the Quality Improvement Organization (QIO), for each hospital is responsible for deciding, during review of inpatient admissions on a case-by-case basis, whether the admission was medically necessary. Medicare law authorizes the QIO to make these judgments, and the judgments are binding for purposes of Medicare coverage. In making these judgments, however, QIOs consider only the medical evidence which was available to the physician at the time an admission decision had to be made. They do not take into account other information (e.g., test results) which became available only after admission, except in cases where considering the post-admission information would support a finding that an admission was medically necessary.

Refer to Parts 4 and 7 of the QIO Manual with regard to initial determinations for these services. The QIO will review the swing bed services in these PPS hospitals as well.

NOTE: When patients requiring extended care services are admitted to beds in a hospital, they are considered inpatients of the hospital. In such cases, the services furnished in the hospital will not be considered extended care services, and payment may not be made under the program for such services unless the services are extended care services furnished pursuant to a swing bed agreement granted to the hospital by the Secretary of Health and Human Services.

## *100-2,1,10.1.4*
### Charges for Deluxe Private Room
A3-3101.1.D, HO-210.1.D

Beneficiaries found to need a private room (either because they need isolation for medical reasons or because they need immediate admission when no other accommodations are available) may be assigned to any of the provider's private rooms. They do not have the right to insist on the private room of their choice, but their preferences should be given the same consideration as if they were paying all provider charges themselves. The program does not, under any circumstances, pay for personal comfort items. Thus, the program does not pay for deluxe accommodations and/or services. These would include a suite, or a room substantially more spacious than is required for treatment, or specially equipped or decorated, or serviced for the comfort and convenience of persons willing to pay a differential for such amenities. If the beneficiary (or representative) requests such deluxe accommodations, the provider should advise that there will be a charge, not covered by Medicare, of a specified amount per day (not exceeding the differential defined in the next sentence); and may charge the beneficiary that amount for each day he/she occupies the deluxe accommodations. The maximum amount the provider may charge the beneficiary for such accommodations is the differential between the most prevalent private room rate at the time of admission and the customary charge for the room occupied. Beneficiaries may not be charged this differential if they (or their representative) do not request the deluxe accommodations.

# APPENDIX 4 — PUB 100 REFERENCES

The beneficiary may not be charged such a differential in private room rates if that differential is based on factors other than personal comfort items. Such factors might include differences between older and newer wings, proximity to lounge, elevators or nursing stations, desirable view, etc. Such rooms are standard 1-bed units and not deluxe rooms for purposes of these instructions, even though the provider may call them deluxe and have a higher customary charge for them. No additional charge may be imposed upon the beneficiary who is assigned to a room that may be somewhat more desirable because of these factors.

## 100-2,1,40

### Supplies, Appliances, and Equipment

Supplies, appliances, and equipment, which are ordinarily furnished by the hospital for the care and treatment of the beneficiary solely during the inpatient hospital stay, are covered inpatient hospital services.

Under certain circumstances, supplies, appliances, and equipment used during the beneficiary's inpatient stay are covered under Part A even though the supplies, appliances and equipment leave the hospital with the patient upon discharge. These are circumstances in which it would be unreasonable or impossible from a medical standpoint to limit the patient's use of the item to the periods during which the individual is an inpatient. Examples of items covered under this rule are:

- Items permanently installed in or attached to the patient's body while an inpatient, such as cardiac valves, cardiac pacemakers, and artificial limbs; and
- Items which are temporarily installed in or attached to the patient's body while an inpatient, and which are also necessary to permit or facilitate the patient's release from the hospital, such as tracheotomy or drainage tubes.

Hospital "admission packs" containing primarily toilet articles, such as soap, toothbrushes, toothpaste, and combs, are covered under Part A if routinely furnished by the hospital to all its inpatients. If not routinely furnished to all patients, the packs are not covered. In that situation, the hospital may charge beneficiaries for the pack, but only if they request it with knowledge of what they are requesting and what the charge to them will be.

Supplies, appliances, and equipment furnished to an inpatient for use only outside the hospital are not, in general, covered as inpatient hospital services. However, a temporary or disposable item, which is medically necessary to permit or facilitate the patient's departure from the hospital and is required until the patient can obtain a continuing supply, is covered as an inpatient hospital service.

Oxygen furnished to hospital inpatients is covered under Part A as an inpatient supply.

## 100-2,10,20

### Coverage Guidelines for Ambulance Service Claims

B3-2125

Payment may be made for expenses incurred by a patient for ambulance service provided conditions l, 2, and 3 in the left-hand column have been met. The right-hand column indicates the documentation needed to establish that the condition has been met.

| Conditions | Review Action |
|---|---|
| 1. Patient was transported by an approved supplier of ambulance services. | 1. Ambulance supplier is listed in the table of approved ambulance companies (§10.1.3) |
| 2. The patient was suffering from an illness or injury, which contraindicated transportation by other means. (§10.2) | 2. (a) The contractor presumes the requirement was met if the submitted documentation indicates that the patient:<br><br>• Was transported in an emergency situation, e.g., as a result of an accident, injury or acute illness, or<br><br>• Needed to be restrained to prevent injury to the beneficiary or others; or<br><br>• Was unconscious or in shock; or<br><br>• Required oxygen or other emergency treatment during transport to the nearest appropriate facility; or<br><br>• Exhibits signs and symptoms of acute respiratory distress or cardiac distress such as shortness of breath or chest pain; or<br><br>• Exhibits signs and symptoms that indicate the possibility of acute stroke; or<br><br>• Had to remain immobile because of a fracture that had not been set or the possibility of a fracture; or<br><br>• Was experiencing severe hemorrhage; or<br><br>• Could be moved only by stretcher; or<br><br>• Was bed-confined before and after the ambulance trip.<br><br>(b) In the absence of any of the conditions listed in (a)above additional documentation should be obtained to establish medical need where the evidence indicates the existence of the circumstances listed below:<br><br>(i) Patient's condition would not ordinarily require movement by stretcher, or<br><br>(ii) The individual was not admitted as a hospital inpatient (except in accident cases), or<br><br>(iii) The ambulance was used solely because other means of transportation were unavailable, or |

| Conditions | Review Action |
|---|---|
| | (iv) The individual merely needed assistance in getting from his room or home to a vehicle. |
| | (c) Where the information indicates a situation not listed in 2(a) or 2(b) above, refer the case to your supervisor. |
| 3. The patient was transported from and to points listed below. | 3. Claims should show the ZIP code of the point of pickup |
| (a) From patient's residence (or other place where need arose) to hospital or skilled nursing facility. | (a)<br>i. Condition met if trip began within the institution's service area as shown in the carrier's locality guide<br>ii. Condition met where the trip began outside the institution's service area if the institution was the nearest one with appropriate facilities. |

NOTE: A patient's residence is the place where he or she makes his/her home and dwells permanently, or for an extended period of time. A skilled nursing facility is one, which is listed in the Directory of Medical Facilities as a participating SNF or as an institution which meets §1861(j)(1) of the Act.

NOTE: A claim for ambulance service to a participating hospital or skilled nursing facility should not be denied on the grounds that there is a nearer nonparticipating institution having appropriate facilities.

| Conditions | Review Action |
|---|---|
| (b) Skilled nursing facility to a hospital or hospital to a skilled nursing facility. | (b)<br>(i) Condition met if the ZIP code of the pickup point is within the service area of the destination as shown in the carrier's locality guide.<br>(ii) Condition met where the ZIP code of the pickup point is outside the service area of the destination if the destination institution was the nearest appropriate facility. |
| (c) Hospital to hospital or skilled nursing facility to skilled nursing facility. | (c) Condition met if the discharging institution was not an appropriate facility and the admitting institution was the nearest appropriate facility. |

| Conditions | Review Action |
|---|---|
| (d) From a hospital or skilled nursing facility to patient's residence. | (d)<br>(i) Condition met if patient's residence is within the institution's service area as shown in the carrier's locality guide.<br>(ii) Condition met where the patient's residence is outside the institution's service area if the institution was the nearest appropriate facility. |
| (e) Round trip for hospital or participating skilled nursing facility inpatients to the nearest hospital or nonhospital treatment facility. | (e) Condition met if the reasonable and necessary diagnostic or therapeutic service required by patient's condition is not available at the institution where the beneficiary is an inpatient. |

NOTE: Ambulance service to a physician's office or a physician-directed clinic is not covered. See §10.3.7 above, where a stop is made at a physician's office en route to a hospital and §10.3.3 for additional exceptions.)

| Conditions | Review Action |
|---|---|
| 4. Ambulance services involving hospital admissions in Canada or Mexico are covered (Medicare Claims Processing Manual, Chapter 1, "General Billing Requirements, " §§10.1.3.) if the following conditions are met: | (a) The foreign hospitalization has been determined to be covered; and<br>(b) The ambulance service meets the coverage requirements set forth in §§10-10.3. If the foreign hospitalization has been determined to be covered on the basis of emergency services (See the Medicare Claims Processing Manual, Chapter 1, "General Billing Requirements," §10.1.3), the necessity requirement (§10.2 ) and the destination requirement (§10.3 ) are considered met. |
| 5. The carrier will make partial payment for otherwise covered ambulance service, which exceeded limits defined in item | (a) From the pickup point to the nearest appropriate facility, or<br>(b) From the nearest appropriate facility to the beneficiary's residence where he or she is being returned home from a distant institution. |
| 6. The carrier will base the payment on the amount payable had the patient been transported: | |

## 100-2,13,30
### Rural Health Clinic and Federally Qualified Health Center Service Defined

Payments for covered RHC/FQHC services furnished to Medicare beneficiaries are made on the basis of an all-inclusive rate per covered visit (except for pneumococcal and influenza vaccines and their administration, which is paid at 100 percent of reasonable cost). The term "visit" is defined as a face-to-face encounter between the patient and a physician, physician assistant, nurse practitioner, certified nurse midwife, visiting nurse, clinical psychologist, or clinical social worker during which an RHC/FQHC service is rendered. As a result of section 5114 of the Deficit Reduction Act of 2005 (DRA), the FQHC definition of a face-to-face encounter is expanded to include encounters with qualified practitioners of Outpatient Diabetes Self-Management Training Services (DSMT) and medical nutrition therapy ( MNT) services when the FQHC meets all relevant program requirements for the provision of such services.

Encounters with (1) more than one health professional; and (2) multiple encounters with the same health professional which take place on the same day and at a single location, constitute a single visit. An exception occurs in cases in which the patient, subsequent to the first encounter, suffers an illness or injury requiring additional diagnosis or treatment.

## 100-2,15,100
### Surgical Dressings, Splints, Casts, and Other Devices Used for Reductions of Fractures and Dislocations
B3-2079, A3-3110.3, HO-228.3

Surgical dressings are limited to primary and secondary dressings required for the treatment of a wound caused by, or treated by, a surgical procedure that has been performed by a physician or other health care professional to the extent permissible under State law. In addition, surgical dressings required after debridement of a wound are also covered, irrespective of the type of debridement, as long as the debridement was reasonable and necessary and was performed by a health care professional acting within the scope of his/her legal authority when performing this function. Surgical dressings are covered for as long as they are medically necessary. Primary dressings are therapeutic or protective coverings applied directly to wounds or lesions either on the skin or caused by an opening to the skin. Secondary dressing materials that serve a therapeutic or protective function and that are needed to secure a primary dressing are also covered. Items such as adhesive tape, roll gauze, bandages, and disposable compression material are examples of secondary dressings. Elastic stockings, support hose, foot coverings, leotards, knee supports, surgical leggings, gauntlets, and pressure garments for the arms and hands are examples of items that are not ordinarily covered as surgical dressings. Some items, such as transparent film, may be used as a primary or secondary dressing. If a physician, certified nurse midwife, physician assistant, nurse practitioner, or clinical nurse specialist applies surgical dressings as part of a professional service that is billed to Medicare, the surgical dressings are considered incident to the professional services of the health care practitioner. (See Sec. 60.1, 180, 190, 200, and 210.) When surgical dressings are not covered incident to the services of a health care practitioner and are obtained by the patient from a supplier (e.g., a drugstore, physician, or other health care practitioner that qualifies as a supplier) on an order from a physician or other health care professional authorized under State law or regulation to make such an order, the surgical dressings are covered separately under Part B. Splints and casts, and other devices used for reductions of fractures and dislocations are covered under Part B of Medicare. This includes dental splints.

## 100-2,15,110
### Durable Medical Equipment - General
B3-2100, A3-3113, HO-235, HHA-220

Expenses incurred by a beneficiary for the rental or purchases of durable medical equipment (DME) are reimbursable if the following three requirements are met:

- The equipment meets the definition of DME (Sec.110.1);
- The equipment is necessary and reasonable for the treatment of the patient's illness or injury or to improve the functioning of his or her malformed body member (Sec.110.1); and
- The equipment is used in the patient's home. The decision whether to rent or purchase an item of equipment generally resides with the beneficiary, but the decision on how to pay rests with CMS. For some DME, program payment policy calls for lump sum payments and in others for periodic payment. Where covered DME is furnished to a beneficiary by a supplier of services other than a provider of services, the DMERC makes the reimbursement. If a provider of services furnishes the equipment, the intermediary makes the reimbursement. The payment method is identified in the annual fee schedule update furnished by CMS. The CMS issues quarterly updates to a fee schedule file that contains rates by HCPCS code and also identifies the classification of the HCPCS code within the following categories. Category Code Definition IN Inexpensive and Other Routinely Purchased Items FS Frequently Serviced Items CR Capped Rental Items OX Oxygen and Oxygen Equipment OS Ostomy, Tracheostomy & Urological Items SD Surgical Dressings PO Prosthetics & Orthotics SU Supplies TE Transcutaneous Electrical Nerve Stimulators The DMERCs, carriers, and intermediaries, where appropriate, use the CMS files to determine payment rules. See the Medicare Claims Processing Manual, Chapter 20, "Durable Medical Equipment, Surgical Dressings and Casts, Orthotics and Artificial Limbs, and Prosthetic Devices," for a detailed description of payment rules for each classification. Payment may also be made for repairs, maintenance, and delivery of equipment and for expendable and nonreusable items essential to the effective use of the equipment subject to the conditions in Sec.110.2. See the Medicare Benefit Policy Manual, Chapter 11, "End Stage Renal Disease," for hemodialysis equipment and supplies.

## 100-2,15,110.1
### Definition of Durable Medical Equipment
B3-2100.1, A3-3113.1, HO-235.1, HHA-220.1, B3-2100.2, A3-3113.2, HO-235.2, HHA-220.2

- Durable medical equipment is equipment which:
- Can withstand repeated use;
- Is primarily and customarily used to serve a medical purpose;
- Generally is not useful to a person in the absence of an illness or injury; and
- Is appropriate for use in the home.

All requirements of the definition must be met before an item can be considered to be durable medical equipment. The following describes the underlying policies for determining whether an item meets the definition of DME and may be covered.

## A. Durability

An item is considered durable if it can withstand repeated use, i.e., the type of item that could normally be rented. Medical supplies of an expendable nature, such as incontinent pads, lambs wool pads, catheters, ace bandages, elastic stockings, surgical facemasks, irrigating kits, sheets, and bags are not considered "durable" within the meaning of the definition. There are other items that, although durable in nature, may fall into other coverage categories such as supplies, braces, prosthetic devices, artificial arms, legs, and eyes.

## B. Medical Equipment

Medical equipment is equipment primarily and customarily used for medical purposes and is not generally useful in the absence of illness or injury. In most instances, no development will be needed to determine whether a specific item of equipment is medical in nature. However, some cases will require development to determine whether the item constitutes medical equipment. This development would include the advice of local medical organizations (hospitals, medical schools, medical societies) and specialists in the field of physical medicine and rehabilitation. If the equipment is new on the market, it may be necessary, prior to seeking professional advice, to obtain information from the supplier or manufacturer explaining the design, purpose, effectiveness and method of using the equipment in the home as well as the results of any tests or clinical studies that have been conducted.

   1. Equipment Presumptively

     MedicalItems such as hospital beds, wheelchairs, hemodialysis equipment, iron lungs, respirators, intermittent positive pressure breathing machines, medical regulators, oxygen tents, crutches, canes, trapeze bars, walkers, inhalators, nebulizers, commodes, suction machines, and traction equipment presumptively constitute medical equipment. (Although hemodialysis equipment is covered as a prosthetic device (Sec.120), it also meets the definition of DME, and reimbursement for the rental or purchase of such equipment for use in the beneficiary's home will be made only under the provisions for payment applicable to DME. See the Medicare Benefit Policy Manual, Chapter 11, "End Stage Renal Disease," Sec.30.1, for coverage of home use of hemodialysis.) NOTE: There is a wide variety in types of respirators and suction machines. The DMERC's medical staff should determine whether the apparatus specified in the claim is appropriate for home use.

   2. Equipment Presumptively Nonmedical

     Equipment which is primarily and customarily used for a nonmedical purpose may not be considered "medical" equipment for which payment can be made under the medical insurance program. This is true even though the item has some remote medically related use. For example, in the case of a cardiac patient, an air conditioner might possibly be used to lower room temperature to reduce fluid loss in the patient and to restore an environment conducive to maintenance of the proper fluid balance. Nevertheless, because the primary and customary use of an air conditioner is a nonmedical one, the air conditioner cannot be deemed to be medical equipment for which payment can be made. Other devices and equipment used

for environmental control or to enhance the environmental setting in which the beneficiary is placed are not considered covered DME. These include, for example, room heaters, humidifiers, dehumidifiers, and electric air cleaners. Equipment which basically serves comfort or convenience functions or is primarily for the convenience of a person caring for the patient, such as elevators, stairway elevators, and posture chairs, do not constitute medical equipment. Similarly, physical fitness equipment (such as an exercycle), first-aid or precautionary-type equipment (such as preset portable oxygen units), self-help devices (such as safety grab bars), and training equipment (such as Braille training texts) are considered nonmedical in nature.

   3. Special Exception Items

     Specified items of equipment may be covered under certain conditions even though they do not meet the definition of DME because they are not primarily and customarily used to serve a medical purpose and/or are generally useful in the absence of illness or injury. These items would be covered when it is clearly established that they serve a therapeutic purpose in an individual case and would include:

     a. Gel pads and pressure and water mattresses (which generally serve a preventive purpose) when prescribed for a patient who had bed sores or there is medical evidence indicating that they are highly susceptible to such ulceration; and

     b. Heat lamps for a medical rather than a soothing or cosmetic purpose, e.g., where the need for heat therapy has been established.

In establishing medical necessity for the above items, the evidence must show that the item is included in the physician's course of treatment and a physician is supervising its use.

NOTE: The above items represent special exceptions and no extension of coverage to other items should be inferred

## C. Necessary and Reasonable

Although an item may be classified as DME, it may not be covered in every instance. Coverage in a particular case is subject to the requirement that the equipment be necessary and reasonable for treatment of an illness or injury, or to improve the functioning of a malformed body member. These considerations will bar payment for equipment which cannot reasonably be expected to perform a therapeutic function in an individual case or will permit only partial therapeutic function in an individual case or will permit only partial payment when the type of equipment furnished substantially exceeds that required for the treatment of the illness or injury involved. See the Medicare Claims Processing Manual, Chapter 1, "General Billing Requirements;" Sec.60, regarding the rules for providing advance beneficiary notices (ABNs) that advise beneficiaries, before items or services actually are furnished, when Medicare is likely to deny payment for them. ABNs allow beneficiaries to make an informed consumer decision about receiving items or services for which they may have to pay out-of-pocket and to be more active participants in their own health care treatment decisions.

   1. Necessity for the Equipment

     Equipment is necessary when it can be expected to make a meaningful contribution to the treatment of the patient's illness or injury or to the improvement of his or her malformed body member. In most cases the physician's prescription for the equipment and other medical information available to the DMERC will be sufficient to establish that the equipment serves this purpose.

2. Reasonableness of the Equipment
Even though an item of DME may serve a useful medical purpose, the DMERC or intermediary must also consider to what extent, if any, it would be reasonable for the Medicare program to pay for the item prescribed. The following considerations should enter into the determination of reasonableness:

1. Would the expense of the item to the program be clearly disproportionate to the therapeutic benefits which could ordinarily be derived from use of the equipment?

2. Is the item substantially more costly than a medically appropriate and realistically feasible alternative pattern of care?

3. Does the item serve essentially the same purpose as equipment already available to the beneficiary?

3. Payment Consistent With What is Necessary and Reasonable
Where a claim is filed for equipment containing features of an aesthetic nature or features of a medical nature which are not required by the patient's condition or where there exists a reasonably feasible and medically appropriate alternative pattern of care which is less costly than the equipment furnished, the amount payable is based on the rate for the equipment or alternative treatment which meets the patient's medical needs. The acceptance of an assignment binds the supplier-assignee to accept the payment for the medically required equipment or service as the full charge and the supplier-assignee cannot charge the beneficiary the differential attributable to the equipment actually furnished.

4. Establishing the Period of Medical Necessity
Generally, the period of time an item of durable medical equipment will be considered to be medically necessary is based on the physician's estimate of the time that his or her patient will need the equipment. See the Medicare Program Integrity Manual, Chapters 5 and 6, for medical review guideline

### D. Definition of a Beneficiary's Home
For purposes of rental and purchase of DME a beneficiary's home may be his/her own dwelling, an apartment, a relative's home, a home for the aged, or some other type of institution. However, an institution may not be considered a beneficiary's home if it:

- Meets at least the basic requirement in the definition of a hospital, i.e., it is primarily engaged in providing by or under the supervision of physicians, to inpatients, diagnostic and therapeutic services for medical diagnosis, treatment, and care of injured, disabled, and sick persons, or rehabilitation services for the rehabilitation of injured, disabled, or sick persons; or

- Meets at least the basic requirement in the definition of a skilled nursing facility, i.e., it is primarily engaged in providing to inpatients skilled nursing care and related services for patients who require medical or nursing care, or rehabilitation services for the rehabilitation of injured, disabled, or sick persons.

Thus, if an individual is a patient in an institution or distinct part of an institution which provides the services described in the bullets above, the individual is not entitled to have separate Part B payment made for rental or purchase of DME. This is because

such an institution may not be considered the individual's home. The same concept applies even if the patient resides in a bed or portion of the institution not certified for Medicare.

If the patient is at home for part of a month and, for part of the same month is in an institution that cannot qualify as his or her home, or is outside the U.S., monthly payments may be made for the entire month. Similarly, if DME is returned to the provider before the end of a payment month because the beneficiary died in that month or because the equipment became unnecessary in that month, payment may be made for the entire month.

## 100-2,15,110.2
### Repairs, Maintenance, Replacement, and Delivery
Under the circumstances specified below, payment may be made for repair, maintenance, and replacement of medically required DME, including equipment which had been in use before the user enrolled in Part B of the program. However, do not pay for repair, maintenance, or replacement of equipment in the frequent and substantial servicing or oxygen equipment payment categories. In addition, payments for repair and maintenance may not include payment for parts and labor covered under a manufacturer's or supplier's warranty.

### A. Repairs
To repair means to fix or mend and to put the equipment back in good condition after damage or wear. Repairs to equipment which a beneficiary owns are covered when necessary to make the equipment serviceable. However, do not pay for repair of previously denied equipment or equipment in the frequent and substantial servicing or oxygen equipment payment categories. If the expense for repairs exceeds the estimated expense of purchasing or renting another item of equipment for the remaining period of medical need, no payment can be made for the amount of the excess. (See subsection C where claims for repairs suggest malicious damage or culpable neglect.) Since renters of equipment recover from the rental charge the expenses they incur in maintaining in working order the equipment they rent out, separately itemized charges for repair of rented equipment are not covered. This includes items in the frequent and substantial servicing, oxygen equipment, capped rental, and inexpensive or routinely purchased payment categories which are being rented. A new Certificate of Medical Necessity (CMN) and/or physician's order is not needed for repairs. For replacement items, see Subsection C below.

### B. Maintenance
Routine periodic servicing, such as testing, cleaning, regulating, and checking of the beneficiary's equipment, is not covered. The owner is expected to perform such routine maintenance rather than a retailer or some other person who charges the beneficiary. Normally, purchasers of DME are given operating manuals which describe the type of servicing an owner may perform to properly maintain the equipment. It is reasonable to expect that beneficiaries will perform this maintenance. Thus, hiring a third party to do such work is for the convenience of the beneficiary and is not covered. However, more extensive maintenance which, based on the manufacturers' recommendations, is to be performed by authorized technicians, is covered as repairs for medically necessary equipment which a beneficiary owns. This might include, for example, breaking down sealed components and performing tests which require specialized testing equipment not available to the beneficiary. Do not pay for maintenance of purchased items that require frequent and substantial servicing or oxygen equipment. Since renters of equipment recover from the rental charge the expenses they incur in maintaining in working order the

equipment they rent out, separately itemized charges for maintenance of rented equipment are generally not covered. Payment may not be made for maintenance of rented equipment other than the maintenance and servicing fee established for capped rental items. For capped rental items which have reached the 15-month rental cap, contractors pay claims for maintenance and servicing fees after 6 months have passed from the end of the final paid rental month or from the end of the period the item is no longer covered under the supplier's or manufacturer's warranty, whichever is later. See the Medicare Claims Processing Manual, Chapter 20, "Durable Medical Equipment, Prosthetics and Orthotics, and Supplies (DMEPOS)," for additional instruction and an example. A new CMN and/or physician's order is not needed for covered maintenance.

### C. Replacement
Replacement refers to the provision of an identical or nearly identical item. Situations involving the provision of a different item because of a change in medical condition are not addressed in this section.

Equipment which the beneficiary owns or is a capped rental item may be replaced in cases of loss or irreparable damage. Irreparable damage refers to a specific accident or to a natural disaster (e.g., fire, flood). A physician's order and/or new Certificate of Medical Necessity (CMN), when required, is needed to reaffirm the medical necessity of the item.

Irreparable wear refers to deterioration sustained from day-to-day usage over time and a specific event cannot be identified. Replacement of equipment due to irreparable wear takes into consideration the reasonable useful lifetime of the equipment. If the item of equipment has been in continuous use by the patient on either a rental or purchase basis for the equipment's useful lifetime, the beneficiary may elect to obtain a new piece of equipment. Replacement may be reimbursed when a new physician order and/or new CMN, when required, is needed to reaffirm the medical necessity of the item.

The reasonable useful lifetime of durable medical equipment is determined through program instructions. In the absence of program instructions, carriers may determine the reasonable useful lifetime of equipment, but in no case can it be less than 5 years. Computation of the useful lifetime is based on when the equipment is delivered to the beneficiary, not the age of the equipment. Replacement due to wear is not covered during the reasonable useful lifetime of the equipment. During the reasonable useful lifetime, Medicare does cover repair up to the cost of replacement (but not actual replacement) for medically necessary equipment owned by the beneficiary. (See subsection A.)

Charges for the replacement of oxygen equipment, items that require frequent and substantial servicing or inexpensive or routinely purchased items which are being rented are not covered. Cases suggesting malicious damage, culpable neglect, or wrongful disposition of equipment should be investigated and denied where the DMERC determines that it is unreasonable to make program payment under the circumstances. DMERCs refer such cases to the program integrity specialist in the RO.

### D. Delivery
Payment for delivery of DME whether rented or purchased is generally included in the fee schedule allowance for the item. See Pub. 100-04, Medicare Claims Processing Manual, Chapter 20, "Durable Medical Equipment, Prosthetics and Orthotics, and Supplies (DMEPOS)," for the rules that apply to making reimbursement for exceptional cases.

### 100-2,15,110.3
#### Coverage of Supplies and Accessories
B3-2100.5, A3-3113.4, HO-235.4, HHA-220.5 B3-2100.5, A3-3113.4, HO-235.4, HHA-220.5

Payment may be made for supplies, e.g., oxygen, that are necessary for the effective use of durable medical equipment. Such supplies include those drugs and biologicals which must be put directly into the equipment in order to achieve the therapeutic benefit of the durable medical equipment or to assure the proper functioning of the equipment, e.g., tumor chemotherapy agents used with an infusion pump or heparin used with a home dialysis system. However, the coverage of such drugs or biologicals does not preclude the need for a determination that the drug or biological itself is reasonable and necessary for treatment of the illness or injury or to improve the functioning of a malformed body member. In the case of prescription drugs, other than oxygen, used in conjunction with durable medical equipment, prosthetic, orthotics, and supplies (DMEPOS) or prosthetic devices, the entity that dispenses the drug must furnish it directly to the patient for whom a prescription is written. The entity that dispenses the drugs must have a Medicare supplier number, must possess a current license to dispense prescription drugs in the State in which the drug is dispensed, and must bill and receive payment in its own name. A supplier that is not the entity that dispenses the drugs cannot purchase the drugs used in conjunction with DME for resale to the beneficiary. Reimbursement may be made for replacement of essential accessories such as hoses, tubes, mouthpieces, etc., for necessary DME, only if the beneficiary owns or is purchasing the equipment. Payment may be made for supplies, e.g., oxygen, that are necessary for the effective use of durable medical equipment. Such supplies include those drugs and biologicals which must be put directly into the equipment in order to achieve the therapeutic benefit of the durable medical equipment or to assure the proper functioning of the equipment, e.g., tumor chemotherapy agents used with an infusion pump or heparin used with a home dialysis system. However, the coverage of such drugs or biologicals does not preclude the need for a determination that the drug or biological itself is reasonable and necessary for treatment of the illness or injury or to improve the functioning of a malformed body member. In the case of prescription drugs, other than oxygen, used in conjunction with durable medical equipment, prosthetic, orthotics, and supplies (DMEPOS) or prosthetic devices, the entity that dispenses the drug must furnish it directly to the patient for whom a prescription is written. The entity that dispenses the drugs must have a Medicare supplier number, must possess a current license to dispense prescription drugs in the State in which the drug is dispensed, and must bill and receive payment in its own name. A supplier that is not the entity that dispenses the drugs cannot purchase the drugs used in conjunction with DME for resale to the beneficiary. Reimbursement may be made for replacement of essential accessories such as hoses, tubes, mouthpieces, etc., for necessary DME, only if the beneficiary owns or is purchasing the equipment.

### 100-2,15,120
#### Prosthetic Devices
B3-2130, A3-3110.4, HO-228.4, A3-3111, HO-229

#### A. General
Prosthetic devices (other than dental) which replace all or part of an internal body organ (including contiguous tissue), or replace all or part of the function of a permanently inoperative or

malfunctioning internal body organ are covered when furnished on a physician's order. This does not require a determination that there is no possibility that the patient's condition may improve sometime in the future. If the medical record, including the judgment of the attending physician, indicates the condition is of long and indefinite duration, the test of permanence is considered met. (Such a device may also be covered under Sec.60.l as a supply when furnished incident to a physician's service.)

Examples of prosthetic devices include artificial limbs, parenteral and enteral (PEN) nutrition, cardiac pacemakers, prosthetic lenses (see subsection B), breast prostheses (including a surgical brassiere) for postmastectomy patients, maxillofacial devices, and devices which replace all or part of the ear or nose. A urinary collection and retention system with or without a tube is a prosthetic device replacing bladder function in case of permanent urinary incontinence. The foley catheter is also considered a prosthetic device when ordered for a patient with permanent urinary incontinence. However, chucks, diapers, rubber sheets, etc., are supplies that are not covered under this provision. Although hemodialysis equipment is a prosthetic device, payment for the rental or purchase of such equipment in the home is made only for use under the provisions for payment applicable to durable medical equipment.

An exception is that if payment cannot be made on an inpatient's behalf under Part A, hemodialysis equipment, supplies, and services required by such patient could be covered under Part B as a prosthetic device, which replaces the function of a kidney. See the Medicare Benefit Policy Manual, Chapter 11, "End Stage Renal Disease," for payment for hemodialysis equipment used in the home. See the Medicare Benefit Policy Manual, Chapter 1, "Inpatient Hospital Services," Sec.10, for additional instructions on hospitalization for renal dialysis.

NOTE: Medicare does not cover a prosthetic device dispensed to a patient prior to the time at which the patient undergoes the procedure that makes necessary the use of the device. For example, the carrier does not make a separate Part B payment for an intraocular lens (IOL) or pacemaker that a physician, during an office visit prior to the actual surgery, dispenses to the patient for his or her use. Dispensing a prosthetic device in this manner raises health and safety issues. Moreover, the need for the device cannot be clearly established until the procedure that makes its use possible is successfully performed. Therefore, dispensing a prosthetic device in this manner is not considered reasonable and necessary for the treatment of the patient's condition.

Colostomy (and other ostomy) bags and necessary accouterments required for attachment are covered as prosthetic devices. This coverage also includes irrigation and flushing equipment and other items and supplies directly related to ostomy care, whether the attachment of a bag is required.

Accessories and/or supplies which are used directly with an enteral or parenteral device to achieve the therapeutic benefit of the prosthesis or to assure the proper functioning of the device may also be covered under the prosthetic device benefit subject to the additional guidelines in the Medicare National Coverage Determinations Manual.

Covered items include catheters, filters, extension tubing, infusion bottles, pumps (either food or infusion), intravenous (I.V.) pole, needles, syringes, dressings, tape, Heparin Sodium (parenteral only), volumetric monitors (parenteral only), and parenteral and enteral nutrient solutions. Baby food and other regular grocery products that can be blenderized and used with the enteral system are not covered. Note that some of these items, e.g., a food pump and an I.V. pole, qualify as DME. Although coverage of the enteral and parenteral nutritional therapy systems is provided on the basis of the prosthetic device benefit, the payment rules relating to lump sum or monthly payment for DME apply to such items.

The coverage of prosthetic devices includes replacement of and repairs to such devices as explained in subsection D.

Finally, the Benefits Improvement and Protection Act of 2000 amended Sec.1834(h)(1) of the Act by adding a provision (1834 (h)(1)(G)(i)) that requires Medicare payment to be made for the replacement of prosthetic devices which are artificial limbs, or for the replacement of any part of such devices, without regard to continuous use or useful lifetime restrictions if an ordering physician determines that the replacement device, or replacement part of such a device, is necessary.

Payment may be made for the replacement of a prosthetic device that is an artificial limb, or replacement part of a device if the ordering physician determines that the replacement device or part is necessary because of any of the following:

1. A change in the physiological condition of the patient;

2. An irreparable change in the condition of the device, or in a part of the device; or

3. The condition of the device, or the part of the device, requires repairs and the cost of such repairs would be more than 60 percent of the cost of a replacement device, or, as the case may be, of the part being replaced.

This provision is effective for items replaced on or after April 1, 2001. It supersedes any rule that that provided a 5-year or other replacement rule with regard to prosthetic devices.

### B. Prosthetic Lenses

The term "internal body organ" includes the lens of an eye. Prostheses replacing the lens of an eye include post-surgical lenses customarily used during convalescence from eye surgery in which the lens of the eye was removed. In addition, permanent lenses are also covered when required by an individual lacking the organic lens of the eye because of surgical removal or congenital absence. Prosthetic lenses obtained on or after the beneficiary's date of entitlement to supplementary medical insurance benefits may be covered even though the surgical removal of the crystalline lens occurred before entitlement.

1. Prosthetic Cataract Lenses
   One of the following prosthetic lenses or combinations of prosthetic lenses furnished by a physician (see Sec.30.4 for coverage of prosthetic lenses prescribed by a doctor of optometry) may be covered when determined to be reasonable and necessary to restore essentially the vision provided by the crystalline lens of the eye:

• Prosthetic bifocal lenses in frames;

• Prosthetic lenses in frames for far vision, and prosthetic lenses in frames for near vision; or

• When a prosthetic contact lens(es) for far vision is prescribed (including cases of binocular and monocular aphakia), make payment for the contact lens(es) and prosthetic lenses in frames for near vision to be worn at the same time as the contact lens(es), and prosthetic lenses in frames to be worn when the contacts have been removed.

Lenses which have ultraviolet absorbing or reflecting properties may be covered, in lieu of payment for regular (untinted) lenses, if it has been determined that such lenses are medically reasonable and necessary for the individual patient. Medicare does not cover cataract sunglasses obtained in addition to the regular (untinted) prosthetic lenses since the sunglasses duplicate the restoration of vision function performed by the regular prosthetic lenses.

2. Payment for Intraocular Lenses (IOLs) Furnished in Ambulatory Surgical Centers (ASCs) Effective for services furnished on or after March 12, 1990, payment for intraocular lenses (IOLs) inserted during or subsequent to cataract surgery in a Medicare certified ASC is included with the payment for facility services that are furnished in connection with the covered surgery. Refer to the Medicare Claims Processing Manual, Chapter 14, "Ambulatory Surgical Centers," for more information.

3. Limitation on Coverage of Conventional Lenses One pair of conventional eyeglasses or conventional contact lenses furnished after each cataract surgery with insertion of an IOL is covered.

### C. Dentures
Dentures are excluded from coverage. However, when a denture or a portion of the denture is an integral part (built-in) of a covered prosthesis (e.g., an obturator to fill an opening in the palate), it is covered as part of that prosthesis.

### D. Supplies, Repairs, Adjustments, and Replacement
Supplies are covered that are necessary for the effective use of a prosthetic device (e.g., the batteries needed to operate an artificial larynx). Adjustment of prosthetic devices required by wear or by a change in the patient's condition is covered when ordered by a physician. General provisions relating to the repair and replacement of durable medical equipment in Sec.110.2 for the repair and replacement of prosthetic devices are applicable. (See the Medicare Benefit Policy Manual, Chapter 16, "General Exclusions from Coverage," Sec.40.4, for payment for devices replaced under a warranty.) Replacement of conventional eyeglasses or contact lenses furnished in accordance with Sec.120.B.3 is not covered. Necessary supplies, adjustments, repairs, and replacements are covered even when the device had been in use before the user enrolled in Part B of the program, so long as the device continues to be medically required.

## 100-2,15,130
### Leg, Arm, Back, and Neck Braces, Trusses, and Artificial Legs, Arms, and Eyes
B3-2133, A3-3110.5, HO-228.5, AB-01-06 dated 1/18/01

These appliances are covered under Part B when furnished incident to physicians' services or on a physician's order. A brace includes rigid and semi-rigid devices which are used for the purpose of supporting a weak or deformed body member or restricting or eliminating motion in a diseased or injured part of the body. Elastic stockings, garter belts, and similar devices do not come within the scope of the definition of a brace. Back braces include, but are not limited to, special corsets, e.g., sacroiliac, sacrolumbar, dorsolumbar corsets, and belts. A terminal device (e.g., hand or hook) is covered under this provision whether an artificial limb is required by the patient. Stump stockings and harnesses (including replacements) are also covered when these appliances are essential to the effective use of the artificial limb.

Adjustments to an artificial limb or other appliance required by wear or by a change in the patient's condition are covered when ordered by a physician.

Adjustments, repairs and replacements are covered even when the item had been in use before the user enrolled in Part B of the program so long as the device continues to be medically required.

## 100-2,15,140
### Therapeutic Shoes for Individuals with Diabetes
B3-2134

Coverage of therapeutic shoes (depth or custom-molded) along with inserts for individuals with diabetes is available as of May 1, 1993. These diabetic shoes are covered if the requirements as specified in this section concerning certification and prescription are fulfilled. In addition, this benefit provides for a pair of diabetic shoes even if only one foot suffers from diabetic foot disease. Each shoe is equally equipped so that the affected limb, as well as the remaining limb, is protected. Claims for therapeutic shoes for diabetics are processed by the Durable Medical Equipment Regional Carriers (DMERCs). Therapeutic shoes for diabetics are not DME and are not considered DME nor orthotics, but a separate category of coverage under Medicare Part B. (See Sec.1861(s)(12) and Sec.1833(o) of the Act.)

### A. Definitions
The following items may be covered under the diabetic shoe benefit:

1. Custom-Molded ShoesCustom-molded shoes are shoes that:

- Are constructed over a positive model of the patient's foot;
- Are made from leather or other suitable material of equal quality;
- Have removable inserts that can be altered or replaced as the patient's condition warrants; and
- Have some form of shoe closure.

2. Depth Shoes

Depth shoes are shoes that:

- Have a full length, heel-to-toe filler that, when removed, provides a minimum of 3/16 inch of additional depth used to accommodate custom-molded or customized inserts;
- Are made from leather or other suitable material of equal quality;
- Have some form of shoe closure; and
- Are available in full and half sizes with a minimum of three widths so that the sole is graded to the size and width of the upper portions of the shoes according to the American standard last sizing schedule or its equivalent. (The American standard last sizing schedule is the numerical shoe sizing system used for shoes sold in the United States.)

3. Inserts

Inserts are total contact, multiple density, removable inlays that are directly molded to the patient's foot or a model of the patient's foot and that are made of a suitable material with regard to the patient's condition.

# APPENDIX 4 — PUB 100 REFERENCES

## B. Coverage

1. Limitations

   For each individual, coverage of the footwear and inserts is limited to one of the following within one calendar year:

   - No more than one pair of custom-molded shoes (including inserts provided with such shoes) and two additional pairs of inserts; or

   - No more than one pair of depth shoes and three pairs of inserts (not including the noncustomized removable inserts provided with such shoes).

2. Coverage of Diabetic Shoes and Brace

   Orthopedic shoes, as stated in the Medicare Claims Processing Manual, Chapter 20, "Durable Medical Equipment, Surgical Dressings and Casts, Orthotics and Artificial Limbs, and Prosthetic Devices," generally are not covered. This exclusion does not apply to orthopedic shoes that are an integral part of a leg brace. In situations in which an individual qualifies for both diabetic shoes and a leg brace, these items are covered separately. Thus, the diabetic shoes may be covered if the requirements for this section are met, while the brace may be covered if the requirements of Sec.130 are met.

3. Substitution of Modifications for Inserts

   An individual may substitute modification(s) of custom-molded or depth shoes instead of obtaining a pair(s) of inserts in any combination. Payment for the modification(s) may not exceed the limit set for the inserts for which the individual is entitled. The following is a list of the most common shoe modifications available, but it is not meant as an exhaustive list of the modifications available for diabetic shoes:

Rigid Rocker Bottoms - These are exterior elevations with apex positions for 51 percent to 75 percent distance measured from the back end of the heel. The apex is a narrowed or pointed end of an anatomical structure. The apex must be positioned behind the metatarsal heads and tapered off sharply to the front tip of the sole. Apex height helps to eliminate pressure at the metatarsal heads. Rigidity is ensured by the steel in the shoe. The heel of the shoe tapers off in the back in order to cause the heel to strike in the middle of the heel;

   - Roller Bottoms (Sole or Bar) - These are the same as rocker bottoms, but the heel is tapered from the apex to the front tip of the sole;

   - Metatarsal Bars- An exterior bar is placed behind the metatarsal heads in order to remove pressure from the metatarsal heads. The bars are of various shapes, heights, and construction depending on the exact purpose;

   - Wedges (Posting) - Wedges are either of hind foot, fore foot, or both and may be in the middle or to the side. The function is to shift or transfer weight bearing upon standing or during ambulation to the opposite side for added support, stabilization, equalized weight distribution, or balance; and

   - Offset Heels- This is a heel flanged at its base either in the middle, to the side, or a combination, that is then extended upward to the shoe in order to stabilize extreme positions of the hind foot. Other modifications to diabetic shoes include, but are not limited to, flared heels, Velcro closures, and inserts for missing toes.

4. Separate Inserts Inserts may be covered and dispensed independently of diabetic shoes if the supplier of the shoes verifies in writing that the patient has appropriate footwear into which the insert can be placed. This footwear must meet the definitions found above for depth shoes and custom-molded shoes.

## C. Certification

The need for diabetic shoes must be certified by a physician who is a doctor of medicine or a doctor of osteopathy and who is responsible for diagnosing and treating the patient's diabetic systemic condition through a comprehensive plan of care. This managing physician must:

   - Document in the patient's medical record that the patient has diabetes;

   - Certify that the patient is being treated under a comprehensive plan of care for diabetes, and that the patient needs diabetic shoes; and

   - Document in the patient's record that the patient has one or more of the following conditions:

   - Peripheral neuropathy with evidence of callus formation;
     - History of pre-ulcerative calluses;
     - History of previous ulceration;
     - Foot deformity;
     - Previous amputation of the foot or part of the foot; or
     - Poor circulation.

## D. Prescription

Following certification by the physician managing the patient's systemic diabetic condition, a podiatrist or other qualified physician who is knowledgeable in the fitting of diabetic shoes and inserts may prescribe the particular type of footwear necessary.

## E. Furnishing

Footwear The footwear must be fitted and furnished by a podiatrist or other qualified individual such as a pedorthist, an orthotist, or a prosthetist. The certifying physician may not furnish the diabetic shoes unless the certifying physician is the only qualified individual in the area. It is left to the discretion of each carrier to determine the meaning of "in the area."

## *100-2,15,150*
## Dental Services
B3-2136

As indicated under the general exclusions from coverage, items and services in connection with the care, treatment, filling, removal, or replacement of teeth or structures directly supporting the teeth are not covered. "Structures directly supporting the teeth" means the periodontium, which includes the gingivae, dentogingival junction, periodontal membrane, cementum of the teeth, and alveolar process.

In addition to the following, see Pub 100-01, the Medicare General Information, Eligibility, and Entitlement Manual, Chapter 5, Definitions and Pub 3, the Medicare National Coverage Determinations Manual for specific services which may be covered when furnished by a dentist. If an otherwise noncovered procedure or service is performed by a dentist as incident to and as an integral part of a covered procedure or service performed by the dentist, the total service performed by the dentist on such an occasion is covered.

EXAMPLE 1: The reconstruction of a ridge performed primarily to prepare the mouth for dentures is a noncovered procedure. However, when the reconstruction of a ridge is performed as a result of and at the same time as the surgical removal of a tumor (for other than dental purposes), the totality of surgical procedures is a covered service.

Appendix 4 — Pub 100 References

EXAMPLE 2: Medicare makes payment for the wiring of teeth when this is done in connection with the reduction of a jaw fracture.

The extraction of teeth to prepare the jaw for radiation treatment of neoplastic disease is also covered. This is an exception to the requirement that to be covered, a noncovered procedure or service performed by a dentist must be an incident to and an integral part of a covered procedure or service performed by the dentist. Ordinarily, the dentist extracts the patient's teeth, but another physician, e.g., a radiologist, administers the radiation treatments.

When an excluded service is the primary procedure involved, it is not covered, regardless of its complexity or difficulty. For example, the extraction of an impacted tooth is not covered. Similarly, an alveoplasty (the surgical improvement of the shape and condition of the alveolar process) and a frenectomy are excluded from coverage when either of these procedures is performed in connection with an excluded service, e.g., the preparation of the mouth for dentures. In a like manner, the removal of a torus palatinus (a bony protuberance of the hard palate) may be a covered service. However, with rare exception, this surgery is performed in connection with an excluded service, i.e., the preparation of the mouth for dentures. Under such circumstances, Medicare does not pay for this procedure.

Dental splints used to treat a dental condition are excluded from coverage under 1862(a)(12) of the Act. On the other hand, if the treatment is determined to be a covered medical condition (i.e., dislocated upper/lower jaw joints), then the splint can be covered.

Whether such services as the administration of anesthesia, diagnostic x-rays, and other related procedures are covered depends upon whether the primary procedure being performed by the dentist is itself covered. Thus, an x-ray taken in connection with the reduction of a fracture of the jaw or facial bone is covered. However, a single x-ray or x-ray survey taken in connection with the care or treatment of teeth or the periodontium is not covered.

Medicare makes payment for a covered dental procedure no matter where the service is performed. The hospitalization or nonhospitalization of a patient has no direct bearing on the coverage or exclusion of a given dental procedure.

Payment may also be made for services and supplies furnished incident to covered dental services. For example, the services of a dental technician or nurse who is under the direct supervision of the dentist or physician are covered if the services are included in the dentist's or physician's bill.

## 100-2,15,230

### Practice of Physical Therapy, Occupational Therapy, and Speech-Language Pathology

**A. Group Therapy Services.**
Contractors pay for outpatient physical therapy services (which includes outpatient speech-language pathology services) and outpatient occupational therapy services provided simultaneously to two or more individuals by a practitioner as group therapy services (97150). The individuals can be, but need not be performing the same activity. The physician or therapist involved in group therapy services must be in constant attendance, but one-on-one patient contact is not required.

**B. Therapy Students**
1. General
Only the services of the therapist can be billed and paid under Medicare Part B. The services performed by a

student are not reimbursed even if provided under "line of sight" supervision of the therapist; however, the presence of the student "in the room" does not make the service unbillable. Pay for the direct (one-to-one) patient contact services of the physician or therapist provided to Medicare Part B patients. Group therapy services performed by a therapist or physician may be billed when a student is also present "in the room".

EXAMPLES:

Therapists may bill and be paid for the provision of services in the following scenarios:

- The qualified practitioner is present and in the room for the entire session. The student participates in the delivery of services when the qualified practitioner is directing the service, making the skilled judgment, and is responsible for the assessment and treatment.

- The qualified practitioner is present in the room guiding the student in service delivery when the therapy student and the therapy assistant student are participating in the provision of services, and the practitioner is not engaged in treating another patient or doing other tasks at the same time

- The qualified practitioner is responsible for the services and as such, signs all documentation. (A student may, of course, also sign but it is not necessary since the Part B payment is for the clinician's service, not for the student's services).

2. Therapy Assistants as Clinical Instructors
Physical therapist assistants and occupational therapy assistants are not precluded from serving as clinical instructors for therapy students, while providing services within their scope of work and performed under the direction and supervision of a licensed physical or occupational therapist to a Medicare beneficiary.

3. Services Provided Under Part A and Part B
The payment methodologies for Part A and B therapy services rendered by a student are different. Under the MPFS (Medicare Part B), Medicare pays for services provided by physicians and practitioners that are specifically authorized by statute. Students do not meet the definition of practitioners under Medicare Part B. Under SNF PPS, payments are based upon the case mix or Resource Utilization Group (RUG) category that describes the patient. In the rehabilitation groups, the number of therapy minutes delivered to the patient determines the RUG category. Payment levels for each category are based upon the costs of caring for patients in each group rather than providing pecific payment for each therapy service as is done in Medicare Part B.

## 100-2,15,280.1

### Glaucoma Screening

**A. Conditions of Coverage**
The regulations implementing the Benefits Improvements and Protection Act of 2000, Sec.102, provide for annual coverage for glaucoma screening for beneficiaries in the following high risk categories:

- Individuals with diabetes mellitus;

- Individuals with a family history of glaucoma; or

- African-Americans age 50 and over. In addition, beginning with dates of service on or after January 1, 2006, 42 CFR

410.23(a)(2), revised, the definition of an eligible beneficiary in a high-risk category is expanded to include:

- Hispanic-Americans age 65 and over.

Medicare will pay for glaucoma screening examinations where they are furnished by or under the direct supervision in the office setting of an ophthalmologist or optometrist, who is legally authorized to perform the services under State law. Screening for glaucoma is defined to include:

- A dilated eye examination with an intraocular pressure measurement; and

- A direct ophthalmoscopy examination, or a slit-lamp biomicroscopic examination.

Payment may be made for a glaucoma screening examination that is performed on an eligible beneficiary after at least 11 months have passed following the month in which the last covered glaucoma screening examination was performed.

The following HCPCS codes apply for glaucoma screening:

G0117   Glaucoma screening for high-risk patients furnished by an optometrist or ophthalmologist; and

G0118   Glaucoma screening for high-risk patients furnished under the direct supervision of an optometrist or ophthalmologist.

The type of service for the above G codes is: TOS Q.

For providers who bill intermediaries, applicable types of bill for screening glaucoma services are 13X, 22X, 23X, 71X, 73X, 75X, and 85X. The following revenue codes should be reported when billing for screening glaucoma services:

- Comprehensive outpatient rehabilitation facilities (CORFs), critical access hospitals (CAHs), skilled nursing facilities (SNFs), independent and provider-based RHCs and free standing and provider-based FQHCs bill for this service under revenue code 770. CAHs electing the optional method of payment for outpatient services report this service under revenue codes 96X, 97X, or 98X.

- Hospital outpatient departments bill for this service under any valid/appropriate revenue code. They are not required to report revenue code 770.

### B. Calculating the Frequency
Once a beneficiary has received a covered glaucoma screening procedure, the beneficiary may receive another procedure after 11 full months have passed. To determine the 11-month period, start the count beginning with the month after the month in which the previous covered screening procedure was performed.

### C. Diagnosis Coding Requirements
Providers bill glaucoma screening using screening ("V") code V80.1 (Special Screening for Neurological, Eye, and Ear Diseases, Glaucoma). Claims submitted without a screening diagnosis code may be returned to the provider as unprocessable.

### D. Payment Methodology
1. Carriers
   Contractors pay for glaucoma screening based on the Medicare physician fee schedule. Deductible and coinsurance apply. Claims from physicians or other providers where assignment was not taken are subject to the Medicare limiting charge (refer to the Medicare Claims Processing Manual, Chapter 12, "Physician/Non-physician Practitioners," for more information about the Medicare limiting charge).

2. Intermediaries
   Payment is made for the facility expense as follows:

- Independent and provider-based RHC/free standing and provider-based FQHC - payment is made under the all inclusive rate for the screening glaucoma service based on the visit furnished to the RHC/FQHC patient;

- CAH - payment is made on a reasonable cost basis unless the CAH has elected the optional method of payment for outpatient services in which case, procedures outlined in the Medicare Claims Processing Manual, Chapter 3, Sec.30.1.1, should be followed;

- CORF - payment is made under the Medicare physician fee schedule;

- Hospital outpatient department - payment is made under outpatient prospective payment system (OPPS);

- Hospital inpatient Part B - payment is made under OPPS;

- SNF outpatient - payment is made under the Medicare physician fee schedule (MPFS); and

- SNF inpatient Part B - payment is made under MPFS. Deductible and coinsurance apply.

### E. Special Billing Instructions for RHCs and FQHCs
Screening glaucoma services are considered RHC/FQHC services. RHCs and FQHCs bill the contractor under bill type 71X or 73X along with revenue code 770 and HCPCS codes G0117 or G0118 and RHC/FQHC revenue code 520 or 521 to report the related visit. Reporting of revenue code 770 and HCPCS codes G0117 and G0118 in addition to revenue code 520 or 521 is required for this service in order for CWF to perform frequency editing.

Payment should not be made for a screening glaucoma service unless the claim also contains a visit code for the service. Therefore, the contractor installs an edit in its system to assure payment is not made for revenue code 770 unless the claim also contains a visit revenue code (520 or 521).

## 100-2,15,290
### Foot Care

### A. Treatment of Subluxation of Foot
Subluxations of the foot are defined as partial dislocations or displacements of joint surfaces, tendons ligaments, or muscles of the foot. Surgical or nonsurgical treatments undertaken for the sole purpose of correcting a subluxated structure in the foot as an isolated entity are not covered.

However, medical or surgical treatment of subluxation of the ankle joint (talo-crural joint) is covered. In addition, reasonable and necessary medical or surgical services, diagnosis, or treatment for medical conditions that have resulted from or are associated with partial displacement of structures is covered. For example, if a patient has osteoarthritis that has resulted in a partial displacement of joints in the foot, and the primary treatment is for the osteoarthritis, coverage is provided.

### B. Exclusions from Coverage
The following foot care services are generally excluded from coverage under both Part A and Part B. (See Sec.290.F and Sec.290.G for instructions on applying foot care exclusions.)

1. Treatment of Flat Foot
   The term "flat foot" is defined as a condition in which one or more arches of the foot have flattened out. Services or devices directed toward the care or correction of such conditions, including the prescription of supportive devices, are not covered.

2. Routine Foot Care

Except as provided above, routine foot care is excluded from coverage. Services that normally are considered routine and not covered by Medicare include the following:

- The cutting or removal of corns and calluses;

- The trimming, cutting, clipping, or debriding of nails; and

- Other hygienic and preventive maintenance care, such as cleaning and soaking the feet, the use of skin creams to maintain skin tone of either ambulatory or bedfast patients, and any other service performed in the absence of localized illness, injury, or symptoms involving the foot.

3. Supportive Devices for Feet

Orthopedic shoes and other supportive devices for the feet generally are not covered. However, this exclusion does not apply to such a shoe if it is an integral part of a leg brace, and its expense is included as part of the cost of the brace. Also, this exclusion does not apply to therapeutic shoes furnished to diabetics.

### C. Exceptions to Routine Foot Care Exclusion

1. Necessary and Integral Part of Otherwise Covered Services

In certain circumstances, services ordinarily considered to be routine may be covered if they are performed as a necessary and integral part of otherwise covered services, such as diagnosis and treatment of ulcers, wounds, or infections.

2. Treatment of Warts on Foot

The treatment of warts (including plantar warts) on the foot is covered to the same extent as services provided for the treatment of warts located elsewhere on the body.

3. Presence of Systemic Condition

The presence of a systemic condition such as metabolic, neurologic, or peripheral vascular disease may require scrupulous foot care by a professional that in the absence of such condition(s) would be considered routine (and, therefore, excluded from coverage). Accordingly, foot care that would otherwise be considered routine may be covered when systemic condition(s) result in severe circulatory embarrassment or areas of diminished sensation in the individual's legs or feet. (See subsection A.)

In these instances, certain foot care procedures that otherwise are considered routine (e.g., cutting or removing corns and calluses, or trimming, cutting, clipping, or debriding nails) may pose a hazard when performed by a nonprofessional person on patients with such systemic conditions. (See Sec.290.G for procedural instructions.)

4. Mycotic Nails

In the absence of a systemic condition, treatment of mycotic nails may be covered.

The treatment of mycotic nails for an ambulatory patient is covered only when the physician attending the patient's mycotic condition documents that (1) there is clinical evidence of mycosis of the toenail, and (2) the patient has marked limitation of ambulation, pain, or secondary infection resulting from the thickening and dystrophy of the infected toenail plate.

The treatment of mycotic nails for a nonambulatory patient is covered only when the physician attending the patient's mycotic condition documents that (1) there is clinical evidence of mycosis of the toenail, and (2) the patient suffers from pain or secondary infection resulting from the thickening and dystrophy of the infected toenail plate.

For the purpose of these requirements, documentation means any written information that is required by the carrier in order for services to be covered. Thus, the information submitted with claims must be substantiated by information found in the patient's medical record. Any information, including that contained in a form letter, used for documentation purposes is subject to carrier verification in order to ensure that the information adequately justifies coverage of the treatment of mycotic nails.

### D. Systemic Conditions That Might Justify Coverage

Although not intended as a comprehensive list, the following metabolic, neurologic, and peripheral vascular diseases (with synonyms in parentheses) most commonly represent the underlying conditions that might justify coverage for routine foot care.

- Diabetes mellitus *
- Arteriosclerosis obliterans (A.S.O., arteriosclerosis of the extremities, occlusive peripheral arteriosclerosis)
- Buerger's disease (thromboangiitis obliterans)
- Chronic thrombophlebitis *
- Peripheral neuropathies involving the feet -
- Associated with malnutrition and vitamin deficiency *
  - Malnutrition (general, pellagra)
  - Alcoholism
  - Malabsorption (celiac disease, tropical sprue)
  - Pernicious anemia
- Associated with carcinoma *
- Associated with diabetes mellitus *
- Associated with drugs and toxins *
- Associated with multiple sclerosis *
- Associated with uremia (chronic renal disease) *
- Associated with traumatic injury
- Associated with leprosy or neurosyphilis
- Associated with hereditary disorders
- Hereditary sensory radicular neuropathy
- Angiokeratoma corporis diffusum (Fabry's)
- Amyloid neuropathy

When the patient's condition is one of those designated by an asterisk (*), routine procedures are covered only if the patient is under the active care of a doctor of medicine or osteopathy who documents the condition.

### E. Supportive Devices for Feet

Orthopedic shoes and other supportive devices for the feet generally are not covered. However, this exclusion does not apply to such a shoe if it is an integral part of a leg brace, and its expense is included as part of the cost of the brace. Also, this exclusion does not apply to therapeutic shoes furnished to diabetics.

### F. Presumption of Coverage

In evaluating whether the routine services can be reimbursed, a presumption of coverage may be made where the evidence available discloses certain physical and/or clinical findings consistent with the diagnosis and indicative of severe peripheral involvement. For purposes of applying this presumption the following findings are pertinent:

Class A Findings
    Nontraumatic amputation of foot or integral skeletal portion thereof.

Class B Findings
    Absent posterior tibial pulse;

    Advanced trophic changes as: hair growth (decrease or absence) nail changes (thickening) pigmentary changes (discoloration) skin texture (thin, shiny) skin color (rubor or redness) (Three required); and

Absent dorsalis pedis pulse.

Class C Findings
    Claudication;

    Temperature changes (e.g., cold feet);

    Edema;

    Paresthesias (abnormal spontaneous sensations in the feet); and

    Burning.

The presumption of coverage may be applied when the physician rendering the routine foot care has identified:

1. A Class A finding;

2. Two of the Class B findings; or

3. One Class B and two Class C findings.

Cases evidencing findings falling short of these alternatives may involve podiatric treatment that may constitute covered care and should be reviewed by the intermediary's medical staff and developed as necessary.

For purposes of applying the coverage presumption where the routine services have been rendered by a podiatrist, the contractor may deem the active care requirement met if the claim or other evidence available discloses that the patient has seen an M.D. or D.O. for treatment and/or evaluation of the complicating disease process during the 6-month period prior to the rendition of the routine-type services. The intermediary may also accept the podiatrist's statement that the diagnosing and treating M.D. or D.O. also concurs with the podiatrist's findings as to the severity of the peripheral involvement indicated.

Services ordinarily considered routine might also be covered if they are performed as a necessary and integral part of otherwise covered services, such as diagnosis and treatment of diabetic ulcers, wounds, and infections.

**G. Application of Foot Care Exclusions to Physician's Services**
The exclusion of foot care is determined by the nature of the service. Thus, payment for an excluded service should be denied whether performed by a podiatrist, osteopath, or a doctor of medicine, and without regard to the difficulty or complexity of the procedure.

When an itemized bill shows both covered services and noncovered services not integrally related to the covered service, the portion of charges attributable to the noncovered services should be denied. (For example, if an itemized bill shows surgery for an ingrown toenail and also removal of calluses not necessary for the performance of toe surgery, any additional charge attributable to removal of the calluses should be denied.)

In reviewing claims involving foot care, the carrier should be alert to the following exceptional situations:

1. Payment may be made for incidental noncovered services performed as a necessary and integral part of, and secondary to, a covered procedure. For example, if trimming of toenails is required for application of a cast to a fractured foot, the carrier need not allocate and deny a portion of the charge for the trimming of the nails. However, a separately itemized charge for such excluded service should be disallowed. When the primary procedure is covered the administration of anesthesia necessary for the performance of such procedure is also covered.

2. Payment may be made for initial diagnostic services performed in connection with a specific symptom or complaint if it seems likely that its treatment would be covered even though the resulting diagnosis may be one requiring only noncovered care.

The name of the M.D. or D.O. who diagnosed the complicating condition must be submitted with the claim. In those cases, where active care is required, the approximate date the beneficiary was last seen by such physician must also be indicated.

NOTE: Section 939 of P.L. 96-499 removed "warts" from the routine foot care exclusion effective July 1, 1981.

Relatively few claims for routine-type care are anticipated considering the severity of conditions contemplated as the basis for this exception. Claims for this type of foot care should not be paid in the absence of convincing evidence that nonprofessional performance of the service would have been hazardous for the beneficiary because of an underlying systemic disease. The mere statement of a diagnosis such as those mentioned in Sec.D above does not of itself indicate the severity of the condition. Where development is indicated to verify diagnosis and/or severity the carrier should follow existing claims processing practices which may include review of carrier's history and medical consultation as well as physician contacts.

The rules in Sec.290.F concerning presumption of coverage also apply.

Codes and policies for routine foot care and supportive devices for the feet are not exclusively for the use of podiatrists. These codes must be used to report foot care services regardless of the specialty of the physician who furnishes the services. Carriers must instruct physicians to use the most appropriate code available when billing for routine foot care.

## 100-2,15,290

**Foot Care**
Subluxations of the foot are defined as partial dislocations or displacements of joint surfaces, tendons ligaments, or muscles of the foot. Surgical or nonsurgical treatments undertaken for the sole purpose of correcting a subluxated structure in the foot as an isolated entity are not covered.

However, medical or surgical treatment of subluxation of the ankle joint (talo-crural joint) is covered. In addition, reasonable and necessary medical or surgical services, diagnosis, or treatment for medical conditions that have resulted from or are associated with partial displacement of structures is covered. For example, if a patient has osteoarthritis that has resulted in a partial displacement of joints in the foot, and the primary treatment is for the osteoarthritis, coverage is provided.

**B. Exclusions from Coverage**
The following foot care services are generally excluded from coverage under both Part A and Part B. (See Sec.290.F and Sec.290.G for instructions on applying foot care exclusions.)

1. Treatment of Flat Foot The term "flat foot" is defined as a condition in which one or more arches of the foot have

flattened out. Services or devices directed toward the care or correction of such conditions, including the prescription of supportive devices, are not covered.

2. Routine Foot Care Except as provided above, routine foot care is excluded from coverage. Services that normally are considered routine and not covered by Medicare include the following: The cutting or removal of corns and calluses; The trimming, cutting, clipping, or debriding of nails; and Other hygienic and preventive maintenance care, such as cleaning and soaking the feet, the use of skin creams to maintain skin tone of either ambulatory or bedfast patients, and any other service performed in the absence of localized illness, injury, or symptoms involving the foot.

3. Supportive Devices for Feet Orthopedic shoes and other supportive devices for the feet generally are not covered.

However, this exclusion does not apply to such a shoe if it is an integral part of a leg brace, and its expense is included as part of the cost of the brace. Also, this exclusion does not apply to therapeutic shoes furnished to diabetics.

## C. Exceptions to Routine Foot Care Exclusion

1. Necessary and Integral Part of Otherwise Covered Services In certain circumstances, services ordinarily considered to be routine may be covered if they are performed as a necessary and integral part of otherwise covered services, such as diagnosis and treatment of ulcers, wounds, or infections.

2. Treatment of Warts on Foot The treatment of warts (including plantar warts) on the foot is covered to the same extent as services provided for the treatment of warts located elsewhere on the body.

3. Presence of Systemic Condition The presence of a systemic condition such as metabolic, neurologic, or peripheral vascular disease may require scrupulous foot care by a professional that in the absence of such condition(s) would be considered routine (and, therefore, excluded from coverage).

Accordingly, foot care that would otherwise be considered routine may be covered when systemic condition(s) result in severe circulatory embarrassment or areas of diminished sensation in the individual's legs or feet. (See subsection A.) In these instances, certain foot care procedures that otherwise are considered routine (e.g., cutting or removing corns and calluses, or trimming, cutting, clipping, or debriding nails) may pose a hazard when performed by a nonprofessional person on patients with such systemic conditions. (See Sec.290.G for procedural instructions.) 4. Mycotic Nails In the absence of a systemic condition, treatment of mycotic nails may be covered.

The treatment of mycotic nails for an ambulatory patient is covered only when the physician attending the patient's mycotic condition documents that (1) there is clinical evidence of mycosis of the toenail, and (2) the patient has marked limitation of ambulation, pain, or secondary infection resulting from the thickening and dystrophy of the infected toenail plate.

The treatment of mycotic nails for a nonambulatory patient is covered only when the physician attending the patient's mycotic condition documents that (1) there is clinical evidence of mycosis of the toenail, and (2) the patient suffers from pain or secondary infection resulting from the thickening and dystrophy of the infected toenail plate.

For the purpose of these requirements, documentation means any written information that is required by the carrier in order for services to be covered. Thus, the information submitted with claims must be substantiated by information found in the patient's medical record. Any information, including that contained in a form letter, used for documentation purposes is subject to carrier verification in order to ensure that the information adequately justifies coverage of the treatment of mycotic nails.

## D. Systemic Conditions That Might Justify Coverage

Although not intended as a comprehensive list, the following metabolic, neurologic, and peripheral vascular diseases (with synonyms in parentheses) most commonly represent the underlying conditions that might justify coverage for routine foot care.

Diabetes mellitus * Arteriosclerosis obliterans (A.S.O., arteriosclerosis of the extremities, occlusive peripheral arteriosclerosis) Buerger's disease (thromboangiitis obliterans) Chronic thrombophlebitis * Peripheral neuropathies involving the feet - Associated with malnutrition and vitamin deficiency * Malnutrition (general, pellagra) Alcoholism Malabsorption (celiac disease, tropical sprue) Pernicious anemia Associated with carcinoma * Associated with diabetes mellitus * Associated with drugs and toxins * Associated with multiple sclerosis * Associated with uremia (chronic renal disease) * Associated with traumatic injury Associated with leprosy or neurosyphilis Associated with hereditary disorders Hereditary sensory radicular neuropathy Angiokeratoma corporis diffusum (Fabry's) Amyloid neuropathy When the patient's condition is one of those designated by an asterisk (*), routine procedures are covered only if the patient is under the active care of a doctor of medicine or osteopathy who documents the condition.

## E. Supportive Devices for Feet

Orthopedic shoes and other supportive devices for the feet generally are not covered.However, this exclusion does not apply to such a shoe if it is an integral part of a leg brace, and its expense is included as part of the cost of the brace. Also, this exclusion does not apply to therapeutic shoes furnished to diabetics.

## F. Presumption of Coverage

In evaluating whether the routine services can be reimbursed, a presumption of coverage may be made where the evidence available discloses certain physical and/or clinical findings consistent with the diagnosis and indicative of severe peripheral involvement. For purposes of applying this presumption the following findings are pertinent:

Class A Findings

Nontraumatic amputation of foot or integral skeletal portion thereof.

Class B Findings

Absent posterior tibial pulse; Advanced trophic changes as: hair growth (decrease or absence) nail changes (thickening) pigmentary changes (discoloration) skin texture (thin, shiny) skin color (rubor or redness) (Three required);

and Absent dorsalis pedis pulse.

Class C Findings

Claudication;

Temperature changes (e.g., cold feet);

Edema;

Paresthesias (abnormal spontaneous sensations in the feet); and

Burning.

The presumption of coverage may be applied when the physician rendering the routine foot care has identified:

1. A Class A finding;

2. Two of the Class B findings; or

3. One Class B and two Class C findings.

Cases evidencing findings falling short of these alternatives may involve podiatric treatment that may constitute covered care and should be reviewed by the intermediary's medical staff and developed as necessary.

For purposes of applying the coverage presumption where the routine services have been rendered by a podiatrist, the contractor may deem the active care requirement met if the claim or other evidence available discloses that the patient has seen an M.D. or D.O. for treatment and/or evaluation of the complicating disease process during the 6-month period prior to the rendition of the routine-type services. The intermediary may also accept the podiatrist's statement that the diagnosing and treating M.D. or D.O. also concurs with the podiatrist's findings as to the severity of the peripheral involvement indicated.

Services ordinarily considered routine might also be covered if they are performed as a necessary and integral part of otherwise covered services, such as diagnosis and treatment of diabetic ulcers, wounds, and infections.

**G. Application of Foot Care Exclusions to Physician's Services**
The exclusion of foot care is determined by the nature of the service. Thus, payment for an excluded service should be denied whether performed by a podiatrist, osteopath, or a doctor of medicine, and without regard to the difficulty or complexity of the procedure.

When an itemized bill shows both covered services and noncovered services not integrally related to the covered service, the portion of charges attributable to the noncovered services should be denied. (For example, if an itemized bill shows surgery for an ingrown toenail and also removal of calluses not necessary for the performance of toe surgery, any additional charge attributable to removal of the calluses should be denied.) In reviewing claims involving foot care, the carrier should be alert to the following exceptional situations:

1. Payment may be made for incidental noncovered services performed as a necessary and integral part of, and secondary to, a covered procedure. For example, if trimming of toenails is required for application of a cast to a fractured foot, the carrier need not allocate and deny a portion of the charge for the trimming of the nails. However, a separately itemized charge for such excluded service should be disallowed. When the primary procedure is covered the administration of anesthesia necessary for the performance of such procedure is also covered.

2. Payment may be made for initial diagnostic services performed in connection with a specific symptom or complaint if it seems likely that its treatment would be covered even though the resulting diagnosis may be one requiring only noncovered care.

The name of the M.D. or D.O. who diagnosed the complicating condition must be submitted with the claim. In those cases, where active care is required, the approximate date the beneficiary was last seen by such physician must also be indicated.

NOTE: Section 939 of P.L. 96-499 removed "warts" from the routine foot care exclusion effective July 1, 1981.

Relatively few claims for routine-type care are anticipated considering the severity of conditions contemplated as the basis for this exception. Claims for this type of foot care should not be paid in the absence of convincing evidence that nonprofessional performance of the service would have been hazardous for the beneficiary because of an underlying systemic disease. The mere statement of a diagnosis such as those mentioned in Sec.D above does not of itself indicate the severity of the condition. Where development is indicated to verify diagnosis and/or severity the carrier should follow existing claims processing practices, which may include review of carrier's history and medical consultation as well as physician contacts.

The rules in Sec.290.F concerning presumption of coverage also apply.

Codes and policies for routine foot care and supportive devices for the feet are not exclusively for the use of podiatrists. These codes must be used to report foot care services regardless of the specialty of the physician who furnishes the services. Carriers must instruct physicians to use the most appropriate code available when billing for routine foot care.

## 100-2,15,300
## Diabetes Self-Management Training Services
Section 4105 of the Balanced Budget Act of 1997 permits Medicare coverage of diabetes self-management training (DSMT) services when these services are furnished by a certified provider who meets certain quality standards. This program is intended to educate beneficiaries in the successful self-management of diabetes. The program includes instructions in self-monitoring of blood glucose; education about diet and exercise; an insulin treatment plan developed specifically for the patient who is insulin-dependent; and motivation for patients to use the skills for self-management.

Diabetes self-management training services may be covered by Medicare only if the treating physician or treating qualified non-physician practitioner who is managing the beneficiary's diabetic condition certifies that such services are needed. The referring physician or qualified non-physician practitioner must maintain the plan of care in the beneficiary's medical record and documentation substantiating the need for training on an individual basis when group training is typically covered, if so ordered. The order must also include a statement signed by the physician that the service is needed as well as the following:

• The number of initial or follow-up hours ordered (the physician can order less than 10 hours of training);

• The topics to be covered in training (initial training hours can be used for the full initial training program or specific areas such as nutrition or insulin training); and

• A determination that the beneficiary should receive individual or group training.

The provider of the service must maintain documentation in a file that includes the original order from the physician and any special conditions noted by the physician.

When the training under the order is changed, the training order/referral must be signed by the physician or qualified non-physician practitioner treating the beneficiary and maintained in the beneficiary's file in the DSMT's program records.

NOTE: All entities billing for DSMT under the fee-for-service payment system or other payment systems must meet all national coverage requirements.

### 100-2,15,300.2
### Certified Providers

A designated certified provider bills for DSMT provided by an accredited DSMT program. Certified providers must submit a copy of their accreditation certificate to the contractor. The statute states that a "certified provider" is a physician or other individual or entity designated by the Secretary that, in addition to providing outpatient self-management training services, provides other items and services for which payment may be made under title XVIII, and meets certain quality standards. The CMS is designating all providers and suppliers that bill Medicare for other individual services such as hospital outpatient departments, renal dialysis facilities, physicians and durable medical equipment suppliers as certified. All suppliers/providers who may bill for other Medicare services or items and who represent a DSMT program that is accredited as meeting quality standards can bill and receive payment for the entire DSMT program. Registered dietitians are eligible to bill on behalf of an entire DSMT program on or after January 1, 2002, as long as the provider has obtained a Medicare provider number. A dietitian may not be the sole provider of the DSMT service.

The CMS will not reimburse services on a fee-for-service basis rendered to a beneficiary under Part A.

NOTE: While separate payment is not made for this service to Rural Health Clinics (RHCs), the service is covered but is considered included in the all-inclusive encounter rate. Effective January 1, 2006, payment for DSMT provided in a Federally Qualified Health Clinic (FQHC) that meets all of the requirements identified in Pub. 100-04, chapter 18, section 120 may be made in addition to one other visit the beneficiary had during the same day.

All DSMT programs must be accredited as meeting quality standards by a CMS approved national accreditation organization. Currently, CMS recognizes the American Diabetes Association and the Indian Health Service as approved national accreditation organizations. Programs without accreditation by a CMS-approved national accreditation organization are not covered. Certified providers may be asked to submit updated accreditation documents at any time or to submit outcome data to an organization designated by CMS.

Enrollment of DMEPOS Suppliers The DMEPOS suppliers are reimbursed for diabetes training through local carriers. In order to file claims for DSMT, a DMEPOS supplier must be enrolled in the Medicare program with the National Supplier Clearinghouse (NSC). The supplier must also meet the quality standards of a CMS-approved national accreditation organization as stated above. DMEPOS suppliers must obtain a provider number from the local carrier in order to bill for DSMT.

The carrier requires a completed Form CMS-855, along with an accreditation certificate as part of the provider application process. After it has been determined that the quality standards are met, a billing number is assigned to the supplier. Once a supplier has received a provider identification (PIN) number, the supplier can begin receiving reimbursement for this service.

Carriers should contact the National Supplier Clearinghouse (NSC) according to the instruction in Pub 100-08, the Medicare Program Integrity Manual, Chapter 10, "Healthcare Provider/Supplier Enrollment," to verify an applicant is currently enrolled and eligible to receive direct payment from the Medicare program.

The applicant is assigned specialty 87.

Any DMEPOS supplier that has its billing privileges deactivated or revoked by the NSC will also have the billing number deactivated by the carrier.

### 100-2,15,300.3
### Frequency of Training

#### A - Initial Training

The initial year for DSMT is the 12 month period following the initial date.

Medicare will cover initial training that meets the following conditions:

- Is furnished to a beneficiary who has not previously received initial or follow-up training under HCPCS codes G0108 or G0109;
- Is furnished within a continuous 12-month period;
- Does not exceed a total of 10 hours* (the 10 hours of training can be done in any combination of 1/2 hour increments);
- With the exception of 1 hour of individual training, training is usually furnished in a group setting, which can contain other patients besides Medicare beneficiaries, and;
- One hour of individual training may be used for any part of the training including insulin training.

* When a claim contains a DSMT HCPCS code and the associated units cause the total time for the DSMT initial year to exceed '10' hours, a CWF error will set.

#### B - Follow-Up Training

Medicare covers follow-up training under the following conditions:

- No more than 2 hours individual or group training per beneficiary per year;
- Group training consists of 2 to 20 individuals who need not all be Medicare beneficiaries;
- Follow-up training for subsequent years is based on a 12 month calendar after completion of the full 10 hours of initial training;
- Follow-up training is furnished in increments of no less than one-half hour*; and
- The physician (or qualified non-physician practitioner) treating the beneficiary must document in the beneficiary's medical record that the beneficiary is a diabetic.

*When a claim contains a DSMT HCPCS code and the associated units cause the total time for any follow-up year to exceed 2 hours, a CWF error will set.

### 100-2,15,300.4
### Coverage Requirements for Individual Training

Medicare covers training on an individual basis for a Medicare beneficiary under any of the following conditions:

- No group session is available within 2 months of the date the training is ordered;

- The beneficiary's physician (or qualified non-physician practitioner) documents in the beneficiary's medical record that the beneficiary has special needs resulting from conditions, such as severe vision, hearing or language limitations or other such special conditions as identified by the treating physician or non-physician practitioner, that will hinder effective participation in a group training session; or
- The physician orders additional insulin training.

The need for individual training must be identified by the physician or non-physician practitioner in the referral.

NOTE: If individual training has been provided to a Medicare beneficiary and subsequently the carrier or intermediary determines that training should have been provided in a group, carriers and intermediaries down-code the reimbursement from individual to the group level and provider education would be the appropriate actions instead of denying the service as billed.

## 100-2,15,50
### Drugs and Biologicals
B3-2049, A3-3112.4.B, HO-230.4.B

The Medicare program provides limited benefits for outpatient drugs. The program covers drugs that are furnished "incident to" a physician's service provided that the drugs are not usually self-administered by the patients who take them.

Generally, drugs and biologicals are covered only if all of the following requirements are met:

- They meet the definition of drugs or biologicals (see Sec.50.1);
- They are of the type that are not usually self-administered. (see Sec.50.2);
- They meet all the general requirements for coverage of items as incident to a physician's services (see Sec.Sec.50.1 and 50.3);
- They are reasonable and necessary for the diagnosis or treatment of the illness or injury for which they are administered according to accepted standards of medical practice (see Sec.50.4);
- They are not excluded as noncovered immunizations (see Sec.50.4.4.2); and
- They have not been determined by the FDA to be less than effective. (See Sec.Sec.50.4.4).

Medicare Part B does generally not cover drugs that can be self-administered, such as those in pill form, or are used for self-injection. However, the statute provides for the coverage of some self-administered drugs. Examples of self-administered drugs that are covered include blood-clotting factors, drugs used in immunosuppressive therapy, erythropoietin for dialysis patients, osteoporosis drugs for certain homebound patients, and certain oral cancer drugs. (See Sec.110.3 for coverage of drugs, which are necessary to the effective use of Durable Medical Equipment (DME) or prosthetic devices.)

## 100-2,15,50.2
### Determining Self-Administration of Drug or Biological
AB-02-072, AB-02-139, B3-2049.2

The Medicare program provides limited benefits for outpatient prescription drugs. The program covers drugs that are furnished "incident to" a physician's service provided that the drugs are not usually self-administered by the patients who take them. Section 112 of the Benefits, Improvements & Protection Act of 2000

(BIPA) amended sections 1861(s)(2)(A) and 1861(s)(2)(B) of the Act to redefine this exclusion. The prior statutory language referred to those drugs "which cannot be self-administered." Implementation of the BIPA provision requires interpretation of the phrase "not usually self-administered by the patient".

### A. Policy
Fiscal intermediaries and carriers are instructed to follow the instructions below when applying the exclusion for drugs that are usually self-administered by the patient. Each individual contractor must make its own individual determination on each drug. Contractors must continue to apply the policy that not only the drug is medically reasonable and necessary for any individual claim, but also that the route of administration is medically reasonable and necessary. That is, if a drug is available in both oral and injectable forms, the injectable form of the drug must be medically reasonable and necessary as compared to using the oral form.

For certain injectable drugs, it will be apparent due to the nature of the condition(s) for which they are administered or the usual course of treatment for those conditions, they are, or are not, usually self-administered. For example, an injectable drug used to treat migraine headaches is usually self-administered. On the other hand, an injectable drug, administered at the same time as chemotherapy, used to treat anemia secondary to chemotherapy is not usually self-administered.

### B. Administered
The term "administered" refers only to the physical process by which the drug enters the patient's body. It does not refer to whether the process is supervised by a medical professional (for example, to observe proper technique or side-effects of the drug). Only injectable (including intravenous) drugs are eligible for inclusion under the "incident to" benefit. Other routes of administration including, but not limited to, oral drugs, suppositories, topical medications are all considered to be usually self-administered by the patient.

### C. Usually
For the purposes of applying this exclusion, the term "usually" means more than 50 percent of the time for all Medicare beneficiaries who use the drug. Therefore, if a drug is self-administered by more than 50 percent of Medicare beneficiaries, the drug is excluded from coverage and the contractor may not make any Medicare payment for it. In arriving at a single determination as to whether a drug is usually self-administered, contractors should make a separate determination for each indication for a drug as to whether that drug is usually self-administered.

After determining whether a drug is usually self-administered for each indication, contractors should determine the relative contribution of each indication to total use of the drug (i.e., weighted average) in order to make an overall determination as to whether the drug is usually self-administered. For example, if a drug has three indications, is not self-administered for the first indication, but is self administered for the second and third indications, and the first indication makes up 40 percent of total usage, the second indication makes up 30 percent of total usage, and the third indication makes up 30 percent of total usage, then the drug would be considered usually self-administered.

Reliable statistical information on the extent of self-administration by the patient may not always be available. Consequently, CMS offers the following guidance for each contractor's consideration in making this determination in the absence of such data:

1. Absent evidence to the contrary, presume that drugs delivered intravenously are not usually self-administered by the patient.

2. Absent evidence to the contrary, presume that drugs delivered by intramuscular injection are not usually self-administered by the patient. (Avonex, for example, is delivered by intramuscular injection, not usually self-administered by the patient.) The contractor may consider the depth and nature of the particular intramuscular injection in applying this presumption. In applying this presumption, contractors should examine the use of the particular drug and consider the following factors:

3. Absent evidence to the contrary, presume that drugs delivered by subcutaneous injection are self-administered by the patient. However, contractors should examine the use of the particular drug and consider the following factors:

   A. Acute Condition - Is the condition for which the drug is used an acute condition? If so, it is less likely that a patient would self-administer the drug. If the condition were longer term, it would be more likely that the patient would self-administer the drug.

   B. Frequency of Administration - How often is the injection given? For example, if the drug is administered once per month, it is less likely to be self-administered by the patient. However, if it is administered once or more per week, it is likely that the drug is self-administered by the patient. In some instances, carriers may have provided payment for one or perhaps several doses of a drug that would otherwise not be paid for because the drug is usually self-administered. Carriers may have exercised this discretion for limited coverage, for example, during a brief time when the patient is being trained under the supervision of a physician in the proper technique for self-administration. Medicare will no longer pay for such doses. In addition, contractors may no longer pay for any drug when it is administered on an outpatient emergency basis, if the drug is excluded because it is usually self-administered by the patient.

## D. Definition of Acute Condition

For the purposes of determining whether a drug is usually self-administered, an acute condition means a condition that begins over a short time period, is likely to be of short duration and/or the expected course of treatment is for a short, finite interval. A course of treatment consisting of scheduled injections lasting less than two weeks, regardless of frequency or route of administration, is considered acute. Evidence to support this may include Food and Drug administration (FDA) approval language, package inserts, drug compendia, and other information.

## E. By the Patient

The term "by the patient" means Medicare beneficiaries as a collective whole. The carrier includes only the patients themselves and not other individuals (that is, spouses, friends, or other care-givers are not considered the patient). The determination is based on whether the drug is self-administered by the patient a majority of the time that the drug is used on an outpatient basis by Medicare beneficiaries for medically necessary indications.

The carrier ignores all instances when the drug is administered on an inpatient basis. The carrier makes this determination on a drug-by-drug basis, not on a beneficiary-by-beneficiary basis. In evaluating whether beneficiaries as a collective whole self-administer, individual beneficiaries who do not have the capacity to self-administer any drug due to a condition other than the condition for which they are taking the drug in question are not considered. For example, an individual afflicted with paraplegia or advanced dementia would not have the capacity to self-administer any injectable drug, so such individuals would not be included in the population upon which the determination for self-administration by the patient was based. Note that some individuals afflicted with a less severe stage of an otherwise debilitating condition would be included in the population upon which the determination for "self-administered by the patient" was based; for example, an early onset of dementia.

## F. Evidentiary Criteria

Contractors are only required to consider the following types of evidence: peer reviewed medical literature, standards of medical practice, evidence-based practice guidelines, FDA approved label, and package inserts. Contractors may also consider other evidence submitted by interested individuals or groups subject to their judgment.

Contractors should also use these evidentiary criteria when reviewing requests for making a determination as to whether a drug is usually self-administered, and requests for reconsideration of a pending or published determination.

Please note that prior to the August 1, 2002, one of the principal factors used to determine whether a drug was subject to the self-administered exclusion was whether the FDA label contained instructions for self-administration. However, CMS notes that under the new standard, the fact that the FDA label includes instructions for self-administration is not, by itself, a determining factor that a drug is subject to this exclusion.

## G. Provider Notice of Noncovered Drugs

Contractors must describe on their Web site the process they will use to determine whether a drug is usually self-administered and thus does not meet the "incident to" benefit category. Contractors must publish a list of the injectable drugs that are subject to the self-administered exclusion on their Web site, including the data and rationale that led to the determination. Contractors will report the workload associated with developing new coverage statements in CAFM 21208.

Contractors must provide notice 45 days prior to the date that these drugs will not be covered. During the 45-day time period, contractors will maintain existing medical review and payment procedures. After the 45-day notice, contractors may deny payment for the drugs subject to the notice.

Contractors must not develop local medical review policies (LMRPs) for this purpose because further elaboration to describe drugs that do not meet the ‚Äòincident to' and the ‚Äònot usually self-administered' provisions of the statute are unnecessary. Current LMRPs based solely on these provisions must be withdrawn. LMRPs that address the self-administered exclusion and other information may be reissued absent the self-administered drug exclusion material. Contractors will report this workload in CAFM 21206. However, contractors may continue to use and write LMRPs to describe reasonable and necessary uses of drugs that are not usually self-administered.
H. Conferences Between Contractors Contractors' Medical Directors may meet and discuss whether a drug is usually self-administered without reaching a formal consensus. Each contractor uses its discretion as to whether or not it will participate in such discussions. Each contractor must make its

own individual determinations, except that fiscal intermediaries may, at their discretion, follow the determinations of the local carrier with respect to the self-administered exclusion.

### I. Beneficiary Appeals
If a beneficiary's claim for a particular drug is denied because the drug is subject to the "self-administered drug" exclusion, the beneficiary may appeal the denial. Because it is a "benefit category" denial and not a denial based on medical necessity, an Advance Beneficiary Notice (ABN) is not required. A "benefit category" denial (i.e., a denial based on the fact that there is no benefit category under which the drug may be covered) does not trigger the financial liability protection provisions of Limitation On Liability (under Sec.1879 of the Act). Therefore, physicians or providers may charge the beneficiary for an excluded drug.

### J. Provider and Physician Appeals
A physician accepting assignment may appeal a denial under the provisions found in Chapter 29 of the Medicare Claims Processing Manual.

### K. Reasonable and Necessary
Carriers and fiscal intermediaries will make the determination of reasonable and necessary with respect to the medical appropriateness of a drug to treat the patient's condition. Contractors will continue to make the determination of whether the intravenous or injection form of a drug is appropriate as opposed to the oral form. Contractors will also continue to make the determination as to whether a physician's office visit was reasonable and necessary. However, contractors should not make a determination of whether it was reasonable and necessary for the patient to choose to have his or her drug administered in the physician's office or outpatient hospital setting. That is, while a physician's office visit may not be reasonable and necessary in a specific situation, in such a case an injection service would be payable.

### L. Reporting Requirements
Each carrier and intermediary must report to CMS, every September 1 and March 1, its complete list of injectable drugs that the contractor has determined are excluded when furnished incident to a physician's service on the basis that the drug is usually self-administered. The CMS anticipates that contractors will review injectable drugs on a rolling basis and publish their list of excluded drugs as it is developed. For example, contractors should not wait to publish this list until every drug has been reviewed.

Contractors must send their exclusion list to the following e-mail address: drugdata@cms.hhs.gov a template that CMS will provide separately, consisting of the following data elements in order:

1. Carrier Name
2. State
3. Carrier ID#
4. HCPCS
5. Descriptor
6. Effective Date of Exclusion
7. End Date of Exclusion
8. Comments

Any exclusion list not provided in the CMS mandated format will be returned for correction. To view the presently mandated CMS format for this report, open the file located at: http://cms.hhs.gov/manuals/pm_trans/AB02_139a

### 100-2,15,50.4.2
### Unlabeled Use of Drug
B3-2049.3

An unlabeled use of a drug is a use that is not included as an indication on the drug's label as approved by the FDA. FDA approved drugs used for indications other than what is indicated on the official label may be covered under Medicare if the carrier determines the use to be medically accepted, taking into consideration the major drug compendia, authoritative medical literature and/or accepted standards of medical practice. In the case of drugs used in an anti-cancer chemotherapeutic regimen, unlabeled uses are covered for a medically accepted indication as defined in Sec.50.5. These decisions are made by the contractor on a case-by-case basis.

### 100-2,15,50.5
### Self-Administered Drugs and Biologicals
B3-2049.5

Medicare Part B does not cover drugs that are usually self-administered by the patient unless the statute provides for such coverage. The statute explicitly provides coverage, for blood clotting factors, drugs used in immunosuppressive therapy, erythropoietin for dialysis patients, certain oral anti-cancer drugs and anti-emetics used in certain situations.

### 100-2,16,10
### General Exclusions From Coverage
A3-3150, HO-260, HHA-232, B3-2300

No payment can be made under either the hospital insurance or supplementary medical insurance program for certain items and services, when the following conditions exist:

- Not reasonable and necessary (Sec.20);
- No legal obligation to pay for or provide (Sec.40);
- Paid for by a governmental entity (Sec.50);
- Not provided within United States (Sec.60);
- Resulting from war (Sec.70);
- Personal comfort (Sec.80);
- Routine services and appliances (Sec.90);
- Custodial care (Sec.110);
- Cosmetic surgery (Sec.120);
- Charges by immediate relatives or members of household (Sec.130);
- Dental services (Sec.140);
- Paid or expected to be paid under workers' compensation (Sec.150);
- Nonphysician services provided to a hospital inpatient that were not provided directly or arranged for by the hospital (Sec.170);
- Services Related to and Required as a Result of Services Which are not Covered Under Medicare (Sec.180);
- Excluded foot care services and supportive devices for feet (Sec.30); or
- Excluded investigational devices (See Chapter 14, Sec.30).

### 100-2,16,140
### Dental Services Exclusion
A3-3162, HO-260.13, B3-2336

Items and services in connection with the care, treatment, filling, removal, or replacement of teeth, or structures directly supporting the teeth are not covered. Structures directly supporting the teeth mean the periodontium, which includes the gingivae, dentogingival junction, periodontal membrane, cementum, and alveolar process. However, payment may be made for certain other services of a dentist. (See the Medicare Benefit Policy Manual, Chapter 15, "Covered Medical and Other Health Services," Sec.150.)

The hospitalization or nonhospitalization of a patient has no direct bearing on the coverage or exclusion of a given dental procedure.

When an excluded service is the primary procedure involved, it is not covered regardless of its complexity or difficulty. For example, the extraction of an impacted tooth is not covered. Similarly, an alveoplasty (the surgical improvement of the shape and condition of the alveolar process) and a frenectomy are excluded from coverage when either of these procedures is performed in connection with an excluded service, e.g., the preparation of the mouth for dentures. In like manner, the removal of the torus palatinus (a bony protuberance of the hard palate) could be a covered service. However, with rare exception, this surgery is performed in connection with an excluded service, i.e., the preparation of the mouth for dentures. Under such circumstances, reimbursement is not made for this purpose.

The extraction of teeth to prepare the jaw for radiation treatments of neoplastic disease is also covered. This is an exception to the requirement that to be covered, a noncovered procedure or service performed by a dentist must be an incident to and an integral part of a covered procedure or service performed by the dentist. Ordinarily, the dentist extracts the patient's teeth, but another physician, e.g., a radiologist, administers the radiation treatments.

Whether such services as the administration of anesthesia, diagnostic x-rays, and other related procedures are covered depends upon whether the primary procedure being performed by the dentist is covered. Thus, an x-ray taken in connection with the reduction of a fracture of the jaw or facial bone is covered. However, a single x-ray or xray survey taken in connection with the care or treatment of teeth or the periodontium is not covered.

See also the Medicare Benefit Policy Manual, Chapter 1, "Inpatient Hospital Services, Sec.70, and Chapter 15, "Covered Medical and Other Health Services," Sec.150 for additional information on dental services.

## 100-2,16,20
### Services Not Reasonable and Necessary
A3-3151, HO-260.1, B3-2303, AB-00-52 - 6/00

Items and services which are not reasonable and necessary for the diagnosis or treatment of illness or injury or to improve the functioning of a malformed body member are not covered, e.g., payment cannot be made for the rental of a special hospital bed to be used by the patient in their home unless it was a reasonable and necessary part of the patient's treatment. See also Sec.80.

A health care item or service for the purpose of causing, or assisting to cause, the death of any individual (assisted suicide) is not covered. This prohibition does not apply to the provision of an item or service for the purpose of alleviating pain or discomfort, even if such use may increase the risk of death, so long as the item or service is not furnished for the specific purpose of causing death.

## 100-2,16,90
### Routine Services and Appliances
A3-3157, HO-260.7, B3-2320, R-1797A3 - 5/00

Routine physical checkups; eyeglasses, contact lenses, and eye examinations for the purpose of prescribing, fitting, or changing eyeglasses; eye refractions by whatever practitioner and for whatever purpose performed; hearing aids and examinations for hearing aids; and immunizations are not covered.

The routine physical checkup exclusion applies to (a) examinations performed without relationship to treatment or diagnosis for a specific illness, symptom, complaint, or injury; and (b) examinations required by third parties such as insurance companies business establishments, or Government agencies.

If the claim is for a diagnostic test or examination performed solely for the purpose of establishing a claim under title IV of Public Law 91-173, "Black Lung Benefits," the service is not covered under Medicare and the claimant should be advised to contact their Social Security office regarding the filing of a claim for reimbursement under the "Black Lung" program.

The exclusions apply to eyeglasses or contact lenses, and eye examinations for the purpose of prescribing, fitting, or changing eyeglasses or contact lenses for refractive errors. The exclusions do not apply to physicians' services (and services incident to a physicians' service) performed in conjunction with an eye disease, as for example, glaucoma or cataracts, or to post-surgical prosthetic lenses which are customarily used during convalescence from eye surgery in which the lens of the eye was removed, or to permanent prosthetic lenses required by an individual lacking the organic lens of the eye whether by surgical removal or congenital disease. Such prosthetic lens is a replacement for an internal body organ - the lens of the eye. (See the Medicare Benefit Policy Manual, Chapter 15, "Covered Medical and Other Health Services," Sec.120). Expenses for all refractive procedures, whether performed by an ophthalmologist (or any other physician) or an optometrist and without regard to the reason for performance of the refraction, are excluded from coverage.

### A. Immunizations
Vaccinations or inoculations are excluded as immunizations unless they are either

Directly related to the treatment of an injury or direct exposure to a disease or condition, such as antirabies treatment, tetanus antitoxin or booster vaccine, botulin antitoxin, antivenin sera, or immune globulin. (In the absence of injury or direct exposure, preventive immunization (vaccination or inoculation) against such diseases as smallpox, polio, diphtheria, etc., is not covered.); or

Specifically covered by statute, as described in the Medicare Benefit Policy Manual, Chapter 15, "Covered Medical and Other Health Services," Sec.50.

### B. Antigens
Prior to the Omnibus Reconciliation Act of 1980, a physician who prepared an antigen for a patient could not be reimbursed for that service unless the physician also administered the antigen to the patient. Effective January 1, 1981, payment may be made for a reasonable supply of antigens that have been prepared for a particular patient even though they have not been administered to the patient by the same physician who prepared them if:

The antigens are prepared by a physician who is a doctor of medicine or osteopathy, and "The physician who prepared the antigens has examined the patient and has determined a plan of treatment and a dosage regimen.

A reasonable supply of antigens is considered to be not more than a 12-week supply of antigens that has been prepared for a particular patient at any one time. The purpose of the reasonable supply limitation is to assure that the antigens retain their potency and effectiveness over the period in which they are to be administered to the patient. (See the Medicare Benefit Policy Manual, Chapter 15, "Covered Medical and Other Health Services," Sec.50.4.4.2)

## 100-2,6,10
### Medical and Other Health Services Furnished to Inpatients of Participating Hospitals

Payment may be made under Part B for physician services and for the nonphysician medical and other health services listed below when furnished by a participating hospital (either directly or under arrangements) to an inpatient of the hospital, but only if payment for these services cannot be made under Part A.

In PPS hospitals, this means that Part B payment could be made for these services if:

- No Part A prospective payment is made at all for the hospital stay because of patient exhaustion of benefit days before admission;
- The admission was disapproved as not reasonable and necessary (and waiver of liability payment was not made);
- The day or days of the otherwise covered stay during which the services were provided were not reasonable and necessary (and no payment was made under waiver of liability);
- The patient was not otherwise eligible for or entitled to coverage under Part A (See the Medicare Benefit Policy Manual, Chapter 1, Sec.150, for services received as a result of noncovered services); or
- No Part A day outlier payment is made (for discharges before October 1997) for one or more outlier days due to patient exhaustion of benefit days after admission but before the case's arrival at outlier status, or because outlier days are otherwise not covered and waiver of liability payment is not made.

However, if only day outlier payment is denied under Part A (discharges before October 1997), Part B payment may be made for only the services covered under Part B and furnished on the denied outlier days.

In non-PPS hospitals, Part B payment may be made for services on any day for which Part A payment is denied (i.e., benefit days are exhausted; services are not at the hospital level of care; or patient is not otherwise eligible or entitled to payment under Part A).

Services payable are:

- Diagnostic x-ray tests, diagnostic laboratory tests, and other diagnostic tests;
- X-ray, radium, and radioactive isotope therapy, including materials and services of technicians;
- Surgical dressings, and splints, casts, and other devices used for reduction of fractures and dislocations;
- Prosthetic devices (other than dental) which replace all or part of an internal body organ (including contiguous tissue), or all or part of the function of a permanently inoperative or malfunctioning internal body organ, including replacement or repairs of such devices;
- Leg, arm, back, and neck braces, trusses, and artificial legs, arms, and eyes including adjustments, repairs, and replacements required because of breakage, wear, loss, or a change in the patient's physical condition;
- Outpatient physical therapy, outpatient speech-language pathology services, and outpatient occupational therapy (see the Medicare Benefit Policy Manual, Chapter 15, "Covered Medical and Other Health Services," Sec.Sec.220 and 230);
- Screening mammography services;
- Screening pap smears;
- Influenza, pneumococcal pneumonia, and hepatitis B vaccines;
- Colorectal screening;
- Bone mass measurements;
- Diabetes self-management;
- Prostate screening;
- Ambulance services;
- Hemophilia clotting factors for hemophilia patients competent to use these factors without supervision);
- Immunosuppressive drugs;
- Oral anti-cancer drugs;
- Oral drug prescribed for use as an acute anti-emetic used as part of an anti-cancer chemotherapeutic regimen; and
- Epoetin Alfa (EPO).

Coverage rules for these services are described in the Medicare Benefit Policy Manual, Chapters: 11, "End Stage Renal Disease (ESRD);" 14, "Medical Devices;" or 15, "Medical and Other Health Services."

For services to be covered under Part A or Part B, a hospital must furnish nonphysician services to its inpatients directly or under arrangements. A nonphysician service is one which does not meet the criteria defining physicians' services specifically provided for in regulation at 42 CFR 415.102. Services "incident to" physicians' services (except for the services of nurse anesthetists employed by anesthesiologists) are nonphysician services for purposes of this provision. This provision is applicable to all hospitals participating in Medicare, including those paid under alternative arrangements such as State cost control systems, and to emergency hospital services furnished by nonparticipating hospitals.

In all hospitals, every service provided to a hospital inpatient other than those listed in the next paragraph must be treated as an inpatient hospital service to be paid for under Part A, if Part A coverage is available and the beneficiary is entitled to Part A. This is because every hospital must provide directly or arrange for any nonphysician service rendered to its inpatients, and a hospital can be paid under Part B for a service provided in this manner only if Part A coverage does not exist.

These services, when provided to a hospital inpatient, may be covered under Part B, even though the patient has Part A coverage for the hospital stay. This is because these services are covered under Part B and not covered under Part A. They are:

- Physicians' services (including the services of residents and interns in unapproved teaching programs);
- Influenza vaccine;
- Pneumoccocal vaccine and its administration;

- Hepatitis B vaccine and its administration;
- Screening mammography services;
- Screening pap smears and pelvic exams;
- Colorectal screening;
- Bone mass measurements;
- Diabetes self management training services; and
- Prostate screening.

However, note that in order to have any Medicare coverage at all (Part A or Part B), any nonphysician service rendered to a hospital inpatient must be provided directly or arranged for by the hospital.

## 100-2,6,20.6
### Outpatient Observation Services

**A. Outpatient Observation Services Defined**
Observation care is a well-defined set of specific, clinically appropriate services, which include ongoing short term treatment, assessment, and reassessment before a decision can be made regarding whether patients will require further treatment as hospital inpatients or if they are able to be discharged from the hospital. Observation status is commonly assigned to patients who present to the emergency department and who then require a significant period of treatment or monitoring in order to make a decision concerning their admission or discharge.

Observation services are covered only when provided by the order of a physician or another individual authorized by State licensure law and hospital staff bylaws to admit patients to the hospital or to order outpatient tests. In the majority of cases, the decision whether to discharge a patient from the hospital following resolution of the reason for the observation care or to admit the patient as an inpatient can be made in less than 48 hours, usually in less than 24 hours. In only rare and exceptional cases do reasonable and necessary outpatient observation services span more than 48 hours.

Hospitals may bill for patients who are directly admitted to the hospital for outpatient observation services. A "direct admission" occurs when a physician in the community refers a patient to the hospital for observation, bypassing the clinic or emergency department (ED). Effective for services furnished on or after January 1, 2003, hospitals may bill for patients directly admitted for observation services.

See, the Medicare Claims Processing Manual, Pub. 100-04, chapter 4, section 290, at http://www.cms.hhs.gov/manuals/downloads/clm104c04.pdf for billing and payment instructions for outpatient observation services.

**B. Coverage of Outpatient Observation Services**

When a physician orders that a patient be placed under observation care, the patient's status is that of an outpatient. The purpose of observation is to determine the need for further treatment or for inpatient admission. Thus, a patient receiving observation services may improve and be released, or be admitted as an inpatient (see Pub. 100-02, Medicare Benefit Policy Manual, Chapter 1, Section 10 "Covered Inpatient Hospital Services Covered Under Part A" at http://www.cms.hhs.gov/manuals/Downloads/bp102c01.pdf ). For more information on correct reporting of observation services, see the Medicare Claims Processing Manual, Pub. 100-04, chapter 4, section 290.2.2.)

All hospital observation services, regardless of the duration of the observation care, that are medically reasonable and necessary are covered by Medicare. Observation services are reported using HCPCS code G0378 (Hospital observation service, per hour). Beginning January 1, 2008, HCPCS code G0378 for hourly observation services is assigned status indicator N, signifying that its payment is always packaged. No separate payment is made for observation services reported with HCPCS code G0378. In most circumstances, observation services are supportive and ancillary to the other separately payable services provided to a patient. In certain circumstances when observation care is billed in conjunction with a high level clinic visit (Level 5), high level emergency department visit (Level 4 or 5), critical care services, or direct admission to observation as an integral part of a patient's extended encounter of care, payment may be made for the entire extended care encounter through one of two composite APCs when certain criteria are met. For information about billing and payment methodology for observation services in years prior to CY 2008, see the Medicare Claims Processing Manual, Pub. 100-04, chapter 4, sections 290.3-290.4. For information about payment for extended assessment and management under composite APCs, see section 290.5.

Payment for all reasonable and necessary observation services is packaged into the payments for other separately payable services provided to the patient in the same encounter. Observation services that are packaged through assignment of status indicator N are covered OPPS services. Since the payment for these services is included in the APC payment for other separately payable services on the claim, hospitals must not bill Medicare beneficiaries directly for the packaged services.

**C. Services Not Covered by Medicare and Notification to the Beneficiary**
In making the determination whether an ABN can be used to shift liability to a beneficiary for the cost of non-covered items or services related to an encounter that includes observation care, the provider should follow a two step process. First, the provider must decide whether the item or service meets either the definition of observation care or would be otherwise covered. If the item or service does not meet the definitional requirements of any Medicare-covered benefit under Part B, then the item or service is not covered by Medicare and an ABN is not required to shift the liability to the beneficiary. However, the provider may choose to provide voluntary notification for these items or services.

Second, if the item or service meets the definition of observation services or would be otherwise covered, then the provider must decide whether the item or service is "reasonable and necessary" for the beneficiary on the occasion in question, or if the item or service exceeds any frequency limitation for the particular benefit or falls outside of a timeframe for receipt of a particular benefit. In these cases, the ABN would be used to shift the liability to the beneficiary (see the Medicare Claims Processing Manual; Pub. 100-04, Chapter 30, "Financial Liability Protections," Section 20, at http://www.cms.hhs.gov/manuals/downloads/clm104c30.pdf for information regarding Limitation On Liability (LOL) Under Sec.1879 Where Medicare Claims Are Disallowed).

If an ABN is not issued to the beneficiary, the provider may be held liable for the cost of the item or service unless the provider/supplier is able to demonstrate that they did not know and could not have reasonably been expected to know that Medicare would not pay for the item or service.

### 100-3,240.4
## NCD for Continuous Positive Airway Pressure (CPAP) Therapy For Obstructive Sleep Apnea (OSA) (240.4)

**B. Nationally Covered Indications**

Effective for claims with dates of service on and after March 13, 2008, the Centers for Medicare & Medicaid Services (CMS) determines that CPAP therapy when used in adult patients with OSA is considered reasonable and necessary under the following situations:

1. The use of CPAP is covered under Medicare when used in adult patients with OSA. Coverage of CPAP is initially limited to a 12-week period to identify beneficiaries diagnosed with OSA as subsequently described who benefit from CPAP. CPAP is subsequently covered only for those beneficiaries diagnosed with OSA who benefit from CPAP during this 12-week period.

2. The provider of CPAP must conduct education of the beneficiary prior to the use of the CPAP device to ensure that the beneficiary has been educated in the proper use of the device. A caregiver, for example a family member, may be compensatory, if consistently available in the beneficiary's home and willing and able to safely operate the CPAP device.

3. A positive diagnosis of OSA for the coverage of CPAP must include a clinical evaluation and a positive:

   a. attended PSG performed in a sleep laboratory; or

   b. unattended HST with a Type II home sleep monitoring device; or

   c. unattended HST with a Type III home sleep monitoring device; or

   d. unattended HST with a Type IV home sleep monitoring device that measures at least 3 channels.

4. The sleep test must have been previously ordered by the beneficiaryÔø¾s treating physician and furnished under appropriate physician supervision.

5. An initial 12-week period of CPAP is covered in adult patients with OSA if either of the following criterion using the AHI or RDI are met:

   a. AHI or RDI greater than or equal to 15 events per hour, or

   b. AHI or RDI greater than or equal to 5 events and less than or equal to 14 events per hour with documented symptoms of excessive daytime sleepiness, impaired cognition, mood disorders or insomnia, or documented hypertension, ischemic heart disease, or history of stroke.

6. The AHI or RDI is calculated on the average number of events of per hour. If the AHI or RDI is calculated based on less than 2 hours of continuous recorded sleep, the total number of recorded events to calculate the AHI or RDI during sleep testing must be at a minimum the number of events that would have been required in a 2-hour period.

7. Apnea is defined as a cessation of airflow for at least 10 seconds. Hypopnea is defined as an abnormal respiratory event lasting at least 10 seconds with at least a 30% reduction in thoracoabdominal movement or airflow as compared to baseline, and with at least a 4% oxygen desaturation.

8. Coverage with Evidence Development (CED): Medicare provides the following limited coverage for CPAP in adult beneficiaries who do not qualify for CPAP coverage based on criteria 1-7 above. A clinical study seeking Medicare payment for CPAP provided to a beneficiary who is an enrolled subject in that study must address one or more of the following questions

   a. In Medicare-aged subjects with clinically identified risk factors for OSA, how does the diagnostic accuracy of a clinical trial of CPAP compare with PSG and Type II, III & IV HST in identifying subjects with OSA who will respond to CPAP?

   b. In Medicare-aged subjects with clinically identified risk factors for OSA who have not undergone confirmatory testing with PSG or Type II, III & IV HST, does CPAP cause clinically meaningful harm?

The study must meet the following additional standards:

   c. The principal purpose of the research study is to test whether a particular intervention potentially improves the participantsÔø¾ health outcomes.

   d. The research study is well-supported by available scientific and medical information or it is intended to clarify or establish the health outcomes of interventions already in common clinical use.

   e. The research study does not unjustifiably duplicate existing studies.

   f. The research study design is appropriate to answer the research question being asked in the study.

   g. The research study is sponsored by an organization or individual capable of executing the proposed study successfully.

   h. The research study is in compliance with all applicable Federal regulations concerning the protection of human subjects found at 45 CFR Part 46. If a study is Food and Drug Administration-regulated, it also must be in compliance with 21 CFR Parts 50 and 56.

   i. All aspects of the research study are conducted according to the appropriate standards of scientific integrity.

   j. The research study has a written protocol that clearly addresses, or incorporates by reference, the Medicare standards.

   k. The clinical research study is not designed to exclusively test toxicity or disease pathophysiology in healthy individuals. Trials of all medical technologies measuring therapeutic outcomes as one of the objectives meet this standard only if the disease or condition being studied is life-threatening as defined in 21 CFR Ôø¾ 312.81(a) and the patient has no other viable treatment options.

   l. The clinical research study is registered on the ClinicalTrials.gov Web site by the principal sponsor/investigator prior to the enrollment of the first study subject.

   m. The research study protocol specifies the method and timing of public release of all pre-specified outcomes to be measured, including release of outcomes if outcomes are negative or study is terminated early. The results must be made public within 24 months of the end of data collection. If a report is planned for publication in a peer-reviewed journal, then that initial release may be an abstract that meets the requirements of the International

Committee of Medical Journal Editors. However, a full report of the outcomes must be made public no later than 3 years after the end of data collection.

n. The research study protocol must explicitly discuss subpopulations affected by the treatment under investigation, particularly traditionally underrepresented groups in clinical studies, how the inclusion and exclusion criteria affect enrollment of these populations, and a plan for the retention and reporting of said populations in the trial. If the inclusion and exclusion criteria are expected to have a negative effect on the recruitment or retention of underrepresented populations, the protocol must discuss why these criteria are necessary.

o. The research study protocol explicitly discusses how the results are or are not expected to be generalizable to the Medicare population to infer whether Medicare patients may benefit from the intervention. Separate discussions in the protocol may be necessary for populations eligible for Medicare due to age, disability, or Medicaid eligibility.

**C.   Nationally Non-covered Indications**

Effective for claims with dates of services on and after March 13, 2008, other diagnostic tests for the diagnosis of OSA, other than those noted above for prescribing CPAP, are not sufficient for the coverage of CPAP.

**D.   Other**

N/A

(This NCD last reviewed March

## 100-4,1,10.1.4.1

### Physician and Ambulance Services Furnished in Connection With Covered Foreign Inpatient Hospital Services

Payment is made for necessary physician and ambulance services that meet the other coverage requirements of the Medicare program, and are furnished in connection with and during a period of covered foreign hospitalization.

**A. Coverage of Physician and Ambulance Services Furnished Outside the U.S.**

Where inpatient services in a foreign hospital are covered, payment may also be made for

- Physicians' services furnished to the beneficiary while he/she is an inpatient,

- Physicians' services furnished to the beneficiary outside the hospital on the day of his/her admission as an inpatient, provided the services were for the same condition for which the beneficiary was hospitalized (including the services of a Canadian ship's physician who furnishes emergency services in Canadian waters on the day the patient is admitted to a Canadian hospital for a covered emergency stay and,

- Ambulance services, where necessary, for the trip to the hospital in conjunction with the beneficiary's admission as an inpatient. Return trips from a foreign hospital are not covered.

In cases involving foreign ambulance services, the general requirements in Chapter 15 are also applicable, subject to the following special rules:

- If the foreign hospitalization was determined to be covered on the basis of emergency services, the medical necessity requirements outlined in Chapter 15 are considered met.

- The definition of:

- physician

- for purposes of coverage of services furnished outside the U.S., is expanded to include a foreign practitioner, provided the practitioner is legally licensed to practice in the country in which the services are furnished.

- Only the enrollee can file for Part B benefits; the assignment method may not be used.

- Where the enrollee is deceased, the rules for settling Part B underpayments are applicable. Payment is made to the foreign physician or foreign ambulance company on an unpaid bill provided the physician or ambulance company accepts the payment as the full charge for the service, or payment an be made to a person who has agreed to assume legal liability to pay the physician or supplier. Where the bill is paid, payment may be made in accordance with Medicare regulations. The regular deductible and coinsurance requirements apply to physicians' and ambulance service

## 100-4,1,30.3.5

### Effect of Assignment Upon Purchase of Cataract Glasses FromParticipating Physician or Supplier on Claims Submitted to Carriers

B3-3045.4

A pair of cataract glasses is comprised of two distinct products: a professional product (the prescribed lenses) and a retail commercial product (the frames). The frames serve not only as a holder of lenses but also as an article of personal apparel. As such, they are usually selected on the basis of personal taste and style. Although Medicare will pay only for standard frames, most patients want deluxe frames. Participating physicians and suppliers cannot profitably furnish such deluxe frames unless they can make an extra (noncovered) charge for the frames even though they accept assignment.

Therefore, a participating physician or supplier (whether an ophthalmologist, optometrist, or optician) who accepts assignment on cataract glasses with deluxe frames may charge the Medicare patient the difference between his/her usual charge to private pay patients for glasses with standard frames and his/her usual charge to such patients for glasses with deluxe frames, in addition to the applicable deductible and coinsurance on glasses with standard frames, if all of the following requirements are met:

A. The participating physician or supplier has standard frames available, offers them for saleto the patient, and issues and ABN to the patient that explains the price and other differences between standard and deluxe frames. Refer to Chapter 30.

B. The participating physician or supplier obtains from the patient (or his/her representative) and keeps on file the following signed and dated statement:

_____

Name of Patient                           Medicare Claim Number

Having been informed that an extra charge is being made by the physician or supplier for deluxe frames, that this extra charge is not covered by Medicare, and that standard frames are available for purchase from the physician or supplier at no extra charge, I have chosen to purchase deluxe frames.

_____

Signature                                          Date

C. The participating physician or supplier itemizes on his/her claim his/her actual charge for the lenses, his/her actual charge for the standard frames, and his/her actual extra charge for the deluxe frames (charge differential). Once the assigned claim for deluxe frames has been processed, the carrier will follow the ABN instructions as described in Sec.60.

## 100-4,11,30.3

### Data Required on Claim to FI

See Pub. 100-02, Chapter 9, Secs.10 & 20.2 for coverage requirements for Hospice benefits. This section addresses only the submittal of claims. See section 20, of this chapter for information on Notice of Election (NOE) transaction types (81A,C,E and 82A,C,E).

Before billing, the hospice must submit an admission notice to the FI (see section 20). The Social Security Act at Sec.1862 (a)(22) requires that all claims for Medicare payment must be submitted in an electronic form specified by the Secretary of Health and Human Services, unless an exception described at Sec.1862 (h) applies. The electronic form required for billing hospice services is the ANSI X12N 837 Institutional claim transaction. Since the data structure of the 837 transaction is difficult to express in narrative form and to provide assistance to small providers excepted from the electronic claim requirement, the instructions below are given relative to the data element names on the UB-04 (Form CMS-1450) hardcopy form. Each data element name is shown in bold type. Information regarding the form locator numbers that correspond to these data element names and a table to crosswalk UB-04 form locators to the 837 transaction is found in Chapter 25.

Because claim formats serve the needs of many payers, some data elements may not be needed by a particular payer. Detailed information is given only for items required for Medicare hospice claims. Items not listed need not be completed although hospices may complete them when billing multiple payers.

**Provider Name, Address, and Telephone Number** The hospice enters this information for their agency.

**Type of Bill** This three-digit alphanumeric code gives three specific pieces of information. The first digit identifies the type of facility. The second classifies the type of care. The third indicates the sequence of this bill in this particular benefit period. It is referred to as a "frequency" code.

Code Structure

| 1st Digit - Type of Facility |
| --- |
| 8 - Special facility (Hospice) |

| 2nd Digit - Classification (Special Facility Only) |
| --- |
| 1 - Hospice (Nonhospital based) |
| 2 - Hospice (Hospital based) |

| 3rd Digit Frequency | Definition |
| --- | --- |
| 0 - Nonpayment/Zero Claims | Used when no payment from Medicare is anticipated. |
| I - Admit Through Discharge Claim | This code is used for a bill encompassing an entire course of hospice treatment for which the provider expects payment from the payer, i.e., no further bills will be submitted for this patient. |

| 3rd Digit Frequency | Definition |
| --- | --- |
| 2 - Interim - First Claim | This code is used for the first of an expected series of payment bills for a hospice course of treatment. |
| 3 - Interim - Continuing Claim | This code is used when a payment bill for a hospice course of treatment has already been submitted and further bills are expected to be submitted. |
| 4 - Interim - Last Claim | This code is used for a payment bill that is the last of a series for a hospice course of treatment. The "Through" date of this bill (FL 6) is the discharge date, transfer date, or date of death. |
| 5 - Late Charges | Use this code for late charges that need to be billed. Late charges can be submitted only for revenue codes not on the original bill. For additional information on late charge bills see Chapter 3. |
| 7 - Replacement of Prior Claim | This code is used by the provider when it wants to correct (other than late charges) a previously submitted bill. This is the code used on the corrected or "new" bill. For additional information on replacement bills see Chapter 3. |
| 8 - Void/Cancel of a Prior Claim | This code is used to cancel a previously processed claim. For additional information on void/cancel bills see Chapter 3. |

**Statement Covers Period** (From-Through)

The hospice shows the beginning and ending dates of the period covered by this bill in numeric fields (MM-DD-YY). The hospice does not show days before the patient's entitlement began. Since the 12-month hospice "cap period" (see Sec.80.2) ends each year on October 31, hospices must submit separate bills for October and November.

**Patient Name/Identifier**

The hospice enters the beneficiary's name exactly as it appears on the Medicare card.

**Patient Address**

**Patient Birth date**

**Patient Sex**

The hospice enters the appropriate address, date of birth and gender information describing the beneficiary.

Admission/Start of Care Date

The hospice enters the admission date, which must be the same date as the effective date of the hospice election or change of election. The date of admission may not precede the physician's certification by more than 2 calendar days.

The admission date stays the same on all continuing claims for the same hospice election.

The hospice enters the month, day, and year numerically as MM-DD-YY.

Patient Discharge Status

This code indicates the patient's status as of the "Through" date (FL 6) of the billing period. The hospice enters the most appropriate NUBC approved code.

The codes most commonly used on hospice claims include:

01 Discharged to home or self care

30 Still patient  40 Expired at home

41 Expired in a medical facility, such as a hospital, SNF, ICF or freestanding hospice

42 Expired - place unknown

50 Discharged/Transferred to Hospice - home

51 Discharged/Transferred to Hospice - medical facility

## Condition Codes

The hospice enters any appropriate NUBC approved code(s) identifying conditions related to this bill that may affect processing.

Codes listed below are only those most frequently applicable to hospice claims. For a complete list of codes, see Chapter 25.

| | | |
|---|---|---|
| 07 | Treatment of Non-terminal Condition for Hospice | Code indicates the patient has elected hospice care but the provider is not treating the terminal condition, and is, therefore, requesting regular Medicare payment. |
| 20 | Beneficiary Requested Billing | Code indicates the provider realizes the services on this bill are at a noncovered level of care or otherwise excluded from coverage, but the beneficiary has requested a formal determination. |
| 21 | Billing for Denial Notice | Code indicates the provider realizes services are at a noncovered level of care or excluded, but requests a denial notice from Medicare in order to bill Medicaid or other insurers. |

## Occurrence Codes and Dates

The hospice enters any appropriate NUBC approved code(s) and associated date(s) defining specific event(s) relating to this billing period. Event codes are two numeric digits, and dates are six numeric digits (MM-DD-YY). If there are more occurrences than there are spaces on the form, use FL 36 (occurrence span) to record additional occurrences and dates.

Codes listed below are only those most frequently applicable to hospice claims. For a complete list of codes, see Chapter 25.

| Code | Title | Definition |
|---|---|---|
| 23 | Cancellation of Hospice Election Period (FI USE Only) | Code indicates date on which a hospice period of election is cancelled by an FI as opposed to revocation by the beneficiary. |
| 24 | Date Insurance Denied | Code indicates the date of receipt of a denial of coverage by a higher priority payer. |

| Code | Title | Definition |
|---|---|---|
| 27 | Date of Hospice Certification or Re-Certification | Code indicates the date of certification or re-certification of the hospice benefit period, beginning with the first 2 initial benefit periods of 90 days each and the subsequent 60-day benefit periods. Note regarding transfers from one hospice to another hospice: If a patient is in the first certification period when they transfer to another hospice, the receiving hospice would use the same certification date as the previous hospice until the next certification period. However, if they were in the next certification at the time of transfer, then they would enter that date in the Occurrence Code 27 and date. |
| 42 | Date of Termination of Hospice Benefit | Enter code to indicate the date on which beneficiary terminated his/her election to receive hospice benefits. This code can be used only when the beneficiary has revoked the benefit, has been decertified or discharged. It cannot be used in transfer situations. |

## Occurrence Span Code and Dates

The hospice enters any appropriate NUBC approved code(s) and associated beginning and ending date(s) defining a specific event relating to this billing period are shown. Event codes are two alphanumeric digits and dates are shown numerically as MM-DD-YY.

Codes listed below are only those most frequently applicable to hospice claims. For a complete list of codes, see Chapter 25.

| Code | Title | Definition |
|---|---|---|
| M2 | Dates of Inpatient Respite Care | Code indicates From/Through dates of a period of inpatient respite care for hospice patients to differentiate separate respite periods of less than 5 days each. M2 is used when respite care is provided more than once during a benefit period. |
| 77 | Provider Liability - Utilization Charged | Code indicates From/Through dates for a period of non-covered hospice care for which the provider accepts payment liability (other than for medical necessity or custodial care). |

Hospices must use occurrence span code 77 to identify days of care that are not covered by Medicare due to untimely physician recertification. This is particularly important when the non-covered days fall at the beginning of a billing period.

## Value Codes and Amounts

The hospice enters any appropriate NUBC approved code(s) and the associated value amounts identifying numeric information related to this bill that may affect processing.

The most commonly used value codes on hospice claims are value codes 61 and G8, which are used to report the location of the site of hospice services. Otherwise, value codes are commonly used only to indicate Medicare is secondary to another payer. For detailed information on reporting Medicare secondary payer information, see the Medicare Secondary Payer Manual.

| Code | Title | Definition |
|------|-------|------------|
| 61 | Place of Residence where Service is Furnished (Routine Home Care and Continuous Home Care) | MSA or Core-Based Statistical Area (CBSA) number (or rural State code) of the location where the hospice service is delivered. A residence can be an inpatient facility if an individual uses that facility as a place of residence. It is the level of care that is required and not the location where hospice services are provided that determines payment. In other words, if an individual resides in a freestanding hospice facility and requires routine home care, then claims are submitted for routine home care. Hospices must report value code 61 when billing revenue codes 0651 and 0652. |
| G8 | Facility where Inpatient Hospice Service is Delivered (General Inpatient and Inpatient Respite Care). | MSA or Core Based Statistical Area (CBSA) number (or rural State code) of the facility where inpatient hospice services are delivered. Hospices must report value code G8 when billing revenue codes 0655 and 0656. |

If hospice services are provided to the beneficiary in more than one CBSA area during the billing period, the hospice reports the CBSA that applies at the end of the billing period. This applies for either routine home care and continuous home care (e.g., the beneficiary's residence changes between locations in different CBSAs) or for general inpatient and inpatient respite care (e.g., the beneficiary is served in inpatient facilities in different CBSAs).

## Revenue Codes

The hospice assigns a revenue code for each type of service provided and enter the appropriate four-digit numeric revenue code to explain each charge.

For claims with dates of service before July 1, 2008, hospices only reported the revenue codes in the table below. Effective on claims with dates of service on or after January 1, 2008, additional revenue codes will be reported describing the visits

provided under each level of care. However, Medicare payment will continue to be reflected only on claim lines with the revenue codes in this table.

| Code | Description | Standard Abbreviation |
|------|-------------|------------------------|
| 0651* | Routine Home Care | RTN Home |
| 0652* | Continuous Home Care | CTNS Home  A minimum of 8 hours of primarily nursing care within a 24-hour period. The 8-hours of care does not need to be continuous within the 24-hour period, but a need for an aggregate of 8 hours of primarily nursing care is required. Nursing care must be provided by a registered nurse or a licensed practical nurse. If skilled intervention is required for less than 8 aggregate hours (or less than 32 units) within a 24 hour period, then the care rendered would be covered as a routine home care day. Services provided by a nurse practitioner as the attending physician are not included in the CHC computation nor is care that is not directly related to the crisis included in the computation. CHC billing should reflect direct patient care during a period of crisis and should not reflect time related to staff working hours, time taken for meal breaks, time used for educating staff, time used to report etc. |
| 0655*** | Inpatient Respite Care | IP Respite |
| 0656*** | General Inpatient Care | GNL IP |
| 0657** | Physician Services | PHY SER (must be accompanied by a physician procedure code) |

\*      Reporting of value code 61 is required with these revenue codes.
\*\*    Reporting of modifier GV is required with this revenue code when billing physician services performed by a nurse practitioner.
\*\*\*  Reporting of value code G8 is required with these revenue codes.

NOTE: Hospices use revenue code 0657 to identify hospice charges for services furnished to patients by physician or nurse practitioner employees, or physicians or nurse practitioners receiving compensation from the hospice. Physician services performed by a nurse practitioner require the addition of the modifier GV in conjunction with revenue code 0657. Procedure codes are required in order for the FI to determine the reimbursement rate for the physician services. Appropriate procedure codes are available from the FI.

Effective on claims with dates of service on or after July 1, 2008, hospices must report the number of visits that were provided to the beneficiary in the course of delivering the hospice levels of care billed with the codes above. Charges for these codes will be reported on the appropriate level of care line. Total number of patient care visits is to be reported by the discipline (registered nurse, nurse practitioner, licensed nurse, home health aide (also known as a hospice aide), social worker, physician or nurse practitioner serving as the beneficiary's attending physician) for each week at each location of service. If visits are provided in multiple sites, a separate line for each site and for each discipline will be required. The total number of visits does not imply the total number of activities or interventions provided. If patient care visits in a particular discipline are not provided under a given level of care or service location, do not report a line for the corresponding revenue code.

To constitute a visit, the discipline, (as defined above) must have provided care to the beneficiary. Services provided by a social worker to the beneficiary's family also constitute a visit. For example, phone calls, documentation in the medical/clinical record, interdisciplinary group meetings, obtaining physician orders, rounds in a facility or any other activity that is not related to the provision of items or services to a beneficiary, do not count towards a visit to be placed on the claim. In addition, the visit must be reasonable and necessary for the palliation and management of the terminal illness and related conditions as described in the patient's plan of care.

Example 1: Week 1: A visit by the RN was made to the beneficiary's home on Monday and Wednesday where the nurse assessed the patient, verified effect of pain medications, provided patient teaching, obtained vital signs and documented in the medical record. A
home health aide assisted the patient with a bath on Tuesday and Thursday. There were no social work or physician visits. Thus for that week there were 2 visits provided by the nurse and 2 by the home health aide. Since there were no visits by the social worker or by the physician, there would not be any line items for each of those disciplines.

Example 2: If a hospice patient is receiving routine home care while residing in a nursing home, the hospice would record visits for all of its physicians, nurses, social workers, and home health aides who visit the patient to provide care for the palliation and management of the terminal illness and related conditions, as described in the patient's plan of care. In this example the nursing home is acting as the patient's home. Only the patient care provided by the hospice staff constitutes a visit.

Hospices must enter the following revenue codes, when applicable: 055X Skilled Nursing

Required detail: The earliest date of service this discipline was provided during the delivery of each level of care in each service location, service units which represent the number of visits provided in that location, and a charge amount.

• 056X Medical Social Services

Required detail: The earliest date of service this discipline was provided during the delivery of each level of care in each service location, service units which represent the number of visits provided in that location, and a charge amount.

• 057X Home Health Aide

Required detail: The earliest date of service this discipline was provided during the delivery of each level of care in each service location, service units which represent the number of visits provided in that location, and a charge amount.

Hospices should follow NUBC coding guidelines for the use of the appropriate fourth position (the "X") when reporting these revenue codes.

Visits by registered nurses, licensed vocational nurses and nurse practitioners (unless the nurse practitioner is acting as the beneficiary's attending physician) are reported under revenue code 055X.

All visits to provide care related to the palliation and management of the terminal illness or related conditions, whether provided by hospice employees or provided under arrangement, must be reported. The one exception is related to General Inpatient Care. CMS is not requiring hospices to report visit data at this time for visits made by non-hospice staff providing General Inpatient Care in contract facilities. However, General Inpatient Care visits related to the palliation and management of the terminal illness or related conditions provided by hospice staff in contract facilities must be reported , and all General Inpatient Care visits related to the palliation and management of the terminal illness or related conditions provided in hospice-owned facilities must be reported.

HCPCS/Accommodation Rates/HIPPS Rate Codes

For services provided on or before December 31, 2006, HCPCS codes are required only to report procedures on service lines for attending physician services (revenue 657). Level of care revenue codes (651, 652, 655 or 656) do not require HCPCS coding.

For services provided on or after January 1, 2007, hospices must also report a HCPCS code along with each level of care revenue code (651, 652, 655 and 656) to identify the type of service location where that level of care was provided.

The following HCPCS codes will be used to report the type of service location for hospice services:

| HCPCS Code | Definition |
|---|---|
| Q5001 | HOSPICE CARE PROVIDED IN PATIENT'S HOME/RESIDENCE |
| Q5002 | HOSPICE CARE PROVIDED IN ASSISTED LIVING FACILITY |
| Q5003 | HOSPICE CARE PROVIDED IN NURSING LONG TERM CARE FACILITY (LTC) OR NON-SKILLED NURSING FACILITY (NF) |
| Q5004 | HOSPICE CARE PROVIDED IN SKILLED NURSING FACILITY (SNF) |
| Q5005 | HOSPICE CARE PROVIDED IN INPATIENT HOSPITAL |
| Q5006 | HOSPICE CARE PROVIDED IN INPATIENT HOSPICE FACILITY |
| Q5007 | HOSPICE CARE PROVIDED IN LONG TERM CARE HOSPITAL (LTCH) |
| Q5008 | HOSPICE CARE PROVIDED IN INPATIENT PSYCHIATRIC FACILITY |
| Q5009 | HOSPICE CARE PROVIDED IN PLACE NOT OTHERWISE SPECIFIED (NOS) |

If care is rendered at multiple locations, each location is to be identified on the claim with a corresponding HCPCS code. For example, routine home care may be provided for a portion of the billing period in the patient's residence and another portion in an assisted living facility. In this case, report one revenue code 651 line with HCPCS code Q5001 and the number of days of routine home care provided in the residence and another revenue code 651 line with HCPCS code Q5002 and the number of days of routine home care provided in the assisted living facility.

- Q5003 is to be used for skilled nursing facility residents in a non Medicare covered stay and nursing facility residents.

- Q5004 is to be used for skilled nursing facility residents in a Medicare covered stay.

These service location HCPCS codes are not required on revenue code lines describing the visits provided under each level of care (e.g. 055X, 056X, 057X).

Service Date  The HIPAA standard 837 Institutional claim format requires line item dates of service for all outpatient claims. Medicare classifies hospice claims as outpatient claims (see Chapter 1, Sec.60.4). For services provided on or before December 31, 2006, CMS allows hospices to satisfy the line item date of service requirement by placing any valid date within the FL 6 Statement Covers Period dates on line items on hospice claims.

For services provided on or after January 1, 2007, service date reporting requirements will vary between continuous home care lines (revenue code 652) and other revenue code lines.

Revenue code 652 - report a separately dated line item for each day that continuous home care is provided, reporting the number of hours, or parts of hours rounded to 15-minute increments, of continuous home care that was provided on that date.

Other payment revenue codes - report a separate line for each level of care provided at each service location type, as described in the instructions for HCPCS coding reported above. Hospices report the earliest date that each level of care was provided at each service location. Attending physician services should be individually dated, reporting the date that each HCPCS code billed was delivered.

Non-payment service revenue codes - report dates as described in the table above under Revenue Codes.

### Service Units
The hospice enters the number of units for each type of service. Units are measured in days for revenue codes 651, 655, and 656, in hours for revenue code 652, and in procedures for revenue code 657. For services provided on or after January 1, 2007, hours for revenue code 652 are reported in 15-minute increments. For services provided on or after January 1, 2008, units for visit discipline revenue codes are measured by the number of visits.

### Total Charges
The hospice enters the total charge for the service described on each revenue code line. This information is being collected for purposes of research and will not affect the amount of reimbursement.

### Payer Name
The hospice identifies the appropriate payer(s) for the claim.

National Provider Identifier - Billing Provider

The hospice enters its own National Provider Identifier (NPI).

### Principal Diagnosis Code
The hospice enters diagnosis coding as required by ICD-9-CM Coding Guidelines. Hospices may not report V-codes as the primary diagnosis on hospice claims. The principal diagnosis code describes the terminal illness of the hospice patient and V-codes do not describe terminal conditions.

### Other Diagnosis Codes
The hospice enters diagnosis coding as required by ICD-9-CM Coding Guidelines.

### Attending Provider Name and Identifiers
The hospice enters the National Provider Identifier (NPI) and name of the physician currently responsible for certifying the terminal illness, and signing the individual's plan of care for medical care and treatment.

### Other Provider Name and Identifiers
If the attending physician is a nurse practitioner, the hospice enters the NPI and name of the nurse practitioner.

## 100-4,11,40.1.3.1
### Care Plan Oversight
Care plan oversight (CPO) exists where there is physician supervision of patients under care of hospices that require complex and multidisciplinary care modalities involving regular physician development and/or revision of care plans. Implicit in the concept of CPO is the expectation that the physician has coordinated an aspect of the patient's care with the hospice during the month for which CPO services were billed.

For a physician or NP employed by or under arrangement with a hospice agency, CPO functions are incorporated and are part of the hospice per diem payment and as such may not be separately billed.

For information on separately billable CPO services by the attending physician or nurse practitioner see Chapter 12, 180 of this manual.

## 100-4,12,180
### Care Plan Oversight Services
The Medicare Benefit Policy Manual, Chapter 15, contains requirements for coverage for medical and other health services including those of physicians and non-physician practitioners.

Care plan oversight (CPO) is the physician supervision of a patient receiving complex and/or multidisciplinary care as part of Medicare-covered services provided by a participating home health agency or Medicare approved hospice.

CPO services require complex or multidisciplinary care modalities involving:  Regular physician development and/or revision of care plans;  Review of subsequent reports of patient status;  Review of related laboratory and other studies;  Communication with other health professionals not employed in the same practice who are involved in the patient's care;  Integration of new information into the medical treatment plan; and/or  Adjustment of medical therapy.

The CPO services require recurrent physician supervision of a patient involving 30 or more minutes of the physician's time per month. Services not countable toward the 30 minutes threshold that must be provided in order to bill for CPO include, but are not limited to:  Time associated with discussions with the patient, his or her family or friends to adjust medication or treatment;  Time spent by staff getting or filing charts;  Travel time; and/or  Physician's time spent telephoning prescriptions into the pharmacist unless the telephone conversation involves discussions of pharmaceutical therapies.

Implicit in the concept of CPO is the expectation that the physician has coordinated an aspect of the patient's care with the home health agency or hospice during the month for which CPO services were billed. The physician who bills for CPO must be the same physician who signs the plan of care.

Nurse practitioners, physician assistants, and clinical nurse specialists, practicing within the scope of State law, may bill for care plan oversight. These non-physician practitioners must have been providing ongoing care for the beneficiary through evaluation and management services. These non-physician practitioners may not bill for CPO if they have been involved only with the delivery of the Medicare-covered home health or hospice service.

## A. Home Health CPO

Non-physician practitioners can perform CPO only if the physician signing the plan of care provides regular ongoing care under the same plan of care as does the NPP billing for CPO and either: The physician and NPP are part of the same group practice; or If the NPP is a nurse practitioner or clinical nurse specialist, the physician signing the plan of care also has a collaborative agreement with the NPP; or If the NPP is a physician assistant, the physician signing the plan of care is also the physician who provides general supervision of physician assistant services for the practice.

Billing may be made for care plan oversight services furnished by an NPP when: The NPP providing the care plan oversight has seen and examined the patient; The NPP providing care plan oversight is not functioning as a consultant whose participation is limited to a single medical condition rather than multidisciplinary coordination of care; and The NPP providing care plan oversight integrates his or her care with that of the physician who signed the plan of care.

NPPs may not certify the beneficiary for home health care.

## B. Hospice CPO

The attending physician or nurse practitioner (who has been designated as the attending physician) may bill for hospice CPO when they are acting as an "attending physician".

An "attending physician" is one who has been identified by the individual, at the time he/she elects hospice coverage, as having the most significant role in the determination and delivery of their medical care. They are not employed nor paid by the hospice. The care plan oversight services are billed using Form CMS-1500 or electronic equivalent.

For additional information on hospice CPO, see Chapter 11, 40.1.3.1 of this manual.

## 100-4,12,180.1

### Care Plan Oversight Billing Requirements

#### A. Codes for Which Separate Payment May Be Made

Effective January 1, 1995, separate payment may be made for CPO oversight services for 30 minutes or more if the requirements specified in the Medicare Benefits Policy Manual, Chapter 15 are met.

Providers billing for CPO must submit the claim with no other services billed on that claim and may bill only after the end of the month in which the CPO services were rendered. CPO services may not be billed across calendar months and should be submitted (and paid) only for one unit of service.

Physicians may bill and be paid separately for CPO services only if all the criteria in the Medicare Benefit Policy Manual, Chapter 15 are met.

#### B. Physician Certification and Recertification of Home Health Plans of Care

Effective 2001, two new HCPCS codes for the certification and recertification and development of plans of care for Medicare-covered home health services were created.

See the Medicare General Information, Eligibility, and Entitlement Manual, Pub. 100-01, Chapter 4, "Physician Certification and Recertification of Services," 10-60, and the Medicare Benefit Policy Manual, Pub. 100-02, Chapter 7, "Home Health Services", 30.

The home health agency certification code can be billed only when the patient has not received Medicare-covered home health services for at least 60 days. The home health agency recertification code is used after a patient has received services for at least 60 days (or one certification period) when the physician signs the certification after the initial certification period. The home health agency recertification code will be reported only once every 60 days, except in the rare situation when the patient starts a new episode before 60 days elapses and requires a new plan of care to start a new episode.

#### C. Provider Number of Home Health Agency (HHA) or Hospice

For claims for CPO submitted on or after January 1, 1997, physicians must enter on the Medicare claim form the 6-character Medicare provider number of the HHA or hospice providing Medicare-covered services to the beneficiary for the period during which CPO services was furnished and for which the physician signed the plan of care. Physicians are responsible for obtaining the HHA or hospice Medicare provider numbers.

Additionally, physicians should provide their UPIN to the HHA or hospice furnishing services to their patient.

NOTE: There is currently no place on the HIPAA standard ASC X12N 837 professional format to specifically include the HHA or hospice provider number required for a care plan oversight claim. For this reason, the requirement to include the HHA or hospice provider number on a care plan oversight claim is temporarily waived until a new version of this electronic standard format is adopted under HIPAA and includes a place to provide the HHA and hospice provider numbers for care plan oversight claims.

## 100-4,12,190.3

### List of Medicare Telehealth Services

The use of a telecommunications system may substitute for a face-to-face, "hands on" encounter for consultation, office visits, individual psychotherapy, pharmacologic management, psychiatric diagnostic interview examination, end stage renal disease related services, and individual medical nutrition therapy. These services and corresponding current procedure terminology (CPT) or Healthcare Common Procedure Coding System (HCPCS) codes are listed below.

Consultations (CPT codes 99241 - 99275) - Effective October 1, 2001 - December 31, 2005; Consultations (CPT codes 99241 - 99255) - Effective January 1, 2006; Office or other outpatient visits (CPT codes 99201 - 99215); Individual psychotherapy (CPT codes 90804 - 90809); Pharmacologic management (CPT code 90862); and Psychiatric diagnostic interview examination (CPT code 90801) - Effective March 1, 2003.

End Stage Renal Disease (ESRD) related services (HCPCS codes G0308, G0309, G0311, G0312, G0314, G0315, G0317, and G0318) - Effective January 1, 2005.

Individual Medical Nutrition Therapy (HCPCS codes G0270, 97802, and 97803) (Effective January 1, 2006).

Neurobehavioral status exam (CPT code 96116) (Effective January 1, 2008).

## 100-4,12,190.7
### Contractor Editing of Telehealth Claims

Medicare telehealth services (as listed in section 190.3) are billed with either the "GT" or "GQ" modifier. The contractor shall approve covered telehealth services if the physician or practitioner is licensed under State law to provide the service. Contractors must familiarize themselves with licensure provisions of States for which they process claims and disallow telehealth services furnished by physicians or practitioners who are not authorized to furnish the applicable telehealth service under State law. For example, if a nurse practitioner is not licensed to provide individual psychotherapy under State law, he or she would not be permitted to receive payment for individual psychotherapy under Medicare. The contractor shall install edits to ensure that only properly licensed physicians and practitioners are paid for covered telehealth services.

If a contractor receives claims for professional telehealth services coded with the "GQ" modifier (representing "via asynchronous telecommunications system"), it shall approve/pay for these services only if the physician or practitioner is affiliated with a Federal telemedicine demonstration conducted in Alaska or Hawaii. The contractor may require the physician or practitioner at the distant site to document his or her participation in a Federal telemedicine demonstration program conducted in Alaska or Hawaii prior to paying for telehealth services provided via asynchronous, store and forward technologies.

If a contractor denies telehealth services because the physician or practitioner may not bill for them, the contractor uses MSN message 21.18: "This item or service is not covered when performed or ordered by this practitioner." The contractor uses remittance advice message 52 when denying the claim based upon MSN message 21.18.

If a service is billed with one of the telehealth modifiers and the procedure code is not designated as a covered telehealth service, the contractor denies the service using MSN message 9.4: "This item or service was denied because information required to make payment was incorrect." The remittance advice message depends on what is incorrect, e.g., B18 if procedure code or modifier is incorrect, 125 for submission billing errors, 4-12 for difference inconsistencies. The contractor uses B18 as the explanation for the denial of the claim.

The only claims from institutional facilities that FIs shall pay for telehealth services at the distant site, except for MNT services, are for physician or practitioner services when the distant site is located in a CAH that has elected Method II, and the physician or practitioner has reassigned his/her benefits to the CAH. The CAH bills its regular FI for the professional services provided at the distant site via a telecommunications system, in any of the revenue codes 096x, 097x or 098x. All requirements for billing distant site telehealth services apply.

Claims from hospitals or CAHs for MNT services are submitted to the hospital's or CAH's regular FI. Payment is based on the non-facility amount on the Medicare Physician Fee Schedule for the particular HCPCS codes.

## 100-4,12,210.1
### Application of Limitation
B3-2472 - 2472.5

### A. Status of Patient
The limitation is applicable to expenses incurred in connection with the treatment of an individual who is not an inpatient of a hospital. Thus, the limitation applies to mental health services furnished to a person in a physician's office, in the patient's home, in a skilled nursing facility, as an outpatient, and so forth. The term "hospital" in this context means an institution, which is primarily engaged in providing to inpatients, by or under the supervision of physician(s): Diagnostic and therapeutic services for medical diagnosis, treatment and care of injured, disabled, or sick persons; Rehabilitation services for injured, disabled, or sick persons; or Psychiatric services for the diagnosis and treatment of mentally ill patients.

### B. Disorders Subject to Limitation
The term "mental, psychoneurotic, and personality disorders" is defined as the specific psychiatric conditions described in the American Psychiatric Association's (APA) "Diagnostic and Statistical Manual of Mental Disorders, Third Edition - Revised (DSMIII- R)." When the treatment services rendered are both for a psychiatric condition as defined in the DSM-III-R and one or more nonpsychiatric conditions, separate the expenses for the psychiatric aspects of treatment from the expenses for the nonpsychiatric aspects of treatment. However, in any case in which the psychiatric treatment component is not readily distinguishable from the nonpsychiatric treatment component, all of the expenses are allocated to whichever component constitutes the primary diagnosis.

1. Diagnosis Clearly Meets Definition - If the primary diagnosis reported for a particular service is the same as or equivalent to a condition described in the APA's DSM-III-R, the expense for the service is subject to the limitation except as described in subsection D.

2. Diagnosis Does Not Clearly Meet Definition - When it is not clear whether the primary diagnosis reported meets the definition of mental, psychoneurotic, and personality disorders, it may be necessary to contact the practitioner to clarify the diagnosis. In deciding whether contact is necessary in a given case, give consideration to such factors as the type of services rendered, the diagnosis, and the individual's previous utilization history.

### C. Services Subject to Limitation
Carriers apply the limitation to claims for professional services that represent mental health treatment furnished to individuals who are not hospital inpatients by physicians, clinical psychologists, clinical social workers, and other allied health professionals.

Items and supplies furnished by physicians or other mental health practitioners in connection with treatment are also subject to the limitation. (The limitation also applies to CORF claims processed by intermediaries.) Carriers apply the limitation only to treatment services. It does not apply to diagnostic services as described in subsection D. Testing services performed to evaluate a patient's progress during treatment are considered part of treatment and are subject to the limitation.

### D. Services Not Subject to Limitation
1. Diagnosis of Alzheimer's Disease or Related Disorder - When the primary diagnosis reported for a particular service is Alzheimer's Disease (coded 331.0 in the "International Classification of Diseases, 9th Revision") or Alzheimer's or other disorders coded 290.XX in the APA's DSM-III-R, carriers look to the nature of the service that has been rendered in determining whether it is subject to the limitation. Typically, treatment provided to a patient with a diagnosis of Alzheimer's Disease or a related disorder represents medical management of the patient's condition (rather than psychiatric treatment) and is not

subject to the limitation. However, when the primary treatment rendered to a patient with such a diagnosis is psychotherapy, it is subject to the limitation.

2. Brief Office Visits for Monitoring or Changing Drug Prescriptions - Brief office visits for the sole purpose of monitoring or changing drug prescriptions used in the treatment of mental, psychoneurotic and personality disorders are not subject to the limitation. These visits are reported using HCPCS code M0064 (brief office visit for the sole purpose of monitoring or changing drug prescriptions used in the treatment of mental, psychoneurotic, and personality disorders). Claims where the diagnosis reported is a mental, psychoneurotic, or personality disorder (other than a diagnosis specified in subsection A) are subject to the limitation except for the procedure identified by HCPCS code M0064.

3. Diagnostic Services - Carriers do not apply the limitation to tests and evaluations performed to establish or confirm the patient's diagnosis. Diagnostic services include psychiatric or psychological tests and interpretations, diagnostic consultations, and initial evaluations.

An initial visit to a practitioner for professional services often combines diagnostic evaluation and the start of therapy. Such a visit is neither solely diagnostic nor solely therapeutic. Therefore, carriers deem the initial visit to be diagnostic so that the limitation does not apply. Separating diagnostic and therapeutic components of a visit is not administratively feasible, unless the practitioner already has separately identified them on the bill. Determining the entire visit to be therapeutic is not justifiable since some diagnostic work must be done before even a tentative diagnosis can be made and certainly before therapy can be instituted. Moreover, the patient should not be disadvantaged because therapeutic as well as diagnostic services were provided in the initial visit. In the rare cases where a practitioner's diagnostic services take more than one visit, carriers do not apply the limitation to the additional visits. However, it is expected such cases are few. Therefore, when a practitioner bills for more than one visit for professional diagnostic services, carriers request documentation to justify the reason for more than one diagnostic visit.

4. Partial Hospitalization Services Not Directly Provided by Physician - The limitation does not apply to partial hospitalization services that are not directly provided by a physician. These services are billed by hospitals and community mental health centers (CMHCs) to intermediaries.

### E. Computation of Limitation
Carriers determine the Medicare allowed payment amount for services subject to the limitation.

They:

- Multiply this amount by 0.625;
- Subtract any unsatisfied deductible; and,
- Multiply the remainder by 0.8 to obtain the amount of Medicare payment.

The beneficiary is responsible for the difference between the amount paid by Medicare and the full allowed amount.

EXAMPLE A:

A beneficiary is referred to a Medicare participating psychiatrist who performs a diagnostic evaluation that costs $350. Those services are not subject to the limitation, and they satisfy the deductible. The psychiatrist then conducts 10 weekly therapy sessions for which he/she charges $125 each. The Medicare allowed amount is $90 each, for a total of $900.

Apply the limitation by multiplying 0.625 times $900, which equals $562.50.

Apply regular 20 percent coinsurance by multiplying 0.8 times $562.50, which equals $450 (the amount of Medicare payment).

The beneficiary is responsible for $450 (the difference between Medicare payment and the allowed amount).

EXAMPLE B:

A beneficiary was an inpatient of a psychiatric hospital and was discharged on January 1, 1992. During his/her inpatient stay he/she was diagnosed and therapy was begun under a treatment team that included a clinical psychologist. He/she received post-discharge therapy from the psychologist for 12 sessions, at which point the psychologist administered testing that showed the patient had recovered sufficiently to warrant termination of therapy. The allowed amount for the therapy sessions was $80 each, and the amount for the testing was $125, for a total of $1085. All services in 1992 were subject to the limitation, since the diagnosis had been completed in the hospital and the subsequent testing was a part of therapy.

Apply the limitation by multiplying 0.625 times $1085, which gives $678.13.

Since the deductible must be met for 1992, subtract $100 from $678.13, for a remainder of $578.13.

Determine Medicare payment by multiplying the remainder by 0.8, which equals $462.50.

The beneficiary is responsible for $622.50.

## 100-4,12,30.4
### Cardiovascular System (Codes 92950-93799)

#### A. Echocardiography Contrast Agents
Effective October 1, 2000, physicians may separately bill for contrast agents used in echocardiography. Physicians should use HCPCS Code A9700 (Supply of Injectable Contrast Material for Use in Echocardiography, per study). The type of service code is 9. This code will be carrier-priced.

#### B. Electronic Analyses of Implantable Cardioverter-defibrillators and Pacemakers
The CPT codes 93731, 93734, 93741 and 93743 are used to report electronic analyses of single or dual chamber pacemakers and single or dual chamber implantable cardioverterdefibrillators. In the office, a physician uses a device called a programmer to obtain information about the status and performance of the device and to evaluate the patient's cardiac rhythm and response to the implanted device. Advances in information technology now enable physicians to evaluate patients with implanted cardiac devices without requiring the patient to be present in the physician's office. Using a manufacturer's specific monitor/transmitter, a patient can send complete device data and specific cardiac data to a distant receiving station or secure Internet server. The electronic analysis of cardiac device data that is remotely obtained provides immediate and long-term data on the device and clinical data on the patient's cardiac functioning equivalent to that obtained during an in-office evaluation. Physicians should report the electronic analysis of an implanted cardiac device

using remotely obtained data as described above with CPT code 93731, 93734, 93741 or 93743, depending on the type of cardiac device implanted in the patient.

## 100-4,12,60
### Payment for Pathology Services
B3-15020, AB-01-47 (CR1499)

### A. General Payment Rule
Payment may be made under the fee schedule for the professional component of physician laboratory or physician pathology services furnished to hospital inpatients or outpatients by hospital physicians or by independent laboratories, if they qualify as the reassignee for the physician service.. Payment may be made under the fee schedule, as noted below, for the technical component (TC) of pathology services furnished by an independent laboratory to hospital inpatients or outpatients. Payment may be made under the fee schedule for the technical component of physician pathology services furnished by an independent laboratory, or a hospital if it is acting as an independent laboratory, to non-hospital patients. The Medicare physician fee schedule identifies those physician laboratory or physician pathology services that have a technical component service.

CMS published a final regulation in 1999 that would no longer allow independent laboratories to bill under the physician fee schedule for the TC of physician pathology services. The implementation of this regulation was delayed by Section 542 of the Benefits and Improvement and Protection Act of 2000 (BIPA). Section 542 allows the Medicare carrier to continue to pay for the TC of physician pathology services when an independent laboratory furnishes this service to an inpatient or outpatient of a covered hospital. This provision is applicable to TC services furnished in 2001, 2002, 2003, 2004, 2005 or 2006.

For this provision, a covered hospital is a hospital that had an arrangement with an independent laboratory that was in effect as of July 22, 1999, under which a laboratory furnished the TC of physician pathology services to fee-for-service Medicare beneficiaries who were hospital inpatients or outpatients, and submitted claims for payment for the TC to a carrier. The TC could have been submitted separately or combined with the professional component and reported as a combined service.

The term, fee-for-service Medicare beneficiary, means an individual who:

- Is entitled to benefits under Part A or enrolled under Part B of title XVIII or both; and
- Is not enrolled in any of the following: A Medicare + Choice plan under Part C of such title; a plan offered by an eligible organization under 1876 of the Social Security Act; a program of all-inclusive care for the elderly under 1894; or a social health maintenance organization demonstration project established under Section 4108 of the Omnibus Budget Reconciliation Act of 1987.

In implementing Section 542, the carriers should consider as independent laboratories those entities that it has previously recognized as independent laboratories. An independent laboratory that has acquired another independent laboratory that had an arrangement of July 22, 1999, with a covered hospital, can bill the TC of physician pathology services for that hospital's inpatients and outpatients under the physician fee schedule.

An independent laboratory that furnishes the TC of physician pathology services to inpatients or outpatients of a hospital that is not a covered hospital may not bill the carrier for the TC of physician pathology services during the time 542 is in effect.

If the arrangement between the independent laboratory and the covered hospital limited the provision of TC physician pathology services to certain situations or at particular times, then the independent laboratory can bill the carrier only for these limited services.

The carrier shall require independent laboratories that had an arrangement, on or prior to July 22, 1999 with a covered hospital, to bill for the technical component of physician pathology services to provide a copy of this agreement, or other documentation substantiating that an arrangement was in effect between the hospital and the independent laboratory as of this date. The independent laboratory must submit this documentation for each covered hospital that the independent laboratory services.

See Chapter 16 for additional instruction on laboratory services including clinical diagnostic laboratory services.

Physician laboratory and pathology services are limited to:

- Surgical pathology services;
- Specific cytopathology, hematology and blood banking services that have been identified to require performance by a physician and are listed below;
- Clinical consultation services that meet the requirements in subsection D below; and
- Clinical laboratory interpretation services that meet the requirements and which are specifically listed in subsection E below.

### B. Surgical Pathology Services
Surgical pathology services include the gross and microscopic examination of organ tissue performed by a physician, except for autopsies, which are not covered by Medicare. Surgical pathology services paid under the physician fee schedule are reported under the following CPT codes:

88300, 88302, 88304, 88305, 88307, 88309, 88311, 88312, 88313, 88314, 88318, 88319, 88321, 88323, 88325, 88329, 88331, 88332, 88342, 88346, 88347, 88348, 88349, 88355, 88356, 88358, 88361, 88362, 88365, 88380.

Depending upon circumstances and the billing entity, the carriers may pay professional component, technical component or both.

### C. Specific Hematology, Cytopathology and Blood Banking Services
Cytopathology services include the examination of cells from fluids, washings, brushings or smears, but generally excluding hematology. Examining cervical and vaginal smears are the most common service in cytopathology. Cervical and vaginal smears do not require interpretation by a physician unless the results are or appear to be abnormal. In such cases, a physician personally conducts a separate microscopic evaluation to determine the nature of an abnormality. This microscopic evaluation ordinarily does require performance by a physician. When medically necessary and when furnished by a physician, it is paid under the fee schedule.

These codes include 88104, 88106, 88107, 88108, 88112, 88125, 88141, 88160, 88161, 88162, 88172, 88173, 88180, 88182.

For services furnished prior to January 1, 1999, carriers pay separately under the physician fee schedule for the interpretation of an abnormal pap smear furnished to a hospital inpatient by a physician. They must pay under the clinical laboratory fee schedule for pap smears furnished in all other situations. This policy also applies to screening pap smears requiring a physician interpretation. For services furnished on or after January 1, 1999, carriers allow separate payment for a physician's interpretation of a pap smear to any patient (i.e., hospital or non-hospital) as long as: (1) the laboratory's screening personnel suspect an abnormality; and (2) the physician reviews and interprets the pap smear.

This policy also applies to screening pap smears requiring a physician interpretation and described in the National Coverage Determination Manual and Chapter 18. These services are reported under codes P3000 or P3001.

Physician hematology services include microscopic evaluation of bone marrow aspirations and biopsies. It also includes those limited number of peripheral blood smears which need to be referred to a physician to evaluate the nature of an apparent abnormality identified by the technologist. These codes include 85060, 38220, 85097, and 38221.

Carriers pay the professional component for the interpretation of an abnormal blood smear (code 85060) furnished to a hospital inpatient by a hospital physician or an independent laboratory.

For the other listed hematology codes, payment may be made for the professional component if the service is furnished to a patient by a hospital physician or independent laboratory. In addition, payment may be made for these services furnished to patients by an independent laboratory.

Codes 38220 and 85097 represent professional-only component services and have no technical component values.

Blood banking services of hematologists and pathologists are paid under the physician fee schedule when analyses are performed on donor and/or patient blood to determine compatible donor units for transfusion where cross matching is difficult or where contamination with transmissible disease of donor is suspected.

The blood banking codes are 86077, 86078, and 86079 and represent professional component only services. These codes do not have a technical component.

## D. Clinical Consultation Services

- Clinical consultations are paid under the physician fee schedule only if they:
- Are requested by the patient's attending physician;
- Relate to a test result that lies outside the clinically significant normal or expected range in view of the condition of the patient;
- Result in a written narrative report included in the patient's medical record; and
- Require the exercise of medical judgment by the consultant physician.

Clinical consultations are professional component services only. There is no technical component. The clinical consultation codes are 80500 and 80502.

Routine conversations held between a laboratory director and an attending physician about test orders or results do not qualify as consultations unless all four requirements are met. Laboratory personnel, including the director, may from time to time contact attending physicians to report test results or to suggest additional testing or be contacted by attending physicians on similar matters. These contacts do not constitute clinical consultations. However, if in the course of such a contact, the attending physician requests a consultation from the pathologist, and if that consultation meets the other criteria and is properly documented, it is paid under the fee schedule.

EXAMPLE: A pathologist telephones a surgeon about a patient's suitability for surgery based on the results of clinical laboratory test results. During the course of their conversation, the surgeon ask the pathologist whether, based on test results, patient history and medical records, the patient is a candidate for surgery. The surgeon's request requires the pathologist to render a medical judgment and provide a consultation. The athologist follows up his/her oral advice with a written report and the surgeon notes in the patient's medical record that he/she requested a consultation. This consultation is paid under the fee schedule.

In any case, if the information could ordinarily be furnished by a nonphysician laboratory specialist, the service of the physician is not a consultation payable under the fee schedule.

See the Program Integrity Manual for guidelines for related data analysis to identify inappropriate patterns of billing for consultations.

## E. Clinical Laboratory Interpretation Services

Only clinical laboratory interpretation services listed below and which meet the criteria in subsections D.1, D.3, and D.4 for clinical consultations and, as a result, are billable under the fee schedule. These services are reported under the clinical laboratory code with modifier 26. These services can be paid under the physician fee schedule if they are furnished to a patient by a hospital pathologist or an independent laboratory. Note that a hospital's standing order policy can be used as a substitute for the individual request by the patient's attending physician. Carriers are not allowed to revise CMS's list to accommodate local medical practice. The CMS periodically reviews this list and adds or deletes clinical laboratory codes as warranted.

Clinical Laboratory Interpretation Services

| Code | Definition |
|------|-----------|
| 83020 | Hemoglobin; electrophoresis |
| 83912 | Nucleic acid probe, with electrophoresis, with examination and report |
| 84165 | Protein, total, serum; electrophoretic fractionation and quantitation |
| 84181 | Protein; Western Blot with interpretation and report, blood or other body fluid |
| 84182 | Protein; Western Blot, with interpretation and report, blood or other body fluid, immunological probe for band identification; each |
| 85390 | Fibrinolysin; screening |
| 85576 | Platelet; aggregation (in vitro), any agent |
| 86255 | Fluorescent antibody; screen |
| 86256 | Fluorescent antibody; titer |
| 86320 | Immunoelectrophoresis; serum, each specimen |
| 86325 | Immunoelectrophoresis; other fluids (e.g.urine) with concentration, each specimen |
| 86327 | Immunoelectrophoresis; crossed (2 dimensional assay) |
| 86334 | Immunofixation electrophoresis |
| 87164 | Dark field examination, any source (e.g. penile, vaginal, oral, skin); includes specimen collection |

# APPENDIX 4 — PUB 100 REFERENCES

| Code | Definition |
|------|------------|
| 87207 | Smear, primary source, with interpretation; special stain for inclusion bodies or intracellular parasites (e.g. malaria, kala azar, herpes) |
| 88371 | Protein analysis of tissue by Western Blot, with interpretation and report. |
| 88372 | Protein analysis of tissue by Western Blot, immunological probe for band identification, each |
| 89060 | Crystal identification by light microscopy with or without polarizing lens analysis, any body fluid (except urine) |

## 100-4,13,140
### Bone Mass Measurements (BMMs)

Sections H1861(s)(15)H and H(rr)(1)H of the Social Security Act (the Act) (as added by 4106 of the Balanced Budget Act (BBA) of 1997) standardize Medicare coverage of medically necessary bone mass measurements by providing for uniform coverage under Medicare Part B. This coverage is effective for claims with dates of service furnished on or after July 1, I998.

Effective for dates of service on and after January 1, 2007, the CY 2007 Physician Fee Schedule final rule expanded the number of beneficiaries qualifying for BMM by reducing the dosage requirement for glucocorticoid (steroid) therapy from 7.5 mg of prednisone per day to 5.0 mg. It also changed the definition of BMM by removing coverage for a single-photon absorptiometry as it is not considered reasonable and necessary under section 1862 (a)(1)(A) of the Act. Finally, it required that in the case of monitoring and confirmatory baseline BMMs, they be performed with a dual-energy xray absorptiometry (axial) test.

Conditions of Coverage for BMMs are located in Pub.100-02, Medicare Benefit Policy Manual, chapter 15.

## 100-4,13,40.1.2
### HCPCS Coding Requirements

Providers must report HCPCS codes when submitting claims for MRA of the chest, abdomen, head, neck or peripheral vessels of lower extremities. The following HCPCS codes should be used to report these services:

| MRA of head | 70544, 70544-26, 70544-TC |
|-------------|---------------------------|
| MRA of head | 70545, 70545-26, 70545-TC |
| MRA of head | 70546, 70546-26, 70546-TC |
| MRA of neck | 70547, 70547-26, 70547-TC |
| MRA of neck | 70548, 70548-26, 70548-TC |
| MRA of neck | 70549, 70549-26, 70549-TC |
| MRA of chest | 71555, 71555-26, 71555-TC |
| MRA of pelvis | 72198, 72198-26, 72198-TC |
| MRA of abdomen (dates of service on or after July 1, 2003) - see below. | 74185, 74185-26, 74185-TC |
| MRA of peripheral vessels of lower extremities | 73725, 73725-26, 73725-TC |

Hospitals subject to OPPS should report the following C codes in place of the above HCPCS codes as follows:

- MRA of chest 71555: C8909 - C8911
- MRA of abdomen 74185: C8900 - C8902

- MRA of peripheral vessels of lower extremities 73725: C8912 - C8914

For claims with dates of service on or after July 1, 2003, coverage under this benefit has been expanded for the use of MRA for diagnosing pathology in the renal or aortoiliac arteries. The following HCPCS code should be used to report this expanded coverage of MRA:

- MRA, pelvis, with or without contrast material(s) 72198, 72198-26, 72198-TC

Hospitals subject to OPPS report the following C codes in place of HCPCS code 72198:

- MRA, pelvis, with or without contrast material(s) 72198: C8918 - C8920

Providers utilizing the UB-92 flat file, use record type 61, HCPCS code (Field No. 6) to report HCPCS/CPT code. Providers utilizing the hard copy UB-92, report the HCPCS/CPT code in FL 44 "HCPCS/Rates." Providers utilizing the Medicare A 837 Health Care Claim version 3051 implementations 3A.01 and 1A.C1, report the HCPCS/CPT in 2-395-SV202-02.

## 100-4,13,60.14
### Billing Requirements for PET Scans for Non-Covered Indications

For services performed on or after January 28, 2005, contractors shall accept claims with the following HCPCS code for non-covered PET indications:

- - G0235: PET imaging, any site not otherwise specified

Short Descriptor: PET not otherwise specified

Type of Service: 4

NOTE:This code is for a non-covered service.

## 100-4,13,60.3
### PET Scan Qualifying Conditions and HCPCS Code Chart

Below is a summary of all covered PET scan conditions, with effective dates.

NOTE: The G codes below except those a # can be used to bill for PET Scan services through January 27, 2005. Effective for dates of service on or after January 28, 2005, providers must bill for PET Scan services using the appropriate CPT codes. See section 60.3.1. The G codes with a # can continue to be used for billing after January 28, 2005 and these remain non-covered by Medicare. (NOTE: PET Scanners must be FDA-approved.)

| Conditions | Coverage Effective Date | ****HCPCS / CPT |
|------------|------------------------|-----------------|
| *Myocardial perfusion imaging (following previous PET G0030-G0047) single study, rest or stress (exercise and/or pharmacologic) | 3/14/95 | G0030 |
| *Myocardial perfusion imaging (following previous PET G0030-G0047) multiple studies, rest or stress (exercise and/or pharmacologic) | 3/14/95 | G0031 |
| *Myocardial perfusion imaging (following rest SPECT, 78464); single study, rest or stress (exercise and/or pharmacologic) | 3/14/95 | G0032 |

| Conditions | Coverage Effective Date | ****HCPCS / CPT |
|---|---|---|
| *Myocardial perfusion imaging (following rest SPECT 78464); multiple studies, rest or stress (exercise and/or pharmacologic) | 3/14/95 | G0033 |
| *Myocardial perfusion (following stress SPECT 78465); single study, rest or stress (exercise and/or pharmacologic) | 3/14/95 | G0034 |
| *Myocardial Perfusion Imaging (following stress SPECT 78465); multiple studies, rest or stress (exercise and/or pharmacologic) | 3/14/95 | G0035 |
| *Myocardial Perfusion Imaging (following coronary angiography 93510-93529); single study, rest or stress (exercise and/or pharmacologic) | 3/14/95 | G0036 |
| *Myocardial Perfusion Imaging, (following coronary angiography), 93510-93529); multiple studies, rest or stress (exercise and/or pharmacologic) | 3/14/95 | G0037 |
| *Myocardial Perfusion Imaging (following stress planar myocardial perfusion, 78460); single study, rest or stress (exercise and/or pharmacologic) | 3/14/95 | G0038 |
| *Myocardial Perfusion Imaging (following stress planar myocardial perfusion, 78460); multiple studies, rest or stress (exercise and/or pharmacologic) | 3/14/95 | G0039 |
| *Myocardial Perfusion Imaging (following stress echocardiogram 93350); single study, rest or stress (exercise and/or pharmacologic) | 3/14/95 | G0040 |
| *Myocardial Perfusion Imaging (following stress echocardiogram, 93350); multiple studies, rest or stress (exercise and/or pharmacologic) | 3/14/95 | G0041 |
| *Myocardial Perfusion Imaging (following stress nuclear ventriculogram 78481 or 78483); single study, rest or stress (exercise and/or pharmacologic) | 3/14/95 | G0042 |

| Conditions | Coverage Effective Date | ****HCPCS / CPT |
|---|---|---|
| *Myocardial Perfusion Imaging (following stress nuclear ventriculogram 78481 or 78483); multiple studies, rest or stress (exercise and/or pharmacologic) | 3/14/95 | G0043 |
| *Myocardial Perfusion Imaging (following stress ECG, 93000); single study, rest or stress (exercise and/or pharmacologic) | 3/14/95 | G0044 |
| *Myocardial perfusion (following stress ECG, 93000), multiple studies; rest or stress (exercise and/or pharmacologic) | 3/14/95 | G0045 |
| *Myocardial perfusion (following stress ECG, 93015), single study; rest or stress (exercise and/or pharmacologic) | 3/14/95 | G0046 |
| *Myocardial perfusion (following stress ECG, 93015); multiple studies, rest or stress (exercise and/or pharmacologic) | 3/14/95 | G0047 |
| PET imaging regional or whole body; single pulmonary nodule | 1/1/98 | G0125 |
| Lung cancer, non-small cell (PET imaging whole body) Diagnosis, Initial Staging, Restaging | 7/1/01 | G0210 G0211 G0212 |
| Colorectal cancer (PET imaging whole body) Diagnosis, Initial Staging, Restaging | 7/1/01 | G0213 G0214 G0215 |
| Melanoma (PET imaging whole body) Diagnosis, Initial Staging, Restaging | 7/1/01 | G0216 G0217 G0218 |
| Melanoma for non-covered indications Lymphoma (PET imaging whole body) | 7/1/01 | #G0219 |
| Diagnosis, Initial Staging, Restaging | 7/1/01 | G0220 G0221 G0222 |
| Head and neck cancer; excluding thyroid and CNS cancers (PET imaging whole body or regional) Diagnosis, Initial Staging, Restaging | 7/1/01 | G0223 G0224 G0225 |

# APPENDIX 4 — PUB 100 REFERENCES

## 100-4,13,60.3.1
### Appropriate CPT Codes Effective for PET Scans for Services Performed on or After January 28, 2005

NOTE: All PET scan services require the use of a radiopharmaceutical diagnostic imaging agent (tracer). The applicable tracer code should be billed when billing for a PET scan service. See section 60.3.2 below for applicable tracer codes.

| CPT Code | Description |
|---|---|
| 78459 | Myocardial imaging, positron emission tomography (PET), metabolic evaluation |
| 78491 | Myocardial imaging, positron emission tomography (PET), perfusion, single study at rest or stress |
| 78492 | Myocardial imaging, positron emission tomography (PET), perfusion, multiple studies at rest and/or stress |
| 78608 | Brain imaging, positron emission tomography (PET); metabolic evaluation |
| 78811 | Tumor imaging, positron emission tomography (PET); limited area (eg, chest, head/neck) |
| 78812 | Tumor imaging, positron emission tomography (PET); skull base to mid-thigh |
| 78813 | Tumor imaging, positron emission tomography (PET); whole body |
| 78814 | Tumor imaging, positron emission tomography (PET) with concurrently acquired computed tomography (CT) for attenuation correction and anatomical localization; limited area (eg, chest, head/neck) |
| 78815 | Tumor imaging, positron emission tomography (PET) with concurrently acquired computed tomography (CT) for attenuation correction and anatomical localization; skull base to mid-thigh |
| 78816 | Tumor imaging, positron emission tomography (PET) with concurrently acquired computed tomography (CT) for attenuation correction and anatomical localization; whole body |

## 100-4,13,60.3.2
### Tracer Codes Required for PET Scans

The following tracer codes are applicable only to CPT 78491 and 78492. They can not be reported with any other code.

Institutional providers billing the fiscal intermediary.

| HCPCS | Description |
|---|---|
| *A9555 | Rubidium Rb-82, Diagnostic, Per study dose, Up To 60 Millicuries |
| * Q3000 (Deleted effective 12/31/05) | Supply of Radiopharmaceutical Diagnostic Imaging Agent, Rubidium Rb-82, per dose |
| A9526 | Nitrogen N-13 Ammonia, Diagnostic, Per study dose, Up To 40 Millicuries |

NOTE: For claims with dates of service prior to 1/01/06, providers report Q3000 for supply of radiopharmaceutical diagnostic imaging agent, Rubidium Rb-82. For claims with dates of service 1/01/06 and later, providers report A9555 for radiopharmaceutical diagnostic imaging agent, Rubidium Rb-82 in place of Q3000.

Physicians / practitioners billing the carrier:

| HCPCS | Description |
|---|---|
| *A4641 | Supply of Radiopharmaceutical Diagnostic Imaging Agent, Not Otherwise Classified |
| A9526 | Nitrogen N-13 Ammonia, Diagnostic, Per study dose, Up To 40 Millicuries |
| A9555 | Rubidium Rb-82, Diagnostic, Per study dose, Up To 60 Millicuries |

*NOTE: Effective January 1, 2008, tracer code A4641 is not applicable for PET Scans.

The following tracer codes are applicable only to CPT 78459, 78608, 78811-78816. They can not be reported with any other code:

Institutional providers billing the fiscal intermediary:

| HCPCS | Description |
|---|---|
| * A9552 | Fluorodeoxyglucose F18, FDG, Diagnostic, Per study dose, Up to 45 Millicuries |
| * C1775 (Deleted effective 12/31/05) | Supply of Radiopharmaceutical Diagnostic Imaging Agent, Fluorodeoxyglucose F18, (2-Deoxy-2-18F Fluoro-D-Glucose), Per dose (4-40 Mci/Ml) |
| **A4641 | Supply of Radiopharmaceutical Diagnostic Imaging Agent, Not Otherwise Classified |

* NOTE: For claims with dates of service prior to 1/01/06, OPPS hospitals report C1775 for supply of radiopharmaceutical diagnostic imaging agent, Fluorodeoxyglucose F18. For claims with dates of service 1/01/06 and later, providers report A9552 for radiopharmaceutical diagnostic imaging agent, Fluorodeoxyglucose F18 in place of C1775.

** NOTE: Effective January 1, 2008, tracer code A4641 is not applicable for PET Scans.

Physicians / practitioners billing the carrier:

| HCPCS | Description |
|---|---|
| A9552 | Fluorodeoxyglucose F18, FDG, Diagnostic, Per study dose, Up to 45 Millicuries |
| *A4641 | Supply of Radiopharmaceutical Diagnostic Imaging Agent, Not Otherwise Classified |

*NOTE: Effective January 1, 2008, tracer code A4641 is not applicable for PET Scans.

## 100-4,13,60.7.1
### Darbepoetin Alfa (Aranesp) Facility Billing Requirements

Revenue code 0636 is used to report Aranesp.

The HCPCS code for aranesp must be included: HCPCS HCPCS Description Dates of Service Q4054 Injection, darbepoetin alfa, 1mcg (for ESRD on Dialysis) 1/1/2004 through 12/31/2005 J0882 Injection, darbepoetin alfa, 1mcg (for ESRD on Dialysis)

1/1/2006 to present The hematocrit reading taken prior to the last administration of Aranesp during the billing period must also be reported on the UB-92/Form CMS-1450 with value code 49. For claims with dates of service on or after April 1, 2006, a hemoglobin reading may be reported on Aranesp claims using value code 48.

Effective January 1, 2006 the definition of value code 48 and 49 used to report the hemoglobin and hematocrit readings are changed to indicate the patient's most recent reading taken before the start of the billing period.

To report a hematocrit or hemoglobin reading for a new patient on or after January 1, 2006, the provider should report the reading that prompted the treatment of darbepoetin alfa. The provider may use results documented on form CMS 2728 or the patient's medical records from a transferring facility.

The payment allowance for Aranesp is the only allowance for the drug and its administration when used for ESRD patients. Effective January 1, 2005, the cost of supplies to administer Aranesp may be billed to the FI. HCPCS A4657 and Revenue Code 270 should be used to capture the charges for syringes used in the administration of Aranesp. The maximum number of administrations of Aranesp for a billing cycle is 5 times in 30/31days.

## 100-4,16,10
### Background
B3-2070, B3-2070.1, B3-4110.3, B3-5114

Diagnostic X-ray, laboratory, and other diagnostic tests, including materials and the services of technicians, are covered under the Medicare program. Some clinical laboratory procedures or tests require Food and Drug Administration (FDA) approval before coverage is provided.

A diagnostic laboratory test is considered a laboratory service for billing purposes, regardless of whether it is performed in:

- A physician's office, by an independent laboratory;
- By a hospital laboratory for its outpatients or nonpatients;
- In a rural health clinic; or
- In an HMO or Health Care Prepayment Plan (HCPP) for a patient who is not a member.

When a hospital laboratory performs laboratory tests for nonhospital patients, the laboratory is functioning as an independent laboratory, and still bills the fiscal intermediary (FI). Also, when physicians and laboratories perform the same test, whether manually or with automated equipment, the services are deemed similar. Laboratory services furnished by an independent laboratory are covered under SMI if the laboratory is an approved Independent Clinical Laboratory. However, as is the case of all diagnostic services, in order to be covered these services must be related to a patient's illness or injury (or symptom or complaint) and ordered by a physician. A small number of laboratory tests can be covered as a preventive screening service.

See the Medicare Benefit Policy Manual, Chapter 15, for detailed coverage requirements.

See the Medicare Program Integrity Manual, Chapter 10, for laboratory/supplier enrollment guidelines.

See the Medicare State Operations Manual for laboratory/supplier certification requirements.

## 100-4,16,60.2
### Travel Allowance
In addition to a specimen collection fee allowed under Sec.60.1, Medicare, under Part B, covers a specimen collection fee and travel allowance for a laboratory technician to draw a specimen from either a nursing home patient or homebound patient under Sec.1833(h)(3) of the Act and payment is made based on the clinical laboratory fee schedule. The travel allowance is intended to cover the estimated travel costs of collecting a specimen and to reflect the technician's salary and travel costs.

The additional allowance can be made only where a specimen collection fee is also payable, i.e., no travel allowance is made where the technician merely performs a messenger service to pick up a specimen drawn by a physician or nursing home personnel. The travel allowance may not be paid to a physician unless the trip to the home, or to the nursing home was solely for the purpose of drawing a specimen. Otherwise travel costs are considered to be associated with the other purposes of the trip. The travel allowance is not distributed by CMS. Instead, the carrier must calculate the travel allowance for each claim using the following rules for the particular Code. The following HCPCS codes are used for travel allowances:

- Per Mile Travel Allowance (P9603)
- The minimum "per mile travel allowance" is $1.035. The per mile travel allowance is to be used in situations where the average trip to patients' homes is longer than 20 miles round trip, and is to be pro-rated in situations where specimens are drawn or picked up from non-Medicare patients in the same trip. - one way, in connection with medically necessary laboratory specimen collection drawn from homebound or nursing home bound patient; prorated miles actually traveled (carrier allowance on per mile basis); or
- The per mile allowance was computed using the Federal mileage rate plus an additional 45 cents a mile to cover the technician's time and travel costs. Contractors have the option of establishing a higher per mile rate in excess of the minimum (1.035 cents a mile in CY 2008) if local conditions warrant it. The minimum mileage rate will be reviewed and updated in conjunction with the clinical lab fee schedule as needed. At no time will the laboratory be allowed to bill for more miles than are reasonable or for miles not actually traveled by the laboratory technician.

Example 1: In CY 2008, a laboratory technician travels 60 miles round trip from a lab in a city to a remote rural location, and back to the lab to draw a single Medicare patient's blood. The total reimbursement would be $62.10 (60 miles x 1.035 cents a mile), plus the specimen collection fee.

Example 2: In CY 2008, a laboratory technician travels 40 miles from the lab to a

Medicare patient's home to draw blood, and then travels an additional 10 miles to a non- Medicare patient's home and then travels 30 miles to return to the lab. The total miles traveled would be 80 miles. The claim submitted would be for one half of the miles traveled or $41.40 (40 x 1.035), plus the specimen collection fee.

### Flat Rate (P9604)
The CMS will pay a minimum of $9.55 one way flat rate travel allowance. The flat rate travel allowance is to be used in areas where average trips are less than 20 miles round trip. The flat rate travel fee is to be pro-rated for more than one blood drawn at the same address, and for stops at the homes of Medicare

and non-Medicare patients. The laboratory does the pro-ration when the claim is submitted based on the number of patients seen on that trip. The specimen collection fee will be paid for each patient encounter.

This rate is based on an assumption that a trip is an average of 15 minutes and up to 10 miles one way. It uses the Federal mileage rate and a laboratory technician's time of $17.66 an hour, including overhead. Contractors have the option of establishing a flat rate in excess of the minimum of $9.55, if local conditions warrant it. The minimum national flat rate will be reviewed and updated in conjunction with the clinical laboratory fee schedule, as necessitated by adjustments in the Federal travel allowance and salaries.

The claimant identifies round trip travel by use of the LR modifier

Example 3: A laboratory technician travels from the laboratory to a single Medicare patient's home and returns to the laboratory without making any other stops. The flat rate would be calculated as follows: 2 x $9.55 for a total trip reimbursement of $19.10, plus the specimen collection fee.

Example 4: A laboratory technician travels from the laboratory to the homes of five patients to draw blood, four of the patients are Medicare patients and one is not. An additional flat rate would be charged to cover the 5 stops and the return trip to the lab (6 x $9.55 = $57.30). Each of the claims submitted would be for $11.46 ($57.30 /5 = $11.46). Since one of the patients is non-Medicare, four claims would be submitted for $11.46 each, plus the specimen collection fee for each.

Example 5: A laboratory technician travels from a laboratory to a nursing home and draws blood from 5 patients and returns to the laboratory. Four of the patients are on Medicare and one is not. The $9.55 flat rate is multiplied by two to cover the return trip to the laboratory (2 x $9.55 = $19.10) and then divided by five (1/5 of $19.10 = $3.82).

Since one of the patients is non-Medicare, four claims would be submitted for $3.82 each, plus the specimen collection fee.

If a carrier determines that it results in equitable payment, the carrier may extend the former payment allowances for additional travel (such as to a distant rural nursing home) to all circumstances where travel is required. This might be appropriate, for example, if the carrier's former payment allowance was on a per mile basis. Otherwise, it should establish an appropriate allowance and inform the suppliers in its service area. If a carrier decides to establish a new allowance, one method is to consider developing a travel allowance consisting of:

- The current Federal mileage allowance for operating personal automobiles, plus a personnel allowance per mile to cover personnel costs based upon an estimate of average hourly wages and average driving speed.

Carriers must prorate travel allowance amounts claimed by suppliers by the number of patients (including Medicare and non-Medicare patients) from whom specimens were drawn on a given trip.

The carrier may determine that payment in addition to the routine travel allowance determined under this section is appropriate if:

- The patient from whom the specimen must be collected is in a nursing home or is homebound; and

- The clinical laboratory tests are needed on an emergency basis outside the general business hours of the laboratory making the collection.

Subsequent updated travel allowance amounts will be issued by CMS via Recurring Update Notification (RUN) on an annual basis.

### 100-4,18,10.2.1

### Healthcare Common Procedure Coding System (HCPCS) andDiagnosis Codes

Vaccines and their administration are reported using separate codes. The following codes are for reporting the vaccines only.

| HCPCS | Definition |
|---|---|
| 90655 | Influenza virus vaccine, split virus, preservative free, for children 6-35 months of age, for intramuscular use; |
| 90656 | Influenza virus vaccine, split virus, preservative free, for use in individuals 3 years and above, for intramuscular use; |
| 90657 | Influenza virus vaccine, split virus, for children 6-35 months of age, for intramuscular use; |
| 90658 | Influenza virus vaccine, split virus, for use in individuals 3 years of age and above, for intramuscular use; |
| 90659 | Influenza virus vaccine, whole virus, for intramuscular or jet injection use (Discontinued December 31, 2003); |
| 90660 | Influenza virus vaccine, live, for intranasal use; |
| 90669 | Pneumococcal conjugate vaccine, polyvalent, for children under 5 years, for intramuscular use |
| 90732 | Pneumococcal polysaccharide vaccine, 23-valent, adult or immunosuppressed patient dosage, for use in individuals 2 years or older, for subcutaneous or intramuscular use; |
| 90740 | Hepatitis B vaccine, dialysis or immunosuppressed patient dosage (3 dose schedule), for intramuscular use; |
| 90743 | Hepatitis B vaccine, adolescent (2 dose schedule), for intramuscular use; |
| 90744 | Hepatitis B vaccine, pediatric/adolescent dosage (3 dose schedule), for intramuscular use; |
| 90746 | Hepatitis B vaccine, adult dosage, for intramuscular use; and |
| 90747 | Hepatitis B vaccine, dialysis or immunosuppressed patient dosage (4 dose schedule), for intramuscular use. |

The following codes are for reporting administration of the vaccines only. The administration of the vaccines is billed using:

| HCPCS | Defintion |
|---|---|
| G0008 | Administration of influenza virus vaccine; |
| G0009 | Administration of pneumococcal vaccine; and |
| *G0010 | Administration of hepatitis B vaccine. |
| *90471 | Immunization administration. (For OPPS hospitals billing for the hepatitis B vaccine administration) |
| *90472 | Each additional vaccine. (For OPPS hospitals billing for the hepatitis B vaccine administration) |

\* NOTE: For claims with dates of service prior to January 1, 2006, OPPS and non-OPPS hospitals report G0010 for Hepatitis B vaccine administration. For claims with dates of service January 1, 2006 and later, OPPS hospitals report 90471 or 90472 for hepatitis B vaccine administration as appropriate in place of G0010.

One of the following diagnosis codes must be reported as appropriate. If the sole purpose for the visit is to receive a vaccine or if a vaccine is the only service billed on a claim the applicable following diagnosis code may be used.

| Diagnosis Code | Description |
|---|---|
| V03.82 | Pneumococcus |
| V04.81** | Influenza |
| V06.6*** | Pneumococcus and Influenza |
| V05.3 | Hepatitis B |

**Effective for influenza virus claims with dates of service October 1, 2003 and later.

***Effective October 1, 2006, providers may report diagnosis code V06.6 on claims for pneumococcus and/or influenza virus vaccines when the purpose of the visit was to receive both vaccines.

If a diagnosis code for pneumococcus, hepatitis B, or influenza virus vaccination is not reported on a claim, contractors may not enter the diagnosis on the claim. Contractors must follow current resolution processes for claims with missing diagnosis codes.

If the diagnosis code and the narrative description are correct, but the HCPCS code is incorrect, the carrier or intermediary may correct the HCPCS code and pay the claim. For example, if the reported diagnosis code is V04.81 and the narrative description (if annotated on the claim) says "flu shot" but the HCPCS code is incorrect, contractors may change the HCPCS code and pay for the flu vaccine. Effective October 1, 2006, carriers/AB MACs should follow the instructions in Pub. 100-04, Chapter 1, Section 80.3.2.1.1 (Carrier Data Element Requirements) for claims submitted without a HCPCS code.

Claims for Hepatitis B vaccinations must report the I.D. Number of referring physician. In addition, if a doctor of medicine or osteopathy does not order the influenza virus vaccine, the intermediary claims require:

UPIN code SLF000 to be reported on claims submitted prior to the date when Medicare will no longer accept identifiers other than NPIs, or

The provider's own NPI to be reported in the NPI field for the attending physician on claims submitted when NPI requirements are implemented.

## 100-4,18,10.2.2.1

### FI Payment for Pneumococcal Pneumonia Virus, InfluenzaVirus, and Hepatitis B Virus Vaccines and Their Administration

Payment for Vaccines

Payment for all of these vaccines is on a reasonable cost basis for hospitals, home health agencies (HHAs), skilled nursing facilities (SNFs), critical access hospitals (CAHs), and hospital-based renal dialysis facilities (RDFs). Payment for comprehensive outpatient rehabilitation facilities (CORFs), Indian Health Service hospitals (IHS), IHS CAHs and independent RDFs is based on 95 percent of the average wholesale price (AWP). Section 10.2.4 of this chapter contains information on payment of these vaccines when provided by RDFs or hospices. See Sec.10.2.2.2 for payment to independent and provider- based Rural Health Centers and Federally Qualified Health Clinics.

Payment for these vaccines is as follows:

| Facility | Type of Bill | Payment |
|---|---|---|
| Hospitals, other than Indian Health Service (IHS) Hospitals and Critical Access Hospitals (CAHs) | 12x, 13x | Reasonable cost |
| IHS Hospitals | 12x, 13x, 83x | 95% of AWP |
| IHS CAHs | 85x | 95% of AWP |
| CAHs | 85x | Reasonable cost |
| Method I and Method II | | |
| Skilled Nursing Facilities | 22x, 23x | Reasonable cost |
| Home Health Agencies | 34x | Reasonable cost |
| Comprehensive Outpatient Rehabilitation Facilities | 75x | 95% of the AWP |
| Independent Renal Dialysis Facilities | 72x | 95% of the AWP |
| Hospital-based Renal Dialysis Facilities | 72x | Reasonable cost |

**Payment for Vaccine Administration**

Payment for the administration of Influenza Virus and PPV vaccines is as follows:

| Facility | Type of Bill | Payment |
|---|---|---|
| Hospitals, other than IHS Hospitals and CAHs | 12x, 13x | Outpatient Prospective Payment System (OPPS) for hospitals subject to OPPS Reasonable cost for hospitals not subject to OPPS |
| IHS Hospitals | 12x, 13x, 83x | MPFS as indicated in guidelines below. |
| IHS CAHs | 85x | MPFS as indicated in guidelines below. |
| CAHs | 85x | Reasonable cost |
| Method I and II | | |
| Skilled Nursing Facilities | 22x, 23x | MPFS as indicated in the guidelines below |
| Home Health Agencies | 34x | OPPS |
| Comprehensive Outpatient Rehabilitation Facilities | 75x | MPFS as indicated in the guidelines below |
| Independent RDFs | 72x | MPFS as indicated in the guidelines below |
| Hospital-based RDFs | 72x | Reasonable cost |

Guidelines for pricing PPV and Influenza vaccine administration under the MPFS.

# APPENDIX 4 — PUB 100 REFERENCES

Make reimbursement based on the rate in the MPFS associated with the CPT code 90782 or 90471 as follows:

| HCPCS code | Effective prior to March 1, 2003 | Effective on and after March 1, 2003 |
|---|---|---|
| G0008 | 90782 | 90471 |
| G0009 | 90782 | 90471 |

See Sec.10.2.2.2 for payment to independent and provider based Rural Health Centers and Federally Qualified Health Clinics.

Payment for the administration of Hepatitis B vaccine is as follows:

| Facility | Type of Bill | Payment |
|---|---|---|
| Hospitals other than IHS hospitals and CAHs | 12x, 13x | Outpatient Prospective Payment System (OPPS) for hospitals subject to OPPS Reasonable cost for hospitals not subject to OPPS |
| IHS Hospitals | 12x, 13x, 83x | MPFS as indicated in the guidelines below |
| CAHs Method I and II | 85x | Reasonable cost |
| IHS CAHs | 85x | MPFS as indicated in guidelines below. |
| Skilled Nursing Facilities | 22x, 23x | MPFS as indicated in the chart below |
| Home Health Agencies | 34x | OPPS |
| Comprehensive Outpatient Rehabilitation Facilities | 75x | MPFS as indicated in the guidelines below |
| Independent RDFs | 72x | MPFS as indicated in the chart below |
| Hospital-based RDFs | 72x | Reasonable cost |

Guidelines for pricing Hepatitis B vaccine administration under the MPFS.

Make reimbursement based on the rate in the MPFS associated with the CPT code 90782 or 90471 as follows:

| HCPCS code | Effective prior to March 1, 2003 | Effective on and after March 1, 2003 |
|---|---|---|
| G0010 | 90782 | 90471 |

See Sec.10.2.2.2 for payment to independent and provider based Rural Health Centers and Federally Qualified Health Clinics.

## 100-4, 18, 10.2.2.1
### FI/AB MAC Payment for Pneumococcal Pneumonia Virus, Influenza Virus, and Hepatitis B Virus Vaccines and Their Administration
Payment for Vaccines

Payment for all of these vaccines is on a reasonable cost basis for hospitals, home health agencies (HHAs), skilled nursing facilities (SNFs), critical access hospitals (CAHs), and hospital-based renal dialysis facilities (RDFs). Payment for comprehensive outpatient rehabilitation facilities (CORFs), Indian Health Service hospitals (IHS), IHS CAHs and independent RDFs is based on 95 percent of the average wholesale price (AWP). Section 10.2.4 of this chapter contains information on payment of these vaccines when provided by RDFs or hospices. See Sec.10.2.2.2 for payment to independent and provider- based Rural Health Centers and Federally Qualified Health Clinics.

Payment for these vaccines is as follows:

| Facility | Type of Bill | Payment |
|---|---|---|
| Hospitals, other than Indian Health Service (IHS) Hospitals and Critical Access Hospitals (CAHs) | 12x, 13x | Reasonable cost |
| IHS Hospitals | 12x, 13x, 83x | 95% of AWP |
| IHS CAHs | 85x | 95% of AWP |
| CAHs Method I and Method II | 85x | Reasonable cost |
| Skilled Nursing Facilities | 22x, 23x | Reasonable cost |
| Home Health Agencies | 34x | Reasonable cost |
| Comprehensive Outpatient Rehabilitation Facilities | 75x | 95% of the AWP |
| Independent Renal Dialysis Facilities | 72x | 95% of the AWP |
| Hospital-based Renal Dialysis | 72x | Reasonable cost |

**Payment for Vaccine Administration**
Payment for the administration of influenza virus and pneumococcal vaccines is as follows:

| Facility | Type of Bill | Payment |
|---|---|---|
| Hospitals, other than IHS Hospitals and CAHs | 12x, 13x | Outpatient Prospective Payment System (OPPS) for hospitals subject to OPPS |
| Reasonable cost for hospitals not subject to OPPS IHS Hospitals | 12x, 13x, 83x | MPFS as indicated in guidelines below. |
| IHS CAHs | 85x | MPFS as indicated in guidelines below. |
| CAHs Method I and II | 85x | Reasonable cost |
| Skilled Nursing Facilities | 22x, 23x | MPFS as indicated in the guidelines below |
| Home Health Agencies | 34x | OPPS |
| Comprehensive Outpatient Rehabilitation Facilities | 75x | MPFS as indicated in the guidelines below |
| Independent RDFs | 72x | MPFS as indicated in the guidelines below |
| Hospital-based RDFs | 72x | Reasonable cost |

Guidelines for pricing pneumococcal and influenza virus vaccine administration under the MPFS.

Make reimbursement based on the rate in the MPFS associated with the CPT code 90782 or 90471 as follows:

| HCPCS code | Effective prior to March 1, 2003 | Effective on and after March 1, 2003 |
|---|---|---|
| G0008 | 90782 | 90471 |
| G0009 | 90782 | 90471 |

See Sec.10.2.2.2 for payment to independent and provider based Rural Health Centers and Federally Qualified Health Clinics.

Payment for the administration of hepatitis B vaccine is as follows:

| Facility | Type of Bill | Payment |
|---|---|---|
| Hospitals other than IHS hospitals and CAHs | 12x, 13x | Outpatient Prospective Payment System (OPPS) for hospitals subject to OPPS |
| Reasonable cost for hospitals not subject to OPPS IHS Hospitals | 12x, 13x, 83x | MPFS as indicated in the guidelines below |
| CAHs Method I and II | 85x | Reasonable cost |
| IHS CAHs | 85x | MPFS as indicated in guidelines below. |
| Skilled Nursing Facilities | 22x, 23x | MPFS as indicated in the chart below |
| Home Health Agencies | 34x | OPPS |
| Comprehensive Outpatient Rehabilitation Facilities | 75x | MPFS as indicated in the guidelines below |
| Independent RDFs | 72x | MPFS as indicated in the chart below |
| Hospital-based RDFs | 72x | Reasonable cost |

Guidelines for pricing hepatitis B vaccine administration under the MPFS.

Make reimbursement based on the rate in the MPFS associated with the CPT code 90782 or 90471 as follows:

| HCPCS code | Effective prior to March 1, 2003 | Effective on and after March 1, 2003 |
|---|---|---|
| G0010 | 90782 | 90471 |

See Sec.10.2.2.2 for payment to independent and provider based Rural Health Centers and Federally Qualified Health Clinics.

## *100-4,18,10.2.5.2*
### Carrier/AB MAC Payment Requirements

Payment for pneumococcal, influenza virus, and hepatitis B vaccines follows the same standard rules that are applicable to any injectable drug or biological. (See chapter 17 for procedures for determining the payment rates for pneumococcal and influenza virus vaccines.) Effective for claims with dates of service on or after February 1, 2001, Sec.114, of the Benefits Improvement and Protection Act of 2000 mandated that all drugs and biologicals be paid based on mandatory assignment. Therefore, all providers of influenza virus and pneumococcal vaccines must accept assignment for the vaccine.

Prior to March 1, 2003, the administration of pneumococcal, influenza virus, and hepatitis B vaccines, (HCPCS codes G0008, G0009, and G0010), though not reimbursed directly through the MPFS, were reimbursed at the same rate as HCPCS code 90782 on the MPFS for the year that corresponded to the date of service of the claim.

Prior to March 1, 2003, HCPCS codes G0008, G0009, and G0010 are reimbursed at the same rate as HCPCS code 90471. Assignment for the administration is not mandatory, but is applicable should the provider be enrolled as a provider type "Mass Immunization Roster Biller," submits roster bills, or participates in the centralized billing program.

Carriers/AB MACs may not apply the limiting charge provision for pneumococcal, influenza virus vaccine, or hepatitis B vaccine and their administration in accordance with Secs.1833(a)(1) and 1833(a)(10)(A) of the Social Security Act (the Act.) The administration of the influenza virus vaccine is covered in the influenza virus vaccine benefit under Sec.1861(s)(10)(A) of the Act, rather than under the physicians' services benefit. Therefore, it is not eligible for the 10 percent Health Professional Shortage Area (HPSA) incentive payment or the 5 percent Physician Scarcity Area (PSA) incentive payment.

No Legal Obligation to Pay  Nongovernmental entities that provide immunizations free of charge to all patients, regardless of their ability to pay, must provide the immunizations free of charge to Medicare beneficiaries and may not bill Medicare. (See Pub. 100-02, Medicare Benefit Policy Manual, chapter 16.) Thus, for example, Medicare may not pay for influenza virus vaccinations administered to Medicare beneficiaries if a physician provides free vaccinations to all non-Medicare patients or where an employer offers free vaccinations to its employees. Physicians also may not charge Medicare beneficiaries more for a vaccine than they would charge non-Medicare patients. (See Sec.1128(b)(6)(A) of the Act.)

When an employer offers free vaccinations to its employees, it must also offer the free vaccination to an employee who is also a Medicare beneficiary. It does not have to offer free vaccinations to its non-Medicare employees.

Nongovernmental entities that do not charge patients who are unable to pay or reduce their charges for patients of limited means, yet expect to be paid if the patient has health insurance coverage for the services provided, may bill Medicare and expect payment.

Governmental entities (such as PHCs) may bill Medicare for pneumococcal, hepatitis B, and influenza virus vaccines administered to Medicare beneficiaries when services are rendered free of charge to non-Medicare beneficiaries.

## 100-4,18,10.3.1.1

### Centralized Billing for Influenza Virus and Pneumococcal Vaccines to Medicare Carriers/AB MACs

The CMS currently authorizes a limited number of providers to centrally bill for influenza virus and pneumococcal immunization claims. Centralized billing is an optional program available to providers who qualify to enroll with Medicare as the provider type "Mass Immunization Roster Biller," as well as to other individuals and entities that qualify to enroll as regular Medicare providers. Centralized billers must roster bill, must accept assignment, and must bill electronically.

To qualify for centralized billing, a mass immunizer must be operating in at least three payment localities for which there are three different contractors processing claims. Individuals and entities providing the vaccine and administration must be properly licensed in the State in which the immunizations are given and the contractor must verify this through the enrollment process.

Centralized billers must send all claims for influenza virus and pneumococcal immunizations to a single contractor for payment, regardless of the jurisdiction in which the vaccination was administered. (This does not include claims for the Railroad Retirement Board, United Mine Workers or Indian Health Services. These claims must continue to go to the appropriate processing entity.) Payment is made based on the payment locality where the service was provided. This process is only available for claims for the influenza virus and pneumococcal vaccines and their administration. The general coverage and coding rules still apply to these claims.

This section applies only to those individuals and entities that provide mass immunization services for influenza virus and pneumococcal vaccinations and that have been authorized by CMS to centrally bill. All other providers, including those individuals and entities that provide mass immunization services that are not authorized to centrally bill, must continue to bill for these claims to their regular carrier/AB MAC per the instructions in Sec.10.3.1 of this chapter.

The claims processing instructions in this section apply only to the designated processing contractor. However, all carriers/AB MACs must follow the instructions in Sec.10.3.1.1.J, below, "Provider Education Instructions for All Carriers/AB MACs." A. Processing Contractor Trailblazers Health Enterprises is designated as the sole contractor for the payment of influenza virus and pneumococcal claims for centralized billers from October 1, 2000, through the length of the contract. The CMS central office will notify centralized billers of the appropriate contractor to bill when they receive their notification of acceptance into the centralized billing program.

### B. Request for Approval

Approval to participate in the CMS centralized billing program is a two part approval process. Individuals and corporations who wish to enroll as a CMS mass immunizer centralized biller must send their request in writing. CMS will complete Part 1 of the approval process by reviewing preliminary demographic information included in the request for participation letter. Completion of Part 1 is not approval to set up vaccination clinics, vaccinate beneficiaries, and bill Medicare for reimbursement. All new participants must complete Part 2 of the approval process (Form CMS-855 Application) before they may set up vaccination clinics, vaccinate Medicare beneficiaries, and bill Medicare for reimbursement. If an individual or entity's request is approved for centralized billing, the approval is limited to 12 months from September to August 31 of the next year. It is the responsibility of the centralized biller to reapply for approval each year. The designated contractor shall provide in writing to CMS and approved centralized billers notification of completion and approval of Part 2 of the approval process. The designated contractor may not process claims for any centralized biller who has not completed Parts 1 and 2 of the approval process. If claims are submitted by a provider who has not received approval of Parts 1 and 2 of the approval process to participate as a centralized biller, the contractor must return the claims to the provider to submit to the local carrier/AB MAC for payment.

### C. Notification of Provider Participation to the Processing Contractor

Before September 1 of every year, CMS will provide the designated contractor with the names of the entities that are authorized to participate in centralized billing for the 12 month period beginning September 1 and ending August 31 of the next year.

### D. Enrollment

Though centralized billers may already have a Medicare provider number, for purposes of centralized billing, they must also obtain a provider number from the processing contractor for centralized billing through completion of the Form CMS-855 (Provider Enrollment Application). Providers/suppliers are encouraged to apply to enroll as a centralized biller early as possible. Applicants who have not completed the entire enrollment process and received approval from CMS and the designated contractor to participate as a Medicare mass immunizer centralized biller will not be allowed to submit claims to Medicare for reimbursement.

Whether an entity enrolls as a provider type "Mass Immunization Roster Biller" or some other type of provider, all normal enrollment processes and procedures must be followed. Authorization from CMS to participate in centralized billing is dependent upon the entity's ability to qualify as some type of Medicare provider. In addition, as under normal enrollment procedures, the contractor must verify that the entity is fully qualified and certified per State requirements in each State in which they plan to operate.

The contractor will activate the provider number for the 12-month period from September 1 through August 31 of the following year. If the provider is authorized to participate in the centralized billing program the next year, the contractor will extend the activation of the provider number for another year. The entity need not re-enroll with the contractor every year. However, should there be changes in the States in which the entity plans to operate, the contractor will need to verify that the entity meets all State certification and licensure requirements in those new States.

### E. Electronic Submission of Claims on Roster Bills

Centralized billers must agree to submit their claims on roster bills in an Electronic Media Claims standard format using the appropriate version of American National Standards Institute (ANSI) format. Contractors should refer to the appropriate ANSI Implementation Guide to determine the correct location for this information on electronic claims. The processing contractor must provide instructions on acceptable roster billing formats to the approved centralized billers. Paper claims will not be accepted.

### F. Required Information on Roster Bills for Centralized Billing

In addition to the roster billing instructions found in Sec.10.3.1 of this chapter, centralized billers must complete on the electronic format the area that corresponds to Item 32 and 33 on Form CMS 1500 (08-05). The contractor must use the ZIP Code in Item 32 to determine the payment locality for the claim. Item 33 must be completed to report the provider of service/supplier's billing name, address, ZIP Code, and telephone number. In addition, the NPI of the billing provider or group must be appropriately reported.

For electronic claims, the name, address, and ZIP Code of the facility are reported in:

- The HIPAA compliant ANSI X12N 837: Claim level loop 2310D NM101=FA. When implemented, the facility (e.g., hospitals) NPI will be captured in the loop 2310D NM109 (NM108=XX) if one is available. Prior to NPI, enter the tax information in loop 2310D NM109 (NM108=24 or 34) and enter the Medicare legacy facility identifier in loop 2310D REF02 (REF01=1C). Report the address, city, state, and ZIP Code in loop 2310D N301 and N401, N402, and N403. Facility data is not required to be reported at the line level for centralized billing.

### G. Payment Rates and Mandatory Assignment

The payment rates for the administration of the vaccinations are based on the Medicare Physician Fee Schedule (MPFS) for the appropriate year. Payment made through the MPFS is based on geographic locality. Therefore, payments vary based on the geographic locality where the service was performed.

The HCPCS codes G0008 and G0009 for the administration of the vaccines are not paid on the MPFS. However, prior to March 1, 2003, they must be paid at the same rate as HCPCS code 90782, which is on the MPFS. The designated contractor must pay per the correct MPFS file for each calendar year based on the date of service of the claim. Beginning March 1, 2003, HCPCS codes G0008, G0009, and G0010 are to be reimbursed at the same rate as HCPCS code 90471.

In order to pay claims correctly for centralized billers, the designated contractor must have the correct name and address, including ZIP Code, of the entity where the service was provided.

The following remittance advice and Medicare Summary Notice (MSN) messages apply:

- Claim adjustment reason code 16, "Claim/service lacks information which is needed for adjudication. At least one Remark Code must be provided (may be comprised of either the Remittance Advice Remark Code or NCPDP Reject Reason Code.)" and Remittance advice remark code MA114, "Missing/incomplete/invalid information on where the services were furnished." and MSN 9.4 - "This item or service was denied because information required to make payment was incorrect." The payment rates for the vaccines must be determined by the standard method used by Medicare for reimbursement of drugs and biologicals. (See chapter 17 for procedures for determining the payment rates for vaccines.) Effective for claims with dates of service on or after February 1, 2001, Sec.114, of the Benefits Improvement and Protection Act of 2000 mandated that all drugs and biologicals be paid based on mandatory assignment. Therefore, all providers of influenza virus and pneumococcal vaccines must accept assignment for the vaccine. In addition, as a requirement for both centralized billing and roster billing, providers must agree to accept assignment for the administration of the vaccines as well. This means that they must agree to accept the amount that Medicare pays for the vaccine and the administration. Also, since there is no coinsurance or deductible for the influenza virus and pneumococcal

benefit, accepting assignment means that Medicare beneficiaries cannot be charged for the vaccination.

### H. Common Working File Information

To identify these claims and to enable central office data collection on the project, special processing number 39 has been assigned. The number should be entered on the HUBC claim record to CWF in the field titled Demonstration Number.

### I. Provider Education Instructions for the Processing Contractor

The processing contractor must fully educate the centralized billers on the processes for centralized billing as well as for roster billing. General information on influenza virus and pneumococcal coverage and billing instructions is available on the CMS Web site for providers.

### J. Provider Education Instructions for All Carriers/AB MACs

By April 1 of every year, all carriers/AB MACs must publish in their bulletins and put on their Web sites the following notification to providers. Questions from interested providers should be forwarded to the central office address below. Carriers/AB MACs must enter the name of the assigned processing contractor where noted before sending.

#### NOTIFICATION TO PROVIDERS

Centralized billing is a process in which a provider, who provides mass immunization services for influenza virus and pneumococcal pneumonia virus (PPV) immunizations, can send all claims to a single contractor for payment regardless of the geographic locality in which the vaccination was administered. (This does not include claims for the Railroad Retirement Board, United Mine Workers or Indian Health Services. These claims must continue to go to the appropriate processing entity.) This process is only available for claims for the influenza virus and pneumococcal vaccines and their administration. The administration of the vaccinations is reimbursed at the assigned rate based on the Medicare physician fee schedule for the appropriate locality. The vaccines are reimbursed at the assigned rate using the Medicare standard method for reimbursement of drugs and biologicals.

Individuals and entities interested in centralized billing must contact CMS central office, in writing, at the following address by June 1 of the year they wish to begin centrally billing.

Center for Medicare & Medicaid Services  Division of Practitioner Claims Processing  Provider Billing and Education Group  7500 Security Boulevard  Mail Stop C4-10-07  Baltimore, Maryland 21244  By agreeing to participate in the centralized billing program, providers agree to abide by the following criteria.

#### CRITERIA FOR CENTRALIZED BILLING

To qualify for centralized billing, an individual or entity providing mass immunization services for influenza virus and pneumococcal vaccinations must provide these services in at least three payment localities for which there are at least three different contractors processing claims.

Individuals and entities providing the vaccine and administration must be properly licensed in the State in which the immunizations are given.

Centralized billers must agree to accept assignment (i.e., they must agree to accept the amount that Medicare pays for the vaccine and the administration).

NOTE: The practice of requiring a beneficiary to pay for the vaccination upfront and to file their own claim for reimbursement is inappropriate. All Medicare providers are required to file claims on behalf of the beneficiary per Sec.1848(g)(4)(A) of the Social Security Act and centralized billers may not collect any payment.

The contractor assigned to process the claims for centralized billing is chosen at the discretion of CMS based on such considerations as workload, user-friendly software developed by the contractor for billing claims, and overall performance. The assigned contractor for this year is [Fill in name of contractor.]

The payment rates for the administration of the vaccinations are based on the Medicare physician fee schedule (MPFS) for the appropriate year. Payment made through the MPFS is based on geographic locality. Therefore, payments received may vary based on the geographic locality where the service was performed. Payment is made at the assigned rate.

The payment rates for the vaccines are determined by the standard method used by Medicare for reimbursement of drugs and biologicals. Payment is made at the assigned rate.

Centralized billers must submit their claims on roster bills in an approved Electronic Media Claims standard format. Paper claims will not be accepted.

Centralized billers must obtain certain information for each beneficiary including name, health insurance number, date of birth, sex, and signature. [Fill in name of contractor] must be contacted prior to the season for exact requirements. The responsibility lies with the centralized biller to submit correct beneficiary Medicare information (including the beneficiary's Medicare Health Insurance Claim Number) as the contractor will not be able to process incomplete or incorrect claims.

Centralized billers must obtain an address for each beneficiary so that a Medicare Summary Notice (MSN) can be sent to the beneficiary by the contractor. Beneficiaries are sometimes confused when they receive an MSN from a contractor other than the contractor that normally processes their claims which results in unnecessary beneficiary inquiries to the Medicare contractor. Therefore, centralized billers must provide every beneficiary receiving an influenza virus or pneumococcal vaccination with the name of the processing contractor. This notification must be in writing, in the form of a brochure or handout, and must be provided to each beneficiary at the time he or she receives the vaccination.

Centralized billers must retain roster bills with beneficiary signatures at their permanent location for a time period consistent with Medicare regulations. [Fill in name of contractor] can provide this information.

Though centralized billers may already have a Medicare provider number, for purposes of centralized billing, they must also obtain a provider number from [Fill in name of contractor]. This can be done by completing the Form CMS-855 (Provider Enrollment Application), which can be obtained from [Fill in name of contractor].

If an individual or entity's request for centralized billing is approved, the approval is limited to the 12 month period from September 1 through August 31 of the following year. It is the responsibility of the centralized biller to reapply to CMS CO for approval each year by June 1. Claims will not be processed for any centralized biller without permission from CMS.

Each year the centralized biller must contact [Fill in name of contractor] to verify understanding of the coverage policy for the administration of the pneumococcal vaccine, and for a copy of the warning language that is required on the roster bill.

The centralized biller is responsible for providing the beneficiary with a record of the pneumococcal vaccination.

The information in items 1 through 8 below must be included with the individual or entity's annual request to participate in centralized billing:

1. Estimates for the number of beneficiaries who will receive influenza virus vaccinations;

2. Estimates for the number of beneficiaries who will receive pneumococcal vaccinations;

3. The approximate dates for when the vaccinations will be given;

4. A list of the States in which influenza virus and pneumococcal clinics will be held;

5. The type of services generally provided by the corporation (e.g., ambulance, home health, or visiting nurse);

6. Whether the nurses who will administer the influenza virus and pneumococcal vaccinations are employees of the corporation or will be hired by the corporation specifically for the purpose of administering influenza virus and pneumococcal vaccinations;

7. Names and addresses of all entities operating under the corporation's application;

8. Contact information for designated contact person for centralized billing program.

## 100-4,18,10.4.1

In order to prevent duplicate payment by the same FI/AB MAC, CWF edits by line item on the FI/AB MAC number, the beneficiary Health Insurance Claim (HIC) number, and the date of service, the influenza virus procedure codes 90657, 90658, or 90659, the pneumonia procedure code 90732, and the administration codes G0008 or G0009.

If CWF receives a claim with either HCPCS codes 90657, 90658 or 90659, and it already has on record a claim with the same HIC number, same FI/AB MAC number, same date of service, and any one of those HCPCS codes, the second claim submitted to CWF rejects.

If CWF receives a claim with HCPCS code 90732 and it already has on record a claim with the same HIC number, same FI/AB MAC number, same date of service, and the same HCPCS code, the second claim submitted to CWF rejects when all four items match.

If CWF receives a claim with HCPCS administration codes G0008 or G0009 and it already has on record a claim with the same HIC number, same FI/AB MAC number, same date of service, and same procedure code, CWF rejects the second claim submitted when all four items match.

CWF returns to the FI/AB MAC a reject code "7262" for this edit. FIs/AB MACs must deny the second claim and use the same messages they currently use for the denial of duplicate claims.

## 100-4,18,120.1

### Coding and Payment of DSMT Services

The following HCPCS codes are used to report DSMT: G0108 - Diabetes outpatient self-management training services, individual, per 30 minutes.

G0109 - Diabetes outpatient self-management training services, group session (2 or more), per 30 minutes.

The type of service for these codes is 1.

| Type of Facility | Payment Method | Type of Bill |
|---|---|---|
| Physician (billed to the carrier) | MPFS | NA |
| Hospitals subject to OPPS | MPFS | 12X, 13X |
| Method I and Method II Critical Access Hospitals (CAHs) (technical services) | 101% of reasonable cost | 12X and 85X |
| Indian Health Service (IHS) providers billing hospital outpatient Part B | OMB-approved outpatient per visit all inclusive rate (AIR) | 13X |
| IHS providers billing inpatient Part B | All-inclusive inpatient ancillary per diem rate | 12X |
| IHS CAHs billing outpatient Part B | 101% of the all-inclusive facility specific per visit rate | 85X |
| IHS CAHs billing inpatient Part B | 101% of the all-inclusive facility specific per diem rate | 12X |
| FQHCs* | All-inclusive encounter rate with other qualified services. Separate visit payment available with HCPCS. | 73X |
| Skilled Nursing Facilities ** | MPFS non-facility rate | 22X, 23X |
| Maryland Hospitals under jurisdiction of the Health Services Cost Review Commission (HSCRC) | 94% of provider submitted charges in accordance with the terms of the Maryland Waiver | 12X, 13X |
| Home Health Agencies (can be billed only if the service is provided outside of the treatment plan) | MPFS non-facility rate | 34X |

* Effective January 1, 2006, payment for DSMT provided in an FQHC that meets all of the requirements as above, may be made in addition to one other visit the beneficiary had during the same day, if this qualifying visit is billed on TOB 73X, with HCPCS G0108 or G0109, and revenue codes 0520, 0521, 0522, 0524, 0525, 0527, 0528, or 0900.

** The SNF consolidated billing provision allows separate part B payment for training services for beneficiaries that are in skilled Part A SNF stays, however, the SNF must submit these services on a 22 bill type. Training services provided by other provider types must be reimbursed by X the SNF.

NOTE: An ESRD facility is a reasonable site for this service, however, because it is required to provide dietician and nutritional services as part of the care covered in the composite rate, ESRD facilities are not allowed to bill for it separately and do not receive separate reimbursement. Likewise, an RHC is a reasonable site for this service, however it must be provided in an RHC with other qualifying services and paid at the all-inclusive encounter rate.

Deductible and co-insurance apply.

## 100-4,18,20.4
### Billing Requirements - FI/A/B MAC Claims

Contractors use the weekly-updated MQSA file to verify that the billing facility is certified by the FDA to perform mammography services, and has the appropriate certification to perform the type of mammogram billed (film and/or digital). (See Sec.20.1.) FIs/A/B MACs use the provider number submitted on the claim to identify the facility and use the MQSA data file to verify the facility's certification(s). FIs/A/B MACs complete the following activities in processing mammography claims:

If the provider number on the claim does not correspond with a certified mammography facility on the MQSA file, then intermediaries/A/B MACs deny the claim.

When a film mammography HCPCS code is on a claim, the claim is checked for a "1" film indicator.

If a film mammography HCPCS code comes in on a claim and the facility is certified for film mammography, the claim is paid if all other relevant Medicare criteria are met.

If a film mammography HCPCS code is on a claim and the facility is certified for digital mammography only, the claim is denied.

When a digital mammography HCPCS code is on a claim, the claim is checked for "2" digital indicator.

If a digital mammography HCPCS code is on a claim and the facility is certified for digital mammography, the claim is paid if all other relevant Medicare criteria are met.

If a digital mammography HCPCS code is on a claim and the facility is certified for film mammography only, the claim is denied.

NOTE: The Common Working File (CWF) no longer receives the mammography file for editing purposes.

Except as provided in the following sections for RHCs and FQHCs, the following procedures apply to billing for screening mammographies: The technical component portion of the screening mammography is billed on Form CMS-1450 under bill type 12X, 13X, 14X**, 22X, 23X or 85X using revenue code 0403 and HCPCS code 77057* (76092*).

The technical component portion of the diagnostic mammography is billed on Form CMS-1450 under bill type 12X, 13X, 14X**, 22X, 23X or 85X using revenue code 0401 and HCPCS code 77055* (76090*), 77056* (76091*), G0204 and G0206.

Separate bills are required for claims for screening mammographies with dates of service prior to January 1, 2002. Providers include on the bill only charges for the screening mammography. Separate bills are not required for claims for screening mammographies with dates of service on or after January 1, 2002.

See separate instructions below for rural health clinics (RHCs) and federally qualified health centers (FQHCs).

* For claims with dates of service prior to January 1, 2007, providers report CPT codes 76090, 76091, and 76092. For claims with dates of service January 1, 2007 and later, providers report CPT codes 77055, 77056, and 77057 respectively.

# APPENDIX 4 — PUB 100 REFERENCES

** For claims with dates of service April 1, 2005 and later, hospitals bill for all mammography services under the 13X type of bill or for dates of service April 1, 2007 and later, 12X or 13X as appropriate. The 14X type of bill is no longer applicable. Appropriate bill types for providers other than hospitals are 22X, 23X, and 85X.

In cases where screening mammography services are self-referred and as a result an attending physician NPI is not available, the provider shall duplicate their facility NPI in the attending physician identifier field on the claim.

## 100-4, 18, 60.1
### Payment
Payment (contractor) is under the MPFS except as follows:

- Fecal occult blood tests (82270* (G0107*) and G0328) are paid under the clinical diagnostic lab fee schedule except reasonable cost is paid to all non-OPPS hospitals, including CAHs, but not IHS hospitals billing on TOB 83x. IHS hospitals billing on TOB 83x are paid the ASC payment amount. Other IHS hospitals (billing on TOB 13x) are paid the OMB approved AIR, or the facility specific per visit amount as applicable. Deductible and coinsurance do not apply for these tests. See section A below for payment to Maryland waiver on TOB 13X. Payment from all hospitals for non-patient laboratory specimens on TOB 14X will be based on the clinical diagnostic fee schedule, including CAHs and Maryland waiver hospitals

Flexible sigmoidoscopy (code G0104) is paid under OPPS for hospital outpatient departments and on a reasonable cost basis for CAHs; or current payment methodologies for hospitals not subject to OPPS.

Colonoscopies (G0105 and G0121) and barium enemas (G0106 and G0120) are paid under OPPS for hospital outpatient departments and on a reasonable costs basis for CAHs or current payment methodologies for hospitals not subject to OPPS. Also colonoscopies may be done in an Ambulatory Surgical Center (ASC) and when done in an ASC the ASC rate applies. The ASC rate is the same for diagnostic and screening colonoscopies. The ASC rate is paid to IHS hospitals when the service is billed on TOB 83x.

Prior to January 1, 2007, deductible and coinsurance apply to HCPCS codes G0104, G0105, G0106, G0120, and G0121. Beginning with services provided on or after January 1, 2007, Section 5113 of the Deficit Reduction Act of 2005 waives the requirement of the annual Part B deductible for these screening services. Coinsurance still applies. Coinsurance and deductible applies to the diagnostic colorectal service codes listed below.

The following screening codes must be paid at rates consistent with the diagnostic codes indicated.

| Screening Code | Diagnostic Code |
| --- | --- |
| G0104 | 45330 |
| G0105 and G0121 | 45378 |
| G0106 and G0120 | 74280 |

### A. Special Payment Instructions for TOB 13X Maryland Waiver Hospitals
For hospitals in Maryland under the jurisdiction of the Health Services Cost Review Commission, screening colorectal services HCPCS codes G0104, G0105, G0106, 82270* (G0107*), G0120, G0121 and G0328 are paid according to the terms of the waiver, that is 94% of submitted charges minus any unmet existing deductible, co-insurance and non-covered charges. Maryland Hospitals bill TOB 13X for outpatient colorectal cancer screenings.

### B. Special Payment Instructions for Non-Patient Laboratory Specimen (TOB 14X) for all hospitals
Payment for colorectal cancer screenings (82270* (G0107*) and G0328) to a hospital for a non-patient laboratory specimen (TOB 14X), is the lesser of the actual charge, the fee schedule amount, or the National Limitation Amount (NLA), (including CAHs and Maryland Waiver hospitals). Part B deductible and coinsurance do not apply.

*NOTE: For claims with dates of service prior to January 1, 2007, physicians, suppliers, and providers report HCPCS code G0107. Effective January 1, 2007, code G0107 is discontinued and replaced with CPT code 82270.

## 100-4, 18, 60.2
### HCPCS Codes, Frequency Requirements, and Age Requirements (If Applicable)
Effective for services furnished on or after January 1, 1998, the following codes are used for colorectal cancer screening services:

- 82270* (G0107*) - Colorectal cancer screening; fecal-occult blood tests, 1-3 simultaneous determinations;
- G0104 - Colorectal cancer screening; flexible sigmoidoscopy;
- G0105 - Colorectal cancer screening; colonoscopy on individual at high risk;
- G0106 - Colorectal cancer screening; barium enema; as an alternative to G0104, screening sigmoidoscopy;
- G0120 - Colorectal cancer screening; barium enema; as an alternative to G0105, screening colonoscopy.

Effective for services furnished on or after July 1, 2001, the following codes are used for colorectal cancer screening services:

- G0121 - Colorectal cancer screening; colonoscopy on individual not meeting criteria for high risk. Note that the description for this code has been revised to remove the term "noncovered."
- G0122 - Colorectal cancer screening; barium enema (noncovered).

Effective for services furnished on or after January 1, 2004, the following code is used for colorectal cancer screening services as an alternative to 82270* (G0107*):

- G0328 - Colorectal cancer screening; immunoassay, fecal-occult blood test, 1-3 simultaneous determinations

*NOTE: For claims with dates of service prior to January 1, 2007, physicians, suppliers, and providers report HCPCS code G0107. Effective January 1, 2007, code G0107 is discontinued and replaced with CPT code 82270.

- G0104 - Colorectal Cancer Screening; Flexible Sigmoidoscopy

Screening flexible sigmoidoscopies (code G0104) may be paid for beneficiaries who have attained age 50, when performed by a doctor of medicine or osteopathy at the frequencies noted below.

For claims with dates of service on or after January 1, 2002, contractors pay for screening flexible sigmoidoscopies (code G0104) for beneficiaries who have attained age 50 when these services were performed by a doctor of medicine or osteopathy, or by a physician assistant, nurse practitioner, or clinical nurse specialist (as defined in Sec.1861(aa)(5) of the Act and in the Code of Federal Regulations at42 CFR 410.74,410.75, and410.76) at the frequencies noted above. For claims with dates of service prior to January 1, 2002, contractors pay for these services under the conditions noted only when a doctor of medicine or osteopathy performs them.

For services furnished from January 1, 1998, through June 30, 2001, inclusive:

- Once every 48 months (i.e., at least 47 months have passed following the month in which the last covered screening flexible sigmoidoscopy was done).
- For services furnished on or after July 1, 2001:
- Once every 48 months as calculated above unless the beneficiary does not meet the criteria for high risk of developing colorectal cancer (refer to Sec.60.3 of this chapter) and he/she has had a screening colonoscopy (code G0121) within the preceding 10 years. If such a beneficiary has had a screening colonoscopy within the preceding 10 years, then he or she can have covered a screening flexible sigmoidoscopy only after at least 119 months have passed following the month that he/she received the screening colonoscopy (code G0121).

NOTE:If during the course of a screening flexible sigmoidoscopy a lesion or growth is detected which results in a biopsy or removal of the growth; the appropriate diagnostic procedure classified as a flexible sigmoidoscopy with biopsy or removal should be billed and paid rather than code G0104.

G0105 - Colorectal Cancer Screening; Colonoscopy on Individual at High Risk

Screening colonoscopies (code G0105) may be paid when performed by a doctor of medicine or osteopathy at a frequency of once every 24 months for beneficiaries at high risk for developing colorectal cancer (i.e., at least 23 months have passed following the month in which the last covered G0105 screening colonoscopy was performed). Refer to Sec.60.3of this chapter for the criteria to use in determining whether or not an individual is at high risk for developing colorectal cancer.

NOTE:If during the course of the screening colonoscopy, a lesion or growth is detected which results in a biopsy or removal of the growth, the appropriate diagnostic procedure classified as a colonoscopy with biopsy or removal should be billed and paid rather than code G0105.

**A. Colonoscopy Cannot be Completed Because of Extenuating Circumstances**
1. FIs

When a covered colonoscopy is attempted but cannot be completed because of extenuating circumstances, Medicare will pay for the interrupted colonoscopy as long as the coverage conditions are met for the incomplete procedure. However, the frequency standards associated with screening colonoscopies will not be applied by CWF. When a covered colonoscopy is next attempted and completed, Medicare will pay for that colonoscopy according to its payment methodology for this procedure as long as coverage conditions are met, and the frequency standards will be applied by CWF. This policy is applied to both screening and diagnostic colonoscopies.

When submitting a facility claim for the interrupted colonoscopy, providers are to suffix the colonoscopy HCPCS codes with a modifier of "-73" or "-74" as appropriate to indicate that the procedure was interrupted. Payment for covered incomplete screening colonoscopies

shall be consistent with payment methodologies currently in place for complete screening colonoscopies, including those contained in42 CFR 419.44(b). In situations where a critical access hospital (CAH) has elected payment Method II for CAH patients, payment shall be consistent with payment methodologies currently in place as outlined in Chapter 3. As such, instruct CAHs that elect Method II payment to use modifier "-53" to identify an incomplete screening colonoscopy (physician professional service(s) billed in revenue code 096X, 097X, and/or 098X). Such CAHs will also bill the technical or facility component of the interrupted colonoscopy in revenue code 075X (or other appropriate revenue code) using the "-73" or "-74" modifier as appropriate.

Note that Medicare would expect the provider to maintain adequate information in the patient's medical record in case it is needed by the contractor to document the incomplete procedure.

2. Carriers

When a covered colonoscopy is attempted but cannot be completed because of extenuating circumstances (see Chapter 12), Medicare will pay for the interrupted colonoscopy at a rate consistent with that of a flexible sigmoidoscopy as long as coverage conditions are met for the incomplete procedure. When a covered colonoscopy is next attempted and completed, Medicare will pay for that colonoscopy according to its payment methodology for this procedure as long as coverage conditions are met. This policy is applied to both screening and diagnostic colonoscopies.

When submitting a claim for the interrupted colonoscopy, professional providers are to suffix the colonoscopy code with a modifier of "-53" to indicate that the procedure was interrupted. When submitting a claim for the facility fee associated with this procedure, Ambulatory Surgical Centers (ASCs) are to suffix the colonoscopy code with "-73" or "-74" as appropriate. Payment for covered screening colonoscopies, including that for the associated ASC facility fee when applicable, shall be consistent with payment for diagnostic colonoscopies, whether the procedure is complete or incomplete.

Note that Medicare would expect the provider to maintain adequate information in the patient's medical record in case it is needed by the contractor to document the incomplete procedure.

- G0106 - Colorectal Cancer Screening; Barium Enema; as an Alternative to G0104, Screening Sigmoidoscopy

Screening barium enema examinations may be paid as an alternative to a screening sigmoidoscopy (code G0104). The same frequency parameters for screening sigmoidoscopies (see those codes above) apply. In the case of an individual aged 50 or over, payment may be made for a screening barium enema examination (code G0106) performed after at least 47 months have passed following the month in which the last screening barium enema or screening flexible sigmoidoscopy was performed. For example, the beneficiary received a screening barium enema examination as an alternative to a screening flexible sigmoidoscopy in January 1999. Start counts beginning February 1999. The beneficiary is eligible for another screening barium enema in January 2003. The screening barium enema must be ordered in writing after a determination that the test is the appropriate screening test. Generally, it is expected that this will be a screening double contrast enema unless the individual is unable to withstand such an exam. This means that in the case of a particular individual, the attending physician must determine that the estimated screening potential for the barium enema is equal to or greater than the screening potential that has been estimated for a screening flexible sigmoidoscopy for the same individual. The screening single contrast barium enema also requires a written order from the beneficiary's attending physician in the same manner as described above for the screening double contrast barium enema examination.

- 82270* (G0107*) - Colorectal Cancer Screening; Fecal-Occult Blood Test, 1-3 Simultaneous Determinations

Effective for services furnished on or after January 1, 1998, screening FOBT (code 82270* (G0107*) may be paid for beneficiaries who have attained age 50, and at a frequency of once every 12 months (i.e., at least 11 months have passed following the month in which the last covered screening FOBT was performed). This screening FOBT means a guaiac-based test for peroxidase activity, in which the beneficiary completes it by taking samples from two different sites of three consecutive stools. This screening requires a written order from the beneficiary's attending physician. (The term "attending physician" is defined to mean a doctor of medicine or osteopathy (as defined in Sec.1861(r)(1)of the Act) who is fully knowledgeable about the beneficiary's medical condition, and who would be responsible for using the results of any examination performed in the overall management of the beneficiary's specific medical problem.)

Effective for services furnished on or after January 1, 2004, payment may be made for a immunoassay-based FOBT (G0328, described below) as an alternative to the guaiacbased FOBT, 82270* (G0107*). Medicare will pay for only one covered FOBT per year, either 82270* (G0107*) or G0328, but not both.

*NOTE: For claims with dates of service prior to January 1, 2007, physicians, suppliers, and providers report HCPCS code G0107. Effective January 1, 2007, code G0107 is discontinued and replaced with CPT code 82270.

- G0328 - Colorectal Cancer Screening; Immunoassay, Fecal-Occult Blood Test, 1-3 Simultaneous Determinations

Effective for services furnished on or after January 1, 2004, screening FOBT, (code G0328) may be paid as an alternative to 82270* (G0107*) for beneficiaries who have attained age 50. Medicare will pay for a covered FOBT (either 82270* (G0107*) or G0328, but not both) at a frequency of once every 12 months (i.e., at least 11 months have passed following the month in which the last covered screening FOBT was performed). Screening FOBT, immunoassay, includes the use of a spatula to collect the appropriate number of samples or the use of a special brush for the collection of samples, as determined by the individual manufacturer's instructions. This screening requires a written order from the beneficiary's attending physician. (The term "attending physician" is defined to mean a doctor of medicine or osteopathy (as defined in Sec.1861(r)(1) of the Act) who is fully knowledgeable about the beneficiary's medical condition, and who would be responsible for using the results of any examination performed in the overall management of the beneficiary's specific medical problem.)

- G0120 - Colorectal Cancer Screening; Barium Enema; as an Alternative to or G0105, Screening Colonoscopy

Screening barium enema examinations may be paid as an alternative to a screening colonoscopy (code G0105) examination. The same frequency parameters for screening colonoscopies (see those codes above) apply. In the case of an individual who is at high risk for colorectal cancer, payment may

be made for a screening barium enema examination (code G0120) performed after at least 23 months have passed following the month in which the last screening barium enema or the last screening colonoscopy was performed. For example, a beneficiary at high risk for developing colorectal cancer received a screening barium enema examination (code G0120) as an alternative to a screening colonoscopy (code G0105) in January 2000. Start counts beginning February 2000. The beneficiary is eligible for another screening barium enema examination (code G0120) in January 2002. The screening barium enema must be ordered in writing after a determination that the test is the appropriate screening test. Generally, it is expected that this will be a screening double contrast barium enema unless the individual is unable to withstand such an exam. This means that in the case of a particular individual, the attending physician must determine that the estimated screening potential for the barium enema is equal to or greater than the screening potential that has been estimated for a screening colonoscopy, for the same individual. The screening single contrast barium enema also requires a written order from the beneficiary's attending physician in the same manner as described above for the screening double contrast barium enema examination.

- G0121 - Colorectal Screening; Colonoscopy on Individual Not Meeting Criteria for High Risk - Applicable On and After July 1, 2001

Effective for services furnished on or after July 1, 2001, screening colonoscopies (code G0121) performed on individuals not meeting the criteria for being at high risk for developing colorectal cancer (refer to Sec.60.3 of this chapter) may be paid under the following conditions:

- At a frequency of once every 10 years (i.e., at least 119 months have passed following the month in which the last covered G0121 screening colonoscopy was performed.)

If the individual would otherwise qualify to have covered a G0121 screening colonoscopy based on the above but has had a covered screening flexible sigmoidoscopy (code G0104), then he or she may have covered a G0121 screening colonoscopy only after at least 47 months have passed following the month in which the last covered G0104 flexible sigmoidoscopy was performed.

NOTE:If during the course of the screening colonoscopy, a lesion or growth is detected which results in a biopsy or removal of the growth, the appropriate diagnostic procedure classified as a colonoscopy with biopsy or removal should be billed and paid rather than code G0121.

- G0122 - Colorectal Cancer Screening; Barium Enema

The code is not covered by Medicare.

### *100-4,18,60.6*

### Billing Requirements for Claims Submitted to FIs

Follow the general bill review instructions in Chapter 25. Hospitals use the ANSI X12N 837I to bill the FI or on the hardcopy Form CMS-1450. Hospitals bill revenue codes and HCPCS codes as follows:

| Screening Test/ Procedure | Revenue Code | HCPCS Code | TOB |
|---|---|---|---|
| Fecal Occult blood test | 030X | 82270*** (G0107***), G0328 | 13X, 14X**, 22X, 23X, 83X, 85X |

| Screening Test/ Procedure | Revenue Code | HCPCS Code | TOB |
|---|---|---|---|
| Barium enema | 032X | G0106, G0120, G0122 | 13X, 22X, 23X, 85X**** |
| Flexible Sigmoidoscopy | * | G0104 | 13X, 22X, 23X, 83X, 85X**** |
| Colonoscopy-high risk | * | G0105, G0121 | 13X, 22X, 23X, 83X, 85X**** |

\* The appropriate revenue code when reporting any other surgical procedure.

\*\* 14X is only applicable for non-patient laboratory specimens.

\*\*\* For claims with dates of service prior to January 1, 2007, physicians, suppliers, and providers report HCPCS code G0107. Effective January 1, 2007, code G0107, is discontinued and replaced with CPT code 82270.

\*\*\*\* CAHs that elect Method II bill revenue code 096X, 097X, and/or 098X for professional services and 075X (or other appropriate revenue code) for the technical or facility component.

A Special Billing Instructions for Hospital Inpatients

When these tests/procedures are provided to inpatients of a hospital, they are covered under this benefit. However, the provider bills on bill type 13X using the discharge date of the hospital stay to avoid editing in the Common Working File (CWF) as a result of the hospital bundling rules.

## 100-4,20,100.2.2

### Evidence of Medical Necessity for Parenteral and Enteral Nutrition (PEN) Therapy

The PEN coverage is determined by information provided by the treating physician and the PEN supplier. A completed certification of medical necessity (CMN) must accompany and support initial claims for PEN to establish whether coverage criteria are met and to ensure that the PEN therapy provided is consistent with the attending or ordering physician's prescription.

Contractors ensure that the CMN contains pertinent information from the treating physician. Uniform specific medical data facilitate the review and promote consistency in coverage determinations and timelier claims processing.The medical and prescription information on a PEN CMN can be most appropriatelycompleted by the treating physician or from information in the patient's records by an employee of the physician for the physician's review and signature.

Although PEN suppliers sometimes may assist in providing the PEN services, they cannot complete the CMN since they do not have the same access to patient information needed to properly enter medical or prescription information. Contractors use appropriate professional relations issuances, training sessions, and meetings to ensure that all persons and PEN suppliers are aware of this limitation of their role. When properly completed, the PEN CMN includes the elements of a prescription as well as other data needed to determine whether Medicare coverage is possible. This practice will facilitate prompt delivery of PEN services and timely submittal of the related claim.

## 100-4,20,160.1

### Billing for Total Parenteral Nutrition and Enteral NutritionFurnished to Part B Inpatients

A3-3660.6, SNF-544, SNF-559, SNF-260.4, SNF-261, HHA-403, HO-438, HO-229

Inpatient Part A hospital or SNF care includes total parenteral nutrition (TPN) systems and enteral nutrition (EN).

For inpatients for whom Part A benefits are not payable (e.g., benefits are exhausted or the beneficiary is entitled to Part B only), total parenteral nutrition (TPN) systems and enteral nutrition (EN) delivery systems are covered by Medicare as prosthetic devices when the coverage criteria are met. When these criteria are met, the medical equipment and medical supplies (together with nutrients) being used comprise covered prosthetic devices for coverage purposes rather than durable medical equipment. However, reimbursement rules relating to DME continue to apply to such items.

When a facility supplies TPN or EN systems that meet the criteria for coverage as a prosthetic device to an inpatient whose care is not covered under Part A, the facility must bill one of the DMERCs. Additionally, HHAs, SNFs, and hospitals that provide PEN supplies, equipment and nutrients as a prosthetic device under Part B must use the CMS-1500 or the related NSF or ANSI ASC X12N 837 format to bill the appropriate DMERC. The DMERC is determined according to the residence of the beneficiary. Refer to Sec.10 for jurisdiction descriptions.

FIs return claims containing PEN charges for Part B services where the bill type is 12x,

13x, 22x, 23x, 32x, 33x, or 34x with instructions to the provider to bill the DMERC.

## 100-4,3,10.4

### Payment of Nonphysician Services for Inpatients

All items and nonphysician services furnished to inpatients must be furnished directly by the hospital or billed through the hospital under arrangements. This provision applies to all hospitals, regardless of whether they are subject to PPS.

Other Medical Items, Supplies, and Services the following medical items, supplies, and services furnished to inpatients are covered under Part A. Consequently, they are covered by the prospective payment rate or reimbursed as reasonable costs under Part A to hospitals excluded from PPS.

- Laboratory services (excluding anatomic pathology services and certain clinical pathology services);
- Pacemakers and other prosthetic devices including lenses, and artificial limbs, knees, and hips;
- Radiology services including computed tomography (CT) scans furnished to inpatients by a physician's office, other hospital, or radiology clinic;
- Total parenteral nutrition (TPN) services; and
- Transportation, including transportation by ambulance, to and from another hospital or freestanding facility to receive specialized diagnostic or therapeutic services not available at the facility where the patient is an inpatient.

The hospital must include the cost of these services in the appropriate ancillary service cost center, i.e., in the cost of the diagnostic or therapeutic service. It must not show them separately under revenue code 0540.

## EXCEPTIONS

Pneumococcal Vaccine -is payable under Part B only and is billed by the hospital on the Form CMS-1450.

Ambulance Service For purposes of this section "hospital inpatient" means beneficiary who has been formally admitted it does not include a beneficiary who is in the process of being transferred from one hospital to another. Where the patient is transferred from one hospital to another, and is admitted as an inpatient to the second, the ambulance service is payable under only Part B. If transportation is by a hospital owned and operated ambulance, the hospital bills separately on Form CMS-1450 as appropriate. Similarly, if the hospital arranges for the ambulance transportation with an ambulance operator, including paying the ambulance operator, it bills separately. However, if the hospital does not assume any financial responsibility, the billing is to the carrier by the ambulance operator or beneficiary, as appropriate, if an ambulance is used for the transportation of a hospital inpatient to another facility for diagnostic tests or special treatment the ambulance trip is considered part of the DRG, and not separately billable, if the resident hospital is under PPS.

Part B Inpatient Services Where Part A benefits are not payable, payment maybe made to the hospital under Part B for certain medical and other health services. See Chapter 4 for a description of Part B inpatient services.

Anesthetist Services "Incident to" Physician Services

If a physician's practice was to employ anesthetists and to bill on a reasonable charge basis for these services and that practice was in effect as of the last day of the hospital's most recent 12-month cost reporting period ending before September 30, 1983, the physician may continue that practice through cost reporting periods beginning October 1, 1984. However, if the physician chooses to continue this practice, the hospital may not add costs of the anesthetist's service to its base period costs for purposes of its transition payment rates. If it is the existing or new practice of the physician to employ certified registered nurse anesthetists (CRNAs) and other qualified anesthetists and include charges for their services in the physician bills for anesthesiology services for the hospital's cost report periods beginning on or after October 1, 1984, and before October 1, 1987, the physician may continue to do so.

## B. Exceptions/Waivers

These provisions were waived before cost reporting periods beginning on or after October1, 1986, under certain circumstances. The basic criteria for waiver was that services furnished by outside suppliers are so extensive that a sudden change in billing practices would threaten the stability of patient care. Specific criteria for waiver and processing procedures are in Sec.2804 of the Provider Reimbursement Manual (CMS Pub. 15-1).

## *100-4,3,20.7.3*
## Payment for Blood Clotting Factor Administered to Hemophilia Patients

Section 6011 of Public Law (P.L.) 101-239 amended Sec.1886(a)(4) of the Social Security Act (the Act) to provide that prospective payment system (PPS) hospitals receive anadditional payment for the costs of administering blood clotting factor to Medicare hemophiliacs who are hospital inpatients. Section 6011(b) of P.L. 101.239 specified that the payment be based on a predetermined price per unit of clotting factor multiplied by the number of units provided. This add-on payment originally was effective for blood clotting factors furnished on or after June 19, 1990, and before December 19,

1991. Section 13505 of P. L. 103-66 amended Sec.6011 (d) of P.L. 101-239 to extend the period covered by the add-on payment for blood clotting factors administered to Medicare inpatients with hemophilia through September 30, 1994. Section 4452 of P.L. 105-33 amended Sec.6011(d) of P.L. 101-239 to reinstate the add-on payment for the costs of administering blood clotting factor to Medicare beneficiaries who have hemophilia and who are hospital inpatients for discharges occurring on or after October 1, 1998.

Local carriers shall process non-institutional blood clotting factor claims.

The FIs shall process institutional blood clotting factor claims payable under either Part A or Part B.

### A. Inpatient Bills

Under the Inpatient Prospective Payment System (PPS), hospitals receive a special add-on payment for the costs of furnishing blood clotting factors to Medicare beneficiaries with hemophilia, admitted as inpatients of PPS hospitals. The clotting factor add-on payment is calculated using the number of units (as defined in the HCPCS code long descriptor) billed by the provider under special instructions for units of service.

The PPS Pricer software does not calculate the payment amount. The Fiscal Intermediary Standard System (FISS) calculates the payment amount and subtracts the charges from those submitted to Pricer so that the clotting factor charges are not included in cost outlier computations.

Blood clotting factors not paid on a cost or PPS basis are priced as a drug/biological under the Medicare Part B Drug Pricing File effective for the specific date of service. As of January 1, 2005, the average sales price (ASP) plus 6 percent shall be used.

If a beneficiary is in a covered Part A stay in a PPS hospital, the clotting factors are paid in addition to the DRG/HIPPS payment (For FY 2004, this payment is based on 95 percent of average wholesale price.) For a SNF subject to SNF/PPS, the payment is bundled into the SNF/PPS rate.

For SNF inpatient Part A, there is no add-on payment for blood clotting factors.

The codes for blood-clotting factors are found on the Medicare Part B Drug Pricing File. This file is distributed on a quarterly basis.

For discharges occurring on or after October 1, 2000, and before December 31, 2005, report HCPCS Q0187 based on 1 billing unit per 1.2 mg. Effective January 1, 2006, HCPCS code J7189 replaces Q0187 and is defined as 1 billing unit per 1 microgram (mcg).

The examples below include the HCPCS code and indicate the dosage amount specified in the descriptor of that code. Facilities use the units field as a multiplier to arrive at the dosage amount.

### EXAMPLE 1
HCPCS Drug Dosage

J7189 Factor VIIa 1 mcg

Actual dosage: 13,365 mcg

On the bill, the facility shows J7189 and 13,365 in the units field (13,365 mcg divided by 1 mcg = 13,365 units).

NOTE:The process for dealing with one international unit (IU) is the same as the process for dealing with one microgram.

### EXAMPLE 2
HCPCS Drug Dosage

J9355 Trastuzumab 10 mg

Actual dosage: 140 mg

On the bill, the facility shows J9355 and 14 in the units field (140 mg divided by 10mg = 14 units). When the dosage amount is greater than the amount indicated for the HCPCS code, the facility rounds up to determine units. When the dosage amount is less than the amount indicated for the HCPCS code, use 1 as the unit of measure.

### EXAMPLE 3

HCPCS Drug Dosage

J3100 Tenecteplase 50 mg

Actual Dosage: 40 mg

The provider would bill for 1 unit, even though less than 1 full unit was furnished.

At times, the facility provides less than the amount provided in a single use vial and there is waste, i.e.; some drugs may be available only in packaged amounts that exceed the needs of an individual patient. Once the drug is reconstituted in the hospital's pharmacy, it may have a limited shelf life. Since an individual patient may receive less than the fully reconstituted amount, we encourage hospitals to schedule patients in such a way that the hospital can use the drug most efficiently. However, if the hospital must discard the remainder of a vial after administering part of it to a Medicare patient, the provider may bill for the amount of drug discarded plus the amount administered.

### Example 1:

Drug X is available only in a 100-unit size. A hospital schedules three Medicare patients to receive drug X on the same day within the designated shelf life of the product. An appropriate hospital staff member administers 30 units to each patient. The remaining 10 units are billed to Medicare on the account of the last patient. Therefore, 30 units are billed on behalf of the first patient seen and 30 units are billed on behalf of the second patient seen. Forty units are billed on behalf of the last patient seen because the hospital had to discard 10 units at that point.

### Example 2:

An appropriate hospital staff member must administer 30 units of drug X to a Medicare patient, and it is not practical to schedule another patient who requires the same drug. For example, the hospital has only one patient who requires drug X, or the hospital sees the patient for the first time and did not know the patient's condition. The hospital bills for 100 units on behalf of the patient, and Medicare pays for 100 units.

When the number of units of blood clotting factor administered to hemophiliac inpatients exceeds 99,999, the hospital reports the excess as a second line for revenue code 0636 and repeats the HCPCS code. One hundred thousand fifty (100,050) units are reported on one line as 99,999, and another line shows 1,051.

Revenue Code 0636 is used. It requires HCPCS. Some other inpatient drugs continue to be billed without HCPCS codes under pharmacy.

No changes in beneficiary notices are required. Coverage is applicable to hospital Part A claims only. Coverage is also applicable to inpatient Part B services in SNFs and all types of hospitals, including CAHs. Separate payment is not made to SNFs for beneficiaries in an inpatient Part A stay.

### B. FI Action

The FI is responsible for the following:

- It accepts HCPCS codes for inpatient services;

- It edits to require HCPCS codes with Revenue Code 0636. Multiple iterations of the revenue code are possible with the same or different HCPCS codes. It does not edit units except to ensure a numeric value;

- It reduces charges forwarded to Pricer by the charges for hemophilia clotting factors in revenue code 0636. It retains the charges and revenue and HCPCS codes for CWF; and

- It modifies data entry screens to accept HCPCS codes for hospital (including CAH) swing bed, and SNF inpatient claims (bill types 11X, 12X, 18x, 21x and, 22x).

The September 1, 1993, IPPS final rule (58 FR 46304) states that payment will be made for the blood clotting factor only if an ICD-9-CM diagnosis code for hemophilia is included on the bill.

Since inpatient blood-clotting factors are covered only for beneficiaries with hemophilia, the FI must ensure that one of the following hemophilia diagnosis codes is listed on the bill before payment is made:

- 286.0 Congenital factor VIII disorder
- 286.1 Congenital factor IX disorder
- 286.2 Congenital factor IX disorder
- 286.3 Congenital deficiency of other clotting factor
- 286.4 von Willebrands' disease

Effective for discharges on or after August 1, 2001, payment may also be made if one of the following diagnosis codes is reported:

- 286.5 Hemorrhagic disorder due to circulating anticoagulants
- 286.7 Acquired coagulation factor deficiency

### C. Part A Remittance Advice

1. X12.835 Ver. 003030M

For remittance reporting PIP and/or non-PIP payments, the Hemophilia Add on will be reported in a claims level 2-090-CAS segment (CAS is the element identifier) exhibiting an "OA" Group Code and adjustment reason code "97" (payment is included in the allowance for the basic service/ procedure) followed by the associated dollar amount (POSITIVE) and units of service. For this version of the 835, "OA" group coded line level CAS segments are informational and are not included in the balancing routine. The Hemophilia Add On amount will always be included in the 2-010-CLP04 Claim Payment Amount.

For remittance reporting PIP payments, the Hemophilia Add On will also be reported in the provider level adjustment (element identifier PLB) segment with the provider level adjustment reason code "CA" (Manual claims adjustment) followed by the associated dollar amount (NEGATIVE).

NOTE: A data maintenance request will be submitted to ANSI ASC X12 for a new PLB adjustment reason code specifically for PIP payment Hemophilia Add On situations for future use. However, continue to use adjustment reason code "CA" until further notice.

The FIs enter MA103 (Hemophilia Add On) in an open MIA (element identifier) remark code data element. This will alert the provider that the reason code 97 and PLB code "CA" adjustments are related to the Hemophilia Add On.

2. X12.835 Ver. 003051

For remittances reporting PIP and/or non-PIP payments, Hemophilia Add On information will be reported in the claim level 2-062-AMT and 2-064-QTY segments. The 2-062-AMTO1 element will carry a "ZK" (Federal Medicare claim MANDATE - Category 1) qualifier code followed by the total claim level Hemophilia Add On amount (POSITIVE). The 2-064QTY01 element will carry a "FL" (Units) qualifier code followed by the number of units approved for the Hemophilia Add On for the claim. The Hemophilia Add On amount will always be included in the 2-010-CLP04 Claim Payment Amount.

NOTE: A data maintenance request will be submitted to ANSI ASC X12 for a new AMT qualifier code specifically for the Hemophilia Add On for future use. However, continue to use adjustment reason code "ZK" until further notice.

For remittances reporting PIP payments, the Hemophilia Add On will be reported in the provider level adjustment PLB segment with the provider level adjustment reason "ZZ" followed by the associated dollar amount (NEGATIVE).

NOTE: A data maintenance request will be submitted to ANSI ASC X12 for a new PLB, adjustment reason code specifically for the Hemophilia Add On for future use. However, continue to use PLB adjustment reason code "ZZ" until further notice. The FIs enter MA103 (Hemophilia Add On) in an open MIA remark code data element. This will alert the provider that the ZK, FL and ZZ entries are related to the Hemophilia Add On. (Effective with version 4010 of the 835, report ZK in lieu of FL in the QTY segment.)

   3. Standard Hard Copy Remittance Advice

For paper remittances reporting non-PIP payments involving Hemophilia Add On, add a "Hemophilia Add On" category to the end of the "Pass Thru Amounts" listings in the "Summary" section of the paper remittance. Enter the total of the Hemophilia Add On amounts due for the claims covered by this remittance next to the Hemophilia Add On heading.

The FIs add the Remark Code "MA103" (Hemophilia Add On) to the remittance advice under the REM column for those claims that qualify for Hemophilia Add On payments.

This will be the full extent of Hemophilia Add On reporting on paper remittance notices; providers wishing more detailed information must subscribe to the Medicare Part A specifications for the ANSI ASC X12N 835, where additional information is available.

See chapter 22, for detailed instructions and definitions.

## 100-4,3,40.2.2
### Charges to Beneficiaries for Part A Services
The hospital submits a bill even where the patient is responsible for a deductible which covers the entire amount of the charges for non-PPS hospitals, or in PPS hospitals, where the DRG payment amount will be less than the deductible.

A hospital receiving payment for a covered hospital stay (or PPS hospital that includes at least one covered day, or one treated as covered under guarantee of payment or limitation on liability) may charge the beneficiary, or other person, for items and services furnished during the stay only as described in subsections A through H. If limitation of liability applies, a beneficiary's liability for payment is governed by the limitation

on liability notification rules in Chapter 30 of this manual. For related notices for inpatient hospitals, see CMS Transmittal 594, Change Request3903, dated June 24, 2005.

### A. Deductible and Coinsurance
The hospital may charge the beneficiary or other person for applicable deductible and coinsurance amounts. The deductible is satisfied only by charges for covered services. The FI deducts the deductible and coinsurance first from the PPS payment. Where the deductible exceeds the PPS amount, the excess will be applied to a subsequent payment to the hospital. (See Chapter 3 of the Medicare General Information, Eligibility, and Entitlement Manual for specific policies.)

### B. Blood Deductible
The Part A blood deductible provision applies to whole blood and red blood cells, and reporting of the number of pints is applicable to both PPS and non-PPS hospitals. (See Chapter 3 of the Medicare General Information, Eligibility, and Entitlement Manual for specific policies.) Hospitals shall report charges for red blood cells using revenue code 381, and charges for whole blood using revenue code 382.

### C. Inpatient Care No Longer Required
The hospital may charge for services that are not reasonable and necessary or that constitute custodial care. Notification may be required under limitation of liability. See CMS Transmittal 594, Change Request3903, dated June 24, 2005, section V. of the attachment, for specific notification requirements. Note this transmittal will be placed in Chapter 30 of this manual at a future point. Chapter 1, section 150 of this manual also contains related billing information in addition to that provided below.

In general, after proper notification has occurred, and assuming an expedited decision is received from a Quality Improvement Organization (QIO), the following entries are required on the bill the hospital prepares:

- Occurrence code 31 (and date) to indicate the date the hospital notified the patient in accordance with the first bullet above;

- Occurrence span code 76 (and dates) to indicate the period of noncovered care for which it is charging the beneficiary;

- Occurrence span code 77 (and dates) to indicate the period of noncovered care for which the provider is liable, when it is aware of this prior to billing; and

- Value code 31 (and amount) to indicate the amount of charges it may bill the beneficiary for days for which inpatient care was no longer required. They are included as noncovered charges on the bill.

### D. Change in the Beneficiary's Condition
If the beneficiary remains in the hospital after receiving notice as described in subsection C, and the hospital, the physician who concurred in the hospital's determination, or the QIO, subsequently determines that the beneficiary again requires inpatient hospital care, the hospital may not charge the beneficiary or other person for services furnished after the beneficiary again required inpatient hospital care until proper notification occurs (see subsection C).

If a patient who needs only a SNF level of care remains in the hospital after the SNF bed becomes available, and the bed ceases to be available, the hospital may continue to charge the beneficiary. It need not provide the beneficiary with another notice when the patient chose not to be discharged to the SNF bed.

## E. Admission Denied

If the entire hospital admission is determined to be not reasonable or necessary, limitation of liability may apply. See 2005 CMS transmittal 594, section V. of the attachment, for specific notification requirements.

NOTE: This transmittal will be placed in Chapter 30 of this manual at a future point.

In such cases the following entries are required on the bill:

- Occurrence code 31 (and date) to indicate the date the hospital notified the beneficiary.

- Occurrence span code 76 (and dates) to indicate the period of noncovered care for which the hospital is charging the beneficiary.

- Occurrence span code 77 (and dates) to indicate any period of noncovered care for which the provider is liable (e.g., the period between issuing the notice and the time it may charge the beneficiary) when the provider is aware of this prior to billing.

- Value code 31 (and amount) to indicate the amount of charges the hospital may bill the beneficiary for hospitalization that was not necessary or reasonable. They are included as noncovered charges on the bill.

## F. Procedures, Studies and Courses of Treatment That Are Not Reasonable or Necessary

If diagnostic procedures, studies, therapeutic studies and courses of treatment are excluded from coverage as not reasonable and necessary (even though the beneficiary requires inpatient hospital care) the hospital may charge the beneficiary or other person for the services or care according the procedures given in CMS Transmittal 594, Change Request3903, dated June 24, 2005.

The following bill entries apply to these circumstances:

- Occurrence code 32 (and date) to indicate the date the hospital provided the notice to the beneficiary.

- Value code 31 (and amount) to indicate the amount of such charges to be billed to the beneficiary. They are included as noncovered charges on the bill.

## G. Nonentitlement Days and Days after Benefits Exhausted

If a hospital stay exceeds the day outlier threshold, the hospital may charge for some, or all, of the days on which the patient is not entitled to Medicare Part A, or after the Part A benefits are exhausted (i.e., the hospital may charge its customary charges for services furnished on those days). It may charge the beneficiary for the lesser of:

- The number of days on which the patient was not entitled to benefits or after the benefits were exhausted; or

- The number of outlier days. (Day outliers were discontinued at the end of FY 1997.)

If the number of outlier days exceeds the number of days on which the patient was not entitled to benefits, or after benefits were exhausted, the hospital may charge for all days on which the patient was not entitled to benefits or after benefits were exhausted. If the number of days on which the beneficiary was not entitled to benefits, or after benefits were exhausted, exceeds the number of outlier days, the hospital determines the days for which it may charge by starting with the last day of the stay (i.e., the day before the day of discharge) and identifying and counting off in reverse order, days on which the patient was not entitled to benefits or after the benefits were exhausted, until

the number of days counted off equals the number of outlier days. The days counted off are the days for which the hospital may charge.

## H. Contractual Exclusions

In addition to receiving the basic prospective payment, the hospital may charge the beneficiary for any services that are excluded from coverage for reasons other than, or in addition to, absence of medical necessity, provision of custodial care, nonentitlement to Part A, or exhaustion of benefits. For example, it may charge for most cosmetic and dental surgery.

## I. Private Room Care

Payment for medically necessary private room care is included in the prospective payment. Where the beneficiary requests private room accommodations, the hospital must inform the beneficiary of the additional charge. (See the Medicare Benefit Policy Manual, Chapter 1.) When the beneficiary accepts the liability, the hospital will supply the service, and bill the beneficiary directly. If the beneficiary believes the private room was medically necessary, the beneficiary has a right to a determination and may initiate a Part A appeal.

## J. Deluxe Item or Service

Where a beneficiary requests a deluxe item or service, i.e., an item or service which is more expensive than is medically required for the beneficiary's condition, the hospital may collect the additional charge if it informs the beneficiary of the additional charge. That charge is the difference between the customary charge for the item or service most commonly furnished by the hospital to private pay patients with the beneficiary's condition, and the charge for the more expensive item or service requested. If the beneficiary believes that the more expensive item or service was medically necessary, the beneficiary has a right to a determination and may initiate a Part A appeal.

## K - Inpatient Acute Care Hospital Admission Followed By a Death or Discharge Prior To Room Assignment

A patient of an acute care hospital is considered an inpatient upon issuance of written doctor's orders to that effect. If a patient either dies or is discharged prior to being assigned and/or occupying a room, a hospital may enter an appropriate room and board charge on the claim. If a patient leaves of their own volition prior to being assigned and/or occupying a room, a hospital may enter an appropriate room and board charge on the claim as well as a patient status code 07 which indicates they left against medical advice. A hospital is not required to enter a room and board charge, but failure to do so may have a minimal impact on future DRG weight calculations.

## *100-4,3,40.3*

## Outpatient Services Treated as Inpatient Services

A3-3610.3, HO-415.6, HO-400D, A-03-008, A-03-013, A-03-054

### A. Outpatient Services Followed by Admission Before Midnight of the Following Day (Effective For Services Furnished Before October 1, 1991)

When a beneficiary receives outpatient hospital services during the day immediately preceding the hospital admission, the outpatient hospital services are treated as inpatient services if the beneficiary has Part A coverage. Hospitals and FIs apply this provision only when the beneficiary is admitted to the hospital before midnight of the day following receipt of outpatient services. The day on which the patient is formally admitted as an inpatient is counted as the first inpatient day.

# APPENDIX 4 — PUB 100 REFERENCES

When this provision applies, services are included in the applicable PPS payment and not billed separately. When this provision applies to hospitals and units excluded from the hospital PPS, services are shown on the bill and included in the Part A payment. See Chapter 1 for FI requirements for detecting duplicate claims in such cases.

### B. Preadmission Diagnostic Services (Effective for Services Furnished On or After January 1, 1991)

Diagnostic services (including clinical diagnostic laboratory tests) provided to a beneficiary by the admitting hospital, or by an entity wholly owned or wholly operated by the admitting hospital (or by another entity under arrangements with the admitting hospital), within 3 days prior to and including the date of the beneficiary's admission are deemed to be inpatient services and included in the inpatient payment, unless there is no Part A coverage. For example, if a patient is admitted on a Wednesday, outpatient services provided by the hospital on Sunday, Monday, Tuesday, or Wednesday are included in the inpatient Part A payment.

This provision does not apply to ambulance services and maintenance renal dialysis services (see the Medicare Benefit Policy Manual, Chapters 10 and 11, respectively). Additionally, Part A services furnished by skilled nursing facilities, home health agencies, and hospices are excluded from the payment window provisions.

For services provided before October 31, 1994, this provision applies to both hospitals subject to the hospital inpatient prospective payment system (IPPS) as well as those hospitals and units excluded from IPPS.

For services provided on or after October 31, 1994, for hospitals and units excluded from IPPS, this provision applies only to services furnished within one day prior to and including the date of the beneficiary's admission. The hospitals and units that are excluded from IPPS are: psychiatric hospitals and units; inpatient rehabilitation facilities (IRF) and units; long-term care hospitals (LTCH); children's hospitals; and cancer hospitals.

Critical access hospitals (CAHs) are not subject to the 3-day (nor 1-day) DRG payment window.

An entity is considered to be "wholly owned or operated" by the hospital if the hospital is the sole owner or operator. A hospital need not exercise administrative control over a facility in order to operate it. A hospital is considered the sole operator of the facility if the hospital has exclusive responsibility for implementing facility policies (i.e., conducting or overseeing the facility's routine operations), regardless of whether it also has the authority to make the policies.

For this provision, diagnostic services are defined by the presence on the bill of the following revenue and/or CPT codes:

- 0254 - Drugs incident to other diagnostic services
- 0255 - Drugs incident to radiology
- 030X - Laboratory
- 031X - Laboratory pathological
- 032X - Radiology diagnostic
- 0341, 0343 - Nuclear medicine, diagnostic/Diagnostic Radiopharmaceuticals
- 035X - CT scan
- 0371 - Anesthesia incident to Radiology
- 0372 - Anesthesia incident to other diagnostic services
- 040X - Other imaging services
- 046X - Pulmonary function
- 0471 - Audiology diagnostic
- 0481, 0489- Cardiology, Cardiac Catheter Lab/Other Cardiology with CPT codes 93501, 93503, 93505, 93508, 93510, 93526, 93541, 93542, 93543, 93544, 93556, 93561, or 93562 diagnostic
- 0482- Cardiology, Stress Test
- 0483- Cardiology, Echocardiology
- 053X - Osteopathic services
- 061X - MRT
- 062X - Medical/surgical supplies, incident to radiology or other diagnostic services
- 073X - EKG/ECG
- 074X - EEG
- 0918- Testing- Behavioral Health
- 092X - Other diagnostic services

The CWF rejects services furnished January 1, 1991, or later when outpatient bills for diagnostic services with through dates or last date of service (occurrence span code 72) fall on the day of admission or any of the 3 days immediately prior to admission to an IPPS or IPPS-excluded hospital. This reject applies to the bill in process, regardless of whether the outpatient or inpatient bill is processed first. Hospitals must analyze the two bills and report appropriate corrections. For services on or after October 31, 1994, for hospitals and units excluded from IPPS, CWF will reject outpatient diagnostic bills that occur on the day of or one day before admission. For IPPS hospitals, CWF will continue to reject outpatient diagnostic bills for services that occur on the day of or any of the 3 days prior to admission. Effective for dates of service on or after July 1, 2008, CWF will reject diagnostic services when the line item date of service (LIDOS) falls on the day of admission or any of the 3 days immediately prior to an admission to an IPPS hospital or on the day of admission or one day prior to admission for hospitals excluded from IPPS.

Hospitals in Maryland that are under the jurisdiction of the Health Services Cost Review Commission are subject to the 3-day payment window.

### C. Other Preadmission Services (Effective for Services Furnished On or After October 1, 1991)

Nondiagnostic outpatient services that are related to a patient's hospital admission and that are provided by the hospital, or by an entity wholly owned or wholly operated by the admitting hospital (or by another entity under arrangements with the admitting hospital), to the patient during the 3 days immediately preceding and including the date of the patient's admission are deemed to be inpatient services and are included in the inpatient payment. Effective March 13, 1998, we defined nondiagnostic preadmission services as being related to the admission only when there is an exact match (for all digits) between the ICD-9-CM principal diagnosis code assigned for both the preadmission services and the inpatient stay. Thus, whenever Part A covers an admission, the hospital may bill nondiagnostic preadmission services to Part B as outpatient services only if they are not related to the admission. The FI shall assume, in the absence of evidence to the contrary, that such bills are not admission related and, therefore, are not deemed to be inpatient (Part A) services. If there are both diagnostic and nondiagnostic preadmission services and the nondiagnostic services are unrelated to the admission, the hospital may separately bill the nondiagnostic preadmission services to Part B. This provision applies only when the patient has Part A coverage. This provision does not apply to ambulance services and maintenance renal dialysis. Additionally, Part A services furnished by skilled nursing facilities, home health agencies, and hospices are excluded from the payment window provisions.

For services provided before October 31, 1994, this provision applies to both hospitals subject to IPPS as well as those hospitals and units excluded from IPPS (see section B above).

For services provided on or after October 31, 1994, for hospitals and units excluded from IPPS, this provision applies only to services furnished within one day prior to and including the date of the beneficiary's admission.

Critical access hospitals (CAHs) are not subject to the 3-day (nor 1-day) DRG payment window.

Hospitals in Maryland that are under the jurisdiction of the Health Services Cost Review Commission are subject to the 3-day payment window.

Effective for dates of service on or after July 1, 2008, CWF will reject therapeutic services when the line item date of service (LIDOS) falls on the day of admission or any of the 3 days immediately prior to an admission to an IPPS hospital or on the day of admission or one day prior to admission for hospitals excluded from IPPS.

## 100-4,32,100
### Billing Requirements for Expanded Coverage of Cochlear Implantation

Effective for dates of services on and after April 4, 2005, the Centers for Medicare & Medicaid Services (CMS) has expanded the coverage for cochlear implantation to cover moderate-to-profound hearing loss in individuals with hearing test scores equal to or less than 40% correct in the best aided listening condition on tape-recorded tests of open-set sentence recognition and who demonstrate limited benefit from amplification. (See Publication 100-03, chapter 1, section 50.3, for specific coverage criteria).

In addition CMS is covering cochlear implantation for individuals with open-set sentence recognition test scores of greater than 40% to less than or equal to 60% correct but only when the provider is participating in, and patients are enrolled in, either:

- A Food and Drug Administration (FDA)-approved category B investigational device exemption (IDE) clinical trial; or
- A trial under the CMS clinical trial policy (see Pub. 100-03, section 310.1); or
- A prospective, controlled comparative trial approved by CMS as consistent with the evidentiary requirements for national coverage analyses and meeting specific quality standards.

## 100-4,32,50
### Deep Brain Stimulation for Essential Tremor and Parkinson's Disease

Deep brain stimulation (DBS) refers to high-frequency electrical stimulation of anatomic regions deep within the brain utilizing neurosurgically implanted electrodes. These DBS electrodes are stereotactically placed within targeted nuclei on one (unilateral) or both (bilateral) sides of the brain. There are currently three targets for DBS -- the thalamic ventralis intermedius nucleus (VIM), subthalamic nucleus (STN) and globus pallidus interna (GPi).

Essential tremor (ET) is a progressive, disabling tremor most often affecting the hands. ET may also affect the head, voice and legs. The precise pathogenesis of ET is unknown. While it may start at any age, ET usually peaks within the second and sixth

decades. Beta-adrenergic blockers and anticonvulsant medications are usually the first line treatments for reducing the severity of tremor. Many patients, however, do not adequately respond or cannot tolerate these medications. In these medically refractory ET patients, thalamic VIM DBS may be helpful for symptomatic relief of tremor.

Parkinson's disease (PD) is an age-related progressive neurodegenerative disorder involving the loss of dopaminergic cells in the substantia nigra of the midbrain. The disease is characterized by tremor, rigidity, bradykinesia and progressive postural instability. Dopaminergic medication is typically used as a first line treatment for reducing the primary symptoms of PD. However, after prolonged use, medication can become less effective and can produce significant adverse events such as dyskinesias and other motor function complications. For patients who become unresponsive to medical treatments and/or have intolerable side effects from medications, DBS for symptom relief may be considere

## 100-4,4,160
### Clinic and Emergency Visits

CMS has acknowledged from the beginning of the OPPS that CMS believes that CPT Evaluation and Management (E/M) codes were designed to reflect the activities of physicians and do not describe well the range and mix of services provided by hospitals during visits of clinic and emergency department patients. While awaiting the development of a national set of facility-specific codes and guidelines, providers should continue to apply their current internal guidelines to the existing CPT codes. Each hospital's internal guidelines should follow the intent of the CPT code descriptors, in that the guidelines should be designed to reasonably relate the intensity of hospital resources to the different levels of effort represented by the codes. Hospitals should ensure that their guidelines accurately reflect resource distinctions between the five levels of codes.

Effective January 1, 2007, CMS is distinguishing between two types of emergency departments: Type A emergency departments and Type B emergency departments.

A Type A emergency department is defined as an emergency department that is available 24 hours a day, 7 days a week and is either licensed by the State in which it is located under applicable State law as an emergency room or emergency department or it is held out to the public (by name, posted signs, advertising, or other means) as a place that provides care for emergency medical conditions on an urgent basis without requiring a previously scheduled appointment.

A Type B emergency department is defined as an emergency department that meets the definition of a "dedicated emergency department" as defined in 42 CFR 489.24 under the EMTALA regulations. It must meet at least one of the following requirements: (1) It is licensed by the State in which it is located under applicable State law as an emergency room or emergency department; (2) It is held out to the public (by name, posted signs, advertising, or other means) as a place that provides care for emergency medical conditions on an urgent basis without requiring a previously scheduled appointment; or (3) During the calendar year immediately preceding the calendar year in which a determination under 42 CFR 489.24 is being made, based on a representative sample of patient visits that occurred during that calendar year, it provides at least one-third of all of its outpatient visits for the treatment of emergency medical conditions on an urgent basis without requiring a previously scheduled appointment.

Hospitals must bill for visits provided in Type A emergency departments using CPT emergency department E/M codes. Hospitals must bill for visits provided in Type B emergency departments using the G-codes that describe visits provided in Type B emergency departments.

Hospitals that will be billing the new Type B ED visit codes may need to update their internal guidelines to report these codes.

Emergency department and clinic visits are paid in some cases separately and in other cases as part of a composite APC payment. See section 10.2.1 of this chapter for further details.

## 100-4,4,160.1
### Critical Care Services

Beginning January 1, 2007, critical care services will be paid at two levels, depending on the presence or absence of trauma activation. Providers will receive one payment rate for critical care without trauma activation and will receive additional payment when critical care is associated with trauma activation.

To determine whether trauma activation occurs, follow the National Uniform Billing Committee (NUBC) guidelines in the Claims Processing Manual, Pub 100-04, Chapter 25, Sec.75.4 related to the reporting of the trauma revenue codes in the 68x series. The revenue code series 68x can be used only by trauma centers/hospitals as licensed or designated by the state or local government authority authorized to do so, or as verified by the American College of Surgeons. Different subcategory revenue codes are reported by designated Level 1-4 hospital trauma centers. Only patients for whom there has been prehospital notification based on triage information from prehospital caregivers, who meet either local, state or American College of Surgeons field triage criteria, or are delivered by inter-hospital transfers, and are given the appropriate team response can be billed a trauma activation charge.

When critical care services are provided without trauma activation, the hospital may bill CPT code 99291, Critical care, evaluation and management of the critically ill or critically injured patient; first 30-74 minutes (and 99292, if appropriate). If trauma activation occurs under the circumstances described by the NUBC guidelines that would permit reporting a charge under 68x, the hospital may also bill one unit of code G0390, which describes trauma activation associated with hospital critical care services. Revenue code 68x must be reported on the same date of service. The OCE will edit to ensure that G0390 appears with revenue code 68x on the same date of service and that only one unit of G0390 is billed. CMS believes that trauma activation is a one-time occurrence in association with critical care services, and therefore, CMS will only pay for one unit of G0390 per day.

The CPT code 99291 is defined by CPT as the first 30-74 minutes of critical care. This 30 minute minimum has always applied under the OPPS. The CPT code 99292, Critical care, evaluation and management of the critically ill or critically injured patient; each additional 30 minutes, remains a packaged service under the OPPS, so that hospitals do not have the ongoing administrative burden of reporting precisely the time for each critical service provided. As the CPT guidelines indicate, hospitals that provide less than 30 minutes of critical care should bill for a visit, typically an emergency department visit, at a level consistent with their own internal guidelines.

Under the OPPS, the time that can be reported as critical care is the time spent by a physician and/or hospital staff engaged in active face-to-face critical care of a critically ill or critically injured patient. If the physician and hospital staff or multiple hospital staff members are simultaneously engaged in this active face-to-face care, the time involved can only be counted once.

In CY 2007 hospitals may continue to report a charge with RC 68x without any HCPCS code when trauma team activation occurs. In order to receive additional payment when critical care services are associated with trauma activation, the hospital must report G0390 on the same date of service as RC 68x, in addition to CPT code 99291 (or 99292, if appropriate.)

In CY 2007 hospitals should continue to report 99291 (and 99292 as appropriate) for critical care services furnished without trauma team activation. CPT 99291 maps to APC 0617 (Critical Care). (CPT 99292 is packaged and not paid separately, but should be reported if provided.)

Critical care services are paid in some cases separately and in other cases as part of a composite APC payment. See Section 10.2.1 of this chapter for further details.

## 100-4,4,200.1
### Billing for Corneal Tissue

Corneal tissue will be paid on a cost basis, not under OPPS. To receive cost based reimbursement hospitals must bill charges for corneal tissue using HCPCS code V2785.

## 100-4,4,200.3.4
### Billing for Linear Accelerator (Robotic Image-Guided and
Non-Robotic Image-Guided) SRS Planning and Delivery

Effective for services furnished on or after January 1, 2006, hospitals must bill using existing CPT codes that most accurately describe the service furnished for both robotic and non-robotic image-guided SRS planning. For robotic image-guided SRS delivery, hospitals must bill using HCPCS code G0039 for the first session and HCPCS code G0340 for the second through the fifth sessions. For non-robotic image-guided SRS delivery, hospitals must bill G0173 for delivery if the delivery occurs in one session, and G0251 for delivery per session (not to exceed five sessions) if delivery occurs during multiple sessions.

Linear Accelerator-Based Robotic Image-Guided SRS Planning Use existing CPT codes Delivery G0339 (complete, 1P st P session) G0340 (2P nd P - 5P th P session) Linear Accelerator-Based Non-Robotic Image-Guided SRS Planning Use existing CPT codes Delivery G0173 (single session) G0251 (multiple) G0173 Linear accelerator based stereotactic radiosurgery, delivery including collimator changes and custom plugging, complete course of treatment in one session, all lesions.

- G0251 Linear accelerator based stereotactic radiosurgery, delivery including collimator changes and custom plugging, fractionated treatment, all lesions, per session, maximum 5 sessions per course of treatment.

- G0339 Image-guided robotic linear accelerator-based stereotactic radiosurgery, complete course of therapy in one session or first session of fractionated treatment.

- G0340 Image-guided robotic linear accelerator-based stereotactic radiosurgery, delivery including collimator changes and custom plugging, fractionated treatment, all lesions, per session, second through fifth sessions, maximum five sessions per course of treatment.

## 100-4,4,200.4
### Billing for Amniotic Membrane

Hospitals should report HCPCS code V2790 (Amniotic membrane for surgical reconstruction, per procedure) to report amniotic membrane tissue when the tissue is used. A specific procedure code associated with use of amniotic membrane tissue is CPT code 65780 (Ocular surface reconstruction; amniotic membrane transplantation).

Payment for the amniotic membrane tissue is packaged into payment for CPT code 65780 or other procedures with which the amniotic membrane is used.

## 100-4,4,200.6
### Billing and Payment for Alcohol and/or Substance Abuse Assessment and Intervention Services

For CY 2008, the CPT Editorial Panel has created two new Category I CPT codes for reporting alcohol and/or substance abuse screening and intervention services. They are CPT code 99408 (Alcohol and/or substance (other than tobacco) abuse structured screening (e.g., AUDIT, DAST), and brief intervention (SBI) services; 15 to 30 minutes); and CPT code 99409 (Alcohol and/or substance (other than tobacco) abuse structured screening (e.g., AUDIT, DAST), and brief intervention (SBI) services; greater than 30 minutes). However, screening services are not covered by Medicare without specific statutory authority, such as has been provided for mammography, diabetes, and colorectal cancer screening. Therefore, beginning January 1, 2008, the OPPS recognizes two parallel G-codes (HCPCS codes G0396 and G0397) to allow for appropriate reporting and payment of alcohol and substance abuse structured assessment and intervention services that are not provided as screening services, but that are performed in the context of the diagnosis or treatment of illness or injury.

Contractors shall make payment under the OPPS for HCPCS code G0396 (Alcohol and/or substance (other than tobacco) abuse structured assessment (e.g., AUDIT, DAST) and brief intervention, 15 to 30 minutes) and HCPCS code G0397, (Alcohol and/or substance(other than tobacco) abuse structured assessment (e.g., AUDIT, DAST) and intervention greater than 30 minutes), only when reasonable and necessary (i.e., when the service is provided to evaluate patients with signs/symptoms of illness or injury) as per section 1862(a)(1)(A) of the Act.

HCPCS codes G0396 and G0397 are to be used for structured alcohol and/or substance (other than tobacco) abuse assessment and intervention services that are distinct from other clinic and emergency department visit services performed during the same encounter. Hospital resources expended performing services described by HCPCS codes G0396 and G0397 may not be counted as resources for determining the level of a visit service and vice versa (i.e., hospitals may not double count the same facility resources in order to reach a higher level clinic or emergency department visit). However, alcohol and/or substance structured assessment or intervention services lasting less than 15 minutes should not be reported using these HCPCS codes, but the hospital resources expended should be included in determining the level of the visit service reported.

## 100-4,4,200.7.2
### Cardiac Echocardiography With Contrast

Hospitals are instructed to bill for echocardiograms with contrast using the applicable HCPCS code(s) included in Table 200.7.2 below. Hospitals should also report the appropriate units of the HCPCS codes for the contrast agents used in the performance of the echocardiograms.

Table 200.7.2 - HCPCS Codes For Echocardiograms With Contrast HCPCS Long Descriptor C8921 Transthoracic echocardiography with contrast for congenital cardiac anomalies; complete C8922 Transthoracic echocardiography with contrast for congenital cardiac anomalies; follow-up or limited study C8923 Transthoracic echocardiography with contrast, realtime with image documentation (2D) with or without HCPCS Long Descriptor M-mode recording; complete C8924 Transthoracic echocardiography with contrast, realtime with image documentation (2D) with or without M-mode recording; follow-up or limited study C8925 Transesophageal echocardiography (TEE) with contrast, real time with image documentation (2D) (with or without M-mode recording); including probe placement, image acquisition, interpretation and report C8926 Transesophageal echocardiography (TEE) with contrast for congenital cardiac anomalies; including probe placement, image acquisition, interpretation and report C8927 Transesophageal echocardiography (TEE) with contrast for monitoring purposes, including probe placement, real time 2-dimensional image acquisition and interpretation leading to ongoing (continuous) assessment of (dynamically changing) cardiac pumping function and to therapeutic measures on an immediate time basis C8928 Transthoracic echocardiography with contrast, realtime with image documentation (2D), with or without M-mode recording, during rest and cardiovascular stress test using treadmill, bicycle exercise and/or pharmacologically induced stress, with interpretation and report

## 100-4,4,230.2.1
### Administration of Drugs Via Implantable or Portable Pumps

for Implantable or Portable Pumps 2005 CPT Final CY 2006 OPPS 2005 CPT 2005 Description Code Description SI APC n/a n/a C8957 Intravenous infusion for therapy/diagnosis; initiation of prolonged infusion (more than 8 hours), requiring use of portable or implantable pump S 0120 96414 Chemotherapy administration, intravenous; infusion technique, initiation of prolonged infusion (more than 8 hours), requiring the use of a portable or implantable pump 96416 Chemotherapy administration, intravenous infusion technique; initiation of prolonged chemotherapy infusion (more than 8 hours), requiring use of portable or implantable pump S 0117 96425 Chemotherapy administration, infusion technique, initiation of prolonged infusion (more than 8 hours), requiring the use of a portable or implantable pump) 96425 Chemotherapy administration, intra-arterial; infusion technique, initiation of prolonged infusion (more than 8 hours), requiring the use of a portable or implantable pump S 0117 96520 Refilling and maintenance of portable pump 96521 Refilling and maintenance of portable pump T 0125 2005 CPT Final CY 2006 OPPS 2005 CPT 2005 Description Code Description SI APC 96530 Refilling and maintenance of implantable pump or reservoir for drug delivery, systemic [e.g. Intravenous, intra-arterial] 96522 Refilling and maintenance of implantable pump or reservoir for drug delivery, systemic (e.g., intravenous, intra-arterial) T 0125 n/a n/a 96523 Irrigation of implanted venous access device for drug delivery systems N - Hospitals are to report HCPCS code C8957 and CPT codes 96416 and 96425 to indicate the initiation of a prolonged infusion that requires the use of an implantable or portable pump. CPT codes 96521, 92522, and 96523 should be used by hospitals to indicate refilling and maintenance of drug delivery systems or irrigation of implanted venous access devices for such systems, and may be reported for the servicing of devices used for therapeutic drugs other than chemotherapy.

## 100-4,4,230.2.3
### Non-Chemotherapy Drug Administration
Table 5: CY 2006 OPPS Non-Chemotherapy Drug Administration -Intravenous Infusion Technique

| 2005 CPT | Final CY 2006 OPPS | 2005 CPT | 2005 Desc | Code | Desc | SI | APC |
|---|---|---|---|---|---|---|---|
| 90780 | Intravenous infusion for therapy/diagnosis, administered by physician or under direct supervision of physician; up to one hour\ | C8950 | Intravenous infusion for therapy/diagnosis; up to 1 hour | S | 0120 | | |
| 90781 | Intravenous infusion for therapy/diagnosis, administered by physician or under direct supervision of physician; each additional hour, up to eight (8) hours (List separately in addition to code for primary procedure) | C8951 | Intravenous infusion for therapy/diagnosis; each additional hour (List separately in addition to C8950) | N | - | n/a | n/a |
| | | C8957 | Intravenous infusion for therapy/diagnosis; initiation of prolonged infusion (more than 8 hours), requiring use of portable or implantable pump | S | 120 | | |

Hospitals are to report HCPCS code C8950 to indicate an infusion of drugs other than anti-neoplastic drugs furnished on or after January 1, 2006 (except as noted at 230.2.2(A) above). HCPCS code C8951 should be used to report all additional infusion hours, with no limit on the number of hours billed per line. Medically necessary separate therapeutic or diagnostic hydration services should be reported with C8950 and C8951, as these are considered intravenous infusions for therapy/diagnosis.

HCPCS codes C8950 and C8951 should not be reported when the infusion is a necessary and integral part of a separately payable OPPS procedure.

When more than one nonchemotherapy drug is infused, hospitals are to code HCPCS codes C8950 and C8951 (if necessary) to report the total duration of an infusion, regardless of the number of substances or drugs infused. Hospitals are reminded to bill separately for each drug infused, in addition to the drug administration services.

The OCE pays one APC for each encounter reported by HCPCS code C8950, and only pays one APC for C8950 per day (unless Modifier 59 is used). Payment for additional hours of infusion reported by HCPCS code C8951 is packaged into the payment for the initial infusion. While no separate payment will be made for units of HCPCS code C8951, hospitals are instructed to report all codes that appropriately describe the services provided and the corresponding charges so that CMS may capture specific historical hospital cost data for future payment rate setting activities.

OCE logic assumes that all services for non-chemotherapy infusions billed on the same date of service were provided during the same encounter. Where a beneficiary makes two separate visits to the hospital for non-chemotherapy infusions in the same day, hospitals are to report modifier 59 for non-chemotherapy infusion codes during the second encounter that were also furnished in the first encounter. The OCE identifies modifier 59 and pays up to a maximum number of units per day, as listed in Table 1.

**EXAMPLE 1**
A beneficiary receives infused drugs that are not anti-neoplastic drugs (including hydrating solutions) for 2 hours. The hospital reports one unit of HCPCS code C8950 and one unit of HCPCS code C8951. The OCE will pay one unit of APC 0120. Payment for the unit of HCPCS code C8951 is packaged into the payment for one unit of APC 0120. (NOTE: See 230.1 for drug billing instructions.)

**EXAMPLE 2**
A beneficiary receives infused drugs that are not anti-neoplastic drugs (including hydrating solutions) for 12 hours. The hospital reports one unit of HCPCS code C8950 and eleven units of HCPCS code C8951. The OCE will pay one unit of APC 0120. Payment for the 11 units of HCPCS code C8951 is packaged into the payment for one unit of APC 0120. (NOTE: See 230.1 for drug billing instructions.)

**EXAMPLE 3**
A beneficiary experiences multiple attempts to initiate an intravenous infusion before a successful infusion is started 20 minutes after the first attempt. Once started, the infusion lasts one hour. The hospital reports one unit of HCPCS code C8950 to identify the 1 hour of infusion time. The 20 minutes spent prior to the infusion attempting to establish an IV line are not separately billable in the OPPS. The OCE pays one unit of APC 0120. (NOTE: See 230.1 for drug billing instructions.)

**B. Administration of Non-Chemotherapy Drugs by a Route Other Than Intravenous Infusion**
Table 6: CY 2006 OPPS Non-Chemotherapy Drug Administration -Route Other Than Intravenous Infusion

| 2005 CPT | Final CY 2006 OPPS | 2005 CPT | 2005 Description | Code | Desc | SI | APC |
|---|---|---|---|---|---|---|---|
| 90784 | Therapeutic, prophylactic or diagnostic injection (specify material injected); intravenous | C8952 | Therapeutic, prophylactic or diagnostic injection; intravenous push | X | 0359 | | |
| 90782 | Therapeutic, prophylactic or diagnostic injection (specify material injected); subcutaneous or intramuscular | 90772 | Therapeutic, prophylactic or diagnostic injection (specify substance or drug); subcutaneous or intramuscular | X | 0353 | | |
| 90783 | Therapeutic, prophylactic or diagnostic injection (specify material injected); intra-arterial | 90773 | Therapeutic, prophylactic or diagnostic injection (specify substance or drug); intra-arterial | X | 0359 | | |
| 90779 | Unlisted therapeutic, prophylactic or diagnostic intravenous or intra-arterial, injection or infusion | 90779 | Unlisted therapeutic, prophylactic or diagnostic intravenous or intra-arterial injection or infusion | X | 0352 | | |

## 100-4,4,231.4
### Billing for Split Unit of Blood

HCPCS code P9011 was created to identify situations where one unit of blood or a blood product is split and some portion of the unit is transfused to one patient and the other portions are transfused to other patients or to the same patient at other times. When a patient receives a transfusion of a split unit of blood or blood product, OPPS providers should bill P9011 for the blood product transfused, as well as CPT 86985 (Splitting, blood products) for each splitting procedure performed to prepare the blood product for a specific patient.

Providers should bill split units of packed red cells and whole blood using Revenue Code 389 (Other blood), and should not use Revenue Codes 381 (Packed red cells) or 382 (Whole blood). Providers should bill split units of other blood products using the applicable revenue codes for the blood product type, such as 383 (Plasma) or 384 (Platelets), rather than 389. Reporting revenue codes according to these specifications will ensure the Medicare beneficiary's blood deductible is applied correctly.

EXAMPLE: OPPS provider splits off a 100cc aliquot from a 250 cc unit of leukocytereduced red blood cells for a transfusion to Patient X. The hospital then splits off an 80cc aliquot of the remaining unit for a transfusion to Patient Y. At a later time, the remaining 70cc from the unit is transfused to Patient Z.

In billing for the services for Patient X and Patient Y, the OPPS provider should report the charges by billing P9011 and 86985 in addition to the CPT code for the transfusion service, because a specific splitting service was required to prepare a split unit for transfusion to each of those patients. However, the OPPS provider should report only P9011 and the CPT code for the transfusion service for Patient Z because no additional splitting was necessary to prepare the split unit for transfusion to Patient Z. The OPPS provider should bill Revenue Code 0389 for each split unit of the leukocyte-reduced red blood cells that was transfused.

## 100-4,4,240
### Inpatient Part B Hospital Services

Inpatient Part B services which are paid under OPPS include:

- Diagnostic x-ray tests, and other diagnostic tests (excluding clinical diagnostic laboratory tests);

- X-ray, radium, and radioactive isotope therapy, including materials and services of technicians;

- Surgical dressings applied during an encounter at the hospital and splints, casts, and other devices used for reduction of fractures and dislocations (splints and casts, etc., include dental splints);

- Implantable prosthetic devices;

- Hepatitis B vaccine and its administration, and certain preventive screening services (pelvic exams, screening sigmoidoscopies, screening colonoscopies, bone mass measurements, and prostate screening.)
  - Bone Mass measurements;
  - Prostate screening;
  - Immunosuppressive drugs;
  - Oral anti-cancer drugs;
  - Oral drug prescribed for use as an acute anti-emetic used as part of an anti-cancer chemotherapeutic regimen; and
  - Epoetin Alfa (EPO)

NOTE: Payment for some of these services is packaged into the payment rate of other separately payable services.

Inpatient Part B services paid under other payment methods include:

- Clinical diagnostic laboratory tests, prosthetic devices other than implantable ones and other than dental which replace all or part of an internal body organ (including contiguous tissue), or all or part of the function of a permanently inoperative or malfunctioning internal body organ, including replacement or repairs of such devices;

- Leg, arm, back and neck braces; trusses and artificial legs; arms and eyes including adjustments, repairs, and replacements required because of breakage, wear, loss, or a change in the patient's physical condition; take home surgical dressings; outpatient physical therapy; outpatient occupational therapy; and outpatient speech-language pathology services;

- Ambulance services;

- Screening pap smears, screening colorectal tests, and screening mammography;

- Influenza virus vaccine and its administration, pneumococcal vaccine and its administration;
- Diabetes self-management;
- Hemophilia clotting factors for hemophilia patients competent to use these factors without supervision).

See Chapter 6 of the Medicare Benefit Policy Manual for a discussion of the circumstances under which the above services may be covered as Part B Inpatient services.

## 100-4,4,290.1
### Observation Services Overview

Observation care is a well-defined set of specific, clinically appropriate services, which include ongoing short term treatment, assessment, and reassessment, that are furnished while a decision is being made regarding whether patients will require further treatment as hospital inpatients or if they are able to be discharged from the hospital. Observation status is commonly assigned to patients who present to the emergency department and who then require a significant period of treatment or monitoring in order to make a decision concerning their admission or discharge. Observation services are covered only when provided by the order of a physician or another individual authorized by State licensure law and hospital staff bylaws to admit patients to the hospital or to order outpatient services.

Observation services must also be reasonable and necessary to be covered by Medicare. In only rare and exceptional cases do reasonable and necessary outpatient observation services span more than 48 hours. In the majority of cases, the decision whether to discharge a patient from the hospital following resolution of the reason for the observation care or to admit the patient as an inpatient can be made in less than 48 hours, usually in less than 24 hours.

## 100-4,4,290.2.2
### Reporting Hours of Observation

Observation time begins at the clock time documented in the patient's medical record, which coincides with the time the patient is placed in a bed for the purpose of initiating observation care in accordance with a physician's order. . Hospitals should round to the nearest hour. For example, a patient who was placed in an observation bed at 3:03 p.m. according to the nurses' notes and discharged to home at 9:45 p.m. should have a "7" placed in the units field of the reported observation HCPCS code.

General standing orders for observation services following all outpatient surgery are not recognized. Hospitals should not report as observation care, services that are part of another Part B service, such as postoperative monitoring during a standard recovery period (e.g., 4-6 hours), which should be billed as recovery room services. Similarly, in the case of patients who undergo diagnostic testing in a hospital outpatient department, routine preparation services furnished prior to the testing and recovery afterwards are included in the payments for those diagnostic services. Observation services should not be billed concurrently with diagnostic or therapeutic services for which active monitoring is a part of the procedure (e.g., colonoscopy, chemotherapy). In situations where such a procedure interrupts observation services, hospitals would record for each period of observation services the beginning and ending times during the hospital outpatient encounter and add the length of time for the periods of observation services together to reach the total number of units reported on the claim for the hourly observation services HCPCS code G0378 (Hospital observation service, per hour).

Observation time ends when all medically necessary services related to observation care are completed. For example, this could be before discharge when the need for observation has ended, but other medically necessary services not meeting the definition of observation care are provided (in which case, the additional medically necessary services would be billed separately or included as part of the emergency department or clinic visit). Alternatively, the end time of observation services may coincide with the time the patient is actually discharged from the hospital or admitted as an inpatient.

Observation time may include medically necessary services and follow-up care provided after the time that the physician writes the discharge order, but before the patient is discharged. However, reported observation time would not include the time patients remain in the observation area after treatment is finished for reasons such as waiting for transportation home.

If a period of observation spans more than 1 calendar day, all of the hours for the entire period of observation must be included on a single line and the date of service for that line is the date that observation care begins.

## 100-4,4,290.5.1
### Billing and Payment for Observation Services Beginning January 1, 2008

Observation services are reported using HCPCS code G0378 (Hospital observation service, per hour). Beginning January 1, 2008, HCPCS code G0378 for hourly observation services is assigned status indicator N, signifying that its payment is always packaged. No separate payment is made for observation services reported with HCPCS code G0378, and APC 0339 is deleted as of January 1, 2008. In most circumstances, observation services are supportive and ancillary to the other services provided to a patient. In certain circumstances when observation care is billed in conjunction with a high level clinic visit (Level 5), high level emergency department visit (Level 4 or 5), critical care services, or direct admission as an integral part of a patient's extended encounter of care, payment may be made for the entire extended care encounter through one of two composite APCs when certain criteria are met. For information about payment for extended assessment and management composite APCs, see Sec.10.2.1 (Composite APCs) of this chapter.

APC 8002 (Level I Extended Assessment and Management Composite) describes an encounter for care provided to a patient that includes a high level (Level 5) clinic visit or direct admission to observation in conjunction with observation services of substantial duration (8 or more hours). APC 8003 (Level II Extended Assessment and Management Composite) describes an encounter for care provided to a patient that includes a high level (Level 4 or 5) emergency department visit or critical care services in conjunction with observation services of substantial duration. There is no limitation on diagnosis for payment of these composite APCs; however, composite APC payment will not be made when observation services are reported in association with a surgical procedure (T status procedure) or the hours of observation care reported are less than 8. The I/OCE evaluates every claim received to determine if payment through a composite APC is appropriate. If payment through a composite APC is inappropriate, the I/OCE, in conjunction with the Pricer, determines the appropriate status indicator, APC, and payment for every code on a claim.

All of the following requirements must be met in order for a hospital to receive an APC payment for an extended assessment and management composite APC:

---

1. Observation Time

   a. Observation time must be documented in the medical record.

   b. A beneficiary's time in observation (and hospital billing) begins with the beneficiary's admission to an observation bed.

   c. A beneficiary's time in observation (and hospital billing) ends when all clinical or medical interventions have been completed, including follow-up care furnished by hospital staff and physicians that may take place after a physician has ordered the patient be released or admitted as an inpatient.

   d. The number of units reported with HCPCS code G0378 must equal or exceed 8 hours.

2. Additional Hospital Services

   a. The claim for observation services must include one of the following services in addition to the reported observation services. The additional services listed below must have a line item date of service on the same day or the day before the date reported for observation: An emergency department visit (CPT code 99284 or 99285) or A clinic visit (CPT code 99205 or 99215); or Critical care (CPT code 99291); or Direct admission to observation reported with HCPCS code G0379 (APC 0604) must be reported on the same date of service as the date reported for observation services.

   b. No procedure with a T status indicator can be reported on the same day or day before observation care is provided.

3. Physician Evaluation

   a. The beneficiary must be in the care of a physician during the period of observation, as documented in the medical record by admission, discharge, and other appropriate progress notes that are timed, written, and signed by the physician.

   b. The medical record must include documentation that the physician explicitly assessed patient risk to determine that the beneficiary would benefit from observation care.

Criteria 1 and 3 related to observation care beginning and ending time and physician evaluation apply regardless of whether the hospital believes that observation services will be packaged or will meet the criteria for extended assessment and management composite payment.

Only observation services that are billed on a 13X bill type may be considered for a composite APC payment.

Non-repetitive services provided on the same day as either direct admission to observation care or observation services must be reported on the same claim because the OCE claim-by-claim logic cannot function properly unless all services related to the episode of observation care, including hospital clinic visits, emergency department visits, critical care services, and T status procedures, are reported on the same claim.

Additional guidance can be found in Change Request 4047, Transmittal 763, issued on November 25, 2005.

If a claim for services providing during an extended assessment and management encounter including observation care does not meet all of the requirements listed above, then the usual APC logic will apply to separately payable items and services on the claim; the special logic for direct admission will apply, and payment for the observation care will be packaged into payments for other separately payable services provided to the beneficiary in the same encounter.

## 100-4,5,10.2

### A. Financial Limitation Prior to the Balanced Budget Refinement Act (BBRA)

Section 4541(a)(2) of the Balanced Budget Act (BBA) (P.L. 105-33) of 1997, which added ¬ß1834(k)(5) to the Act, required payment under a prospective payment system for outpatient rehabilitation services (except those furnished by or under arrangements with a hospital). Outpatient rehabilitation services include the following services:

- Physical therapy (which includes outpatient speech-language pathology); and
- Occupational therapy.

Section 4541(c) of the BBA required application of a financial limitation to all outpatient rehabilitation services (except those furnished by or under arrangements with a hospital). In 1999, an annual per beneficiary limit of $1,500 applied to all outpatient physical therapy services (including speech-language pathology services). A separate limit applied to all occupational therapy services. The limit is based on incurred expenses and includes applicable deductible and coinsurance. The BBA provided that the limits be indexed by the Medicare Economic Index (MEI) each year beginning in 2002.

The limitation is based on therapy services the Medicare beneficiary receives, not the type of practitioner who provides the service. Physical therapists, speech-language pathologists, occupational therapists as well as physicians and certain nonphysician practitioners could render a therapy service.

As a transitional measure, effective in 1999, providers/suppliers were instructed to keep track of the allowed incurred expenses. This process was put in place to assure providers/suppliers did not bill Medicare for patients who exceeded the annual limitations for physical therapy, and for occupational therapy services rendered by individual providers/suppliers. In 2003 and later, the limitation was applied through CMS systems.

### B. Moratoria and Exceptions for Therapy Claims

Section 221 of the BBRA of 1999 placed a 2-year moratorium on the application of the financial limitation for claims for therapy services with dates of service January 1, 2000, through December 31, 2001.

Section 421 of the Medicare, Medicaid, and SCHIP Benefits Improvement and Protection Act (BIPA) of 2000, extended the moratorium on application of the financial limitation to claims for outpatient rehabilitation services with dates of service January 1, 2002, through December 31, 2002. Therefore, the moratorium was for a 3-year period and applied to outpatient rehabilitation claims with dates of service January 1, 2000, through December 31, 2002.

In 2003, there was not a moratorium on therapy caps. Implementation was delayed until September 1, 2003. Therapy caps were in effect for services rendered on September 1, 2003 through December 7, 2003.

Congress re-enacted a moratorium on financial limitations on outpatient therapy services on December 8, 2003 that extended through December 31, 2005. Caps were implemented again on January 1, 2006 and policies were modified to allow exceptions as directed by the Deficit Reduction Act of 2005 only for calendar year 2006. The Tax Relief and Health Care Act of 2006 extended the cap exceptions process through calendar year

2007. The Medicare, Medicaid, and SCHIP Extension Act of 2007 extended the cap exceptions process for services furnished through June 30, 2008.

Future exceptions. The cap exception for therapy services billed by outpatient hospitals was part of the original legislation and applies as long as caps are in effect. Exceptions to caps based on the medical necessity of the service are in effect only when Congress legislates the exceptions, as they did for 2007. References to the exceptions process in subsection C of this section apply only when the exceptions are in effect.

## C. Application of Financial Limitations

Financial limitations on outpatient therapy services, as described above, began for therapy services rendered on or after on January 1, 2006. See C 1 to C 7 of this section when exceptions to therapy caps apply. The limits were $1740 in 2006 and $1780 in 2007. For 2008, the annual limit on the allowed amount for outpatient physical therapy and speech-language pathology combined is $1810; the limit for occupational therapy is $1810. Limits apply to outpatient Part B therapy services from all settings except outpatient hospital (place of service code 22 on carrier claims) and hospital emergency room (place of service code 23 on carrier claims). These excluded hospital services are reported on types of bill 12x or 13x on intermediary claims.

Contractors apply the financial limitations to the Medicare Physician Fee Schedule (MPFS) amount (or the amount charged if it is smaller) for therapy services for each beneficiary.

As with any Medicare payment, beneficiaries pay the coinsurance (20 percent) and any deductible that may apply. Medicare will pay the remaining 80 percent of the limit after the deductible is met. These amounts will change each calendar year. Medicare Contractors shall publish the financial limitation amount in educational articles. It is also available at 1-800-Medicare.

Medicare shall apply these financial limitations in order, according to the dates when the claims were received. When limitations apply, the Common Working File (CWF) tracks the limits. Shared System Maintainers are not responsible for tracking the dollar amounts of incurred expenses of rehabilitation services for each therapy limit.

In processing claims where Medicare is the secondary payer, the shared system takes the lowest secondary payment amount from MSPPAY and sends this amount on to CWF as the amount applied to therapy limits.

1. Exceptions to Therapy Caps - General

   The Tax Relief and Health Care Act of 2006 directed CMS to extend a process to allow for exceptions to the caps for services received in CY2007 in cases where continued therapy services are medically necessary. The following policies concerning exceptions to caps due to medical necessity apply only when the exceptions process is in effect. With the exception of the use of the KX modifier, the guidance in this section concerning medical necessity applies as well to services provided before caps are reached.

   Instructions for contractors to manage automatic process for exceptions will be found in the Program Integrity Manual, chapter 3, section 3.4.1.2. Provider and supplier information concerning exceptions is in this manual and in IOM Pub. 100-02, chapter 15, section 220.3. Exceptions shall be identified by a modifier on the claim and supported by documentation.

Since the providers and suppliers will take an active role in obtaining an exception for a beneficiary, this manual section is written to address them as well as Medicare contractors.

The beneficiary may qualify for use of the cap exceptions at any time during the episode when documented medically necessary services exceed caps. All covered and medically necessary services qualify for exceptions to caps.

In 2006, the Exception Processes fell into two categories, Automatic Process Exceptions, and Manual Process Exceptions. Beginning January 1, 2007, there is no manual process for exceptions. All services that require exceptions to caps shall be processed using the automatic process. All requests for exception are in the form of a KX modifier added to claim lines. (See subsection C6 for use of the KX modifier.)

Use of the automatic process for exceptions increases the responsibility of the provider/supplier for determining and documenting that services are appropriate.

Also, use of the automatic process for exception does not exempt services from manual or other medical review processes as described in 100-08, Chapter 3, Section 3.4.1.1.1. Rather, atypical use of the automatic exception process may invite contractor scrutiny. Particular care should be taken to document improvement and avoid billing for services that do not meet the requirements for skilled services, or for services which are maintenance rather than rehabilitative treatment (See Pub. 100-02, chapter 15, sections 220.2, 220.3, and 230).

The KX modifier, described in subsection C6, is added to claim lines to indicate that the clinician attests that services are medically necessary and justification is documented in the medical record.

2. Automatic Process Exceptions

   The term "automatic process exceptions" indicates that the claims processing for the exception is automatic, and not that the exception is automatic. An exception may be made when the patient's condition is justified by documentation indicating that the beneficiary requires continued skilled therapy, i.e., therapy beyond the amount payable under the therapy cap, to achieve their prior functional status or maximum expected functional status within a reasonable amount of time.

   No special documentation is submitted to the contractor for automatic process exceptions. The clinician is responsible for consulting guidance in the Medicare manuals and in the professional literature to determine if the beneficiary may qualify for the automatic process exception when documentation justifies medically necessary services above the caps. The clinician's opinion is not binding on the Medicare contractor who makes the final determination concerning whether the claim is payable.

   Documentation justifying the services shall be submitted in response to any Additional Documentation Request (ADR) for claims that are selected for medical review. Follow the documentation requirements in Pub. 100-02, chapter 15, section 220.3. If medical records are requested for review, clinicians may include, at their discretion, a summary that specifically addresses the justification for therapy cap exception.

In making a decision about whether to utilize the automatic process exception, clinicians shall consider, for example, whether services are appropriate to--

- The patient's condition including the diagnosis, complexities and severity (A list of the excepted evaluation codes are in C.2.a. A list of the ICD-9 codes for conditions and complexities that might qualify a beneficiary for exception to caps is in 10.2 C3. The list is a guideline and neither assures that services on the list will be excepted nor limits provision of covered and medically necessary services for conditions not on the list);
- The services provided including their type, frequency and duration;
- The interaction of current active conditions and complexities that directly and significantly influence the treatment such that it causes services to exceed caps.

In addition, the following should be considered before using the automatic exception process:

a. Exceptions for Services

Evaluation. The CMS will except therapy evaluations from caps after the therapy caps are reached when evaluation is necessary, e.g., to determine if the current status of the beneficiary requires therapy services. For example, the following evaluation procedures may be appropriate:

92506, 92597, 92607, 92608, 92610, 92611, 92612, 92614, 92616, 96105, 97001, 97002, 97003, 97004.

These codes will continue to be reported as outpatient therapy procedures as described in the Claims Processing Manual, Chapter 5, Section 20(B) "Applicable Outpatient Rehabilitation HCPCS Codes." They are not diagnostic tests. Definition of evaluations and documentation is found in Pub 100-02, sections 220 and 230.

Other Services. There are a number of sources that suggest the amount of certain services that may be typical, either per service, per episode, per condition, or per discipline. For example, see the CSC- Utilization and Edit Report, 2006, Appendices at www.cms.hhs.gov/TherapyServices (Studies and Reports). Professional literature and guidelines from professional associations also provide a basis on which to estimate whether the type, frequency and intensity of services are appropriate to an individual. Clinicians and contractors should utilize available evidence related to the patient's condition to justify provision of medically necessary services to individual beneficiaries, especially when they exceed caps. Contractors shall not limit medically necessary services that are justified by scientific research applicable to the beneficiary. Neither contractors nor clinicians shall utilize professional literature and scientific reports to justify payment for continued services after an individual's goals have been met earlier than is typical. Conversely, professional literature and scientific reports shall not be used as justification to deny payment to patients whose needs are greater than is typical or when the patient's condition is not represented by the literature.

b. Exceptions for Conditions or Complexities Identified by ICD-9 codes.

Clinicians may utilize the automatic process for exception for any diagnosis for which they can justify services exceeding the cap. Based upon analysis of claims data, research and evidence based practice guidelines, CMS has identified conditions and complexities represented by ICD-9 codes that may be more likely than others to require therapy services that exceed therapy caps. This list appears in 10.2 C3. Clinicians may use the automatic process of exception for beneficiaries who do not have a condition or complexity on this list when they justify the provision of therapy services that exceed caps for that patient's condition.

NOT ALL patients who have a condition or complexity on the list are "automatically" excepted from therapy caps. See Pub. 100-02, chapter 15, section 230.3 for documenting the patient's condition and complexities. Contractors may scrutinize claims from providers whose services exceed caps more frequently than is typical.

Regardless of the condition, the patient must also meet other requirements for coverage. For example, the patient must require skilled treatment for a covered, medically necessary service; the services must be appropriate in type, frequency and duration for the patient's condition and service must be documented appropriately. Guidelines for utilization of therapy services may be found in Medicare manuals, Local Coverage Determinations of Medicare contractors, and professional guidelines issued by associations and states.

Bill the most relevant diagnosis. As always, when billing for therapy services, the ICD-9 code that best relates to the reason for the treatment shall be on the claim, unless there is a compelling reason. For example, when a patient with diabetes is being treated for gait training due to amputation, the preferred diagnosis is abnormality of gait (which characterizes the treatment). Where it is possible in accordance with State and local laws and the contractors Local Coverage Determinations, avoid using vague or general diagnoses. When a claim includes several types of services, or where the physician/NPP must supply the diagnosis, it may not be possible to use the most relevant therapy code in the primary position. In that case, the relevant code should, if possible, be on the claim in another position.

Codes representing the medical condition that caused the treatment are used when there is no code representing the treatment. Complicating conditions are preferably used in non-primary positions on the claim and are billed in the primary position only in the rare circumstance that there is no more relevant code.

The condition or complexity that caused treatment to exceed caps must be related to the therapy goals and must either be the condition that is being treated or a complexity that directly and significantly impacts the rate of recovery of the condition being treated such that it is appropriate to exceed the caps. Codes marked as complexities represented by ICD-9 codes on the list below are unlikely to require therapy services that would exceed the caps unless they occur in a patient who also has another condition (either listed or not

# APPENDIX 4 — PUB 100 REFERENCES

listed). Therefore, documentation for an exception should indicate how the complexity (or combination of complexities) directly and significantly affects treatment for a therapy condition. For example, if the condition underlying the reason for therapy is V43.64, hip replacement, the treatment may have a goal to ambulate 60' with stand-by assistance and a KX modifier may be appropriate for gait training (assuming the severity of the patient is such that the services exceed the cap). Alternatively, it would not be appropriate to use the KX modifier for a patient who recovered from hip replacement last year and is being treated this year for a sprain of a severity which does not justify extensive therapy exceeding caps.

3. ICD-9 Codes That are Likely to Qualify for the Automatic Process Therapy Cap Exception Based Upon Clinical Condition or Complexity

When using this table, refer to the ICD-9 code book for coding instructions. Some contractors' Local Coverage Determinations do not allow the use of some of the codes on this list in the primary diagnosis position on a claim. If the contractor has determined that these codes do not characterize patients who require medically necessary services, providers/suppliers may not use these codes, but must utilize a billable diagnosis code allowed by their contractor to describe the patient's condition. Contractors shall not apply therapy caps to services based on the patient's condition, but only on the medical necessity of the service for the condition. If a service would be payable before the cap is reached and is still medically necessary after the cap is reached, that service is excepted. Providers/suppliers may use the automatic process for exception for medically necessary services when the patient has a billable condition that is not on the list below. The diagnosis on the list below may be put in a secondary position on the claim and/or in the medical records, as the contractor directs.

When two codes are listed in the left cell in a row, all the codes between them are also eligible for exception. If one code is in the cell, only that one code is likely to qualify for exception. The descriptions in the table are not always identical to those in the ICD-9 code book, but may be summaries. Contact your contractor for interpretation if you are not sure that a condition or complexity is applicable for automatic process exception.

It is very important to recognize that most of the conditions on this list would not ordinarily result in services exceeding the cap. Use the KX modifier only in cases where the condition of the individual patient is such that services are APPROPRIATELY provided in an episode that exceeds the cap. In most cases, the severity of the condition, comorbidities, or complexities will contribute to the necessity of services exceeding the cap, and these should be documented. Routine use of the KX modifier for all patients with these conditions will likely show up on data analysis as aberrant and invite inquiry. Be sure that documentation is sufficiently detailed to support the use of the modifier.

The following ICD-9 codes describe the conditions (etiology or underlying medical conditions) that may result in excepted conditions (marked X) and complexities (marked *) that MIGHT cause medically necessary therapy services to qualify for the automatic process exception for each discipline separately. When the field corresponding

to the therapy discipline treating and the diagnosis code is marked with a dash (‚Äì) services by that discipline are not appropriate for that diagnosis and, therefore, services do not qualify for exception to caps.

These codes are grouped only to facilitate reference to them. The codes may be used only when the code is applicable to the condition being actively treated. For example, an exception should not be claimed for a diagnosis of hip replacement when the service provided is for an unrelated dysphagia.

| ICD-9 Cluster | ICD-9 (Cluster) Description | PT | OT | SLP |
|---|---|---|---|---|
| V43.61-V43.69 | Joint Replacement | X | X | -- |
| V45.4 | Arthrodesis Status | * | * | -- |
| V45.81-V45.82 and V45.89 | Other Postprocedural Status | * | * | -- |
| V49.61-V49.67 | Upper Limb Amputation Status | X | X | -- |
| V49.71-V49.77 | Lower Limb Amputation Status | X | X | -- |
| V54.10-V54.29 | Aftercare for Healing Traumatic or Pathologic Fracture | X | X | -- |
| V58.71-V58.78 | Aftercare Following Surgery to Specified Body Systems, Not Elsewhere Classified | * | * | * |
| 244.0-244.9 | Acquired Hypothyroidism | * | * | * |
| 250.00-251.9 | Diabetes Mellitus and Other Disorders of Pancreatic Internal Secretion | * | * | * |
| 276.0-276.9 | Disorders of Fluid, Electrolyte, and Acid-Base Balance | * | * | * |
| 278.00-278.01 | Obesity and Morbid Obesity | * | * | * |
| 280.0-289.9 | Diseases of the blood and blood-forming organs | * | * | * |
| 290.0-290.43 | Dementias | * | * | * |
| 294.0-294.9 | Persistent Mental Disorders due to Conditions Classified Elsewhere | * | * | * |
| 295.00-299.91 | Other Psychoses | * | * | * |
| 300.00-300.9 | Anxiety, Disassociative and Somatoform Disorders | * | * | * |
| 310.0-310.9 | Specific Nonpsychotic Mental Disorders due to Brain Damage | * | * | * |
| 311 | Depressive Disorder, Not Elsewhere Classified | * | * | * |

X  Automatic (only ICD-9 needed on claim)
*  Complexity (requires another ICD-9 on claim)
-- Does not serve as qualifying ICD-9 on claim

| ICD-9 Cluster | ICD-9 (Cluster) Description | PT | OT | SLP |
|---|---|---|---|---|
| 315.00-315.9 | Specific delays in Development | * | * | * |
| 317 | Mild Mental Retardation | * | * | * |
| 320.0-326 | Inflammatory Diseases of the Central Nervous System | * | * | * |
| 330.0-337.9 | Hereditary and Degenerative Diseases of the Central Nervous System | X | X | X |
| 340-345.91 and 348.0-349.9 | Other Disorders of the Central Nervous System | X | X | X |
| 353.0-359.9 | Disorders of the Peripheral Nervous system | X | X | -- |
| 365.00-365.9 | Glaucoma | * | * | * |
| 369.00-369.9 | Blindness and Low Vision | * | * | * |
| 386.00-386.9 | Vertiginous Syndromes and Other Disorders of Vestibular System | * | * | * |
| 389.00-389.9 | Hearing Loss | * | * | * |
| 401.0-405.99 | Hypertensive Disease | * | * | * |
| 410.00-414.9 | Ischemic Heart Disease | * | * | * |
| 415.0-417.9 | Diseases of Pulmonary Circulation | * | * | * |
| 420.0-429.9 | Other Forms of Heart Disease | * | * | * |
| 430-438.9 | Cerebrovascular Disease | X | X | X |
| 440.0-448.9 | Diseases of Arteries, Arterioles, and Capillaries | * | * | * |
| 451.0-453.9 and 456.0-459.9 | Diseases of Veins and Lymphatics, and Other Diseases of Circulatory System | * | * | * |
| 465.0-466.19 | Acute Respiratory Infections | * | * | * |
| 478.30-478.5 | Paralysis, Polyps, or Other Diseases of Vocal Cords | * | * | * |
| 480.0-486 | Pneumonia | * | * | * |
| 490-496 | Chronic Obstructive Pulmonary Disease and Allied Conditions | * | * | * |
| 507.0-507.8 | Pneumonitis due to solids and liquids | * | * | * |
| 510.0-519.9 | Other Diseases of Respiratory System | * | * | * |
| 560.0-560.9 | Intestinal Obstruction Without Mention of Hernia | * | * | * |
| 578.0-578.9 | Gastrointestinal Hemorrhage | * | * | * |

X  Automatic (only ICD-9 needed on claim)
*  Complexity (requires another ICD-9 on claim)
--  Does not serve as qualifying ICD-9 on claim

| ICD-9 Cluster | ICD-9 (Cluster) Description | PT | OT | SLP |
|---|---|---|---|---|
| 584.5-586 | Renal Failure and Chronic Kidney Disease | * | * | * |
| 590.00-599.9 | Other Diseases of Urinary System | * | * | * |
| 682.0-682.8 | Other Cellulitis and Abscess | * | * | -- |
| 707.00-707.9 | Chronic Ulcer of Skin | * | * | * |
| 710.0-710.9 | Diffuse Diseases of Connective Tissue | * | * | * |
| 711.00-711.99 | Arthropathy Associated with Infections | * | * | -- |
| 712.10-713.8 | Crystal Arthropathies and Arthropathy Associated with Other Disorders Classified Elsewhere | * | * | -- |
| 714.0-714.9 | Rheumatoid Arthritis and Other Inflammatory Polyarthropathies | * | * | -- |
| 715.00-715.98 | Osteoarthrosis and Allied Disorders (Complexity except as listed below) | * | * | -- |
| 715.09 | Osteoarthritis and allied disorders, multiple sites | X | X | -- |
| 715.11 | Osteoarthritis, localized, primary, shoulder region | X | X | -- |
| 715.15 | Osteoarthritis, localized, primary, pelvic region and thigh | X | X | -- |
| 715.16 | Osteoarthritis, localized, primary, lower leg | X | X | -- |
| 715.91 | Osteoarthritis, unspecified id gen. or local, shoulder | X | X | -- |
| 715.96 | Osteoarthritis, unspecified if gen. or local, lower leg | X | X | -- |
| 716.00-716.99 | Other and Unspecified Arthropathies | * | * | -- |
| 717.0-717.9 | Internal Derangement of Knee | * | * | -- |
| 718.00-718.99 | Other Derangement of Joint (Complexity except as listed below) | * | * | -- |
| 718.49 | Contracture of Joint, Multiple Sites | X | X | -- |
| 719.00-719.99 | Other and Unspecified Disorders of Joint (Complexity except as listed below) | * | * | -- |
| 719.7 | Difficulty Walking | X | X | -- |
| 720.0-724.9 | Dorsopathies | * | * | -- |

X  Automatic (only ICD-9 needed on claim)
*  Complexity (requires another ICD-9 on claim)
--  Does not serve as qualifying ICD-9 on claim

| ICD-9 Cluster | ICD-9 (Cluster) Description | PT | OT | SLP |
|---|---|---|---|---|
| 725-729.9 | Rheumatism, Excluding Back (Complexity except as listed below) | * | * | -- |
| 726.10-726.19 | Rotator Cuff Disorder and Allied Syndromes | X | X | -- |
| 727.61-727.62 | Rupture of Tendon, Nontraumatic | X | X | -- |
| 730.00-739.9 | Osteopathies, Chondropathies, and Acquired Musculoskeletal Deformities (Complexity except as listed below) | * | * | -- |
| 733.00 | Osteoporosis | X | X | -- |
| 741.00-742.9 and 745.0-748.9 and 754.0-756.9 | Congenital Anomalies | * | * | * |
| 780.31-780.39 | Convulsions | * | * | * |
| 780.71-780.79 | Malaise and Fatigue | * | * | * |
| 780.93 | Memory Loss | * | * | * |
| 781.0-781.99 | Symptoms Involving Nervous and Musculoskeletal System (Complexity except as listed below) | * | * | * |
| 781.2 | Abnormality of Gait | X | X | -- |
| 781.3 | Lack of Coordination | X | X | -- |
| 783.0-783.9 | Symptoms Concerning Nutrition, Metabolism, and Development | * | * | * |
| 784.3-784.69 | Aphasia, Voice and Other Speech Disturbance, Other Symbolic Dysfunction | * | * | X |
| 785.4 | Gangrene | * | * | -- |
| 786.00-786.9 | Symptoms involving Respiratory System and Other Chest Symptoms | * | * | * |
| 787.2 | Dysphagia | * | * | X |
| 800.00-828.1 | Fractures (Complexity except as listed below) | * | * | -- |
| 806.00-806.9 | Fracture of Vertebral Column With Spinal Cord Injury | X | X | -- |
| 810.11-810.13 | Fracture of Clavicle | X | X | -- |
| 811.00-811.19 | Fracture of Scapula | X | X | -- |
| 812.00-812.59 | Fracture of Humerus | X | X | -- |
| 813.00-813.93 | Fracture of Radius and Ulna | X | X | -- |
| 820.00-820.9 | Fracture of Neck of Femue | X | X | -- |

X  Automatic (only ICD-9 needed on claim)
*  Complexity (requires another ICD-9 on claim)
--  Does not serve as qualifying ICD-9 on claim

| ICD-9 Cluster | ICD-9 (Cluster) Description | PT | OT | SLP |
|---|---|---|---|---|
| 821.00-821.39 | Fracture of Other and Unspecified Parts of Femur | X | X | -- |
| 828.0-828.1 | Multiple Fractures Involving Both Lower Limbs, Lower with Upper Limb, and Lower Limb(s) with Rib(s) and Sternum | X | X | -- |
| 830.0-839.9 | Dislocations | X | X | -- |
| 840.0-848.8 | Sprains and Strains of Joints and Adjacent Muscles | * | * | -- |
| 851.00-854.19 | Intracranial Injury, excluding those with Skull Fracture | X | X | X |
| 888.00-884.2 | Open Wound of Upper Limb | * | * | -- |
| 885.0-887.7 | Traumatic Amputation, Thumb(s), Finger(s), Arm and Hand (complete)(partial) | X | X | -- |
| 890.0-894.2 | Open Wound Lower Limb | * | * | -- |
| 895.0-897.7 | Traumatic Amputation, Toe(s), Foot/Feet, Leg(s) (complete) (partial) | * | * | -- |
| 905.0-905.9 | Late Effects of Musculoskeletal and Connective Tissue Injuries | * | * | * |
| 907.0-907.9 | Late Effect of Injuries to the Nervous System | * | * | * |
| 941.00-949.5 | Burns | * | * | * |
| 952.00-952.9 | Spinal Cord Injury Without Evidence of Spinal Bone Injury | X | X | X |
| 953.0-953.8 | Injury to Nerve Roots and Spinal Plexus | X | X* | -- |
| 959.01 | Head Injury, Unspecified | X | X | X |

X  Automatic (only ICD-9 needed on claim)
*  Complexity (requires another ICD-9 on claim)
--  Does not serve as qualifying ICD-9 on claim

## 100-4,8,60.4.1
### Epoetin Alfa (EPO) Facility Billing Requirements

Revenue codes required for reporting EPO:

| Revenue Codes Dates of Service | Bill Type 72x | Bill Type 12x | Bill type 13x | Bill type 85x |
|---|---|---|---|---|
| 0634 - administrations under 10,000 units | 1/1/04 - present | 4/1/06 - present | 1/1/04 - present | 1/1/04 - present |
| 0635 - administrations of 10,000 units or more | 1/1/04 - present | 4/1/06 - present | 1/1/04 - present | 1/1/04 - present |

| Revenue Codes Dates of Service | Bill Type 72x | Bill Type 12x | Bill type 13x | Bill type 85x |
|---|---|---|---|---|
| 0636 - detailed drug coding | N/A | 1/1/04 - 3/31/06 | N/A | |

N/A   For additional hospital billing instructions related to bill types 12x, 13x and 85x see also sections 60.4.3.1 and 60.4.3.2 of this chapter.

The HCPCS code for EPO must be included:

| HCPCS | HCPCS Description | Dates of Service |
|---|---|---|
| Q4055 | Injection, Epoetin alfa, 1,000 units (for ESRD on Dialysis) | 1/1/2004 through 12/31/2005 |
| J0886 | Injection, Epoetin alfa, 1,000 units (for ESRD on Dialysis) | 1/1/2006 through 12/31/2006 |
| Q4081 | 1 Injection, Epoetin alfa, 100 | 1/1/2007 to present |

The number of units of EPO administered during the billing period is reported with value code 68. Medicare no longer requires value code 68 for claims with dates of service on or after January 1, 2008. Each administration of epoetin alfa (EPO) is reported on a separate line item with the units reported used as a multiplier by the dosage description in the HCPCS to arrive at the dosage per administration.

Append the GS modifier to report a line item that represents an administration of EPO at the reduced dosage following existing instructions in section 60.4 of this chapter. The hematocrit reading taken prior to the last administration of EPO during the billing period must also be reported on the UB-92/Form CMS-1450 with value code 49. Effective January 1, 2006 the definition of value code 49 used to report the hematocrit reading is changed to indicate the patient's most recent hematocrit reading taken before the start of the billing period.

The hemoglobin reading taken during the billing period must be reported on the UB- 92/Form CMS-1450 with value code 48. Effective January 1, 2006 the definition of value code 48 used for the hemoglobin reading is changed to indicate the patient's most recent hemoglobin reading taken before the start of the billing period.

To report a hemoglobin or hematocrit reading for a new patient on or after January 1, 2006, the provider should report the reading that prompted the treatment of epoetin alfa. The provider may use results documented on form CMS 2728 or the patient's medical records from a transferring facility.

The maximum number of administrations of EPO for a billing cycle is 13 times in 30 days and 14 times in 31 days.

# APPENDIX 5 — NEW, CHANGED, DELETED, AND REINSTATED HCPCS CODES FOR 2009

### New Codes

| | | | | |
|---|---|---|---|---|
| A6545 | A9284 | A9580 | C8929 | C8930 |
| C9245 | C9246 | C9247 | C9248 | C9356 |
| C9358 | C9359 | C9898 | C9899 | D0417 |
| D0418 | D3222 | D5991 | E0487 | E0656 |
| E0657 | E0770 | E1354 | E1356 | E1357 |
| E1358 | E2230 | E2231 | E2295 | G0398 |
| G0399 | G0400 | G0402 | G0403 | G0404 |
| G0405 | G0406 | G0407 | G0408 | G0409 |
| G0410 | G0411 | G0412 | G0413 | G0414 |
| G0415 | G0416 | G0417 | G0418 | G0419 |
| G8485 | G8486 | G8487 | G8488 | G8489 |
| G8490 | G8491 | G8492 | G8493 | G8494 |
| G8495 | G8496 | G8497 | G8498 | G8499 |
| G8500 | G8501 | G8502 | G8503 | G8504 |
| G8505 | G8506 | G8507 | G8508 | G8509 |
| G8510 | G8511 | G8512 | G8513 | G8514 |
| G8515 | G8516 | G8517 | G8518 | G8519 |
| G8520 | G8521 | G8522 | G8523 | G8524 |
| G8525 | G8526 | G8527 | G8528 | G8529 |
| G8530 | G8531 | G8532 | G8533 | G8534 |
| G8535 | G8536 | G8537 | G8538 | G8539 |
| G8540 | G8541 | G8542 | G8543 | G8544 |
| J0641 | J1267 | J1453 | J1459 | J1930 |
| J1953 | J2785 | J3101 | J3300 | J7186 |
| J7606 | J8705 | J9033 | J9207 | J9330 |
| K0672 | L0113 | L6711 | L6712 | L6713 |
| L6714 | L6721 | L6722 | L8604 | Q4100 |
| Q4101 | Q4102 | Q4103 | Q4104 | Q4105 |
| Q4106 | Q4107 | Q4108 | Q4109 | Q4110 |
| Q4111 | Q4112 | Q4113 | Q4114 | S2118 |
| S2270 | S3628 | S3711 | S3860 | S3861 |
| S3862 | S9433 | | | |

### Changed Codes

| | | | | |
|---|---|---|---|---|
| A6010 | A6011 | A6021 | A6022 | A6023 |
| A6024 | A6196 | A6197 | A6198 | A6199 |
| A6203 | A6204 | A6205 | A6206 | A6207 |
| A6208 | A6209 | A6210 | A6211 | A6212 |
| A6213 | A6214 | A6215 | A6219 | A6220 |
| A6221 | A6222 | A6223 | A6224 | A6228 |
| A6229 | A6230 | A6231 | A6232 | A6233 |
| A6234 | A6235 | A6236 | A6237 | A6238 |
| A6239 | A6240 | A6241 | A6242 | A6243 |
| A6244 | A6245 | A6246 | A6247 | A6248 |
| A6251 | A6252 | A6253 | A6254 | A6255 |
| A6256 | A6257 | A6258 | A6259 | A6260 |
| A6261 | A6262 | A6266 | A6407 | A9502 |
| C8921 | C8922 | C8923 | C8924 | C8925 |
| C8926 | C8927 | C8928 | D0486 | D1203 |
| D1204 | D3310 | D3320 | D3330 | D4210 |
| D4211 | D4240 | D4241 | D4260 | D4261 |
| D5211 | D5212 | E0764 | G0129 | G0248 |
| G0250 | G0275 | G8417 | G8418 | G8419 |
| G8420 | G8427 | G8428 | G8429 | G8430 |
| G8431 | G8433 | G8437 | G8438 | G8439 |
| G8440 | G8446 | G8447 | G8448 | G8457 |
| G8485 | G8486 | G8487 | J0270 | J0348 |
| J1572 | J2788 | J2790 | J3301 | J7639 |
| J9000 | J9001 | J9010 | J9015 | J9017 |
| J9020 | J9040 | J9045 | J9050 | J9098 |
| J9100 | J9110 | J9120 | J9150 | J9151 |
| J9160 | J9165 | J9170 | J9181 | J9185 |
| J9190 | J9200 | J9201 | J9206 | J9208 |
| J9209 | J9211 | J9213 | J9214 | J9215 |
| J9216 | J9230 | J9265 | J9266 | J9268 |
| J9270 | J9300 | J9310 | J9320 | J9340 |
| J9350 | J9355 | J9357 | J9360 | J9390 |
| J9600 | K0669 | K0899 | L3905 | L4360 |
| L8681 | L8689 | L8695 | | |

### Deleted Codes

| | | | | |
|---|---|---|---|---|
| C9003 | C9237 | C9238 | C9239 | C9240 |
| C9723 | G0297 | G0300 | G0308 | G0309 |
| G0310 | G0311 | G0312 | G0313 | G0314 |
| G0315 | G0316 | G0317 | G0318 | G0319 |
| G0320 | G0321 | G0322 | G0323 | G0324 |
| G0325 | G0326 | G0327 | G0332 | G0344 |
| G0366 | G0367 | G0368 | G0377 | G0394 |
| J1751 | J1752 | J3100 | J7340 | J7341 |
| J7342 | J7343 | J7344 | J7346 | J7347 |
| J7348 | J7349 | J7602 | J7603 | J9182 |
| L2860 | L3890 | L5993 | L5994 | L5995 |
| L7611 | L7612 | L7613 | L7614 | L7621 |
| L7622 | S0141 | S0143 | S2075 | S2076 |
| S2077 | S2135 | S9092 | | |

### Reinstated Codes

| | | | |
|---|---|---|---|
| J7611 | J7612 | J7613 | J7614 |

# APPENDIX 6 — PLACE OF SERVICE AND TYPE OF SERVICE

## *Place-of-Service Codes for Professional Claims*

### Database (last updated September 25, 2007)

Listed below are place of service codes and descriptions. These codes should be used on professional claims to specify the entity where service(s) were rendered. Check with individual payers (e.g., Medicare, Medicaid, other private insurance) for reimbursement policies regarding these codes. If you would like to comment on a code(s) or description(s), please send your request to posinfo@cms.hhs.gov.

| | | |
|---|---|---|
| 01 | Pharmacy | A facility or location where drugs and other medically related items and services are sold, dispensed, or otherwise provided directly to patients. |
| 02 | Unassigned | N/A |
| 03 | School | A facility whose primary purpose is education. |
| 04 | Homeless shelter | A facility or location whose primary purpose is to provide temporary housing to homeless individuals (e.g., emergency shelters, individual or family shelters). |
| 05 | Indian Health Service freestanding facility | A facility or location, owned and operated by the Indian Health Service, which provides diagnostic, therapeutic (surgical and non-surgical), and rehabilitation services to American Indians and Alaska natives who do not require hospitalization. |
| 06 | Indian Health Service provider-based facility | A facility or location, owned and operated by the Indian Health Service, which provides diagnostic, therapeutic (surgical and nonsurgical), and rehabilitation services rendered by, or under the supervision of, physicians to American Indians and Alaska natives admitted as inpatients or outpatients. |
| 07 | Tribal 638 freestanding facility | A facility or location owned and operated by a federally recognized American Indian or Alaska native tribe or tribal organization under a 638 agreement, which provides diagnostic, therapeutic (surgical and nonsurgical), and rehabilitation services to tribal members who do not require hospitalization. |
| 08 | Tribal 638 Provider-based Facility | A facility or location owned and operated by a federally recognized American Indian or Alaska native tribe or tribal organization under a 638 agreement, which provides diagnostic, therapeutic (surgical and nonsurgical), and rehabilitation services to tribal members admitted as inpatients or outpatients. |
| 09 | Prison/correctional facility | A prison, jail, reformatory, work farm, detention center, or any other similar facility maintained by either federal, state or local authorities for the purpose of confinement or rehabilitation of adult or juvenile criminal offenders. |
| 10 | Unassigned | N/A |
| 11 | Office | Location, other than a hospital, skilled nursing facility (SNF), military treatment facility, community health center, State or local public health clinic, or intermediate care facility (ICF), where the health professional routinely provides health examinations, diagnosis, and treatment of illness or injury on an ambulatory basis. |
| 12 | Home | Location, other than a hospital or other facility, where the patient receives care in a private residence. |
| 13 | Assisted living facility | Congregate residential facility with self-contained living units providing assessment of each resident's needs and on-site support 24 hours a day, 7 days a week, with the capacity to deliver or arrange for services including some health care and other services. |
| 14 | Group home | A residence, with shared living areas, where clients receive supervision and other services such as social and/or behavioral services, custodial service, and minimal services (e.g., medication administration). |
| 15 | Mobile unit | A facility/unit that moves from place-to-place equipped to provide preventive, screening, diagnostic, and/or treatment services. |
| 16 | Temporary lodging | A short-term accommodation such as a hotel, campground, hostel, cruise ship or resort where the patient receives care, and which is not identified by any other POS code. |

**17-19** Unassigned — N/A

**20** Urgent care facility — Location, distinct from a hospital emergency room, an office, or a clinic, whose purpose is to diagnose and treat illness or injury for unscheduled, ambulatory patients seeking immediate medical attention.

**21** Inpatient hospital — A facility, other than psychiatric, which primarily provides diagnostic, therapeutic (both surgical and nonsurgical), and rehabilitation services by, or under, the supervision of physicians to patients admitted for a variety of medical conditions.

**22** Outpatient hospital — A portion of a hospital which provides diagnostic, therapeutic (both surgical and nonsurgical), and rehabilitation services to sick or injured persons who do not require hospitalization or institutionalization.

**23** Emergency room—hospital — A portion of a hospital where emergency diagnosis and treatment of illness or injury is provided.

**24** Ambulatory surgical center — A freestanding facility, other than a physician's office, where surgical and diagnostic services are provided on an ambulatory basis.

**25** Birthing center — A facility, other than a hospital's maternity facilities or a physician's office, which provides a setting for labor, delivery, and immediate post-partum care as well as immediate care of new born infants.

**26** Military treatment facility — A medical facility operated by one or more of the uniformed services. Military treatment facility (MTF) also refers to certain former U.S. Public Health Service (USPHS) facilities now designated as uniformed service treatment facilities (USTF).

**27-30** Unassigned — N/A

**31** Skilled nursing facility — A facility which primarily provides inpatient skilled nursing care and related services to patients who require medical, nursing, or rehabilitative services but does not provide the level of care or treatment available in a hospital.

**32** Nursing facility — A facility which primarily provides to residents skilled nursing care and related services for the rehabilitation of injured, disabled, or sick persons, or, on a regular basis, health-related care services above the level of custodial care to other than mentally retarded individuals.

**33** Custodial care facility — A facility which provides room, board, and other personal assistance services, generally on a long-term basis, and which does not include a medical component.

**34** Hospice — A facility, other than a patient's home, in which palliative and supportive care for terminally ill patients and their families are provided.

**35-40** Unassigned — N/A

**41** Ambulance—land — A land vehicle specifically designed, equipped and staffed for lifesaving and transporting the sick or injured.

**42** Ambulance—air or water — An air or water vehicle specifically designed, equipped and staffed for lifesaving and transporting the sick or injured.

**43-48** Unassigned — N/A

**49** Independent clinic — A location, not part of a hospital and not described by any other place-of-service code, that is organized and operated to provide preventive, diagnostic, therapeutic, rehabilitative, or palliative services to outpatients only.

**50** Federally qualified health center — A facility located in a medically underserved area that provides Medicare beneficiaries preventive primary medical care under the general direction of a physician.

**51** Inpatient psychiatric facility — A facility that provides inpatient psychiatric services for the diagnosis and treatment of mental illness on a 24-hour basis, by or under the supervision of a physician.

**52** Psychiatric facility-partial hospitalization — A facility for the diagnosis and treatment of mental illness that provides a planned therapeutic program for patients who do not require full time hospitalization, but who need broader programs than are possible from outpatient visits to a hospital-based or hospital-affiliated facility.

| 53 | Community mental health center | A facility that provides the following services: outpatient services, including specialized outpatient services for children, the elderly, individuals who are chronically ill, and residents of the CMHC's mental health services area who have been discharged from inpatient treatment at a mental health facility; 24 hour a day emergency care services; day treatment, other partial hospitalization services, or psychosocial rehabilitation services; screening for patients being considered for admission to state mental health facilities to determine the appropriateness of such admission; and consultation and education services. |
| 54 | Intermediate care facility/mentally retarded | A facility which primarily provides health-related care and services above the level of custodial care to mentally retarded individuals but does not provide the level of care or treatment available in a hospital or SNF. |
| 55 | Residential substance abuse treatment facility | A facility which provides treatment for substance (alcohol and drug) abuse to live-in residents who do not require acute medical care. Services include individual and group therapy and counseling, family counseling, laboratory tests, drugs and supplies, psychological testing, and room and board. |
| 56 | Psychiatric residential treatment center | A facility or distinct part of a facility for psychiatric care which provides a total 24-hour therapeutically planned and professionally staffed group living and learning environment. |
| 57 | Non-residential substance abuse treatment facility | A location which provides treatment for substance (alcohol and drug) abuse on an ambulatory basis. Services include individual and group therapy and counseling, family counseling, laboratory tests, drugs and supplies, and psychological testing. |
| 58-59 | Unassigned | N/A |
| 60 | Mass immunization center | A location where providers administer pneumococcal pneumonia and influenza virus vaccinations and submit these services as electronic media claims, paper claims, or using the roster billing method. This generally takes place in a mass immunization setting, such as, a public health center, pharmacy, or mall but may include a physician office setting. |
| 61 | Comprehensive inpatient rehabilitation facility | A facility that provides comprehensive rehabilitation services under the supervision of a physician to inpatients with physical disabilities. Services include physical therapy, occupational therapy, speech pathology, social or psychological services, and orthotics and prosthetics services. |
| 62 | Comprehensive outpatient rehabilitation facility | A facility that provides comprehensive rehabilitation services under the supervision of a physician to outpatients with physical disabilities. Services include physical therapy, occupational therapy, and speech pathology services. |
| 63-64 | Unassigned | N/A |
| 65 | End-stage renal disease treatment facility | A facility other than a hospital, which provides dialysis treatment, maintenance, and/or training to patients or caregivers on an ambulatory or home-care basis. |
| 66-70 | Unassigned | N/A |
| 71 | Public health clinic | A facility maintained by either state or local health departments that provides ambulatory primary medical care under the general direction of a physician. |
| 72 | Rural health clinic | A certified facility which is located in a rural medically underserved area that provides ambulatory primary medical care under the general direction of a physician. |
| 73-80 | Unassigned | N/A |
| 81 | Independent laboratory | A laboratory certified to perform diagnostic and/or clinical tests independent of an institution or a physician's office. |
| 82-98 | Unassigned | N/A |
| 99 | Other place of service | Other place of service not identified above. |

## Type of Service

### Common Working File Type of Service (TOS) Indicators

For submitting a claim to the Common Working File (CWF), use the following table to assign the proper TOS. Some procedures may have more than one applicable TOS. CWF will reject alerts on codes with incorrect TOS designations. CWF is rejecting codes with incorrect TOS designations.

The only exceptions to this table are:

- Surgical services billed for dates of service through December 31, 2007, containing the ASC facility service modifier SG must be reported as TOS F. Effective for services on or after January 1, 2008, the SG modifier is no longer applicable for Medicare services. ASC providers should discontinue applying the SG modifier on ASC facility claims. The indicator F does not appear in the TOS table because its use depends upon claims submitted with POS 24 (ASC facility) from an ASC (specialty 49). This became effective for dates of service January 1, 2008, or after.

- Surgical services billed with an assistant-at-surgery modifier (80-82, AS,) must be reported with TOS 8. The 8 indicator does not appear on the TOS table because its use is dependent upon the use of the appropriate modifier. (See Pub. 100-4 *Medicare Claims Processing Manual,* chapter 12, "Physician/Practitioner Billing," for instructions on when assistant-at-surgery is allowable.)

- Psychiatric treatment services that are subject to the outpatient mental health treatment limitation should be reported with TOS T.

- TOS H appears in the list of descriptors. However, it does not appear in the table. In CWF, "H" is used only as an indicator for hospice. The carrier should not submit TOS H to CWF at this time.

- For outpatient services, when a transfusion medicine code appears on a claim that also contains a blood product, the service is paid under reasonable charge at 80 percent; coinsurance and deductible apply. When transfusion medicine codes are paid under the clinical laboratory fee schedule they are paid at 100 percent; coinsurance and deductible do not apply.

Note: For injection codes with more than one possible TOS designation, use the following guidelines when assigning the TOS:

When the choice is L or 1:

- Use TOS L when the drug is used related to ESRD; or

- Use TOS 1 when the drug is not related to ESRD and is administered in the office.

When the choice is G or 1:

- Use TOS G when the drug is an immunosuppressive drug; or

- Use TOS 1 when the drug is used for other than immunosuppression.

When the choice is P or 1:

- Use TOS P if the drug is administered through durable medical equipment (DME); or

- Use TOS 1 if the drug is administered in the office.

The place of service or diagnosis may be considered when determining the appropriate TOS. The descriptors for each of the TOS codes listed in the following table are:

| | |
|---|---|
| 0 | Whole blood |
| 1 | Medical care |
| 2 | Surgery |
| 3 | Consultation |
| 4 | Diagnostic radiology |
| 5 | Diagnostic laboratory |
| 6 | Therapeutic radiology |
| 7 | Anesthesia |
| 8 | Assistant at surgery |
| 9 | Other medical items or services |
| A | Used DME |
| B | High risk screening mammography |
| C | Low risk screening mammography |
| D | Ambulance |
| E | Enteral/parenteral nutrients/supplies |
| F | Ambulatory surgical center (facility usage for surgical services) |
| G | Immunosuppressive drugs |
| H | Hospice |
| J | Diabetic shoes |
| K | Hearing items and services |
| L | ESRD supplies |
| M | Monthly capitation payment for dialysis |
| N | Kidney donor |
| P | Lump sum purchase of DME, prosthetics, orthotics |
| Q | Vision items or services |
| R | Rental of DME |
| S | Surgical dressings or other medical supplies |
| T | Outpatient mental health treatment limitation |
| U | Occupational therapy |
| V | Pneumococcal/flu vaccine |
| W | Physical therapy |

## Berenson-Eggers Type of Service (BETOS) Codes

The BETOS coding system was developed primarily for analyzing the growth in Medicare expenditures. The coding system covers all HCPCS codes; assigns a HCPCS code to only one BETOS code; consists of readily understood clinical categories (as opposed to statistical or financial categories); consists of categories that permit objective assignment; is stable over time; and is relatively immune to minor changes in technology or practice patterns.

**BETOS Codes and Descriptions:**

**1. Evaluation and Management**

1. M1A   Office visits—new
2. M1B  Office visits—established
3. M2A  Hospital visit—initial
4. M2B  Hospital visit—subsequent
5. M2C  Hospital visit—critical care
6. M3    Emergency room visit
7. M4A  Home visit
8. M4B  Nursing home visit
9. M5A  Specialist—pathology
10. M5B  Specialist—psychiatry
11. M5C  Specialist—ophthalmology
12. M5D  Specialist—other
13. M6    Consultations

**2. Procedures**

1. P0    Anesthesia
2. P1A  Major procedure—breast
3. P1B  Major procedure—colectomy
4. P1C  Major procedure—cholecystectomy
5. P1D  Major procedure—TURP
6. P1E  Major procedure—hysterectomy
7. P1F  Major procedure—explor/decompr/excis disc
8. P1G  Major procedure—other
9. P2A  Major procedure, cardiovascular—CABG
10. P2B  Major procedure, cardiovascular—aneurysm repair
11. P2C  Major procedure, cardiovascular—thromboendarterectomy
12. P2D  Major procedure, cardiovascular—coronary angioplasty (PTCA)
13. P2E  Major procedure, cardiovascular—pacemaker insertion
14. P2F  Major procedure, cardiovascular—other
15. P3A  Major procedure, orthopedic—hip fracture repair
16. P3B  Major procedure, orthopedic—hip replacement
17. P3C  Major procedure, orthopedic—knee replacement
18. P3D  Major procedure, orthopedic—other
19. P4A  Eye procedure—corneal transplant
20. P4B  Eye procedure—cataract removal/lens insertion
21. P4C  Eye procedure—retinal detachment
22. P4D  Eye procedure—treatment of retinal lesions
23. P4E  Eye procedure—other
24. P5A  Ambulatory procedures—skin
25. P5B  Ambulatory procedures—musculoskeletal
26. P5C  Ambulatory procedures—groin hernia repair
27. P5D  Ambulatory procedures—lithotripsy
28. P5E  Ambulatory procedures—other
29. P6A  Minor procedures—skin
30. P6B  Minor procedures—musculoskeletal
31. P6C  Minor procedures—other (Medicare fee schedule)
32. P6D  Minor procedures—other (non-Medicare fee schedule)
33. P7A  Oncology—radiation therapy
34. P7B  Oncology—other
35. P8A  Endoscopy—arthroscopy
36. P8B  Endoscopy—upper gastrointestinal
37. P8C  Endoscopy—sigmoidoscopy
38. P8D  Endoscopy—colonoscopy
39. P8E  Endoscopy—cystoscopy
40. P8F  Endoscopy—bronchoscopy
41. P8G  Endoscopy—laparoscopic cholecystectomy
42. P8H  Endoscopy—laryngoscopy
43. P8I  Endoscopy—other
44. P9A  Dialysis services (Medicare fee schedule)
45. P9B  Dialysis services (non-Medicare fee schedule)

**3. Imaging**

1. I1A   Standard imaging—chest
2. I1B   Standard imaging—musculoskeletal
3. I1C   Standard imaging—breast
4. I1D   Standard imaging—contrast gastrointestinal
5. I1E   Standard imaging—nuclear medicine
6. I1F   Standard imaging—other

7. I2A Advanced imaging—CAT/CT/CTA; brain/head/neck

8. I2B Advanced imaging—CAT/CT/CTA; other

9. I2C Advanced imaging—MRI/MRA; brain/head/neck

10. I2D Advanced imaging—MRI/MRA; other

11. I3A Echography—eye

12. I3B Echography—abdomen/pelvis

13. I3C Echography—heart

14. I3D Echography—carotid arteries

15. I3E Echography—prostate, transrectal

16. I3F Echography—other

17. I4A Imaging/procedure—heart, including cardiac catheterization

18. I4B Imaging/procedure—other

4. **Tests**

1. T1A Lab tests—routine venipuncture (non-Medicare fee schedule)

2. T1B Lab tests—automated general profiles

3. T1C Lab tests—urinalysis

4. T1D Lab tests—blood counts

5. T1E Lab tests—glucose

6. T1F Lab tests—bacterial cultures

7. T1G Lab tests—other (Medicare fee schedule)

8. T1H Lab tests—other (non-Medicare fee schedule)

9. T2A Other tests—electrocardiograms

10. T2B Other tests—cardiovascular stress tests

11. T2C Other tests—EKG monitoring

12. T2D Other tests—other

5. **Durable Medical Equipment**

1. D1A Medical/surgical supplies

2. D1B Hospital beds

3. D1C Oxygen and supplies

4. D1D Wheelchairs

5. D1E Other DME

6. D1F Prosthetic/orthotic devices

7. D1G Drugs administered through DME

6. **Other**

1. O1A Ambulance

2. O1B Chiropractic

3. O1C Enteral and parenteral

4. O1D Chemotherapy

5. O1E Other drugs

6. O1F Hearing and speech services

7. O1G Immunizations/vaccinations

7. **Exceptions/Unclassified**

1. Y1 Other—Medicare fee schedule

2. Y2 Other—Non-Medicare fee schedule

3. Z1 Local codes

4. Z2 Undefined codes

# APPENDIX 7 — NATIONAL AVERAGE PAYMENT TABLE FOR HCPCS

The following table represents commercial and/or Medicare national average payment (NAP) for services, supplies (DME, orthotics, prosthetics, etc.) drugs, biologicals, and nonphysician procedures using HCPCS Level II codes. Not all HCPCS Level II codes are included in this listing since data concerning the commercial and Medicare national average payments were not available. Please remember these are benchmarks and/or average payments and do not represent actual payment applicable to specific carriers, localities, or third-party payers. The dollar amounts should be used as a broad benchmark tool only.

For the commercial values, the 60th percentile value for the code was calculated by ranking each data point across the nation and calculating the 60th percentile when there were frequencies greater than or equal to 50.

The Medicare data shown is the average of the floor and ceiling limits from the Medicare DMEPOS fee schedule or the National Limitation Amount from the Medicare Clinical Lab Fee Schedule.

| Proc | Mod | Commercial | Medicare | Proc | Mod | Commercial | Medicare | Proc | Mod | Commercial | Medicare |
|------|-----|-----------|----------|------|-----|-----------|----------|------|-----|-----------|----------|
| A0021 | | 4.10 | 0.00 | A0431 | | 8800.00 | 0.00 | A4244 | | 1.26 | 0.00 |
| A0080 | | 1.50 | 0.00 | A0432 | | 557.20 | 0.00 | A4245 | | 2.10 | 0.00 |
| A0090 | | 0.50 | 0.00 | A0433 | | 835.50 | 0.00 | A4246 | | 5.00 | 0.00 |
| A0100 | | 3.30 | 0.00 | A0434 | | 1370.30 | 0.00 | A4247 | | 8.75 | 0.00 |
| A0110 | | 60.00 | 0.00 | A0435 | | 32.90 | 0.00 | A4248 | | 4.50 | 0.00 |
| A0120 | | 25.00 | 0.00 | A0436 | | 80.00 | 0.00 | A4250 | | 15.00 | 0.00 |
| A0130 | | 34.50 | 0.00 | A0888 | | 10.50 | 0.00 | A4253 | NU | 51.50 | 0.00 |
| A0140 | | 179.00 | 0.00 | A0998 | | 160.00 | 0.00 | A4255 | | 0.00 | 3.80 |
| A0160 | | 0.41 | 0.00 | A4206 | | 0.28 | 0.00 | A4256 | | 14.30 | 10.58 |
| A0170 | | 36.60 | 0.00 | A4207 | | 1.00 | 0.00 | A4257 | | 0.00 | 11.80 |
| A0180 | | 74.40 | 0.00 | A4208 | | 0.25 | 0.00 | A4258 | | 28.00 | 16.70 |
| A0190 | | 10.90 | 0.00 | A4209 | | 0.50 | 0.00 | A4259 | | 18.00 | 0.00 |
| A0200 | | 49.10 | 0.00 | A4210 | | 978.35 | 0.00 | A4261 | | 26.00 | 0.00 |
| A0210 | | 10.40 | 0.00 | A4211 | | 1.10 | 0.00 | A4262 | | 1.00 | 0.00 |
| A0225 | | 824.00 | 0.00 | A4212 | | 14.00 | 0.00 | A4263 | | 60.02 | 0.00 |
| A0380 | | 10.00 | 0.00 | A4213 | | 1.23 | 0.00 | A4265 | | 5.00 | 3.14 |
| A0382 | | 25.00 | 0.00 | A4215 | | 0.60 | 0.00 | A4266 | | 58.00 | 0.00 |
| A0384 | | 28.23 | 0.00 | A4216 | | 0.55 | 0.42 | A4267 | | 0.38 | 0.00 |
| A0390 | | 10.00 | 0.00 | A4217 | AU | 0.00 | 2.90 | A4268 | | 1.30 | 0.00 |
| A0392 | | 45.00 | 0.00 | A4217 | | 3.77 | 2.90 | A4270 | | 17.50 | 0.00 |
| A0394 | | 40.00 | 0.00 | A4218 | | 2.70 | 0.00 | A4280 | | 5.17 | 5.57 |
| A0396 | | 60.00 | 0.00 | A4220 | | 65.00 | 0.00 | A4290 | | 225.00 | 0.00 |
| A0398 | | 14.57 | 0.00 | A4221 | | 26.76 | 20.94 | A4300 | | 15.60 | 0.00 |
| A0420 | | 43.00 | 0.00 | A4222 | | 64.98 | 43.23 | A4301 | | 13.50 | 0.00 |
| A0422 | | 60.00 | 0.00 | A4223 | | 111.80 | 0.00 | A4305 | | 22.88 | 0.00 |
| A0424 | | 143.00 | 0.00 | A4230 | | 11.60 | 0.00 | A4306 | | 28.10 | 0.00 |
| A0425 | | 11.00 | 0.00 | A4231 | | 7.40 | 0.00 | A4310 | | 9.97 | 7.14 |
| A0426 | | 598.05 | 0.00 | A4232 | | 3.30 | 0.00 | A4311 | | 14.84 | 13.73 |
| A0427 | | 657.14 | 0.00 | A4233 | NU | 14.80 | 0.74 | A4312 | | 27.06 | 16.69 |
| A0428 | | 425.06 | 0.00 | A4234 | NU | 7.50 | 3.36 | A4313 | | 25.00 | 17.13 |
| A0429 | | 475.06 | 0.00 | A4235 | NU | 11.00 | 2.17 | A4314 | | 29.97 | 23.40 |
| A0430 | | 6100.00 | 0.00 | A4236 | NU | 4.10 | 1.56 | A4315 | | 40.85 | 24.41 |

# APPENDIX 7 — NATIONAL AVERAGE PAYMENT TABLE FOR HCPCS

| Proc | Mod | Commercial | Medicare | Proc | Mod | Commercial | Medicare | Proc | Mod | Commercial | Medicare |
|------|-----|-----------|----------|------|-----|-----------|----------|------|-----|-----------|----------|
| A4316 | | 40.00 | 26.27 | A4380 | | 0.00 | 34.53 | A4427 | | 4.05 | 2.57 |
| A4320 | | 6.05 | 4.93 | A4381 | | 8.33 | 4.27 | A4428 | | 11.72 | 6.02 |
| A4321 | | 9.00 | 0.00 | A4382 | | 0.00 | 22.78 | A4429 | | 9.90 | 7.63 |
| A4322 | | 3.50 | 2.81 | A4383 | | 51.37 | 26.08 | A4430 | | 14.87 | 7.88 |
| A4326 | | 18.23 | 9.98 | A4384 | | 11.54 | 8.90 | A4431 | | 8.22 | 5.76 |
| A4327 | | 0.00 | 41.28 | A4385 | | 8.24 | 4.72 | A4432 | | 6.13 | 3.32 |
| A4328 | | 11.70 | 9.67 | A4387 | | 3.60 | 0.00 | A4433 | | 6.37 | 3.09 |
| A4330 | | 6.26 | 6.62 | A4388 | | 7.57 | 4.04 | A4434 | | 6.65 | 3.48 |
| A4331 | | 4.00 | 2.94 | A4389 | | 11.90 | 5.76 | A4450 | AU | 0.00 | 0.09 |
| A4332 | | 0.17 | 0.11 | A4390 | | 14.87 | 8.89 | A4450 | AV | 0.00 | 0.09 |
| A4333 | | 3.03 | 2.04 | A4391 | | 10.57 | 6.54 | A4450 | AW | 0.00 | 0.10 |
| A4334 | | 6.95 | 4.56 | A4392 | | 12.25 | 7.57 | A4450 | | 0.13 | 0.00 |
| A4335 | | 0.20 | 0.00 | A4393 | | 15.37 | 8.36 | A4452 | AU | 0.00 | 0.34 |
| A4338 | | 15.00 | 11.34 | A4394 | | 3.60 | 2.39 | A4452 | AV | 0.00 | 0.34 |
| A4340 | | 41.00 | 29.37 | A4395 | | 0.08 | 0.05 | A4452 | AW | 0.00 | 0.37 |
| A4344 | | 19.00 | 14.82 | A4396 | | 70.99 | 37.45 | A4452 | | 0.45 | 0.00 |
| A4346 | | 25.01 | 18.12 | A4397 | | 7.72 | 4.43 | A4455 | | 1.70 | 1.33 |
| A4349 | | 2.70 | 1.87 | A4398 | | 18.90 | 12.78 | A4458 | | 10.00 | 0.00 |
| A4351 | | 2.25 | 1.68 | A4399 | | 16.03 | 11.34 | A4461 | | 3.90 | 3.05 |
| A4352 | | 7.60 | 5.94 | A4400 | | 53.21 | 45.21 | A4463 | | 17.00 | 12.31 |
| A4353 | | 9.50 | 6.48 | A4402 | | 2.00 | 1.48 | A4465 | | 14.00 | 0.00 |
| A4354 | | 12.50 | 10.92 | A4404 | | 2.74 | 1.57 | A4481 | | 0.47 | 0.35 |
| A4355 | | 10.00 | 8.24 | A4405 | | 4.69 | 3.15 | A4483 | | 10.50 | 0.00 |
| A4356 | | 56.13 | 42.21 | A4406 | | 9.10 | 5.31 | A4490 | | 7.48 | 0.00 |
| A4357 | | 12.20 | 8.98 | A4407 | | 14.44 | 8.11 | A4495 | | 12.50 | 0.00 |
| A4358 | | 8.84 | 6.14 | A4408 | | 11.17 | 9.13 | A4500 | | 10.38 | 0.00 |
| A4361 | | 20.39 | 16.99 | A4409 | | 10.45 | 5.76 | A4510 | | 19.50 | 0.00 |
| A4362 | | 4.89 | 3.20 | A4410 | | 11.27 | 8.36 | A4520 | | 1.10 | 0.00 |
| A4363 | | 4.10 | 2.19 | A4411 | | 8.10 | 4.72 | A4550 | | 45.01 | 0.00 |
| A4364 | | 4.00 | 2.71 | A4412 | | 9.00 | 2.50 | A4554 | | 2.25 | 0.00 |
| A4365 | | 18.70 | 10.47 | A4413 | | 9.12 | 5.09 | A4556 | | 10.50 | 11.23 |
| A4366 | | 1.86 | 1.21 | A4414 | | 8.22 | 4.56 | A4557 | | 23.00 | 19.52 |
| A4367 | | 13.79 | 6.80 | A4415 | | 7.63 | 5.55 | A4558 | | 7.00 | 5.04 |
| A4368 | | 0.43 | 0.24 | A4416 | | 4.47 | 2.55 | A4559 | | 8.00 | 0.10 |
| A4369 | | 3.90 | 2.24 | A4417 | | 4.07 | 3.44 | A4561 | | 36.80 | 21.33 |
| A4371 | | 6.00 | 3.38 | A4418 | | 2.53 | 1.68 | A4562 | | 64.99 | 53.05 |
| A4372 | | 8.00 | 3.87 | A4419 | | 2.93 | 1.61 | A4565 | | 14.00 | 0.00 |
| A4373 | | 11.67 | 5.81 | A4421 | | 0.20 | 0.00 | A4570 | | 25.01 | 0.00 |
| A4375 | | 17.18 | 15.89 | A4422 | | 0.21 | 0.11 | A4575 | | 775.00 | 0.00 |
| A4376 | | 53.30 | 44.01 | A4423 | | 2.92 | 1.72 | A4580 | | 58.00 | 0.00 |
| A4377 | | 7.74 | 3.97 | A4424 | | 6.47 | 4.40 | A4590 | | 49.99 | 0.00 |
| A4378 | | 29.93 | 28.45 | A4425 | | 4.97 | 3.31 | A4595 | | 32.45 | 26.65 |
| A4379 | | 15.02 | 13.90 | A4426 | | 4.20 | 2.53 | A4604 | NU | 75.00 | 61.80 |

| Proc | Mod | Commercial | Medicare | Proc | Mod | Commercial | Medicare | Proc | Mod | Commercial | Medicare |
|------|-----|-----------|----------|------|-----|-----------|----------|------|-----|-----------|----------|
| A4605 | NU | 40.00 | 15.17 | A4640 | UE | 0.00 | 41.50 | A5053 | | 1.73 | 1.61 |
| A4606 | | 68.00 | 0.00 | A4642 | | 4.30 | 0.00 | A5054 | | 2.63 | 1.66 |
| A4608 | | 0.00 | 53.79 | A4651 | | 2.50 | 0.00 | A5055 | | 1.93 | 1.33 |
| A4611 | NU | 0.00 | 181.72 | A4653 | | 50.00 | 0.00 | A5061 | | 5.59 | 3.26 |
| A4611 | RR | 0.00 | 18.84 | A4657 | | 0.80 | 0.00 | A5062 | | 3.40 | 2.06 |
| A4611 | UE | 0.00 | 136.29 | A4660 | | 20.01 | 0.00 | A5063 | | 4.17 | 2.50 |
| A4612 | NU | 0.00 | 73.94 | A4663 | | 32.00 | 0.00 | A5071 | | 7.95 | 5.56 |
| A4612 | RR | 0.00 | 7.53 | A4670 | | 89.79 | 0.00 | A5072 | | 3.74 | 3.26 |
| A4612 | UE | 0.00 | 56.38 | A4671 | | 33.70 | 0.00 | A5073 | | 5.63 | 2.94 |
| A4613 | NU | 0.00 | 133.40 | A4672 | | 18.50 | 0.00 | A5081 | | 3.07 | 3.06 |
| A4613 | RR | 0.00 | 13.35 | A4673 | | 44.70 | 0.00 | A5082 | | 12.25 | 11.00 |
| A4613 | UE | 0.00 | 96.47 | A4674 | | 2.00 | 0.00 | A5083 | | 0.50 | 0.59 |
| A4614 | | 35.00 | 22.00 | A4690 | | 623.91 | 0.00 | A5093 | | 3.28 | 1.81 |
| A4615 | | 2.96 | 0.77 | A4706 | | 10.00 | 0.00 | A5102 | | 42.54 | 20.89 |
| A4616 | | 0.52 | 0.08 | A4707 | | 17.10 | 0.00 | A5105 | | 49.00 | 37.71 |
| A4617 | | 10.00 | 3.32 | A4709 | | 12.00 | 0.00 | A5112 | | 43.32 | 32.03 |
| A4618 | NU | 16.50 | 8.23 | A4714 | | 16.20 | 0.00 | A5113 | | 6.50 | 4.35 |
| A4618 | RR | 0.00 | 0.95 | A4719 | | 31.00 | 0.00 | A5114 | | 10.50 | 8.27 |
| A4618 | UE | 0.00 | 6.17 | A4720 | | 23.30 | 0.00 | A5120 | AU | 0.00 | 0.23 |
| A4619 | | 1.19 | 1.12 | A4721 | | 60.20 | 0.00 | A5120 | AV | 0.00 | 0.25 |
| A4620 | | 5.00 | 0.67 | A4722 | | 63.20 | 0.00 | A5120 | | 0.40 | 0.00 |
| A4623 | | 10.02 | 6.06 | A4723 | | 34.80 | 0.00 | A5121 | | 8.00 | 6.90 |
| A4624 | NU | 3.30 | 2.44 | A4725 | | 32.00 | 0.00 | A5122 | | 13.20 | 11.89 |
| A4625 | | 8.70 | 6.41 | A4726 | | 75.80 | 0.00 | A5126 | | 1.79 | 1.22 |
| A4626 | | 4.45 | 2.95 | A4728 | | 109.00 | 0.00 | A5131 | | 21.64 | 14.67 |
| A4627 | | 26.00 | 0.00 | A4730 | | 3.10 | 0.00 | A5200 | | 22.26 | 10.46 |
| A4628 | NU | 4.70 | 3.46 | A4736 | | 33.60 | 0.00 | A5500 | | 75.00 | 66.76 |
| A4629 | | 5.91 | 4.29 | A4737 | | 4.70 | 0.00 | A5501 | | 274.97 | 200.25 |
| A4630 | NU | 6.50 | 5.78 | A4740 | | 17.10 | 0.00 | A5503 | | 41.01 | 29.70 |
| A4633 | NU | 0.00 | 37.96 | A4750 | | 15.00 | 0.00 | A5504 | | 40.63 | 29.70 |
| A4634 | | 0.40 | 0.00 | A4755 | | 11.00 | 0.00 | A5505 | | 41.01 | 29.70 |
| A4635 | NU | 0.00 | 4.74 | A4760 | | 20.00 | 0.00 | A5506 | | 45.00 | 29.70 |
| A4635 | RR | 0.00 | 0.64 | A4765 | | 10.30 | 0.00 | A5507 | | 0.00 | 29.70 |
| A4635 | UE | 0.00 | 3.14 | A4770 | | 10.80 | 0.00 | A5508 | | 26.00 | 0.00 |
| A4636 | NU | 0.00 | 3.90 | A4772 | | 28.00 | 0.00 | A5510 | | 50.00 | 0.00 |
| A4636 | RR | 0.00 | 0.40 | A4860 | | 5.30 | 0.00 | A5512 | | 34.99 | 27.24 |
| A4636 | UE | 0.00 | 2.84 | A4911 | | 11.20 | 0.00 | A5513 | | 45.19 | 40.65 |
| A4637 | NU | 3.00 | 1.97 | A4927 | | 6.00 | 0.00 | A6010 | | 31.61 | 28.64 |
| A4637 | RR | 0.00 | 0.28 | A4928 | | 0.30 | 0.00 | A6011 | | 2.50 | 2.11 |
| A4637 | UE | 0.00 | 1.49 | A4930 | | 1.01 | 0.00 | A6021 | | 24.30 | 19.45 |
| A4639 | NU | 0.00 | 265.67 | A4931 | | 5.00 | 0.00 | A6022 | | 25.21 | 19.45 |
| A4640 | NU | 75.03 | 58.57 | A5051 | | 3.01 | 1.92 | A6023 | | 0.00 | 176.03 |
| A4640 | RR | 0.00 | 5.97 | A5052 | | 2.00 | 1.38 | A6024 | | 7.53 | 5.73 |

# APPENDIX 7 — NATIONAL AVERAGE PAYMENT TABLE FOR HCPCS

| Proc | Mod | Commercial | Medicare | Proc | Mod | Commercial | Medicare | Proc | Mod | Commercial | Medicare |
|------|-----|-----------|----------|------|-----|-----------|----------|------|-----|-----------|----------|
| A6025 | | 40.01 | 0.00 | A6241 | | 0.00 | 2.38 | A6455 | | 1.14 | 1.29 |
| A6154 | | 22.55 | 13.30 | A6242 | | 6.80 | 5.62 | A6456 | | 1.54 | 1.19 |
| A6196 | | 8.25 | 6.80 | A6243 | | 12.31 | 11.39 | A6457 | | 1.37 | 1.06 |
| A6197 | | 19.89 | 15.21 | A6244 | | 47.11 | 36.34 | A6502 | | 0.20 | 0.00 |
| A6198 | | 59.70 | 0.00 | A6245 | | 8.00 | 6.73 | A6504 | | 191.60 | 0.00 |
| A6199 | | 6.30 | 4.90 | A6246 | | 15.00 | 9.18 | A6506 | | 167.50 | 0.00 |
| A6200 | | 9.50 | 0.00 | A6247 | | 23.10 | 22.00 | A6507 | | 138.20 | 0.00 |
| A6201 | | 21.99 | 0.00 | A6248 | | 19.38 | 15.02 | A6509 | | 325.00 | 0.00 |
| A6202 | | 34.99 | 0.00 | A6250 | | 11.50 | 0.00 | A6511 | | 369.00 | 0.00 |
| A6203 | | 4.68 | 3.10 | A6251 | | 2.03 | 1.84 | A6530 | | 38.70 | 0.00 |
| A6204 | | 7.50 | 5.77 | A6252 | | 3.40 | 3.01 | A6531 | AW | 0.00 | 40.03 |
| A6205 | | 50.00 | 0.00 | A6253 | | 7.25 | 5.87 | A6531 | | 43.27 | 0.00 |
| A6206 | | 7.00 | 0.00 | A6254 | | 2.00 | 1.12 | A6532 | AW | 0.00 | 56.39 |
| A6207 | | 7.49 | 6.79 | A6255 | | 6.06 | 2.81 | A6532 | | 44.99 | 0.00 |
| A6208 | | 35.00 | 0.00 | A6256 | | 17.00 | 0.00 | A6533 | | 51.50 | 0.00 |
| A6209 | | 8.10 | 6.92 | A6257 | | 1.14 | 1.42 | A6534 | | 65.00 | 0.00 |
| A6210 | | 22.50 | 18.43 | A6258 | | 5.15 | 3.98 | A6535 | | 104.00 | 0.00 |
| A6211 | | 36.89 | 27.17 | A6259 | | 13.12 | 10.12 | A6536 | | 42.50 | 0.00 |
| A6212 | | 10.00 | 8.98 | A6260 | | 1.98 | 0.00 | A6537 | | 75.00 | 0.00 |
| A6213 | | 19.34 | 0.00 | A6261 | | 9.79 | 0.00 | A6538 | | 84.00 | 0.00 |
| A6214 | | 11.24 | 9.52 | A6262 | | 0.92 | 0.00 | A6539 | | 161.90 | 0.00 |
| A6215 | | 0.70 | 0.00 | A6266 | | 1.96 | 1.78 | A6540 | | 125.00 | 0.00 |
| A6216 | | 0.07 | 0.05 | A6402 | | 0.15 | 0.11 | A6541 | | 152.80 | 0.00 |
| A6217 | | 0.60 | 0.00 | A6403 | | 0.53 | 0.40 | A6542 | | 180.30 | 0.00 |
| A6218 | | 1.00 | 0.00 | A6404 | | 0.66 | 0.00 | A6543 | | 108.80 | 0.00 |
| A6219 | | 1.16 | 0.88 | A6407 | | 2.00 | 1.74 | A6549 | | 65.00 | 0.00 |
| A6220 | | 3.07 | 2.39 | A6410 | | 0.52 | 0.36 | A6550 | | 52.00 | 25.37 |
| A6221 | | 5.00 | 0.00 | A6411 | | 5.00 | 0.00 | A7000 | NU | 12.74 | 8.83 |
| A6222 | | 2.33 | 1.97 | A6412 | | 0.34 | 0.00 | A7001 | NU | 39.99 | 30.60 |
| A6223 | | 2.89 | 2.24 | A6441 | | 0.87 | 0.62 | A7002 | NU | 5.00 | 3.55 |
| A6224 | | 4.34 | 3.34 | A6442 | | 0.21 | 0.16 | A7003 | NU | 4.00 | 2.54 |
| A6228 | | 3.30 | 0.00 | A6443 | | 0.34 | 0.27 | A7004 | NU | 2.00 | 1.67 |
| A6229 | | 4.00 | 3.34 | A6444 | | 0.77 | 0.52 | A7005 | NU | 39.00 | 28.52 |
| A6231 | | 5.00 | 4.33 | A6445 | | 0.48 | 0.30 | A7006 | NU | 10.00 | 8.83 |
| A6232 | | 8.03 | 6.37 | A6446 | | 0.50 | 0.38 | A7007 | NU | 7.55 | 4.27 |
| A6233 | | 9.87 | 17.75 | A6447 | | 0.67 | 0.62 | A7008 | NU | 12.39 | 10.18 |
| A6234 | | 7.85 | 6.05 | A6448 | | 1.41 | 1.08 | A7009 | NU | 0.00 | 38.89 |
| A6235 | | 17.17 | 15.56 | A6449 | | 2.09 | 1.62 | A7010 | NU | 25.00 | 21.82 |
| A6236 | | 28.00 | 25.21 | A6450 | | 6.50 | 0.00 | A7011 | | 20.00 | 0.00 |
| A6237 | | 11.10 | 7.32 | A6451 | | 10.00 | 0.00 | A7012 | NU | 5.00 | 3.50 |
| A6238 | | 27.35 | 21.08 | A6452 | | 6.42 | 5.47 | A7013 | NU | 1.20 | 0.77 |
| A6239 | | 50.80 | 0.00 | A6453 | | 0.76 | 0.57 | A7014 | NU | 5.36 | 4.16 |
| A6240 | | 11.58 | 11.32 | A6454 | | 1.03 | 0.71 | A7015 | NU | 3.20 | 1.74 |

# APPENDIX 7 — NATIONAL AVERAGE PAYMENT TABLE FOR HCPCS

| Proc | Mod | Commercial | Medicare | Proc | Mod | Commercial | Medicare | Proc | Mod | Commercial | Medicare |
|------|-----|-----------|----------|------|-----|-----------|----------|------|-----|-----------|----------|
| A7016 | NU | 10.00 | 6.71 | A7525 | | 5.60 | 1.92 | A9554 | | 229.00 | 0.00 |
| A7017 | NU | 0.00 | 123.99 | A7526 | | 8.25 | 3.12 | A9555 | | 370.00 | 0.00 |
| A7017 | RR | 0.00 | 12.40 | A7527 | | 31.90 | 3.31 | A9556 | | 46.01 | 0.00 |
| A7017 | UE | 0.00 | 92.98 | A8000 | NU | 0.00 | 141.85 | A9557 | | 550.00 | 0.00 |
| A7018 | | 0.76 | 0.35 | A8000 | RR | 0.00 | 14.18 | A9558 | | 117.00 | 0.00 |
| A7025 | NU | 0.00 | 402.32 | A8000 | UE | 0.00 | 106.41 | A9560 | | 137.00 | 0.00 |
| A7026 | NU | 0.00 | 26.60 | A8001 | NU | 0.00 | 141.85 | A9561 | | 48.00 | 0.00 |
| A7027 | NU | 306.00 | 172.53 | A8001 | RR | 0.00 | 14.18 | A9562 | | 250.00 | 0.00 |
| A7028 | NU | 0.00 | 45.83 | A8001 | UE | 0.00 | 106.41 | A9565 | | 656.60 | 0.00 |
| A7029 | NU | 0.00 | 18.72 | A9275 | | 1.00 | 0.00 | A9567 | | 55.00 | 0.00 |
| A7030 | NU | 325.97 | 174.49 | A9276 | | 35.00 | 0.00 | A9576 | | 5.30 | 0.00 |
| A7031 | NU | 112.02 | 64.54 | A9277 | | 649.00 | 0.00 | A9577 | | 8.60 | 0.00 |
| A7032 | NU | 63.01 | 37.49 | A9279 | | 100.00 | 0.00 | A9578 | | 4.00 | 0.00 |
| A7033 | NU | 46.80 | 26.28 | A9281 | | 30.00 | 0.00 | A9579 | | 6.00 | 0.00 |
| A7034 | NU | 199.98 | 108.82 | A9282 | | 400.00 | 0.00 | A9605 | | 3154.00 | 0.00 |
| A7035 | NU | 60.01 | 36.77 | A9500 | | 180.00 | 0.00 | A9698 | | 80.00 | 0.00 |
| A7036 | NU | 30.94 | 16.84 | A9502 | | 200.00 | 0.00 | A9700 | | 200.00 | 0.00 |
| A7037 | NU | 51.50 | 37.95 | A9503 | | 58.00 | 0.00 | A9901 | | 25.00 | 0.00 |
| A7038 | NU | 7.25 | 4.99 | A9505 | | 100.00 | 0.00 | A9999 | | 7.50 | 0.00 |
| A7039 | NU | 19.51 | 14.18 | A9507 | | 3568.80 | 0.00 | B4034 | | 7.50 | 0.00 |
| A7040 | | 0.00 | 42.18 | A9508 | | 47.10 | 0.00 | B4035 | | 19.23 | 0.00 |
| A7041 | | 0.00 | 79.24 | A9509 | | 0.20 | 0.00 | B4036 | | 11.29 | 0.00 |
| A7042 | | 0.00 | 191.29 | A9510 | | 117.00 | 0.00 | B4081 | | 49.25 | 0.00 |
| A7043 | | 69.86 | 30.01 | A9512 | | 3.00 | 0.00 | B4082 | | 36.00 | 0.00 |
| A7044 | NU | 199.99 | 111.84 | A9516 | | 0.20 | 0.00 | B4083 | | 2.06 | 0.00 |
| A7045 | NU | 26.00 | 18.01 | A9517 | | 42.00 | 0.00 | B4086 | | 34.65 | 0.00 |
| A7045 | RR | 0.00 | 1.81 | A9521 | | 995.00 | 0.00 | B4087 | | 45.00 | 0.00 |
| A7045 | UE | 0.00 | 13.51 | A9524 | | 165.00 | 0.00 | B4088 | | 158.40 | 0.00 |
| A7046 | NU | 37.45 | 18.05 | A9526 | | 278.00 | 0.00 | B4100 | | 0.90 | 0.00 |
| A7501 | | 0.00 | 97.16 | A9527 | | 68.20 | 0.00 | B4102 | | 3.00 | 0.00 |
| A7502 | | 0.00 | 46.17 | A9528 | | 329.57 | 0.00 | B4103 | | 5.10 | 0.00 |
| A7503 | | 23.35 | 10.48 | A9529 | | 51.00 | 0.00 | B4104 | | 0.10 | 0.00 |
| A7504 | | 1.33 | 0.62 | A9530 | | 42.80 | 0.00 | B4149 | | 2.19 | 0.00 |
| A7505 | | 6.25 | 4.33 | A9531 | | 8.00 | 0.00 | B4150 | | 1.04 | 0.00 |
| A7506 | | 0.42 | 0.31 | A9537 | | 78.90 | 0.00 | B4152 | | 0.98 | 0.00 |
| A7507 | | 2.60 | 2.31 | A9538 | | 50.00 | 0.00 | B4153 | | 4.50 | 0.00 |
| A7508 | | 3.00 | 2.66 | A9539 | | 40.00 | 0.00 | B4154 | | 1.61 | 0.00 |
| A7509 | | 2.00 | 1.31 | A9540 | | 54.00 | 0.00 | B4155 | | 1.57 | 0.00 |
| A7520 | | 131.01 | 43.92 | A9541 | | 65.00 | 0.00 | B4157 | | 4.80 | 0.00 |
| A7521 | | 94.10 | 43.52 | A9547 | | 824.85 | 0.00 | B4158 | | 2.10 | 0.00 |
| A7522 | | 0.00 | 41.78 | A9548 | | 448.20 | 0.00 | B4159 | | 1.90 | 0.00 |
| A7523 | | 5.00 | 0.00 | A9550 | | 36.00 | 0.00 | B4160 | | 2.40 | 0.00 |
| A7524 | | 0.00 | 71.60 | A9552 | | 600.00 | 0.00 | B4161 | | 4.10 | 0.00 |

| Proc | Mod | Commercial | Medicare | Proc | Mod | Commercial | Medicare | Proc | Mod | Commercial | Medicare |
|------|-----|-----------|----------|------|-----|-----------|----------|------|-----|-----------|----------|
| B4162 | | 3.10 | 0.00 | E0110 | NU | 90.88 | 71.77 | E0148 | NU | 158.96 | 117.52 |
| B4178 | | 125.00 | 0.00 | E0110 | RR | 21.00 | 14.79 | E0148 | RR | 25.00 | 11.77 |
| B4180 | | 99.99 | 0.00 | E0110 | UE | 0.00 | 53.82 | E0148 | UE | 0.00 | 88.14 |
| B4185 | | 17.20 | 0.00 | E0111 | NU | 54.01 | 49.27 | E0149 | NU | 259.92 | 206.46 |
| B4189 | | 244.94 | 0.00 | E0111 | RR | 0.00 | 7.80 | E0149 | RR | 31.24 | 20.65 |
| B4193 | | 378.21 | 0.00 | E0111 | UE | 0.00 | 38.02 | E0149 | UE | 0.00 | 154.84 |
| B4197 | | 450.13 | 0.00 | E0112 | NU | 40.00 | 34.23 | E0153 | NU | 90.99 | 64.18 |
| B4199 | | 499.86 | 0.00 | E0112 | RR | 0.00 | 9.19 | E0153 | RR | 0.00 | 7.25 |
| B4216 | | 10.65 | 0.00 | E0112 | UE | 0.00 | 26.12 | E0153 | UE | 0.00 | 48.13 |
| B4220 | | 17.83 | 0.00 | E0113 | NU | 50.00 | 19.55 | E0154 | NU | 103.02 | 65.22 |
| B4222 | | 20.00 | 0.00 | E0113 | RR | 0.00 | 4.77 | E0154 | RR | 11.04 | 7.92 |
| B4224 | | 48.48 | 0.00 | E0113 | UE | 0.00 | 14.67 | E0154 | UE | 0.00 | 49.55 |
| B5100 | | 11.50 | 0.00 | E0114 | NU | 59.00 | 43.65 | E0155 | NU | 56.29 | 29.20 |
| B9000 | RR | 112.68 | 0.00 | E0114 | RR | 15.00 | 7.93 | E0155 | RR | 5.00 | 3.56 |
| B9002 | NU | 1487.06 | 0.00 | E0114 | UE | 0.00 | 33.00 | E0155 | UE | 0.00 | 22.25 |
| B9002 | RR | 209.96 | 0.00 | E0116 | NU | 39.99 | 25.66 | E0156 | NU | 31.03 | 24.45 |
| B9004 | RR | 584.82 | 0.00 | E0116 | RR | 0.00 | 5.00 | E0156 | RR | 5.00 | 3.13 |
| B9006 | RR | 554.97 | 0.00 | E0116 | UE | 0.00 | 19.32 | E0156 | UE | 0.00 | 18.36 |
| C1300 | | 550.00 | 0.00 | E0117 | NU | 0.00 | 178.26 | E0157 | NU | 0.00 | 75.78 |
| C1713 | | 720.00 | 0.00 | E0117 | RR | 0.00 | 17.82 | E0157 | RR | 0.00 | 8.32 |
| C1715 | | 60.00 | 0.00 | E0117 | UE | 0.00 | 133.71 | E0157 | UE | 0.00 | 56.84 |
| C1717 | | 115.50 | 0.00 | E0118 | | 38.10 | 0.00 | E0158 | NU | 40.01 | 29.77 |
| C1718 | | 227.00 | 0.00 | E0130 | NU | 90.56 | 64.97 | E0158 | RR | 0.00 | 3.29 |
| C1726 | | 160.00 | 0.00 | E0130 | RR | 0.00 | 15.56 | E0158 | UE | 0.00 | 22.47 |
| C1751 | | 23.00 | 0.00 | E0130 | UE | 0.00 | 50.63 | E0159 | NU | 22.88 | 16.53 |
| C1758 | | 65.30 | 0.00 | E0135 | NU | 104.97 | 77.55 | E0159 | RR | 0.00 | 1.71 |
| C1760 | | 798.00 | 0.00 | E0135 | RR | 25.00 | 15.97 | E0159 | UE | 0.00 | 12.40 |
| C1769 | | 136.80 | 0.00 | E0135 | UE | 0.00 | 59.50 | E0160 | NU | 0.00 | 30.58 |
| C1781 | | 500.00 | 0.00 | E0140 | NU | 363.01 | 333.66 | E0160 | RR | 0.00 | 4.01 |
| C1879 | | 96.00 | 0.00 | E0140 | RR | 0.00 | 33.38 | E0160 | UE | 0.00 | 22.91 |
| C1887 | | 45.00 | 0.00 | E0140 | UE | 0.00 | 250.25 | E0161 | NU | 0.00 | 24.27 |
| C1894 | | 138.00 | 0.00 | E0141 | NU | 125.05 | 106.65 | E0161 | RR | 0.00 | 3.30 |
| C2641 | | 220.00 | 0.00 | E0141 | RR | 0.00 | 20.69 | E0161 | UE | 0.00 | 18.17 |
| C9003 | | 9.30 | 0.00 | E0141 | UE | 0.00 | 79.99 | E0162 | NU | 0.00 | 134.78 |
| C9113 | | 58.40 | 0.00 | E0143 | NU | 144.92 | 111.22 | E0162 | RR | 0.00 | 14.15 |
| C9233 | | 2800.00 | 0.00 | E0143 | RR | 30.00 | 19.97 | E0162 | UE | 0.00 | 104.53 |
| C9240 | | 150.90 | 0.00 | E0143 | UE | 0.00 | 83.23 | E0163 | NU | 130.03 | 102.02 |
| E0100 | NU | 25.00 | 19.49 | E0144 | NU | 339.97 | 294.57 | E0163 | RR | 27.21 | 22.60 |
| E0100 | RR | 7.00 | 5.50 | E0144 | RR | 0.00 | 29.47 | E0163 | UE | 0.00 | 78.67 |
| E0100 | UE | 0.00 | 15.54 | E0144 | UE | 0.00 | 220.92 | E0165 | NU | 304.43 | 0.00 |
| E0105 | NU | 55.01 | 45.43 | E0147 | NU | 574.58 | 531.70 | E0165 | RR | 25.00 | 17.19 |
| E0105 | RR | 12.50 | 8.20 | E0147 | RR | 0.00 | 53.17 | E0167 | NU | 12.50 | 11.10 |
| E0105 | UE | 0.00 | 35.02 | E0147 | UE | 0.00 | 398.80 | E0167 | RR | 0.00 | 1.17 |

| Proc | Mod | Commercial | Medicare | Proc | Mod | Commercial | Medicare | Proc | Mod | Commercial | Medicare |
|------|-----|-----------|----------|------|-----|-----------|----------|------|-----|-----------|----------|
| E0167 | UE | 0.00 | 8.36 | E0200 | RR | 0.00 | 9.96 | E0249 | NU | 150.02 | 92.13 |
| E0168 | NU | 205.25 | 139.60 | E0200 | UE | 0.00 | 55.03 | E0249 | RR | 0.00 | 10.13 |
| E0168 | RR | 28.00 | 14.03 | E0202 | RR | 129.32 | 57.92 | E0249 | UE | 0.00 | 69.10 |
| E0168 | UE | 0.00 | 104.69 | E0203 | | 295.00 | 0.00 | E0250 | RR | 181.99 | 90.43 |
| E0170 | RR | 0.00 | 148.67 | E0205 | NU | 250.06 | 179.51 | E0251 | RR | 0.00 | 68.53 |
| E0171 | RR | 55.00 | 26.75 | E0205 | RR | 0.00 | 19.74 | E0255 | RR | 149.99 | 108.67 |
| E0175 | NU | 0.00 | 61.27 | E0205 | UE | 0.00 | 134.63 | E0256 | RR | 0.00 | 77.10 |
| E0175 | RR | 0.00 | 6.13 | E0210 | NU | 0.00 | 30.19 | E0260 | NU | 892.50 | 0.00 |
| E0175 | UE | 0.00 | 45.09 | E0210 | RR | 0.00 | 2.84 | E0260 | RR | 194.94 | 0.00 |
| E0181 | NU | 306.23 | 0.00 | E0210 | UE | 0.00 | 22.65 | E0261 | RR | 160.05 | 126.67 |
| E0181 | RR | 35.00 | 24.11 | E0215 | NU | 93.02 | 65.53 | E0265 | NU | 2259.67 | 0.00 |
| E0182 | RR | 35.00 | 24.22 | E0215 | RR | 0.00 | 6.86 | E0265 | RR | 230.55 | 184.89 |
| E0184 | NU | 284.33 | 180.10 | E0215 | UE | 0.00 | 49.16 | E0266 | RR | 203.33 | 164.27 |
| E0184 | RR | 34.99 | 22.73 | E0217 | NU | 595.86 | 459.24 | E0271 | NU | 224.97 | 205.39 |
| E0184 | UE | 0.00 | 138.12 | E0217 | RR | 70.02 | 51.14 | E0271 | RR | 30.01 | 21.33 |
| E0185 | NU | 349.91 | 295.87 | E0217 | UE | 0.00 | 344.40 | E0271 | UE | 0.00 | 160.45 |
| E0185 | RR | 50.50 | 41.57 | E0218 | NU | 449.89 | 0.00 | E0272 | NU | 0.00 | 187.19 |
| E0185 | UE | 0.00 | 227.07 | E0218 | RR | 65.01 | 0.00 | E0272 | RR | 0.00 | 19.55 |
| E0186 | RR | 27.60 | 18.78 | E0220 | NU | 0.00 | 7.84 | E0272 | UE | 0.00 | 139.72 |
| E0187 | RR | 0.00 | 21.47 | E0220 | RR | 0.00 | 0.83 | E0274 | RR | 34.99 | 0.00 |
| E0188 | NU | 59.99 | 24.45 | E0220 | UE | 0.00 | 5.86 | E0275 | NU | 0.00 | 14.16 |
| E0188 | RR | 3.72 | 2.87 | E0225 | NU | 0.00 | 359.50 | E0275 | RR | 0.00 | 1.48 |
| E0188 | UE | 0.00 | 18.36 | E0225 | RR | 0.00 | 35.44 | E0275 | UE | 0.00 | 10.62 |
| E0189 | NU | 75.00 | 48.07 | E0225 | UE | 0.00 | 269.62 | E0276 | NU | 0.00 | 12.31 |
| E0189 | RR | 0.00 | 5.21 | E0230 | NU | 13.50 | 7.85 | E0276 | RR | 0.00 | 1.45 |
| E0189 | UE | 0.00 | 36.06 | E0230 | RR | 0.00 | 0.88 | E0276 | UE | 0.00 | 9.73 |
| E0190 | NU | 50.00 | 0.00 | E0230 | UE | 10.00 | 5.87 | E0277 | NU | 5180.00 | 0.00 |
| E0191 | NU | 15.00 | 9.24 | E0235 | RR | 21.58 | 15.97 | E0277 | RR | 870.73 | 0.00 |
| E0191 | RR | 0.00 | 0.95 | E0236 | NU | 374.97 | 0.00 | E0280 | NU | 0.00 | 35.34 |
| E0191 | UE | 0.00 | 6.90 | E0236 | RR | 64.99 | 40.93 | E0280 | RR | 3.06 | 3.80 |
| E0193 | RR | 1499.79 | 835.70 | E0238 | NU | 27.02 | 25.01 | E0280 | UE | 0.00 | 26.50 |
| E0194 | RR | 3479.87 | 3010.27 | E0238 | RR | 0.00 | 2.52 | E0290 | RR | 0.00 | 69.14 |
| E0196 | RR | 39.00 | 30.06 | E0238 | UE | 0.00 | 18.39 | E0291 | RR | 0.00 | 50.23 |
| E0197 | NU | 329.03 | 204.96 | E0239 | NU | 0.00 | 416.10 | E0292 | RR | 0.00 | 77.74 |
| E0197 | RR | 30.01 | 28.28 | E0239 | RR | 0.00 | 41.62 | E0293 | RR | 0.00 | 66.15 |
| E0197 | UE | 0.00 | 180.04 | E0239 | UE | 0.00 | 312.09 | E0294 | RR | 200.00 | 120.85 |
| E0198 | NU | 0.00 | 204.96 | E0240 | NU | 50.00 | 0.00 | E0295 | RR | 176.01 | 117.80 |
| E0198 | RR | 0.00 | 21.23 | E0241 | | 34.99 | 0.00 | E0296 | RR | 249.97 | 151.89 |
| E0198 | UE | 0.00 | 155.53 | E0243 | | 55.01 | 0.00 | E0297 | RR | 212.95 | 130.12 |
| E0199 | NU | 40.26 | 29.65 | E0244 | | 60.00 | 0.00 | E0300 | NU | 0.00 | 2625.73 |
| E0199 | RR | 0.00 | 2.95 | E0245 | | 75.01 | 0.00 | E0300 | RR | 0.00 | 262.57 |
| E0199 | UE | 0.00 | 22.24 | E0247 | NU | 115.02 | 0.00 | E0300 | UE | 0.00 | 1969.29 |
| E0200 | NU | 0.00 | 73.34 | E0248 | NU | 194.00 | 0.00 | E0301 | RR | 679.98 | 250.42 |

# APPENDIX 7 — NATIONAL AVERAGE PAYMENT TABLE FOR HCPCS

| Proc | Mod | Commercial | Medicare | Proc | Mod | Commercial | Medicare | Proc | Mod | Commercial | Medicare |
|------|-----|-----------|----------|------|-----|-----------|----------|------|-----|-----------|----------|
| E0302 | RR | 0.00 | 661.78 | E0480 | RR | 81.01 | 40.65 | E0605 | NU | 0.00 | 24.45 |
| E0303 | RR | 374.91 | 281.18 | E0482 | RR | 695.95 | 397.77 | E0605 | RR | 0.00 | 2.84 |
| E0304 | RR | 60.00 | 712.87 | E0483 | RR | 1263.32 | 983.40 | E0605 | UE | 0.00 | 20.14 |
| E0305 | NU | 166.62 | 0.00 | E0484 | NU | 75.00 | 34.15 | E0606 | RR | 0.00 | 21.22 |
| E0305 | RR | 23.00 | 16.46 | E0484 | RR | 0.00 | 3.42 | E0607 | NU | 92.01 | 66.82 |
| E0310 | NU | 184.99 | 179.58 | E0484 | UE | 0.00 | 25.63 | E0607 | RR | 15.00 | 6.68 |
| E0310 | RR | 37.00 | 21.06 | E0486 | NU | 2000.00 | 0.00 | E0607 | UE | 0.00 | 50.10 |
| E0310 | UE | 0.00 | 135.89 | E0500 | RR | 140.98 | 101.54 | E0610 | NU | 0.00 | 220.02 |
| E0316 | RR | 0.00 | 195.44 | E0550 | NU | 625.09 | 0.00 | E0610 | RR | 0.00 | 23.21 |
| E0325 | NU | 9.54 | 9.35 | E0550 | RR | 69.45 | 46.37 | E0610 | UE | 0.00 | 165.04 |
| E0325 | RR | 0.00 | 1.40 | E0555 | NU | 7.50 | 0.00 | E0615 | NU | 0.00 | 442.91 |
| E0325 | UE | 0.00 | 6.19 | E0560 | NU | 0.00 | 158.66 | E0615 | RR | 0.00 | 54.12 |
| E0326 | NU | 0.00 | 9.72 | E0560 | RR | 21.09 | 18.60 | E0615 | UE | 0.00 | 332.19 |
| E0326 | RR | 0.00 | 1.10 | E0560 | UE | 0.00 | 118.99 | E0617 | RR | 0.00 | 281.25 |
| E0326 | UE | 0.00 | 7.28 | E0561 | NU | 175.99 | 98.98 | E0618 | RR | 350.06 | 259.33 |
| E0371 | RR | 550.09 | 411.15 | E0561 | RR | 16.89 | 9.89 | E0619 | RR | 358.00 | 0.00 |
| E0372 | RR | 700.04 | 498.89 | E0561 | UE | 0.00 | 74.22 | E0620 | NU | 0.00 | 808.81 |
| E0373 | RR | 649.74 | 568.39 | E0562 | NU | 409.92 | 278.63 | E0620 | RR | 0.00 | 80.88 |
| E0424 | RR | 394.99 | 0.00 | E0562 | RR | 48.01 | 27.85 | E0620 | UE | 0.00 | 606.61 |
| E0431 | RR | 70.01 | 0.00 | E0562 | UE | 0.00 | 208.97 | E0621 | NU | 171.99 | 88.79 |
| E0434 | RR | 74.99 | 0.00 | E0565 | RR | 102.01 | 56.44 | E0621 | RR | 13.19 | 8.56 |
| E0439 | RR | 402.38 | 0.00 | E0570 | NU | 250.00 | 0.00 | E0621 | UE | 0.00 | 66.94 |
| E0441 | | 159.73 | 0.00 | E0570 | RR | 25.86 | 0.00 | E0627 | NU | 424.06 | 312.02 |
| E0442 | | 104.59 | 0.00 | E0571 | RR | 35.00 | 27.72 | E0627 | RR | 0.00 | 31.21 |
| E0443 | | 27.03 | 0.00 | E0572 | RR | 0.00 | 35.24 | E0627 | UE | 0.00 | 234.03 |
| E0444 | | 17.00 | 0.00 | E0574 | RR | 54.99 | 37.24 | E0628 | NU | 350.95 | 312.02 |
| E0445 | | 498.00 | 0.00 | E0575 | NU | 750.42 | 0.00 | E0628 | RR | 0.00 | 31.21 |
| E0450 | RR | 1218.63 | 882.93 | E0575 | RR | 109.99 | 95.07 | E0628 | UE | 0.00 | 234.03 |
| E0457 | NU | 0.00 | 568.42 | E0580 | NU | 0.00 | 123.99 | E0629 | NU | 349.97 | 305.91 |
| E0457 | RR | 0.00 | 56.84 | E0580 | RR | 0.00 | 12.40 | E0629 | RR | 0.00 | 30.60 |
| E0457 | UE | 0.00 | 426.29 | E0580 | UE | 0.00 | 92.98 | E0629 | UE | 0.00 | 229.41 |
| E0459 | RR | 0.00 | 47.08 | E0585 | RR | 49.99 | 32.44 | E0630 | NU | 1190.02 | 0.00 |
| E0460 | RR | 0.00 | 678.55 | E0600 | NU | 516.08 | 0.00 | E0630 | RR | 120.99 | 94.25 |
| E0461 | RR | 1499.91 | 882.93 | E0600 | RR | 90.99 | 42.36 | E0635 | RR | 169.95 | 113.19 |
| E0462 | RR | 0.00 | 269.55 | E0601 | NU | 1449.89 | 0.00 | E0636 | RR | 0.00 | 975.47 |
| E0463 | RR | 0.00 | 1300.90 | E0601 | RR | 173.00 | 103.33 | E0637 | NU | 3165.13 | 0.00 |
| E0463 | | 1990.00 | 0.00 | E0601 | UE | 850.28 | 0.00 | E0650 | NU | 0.00 | 666.21 |
| E0464 | RR | 0.00 | 1300.90 | E0602 | NU | 0.00 | 27.31 | E0650 | RR | 70.18 | 82.21 |
| E0470 | NU | 3500.67 | 0.00 | E0602 | RR | 0.00 | 2.74 | E0650 | UE | 0.00 | 499.65 |
| E0470 | RR | 416.59 | 237.36 | E0602 | UE | 0.00 | 20.48 | E0651 | NU | 1299.80 | 849.54 |
| E0471 | NU | 7194.17 | 0.00 | E0603 | NU | 210.00 | 0.00 | E0651 | RR | 105.03 | 86.79 |
| E0471 | RR | 819.85 | 594.01 | E0603 | RR | 56.80 | 0.00 | E0651 | UE | 0.00 | 637.16 |
| E0472 | RR | 858.06 | 594.01 | E0604 | RR | 84.99 | 0.00 | E0652 | NU | 6497.98 | 4903.84 |

| Proc | Mod | Commercial | Medicare | Proc | Mod | Commercial | Medicare | Proc | Mod | Commercial | Medicare |
|------|-----|-----------|----------|------|-----|-----------|----------|------|-----|-----------|----------|
| E0652 | RR | 649.78 | 484.66 | E0694 | RR | 0.00 | 409.53 | E0850 | NU | 149.04 | 97.18 |
| E0652 | UE | 0.00 | 3674.59 | E0694 | UE | 0.00 | 3071.49 | E0850 | RR | 30.00 | 13.35 |
| E0655 | NU | 149.98 | 99.83 | E0700 | | 20.00 | 0.00 | E0850 | UE | 0.00 | 72.89 |
| E0655 | RR | 13.17 | 11.73 | E0705 | NU | 66.00 | 50.99 | E0855 | NU | 575.07 | 464.94 |
| E0655 | UE | 0.00 | 74.97 | E0705 | RR | 0.00 | 5.19 | E0855 | RR | 75.02 | 46.49 |
| E0660 | NU | 0.00 | 147.77 | E0705 | UE | 0.00 | 37.34 | E0855 | UE | 0.00 | 348.69 |
| E0660 | RR | 21.00 | 15.39 | E0720 | NU | 459.91 | 340.01 | E0856 | NU | 0.00 | 142.48 |
| E0660 | UE | 0.00 | 110.82 | E0720 | RR | 60.01 | 0.00 | E0856 | RR | 0.00 | 14.27 |
| E0665 | NU | 0.00 | 126.72 | E0730 | NU | 744.93 | 342.77 | E0856 | UE | 0.00 | 106.87 |
| E0665 | RR | 20.00 | 13.02 | E0730 | RR | 99.00 | 0.00 | E0860 | NU | 50.01 | 35.64 |
| E0665 | UE | 0.00 | 95.17 | E0730 | UE | 275.69 | 0.00 | E0860 | RR | 0.00 | 6.02 |
| E0666 | NU | 194.95 | 127.73 | E0731 | NU | 399.91 | 329.94 | E0860 | UE | 0.00 | 27.30 |
| E0666 | RR | 15.00 | 13.17 | E0740 | NU | 627.55 | 483.66 | E0870 | NU | 0.00 | 107.59 |
| E0666 | UE | 0.00 | 95.82 | E0740 | RR | 74.99 | 48.37 | E0870 | RR | 0.00 | 12.40 |
| E0667 | NU | 500.04 | 299.49 | E0740 | UE | 0.00 | 362.77 | E0870 | UE | 0.00 | 81.05 |
| E0667 | RR | 50.01 | 33.82 | E0744 | RR | 0.00 | 84.70 | E0880 | NU | 0.00 | 116.13 |
| E0667 | UE | 0.00 | 224.62 | E0745 | NU | 1139.68 | 0.00 | E0880 | RR | 0.00 | 18.23 |
| E0668 | NU | 499.92 | 408.74 | E0745 | RR | 176.66 | 82.80 | E0880 | UE | 0.00 | 87.90 |
| E0668 | RR | 0.00 | 40.34 | E0747 | NU | 5119.44 | 0.00 | E0890 | NU | 0.00 | 111.38 |
| E0668 | UE | 0.00 | 306.57 | E0748 | NU | 5249.63 | 0.00 | E0890 | RR | 0.00 | 30.37 |
| E0669 | NU | 299.93 | 169.56 | E0760 | NU | 4500.71 | 0.00 | E0890 | UE | 0.00 | 89.72 |
| E0669 | RR | 0.00 | 16.97 | E0762 | NU | 392.30 | 1017.10 | E0900 | NU | 0.00 | 118.51 |
| E0669 | UE | 0.00 | 127.20 | E0762 | RR | 0.00 | 101.72 | E0900 | RR | 0.00 | 25.55 |
| E0671 | NU | 499.92 | 384.20 | E0762 | UE | 0.00 | 762.80 | E0900 | UE | 0.00 | 88.91 |
| E0671 | RR | 0.00 | 38.43 | E0765 | NU | 0.00 | 77.82 | E0910 | RR | 30.50 | 18.50 |
| E0671 | UE | 0.00 | 288.14 | E0765 | RR | 0.00 | 7.80 | E0911 | RR | 56.00 | 46.11 |
| E0672 | NU | 0.00 | 298.53 | E0765 | UE | 0.00 | 58.39 | E0912 | RR | 206.00 | 105.89 |
| E0672 | RR | 0.00 | 29.86 | E0776 | NU | 124.96 | 132.43 | E0920 | RR | 98.99 | 42.68 |
| E0672 | UE | 0.00 | 223.91 | E0776 | RR | 33.99 | 17.25 | E0930 | RR | 0.00 | 42.27 |
| E0673 | NU | 364.93 | 248.06 | E0776 | UE | 0.00 | 97.43 | E0935 | RR | 50.00 | 21.03 |
| E0673 | RR | 62.49 | 24.81 | E0779 | RR | 25.99 | 15.48 | E0936 | | 80.00 | 0.00 |
| E0673 | UE | 0.00 | 186.07 | E0780 | NU | 20.00 | 9.59 | E0940 | RR | 45.00 | 32.16 |
| E0675 | RR | 524.95 | 355.71 | E0781 | RR | 500.04 | 245.01 | E0941 | RR | 46.24 | 40.16 |
| E0691 | NU | 689.71 | 831.20 | E0784 | NU | 6193.53 | 0.00 | E0942 | NU | 28.54 | 18.36 |
| E0691 | RR | 0.00 | 83.12 | E0784 | RR | 521.39 | 386.25 | E0942 | RR | 0.00 | 2.17 |
| E0691 | UE | 0.00 | 623.40 | E0785 | KF | 0.00 | 437.07 | E0942 | UE | 0.00 | 13.77 |
| E0692 | NU | 0.00 | 1043.74 | E0791 | RR | 439.98 | 292.49 | E0944 | NU | 51.99 | 42.44 |
| E0692 | RR | 0.00 | 104.37 | E0840 | NU | 0.00 | 67.79 | E0944 | RR | 0.00 | 4.26 |
| E0692 | UE | 0.00 | 782.82 | E0840 | RR | 0.00 | 15.10 | E0944 | UE | 0.00 | 31.82 |
| E0693 | NU | 2389.49 | 1286.66 | E0840 | UE | 0.00 | 50.81 | E0945 | NU | 0.00 | 41.00 |
| E0693 | RR | 0.00 | 128.67 | E0849 | NU | 125.00 | 476.66 | E0945 | RR | 0.00 | 4.11 |
| E0693 | UE | 0.00 | 965.00 | E0849 | RR | 0.00 | 47.67 | E0945 | UE | 0.00 | 31.74 |
| E0694 | NU | 0.00 | 4095.29 | E0849 | UE | 0.00 | 357.48 | E0946 | RR | 0.00 | 54.73 |

# APPENDIX 7 — NATIONAL AVERAGE PAYMENT TABLE FOR HCPCS

| Proc | Mod | Commercial | Medicare | Proc | Mod | Commercial | Medicare | Proc | Mod | Commercial | Medicare |
|---|---|---|---|---|---|---|---|---|---|---|---|
| E0947 | NU | 0.00 | 560.98 | E0969 | UE | 0.00 | 108.67 | E0995 | UE | 0.00 | 21.07 |
| E0947 | RR | 70.78 | 58.18 | E0971 | NU | 67.52 | 40.14 | E1002 | NU | 5251.10 | 3749.22 |
| E0947 | UE | 0.00 | 420.73 | E0971 | RR | 9.00 | 4.02 | E1002 | RR | 0.00 | 374.92 |
| E0948 | NU | 794.77 | 542.60 | E0971 | UE | 41.99 | 30.12 | E1002 | UE | 0.00 | 2811.91 |
| E0948 | RR | 125.00 | 54.24 | E0973 | NU | 118.05 | 106.35 | E1003 | NU | 0.00 | 4061.96 |
| E0948 | UE | 0.00 | 382.68 | E0973 | RR | 13.00 | 10.13 | E1003 | RR | 0.00 | 406.21 |
| E0950 | NU | 191.39 | 96.16 | E0973 | UE | 0.00 | 79.77 | E1003 | UE | 0.00 | 3046.47 |
| E0950 | RR | 13.01 | 9.63 | E0974 | NU | 86.98 | 72.53 | E1004 | NU | 0.00 | 4503.87 |
| E0950 | UE | 0.00 | 72.12 | E0974 | RR | 9.00 | 7.69 | E1004 | RR | 0.00 | 450.39 |
| E0951 | NU | 22.47 | 17.56 | E0974 | UE | 0.00 | 54.81 | E1004 | UE | 0.00 | 3377.89 |
| E0951 | RR | 2.15 | 1.82 | E0978 | NU | 49.99 | 39.50 | E1005 | NU | 0.00 | 4875.09 |
| E0951 | UE | 0.00 | 13.16 | E0978 | RR | 5.00 | 3.96 | E1005 | RR | 0.00 | 487.51 |
| E0952 | NU | 20.00 | 17.42 | E0978 | UE | 0.00 | 29.29 | E1005 | UE | 0.00 | 3656.32 |
| E0952 | RR | 0.00 | 1.82 | E0980 | NU | 0.00 | 30.58 | E1006 | NU | 0.00 | 5971.53 |
| E0952 | UE | 0.00 | 13.07 | E0980 | RR | 0.00 | 3.06 | E1006 | RR | 0.00 | 597.14 |
| E0955 | NU | 252.79 | 187.02 | E0980 | UE | 0.00 | 22.81 | E1006 | UE | 0.00 | 4478.65 |
| E0955 | RR | 24.99 | 18.72 | E0981 | NU | 71.38 | 43.62 | E1007 | NU | 10283.23 | 8085.68 |
| E0955 | UE | 0.00 | 140.26 | E0981 | RR | 0.00 | 4.44 | E1007 | RR | 0.00 | 808.57 |
| E0956 | NU | 130.96 | 91.19 | E0981 | UE | 0.00 | 33.03 | E1007 | UE | 0.00 | 6064.25 |
| E0956 | RR | 0.00 | 9.13 | E0982 | NU | 95.00 | 47.67 | E1008 | NU | 0.00 | 8086.40 |
| E0956 | UE | 0.00 | 68.39 | E0982 | RR | 0.00 | 4.77 | E1008 | RR | 0.00 | 808.64 |
| E0957 | NU | 175.04 | 127.59 | E0982 | UE | 0.00 | 35.74 | E1008 | UE | 0.00 | 6064.81 |
| E0957 | RR | 0.00 | 12.76 | E0983 | RR | 0.00 | 231.19 | E1010 | NU | 2309.40 | 1058.01 |
| E0957 | UE | 0.00 | 95.69 | E0984 | NU | 0.00 | 1767.29 | E1010 | RR | 0.00 | 105.80 |
| E0958 | RR | 50.00 | 40.36 | E0984 | RR | 0.00 | 164.27 | E1010 | UE | 0.00 | 793.52 |
| E0959 | NU | 0.00 | 40.90 | E0984 | UE | 0.00 | 1363.70 | E1014 | NU | 0.00 | 337.76 |
| E0959 | RR | 8.90 | 4.12 | E0985 | NU | 0.00 | 187.64 | E1014 | RR | 0.00 | 33.78 |
| E0959 | UE | 0.00 | 30.95 | E0985 | RR | 0.00 | 18.78 | E1014 | UE | 0.00 | 253.31 |
| E0960 | NU | 139.97 | 84.16 | E0985 | UE | 0.00 | 140.71 | E1015 | NU | 172.09 | 106.10 |
| E0960 | RR | 0.00 | 8.42 | E0986 | NU | 0.00 | 4499.42 | E1015 | RR | 0.00 | 10.60 |
| E0960 | UE | 0.00 | 63.12 | E0986 | RR | 0.00 | 449.95 | E1015 | UE | 0.00 | 79.57 |
| E0961 | NU | 30.34 | 27.51 | E0986 | UE | 0.00 | 3374.59 | E1016 | NU | 150.00 | 121.46 |
| E0961 | RR | 5.50 | 2.87 | E0990 | NU | 195.05 | 108.63 | E1016 | RR | 0.00 | 12.16 |
| E0961 | UE | 0.00 | 13.75 | E0990 | RR | 14.50 | 12.23 | E1016 | UE | 0.00 | 91.10 |
| E0966 | NU | 107.97 | 66.02 | E0990 | UE | 0.00 | 84.87 | E1020 | NU | 314.90 | 225.16 |
| E0966 | RR | 9.36 | 6.51 | E0992 | NU | 93.01 | 88.02 | E1020 | RR | 29.99 | 22.50 |
| E0966 | UE | 0.00 | 49.51 | E0992 | RR | 0.00 | 8.56 | E1020 | UE | 0.00 | 168.86 |
| E0967 | NU | 73.54 | 60.77 | E0992 | UE | 0.00 | 66.02 | E1028 | NU | 242.98 | 191.05 |
| E0967 | RR | 0.00 | 6.08 | E0994 | NU | 24.49 | 16.31 | E1028 | RR | 26.85 | 19.10 |
| E0967 | UE | 0.00 | 45.56 | E0994 | RR | 0.00 | 1.65 | E1028 | UE | 0.00 | 143.28 |
| E0968 | RR | 0.00 | 16.59 | E0994 | UE | 0.00 | 12.24 | E1029 | NU | 0.00 | 341.83 |
| E0969 | NU | 0.00 | 144.89 | E0995 | NU | 40.26 | 28.12 | E1029 | RR | 0.00 | 34.18 |
| E0969 | RR | 0.00 | 14.35 | E0995 | RR | 0.00 | 2.82 | E1029 | UE | 0.00 | 256.37 |

# APPENDIX 7 — NATIONAL AVERAGE PAYMENT TABLE FOR HCPCS

| Proc | Mod | Commercial | Medicare | Proc | Mod | Commercial | Medicare | Proc | Mod | Commercial | Medicare |
|------|-----|-----------|----------|------|-----|-----------|----------|------|-----|-----------|----------|
| E1030 | NU | 0.00 | 1077.88 | E1226 | UE | 0.00 | 378.51 | E1298 | NU | 0.00 | 391.88 |
| E1030 | RR | 0.00 | 107.79 | E1227 | NU | 0.00 | 256.69 | E1298 | RR | 0.00 | 40.10 |
| E1030 | UE | 0.00 | 808.42 | E1227 | RR | 0.00 | 25.67 | E1298 | UE | 0.00 | 293.90 |
| E1031 | RR | 54.99 | 46.72 | E1227 | UE | 0.00 | 192.54 | E1310 | NU | 0.00 | 1986.35 |
| E1035 | RR | 750.04 | 567.21 | E1228 | RR | 0.00 | 25.92 | E1310 | RR | 0.00 | 169.90 |
| E1037 | RR | 0.00 | 100.36 | E1230 | NU | 2499.28 | 2092.16 | E1310 | UE | 0.00 | 1489.76 |
| E1038 | RR | 54.99 | 16.68 | E1230 | RR | 222.36 | 205.77 | E1340 | | 20.00 | 0.00 |
| E1039 | RR | 56.84 | 31.64 | E1230 | UE | 0.00 | 1654.65 | E1353 | RR | 5.00 | 0.00 |
| E1050 | RR | 0.00 | 94.20 | E1232 | NU | 2535.62 | 1978.03 | E1353 | | 0.00 | 30.41 |
| E1060 | RR | 160.95 | 116.62 | E1232 | RR | 0.00 | 197.81 | E1355 | RR | 20.00 | 0.00 |
| E1070 | RR | 155.01 | 101.32 | E1232 | UE | 0.00 | 1483.54 | E1355 | | 0.00 | 22.90 |
| E1083 | RR | 0.00 | 72.84 | E1233 | NU | 2815.64 | 2049.55 | E1372 | NU | 0.00 | 150.81 |
| E1084 | RR | 130.01 | 90.75 | E1233 | RR | 0.00 | 204.95 | E1372 | RR | 49.00 | 21.92 |
| E1086 | RR | 108.04 | 0.00 | E1233 | UE | 0.00 | 1537.16 | E1372 | UE | 0.00 | 111.63 |
| E1087 | RR | 0.00 | 117.02 | E1234 | NU | 2898.83 | 1784.28 | E1390 | NU | 395.00 | 0.00 |
| E1088 | RR | 192.99 | 139.46 | E1234 | RR | 0.00 | 178.44 | E1390 | RR | 433.88 | 0.00 |
| E1090 | RR | 174.01 | 0.00 | E1234 | UE | 0.00 | 1338.20 | E1390 | UE | 671.30 | 0.00 |
| E1092 | RR | 172.04 | 118.87 | E1235 | NU | 0.00 | 1718.13 | E1391 | RR | 385.07 | 0.00 |
| E1093 | RR | 214.18 | 102.23 | E1235 | RR | 0.00 | 171.82 | E1392 | RR | 64.99 | 0.00 |
| E1100 | RR | 0.00 | 96.03 | E1235 | UE | 0.00 | 1288.59 | E1405 | RR | 0.00 | 234.35 |
| E1110 | RR | 143.01 | 94.04 | E1236 | NU | 1774.58 | 1515.83 | E1406 | RR | 0.00 | 215.39 |
| E1130 | RR | 64.00 | 0.00 | E1236 | RR | 290.00 | 151.58 | E1510 | RR | 1800.00 | 0.00 |
| E1140 | RR | 92.02 | 0.00 | E1236 | UE | 0.00 | 1136.87 | E1594 | RR | 583.20 | 0.00 |
| E1150 | RR | 104.98 | 75.46 | E1237 | NU | 0.00 | 1529.07 | E1610 | RR | 650.00 | 0.00 |
| E1160 | RR | 75.71 | 57.82 | E1237 | RR | 0.00 | 152.91 | E1634 | | 5.60 | 0.00 |
| E1161 | NU | 2958.45 | 2188.64 | E1237 | UE | 0.00 | 1146.82 | E1700 | NU | 0.00 | 318.98 |
| E1161 | RR | 268.70 | 218.87 | E1238 | NU | 2260.53 | 1515.83 | E1700 | RR | 0.00 | 31.29 |
| E1161 | UE | 0.00 | 1641.50 | E1238 | RR | 353.97 | 151.58 | E1700 | UE | 0.00 | 239.24 |
| E1170 | RR | 0.00 | 82.61 | E1238 | UE | 0.00 | 1136.87 | E1701 | | 9.00 | 9.82 |
| E1171 | RR | 0.00 | 74.14 | E1240 | RR | 159.03 | 95.30 | E1702 | | 0.00 | 20.88 |
| E1172 | RR | 0.00 | 90.61 | E1250 | RR | 107.03 | 0.00 | E1800 | RR | 394.97 | 113.32 |
| E1180 | RR | 0.00 | 93.74 | E1260 | RR | 122.04 | 0.00 | E1801 | RR | 248.03 | 119.33 |
| E1190 | RR | 0.00 | 108.29 | E1270 | RR | 144.00 | 73.02 | E1802 | RR | 515.00 | 302.29 |
| E1195 | RR | 0.00 | 116.21 | E1280 | RR | 168.02 | 121.42 | E1805 | RR | 394.98 | 116.87 |
| E1200 | RR | 0.00 | 80.49 | E1285 | RR | 214.02 | 0.00 | E1806 | RR | 172.03 | 97.97 |
| E1220 | | 6849.00 | 0.00 | E1290 | RR | 159.96 | 0.00 | E1810 | RR | 117.75 | 115.24 |
| E1221 | RR | 0.00 | 43.95 | E1295 | RR | 0.00 | 112.36 | E1811 | RR | 185.14 | 124.06 |
| E1222 | RR | 0.00 | 62.71 | E1296 | NU | 0.00 | 454.80 | E1812 | RR | 195.00 | 79.54 |
| E1223 | RR | 0.00 | 68.47 | E1296 | RR | 0.00 | 46.20 | E1815 | RR | 394.98 | 116.87 |
| E1224 | RR | 0.00 | 75.07 | E1296 | UE | 0.00 | 341.10 | E1816 | RR | 0.00 | 126.02 |
| E1225 | RR | 49.98 | 41.81 | E1297 | NU | 0.00 | 96.77 | E1818 | RR | 299.95 | 128.66 |
| E1226 | NU | 600.16 | 504.73 | E1297 | RR | 0.00 | 10.75 | E1820 | NU | 150.01 | 75.61 |
| E1226 | RR | 60.01 | 51.95 | E1297 | UE | 0.00 | 72.57 | E1820 | RR | 0.00 | 7.56 |

**Appendix 7 — National Average Payment Table for HCPCS**

| Proc | Mod | Commercial | Medicare | Proc | Mod | Commercial | Medicare | Proc | Mod | Commercial | Medicare |
|------|-----|-----------|----------|------|-----|-----------|----------|------|-----|-----------|----------|
| E1820 | UE | 0.00 | 56.71 | E2209 | UE | 0.00 | 74.35 | E2226 | RR | 0.00 | 3.51 |
| E1821 | NU | 0.00 | 97.36 | E2210 | NU | 9.10 | 6.06 | E2226 | UE | 0.00 | 26.33 |
| E1821 | RR | 0.00 | 9.72 | E2210 | RR | 0.00 | 0.61 | E2227 | NU | 0.00 | 1451.45 |
| E1821 | UE | 0.00 | 73.03 | E2210 | UE | 0.00 | 4.55 | E2227 | RR | 0.00 | 145.16 |
| E1825 | RR | 394.98 | 116.87 | E2211 | NU | 45.00 | 37.84 | E2227 | UE | 0.00 | 1088.56 |
| E1830 | RR | 394.98 | 116.87 | E2211 | RR | 0.00 | 3.71 | E2228 | NU | 0.00 | 866.04 |
| E1840 | RR | 700.05 | 354.01 | E2211 | UE | 0.00 | 27.11 | E2228 | RR | 0.00 | 86.60 |
| E1841 | RR | 0.00 | 419.03 | E2212 | NU | 7.71 | 5.44 | E2228 | UE | 0.00 | 649.56 |
| E1841 |  | 75.00 | 0.00 | E2212 | RR | 0.00 | 0.57 | E2310 | NU | 1344.83 | 1082.47 |
| E2000 | RR | 143.02 | 47.95 | E2212 | UE | 0.00 | 4.09 | E2310 | RR | 0.00 | 108.25 |
| E2100 | NU | 659.88 | 594.95 | E2213 | NU | 38.07 | 28.13 | E2310 | UE | 0.00 | 811.86 |
| E2100 | RR | 0.00 | 59.50 | E2213 | RR | 5.00 | 2.82 | E2311 | NU | 2650.19 | 2191.51 |
| E2100 | UE | 0.00 | 446.22 | E2213 | UE | 0.00 | 21.08 | E2311 | RR | 0.00 | 219.16 |
| E2101 | NU | 0.00 | 174.42 | E2214 | NU | 42.52 | 33.30 | E2311 | UE | 0.00 | 1643.64 |
| E2101 | RR | 0.00 | 17.45 | E2214 | RR | 0.00 | 3.67 | E2312 | NU | 0.00 | 1865.46 |
| E2101 | UE | 0.00 | 130.82 | E2214 | UE | 0.00 | 24.97 | E2312 | RR | 0.00 | 186.55 |
| E2120 | RR | 283.40 | 262.26 | E2215 | NU | 0.00 | 8.88 | E2312 | UE | 0.00 | 1399.12 |
| E2201 | NU | 390.08 | 345.12 | E2215 | RR | 0.00 | 0.88 | E2313 | NU | 0.00 | 296.24 |
| E2201 | RR | 44.77 | 34.51 | E2215 | UE | 0.00 | 6.64 | E2313 | RR | 0.00 | 29.63 |
| E2201 | UE | 0.00 | 258.85 | E2216 | NU | 125.00 | 0.00 | E2313 | UE | 0.00 | 222.18 |
| E2202 | NU | 0.00 | 438.43 | E2217 | NU | 64.10 | 0.00 | E2321 | NU | 1606.56 | 1469.92 |
| E2202 | RR | 50.00 | 43.85 | E2219 | NU | 58.00 | 38.71 | E2321 | RR | 0.00 | 147.00 |
| E2202 | UE | 0.00 | 328.84 | E2219 | RR | 0.00 | 4.37 | E2321 | UE | 0.00 | 1102.45 |
| E2203 | NU | 480.08 | 443.12 | E2219 | UE | 0.00 | 29.04 | E2322 | NU | 0.00 | 1304.59 |
| E2203 | RR | 0.00 | 44.30 | E2220 | NU | 35.65 | 26.38 | E2322 | RR | 0.00 | 130.46 |
| E2203 | UE | 0.00 | 332.34 | E2220 | RR | 0.00 | 2.55 | E2322 | UE | 0.00 | 978.45 |
| E2204 | NU | 0.00 | 752.40 | E2220 | UE | 0.00 | 20.18 | E2323 | NU | 79.99 | 63.98 |
| E2204 | RR | 0.00 | 75.25 | E2221 | NU | 44.99 | 23.64 | E2323 | RR | 0.00 | 6.40 |
| E2204 | UE | 0.00 | 564.30 | E2221 | RR | 0.00 | 2.39 | E2323 | UE | 0.00 | 47.98 |
| E2205 | NU | 0.00 | 30.22 | E2221 | UE | 0.00 | 17.74 | E2324 | NU | 0.00 | 40.54 |
| E2205 | RR | 0.00 | 3.01 | E2222 | NU | 42.80 | 19.48 | E2324 | RR | 0.00 | 4.04 |
| E2205 | UE | 0.00 | 22.68 | E2222 | RR | 0.00 | 1.94 | E2324 | UE | 0.00 | 30.41 |
| E2206 | NU | 51.60 | 37.63 | E2222 | UE | 0.00 | 14.63 | E2325 | NU | 0.00 | 1245.82 |
| E2206 | RR | 0.00 | 3.76 | E2223 | NU | 0.00 | 5.19 | E2325 | RR | 0.00 | 124.60 |
| E2206 | UE | 0.00 | 28.22 | E2223 | RR | 0.00 | 0.52 | E2325 | UE | 0.00 | 934.37 |
| E2207 | NU | 64.98 | 40.10 | E2223 | UE | 0.00 | 3.90 | E2326 | NU | 0.00 | 321.11 |
| E2207 | RR | 0.00 | 4.02 | E2224 | NU | 0.00 | 90.71 | E2326 | RR | 0.00 | 32.13 |
| E2207 | UE | 0.00 | 30.07 | E2224 | RR | 0.00 | 9.52 | E2326 | UE | 0.00 | 240.82 |
| E2208 | NU | 145.98 | 109.87 | E2224 | UE | 0.00 | 68.04 | E2327 | NU | 0.00 | 2416.45 |
| E2208 | RR | 16.00 | 10.98 | E2225 | NU | 0.00 | 16.10 | E2327 | RR | 0.00 | 241.65 |
| E2208 | UE | 0.00 | 82.41 | E2225 | RR | 0.00 | 1.61 | E2327 | UE | 0.00 | 1812.34 |
| E2209 | NU | 132.02 | 99.13 | E2225 | UE | 0.00 | 12.06 | E2328 | NU | 0.00 | 4583.67 |
| E2209 | RR | 15.00 | 9.94 | E2226 | NU | 69.50 | 35.10 | E2328 | RR | 0.00 | 458.36 |

# APPENDIX 7 — NATIONAL AVERAGE PAYMENT TABLE FOR HCPCS

| Proc | Mod | Commercial | Medicare | Proc | Mod | Commercial | Medicare | Proc | Mod | Commercial | Medicare |
|------|-----|-----------|----------|------|-----|-----------|----------|------|-----|-----------|----------|
| E2328 | UE | 0.00 | 3437.77 | E2367 | NU | 474.84 | 387.65 | E2385 | RR | 0.00 | 4.59 |
| E2329 | NU | 0.00 | 1633.67 | E2367 | RR | 0.00 | 38.77 | E2385 | UE | 0.00 | 34.33 |
| E2329 | RR | 0.00 | 163.37 | E2367 | UE | 0.00 | 290.74 | E2386 | NU | 173.10 | 139.22 |
| E2329 | UE | 0.00 | 1225.26 | E2368 | NU | 0.00 | 477.83 | E2386 | RR | 0.00 | 13.92 |
| E2330 | NU | 0.00 | 3165.44 | E2368 | RR | 0.00 | 47.80 | E2386 | UE | 0.00 | 104.41 |
| E2330 | RR | 0.00 | 316.54 | E2368 | UE | 0.00 | 358.38 | E2387 | NU | 90.00 | 62.43 |
| E2330 | UE | 0.00 | 2374.09 | E2369 | NU | 0.00 | 416.20 | E2387 | RR | 0.00 | 6.25 |
| E2340 | NU | 400.10 | 331.49 | E2369 | RR | 0.00 | 41.63 | E2387 | UE | 0.00 | 46.85 |
| E2340 | RR | 0.00 | 33.16 | E2369 | UE | 0.00 | 312.14 | E2388 | NU | 0.00 | 46.61 |
| E2340 | UE | 0.00 | 248.63 | E2370 | NU | 1000.00 | 742.63 | E2388 | RR | 0.00 | 4.66 |
| E2341 | NU | 0.00 | 497.26 | E2370 | RR | 0.00 | 74.27 | E2388 | UE | 0.00 | 34.97 |
| E2341 | RR | 0.00 | 49.73 | E2370 | UE | 0.00 | 556.96 | E2389 | NU | 0.00 | 25.31 |
| E2341 | UE | 0.00 | 372.95 | E2371 | NU | 0.00 | 139.44 | E2389 | RR | 0.00 | 2.54 |
| E2342 | NU | 528.97 | 414.38 | E2371 | RR | 0.00 | 13.95 | E2389 | UE | 0.00 | 18.97 |
| E2342 | RR | 0.00 | 41.44 | E2371 | UE | 0.00 | 104.58 | E2390 | NU | 0.00 | 39.58 |
| E2342 | UE | 0.00 | 310.79 | E2373 | NU | 0.00 | 650.26 | E2390 | RR | 0.00 | 3.96 |
| E2343 | NU | 0.00 | 663.02 | E2373 | RR | 0.00 | 65.02 | E2390 | UE | 0.00 | 29.67 |
| E2343 | RR | 0.00 | 66.30 | E2373 | UE | 0.00 | 487.70 | E2391 | NU | 50.00 | 18.97 |
| E2343 | UE | 0.00 | 497.26 | E2374 | NU | 0.00 | 493.97 | E2391 | RR | 0.00 | 1.90 |
| E2351 | NU | 0.00 | 646.24 | E2374 | RR | 0.00 | 49.40 | E2391 | UE | 0.00 | 14.23 |
| E2351 | RR | 0.00 | 64.64 | E2374 | UE | 0.00 | 370.49 | E2392 | NU | 80.80 | 49.84 |
| E2351 | UE | 0.00 | 484.67 | E2375 | NU | 1159.00 | 792.32 | E2392 | RR | 0.00 | 5.00 |
| E2360 | NU | 0.00 | 103.92 | E2375 | RR | 0.00 | 79.23 | E2392 | UE | 0.00 | 37.38 |
| E2360 | RR | 0.00 | 10.45 | E2375 | UE | 0.00 | 594.22 | E2394 | NU | 0.00 | 71.00 |
| E2360 | UE | 0.00 | 77.94 | E2376 | NU | 0.00 | 1241.60 | E2394 | RR | 0.00 | 7.12 |
| E2361 | NU | 170.95 | 129.01 | E2376 | RR | 0.00 | 124.17 | E2394 | UE | 0.00 | 53.25 |
| E2361 | RR | 17.43 | 12.91 | E2376 | UE | 0.00 | 931.22 | E2395 | NU | 90.80 | 50.46 |
| E2361 | UE | 0.00 | 96.78 | E2377 | NU | 791.00 | 449.28 | E2395 | RR | 0.00 | 5.05 |
| E2362 | NU | 0.00 | 85.08 | E2377 | RR | 0.00 | 44.92 | E2395 | UE | 0.00 | 37.86 |
| E2362 | RR | 0.00 | 8.51 | E2377 | UE | 0.00 | 336.98 | E2396 | NU | 0.00 | 61.52 |
| E2362 | UE | 0.00 | 63.81 | E2381 | NU | 90.00 | 70.47 | E2396 | RR | 0.00 | 6.60 |
| E2363 | NU | 230.04 | 172.05 | E2381 | RR | 0.00 | 7.06 | E2396 | UE | 0.00 | 46.15 |
| E2363 | RR | 0.00 | 17.22 | E2381 | UE | 0.00 | 52.86 | E2397 | NU | 0.00 | 383.07 |
| E2363 | UE | 0.00 | 129.04 | E2382 | NU | 60.00 | 19.21 | E2397 | RR | 0.00 | 38.31 |
| E2364 | NU | 112.30 | 103.92 | E2382 | RR | 0.00 | 1.92 | E2397 | UE | 0.00 | 287.30 |
| E2364 | RR | 0.00 | 10.45 | E2382 | UE | 0.00 | 14.40 | E2399 | | 1350.00 | 0.00 |
| E2364 | UE | 0.00 | 77.94 | E2383 | NU | 181.10 | 140.49 | E2402 | RR | 3870.70 | 1587.73 |
| E2365 | NU | 149.02 | 103.76 | E2383 | RR | 0.00 | 14.05 | E2500 | NU | 0.00 | 361.73 |
| E2365 | RR | 11.22 | 10.38 | E2383 | UE | 0.00 | 105.37 | E2500 | RR | 0.00 | 36.18 |
| E2365 | UE | 0.00 | 77.84 | E2384 | NU | 81.50 | 74.84 | E2500 | UE | 0.00 | 271.30 |
| E2366 | NU | 300.04 | 243.85 | E2384 | RR | 0.00 | 7.50 | E2502 | NU | 0.00 | 1106.12 |
| E2366 | RR | 0.00 | 24.45 | E2384 | UE | 0.00 | 56.13 | E2502 | RR | 0.00 | 110.62 |
| E2366 | UE | 0.00 | 182.89 | E2385 | NU | 0.00 | 45.79 | E2502 | UE | 0.00 | 829.60 |

# APPENDIX 7 — NATIONAL AVERAGE PAYMENT TABLE FOR HCPCS

| Proc | Mod | Commercial | Medicare | Proc | Mod | Commercial | Medicare | Proc | Mod | Commercial | Medicare |
|------|-----|-----------|----------|------|-----|-----------|----------|------|-----|-----------|----------|
| E2504 | NU | 0.00 | 1459.12 | E2612 | NU | 0.00 | 390.85 | G0141 | | 50.00 | 0.00 |
| E2504 | RR | 0.00 | 145.93 | E2612 | RR | 0.00 | 39.08 | G0143 | | 65.00 | 28.31 |
| E2504 | UE | 0.00 | 1094.32 | E2612 | UE | 0.00 | 293.13 | G0144 | | 45.00 | 29.85 |
| E2506 | NU | 0.00 | 2139.49 | E2613 | NU | 495.00 | 363.56 | G0145 | | 70.00 | 37.01 |
| E2506 | RR | 0.00 | 213.95 | E2613 | RR | 0.00 | 36.36 | G0147 | | 0.00 | 15.90 |
| E2506 | UE | 0.00 | 1604.59 | E2613 | UE | 0.00 | 272.67 | G0148 | | 0.00 | 21.23 |
| E2508 | NU | 0.00 | 3308.37 | E2614 | NU | 367.00 | 503.14 | G0151 | | 50.00 | 0.00 |
| E2508 | RR | 0.00 | 330.85 | E2614 | RR | 0.00 | 50.32 | G0152 | | 50.00 | 0.00 |
| E2508 | UE | 0.00 | 2481.29 | E2614 | UE | 0.00 | 377.37 | G0153 | | 50.00 | 0.00 |
| E2510 | NU | 7392.62 | 6260.63 | E2615 | NU | 646.80 | 418.40 | G0154 | | 35.10 | 0.00 |
| E2510 | RR | 0.00 | 626.06 | E2615 | RR | 0.00 | 41.85 | G0155 | | 100.00 | 0.00 |
| E2510 | UE | 0.00 | 4695.47 | E2615 | UE | 0.00 | 313.79 | G0156 | | 15.00 | 0.00 |
| E2512 | NU | 477.00 | 0.00 | E2616 | NU | 0.00 | 562.94 | G0166 | | 350.00 | 0.00 |
| E2512 | RR | 14.50 | 0.00 | E2616 | RR | 0.00 | 56.30 | G0168 | | 132.00 | 0.00 |
| E2599 | | 145.00 | 0.00 | E2616 | UE | 0.00 | 422.22 | G0175 | | 20.30 | 0.00 |
| E2601 | NU | 97.40 | 56.58 | E2617 | | 1029.60 | 0.00 | G0176 | | 66.50 | 0.00 |
| E2601 | RR | 0.00 | 5.67 | E2618 | | 140.00 | 0.00 | G0177 | | 45.00 | 0.00 |
| E2601 | UE | 0.00 | 42.43 | E2619 | NU | 79.00 | 47.47 | G0179 | | 80.00 | 0.00 |
| E2602 | NU | 0.00 | 110.45 | E2619 | RR | 0.00 | 4.75 | G0180 | | 105.00 | 0.00 |
| E2602 | RR | 0.00 | 11.05 | E2619 | UE | 0.00 | 35.62 | G0181 | | 150.00 | 0.00 |
| E2602 | UE | 0.00 | 82.84 | E2620 | NU | 0.00 | 506.63 | G0182 | | 165.00 | 0.00 |
| E2603 | NU | 250.00 | 140.22 | E2620 | RR | 0.00 | 50.66 | G0202 | | 270.00 | 0.00 |
| E2603 | RR | 0.00 | 14.03 | E2620 | UE | 0.00 | 379.98 | G0204 | | 310.00 | 0.00 |
| E2603 | UE | 0.00 | 105.17 | E2621 | NU | 0.00 | 531.66 | G0206 | | 247.00 | 0.00 |
| E2604 | NU | 0.00 | 174.28 | E2621 | RR | 0.00 | 53.16 | G0237 | | 38.00 | 0.00 |
| E2604 | RR | 0.00 | 17.42 | E2621 | UE | 0.00 | 398.75 | G0238 | | 50.00 | 0.00 |
| E2604 | UE | 0.00 | 130.73 | G0008 | | 20.00 | 0.00 | G0239 | | 35.00 | 0.00 |
| E2605 | NU | 451.40 | 248.98 | G0009 | | 20.00 | 0.00 | G0245 | | 95.00 | 0.00 |
| E2605 | RR | 0.00 | 24.91 | G0010 | | 20.00 | 0.00 | G0246 | | 60.00 | 0.00 |
| E2605 | UE | 0.00 | 186.77 | G0027 | | 19.01 | 9.09 | G0247 | | 56.70 | 0.00 |
| E2606 | NU | 0.00 | 388.44 | G0101 | | 66.01 | 0.00 | G0248 | | 400.00 | 0.00 |
| E2606 | RR | 0.00 | 38.86 | G0102 | | 35.00 | 0.00 | G0249 | | 280.00 | 0.00 |
| E2606 | UE | 0.00 | 291.32 | G0103 | | 83.00 | 25.70 | G0250 | | 23.00 | 0.00 |
| E2607 | NU | 418.00 | 268.11 | G0104 | | 239.98 | 0.00 | G0255 | | 400.00 | 0.00 |
| E2607 | RR | 0.00 | 26.82 | G0105 | | 855.12 | 0.00 | G0260 | | 1408.00 | 0.00 |
| E2607 | UE | 0.00 | 201.09 | G0108 | | 70.00 | 0.00 | G0268 | | 90.00 | 0.00 |
| E2608 | NU | 0.00 | 321.99 | G0109 | | 40.00 | 0.00 | G0269 | | 150.00 | 0.00 |
| E2608 | RR | 0.00 | 32.19 | G0117 | | 53.00 | 0.00 | G0270 | | 35.00 | 0.00 |
| E2608 | UE | 0.00 | 241.49 | G0121 | | 859.77 | 0.00 | G0271 | | 14.40 | 0.00 |
| E2609 | | 981.00 | 0.00 | G0123 | | 58.99 | 28.31 | G0275 | | 39.00 | 0.00 |
| E2611 | NU | 374.80 | 288.93 | G0127 | | 32.00 | 0.00 | G0278 | | 40.00 | 0.00 |
| E2611 | RR | 0.00 | 28.89 | G0128 | | 13.80 | 0.00 | G0281 | | 25.00 | 0.00 |
| E2611 | UE | 0.00 | 216.72 | G0130 | | 100.00 | 0.00 | G0282 | | 30.00 | 0.00 |

| Proc | Mod | Commercial | Medicare | Proc | Mod | Commercial | Medicare | Proc | Mod | Commercial | Medicare |
|------|-----|-----------|----------|------|-----|-----------|----------|------|-----|-----------|----------|
| G0283 | | 30.00 | 0.00 | G8281 | | 100.00 | 0.00 | H0039 | | 24.60 | 0.00 |
| G0288 | | 650.00 | 0.00 | G9001 | | 129.80 | 0.00 | H0040 | | 70.30 | 0.00 |
| G0289 | | 2483.00 | 0.00 | G9002 | | 108.30 | 0.00 | H0045 | | 144.00 | 0.00 |
| G0290 | | 4000.00 | 0.00 | G9007 | | 75.00 | 0.00 | H0047 | | 17.00 | 0.00 |
| G0293 | | 30.00 | 0.00 | G9008 | | 38.50 | 0.00 | H0048 | | 20.00 | 0.00 |
| G0306 | | 34.00 | 10.86 | G9012 | | 12.50 | 0.00 | H1000 | | 75.00 | 0.00 |
| G0307 | | 34.00 | 9.04 | G9016 | | 40.00 | 0.00 | H1001 | | 152.00 | 0.00 |
| G0317 | | 575.00 | 0.00 | G9035 | | 113.00 | 0.00 | H1002 | | 70.00 | 0.00 |
| G0318 | | 480.00 | 0.00 | G9043 | | 37.50 | 0.00 | H1003 | | 16.00 | 0.00 |
| G0319 | | 400.00 | 0.00 | G9044 | | 37.50 | 0.00 | H2000 | | 123.60 | 0.00 |
| G0321 | | 1037.00 | 0.00 | G9051 | | 23.00 | 0.00 | H2010 | | 20.60 | 0.00 |
| G0323 | | 500.00 | 0.00 | G9052 | | 23.00 | 0.00 | H2011 | | 54.00 | 0.00 |
| G0325 | | 47.00 | 0.00 | G9056 | | 23.00 | 0.00 | H2012 | | 75.00 | 0.00 |
| G0326 | | 66.00 | 0.00 | G9066 | | 23.00 | 0.00 | H2014 | | 20.00 | 0.00 |
| G0327 | | 20.00 | 0.00 | G9071 | | 23.00 | 0.00 | H2015 | | 19.30 | 0.00 |
| G0328 | QW | 0.00 | 22.22 | G9072 | | 23.00 | 0.00 | H2016 | | 0.30 | 0.00 |
| G0328 | | 45.00 | 22.22 | G9075 | | 23.00 | 0.00 | H2017 | | 10.00 | 0.00 |
| G0332 | | 133.00 | 0.00 | G9086 | | 23.00 | 0.00 | H2018 | | 75.00 | 0.00 |
| G0333 | | 68.00 | 0.00 | G9098 | | 23.00 | 0.00 | H2019 | | 27.50 | 0.00 |
| G0340 | | 10000.00 | 0.00 | H0001 | | 151.00 | 0.00 | H2020 | | 158.90 | 0.00 |
| G0344 | | 155.00 | 0.00 | H0002 | | 269.00 | 0.00 | H2021 | | 20.10 | 0.00 |
| G0364 | | 41.00 | 0.00 | H0003 | | 50.00 | 0.00 | H2024 | | 35.80 | 0.00 |
| G0365 | | 449.00 | 0.00 | H0004 | | 24.00 | 0.00 | H2025 | | 26.50 | 0.00 |
| G0366 | | 60.00 | 0.00 | H0005 | | 64.00 | 0.00 | H2026 | | 46.90 | 0.00 |
| G0367 | | 38.00 | 0.00 | H0006 | | 18.00 | 0.00 | H2030 | | 2.50 | 0.00 |
| G0368 | | 24.00 | 0.00 | H0010 | | 48.70 | 0.00 | H2032 | | 8.30 | 0.00 |
| G0372 | | 30.00 | 0.00 | H0011 | | 354.00 | 0.00 | H2035 | | 160.00 | 0.00 |
| G0375 | | 25.00 | 0.00 | H0014 | | 250.00 | 0.00 | H2036 | | 350.00 | 0.00 |
| G0376 | | 72.00 | 0.00 | H0015 | | 175.00 | 0.00 | J0120 | | 23.10 | 0.00 |
| G0377 | | 25.00 | 0.00 | H0017 | | 104.10 | 0.00 | J0129 | | 40.00 | 0.00 |
| G0378 | | 33.50 | 0.00 | H0018 | | 240.00 | 0.00 | J0132 | | 2.18 | 0.00 |
| G0379 | | 100.00 | 0.00 | H0019 | | 100.00 | 0.00 | J0133 | | 278.30 | 0.00 |
| G0380 | | 100.00 | 0.00 | H0020 | | 12.90 | 0.00 | J0135 | | 644.28 | 0.00 |
| G0381 | | 120.00 | 0.00 | H0022 | | 73.00 | 0.00 | J0150 | | 54.99 | 0.00 |
| G0382 | | 137.80 | 0.00 | H0023 | | 163.30 | 0.00 | J0152 | | 136.70 | 0.00 |
| G0389 | | 173.00 | 0.00 | H0025 | | 2.70 | 0.00 | J0170 | | 4.00 | 0.00 |
| G0392 | | 5331.00 | 0.00 | H0031 | | 48.00 | 0.00 | J0180 | | 145.01 | 0.00 |
| G0393 | | 3454.00 | 0.00 | H0032 | | 20.00 | 0.00 | J0200 | | 25.00 | 0.00 |
| G0394 | | 15.00 | 4.54 | H0033 | | 15.00 | 0.00 | J0207 | | 1097.66 | 0.00 |
| G8152 | | 1.00 | 0.00 | H0034 | | 23.00 | 0.00 | J0210 | | 24.00 | 0.00 |
| G8271 | | 1.00 | 0.00 | H0035 | | 11.00 | 0.00 | J0215 | | 46.67 | 0.00 |
| G8275 | | 100.00 | 0.00 | H0036 | | 13.10 | 0.00 | J0256 | | 6.50 | 0.00 |
| G8278 | | 100.00 | 0.00 | H0037 | | 200.00 | 0.00 | J0270 | | 3.88 | 0.00 |

| Proc | Mod | Commercial | Medicare | Proc | Mod | Commercial | Medicare | Proc | Mod | Commercial | Medicare |
|------|-----|-----------|----------|------|-----|-----------|----------|------|-----|-----------|----------|
| J0275 | | 38.40 | 0.00 | J0694 | | 13.72 | 0.00 | J1094 | | 1.00 | 0.00 |
| J0278 | | 22.88 | 0.00 | J0696 | | 23.91 | 0.00 | J1100 | | 1.00 | 0.00 |
| J0280 | | 3.00 | 0.00 | J0697 | | 15.00 | 0.00 | J1110 | | 60.01 | 0.00 |
| J0282 | | 0.90 | 0.00 | J0698 | | 25.00 | 0.00 | J1120 | | 33.99 | 0.00 |
| J0285 | | 39.20 | 0.00 | J0702 | | 10.00 | 0.00 | J1160 | | 5.00 | 0.00 |
| J0287 | | 42.50 | 0.00 | J0704 | | 2.00 | 0.00 | J1165 | | 1.01 | 0.00 |
| J0289 | | 54.00 | 0.00 | J0706 | | 5.00 | 0.00 | J1170 | | 2.17 | 0.00 |
| J0290 | | 5.82 | 0.00 | J0710 | | 7.00 | 0.00 | J1180 | | 7.00 | 0.00 |
| J0295 | | 12.28 | 0.00 | J0713 | | 10.16 | 0.00 | J1190 | | 419.91 | 0.00 |
| J0330 | | 0.91 | 0.00 | J0715 | | 13.48 | 0.00 | J1200 | | 3.00 | 0.00 |
| J0348 | | 2.45 | 0.00 | J0720 | | 20.00 | 0.00 | J1212 | | 79.98 | 0.00 |
| J0360 | | 25.00 | 0.00 | J0725 | | 6.00 | 0.00 | J1230 | | 3.50 | 0.00 |
| J0364 | | 3.74 | 0.00 | J0735 | | 89.99 | 0.00 | J1240 | | 6.00 | 0.00 |
| J0390 | | 75.00 | 0.00 | J0740 | | 1864.71 | 0.00 | J1245 | | 40.01 | 0.00 |
| J0456 | | 51.19 | 0.00 | J0743 | | 30.58 | 0.00 | J1250 | | 13.77 | 0.00 |
| J0460 | | 2.00 | 0.00 | J0744 | | 12.76 | 0.00 | J1260 | | 11.77 | 0.00 |
| J0470 | | 65.00 | 0.00 | J0760 | | 15.00 | 0.00 | J1265 | | 3.43 | 0.00 |
| J0475 | | 398.40 | 0.00 | J0770 | | 64.98 | 0.00 | J1270 | | 12.00 | 0.00 |
| J0476 | | 76.52 | 0.00 | J0780 | | 15.00 | 0.00 | J1300 | | 419.00 | 0.00 |
| J0500 | | 25.00 | 0.00 | J0795 | | 8.00 | 0.00 | J1325 | | 26.90 | 0.00 |
| J0515 | | 15.00 | 0.00 | J0800 | | 299.93 | 0.00 | J1327 | | 47.60 | 0.00 |
| J0530 | | 35.00 | 0.00 | J0835 | | 130.03 | 0.00 | J1330 | | 5.00 | 0.00 |
| J0540 | | 56.00 | 0.00 | J0850 | | 1124.13 | 0.00 | J1335 | | 89.75 | 0.00 |
| J0550 | | 91.51 | 0.00 | J0878 | | 0.81 | 0.00 | J1364 | | 9.53 | 0.00 |
| J0560 | | 35.01 | 0.00 | J0881 | | 10.00 | 0.00 | J1380 | | 15.00 | 0.00 |
| J0570 | | 60.01 | 0.00 | J0882 | | 12.00 | 0.00 | J1390 | | 20.00 | 0.00 |
| J0580 | | 102.02 | 0.00 | J0885 | | 23.01 | 0.00 | J1410 | | 79.96 | 0.00 |
| J0583 | | 3.01 | 0.00 | J0886 | | 39.47 | 0.00 | J1435 | | 1.25 | 0.00 |
| J0585 | | 8.00 | 0.00 | J0894 | | 56.01 | 0.00 | J1438 | | 202.00 | 0.00 |
| J0587 | | 15.00 | 0.00 | J0895 | | 28.20 | 0.00 | J1440 | | 356.10 | 0.00 |
| J0592 | | 2.90 | 0.00 | J0900 | | 20.00 | 0.00 | J1441 | | 579.82 | 0.00 |
| J0594 | | 27.00 | 0.00 | J0945 | | 2.50 | 0.00 | J1450 | | 93.11 | 0.00 |
| J0595 | | 10.00 | 0.00 | J0970 | | 32.00 | 0.00 | J1455 | | 11.68 | 0.00 |
| J0600 | | 60.00 | 0.00 | J1000 | | 4.00 | 0.00 | J1457 | | 2.00 | 0.00 |
| J0610 | | 0.12 | 0.00 | J1020 | | 6.00 | 0.00 | J1458 | | 362.40 | 0.00 |
| J0620 | | 25.01 | 0.00 | J1030 | | 11.00 | 0.00 | J1460 | | 3.90 | 0.00 |
| J0630 | | 45.00 | 0.00 | J1040 | | 20.00 | 0.00 | J1470 | | 41.00 | 0.00 |
| J0636 | | 5.80 | 0.00 | J1051 | | 25.00 | 0.00 | J1480 | | 60.00 | 0.00 |
| J0637 | | 64.61 | 0.00 | J1055 | | 80.01 | 0.00 | J1490 | | 71.00 | 0.00 |
| J0640 | | 6.00 | 0.00 | J1056 | | 71.00 | 0.00 | J1520 | | 55.00 | 0.00 |
| J0670 | | 10.00 | 0.00 | J1060 | | 20.00 | 0.00 | J1530 | | 20.00 | 0.00 |
| J0690 | | 5.00 | 0.00 | J1070 | | 12.00 | 0.00 | J1550 | | 144.50 | 0.00 |
| J0692 | | 5.71 | 0.00 | J1080 | | 23.18 | 0.00 | J1560 | | 117.50 | 0.00 |

# APPENDIX 7 — NATIONAL AVERAGE PAYMENT TABLE FOR HCPCS

| Proc | Mod | Commercial | Medicare | Proc | Mod | Commercial | Medicare | Proc | Mod | Commercial | Medicare |
|------|-----|-----------|----------|------|-----|-----------|----------|------|-----|-----------|----------|
| J1561 | | 89.98 | 0.00 | J1885 | | 10.00 | 0.00 | J2425 | | 13.00 | 0.00 |
| J1562 | | 15.00 | 0.00 | J1890 | | 10.00 | 0.00 | J2430 | | 523.90 | 0.00 |
| J1565 | | 35.50 | 0.00 | J1931 | | 28.10 | 0.00 | J2440 | | 6.00 | 0.00 |
| J1566 | | 101.00 | 0.00 | J1940 | | 2.00 | 0.00 | J2460 | | 25.00 | 0.00 |
| J1567 | | 85.00 | 0.00 | J1945 | | 191.04 | 0.00 | J2469 | | 59.98 | 0.00 |
| J1568 | | 94.99 | 0.00 | J1950 | | 619.26 | 0.00 | J2501 | | 16.25 | 0.00 |
| J1569 | | 100.28 | 0.00 | J1955 | | 43.05 | 0.00 | J2503 | | 1506.83 | 0.00 |
| J1570 | | 62.17 | 0.00 | J1956 | | 38.30 | 0.00 | J2504 | | 233.42 | 0.00 |
| J1572 | | 113.40 | 0.00 | J1980 | | 20.00 | 0.00 | J2505 | | 5491.64 | 0.00 |
| J1580 | | 9.00 | 0.00 | J2001 | | 10.00 | 0.00 | J2510 | | 20.00 | 0.00 |
| J1590 | | 2.40 | 0.00 | J2010 | | 13.00 | 0.00 | J2513 | | 6.20 | 0.00 |
| J1595 | | 1959.60 | 0.00 | J2020 | | 64.30 | 0.00 | J2515 | | 25.00 | 0.00 |
| J1600 | | 49.98 | 0.00 | J2060 | | 15.00 | 0.00 | J2540 | | 4.88 | 0.00 |
| J1610 | | 134.98 | 0.00 | J2150 | | 7.00 | 0.00 | J2543 | | 13.50 | 0.00 |
| J1626 | | 25.00 | 0.00 | J2170 | | 15.53 | 0.00 | J2545 | | 114.99 | 0.00 |
| J1630 | | 16.23 | 0.00 | J2175 | | 2.00 | 0.00 | J2550 | | 5.00 | 0.00 |
| J1631 | | 30.99 | 0.00 | J2180 | | 15.00 | 0.00 | J2560 | | 14.00 | 0.00 |
| J1640 | | 17.00 | 0.00 | J2185 | | 8.67 | 0.00 | J2590 | | 6.00 | 0.00 |
| J1642 | | 1.00 | 0.00 | J2210 | | 10.00 | 0.00 | J2597 | | 13.00 | 0.00 |
| J1644 | | 1.00 | 0.00 | J2248 | | 2.46 | 0.00 | J2650 | | 10.00 | 0.00 |
| J1645 | | 27.57 | 0.00 | J2250 | | 2.00 | 0.00 | J2670 | | 50.00 | 0.00 |
| J1650 | | 12.64 | 0.00 | J2260 | | 128.79 | 0.00 | J2675 | | 7.76 | 0.00 |
| J1652 | | 13.74 | 0.00 | J2270 | | 4.30 | 0.00 | J2680 | | 12.00 | 0.00 |
| J1655 | | 9.00 | 0.00 | J2271 | | 12.75 | 0.00 | J2690 | | 5.00 | 0.00 |
| J1670 | | 125.01 | 0.00 | J2275 | | 13.00 | 0.00 | J2700 | | 5.15 | 0.00 |
| J1700 | | 0.44 | 0.00 | J2278 | | 12.78 | 0.00 | J2710 | | 3.08 | 0.00 |
| J1710 | | 10.00 | 0.00 | J2280 | | 35.00 | 0.00 | J2724 | | 31.60 | 0.00 |
| J1720 | | 5.00 | 0.00 | J2300 | | 1.73 | 0.00 | J2725 | | 60.00 | 0.00 |
| J1740 | | 416.66 | 0.00 | J2310 | | 12.65 | 0.00 | J2760 | | 43.00 | 0.00 |
| J1743 | | 547.68 | 0.00 | J2315 | | 2.20 | 0.00 | J2765 | | 4.10 | 0.00 |
| J1745 | | 99.98 | 0.00 | J2320 | | 7.80 | 0.00 | J2770 | | 140.99 | 0.00 |
| J1751 | | 40.00 | 0.00 | J2321 | | 25.00 | 0.00 | J2778 | | 500.18 | 0.00 |
| J1752 | | 40.00 | 0.00 | J2322 | | 40.00 | 0.00 | J2780 | | 4.00 | 0.00 |
| J1756 | | 1.20 | 0.00 | J2323 | | 15.33 | 0.00 | J2783 | | 347.94 | 0.00 |
| J1785 | | 4.00 | 0.00 | J2325 | | 65.00 | 0.00 | J2788 | | 65.01 | 0.00 |
| J1790 | | 6.23 | 0.00 | J2353 | | 216.86 | 0.00 | J2790 | | 157.98 | 0.00 |
| J1800 | | 15.00 | 0.00 | J2354 | | 10.01 | 0.00 | J2792 | | 28.01 | 0.00 |
| J1810 | | 25.00 | 0.00 | J2355 | | 499.89 | 0.00 | J2794 | | 5.67 | 0.00 |
| J1815 | | 0.70 | 0.00 | J2357 | | 18.17 | 0.00 | J2795 | | 0.25 | 0.00 |
| J1817 | | 7.40 | 0.00 | J2360 | | 25.00 | 0.00 | J2800 | | 20.00 | 0.00 |
| J1825 | | 457.35 | 0.00 | J2370 | | 2.00 | 0.00 | J2805 | | 103.95 | 0.00 |
| J1830 | | 119.00 | 0.00 | J2400 | | 15.00 | 0.00 | J2810 | | 0.40 | 0.00 |
| J1840 | | 5.58 | 0.00 | J2405 | | 12.00 | 0.00 | J2820 | | 50.99 | 0.00 |

# APPENDIX 7 — NATIONAL AVERAGE PAYMENT TABLE FOR HCPCS

| Proc | Mod | Commercial | Medicare | Proc | Mod | Commercial | Medicare | Proc | Mod | Commercial | Medicare |
|------|-----|-----------|----------|------|-----|-----------|----------|------|-----|-----------|----------|
| J2850 | | 65.00 | 0.00 | J3471 | | 0.36 | 0.00 | J7507 | | 4.79 | 0.00 |
| J2910 | | 31.00 | 0.00 | J3475 | | 1.10 | 0.00 | J7509 | | 0.92 | 0.00 |
| J2916 | | 15.00 | 0.00 | J3480 | | 1.00 | 0.00 | J7510 | | 0.17 | 0.00 |
| J2920 | | 5.00 | 0.00 | J3485 | | 3.54 | 0.00 | J7511 | | 438.05 | 0.00 |
| J2930 | | 10.16 | 0.00 | J3487 | | 406.92 | 0.00 | J7513 | | 650.22 | 0.00 |
| J2941 | | 65.84 | 0.00 | J3488 | | 359.90 | 0.00 | J7515 | | 1.58 | 0.00 |
| J2950 | | 12.00 | 0.00 | J3530 | | 40.00 | 0.00 | J7516 | | 27.29 | 0.00 |
| J2997 | | 79.99 | 0.00 | J3535 | | 10.30 | 0.00 | J7517 | | 3.72 | 0.00 |
| J3000 | | 7.73 | 0.00 | J7030 | | 14.06 | 0.00 | J7518 | | 3.21 | 0.00 |
| J3010 | | 3.00 | 0.00 | J7040 | | 18.00 | 0.00 | J7520 | | 9.59 | 0.00 |
| J3030 | | 84.99 | 0.00 | J7042 | | 13.00 | 0.00 | J7525 | | 503.95 | 0.00 |
| J3070 | | 25.00 | 0.00 | J7050 | | 15.00 | 0.00 | J7602 | | 0.30 | 0.00 |
| J3105 | | 74.24 | 0.00 | J7060 | | 19.00 | 0.00 | J7603 | | 1.10 | 0.00 |
| J3110 | | 10.65 | 0.00 | J7070 | | 18.00 | 0.00 | J7604 | | 179.80 | 0.00 |
| J3120 | | 16.49 | 0.00 | J7120 | | 25.00 | 0.00 | J7605 | | 6.30 | 0.00 |
| J3130 | | 25.00 | 0.00 | J7130 | | 5.00 | 0.00 | J7607 | | 6.00 | 0.00 |
| J3140 | | 20.00 | 0.00 | J7187 | | 1.40 | 0.00 | J7608 | | 5.60 | 0.00 |
| J3150 | | 2.00 | 0.00 | J7189 | | 1.70 | 0.00 | J7609 | | 0.80 | 0.00 |
| J3230 | | 7.37 | 0.00 | J7190 | | 1.62 | 0.00 | J7610 | | 1.20 | 0.00 |
| J3240 | | 954.39 | 0.00 | J7192 | | 1.47 | 0.00 | J7611 | | 0.95 | 0.00 |
| J3243 | | 59.39 | 0.00 | J7193 | | 1.27 | 0.00 | J7612 | | 5.00 | 0.00 |
| J3250 | | 8.00 | 0.00 | J7195 | | 1.13 | 0.00 | J7613 | | 1.08 | 0.00 |
| J3260 | | 7.75 | 0.00 | J7198 | | 1.47 | 0.00 | J7614 | | 2.50 | 0.00 |
| J3265 | | 6.50 | 0.00 | J7300 | | 500.18 | 0.00 | J7615 | | 2.00 | 0.00 |
| J3285 | | 100.88 | 0.00 | J7302 | | 600.05 | 0.00 | J7620 | | 4.00 | 0.00 |
| J3301 | | 4.00 | 0.00 | J7303 | | 42.02 | 0.00 | J7624 | | 2.10 | 0.00 |
| J3302 | | 1.00 | 0.00 | J7304 | | 17.00 | 0.00 | J7626 | | 6.22 | 0.00 |
| J3303 | | 5.00 | 0.00 | J7307 | | 785.00 | 0.00 | J7627 | | 5.24 | 0.00 |
| J3310 | | 15.00 | 0.00 | J7308 | | 199.97 | 0.00 | J7628 | | 4.00 | 0.00 |
| J3315 | | 666.39 | 0.00 | J7319 | | 261.70 | 0.00 | J7631 | | 0.77 | 0.00 |
| J3320 | | 10.00 | 0.00 | J7321 | | 231.99 | 0.00 | J7633 | | 5.00 | 0.00 |
| J3355 | | 63.18 | 0.00 | J7322 | | 300.10 | 0.00 | J7634 | | 5.00 | 0.00 |
| J3360 | | 3.00 | 0.00 | J7323 | | 225.04 | 0.00 | J7635 | | 0.70 | 0.00 |
| J3370 | | 10.19 | 0.00 | J7324 | | 335.00 | 0.00 | J7636 | | 10.00 | 0.00 |
| J3396 | | 12.00 | 0.00 | J7330 | | 49375.00 | 0.00 | J7637 | | 3.00 | 0.00 |
| J3400 | | 25.00 | 0.00 | J7341 | | 6.00 | 0.00 | J7638 | | 0.40 | 0.00 |
| J3410 | | 2.00 | 0.00 | J7343 | | 55.00 | 0.00 | J7639 | | 27.24 | 0.00 |
| J3411 | | 1.50 | 0.00 | J7344 | | 96.00 | 0.00 | J7640 | | 10.10 | 0.00 |
| J3415 | | 6.00 | 0.00 | J7345 | | 90.00 | 0.00 | J7642 | | 0.60 | 0.00 |
| J3420 | | 2.00 | 0.00 | J7500 | | 1.33 | 0.00 | J7643 | | 0.20 | 0.00 |
| J3430 | | 5.00 | 0.00 | J7501 | | 171.03 | 0.00 | J7644 | | 3.70 | 0.00 |
| J3465 | | 10.14 | 0.00 | J7502 | | 6.36 | 0.00 | J7645 | | 4.20 | 0.00 |
| J3470 | | 50.01 | 0.00 | J7506 | | 0.27 | 0.00 | J7650 | | 1.40 | 0.00 |

# APPENDIX 7 — NATIONAL AVERAGE PAYMENT TABLE FOR HCPCS

| Proc | Mod | Commercial | Medicare | Proc | Mod | Commercial | Medicare | Proc | Mod | Commercial | Medicare |
|------|-----|-----------|----------|------|-----|-----------|----------|------|-----|-----------|----------|
| J7669 | | 1.60 | 0.00 | J9098 | | 781.85 | 0.00 | J9293 | | 643.12 | 0.00 |
| J7674 | | 0.75 | 0.00 | J9100 | | 6.00 | 0.00 | J9300 | | 5298.26 | 0.00 |
| J7682 | | 71.90 | 0.00 | J9110 | | 25.00 | 0.00 | J9303 | | 172.80 | 0.00 |
| J7685 | | 156.03 | 0.00 | J9120 | | 1140.00 | 0.00 | J9305 | | 91.99 | 0.00 |
| J8498 | | 6.00 | 0.00 | J9130 | | 27.00 | 0.00 | J9310 | | 934.70 | 0.00 |
| J8501 | | 57.02 | 0.00 | J9140 | | 48.00 | 0.00 | J9320 | | 305.08 | 0.00 |
| J8520 | | 5.50 | 0.00 | J9150 | | 127.78 | 0.00 | J9340 | | 150.00 | 0.00 |
| J8521 | | 19.61 | 0.00 | J9151 | | 112.03 | 0.00 | J9350 | | 1661.86 | 0.00 |
| J8530 | | 3.56 | 0.00 | J9160 | | 2289.70 | 0.00 | J9355 | | 125.00 | 0.00 |
| J8540 | | 0.33 | 0.00 | J9170 | | 677.99 | 0.00 | J9360 | | 6.00 | 0.00 |
| J8560 | | 97.00 | 0.00 | J9175 | | 8.00 | 0.00 | J9370 | | 31.01 | 0.00 |
| J8597 | | 5.30 | 0.00 | J9178 | | 51.99 | 0.00 | J9375 | | 57.35 | 0.00 |
| J8600 | | 4.73 | 0.00 | J9181 | | 10.00 | 0.00 | J9380 | | 101.20 | 0.00 |
| J8610 | | 3.03 | 0.00 | J9185 | | 574.94 | 0.00 | J9390 | | 155.02 | 0.00 |
| J8700 | | 10.00 | 0.00 | J9190 | | 7.50 | 0.00 | J9395 | | 175.02 | 0.00 |
| J9000 | | 28.00 | 0.00 | J9200 | | 127.52 | 0.00 | K0001 | NU | 417.30 | 0.00 |
| J9001 | | 766.45 | 0.00 | J9201 | | 244.93 | 0.00 | K0001 | RR | 65.00 | 0.00 |
| J9010 | | 991.86 | 0.00 | J9202 | | 625.09 | 0.00 | K0002 | RR | 90.01 | 75.70 |
| J9015 | | 1408.88 | 0.00 | J9206 | | 274.97 | 0.00 | K0003 | NU | 900.85 | 0.00 |
| J9017 | | 572.10 | 0.00 | J9208 | | 199.99 | 0.00 | K0003 | RR | 106.99 | 82.87 |
| J9020 | | 82.39 | 0.00 | J9209 | | 65.00 | 0.00 | K0004 | NU | 1224.50 | 0.00 |
| J9025 | | 10.00 | 0.00 | J9211 | | 825.13 | 0.00 | K0004 | RR | 145.05 | 123.62 |
| J9027 | | 434.97 | 0.00 | J9212 | | 5.83 | 0.00 | K0005 | NU | 2294.32 | 1710.11 |
| J9031 | | 250.03 | 0.00 | J9213 | | 62.59 | 0.00 | K0005 | RR | 200.03 | 171.00 |
| J9035 | | 124.99 | 0.00 | J9214 | | 24.99 | 0.00 | K0005 | UE | 0.00 | 1282.56 |
| J9040 | | 391.22 | 0.00 | J9216 | | 350.17 | 0.00 | K0006 | RR | 143.48 | 116.01 |
| J9041 | | 60.01 | 0.00 | J9217 | | 724.71 | 0.00 | K0007 | NU | 1734.27 | 0.00 |
| J9045 | | 259.98 | 0.00 | J9218 | | 29.10 | 0.00 | K0007 | RR | 199.98 | 165.12 |
| J9050 | | 265.97 | 0.00 | J9219 | | 6000.00 | 0.00 | K0009 | | 4042.50 | 0.00 |
| J9055 | | 115.20 | 0.00 | J9225 | | 6498.00 | 0.00 | K0010 | RR | 425.82 | 394.04 |
| J9060 | | 9.00 | 0.00 | J9230 | | 300.01 | 0.00 | K0011 | NU | 7000.00 | 0.00 |
| J9062 | | 33.99 | 0.00 | J9245 | | 3793.15 | 0.00 | K0011 | RR | 512.33 | 0.00 |
| J9065 | | 102.97 | 0.00 | J9250 | | 1.00 | 0.00 | K0012 | RR | 0.00 | 300.55 |
| J9070 | | 12.00 | 0.00 | J9260 | | 12.00 | 0.00 | K0015 | NU | 181.94 | 168.08 |
| J9080 | | 13.00 | 0.00 | J9261 | | 213.98 | 0.00 | K0015 | RR | 19.99 | 16.82 |
| J9090 | | 35.00 | 0.00 | J9263 | | 20.00 | 0.00 | K0015 | UE | 0.00 | 126.05 |
| J9091 | | 58.01 | 0.00 | J9264 | | 20.00 | 0.00 | K0017 | NU | 61.34 | 47.28 |
| J9092 | | 100.01 | 0.00 | J9265 | | 236.29 | 0.00 | K0017 | RR | 7.89 | 4.73 |
| J9093 | | 11.00 | 0.00 | J9266 | | 3576.00 | 0.00 | K0017 | UE | 0.00 | 35.46 |
| J9094 | | 17.00 | 0.00 | J9268 | | 3766.00 | 0.00 | K0018 | NU | 0.00 | 26.41 |
| J9095 | | 50.01 | 0.00 | J9280 | | 179.97 | 0.00 | K0018 | RR | 0.00 | 2.63 |
| J9096 | | 100.02 | 0.00 | J9290 | | 499.92 | 0.00 | K0018 | UE | 0.00 | 19.83 |
| J9097 | | 206.04 | 0.00 | J9291 | | 915.11 | 0.00 | K0019 | NU | 21.54 | 15.95 |

# APPENDIX 7 — NATIONAL AVERAGE PAYMENT TABLE FOR HCPCS

| Proc | Mod | Commercial | Medicare | Proc | Mod | Commercial | Medicare | Proc | Mod | Commercial | Medicare |
|------|-----|-----------|----------|------|-----|-----------|----------|------|-----|-----------|----------|
| K0019 | RR | 0.00 | 1.59 | K0051 | UE | 0.00 | 36.48 | K0603 | NU | 0.75 | 0.53 |
| K0019 | UE | 0.00 | 11.96 | K0052 | NU | 92.48 | 85.51 | K0604 | NU | 0.00 | 5.64 |
| K0020 | NU | 46.48 | 42.98 | K0052 | RR | 14.32 | 8.55 | K0605 | NU | 0.00 | 13.51 |
| K0020 | RR | 4.65 | 4.30 | K0052 | UE | 0.00 | 64.12 | K0606 | RR | 3200.00 | 2098.09 |
| K0020 | UE | 0.00 | 32.22 | K0053 | NU | 123.04 | 94.36 | K0607 | NU | 0.00 | 179.67 |
| K0037 | NU | 0.00 | 44.55 | K0053 | RR | 15.52 | 9.43 | K0607 | RR | 0.00 | 17.98 |
| K0037 | RR | 0.00 | 3.98 | K0053 | UE | 0.00 | 70.77 | K0607 | UE | 0.00 | 134.75 |
| K0037 | UE | 0.00 | 33.42 | K0056 | NU | 104.61 | 87.97 | K0608 | NU | 0.00 | 112.12 |
| K0038 | NU | 28.87 | 22.44 | K0056 | RR | 10.00 | 8.80 | K0608 | RR | 0.00 | 11.23 |
| K0038 | RR | 0.00 | 2.25 | K0056 | UE | 0.00 | 65.99 | K0608 | UE | 0.00 | 84.09 |
| K0038 | UE | 0.00 | 16.84 | K0065 | NU | 50.00 | 41.13 | K0609 | KF | 0.00 | 827.84 |
| K0039 | NU | 0.00 | 49.84 | K0065 | RR | 0.00 | 4.12 | K0609 | | 0.00 | 745.64 |
| K0039 | RR | 0.00 | 5.00 | K0065 | UE | 0.00 | 30.84 | K0730 | NU | 60.00 | 1594.72 |
| K0039 | UE | 0.00 | 37.38 | K0069 | NU | 124.93 | 92.43 | K0730 | RR | 0.00 | 159.47 |
| K0040 | NU | 83.91 | 69.07 | K0069 | RR | 0.00 | 9.63 | K0730 | UE | 0.00 | 1196.04 |
| K0040 | RR | 9.31 | 6.89 | K0069 | UE | 0.00 | 69.32 | K0733 | NU | 69.00 | 27.95 |
| K0040 | UE | 0.00 | 51.79 | K0070 | NU | 208.94 | 169.43 | K0733 | RR | 0.00 | 2.81 |
| K0041 | NU | 57.48 | 48.95 | K0070 | RR | 0.00 | 16.96 | K0733 | UE | 0.00 | 20.97 |
| K0041 | RR | 0.00 | 4.91 | K0070 | UE | 0.00 | 127.07 | K0734 | NU | 497.20 | 306.61 |
| K0041 | UE | 0.00 | 36.72 | K0071 | NU | 109.30 | 101.06 | K0734 | RR | 0.00 | 30.67 |
| K0042 | NU | 36.42 | 33.70 | K0071 | RR | 0.00 | 10.11 | K0734 | UE | 0.00 | 229.96 |
| K0042 | RR | 5.00 | 3.36 | K0071 | UE | 0.00 | 75.78 | K0735 | NU | 0.00 | 390.15 |
| K0042 | UE | 0.00 | 25.27 | K0072 | NU | 66.02 | 60.83 | K0735 | RR | 0.00 | 39.03 |
| K0043 | NU | 19.54 | 18.07 | K0072 | RR | 0.00 | 6.08 | K0735 | UE | 0.00 | 292.61 |
| K0043 | RR | 0.00 | 1.81 | K0072 | UE | 0.00 | 45.62 | K0736 | NU | 500.00 | 309.13 |
| K0043 | UE | 0.00 | 13.56 | K0073 | NU | 0.00 | 32.19 | K0736 | RR | 0.00 | 30.92 |
| K0044 | NU | 16.64 | 15.39 | K0073 | RR | 0.00 | 3.22 | K0736 | UE | 0.00 | 231.86 |
| K0044 | RR | 0.00 | 1.55 | K0073 | UE | 0.00 | 24.15 | K0737 | NU | 0.00 | 391.33 |
| K0044 | UE | 0.00 | 11.55 | K0077 | NU | 59.02 | 54.44 | K0737 | RR | 0.00 | 39.13 |
| K0045 | NU | 78.98 | 52.38 | K0077 | RR | 0.00 | 5.44 | K0737 | UE | 0.00 | 293.50 |
| K0045 | RR | 7.94 | 5.40 | K0077 | UE | 0.00 | 40.82 | K0738 | | 100.00 | 0.00 |
| K0045 | UE | 0.00 | 39.29 | K0098 | NU | 0.00 | 25.17 | K0800 | NU | 1680.60 | 1195.81 |
| K0046 | NU | 19.54 | 18.07 | K0098 | RR | 0.00 | 2.52 | K0800 | RR | 0.00 | 119.59 |
| K0046 | RR | 2.00 | 1.81 | K0098 | UE | 0.00 | 18.86 | K0800 | UE | 0.00 | 896.86 |
| K0046 | UE | 0.00 | 13.56 | K0105 | NU | 0.00 | 91.98 | K0801 | NU | 0.00 | 1927.91 |
| K0047 | NU | 76.45 | 70.75 | K0105 | RR | 92.00 | 9.19 | K0801 | RR | 0.00 | 192.77 |
| K0047 | RR | 0.00 | 7.10 | K0105 | UE | 0.00 | 68.98 | K0801 | UE | 0.00 | 1445.92 |
| K0047 | UE | 0.00 | 53.04 | K0195 | RR | 25.00 | 19.49 | K0802 | NU | 0.00 | 2181.76 |
| K0050 | NU | 0.00 | 30.07 | K0455 | RR | 0.00 | 245.01 | K0802 | RR | 0.00 | 218.17 |
| K0050 | RR | 0.00 | 3.00 | K0552 | | 7.50 | 2.45 | K0802 | UE | 0.00 | 1636.34 |
| K0050 | UE | 0.00 | 22.56 | K0553 | | 260.00 | 0.00 | K0806 | NU | 8.30 | 1446.62 |
| K0051 | NU | 0.00 | 48.67 | K0601 | NU | 1.80 | 1.02 | K0806 | RR | 0.00 | 144.66 |
| K0051 | RR | 0.00 | 4.90 | K0602 | NU | 14.33 | 5.89 | K0806 | UE | 0.00 | 1084.96 |

| Proc | Mod | Commercial | Medicare | Proc | Mod | Commercial | Medicare | Proc | Mod | Commercial | Medicare |
|------|-----|-----------|----------|------|-----|-----------|----------|------|-----|-----------|----------|
| K0807 | NU | 0.00 | 2195.07 | K0859 | RR | 0.00 | 620.83 | L0625 | | 54.15 | 49.52 |
| K0807 | RR | 0.00 | 219.51 | K0860 | RR | 0.00 | 930.01 | L0626 | | 95.33 | 70.07 |
| K0807 | UE | 0.00 | 1646.32 | K0861 | RR | 0.00 | 525.53 | L0627 | | 469.95 | 369.52 |
| K0808 | NU | 0.00 | 3396.23 | K0862 | RR | 0.00 | 650.98 | L0628 | | 95.02 | 75.41 |
| K0808 | RR | 0.00 | 339.62 | K0863 | RR | 0.00 | 930.01 | L0629 | | 220.00 | 0.00 |
| K0808 | UE | 0.00 | 2547.17 | K0864 | RR | 0.00 | 1106.72 | L0630 | | 200.07 | 145.59 |
| K0813 | RR | 0.00 | 223.15 | L0112 | | 0.00 | 1257.91 | L0631 | | 995.46 | 922.87 |
| K0814 | RR | 0.00 | 285.62 | L0120 | | 29.99 | 24.96 | L0633 | | 339.94 | 257.79 |
| K0815 | RR | 0.00 | 325.26 | L0130 | | 184.95 | 153.48 | L0634 | | 135.00 | 0.00 |
| K0816 | RR | 0.00 | 311.49 | L0140 | | 61.01 | 60.22 | L0635 | | 1176.88 | 900.45 |
| K0820 | RR | 0.00 | 238.34 | L0150 | | 130.97 | 101.66 | L0636 | | 1668.25 | 1332.99 |
| K0821 | RR | 0.00 | 305.96 | L0160 | | 184.99 | 147.33 | L0637 | | 1378.74 | 1054.89 |
| K0822 | RR | 0.00 | 369.77 | L0170 | | 0.00 | 606.68 | L0638 | | 1446.84 | 1185.37 |
| K0822 | | 6695.00 | 0.00 | L0172 | | 159.12 | 119.43 | L0639 | | 1349.47 | 1054.89 |
| K0823 | RR | 0.00 | 372.19 | L0174 | | 312.05 | 258.42 | L0640 | | 1593.38 | 940.44 |
| K0823 | | 6695.00 | 0.00 | L0180 | | 448.50 | 348.56 | L0700 | | 2699.76 | 1901.83 |
| K0824 | RR | 0.00 | 447.95 | L0190 | | 533.23 | 465.99 | L0710 | | 0.00 | 1964.68 |
| K0825 | RR | 0.00 | 410.07 | L0200 | | 642.96 | 485.79 | L0810 | | 2796.00 | 2426.48 |
| K0825 | | 7545.00 | 0.00 | L0210 | | 42.00 | 41.66 | L0820 | | 0.00 | 2032.01 |
| K0826 | RR | 0.00 | 579.91 | L0220 | | 0.00 | 115.21 | L0830 | | 0.00 | 2949.86 |
| K0827 | RR | 0.00 | 493.11 | L0430 | | 0.00 | 1260.49 | L0859 | | 1442.80 | 1146.01 |
| K0828 | RR | 0.00 | 639.01 | L0450 | | 195.98 | 163.50 | L0861 | | 0.00 | 193.72 |
| K0829 | RR | 0.00 | 586.79 | L0454 | | 363.92 | 311.71 | L0960 | | 65.00 | 0.00 |
| K0835 | RR | 0.00 | 375.31 | L0456 | | 880.51 | 893.88 | L0970 | | 129.99 | 107.51 |
| K0836 | RR | 0.00 | 389.20 | L0458 | | 1024.94 | 801.54 | L0972 | | 112.95 | 96.81 |
| K0837 | RR | 0.00 | 447.95 | L0460 | | 1180.36 | 902.19 | L0974 | | 0.00 | 168.42 |
| K0838 | RR | 0.00 | 400.74 | L0462 | | 1265.21 | 1122.17 | L0976 | | 181.02 | 150.42 |
| K0839 | RR | 0.00 | 579.91 | L0464 | | 1631.31 | 1335.93 | L0978 | | 0.00 | 181.08 |
| K0840 | RR | 0.00 | 878.60 | L0466 | | 374.89 | 351.46 | L0980 | | 0.00 | 16.43 |
| K0841 | RR | 0.00 | 399.47 | L0468 | | 512.05 | 431.20 | L0982 | | 0.00 | 15.32 |
| K0842 | RR | 0.00 | 399.47 | L0470 | | 700.20 | 599.75 | L0984 | | 69.98 | 56.32 |
| K0843 | RR | 0.00 | 480.97 | L0472 | | 471.77 | 380.37 | L1000 | | 0.00 | 1909.87 |
| K0848 | RR | 0.00 | 488.81 | L0480 | | 1814.69 | 1339.51 | L1005 | | 3501.08 | 2876.57 |
| K0849 | RR | 0.00 | 469.97 | L0482 | | 1757.97 | 1458.78 | L1010 | | 76.99 | 63.13 |
| K0850 | RR | 0.00 | 567.01 | L0484 | | 1863.49 | 1671.77 | L1020 | | 97.98 | 81.31 |
| K0851 | RR | 0.00 | 545.17 | L0486 | | 2249.56 | 1773.65 | L1025 | | 131.04 | 117.31 |
| K0852 | RR | 0.00 | 655.14 | L0488 | | 1069.18 | 902.19 | L1030 | | 75.00 | 59.84 |
| K0853 | RR | 0.00 | 673.00 | L0490 | | 0.00 | 254.23 | L1040 | | 94.03 | 73.39 |
| K0854 | RR | 0.00 | 891.57 | L0491 | | 0.00 | 690.25 | L1050 | | 83.29 | 78.32 |
| K0855 | RR | 0.00 | 842.22 | L0492 | | 0.00 | 448.19 | L1060 | | 112.02 | 89.97 |
| K0856 | RR | 0.00 | 524.69 | L0621 | | 101.81 | 86.75 | L1070 | | 0.00 | 84.64 |
| K0857 | RR | 0.00 | 535.21 | L0622 | | 350.04 | 243.03 | L1080 | | 0.00 | 52.06 |
| K0858 | RR | 0.00 | 650.98 | L0623 | | 75.00 | 0.00 | L1085 | | 0.00 | 144.80 |

Appendix 7 — National Average Payment Table for HCPCS

**Appendix 7 — National Average Payment Table for HCPCS**

| Proc | Mod | Commercial | Medicare | Proc | Mod | Commercial | Medicare | Proc | Mod | Commercial | Medicare |
|------|-----|-----------|----------|------|-----|-----------|----------|------|-----|-----------|----------|
| L1090 | | 0.00 | 86.23 | L1832 | | 649.86 | 571.92 | L2040 | | 194.06 | 167.02 |
| L1100 | | 0.00 | 149.60 | L1834 | | 846.69 | 730.24 | L2050 | | 0.00 | 448.12 |
| L1110 | | 0.00 | 240.26 | L1836 | | 149.99 | 119.92 | L2060 | | 0.00 | 546.17 |
| L1120 | | 31.99 | 37.36 | L1840 | | 1209.17 | 864.97 | L2070 | | 0.00 | 126.51 |
| L1200 | | 1869.41 | 1473.93 | L1843 | | 903.41 | 806.42 | L2080 | | 0.00 | 338.36 |
| L1210 | | 294.08 | 246.15 | L1844 | | 1664.93 | 1495.80 | L2090 | | 0.00 | 412.50 |
| L1220 | | 244.99 | 208.41 | L1845 | | 940.13 | 768.89 | L2106 | | 449.88 | 639.60 |
| L1230 | | 0.00 | 534.75 | L1846 | | 1257.94 | 1050.90 | L2108 | | 1018.23 | 1005.11 |
| L1240 | | 88.03 | 73.05 | L1847 | | 582.01 | 516.93 | L2112 | | 475.17 | 438.89 |
| L1250 | | 79.99 | 67.96 | L1850 | | 296.19 | 270.78 | L2114 | | 544.84 | 546.02 |
| L1260 | | 85.03 | 71.17 | L1855 | | 1191.15 | 0.00 | L2116 | | 650.03 | 669.69 |
| L1270 | | 80.02 | 72.89 | L1858 | | 1299.77 | 0.00 | L2126 | | 0.00 | 1126.46 |
| L1280 | | 110.79 | 81.15 | L1860 | | 0.00 | 1009.44 | L2128 | | 1817.40 | 1613.07 |
| L1290 | | 85.03 | 73.94 | L1880 | | 655.34 | 0.00 | L2132 | | 0.00 | 758.85 |
| L1300 | | 2015.66 | 1571.40 | L1900 | | 286.94 | 253.78 | L2134 | | 0.00 | 909.84 |
| L1310 | | 0.00 | 1616.97 | L1901 | | 20.00 | 15.90 | L2136 | | 0.00 | 1112.49 |
| L1500 | | 0.00 | 1786.85 | L1902 | | 85.03 | 75.10 | L2180 | | 133.02 | 110.17 |
| L1510 | | 0.00 | 1130.44 | L1904 | | 477.17 | 442.37 | L2182 | | 102.17 | 86.22 |
| L1520 | | 0.00 | 2146.11 | L1906 | | 120.04 | 113.13 | L2184 | | 139.97 | 116.53 |
| L1600 | | 157.04 | 121.22 | L1907 | | 620.76 | 505.72 | L2186 | | 184.05 | 141.62 |
| L1610 | | 0.00 | 41.30 | L1910 | | 301.95 | 251.57 | L2188 | | 0.00 | 281.74 |
| L1620 | | 149.98 | 126.04 | L1920 | | 362.90 | 328.87 | L2190 | | 0.00 | 82.16 |
| L1630 | | 0.00 | 159.41 | L1930 | | 250.02 | 222.54 | L2192 | | 0.00 | 335.42 |
| L1640 | | 0.00 | 434.07 | L1932 | | 1005.00 | 802.00 | L2200 | | 55.01 | 44.73 |
| L1650 | | 249.05 | 217.80 | L1940 | | 549.84 | 465.23 | L2210 | | 76.00 | 63.24 |
| L1652 | | 345.07 | 320.38 | L1945 | | 1114.22 | 870.81 | L2220 | | 93.03 | 77.04 |
| L1660 | | 194.00 | 160.99 | L1950 | | 907.76 | 700.69 | L2230 | | 86.99 | 72.18 |
| L1680 | | 0.00 | 1146.19 | L1951 | | 989.94 | 754.80 | L2232 | | 120.00 | 87.95 |
| L1685 | | 0.00 | 1118.96 | L1960 | | 629.20 | 521.43 | L2240 | | 0.00 | 78.67 |
| L1686 | | 1034.80 | 858.11 | L1970 | | 836.13 | 669.38 | L2250 | | 382.23 | 334.27 |
| L1690 | | 1980.36 | 1737.95 | L1971 | | 461.15 | 421.27 | L2260 | | 226.95 | 188.58 |
| L1700 | | 0.00 | 1436.57 | L1980 | | 416.06 | 345.25 | L2265 | | 134.04 | 110.78 |
| L1710 | | 0.00 | 1681.67 | L1990 | | 499.95 | 419.32 | L2270 | | 60.00 | 50.52 |
| L1720 | | 0.00 | 1239.59 | L2000 | | 1061.28 | 954.15 | L2275 | | 148.03 | 117.99 |
| L1730 | | 0.00 | 1064.69 | L2005 | | 4358.40 | 3683.74 | L2280 | | 514.02 | 425.97 |
| L1755 | | 0.00 | 1489.37 | L2010 | | 0.00 | 869.80 | L2300 | | 0.00 | 253.28 |
| L1800 | | 75.00 | 62.58 | L2020 | | 1277.13 | 1098.42 | L2310 | | 0.00 | 115.73 |
| L1810 | | 104.97 | 92.65 | L2030 | | 0.00 | 952.98 | L2320 | | 232.94 | 193.55 |
| L1815 | | 102.45 | 91.13 | L2034 | | 0.00 | 1841.66 | L2330 | | 457.56 | 369.38 |
| L1820 | | 141.52 | 121.98 | L2035 | | 207.74 | 156.67 | L2335 | | 0.00 | 213.71 |
| L1825 | | 58.98 | 51.73 | L2036 | | 2142.40 | 1745.32 | L2340 | | 510.03 | 420.44 |
| L1830 | | 90.02 | 82.30 | L2037 | | 1889.46 | 1566.84 | L2350 | | 1006.11 | 838.22 |
| L1831 | | 285.97 | 264.52 | L2038 | | 0.00 | 1344.97 | L2360 | | 62.98 | 48.68 |

| Proc | Mod | Commercial | Medicare | Proc | Mod | Commercial | Medicare | Proc | Mod | Commercial | Medicare |
|------|-----|-----------|----------|------|-----|-----------|----------|------|-----|-----------|----------|
| L2370 | | 0.00 | 241.49 | L2795 | | 96.00 | 79.93 | L3252 | | 300.08 | 0.00 |
| L2375 | | 114.22 | 106.30 | L2800 | | 111.68 | 100.34 | L3253 | | 80.02 | 0.00 |
| L2380 | | 165.97 | 115.81 | L2810 | | 89.01 | 73.48 | L3254 | | 28.00 | 0.00 |
| L2385 | | 151.95 | 126.00 | L2820 | | 98.97 | 81.69 | L3257 | | 54.99 | 0.00 |
| L2387 | | 221.00 | 155.68 | L2830 | | 107.00 | 88.38 | L3260 | | 30.00 | 0.00 |
| L2390 | | 164.80 | 102.97 | L2840 | | 52.00 | 41.10 | L3265 | | 24.99 | 0.00 |
| L2395 | | 157.47 | 147.19 | L2850 | | 65.02 | 58.25 | L3300 | | 40.00 | 46.86 |
| L2397 | | 132.99 | 105.73 | L2860 | | 330.00 | 0.00 | L3310 | | 88.00 | 73.15 |
| L2405 | | 99.00 | 78.36 | L3000 | | 249.99 | 282.32 | L3320 | | 107.86 | 0.00 |
| L2415 | | 143.97 | 109.17 | L3001 | | 130.04 | 118.87 | L3330 | | 0.00 | 508.64 |
| L2425 | | 145.05 | 128.83 | L3002 | | 175.01 | 145.16 | L3332 | | 15.00 | 66.29 |
| L2430 | | 158.04 | 128.83 | L3003 | | 171.10 | 156.61 | L3334 | | 15.00 | 34.29 |
| L2492 | | 115.98 | 95.93 | L3010 | | 219.40 | 156.61 | L3340 | | 67.00 | 76.60 |
| L2500 | | 0.00 | 296.77 | L3020 | | 209.91 | 178.32 | L3350 | | 29.92 | 20.57 |
| L2510 | | 851.35 | 683.32 | L3030 | | 250.07 | 68.59 | L3360 | | 39.08 | 32.00 |
| L2520 | | 0.00 | 433.36 | L3031 | | 130.00 | 0.00 | L3370 | | 0.00 | 44.57 |
| L2525 | | 1372.73 | 1146.72 | L3040 | | 38.57 | 42.30 | L3380 | | 0.00 | 44.57 |
| L2526 | | 0.00 | 644.34 | L3050 | | 36.99 | 42.30 | L3390 | | 56.55 | 44.57 |
| L2530 | | 267.07 | 221.03 | L3060 | | 65.16 | 66.29 | L3400 | | 60.02 | 36.59 |
| L2540 | | 457.33 | 397.72 | L3070 | | 25.00 | 28.56 | L3410 | | 95.00 | 83.44 |
| L2550 | | 324.93 | 270.18 | L3080 | | 8.00 | 28.56 | L3420 | | 49.01 | 49.15 |
| L2570 | | 0.00 | 448.07 | L3090 | | 15.00 | 36.59 | L3430 | | 52.99 | 144.03 |
| L2580 | | 0.00 | 436.59 | L3100 | | 30.00 | 38.86 | L3440 | | 73.36 | 68.59 |
| L2600 | | 0.00 | 193.20 | L3140 | | 0.00 | 80.02 | L3450 | | 42.60 | 94.86 |
| L2610 | | 367.08 | 228.46 | L3150 | | 90.99 | 73.15 | L3455 | | 0.00 | 36.59 |
| L2620 | | 330.08 | 251.53 | L3170 | | 42.00 | 45.74 | L3460 | | 28.00 | 30.86 |
| L2622 | | 317.87 | 288.48 | L3201 | | 60.61 | 0.00 | L3465 | | 0.00 | 52.59 |
| L2624 | | 399.08 | 311.51 | L3202 | | 52.49 | 0.00 | L3470 | | 0.00 | 56.01 |
| L2627 | | 0.00 | 1612.65 | L3203 | | 58.03 | 0.00 | L3480 | | 45.99 | 56.01 |
| L2628 | | 0.00 | 1576.06 | L3204 | | 53.13 | 0.00 | L3485 | | 28.50 | 0.00 |
| L2630 | | 0.00 | 232.94 | L3206 | | 62.00 | 0.00 | L3500 | | 35.00 | 26.30 |
| L2640 | | 425.50 | 316.13 | L3208 | | 39.99 | 0.00 | L3510 | | 34.99 | 26.30 |
| L2650 | | 0.00 | 112.89 | L3209 | | 50.00 | 0.00 | L3520 | | 0.00 | 28.56 |
| L2660 | | 0.00 | 175.33 | L3211 | | 70.56 | 0.00 | L3530 | | 0.00 | 28.56 |
| L2670 | | 0.00 | 160.47 | L3215 | | 89.99 | 0.00 | L3540 | | 57.02 | 45.74 |
| L2680 | | 0.00 | 147.21 | L3216 | | 115.06 | 0.00 | L3550 | | 0.00 | 8.01 |
| L2750 | | 97.02 | 78.63 | L3219 | | 137.00 | 0.00 | L3560 | | 0.00 | 20.57 |
| L2755 | | 143.40 | 117.43 | L3221 | | 139.94 | 0.00 | L3570 | | 0.00 | 76.60 |
| L2760 | | 69.01 | 57.16 | L3222 | | 175.00 | 0.00 | L3580 | | 65.02 | 58.29 |
| L2768 | | 138.97 | 117.10 | L3224 | | 70.02 | 55.32 | L3590 | | 0.00 | 48.01 |
| L2770 | | 70.00 | 58.09 | L3225 | | 78.01 | 63.64 | L3595 | | 0.00 | 37.71 |
| L2780 | | 77.02 | 63.67 | L3230 | | 303.97 | 0.00 | L3600 | | 103.97 | 68.59 |
| L2785 | | 38.01 | 29.81 | L3250 | | 399.89 | 0.00 | L3610 | | 137.10 | 90.30 |

| Proc | Mod | Commercial | Medicare | Proc | Mod | Commercial | Medicare | Proc | Mod | Commercial | Medicare |
|------|-----|-----------|----------|------|-----|-----------|----------|------|-----|-----------|----------|
| L3620 | | 86.99 | 68.59 | L3905 | | 470.00 | 410.77 | L3965 | UE | 0.00 | 687.58 |
| L3630 | | 114.99 | 90.30 | L3906 | | 350.15 | 363.74 | L3966 | NU | 0.00 | 690.64 |
| L3640 | | 0.00 | 38.86 | L3907 | | 507.39 | 0.00 | L3966 | RR | 0.00 | 69.07 |
| L3650 | | 64.91 | 54.59 | L3908 | | 64.00 | 55.16 | L3966 | UE | 0.00 | 517.98 |
| L3651 | | 64.98 | 53.86 | L3909 | | 18.00 | 11.56 | L3967 | | 0.00 | 1622.52 |
| L3652 | | 216.51 | 162.31 | L3910 | | 453.13 | 0.00 | L3968 | NU | 0.00 | 874.00 |
| L3660 | | 110.99 | 94.62 | L3911 | | 25.00 | 20.27 | L3968 | RR | 0.00 | 87.40 |
| L3670 | | 133.03 | 104.10 | L3912 | | 99.97 | 87.30 | L3968 | UE | 0.00 | 655.50 |
| L3671 | | 0.00 | 737.02 | L3913 | | 202.00 | 221.53 | L3969 | NU | 0.00 | 611.19 |
| L3672 | | 0.00 | 916.54 | L3915 | | 64.00 | 434.80 | L3969 | RR | 0.00 | 61.13 |
| L3673 | | 0.00 | 998.93 | L3916 | | 120.02 | 0.00 | L3969 | UE | 0.00 | 458.38 |
| L3675 | | 175.97 | 143.54 | L3917 | | 96.16 | 86.40 | L3970 | NU | 263.98 | 244.49 |
| L3700 | | 69.01 | 64.26 | L3918 | | 74.01 | 0.00 | L3970 | RR | 0.00 | 24.45 |
| L3701 | | 21.99 | 16.66 | L3919 | | 190.00 | 221.53 | L3970 | UE | 0.00 | 183.37 |
| L3702 | | 250.00 | 236.18 | L3921 | | 246.80 | 262.73 | L3971 | | 0.00 | 1540.13 |
| L3710 | | 148.97 | 113.80 | L3923 | | 39.99 | 80.08 | L3972 | NU | 0.00 | 155.47 |
| L3720 | | 670.18 | 602.10 | L3924 | | 105.01 | 0.00 | L3972 | RR | 0.00 | 15.55 |
| L3730 | | 923.65 | 829.82 | L3925 | | 50.00 | 45.44 | L3972 | UE | 0.00 | 116.60 |
| L3740 | | 1216.30 | 983.82 | L3927 | | 0.00 | 28.61 | L3973 | | 0.00 | 1622.52 |
| L3760 | | 459.88 | 409.05 | L3928 | | 58.99 | 0.00 | L3974 | NU | 0.00 | 131.86 |
| L3762 | | 100.01 | 87.96 | L3929 | | 65.00 | 71.96 | L3974 | RR | 0.00 | 13.20 |
| L3763 | | 450.00 | 602.16 | L3930 | | 65.31 | 0.00 | L3974 | UE | 0.00 | 98.89 |
| L3764 | | 1150.00 | 680.10 | L3931 | | 83.00 | 167.86 | L3975 | | 0.00 | 1374.24 |
| L3765 | | 0.00 | 1048.80 | L3932 | | 47.36 | 0.00 | L3976 | | 0.00 | 1374.24 |
| L3766 | | 0.00 | 1110.61 | L3933 | | 120.00 | 174.53 | L3977 | | 0.00 | 1540.13 |
| L3800 | | 179.99 | 0.00 | L3934 | | 50.01 | 0.00 | L3978 | | 0.00 | 1622.52 |
| L3805 | | 290.11 | 0.00 | L3935 | | 85.00 | 180.71 | L3980 | | 350.01 | 284.59 |
| L3806 | | 350.00 | 670.81 | L3936 | | 85.03 | 0.00 | L3982 | | 356.11 | 343.65 |
| L3807 | | 224.05 | 204.53 | L3938 | | 84.99 | 0.00 | L3984 | | 350.12 | 316.84 |
| L3808 | | 250.00 | 633.49 | L3940 | | 106.43 | 0.00 | L3985 | | 583.80 | 0.00 |
| L3810 | | 71.99 | 0.00 | L3942 | | 74.98 | 0.00 | L3986 | | 500.00 | 0.00 |
| L3820 | | 96.98 | 0.00 | L3946 | | 77.23 | 0.00 | L3995 | | 38.50 | 30.10 |
| L3825 | | 64.39 | 0.00 | L3948 | | 56.99 | 0.00 | L4000 | | 0.00 | 1199.45 |
| L3830 | | 87.80 | 0.00 | L3954 | | 105.02 | 0.00 | L4002 | | 30.00 | 0.00 |
| L3840 | | 63.01 | 0.00 | L3956 | | 87.40 | 0.00 | L4010 | | 0.00 | 631.33 |
| L3845 | | 83.18 | 90.00 | L3960 | | 880.78 | 676.53 | L4020 | | 0.00 | 810.26 |
| L3850 | | 114.79 | 0.00 | L3961 | | 0.00 | 1374.24 | L4030 | | 0.00 | 474.95 |
| L3855 | | 118.99 | 0.00 | L3962 | | 634.21 | 660.48 | L4040 | | 0.00 | 384.00 |
| L3860 | | 152.98 | 0.00 | L3964 | NU | 0.00 | 574.53 | L4045 | | 0.00 | 308.58 |
| L3890 | | 371.50 | 0.00 | L3964 | RR | 0.00 | 57.45 | L4050 | | 0.00 | 388.37 |
| L3900 | | 1382.05 | 1191.12 | L3964 | UE | 0.00 | 430.87 | L4055 | | 0.00 | 251.48 |
| L3901 | | 0.00 | 1479.32 | L3965 | NU | 0.00 | 916.78 | L4060 | | 0.00 | 298.96 |
| L3904 | | 0.00 | 2695.73 | L3965 | RR | 0.00 | 91.70 | L4070 | | 359.93 | 264.74 |

| Proc | Mod | Commercial | Medicare | Proc | Mod | Commercial | Medicare | Proc | Mod | Commercial | Medicare |
|------|-----|-----------|----------|------|-----|-----------|----------|------|-----|-----------|----------|
| L4080 | | 0.00 | 95.15 | L5500 | | 0.00 | 1287.17 | L5649 | | 2438.46 | 1908.15 |
| L4090 | | 0.00 | 84.95 | L5505 | | 0.00 | 1743.17 | L5650 | | 590.01 | 489.26 |
| L4100 | | 123.03 | 98.12 | L5510 | | 0.00 | 1459.09 | L5651 | | 1452.35 | 1203.57 |
| L4110 | | 99.46 | 79.78 | L5520 | | 0.00 | 1441.23 | L5652 | | 526.91 | 436.94 |
| L4130 | | 0.00 | 466.72 | L5530 | | 2173.36 | 1731.06 | L5653 | | 0.00 | 583.28 |
| L4205 | | 30.00 | 0.00 | L5535 | | 0.00 | 1699.56 | L5654 | | 412.50 | 332.37 |
| L4210 | | 40.00 | 0.00 | L5540 | | 2364.54 | 1813.96 | L5655 | | 339.93 | 265.83 |
| L4350 | | 89.43 | 84.09 | L5560 | | 0.00 | 1947.88 | L5656 | | 0.00 | 371.77 |
| L4360 | | 299.93 | 260.47 | L5570 | | 0.00 | 2025.11 | L5658 | | 0.00 | 364.40 |
| L4370 | | 190.00 | 177.60 | L5580 | | 0.00 | 2364.17 | L5661 | | 0.00 | 609.89 |
| L4380 | | 124.99 | 101.05 | L5585 | | 0.00 | 2564.22 | L5665 | | 618.82 | 513.16 |
| L4386 | | 175.04 | 142.50 | L5590 | | 3055.69 | 2409.25 | L5666 | | 93.02 | 70.16 |
| L4392 | | 27.01 | 21.12 | L5595 | | 0.00 | 4035.40 | L5668 | | 129.97 | 101.21 |
| L4394 | | 0.00 | 15.41 | L5600 | | 0.00 | 4456.29 | L5670 | | 327.94 | 271.95 |
| L4396 | | 180.00 | 150.56 | L5610 | | 0.00 | 2074.97 | L5671 | | 625.09 | 498.51 |
| L4398 | | 92.01 | 69.31 | L5611 | | 1801.20 | 1614.74 | L5672 | | 0.00 | 298.85 |
| L5000 | | 600.10 | 506.38 | L5613 | | 2698.47 | 2456.11 | L5673 | | 848.83 | 669.69 |
| L5010 | | 1499.67 | 1220.13 | L5614 | | 0.00 | 1519.55 | L5676 | | 437.95 | 363.17 |
| L5020 | | 2395.08 | 1986.14 | L5616 | | 0.00 | 1361.16 | L5677 | | 493.88 | 494.15 |
| L5050 | | 2902.45 | 2300.04 | L5617 | | 0.00 | 507.07 | L5678 | | 48.01 | 39.80 |
| L5060 | | 0.00 | 2768.12 | L5618 | | 361.99 | 281.86 | L5679 | | 732.80 | 558.06 |
| L5100 | | 3019.52 | 2329.30 | L5620 | | 354.06 | 278.63 | L5680 | | 401.06 | 305.05 |
| L5105 | | 0.00 | 3481.63 | L5622 | | 438.13 | 363.33 | L5681 | | 1404.11 | 1184.81 |
| L5150 | | 0.00 | 3519.45 | L5624 | | 456.87 | 364.36 | L5682 | | 0.00 | 626.77 |
| L5160 | | 0.00 | 3828.04 | L5626 | | 603.76 | 477.84 | L5683 | | 1424.96 | 1184.81 |
| L5200 | | 0.00 | 3310.78 | L5628 | | 0.00 | 483.89 | L5684 | | 58.02 | 48.24 |
| L5210 | | 0.00 | 2431.94 | L5629 | | 384.09 | 318.50 | L5685 | | 175.00 | 115.34 |
| L5220 | | 0.00 | 2764.35 | L5630 | | 0.00 | 449.79 | L5686 | | 0.00 | 51.20 |
| L5230 | | 0.00 | 3812.58 | L5631 | | 531.02 | 440.35 | L5688 | | 75.00 | 61.22 |
| L5250 | | 0.00 | 5200.02 | L5632 | | 276.72 | 222.53 | L5690 | | 0.00 | 98.07 |
| L5270 | | 0.00 | 5154.47 | L5634 | | 0.00 | 304.86 | L5692 | | 191.81 | 133.18 |
| L5280 | | 0.00 | 5102.92 | L5636 | | 0.00 | 255.37 | L5694 | | 218.96 | 181.82 |
| L5301 | | 3113.72 | 2301.11 | L5637 | | 401.50 | 289.53 | L5695 | | 201.94 | 163.44 |
| L5311 | | 0.00 | 3305.79 | L5638 | | 0.00 | 487.74 | L5696 | | 0.00 | 185.43 |
| L5321 | | 4167.25 | 3293.97 | L5639 | | 0.00 | 1123.66 | L5697 | | 0.00 | 80.46 |
| L5331 | | 0.00 | 4661.09 | L5640 | | 0.00 | 640.85 | L5698 | | 141.03 | 104.54 |
| L5341 | | 0.00 | 5065.13 | L5642 | | 0.00 | 620.94 | L5699 | | 0.00 | 186.87 |
| L5400 | | 0.00 | 1206.21 | L5643 | | 0.00 | 1559.88 | L5700 | | 3463.45 | 2744.60 |
| L5410 | | 0.00 | 418.74 | L5644 | | 0.00 | 591.95 | L5701 | | 4158.35 | 3407.65 |
| L5420 | | 0.00 | 1523.38 | L5645 | | 964.30 | 799.66 | L5702 | | 0.00 | 4354.26 |
| L5430 | | 0.00 | 504.33 | L5646 | | 0.00 | 549.12 | L5703 | | 0.00 | 2096.49 |
| L5450 | | 495.00 | 408.31 | L5647 | | 960.72 | 797.22 | L5704 | | 648.20 | 527.72 |
| L5460 | | 0.00 | 546.49 | L5648 | | 0.00 | 659.83 | L5705 | | 1157.67 | 930.98 |

**Appendix 7 — National Average Payment Table for HCPCS**

| Proc | Mod | Commercial | Medicare | Proc | Mod | Commercial | Medicare | Proc | Mod | Commercial | Medicare |
|------|-----|-----------|----------|------|-----|-----------|----------|------|-----|-----------|----------|
| L5706 | | 0.00 | 913.36 | L5960 | | 0.00 | 966.18 | L6382 | | 0.00 | 1483.94 |
| L5707 | | 0.00 | 1239.78 | L5962 | | 709.91 | 589.10 | L6384 | | 0.00 | 1910.83 |
| L5710 | | 0.00 | 360.46 | L5964 | | 1131.85 | 938.60 | L6386 | | 0.00 | 402.48 |
| L5711 | | 0.00 | 523.31 | L5966 | | 0.00 | 1196.00 | L6388 | | 0.00 | 440.60 |
| L5712 | | 0.00 | 431.85 | L5968 | | 0.00 | 3272.35 | L6400 | | 0.00 | 2325.53 |
| L5714 | | 0.00 | 419.20 | L5970 | | 251.00 | 203.54 | L6450 | | 0.00 | 3089.90 |
| L5716 | | 0.00 | 730.45 | L5971 | | 0.00 | 203.54 | L6500 | | 0.00 | 3092.44 |
| L5718 | | 0.00 | 912.99 | L5972 | | 464.09 | 353.21 | L6550 | | 0.00 | 3821.68 |
| L5722 | | 0.00 | 904.87 | L5974 | | 287.05 | 233.55 | L6570 | | 0.00 | 4386.55 |
| L5724 | | 0.00 | 1512.75 | L5975 | | 549.86 | 417.47 | L6580 | | 0.00 | 1566.61 |
| L5726 | | 0.00 | 1743.41 | L5976 | | 699.28 | 561.26 | L6582 | | 0.00 | 1379.35 |
| L5728 | | 0.00 | 2384.75 | L5978 | | 378.91 | 292.48 | L6584 | | 0.00 | 2051.33 |
| L5780 | | 0.00 | 1147.44 | L5979 | | 2757.66 | 2286.81 | L6586 | | 0.00 | 1887.59 |
| L5781 | | 4477.56 | 3603.07 | L5980 | | 4591.04 | 3715.91 | L6588 | | 0.00 | 2832.77 |
| L5782 | | 0.00 | 3798.45 | L5981 | | 3619.47 | 2886.54 | L6590 | | 0.00 | 2636.73 |
| L5785 | | 639.16 | 520.70 | L5982 | | 0.00 | 579.39 | L6600 | | 0.00 | 188.00 |
| L5790 | | 868.98 | 720.62 | L5984 | | 723.67 | 570.94 | L6605 | | 0.00 | 185.62 |
| L5795 | | 0.00 | 1076.07 | L5985 | | 334.41 | 255.91 | L6610 | | 0.00 | 166.86 |
| L5810 | | 0.00 | 487.94 | L5986 | | 777.02 | 635.09 | L6611 | | 0.00 | 370.76 |
| L5811 | | 0.00 | 730.93 | L5987 | | 8516.79 | 6477.98 | L6615 | | 222.06 | 174.11 |
| L5812 | | 683.20 | 566.55 | L5988 | | 2329.11 | 1798.93 | L6616 | | 77.98 | 65.01 |
| L5814 | | 4407.62 | 3344.35 | L5990 | | 2142.63 | 1633.70 | L6620 | | 0.00 | 303.88 |
| L5816 | | 0.00 | 852.32 | L5995 | | 850.00 | 0.00 | L6621 | | 0.00 | 2059.73 |
| L5818 | | 0.00 | 962.45 | L6000 | | 0.00 | 1331.63 | L6623 | | 0.00 | 642.88 |
| L5822 | | 0.00 | 1706.67 | L6010 | | 0.00 | 1481.88 | L6624 | | 0.00 | 3391.38 |
| L5824 | | 0.00 | 1536.96 | L6020 | | 0.00 | 1381.63 | L6625 | | 0.00 | 533.03 |
| L5826 | | 0.00 | 2829.82 | L6025 | | 0.00 | 7206.16 | L6628 | | 0.00 | 480.11 |
| L5828 | | 3412.90 | 2830.17 | L6050 | | 0.00 | 1903.82 | L6629 | | 192.19 | 146.63 |
| L5830 | | 0.00 | 1901.73 | L6055 | | 0.00 | 2653.44 | L6630 | | 260.99 | 216.00 |
| L5840 | | 0.00 | 3396.89 | L6100 | | 2468.01 | 1928.86 | L6632 | | 83.99 | 65.12 |
| L5845 | | 2127.18 | 1614.04 | L6110 | | 0.00 | 2045.88 | L6635 | | 0.00 | 176.52 |
| L5848 | | 1228.14 | 968.33 | L6120 | | 0.00 | 2384.19 | L6637 | | 0.00 | 368.00 |
| L5850 | | 155.01 | 128.21 | L6130 | | 0.00 | 2594.44 | L6638 | | 0.00 | 2251.92 |
| L5855 | | 0.00 | 309.52 | L6200 | | 0.00 | 2734.12 | L6639 | | 0.00 | 1373.41 |
| L5856 | | 25505.40 | 21648.61 | L6205 | | 0.00 | 3649.61 | L6640 | | 0.00 | 280.74 |
| L5857 | | 0.00 | 7701.93 | L6250 | | 0.00 | 2691.28 | L6641 | | 196.45 | 160.78 |
| L5858 | | 20445.35 | 16736.01 | L6300 | | 0.00 | 3733.86 | L6642 | | 0.00 | 217.93 |
| L5910 | | 438.00 | 362.98 | L6310 | | 0.00 | 3041.31 | L6645 | | 0.00 | 319.94 |
| L5920 | | 640.82 | 531.76 | L6320 | | 0.00 | 1712.72 | L6646 | | 0.00 | 2840.17 |
| L5925 | | 466.99 | 336.75 | L6350 | | 0.00 | 3925.58 | L6647 | | 0.00 | 467.59 |
| L5930 | | 3864.02 | 3050.44 | L6360 | | 0.00 | 3192.22 | L6648 | | 0.00 | 2929.24 |
| L5940 | | 617.08 | 502.72 | L6370 | | 0.00 | 2035.57 | L6650 | | 0.00 | 339.24 |
| L5950 | | 947.76 | 779.73 | L6380 | | 0.00 | 1152.81 | L6655 | | 93.01 | 75.29 |

| Proc | Mod | Commercial | Medicare | Proc | Mod | Commercial | Medicare | Proc | Mod | Commercial | Medicare |
|------|-----|-----------|----------|------|-----|-----------|----------|------|-----|-----------|----------|
| L6660 | | 124.99 | 91.99 | L6925 | | 0.00 | 7721.75 | L7600 | | 90.00 | 0.00 |
| L6665 | | 62.98 | 46.16 | L6930 | | 0.00 | 6729.96 | L7611 | | 0.00 | 605.42 |
| L6670 | | 0.00 | 48.07 | L6935 | | 9410.46 | 7866.31 | L7612 | | 0.00 | 1114.71 |
| L6672 | | 0.00 | 168.99 | L6940 | | 0.00 | 8793.12 | L7613 | | 0.00 | 1406.86 |
| L6675 | | 145.04 | 120.36 | L6945 | | 0.00 | 10229.78 | L7614 | | 0.00 | 1191.60 |
| L6676 | | 0.00 | 121.55 | L6950 | | 0.00 | 9994.62 | L7621 | | 0.00 | 2117.96 |
| L6677 | | 0.00 | 267.13 | L6955 | | 0.00 | 11969.92 | L7622 | | 0.00 | 1825.84 |
| L6680 | | 310.55 | 232.53 | L6960 | | 0.00 | 12072.57 | L7900 | | 495.03 | 482.93 |
| L6682 | | 365.98 | 257.09 | L6965 | | 0.00 | 14203.95 | L8000 | | 43.01 | 36.59 |
| L6684 | | 0.00 | 349.35 | L6970 | | 0.00 | 14617.17 | L8001 | | 129.97 | 112.95 |
| L6686 | | 0.00 | 591.68 | L6975 | | 0.00 | 16015.78 | L8002 | | 170.00 | 148.57 |
| L6687 | | 697.11 | 578.09 | L7007 | | 5180.90 | 3448.67 | L8010 | | 75.06 | 0.00 |
| L6688 | | 0.00 | 530.92 | L7008 | | 0.00 | 5427.85 | L8015 | | 60.00 | 54.10 |
| L6689 | | 0.00 | 675.29 | L7009 | | 0.00 | 3518.74 | L8020 | | 194.99 | 201.06 |
| L6690 | | 0.00 | 689.14 | L7040 | | 0.00 | 2825.41 | L8030 | | 315.00 | 316.18 |
| L6691 | | 0.00 | 345.95 | L7045 | | 0.00 | 1619.91 | L8035 | | 3600.88 | 3299.10 |
| L6692 | | 0.00 | 560.47 | L7170 | | 0.00 | 5876.47 | L8040 | KM | 0.00 | 2118.81 |
| L6693 | | 0.00 | 2556.53 | L7180 | | 0.00 | 32739.30 | L8040 | KN | 0.00 | 892.13 |
| L6694 | | 909.20 | 669.69 | L7181 | | 0.00 | 36081.39 | L8040 | | 0.00 | 2230.33 |
| L6695 | | 0.00 | 558.06 | L7185 | | 0.00 | 5950.71 | L8041 | KM | 0.00 | 2553.88 |
| L6696 | | 0.00 | 1184.81 | L7186 | | 0.00 | 8865.10 | L8041 | KN | 0.00 | 1075.32 |
| L6697 | | 0.00 | 1184.81 | L7190 | | 0.00 | 7571.15 | L8041 | | 0.00 | 2688.30 |
| L6698 | | 0.00 | 498.51 | L7191 | | 0.00 | 9263.51 | L8042 | KM | 0.00 | 2869.52 |
| L6703 | | 456.00 | 325.81 | L7260 | | 0.00 | 1972.37 | L8042 | KN | 0.00 | 1208.22 |
| L6704 | | 786.00 | 586.93 | L7261 | | 0.00 | 3590.48 | L8042 | | 0.00 | 3020.55 |
| L6706 | | 754.00 | 349.70 | L7266 | | 0.00 | 992.27 | L8043 | KM | 0.00 | 3213.87 |
| L6707 | | 0.00 | 1288.91 | L7272 | | 0.00 | 2023.22 | L8043 | KN | 0.00 | 1353.21 |
| L6708 | | 0.00 | 838.31 | L7274 | | 7397.53 | 5756.29 | L8043 | | 0.00 | 3383.03 |
| L6709 | | 0.00 | 1214.21 | L7360 | | 0.00 | 227.90 | L8044 | KM | 0.00 | 3558.22 |
| L6805 | | 0.00 | 340.99 | L7362 | | 0.00 | 251.09 | L8044 | KN | 0.00 | 1498.20 |
| L6810 | | 0.00 | 186.95 | L7364 | | 0.00 | 399.36 | L8044 | | 0.00 | 3745.48 |
| L6881 | | 0.00 | 3681.47 | L7366 | | 0.00 | 537.95 | L8045 | KM | 0.00 | 2341.31 |
| L6882 | | 3662.54 | 2792.58 | L7367 | | 450.27 | 350.59 | L8045 | KN | 0.00 | 985.81 |
| L6883 | | 0.00 | 1590.39 | L7368 | | 577.14 | 454.49 | L8045 | | 0.00 | 2464.54 |
| L6884 | | 0.00 | 2237.45 | L7400 | | 369.00 | 276.00 | L8046 | KM | 0.00 | 2295.63 |
| L6885 | | 0.00 | 3192.22 | L7401 | | 0.00 | 308.97 | L8046 | KN | 0.00 | 966.57 |
| L6890 | | 223.01 | 170.47 | L7402 | | 0.00 | 333.67 | L8046 | | 0.00 | 2416.45 |
| L6895 | | 699.93 | 559.63 | L7403 | | 465.00 | 331.63 | L8047 | KM | 0.00 | 1176.51 |
| L6900 | | 0.00 | 1513.80 | L7404 | | 0.00 | 500.51 | L8047 | KN | 0.00 | 495.37 |
| L6905 | | 0.00 | 1471.46 | L7405 | | 0.00 | 654.59 | L8047 | | 0.00 | 1238.42 |
| L6910 | | 0.00 | 1433.50 | L7500 | | 101.00 | 0.00 | L8300 | | 81.59 | 84.54 |
| L6915 | | 0.00 | 627.41 | L7510 | | 41.00 | 0.00 | L8310 | | 120.04 | 133.48 |
| L6920 | | 0.00 | 6688.48 | L7520 | | 36.00 | 0.00 | L8320 | | 0.00 | 53.58 |

**Appendix 7 — National Average Payment Table for HCPCS**

| Proc | Mod | Commercial | Medicare | Proc | Mod | Commercial | Medicare | Proc | Mod | Commercial | Medicare |
|------|-----|-----------|----------|------|-----|-----------|----------|------|-----|-----------|----------|
| L8330 | | 0.00 | 49.48 | L8631 | | 0.00 | 1981.68 | Q0083 | | 95.04 | 0.00 |
| L8400 | | 20.20 | 15.78 | L8641 | | 0.00 | 350.82 | Q0084 | | 250.03 | 0.00 |
| L8410 | | 25.25 | 20.76 | L8642 | | 0.00 | 284.55 | Q0085 | | 300.00 | 0.00 |
| L8415 | | 24.99 | 21.48 | L8658 | | 0.00 | 305.88 | Q0091 | | 55.00 | 0.00 |
| L8417 | | 89.00 | 67.69 | L8659 | | 0.00 | 1738.12 | Q0092 | | 18.00 | 0.00 |
| L8420 | | 25.01 | 19.50 | L8670 | | 0.00 | 502.09 | Q0111 | | 18.00 | 5.96 |
| L8430 | | 27.99 | 22.18 | L8680 | | 700.00 | 418.44 | Q0112 | | 18.00 | 5.96 |
| L8435 | | 27.23 | 21.07 | L8681 | | 2000.00 | 1081.18 | Q0113 | | 0.00 | 7.56 |
| L8440 | | 54.00 | 41.92 | L8682 | | 0.00 | 5430.64 | Q0114 | | 22.00 | 9.99 |
| L8460 | | 80.98 | 66.80 | L8683 | | 0.00 | 4780.20 | Q0115 | | 30.00 | 13.83 |
| L8465 | | 62.01 | 48.89 | L8684 | | 0.00 | 682.45 | Q0144 | | 21.99 | 0.00 |
| L8470 | | 8.00 | 6.70 | L8685 | | 0.00 | 11911.98 | Q0163 | | 1.00 | 0.00 |
| L8480 | | 11.00 | 9.22 | L8686 | | 0.00 | 7600.80 | Q0164 | | 0.80 | 0.00 |
| L8485 | | 14.00 | 11.15 | L8687 | | 26812.00 | 15502.26 | Q0165 | | 1.00 | 0.00 |
| L8500 | | 625.07 | 661.42 | L8688 | | 0.00 | 9891.69 | Q0166 | | 63.06 | 0.00 |
| L8501 | | 145.03 | 121.07 | L8689 | | 5045.00 | 1553.71 | Q0167 | | 7.73 | 0.00 |
| L8505 | | 26.00 | 0.00 | L8690 | | 0.00 | 4284.90 | Q0168 | | 12.82 | 0.00 |
| L8507 | | 47.99 | 37.72 | L8691 | | 0.00 | 2401.83 | Q0169 | | 2.50 | 0.00 |
| L8509 | | 130.00 | 98.34 | L8695 | | 0.00 | 15.01 | Q0170 | | 1.00 | 0.00 |
| L8510 | | 0.00 | 227.55 | M0064 | | 54.35 | 0.00 | Q0173 | | 0.94 | 0.00 |
| L8511 | | 0.00 | 65.50 | M0076 | | 200.20 | 0.00 | Q0179 | | 67.99 | 0.00 |
| L8512 | | 1.44 | 1.96 | M0300 | | 105.00 | 0.00 | Q0180 | | 82.80 | 0.00 |
| L8513 | | 4.17 | 4.68 | P2038 | | 0.00 | 7.02 | Q0480 | | 0.00 | 81123.55 |
| L8514 | | 0.00 | 84.92 | P3000 | | 21.00 | 14.76 | Q0481 | | 0.00 | 13088.34 |
| L8515 | | 50.00 | 56.84 | P3001 | | 25.00 | 0.00 | Q0482 | | 0.00 | 4099.52 |
| L8600 | | 1000.08 | 625.83 | P7001 | | 27.00 | 0.00 | Q0483 | | 0.00 | 16888.16 |
| L8603 | | 499.98 | 395.20 | P9016 | | 423.80 | 0.00 | Q0484 | | 0.00 | 3279.63 |
| L8606 | | 300.03 | 198.18 | P9021 | | 286.60 | 0.00 | Q0485 | | 0.00 | 316.65 |
| L8609 | | 0.00 | 5868.64 | P9022 | | 160.70 | 0.00 | Q0486 | | 0.00 | 263.54 |
| L8610 | | 569.85 | 586.61 | P9033 | | 1800.00 | 0.00 | Q0487 | | 0.00 | 307.47 |
| L8612 | | 658.79 | 609.39 | P9035 | | 1179.90 | 0.00 | Q0488 | | 112.50 | 0.00 |
| L8613 | | 0.00 | 257.71 | P9037 | | 1772.00 | 0.00 | Q0489 | | 0.00 | 14641.12 |
| L8614 | | 0.00 | 17417.81 | P9040 | | 693.00 | 0.00 | Q0490 | | 0.00 | 633.30 |
| L8615 | | 350.00 | 406.24 | P9041 | | 19.21 | 0.00 | Q0491 | | 0.00 | 995.62 |
| L8616 | | 100.00 | 94.62 | P9045 | | 56.03 | 0.00 | Q0492 | | 0.00 | 80.21 |
| L8617 | | 0.00 | 82.64 | P9047 | | 125.04 | 0.00 | Q0493 | | 0.00 | 228.39 |
| L8618 | | 28.00 | 23.62 | P9053 | | 1820.00 | 0.00 | Q0494 | | 0.00 | 193.26 |
| L8619 | | 6802.24 | 7476.41 | P9058 | | 860.00 | 0.00 | Q0495 | | 0.00 | 3762.40 |
| L8621 | | 0.60 | 0.56 | P9603 | | 1.00 | 0.00 | Q0496 | | 0.00 | 1350.39 |
| L8622 | | 3.80 | 0.30 | P9604 | | 5.61 | 0.00 | Q0497 | | 0.00 | 421.67 |
| L8623 | | 69.00 | 58.27 | P9612 | | 30.00 | 0.00 | Q0498 | | 0.00 | 462.67 |
| L8624 | | 150.00 | 145.25 | P9615 | | 22.00 | 0.00 | Q0499 | | 0.00 | 150.32 |
| L8630 | | 0.00 | 337.65 | Q0081 | | 120.02 | 0.00 | Q0500 | | 0.00 | 27.50 |

| Proc | Mod | Commercial | Medicare | Proc | Mod | Commercial | Medicare | Proc | Mod | Commercial | Medicare |
|------|-----|-----------|----------|------|-----|-----------|----------|------|-----|-----------|----------|
| Q0501 | | 0.00 | 460.00 | Q4040 | | 49.97 | 0.00 | Q9959 | | 1.00 | 0.00 |
| Q0502 | | 0.00 | 585.64 | Q4041 | | 32.00 | 0.00 | Q9960 | | 4.20 | 0.00 |
| Q0503 | | 0.00 | 1171.29 | Q4042 | | 74.97 | 0.00 | Q9961 | | 1.00 | 0.00 |
| Q0504 | | 0.00 | 618.07 | Q4044 | | 59.98 | 0.00 | Q9962 | | 1.70 | 0.00 |
| Q0510 | | 50.00 | 0.00 | Q4045 | | 25.00 | 0.00 | Q9963 | | 1.20 | 0.00 |
| Q0511 | | 24.00 | 0.00 | Q4046 | | 50.01 | 0.00 | Q9964 | | 100.00 | 0.00 |
| Q0512 | | 16.00 | 0.00 | Q4048 | | 27.99 | 0.00 | Q9965 | | 2.50 | 0.00 |
| Q0513 | | 68.40 | 0.00 | Q4049 | | 22.03 | 0.00 | Q9966 | | 2.00 | 0.00 |
| Q0514 | | 84.50 | 0.00 | Q4079 | | 13.30 | 0.00 | Q9967 | | 1.20 | 0.00 |
| Q0515 | | 4.00 | 0.00 | Q4080 | | 72.31 | 0.00 | R0070 | | 130.00 | 0.00 |
| Q1003 | | 50.00 | 0.00 | Q4081 | | 1.30 | 0.00 | R0075 | | 69.98 | 0.00 |
| Q2009 | | 7.97 | 0.00 | Q4082 | | 2036.20 | 0.00 | S0020 | | 10.00 | 0.00 |
| Q3001 | | 88.00 | 0.00 | Q4083 | | 200.03 | 0.00 | S0023 | | 3.00 | 0.00 |
| Q3014 | | 30.00 | 0.00 | Q4084 | | 285.06 | 0.00 | S0028 | | 3.71 | 0.00 |
| Q3025 | | 125.00 | 0.00 | Q4085 | | 197.98 | 0.00 | S0030 | | 27.50 | 0.00 |
| Q3026 | | 45.70 | 0.00 | Q4086 | | 299.95 | 0.00 | S0032 | | 21.56 | 0.00 |
| Q4005 | | 41.98 | 0.00 | Q4087 | | 102.17 | 0.00 | S0034 | | 122.30 | 0.00 |
| Q4006 | | 63.08 | 0.00 | Q4088 | | 95.68 | 0.00 | S0039 | | 14.00 | 0.00 |
| Q4007 | | 20.01 | 0.00 | Q4091 | | 70.01 | 0.00 | S0040 | | 14.16 | 0.00 |
| Q4008 | | 36.02 | 0.00 | Q4092 | | 81.05 | 0.00 | S0073 | | 17.67 | 0.00 |
| Q4009 | | 25.99 | 0.00 | Q4093 | | 0.20 | 0.00 | S0077 | | 3.27 | 0.00 |
| Q4010 | | 50.02 | 0.00 | Q4094 | | 1.00 | 0.00 | S0080 | | 118.48 | 0.00 |
| Q4011 | | 14.99 | 0.00 | Q4095 | | 375.00 | 0.00 | S0081 | | 2.17 | 0.00 |
| Q4012 | | 28.01 | 0.00 | Q5001 | | 154.00 | 0.00 | S0088 | | 47.50 | 0.00 |
| Q4013 | | 34.99 | 0.00 | Q5002 | | 155.00 | 0.00 | S0090 | | 11.75 | 0.00 |
| Q4014 | | 53.02 | 0.00 | Q5003 | | 7.50 | 0.00 | S0091 | | 79.00 | 0.00 |
| Q4016 | | 28.00 | 0.00 | Q5004 | | 131.50 | 0.00 | S0092 | | 83.12 | 0.00 |
| Q4017 | | 28.00 | 0.00 | Q5005 | | 617.00 | 0.00 | S0109 | | 0.17 | 0.00 |
| Q4018 | | 51.00 | 0.00 | Q5006 | | 683.70 | 0.00 | S0122 | | 78.00 | 0.00 |
| Q4019 | | 14.00 | 0.00 | Q5009 | | 130.70 | 0.00 | S0126 | | 77.91 | 0.00 |
| Q4020 | | 30.00 | 0.00 | Q9945 | | 1.00 | 0.00 | S0128 | | 82.09 | 0.00 |
| Q4021 | | 30.00 | 0.00 | Q9946 | | 2.00 | 0.00 | S0132 | | 166.78 | 0.00 |
| Q4022 | | 45.01 | 0.00 | Q9947 | | 2.50 | 0.00 | S0136 | | 1.27 | 0.00 |
| Q4023 | | 14.00 | 0.00 | Q9948 | | 1.00 | 0.00 | S0142 | | 16.00 | 0.00 |
| Q4024 | | 26.75 | 0.00 | Q9949 | | 1.20 | 0.00 | S0143 | | 97.10 | 0.00 |
| Q4030 | | 108.05 | 0.00 | Q9950 | | 1.00 | 0.00 | S0145 | | 1242.00 | 0.00 |
| Q4031 | | 25.42 | 0.00 | Q9951 | | 1.00 | 0.00 | S0146 | | 100.00 | 0.00 |
| Q4032 | | 60.98 | 0.00 | Q9952 | | 6.00 | 0.00 | S0155 | | 24.20 | 0.00 |
| Q4034 | | 95.48 | 0.00 | Q9953 | | 35.00 | 0.00 | S0162 | | 384.46 | 0.00 |
| Q4036 | | 71.02 | 0.00 | Q9954 | | 30.00 | 0.00 | S0164 | | 15.00 | 0.00 |
| Q4037 | | 80.00 | 0.00 | Q9956 | | 198.00 | 0.00 | S0170 | | 8.24 | 0.00 |
| Q4038 | | 91.02 | 0.00 | Q9957 | | 98.98 | 0.00 | S0171 | | 0.56 | 0.00 |
| Q4039 | | 30.00 | 0.00 | Q9958 | | 250.00 | 0.00 | S0180 | | 750.00 | 0.00 |

# APPENDIX 7 — NATIONAL AVERAGE PAYMENT TABLE FOR HCPCS

| Proc | Mod | Commercial | Medicare | Proc | Mod | Commercial | Medicare | Proc | Mod | Commercial | Medicare |
|------|-----|-----------|----------|------|-----|-----------|----------|------|-----|-----------|----------|
| S0181 | | 39.99 | 0.00 | S1015 | | 25.00 | 0.00 | S5145 | | 49.50 | 0.00 |
| S0187 | | 1.90 | 0.00 | S1016 | | 30.00 | 0.00 | S5150 | | 4.80 | 0.00 |
| S0189 | | 32.00 | 0.00 | S1040 | | 2700.00 | 0.00 | S5151 | | 250.00 | 0.00 |
| S0190 | | 99.99 | 0.00 | S2068 | | 25000.00 | 0.00 | S5161 | | 31.50 | 0.00 |
| S0191 | | 3.00 | 0.00 | S2075 | | 2584.00 | 0.00 | S5165 | | 100.80 | 0.00 |
| S0199 | | 630.00 | 0.00 | S2077 | | 1000.00 | 0.00 | S5170 | | 6.60 | 0.00 |
| S0201 | | 16.00 | 0.00 | S2083 | | 350.00 | 0.00 | S5498 | | 14.00 | 0.00 |
| S0207 | | 750.00 | 0.00 | S2114 | | 2433.00 | 0.00 | S5501 | | 20.00 | 0.00 |
| S0208 | | 525.00 | 0.00 | S2135 | | 345.00 | 0.00 | S5502 | | 100.00 | 0.00 |
| S0209 | | 3.00 | 0.00 | S2140 | | 250.00 | 0.00 | S5517 | | 53.60 | 0.00 |
| S0215 | | 2.30 | 0.00 | S2900 | | 1500.00 | 0.00 | S5518 | | 10.00 | 0.00 |
| S0220 | | 134.50 | 0.00 | S3005 | | 60.00 | 0.00 | S5520 | | 75.00 | 0.00 |
| S0257 | | 20.00 | 0.00 | S3600 | | 25.00 | 0.00 | S5521 | | 120.00 | 0.00 |
| S0260 | | 75.00 | 0.00 | S3620 | | 40.00 | 0.00 | S5522 | | 300.00 | 0.00 |
| S0265 | | 75.00 | 0.00 | S3820 | | 3120.00 | 0.00 | S5523 | | 130.00 | 0.00 |
| S0302 | | 10.00 | 0.00 | S3822 | | 385.00 | 0.00 | S5550 | | 0.20 | 0.00 |
| S0315 | | 142.50 | 0.00 | S3823 | | 460.00 | 0.00 | S5565 | | 0.40 | 0.00 |
| S0316 | | 92.00 | 0.00 | S3830 | | 2050.00 | 0.00 | S8037 | | 1400.00 | 0.00 |
| S0317 | | 183.20 | 0.00 | S3854 | | 3650.00 | 0.00 | S8085 | | 475.00 | 0.00 |
| S0341 | | 11.70 | 0.00 | S3900 | | 85.00 | 0.00 | S8092 | | 370.00 | 0.00 |
| S0346 | | 265.00 | 0.00 | S4011 | | 6000.00 | 0.00 | S8096 | | 35.00 | 0.00 |
| S0347 | | 125.00 | 0.00 | S4016 | | 2000.00 | 0.00 | S8100 | | 15.00 | 0.00 |
| S0390 | | 75.00 | 0.00 | S4022 | | 2000.00 | 0.00 | S8101 | | 46.00 | 0.00 |
| S0395 | | 63.00 | 0.00 | S4035 | | 6.10 | 0.00 | S8110 | | 45.00 | 0.00 |
| S0500 | | 89.00 | 0.00 | S4042 | | 500.00 | 0.00 | S8120 | | 1.50 | 0.00 |
| S0504 | | 120.00 | 0.00 | S4981 | | 150.00 | 0.00 | S8121 | | 2.00 | 0.00 |
| S0512 | | 95.00 | 0.00 | S4989 | | 525.00 | 0.00 | S8186 | | 27.50 | 0.00 |
| S0516 | | 79.00 | 0.00 | S4993 | | 28.00 | 0.00 | S8262 | | 1500.00 | 0.00 |
| S0580 | | 30.00 | 0.00 | S5010 | | 26.20 | 0.00 | S8265 | | 79.70 | 0.00 |
| S0581 | | 73.50 | 0.00 | S5011 | | 13.40 | 0.00 | S8415 | | 130.00 | 0.00 |
| S0592 | | 45.00 | 0.00 | S5013 | | 21.00 | 0.00 | S8422 | | 150.00 | 0.00 |
| S0605 | | 25.00 | 0.00 | S5100 | | 6.00 | 0.00 | S8423 | | 165.00 | 0.00 |
| S0610 | | 250.00 | 0.00 | S5101 | | 6.50 | 0.00 | S8424 | | 8.50 | 0.00 |
| S0612 | | 175.00 | 0.00 | S5102 | | 59.30 | 0.00 | S8426 | | 278.10 | 0.00 |
| S0613 | | 45.00 | 0.00 | S5105 | | 80.00 | 0.00 | S8427 | | 150.00 | 0.00 |
| S0618 | | 100.00 | 0.00 | S5110 | | 10.00 | 0.00 | S8428 | | 55.00 | 0.00 |
| S0620 | | 42.00 | 0.00 | S5111 | | 70.00 | 0.00 | S8429 | | 36.00 | 0.00 |
| S0621 | | 69.00 | 0.00 | S5116 | | 70.00 | 0.00 | S8430 | | 33.10 | 0.00 |
| S0625 | | 350.00 | 0.00 | S5120 | | 4.60 | 0.00 | S8431 | | 10.90 | 0.00 |
| S0630 | | 50.00 | 0.00 | S5125 | | 2.40 | 0.00 | S8450 | | 16.00 | 0.00 |
| S0800 | | 1580.00 | 0.00 | S5126 | | 61.30 | 0.00 | S8451 | | 35.00 | 0.00 |
| S0820 | | 200.00 | 0.00 | S5135 | | 4.50 | 0.00 | S8452 | | 35.00 | 0.00 |
| S1001 | | 29.00 | 0.00 | S5140 | | 53.40 | 0.00 | S8490 | | 0.40 | 0.00 |

| Proc | Mod | Commercial | Medicare | Proc | Mod | Commercial | Medicare | Proc | Mod | Commercial | Medicare |
|------|-----|-----------|----------|------|-----|-----------|----------|------|-----|-----------|----------|
| S8948 | | 45.00 | 0.00 | S9341 | | 20.00 | 0.00 | S9484 | | 60.00 | 0.00 |
| S8950 | | 40.90 | 0.00 | S9342 | | 23.00 | 0.00 | S9485 | | 488.00 | 0.00 |
| S8990 | | 50.00 | 0.00 | S9343 | | 22.40 | 0.00 | S9490 | | 229.90 | 0.00 |
| S8999 | | 200.00 | 0.00 | S9345 | | 35.60 | 0.00 | S9494 | | 140.00 | 0.00 |
| S9001 | | 80.00 | 0.00 | S9346 | | 60.00 | 0.00 | S9497 | | 264.70 | 0.00 |
| S9061 | | 50.00 | 0.00 | S9347 | | 110.00 | 0.00 | S9500 | | 150.00 | 0.00 |
| S9075 | | 50.00 | 0.00 | S9348 | | 83.00 | 0.00 | S9501 | | 168.00 | 0.00 |
| S9083 | | 130.00 | 0.00 | S9349 | | 460.00 | 0.00 | S9502 | | 192.00 | 0.00 |
| S9088 | | 75.00 | 0.00 | S9351 | | 695.00 | 0.00 | S9503 | | 170.00 | 0.00 |
| S9090 | | 150.00 | 0.00 | S9353 | | 420.00 | 0.00 | S9504 | | 180.00 | 0.00 |
| S9092 | | 90.00 | 0.00 | S9355 | | 100.00 | 0.00 | S9529 | | 50.00 | 0.00 |
| S9097 | | 145.00 | 0.00 | S9357 | | 60.00 | 0.00 | S9537 | | 55.00 | 0.00 |
| S9098 | | 240.00 | 0.00 | S9359 | | 150.00 | 0.00 | S9538 | | 400.00 | 0.00 |
| S9109 | | 25.00 | 0.00 | S9361 | | 70.50 | 0.00 | S9558 | | 30.50 | 0.00 |
| S9122 | | 27.00 | 0.00 | S9363 | | 93.00 | 0.00 | S9559 | | 85.00 | 0.00 |
| S9123 | | 52.00 | 0.00 | S9364 | | 170.00 | 0.00 | S9560 | | 399.00 | 0.00 |
| S9124 | | 42.00 | 0.00 | S9365 | | 250.00 | 0.00 | S9562 | | 110.00 | 0.00 |
| S9125 | | 27.30 | 0.00 | S9366 | | 300.00 | 0.00 | S9590 | | 41.00 | 0.00 |
| S9126 | | 161.00 | 0.00 | S9367 | | 325.00 | 0.00 | S9900 | | 18.00 | 0.00 |
| S9127 | | 156.00 | 0.00 | S9368 | | 200.00 | 0.00 | S9970 | | 291.70 | 0.00 |
| S9128 | | 125.00 | 0.00 | S9370 | | 75.00 | 0.00 | S9975 | | 81.90 | 0.00 |
| S9129 | | 125.00 | 0.00 | S9372 | | 69.00 | 0.00 | S9981 | | 25.00 | 0.00 |
| S9131 | | 125.00 | 0.00 | S9373 | | 85.00 | 0.00 | S9982 | | 0.80 | 0.00 |
| S9140 | | 156.00 | 0.00 | S9374 | | 88.00 | 0.00 | S9986 | | 35.00 | 0.00 |
| S9141 | | 181.00 | 0.00 | S9375 | | 105.00 | 0.00 | S9989 | | 55.70 | 0.00 |
| S9145 | | 429.40 | 0.00 | S9376 | | 125.00 | 0.00 | S9992 | | 29.00 | 0.00 |
| S9150 | | 0.20 | 0.00 | S9377 | | 365.00 | 0.00 | S9996 | | 17.40 | 0.00 |
| S9208 | | 205.00 | 0.00 | S9401 | | 25.00 | 0.00 | S9999 | | 6.30 | 0.00 |
| S9211 | | 85.00 | 0.00 | S9430 | | 20.00 | 0.00 | T1000 | | 11.50 | 0.00 |
| S9212 | | 43.80 | 0.00 | S9434 | | 9.00 | 0.00 | T1001 | | 40.00 | 0.00 |
| S9213 | | 205.00 | 0.00 | S9435 | | 28.50 | 0.00 | T1002 | | 7.70 | 0.00 |
| S9214 | | 300.00 | 0.00 | S9436 | | 100.00 | 0.00 | T1003 | | 10.00 | 0.00 |
| S9325 | | 75.00 | 0.00 | S9441 | | 25.00 | 0.00 | T1004 | | 11.30 | 0.00 |
| S9326 | | 149.00 | 0.00 | S9442 | | 60.00 | 0.00 | T1005 | | 3.90 | 0.00 |
| S9327 | | 159.10 | 0.00 | S9443 | | 50.00 | 0.00 | T1007 | | 270.00 | 0.00 |
| S9328 | | 55.00 | 0.00 | S9449 | | 135.00 | 0.00 | T1013 | | 19.70 | 0.00 |
| S9329 | | 125.00 | 0.00 | S9452 | | 39.00 | 0.00 | T1015 | | 54.00 | 0.00 |
| S9330 | | 130.00 | 0.00 | S9455 | | 108.00 | 0.00 | T1016 | | 25.00 | 0.00 |
| S9331 | | 85.00 | 0.00 | S9460 | | 156.00 | 0.00 | T1017 | | 33.00 | 0.00 |
| S9335 | | 500.00 | 0.00 | S9465 | | 185.90 | 0.00 | T1018 | | 12.20 | 0.00 |
| S9336 | | 144.70 | 0.00 | S9470 | | 85.00 | 0.00 | T1019 | | 3.90 | 0.00 |
| S9338 | | 91.00 | 0.00 | S9475 | | 125.00 | 0.00 | T1020 | | 121.50 | 0.00 |
| S9340 | | 25.00 | 0.00 | S9480 | | 175.00 | 0.00 | T1021 | | 9.50 | 0.00 |

Appendix 7 — National Average Payment Table for HCPCS

# APPENDIX 7 — NATIONAL AVERAGE PAYMENT TABLE FOR HCPCS

| Proc | Mod | Commercial | Medicare | Proc | Mod | Commercial | Medicare | Proc | Mod | Commercial | Medicare |
|------|-----|-----------|----------|------|-----|-----------|----------|------|-----|-----------|----------|
| T1023 | | 22.50 | 0.00 | T4528 | | 1.10 | 0.00 | V2211 | | 80.02 | 74.02 |
| T1024 | | 25.90 | 0.00 | T4529 | | 1.00 | 0.00 | V2212 | | 71.01 | 76.43 |
| T1025 | | 176.00 | 0.00 | T4530 | | 1.10 | 0.00 | V2213 | | 0.00 | 77.20 |
| T1027 | | 7.20 | 0.00 | T4531 | | 1.10 | 0.00 | V2214 | | 89.98 | 83.92 |
| T1028 | | 29.80 | 0.00 | T4532 | | 0.90 | 0.00 | V2215 | | 104.98 | 85.19 |
| T1030 | | 150.00 | 0.00 | T4533 | | 1.00 | 0.00 | V2218 | | 0.00 | 101.38 |
| T1031 | | 105.00 | 0.00 | T4534 | | 1.10 | 0.00 | V2219 | | 46.99 | 44.63 |
| T1502 | | 15.00 | 0.00 | T4535 | | 0.70 | 0.00 | V2220 | | 55.00 | 36.19 |
| T2001 | | 10.00 | 0.00 | T4537 | | 20.00 | 0.00 | V2221 | | 92.02 | 88.53 |
| T2002 | | 1.00 | 0.00 | T4541 | | 0.50 | 0.00 | V2299 | | 115.00 | 0.00 |
| T2003 | | 10.00 | 0.00 | T4542 | | 0.50 | 0.00 | V2300 | | 99.97 | 65.41 |
| T2007 | | 25.00 | 0.00 | T5999 | | 17.10 | 0.00 | V2301 | | 104.50 | 77.10 |
| T2014 | | 26.50 | 0.00 | V2020 | | 105.99 | 62.84 | V2302 | | 112.52 | 82.18 |
| T2015 | | 11.30 | 0.00 | V2025 | | 108.00 | 0.00 | V2303 | | 84.51 | 64.37 |
| T2016 | | 118.50 | 0.00 | V2100 | | 45.01 | 39.26 | V2304 | | 86.49 | 67.34 |
| T2017 | | 3.60 | 0.00 | V2101 | | 50.01 | 41.36 | V2305 | | 92.47 | 78.03 |
| T2018 | | 128.80 | 0.00 | V2102 | | 65.01 | 58.20 | V2306 | | 0.00 | 80.35 |
| T2019 | | 3.00 | 0.00 | V2103 | | 44.49 | 34.09 | V2307 | | 93.98 | 76.07 |
| T2020 | | 45.00 | 0.00 | V2104 | | 45.01 | 37.75 | V2308 | | 122.48 | 79.72 |
| T2021 | | 5.90 | 0.00 | V2105 | | 59.99 | 41.10 | V2309 | | 0.00 | 86.85 |
| T2022 | | 200.00 | 0.00 | V2106 | | 68.99 | 45.61 | V2310 | | 0.00 | 85.82 |
| T2023 | | 168.80 | 0.00 | V2107 | | 52.00 | 43.38 | V2311 | | 109.03 | 89.30 |
| T2024 | | 90.00 | 0.00 | V2108 | | 52.51 | 44.92 | V2312 | | 137.47 | 89.81 |
| T2025 | | 30.00 | 0.00 | V2109 | | 61.51 | 49.69 | V2313 | | 0.00 | 100.30 |
| T2031 | | 114.60 | 0.00 | V2110 | | 59.49 | 49.04 | V2314 | | 116.53 | 107.72 |
| T2032 | | 510.00 | 0.00 | V2111 | | 89.00 | 51.12 | V2315 | | 0.00 | 119.59 |
| T2033 | | 276.10 | 0.00 | V2112 | | 60.01 | 55.80 | V2318 | | 0.00 | 147.01 |
| T2034 | | 89.10 | 0.00 | V2113 | | 84.99 | 62.89 | V2319 | | 50.49 | 49.77 |
| T2038 | | 11.80 | 0.00 | V2114 | | 81.00 | 68.12 | V2320 | | 74.50 | 52.50 |
| T2042 | | 180.00 | 0.00 | V2115 | | 99.97 | 74.14 | V2321 | | 0.00 | 117.88 |
| T2043 | | 46.00 | 0.00 | V2118 | | 0.00 | 73.50 | V2399 | | 158.00 | 0.00 |
| T2044 | | 170.00 | 0.00 | V2121 | | 121.99 | 75.88 | V2410 | | 90.03 | 89.87 |
| T2045 | | 710.80 | 0.00 | V2200 | | 55.99 | 51.38 | V2430 | | 150.53 | 108.31 |
| T2046 | | 156.60 | 0.00 | V2201 | | 60.00 | 56.00 | V2499 | | 100.00 | 0.00 |
| T2048 | | 13.90 | 0.00 | V2202 | | 64.49 | 65.90 | V2500 | | 98.03 | 81.46 |
| T2049 | | 2.80 | 0.00 | V2203 | | 58.61 | 51.84 | V2501 | | 110.01 | 124.08 |
| T4521 | | 1.00 | 0.00 | V2204 | | 60.01 | 54.19 | V2502 | | 180.04 | 152.86 |
| T4522 | | 0.90 | 0.00 | V2205 | | 62.50 | 58.59 | V2503 | | 180.01 | 140.78 |
| T4523 | | 1.10 | 0.00 | V2206 | | 60.09 | 62.95 | V2510 | | 109.98 | 111.21 |
| T4524 | | 1.10 | 0.00 | V2207 | | 65.02 | 57.26 | V2511 | | 149.97 | 159.78 |
| T4525 | | 0.90 | 0.00 | V2208 | | 64.01 | 60.10 | V2512 | | 169.97 | 188.80 |
| T4526 | | 1.10 | 0.00 | V2209 | | 62.50 | 64.71 | V2513 | | 150.05 | 158.51 |
| T4527 | | 1.20 | 0.00 | V2210 | | 89.49 | 71.37 | V2520 | | 114.00 | 104.53 |

| Proc | Mod | Commercial | Medicare | Proc | Mod | Commercial | Medicare | Proc | Mod | Commercial | Medicare |
|------|-----|-----------|----------|------|-----|-----------|----------|------|-----|-----------|----------|
| V2521 | | 160.03 | 181.98 | V2755 | | 15.00 | 16.65 | V5110 | | 399.96 | 0.00 |
| V2522 | | 159.99 | 177.09 | V2756 | | 3.00 | 0.00 | V5130 | | 2200.00 | 0.00 |
| V2523 | | 143.95 | 150.92 | V2760 | | 15.50 | 16.06 | V5140 | | 2299.70 | 0.00 |
| V2530 | | 0.00 | 223.53 | V2761 | | 30.00 | 0.00 | V5160 | | 599.99 | 0.00 |
| V2531 | | 499.87 | 490.71 | V2762 | | 50.51 | 53.68 | V5241 | | 300.00 | 0.00 |
| V2599 | | 67.50 | 0.00 | V2770 | | 0.00 | 19.56 | V5244 | | 2095.00 | 0.00 |
| V2600 | | 136.00 | 0.00 | V2780 | | 13.50 | 12.56 | V5247 | | 1950.00 | 0.00 |
| V2623 | | 2199.95 | 899.63 | V2781 | | 105.00 | 0.00 | V5250 | | 3000.00 | 0.00 |
| V2624 | | 74.99 | 61.01 | V2782 | | 46.01 | 57.97 | V5251 | | 1435.50 | 0.00 |
| V2625 | | 500.14 | 370.94 | V2783 | | 69.98 | 65.37 | V5252 | | 2700.00 | 0.00 |
| V2626 | | 400.00 | 199.96 | V2784 | | 40.00 | 42.51 | V5253 | | 2700.00 | 0.00 |
| V2627 | | 2349.86 | 1291.39 | V2785 | | 3150.00 | 0.00 | V5254 | | 2800.00 | 0.00 |
| V2628 | | 449.94 | 304.92 | V2786 | | 75.00 | 0.00 | V5255 | | 2100.00 | 0.00 |
| V2629 | | 1200.00 | 0.00 | V2788 | | 1195.00 | 0.00 | V5256 | | 1770.00 | 0.00 |
| V2630 | | 325.00 | 0.00 | V2797 | | 10.00 | 0.00 | V5257 | | 2250.00 | 0.00 |
| V2632 | | 386.00 | 0.00 | V5008 | | 99.99 | 0.00 | V5258 | | 3800.00 | 0.00 |
| V2700 | | 69.00 | 43.91 | V5010 | | 120.01 | 0.00 | V5259 | | 1990.00 | 0.00 |
| V2702 | | 12.50 | 0.00 | V5011 | | 133.77 | 0.00 | V5260 | | 2000.00 | 0.00 |
| V2710 | | 80.01 | 64.26 | V5014 | | 198.02 | 0.00 | V5261 | | 2950.00 | 0.00 |
| V2715 | | 12.04 | 11.65 | V5020 | | 95.01 | 0.00 | V5264 | | 60.00 | 0.00 |
| V2718 | | 34.99 | 28.62 | V5030 | | 1799.85 | 0.00 | V5265 | | 45.00 | 0.00 |
| V2730 | | 35.00 | 21.14 | V5050 | | 1649.25 | 0.00 | V5266 | | 1.10 | 0.00 |
| V2744 | | 40.01 | 16.44 | V5060 | | 1600.20 | 0.00 | V5267 | | 9.00 | 0.00 |
| V2745 | | 12.50 | 10.29 | V5090 | | 399.92 | 0.00 | V5275 | | 43.00 | 0.00 |
| V2750 | | 43.01 | 19.13 | V5100 | | 2599.78 | 0.00 | | | | |